MW01126161

THE CRISIS
OF
DEMOCRATIC
CAPITALISM

ALSO BY MARTIN WOLF

*The Shifts and the Shocks: What We've Learned—and
Have Still to Learn—from the Financial Crisis*

Fixing Global Finance

Why Globalization Works

The Resistible Appeal of Fortress Europe

India's Exports

THE CRISIS

OF

DEMOCRATIC

CAPITALISM

Martin Wolf

PENGUIN PRESS

NEW YORK

2023

PENGUIN PRESS
An imprint of Penguin Random House LLC
penguinrandomhouse.com

Copyright © 2023 by Martin Wolf
Penguin Random House supports copyright. Copyright fuels
creativity, encourages diverse voices, promotes free speech, and
creates a vibrant culture. Thank you for buying an authorized
edition of this book and for complying with copyright laws by
not reproducing, scanning, or distributing any part of it in any
form without permission. You are supporting writers and
allowing Penguin Random House to continue to publish
books for every reader.

Text Credits
Page 198: Excerpt from 'Illiberal Democracy or Undemocratic
Liberalism?" from *Project Syndicate*, 2016, by Yascha Mounk.
Used by permission.
Page 221: Letter from J. M. Keynes to F. W. Pethick-Lawrence,
June 21, 1942 (PETH 2/218). Used by permission of
The Master and Fellows of Trinity College, Cambridge.
Page 238: Excerpt from "How Far Will International Economic
Integration Go?" from *Journal of Economic Perspectives*,
Winter 2000, by Dani Rodrik. Used by permission.

Image Credits
Page 98: Data for figure 19, "Decadal average growth rate of
output per hour"—Total Economy Database, The Conference
Board, May 2017.
Page 100: Data for figure 20, "Private debt over GDP in mature
economies"—IIF Global Debt Monitor.
Page 188: Data for table 3, "The three dimensions of British
political loyalties"— Electoral Calculus.
Page 189: Data for table 4, "The seven tribes of modern British
politics"—Electoral Calculus.

LIBRARY OF CONGRESS CATALOGING-IN-PUBLICATION DATA

Names: Wolf, Martin, 1946– author.
Title: The crisis of democratic capitalism / Martin Wolf.
Description: New York: Penguin Press, [2023] |
Includes bibliographical references and index.
Identifiers: LCCN 2022035909 (print) |
LCCN 2022035910 (ebook) |
ISBN 9780735224216 (hardcover) | ISBN 9780735224223 (ebook)
Subjects: LCSH: Democracy—Economic aspects. |
Capitalism—Political aspects.
Classification: LCC JC423.W564 2023 (print) |
LCC JC423 (ebook) |
DDC 330.12/2—dc23/eng/20221117
LC record available at https://lccn.loc.gov/2022035909
LC ebook record available at https://lccn.loc.gov/2022035910

Printed in the United States of America
1st Printing

Designed by Amanda Dewey

For my beloved grandchildren, Zach, Rebecca, Alexander, Anna, Abigail, and Eden.

May their generation do a better job than mine has.

ΜΗΔΕΝ ΑΓΑΝ

(Nothing in excess)

*—This famous text appears
at the shrine of Apollo at Delphi.*

CONTENTS

———————————■———————————

Why I Wrote This Book

History does not repeat itself, but it rhymes.
—*Attributed to Mark Twain*[1]

My opinions have altered as the world has unfolded. I make no apologies for this. Those who have not changed their opinions over a lifetime do not think. But my values have not altered. I inherited them from my parents, both refugees from Hitler's Europe. I believe in democracy and so in the obligations of citizenship, in individual liberty and so in the freedom of opinion, and in the Enlightenment and so in the primacy of truth. The role of the fourth estate is, in my view, to serve these great causes. I am proud to have been one of its servants."[2]

I made these remarks in New York on June 27, 2019, when I received the Gerald Loeb Lifetime Achievement Award for business journalism. They are my credo. This book is witness to where those unchanging values and evolving opinions have brought me at the beginning of the third decade of the twenty-first century.

In the middle of the eighth decade of my life, I see a long historical circle—a circle that includes not just my life but also those of my parents. This story of two generations began on April 23, 1910, with the birth of my father, Edmund Wolf, in the Polish city of

Rzeszów, then part of the Austro-Hungarian Empire. By then the potent nineteenth-century mixture of industrialization, urbanization, class conflict, nationalism, imperialism, racism, and great-power rivalry had been at work for a long time. Four years later, the First World War, the conflict that was to demolish European stability, began. My grandfather, Ignatz, fearful of the arrival of Russian armies, moved his family to Vienna, where my father grew up. My mother, Rebecca Wolf (née Wijnschenk), was born in Amsterdam on August 30, 1918, just over two months before the First World War ended, although the Netherlands itself remained neutral. The Bolshevik revolution was just over nine months old when she was born.

Monarchs fled. European empires fell. A new world was born. But the hopes that it would be a better one proved a fantasy. In its place came the chaos of the interwar years: in the 1920s, hyperinflations, a fragile and unbalanced economic recovery, and battles among democrats, communists, and fascists; in the 1930s, the Great Depression, the collapse of the gold standard, the rise to power of Adolf Hitler in Germany and Franklin Delano Roosevelt in the US, Japanese militarism, Stalin's show trials, the Spanish civil war, appeasement, and at the end of the decade, the Second World War. This surely had been a time of trouble.

My father, rightly fearful of what Hitler's Germany intended, left Austria in 1937. My mother fled the Netherlands with her parents and siblings in May 1940, as the Nazis invaded. My parents met in wartime London in the autumn of 1942, at a party given by Dutch Jewish friends of my mother to celebrate the return from internment of my father's closest friend, who had been interned in Australia as an "enemy alien," while my father had been similarly interned in Canada. My parents' marriage on October 21, 1943, led to my birth on August 16, 1946, and so to my life as a man brought up and educated in Britain. I have also spent all but sixteen years of this life as a Londoner.

Without the Second World War and the genocidal anti-Semitism of the Third Reich, my Austrian-Jewish father and my Dutch-Jewish mother would never have met. I and my brother, born in 1948, are, like many millions of others, children of catastrophe. My parents and their immediate families escaped the wreck. My father's family (his parents, brother, sister, and his brother's wife and daughter) did so by managing, with difficulty, to reach Palestine in 1939. My mother's family did so by reaching an English fishing port on a trawler in May 1940. Their wider families of aunts, uncles, and cousins were murdered almost to the last individual. My mother's family had been large: her father, born poor in Amsterdam, was one of nine siblings. She told me that about thirty of her close relatives died during the Shoah, or Holocaust, as it is more usually known. She almost never spoke of this catastrophe. But I was aware that my parents' history was not like that of the other adults I knew, except for my parents' closest friends, who shared similar histories as refugees.

Not infrequently, people who read or hear me complain of my pessimism. To this criticism, I give three responses. The first is that my pessimism has made most of the surprises I have experienced pleasant ones. The second is that my biggest mistakes have come from overoptimism, most recently over the wisdom of finance and the good sense of electorates. The third and probably most important response is that my existence is due to the decisions of two pessimistic men: my father and my mother's father. My father took the opportunity afforded by the royalties he earned from early successes as a playwright in Vienna to leave for London on the way, he hoped, to America. My grandfather, who had left school in Amsterdam as a child and became a successful fish merchant in Ijmuiden on the coast of North Holland, was not only realistic, but also able to make quick decisions. As soon as the Germans invaded his country, he obtained a trawler and a captain (being a well-known fish merchant, he presumably found this not too difficult) and invited his relatives to join him and his family. He waited for some hours, but none of them came. In the end, the captain told him they had to go, presumably because of the speed of the German advance. My grandfather's combination of pessimism with quick wits saved his own family. But almost all their relatives perished. Pessimism saved him.

Yet these answers, while true, are not the whole story. My family history makes me aware of the fragility of civilization. Any moderately well-informed Jew should know this. But the connection to the Shoah reinforces it. Homo sapiens is prone to orgies of stupidity, brutality, and destruction. Humans naturally separate people into those who belong to "their" tribe and outsiders. They slaughter the latter gleefully. They have always done so. I have never taken peace, stability, or freedom for granted and regard those who do as fools.

My childhood was, nevertheless, secure. I loved and trusted my parents—and rightly so. Postwar England was shabby: I still remember the bomb sites in the City of London. But the country felt to me stable, peaceful, democratic, and free. The Cold War was a shadow upon us and at some points, notably the Cuban missile crisis of 1962, was even terrifying. Yet the world seemed solid as I grew up.

My parents died in the 1990s, my mother in 1993 and my father in 1997. The world in which they died was far better than that of their youth and early adulthood. Their belief in a democratic and largely peaceful world seemed vindicated. The totalitarian shadows over Europe had vanished. Democracy was triumphant. Communist central and eastern Europe had emerged from behind the Iron Curtain. Europe was on its way to reunification. It even seemed conceivable that Russia was moving toward integration into a world of democracy and individual freedom. The great schisms—ideological, political, and economic—of the twentieth century and indeed back to the French Revolution seemed over.

Subsequent events have shown that this confidence was built on fragile foundations. Liberalized finance proved unstable. I realized this during the Asian financial crisis, as I explained in my book *Why Globalization Works*.[3] But the concern became even more compelling after the global financial crisis and Great Recession of 2007–09, which were the focus of a subsequent book, *The Shifts and the Shocks*. Moreover, the world economy was generating destabilizing macroeconomic imbalances. This was the theme of my *Fixing Global Finance*, written before *The Shifts and the Shocks*.[4] The financial instability we were seeing resulted, I argued, from the inability of the international monetary system to handle large net (and gross) cross-border capital flows in a reasonably safe manner. Moreover, financial instability was only one of the failings of Western economies. Also important were rising inequality, increasing personal insecurity, and slowing economic growth, especially after the Great Recession. Finally, largely as a result of all these calamities, partly brought about by their own moral and intellectual failings, ruling elites—commercial, cultural, intellectual, political, and administrative—lost credibility in the eyes of the public.

Equally large shifts occurred in politics. The first big shock was the attacks on the US on September 11, 2001, which were followed by wars in Iraq and Afghanistan. The biggest change of all was a counterpart of the economic success of globalization, namely, the rise of China and, to a much lesser extent, India. This created a shift in the balance of global economic and so political power, away from the US and the liberal West toward China and its system of bureaucratic absolutism. Yet this was far from the only way in which global politics changed. As the twenty-first century progressed, we saw a shift away from liberal democracy toward systems that some have called "illiberal democracy" but might be better described as "demagogic autocracy." In a recent book, the Russian economist Sergei Guriev and the American political scientist Daniel Treisman call these systems "spin dictatorships," to distinguish them from the "fear dictatorships" of old.[5] Alas, the shift toward demagogic or "spin" systems is to be seen—so far, in nascent form—not only in new democracies, but also in some of the world's most established democracies, notably the US, where Donald Trump remained an embodiment of the aspiration for arbitrary power even after his defeat in 2020.[6] The rise of Trump, along with that of Boris Johnson in the UK, undermined the international credibility of the two countries and weakened Western cohesion.

Above all, their demagogic approach to politics undermined the rule of law, the commitment to truth, and the credibility of international agreements, all fundamental underpinnings of liberal democracy. Outright despotism is the probable end point.

Today's challenges are beginning to look as significant as those of the first half of the twentieth century. We see fundamental shifts in global power—then from the UK and France toward Germany and the US, now from the US to China. We see huge crises—then the world wars, Spanish flu, the hyperinflations of central Europe in the early 1920s and the Great Depression of the 1930s, now the Great Recession, COVID-19, and Russia's invasion of Ukraine in February 2022. We see a collapse of democracies and rise of authoritarianism—then in Germany, Italy, Spain, and other continental countries, now in the fragile democracies of developing countries and postcommunist countries in central and eastern Europe (including Russia). But this time, liberal democracy has been shaken even in Trump's US and Brexit Britain, countries that carried the banner of liberal democracy throughout the twentieth century.[7] Above all, we confront the risks of nuclear war and runaway climate change, the former largely unimagined before the 1940s and the latter barely considered before the 1980s.

We might have avoided the biggest mistakes of the first half of the twentieth century. But my parents would surely have heard loud echoes of their past. Not least among these has been Putin's determination to restore the Russian empire by force, so painfully reminiscent of Hitler's desire to bring the German-speaking peoples of Europe together under his totalitarian rule. Even war between Russia and NATO has become less inconceivable.

This book is a response to this new and troubling era. Its central argument is simple: when we look closely at what is happening in our economies and our polities, we must recognize the need for substantial change if core Western values of freedom, democracy, and the Enlightenment are to survive. But in so doing, we must also remember that reform is not revolution, but its opposite. It is not just impossible, but wrong, to try to re-create a society from scratch, as if its history counted for nothing. The outcome of such attempts has always been destruction and despotism. Only unbridled power can deliver a revolutionary overthrow of the existing order. But unbridled power is by its nature destructive: it shatters the security on which productive human relations can be based and decent lives lived. As Edmund Burke wrote in his response to the French Revolution, society is a "partnership not only between those who are living, but between those who are living, those who are dead, and those who are to be born."[8] Change is essential, both at home and abroad, but it must build on what is. Indeed, one cannot start anywhere else.

The motto of this book is "Never too much," as the ancient Greeks used to say.[9] The health of our societies depends on sustaining a delicate balance between the economic and the political, the individual and the collective, the national and the global. But that balance is broken. Our economy has destabilized our politics and vice versa. We are no longer able to combine the operations of the market economy with stable liberal democracy. A big part of the reason for this is that the economy is not delivering the security and widely shared prosperity expected by large parts of our societies. One symptom of this disappointment is a widespread loss of confidence in elites. Another is rising populism and authoritarianism. Another is the rise of identity politics of both left and right. Yet another is loss of trust in the notion of truth. Once this last happens, the possibility of informed and rational debate among citizens, the very foundation of democracy, has evaporated. In *The Great Transformation*, published in 1944, the same year as Friedrich Hayek's *The Road to Serfdom*, Karl Polanyi argued that human beings would not long tolerate living under a truly free market system.[10] Experience of the past four decades has vindicated this point of view.

This need to reform the relationship between democratic politics and the market economy is not driven purely by domestic tensions, important though they are. It is made more urgent by the rise of autocracy worldwide and, above all, by the apparent success of China's despotic capitalism. Western nations must improve their economic, social, and political performance in response.

Even though domestic reform is essential, if we are to strengthen the solidarity on which the health of all societies depends, reform cannot be limited to the domestic. No country is an island. Indeed, never before in history have we so clearly shared a common destiny on our fragile planet. This tribal species has created problems that its tribalism will only make worse. Any insistence on a narrow and exclusive national sovereignty, democratic or not, will fail to protect citizens. COVID-19 has demonstrated this. Trump declared "America First." But the pandemic has demonstrated that even a country as powerful as America cannot fix its problems on its own. The same is true, to a far greater extent, of climate.

We should want democracy, the market economy, and the spirit of free inquiry to thrive in a new age. Currently, they are not. In trying to decide what we must do, I can only distill lessons from the events of my lifetime and those that came before it. But the aim is clear: we must resolve, as Abraham Lincoln stated in the Gettysburg Address, that "government of the people, by the people, for the people, shall not perish from the earth." Democracy is always imperfect. But tyranny is never the answer. It is up to each generation to resist its siren song. This is not happening to the extent I once took for granted. On the contrary, many are succumbing.

I have dedicated this book to my six grandchildren, Zach, Rebecca, Alexander, Anna, Abigail, and Eden. Now in my seventy-sixth year, I cannot have many left. But the children can reasonably hope to see the twenty-second century. I fear for what the world might then look like. I recognize the dangers of environmental catastrophe and thermonuclear war. But I fear just as much that they will end up in an Orwellian world of lies and oppression. This is the world emerging in China and in many other countries, even in leading democracies.

The twentieth was a century of monstrous dictators. The dictators have returned, if not ones as monstrous as the worst of the previous century. But Xi Jinping is one, as is Vladimir Putin. Donald Trump, Narendra Modi, and Jair Bolsonaro are would-be dictators. Given the size of their populations and economies, these are five of the world's most important countries. With such leaders comes nightfall, for their goal is unbridled power. States that serve only power are a dead end. Humanity escaped that destiny in the twentieth century. But it was a close-run thing. Will it escape once again in the twenty-first?

———■———

CHAPTER ONE

The Fire This Time[1]

What we may be witnessing is not just the end of the
Cold War, or the passing of a particular period of
post-war history, but the end of history as such: that is,
the end point of mankind's ideological evolution
and the universalization of Western liberal democracy
as the final form of human government.
—*Francis Fukuyama*[2]

When Francis Fukuyama wrote his essay "The End of History?," published as the Cold War ended, in 1989, many agreed with him that the Western synthesis of liberal democracy with the free market had won a decisive victory over its ideological enemies. The end of the last totalitarian ideology seemed to many not just an extraordinary and surprising event, but one that promised a better future for humanity. The era of totalitarian coercion and mass murder was over. Freedom—political and economic—had won.

Neither liberal democracy nor free-market capitalism seems at all triumphant today. This is true not just in developing, emerging, or former communist countries, but even in established Western democracies. Economic failings have shaken faith in global capitalism. Political failings have undermined trust in liberal democracy. The ascent of China, whose ruling communist party has rejected the link between capitalism and democracy, has also shaken the confidence *of* the West and confidence *in* the West.

Liberal democracy and free-market capitalism are both now in question. On the nationalist right, Donald Trump in the US, Nigel Farage in the UK, Marine Le Pen in France, Matteo Salvini in Italy, Geert Wilders in the Netherlands, and Heinz-Christian Strache in Austria are shaping—or have shaped—political debate, even when not in power. Self-proclaimed "illiberal democrats"—a euphemism for authoritarians—have come to power in Hungary and Poland, two of the countries that benefited from the fall of the Soviet empire and the opportunity to enter the EU.[3] Following the political example of Vladimir Putin in Russia, Hungary's Viktor Orban and Poland's Jaroslaw Kaczynski set their embattled nations against the world and a purported "will of the people" against individual rights. These various leaders also object to at least one aspect (and frequently more than one) of contemporary global capitalism, be it free trade, free flows of capital, or relatively free movement of people. Inevitably, opposition to those things has also turned into suspicion of the European Union.

Crucially, the US possessed in Donald Trump a president who admired "strong men" and the politics of strong men, hated the free press, was indifferent to the survival of the Western alliance, intensely disliked the EU, was fiercely protectionist, and was happy to intervene arbitrarily in the decisions of individual businesses.[4] He had no ideological attachments to liberal democracy or free-market capitalism. He was populist, instinctively authoritarian, and nationalist. Worst of all, he promulgated the "big lie" that he won the November 2020 presidential election, which he lost by a large margin, thereby undermining the foundations of American democracy. Moreover, the US is not just any country: it is the creator of the post–Second World War liberal world order. Trump lacked the character, intellect, and knowledge needed to be president of a great democratic republic. His rise to power in 2016 and continuing influence over the Republican Party after his defeat in 2020 was (and remains) a worrying failure of the world's most important democracy.

This book will argue that economic disappointment is one of the chief explanations for the rise of left- and right-wing populism in high-income democracies.[5] Many point instead to cultural factors: status anxiety, religious belief, or outright racism. These are indeed important background conditions. But they would not have affected societies so deeply if the economy had performed better. Furthermore, many of these supposedly cultural changes are also related to what has been happening economically: the impact of deindustrialization on the labor force and the pressures of economic migration on established populations are among the important examples. People expect the economy to deliver reasonable levels of prosperity and opportunity to themselves and their children. When it does not, relative to those expectations, they become frustrated and resentful. That is what has happened. Many people in high-income countries condemn the global capitalism of the past three of four decades for these disappointing outcomes. Instead of delivering prosperity and steady progress, it has generated soaring inequality, dead-end jobs, and macroeconomic instability. Predictably, they frequently blame this disappointment on outsiders—minorities at home and foreigners. Thus, one of the points on which populists of both left and right agree is the need to limit international trade. Many also see a need to restrict the movement of capital and workers.

In short, the liberal democracy and global capitalism that were triumphant three decades ago have lost legitimacy. This matters, because these are respectively the political and economic operating systems of today's West. Democracy vests sovereignty in electorates defined by citizenship. Capitalism vests decision-making in owners and managers of private businesses engaged in global competition. The potential for conflict between these political and economic systems is self-evident: democratic politics are national, while market economics are global; and democratic politics are based on the egalitarian idea of one person, one vote, while market economics is founded on the inegalitarian idea that successful competitors reap the rewards.

Today, the synthesis of democracy and capitalism—"democratic capitalism"—is in crisis.[6] The nature of that crisis and what should be done in response to it are the central themes of this book. The discussion focuses on the fate of democratic capitalism in the West, though it is not limited to that, since the future of the West cannot be separated from what is happening in the rest of the world. But the West is the heartland of democratic capitalism. Meanwhile, China, the world's rising superpower, stands for a very different way of managing the links between political power and wealth generation, one we might call "authoritarian capitalism" or "bureaucratic capitalism." Elsewhere, we see the emergence in countries like Brazil, India, Turkey, or even Russia of what might be called "demagogic capitalism" or "demagogic autocratic capitalism." The Western system of democratic capitalism does, however, remain the world's most successful political and economic system, in terms of its proven ability to generate prosperity, freedom, and measured happiness. It has also survived great challenges in the past, notably in the 1930s and 1940s, and then again during the Cold War. But it now needs to change again. It must, above all, find a new equilibrium between the market economy and democratic politics. If it does not do so, liberal democracy may collapse.

What do I mean by the terms *democracy* and *capitalism*? By *democracy*, I mean its dominant contemporary form—universal suffrage, representative democracy.[7] Thus, those who want to limit or narrow suffrage are acting antidemocratically.

To be more complete, I mean by *democracy* what Fukuyama called "liberal democracy." The distinguished political scientist Larry Diamond, of the Hoover Institution, argues that liberal democracy has four individually necessary and collectively sufficient elements: free and fair elections; active participation of people, as citizens, in civic life; protection of the civil and human rights of all citizens equally; and a rule of law that binds all citizens equally.[8] All these elements are necessary and, in combination, sufficient to make a democracy liberal. Note the emphasis above on "citizens." A liberal democracy is exclusive: it includes citizens, but excludes noncitizens. This does not mean noncitizens—foreigners and immigrants—lack all rights; far from it. It means they lack the political rights of citizens.

Crucially, liberal democracy is *not* just a way of deciding who runs the state, though it is that: the term also defines the sort of state it is. As John Stuart Mill insisted in his *Considerations on Representative Government*, democracy is, or should be, characterized by "liberty of discussion, whereby not merely a few individuals in succession, but the whole public, are made, to a certain extent, participants in the government, and sharers in the instruction and mental exercise derived from it."[9] For a liberal democracy to work, then, citizens must be entitled to express their opinions, and fellow citizens must be prepared to tolerate opinions they disagree with and the people who hold them. In the terminology of Isaiah Berlin, as citizens, people enjoy *negative liberty*—the right to make up their own minds, free from coercion—and *positive liberty*—the right to participate in public life, including by voting.[10] Such a political system is inherently pluralist.[11] It cares about the political rights of minorities because it cares about the political rights of *all* citizens.

In essence, a liberal democracy is a competition for power between parties that accept the legitimacy of defeat. It is a "civilized civil war." Force is not permitted. But this means that winners do not seek to destroy the losers. A system in which gangsters seek to kill their opponents, trample on the rights of individuals, suppress the free press, and benefit financially from office, yet go through the motions of running rigged elections, is *not* liberal democracy. Nor is "illiberal democracy" democracy either.[12] Such a system should be called what it is: at best, a dictatorship of the majority, and at worst, "plebiscitary dictatorship." Putin's rule over Russia is a plebiscitary dictatorship, as is Erdogan's over Turkey and Orban's over Hungary. Indeed, increasingly these are just dictatorships, without qualification.

By *capitalism*, I mean an economy in which markets, competition, private economic initiative, and private property play central roles. This system is "market capitalism." The size, scope, and nature of government, with respect to regulatory intervention, taxation, and spending, vary across capitalist countries. Government intervention has also tended to intensify over time as societies became more democratic. This was inevitable, as the franchise widened to include people without significant assets. But it also reflected the growing complexity of economic life and the pervasiveness of what economists call "market imperfections"—situations in which market incentives may lead to socially or economically damaging results.

Yet, as was the case with "liberal democracy," the state, be it large and relatively intrusive or not, must be law-governed. Without the rule of law, there can be no market capitalism, just larceny. Moreover, capitalist economies, thus defined, are also (and have always been) open to global trade and capital flows, at least to some degree. Capitalism is never entirely national, because the wider world offers a host of opportunities for profitable exchange.

More narrowly, by *market capitalism* I mean the form of market economy that has emerged over the past seventy years and particularly over the past forty, for which the word *globalization* provides a shorthand description.[13] In their economic lives, just as in their political ones, people should possess *freedom from* arbitrary coercion, especially but not exclusively, from the state, and *freedom to* buy and sell their labor and anything else they may legitimately own. Again, as is also true in political life, such freedoms are not absolute, but must be bounded by regulatory, legislative, and constitutional limits.

The rule of law is an essential shared underpinning of democracy and capitalism because it protects the freedoms essential to both. This means that "all persons and authorities within the state, whether public or private, should be bound by and entitled to the benefit of laws publicly made, taking effect (generally) in the future and publicly administered in the courts."[14] If some individuals or institutions are above the law, nobody without such privileges can be secure in exercising their freedoms. The law must be universally binding and protecting if liberal democracy and market capitalism are to thrive.

Both liberal democracy and market capitalism share a core value: a belief in the value and legitimacy of human agency, in political and economic life. In these respects, both systems rest on "liberal" ideas. But the workability of democratic capitalism also depends on the presence of certain virtues in the population at large and especially in elites. Neither politics nor the economy will function without a substantial degree of honesty, trustworthiness, self-restraint, truthfulness, and loyalty to shared political, legal, and other institutions. In the absence of these virtues, a cycle of mistrust will corrode social, political, and economic relations.

In short, the political and economic systems depend for their success on the prevalence of fundamental norms of behavior or, as they are sometimes called, "social capital." Today, however, liberal democracy and market capitalism are individually sick, and the balance between them has broken. The last chapter of my previous book, *The Shifts and the Shocks*, on the global financial crisis, bore the title "The Fire Next Time."[15] The penultimate paragraph of that book argued that "the loss of confidence in the competence and probity of elites inevitably reduces trust in democratic legitimacy. People feel even more than before that the country is not being governed for them, but for a narrow segment of well-connected insiders who reap most of the gains and, when things go wrong, are not just shielded from loss but impose massive costs on everybody else. This creates outraged populism, on both the left and the right. Yet willingness to accept shared sacrifice is likely to be still more important in the years ahead than it was before the crisis. The economies of the Western world are poorer than they imagined ten years ago. They must look forward to a long period of retrenchment. Making that both be and appear fair matters."[16]

I was wrong: the fire is not next time; it is now. Moreover, COVID and the impact of Russia's war on Ukraine has made it burn even hotter. The fire is in substantial part the ignition of the slow-burning anger left by the last financial and economic crisis, coming, as that did, after a long period of mediocre performance and wrenching social changes in Western countries. Trump was a product of this process. He promised to drain the swamp, but, inevitably, made it an even worse quagmire. By his actions, his cynicism justified itself. It is conceivable that, as economies recover from the financial crisis and the pandemic, the fire will burn out. But that now seems almost inconceivable. Democratic global capitalism is caught between an unsatisfactory present and an even less satisfactory future of protectionism, populism, and plutocracy, culminating, possibly soon, in autocracy, most significantly in the US.

Restoring health to the Western system is among our biggest challenges. We may not succeed. But nothing good will be achieved if nothing is attempted. The rest of the book elaborates this argument. Part I analyzes the relationship between politics and economics and especially between democracy and capitalism, as I have defined them, in both theory and history. Part II goes on to examine what has gone wrong in the capitalist economy and the democratic polity, as a result of the closely connected rise of predatory capitalism and demagogic politics. Part III analyzes the reforms needed if we are to create a more inclusive and successful economy and healthier democracies. Part IV then looks at how a reinvigorated alliance of democratic capitalist states should engage in the world to defend themselves, promote their core values, and protect global peace, prosperity, and the planet. Finally, the Conclusion returns to the core issue, namely, the responsibility of elites for safeguarding the fragile achievements of democratic capitalism, before they disappear in an incoming tide of plutocratic populism and tyranny.

Part I

---◼---

ON CAPITALISM
AND DEMOCRACY

Prologue to Part I

Democracy and the market have something fundamental in common: the idea of equality of status. In a democracy, everybody has the right to a voice in public affairs. In a free market, everybody has the right to buy and sell what they own. Market economies, with supportive governments, have created enormous increases in wealth and economic opportunity. They have also transformed economic and political systems.

In premodern agrarian economies, it was usually straightforward to exclude the greater part of the population from any role in guiding the polity. Indeed, anything else was usually considered unthinkable. In a modern market economy, the reverse became the case. It became necessary or at least highly advisable to share power. This, then, is why the evolution of wealthy market economies has brought with it, albeit slowly and painfully, greater political inclusion, culminating in universal adult suffrage.

Over the past four decades, democracy has gone global. Never before have there been as many democracies and never before has the proportion of states that are democratic been as high as today. Unfortunately, this progress has stalled, partially even gone into reverse, since the early part of this century, in what is sometimes called "a democratic recession."

Chapter 2 looks at the underlying relationship between democracy and the market economy. Chapter 3 examines what has happened over the past two centuries in practice.

Symbiotic Twins: Politics and Economics in Human History

Man is by nature a political animal in a sense in which
a bee is not, or any other gregarious animal.
—*Aristotle*[1]

Economics provides the principal rationale for human cooperation. Politics provides the framework within which that cooperation works. Economics and politics are necessarily symbiotic.
What, then, is the relationship between market capitalism and liberal
democracy? The answer is that capitalism cannot survive in the long
run without a democratic polity, and democracy cannot survive in the
long run without a market economy. We might then think of market
capitalism and liberal democracy as the "complementary opposites"—
the "yin and yang"—of the world created by the market economy and
modern science and technology. They are married to each other. But
theirs is also a difficult marriage. Managing this productive, yet
fraught, relationship requires awareness of these realities. Why and
how this is so is the topic of this chapter.

How Economics and Politics Intertwine

The economy human beings have created is complex, adaptable, and innovative. Yet it exists to do something simple: provide the resources people need to thrive. We talk of "earning our living" for good reason. Since humans are imaginative, they also constantly redefine what a "living" is. It always means thriving within one's society. But today that no longer just means sufficient food, shelter, clothing, and heating. In the high-income economies of today, it includes a range of goods and services unimaginable to anybody born two centuries ago. One estimate suggests that today we have access to something of the order of ten billion different goods and services.[2]

All the resources on which the human economy depends come from our planet and sun: the economy is embedded in nature, a truth that economists foolishly forgot. Yet the economy is also embedded in human society. By cooperating, human beings can support themselves and their families vastly better than they would be able to do on their own. That has been true since our hunter-gatherer ancestors. Cooperation allowed humans to create a complex division of labor and outcompete other animals far stronger and faster than they are.

The historian Ian Morris of Stanford University has provided estimates of "energy capture" per head for advanced societies.[3] His data suggest that two economic revolutions have occurred since Homo sapiens emerged in Africa some 200,000–300,000 years ago.[4] The first was the slow shift from hunter-gatherer to agricultural economies. The second was the far swifter shift from predominantly agricultural to industrial economies. The agricultural revolution increased energy capture per head roughly sevenfold at its peak, relative to preagrarian societies. By 2000, the industrial revolution had raised energy capture per head another sevenfold relative to the agrarian past (see figure 1). In 2022, the human economy supported 7.9 billion people (and rising), up from roughly 1 billion in 1800 at the dawn of the industrial revolution, and maybe just 4 million 10,000 years ago at the dawn of the agricultural revolution. The recent increase in energy capture, driven by our extraction of fossilized sunlight, as opposed to the incident sunlight that drove preindustrial economies, is also why we now have a climate problem.

FIGURE 1. ENERGY CAPTURE PER HEAD AND PER DAY (KILOCALORIES)
(Source: Ian Morris)

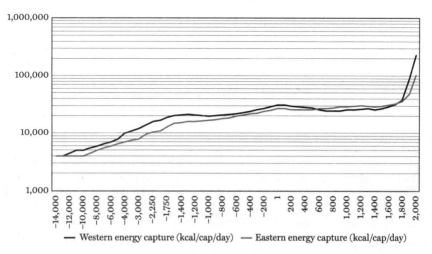

— Western energy capture (kcal/cap/day)   — Eastern energy capture (kcal/cap/day)

Humans have prospered mightily, while other primates have not: the planet contains fewer than 300,000 chimpanzees, 200,000 western gorillas, and 70,000 orangutans.[5] Human beings and the livestock they rear make up 96 percent of the mass of all mammals on the planet.[6] Life on earth, it is argued, has entered a "sixth extinction," with extinction rates thought to be 100 to 1,000 times higher than their background rate over the past tens of millions of years.[7] We can even think of the human economy as a giant cuckoo's hatchling now crowding many other species out of the planetary nest, while also fouling the nest itself, via climate change.

In its own terms, the modern human economy has been an astounding success. It has not only supported an ever-rising population (figure 2), but has given individual humans a far higher average standard of living than ever before (figure 3).[8] Between 1820 and 2008,

FIGURE 2. WORLD POPULATION (MILLIONS; SPLINE INTERPOLATION UNTIL 1950)
(Source: Our World in Numbers)

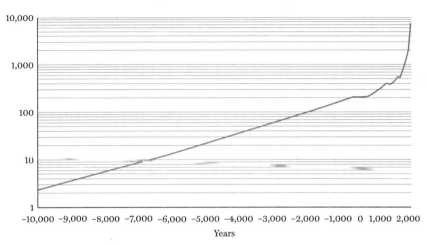

the human economy expanded more than seventyfold, in real terms.[9] This expansion in human economic activity also brought enormous increases in inequality among countries: some prospered; others did not. In 1820, the average real income of the richest country in the world was about five times that of the poorest. By 2017, the ratio of average real income in the richest large country (the US) to the poorest (the Democratic Republic of the Congo) was 70 to 1.[10]

FIGURE 3. GDP PER HEAD
(PURCHASING POWER PARITY; 1990 INTERNATIONAL DOLLARS)
(Source: Maddison Project; Conference Board)

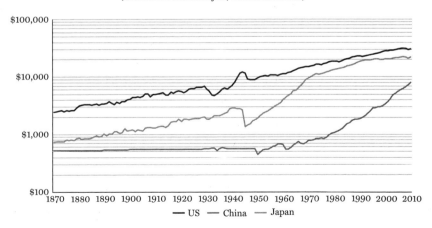

The three epochs of the human economy have come with distinct forms of social organization. The essential characteristic of the ancestral hunter-gatherer bands was cooperation through custom and personal relationships, that of the most powerful agrarian states was cooperation through coercion and hierarchy, and that of the most successful modern economies is cooperation through decentralized competition and democratic consent.

In a hunter-gatherer band, politics and economics fused. It was a large family. In this world, territory was readily available and access to it was either uncontrolled or managed by sanctified custom. Little permanent or fixed property existed and most property was personal (tools, weapons, clothing, and ornaments). Decision-making was informal and fluid, though some—the wiser, the more intelligent, the braver, and the more skilled—had more authority and influence than others. Such a band worked because everybody knew who belonged, was entitled to its protection, and could be trusted. The primary group was an extended family, including those taken in through marriage. To break the band's rules and customs was to risk banishment—a terrifying sanction.

Humanity's most remarkable characteristic is the ability to turn what it has imagined—gods, tribes, states, nations, money, companies—into social reality.[11] Our world is full of entities that are both real and invisible. "France" is an idea or, more precisely, many ideas. So is "God," "the gods," "the law," "the dollar," "the president," "Exxon," and "the Treaty of Rome." Humans may live in the physical world, like other animals, but their imagination gives the social world that controls our interaction with the physical world its form and movement. The first such imagined social and political entities were the tribes into which hunter-gatherer bands merged. A tribe was thought of as a family writ large. To give the tribe reality, people imagined the presence of long-dead ancestors.[12] These, then, were the first of humanity's "imagined communities." Nation-states are the predominant contemporary exemplars.[13]

Agriculture brought a far more complex division of labor and more sophisticated ideas, roles, and institutions. The details depended on the technology, terrain, reliance on trade, nature of warfare, and religious ideas. Behind the diversity, however, a remorseless logic drove the development of these new states: valuable and relatively immovable resources—workers, land, crops, irrigation systems, and stores of food—needed to be protected from bandits, external and internal. Agriculture also generated the resources needed to support the people providing that security, who inevitably became both protectors and predators.[14] The bigger and richer the states they created, the greater the power, wealth, and glory of these predatory protectors. Even if a state had no desire for expansion, it was vulnerable to others who did. War became a semipermanent activity of agrarian states. Not surprisingly, their leaders were also often warriors.

■ ■ ■

The late S. E. Finer suggested there are four potential players in the resulting games of domestic power: "the palace" (the royal house and its servants); "the nobility" (generally both landowners and warriors); "the church" in some form (as a source of religious legitimacy); and, finally, "the forum" (the body of citizens).[15] The palace polity was the predominant form. The great empires—the Persian, Chinese, and Roman—became the pinnacles of monarchical power. Agrarian states were also mostly "patrimonial": they were thought of as the property of the ruler and his family.[16] Wealth was concentrated in the hands of the royal family, though senior officials, priests, soldiers, and noble landowners often shared in the spoils. The most important of the nobles were also often close relatives of the monarch.

Human and animal labor provided the motive power for the economy. Thus, those at the top of society lived off the forced labor of those below them, the heavily taxed peasants, serfs tied to the soil, and slaves. Slavery was not an invention of European colonizers, as some seem to imagine. It was a nigh on universal institution. Stanford's Walter

Scheidel argues that such "pre-modern states generated unprecedented opportunities for the accumulation and concentration of material resources in the hands of the few, both by providing a measure of protection for commercial activities and by opening up new sources of personal gain for those most closely associated with the exercise of political power."[17] The degree of inequality frequently reached the limit set by the need to leave the laboring poor with a subsistence income.[18]

These societies, then, were often almost as unequal as it was possible for them to be. Given these inequalities, the shift from the hunter-gatherer band to the agrarian state probably led to a lower standard of living and more cramped lives for the great mass of the people. But it also led to the survival of far more people. Once the agrarian revolution had occurred, there was no way back. Traditional hunter-gatherers were driven onto marginal land, conquered, or wiped out. Mounted nomads, in contrast, were able to develop effective predation on agrarian societies. Think of the Scythians, Huns, and Mongols, who descended on their horses from the Eurasian grasslands onto the settled populations to their south and west.

As Finer notes, the states of the agrarian societies were not identical. In some cases, their army consisted of the entire body of adult freemen (as in some of the city-states of ancient Greece and republican Rome). Such armies could constrain the centralization of power, at least for a while, and so create the "forum polities." A merchant class (notably in the prosperous "free cities" of Italy and northern Europe) was another potential constraint, particularly if the state depended on the taxes it could raise from these wealth creators and the latter operated across frontiers. Religious authority (such as that of the Roman Catholic Church) could provide yet another barrier to absolute power, particularly if the priests determined the monarch's legitimacy. Not coincidentally, the Western democracies originated out of medieval polities characterized by a complex balance of power among the palace, church, nobility, and free cities, with no ruler able to establish a centralized empire similar to the old Roman Empire.[19]

Any legal constraint imposed on the king could benefit ordinary people (in principle and, to some extent, even in practice), as well as the aristocrats. The Roman Republic—the paradigmatic forum polity— had elected officials and a precise division of power, with two holders of each magistracy, except in extreme crises, when an all-powerful "dictator" was chosen. A different version of the idea of representation emerged from a rebellion against the English king Henry III, led by Simon de Montfort. This resulted in the summoning of a parliament, which included not just the nobility, but representatives of "the commons" (two knights from each shire and two burgesses from each borough), in 1264.[20] In the seventeenth century, that parliament was strong and legitimate enough to defeat the monarchy in a civil war and execute the king. The representative parliament created the foundations on which modern representative democracies could ultimately be built.

England's subsequent role as world-girdling imperial power and first industrial country turned these developments in a small island on the western edge of Eurasia into events of global significance. They contributed to the birth of modern forms of democratic governance. Parliaments and the political parties that accompany them professionalized politics. They also facilitated the emergence of democratic rule in large and populous states. On these foundations—professional government, a rule of law, and electoral politics—today's liberal democracies were ultimately built.

How Market Capitalism Succeeded

The driving force behind the transformation in prosperity over the past two centuries was an economy that rewarded people for developing new commercial ideas in competition with one another. This was the system of "creative destruction" described by the Austrian economist Joseph Schumpeter.[21] A crucial element was the emergence of a fully monetized economy. The contemporary notion of an "industrious revolution" that preceded the industrial revolution is founded on the idea that households increasingly participated in market transactions for the sale of their labor in return for money, which then allowed them to purchase the commodities they needed. The existence of such markets made possible a reduction in the self-sufficiency of households, encouraging specialization and so creating ever greater market demand.[22] Policy makers also consciously created some particularly important markets, notably those in land and labor.[23]

As these markets developed, the old practices of forced labor became increasingly redundant. After long struggles, serfdom and slavery were both abolished. This was a huge and undeniable advance in human freedom, though in places where slavery coincided with a color bar, the liberation remained incomplete, as in the southern states of the US, where it was transformed into a division of caste. In time, even the age-old subordination of women began to erode, as they gained economic independence and political rights.

A large part of the debate on what began the rapid growth of the modern era is of the "how many angels can dance on the head of a pin?" variety. Some, for example, emphasize the availability of resources.[24] Others emphasize institutions.[25] Others emphasize ideas about what people are entitled to do as well as about what works.[26] Yet others emphasize changing prices of factors of production, notably of labor.[27] Others again point to racialized slavery, as both an institution and an extreme form of exploitation. Yet the notion that there should be just one cause seems absurd. Ideas animate institutions. They also show people how to exploit resources, including human resources. This said, the marriage of the market to technology was crucial. The industrial transformation it caused was a great turning point in human economic history.

The socially and economically destabilizing rise of the market economy brought forth, in reaction, an alternative ideology, that of the socialist planned economy. The twentieth century delivered a decisive test of the merits of the market economy against the planned socialist alternative. It was not a test of some form of "pure" market capitalism against a planned alternative. On the contrary, capitalism had itself evolved, with the rise of welfare states and active developmental states. But the contrast between the economic performances of West Germany and East Germany, North Korea and South Korea, western Europe and eastern Europe, Taiwan and Maoist China proved decisive. It even persuaded the Soviet and Chinese communists themselves. Mikhail Gorbachev's "perestroika" and Deng Xiaoping's "reform and opening up" were the result. Deng knew well what he was doing and why. He looked at Hong Kong, Singapore, South Korea, and Taiwan and realized that this was the path China itself needed to follow.

History proved him spectacularly correct. Without the market, economies can generate neither the information nor the incentives needed to be dynamic. It was, accordingly, only after Deng's reforms that China began its staggering economic progress (see figure 3). Much the same is true of India's slow reforms in the 1980s and far faster reforms in the 1990s. In neither case did a competitive domestic economy exist prior to the reforms—in China not at all and in India only to a limited extent, given the stifling restrictions on business activity (the so-called Permit Raj, or License Raj).[28] The dynamic market economy, increasingly open to the world, proved a remarkable engine for sustained advance.

In sum, market capitalism drove economic growth. It started in countries that supplied enough of the basic preconditions for such a revolution: stable property rights; a commitment to scientific and technical progress; and a belief in the right of everybody in the country (initially only white men, but ultimately everybody) to make their way in the world on their merits.[29] This, then, began a process of rising output per head, unequally shared but still shared quite widely in the countries where that revolution began. This was an economic and social revolution that unfolded and spread over the succeeding centuries. It was brutal and exploitative. It was also transformative.

How Market Capitalism Married
Liberal Democracy

In the more economically successful countries, the rise of the market economy generated growing pressures for universal suffrage democracy. It is impossible to believe so profound a political transformation, from the societies run by monarchs and aristocrats of the eighteenth century to the universal suffrage democracies of the twentieth, was a mere accident. So why did this happen? The answers come in terms of ideology, aspirations, empowerment, elite self-interest, and finally, influence.

First, *ideology*. However different they may seem from each other, market capitalism and liberal democracy rest on the same underlying philosophical values. As Larry Siedentop argues, "Western beliefs privilege the idea of equality—of a premise that excludes permanent inequalities of states and ascriptions of authoritative opinion to any person or group—which underpins the secular state and the idea of fundamental or 'natural' rights. Thus, the only birth-right recognized by the liberal tradition is individual freedom."[30] The core belief underpinning a market economy is the right of individuals to change jobs, create businesses, lend and borrow money, and spend how and where they wish. It is an individualistic creed.

Historically, most civilized states rejected this notion of equality of status. Those with power were held to be inherently superior to those without it, as white southerners believed in relation to their enslaved Africans. Moreover, access to power brought wealth, while the absence of power guaranteed poverty. Even if, occasionally, people without political power achieved wealth, perhaps as merchants, they were always at risk of having it seized by a monarch or lord. Power and wealth were intimately connected, and both were frequently the fruit of ascribed, not earned, status. This was particularly true when ownership of land (and so control over the people who worked it) was simultaneously the principal fruit of power and the chief source of wealth. The erosion of the idea of ascribed status in the modern society and economy changed all this. It took too long for that to become evident. But it did do so, in the end.

Crucially, once the notion of the equality of legal status had replaced the old one of the sanctity of inherited status, it became far more difficult to limit political rights. If all adult men (or, as was later understood, all adult men and women) had equal rights to read and learn, buy and sell, innovate and prosper and so benefit themselves, how could they not also have equal rights of political representation?[31] Attempts were long made to limit suffrage on grounds of wealth, race, or gender. But all of these demarcations came to seem arbitrary. Everybody should be entitled to a voice in politics because everybody is affected by political decisions, and everybody has interests to defend.

A limited franchise will always seem arbitrary and oppressive. What one would have is rule by the wealthiest or most powerful, not the "best," unless one accepts the beneficiaries' biased view of who are the best. Being arbitrary and unfair, the resulting franchise will fail to obtain the consent of the governed. The wider the franchise, the more oppressive the remaining restrictions become: how, for example, could one justify the denial of the vote to an educated woman when an uneducated man had it? How, similarly, could such rights be ascribed arbitrarily only to people of a certain skin color? That was transparently ridiculous. The obvious locus of sovereignty is *the adult population as a whole*, exercising its power either through direct votes or through indirect votes (via representative parliaments) or through lots (sortition).[32]

The shared idea underlying both the market and democracy is the right of people to shape their own lives wherever choices need to be made, individually and collectively. That does not guarantee equality of achievement or outcome. In a democratic political system, power is not distributed equally, and in a market economy, wealth is most certainly not distributed equally. Yet those with political power are *accountable to* citizens, not just (as the Chinese Communist Party and, before it, the Chinese imperial state believed) *responsible for* them. Similarly, those who participate in markets must respond to the decisions of customers. Thus, the market and democracy both rest on the proposition that people's choices have inherent value. This ideal of equality of status among all adult citizens is one of the great moral and practical achievements of democratic modernity.

Second, *aspirations*. As Benjamin Friedman of Harvard University has argued, "a rising standard of living fosters openness, tolerance and democracy."[33] With machines doing much of the physical labor, the age-old exploitation of the drudgery of others became increasingly unnecessary. Serfdom and slavery, being no longer economically necessary, as well as increasingly abhorrent, were ultimately abolished. This general rise in prosperity also created a more self-confident and better-educated population that was increasingly unwilling to be subject to the political whims of those with higher ascribed status or greater wealth. In the UK, for example, the resulting political changes began with the demands of the middle classes for parliamentary representation, which was largely achieved in the Great Reform Act of 1832.[34] In the US, property qualifications for white men started to be eliminated even earlier.[35] As people became better off, their aims also changed. Instead of a life concerned mainly with survival, they became increasingly interested in securing more rewarding lives for themselves and their families. This aspiration naturally included a desire for a voice in social and political life. The formation of social groups in which people increasingly had the time to participate also strengthened the political salience of such desires.

Third, *empowerment*. The social upheavals associated with the market revolution included mass urbanization, the development of factories, and the rise of an organized working class. The institutions that emerged from this upheaval, notably trade unions, played a political role that had been impossible for the peasantry, who were scattered over the land and ceaselessly and brutally suppressed by the landowning warrior class and its parasitic descendants. The new groupings also acted to protect themselves from the injustice, and insecurity associated with the rise of the capitalist economy. They found much of that protection in democratic politics.[36]

Fourth, *elite self-interest*. Industrialized warfare was another fruit of the industrial revolution. States needed motivated and literate soldiers and, they discovered, also the labor of women, who became the "home front" in both world wars. The need for—and possibility of—full mobilization of the population dramatically accelerated the shift toward universal adult suffrage. In many countries, not coincidentally, female suffrage directly followed the First World War. The new economy also demanded an educated workforce. This meant not just education, but education in "national values." In this way, nationalism played a crucial role in the creation of a modern state and economy. Over time, the spread of education led to the widespread dissemination of newspapers and the creation of a politically engaged populace. The expansion of education could also be justified politically. Thus, Lord Sherbrooke, a British aristocratic politician of the nineteenth century, responded to the passing of the Reform Act of 1867, which greatly widened the franchise, by arguing that "it will be absolutely necessary that you should prevail on our future masters [the newly enfranchised] to learn their letters."[37] This notion was popularly summarized as "We must educate our masters." The education promoted for such reasons was, in turn, essential to rising prosperity.

Yet, elite self-interest could cut both ways. While there were indeed powerful forces working toward democratization in the industrializing economies of the nineteenth and early twentieth centuries, democratization was not the universal outcome; far from it. The contrast between the United Kingdom and Germany is particularly striking, though a similar contrast exists between northern and southern Europe. Harvard's Daniel Ziblatt notes the point that "the relationship between a pre-existing concentration of social power, on the one hand,

and inclusive political democracy, on the other, is inherently tension ridden." The difference between the successful transitions and the failures was "the ability of old-regime elites to forge a strong 'conservative political party,' a party that represents their interests in the new regime." This, he concludes, "is an essential factor in democratic development."[38] The ability and willingness of oligarchies to create and sustain effective political coalitions while tolerating genuine democracy is central to the story in this book. This is not an outdated story. On the contrary, it is very much the story of today.

Finally, *influence*. The great power of the nineteenth century was the UK, and the great power of the twentieth century was the US, both of which were liberal societies, at least in principle, economically and politically. The progress of these powers toward universal suffrage liberal democracy, though halting, slow, and difficult (and in the case of African Americans disgraceful), was largely internally driven. Their military power in turn determined the outcomes of the two world wars and the Cold War. The US was able to force radical political changes on Germany and Japan. It failed, alas, in post–Soviet Russia, where the changes were far shallower than in post–World War II Germany and Japan, because the Soviet defeat had been peaceful, and the country was never occupied.

While market-driven economic advances created powerful forces in favor of the emergence of democratic political rights, this outcome might not have been inevitable. Without the First World War, would an authoritarian German Empire have continued its economic advance, or would the further development of its economy have led to democratization? The latter is at least quite plausible. After all, we have seen the emergence of (fairly) liberal democracies out of authoritarianism more recently, in the case of Taiwan and South Korea, both also highly economically successful. The Communist Party of China is betting on the opposite, however, namely that market-driven prosperity will reinforce, rather than undermine, the rule of an autocratic party. It is too soon to tell whether this will be true. Successful

Chinese capitalists might in the long run exercise some influence in favor of legal and civil rights, even in China, perhaps because the economy turns out to stagnate under the growing repression of the Xi regime. Alternatively, the exercise of arbitrary state power might ruin its market capitalism.

Marriage of Markets to Democracy— for Better or Worse

It is no accident, then, that the high-income democracies have market economies, just as it was no accident that market economies brought forth universal suffrage democracy. But this marriage between these complementary opposites—the self-seeking of competitive markets to the collective decision-making of democracy—is always fragile. Above all, the survival of liberal democracy depends on the separation of control over economic resources from political power. Being hugely rich must be neither a necessary nor a sufficient condition for holding political power; and similarly, in a competitive market economy holding political power must be neither a necessary nor a sufficient condition for acquiring wealth. Just expressing it this way indicates how fragile such a system has to be. But it also indicates how different these relationships are from those in the hierarchical societies of old, in which wealth and power were two sides of one coin.

It is easy to see why the separation of power from wealth must hold by considering the opposite possibility. Suppose that wealth comes from gaining political power directly or from the favors of those who possess it. Then this can no longer be a competitive market economy in which wealth comes from success in attracting and serving customers. Wealth will come instead from being powerful or serving the powerful. This will become "crony capitalism" or "connections capitalism," in which the political system is exploited for the personal gain of the powerful and their relatives, favorites, and supporters. Now suppose, alternatively, that wealth buys office or the support of those who hold office. Then the political system will be a plutocracy, not a democracy. These plutocrats will surely destroy the competitive market economy, too: the one thing they will not tolerate is upstart competitors. Thus, democratic capitalism demands the separation of power from wealth and so of politics from the economy (and vice versa). Where this separation has not worked, as in so many emerging and developing countries, neither democratic politics nor the market economy tends to thrive: being so closely intertwined, the political and economic systems strangle each other.

There are two main ways in which this delicate balance between politics and market can be destroyed: state control over the economy, and capitalist control over the state.

The extreme form of state control over the economy is socialism, defined here as a system in which the state owns, and the government controls, the principal means of production. Those who control the government will also control *all* economically valuable resources. In such a society, competitive politics will be impossible. If people are to act politically, they need resources of their own (individually or collectively) as well as the ability to influence and inform public opinion. If that is to happen, there need to be independent media organizations. The independence from government control implied by these preconditions for competitive democracy demands a plural market economy, with legally protected private property.[39]

Socialism makes this impossible. Those who control the state will also control the economy. Since they will control both the economy and the government, they will control politics. There can then be no fair competition either *for* political power or *in* economic activity. Thus, the idea of a socialist democracy is a chimera, a will-o'-the-wisp. Such a combination of economic and political power will end up, sooner or later, like the Venezuela of Hugo Chavez and Nicolas Maduro or the Soviet state. Even in China, arbitrary state power makes all private property insecure and so threatens the market economy.

The motivations of those who hold power also matter. In a market economy, loss of power does not necessarily mean loss of wealth or income: one can always work in the private sector, possibly for higher pay. But if the state controls the wealth, the powerful cannot afford to lose power, because there is no private sector for them to go to. The stakes of democratic politics become too high if there is not a large economic sphere independent of politics. Instead of a civilized civil war, politics then becomes a war of survival. Moreover, the holders of power in a socialist state must also find it relatively easy to prevent such a loss of power, because they control all aspects of the economy. Full socialism is inherently antidemocratic and anticompetitive. This is because, at bottom, it is yet another system in which political power and control over valuable resources are fused.

Socialism is an extreme example of state control. But any elected leader who manages to subvert the legal and regulatory institutions that police the borderline between politics and the economy can gain effective control of the state's wealth, as well as the wealth of what then becomes only a notionally private sector. This leads to the crony capitalism evident in Putin's Russia or Orban's Hungary. In such a system the ruler can neither risk losing power nor, without a coup or abdication, be deprived of it, since he controls the machinery of politics and the wealth of the country. In such a system, the private economy exists on the sufferance of the state. It has no independent existence.

The second route to disaster is the opposite, not the capture of the economy by those who control the state, but the capture of the state by those who control the economy. What happens is, yet again, a fusion of economic and political power, but this time it comes from the former to the latter rather than from the latter to the former. Plutocracy is the natural outcome of a form of predatory capitalism that generates huge inequalities of income and wealth. As wealth and economic power become increasingly concentrated, liberal democracy inevitably comes under threat, as is happening today, particularly in the US, the most important democracy of all. But as plutocracy rises, there is also a good chance that the people will elect an autocrat, who turns out to be more rapacious and brutal than any of those plutocrats. In this way, plutocracy can result in autocracy. There are many contemporary examples. In sum, capitalism may lead to democracy, as argued in the previous section, but may then destroy it.

In sum, competitive markets do indeed protect democratic politics. This does not mean that economic and political freedoms are the same: the freedom to transact is different from the freedom to act politically. It is the difference between the right of people to influence what happens by engaging in, or disengaging from, a market (sometimes called "exit") and the right of people to influence what happens by expressing their opinion (sometimes called "voice").[40] These are two aspects of freedom—the freedom to make choices in the economy and the freedom to act in politics. But the two kinds of freedom are connected. It is no accident that competitive electoral politics occur only in countries with legally protected private economic activity. Democratic capitalism, always fragile, is the only form of democracy we are likely to see.

A degree of separation of the economic from the political systems and their protection from each other by independent institutions, accepted norms, and binding rules is a necessary condition for either system to function properly. Thus, these two partners in the marriage of capitalism with democracy need each other. But they must also allow each other a properly independent existence. It is this fragile balance that needs to be maintained if either is to thrive and their fusion—democratic capitalism—is to survive.

Making the Difficult Marriage Work

In their book *The Narrow Corridor*, Daron Acemoglu and James Robinson offer a complementary perspective on the fragile balances that allow a free society to work.[41] The challenge, they argue, is created by the need for a state—the "Leviathan" in the terminology of the seventeenth-century political philosopher Thomas Hobbes—strong enough to provide security and protection to the people, but not so strong as to deprive them of their freedoms. There is, then, a narrow corridor between the two extremes where the interaction between the state and civil society works. It is where a "shackled," but strong, Leviathan and an engaged civil society exist side by side.[42] In other words, it is the liberal democracy discussed above.

Consider how societies may depart from this corridor. At one extreme, the departure will go toward a more "despotic Leviathan," which controls everything and crushes civil society. In such a polity, there may be notionally private businesses, but they exist only on sufferance, because Leviathan grants no rights, only privileges that may be withdrawn at will. The most prominent contemporary example of such a state is China. At the other extreme, the state is what Acemoglu and Robinson call a "paper Leviathan." A paper Leviathan is both ineffective and oppressive. It fails to provide the essential services needed by the public, while its capacities are at the service of a predatory elite. Many Latin American countries fall into this category.

Paper Leviathans are quite similar to "neopatrimonial" states, that is, ones in which political power gives control over almost all the surplus generated by the economy. Putin's Russia is a neopatrimonial state.[43] That has also been the story of many postcolonial countries, especially those possessing "point source" (and so relatively controllable) commodities, such as oil and gas. In those cases, political power has given a privileged few the access to the bulk of the country's surplus wealth: think Angola or Nigeria. The results have been poor economic performance, extreme inequality, unstable polities, and dictatorships. Again, those with power cannot afford to lose elections in such economies, since their livelihoods depend on holding on to it. This is a recipe for unstable and violent politics. Too much is at stake for any other form of politics.

In the modern era, communist states have been the principal examples of despotic Leviathans. The hypercentralized Soviet version failed and ultimately collapsed. But the Chinese answer—an updated form of the age-old Chinese bureaucratic polity, alongside a form of market capitalism—appears to thrive, at least for the moment. As such, it may seem to offer the most credible alternative to democratic capitalism. But two essential qualifications must be made: the Chinese state has a unique history, and the economy is still quite poor. It is very unlikely that the Chinese model will be relevant elsewhere, except perhaps in Vietnam.

Several important aspects of the fragility of democratic capitalism are illuminated by this perspective. The first and most obvious is that democracy and a dynamic market economy depend on the existence of a shackled Leviathan—that is, a law-governed and effective state. The second is that there will be no shackled Leviathan without a balance between the political (democratic) and economic (market) aspects of civil society's engagement with the state. The third is that creating and sustaining the politics and economics of a shackled Leviathan is difficult and rare: having elections or liberalizing the economy is far from enough. That is why many attempts at democracy have failed. The last is that one of the most plausible ways for a society to leave the narrow corridor, in either direction, is for the balance between the state, people, and economy to break down. The walls keeping power and wealth apart may crumble, delivering plutocracy, demagogy, or autocracy, and so a departure from the narrow corridor.

How, in practice, have countries managed to stay in the narrow corridor? The answer is by compromise and cooperation among the social, economic, and political actors in democratic capitalism. Four aspects of this process of compromise and cooperation are particularly significant.

First, capitalist competition is *not* a free-for-all. A free-for-all is a synonym for gangsterism: Russia under Boris Yeltsin, for example. Proper market competition requires active cooperation in agreeing to the rules of the game. Politics are not the only way to set those rules. Many are set by actors in civil society via pressure from activists, employee trade unions, shareholders, or the media. But many of the rules of a complex modern economy are set by the state. It follows that these have to be set by a state that is not captured by the most powerful actors in the economy.

Second, the rules of the game are necessarily complex and evolving. They include the rules that created and then govern the most important actors in the contemporary market economy—corporations. They also include the rules governing the operation of markets: property rights, including intellectual property rights; labor markets; capital markets; competition and monopoly; environmental protection; international trade; and so on and so forth. Moreover, many of these rules take the form of regulations created and run by independent bureaucracies. As the economy has become more complex and intrusive, and politics have become more democratic and demanding, these rules and regulations have, inevitably and rightly, become more onerous. Yet they also may create excessive costs. Getting this balance right is an essential part of modern politics.

Third, a vast number of these rules are agreed upon internationally, to reflect the inescapably cross-border nature of a market economy. Competitive capitalism is global capitalism. The need for international agreement was already understood in the nineteenth century. Today, there exists a vast number of internationally agreed rules that reflect the countless international repercussions of economic activity. The UK, for example, has signed over 14,000 treaties, many of which have economic implications.[44] Internationally agreed rules govern trade, banking and finance, intellectual property, product standards, travel, transport, telecommunications, the mail, the internet, and a host of other activities. Democratic accountability is essential. But sovereignty does not mean absolute control, because sovereignty ends at the border, even for superpowers.

Finally, and probably most crucially, a democratic electorate will

demand a degree of economic security. The idea that economic outcomes will be a matter of indifference to the public at large will not
survive in a universal suffrage democracy. People will demand insurance against unemployment, ill health, and old age. They will expect
the state to help educate their children. They will demand laws that
protect them from exploitation. They will expect action to limit macroeconomic instability. They will want the state to impose a limit to
inequality of outcomes. Not least, they will expect the most economically successful and affluent to pay substantial taxes. Universal
suffrage democracy leads to a big government by the standards of the
nineteenth century. Such governments are consistent with the survival
of competitive capitalism. The libertarian version of capitalism is,
however, incompatible with universal suffrage democracy. People who
want the former must openly admit their opposition to the latter.

Lessons from the Ancients on Democratic Fragility

We can also learn from the ancient Greeks about the fragility of democracy. Some of their most famous authors were hostile to the idea
of rule by the uneducated masses. This is the argument of Plato's
Republic.[45]

We do not have to agree with Plato's conservative perspective or
his belief in philosopher kings (so similar to Confucianism), to realize
that his warnings about oligarchy, democracy, demagogy, and tyranny
are relevant to today's very different world. Plato argued that a reaction against a certain sort of oligarchy (plutocracy) risks turning democracy into tyranny. This is arguably what we witnessed in the US
under the presidency of Donald Trump.[46] Similar things have been
happening in other countries.

More precisely, Plato argued that ordinary people would seek a
protector against the wealthy. How would such a "protector" behave?

"[H]aving a mob entirely at his disposal, he is not restrained from shedding the blood of kinsmen; by the favorite method of false accusation he brings them into court and murders them; . . . some he kills and others he banishes, at the same time hinting at the abolition of debts and partition of lands; and after this, what will be his destiny? Must he not either perish at the hands of his enemies, or from being a man becomes a wolf—that is a tyrant."[47]

Plato's argument is (predictably) conservative.[48] Yet, underneath his antidemocratic prejudices lies a point that is correct. Very often the future tyrant presents himself (they have almost always been men) as the protector of the people against its enemies. Julius Caesar, the military despot whose heir (Octavian, later Augustus) terminated the Roman Republic, was leader of the popular party ("populares"), the party supposedly favoring the plebeians. As Plato warned, the "protector" of the people (his heir, in fact) then became the wolf.

Plato's idea that insecurity and fear are gateways to tyranny are correct. Stable, prosperous societies are unlikely to succumb to despotism from within, though they may be conquered from without. But societies riven by internal conflicts are quite likely to fall before a tyrant. In practice, as Plato also notes, the fear is often of the domestic elite or at least elements of that elite. The people then turn to someone who presents himself as their protector. But this protector is often an empty human being consumed with ambition.[49] Vested with power by the people, he turns himself into a despot. Historically, such a "protector" has often been a war leader, or at least a general—that is, a "man on a white horse" (Caesar, Napoleon, Francisco Franco, and so forth).[50]

I have labeled the approach to politics that brought Trump to power "pluto-populism"—the exploitation of populist themes for plutocratic ends.[51] Trump is a logical outcome of the pluto-populism of the Republican Party. He captured the party in the name of the people. Yet whether Trump started out as servant or opponent of the plutocracy (he was in fact both), his core characteristic had always been rejection of constraints. Such a leader is as old as democracy itself. Plato would have recognized him at once as just another example of the demagogue as purported "protector" and would-be tyrant.

Aristotle, too, was suspicious of democracy.[52] By this, he meant a system in which the will of the people was unconstrained. We might call that system "demagogy," "illiberal democracy," or "tyranny of the majority." For Aristotle, the system we have, with representative elections, constitutional protections, and individual rights, would not be democracy. Supporters of liberal democracy should, however, agree with Aristotle that a system in which "the will of the people," as expressed in a vote on a particular date, is the final word, forever, is not liberal democracy.[53] It is rather a road to tyranny—a plebiscitary dictatorship, to be more precise. Constitutional constraints on temporary majorities are not antidemocratic, but an essential safeguard of democracy.

As both Plato and Aristotle noted, great inequality conflicts with the egalitarian premises of democratic government. This makes plutocracy—a system neither of these philosophers favored—a threat to democracy. But the ancient authors (by definition, members of a literate elite) also complained about the irresponsibility of the demagogues whom ordinary people favored. Similar rhetoric comes from conservatives today, when they protest against the irresponsibility of excessive "entitlement spending," exorbitant taxation, and the potential bankruptcy of the state. These are age-old lines of conflict in states with highly unequal distributions of income and some form of democratic constitution.

Democratic Capitalism and National Identity

Democratic capitalism (the combination of liberal democracy with market capitalism) has proved a good answer—indeed, an inspiring one—to the challenges of creating trust-based economies and politics in which personal freedom and political rights are protected. In this system, politics are protected from the economy by being fenced in by norms, independent institutions, and laws governing elections, corruption, and the role of the state; and the economy is protected from politics by norms, independent institutions, and laws that protect rights to own and transact. This complex relationship between the market economy and the democratic polity is prone to failure, as we have seen.

Loyalty to the political community over loyalty to its component parts is a necessary condition for the health of any democratic political system. That depends on thinking of oneself as a citizen. That is exceptionally important for democracies, because a necessary condition is willingness to accept the loss of elections. Defeat is bearable only if the people who outvote you are people you trust. If not, civil war threatens. Nationhood—the creation of a notional family among tens of millions or even hundreds of millions of people who are unrelated and mostly will never know one another—is a powerful way of creating such a sense of identity. This sense of identity—of mutual belonging—then shapes a "demos": a people. People have fought and died for such imagined communities in the tens of millions.

In our modern world, then, we see a tension. Our economic institutions are designed to allow us to transact freely and with confidence with strangers not just in our own country, but all over the world. In contemporary economics, reliable institutions, including the rule of law, underpin trust. In contemporary politics, too, reliable institutions, including the rule of law, but also the notion of a national community, a "demos," underpin trust. The more the development of the economy disrupts that national identity, the more fraught politics and so economics, too, will become, and the harder it becomes to maintain the relationship between market capitalism and democracy.

This danger is now present across large parts of the world. Moreover, if authoritarianism of some kind were to replace liberal democracy, competitive market capitalism would be unlikely to survive. A corrupt form of neopatrimonialism would become far more likely. This is no remote danger. It is what Trump and his ilk embody.

The great story of democratic capitalism—the fragile marriage between competitive market capitalism and liberal democracy—may end quite soon. Do not assume otherwise. That would be foolishly complacent. What might be done about this looming danger will be the subject of part III of this book.

CHAPTER THREE

The Evolution of Democratic Capitalism

It is true that we are called a democracy, for the
administration is in the hands of the many and not of
the few. But while there exists equal justice to all and
alike in their private disputes, the claim of excellence
is also recognized; and when a citizen is in any way
distinguished, he is preferred to the public service, not
as a matter of privilege, but as the reward of merit.
Neither is poverty an obstacle, but a man may benefit
his country whatever the obscurity of his condition.
—*Thucydides*[1]

Universal suffrage representative democracy evolved over the
last two centuries. This form of democracy was the product
of a long struggle. Market capitalism demanded a more egalitarian politics. The force of this egalitarian idea of equality of status
spread throughout society, delegitimizing class and sex, and ultimately
race, as categories for determining political and social rights. The outcome was equal political rights for all adult citizens of a democratic
state.

The previous chapter argued that market capitalism and liberal
democracy are the "complementary opposites"—the "yin and yang"—

of our world. But, potentially, complementary opposites may become mutually destructive if the balance between them is not maintained. This chapter will provide an overview of the development of democracy and capitalism, as well as of the relationship between the two over the last two centuries, before turning, in part II of the book, to how the relationship between the two, always difficult, has indeed become dangerously unbalanced over the past four decades.

Brief History of Liberal Democracy

Democracy is not a new idea. As noted in chapter 2, governments accountable to—or even directed by—a sizable portion of the governed have existed in the past, most famously in Athens twenty-five hundred years ago. Monarchies destroyed some, as happened to Athens, conquered by the Macedonia of Philip II. Civil war destroyed others, as happened to the Roman Republic, which ended in the military dictatorship known as the Roman Empire. Athens and Rome had highly restricted franchises, excluding women and slaves. Rome's republic was also highly oligarchic. Nevertheless, these systems made rulers accountable and offered humble citizens opportunities to participate in public affairs, as Pericles claimed (in words reported, or perhaps put into his mouth, by Thucydides). These systems were different in these respects from the autocracies, theocracies, and aristocracies that have run most organized states over the past several thousand years. They perished.

Until the last two centuries or so, the idea of government directed by—or accountable to—a large portion of the public had little reality.[2] As noted in the previous chapter, the rise of such political systems to global significance is one of the revolutionary transformations of the period since the industrial revolution. A somewhat earlier one was the emergence of a global capitalist economy. In neither case has the movement been linear. The aim of this chapter is to demonstrate this historical linkage empirically, thereby complementing the more theoretical discussion of chapter 2.

Universal suffrage, representative, liberal democracy—what the West now means by democracy—is, even by the standards of humanity's brief experience with literate civilizations, a political mayfly. It first saw the light of day when New Zealand granted full suffrage (including to women) in 1893. Finland did so in 1906, Norway in 1913, Denmark in 1915, Germany, the Netherlands, and Sweden in 1919 (though Germany then notoriously lost its democracy between 1933 and 1945), Ireland in 1923, the UK in 1928 (though the peculiar university constituencies survived until 1950), Spain in 1933 (though female suffrage was then revoked by the Franco regime in 1937 and reinstated only after his death, in 1977), Austria, France, and Italy in 1945, Japan in 1947, Belgium in 1948, Canada in 1960 (when aboriginal Canadians acquired the vote), Australia in 1962 (when aboriginal Australians acquired the vote), and the US in 1965 (when the vote was extended to African Americans throughout the South, though restrictions on voting by ex-felons in some states have strongly discriminatory effects, and voter suppression and racial gerrymandering are also rife), Portugal in 1974, Switzerland in 1990 (with full suffrage at the federal level in 1971, but the last holdout canton was compelled to grant the vote to women only as late as 1990), and Taiwan in 1996.[3] It really is a remarkably recent development.

Arguably, the above list of countries and dates is too purist. As Larry Diamond of the Hoover Institution rightly notes: "democracy is in many ways a continuous variable."[4] It falls on a continuum, not only in terms of the suffrage, but also in terms of institutional protections for the opposition, freedom of the media, and so forth. To take the suffrage alone, the extent to which the UK could be deemed democratic rose over a century, prior to full universal adult suffrage in 1928, as a series of legislative acts in the nineteenth and early twentieth centuries lifted restrictions on voting by religion, wealth, and gender. The further extension of the franchise to those over eighteen occurred only in 1970. Yet a wide suffrage of adult males is less undemocratic than if voting is restricted to a tiny proportion of property holders. Full suffrage of adult men and women is more democratic than if suffrage is restricted to men alone, even if ethnic minorities are still excluded. So the widening of the suffrage progressed in stages.

Realistically, democracy must be defined by a composite measure. That is what the Polity IV database from the Center for Systemic Peace does in assessing the rise of democracy since 1800.[5] At that early date, it judges, there were no democracies. Even in countries where elections did occur, the electorate made up a very small portion of the population: even in the US, for example, established as a republic, voting was restricted to white male property owners. When George Washington was elected president, only 6 percent of the population of the United States could vote.[6]

According to the Polity IV database, the number of countries with reasonably democratic regimes rose from zero in 1800 to 12 in 1900 (though New Zealand was the only country with universal suffrage) and then shot up to 24 in 1922. Subsequently, the number collapsed to just 9 in 1940. The number of autocracies jumped from 10 in 1922, to 19 in 1929, and then on to 27 in 1940. The number of democracies was back to 18 in 1946 and then 23 in 1950. By 1989, it had reached 48. Thereupon, it jumped, quite suddenly, to 76 in 1994 and went on rising, to reach 97 in 2016. (See figure 4.)

Also remarkable was the collapse in the number of autocracies over four decades, from a peak of 89 in 1977 to 62 in 1989 and then 35 in 1994 and 21 in 2016. While the collapse in the number of autocracies is welcome, less so is the rise in the number of what Polity IV calls "anocracies"—countries with incoherent, unstable, and ineffective governments. The number of anocracies has risen from 21 in 1984 and 39 in 1989 to 49 in 2016. In many cases, therefore, the fall of autocracy bequeathed not democracy but chaos, as in Libya and many other countries. Too often, it turns out, the opposite of autocracy is not democracy but brutal anarchy.

FIGURE 4. GLOBAL TRENDS IN GOVERNANCE
(Source: Center for Systemic Peace, Polity IV dataset)

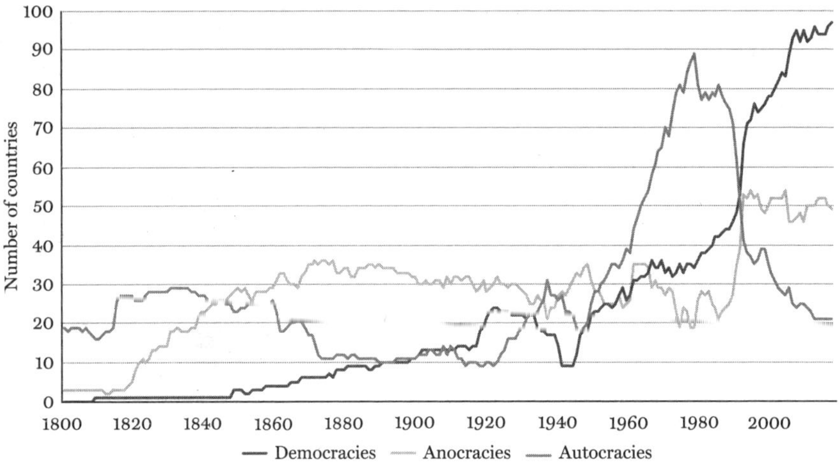

Yet there are also far more states now than a century or more ago, as a result of the disappearance of colonial empires and the birth of a multiplicity of new states. Only 22 states appear in the Polity IV database for 1800. For 1945, there were 67. For 2016, there were 167. It is vital, therefore, to consider the *proportion* of states that are democracies. This rose from zero in 1800 to 22 percent in 1900, 36 percent in 1922, then down to 14 percent in 1940, back up to 33 percent in 1989, 47 percent in 1994, and 58 percent in 2016. The proportion of outright autocracies also fell from 43 percent in 1989 (virtually the same as it had been in 1940, but well down from the 63 percent in 1977) to just 13 percent in 2016. But the proportion of anocratic states has remained high. Chaos might now be a bigger enemy of democracy than autocracy. (See figure 5.)

So, what is the story?

The industrial revolution began in a world of autocracies or narrow oligarchies. In the nineteenth century, the number of countries with moderately wide franchises rose. The victory of the Western allies in World War I and subsequent collapse of the defeated autocracies led to a jump in the number of democracies. The franchise was also

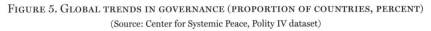

FIGURE 5. GLOBAL TRENDS IN GOVERNANCE (PROPORTION OF COUNTRIES, PERCENT)
(Source: Center for Systemic Peace, Polity IV dataset)

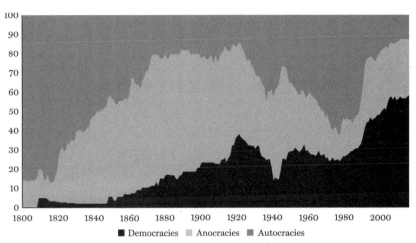

■ Democracies ■ Anocracies ■ Autocracies

widened in many countries at that time, particularly to adult females, in part because women played a big role in the war efforts. But the chaotic political legacy of World War I and the Great Depression was devastating for fragile new democracies. Their number more than halved and dictatorships took their place. After the end of the Second World War, the number of democracies began its long upswing, as the allies liberated western Europe from the Nazis, and colonial empires disappeared. Indian independence in 1947 was a watershed moment for that. But the swiftest increase in the number of democracies came after the fall of the Soviet Union. That marked a true age of democratic transformation.

The Great Recession, which followed the transatlantic financial crisis of 2007–12, did not do anything like the same damage to democracy as the Great Depression did, perhaps because it was better managed. (At the time of writing this, in mid-2022, few have much idea what the longer-term political impact of COVID-19 might be. But it has further reduced confidence in the authorities, with a few exceptions.) The relatively successful policy response to the global financial crisis (at least compared with the abject failure in the 1930s) should take some of the credit. Nevertheless, the rise in the number of democracies has halted and the quality of many—including the US, which had long been in the vanguard of democracy worldwide—is deteriorating. Indeed, it is possible the problem began a little earlier. Already in 2015, Diamond argued that "the world has been in a mild but protracted democratic recession since 2006."[7] Moreover, this democratic recession is multifaceted. It includes "the instability and stagnation of democracies, but also the incremental decline of democracy in 'gray zone' countries (which defy easy classification as to whether or not they are democracies), the deepening authoritarianism in the non-democracies, and the decline in the functioning and self-confidence of the world's established, rich democracies."[8]

In a similar vein, Freedom House, which adds measures of personal freedom to those of the political processes, is alarmed. In its 2021 report, for example, it stated:

> As a lethal pandemic, economic and physical insecurity, and violent conflict ravaged the world in 2020, democracy's defenders sustained heavy new losses in their struggle against authoritarian foes, shifting the international balance in favor of tyranny. Incumbent leaders increasingly used force to crush opponents and settle scores, sometimes in the name of public health, while beleaguered activists— lacking effective international support—faced heavy jail sentences, torture, or murder in many settings.
>
> These withering blows marked the 15th consecutive year of decline in global freedom. The countries experiencing deterioration outnumbered those with improvements by the largest margin recorded since the negative trend began in 2006. The long democratic recession is deepening.[9]

Indeed, after Trump's attempted coup against the 2020 presidential election in the US and, still more important, after the Republican Party's decision to support him in condemning the outcome of the election as illegitimate, without evidence, a "democratic recession" no longer seemed the right phrase. "On the verge of a democratic depression" seemed a better description of the state of US and global democracy in 2021.[10] Above all, in 2016, the US had elected a man to serve as their president who not only had no idea what a liberal democracy was but despised the idea: winning and holding power was all. One must assume that those who voted for him agreed. With such an opposition, Joe Biden's attempt to revive the reputation of his country for democratic principle seemed quite likely to fail.

In a seminal 2016 paper, Roberto Foa and Yascha Mounk detailed with frightening clarity the erosion of belief in the core institutions of democracy:

> Over the last three decades, trust in political institutions such as parliaments or the courts has precipitously declined across the established democracies of North America and Western Europe. So has voter turnout. As party identification has weakened and party membership has declined, citizens have become less willing to stick with establishment parties. Instead, voters increasingly endorse single-issue movements, vote for populist candidates, or support "anti-system" parties that define themselves in opposition to the status quo. Even in some of the richest and most politically stable regions of the world, it seems as though democracy is in a state of serious disrepair.[11]

This is not just a matter of dissatisfaction with specific parties or governments, but rather with democratic regimes themselves. The World Values Survey Waves 5 and 6 (2005–14) showed that the proportion of people who believed it was essential to live in a democracy had collapsed. Of those born in the 1940s, just under 60 percent of Europeans and just over 60 percent of Americans believed it was essential to live in a democracy. For those born in the 1980s, the proportions were down to close to 45 percent and 30 percent, respectively. This was a cohort effect, not an age effect. The more recent cohorts appeared to be disenchanted and uninterested. Amazingly (and frighteningly) in 2011, 24 percent of US "millennials" (then in their late teens or early twenties) thought democracy a "bad" or "very bad" way to run a country.[12]

Not only did younger cohorts seem less committed to the idea of democracy, but interest in politics had markedly declined among them. Worst of all, evidence of rising support for authoritarianism also existed. In the US, for example, the proportion of citizens that thought it would be a "good" or "very good" thing for the army to rule had jumped from one in sixteen in 1995 to one in six in 2014. The relatively well-off had hugely increased their support for the idea of army rule. In the mid-1990s only 5 percent of upper-income citizens thought army rule would be a "good" or "very good" idea. By 2014, that had risen to 16 percent.

In all, we could see a marked shift toward belief in that ancient chimera, a "strong leader," with the biggest shifts in this direction among the younger cohorts and the well-off. In the latter case, many may wish to keep the grubby hands of the "hoi polloi" (the masses) off "their" money. As we considered in the previous chapter and will consider further below, once inequality becomes large enough, nothing is more likely than that the wealthy few will struggle to repress the democratic representation of the poor many.

Subsequent research confirmed this dire picture. A study published in 2020, for example, found that of the world's "democratic citizenry," which totaled 1.9 billion people, only a little over 2 percent lived in countries where more than three quarters of citizens were satisfied with their democracy. Another 21 percent lived in countries where between a half and three quarters of the citizenry were satisfied. But 57 percent lived in countries where only between a quarter and a half were satisfied, a group of countries that included France, Japan, Spain, the UK, and the US. Finally, 20 percent lived in countries where less than a quarter of the citizens were satisfied with their democracy. This was a picture of grim disenchantment.[13]

All this suggests that democracy has become fragile, not just in relatively poor democracies (such as those in sub-Saharan Africa), in middle-income countries with huge social, cultural, or ethnic divisions (such as Brazil, India, the Philippines, or Turkey), or in countries that have shifted only relatively recently from authoritarianism to democracy (such as Hungary and Poland), but even in well-established and prosperous Western democracies. Moreover, as Diamond wrote, "Much of the post–World War II liberal order is rooted in US leadership, so too is democracy worldwide anchored in democracy in America."[14] The withdrawal of the US from defending democracy under Donald Trump, his hostility to democratic allies and democratic norms, and his contempt for the liberal global economic order are potentially transformative events.

Democracy has disappeared in the past. It would be silly to assume it could not do so again. If it does, we will live in a world of arbitrary despotism, unbridled corruption and self-dealing, intimidation, and endless state-manufactured lies. We will live in a world in which the people are treated as perpetual children by whichever set of thugs is in charge.

Brief History of Market Capitalism[15]

Liberal democracy has swept across the world over the past two centuries but has done so with advances and retreats. Today, it is in a retreat. What, then, has been the evolution of market capitalism, especially in today's high-income countries?[16] The answer is more complex, but the broad story is not dissimilar.

The discussion below will separate domestic from global capitalism. In general, while capitalism has evolved in consistent directions, it has also gone through cycles of less and more government intervention. Today, we are moving into an era of greater government intervention, notably in regard to global integration. Thus, the spread of global capitalism has slowed, even reversed, and with COVID-19 and the breakdown in relations between the US and China, it seems likely to go into further retreat. This, then, is much the same story as for democracy. It is a troubled era for both systems.

Cycles of capitalism

Capitalism is not static, but rather a dynamic, even protean, system, which evolves in response to market and technological opportunities and also to political and social pressures. It has always been so. Provided the core attributes of competitive markets and protection of private property are maintained, the system itself—defined to include the institutional framework, relationship with civil society, and government policy—can alter profoundly.

Arguably, the most significant historical transformation of capitalism has been the shift from small businesses with unlimited liability of owner-managers to the limited liability corporation (in US parlance) or company (in the UK's), with their professional managements. The aim of this highly significant institutional innovation was to create business entities that could finance and manage the new economic activities, which were characterized by huge economies of scale and correspondingly enormous capital requirements. In this way, capital and credit could be combined into eternal entities with a legal personality, indeed an economic life, all their own. In the middle of the nineteenth century, the UK allowed creation of such companies by a simple act of registration. This social and legal innovation was then copied in many other countries.[17]

The company has been a staggeringly successful innovation. But it has also turned out to be something of a Faustian bargain.

On the positive side, companies have become the heart of the modern economy: in the US, for example, corporations generated 56 percent of GDP in the first quarter of 2021.[18] Conceptually, a company is a system of command and control embedded within competitive markets.[19] Companies' success comes from their ability to coordinate resources and serve markets worldwide. They have, in the process, created and managed an immensely complex global division of labor. The birth of the company has also led to the creation of cadres of well-schooled and competent managers.[20] Companies generate the bulk of the innovation in our economies.[21] They have valuable brands and reputations to protect, which encourages them to behave responsibly. In sum, companies are engines of prosperity.

Yet, on the negative side, companies also possess enormous economic and political power, which they can and do abuse. Adam Smith himself was concerned that managers would ignore the interests of owners. More significantly, their scale and mobility create significant market power.[22] In addition, companies have been granted the privileges of personhood, including the political privileges of citizens.[23] Yet being so mobile and flexible, they can afford to be indifferent to the fate of their workers and the countries in which they are located and so become sophisticated avoiders of taxes and regulations.[24] Moreover, judicial systems find it almost impossible to hold them or their executives criminally liable, even in the event of significant malfeasance. Shareholders bear the cost of fines imposed as a result of mistakes made by executives, even though the former frequently have limited ability to control the latter. In addition, partly guided by Milton Friedman's influential views of the goals of the company, its dominant purpose was long held to be maximizing shareholder value, to the exclusion of other objectives.[25] This can encourage behavior that borders on the sociopathic.

The invention of the company brought with it other institutional developments. Luca Pacioli invented double-entry bookkeeping in the late fifteenth century. But the training and certification of accountants emerged only in the nineteenth century.[26] In the twentieth century, official accounting standards, such as Generally Accepted Accounting Principles in the US and International Financial Reporting Standards were introduced. The primary aim of both was to clarify the performance of companies increasingly owned by outside shareholders.

Finance also evolved dramatically. The creation of limited liability joint stock banks in the nineteenth century changed the financing of companies, as did corporate bond markets. Institutional share ownership via unit trusts (mutual funds in the US), investment trusts, pension funds, and, more recently, exchange traded funds shifted the meaning of ownership. From a commitment to the long-term health of a specific business a title of "ownership" became little more than a liquid financial asset. A still greater degree of detachment from committed ownership occurred with the emergence of the index fund, whose point was diversifying risk and so limiting exposure to (and interest in the health of) any specific business. The result is "detached capitalism." Private equity and venture capital may be viewed as partial counterweights to these developments. Such institutional developments also caused the ceaseless reshaping of companies via an active market in corporate control through mergers and (often hostile) takeovers.

The rise of capitalism also created powerful countervailing forces. Among the most important were trade unions. Thus, during the nineteenth and early twentieth centuries, a sizable part of the labor force released by the rising productivity in agriculture found employment in large-scale manufacturing and mining. These valuable stocks of physical capital had to be in constant use if their owners were to achieve the desired returns. These huge and concentrated labor forces were also relatively easy to organize; after long and bitter struggles, trade unions organized large parts of the labor force. Since strikes could inflict huge losses, they held leverage over employers.[27] In the end, they forced companies to share the exceptional profits generated by these productive new economic organizations with their workforces.[28]

Trade unions also played a political role by creating (as with the UK's Labour Party) or supporting (as with the Democrats in the US) center-left and left-wing political parties. These parties in turn shaped politics in the new era of wide and then universal suffrage. These new trade unions were also able to finance and organize political activity.

This new political power forced business owners to share their profits, via taxation of incomes and wealth. These developments in turn created a well-paid industrial working class (which Americans call the middle class).

Yet much the most powerful countervailing force is the state. The state's role had long been to create the legal and regulatory environment within which a capitalist economy could operate—no rule of law, no market capitalism. But as standards of living grew to unprecedented levels, so did the resources available to the state. As the supply capacity of the state expanded, so did the demands upon it from the widening electorate, which was increasingly under the influence of the new mass trade unions and political parties. Voters demanded spending on education (as did business). They demanded spending on insurance against unemployment, penury in old age, and ill health. They demanded a modern infrastructure. They demanded full employment. They demanded regulation of the environment, labor markets, worker safety, soundness of financial institutions, anticompetitive behavior, product safety, and international commerce.

TABLE 1: SHARE OF GENERAL GOVERNMENT SPENDING IN GDP

	1870	1913	1937	1960	1980	2001	2019
Australia	18.3%	16.5%	14.8%	21.2%	31.6%	35.8%	38.3%
Belgium		13.8%	21.8%	30.3%	58.6%	49.4%	52.1%
France	12.6%	17.0%	29.0%	34.6%	46.1%	51.7%	55.5%
Germany		14.8%	34.1%	32.4%	47.9%	47.4%	45.2%
Italy	11.9%	11.1%	24.5%	30.1%	41.9%	47.3%	48.6%
Japan		8.3%	25.4%	17.5%	32.0%	35.5%	37.2%
Netherlands	9.1%	9.0%	19.0%	33.7%	55.2%	42.1%	41.3%
Norway	5.9%	9.3%	11.8%	29.9%	37.5%	43.3%	51.6%
Sweden	5.7%	10.4%	16.5%	31.0%	60.1%	51.7%	48.3%
UK	9.4%	12.7%	30.0%	32.2%	43.0%	34.8%	38.9%
US	7.3%	7.5%	19.7%	27.0%	31.8%	32.8%	35.7%

Source: WP/00/44, IMF World Economic Outlook Database

What voters demanded, governments delivered. As table 1 shows, the share of government spending in GDP has risen enormously since 1870, which was the dawn of the age of democratic capitalism. In the US, for example, that ratio rose from 7 percent to 27 percent in 1960 and then 36 percent in 2019. Yet the US share was the lowest of these countries. Some of these countries were spending close to half of GDP in 2019, just before the COVID-19 pandemic. The bulk of this increase in spending was for education, health, and social security (particularly pensions). The big jumps in public spending occurred during the First World War, the Great Depression, the Second World War, and the post-war period. After 1980, the spending of nearly all these governments stopped growing much if at all relative to GDP. The spending share even shrank a little in many (see table 2). Today, big governments seem to have reached limits—political, economic, or possibly both: the shrinkage of the state in the Netherlands and Sweden is particularly striking.

TABLE 2: RISE IN THE SHARE OF GOVERNMENT SPENDING IN GDP

	1913–1980	1980–2019	1913–2019
Australia	15.1%	6.7%	21.8%
Belgium	44.8%	-6.5%	38.3%
France	29.1%	9.4%	38.5%
Germany	33.1%	-2.7%	30.4%
Italy	30.8%	6.7%	37.5%
Japan	23.7%	5.2%	28.9%
Netherlands	46.2%	-13.9%	32.3%
Norway	28.2%	14.1%	42.3%
Sweden	49.7%	-11.8%	37.9%
UK	30.3%	-4.1%	26.2%
US	24.3%	3.9%	28.2%

Source: IMF World Economic Outlook Database data collected for table 1

The emergence of capitalism and democracy within broadly liberal societies—societies that treasure the principles of individual choice, free inquiry, and tolerance for others—did, of course, stimulate passionate discussion. Thinkers, historians, and polemicists, from Adam Smith and Karl Marx to John Maynard Keynes and Amartya Sen, have all engaged in such debates. In the high-income countries, however, the anticapitalist and antidemocratic ideas of the extreme left and authoritarian right have failed to take lasting hold, at least so far. The debate in these democracies has mainly been between "capitalism skeptics" of the left and "capitalism supporters" of the right, with both sides claiming to be pro-democracy. The result on the ground has been a compromise, with the dynamism of capitalism balanced by the intrusions of the state.

The interaction of ideas with events produced swings in the balance between market and government over the past one and a half centuries, from laissez-faire to a mixture of egalitarianism and interventionism, then back toward freer markets (described as neoliberalism by its opponents), and finally back toward somewhat greater interventionism.

The story starts with the predominantly free-market economies of the mid- to late nineteenth century (though the notion of industrial policy already existed in the catch-up powers, such as the US and, later, Germany and Japan). Already at that time, critical voices were growing louder. The First World War then brought a substantial state takeover of the economies of the combatants, as well as the communist revolution in Russia. The success of "war socialism" was widely seen as justifying planning of the economy, an idea subsequently taken to its limits by Joseph Stalin. His first five-year plan covered the years 1928–32. The aim was to achieve forced industrialization by means of central planning of an entirely state-owned economy.[29] This approach became highly influential across the world after the Second World War, mostly in a diluted form, as the Soviet empire expanded and as developing countries, many of them freed from colonial empires after 1945, adopted ostensibly similar five-year development plans.

The agonies of the First World War strengthened the hold of

socialist and nationalist ideas in Europe, on the far left and the authoritarian right. The failure to restore a stable global economy after the First World War and the economic collapse in the early 1930s severely damaged belief in the self-equilibrating properties of an economy driven by self-interest. The Great Depression then led to the abandonment of the old gold standard—a hallowed part of that self-equilibrating system—by many countries, notably including the UK in 1931. It also led to the New Deal in the US, the Nazis' controlled economy in Germany, and finally World War II. The war further increased state control of economies of high-income countries, with total mobilization of resources for the war effort, notably in the UK.

By the late-1940s, Keynesian ideas of macroeconomic stabilization had achieved great influence, though not universal acceptance, especially in the US and postwar Germany. These ideas were to be seen in the objectives and policies of the International Monetary Fund, agreed at Bretton Woods, New Hampshire, in July 1944.[30] Many essential industries, such as railways, coal mining, and the main utilities, were nationalized (though not in the US). Government spending had increased both hugely and irreversibly. Tax rates on high incomes and wealth also reached punitive levels: thus, "in the 1930s, US policy makers invented—and then for almost half a century applied—top marginal income tax rates of 90 percent on the highest income earners. Corporate profits were taxed at 50 percent; large estates at close to 80 percent."[31] In the UK, the top rate of income tax reached 99.25 percent during the Second World War and was around 90 percent during the 1950s and 1960s.[32]

These economies were, however, at most "mixed economies," not socialized ones. In all, however, the old laissez-faire approach to the market economy had been largely discredited. France even adopted a widely admired system of "indicative planning." In Europe, the closest to the old set of ideas were those of the social market economy, introduced in Germany. This embraced the old principles of private property, competition, and monetary stability, but also accepted social protection. Ludwig Erhard was the guiding force in introducing this policy system, first in the parts of Germany occupied by Western powers and then as finance minister of West Germany. It was an enormous and hugely influential success.

The period of the Keynesian mixed economy lasted until the 1970s. The combination of high inflation with high unemployment in the latter decade discredited Keynesian macroeconomics, while the combination of arbitrary price controls with weak profitability of companies, slowing productivity growth and poor performance of nationalized industries, discredited what was increasingly seen as an unworkably interventionist approach to the economy. The outcome was the "Reagan-Thatcher counterrevolution," introduced by Ronald Reagan, elected US president in 1980, and Margaret Thatcher, elected UK prime minister in 1979. In the field of development economics, a not dissimilar set of ideas came to be known (rather misleadingly) as the "Washington Consensus."[33] The core ideas of this counterrevolution were control of inflation through control over monetary aggregates and then through inflation targeting, deregulation—especially of product, labor, and financial markets—lower marginal tax rates, and privatization of nationalized companies. This represented a very partial turn toward laissez-faire. But governments remained very large, on all dimensions, the welfare state was not rolled back to any significant degree, and regulation in some important areas, notably the environment, even tended to increase. Nevertheless, the era of the mixed economy of the 1950s, 1960s, and 1970s changed into one of freer markets in the 1980s, 1990s, and early 2000s. The startling collapse of the Soviet Union and its empire between 1989 and 1991 reinforced this shift worldwide.

A series of financial crises in emerging economies, notably the Asian crisis of 1997–99, shook confidence in deregulated financial markets. But these could be blamed on unworkable fixed-exchange-rate regimes and crony capitalism. However, the transatlantic financial crisis of 2007–12 occurred in the core of the global financial system.

This could not be so easily explained away. The response consisted of massive bailouts and substantial reregulation of the financial system. Business groups even started to shift away from their adherence to the mantra of "shareholder value maximization." Notably, the Business Roundtable, which represents 181 of the world's largest multinational companies, stated in 2019, "While each of our individual companies serves its own corporate purpose, we share a fundamental commitment to all our stakeholders."[34] Finally, COVID-19 brought another round of government intervention. The active state had returned.

In the long run, we can identify both a trend and a cycle in capitalism and its place in wider society. The trend has been toward a depersonalized and institutionalized capitalism, with the emergence of multinational corporations and regulated financial markets, and also of bigger and more intrusive states. Behind this trend has been a ceaseless debate over how society should be organized and, in particular, over the relationship between markets and government and also between companies and the rest of civil society. The cycle has been between reliance on free markets and reliance on active government intervention. Right now, we seem to be moving back toward the latter, though the shift is slow and modest by the standards of earlier periods, notably the 1930s. The disruptions caused by COVID, the Ukraine war, and the fundamental breakdown in relations between the US and China seem likely to accelerate this ongoing shift.

Cycles of globalization

A country is inherently a political rather than an economic entity. Yet this does not mean that countries do not matter economically. Almost nothing could be further from the truth. It does mean that the market economy is not purely national. Capitalism turbocharged this reality by making the exploitation of new resources and new markets a point of competition among capitalists and, frequently, among their governments as well.

Karl Marx and Friedrich Engels understood this. In the *Communist Manifesto*, one of the most important documents of the nineteenth century, they described the emerging capitalist economy brilliantly:

> The bourgeoisie has through its exploitation of the world market given a cosmopolitan character to production and consumption in every country. To the great chagrin of Reactionists, it has drawn from under the feet of industry the national ground on which it stood. All old-established national industries have been destroyed or are daily being destroyed. They are dislodged by new industries, whose introduction becomes a life and death question for all civilized nations, by industries that no longer work up indigenous raw material, but raw material drawn from the remotest zones; industries whose products are consumed, not only at home, but in every quarter of the globe. In place of the old wants, satisfied by the production of the country, we find new wants, requiring for their satisfaction the products of distant lands and climes. In place of the old local and national seclusion and self-sufficiency, we have intercourse in every direction, universal inter-dependence of nations. And as in material, so also in intellectual production. The intellectual creations of individual nations become common property. National one-sidedness and narrow-mindedness become more and more impossible, and from the numerous national and local literatures, there arises a world literature.[35]

Capitalism is inherently global: profit-seeking capitalists will pursue their goals abroad, if allowed to do so, since that is where many good opportunities lie. Just as there had been democracies and republics before the modern era, so was there international commerce. Even before the European voyages of discovery of the fifteenth and sixteenth centuries, there existed a "complex pattern of linkages among wool from England and Spain, woolen cloth from Flanders and Italy, furs from Eastern Europe, gold from West Africa, cotton textiles and pepper from India, fine spices such as cloves and nutmeg from Southeast Asia and silk and porcelain from China that existed from at least a thousand years ago."[36] At that time, the most advanced parts of the global economy were China and the Muslim world. The silk route from China, the first long-distance trading system, originated with the Han Empire, two centuries before the Common Era.[37]

The difference in motivation between the Chinese, who felt they had little need of imports from the rest of the world, and the Europeans, who desired eastern commodities, explains why it was not the Ming Dynasty fleets of admiral Zheng He in the early fifteenth century, but those of Vasco de Gama (to India) and Cristoforo Colombo (to the Americas, while seeking a route to the Indies), in the late fifteenth century that created the first global economic network.[38] The subsequent period between 1500 and 1800 is sometimes thought of as the age of mercantilism. It was an era of competition among European states aimed at promoting exports and creating and protecting trade monopolies. In the seventeenth and eighteenth centuries, the Dutch and British East India companies played a powerful role not just in global trade, but in politics, in their homes and around the Indian Ocean. Adam Smith wrote The Wealth of Nations as an attack on this mercantilist system.[39]

Yet, while European explorers had brought the hitherto separate continents of North and South America into the global economic and political systems, European commerce did not dominate the world even during the mercantilist era. The Chinese, Indian, and Turkish empires continued to play a large role. Indeed, for the Europeans, a big part of the value of the Americas was that it provided silver with which to purchase goods from Asia, since they could offer little else of value to those sophisticated economies.

Trade grew faster than world output between 1500 and 1800.[40] Nevertheless, the ratio of trade to output is estimated at between 2 percent and 10 percent in 1820, far below levels subsequently reached in the late nineteenth and early twentieth centuries, let alone today (see figure 6).[41] The trade was also predominantly in noncompeting goods, though Europeans did manage to develop import-substituting industries in porcelain and textiles.

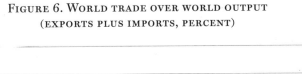

FIGURE 6. WORLD TRADE OVER WORLD OUTPUT
(EXPORTS PLUS IMPORTS, PERCENT)

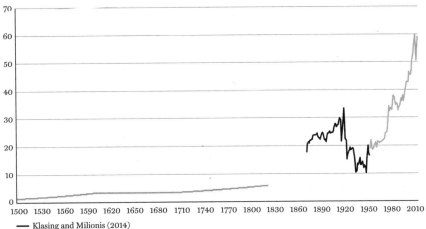

— Klasing and Milionis (2014)
— Penn World Tables (version 8.1)
— Midpoint between estimated upper and lower bounds (Estavadeordal, Frantz and Taylor, 2003)

The British textile industry—whose consequences included the development of cotton plantations worked by African slaves in the southern United States—was an early product of the industrial revolution. That was the beginning of the era of "Promethean growth," in which exploitation of fossil fuels and advances in technology successively transformed economies, societies, and politics.[42] This was also the era of the capitalist revolution, of which Marx and Engels wrote: "[The bourgeoisie] has been the first to show what man's activity can bring about. It has accomplished wonders far surpassing Egyptian pyramids, Roman aqueducts, and Gothic cathedrals; it has conducted expeditions that put in the shade all former Exoduses of nations and crusades."[43]

In the nineteenth century, this global capitalism generated what is sometimes called "the first globalization" (which ended with the First World War) to differentiate it from the "second globalization" of the 1980s, 1990s, and early 2000s. In addition to technological advances, notably in transport and communications (the railway, steamship, and transcontinental cable), the policies of the mercantilist era were dismantled and trade barriers liberalized, especially in the second half of the nineteenth century. A decisive impulse was the UK's adoption of unilateral free trade in 1846 and the subsequent treaties among the European powers to liberalize trade.[44] In that century, global commodity markets became integrated for the first time, as commodity prices converged under the forces of global competition.[45] There was, however, a modest reversal toward protectionism in the last two decades of the century.

The volume of world trade also grew faster than world output, which itself expanded far more quickly than ever before and, in the industrializing parts of the world, also generated sustained increases in real incomes per head, again, for the first time in history. By the First World War, the ratio of world trade to output (measured at purchasing power) had reached 30 percent, up from 20 percent in 1870, a ratio not seen again until the late 1970s. (See figure 6). As two experts write, "By 1913, international commodity markets were vastly more integrated than they had been in 1750; world trade accounted for a far higher share of world output; and a far broader range of goods, including commodities with a high bulk-to-value ratio, was being transported between countries."[46] Moreover, they add, "By the late nineteenth century there was a stark distinction between industrial and primary producing economies."[47] This was part of "the great divergence" between the rapidly industrializing countries of western Europe and North America and the relatively stagnant economies of the rest of the world, notably including almost all of Asia (except Japan in the second half of the nineteenth century).[48]

■ ■ ■

Already in the late nineteenth century, nationalism, protectionism, militarism, imperialism, socialism, and communism were both competing and cooperating with one another, while attacking nineteenth-century liberalism.[49] While the essential features of the late-nineteenth-century economic system—the gold standard and liberal trade (including the UK's free trade)—survived until the eve of the First World War, the war washed them away, never to return. Despite attempts, the corpse of the nineteenth-century system could not be revived. In the interwar period, trade fell sharply, both absolutely and relative to world GDP, as a result of crippling protection and the Great Depression, coupled with post–First World War political fragility. The US, the reluctant new global economic hegemon, introduced the highly protectionist Smoot-Hawley tariff in 1930. The UK abandoned its long-standing policy of unilateral free trade and the gold standard in 1931, both for good. After 1933, Nazi Germany introduced comprehensive quantitative controls on trade, creating what one economist calls a "pernicious bilateralism."[50]

After the Second World War, world trade revived, to reach unparalleled heights. Yet the post–Second World War era differed from that of the nineteenth century in important respects. International institutions were created to contain and manage domestic policy making, in the interests of all. Important events on this journey were: establishment of the International Monetary Fund and the World Bank at the Bretton Woods Conference in 1944; the General Agreement on Tariffs and Trade in 1946 (which led to a series of global trade rounds that culminated in the Uruguay Round, the eighth such round, completed in 1994); creation of the Organization for European Economic Co-operation (later the Organization for Economic Co-operation and Development), designed to administer the Marshall Plan, in 1948; creation of the European Economic Community in 1957; creation of the World Trade Organization in 1995; and China's accession to the WTO in 2001.

The initial thrust of these developments, consciously encouraged by an enlightened US, was to open western European economies, first to one another and then to the wider world. In the 1980s and 1990s, however, the trade liberalization effort was not only extended to but enthusiastically embraced by many developing and emerging economies. This included China, whose policy of "reform and opening up" went back to Deng Xiaoping's rise to power in 1978, and India, in the aftermath of the foreign exchange crisis of 1991. These, then, were the crucial steps on the way to the "second globalization," with its explosive growth of world trade, which reached a peak of 60 percent of world output in 2008 at the time of the transatlantic financial crisis.[51]

The technological revolution in transportation played a huge part in the first globalization. The transformation of transport has been less significant in the second globalization. The main transport changes here were the invention of the container ship and commercial jet aviation, both in the 1950s. These were important developments, just not quite as important as the invention of the railway and the steam ship in the nineteenth century. The driving force behind the explosive growth of world trade has rather been the liberalization of trade barriers and the fall in the cost of communication and data processing, which made possible an unprecedented integration of production across the globe.

In the high-income economies, visible trade barriers had fallen to very low levels prior to their reversal in the presidency of Donald Trump.[52] Nearly all emerging and developing countries still have substantially higher barriers to trade than high-income countries, partly because they postponed liberalization until the late twentieth century. In 2010, average unweighted mean tariffs on imports of manufactures were a mere 2.6 percent in high-income countries, but 6.1 percent in the world as a whole, 6.8 percent in developing countries in the East Asia and Pacific region, 7.2 percent in middle-income developing countries, 8.7 percent in developing countries in Latin America and the Caribbean, 9.7 percent in South Asia, and 11.6 percent in low-income developing countries.[53]

The explosive growth of world trade halted with the transatlantic financial crisis of 2007–12. Since then, there has not been a trade collapse, as in the 1930s, but stagnation. As the International Monetary Fund noted in 2016, "Between 1985 and 2007, real world trade grew on average twice as fast as global GDP, whereas over the past four years, it has barely kept pace."[54] Average annual growth of world trade fell from 6.5 percent between 1965 and 2011 to 3.3 percent between

2012 and 2019. The average growth of world output was 3.5 percent in the second period.[55] Thus, not only did the rate of growth of world trade fall sharply even before COVID-19 hit the world economy, but the gap between the growth of trade and output also narrowed sharply. This was not an era of deglobalization, at least in trade. But globalization slowed sharply.[56]

One explanation is that liberalization had run out of steam. The last global trade liberalization was the Uruguay Round, completed in the mid-1990s. The only significant liberalizing event since then was the accession of China to the WTO in 2001. After that, a series of important attempts—the Doha Round of multilateral trade negotiations, the Trans-Pacific Partnership (TPP) (rejected by Donald Trump in early 2017), and the Transatlantic Trade and Investment Partnership (TTIP, between the US and EU)—failed, were rejected, or languished.[57] Trump's repudiation of the TPP was unsurprising: he is a convinced protectionist who claimed that "protection will lead to great prosperity and strength" in his inaugural address on January 20, 2017.[58] His subsequent actions, notably his trade war against China, were indeed protectionist, a violation of WTO rules, and, not least, economically foolish.[59]

Even under Biden, no early reversal of Donald Trump's protectionist trade policies occurred.[60] There were, it is true, two successful efforts at multilateral trade liberalization: the Comprehensive and Progressive Agreement for Trans-Pacific Partnership (CPTPP), signed in January 2018, which included all eleven members of the planned TPP apart from the US;[61] and the Regional Comprehensive Economic Partnership (RCEP), agreed in November 2020.[62] The principal protagonist of the CPTPP was Japan, and the principal protagonist of RCEP was China, though it did include Japan and South Korea. Neither agreement seems likely to have significant effects on trade.

A further explanation for the slowdown in trade is exhaustion of opportunities. From the 1990s, an important driver of world trade was the unbundling of global value chains—the division of production into successive stages located in different countries. This can be measured by the import content in a country's exports, together with the domestic content of exports used by trading partners in their own exports, all divided by gross exports. This ratio rose sharply until 2008, but then stagnated.

Brexit, too, represented deglobalization of trade.[63] The UK ended up with higher barriers to trade with its EU (and European Economic Area) partners than if it had remained a member. Given the fact that 43 percent of UK exports went to EU markets in 2016, at the time of the referendum, it was inconceivable that other forms of liberalization would offset this loss of market access, even in the medium term.[64]

The nature of trade also changed over time. The old days of predominantly national businesses disappeared. In their place came global corporations. The "systems integrators," the global corporations, few in number and predominantly Western, that own both the relevant intellectual property and the capacity to organize global production and distribution came to dominate much of global trade and derive much of the gains from it.[65]

During the first globalization, in the late nineteenth century, the fall in the costs of transport of goods drove what was then an unprecedentedly rapid growth of world trade.[66] This facilitated a global exchange of manufactures against natural resources and agricultural products, the latter mainly from the Americas and Australasia, but also from poorer countries incorporated within colonial empires. In that era, it had been impossible to unbundle manufacturing. To compete in any given industry, a country had to master all the necessary skills. As a result, manufacturing, and with it the consequent gains from economies of scale and learning-by-doing, were concentrated in high-income economies. Modestly skilled workers in these countries enjoyed privileged access to the fruits of the knowledge developed within their economies and so shared a significant part of these gains—achieving, as a result, rising real incomes and substantial political influence.[67]

Until a few decades ago, the only way to break into this charmed circle was to develop competitive industries of one's own. Japan managed this and so, subsequently, did Taiwan and South Korea. But these were exceptional cases. In the second globalization, however, global communications became so reliable and cheap that it was possible to unbundle the production process across great distances. This allowed the production of components and final assembly to be spread across the world, under the control of manufacturers (or buyers) with the relevant knowledge. As an influential scholar put it, US workers "are not competing with Mexican labor, Mexican capital and Mexican technology as they did in the 1970s. They are competing with a nearly unbeatable combination of US know-how and Mexican wages."[68] One indicator of this change was the rise in the share of foreign value added in countries' gross exports during the years of peak globalization, shown in figure 7. It had become far harder to identify the national origin of exports as trade in inputs became more intense. A more global form of market capitalism replaced the more national capitalism of old.

FIGURE 7. FOREIGN VALUE ADDED SHARE OF GROSS EXPORTS (PERCENT)
(Source: OECD)

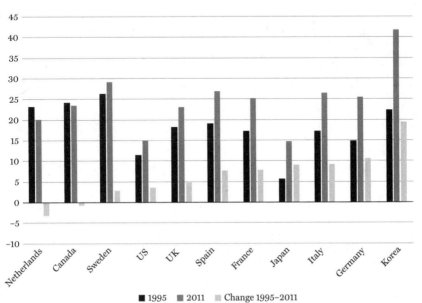

■ 1995 ■ 2011 ■ Change 1995–2011

This development has not been limited to goods. It also applies to services whose activities can easily be distributed across the globe, such as finance. An important consequence has been a widening divergence of interest between nationally bound workers on the one hand, and global corporations on the other. In the first globalization and even after the Second World War, workers and corporations had shared interests against workers and corporations of other countries. In the second globalization, this was much less true. That, combined with the reduction in employment in manufacturing as a result of rapid productivity growth and the decline of trade unions, cast much of the old, relatively well paid and predominantly male working class adrift, with huge political consequences.[69]

Only a relatively small number of developing economies took full advantage of these new opportunities. The big successes were all in Asia. After its leaders' decision to open up the economy, the biggest success of all was China's. The rise of China created not just a new pole for world trade, but a new superpower. Yet this change must also be kept in proportion. If we look at shares of global gross domestic product at market prices, China's share jumped from 2 percent in 1990 to 16 percent in 2019. But the share of the high-income countries was still 60 percent in 2019 (down from 78 percent in 1990), with the US and the EU (the UK excluded) accounting for 25 and 18 percent, respectively.[70] Similarly, despite growing rapidly, China's share in global merchandise imports was only 13 percent in 2019, while the US and EU (excluding both intra-EU trade and the UK) still accounted for 30 percent of world imports.[71]

Nevertheless, the entry of China into the world economy had an unexpectedly large negative impact on US employment in manufacturing. It is estimated that import competition from China between 1999 and 2011 cost in the range of 2 to 2.4 million jobs.[72] This would have been roughly half of the actual job losses in manufacturing over that period: significant, but not overwhelming. Furthermore, jobs in manufacturing stabilized after that. But the local impact of job losses, again in the US, was longer lasting and more negative than might have been expected. Thus, concludes another study, "Adjustment in local labor markets is remarkably slow, with wages and labor-force participation rates remaining depressed and unemployment rates remaining elevated for at least a full decade after the China trade shock commences. Exposed workers experience greater job churning and reduced lifetime income."[73] This "China shock" was politically salient and, in the context of the US refusal to provide effective support and adjustment assistance to the people who have lost their jobs, their families, or the communities in which they live, was inevitably and rightly so. It was not surprising, therefore, that this new dynamic of world trade brought—or at least helped bring—Trump to power. It was no surprise either that his protectionist actions were popular. Protection against imports is the only form of industrial assistance that Americans have generally regarded as legitimate. It also shifts the blame for predominantly domestic policy failure onto foreigners and, worse, in this case, the "yellow peril."

Now let us turn to the story of finance. Over the past two centuries, it rhymes with that of global trade—up, down, up, and after the transatlantic financial crisis, not merely stagnant but sharply down.[74]

Barriers to the flow of capital across borders fell dramatically in the nineteenth century, and flows of capital became enormous. Behind this were huge improvements in communications, especially the development of submarine cables and the security for investors created by the combination of the gold standard, British capital markets, and British power. Holdings of financial assets by foreigners was still just 7 percent of world output in 1870, but reached 19 percent by 1900, roughly where they remained in 1914. They then collapsed to 8 percent of world output in 1930 and on down to 5 percent in 1945. Exchange controls were adopted by many countries in the 1930s. The UK itself adopted them during World War II. They remained in effect on current transactions until 1961 and on capital transactions until 1979.[75] After World War II, capital flows rose again. The stock of foreign-held assets had reached 25 percent of world output by 1980, thus returning to where they had been in 1900. But they then reached 110 percent of world output in 2000 and an astonishing 185 percent in 2007, the year when the transatlantic financial crisis hit.[76] They then fell modestly back to 183 percent in 2016.[77]

A different way of looking at integration of capital markets is in terms of current account surpluses and deficits (which also represent net outflows and inflows of capital for countries). Between 1870 and 1889, Argentina, then a dynamic emerging economy, ran a current account deficit (that is, net capital inflow) averaging 19 percent of gross domestic product—an astonishingly large figure. It then averaged 6.2 percent of GDP between 1890 and 1913. Australia and Canada were also huge capital importers at that time. Meanwhile, the UK's current account surplus averaged 4.6 percent of GDP between 1870 and 1913.[78] At its peak, British net overseas investment ran at 9 percent of GDP, well over half its capital accumulation at the time, while British claims on the rest of the world reached twice GDP.[79] No other large economy has had such high levels of cross-border net ownership of capital relative to its economy.

During the second globalization, current account surpluses and deficits became significant yet again. Between 1997 and 2007, for example, China's current account surplus averaged 4 percent of its rapidly growing GDP, and Germany's averaged 3 cent of GDP. China's surplus ultimately reached 8 percent of GDP in 2006, 10 percent in 2007, and 9 percent in 2008. Between 2008 and 2017, China's current account surplus averaged 3 percent of GDP, while Germany's averaged 7 percent of GDP, even bigger than the UK's in the heyday of the first globalization. Germany's surplus was even over 8 percent of GDP in 2015, 2016, and 2017.[80]

The big difference between the early twenty-first century and the early twentieth is who were the net borrowers. In the late nineteenth century, the net flow of finance went into ownership of real assets, often infrastructure and mines, in the emerging countries of that time with good investment opportunities, predominantly countries with surplus land, such as Argentina, Australia, Canada, and the US. This time the net flow mainly went to high-income countries in order to finance (debt-fueled) consumption, unsustainable housing booms, or both. The countries with the best opportunities for investment nowadays are the fast-growing Asian countries whose principal resource was (and is) cheap, hardworking labor. After the shock of the Asian financial crisis in 1997–98, these countries, which include China, chose to run current account surpluses and so became net exporters of capital, partly in order to accumulate reserves as a way to insure themselves against shocks emanating from the dollar-based global financial system.[81]

This shifted the biggest deficits onto a limited number of high-income countries. In absolute terms, the US has been far and away the biggest net borrower. This was something Donald Trump's administration emphasized with displeasure.[82] Between 1997 and 2007 the US current account deficit averaged 4 percent of GDP. Between 2008 and 2017, it still averaged close to 3 percent of GDP. Spain also ran large and persistent current account deficits before the crisis, as did the UK between 1997 and 2007. Overall, high-income countries ran average current account deficits of 0.5 percent of global GDP between 1997 and 2007 and were then in balance, on average, between 2008 and 2017. Meanwhile, emerging and developing countries of East Asia and the Pacific consistently ran surpluses. These averaged 0.2 percent of global GDP between 1997 and 2007 and then 0.3 percent of global GDP between 2008 and 2017.[83]

In sum, this time, finance has increasingly created net flows of resources among rich countries or even from poor ones to richer ones, thereby becoming an enormously fragile element in the global economy. Indeed, this culminated in a huge financial crisis.

Migration shows much the same pattern as trade and finance: a huge surge in the late nineteenth and early twentieth centuries. In the decade of the 1890s, a high point for population movement, inflows of people into the US were 9 percent of the initial population—equivalent to an immigration of 29 million within a period of ten years today. In Argentina, the comparable figure was 26 percent; in Australia, it was 17 percent. In the same decade, the UK's outflow was 5 percent of the initial population, Spain's 6 percent, and Sweden's 7 percent.

Controls on immigration began to be introduced in the nineteenth and twentieth centuries, notably by the US, much the biggest net recipient of immigrants in absolute terms.[84] Between 1914 and 1945, migration was tightly constrained. After World War II, flows of people into the high-income countries were liberalized, with large increases in the proportion of the foreign-born population in most high-income countries. Nevertheless, controls on movement of people remained far tighter than on movement of goods, many services (other than those requiring movement of providers), and capital. Moreover, the political pressure has in general been in favor of restricting immigration further.[85]

One authoritative analysis of the impact of migration in the nineteenth century concludes that "all of the real wage convergence before World War I was attributable to migration, about two thirds of the GDP per worker convergence and perhaps one half of the GDP per capita convergence."[86] Nothing comparable has happened since then, with the possible exception of migration within the European Union, where free movement of labor is one of the four freedoms guaranteed by the founding treaty. Unfortunately, this principle also became one of the reasons for the UK's vote to leave the EU in the referendum of June 2016. Elsewhere (and from other origins into the EU), immigration into high-income countries is tightly controlled.

Nevertheless, flows of immigration into the high-income countries hit high levels again, even by nineteenth-century standards. In 1911, the foreign-born had been 14.7 percent of the population of the United States and 22 percent of Canada's.[87] European countries were sources of net emigration, not net recipients. In 2019, the high-income democracies with the highest shares of the foreign-born in the population were Australia, Switzerland, New Zealand, Canada, Sweden, Austria, and Ireland (see figure 8). Yet, of these countries, only Austria has had a large backlash against immigrants. Again, the countries with the largest increases in the proportion of foreign-born between 2000 and 2019 were Spain, Ireland, New Zealand, Norway, Austria, Sweden, Switzerland, Belgium, Australia, and Italy. Only in Austria and Italy was the backlash large. The increase in the proportion of foreign-born has certainly been socially and politically significant.[88] But, surprisingly perhaps, given all the political noise there, the increase in the proportion of foreign-born in the US between 2000 and 2016 was the second-*lowest* among high-income countries, ahead only of France, where immigration has also been a very politically salient issue.

FIGURE 8. FOREIGN-BORN AS SHARE OF POPULATION (PERCENT)
(Source: OECD)

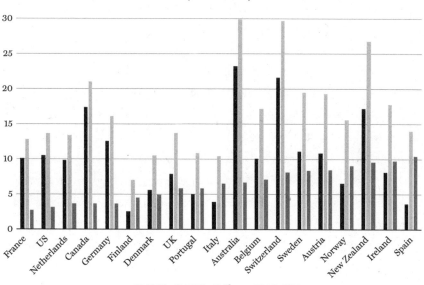

■ 2000   ■ 2019   ▦ Change 2000–2019

The link between the levels of immigration and popular hostility is complex: it reflects the culture of the receiving country, especially embedded racism, the culture and ethnicity of the immigrants, economic conditions in the receiving country, and, not least, the behavior of politicians. The economics of immigration are complex and controversial, too.[89] It is clear, however, that many resent high levels of immigration, for a mixture of cultural, social, and economic reasons. Many also see high levels of immigration as eroding the value of what is, for many citizens of high-income societies, the most valuable asset they own: citizenship.

Yet, at the global level, the movement of people has been both modest and surprisingly stable. In 1960, 2.6 percent of the world's people were living in countries in which they had not been born. By 1990, this was 2.9 percent and in 2010 just 3.1 percent. While there have been large flows of refugees into some developing countries, it is the high-income countries that stand out as receiving large and consistent flows of immigrants in the recent past. Thus, just as in trade and finance, there was a surge in the impact of globalization on high-income democracies in the late twentieth and early twenty-first centuries, and that in turn created a backlash that became quite visible, notably in the US and the UK.

Overall, just as was the case for capitalism itself, globalization—the movement of goods, services, capital, and people across borders—shows cycles within a long-term trend. The trend in this case has been largely driven by technological revolutions and also by organizational changes, especially the rise of global corporations and capital markets. The cycles, however, are determined, as was also true more domestically, by political, economic, and ideological shifts. Recessions, national rivalries, wars, and the rise and fall of socialist, nationalist, and dirigiste attitudes and ideas help explain the degree to which countries are prepared to open up their economies.

Connection between Democracy and Globalization

The pattern of up, down, up, and then down in market capitalism and especially globalization coincides to a quite remarkable degree with that for democratization. (See figure 9.) Globalization and democratization went together in the late nineteenth and early twentieth centuries, in the years before the First World War. The end of the First World War led to a jump in the proportion of democracies. The world economy then deglobalized sharply in the interwar years. Democratization duly followed globalization down, with collapse of trade preceding that in the proportion democracies. Trade and democratization reached a nadir during World War II. Then came the postwar shift toward democratization. A strong recovery in the openness of the world economy followed. Democratization stabilized in the 1960s. Globalization followed in the 1970s. Democratization soared in the 1980s and early 1990s, with globalization following closely behind. Both finally stabilized (or, on some dimensions, declined) after the global financial crisis of the early 2000s.

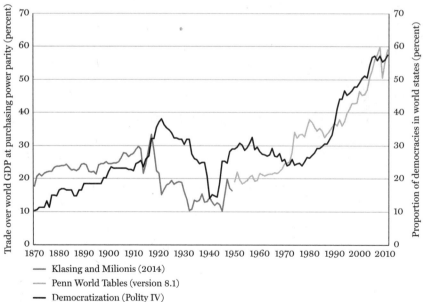

FIGURE 9. GLOBALIZATION AND DEMOCRACY
(Source: Our World in Data and Center for Systemic Peace)

—— Klasing and Milionis (2014)
—— Penn World Tables (version 8.1)
—— Democratization (Polity IV)

This is not to suggest any simple cause and effect between globalization and democracy. The relationship is too complex for that, as indicated in the previous chapter. But periods of market liberalization and expanding globalization have also been ones of optimism. That should have made democracy less conflictual. Periods of rising restrictions on the economy have tended to coincide with economic, political, or other disturbances, when a large proportion of the population feels frightened and angry, which is also bad for liberal democracy. Finally, victories by the democratic powers, as in the First World War, Second World War, and Cold War, have been good for both democracy and globalization.

A different way of looking at how far capitalism correlates with democracy is to look across countries at the relationship between rankings for "economic freedom" and those for "political freedom" at a moment in time.[90] The measure of economic freedom, taken from the Cato Institute, covers the size of government, the legal system, the monetary system, freedom to trade, and the extent and nature of regulation. The measure of political freedom, taken from Freedom House, includes political rights (elections and so forth) and civil liberties (freedom of expression and association, and so forth).

The 30 economically freest countries in 2014 (out of 159, with Venezuela at the bottom) were all among the 60 politically freest countries, with the exceptions of Hong Kong, Singapore, the United Arab Emirates, Qatar, Armenia, and Bahrain. The latter are small autocracies or semiautocracies, with special political characteristics. The list of the 30 most economically free countries includes many important democracies. Italy is the only significant Western democracy not to come in the top 60 countries ranked on economic freedom (it was ranked 69th). Thus, overall, the economically free countries are, with a few (small) exceptions, also leading democracies. Again, if we look at the 30 countries ranked most politically free (out of 204), we find that this list included all the Western democracies, plus Japan (with the US only 28th). Only one of these countries is not among the 60 economically freest countries. Again, not surprisingly, that country is Italy, ranked 29th most politically free. Quite simply, economically free countries tend to be democracies, and vice versa. Liberal capitalism goes together with liberal democracy, not just in theory but also in practice.

Conclusion

The history of modern representative systems of democracy is brief. That of a global capitalist economy is not so much older. But the above discussion highlights some crucial points.

First, over the past two centuries, democracy and capitalism have both evolved substantially. The franchise has been extended dramatically and capitalism has also become vastly more institutionally complex. Most important, the interplay between democratic governments and market capitalism has shaped both.

Second, market capitalism goes across borders. Opportunities for cross-border economic activity have grown over time, as the costs of transport and communications have plummeted.

Third, periods of buoyant global capitalism and periods of democratization have coincided. Similarly, collapses in global capitalism have coincided with periods of retreating democracy.

Fourth, the economy has not been the only factor driving democratization. Also important have been the First World War, the Second World War, and the Cold War. In all three cases, the Western victors pushed for democratization of the losers. After the First World War, the push for a renewal of global capitalism and democratization ultimately failed. After the Second World War, democratization of the losers succeeded.[91] After the Cold War, the results have been very mixed.

Fifth, global capitalism has brought huge economic and social disturbances. The most important of these impacts come from global financial crises.[92]

Sixth, free-market economies go together with democracy. History has not been kind to the hope that one can have a vibrant democracy without a competitive market economy. Equally, there are no important examples of rich capitalist economies that are not also democratic.

Finally, the present condition of Western liberal democracy is deeply worrying. That is in part due to economic failures—slow growth, rising inequality, loss of good jobs. Once again, liberal democracy and global capitalism need to be saved together.

Part II

—■—

WHAT WENT WRONG

Prologue to Part II

As argued in part I, we are now in a "democratic recession" and by *we*, I mean core Western countries, in particular the US. The question is why. The argument in part I was that a democratic capitalist state depends on maintaining a delicate balance between complementary opposites—the market and democracy. These political and economic dimensions of our complex societies may be mutually supportive or mutually destructive. The argument in part II is that the balances between politics and economics, market and state, domestic and global, winners and losers, technological change and ability to adapt to it have been destabilized. The result has not just been populism, but antidemocratic populism. This lost balance must be regained. How to do that will be the focus of part III.

The legitimacy of any system always depends on performance. In the end, people will cease to trust a system that does not work for them. But a system's legitimacy also depends on the relationship between the economically successful and the rest of the population. Even if the system works not too badly in aggregate, the emergency of an excessively large gap in wealth and power is likely to make democracy fragile. It could move a democracy toward outright plutocracy. It could be toward demagogy. Or it could be toward a hybrid, which I call pluto-populism.

The discussion will start in chapter 4 with what has happened domestically within the high-income countries. Chapter 5 analyzes the causes of these changes. Chapter 6 turns to the way politics have changed, especially the dangerous rise of anti-pluralist populism.

CHAPTER FOUR

It's the Economy, Stupid

Those who have a superabundance of good fortune, strength, riches, friends, and so forth, neither wish to submit to rule nor understand how to do so; . . . Those on the other hand who are greatly deficient in these qualities are too subservient. . . . The result is a state not of free men but of slaves and masters, the former full of envy, the latter of contempt. Nothing could be further removed from friendship or from partnership in a state. . . .

It is clear then that the best partnership in a state is the one which operates through the middle people, and also that those states in which the middle element is large, and stronger if possible than the other two together, or at any rate stronger than either of them alone, have every chance of having a well-run constitution.

—*Aristotle*[1]

There are three things necessary for government: weapons, food and trust. If a ruler cannot hold on to all three, he should give up weapons first and food next. Trust should be guarded to the end: without trust we cannot stand.

—*Confucius*

Trust in democratic institutions, the global market economy, and political and economic elites has faded over recent decades, not least in established high-income countries. This has shown itself in protectionism, hostility toward immigration, and, above all, a growing leaning toward authoritarian populism.

What, then, lies at the root of these developments? The principal answer is the hollowing out of the middle classes, identified by Aristotle almost twenty-five hundred years ago as the core constituency for a constitutional democracy. A similar hollowing out of the independent peasantry and the emergence of a class of immensely wealthy generals and capitalists brought about the collapse of the Roman Republic. The reduction in the social and economic status of those in the middle of the income distribution has been the politically crucial economic development of the past four decades inside high-income countries and, above all, inside the US. The impact of this erosion was then made far worse by the shock of the transatlantic financial crisis of 2007–12. COVID-19 seems likely to make things worse, though at the time of writing in mid-2022 this was not yet sure. The result has been to make political and constitutional systems far more fragile.[2]

When a political system becomes fragile in this way, "anything" can happen, including the highly unexpected. That duly happened, notably in the UK vote for Brexit and the election of Donald Trump as US president, in 2016. This was yet another "annus horribilis."[3] But even the EU may be vulnerable: after all, "if economic hard times, inequality, and immigration are key triggers of populist reaction, then the EU is implicated in all three."[4]

Economics of "Status Anxiety"

"Status anxiety" is the most helpful way of thinking about the root cause of the rise in support for populist causes and especially for nationalist politicians (Trump, for example) and goals (Brexit, for example).[5] Who is most prone to such anxiety? The answer is: "those most prone to [it] are likely to be people a few rungs up that hierarchy, namely those whose social status is low enough to generate concern but who still have a significant measure of status to defend. Studies show that the people in this group tend to evince special concern for defending social boundaries; and they are particularly susceptible to last place aversion, namely, concerns about falling to the bottom of the hierarchy."[6] In Western countries, "white" people with relatively modest levels of education feel threatened by racial minorities and immigrants, and men, both white and members of minorities, feel threatened by the rising status of women.

In their book on uncertainty, John Kay and Mervyn King refer to a "reference narrative," a story "which is an expression of our realistic expectations."[7] In this case, important reference narratives failed to come true, creating disappointment, fear, and anger. That is why Trump's "Make America Great *Again*" (my emphasis) was a brilliantly targeted slogan. It is why "Take Back Control," the Brexit slogan, was as well targeted at people who felt they had been losing control over their livelihoods, status, and even country. "Frustrated by the sense that the political class had failed them, many ordinary citizens took the opportunity to vent their fury."[8] Not surprisingly, then, "exit polls indicate that 64 percent of manual workers voted for Brexit compared with 43 percent of managers or professionals; 37 percent voted for Marine Le Pen in the first round of the French presidential elections [in 2017] compared with 14 percent of managers or professionals; and white Americans without a college degree voted for Donald Trump [in 2016] by a margin of almost 20 percent over Hillary Clinton."[9] These are votes for a return to the past by those whose past was at least relatively, if not absolutely, better than their today.

The rising "deaths of despair" among less-educated white people, famously noted by Princeton University's Anne Case and Angus Deaton, also illustrates the woes of downwardly mobile people in the US. Case and Deaton note: "We find marked differences in mortality by race and education, with mortality among white non-Hispanics (males and females) rising for those without a college degree, and falling for those with a college degree. In contrast, mortality rates among blacks and Hispanics have continued to fall, irrespective of educational attainment."[10] Meanwhile, mortality rates in other rich countries continued their fall at the rates that once characterized the US. The "preliminary but plausible" explanation is one of worsening opportunities for those with low levels of education, which creates cumulative disadvantage in the labor market, marriage, child outcomes, and health over generations. A proximate cause of falling life expectancy among these less-educated whites is overprescription of opioids, itself one of the more scandalous failures of a wasteful and venal US health care system.[11] But the demand for such drugs comes from despair, as the great French sociologist Émile Durkheim would have predicted.[12]

How far economic factors affect political inclinations directly, through impoverishment, and how far indirectly, through status anxiety, is unclear. The answer must be a bit of both. People feel the loss of the economic security and social status that a good job gave them. What is clear, however, is that economic conditions influence political views and behavior. Relative income and wealth have always both determined and reflected social status. In a contemporary market-based society, this is still decisively true. Furthermore, today's high-income countries enjoyed huge increases in standards of living in the past. Indeed, in many ways, even the raison d'être of these societies became rising general prosperity, from generation to generation. In the US, this has been called the American dream.[13] Failure to deliver generational improvements in standards of living is for the US to fail as a society. Failure to achieve a generational improvement in one's standard of living is to fail as an individual. As other sources of belonging weaken, and society becomes more atomized, these failures must hurt even more.[14]

In addition, many cultural and social changes have economic roots, which is hardly surprising given the central role of economic activity in shaping, indeed justifying, social and political arrangements. The economy of the mid-twentieth century in the high-income countries, with its armies of unionized, reasonably secure, relatively well paid, and overwhelmingly male industrial workers, was the product of a particular stage of economic development, buttressed by the postwar commitment to full employment. This social and cultural pattern has vanished, together with its economic base. Similarly, declining fertility (partly the result of declining infant mortality), huge reductions in the effort and time needed to look after a household, the declining significance of physical strength as a productive factor, and the rise of the service economy at least partly (in my view, largely) explain the transformation in the economic, social, and political roles of women. Again, the huge gaps in wealth between rich and poor societies and the declining costs of transport and information help explain the recent upsurge in migration from poorer to richer countries. These economically driven changes have also inevitably brought social and cultural transformation. They have, among other things, made less-educated "white" men feel they are foreigners in their own countries and are losing status relative to ethnic minorities, immigrants, and women.

Without being too reductive, we can suggest that cultural markers, including nationality, ethnicity, religion, and other narrower values, become more important when economic status is under threat. In the presidential election campaign of 2008, Barack Obama notoriously declared of people in small towns in the Midwest, hit badly by economic change, that "it's not surprising then they get bitter, they cling to guns or religion or antipathy to people who aren't like them or anti-immigrant sentiment or anti-trade sentiment as a way to explain their frustrations."[15] This was controversial. But it was surely at least partly true. What does the white working class like about Trump? The answer is surely that he respects them (or at least successfully pretends to do so), while, in their view, *everybody else* disrespects them.[16]

How the Economy Moved against the Less Educated

A dominant feature of the period since the early 1980s has been increasing *inequality*, in both wealth and incomes (pretax and posttax).[17] The Organization for Economic Co-operation and Development has noted, "Income inequality in OECD countries is at its highest level for the past half century." Moreover, "Uncertainty and fears of social decline and exclusion have reached the middle classes in many societies."[18] In terms of household disposable incomes (after taxes and subsidies), the UK and the US are the most unequal of the large high-income countries, though New Zealand and Korea are also quite unequal. (See figure 10.)[19]

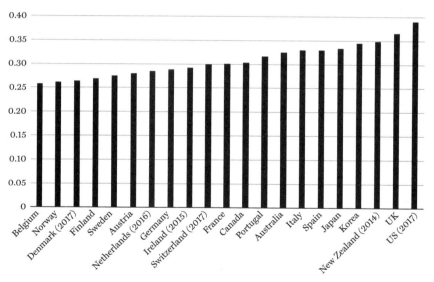

FIGURE 10. INEQUALITY OF HOUSEHOLD DISPOSABLE INCOMES, 2018
(AFTER TAXES AND CASH TRANSFERS) (GINI COEFFICIENT)
(Source: OECD)

Cross-country differences in inequality after taxes and government spending are heavily influenced by both pretax inequality and government policy. (See figure 11.) Inequality was low in Norway in 2010 not only because pretax inequality in household disposable income was low, but because redistribution through the fiscal system was also large. The UK's posttax household disposable incomes were less unequal than those of the US in 2010, even though pretax inequality was even higher. The explanation was that the UK's redistribution effort was substantially greater than that of the US.

FIGURE 11. TAXES, TRANSFERS, AND HOUSEHOLD INCOME INEQUALITY, 2010, RANKED BY IMPACT OF TAXES AND TRANSFERS (GINI COEFFICIENT)
(Source: Janet C. Gornick and Branko Milanovic, LIS Center Research Brief, January 2015)

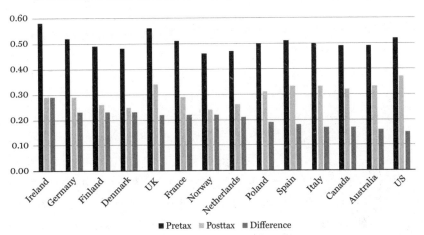

Another way of showing changes over time is the share of the top 10 percent of (pretax) income recipients in the early 1980s and in 2008, the year of the transatlantic financial crisis. A striking feature (see figure 12) is that the countries in which the top 10 percent of recipients had the largest shares in pretax national income in 2008 (the US, Japan, Germany, and the UK) were also those with the biggest increases in these shares between 1981 and 2008. In the US the increase in the share of the top 10 percent in pretax national income between 1981 and 2008 was 9 percentage points. By 2008, the top 10 percent received 44 percent of US pretax national income. In some other countries, notably Spain, the Netherlands, and France, the shares of the top 10 percent in pretax income changed little.

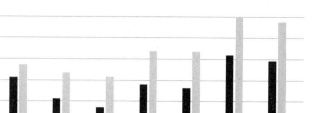

FIGURE 12. SHARES OF THE TOP 10 PERCENT OF INCOME RECIPIENTS
IN PRETAX NATIONAL INCOME (PERCENT)
(Source: World Inequality Database)

One of the most striking aspects of rising inequality has been soaring levels of executive pay and so increasing inequality at the top. According to Deborah Hargreaves of the High Pay Center, "The ratio between average chief executive pay and employee pay in the UK was 129 to 1 in 2016, an increase from 48 to 1 in 1998."[20] In the US, the corresponding ratio was 347 to 1 in 2016, up from 42 to 1 in 1980.[21] "These figures underline the shift in executive remuneration from a reasonably high middle-class salary thirty years ago to untold riches."[22] In effect, these new levels of pay allow an executive to accumulate dynastic wealth in a few short years. Worse, the "bonus culture," which generates these massive incomes, motivates executives who expect to enjoy brief tenures to run their businesses with a view to raising share prices in the short term, at the expense of investment, which brings benefits only in the longer term. The result is to lower productivity growth on which so much ultimately depends (a point to which the discussion returns further on).[23] Similarly, share buybacks, especially buybacks financed by debt, appear to lower corporate investment and weaken corporate balance sheets.[24]

The implications of the rise in inequality in the US, in particular, are startling: over the period 1993 to 2015, the cumulative real growth in incomes of the top 1 percent was 95 percent, compared with 14 percent for the remaining 99 percent. As a result, *the top 1 percent captured 52 percent of the increase in real pretax incomes.* One of the implications of such figures is that GDP growth itself tells little about changes in the welfare of the population. How the benefits of that growth are distributed also matters a great deal. Anybody who takes an Aristotelian view of the role of a thriving middle class in stabilizing a constitutional (or liberal) democracy must be made anxious by such extreme developments.[25]

Wealth is also a source of power. Shareholder control over companies gives direct economic power. Wealth exercises influence via philanthropy, ownership of media, and so forth. But wealth also has a powerful direct influence over politics, by funding parties, supporting candidates, buying political advertising, promoting political causes, and paying for lobbying. Thus, high levels of wealth inequality will, as Aristotle warned, corrode a democratic polity. In France and the UK, the share of the top 10 percent in personal wealth is substantially lower than it was in the early twentieth century, though still high, at a little above 50 percent. In the US, however, the share of the top 10 percent was over 70 percent by 2014. This represented a return to levels in the period before World War II. (See figure 13.) Strikingly, US wealth inequality had become far higher than in the other two countries by the early 1980s. Given the increased inequality of wealth and incomes, evidence of the role of money in US politics is hardly surprising.[26] Democracy is for sale.

A cross-country study at the OECD concluded that "income inequality has a sizable and statistically significant negative impact on growth, and that redistributive policies achieving greater equality in disposable income have no adverse growth consequences. Moreover, . . . it is inequality at the bottom of the distribution that hampers growth."[27] In countries with both rising inequality and low growth, losers will fall behind, not just relatively but absolutely. Unfortunately,

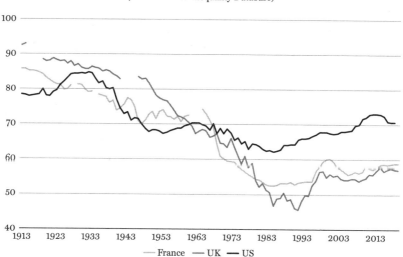

FIGURE 13. SHARE OF TOP 10 PERCENT IN NET PERSONAL WEALTH (PERCENT)
(Source: World Inequality Database)

rising inequality has been quite a general phenomenon.[28] Indeed, Belgium and France were the only high-income economies to have experienced little change in income inequality between the mid-1980s and the end of the first decade of the 2000s.[29]

The evidence shows that the combination of rising inequality with modest real growth in real incomes has indeed meant stagnant real incomes for large parts of the population. In the US, notably, real median household disposable incomes in 2019 (just before the pandemic) were only 10 percent higher than twenty years earlier, while mean real disposable incomes, which are heavily influenced by changes at the top, rose 21 percent over the same period. Between 1984 and 2019, the ratio of median to mean real household incomes in the US fell from 72 percent to 59 percent. Much of that decline had occurred by 2000. (See figure 14.)[30]

There is also evidence of an inverse relationship between inequality and social mobility: the higher the inequality of earnings, the more a son's position in the earnings distribution is correlated with his father's (that is, the higher the economic *immobility*).[31] The late Alan

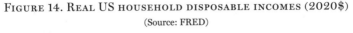

FIGURE 14. REAL US HOUSEHOLD DISPOSABLE INCOMES (2020$)
(Source: FRED)

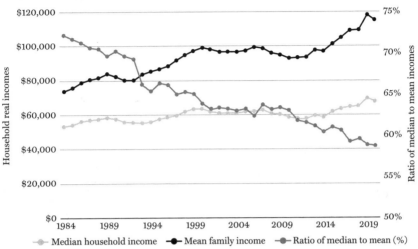

Krueger, chairman of the US Council of Economic Advisers under Barack Obama, called this the "Great Gatsby Curve."[32] (See figure 15.) The impact of a father's relative income on his son's is indeed greater the greater the inequality.[33] Thus, high-inequality countries, such as the US and UK, have lower intergenerational economic mobility. Medium-inequality countries (Italy, Switzerland, France, Canada, and Germany) show a wide range of degrees of economic mobility. Low-inequality countries (the Nordics) have high economic mobility. Yet it is important to note that mobility measured in terms of intergenerational changes in relative earnings is not the same as mobility defined in terms of occupational class. For the latter, the most important determinant of mobility are changes in the structure of the economy, which determine the sorts of jobs it creates and destroys.[34]

Another highly significant longer-term trend has been deindustrialization or, more precisely, the rapid decline in the share of employment in industry. This has happened in every significant high-income country (see figure 16). Naturally, countries with large exports of manufactures (and relatively weak service sectors), such as Germany, Japan, and Italy, have relatively high shares of employment in industry.

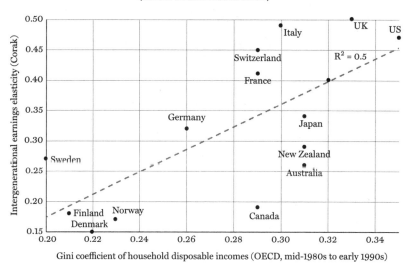

FIGURE 15. "GREAT GATSBY CURVE"
(Source: Corak 2012 and OECD)

Gini coefficient of household disposable incomes (OECD, mid-1980s to early 1990s)

Yet the fall in the share of industry in employment was very substantial even in Germany. The dominant cause of the decline in the share of industry in employment has been rising productivity, not trade: Germany, after all, has consistently run huge trade surpluses in manufactures.[35] Whatever Trump might have suggested with his slogan "Make America Great Again," nostalgia is not a viable economic policy. The promise to bring manufacturing employment back toward shares of half a century ago cannot be delivered: the old industrial way of life is going the way of agriculture, with very high productivity and low employment. (See figure 16.)

Manufacturing industry used to generate a very large number of relatively highly paid and secure jobs for less-educated men. One reason for the relatively high pay was unionization. That, in turn, was made possible by the relative ease of organizing large workforces located in huge plants. The workers consequently had the capacity to inflict damage on the profitability of these capital-intensive businesses, which gave them bargaining power against employers. The loss of industrial jobs has also meant the loss of a way of life. Moreover,

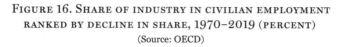

FIGURE 16. SHARE OF INDUSTRY IN CIVILIAN EMPLOYMENT
RANKED BY DECLINE IN SHARE, 1970–2019 (PERCENT)
(Source: OECD)

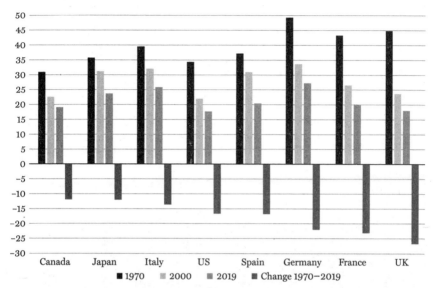

industry was regionally concentrated, often in areas where there were few alternative sources of good jobs. Deindustrialization then became a prime source of regional economic inequality, as regions that had once been in the vanguard of the industrial revolution, usually because they possessed specific resources, particularly coal and iron, fell into long-term decline. This problem has hit all countries in which the manufacturing industry had been important during the industrial revolutions of the nineteenth and early twentieth centuries.

A further important indicator of adverse longer-term structural change has been the falling labor force participation of prime-age men (those between twenty-five and fifty-five years of age). This ratio has declined in all large high-income countries since the 1980s. But the declines were particularly large in Italy and the US. These are the ages when people form families. Work makes most men of that age feel like valuable and productive members of society, able to support their loved ones and sustain successful marriages. That so many men of this age are not even looking for work tells one a great deal about the degree of discouragement. In the US, for example, one in nine men aged twenty-five to fifty-five was not looking for work in 2019, despite the economic recovery over the previous decade. The prime-age male participation rate in the US was even slightly lower than it had been in 2010, just after the financial crisis. It was also the second-lowest of all these countries in 2019. (See figure 17.)

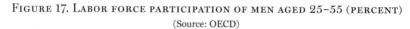

FIGURE 17. LABOR FORCE PARTICIPATION OF MEN AGED 25–55 (PERCENT)
(Source: OECD)

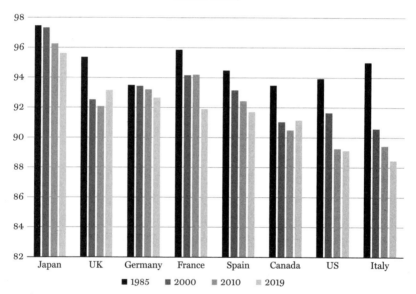

The picture for labor force participation by prime-age women is, at first glance, far more encouraging, with rising participation in most of the larger high-income countries. The striking exception once again is the US. The prime-age female participation rate was lower in 2019 than in 2000. The increase overall since 1985 was far smaller than in any of these other countries. As a result, prime-age female participation in the US has moved from highest of these countries in 1985 to second from the bottom, again ahead only of Italy, in 2019. This is yet another indication of the failure of the US to extend economic opportunity. (See figure 18.)

FIGURE 18. LABOR FORCE PARTICIPATION OF WOMEN AGED 25–55 (PERCENT)
(Source: OECD)

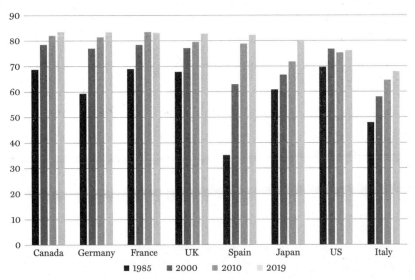

The transformations of labor markets over the past four decades—deindustrialization, deunionization, declining participation, liberalization, and the rise of the "gig economy"—is closely associated with the rise of "precarious" employment.[36] The British economist Guy Standing has summed up what has happened in terms of the emergence of a new social class—the "precariat." Standing asserts, "Although we cannot give anything like precise figures, we may guess that at present, in many countries, at least a quarter of the adult population is in the precariat. This is not just a matter of having insecure employment, of being in jobs of limited duration and with minimal labor protection, although all this is widespread. It is being in a status that offers no sense of career, no sense of secure occupational identity and few, if any, entitlements to the state and enterprise benefits that several generations of those who saw themselves as belonging to the industrial proletariat or the salariat had come to expect as their due."[37]

The most important long-term determinant of prosperity is the level and growth of productivity. In a country with fast increases in productivity, everybody will get better off unless inequality rises very quickly. But in a country with stagnant productivity (such as Italy over the last two decades or the UK over the last one and a half decades), the standard of living can rise for some only if the standard of living of others falls. This then becomes a zero-sum economy: if A wins, B through Z must lose.

In the 1950s and 1960s, productivity growth, measured as growth of output per hour, rose relatively quickly in today's high-income economies. This was the era when continental Europe and, even more, Japan caught up rapidly on US productivity levels. A marked slowdown in productivity growth occurred in the 1970s and 1980s in all the big high-income countries. But the slowdown in the US and UK was relatively small. So productivity growth converged. In the 1990s, productivity growth accelerated somewhat in the US, as a result of the revolution in information technology. In the 2000s, US productivity growth became the fastest of the eight largest high-income economies. In the UK, too, productivity growth in the 1990s was relatively good.

FIGURE 19. DECADAL AVERAGE GROWTH RATE OF OUTPUT PER HOUR
(Source: Conference Board)

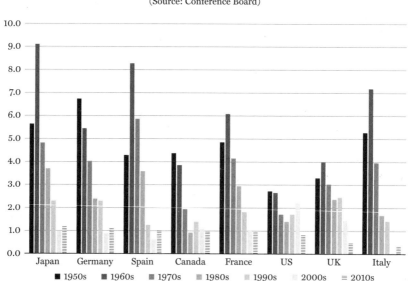

Average productivity growth in the 2010s (between 2010 and 2019) became dismal in all high-income countries. This is important— and depressing. At the bottom of the list for rates of productivity growth after 2010 were the UK and Italy. One explanation for the recent slowdown in productivity growth may be that a significant part of precrisis productivity growth was a delusion. (See figure 19.) That is likely to be particularly true of the financial sector, where it is exceptionally hard to distinguish incomes generated by an unsustainable surge in credit and debt, or some other form of rent extraction, from genuinely higher productivity.[38]

How Crises Destabilized the Economy

In sum, powerful long-term trends created significant economic problems for the high-income democracies. Arguably even more damaging was the crisis that emanated from the core of the global financial system in 2007 and 2008 and proceeded to have a devastating impact on large parts of the world economy.

The proximate cause of the crisis was an explosion of indebtedness, much of it associated with sharp rises in the real prices of property. A significant part of the explanation for this debt explosion was reliance on household debt for sustaining consumption, especially in the US, since the real incomes of so many were stagnating.[39] Behind this were even more profound changes, including the entry of China into the world economy, the liberalization of the financial system, and undue reliance on a monetary policy that targeted only inflation. Ultimately, the financial crisis was the consequence of huge (and insufficiently understood) shifts in the world economy transmitted via a grossly undercapitalized and underregulated financial system.[40] When property prices tumbled in important economies, especially the US, the financial cycle turned and a huge financial crisis erupted. This was followed by a contraction in household and financial sector debt relative to GDP in the mature market economies. That in turn helps explain the weakness of postcrisis economies. Then, with a second crisis—the COVID-19 pandemic—debt exploded upward once again, with as yet unknown consequences. (See figure 20.)

FIGURE 20. PRIVATE DEBT OVER GDP IN MATURE ECONOMIES (PERCENT)
(Source: IIF)

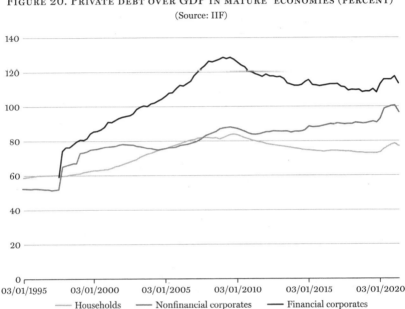

The most obvious legacy of the crisis was the impact on real incomes. Of the group of seven leading high-income countries, plus Spain, only Germany experienced no significant shortfall in GDP per head relative to what would have happened if the 1990–2007 trend in real GDP per head had continued, though this was partly because precrisis growth had been slow. Japan's GDP per head was down 7 percent by 2018, relative to its already feeble 1990–2007 fitted trend annual growth of 1.8 percent; French GDP per head was down 13 percent, relative to its already quite feeble 1990–2007 trend annual growth of 1.6 percent; Canadian and US GDP per head were down 17 percent, relative to 1990–2007 trend annual growth of 2.1 percent and 2.6 percent, respectively; UK and Italian GDP per head were down 22 percent, the former relative to a buoyant 1990–2007 trend annual growth of 2.5 percent, the latter relative to an already miserable trend growth of only 1.4 percent; and Spanish GDP per head was down 24 percent, relative to a 1990–2007 trend annual growth rate of 2.6 percent.[41] (See figure 21.)

In the case of the UK, postcrisis shortfall in real GDP per head is a substantially bigger and more permanent loss than those caused by either of the two world wars or the Great Depression. (After World War II, in fact, the growth of real income accelerated sharply, compared with the interwar years.) Then, of course, came a second huge shock—COVID-19. In 2020, there were huge declines in real GDP per head. Even in 2021, GDP per head was expected to remain 33 percent below the 1990–2007 trend in Spain, 32 percent below in the UK, and 28 percent below in Italy. And in the US, it was forecast to be 21 percent below that earlier trend. These have become extraordinary losses as they have cumulated over time.

FIGURE 21. DEVIATION FROM 1990 TO 2007 EXPONENTIAL TREND
REAL GDP PER HEAD (PERCENT)
(Source: Conference Board)

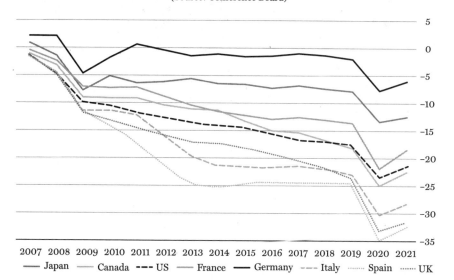

This stagnation in real GDP per head after the financial crisis also had a powerfully negative effect on *household real incomes*. A study by the McKinsey Global Institute showed that, on average, between 65 and 70 percent of all households in high-income countries had flat or falling real incomes from wages and capital between 2005 and 2014 before redistribution by governments.[42] In hard-hit Italy the proportion was 97 percent, in the US 81 percent, and the UK 70 percent. (See figure 22.)

FIGURE 22. PROPORTION OF HOUSEHOLDS WITH FLAT OR FALLING
REAL INCOMES FROM WAGES AND CAPITAL, 2005–14 (PERCENT)
(Source: McKinsey Global Institute)

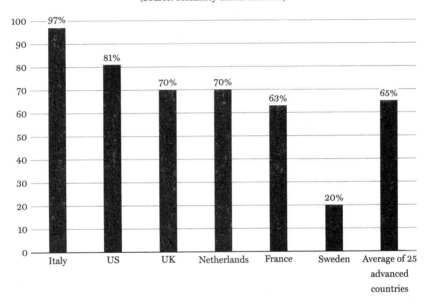

The crisis also had significant effects, in some cases temporary and in other cases long term, on *unemployment*. In the US, for example, the unemployment rate jumped from 4.6 percent in 2007 to 9.6 percent in 2010. In the eurozone, it rose from 7.6 percent in 2007 to a peak of 12.1 percent in 2013 after a substantially lengthier crisis than in the US. Unemployment fell back to low levels quite quickly in the UK and US and remained low throughout in Japan and Germany. But in some other large countries, unemployment reached high or even very high levels and persisted. In Italy, for example, the unemployment rate peaked at 12.8 percent in 2014 (from a precrisis low of 6.2 percent in 2007) but was still 10 percent in 2019. In Spain, the unemployment rate peaked at 26.1 percent in 2013 (from a precrisis low of 8.2 percent in 2007) and was still 14.1 percent in 2019, just before the COVID crisis. (See figure 23.)

FIGURE 23. UNEMPLOYMENT RATES (PERCENT)
(Source: IMF)

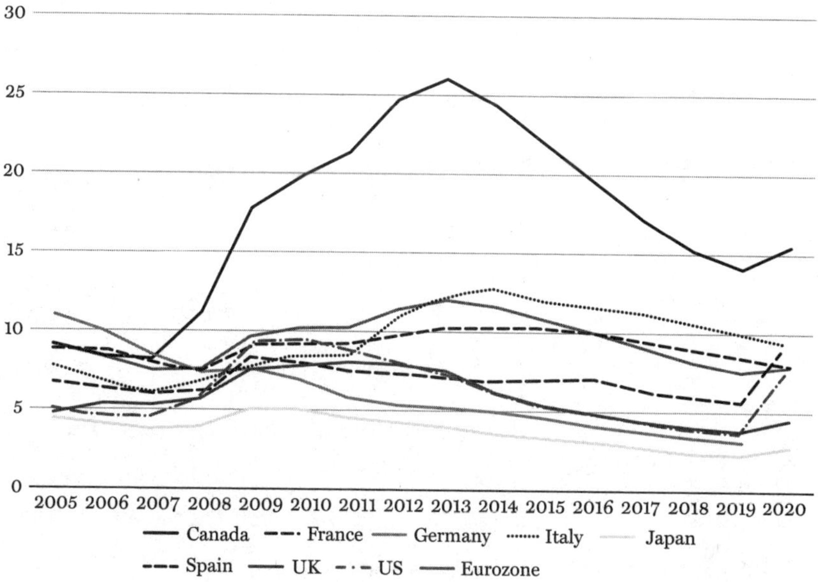

Another important economic impact of the crisis was on the *fiscal position* of affected countries. The recession and subsequent weak recovery led to higher spending and a permanent reduction in revenue relative to precrisis expectations. The loss of revenue from the previously buoyant financial sector was also important, especially in the UK. If we look at the members of the group of seven leading high-income countries, we find that they all imposed significant structural fiscal tightening from peak to trough postcrisis levels. But the structural tightening (this being a measure of "austerity") was largest in the US and UK. Only countries savaged by the eurozone crisis, especially Greece, experienced greater structural fiscal tightening. (See figure 24.)

The unexpected shock of the *financial crisis* shook trust in the

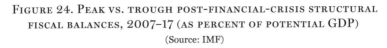

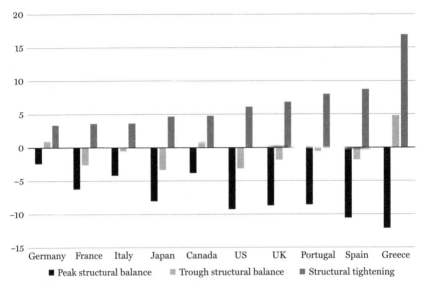

■ Peak structural balance ■ Trough structural balance ■ Structural tightening

wisdom and probity of those running the affected countries' financial, economic, and political systems. Most policy mistakes in economics are invisible to the bulk of the voting public. But the latter could not possibly fail to realize that those in charge had failed to recognize the risks they allowed the financial sector to run. The emperors turned out to be naked. Many members of the public came to believe that these failings were the result not just of stupidity but of the intellectual and moral corruption of decision-makers and opinion formers at all levels—in the financial sector, regulatory bodies, academia, media, and politics. They also saw the resources of the state used to rescue both banks and bankers—the architects, as they saw it, of the disaster—while they (and those they loved) suffered large losses through foreclosure, unemployment, a prolonged period of stagnant or falling real wages, and fiscal austerity. Finally, they also saw that while institutions were forced to pay huge fines, essentially nobody (or nobody of any importance) was punished for what had happened.[43]

At the time of writing, in 2022, it was too soon to be sure about the long-run impact of the COVID-19 pandemic, the second unexpected crisis in less than one and a half decades. A big difference from the financial crisis was that most people viewed this as an act of God. Another was that governments, or at least those with the fiscal and financial resources to do so, responded at once and on an enormous scale. The old line of Ronald Reagan that "the nine most terrifying words in the English language are: I'm from the government and I'm here to help" was forgotten far more completely than had happened even in 2008.[44] Government was very definitely back. Yet another difference was that this time the financial sector boomed almost from the beginning, as central banks and governments poured money into the economies of the high-income countries. Indeed, the concern came to be far more about inflation than about deflation. Yet, despite the differences, COVID reinforced many of the challenges of the postcrisis period. The adoption of new technologies was accelerated. Patterns of work were, as a result, transformed, possibly durably. City centers were hollowed out. Public finances deteriorated. Education was damaged. Domestic inequality worsened. Globally, there were dramatic increases in the numbers of people in extreme poverty. Global cooperation was too weak, especially over vaccination.[45] The legacy of COVID was unknown, but it was likely to be long-lasting.[46]

The consequences of the war in Ukraine were even more uncertain. But it definitely aggravated the supply shocks that COVID-19 had already created, especially in energy and food. Once again, people looked to help from governments. Once again, there was only so much governments could do. What was clear from the beginning of the war, however, was that, as with the pandemic, the answer could not be found in governmental indifference.

Economics, Culture, and Migration

"'How did you go bankrupt?' Bill asked. 'Two ways,' Mike said. 'Gradually and then suddenly.'"[47] These lines by Ernest Hemingway perfectly capture what has happened to the high-income countries. The story started with a lengthy period of rising inequality, weak growth of real incomes for many people in the middle and lower parts of income distributions, poor social mobility in countries with relatively high inequality, deindustrialization, declining labor force participation of prime-age men, weakening productivity growth, rising household indebtedness, and substantial increases in the foreign-born proportion of the population. Then came an unexpected financial crisis, a desperate rescue of the financial system, a cutback in credit availability to households, collapsing house prices (at least in the short run), soaring unemployment, weak recoveries, huge shortfalls in GDP per head relative to historic trends, and prolonged periods of stagnant or declining real incomes for many households, all made worse by fiscal austerity. With this, inevitably, went a collapse of trust in political, technocratic, and business elites.[48] Finally came COVID and the war in Ukraine, further disruptions, whose ultimate results remained uncertain.

The rise of demagogic nationalism and authoritarianism in high-income democracies—the core of today's political crisis—can be attributed in significant part to these economic failures. The problem is not just the economic failures themselves, but that they undermined people's understanding of the future they and their children could aspire to and of how they were valued by the societies to which they belonged. Particularly significant was the huge increase in the inequality of people's condition.[49] Beyond a certain point, this erodes the ability of the mass of citizens to feel part of a shared political project— a democracy. What has been happening demonstrates to them the opposite—the contempt of elites toward ordinary people, who increasingly feel humiliated. It is ironic that the response to this has been to shift toward leaders who are as irresponsible, not to mention malignant, as Trump or Johnson. Malevolent political forces can so easily transform humiliation into anger. But that is hardly a novel discovery.

An alternative to this emphasis on the role of economic change in transforming politics is advanced in a 2016 study of the rise of populism by Ronald Inglehart and Pippa Norris. They argue:

> It would be a mistake to attribute the rise of populism directly to economic inequality alone. Psychological factors seem to play a more important role. Older birth cohorts and less-educated groups support populist parties and leaders that defend traditional cultural values and emphasize nationalistic and xenophobia appeals, rejecting outsiders, and upholding old-fashioned gender roles. Populists support charismatic leaders, reflecting a deep mistrust of the "establishment" and mainstream parties who are led nowadays by educated elites with progressive cultural views on moral issues.[50]

A much narrower view of the cultural origins of the political backlash emphasizes just one element in the list of reasons enumerated by Inglehart and Norris: a nationalistic and xenophobic response to outsiders. In other words, far from being just one change among many others (be it viewed as either economic or cultural), immigration alone matters. Thus, in his influential book, *Whiteshift*, Eric Kaufmann argues:

> Right-wing populism has little to do with economics, but arises largely from ethnic change, caused by immigration, which unsettles the existential security of conservative and order-seeking whites. The issue of Muslim immigration is a force multiplier but not the main driver, playing a backup role in the Trump and Brexit votes and only a minor part in Europe prior to 2004.[51]

The crucial difficulty with primarily cultural explanations is that they fail to provide an answer to the obvious question: Why now?[52]

The changing economic, social, and political role of women, growing social acceptability of homosexuality, transgender rights, and, above all, mass immigration, including of Muslims and "people of color," have been continuing at least since the 1960s and in some countries for longer. Why should all this have become so salient now? (See figure 25.)

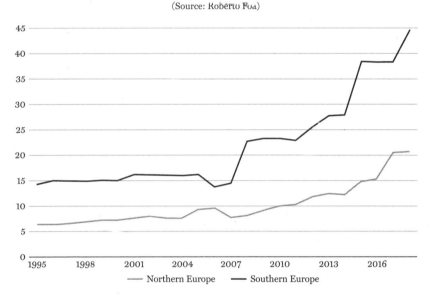

FIGURE 25. VOTE SHARE OF POPULIST PARTIES IN WESTERN EUROPE
(POPULATION-WEIGHTED) (PERCENT)
(Source: Roberto Foa)

The answer surely is that something big happened: the financial crisis and its aftermath. That this made a huge political difference is also consistent with historical research on the political impact of financial crises. Thus, "Political polarization increases after financial crises throughout the nineteenth and twentieth century. Moreover, political parties on the far right appear to be the biggest political beneficiaries of a financial crash. On average, far-right parties have seen an increase in their vote shares of about 30 percent relative to their pre-crisis level in the five years following a systemic financial crisis." The authors of this passage add that "governing becomes more difficult after financial crises, irrespective of which parties are in power." Finally, all these effects "are much more pronounced in financial crises" than in other recessions.[53] Financial crises are turning points, not only economically but also politically, because they are visible to the public and so clearly the fault of certain specific elite institutions and people.

Immigration, too, became far more politically salient in several countries only after the financial crisis, even though increases in foreign-born populations had occurred over many decades. In the UK, for example, the start of the immigration from "new commonwealth" countries was in the 1950s. The race issue then boiled up in Smethwick in the general election of 1964 and again with Enoch Powell's "Rivers of Blood" speech of April 20, 1968.[54] But it cooled down. So why did it boil up again in the Brexit vote? Again, take the case of the US, where the Republicans fell under the sway of a passionate xenophobe who succeeded in gaining power on an anti-immigrant platform. Yet the increase in the foreign-born as a share of the population was strikingly low in the US after 2000 and the share itself modest compared with other apparently similar countries, such as Australia, Canada, and New Zealand.

It seems plausible that immigration became so politically salient because of a financial crisis that originated in the world's most important centers of global finance, which just happen to be London and New York. It was this shock, together with the grossly unfair bailouts of the people who caused the crisis, that persuaded so many Americans that Washington was a "swamp," which Donald Trump alone could drain (evidently, the opposite of the truth). In *Crashed*, a superb account of the financial crisis and its aftermath, Adam Tooze provided a compelling historical overview of the link between the crisis and subsequent political developments, not just in the US and UK, but also in the eurozone and central and eastern Europe.[55] Tooze notes, for example, the damage the crisis did in Hungary, which helped bring Viktor Orban to (apparently permanent) power in 2010.[56] Financial and economic crises crystallized the anger and distrust that had been building up in previous decades over (often interlinked) economic and cultural changes.

The best example of this process is also the most notorious democratic accession to power by a right-wing demagogue ever—that of Adolf Hitler. An enduring and deep well of anti-Semitism had long existed in Germany. The catastrophic defeat in the First World War, postwar political instability, and great inflation of 1923 also shook the stability of German society. Moreover, a wide cultural gap opened up between members of the politically, culturally, and socially conservative German middle, lower middle, and lower classes and the more liberal and adventurous cultural and intellectual circles of the Weimar Republic. All this became tinder waiting to catch fire.

Yet the Great Depression gave the spark. "By 1932, German industrial production had fallen to just 58 percent of its 1928 levels. By the end of 1929 around 1.5 million Germans were without a job; within a year this figure had more than doubled, and by early 1933 a staggering 6 million (26 percent) were out of work."[57] In the federal elections of 1928, the Nazis had won a mere 2.6 percent of the vote. In September 1930, after the financial crisis had begun and the vital American loans had ceased, this had jumped to 18.3 percent. By July 1932, the share had reached 37.3 percent.[58] In March 1933, after the Reichstag fire, it reached 43.9 percent.[59] This switch to the Nazis came almost entirely from Protestant conservatives. Thus, although the desperation created by the Great Depression caused many voters to swing toward the Nazis, those who did so had already identified with the conservative and nationalist cause.[60] Socialists and communists looked for their salvation elsewhere. In this sense, culture mattered, too. But it lay dormant until the spark of the Great Depression was lit.

A remarkable study of the political impact of the failure of Danatbank, then Germany's second-largest bank, in 1931 gives strong support for the interaction of economic distress with cultural predispositions in generating right-wing political extremism. The authors conclude that "Nazi votes surged more in locations more affected by its failure. Radicalization in response to the shock was exacerbated in cities with a history of anti-Semitism. After the Nazis seized power, both pogroms and deportations were more frequent in places affected by the banking crisis. Our results suggest an important synergy between financial distress and cultural predispositions, with far-reaching consequences."[61]

This story also looks similar to the way Republicans chose Trump as their candidate in the 2016 presidential election over establishment Republicans, such as Jeb Bush. History does not repeat itself, but it rhymes. Thus, "the desire for a strong leader who can identify domestic enemies and who promises to do something about them without worrying overmuch about legalities—those germs, mutated to fit the particular local subcultures, are latent in every democratic electorate, waiting for sufficiently widespread human suffering to provide conditions for their explosive spread."[62] But the suffering was essential. It caused a shift from "respectable" leadership to the "unrespectable" version—from Romney in 2012 to Trump in 2016. It is indeed "the economy, stupid."

A different yet telling example of the cultural and political impact of economic failure is contemporary Italy. Productivity is stagnant (see figure 19). GDP per head in 2018 was roughly what it had been two decades earlier. Then the country suffered a huge economic crisis in the 2010s (see figure 21). In this context, one can understand the rise to power of populist politicians and the use by one of them (Matteo Salvini of the Lega) of immigration as a rallying cry. As a result of all this, according to the European Council on Foreign Relations, in no member state of the EU, bar Greece, did the sense of "cohesion" of individuals with the EU fall more sharply between 2007 and 2017 than in Italy. By the latter year, its ranking on this had tumbled to twenty-third of twenty-eight members.[63]

The evidence is clear: if one looks at shifts away from "respectable politicians" toward radical outsiders, especially right-wing populists, the trigger has frequently been economic failure, especially huge financial shocks. One should focus on marginal voters. The committed may choose the party's leader. But those on the margin decide whether he wins. Why did Labour Party voters who once supported Tony Blair, a strongly pro-EU politician, vote for Brexit and Boris Johnson? Why, again, did people who had once voted for Barack Obama vote for Donald Trump? The explanation is that these people had become highly dissatisfied It is the marginal voters—those prepared to change their minds—who decide electoral outcomes.

Plenty of white Americans had sought an ethnonationalist leader such as Trump for decades. Many southern whites had shifted from support for the Democrats to support for the Republicans almost as soon as the former passed the Civil Rights Act of 1964: they were racists. The sort of people who supported George Wallace as a Democrat would happily support Trump as a Republican. Again, a significant number of older English middle- and lower-middle-class conservatives had always opposed membership of the EU, liberal immigration, and contemporary cultural changes. But if Trump or Brexit were to win, a sizable number of people had to *switch* their support toward these causes. A study shows that economic downturns do indeed worsen racial prejudice in the US.[64] Thus, there is "a robust relationship between own-group unemployment and an index of prejudice. We further document significant regional differences in prejudice across different regions of the country and over time."[65] Thus, while some regions do indeed have a permanently higher level of racial prejudice than others, which is consistent with the cultural view, *prejudice also rises with economic insecurity*. Racism is not a fixed quantum, but a variable that moves in line with economic conditions. Members of ethnic groups become more hostile to other groups, the more hostile seems the labor market.

A study of the UK similarly argues that "Austerity caused Brexit." The postcrisis fiscal austerity effectively targeted the "left behind" areas of the UK, which are also more dependent on public spending. Aggregate real government spending on welfare and social protection decreased by around 16 percent per head under the Tories. But real spending per person fell by 46 percent in the most hard-hit districts, which were also the poorest. Ironically, these localities switched toward supporting Brexit and the Tories, even though it was the latter who had inflicted the austerity.[66] Thus, the fiscal "austerity had sizable and timely effects, increasing support for UKIP [the UK Independence Party] across local, national and European elections. The estimates suggest that the referendum might have resulted in a Remain victory had it not been for austerity."[67]

Another fascinating example is Sweden. In support of the cultural hypothesis for right-wing populism, Pippa Norris wrote in 2016 that "populist authoritarian leaders have arisen in several affluent post-industrial 'knowledge' societies, in cradle-to-grave welfare states with some of the best-educated and most secure populations in the world, like Sweden and Denmark—where you'd expect social tolerance and liberal attitudes instead of xenophobic appeals . . . Why? Here's why. Populist authoritarianism can best be explained as a cultural backlash in Western societies against long-term, ongoing social change."[68]

Yet even Sweden has experienced economic shocks and austerity. Thus, "the rapid rise of the [right-wing] Sweden Democrats followed two events that worsened the relative economic standing of large segments of the population. In 2006, a center-right coalition of parties took power and implemented a far-reaching reform agenda of tax cuts and social-insurance austerity aiming to 'make work pay.' Over a mere six years, these reforms led to large shifts in inequality. With earned-income tax credits, incomes continued to grow among labor-market 'insiders' with stable employment [compared to] a stagnation of disposable incomes for labor-market 'outsiders' with unstable or no jobs. The second key event is the 2008 financial crisis that was followed by a 5 percent drop of GDP in a single year. This deep recession drastically increased job insecurity for 'vulnerable' insiders—those with stable employment, but with jobs at higher risk of replacement by automation and other forms of rationalization—relative to 'secure' insiders."[69]

In Sweden, the politicians of the radical right tended to come from groups that experienced lower relative incomes and higher job insecurity. Furthermore, the electoral success of the right-wing Sweden Democrats was strongly correlated with the impact of the economic reforms and the financial crisis across municipalities and precincts within municipalities.[70] Why did people turn to these radical-right politicians? The answer is that the traditional left were insiders and represented insiders: it had become a dominant part of the ruling establishment. "Thus, in an environment of diminished trust, disgruntled voters turned to candidates who shared their economic traits and fates."[71] Finally, the "analysis does not show a link between direct local exposure to immigration and support for the radical right."[72] Instead, "our results rhyme well with the idea that an economic shock which creates insecurity may interact with pre-existing, latent, traits among some voters, and lead them to switch their political allegiance."[73]

Martin Sandbu of the *Financial Times* has concluded—on the evidence, correctly: "What has really happened both in Sweden and elsewhere is that anti-immigrant and illiberal sentiments have been drawn into political service by rising economic insecurity. Even if such attitudes existed, more or less latently, in the past, it is economic change that has turned them into a political force."[74]

Yet while economic forces played an important part in the shift toward populist parties and leaders, they do not explain why populists of the right were more successful than the parties of the left in attracting the support of disenchanted members of the old working class. For this, there are three plausible explanations. First, the established left-of-center parties had largely bought into the economic agenda associated with the disappointed expectations and the financial crisis. They also did not put forward any fundamentally different prospectus from what had been on offer. Second, where that establishment was overthrown by something more revolutionary, as with Jeremy Corbyn's leadership of the Labour Party, it looked a great deal like old-fashioned socialism. By and large, today's working class does not believe it will benefit from an upheaval that seems likely merely to replace corporate bosses with public sector bureaucrats. Indeed, few of them still believe in radical forms of socialism. Finally, the culturally dominant element in left-of-center parties increasingly consists of graduates, academics, public-sector workers, journalists and creative workers, the young, and ethnic minorities. The older and more socially conservative, patriotic, and increasingly disadvantaged members of the working class see little in such parties to attract them.

Health shocks may also spark political extremism. A recent study looked at the impact of Spanish flu on Italian politics in the early 1920s, noting 4.1 million Italians contracted the disease and about 500,000 died. It tested the hypothesis that deaths from the 1918 influenza pandemic contributed to the rise of fascism in Italy. "Our observations," it stated, "were consistent with evidence from other contexts that worsening mortality rates can fuel radical politics. Unequal impacts of pandemics may contribute to political polarization."[75] The COVID pandemic has indeed been divisive on many dimensions. Among other things, it has created intense political divisions over social distancing, lockdowns, mask wearing, and vaccination. In an environment of fear, anxiety, and stress, support for political extremism again seems likely to increase.

Conclusion

Significant long-term economic changes undermined the economic and social positions of important parts of the body politic of high-income countries, especially less-educated (male) workers.[76] Status anxiety is indeed a good way of thinking about this. These longer-term trends had already eroded political loyalties. But the financial crisis was a decisive event. It triggered a cascade away from historic political attachments. It did so in two complementary ways. First, it eroded almost everybody's trust in the establishment, as crises have frequently done in the past. Second, it hit the actual (or perceived) security of vulnerable groups hard, directly and indirectly (via austerity). Politics became more anxious because people were more so. The move from Ronald Reagan's "morning again in America"[77] to Donald Trump's "American carnage"[78] was the result of experience. The chaos of the 1970s could be viewed as a brief interruption in established success. By 2016, things had been going badly for too many for too long to make such confidence credible. In the absence of any confidence in a progressive revolution, the politics of reactionary nostalgia had arrived.[79]

When political allegiances have changed so dramatically, it is implausible to look at long-standing grievances, economic or cultural, as an explanation. Moreover, when one looks at lasting changes, it is similarly implausible to ignore economic change. Suppose there had been no increases in inequality, no deindustrialization, no relative change in the economic position of less-skilled men, and no globalization. Could we then plausibly suppose that the cultural changes would have caused the anger they have? The same applies to immigration. Without rising wage inequality and job insecurity and the shock of the crisis, would it have caused the anger that it has? No. When frightened and insecure, humans go angrily tribal. It is as simple—and as dangerous—as that.

Trust is indispensable to successful government and above all to government by consent.[80] G. K. Chesterton, a British Catholic writer of the late nineteenth and early twentieth centuries, is supposed to have said that "when men stop believing in God they don't believe in nothing; they believe in anything."[81] Similarly, when people reject those in charge, they put their trust not in nobody, but in anybody. Frequently, alas, the people on whom their search alights are charlatans, gangsters, fanatics, or a lethal blend of all three. Institutions are then destroyed, corruption becomes endemic, and the capacity to make sensible policy vanishes. It is even possible for a country to become unreformable. The social and institutional capital needed to renew it disappears and it becomes a failed state. This is the history of Argentina, and more recently (and even worse) of Venezuela. How this political process—foreseen by Aristotle long ago—is working out in the high-income countries is the topic of chapter 6. But first, in chapter 5, we explore the underlying roots of the economic failures. Is globalization to blame or is it something else? If we do not know the causes, we cannot address them.

CHAPTER FIVE

Rise of Rentier Capitalism

> Countries are taking advantage of us, whether they
> think we're very nice or not so smart. They've been
> doing it for many, many years, and we want to end it.
>
> Many of these are friends. Many of these are allies.
> But sometimes allies take advantage of us even more so
> than our non-allies.
>
> All over the world, foreign countries put massive
> tariffs on our products while we put very few, if any, on
> theirs. So we then wonder why we're not doing the
> business we should be doing. And we wonder, maybe
> most importantly, why we had, last year, over an $800
> trillion trade deficit—$800 billion, in terms of a trade
> deficit.
>
> So when you have a number like $800 billion, you
> say to yourself, "Somebody made a lot of bad deals."
> And that's happened over a long period of time.
>
> —*Donald Trump*[1]

C hapter 3 noted that the loss of confidence in democracy has spread even in high-income countries with what were believed to be robust democracies. Chapter 4 argued that this has to do with widespread anxiety, especially in the middle and lower middle classes of these societies. This anxiety, in turn, is heavily influenced by economic disappointments—slow growth, high and rising inequality, deindustrialization, and, more recently, adverse economic shocks.

Such developments have undermined confidence in the competence and probity of elites, convincing a large part of society that the game is rigged against them and persuading them to embrace populist loudmouths, especially nationalist populist loudmouths.

We cannot discuss how to fix *what* has gone wrong without first understanding *why* it has gone wrong. That is the focus of this chapter. The broad conclusion is that why it has gone wrong is not as simple as many suppose. Some of what has happened—the productivity slow-down and the rise of China—was inevitable. Some of what has happened is the result of policy mistakes, in some cases a refusal to help people who were hit by adverse economic changes. Some of the things that are blamed—global trade, for example—are largely innocent. Above all, a good part of what has gone wrong is what Adam Smith warned us against—the tendency of the powerful to rig the economic and political systems against the rest of society. We can remedy our disappointments only if we first understand these complexities.

The Past Is a Foreign Country

After World War II, the Western world experienced a halcyon period. The fast productivity growth of that era, especially in western Europe (apart from the UK) and Japan allowed extraordinarily fast growth in incomes. (See chapter 4, figure 19.) These benefits were also widely shared. Many on the social democratic, or what Americans would call liberal, left believe the great mistake was to abandon the more interventionist state of that period and turn toward free-market economics.[2]

Alas, the opportunities for rapid and equitable growth in the high-income countries in the 1950s and 1960s—the period the French call "les trente glorieuses" from 1945 to 1975—were unsustainable. These countries still held a monopoly of industrial know-how. They had youthful and growing populations. They could take advantage of the innovations of the interwar years and the Second World War.

Exploiting these opportunities generated strong investment and buoyant consumption. Indeed, contrary to what had been widely expected, the big challenge turned out to be containing demand, not promoting it. Those postwar opportunities were particularly abundant in continental Europe and Japan, where it was necessary to undo the physical damage done by the war and possible to follow the US in developing a mass consumer market. The pre–World War II Keynesian notion of "secular stagnation"—chronically deficient demand, first advanced in the late 1930s—was speedily buried, to return over seventy years later, in the 2010s.[3]

This was not just a period of government intervention, as many on the left argue. It was also an era of economic liberalization, especially trade liberalization, under the auspices of the Marshall Plan (established in 1948), the Organization for European Economic Co-operation (also established in 1948), its successor, the Organization for Economic Co-operation and Development (established in 1961), the General Agreement on Tariffs and Trade (agreed in 1947), and the European Economic Community (established in 1957). Thus, for high-income countries, the market opening and trade liberalization of the 1980s and 1990s were at least as much a continuation of the postwar period as a break with it. Indeed, almost all the trade liberalization by high-income countries had already happened by 1980. What changed—and then changed the latter countries—was the trade and market liberalization elsewhere, which injected a huge increase in global competition.

The inflation of the 1970s overthrew the Keynesian consensus of the 1950s and 1960s. This was so, even though the oil price shocks of 1973 and 1979 were also a part of the explanation for the rapid rise in prices. This "stagflation" destroyed belief in a stable trade-off between unemployment and inflation (the so-called "Phillips Curve") that policy makers could exploit.[4] The shift away from Keynesian macroeconomics, toward monetarism and inflation targeting, was a result.

The reaction against the active macroeconomic management of the 1960s. But some such reaction was both inevitable and necessary.

The shifts in the world economy that followed the opening of China (from 1978) and subsequent collapse of the Soviet empire (between 1989 and 1991) and the opening of India (from 1991) could not have been avoided. The world economy is just no longer one of open Western economies and closed developing ones or of a Western monopoly of industrial know-how. This latter change was not only natural, since knowledge spreads, but right, since westerners were hardly entitled to a monopoly of power and wealth forever.

The old "Fordist" economy dominated by giant plants with moderately skilled labor forces and strong trade unions has almost entirely vanished. One result is that university graduates, of whom there are vastly more than ever before, have become the most influential supporters of left-of-center political parties. This also helps explain the rising emphasis of these parties on the causes of "progressive" radicals. Members of the old working class tend to be hostile to the parties' pet causes (such as those of identity or rapid decarbonization in response to climate change) and to the people who advocate them (the young and college educated). Meanwhile, trade unions have greatly weakened and the organized working class atomized. Partly as a result, many erstwhile members of this class now support nationalist causes, such as Brexit, and right-wing demagogues, such as Trump.

Yet even if some industrial production were to be brought home, at great cost, via protection against imports, there would then be ongoing—and probably accelerating—use of robots.[5] The loss by the high-wage economies of their monopoly of advanced industrial know-how is similarly irreversible. These forces have permanently reduced the prospects for high-wage, low- and medium-skilled employment, especially of men. Women are also more trusted in many of the service jobs that increasingly dominate employment, especially caring for children and old people.

While the rent-sharing of the old industrial enterprises in countries that once enjoyed a monopoly of industrial know-how has gone, new and important forms of rent-sharing have emerged from network externalities, especially local network externalities. London, New York, Shanghai, Silicon Valley, and similar places have become hubs of immensely productive businesses.[6] When the factories disappeared in the old industrial locations, so did the incomes they generated and the demand for local services on which much employment depended. The combination of network externalities in some places and deindustrialization in others has driven dramatic increases in regional inequality. Thus, "new analysis by the OECD finds that, in the high-income countries over the past two decades the productivity gap between the top regions and the majority has widened by 60 percent."[7]

Even the welfare state of the mid-twentieth century could be created just once. Only in the US is the welfare state still radically incomplete, particularly in health.[8] Moreover, because the welfare state has already been created, the room for dramatic increases in state spending on the welfare of the citizenry is far smaller today than it was after World War II, though this does not prevent constant pressure to raise spending on all sorts of causes in a higgledy-piggledy and often rather ill-considered way.

In sum, we cannot return to the past. It is indeed a foreign country. Trying to do so cannot be good policy, even though the election of Donald "Make America Great Again" Trump showed it can be good politics. The slowdown in productivity growth, the decline in the growth of human capital, the shift toward low-productivity-growth sectors, the transformation of labor markets, the decline of the old working class, and all the associated social changes are, in many ways, the results of success. But they are also constraints on what can now be expected. As we will discuss in the next section in more detail, the growth potential of the high-income economies has slowed. Our future is just not what it used to be.

Ups and Downs of Innovation and Productivity Growth

The economy of the last two centuries was built on innovation. Without innovation, capital accumulation would just amount to "piling wooden plows on top of existing wooden plows."[9] But technology cannot deliver whatever we want, whenever we want it. In 1800, the world of electricity and the internal combustion engine was out of reach, just as today's world of information and communications technology was out of reach in 1900. People in 2100 may take marvels for granted we cannot now imagine.

This helps explain the ups and downs of productivity growth. Many of the technological transformations of the last two centuries or so were one-offs. In particular, the second industrial revolution of the period from about 1870 to the mid-twentieth century changed so much precisely because so much could then be changed: there was just so much low-hanging fruit.[10] Electricity brought refrigeration, the telephone, the elevator, the skyscraper, air-conditioning, and the early computer. Petroleum brought the internal combustion engine, which delivered cars and aircraft. Chemicals and pharmaceuticals and that most ordinary of miracles, limitless clean running water and sewers, brought revolutionary improvements in health. These innovations then transformed where and how people lived, where and how they worked, and where and how they got around. They also transformed how long people lived, perhaps the most important change of all: Which would you give up first—your iPhone or the decline in the likelihood of your baby's death from 1 in 7 in 1886–90 to 1 in 250 in 2015–20?[11] Yet many of these changes had to be one-offs. Speed went from that of the horse to that of the jet plane. Then, some fifty years ago, the increase in speed halted. Urbanization could also be done only once. The same is true of the collapse in child mortality, the tripling of life expectancy, the ability to control domestic temperatures, and the liberation of people, mostly women, from domestic drudgery.[12]

Not surprisingly, then, innovation at the technological frontier of the world economy, the US, has been slower over the last half century than in the half century before then. (See figure 26.) This has partly been because the economy has been operating on one big innovation engine: information and communication technology. It is a powerful engine. It may turn out to be even more important in the future, with the advent of powerful artificial intelligence. It may in time be joined by transformations in life sciences, materials, and energy systems, as we shift to renewables. But this has not yet happened. There was a brief (and modest) upward blip in growth of total factor productivity in the US in the 1990s, after the introduction of the internet. But this has since passed. COVID has greatly accelerated the use of technologies that facilitate remote working and shopping online. But this is likely to prove a one-off blip, as changes that might have taken ten years were concentrated into a very short period.

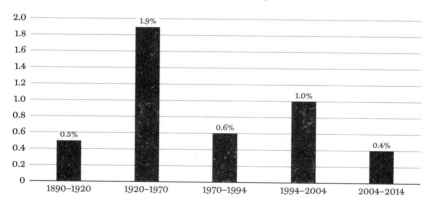

FIGURE 26. ANNUALIZED GROWTH OF US TOTAL FACTOR
PRODUCTIVITY (PERCENT)
(Source: Robert Gordon)

Belief in the limitless potential of technology is almost a secular religion.[13] Not surprisingly, one response of its devotees to the view that innovation is just not what it used to be is that the slowdown is a mirage, because we are mismeasuring GDP. No doubt, we do mismeasure GDP, particularly because it is so hard to quantify quality improvements. But it is difficult to believe that mismeasurement has suddenly become worse than it used to be decades ago. The opposite is far more probable. After all, the statistics we use to measure GDP before 1940 were created after the fact. Again, just as is true of today's digital services, many of the benefits of the new technologies of the past also fell outside measures of GDP: think of a domestic washing machine or dishwasher whose outputs are not measured in GDP, because domestic services are excluded. In all, mismeasurement is not a credible explanation for the productivity slowdown.[14]

Another explanation is a growing divergence in productivity between frontier and laggard firms, because of a lack of competition in the economy.[15] Thus, an OECD study argues that "we find that these patterns of . . . divergence [in total factor productivity] were much more extreme in sectors where pro-competitive product market reforms were least extensive."[16] This seems plausible and has attractive policy implications: push harder for competition.

Yet two other changes—the slowdown in the growth of "human capital" per person and the shift from the production of goods to the production of services as we become richer—provide even more powerful explanations for the slowdown.[17] The first of these shifts is explained by declining fertility and rising longevity, as well as by the inevitable slowing of the rate of improvement in educational standards, once a high proportion of the population has completed university education. The second and probably more important explanation is the enormous improvement in productivity in production of goods, which lowers their relative prices and the share of resources devoted to producing them. So we have inevitably ended up with an ever-larger share of our economies in sectors in which it is relatively hard to raise productivity. We can raise productivity dramatically in services we can turn into "bits." But we cannot do the same in services dependent on face-to-face interaction: the number of adults needed to look after a group of small children has not changed over millennia. Indeed, the number needed to educate them to modern standards has increased enormously.

In all, as Robert Gordon notes, although the impact of the information and communications revolution "was revolutionary, its effect was felt in a limited sphere of human activity, in contrast to [the second industrial revolution of the late nineteenth and early twentieth century], which changed everything. Categories of personal consumption expenditures that felt little effect from the ICT revolution were the purchase of food for consumption at home and away from home, clothing and footwear, motor vehicles and fuel to make them move, furniture, household supplies, and appliances. In 2014, fully two thirds of consumption expenditures went for services, including rent, health care, education, and personal care."[18] Crucially, note that the slowdown in the growth of human capital and the shifts in the structure of the economy toward activities where raising productivity is hard were the results of success. The dynamic capitalist economy of old has just become elderly.

There is, not least, little sign of the sorts of innovations that would generate an explosion in high-wage, rent-sharing jobs for less-skilled people. On the contrary, most of the new jobs being generated as productivity soars in industry, and computers and robots spread across the economy, are in low-skill services. It is hard to raise the productivity of people doing these sorts of jobs. The productivity of couriers is what it is. Only the organization of the deliveries and the number of packages can do anything to alter it. The same is true of caregivers in nursing homes, taxi drivers, cleaners, or servers in restaurants. Moreover, in many such activities, work can easily be "casualized," while many of the workers are immigrants or from marginal communities. Organizing such workers into trade unions is difficult. Along with the liberalization of labor markets and the dwindling away of the old industrial labor force, this helps explain the growth of what the British economist Guy Standing calls the precariat.[19]

In brief, the decline in productivity growth is deep and structural.[20] We have no reason to suppose it will end soon. The qualifications to this are the possibility of an energy revolution, with limitless supply of cheap renewable energy (perhaps including energy from nuclear fusion), as well as further development of artificial intelligence and possible revolutions in material and life sciences. Yet even if productivity growth remains low overall, today's unbalanced innovations may be disruptive. This has already been true of ICT in the recent past: it has raised the relative returns to skilled (graduate) labor and turbocharged globalization, via integration of production, offshoring of services, growing complexity of financial markets, and an explosion of global data flows.[21]

Demographic Change and the World Economy

Demography is another driving force shaping our economies, societies, and politics. It is also slowing growth. Here, two big (and linked) facts stand out: the shift in the structure and growth of world populations; and aging.

Back in 1960, today's high-income countries made up a quarter of the world's population of 3 billion. By 2018, this was down to 16 percent of 7.6 billion. Developing countries' share has risen by a corresponding 9 percentage points. Just under three quarters of this increased share of developing countries was in sub-Saharan Africa, whose population rose from 30 percent of that of all high-income countries in 1960 to 89 percent in 2018 (that is, from 230 million to 1.1 billion). Developing East and South Asia contained 51 percent of the world's people in 2018, up from 48 percent in 1950. China and India each have a larger population than all high-income countries together. India's population has also by now caught up with China's. (See figure 27.)

According to the UN's medium fertility variant, the world's population will reach 9.7 billion in 2050. Sub-Saharan Africa will hold 22 percent of the world's population by then, China and India together 31 percent, developing East and South Asia 48 percent, and today's high-income countries only 14 percent. Of the 1.9 billion increase in the world's population envisaged by UN demographers between 2018 and 2050, an astonishing 53 percent will be in sub-Saharan Africa and another 29 percent in East and South Asia. The share of high-income countries in the increase will be just 3 percent. One implication is that, on the plausible assumption that output per head will converge further, the share of the high-income countries in global GDP will also shrink further. Another is that migration pressure is likely to grow dramatically, particularly from sub-Saharan Africa into Europe.

FIGURE 27. SHIFTING WORLD POPULATION (SHARES IN TOTAL; PERCENT)
(Source: World Bank and UN Medium Fertility Projection)

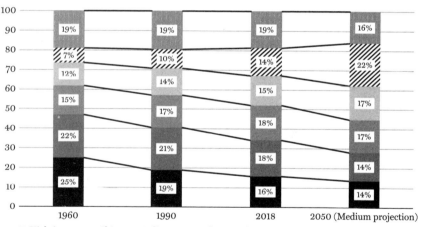

■ High-income ■ China ■ India ▨ Rest of East and South Asia (excluding high-income)
▨ Sub-Saharan Africa ▨ Rest of developing countries

These structural shifts are the first big demographic feature of our world. Aging is the second. In itself, it means higher survival rates into adulthood and longer lives in adulthood. Aging also creates still largely untapped opportunities for longer and more varied working lives and for transmitting the wisdom and experience of the old to the young.

Moreover, the fall in child mortality also allows lower fertility rates, which make it possible for parents to invest more effort and resources in each child and for both of them to pursue their own careers. Clearly, these are all good things. Yet aging also imposes some burdens: rising old-age dependency ratios; an increasing burden of public spending; and, some argue, a vastly greater need for immigrants. (See figure 28 on the rising old-age dependency ratio, notably in Japan and western Europe, though this phenomenon is also now visible in China.)

FIGURE 28. OLD-AGE DEPENDENCY (PERCENT OVER 65 TO AGE 15–64)
(Source: World Bank)

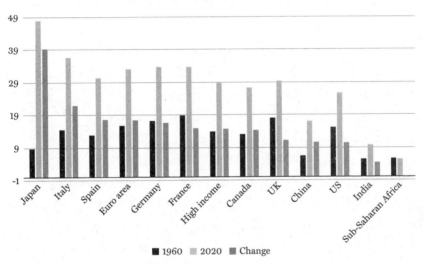

■ 1960   ▨ 2020   ■ Change

The fiscal impact of aging can be mitigated by raising effective retirement ages, but aging will still lead to a rise in the proportion of spending on health and pensions, less economic flexibility, and weakening economic dynamism. This is the reverse side of the coin of rising longevity. Immigration, a widely touted solution, is only a temporary fix, since immigrants age, too. The amount of immigration needed to stabilize the old-age dependency ratio in societies with rising life expectancy and low birth rates is simply colossal.[22] Thus, a United Nations study published in 2000 showed that the population of the EU would need to rise from 400 million (as it then was) to 1.2 billion by 2050 if immigration were to stabilize the old-age dependency ratio. The population of the US would have to rise to more than a billion if the old-age dependency ratio is to be stabilized there. Such levels of immigration are politically and probably practically impossible.[23]

Global Move to the Market

As noted in chapter 3, the decades from about 1980 to 2010 were dominated by the ideal of liberalization. Deng Xiaoping embraced a Chinese version of this set of ideas with his "reform and opening up" in 1978. In high-income countries, the shift was associated with Margaret Thatcher and Ronald Reagan. While the extent to which individual countries moved in this direction differed, the destination was widely agreed upon. Indications of this were abandonment by French president François Mitterrand of his "socialism in one country" in the early 1980s, and the "third-way" politics of Bill Clinton in the US and Tony Blair in the UK in the 1990s and early 2000s.[24] The "single-market" program of the EU of the 1980s can also be viewed in this light. This same idea was embraced by the countries of the former Soviet empire after 1989 and even (albeit temporarily) the Soviet Union itself after 1991. India moved in this direction after 1991 and many other emerging and developing countries have tried to do the same.

The trade-weighted average applied tariff of the high-income countries was, however, already down to 5 percent in 1989, before the Uruguay Round of trade negotiations had been completed. (See figure 29.)[25] The most significant post-1980 liberalizations by high-income countries were in finance (notably, liberalization of exchange controls), and labor, product, and service markets. Crucial, too, were changes in the conception of the corporation toward the profit- or shareholder-value-maximizing model.

In emerging and developing countries, however, the shift toward

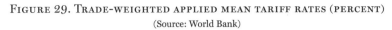

FIGURE 29. TRADE-WEIGHTED APPLIED MEAN TARIFF RATES (PERCENT)
(Source: World Bank)

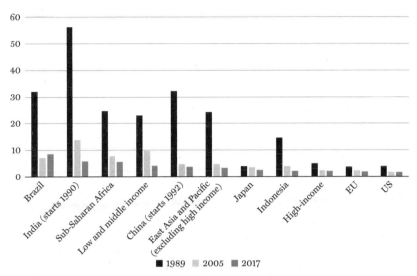

trade openness in the 1980s, 1990s, and early 2000s was a huge turn-
around from the inward-looking, import-substitution-oriented policies
most had previously followed. This greatly increased their imports and
exports, which had large effects on the already open high-income countries. The fall in the trade-weighted average applied tariffs of these
countries was quite remarkable: India's went from 56 percent in 1990
to 6 percent in 2017; China's went from 32 percent in 1989 to 4 percent
in 2017; Brazil's went from 32 percent in 1989 to 9 percent in 2017.

The liberalization of trade by emerging and developing countries,
together with a reinforcing liberalization of inward foreign direct investment, helped the share of global merchandise exports of these
countries to explode upward. If we include the EU's internal trade, the
share of high-income countries in the value of world merchandise exports fell from 80 percent in 1980 to 66 percent in 2019. The share of
emerging and developing countries rose by 14 percentage points, but
China's rise dominated: its share in world merchandise exports rose by
12 percentage points. (See figure 30.)[26]

Thus, at the global level, the crucial step toward entering the world

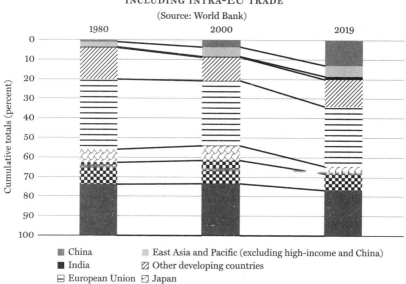

FIGURE 30. SHARES IN WORLD MERCHANDISE EXPORTS BY VALUE, INCLUDING INTRA-EU TRADE

(Source: World Bank)

■ China
■ India
⊟ European Union
▨ US
▨ East Asia and Pacific (excluding high-income and China)
▨ Other developing countries
▨ Japan
■ Other high-income

market was taken by emerging and developing countries. Three things are noteworthy about this epoch-making change: one is that it was in response to argument made by Western countries and institutions over a lengthy period; another is that it followed the remarkable success of a limited number of East Asian economies in doing this (in rough chronological order: Japan, Hong Kong, Taiwan, Singapore, and South Korea); and last, China's decision to follow its smaller neighbors was far and away the most important event in this shift toward the market. But in China's case, it was a move toward a competitive economy under monopoly politics. Indeed, one of the lessons the Chinese learned from what happened to the Soviets was *not* to liberalize politically, but rather to combine continued economic liberalization with strengthened political control by the Communist Party of China. In the longer run, this has created something paradoxical: communist capitalism.

At the time, however, the collapse of the Soviet empire and then of the Soviet Union itself in 1991 reinforced the move toward the market and democracy worldwide. Between then and the financial crises of 2007–12, the ideology of the global market became dominant, though never unquestioned.

How Global Markets Transformed the World Economy

The most important thing that has happened since 1980 is that a huge part of the global "many"—the people of the emerging countries of East and South Asia, who make up roughly half of humanity—spread their economic wings. (See figure 27.) The combination of new technologies with billions of hardworking people and economic opening has transformed the world.

As a result, production in emerging economies now competes directly with that in high-income economies in many sectors. Even when companies based in emerging countries do not compete directly with those of the high-income countries, these emerging countries compete as locations for the use of the capital and know-how possessed by corporations from high-income countries. Emerging economies possess large and rapidly growing markets for goods and services of all kinds. They also offer vast quantities of high-quality human capital, which adds still more to their attraction as locations for production and increasingly also for research. These assets possessed by emerging economies have transformed the incentives confronting the businesses of high-income countries. None of this is going to disappear. On the contrary, the pull of emerging economies is sure to rise still further.

One neat way of illuminating what happened is the "elephant curve" (so called because the first drawing of the curve looked like an elephant head with a raised trunk) invented by Christoph Lakner and Branko Milanovic in 2013.[27] A somewhat more recent version is shown in figure 31.[28] It looks less elephant shaped, mainly because the top percentile has been stretched out dramatically.

The new chart now shows four main things. First, over the period

1980 to 2016, pretax real incomes rose across the global income distribution. Second, real incomes grew by 75 percent or more for the global lower-middle income class, from the 15th to the 45th percentile. Most of these people were in Asia and especially in China. Third, real incomes grew by 50 percent or less for the global upper-middle class—those in the 60th to 95th percentile. Many of these people were in the lower and middle classes of high-income countries. Finally, the top percentile did sensationally well, with progressively tinier slices doing better than the already tiny slices below them: the real incomes of the global top thousandth rose by 235 percent, while those of the thousandth below them rose by "only" 166 percent, across much of the global income distribution, but not at the very top. The top 1 percent of the global income distribution captured 27 percent of the increment in global real pretax incomes, while the bottom 50 percent captured only 12 percent.[29]

FIGURE 31. THE "ELEPHANT CURVE" OF GLOBAL
INEQUALITY AND GROWTH, 1980–2016
(Source: World Inequality Database)

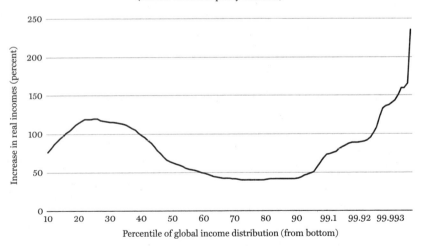

Even so, established high-income countries retain the lion's share of world output. At market prices, the share of high-income countries in world output was still 59 percent in 2019. (See figure 32.) At purchasing power parity (PPP), which greatly increases the share of developing countries, given their low wages, the share of established high-income countries was 40 percent in 2019. Since the share of these countries in world population was about 16 percent (see figure 27), their output per head remained far higher than in developing countries. But the shifts between 2000 and 2019 were significant: at market prices, the share of the established high-income countries fell by 20 percentage points; at PPP, it fell by 17 percentage points. Over the same period, the share of emerging and developing countries in world output at market prices almost doubled, from 21 to 41 percent of the world total. Amazingly, China accounted for 66 percent of that increased share. The share of this Asian giant in the world's total output (at market prices) jumped from 4 to 16 percent in those nineteen years. A new economic superpower had been born. At market prices, its economy was still smaller than those of the US or EU, but at PPP, its economy had already become bigger than those of the US or EU by 2015.[30]

FIGURE 32. SHARES IN WORLD GDP AT MARKET PRICES (PERCENT)
(Source: IMF)

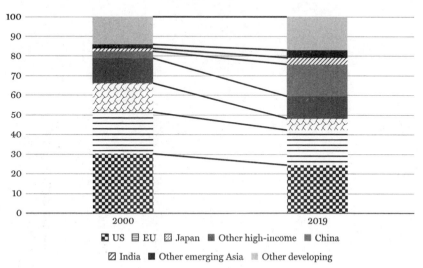

This means something quite straightforward, yet, for some, very disturbing: the long divergence in output per head, standards of living, and so economic, military, and political power between today's high-income countries and the biggest emerging countries—China, above all—has gone into reverse. Moreover, it has done so quite quickly. The relative position of the established high-income countries has been in decline. This was quite natural. But it has hurt.

Yet this convergence was also very incomplete. If we take the seven largest emerging economies at purchasing power parity, we find that three (Brazil, Mexico, and Russia) were either very little more productive or even less productive relative to the leader (the US) in 2019 than they had been in 1992. But four were substantially more productive relative to the US (China, India, Indonesia, and Turkey). China's was the most remarkable story: in 1992, its output per head at purchasing power parity was a mere 5 percent of US levels. By 2019, this ratio had risen to 25 percent. (See figure 33.) There is potential for further catch-up. Whether it will be exploited we do not know: China has many challenges ahead. But if its GDP per head at purchasing power parity were to be 50 percent of US levels in twenty-five years, its economy would be almost as big as those of the US and EU together. That would indeed be transformative.

FIGURE 33. GDP PER HEAD AT CURRENT PURCHASING POWER PARITY
RELATIVE TO US, RANKED BY PERCENTAGE POINT CHANGE
(Source: IMF)

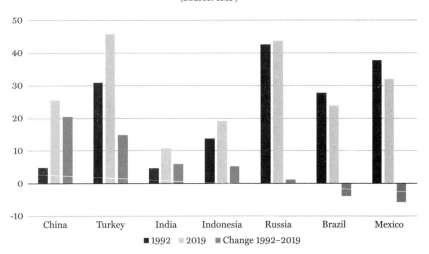

Technology, Globalization, and Immigration

Where do the processes we have just discussed fit into the overall story of adverse economic changes and especially the hollowing out of the middle classes in high-income countries discussed in chapter 4? Let us consider seven aspects of globalization: loyalties, business capital, finance, trade, technology, migration, and ideas.

Globalization corrodes the loyalty of businesses to the countries in which they were initially built. It has created what the late Samuel Huntington supposedly called Davos man.[31] Multinational companies with multinational share registers, employing multinational staffs and producing in many countries for consumers located in many countries, are at least semiglobal, even though nearly all continue to have a national character, especially ones rooted in the bigger high-income economies. Yet they also show their global perspective in their decisions on where to produce, where to pay tax, and so forth. Running against global capitalism has, as a result, become politically popular in the high-income countries now that so many people feel that business has abandoned them. On this, Trump read the political pulse correctly. Boris Johnson did so, too, with his "fuck business." He might have said it at a private event. But he surely meant it.[32]

The ability and willingness of multinational companies to move their capital and know-how across frontiers has been the essential contributor to globalization, and especially their ability to integrate supply chains across borders. This is clearly a decisive advantage for business (and capital) and disadvantage for workers in high-income countries. As noted above, the latter have lost their privileged access to the know-how and capital embedded in the companies they considered their own. This has inevitably affected their bargaining position and their jobs.

The movement of business capital has been an aspect of something vastly bigger—the liberalization of finance. That has exploded in size over the past four decades or so. It has also caused many crises, notably including the Asian crisis of 1997–98 and the transatlantic crisis of 2007–12. The liberalization of finance also forced many countries to abandon fixed exchange rates. The liberalization of finance has raised many concerns apart from financial instability, including tax competition, tax avoidance, tax evasion, and corruption. It is an expression of the power of the financial sector lobby, notes Maurice Obstfeld, former chief economist of the International Monetary Fund, that the possibility of reimposing capital controls or some other sort of curb on cross-border flows has not been considered as seriously as protection against imports, notably in the US.[33]

The expansion of trade in line with comparative advantage, turbocharged by the movement of ideas and capital, offers benefits (greater competition, lower prices, and higher incomes for those with the relevant skills) as well as costs (adjustment to change and, for some, permanent losses of income and employment). Of course, all economic change brings costs of adjustment and, for some, permanent losses. Trade is in no way exceptional in this regard. But adjustment to economic change needs to be managed and losers helped. This is true quite generally, however, not just in relation to changes brought about by trade. It is why localities hard hit by adverse economic changes need assistance in generating new economic activities. It is also why global standards are needed to ensure that trade is not at the expense of good treatment of workers or the environment.

Technological change, especially in transport and communications, has been the main driver of what can be profitably traded. Until the steamship and refrigeration, it was impossible to ship bulk commodities in huge quantities cheaply. Until the truck and van, it was impossible to move goods quickly to the town or even the neighboring village. Until commercial aircraft, it was impossible to move people and high-value items across the world overnight. Until modern information and communications technology, it was impossible to integrate production across great distances seamlessly. Globalization is the child of technological innovation and will continue to be so. Simultaneously, technology is doing to industrial employment what it has done to agriculture: demolishing jobs by raising productivity dramatically. In 1800, 59 percent of French workers were in agriculture. By 2012, the share was under 3 percent.[34] Much the same thing has happened elsewhere. It is close to certain that employment in industry will continue to decline in high-income countries and in many emerging and developing countries as well, as robots and other machines replace industrial workers. Half a century from now, the employment share might be down to just a few percent, or even less. Trade wars cannot stop this.

Labor is a factor of production. Its "owner," like those of other factors of production, wishes to raise its return. One of the ways to do so is to move it, and so himself or herself, to another country, where wages are higher. This, too, can be viewed as movement of "capital" (human capital, in this case) to a better jurisdiction, namely, one that has more complementary economic, social, and political capital. It makes excellent sense for people to do this, just as it does for owners of capital to seek the highest returns through movement of their capital or of the goods and services their capital is able to produce. In addition, since migration is about people, there are other motives that have less (or much less) to do with economics: desire for family reunion and for safety.

In the context of the global movement of ideas, goods and services, and capital, the movement of people is not that big. In 2017, according to the United Nations, 258 million people (3.4 percent of the world population) were international migrants (that is, people who had moved to a foreign country). Of these people, 106 million were born in Asia, 61 million were born in Europe, 38 million were born in Latin America and the Caribbean, and 36 million were African. In 2017, 64 percent of international migrants lived in high-income countries. Refugees account for only 10 percent of international migrants (25.9 million in 2016). The panic over refugees is exaggerated and despicable.[35]

The economic impact of immigration, at recent levels, has been modest. The balance of the evidence suggests that immigration's impact on the earnings and employment opportunities of those already in the country might have been mildly negative, while that on the public finances in high-income countries has been mildly beneficial. Thus, one survey concluded that "the large majority of studies suggest that immigration does not exert significant effects on native labor market outcomes. Even large, sudden inflows of immigrants were not found to reduce native wages or employment significantly."[36] The main reason for this is that immigrants are more likely to be complements than substitutes for existing residents and citizens in the labor market. This is true both of the work they are prepared to do and of the skills they possess (their languages, for example). Similarly, the net fiscal costs of immigrants seem to be very small, at least in the US. In the EU, where benefits are more generous, the net fiscal costs of older and less-skilled immigrants can be larger.[37] Nevertheless, even if net costs to the rest of society are small, the greater part of the gains from migration accrue to the migrants, which is as one would expect.

These aggregative studies suffer from two drawbacks. The first is that migrants are heterogeneous in their motivations, skills, cultures, age, and likelihood of remigration. Ideally, studies would differentiate on all dimensions, which is difficult. Yet it is clear, to take two examples, that the characteristics of people who come for reasons of family reunification or as refugees are likely to be different from those of young people who migrated from central and eastern Europe to the UK, looking for work, or who went from India to the US with high-level technical skills. The second drawback is that none of these studies seem to examine congestion costs. Infrastructure costs associated with rising populations can be handled with additional investment by the public sector. But there are more costs associated with rising populations than this, especially in densely populated countries.

Finally, ideas always move. In contemporary conditions—with high-powered information and communications technologies, huge numbers of foreign students, endless collaborations, and cheap transportation— ideas that used to take decades or even centuries to move across the globe now do so in seconds. The Soviet Union tried hard to control access to the ideas of the world. But it failed. Today, only North Korea is isolated, and it has paid a heavy price. The "Great Firewall of China" is real, but ideas flow across it, especially the ones the leadership wants—those that affect scientific and technological understanding. The flow of innovative ideas unavoidably erodes barriers to knowledge, including intellectual property rights the high-income economies wish to protect. But in the long run, such controls have always failed. China once tried to halt export of the knowledge of how to make silk. The UK once tried to halt export of the knowledge of how to make textile machinery. They failed in the end: ideas flow. It is the ability to create ideas, far more than the ideas themselves, that is valuable. Moreover, the flow of ideas creates value. Yes, free riding on the innovations of others may well reduce incentives to innovate, but it also creates opportunities to use and then develop ideas more rapidly.[38]

We do not know as much as we would like about the balance of effects of these various forces of globalization on the high-income countries, because the processes involved are complex and interactive. Nevertheless, there are a few reasonably clear conclusions.

First, we know about as well as we know anything in applied economics that the impact of global trade on inequality and employment has been modest. This is the broad consensus of the empirical studies by a range of researchers. Thus, "globalization in the form of foreign trade and offshoring has not been a large contributor to rising inequality. Multiple studies of different events around the world point to this conclusion."[39]

Second, there was indeed something of a "China shock" in the US in the first decade of this century. Overall, import competition from China between 1999 and 2011 may have cost in the range of 2 to 2.4 million jobs, which was roughly half of the actual job losses in manufacturing over that period.[40] Moreover, even though "import competition from China did not have large aggregative effects in the US, . . . it had substantially different employment repercussions in different commuting zones."[41] In addition, subsequent "adjustment in local labor markets is remarkably slow, with wages and labor-force participation rates remaining depressed and unemployment rates remaining elevated for at least a full decade after the China trade shock commences. Exposed workers experience greater job churning and reduced lifetime income."[42] This China shock was also politically salient. Given the US's refusal to provide effective support and adjustment assistance to people who lost their jobs, to their families, or to the communities in which they live, that was inevitable. It was not surprising, therefore, that the new dynamic of world trade helped bring Trump to power. It was no surprise either that his protectionist actions were popular.

Third, the impact of technical change has been to raise the demand for skilled people, especially university graduates. This is shown by the fact that relative wages for graduate workers have risen, despite a huge relative increase in their supply, which suggests a countervailing shift in demand toward them. This is the opposite of what would have happened if trade with countries less abundant in skilled workers had been the main agent of change in the labor market. That also would have tended to raise the relative earnings of skilled people in high-income countries, but it would have lowered their shares in employment in all sectors, as employers substituted the now cheaper less-skilled workers for now more-expensive skilled ones. This evidence suggests strongly that the impact of technology on the labor market has dominated that of trade. The difference is political: with trade, it can be blamed on unfair foreigners; with technology, it is a head-on conflict between capital and labor. Capital usually wins, especially in an open world economy.

Fourth, the extent of pre- and posttax inequality (on different measures) and the amount of effort countries make to mitigate pretax inequality, differ substantially across the high-income countries (see figures 10, 11, 12, 13, and 15). Since the policies toward trade and other aspects of globalization have been similar across high-income countries (with the exception of the intense resistance to immigration in South Korea and Japan), globalization cannot be the chief culprit for either levels or changes in inequality. This is particularly true at the top of the income distribution. The differences in experience across high-income countries in both pretax and posttax dimensions indicate that domestic economic institutions and developments, not global ones, have mattered most, including the effectiveness of government response to shifts in competitiveness and the effectiveness of social insurance and other forms of support to those adversely affected by economic change. In the US, people without jobs or skills, living in declining localities, are abandoned to fend for themselves. That is a political choice. Protection—a tax on consumers transferred to protected firms—is proving the most popular form of support, or so Biden's failure to reverse Trump's tariffs suggests. In other high-income countries, the range of potential policy instruments is broader and more effective. It is not the internationally induced changes themselves but rather the shortage of effective policy instruments to deal with them that is so striking in the US.

Macroeconomic Instability

In *The Shifts and the Shocks*, I argued that the macroeconomic fragility plaguing high-income countries was largely due to the reliance on the financial system for generating demand at a time when shifts in the global economy were generating what Larry Summers calls "secular stagnation."[43] The simplest indicator of this phenomenon is the huge secular decline in the ten-year real interest rate. (See figure 34.)[44] We see a sharp fall in long-term real rates in the late 1990s, after the Asian financial crisis, another sharp fall after the 2007–12 global and eurozone financial crises, and a still lower trough during the COVID crisis. Real rates have been negative since the summer of 2011 and averaged –2.9 percent in 2020 and 2021.

FIGURE 34. UK REAL INTEREST RATES
(YIELD ON 10-YEAR INDEX-LINKED GILTS)

So far as aggregate demand is concerned, we can distinguish changes that affect desired savings from those that affect investment, since it is the interaction of the two that determines interest rates needed to ensure full use of existing capacity.

On the side of saving, the big forces have been rising corporate profits as a share of GDP, rising inequality of personal incomes, and extraordinarily high aggregate savings in several high-income and emerging economies, notably Germany, Japan, and China. Rising inequality in the US has resulted in a large increase in the savings of the top 1 percent of the income distribution. (In these calculations, the claims of the wealthy on corporate profits are included.)[45] Similar increases in inequality have raised the propensity to save elsewhere, notably in China and Germany.[46] Meanwhile, structural downside forces on investment have included the already mentioned aging of high-income countries and associated reductions in demand for infrastructure, deindustrialization, and rapid declines in the cost of investment goods, especially in information technology products.

A crucial element in this story was the emergence of China as a huge surplus saver, even though it also had the highest investment rate of any large economy ever. The natural development would have been for capital to flow from the high-income countries to this huge emerging economy, with its gigantic investment needs. In practice, however, the reverse happened: capital flowed (net) upstream from China to the high-income countries, especially the US.[47]

These developments abroad, in China and some other countries, prevented the US from exporting the growing excess savings of its own rich and so running a current account surplus, as late-nineteenth-century UK did in similar domestic conditions. Instead, the reverse happened: the rich of the rest of the world and their governments sought to accumulate what they view as safe US assets, so generating persistent US current account deficits. This meant, necessarily, that the savings of the US rich had to be more than offset by the dis-savings of everybody else in the US (including the US government). Thus, since 1982, the decline in net indebtedness of the rich has been matched by the rise in indebtedness of the bottom 90 percent. This is, incidentally, why the common argument that low interest rates hurt the less well-off is ridiculous. The less well-off are not large net creditors. The rich hold claims on the less rich, not only directly, via their bank deposits and other financial assets, but also via equity in businesses that own such claims.

In the years between the Asian and global financial crises, a huge credit boom, mostly associated with property lending, especially to households in the US and in western, southern, and eastern Europe, temporarily resolved the problem of structurally deficient demand. Thus, the financial system generated an unsustainable surge in investment in property and in household borrowing and spending. After the bust, these sources of demand were replaced by fiscal deficits and spending induced by central-bank-supported rises in asset prices, as monetary policy became even more super-expansionary. Everybody adopted a version of the monetary policy first used by the Bank of Japan in the mid-1990s. (See figure 35.) Also, helpfully, China decided to eliminate its huge current account surplus after the global financial crisis (unlike Germany, alas). But it did so by increasing its debt-fueled investment to close to half of GDP, thus creating a new disequilibrium within its economy, with excessive investment and soaring indebtedness. The real difficulty remains the low share of consumption in China's GDP, which is a consequence of the highly unequal distribution of domestic income. A similar problem exists in Europe, where the large savings surpluses of Germany and some other northern countries are no longer offset by excess spending in peripheral Europe. As a result, the eurozone runs a sizable current account surplus, which must be absorbed elsewhere in the world economy.[48]

FIGURE 35. CENTRAL BANK INTEREST RATES (PERCENT)

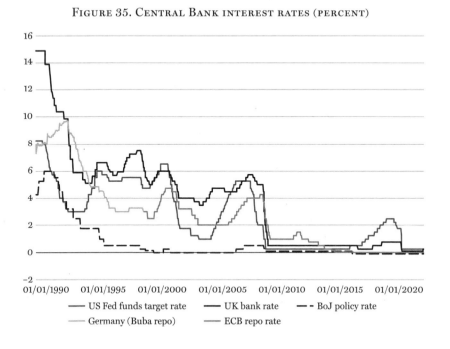

So far, these various responses to the structurally deficient global demand "worked," in the sense that they were better than the alternative of a prolonged slump. But the fact that they had to be employed demonstrates how weak underlying demand has been. Whether this will continue to be the case as the sudden shock of COVID dissipates is highly uncertain. Indeed, the overhang of excess debt from earlier efforts to manage demand in the context of structurally deficient demand made the underlying problem even worse.[49] Debt overhangs depress demand by reducing the ability and willingness of potential borrowers to borrow. Thus, the underlying problems have tended to become worse over time, not better. They are deep-seated, reflecting, as they do, macroeconomic imbalances that are themselves the result of global economic integration, the rise of China, the emergence of a globalized form of rentier capitalism, and increases in income inequality. (See figure 31.) Something must be done about these underlying conditions, a point to which we will return in chapter 8.

It follows from this analysis that global imbalances are telling us something important. Unfortunately, bilateral trade imbalances are just a symptom of the problem. That problem is the structural forces discussed above. A first-order symptom of this has been global imbalances. A second-order symptom is the bilateral surpluses and deficits, on which Trump focused. In his view these reflect bad deals made in the past. The implicit assumption is that a trade deal is a good one if the country ends up selling to a specific partner more than it buys from it, and vice versa. This is idiotic.

First, it is perfectly reasonable for countries to run trade deficits overall, provided the borrowing is affordable. Second, if the borrowing is unaffordable, the only way to fix it is to adjust output and spending in deficit and surplus countries: it is a macroeconomic, not a trade policy, challenge and if it concerns the US, it is a global macroeconomic challenge. Third, overall trade policy is about setting market signals that allow billions of people and tens of thousands of businesses to decide where and how to earn, and spend, their incomes. It is not about making deals aimed at determining how much the people of a country spend on what, and where. That is for a planned, not a market, economy. It cannot work. This is why the US spent so much effort on eliminating bilateralism in Europe after the Second World War.[50] Finally, given overall macroeconomic conditions, a focus on bilateral balances will not shift the overall balance: if, for example, the US stops buying from China, it is likely to buy the same product from some other country; and, again, if the US produces the product at home, it will stop making something else that was previously exported. Focusing on bilateral imbalances when the underlying problem is global macroeconomic disequilibria is like squeezing a balloon: it cannot work.

Toward Rigged Capitalism

The discussion thus far has focused on the big picture—technology, globalization, demography, the distribution of income, and macroeconomic instability. But there is something just as important and possibly far more dangerous: the exploitation of market and political power. We should think of this as the rise of a "rentier economy." This has many aspects: "financialization," corporate (mal-)governance, winner-take-all markets, rents from agglomeration, weaknesses of competition, tax avoidance and evasion, rent seeking, and the erosion of ethical standards.[51] These are principally the outcome of failures of liberalization—above all, a failure to think through the institutional context for markets. The prevailing assumption was that the free pursuit of self-interest is enough on its own: it is not.

Financialization—a hideous, but seemingly inescapable, term for the growing impact of finance—is a characteristic of the economic world of the last four decades, notably in the US and UK. Behind it lies the idea of the economy as just a bundle of tradeable contracts. The rapid liberalization of finance, reinforced by the development of information and communications technology, facilitated a transformation of the economy. Financialization has meant enormous expansion in the scale of financial sector activity, a corresponding expansion in the complexity of financial products, a parallel expansion in the earnings from financial sector activity, and a transformational change in the role of finance in controlling corporate activity.[52] All this has dubious benefits for economic performance. As we shall see, the immense growth of financial activity seems to be far more a vehicle for rent extraction than for productive improvements. It also led directly to the financial crises of 2007–12.

There was an enormous expansion in global private debt in the years running up to the financial crisis of 2007–12, especially of financial sector debt—an indication of the explosion of balance sheets and leverage in the financial sector.[53] This has not been reversed since then, far from it, though its sectoral composition has changed: financial sector debt fell somewhat, relative to global GDP, until the COVID pandemic. Nonfinancial sector corporate debt rose strongly, particularly during the pandemic. Household debt stabilized after the financial crisis, but then jumped during the pandemic. (See figures 36 and 20.) Debt is both the product and the fuel of the financial sector. This explosion in overall debt was matched by one in cross-border financial transactions. In 1995, the total stock of global cross-border foreign direct investment, portfolio equity, debt securities, and other lending was $15 trillion (51 percent of global GDP). By 2007, this had become $103 trillion (185 percent of global GDP). After that, the stock froze, at least up to 2016, when it was 183 percent of global GDP.[54]

A simple indicator of rising complexity is the explosion in the notional and gross market value of over-the-counter derivatives (foreign exchange, interest rates, and equity-linked).[55] Notional values jumped from $72 billion in June 1998 to $653 billion a decade later, and the gross market value jumped from $2.6 billion to $35 billion at the end of 2008. After that, the global crisis blew up the financial system and the world economy. Thereupon, the derivatives music, like the debt expansion, stopped playing. But the market remains huge:

the gross market value at the end of the first quarter of 2021 was $12.6 trillion. (See figure 37.)

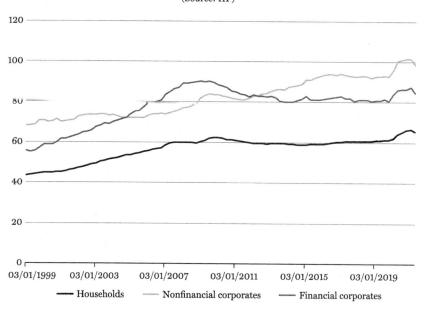

FIGURE 36. GLOBAL PRIVATE DEBT OVER GDP (PERCENT)
(Source: IIF)

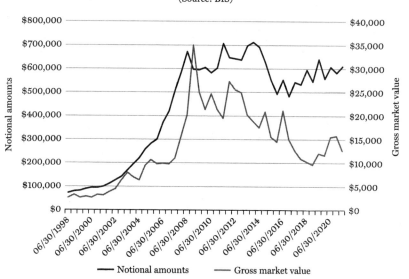

FIGURE 37. NOTIONAL AND MARKET VALUE OF OUTSTANDING
OVER-THE-COUNTER DERIVATIVES ($BILLION)
(Source: BIS)

Also significant was the high share of the financial sector in corporate profits. It may be wondered how much of this represents value added to the economy and how much represents transfers of wealth—that is, rent extraction. The characteristic of banking is that the debts of these institutions are accepted as means of payment: they are money. This means that the financial sector creates its own "fuel." When it makes loans, it simultaneously creates the money with which to pay itself fees and even interest.[56] Thus, in boom times the profits of the financial sector are likely to be at least in part a fictitious product of its aggregate lending. That is precisely what figure 36 suggests. The pre-boom share of finance in total US corporate profits was around 15 percent. This level might or might not have represented value added; it is hard to tell. But the subsequent explosion in profits to over a quarter of the total was both staggering and, as events proved, fictitious (see figure 38). That profits have remained so high subsequent to the crisis must be due in large part to the immense support provided by the authorities, especially the near-zero interest rates that have been in effect for so much of the time, as well as the still gigantic balance sheets of financial institutions.

FIGURE 38. SHARE OF FINANCIAL SECTOR IN
US CORPORATE PROFITS (PERCENT)
(Source: BEA)

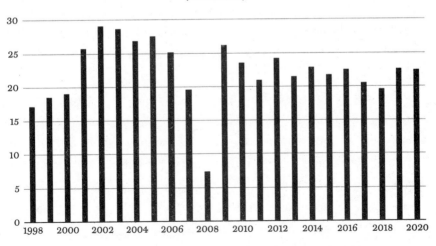

This was all remarkably good for those working in the financial business. One study analyzed the ups and downs of the relative earnings of finance professionals.[57] Their relative earnings peaked in the early part of the last century, before crashing in the 1930s. Relative earnings started to move rapidly upward again, in parallel with financial deregulation, in the 1980s. Also significant in increasing the demand for skills in finance were complex activities, such as initial private offerings (IPOs) and management of credit risk. According to the study, rents—earnings over and above those needed to attract people into the industry—accounted for 30–50 percent of the differential earnings of professionals in finance vis-à-vis the rest of the private sector.

This explosion of financial activity has not done much for productivity growth, which has been quite poor since the 1970s and particularly so since the financial crisis (see figures 19 and 26). This is not surprising. Little of this expansion of financial balance sheets went into financing fresh investment. The great bulk of it went into leveraging balance sheets of households, the nonfinancial corporate sector, and, of course, the financial sector itself. Moreover, much of the most highly rewarded activity of the sector consists of what are likely to be, in whole or part, zero-sum activities: hedging against the volatility created by financial sector activity itself; invention of complex derivatives that conceal embedded risks; and outright gambling.[58] Adair Turner, former chair of the UK's Financial Services Authority, famously described much of this activity as "socially useless."[59] It is quite hard to disagree.[60]

The absence of a positive link between financial activity and economic performance is noteworthy. A paper for the Bank for International Settlements, published in 2014, concluded that "the level of financial development is good only up to a point, after which it becomes a drag on growth, and that a fast-growing financial sector is detrimental to aggregate productivity growth."[61] The explanation for the lack of positive impact is that when the financial sector grows quickly, it hires talented people to manage lending to projects, usually property-related, that can generate collateral for lenders. But lending to the property sector does not aid productivity. It creates "positional goods," such as offices or luxury housing in the centers of big cities.[62] If these skilled people did not work in the financial sector, they might create and manage investments with far higher returns to the economy. They are, after all, mostly numerate and many have backgrounds in science or engineering. Consider, too, the resources being devoted to trading just a microsecond ahead of others—a negative sum activity if ever there was one.[63] The financial sector wastes both human and real resources. It is in large part a rent-extraction machine.

Together with the rise of finance came a profound shift in the aims of the firm, toward maximizing profits, or "shareholder value."[64] This shift had consequences on several dimensions. Particularly important was the idea that corporations should be appendages of financial markets. The role of finance was no longer merely to facilitate investment. Financial considerations were to determine every aspect of corporate behavior—its goals, its internal incentives, and the identity of those in charge. Finance ceased to be a handmaiden of the firm and turned into its mistress.

In 1970, the late Milton Friedman famously declared that "there is one and only one social responsibility of business—to use its resources and engage in activities designed to increase its profits so long as it stays within the rules of the game, which is to say, engages in open and free competition without deception or fraud."[65] If stock markets are efficient, maximizing market capitalization is equivalent to maximizing the present value of profits. Furthermore, in the absence of "market failures" (imperfect information, monopoly, environmental and social spillovers, and so forth), maximizing the value to shareholders should be equivalent to maximizing the value of the firm to society.[66] In this way, the stock market becomes a machine for weighing the value of corporations. Once we accept such ideas, it makes sense to create a direct link between executive rewards and the market value of the business and to have an active market in corporate control, to ensure that the principals (the shareholders) can force their agents (corporate management) to serve their interests.

These propositions remind one of the remark by American humorist H. L. Mencken that "there is always a well-known solution to every human problem—neat, plausible, and wrong."[67] While these ideas do provide a relatively straightforward way to decide on the goals, incentives, and control of companies, they also create big problems.

One is that profit is not a good motivating goal for organizations. It should be a by-product of pursuing other goals, such as making excellent cars or providing reliable advice. If I am told that a business's aim is to make money out of me, I mistrust it. I want to believe it is determined to look after its customers. This is particularly true when it is hard to monitor the quality of what the business offers, which is so often the case, especially in finance.

A deeper problem is that, as Ronald Coase argued in 1937, companies exist precisely *because* markets are imperfect.[68] Instead of markets, we rely on the "relational contracts" characteristic of the firm. Such contracts are based on trust. A couple cannot write a contract covering everything that might happen in their marriage. The same is true of firms. Yet if the relational (or implicit) contract that governs the firm is founded on trust of all committed parties, giving control rights to one party means that many potentially valuable contracts will not be reached.[69] The risks of opportunistic behavior by the controlling parties are too great to allow the needed agreements to be reached.

Moreover, successful corporations generate rents—income over and above the opportunity cost of the factors of production employed. There is no obvious reason why all these rents should accrue to the shareholders and top managers. Moreover, the existence of these rents, combined with the narrow control rights and the manifold principal-agent problems, provides both motives and opportunities for rent-seeking behavior. And that is exactly what we see.

The shift to control of the firm by shareholders who are not engaged in running it also creates a huge collective action problem. Shareholders who own a small fraction of a firm have no incentive to invest in the knowledge necessary to oversee it, especially when they benefit from the privilege of limited liability. Shareholders are also able to insure themselves against failure at any individual company by diversifying their portfolios. Indeed, they are far better able to insure themselves in this way than their workers or even the localities in which they operate. For shareholders, "exit" (that is, selling shares) is almost always a more sensible option than bearing the costs of exercising "voice" (that is, becoming an engaged shareholder). This is true even of most fund managers: the costs of engagement with a company outweigh the benefits for themselves. Worse, fund managements are themselves agents with conflicts of interest vis-à-vis corporate management: while they have a motive to improve the performance of the firms whose shares they own, they may also benefit from obtaining mandates from management, notably rights to manage pension funds. Private equity, activist shareholders, and hostile takeovers may seem partial solutions to these problems. Yet all are blunt tools. Private equity investors, for example, are agents, not principals. They also tend to finance their transactions with high leverage, which creates governance problems, especially when companies come close to bankruptcy. At that point, it makes sense for them to gamble for resurrection, with losses falling on holders of debt.

In practice, then, the shareholder-value-maximizing firm guarantees opportunistic behavior by powerful insiders. This is not a novel complaint. Adam Smith himself argued, "Negligence and profusion, therefore, must always prevail, more or less, in the management of the affairs of such a company [a joint-stock company]."[70] Similarly, John Stuart Mill argued that "experience shows, and proverbs, the expression of popular experience, attest, how inferior is the quality of hired servants, compared with the ministration of those personally interested in the work."[71]

Management has a powerful incentive to rig incentives in its own interests. The most obvious mechanism is to link remuneration to stock market performance, even if that performance has little to do with management's actions. The shorter management's expected term in control and the more difficult it is for outside shareholders to judge what is happening in a large and complex business, the greater the incentive for management to do so. There are many ways to rig rewards: borrow money to buy their company's shares; divert money from long-term investment into stock buybacks; create stock incentive plans that guarantee huge rewards in a rising market, whatever the contributions of management.

The evidence seems overwhelming that the huge rise in managerial rewards (discussed in chapter 4) has had next to nothing to do with corporate performance. Worse, as the British economist Andrew Smithers argues, the incentive schemes that generate these extraordinary rewards are worse than mere rent extraction (though they are that). They distort incentives by encouraging management to increase leverage, thereby making corporate and overall economic performance riskier, and lower spending on fixed investment and research and development.[72] One aspect is the encouragement to short-termism, namely, seeking to raise share prices today rather than the value of the firm over the long term.[73]

The increased pay of top corporate management and the huge increase in rewards in the financial sector also help explain the extraordinary rise in top incomes in a number of countries.[74] One reason to conclude this is the divergence among advanced capitalist countries in both the share of the top 1 percent in pretax incomes and in the increase in that share since 1980. These are, not surprisingly, highest where the shareholder-value revolution has gone furthest: the English-speaking countries—Canada, the UK, and the US. In the US, the share of the top 1 percent reached 18.8 percent in 2019—a jump of 8.3 percentage points from 1981. In the Netherlands, the share was only 6.9 percent in 2019, just 1 percentage point higher than in 1981. (See figure 39.) To put the share of the top 1 percent in the US in context, in 2019 it was 41 percent bigger than that of the entire bottom 50 percent.

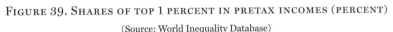

FIGURE 39. SHARES OF TOP 1 PERCENT IN PRETAX INCOMES (PERCENT)
(Source: World Inequality Database)

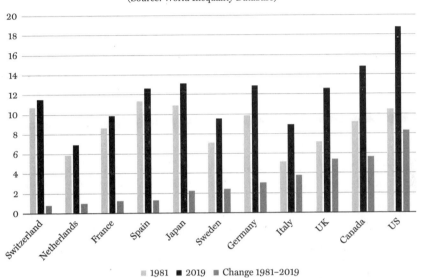

■ 1981   ■ 2019   ■ Change 1981–2019

Important market failures do not exist only within the governance structure of firms. Equally important are failures in the relationship of firms with the outside world. Like all businesses, companies have an incentive to ignore externalities, such as environmental or social damage. If a firm dumps effluent—or its workers, for that matter—others bear the consequences: the family, the community, the state. But there is something inherent in the creation of large firms: monopoly power. The invention of the corporation was a response to the need for very large firms. Size gives market power. This makes it even more likely that companies will be able to raise shareholder value by exploiting others. The increasingly widely accepted view is that even quite small companies have a degree of monopoly power in labor markets.[75] They may also possess some degree of monopoly power over suppliers and consumers.

Certain policies are even intended to increase market power. Among the most important is protection of intellectual property (via copyright and patents, in particular). While there is a case for such protection, it does involve the creation of monopolies. Moreover, companies are powerful institutions. They can influence the law that governs intellectual property, by extending copyright indefinitely, for example. Among the most powerful sources of influence for such extensions was the Disney Corporation.[76] Again the outcome is to create monopoly rents.

Another difficulty is that the firm has a strong interest in internalizing gains while externalizing costs. The victims are members of society at large. Such externalizing can occur in a multitude of important ways. Local and global pollution is perhaps the most obvious and threatening example. But also important is corporate behavior in the labor market. Discrimination among workers imposes social costs, for example. So does shifting all the risks of managing insecurity onto workers or making it more difficult for adults (especially women) to fulfill their roles as parents or caregivers of old people. Perhaps the most obvious example of such risk transfers is that of the financial sector, which creates risk in good times, by increasing leverage, and is rescued by central banks and the government in crises.

The standard counter to such arguments is that the democratic political process can offset such cost externalization by means of regulation, taxes, and subsidies. Yet that assumes a neutral political process in which well-intentioned legislators respond to the choices of well-informed voters. Nothing could be further from reality. In all democratic processes, well-motivated, well-informed, powerful, and concentrated interests outweigh the diffuse interests of bigger but weaker groups.[77] No private interest is more concentrated and more potent than that of large and well-resourced businesses, which duly dominate lobbying in many areas.

A more recent transformation of the market economy, partly driven by digital innovations, is the emergence of winner-take-all markets.[78]

The digital world of zero marginal costs, platform economics, and big data allows the most successful businesses to dominate global markets. The opportunity is now often to sell to advertisers the information they obtain from customers. Superstar individuals also gain: being the world's twentieth most popular blues singer means rather little when everybody in the world can so easily access the performances of the most popular.

The drivers of winner-take-all markets include economies of scale and scope, network effects (both direct and indirect), big data and machine learning, brand loyalties, the high costs of switching, the attraction of specific employers to talented workers, the reputations of founders, and the straightforward economics of agglomeration.[79] The outcome is that these companies are sitting upon monopoly rents that are orders of magnitude bigger than the opportunity cost of the factors of production (land, capital, and human skills) engaged in the business.[80] The twelve most valuable companies in the world in early 2022 included eight technology companies—Apple, Microsoft, Alphabet, Amazon, Meta Platforms, Nividia, Taiwan Semiconductor Manufacturing, and Tencent Holdings—six American, one Chinese, and one Taiwanese. All are monopolies, or near monopolies. One of the others was Berkshire Hathaway, a holding company controlled by Warren Buffett, who sees market power ("moats") as the foundation of market value.[81] Another was Saudi Arabian Oil, a pure rent extractor in the classic definition of that term. The other two were Tesla and JP Morgan. The latter benefited from huge economies of scale and the regulatory moat offered de facto to all large banks. Whether Tesla has durable monopoly power remains to be seen. In brief, a small number of winners that held strong monopoly positions seemed able to shape both the present and the future. Many of these companies were also huge winners from the COVID crisis, which further cemented the economic dominance of giant technology companies. (See figure 40.)

A crucial aspect of the winner-take-all markets of the past four decades has been the divergence of successful metropolitan clusters

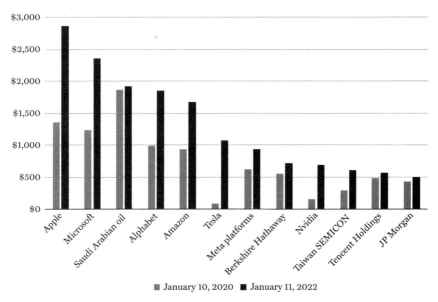

FIGURE 40. MARKET VALUE OF WORLD'S TWELVE MOST VALUABLE COMPANIES JANUARY 10, 2020, AND OF THE SAME COMPANIES JANUARY 11, 2022 ($BILLION)
(Source: Refinitiv)

and declining provincial towns, already noted briefly above.[82] Many big cities—London, New York, Los Angeles, Tokyo, Paris, Milan, Shanghai, Beijing, Mumbai—are thriving.[83] The Chicago Council on Global Affairs notes that forty-two global cities are among the world's 100 largest economies.[84] Meanwhile, once-prosperous industrial towns are crumbling. Contrast London with Sheffield, not so long ago the world's dominant producer of specialty steels. The OECD provides the following brief overview: "The average GDP per worker gap between the top 10 percent (frontier) and the bottom 76 percent regions across OECD countries has grown by almost 60 percent, from $15,200 to $24,000. As a result, one in four persons in the OECD lives in a region that is falling further behind the high-productivity regions in their country."[85]

Clustering is why cities have always been important for economic prosperity.[86] This was true in preindustrial times, again in industrial times, and still more so in today's postindustrial economy. But the cities that succeed have changed. Today, they are engaged in global exchange and are subject to global competition. This compels and rewards specialization while also punishing unsuccessful specialization. The bigger the city and the more diverse its skills, the better its chances of being able to move on from one specialty to the next or even to combine many at the same time. The explosive growth of the "knowledge economy" has further rewarded the concentrations of skills and experience of great metropolises.

Meanwhile, those more specialized cities and towns whose businesses lose out in global competition risk falling into cumulative decline: bright young people leave; new businesses do not enter, because the skills they need are unavailable; and people living on welfare benefits arrive, because accommodation is cheap. The market will not overcome this, because there are so many externalities: ten businesses might thrive where one would fail, but how do the ten businesses coordinate their arrival? This is a classic case for government intervention.

These gains from agglomeration generate huge rents. As Henry George argued, a huge portion of such rents accrues to the owners of land.[87] This is why a land tax is fair (since the owners of land did nothing to earn their wealth) and efficient (because land per se, unlike effort, ingenuity, and saving, cannot be taxed out of existence). The case for land taxes remains strong. But today much of the agglomeration rent accrues to successful urban workers. They gain an income in a productive metropolis over and above what would be needed to persuade them to do the work. Agglomeration rents are ultimately the product of social capital—the rule of law, above all—created by society at large. So, there is a good reason to share these rents out. Instead of continuing to do that, jealousy of London's success was a factor in the vote for Brexit, which will make almost everybody in the UK worse off.[88]

One of the most interesting findings of recent research is the decline in competition, especially in the US.[89] This is partly due to the winner-take-all phenomenon. But it is also to do with changed attitudes to antitrust policy. The thrust of those changes was to ignore concentration if it did not directly harm consumers. Bigness, argued Yale's Robert Bork, the most influential of the analysts, was not inherently bad.[90] The widespread acceptance of this doctrine has had consequences: for example, it allowed the Silicon Valley giants (see figure 38) to buy many potential competitors. Proponents argue that this has led to greater investment in innovation. But it is more likely to have generated excessive market—and other forms of economic—power.

What was happening in the US economy more broadly supports the hypothesis of increased market power. Thus, one can identify seven trends that indicate weak competitive pressure: a clear slowdown in the rate of creation of new businesses and a concomitant increase in the market share of the top firms; reduced fluidity of labor markets, with markedly less job mobility, on all relevant dimensions; a rising share of income going to capital; a rise in the rate of return on capital relative to the yield on safe assets; lower business investment, despite high returns; increased dispersion of rates of return across businesses; and rising wage divergence among workers with similar skills. Among the causes of all this may be undue protection of intellectual property, excessive monopsony power of firms in labor markets, overprotective occupational licensing, and over-restrictive land-use regulation.[91] Yet even more important may be obstacles to competition in the digital economy. An analysis of competition in the digital economy for the UK government concluded that digital markets are subject to "tipping," in which the winner will indeed take all, or most, of a market.[92] This is not true of all digital markets, especially when they interact with the real world; taxi services are an example. But it is true of many.

Thomas Philippon's seminal book, *The Great Reversal*, argues in a similar vein:

First, US markets have become less competitive: concentration is high in many industries, leaders are entrenched, and their profit rates are excessive. Second, this lack of competition has hurt US consumers and workers: it has led to higher prices, lower investment, and lower productivity growth. Third, and contrary to common wisdom, the main explanation is political, not technological: I have traced the decrease in competition to increasing barriers to entry and weak antitrust enforcement, sustained by heavy lobbying and campaign contributions.[93]

These points are supported by what has happened in three crucial industries—finance, health care, and, yet again, "Big Tech."[94] On finance, a startling finding is that the cost of intermediation—how much bankers and brokers charge for taking in savings and transferring them to end users—has remained around 2 percentage points for a century. The US also spends far more on health care than any other high-income country (not much below a fifth of GDP) and yet has far worse health outcomes, because the health system nourishes rent-extracting monopolies: doctors, hospitals, insurance companies, and pharmaceutical businesses all feed at this overflowing trough. Again, the profits of the big technology companies—Amazon, Apple, Google, Facebook, and Microsoft—are in large measure due to monopoly rent. Just consider, for a moment, the pricing of Apple's App Store.[95]

If we are to assess arguments about the emergence of rentier capitalism in the US, we need to compare it with the EU. Many will laugh at the comparison: after all, isn't the EU an economic disaster? When one compares changes in real gross domestic product per head, the answer is no. From 1999 to 2017 real GDP per head rose by 21 percent in the US, 25 percent in the EU, and 19 percent even in the eurozone, despite the damage done by its inept handling of the financial crisis.[96] Levels of inequality and trends in income distribution are also less adverse in the EU than in the US, as noted earlier, so the increases in incomes have also been more evenly shared.

Comparisons between the EU and the US also show that neither profit margins nor market concentration has soared in the EU to the extent they have in the US. The share of wages and salaries in the value-added of business fell by close to 6 percentage points in the US between 2000 and 2015, but not at all in the eurozone.[97] This weakens the hypothesis that technology has been the principal driver of the downward shift in the share of labor incomes. After all, technology (and international trade, for that matter) has affected both sides of the Atlantic roughly equally.

The EU economy is certainly not stronger in all respects. On the contrary, "The US has better universities and a stronger ecosystem for innovation, from venture capital to technological expertise."[98] Nevertheless, competition in product markets has become more effective in the EU over the past two or three decades. This reflects deregulation within the single market—ironically, given Brexit, a UK-driven policy innovation that originated with Margaret Thatcher—and a more aggressive and independent competition policy. The need to preserve and promote competition switched on the two sides of the Atlantic, though the Biden administration has indicated its intention to change that.

A fascinating proposition is that the EU has established more independent regulators than either its individual members or the US would have done. This reflects mutual distrust. Individual states prefer strong independent institutions to being vulnerable to the whims of fellow members. This is particularly beneficial to countries with weak national regulators. The higher an EU member country's product market regulation in 1998, the bigger the subsequent decline in it.[99]

These differences between the US and EU also influence rewards to lobbying. The independence of its regulators makes returns to lobbying relatively low in the EU. Lobbying against deregulation and for favorable regulation is fiercer in the US, because this activity works. Why else would people pay for it?[100]

In sum, important modern economies seem full of monopoly rents.

This is least true where global trade provides competition. But it is very much true in the more sheltered parts of the economy and those dominated by natural monopolies. As Adam Smith warned, incumbent businesses will pursue restraints on competition with great enthusiasm. The difficulty is that it is now too easy for incumbents to buy the political and regulatory protection they desire. The outcome is rentier capitalism.

Exploiting tax loopholes is another significant part of rent extraction. This has several dimensions. The most important are the exploitation of significant corporate tax loopholes and use of tax havens by wealthy individuals.

A huge challenge is tax avoidance by corporations. Corporations (and so also their shareholders) benefit from the range of goods—security, legal systems, infrastructure, educated workforces, and political and social stability—provided by the world's most important liberal democracies. But corporations are also in a perfect position to exploit loopholes in the taxation of companies. This is of great benefit to their shareholders: if profits are lightly taxed (or even untaxed) in the hands of the corporation and then not distributed to shareholders as dividends, they turn into capital gains, which are generally very lightly taxed. This is rightly seen as unfair. That erodes the legitimacy of the tax system and even of the market economy. As the system comes to be seen as rigged, the quality of the jurisdictions on which corporations themselves depend are eroding. They are fouling their own nests.

The biggest challenges within the corporate tax system are base erosion and profit shifting and tax competition. Base erosion and profit shifting refers to the ability of corporations to report profits in low(er)-tax jurisdictions. Important tools for this are: shifting intellectual property into tax havens; charging tax-deductible debt against profits accrued in higher-tax jurisdictions; and rigging transfer prices within the firm, in order to shift profits into low-tax jurisdictions.[101] Digital companies are particularly well suited to shifting profits into low-tax jurisdictions, since the geographical location of their profit-making activities is so hard to determine. Also important users of this strategy are life-science businesses, whose principal assets are intellectual property. Beyond all this, there is a race to the bottom on corporate tax rates driven by competition among jurisdictions. The slashing of the US corporate tax rate under the Trump administration was a consequence of this cross-border competition. The Biden administration reached a global agreement on minimum corporate taxation in late 2021. It is still unclear how effective this will be, perhaps not very.[102]

The sums involved in all this are significant. An IMF study published in 2015 calculated that base erosion and profit shifting reduced long-run annual revenue in OECD member countries by about $450 billion (1 percent of GDP) and in non-OECD countries by slightly over $200 billion (1.3 percent of GDP). These are significant figures in the context of a tax that raised only 2.9 percent of GDP in 2016, on average, in OECD member countries (and just 2 percent in the US in particular).[103] The study also concluded that cuts in corporate tax rates by OECD countries had strong downward effects on rates in other countries, as expected.[104] There has indeed been a dramatic fall in rates over the past four decades. While revenue from corporate taxation has held up relative to other sources of revenue, the share of profits in OECD GDP has been rising. So the average effective rate must have been falling.[105]

One of the most remarkable indicators of base erosion and profit shifting is that US corporations have been reporting profits in Singapore, the British Caribbean, Switzerland, Luxembourg, Bermuda, Ireland, and the Netherlands (in ascending order of significance) equal to 1.4 percent of US GDP, up from about 0.3 percent in 1995. Meanwhile, the share of profits generated in big foreign economies (China, France, Germany, India, Italy, and Japan) has been stuck firmly at 0.2 percent of GDP.[106] Another piece of recent research concluded that "the effective foreign tax rate of U.S. multinationals in sectors other than oil has collapsed since the mid-1990s. While part of this decline is due to the fall of corporate tax rates abroad, by our estimates almost half of it owes to the rise of profit shifting to tax havens. In 2015, about half of the foreign profits of non-oil US multinationals are made in non-haven countries where they face effective tax rates of 27 percent, and about half are booked in tax havens where they face effective rates of 7 percent."[107] This ability of large corporations to shift profits wherever they want, and so avoid taxes, is worse than mere rent extraction. It distorts competition. Smaller domestic firms that do pay tax are greatly disadvantaged by competition from those that do not.

One important piece of recent research notes that 8 percent of world household financial wealth (10 percent of global output) was held offshore in 2007. It finds, as one might expect, that the largest propensities to hold offshore wealth were in corrupt autocracies (Russia and Saudi Arabia) or countries with recent histories of autocratic rule (Argentina and Greece). But it is not restricted to such countries. Other countries with high proportions of offshore wealth in GDP, relative to the global average, are (in descending order) Portugal, Belgium, UK, Germany, and France. Much of this offshore wealth is held by the top 0.01 percent of the wealth distribution (the top 10,000th). Including these data changes the share of the top of the wealth distribution in total wealth: in the UK, for example, roughly a third of the wealth of this tiny group was held offshore in 2007. In all, they held slightly over 5 percent of total UK household financial wealth. No doubt, some tax is paid on these offshore holdings. But how much? "Very little" would be a reasonable guess.[108]

Beyond all this, some features of tax codes create dangerous distortions and inequities. One of the most important examples is the pervasive tax deductibility of interest on debt. This strongly motivates households and corporations to fund themselves through debt rather than equity. That makes the entire economy more vulnerable to financial crises. Another example (albeit a less significant one) is the "carried interest" exemption from income tax. Carried interest includes the performance fees of managers (general partners) of private equity and hedge funds. Under current tax arrangements, these are taxed as capital gains, not as income. This gives some of the most highly rewarded businesspeople in the world their own private (and much lower) tax rates. It is clear, however, that carried interest is not a capital gain. It is a risky income, like that of an author. If it were a capital gain, then there would have to be the possibility of capital losses. But the downside is capped at zero. Thus, it is income. Of course, there may be a case for changing the treatment of variable and uncertain income. But that should apply to all such incomes.[109]

Our economy, far from being a hive of competitive behavior, has created all sorts of opportunities for rent extraction. This has always been so. The powerful have always been rentiers. But sometimes they have provided something of value in return: a degree of social security or stability, for example. In market capitalism, the successful have contributed to economic dynamism. Nevertheless, opportunities for rent extraction have turned out to be far greater than many expected four decades ago. And this has helped generate an extraordinary maldistribution of the gains from growth and left a large part of the population confused, frustrated, and angry.

Moreover, what has happened is not just the exploitation of opportunities for rent extraction. It has included active rent creation and rent seeking via lobbying. Among the most important examples are active lobbying for changes in tax systems that benefit the wealthiest. Another example is lobbying against attempts to bring under control the destabilizing rent extraction and rent seeking by the financial sector. Yet another is the weakness of competition policy. Above all, the wealthy play a dominant role in shaping public policy. Thus, a recent scholarly study of the US concludes that "the majority does not rule—at least not in the causal sense of actually determining policy outcomes. When a majority of citizens disagrees with economic elites or with organized interests, they generally lose."[110] This view is not uncontroversial.[111] But it has much plausibility.

Data on the role of money in US politics are indeed dramatic. Extraordinarily, members of Congress spend about thirty hours a week raising money. That has proved a big step on the journey of the US toward becoming a plutocracy. As former representative Mick Mulvaney stated in April 2018, "If you're a lobbyist who never gave us money, I didn't talk to you. If you're a lobbyist who gave us money, I might talk to you."[112] Corporate lobbying is two to three times bigger in the US than in the EU. Campaign contributions are fifty times larger in America than in EU members.[113]

Extraordinary opportunities create extraordinary temptations. We know that a society built on greed cannot stand.[114] Other moral values of duty, fairness, responsibility, and decency must permeate a successful society. Yet these values cannot occur only outside the market economy. They must permeate the market economy itself. External regulation is essential. But it will never be sufficient if people with market power lack principles other than greed. A lively book on banking, where egregiously bad behavior of all kinds—fraudulent ratings, incomprehensible instruments, gross conflicts of interest, and grotesque irresponsibility—have been pervasive, sums up as follows: "The most driven bankers consider their job a status game. That game consists of lending money, packing and selling on debts, and privatizations. The more business they do, the higher those bankers will rise in the league tables they have constructed their identities around."[115]

This is, once again, not only rent extraction but also rent creation. The fuel of finance is debt or, to be more precise, leverage. The higher the leverage, the greater the prospective returns on equity, but also the greater the risk of failure. From a social point of view, there should be no cost to having far lower ratios of debt to equity. But these would lower returns to equity in good times and so reduce the rewards to financial professionals and financial management.[116] Lower ratios of debt to equity would also greatly reduce the likelihood of crises. But the latter are relatively rare events. When they happen, the industry will argue that they were unforeseeable, which they were not. The industry will also know that the social and economic costs of a financial collapse are so great that the government is sure to try to bail them out. So, for the industry, high leverage is a "heads I win, tails you lose" proposition. After the crisis, many economists argued for much lower leverage in finance. In the end, it fell modestly. Today, the ratio of equity to assets in global banks is mostly between 5 and 6 percent, about twice what it was precrisis. Is this safe? Hardly. These banks will be insolvent if their balance sheets lose around 5 percent of their value. Irresponsible finance creates rent: it lives well off taking risks for which others will ultimately bear the downside costs.[117] There is no doubt that the "too-big-to-fail-or-to-jail" bank must either be ended or be chained.

New Challenges

Already we can see at least three further huge economic challenges facing us: artificial intelligence, climate, and the pandemic. These will shape a possibly still more difficult future.

This is the decade when action needs at last to be taken on global environmental challenges. Climate is the highest priority, but there are others, notably biodiversity, on both land and sea. This is likely to create economic costs, at least in the short to medium run, especially given the huge investment needs.[118] Meeting this challenge is going to be difficult, on at least three levels. First, every significant political actor—countries, the EU as a whole, and in some cases states or cities—will have to work out effective plans and policies for transformation in the generation and use of energy within the next decade. Second, they will also have to gain the political support needed for their implementation. Third, their plans will have to mesh with those of many other countries worldwide, despite radically different constraints and opportunities, since no set of countries can fix this problem on their own. Above all, it cannot be fixed by the high-income countries alone since they generated only some 30 percent of global emissions in 2020. The dominant players are emerging and developing countries, which already generate 70 percent of emissions and will generate all the increase in emissions under all the plausible scenarios for the future. (See figure 41.)

FIGURE 41. SHARES IN GLOBAL EMISSIONS OF CARBON DIOXIDE (PERCENT)
(Source: Global Carbon Project)

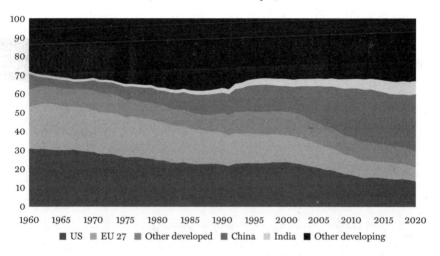

Inevitably, doing all this will exhaust a vast amount of policy and political space. Indeed, as things look today, it seems almost inconceivable that this will happen at all. Yet if nothing much is done in this decade, the task of containing damaging climate change may well be hopeless. Tackling all this requires, not least, close cooperation between China and the US, which generated 44 percent of global emissions of carbon dioxide between them in 2020. Alas, such cooperation seems as elusive as Lewis Carroll's Snark.[119] Instead, we are likely to see all sorts of "climate theater"—actions like forcing people to ride bicycles or recycle rubbish, or banning nuclear power—none of which will be relevant to tackling the great challenge we face. In all, as the outcome of the 2021 United Nations Climate Change Conference shows us, we are far indeed from a workable global solution.[120]

The impact of artificial intelligence is, in a very different way, as controversial as that of climate change. It is conceivable that these new technologies will unsettle our deepest sense of what it is to be human. It seems highly plausible that they will make a huge difference to the workings of our economies and societies, by transforming the roles of workers both by brain and by hand, via the combination of computing, communications, and robotics.[121] It even seems conceivable that, in time, this revolution will lead to a collapse in the market-determined rewards of a large proportion of workers, including educated ones, and correspondingly huge gains to the owners of the relevant capital. Ours would then become a still more deeply unequal rentier economy: the return on the know-how and machines would be owned by a handful of unimaginably rich people, pampered and protected by armies of robotic slaves. Most humans might then become economically redundant.

At worst, most human beings might become as economically irrelevant as the horse, once a ubiquitous means of transport but irrelevant after the invention of the railway and the internal combustion engine. Yet some researchers take a relatively optimistic view on the implications. It is possible, after all, that we will experience no more than further examples of the never-ending adjustments of the last two centuries. Others forecast a far more revolutionary and darker "world without work."[122] At this stage, all we can say is that we do not know. But we need to be able to manage such a revolution, just as we need to develop a plan for our climate.

Finally, the onset of COVID-19 created enormous fiscal deficits almost everywhere, but especially in high-income countries, and so is bequeathing a legacy of higher public debt. It caused high unemployment, some of it temporary but some of it permanent, because some of those laid off are too old or inflexible to find new jobs. It caused economic damage to the young, women (particularly mothers of young children), the less-educated, and members of minority communities and also, crucially, harmed the educations of children and young people. It damaged businesses, on multiple dimensions, which may inflict permanent losses on the level and growth of output. It increased private indebtedness and raised the probability of mass bankruptcies and distress in the financial sector. It damaged the economies of emerging and developing countries and delayed the fight against extreme poverty, possibly for years, partly because of the slow rollout of vaccines across the world. It accelerated changes in the structure of economies away from face-to-face contact and operations dependent on such close contact toward virtual relationships in production and consumption of goods. It may produce lasting changes in patterns of working, buying, and living. It seems to have accelerated deglobalization of goods, while accelerating globalization of the services that can be turned into bits. Finally, it greatly accelerated the breakdown in relations between the US and China, with unknown consequences for economic and political cooperation.[123]

In sum, COVID-19 is going to leave a legacy of challenges and, one might argue, also opportunities. What seems certain is that the post-pandemic economy (when or if we reach that happy state) will be significantly different and more difficult to navigate than was expected as recently as 2019.

Conclusion

This chapter has analyzed what lies behind the economic malaise discussed in chapter 4, as well as some of the challenges that still lie ahead. It argues that the malaise is partly the outcome of profound and inescapable forces, especially the slowdown of productivity growth, unbalanced impact of new technologies, demographic changes, and rise of emerging countries, especially China. It also turns out that international trade is more of a scapegoat than a huge problem. What is a problem, however, is the rise of rentier capitalism, in which a relatively small proportion of the population has successfully captured rents from the economy and uses the resources it has acquired to control the political and even legal systems, especially in the US, the world's most important standard-bearer of democracy.

High inequality, economic insecurity, slow economic growth, and huge financial crises have eroded trust in elites of important high-income societies. This has in turn led to the election of populists and the triumph of populist causes, which usually leads to bad policies. This threatens a vicious downward spiral of bad economics leading to bad policies and back to bad economics. Alas, Latin American economic conditions of high inequality and poor economic performance are producing Latin American outcomes.

As important, these forces are also undermining free societies. When, for example, Trump "ordered" US firms to leave China, he assumed dictatorial powers.[124] But many people like to hear this, because the president was saying that these *American* businesses should be accountable to *American* (that is, his) political priorities. Populism has, once again, married nationalism. Thus, we now see a burgeoning threat to liberal democracy in the heartland of democracy. The discussion turns to the nature and significance of these political developments in chapter 6.

—■—

CHAPTER SIX

Perils of Populism

The alternate domination of one faction over another, sharpened by the spirit of revenge, natural to party dissension, which in different ages and countries has perpetrated the most horrid enormities, is itself a frightful despotism. But this leads at length to a more formal and permanent despotism. The disorders and miseries which result gradually incline the minds of men to seek security and repose in the absolute power of an individual; and sooner or later the chief of some prevailing faction, more able or more fortunate than his competitors, turns this disposition to the purposes of his own elevation, on the ruins of public liberty.

—*George Washington*[1]

As democracy is perfected, the office of the president represents, more and more closely, the inner soul of the people. We move toward a lofty ideal. On some great and glorious day, the plain folks of the land will reach their heart's desire at last, and the White House will be adorned by a downright moron.

—*H. L. Mencken*[2]

No powerful political actor had set out to destroy the American political system itself—until, that is, Trump won the Republican nomination. He was probably the first major party nominee who ran not for president but for autocrat. And he won.

—*Masha Gessen*[3]

Democratic capitalism is now confronted by authoritarian versions. They take two very different forms. One is "demagogic authoritarian capitalism," and the other is "bureaucratic authoritarian capitalism." The former is an internal threat to high-income liberal democracies: this is what they might turn into. The latter is an external threat to high-income liberal democracies: this is what might defeat them. It is, after all, the system that runs China, their most potent rival.

The first version can be seen in Rodrigo Duterte's Philippines, Recep Tayyip Erdogan's Turkey, Jaroslaw Kaczynski's Poland, Viktor Orban's Hungary, Vladimir Putin's Russia, and may be on the way in Jair Bolsonaro's Brazil and Narendra Modi's India. The second version can be seen in China and Vietnam. Such regimes have married the age-old Confucian tradition of a meritocratic and responsive bureaucracy to a communist party-state and market-driven economy. These are quite different from the demagogic version of authoritarian capitalism and pose quite different challenges to the high-income liberal democracies.

The demagogic variant of authoritarianism comes out of electoral majoritarianism taken to destructive limits.[4] The leader of the government uses its (supposedly temporary) power to suppress independent institutions and the opposition and then emerge as an absolute ruler, as Erdogan, Orban, and Putin have done. In this way, liberal democracy mutates into illiberal democracy and then outright dictatorship. This has become the most common way for authoritarian regimes to emerge. Rather than mounting coups or starting revolutions, the would-be autocrat eats up democracy from within, as some wasp larvae eat host spiders.[5] The result tends to be a softish autocracy by the standards of historic fascism or communism. That may make it less repellent to voters, but it is autocracy all the same.

Such regimes de-institutionalize politics: they make it personal.[6] This is government by arbitrary rulers and their courts. Common features of such regimes include a narrow circle of trusted servants, promotion of members of the family, use of referendums as ways of justifying greater power, and the creation of security services personally loyal to the "great leader." What S. E. Finer called "forum government" is thereby converted into palace government and not just any palace government, but one much like Macbeth's.[7] Courtiers in the new autocracies are not infrequently thwarted careerists—thwarted because they are mediocre.[8]

Such a system combines the vices of populism with the evils of despotism. The vices of populism are short-termism, indifference to expertise, and the prioritization of the immediately political over longer-term considerations. The evils of despotism are corruption and arbitrariness. The two together make for economic inefficiency and long-term failure. These regimes tend to be kleptocratic on a grand scale. The kleptocracy breeds in the darkness all authoritarians love. Theirs is the politics of lies, oppression, and theft, hidden under a veneer of love for the people.[9] Ultimately, this form of authoritarianism generates a vicious gangster state. Putin's Russia is the most important contemporary example.

Ivan Krastev and Stephen Holmes argue that authoritarianism of this kind now pervasive in central and eastern Europe, including Russia, should be viewed as a reversal of the post–Cold War rush to imitate the then-triumphant West. The conservative and nationalist demagogues are, they argue, a reaction against that earlier imitation.[10] This depressing view may be correct. Yet it would clearly be absurd for the West to go down such a rabbit hole, since it would be rejecting itself.

Driving such destructive outcomes is among the most important of all human motivations: the will to power. Democratic politics is not only an arena for debate about the future of a society. It is also about acquiring prestige and power. For people with an unbridled will to power, crises are opportunities. The focus in this chapter is on how and why this process has been happening even in the high-income, supposedly "consolidated" democracies of North America and western Europe. If democratic capitalism were to perish there, where would it survive? The election of Donald Trump, a demagogic would-be autocrat, raised this question with great force, as Masha Gessen argues. Something new had happened. Trump's attempt to subvert the 2020 election and the subsequent support of the Republican Party for the big lie of a stolen election has made the danger even more evident. The year 2024 might mark the end of American liberal democracy.

Populism in High-Income Democracies

For established democracies, choosing the demagogic form of authoritarian capitalism should be viewed as an unthinkable defeat. Nevertheless, policy failures, especially the huge financial crisis and its botched aftermath, as well as the upheaval caused by COVID-19, have created this risk even in high-income Western countries. They have done so by undermining the confidence of a sizable proportion of their electorates in their own and their children's futures, as well as in the probity and wisdom of elites. They have also stoked rage and insecurity, already building up in previous decades. Economic failure is not the only reason for this erosion of confidence. But it is a leading cause of the decayed legitimacy of liberal democracy even in high-income countries with long-established democracies.[11] This is reinforced by a (perfectly realistic) belief that those who succeed in the meritocratic race look down on everybody else.[12] To be poorer than expected is bad. To be poorer than expected and despised to boot is worse.

Dry tinder is a fire waiting to happen, but political entrepreneurs need to light the blaze. In normal times, politics remain bounded by conventions and norms. In times of crisis, this may cease to be the case. As the upheaval makes the political system more fragile, the previously unthinkable can arrive. Consolidated democracies, with reasonably competent policy makers, a sense of the boundaries on legitimate behavior, especially among the elites, and a strong commitment to mutual accommodation, are likely to repudiate a would-be dictator. Britain's rejection of Oswald Mosley in the 1930s is an example. But where the legitimacy of democracy is weak and anger is great, a would-be dictator may be voted into power, as in Germany at that time. By suborning constraining institutions—an impartial bureaucracy, the law, and the media—or closing them down altogether, such figures will throttle liberal democracy *and* the liberal market economy.[13] The latter, after all, depends on a neutral rule of law that protects competition and property rights. Both are anathema to the would-be despot and his henchmen.[14]

Populism is a controversial label. Some argue it should be discarded. But it is hard to do so. It is necessary, instead, to define it more precisely. It has two aspects: hostility to elites and rejection of pluralism. In its anti-elite aspect, populism contrasts the virtuous and downtrodden "real" people against corrupt and oppressive elites. In its anti-pluralist aspect, "Put simply, populists do not claim 'We are the 99 percent.' What they imply instead is that 'We are the 100 percent.' . . . What follows from this understanding of populism as an exclusionary form of identity politics is that populism tends to pose a danger to democracy. For democracy requires pluralism and the recognition that we need to find fair terms of living together as free, equal, but also irreducibly diverse citizens. The idea of the single, homogeneous, authentic people is a fantasy."[15]

Anti-elite populists may not be anti-pluralist. But anti-pluralist populists believe there is only one people—the "real" people—and that they and they alone can represent or, more ambitiously, embody it in their own person. Thus, "Think of Nigel Farage celebrating the Brexit vote by claiming that it had been a 'victory for real people' (thus making the 48 percent of the British electorate who had opposed taking the UK out of the European Union somehow less than real—or, put more directly, questioning their status as proper members of the political community)."[16] In the same vein, at a campaign rally in May 2016, Trump announced that "the only important thing is the unification of the people—because the other people don't mean anything."[17] This is fascistic.

If these two beliefs—anti-elitism and anti-pluralism—are combined, one has a regime that denies the legitimacy of political opponents, political parties (other than their own), independent courts, especially independent constitutional courts, an independent bureaucracy, and an independent press. For such populists, "'the people themselves' is a fictional entity outside existing democratic procedures, a homogeneous and morally unified body whose alleged will can be played off against actual election results in democracies."[18] Leaders with attitudes like this want to be above the law and in office forever: they wish to be dictators.

Populist movements are an inevitable feature of democracies, especially in tough times. This does not mean that populists are necessarily popular. Frequently, populists are quite unpopular. But that will not prevent some of them from claiming that they represent the "real" people. Hostility to elites can also frequently be justified. Democracy is, after all, a system intended to give ordinary people a say in the destiny of their country. Moreover, elites frequently do need to be replaced or reformed, because they have failed, morally, practically, or both. Yet there are also risks if power is won with an appeal to the people against elites. The winners may feel entitled to reject competence, even facts, and so destroy the effectiveness of government. Worse, they may seek to discard all constraints imposed by parliaments, courts, and bureaucracies, which are all necessarily run by elites. Anti-elite politics may then turn into tyranny of the majority or, more to the point, tyranny of political entrepreneurs who claim to speak for the majority.

Anti-pluralism is, however, a greater danger than mere hostility to elites. "Le peuple, c'est moi": is this not what America's Donald Trump, Hungary's Viktor Orban, India's Narendra Modi, Turkey's Tayyip Recep Erdogan, and Venezuela's late Hugo Chavez believe (or believed)?[19] If a politician insists that he alone embodies the people's will, all constraining institutions and so the rights of people as individuals to organize and act politically (and in other ways) are in danger.

How does one tell whether such would-be despots are in power? There are four signs: a rejection of or at least a weak commitment to the democratic rules of the game; denial of the legitimacy of political opponents; toleration and encouragement of violence; and willingness to curtail civil liberties of opponents, including the media.[20]

How, moreover, does the elected authoritarian pursue his goals of unbridled and absolute power? First, he subverts the referees, notably prosecutors, the judiciary, election officials, and tax officials. He insists that these officials owe him personal loyalty, not loyalty to their institutions, the government, the constitution, or the country. Second, he hobbles his opponents and any potentially independent figures. An important part of this is control over the media. But the would-be dictator may also simply put opponents in prison on trumped-up charges. He will also use institutions, such as the tax system or libel laws, to attack independent businesspeople and cultural or intellectual figures. Third, the would-be dictator will seek to change the constitution or electoral laws, to make it impossible to mount an electoral challenge. This may not even require a leader. The South in the US did just that under Jim Crow and is seeking to do it once again today. Finally, the leader will exploit or even create crises that entitle him to emergency powers. Security crises are particularly effective ways of reducing normal concerns over violations of due process. The best-known example of exploiting (or creating) an emergency was the Reichstag fire of 1933, which allowed Hitler to assume total power. The Moscow bombings in September 1999 were another example of a convenient security crisis for a would-be despot.[21]

Populists also tend to adopt a demagogic style of politics by whipping up emotions against elites. Their frequently coarse and abusive manner of speaking is a way of demonstrating that the leader not only speaks *for* the people, against the elite, but is *of* the people.[22] Yet politicians who use demagogic tropes about corrupt elites are not necessarily would-be autocrats. Provided they protect orderly government, the rule of law, free speech, and political and civil rights, their activities are not only consistent with democracy but may well defend and promote it. Perhaps the most important exemplar of such a constructive leader in the twentieth century was Franklin Delano Roosevelt. Yet when announcing the second New Deal in 1936, he delivered a speech that contained the following famous words:

> We had to struggle with the old enemies of peace—business and financial monopoly, speculation, reckless banking, class antagonism, sectionalism, war profiteering.
>
> They had begun to consider the Government of the United States as a mere appendage to their own affairs. We know now that Government by organized money is just as dangerous as Government by organized mob.
>
> Never before in all our history have these forces been so united against one candidate as they stand today. They are unanimous in their hate for me—and I welcome their hatred.[23]

This speech is demagogic in style and populist in content. Yet Roosevelt led the most important reforming government in any democracy in the twentieth century, staffed by competent members of the elite during a succession of huge crises. Far from threatening democracy, he saved it. He might be described as a populist. But he was interested in and competent at the central tasks of governing.

We can clarify populism further by distinguishing among left-wing, centrist, and right-wing forms of populism. There is also a parallel distinction to be made between populists who want to promote competent government and those who do not.

Left-wing populists claim to speak for ordinary people against exploitative business and financial elites. They also tend to argue that conventional politicians, bureaucrats, and the legal system are the willing slaves of economic elites. Theirs "is a vertical politics of the bottom and middle arrayed against the top."[24] We have recently seen aspects of this form of populism on the left of the Democratic Party in the US, in the Labour Party under Jeremy Corbyn in the UK, in Podemos in Spain, and Syriza in Greece. Such left-wing populism borders on institutionalized democratic socialism on one side and revolutionary socialism on the other. It is uncertain what sort of government such a party or movement will provide. Syriza's case was a bit of a shock. Nobody, including almost certainly itself, knew what it was going to do when it got into power in January 2015. In the end, however, Alexis Tsipras made his choice for conventional European left-of-center politics (albeit with characteristically clientelistic behavior) and abandoned nearly all his radical ideas, to the disgust of his finance minister, Yanis Varoufakis.

Centrist populists are even more difficult to pin down. Cinque Stelle in Italy was the obvious contemporary example. It framed itself as opposed to conventional politics in all forms and so against the establishment, including traditional parties of the right and left. Its program was exceptionally ill defined, even by populist standards. Founded by a comedian, it embodied a set of naive anarchistic attitudes. In office, the party turned out to be quite conventional, finally abandoning its alliance with Matteo Salvini's right-wing populist Lega and opting for a coalition with the center-left, Partito Democratico (PD), a pillar of the establishment.[25] In the end, its populist campaigning attitudes did not survive the experience of government any more than Syriza's did.

Right-wing populists are, like those on the left, opposed to elites, though, in their case, academic, bureaucratic, and cultural elites are usually the enemy, not economic and financial ones. But right-wing populists not only oppose elites: they are generally xenophobic and hostile to ethnic minorities as well. "Right-wing populists champion the people against an elite that they accuse of coddling a third group, which can consist, for instance, of immigrants, Islamists, or African American militants. Left-wing populism is dyadic. Right-wing populism is triadic. It looks upward, but also down upon an out group."[26] Even this may be too friendly a description of right-wing populists, who are often outright racists. George Wallace, former governor of Alabama, who started his career as an outspoken opponent of racial integration in the American South, and Donald Trump both fall into this category.[27] So, too, does Jean-Marie Le Pen, founder of the National Front in France, Geert Wilders in the Netherlands, and Matteo Salvini in Italy.

Right-wing populists share such attitudes. But their policies vary significantly, from support for a minimal state and laissez-faire at one end to support for a big and generous state at the other. Thus, at one extreme, right-wing populists favor free markets, at least in their own country. Donald Trump is such a populist. In power, he delivered substantial tax cuts for the wealthy and deregulation, especially of environmental protections. Yet this free-market orientation did not apply in two respects, both of which consisted of attacks on despised foreigners: immigration and trade. In these two crucial respects, the appeal to nationalism and ethnic identity overrode free-market instincts. Otherwise, he stuck to traditional Republican policies.[28] But the ability of right-wing populists to deliver the environment needed for a flourishing free-market capitalism tends to be limited by their hostility to institutions, notably independent courts, central banks, and regulatory institutions. At the opposite end of the right-wing spectrum, nationalist populists favor higher spending on welfare programs and substantial economic intervention. A contemporary example is the PiS government in Poland, whose dominant influence is Jaroslaw Kaczynski.[29] Yet even Donald Trump achieved power with promises to protect social security, offer a better plan for medical coverage than

Barack Obama's Affordable Care Act, and rebuild US infrastructure. This is what many of his supporters thought he would provide. But mostly this did not happen.

While these differences among populists of the left, center, and right are significant, we should not exaggerate them. Ultimately, populism is just a means of obtaining power. It does so by declaring itself against elites, though different stripes of populists assail different elites, and in favor of "the people." Especially in times of trouble, this ploy can be very successful. Yet even such relatively less harmful anti-elite populism risks creating a vicious spiral. People vote in (or at least support) a populist politician who insists that ignoring elite "experts" will transform everything for the better. Such promises usually end in failure. But many of their supporters attribute the failure to "traitors"; belief in the effectiveness of institutions diminishes; and finally a post-populist recession causes demoralization, which leads to yet another enfeebling bout of populism. Some countries—Argentina is the paradigmatic example—seem unable to escape from such a spiral of mistrust, failure, and yet more mistrust.

Right-wing populist dictatorships and left-wing populist dictatorships may not feel very different to their victims. Anti-pluralist populism tends toward dictatorship, whatever the ideology. Venezuela's Maduro is a contemporary avatar of a long line of leftist mass murderers. Policy making is likely to be just as arbitrary, oppressive, and lawless in both cases. Not all populists are would-be dictators and not all dictatorships are populist. But all dictatorships, populist or not, are similar in their attitudes to individual rights and the rule of law: they despise them.

A distinction that cuts across the ideological nuances of populism is whether the person in charge actually wishes to govern. In their response to the COVID emergency, Bolsonaro (Brazil) and Trump (the US) showed that they did not really wish to do so, while Orban (Hungary) and Modi (India) showed that they did, though their responses were illiberal, hostile to criticism, and not noticeably effective.[30] Obviously, a hostility to elites can militate against effectiveness. But populist leaders may nevertheless seek to establish reasonably disciplined and effective governments. Alternatively, they may revel in the chaos they create, with nobody knowing from one day to the next what he or she is supposed to do and who (apart from the boss) is responsible for anything. Fortunately, experience with their failures over COVID seems to have diminished the appeal of incompetent populists.[31]

Anti-pluralist populism is a dangerous enemy of liberal democracy, since it regards opposition as treason, fair elections as illegitimate, the rule of law as an odious constraint, free media as a threat, parliaments as impertinent, and anything that constrains the ability of the leader to do whatever he thinks right as intolerable. Anti-elite populism, on its own, should be seen less as a danger and more as a warning. It tells one that substantial parts of the public have become disenchanted. Democracy is rule by consent. If a large portion of the public has withdrawn its consent from existing rulers—by which I mean not just the party in power, but much of the political, economic, bureaucratic, judicial, intellectual, and social elite—then the public may turn to someone who promises to sweep this elite away.

Winds of Political Change

One of the most important political changes of the last few decades has been the breakdown of the old binary political divisions between dominant parties of the center-right, with roots in business (big and small), the professional middle classes, and the self-employed, and parties of the center-left, with roots in the industrial working class and the labor movements of the nineteenth and early twentieth centuries, though also supported by what was once a relatively small "progressive" intelligentsia. In this world, the crucial arguments were over economics, with the right committed to a smaller state and freer enterprise and the left committed to a bigger state and a more managed economy. Moreover, after the huge upheavals of the nineteenth and early twentieth centuries, even these differences had become relatively minor. A broad consensus on the role of the state and the economy existed in the 1950s and 1960s, reinforced by the ideological conflict of the Cold War. Given the challenge from communism, mainstream political parties realized that the survival of democracy depended on sustaining the loyalties of the huge, well-organized, and politically powerful industrial working class. This was particularly true in western Europe, but it was also true in the US.

These binary divisions have now eroded, creating more complex and more fraught politics. In first-past-the-post, or plurality, systems, the result has been more complex coalitions within parties. In proportional systems, it tends to mean more parties and so more complex coalitions among them. One recent analysis, for example, uses cluster analysis (a way of identifying similarities among elements in a big dataset) to identify "seven tribes" of modern British politics (see table 4). Mutatis mutandis, not dissimilar tribes would emerge from such an analysis in other advanced democracies.[32]

The essential idea is that, while in the past there was just one dimension on which voters differed, the economic, there are now two more—national identity and social values. Table 3 illustrates the consequent attitudes, in six cells. The left is still relatively more in favor of high public spending and a more regulated economy, but it is also globalist (especially on free movement of people and international cooperation) and socially liberal.[33] In reverse, the right is in favor of a small state and free enterprise, of national sovereignty and tight control over migration, and also socially conservative.

TABLE 3. THE THREE DIMENSIONS OF BRITISH POLITICAL LOYALTIES
(ELECTORAL CALCULUS)

	Left side	Right side
Economic	Left wing: Higher taxes and spending, more government regulation of business, nationalization	Right wing: Lower taxes and spending, light regulation, private industry, competition and free markets
National	Globalist: Pro-EU, internationalist, cooperate and share sovereignty with other countries, put global interest above national interest	Nationalist: EU-skeptic, put Britain first, have Britain sovereign, controls on immigration, laws made in Britain, not internationally
Social	Socially liberal: Permissive, allow people to "do their own things," accepting of minority rights, multiculturalism	Socially conservative: Traditional, value authority, supporter of dominant culture and "moral majority"

These neat triads are just one possible outcome, however. Indeed, there is no obvious reason why the set of attitudes called left and right in table 3 would coincide. One might expect, instead, that people who believe in free markets would also be globalist and socially liberal. Similarly, one might expect that people who are in favor of national economic regulation and redistribution would also be nationalist and socially conservative. So, although in the two most recent British general elections (2017 and 2019) the Labour Party's position was broadly in the column on the left, and the Conservative Party's in the column on the right (at least relative to Labour's), many voters hold very different combinations of attitudes and values.

This is brought out in table 4. It turns out that only 15 percent of the electorate is strongly to the right on all three dimensions. Only 4 percent are to the far left on all three dimensions, and another 10 percent (the so-called Traditionalists) are somewhat to the left on all three. This leaves 71 percent of the electorate with more eclectic preferences.

TABLE 4. THE SEVEN TRIBES OF MODERN BRITISH POLITICS (ELECTORAL CALCULUS)

Tribe	Economic	National	Social	Description	Proportion of electorate
Strong left	Very left wing	Very globalist	Very liberal	Left intelligentsia	4%
Traditionalists	Fairly left wing	Moderate	Moderate	Traditional Labour working class	10%
Progressive	Mildly left wing	Quite globalist	Liberal	Blairites	11%
Centrists	Average	Average	Average	Mr. and Mrs. Average	24%
Somewheres	Slightly left wing	Strongly nationalist	Strongly conservative	Conservative working class	12%
Kind young capitalists	Quite right wing	Mildly globalist	Mildly liberal	Modern yuppies	24%
Strong right	Very right wing	Nationalist	Conservative	Conservative heartland	15%

This creates obvious dilemmas for parties trying to put together winning coalitions in first-past-the-post elections. The Conservatives, for example, want to get support of the Somewheres, who are nationalist and socially conservative members of the working and lower middle classes.[34] But the economic views of these Somewheres are somewhat to the left: they are in favor of a generous welfare state and government intervention in the economy in their favor. The closer the Conservative Party comes to Somewheres on national and social questions, the more they risk alienating Kind Young Capitalists, who are relatively well educated and are in favor of the free market, globalist, and socially liberal. The closer the Conservative Party comes to Somewheres on economic questions, the more they risk alienating the Strong Right, who are their most loyal supporters. The closer Conservatives come to more moderate (sometimes called "median voter") positions on all three dimensions, in the hope of attracting Centrists, the

more exposed they become to attack from more nationalist and socially conservative politicians, such as Nigel Farage, formerly head of
UKIP (the UK Independence Party) and the Brexit Party. Such politicians might then manage to steal their votes from the Strong Right
and Somewheres. That fear really matters. It was why David Cameron
chose to support a referendum on EU membership in the 2015 general
election. In the 2019 election, the overriding issue of Brexit seems to
have brought many of these groups together. But that was unlikely to
last. Certainly, the Johnson government had difficulties in crafting
policies that satisfied the aspirations of its new Somewhere supporters
and its more traditional, more prosperous pro-market supporters.

The dilemmas for Labour look even worse. Ideologically committed left-wingers make up only 4 percent of the electorate, and its
committed supporters make up only 14 percent. Labour also needs
Blairites and a good proportion of the Centrists and Somewheres, too.
But the patriotic and socially conservative views of the latter are anathema to the far left and unpalatable even to Blairites: Gordon Brown's
notorious description of a woman who challenged him in the 2010
election on immigration as "bigoted" was so revealing.[35] Moreover,
about half the electorate favors the market economy. So, Labour needs
virtually everybody who shares a more critical perspective on the
economy to support it. But the views of its left-wing activists on national and social questions do not match those of a large part of the
working class, though much of the latter remains inclined toward Labour on economic questions. This used to matter less because economic issues were dominant. But they are so no longer.

In the 2019 general election, Labour frightened off those in favor
of the market economy with its economic radicalism, plus a good part
of the patriotic and socially conservative working class with its confu-
sions on Brexit and its globalism on immigration. Thus, in 2019, relative to 2017, there was a particularly large swing against Labour by its
traditional working-class base (Traditionalists in table 4).[36] The vote
share of Labour in this group fell by close to 20 percentage points.

There were also swings away from Labour among the Strong Left, Progressives, and Centrists, but they were smaller than among these Traditionalists. The vote share of Labour in these other three groups (Strong Left, Progressives, and Centrists) fell by around 10 percentage points in each case. The result was an electoral disaster for Labour, which gained only 33 percent of the overall vote, against 44 percent for the Conservatives. If these changes become entrenched, it will be because many traditional working-class Labour people have shifted their political identity in a profound way.

Francis Fukuyama has elaborated the broader significance of these additional dimensions of political disagreement: "Twentieth-century politics had been organized along a left–right spectrum defined by economic issues, the left wanting more equality and the right demanding greater freedom. . . . In the second decade of the twenty-first century, that spectrum appears to be giving way in many regions to one defined by identity. The left has focused less on broad economic equality and more on promoting the interests of a wide variety of groups perceived as being marginalized—blacks, immigrants, women, Hispanics, the LGBT community, refugees, and the like. The right, meanwhile, is redefining itself as patriots who seek to protect traditional national identity, an identity that is often explicitly connected to race, ethnicity, or religion."[37]

Thomas Piketty has provided a fascinating analysis of the evolution of political loyalties in France, the UK, and the US since 1948, using postelection surveys.[38] Most important, in the 1950s and 1960s, "the vote for left-wing (socialist-labour-democratic) parties was associated with lower education and lower income voters. It has gradually become associated with higher education voters."[39] Furthermore, he notes of the US that "the Democratic Party became the party of the educated in a country where the university system is highly stratified and inegalitarian and the disadvantaged have virtually no chance of gaining admission to the most selective colleges and universities."[40] But similar shifts have also occurred in the support for parties of the center-left in France and the UK.

The outcome has been a "multiple-elite" party system or, more precisely, a "binary-elite" party system in the 2000s–2010s: "high-income voters continue to vote for the right, while high-education voters have shifted to supporting the left."[41] This split between a "Merchant Right" and a "Brahmin Left" explains much about contemporary politics. The Brahmin class continues to seek the support of voters by pointing to the exploitative behavior of the commercial elite and the system it runs. But its predominant interest nowadays, Fukuyama argues, seems to lie in rectifying a panoply of injustices over race, ethnicity, gender, and sexual preference and in suppressing opinions on any of these topics that are contrary to its own unchallengeable wisdom. To many of the erstwhile supporters of left-of-center parties, their dominant attitude seems to be dislike for the histories, traditions, values, and even many of the people of their own country. Meanwhile, the merchant elite has successfully sought to win the support of less-educated and poorer voters by emphasizing the intellectual and cultural arrogance, lack of patriotism, hostility to traditional values, lack of loyalty to established ethnicities, and economic ignorance of the Brahmin elite.

The merchant class is doing very well at splitting the old coalition between an educated class of leftist intellectuals and organized labor. It no doubt helps that the former has grown so much bigger as education has spread and public sector employment has increased, and that the latter has become so much weaker as deindustrialization has advanced. The weakening of trade unions as powerful voices for the working class has also made working-class people not just more politically impotent but socially atomized, with tragic social and political consequences. The votes of the relatively less well-off are now split on ethnic and, in some countries, on religious lines. Many victims of adverse economic change also support politicians who emphasize national and cultural identity over economics. Boris Johnson's success in attracting votes in former Labour strongholds in the general election of 2019 demonstrates the opportunity these changes have opened.

The result of these splits is that the old coalition committed to economic redistribution and reform of capitalism has ceased to exist. But the views of the old center-left coalition on economic questions have also diverged. The propensity to vote Remain in the Brexit referendum was positively correlated with wealth, education, and income.[42] Thus, the vote for Leave can also partly be viewed as a vote against liberal economics, for which the EU stood and which the more educated and prosperous, including much of the Brahmin elite, had embraced. Many Brexit voters were also stuck in "left-behind" towns and cities, especially those blighted by the collapse of traditional industries, and so resented the prosperity and divergent cultural norms of economically buoyant metropolitan cities. Thus, the Brexit vote was at least in part a vote against London, just as the vote for Trump was at least in part a vote against the more prosperous coastal cities of the US. In a longer time frame, the collapse of communism—the most radical attempt to eliminate the market economy—has also surely undermined the credibility of more extreme left-wing economic ideas.

Abandoned, as they see it, by traditional left-of-center parties, the less-educated and less well-off members of the old working class are open to populist anti-elitism and to the appeal of charismatic populist leaders. They believe that elites and especially the intellectual elite are hostile not just to their interests, but to their values and ethnic and national identities. Affirmative action in favor of the children of minorities, including relatively recently arrived ethnic minorities, against their own children, is hardly going to be favorably regarded by people who feel themselves to be failing. This does not necessarily make them warm to the traditional merchant elite of big business. But they can be attracted to a leader who sets himself up as opposed to *all* the elites, however fraudulently.

Moreover, the people to whom such a leader appeals are not just the less well-off members of the majority community. Relatively prosperous, but less-educated people were also among Trump's strongest supporters.[43] Indeed, these are core conservative voters everywhere:

owners of small and medium-size businesses, the successful self-employed and skilled craftspeople. Increasingly, education is the dividing line between the left and right, with issues of identity more important to both. Yet, even now, the college educated are a minority of adults everywhere. Among high-income countries in 2014, only in Canada did the share of adults aged 25–64 who have completed tertiary education exceed 50 percent. In the overall adult population it would still be well below 50 percent even there. Even among adults aged 25–34, the number of countries in which graduates were more than half of the population was only seven (South Korea, Japan, Canada, Russia, Luxembourg, Lithuania, and Ireland).

"I love the poorly educated," said Donald Trump at his primary election victory ceremony, in Nevada in February 2016.[44] Fortunately for him and politicians like him, there are still a lot of the less educated (presumably what he meant) and that will continue to be so for a long time.[45] The less attached the less educated are to traditional politics and parties, the more likely they are to be captured by a successful demagogue. That would further weaken the fabric of established parties. At the limit, a party may become no more than a vehicle for its charismatic leader: institutionally, it will have been hollowed out. That seems to be what is happening to the Republican Party today. Its core doctrine seems to be what Germans call Führerprinzip—that is, obedience to the will of the leader.[46] It may be wondered whether Trump will continue to control the Republican base. Maybe someone else will seize their loyalty in time. But it is striking, nevertheless, how completely Trump persuaded his party to buy into his big lie that the election had been stolen. This is an astonishing indication of the moral bankruptcy of the elite of the Republican Party. But this hollowing out of traditional party institutions and hierarchies is not only characteristic of the US. It has also happened in France, with the rise to power of Emmanuel Macron, and before that in Italy, with the rise of Silvio Berlusconi.

Piketty's notion of a conflict between two elites—the intellectual and the commercial—had been previously advanced by Joseph Schumpeter in his classic work, *Capitalism, Socialism and Democracy*, published in 1942.[47] Schumpeter thought that the success of capitalism had brought forth an ever-larger intellectual elite that was anticapitalist in its attitudes and values. Over time, the domination of this new clerisy over opinion would lead to the end of free-market capitalism, which would be replaced by corporatism or outright socialism. Yet it was socialism that collapsed in the late 1980s. Moreover, while parties on the left are indeed dominated by the intelligentsia today, they are also losing their traditional working-class adherents. Schumpeter's idea of a new elite was right. But the way it is working out is not as he imagined.

The rise of populism indicates a move toward political extremes. This is partly the consequences of the failure of orthodox policies to deliver stable prosperity to the bulk of the population over a long period, followed by the shock of the financial crisis. But it is also an expression of the new dimensions of political dispute. Identity is less amenable to the normal democratic political give-and-take than economic policy. Identity and sovereignty are existential questions. That is why the question of Brexit in the UK, questions of immigration and civil rights in the US, and questions of immigration in Europe have been so fraught.

In the British case, what was in substantial part a matter of national identity (whether the UK should remain in the EU) became a prime determinant of political loyalty. In the US, the extremism has gone further. In the words of two centrist scholars back in 2012, "The GOP [Grand Old Party] has become an insurgent outlier in American politics. It is ideologically extreme; scornful of compromise; unmoved by conventional understanding of facts, evidence and science; and dismissive of the legitimacy of its political opposition."[48] Subsequently, extreme opinions have morphed into something even more insidious and dangerous: loyalty to the charismatic leader. Trump was viewed as a king who can do no wrong.[49] Rejection of reason and respect for differences of opinion are incompatible with liberal democracy. The rise of "cancel culture" on the progressive left, while not as dangerous as the attempt of the Trumpian right to create a presidency above the law, displays much the same mixture of arrogance and intolerance: dissent from tribal values is unacceptable. These are profoundly antidemocratic attitudes.

Issue of Immigration

Immigration plays a central role in the populist backlash of the right and the identity politics of the left. Immigration is also quite obviously different from other aspects of globalization. It is special because immigrants are people. An immigrant has a culture, family, attachments, loyalties, a mind, skills, hopes, fears, and everything else that makes a human being. Immigration brings special possibilities and challenges. It is extraordinary that so many people deny this obvious fact.

There is a view among some economists that the economics of free movement of labor are identical to those of trade.[50] That is not so. The economics of trade starts from the assumption that a country can be defined as having given factors of production—land, labor, and sometimes capital. It then shows that the aggregate real incomes accruing to the owners of these factors of production will rise if the country specializes in line with its comparative advantage. (Of course, this ignores the distribution of the gains from trade.) Yet there is no a priori reason to suppose that the welfare of those who lived in the country before the immigration (as well as their descendants) will rise with uncontrolled immigration (and the same applies to uncontrolled capital flows, though the latter have been less politically contentious). It may do so, but it may also fall. Aggregate GDP will increase because there will be more people. Yet that tells one nothing about whether people will on average be better off, since we know that population size does not determine the average prosperity of a country. After all, quite a few countries with small populations have high average incomes per head and quite a few countries with large populations have low incomes per head. Large changes in population will also generate congestion costs and an associated need for expensive investments.

Moreover, it is clear that the people of democracies care about their own citizens and, to a lesser extent, legal residents vastly more than about humanity at large. Even when the UK gave the relatively high ratio of 0.75 percent of GDP in foreign aid, public spending on areas of interest to British citizens was 50 times the transfers to poor foreigners via aid. Many voters seem to think even that is an excessive weighting of foreigners, even though the number of very poor foreigners (with poverty measured by British standards) exceeds the number of British citizens by at least 50 to 1. Thus, their political choices suggest that British citizens regard the value of a fellow citizen as around 2,500 times that of a poor foreigner! The mutual bonds of citizenship are of enormous significance to electorates. Since citizenship matters so much, granting rights of residence, particularly when this is likely to lead to citizenship, also matters enormously. Countries that fail to control immigration in a politically and socially acceptable manner risk a serious backlash.

This is not just "racism." There is good reason to believe that the greater the diversity of a political community, the more difficult it is to sustain the deep trust that is an essential precondition of a thriving and stable democracy. In very different ways, the stories of Lebanon and Belgium are indicative of the difficulties created by ethnic, religious, or other forms of diversity. Sometimes these challenges are successfully managed. But it is foolish to pretend that they do not exist. If a democratic political community is to thrive, there must be an overarching sense of identity that binds everybody.[51]

Threat of "undemocratic liberalism"

Immigration has been an important issue on which elites—in this case, both Brahmin and merchant elites, albeit for different reasons—have invited a backlash. But this has been an aspect of something bigger: "undemocratic liberalism," which may be viewed as the mirror image of illiberal democracy. Yascha Mounk of the Johns Hopkins University's School of Advanced International Studies describes undemocratic liberalism as follows:

> In more and more countries, vast swaths of policy have been cordoned off from democratic contestation. Macroeconomic decisions are made by independent central banks. Trade policy is enshrined in international agreements that result from secretive negotiations conducted within remote institutions. Many controversies about social issues are settled by constitutional courts. In those rare areas, like taxation, where elected representatives retain formal autonomy, the pressures of globalization have attenuated ideological differences between established center-left and center-right parties.
>
> It is hardly surprising, then, that citizens on both sides of the Atlantic feel that they are no longer masters of their political fate. For all intents and purposes, they now live under a regime that is liberal, yet undemocratic: a system in which their rights are mostly respected, but their political preferences are routinely ignored.[52]

A similar critique, this time focused on the EU, is advanced by Oxford University's Jan Zielonka. He argues that a counterrevolution threatens European liberalism: "Under attack is not just the EU but also other symbols of the current order: liberal democracy and neoliberal economics, migration and a multicultural society, historical 'truths' and political correctness, moderate political parties and mainstream media, cultural tolerance and religious neutrality." He blames the counterrevolution on the "liberal project" of "deregulation, marketization, and privatization." But he also condemns the transformation of democracy into technocracy, with ever greater powers delegated to "non-majoritarian institutions—central banks, constitutional courts, regulatory agencies." He is particularly critical of the EU, a non-majoritarian institution led by supposedly enlightened experts.[53] Yet perhaps the biggest problem of all is that the euro has turned into an instrument of domination by creditor countries over debtor countries. Especially during the financial crisis, the eurozone came to look more like an empire than a cooperative relationship among sovereign democracies.

Both authors identify something important. All liberal democracies have constitutional rules, established norms, or both, designed to constrain the power of majorities, be they temporary or not. Some of those constraints are designed to protect the liberties of individuals. Some are designed to protect the rules of the democratic process. Some are intended to protect economic stability or market competition from irresponsible politicians or even to protect the politicians from themselves. Some are intended to establish principles of international cooperation and comity, either to protect economic exchange or to ensure the provision of global public goods. These are—and are intended to be—constraints on democracy. Such constraints are necessary if an unbridled democracy is not to make democracy itself impossible. Democracy cannot mean absolute tyranny of the temporary majority. It is a system of rules and restraints.

Yet, inevitably, such constraints can be seen as unduly burdensome and, at worst, unbearable constraints on sovereignty. In the UK, the inability to limit free movement of people was an important reason for the close vote on Brexit to end up in favor of "Leave." In the eurozone, the rise of populism in southern Europe and in Italy, above all, has much to do with the perfectly correct observation that Italian governments were free only to do what the eurozone rules and the most powerful member state allowed them to do. In the US, the rulings of courts on abortion and marriage rights stimulated a massive illiberal backlash, becoming a salient feature of pluto-populism. Under Trump, the legitimacy of the rules of the World Trade Organization came equally under attack, even though the US played a far bigger role than any other country in the creation of the global trading system. For Trump and his supporters, the Paris climate agreement was equally objectionable.

"Pluto-Populism" and the "Southern Strategy"

Despite the many pressures, most of the high-income Western countries remain liberal democracies with broadly capitalist economies. This is true also of Brexit Britain. The center still holds, at least for now. But the US is somewhat different: it elected a nationalist populist with autocratic ambitions. The story there is unique and, given the size of the US and its historic role, so is its significance.

The shift toward the emphasis on racial identity, nationalism, and the culture wars (over abortion, guns, gender rights, and so forth) that led to Trump's election was not just the result of undemocratic liberalism, elite economic failures, uncomfortable economic developments such as deindustrialization, and cultural changes. It was also the consequence of a specific elite political strategy.

How, after all, does a political party dedicated to the material interests of the top 0.1 percent of the income distribution win and hold power in a universal suffrage democracy?[54] The answer is pluto-populism.[55] This allowed a party that had won the presidency and both houses of Congress in 2016 to put through a tax bill that unambiguously shifted resources from the bottom, middle, and even upper middle of the US income distribution toward the very top, combined with big increases in economic insecurity for the great majority.[56]

This strategy has three elements. The first is to find intellectuals who argue that such policies will lead to a "trickle down" of wealth onto the populace at large. "Supply-side economics" has been the way to argue this.[57] The second element is to foment ethnic and cultural splits among the mass of the population and so, to take the most important example, encourage people to consider themselves "white" or "anti-gay" or "Christian" first and members of the relatively disadvantaged, second, third, or not at all. The third element is to warp the electoral system through vote suppression, gerrymandering, and, above all, elimination of restrictions on the use of money in politics. Of these, the last two should be described as "the Southern strategy" in two senses: first, it was how the elite has historically held power in the South; and second, it was also the strategy on which the Republican Party consciously embarked immediately after passage of civil rights legislation by the Democrats in the 1960s. It has worked, not perfectly, but well enough.[58]

Supply-side economics has proved an excellent political slogan. Yet there is in fact no such relationship between marginal tax rates and the rate of economic growth. That is not surprising. After all, top marginal rates of tax were much higher in the 1950s and 1960s, which were also the decades of fastest growth for high-income democracies. Nor, for that matter, did the tax cuts of the Reagan era unleash a strong upsurge in US economic growth. These simplistic trickle-down ideas are good politics, but questionable economics.[59] The experience with Trump's cuts in corporate taxation are consistent with this. They did not lead to a significant upsurge in real private nonresidential investment. Lowering the corporate tax rate is principally a windfall for shareholders, just as lowering the estate tax is a windfall for inheritors of large estates.

The southern strategy has proved vastly more politically effective than the rhetoric of supply-side economics. The South swung from the Democrats to the Republicans after civil rights laws were enacted. In the process, it also shifted the GOP from being in a quasi-permanent minority in the US House of Representatives from 1933 to 1995 to better than parity with the Democrats since then.[60] In 2019, for example, the Republicans held the governorships of nine of the thirteen states of the Old Confederacy, 23 of their 26 available seats in the Senate, and 101 of their 146 seats in the House of Representatives. From the old days of the Democrats' domination of the South, this was nothing short of a revolution.

It was, however, far more than a stunningly successful regional capture. Yes, the politics of the South in the Union have consistently centered on maintaining systems of racial repression and exploitation. The South was built on slavery. With its refusal to tolerate the secession of the South, the North destroyed the "peculiar institution." The South responded to that defeat with the Jim Crow system of racial repression.[61] Then, a century after the Civil War, the North employed civil rights, legislated under the southerner Lyndon Baines Johnson, together with the help of judgments by the Supreme Court, to destroy Jim Crow.[62] Thereupon, the South started to transplant aspects of its system into the country at large, by embracing (and so transforming) the Republican Party, ironically, the party of Abraham Lincoln and the North's victory in the Civil War. Today, with an enduring majority in the Supreme Court and possessing a strong position in Congress, the Republican Party is well on the way to achieving this objective.[63]

This is a highly successful version of a strategy seen in many other democracies, namely, splitting the less well-off by their racial, ethnic, or cultural identities. Its purest form, however, was achieved in the antebellum South, and its fundamental characteristics have continued ever since. The pre–Civil War South was extremely economically unequal, not just in the population as a whole, which included the slaves, but even among free whites. A standard measure of inequality jumped by 70 percent among the whites between 1774 and 1860: "Any historian looking for the rise of a poor white underclass in the Old South will find it in this evidence."[64] Remarkably, the 1860 census shows that the median wealth of the richest 1 percent of southerners was more than three times that of the richest 1 percent of northerners. The South, ruled by a slave-owning, faux aristocracy of commercial planters, was also far less economically dynamic than the North. Its elite were rent extractors: they lived from exploitation of slave labor and land rent.

So successful was this "plantocracy" in nurturing the doctrine of racial superiority in poor whites that the latter fought and died for the Confederacy in enormous numbers.[65] In the Civil War, whose stated aim was defense of slavery (however much some deny this obvious truth), at least 260,000 Confederate soldiers died (95,000 in combat and 165,000 from disease, accidents, and other causes).[66] This was somewhere between 20 and 35 percent of all the men who served in the Confederate army.[67] Yet a sizable proportion of these men owned no slaves. The identity that came from feelings of racial superiority and fear of racial subordination was sufficient to justify their immense sacrifices.[68] Ultimately, the war brought death or defeat upon them all. Nothing better reveals the political potency of racial identity. Subsequently, of course, racist ideology gave the unhappy world Nazism and the incomparable carnage of the Second World War. Racism works. It plugs into dark aspects of the human character: the search for identity and dominance by "othering" people. What could make that easier than visible difference, such as color, however genetically trivial it evidently is?

A diluted form of the southern system—that is, political division of the relatively less well-off on racial and ethnic lines—has spread throughout the rest of the US. Indeed, it already existed in embryo before the Civil War. But the salience of the issue was increased by the mass emigration of poor and maltreated African Americans from the South to northern cities in the twentieth century. A more recent reason has been the mass immigration of Hispanics.

Here, again, there is an echo of the southern system of plutocratic rule. One of the reasons for the growth of this Hispanic population is the number of undocumented immigrants, recently estimated at 10.5– 12 million.[69] (American-born children of undocumented immigrants are American by birth.) An obvious question is why greater efforts were not made to control this inflow and above all to ensure that businesses do not employ undocumented labor. The answer is that businesses, natural supporters of the Republican Party, oppose such intrusive checks because cheap undocumented labor is profitable. The business wing of the Republican Party (in this case mostly small and medium-size businesses) has, therefore, contributed to—and benefited politically from—the illegal immigration that has spread racial anxiety across the US. According to the US census, the US will be "minority white" (with Hispanics counted as non-white) by 2045.[70] The "whites" know it. This anxiety helped the populist demagogue Donald Trump seize control over the Republican Party, with his promise to build a (largely symbolic) wall on the border with Mexico.

Vote suppression and extreme gerrymandering were important parts of the southern system after the Civil War. These strategies reflected the determination to ensure that African Americans would not gain the political power that should have followed from their numbers in any normal democracy. With a friendlier Republican-appointed Supreme Court, these techniques are—not surprisingly—returning.[71] According to two distinguished American political scientists, "The greatest threat to our democracy today is a Republican Party that plays dirty to win."[72] The right-wing view is that winning overrides playing by the rules of the game. This view is death to democracy.

Such a pluto-populist system requires opinion formers and propagandists to justify, defend, and promote it. In the antebellum South, a remarkably important part was played by Christian churches, which argued that slavery was divinely ordained.[73] White Christians have again played an important part in supporting the Republicans and, more recently, Donald Trump. The Christian right's long-standing support for the Republicans reflects the political salience and so usefulness of the "culture wars" over abortion, gay rights, and so forth, in addition to the racist dog whistles. The transfer of that loyalty to Trump, a man known for his history of sexual license and compulsive lying, is fascinating, though not surprising.[74] White evangelicals have proved to be particularly enthusiastic supporters of Trump, on the principle that the enemy of my enemies is my friend.[75]

Media are also significant. Most of the focus has been on the influence of "new media," on which more later. But old media—especially television and radio—have also been important. Rupert Murdoch's empire has consistently promoted pluto-populist themes. In the US, his significant outlet has been Fox News, whose influence upon Trump has been legendary.[76] Murdoch has a genius for promoting the prosperity of the few by exploiting the prejudices of the many. He also has a remarkable ability to find people who know how to do this for him: most notably, he appointed the late Roger Ailes to run Fox News in 1996.[77] Among radio personalities, the leading right-wing US figure was the late Rush Limbaugh. Limbaugh was not particularly subtle about his racism.[78] He was also a highly influential proponent of the pluto-populist cause.[79] It is hard to exaggerate the damage these people have done to the cause of liberal democracy, and the damage is not over.

Even more indicative of plutocratic influence is the role of money in politics. The Supreme Court's perverse 2010 *Citizens United* decision held that companies are persons and money is speech. By far the largest donors in the US are business lobbies. But rich individuals are also crucial: the top 0.01 percent of individual donors make 40 percent of all contributions. Politics is expensive. Since political donations come overwhelmingly from very big businesses and ultrarich individuals, to whom will the politicians who need these funds listen?[80]

In essence, the marriage of pluto-populism with the politics of the old South is a successful program for welding middle-class and poorer whites to the interests of a sizable part of the commercial elite. This did not even require all that big a change in the Republican Party. Paranoid conservatism was very much present in the party back in the 1950s, when Joseph McCarthy's red baiting dominated the Senate, and the John Birch Society was founded.[81] But a more ambitious conservative program needed a majority and that in turn needed the southern strategy, in both of the senses used above: the shift of the South to the Republicans and the insertion of the politics of ethnic division into the country more broadly. It is hardly an accident that Trump and his supporters took up McCarthy's central theme—that the US government (the "deep state") is full of traitors. This is the theme of right-wing conspiracy theories today, as it was then. The crucial change is that President Eisenhower, an honorable patriot, unlike Trump, did not promote them.

The Brahmin elite of leftist opinion formers have also triggered this shift of the white middle class to the Republicans. Talking about "white privilege" is offensive to many whites, especially those who feel underprivileged and disrespected, as indeed they are. So, of course, is the similar discourse about "male privilege" offensive to men whose poor economic position (in terms of job security and pay) makes it hard for them to play the role of breadwinner that has always sustained marital bonds. Today, strong and stable marriages are increasingly a phenomenon of the upper middle class: according to 2015 data, 64 percent of babies of poor US women were born out of wedlock, while only 36 percent of babies of working-class women and 13 percent of babies of middle- and upper-class women were.[82] Again, much of the new language of gender inclusivity is offensive to a large proportion of the traditionally minded, who are struggling to preserve self-respect in today's more economically challenging environment. People labeled "deplorables" are even more motivated to vote "deplorably."[83] Repelled by the Brahmins and seduced by the plutocrats, many members of the white working or middle classes have shifted to the angry populist right. This has happened throughout much of the West. It happened with devastating effect in the US, with the election of someone unsuited by temperament, character, and intellect to the office of president.

Yet the bargain made by the plutocracy is Faustian. It has been hugely successful, in its own terms: the preferences of the very rich and economically powerful count to an extraordinary extent in US legislation. But there is a catch. What if a politician came along who offered the voters the nationalism, racism, and cultural conservatism, but together with support for higher public spending, fiscal profligacy, hostility to globalization, and, above all, hostility to the norms of liberal democracy, the rule of law, and the post–Second World War US-led order? We know the answer to that no longer hypothetical question. As Stuart Stevens, a Republican consultant, has argued, once upon a time, "Republicans would have said the party stood for some basic principles: fiscal sanity, free trade, strong on Russia, and that character and personal responsibility count. Today it's not that the Republican Party has forgotten these issues and values; instead, it actively opposes all of them."[84] The Republican Party turned out to be a shell, ideologically and institutionally, just waiting to be taken over by a leader who could speak to its voters' fear and anger. The rich obtained their tax cuts. But they were not in control of the man or the forces that delivered them.

This shift in the basis of the Republican Party has a mirror-image shift among the Democrats, with the declining role of trade unions and the rising one of the Brahmin elite, who also figure heavily in the financial and technology sectors. As the declining unions became decreasingly important sources of funding and Republicans were able to attract financial support from business and conservative plutocrats, the Democrats had to obtain funding from these new businesses and more liberal (in the American sense) plutocrats. The way to do this successfully was to go for votes on the basis of cultural and ethnic identity rather than economic interest. After all, even woke billionaires dislike high taxes. In practice, therefore, the political role of money made it difficult for the Democrats to represent the poor effectively, regardless of ethnicity. It is no surprise that more economically radical platforms (universal health care, for example) have not been adopted.

The US, far and away the world's most important democracy, has taken pluto-populism further than any other high-income country. But shadows of it can be seen elsewhere. In the UK, for example, the coalition government argued, falsely, in 2010 that the huge deficits it inherited were the result of irresponsible public spending under Labour, rather than the financial crisis. It then responded by planning to slash the deficits. Moreover, the overwhelming bulk of the subsequent fiscal adjustment (which was close to 10 percent of gross domestic product) came from slashing spending rather than raising taxes.[85] Inevitably, these cuts hit vulnerable people and places particularly hard, with finance of local governments especially badly affected.

Brexit was a brilliant diversion from the realities of high inequality, the financial crisis, and the unbalanced postcrisis fiscal adjustment. It allowed Brexiters to shift the blame for the damage done to the mass of ordinary people off the domestic elites and governments and onto foreigners. It created a merger between the party that imposed this austerity and those most harmed by it, under the standard of national sovereignty. That is what pluto-populism does, whether consciously or not: first, make ordinary people angry and then blame what ails them on foreigners or minorities. Trump used trade and immigration; Johnson used the EU and immigration. The strategy works spectacularly well, helped in Johnson's case by the incompetence of the Labour Party, which no longer understood its own (former) voters. Nevertheless, the Brexiters, though ostensibly anti-elite populists, are not anti-pluralist. The Johnson government did not try to destroy the basis of liberal democracy, though its attitudes toward keeping its promises to foreigners, judicial review, and human rights were decidedly worrying.

Toxic Individualism and Authoritarian Populism

An important contributor to the rise of populist authoritarianism especially in the US is its apparent opposite—hyper-individualism. This ideology has been revealed most clearly during the pandemic, especially in the resistance of many on the right to the idea of "mask mandates" or the requirement to show a "vaccine passport" as a condition for entry into certain crowded places where the pandemic might easily spread. Such hyper-individualism—the belief that one is allowed to do whatever one wishes—is not new. In the US, for example, these attitudes are an aspect of the pioneering spirit on which the country was founded. But it can also be toxic, destroying social bonds and social order, creating instead what Thomas Hobbes called bellum omnium contra omnes—the war of all against all.

In the view of the ancient Romans, such an antisocial version of freedom confused *licentia* (license) with *libertas* (liberty). Thus, "True *libertas* . . . is by no means the unqualified power to do whatever one likes; such power—whether conceded or assumed—is *licentia*, not *libertas*. The necessary prerequisite of *libertas* is the renunciation of self-willed actions; consequently, genuine *libertas* can be enjoyed under the law only."[86] License is not liberty, but the path to tyranny. Sooner or later, Plato's "protector" is likely to emerge, promising "order" and "safety." It is no accident that many people who insist on their right to do as they please in the pandemic are devoted followers of a would-be autocrat like Trump. These are not opposites, but two sides of one coin. License begets tyranny, as it did with the transformation of the disorderly late Roman Republic into the military despotism we know as the Roman Empire. This symbiotic relationship is among the most powerful lessons of history. A democratic republic depends on an ordered liberty, rooted in respect for the law and, still more, for social values.

Changing Roles of Parties and Media

Demagogic populism has been a feature of democratic political systems since ancient Athens. In high-income countries, the seizure of power by anti-pluralist populists has happily been infrequent. The most important precedent was the 1920s and 1930s in Europe, with Mussolini and Hitler. There are big differences between that era and today, in two important respects: political organization and media technology. Political parties and standard media organizations are weaker, and social networks are stronger.

The 1920s and 1930s were an age of machine politics. The rise to power of populist demagogues was engineered through structured political parties. In both cases, the party was a quasi-military organization. Mussolini had his blackshirts and Hitler his brownshirts.[87] Of course, party structures had already emerged in the nineteenth century. Comparable organizations to these do not exist in today's politics in advanced democracies. Leaders either obtain control of existing parties or they have their own, relatively normal, parties, or they set up on their own, as Macron did. As a result, contemporary populism is much less disciplined than its predecessors. It is more bottom-up, anarchic, even nihilistic, though there have been some relatively well-organized groups within parties, such as Momentum in the Labour Party.

The second change is in the nature of media and, above all, in the rise of social media. The rise of fascists and Nazis took place within a world of newspapers and radio. These were one-way media. Once in power, authoritarian governments could control the flow of information to a high degree. Joseph Goebbels, Hitler's propaganda chief, was a master at controlling the narrative. Today's social media, in contrast, are decentralized, allowing the spread of lies, conspiracy theories, opinions, and truths in peer-to-peer networks, with extraordinary ease. In such a system, control over the narrative is far more difficult. Yet, as China shows, it is not impossible for determined authoritarians. The Great Firewall of China and the resulting control over the narrative appear to work.

An important aspect of the new media derives from the fundamental economics of information in the new age: collecting information remains costly, but dissemination is costless. In the old days, it was possible to finance information collection by bundling news with advertising or by state subsidy of some kind, as with the BBC and similar entities. But the new technologies have unbundled news gathering from advertising, with the ads shifting to the technology platforms, which take little responsibility for verifying the information they publish. In the US, "digital ad revenue has grown exponentially, but a majority goes to Facebook and Google rather than to publishers."[88] Thus, half of all display advertising revenue in 2018 went to Facebook (40 percent) and Google (12 percent). Meanwhile, advertising revenue of newspapers has continued to fall. The result is a collapse of the economics of news gathering. The main exception is when the quality of the product and the economic status of the audience make paywalls work. But paywalls have the inevitable consequence of limiting access to high-quality and verified information. This is precisely the sort of news Trump called "fake," by which he meant true and inconvenient. In the UK, *The Guardian* is trying to sustain itself with voluntary contributions. But, overall, given the substantial costs of generating and publishing accurate information and the difficulty of getting paid for it nowadays, the net effect of the information revolution has been ubiquitous, and costless dissemination of noninformation, disinformation, propaganda, and lunatic conspiracy theories.

One way of thinking about the new social media is that they have made it far easier to spread "rumor" (what the Romans called "fama") than before. It is, as a result, also far easier than ever before for the unqualified and unprincipled to influence public opinion. The results are both widespread cynicism about anything one is told, especially by figures of authority, as well as the emergence of passionate adherents of particular opinions in corners of the internet. Yet some things have not changed: it is still possible for political leaders to disseminate their propaganda effectively. Trump was a master at it, via his use of Twitter. It is, however, more difficult to monopolize information today than it used to be, unless one has the resources and determination of the Communist Party of China.

Yascha Mounk, a thoughtful observer, argues, "Over recent years, it has been the populists who have exploited the new technology most effectively to undermine the basic elements of liberal democracy. Unfettered by the constraints of the old media system they have been willing and able to say anything it takes to get elected—to lie, to obfuscate, and to incite hatred against their fellow citizens."[89]

Similarly, the new social media weaponize outrage, since that is how one gains attention.[90] In the view of Martin Gurri, a penetrating analyst of today's technology-enabled nihilism, "The public . . . strives . . . to knock the elites off their high perches into the dust. For the class that rules and speaks on behalf of national institutions to be stripped of authority—to lose the power to persuade—has been a traumatic and terrifying event."[91] Part of the reason so many liked Trump was simply that he was not of the establishment. They were demonstrating their contempt for their rulers.

In the end, it is hard to tell how much difference the new media have made. It is true that social media have weaponized outrage and spread all sorts of fantasies and frauds. It is true that the open and global internet of democracies is open to conscious manipulation by hostile forces, both private and public and both domestic and foreign. It is true, too, that we have little protection against the viral spread of dangerous nonsense, as the rise of the anti-vaccination movement has demonstrated.[92] But it is not clear that this form of intellectual pollution is the main explanation for where we are today. In the right (or rather, wrong) circumstances, poison spreads perfectly well with old technologies—newspapers, books, and radio. The interwar period taught us that. Think of the career of Huey Long, for example. Would Trump have failed to obtain the Republican nomination in the same economic and cultural conditions, but in the absence of today's social media? I suspect he would have succeeded.

What is true, however, is that it would have been hard for him to succeed within the old hierarchical parties. That is indeed a big change. The new media have disseminated populist messages, yet so have the old (newspapers, radio, and television). *Pace* Marshall McLuhan, the medium is not the message.[93] It merely shapes the message. The message itself is distress, fear, and anger. These could well have caused political eruptions even without the new media. In 1848, revolutions spread across Europe like wildfire. It was rather like the Arab Spring and ended up in much the same way, too. Evidently, there were none of our new media at the time.

Can the Democratic Center Hold?

Two years after the pandemic began, it is far too soon to tell how COVID has changed this broad story. Experience with a relatively serious threat seems to have undermined the credibility of populists and increased trust in government. What it has not done is increase confidence in democracy. On balance, it seems, people have shifted toward a desire for competent authoritarian government. Competent authoritarians may be rare. Yet they are potentially even more danger- ous to the future of liberal democracy than incompetents.[94]

Some observers simply despair. Shawn Rosenberg of the University of California, Irvine insists that the task of making people think and behave as conscientious and well-informed citizens is hopeless. Quite simply, "Democratic governance in America (and elsewhere) has not been successful in creating the citizenry it requires. Thus, it is left with citizens who lack the requisite cognitive and emotional capacities to assimilate its cultural definitions and norms, to function in its in- stitutional organizations and to participate in its public sphere."[95] His- torically, he argues, these weaknesses were offset by the control of elites over culture and social and political institutions. But techno- logical, economic, and cultural developments have demolished the gatekeepers or their role in safeguarding the political process. The transformation of the media is one element of this, but a broader breakdown in hierarchies of authority and influence has also occurred.

The people, then, are on their own, but they dislike it. Shorn of natural leaders, they choose self-confident right-wing populists in place of old elites. Thus, says Rosenberg, "The ever-greater structural pen- etration of everyday life by the forces of capitalist markets, democratic politics and globalization have made the complexities of social life and the necessity of individuals to rely on themselves when negotiating those complexities increasingly apparent. Given their inadequate cognitive and emotional abilities to participate in the ways required, the people living in this freer, more equal, more culturally diverse world are left more confused, directionless, alone, and insecure. They feel a commensurately increasing need for an authoritative definition of the world and themselves and authoritative direction of how they must act to secure their place, as individuals and a people, in that world."[96]

That answer is a form of "fascism light." Rosenberg argues that the appeal of right-wing populism to devotion to an idealized nation and a "great leader" supplies a large mass of the people with what democracy cannot: relief from the burden of thinking for themselves in return for absolute loyalty to the leader. This attitude is evidently incompatible with liberal democracy. But, argues Rosenberg, it is going to win. It is far more successful than left-wing populism, because it feeds off fear and anger, while the left promises hope, however unrealistic and ultimately poisonous it may turn out to be. Hope requires trust. Fear does not: it just requires an enemy.

Rosenberg's is a horrifying, but not implausible, dystopian vision. COVID, it seems, might even end up accelerating this shift away from democracy even if it discredits the more foolish authoritarian populists. Certainly, the core democratic institutions do not protect themselves. They need to be protected by people who understand and cherish the values they defend, particularly members of commercial, political, and intellectual elites. Politics must respond to the fear and rage that brought populists to power. But it must not surrender to them.[97] Economic and political reforms are needed if liberal democracy is to be saved. The agenda for reform is the topic of the next part of this book.

Part III

---■---

RENEWING DEMOCRATIC CAPITALISM

Prologue to Part III

B ranko Milanovic, formerly at the World Bank and now at the City University of New York, argues that capitalism is "alone": it has won.[1] No other credible system for organizing production and exchange in a complex modern economy now exists. This is correct. Almost nobody still argues in favor of a centrally planned economy without at least some reliance on market forces and private ownership of productive assets. Yet what sort of capitalism has won? This question arises on two dimensions. First, is it what Milanovic calls "liberal capitalism" and I would call "democratic capitalism," or is it what he calls "political capitalism" and I would call "authoritarian capitalism"?[2] Second, is it to be competitive and dynamic capitalism or is it to be rent-extracting and rigged capitalism? These questions animate part III of the book.

Democracy and market capitalism are being challenged by authoritarian alternatives to the former and state-led alternatives to the latter. The financial crisis, the poor quality of subsequent political leadership, and the inadequate response of many Western democracies to COVID-19 have made this competition more acute. We cannot take it for granted that democratic capitalism—the union of complementary opposites on which contemporary Western society is built—will thrive. It may not even survive.

This "democratic recession" has been the product of social, cultural, and economic developments discussed in part II. Above all, economic failures played a significant role in exacerbating insecurity, anxiety, resentment, and mistrust in substantial parts of the population. This has resulted in the arrival of populist demagogues, who are, in turn, exacerbating the democratic recession of our era. The rise of demagogic populism may prove to be a wake-up call for better policy. But it may also be destructive of sound policy and even of liberal democracy itself. Indeed, the latter outcome hardly looks that far away, notably in the US.

Yet we should remember that universal suffrage democracy has come through many challenges over the past century. So, too, has the market economy. In Europe, the situation looked vastly more hopeless in 1940 than it does today. Leading members of the governing party in the UK then favored peace with Hitler. But those men did not win the argument and, as it turned out, the cause of freedom was not lost, partly because of British defiance and Soviet resistance, but, above all, because of the existence and efforts of the US.

Successful renewal is again possible. It has happened before. To achieve it, there must be imaginative and decent leadership. Yet there must also be ideas. That is what this third section of the book offers.

The underlying thesis is that it will be impossible to combine universal suffrage democracy with a market economy if the former does not appear open to the influence—and the latter does not serve the interests—of the people at large. The democratic societies that have been most successful in achieving these objectives are those I would call "welfare capitalist." In Europe, "social democracy" and the "social market economy" are labels for such a system, though Christian Democrats have embraced welfare capitalism as well. In the US, this would be "liberalism" or perhaps a moderate form of conservatism (now, alas, largely disappeared). Crucially, this type of arrangement appears to be a necessary condition for the long-term survival of universal suffrage democracy. The insecurity that laissez-faire capitalism generates for the great majority who own few assets and are unable to insure or protect themselves against such obvious misfortunes as the unexpected loss of a job or incapacitating illness, is ultimately incompatible with democracy. That is what Western countries had learned by the early to mid-twentieth century. It is what they have learned again over the past four decades. Only autocracy, plutocracy, or some combination of the two is likely to thrive in an economy that generates such insecurity and a polity that shows such indifference.

The work of Torben Iversen of Harvard and David Soskice of the London School of Economics provides a framework for the needed discussion of economic and political reform.[3] Their thesis about how an outward-looking form of democratic capitalism can still thrive has three core elements.

First, in high-income democracies, governments play a central role: they need to ensure that companies are subject to competition, the population is well educated and trained, the infrastructure on which the economy depends is first-rate, and the research that drives technological advance is adequately funded. It has not in fact been the market *against* the state, as many believe, but the market *with* the state. This is true everywhere, albeit to different degrees, across the successful economies.

Second, again, in a stable high-income democracy, the educated and aspirational are a large and politically engaged element in the polity. Such people will tend to vote for parties and people they consider competent. These people provide the solid ground on which democratic politics is built.

Finally, the skills on which sophisticated businesses depend are embedded in networks of people who live in specific locations. The core competences of companies are, as a result, far less mobile than many suppose. Only the relatively less-skilled parts of their operations are genuinely footloose.[4] Indeed, quite a large proportion of the supposed mobility of companies has to do with exploitation of tax loopholes and cheap unskilled labor rather than a shift of the full range of their activities to countries that offer mainly cheap labor, low taxes, and minimal regulation.

Yet this vision of economic interdependence and mutual commitment among politics, business, and the public also illuminates the fragility of modern democratic capitalism. Even if core competences are sticky, the footloose parts of the economy may become big enough to devastate the prospects of large portions of the population, especially of less-skilled and older workers. Again, if economic insecurity starts affecting people who thought they had safe and good jobs, they are likely to feel growing despair. If the government does not know what to do in response to global economic crises, slowing growth, and unexpected shocks, such as COVID-19, trust may collapse. Finally, if business interests and the plutocracy become overwhelmingly powerful, democratic capitalism may fall apart, to be replaced by a plutocratic or autocratic version.

The strengths of democracy are representation and legitimacy, while its weaknesses are ignorance and irresponsibility. The strengths of capitalism are dynamism and flexibility, while its weaknesses are insecurity and inequality. As is true of any marriage, the relationship between liberal democracy and market capitalism may fail. It is sure to do so if the polity or the economy fails to deliver what is needed—political representation and competent government in the case of the polity, and attractive opportunities and widely shared prosperity in the case of the economy.

In good marriages, the strengths of each partner offset the weaknesses of the other. In bad ones, the weaknesses of each partner overwhelm the strengths of the other. Improving the two systems, as well as the balance between them, is, accordingly, the theme of part III of the book. The discussion will start with the economic challenges. Chapter 7 will look at the requirements for a renewal of capitalism. Chapter 8 will explore what such a new New Deal would mean in detail. Finally, chapter 9 will focus on the renewal of democracy.

CHAPTER SEVEN

Renewing Capitalism

Yes to the market economy. No to the market society.
—*Lionel Jospin*[1]

Here I am back again in the Treasury like a recurring decimal—but with one great difference. In 1918 most people's only idea was to get back to pre-1914. No one today feels like that about 1939. That will make an enormous difference when we get down to it.
—*John Maynard Keynes*[2]

As Keynes noted in 1942, the victors of 1918 had tried to recreate much of the pre–First World War economy. They failed. After the Second World War, however, as he predicted, they took a very different approach. The new world they created lasted until the 1980s, when aspects of the nineteenth century's free markets were, perhaps unsurprisingly, restored. Again, after the global financial crisis of 2007–09, an effort was made to restore the precrisis world economy, albeit with some modest reforms. After COVID-19, as after the Second World War, demands for change became more forceful. Realization of the climate emergency made this demand for transformation even more urgent. The big question is whether change will be decisive, as in the middle of the twentieth century, or whether the old and largely failing order will continue, this time with a right-wing populist twist. What makes the latter more likely is that measurable success with reform will be far more difficult to attain this time, partly because societies are far more divided than they were after World War II and partly because the economic opportunities are very much more limited (as discussed in chapters 4 and 5).

The focus of this chapter is on the philosophy of reform. Its guiding light is Karl Popper's idea of "piecemeal social engineering," by which he meant change targeted at remedying specific ills. It rejects both the status quo and revolutionary upheaval.[3] Then, in chapter 8, the discussion turns to specifics.

Reform, Not Revolution

Some aspire to something far more dramatic than mere reform: they aspire to nothing less than anticapitalist revolution. After two big economic crises—the transatlantic financial crisis and then COVID within just twelve years, followed by the shock of Russia's war on Ukraine, not to mention high inequality, slowing growth, a rising tide of authoritarianism, and, above all, increasing concern over environmental constraints, this is hardly surprising. Some of these revolutionaries argue that capitalism is a cancer, economic growth must be halted, and human beings should embrace a preindustrial, even preagrarian, way of living.[4] Thus, Jason Hickel, an economic anthropologist, writes in Less Is More that "we need high-income countries to scale down excess energy and material use; we need a rapid transition to renewables; and we need to shift to a post-capitalist economy that's focused on human well-being and ecological stability rather than on perpetual growth. But we also need more than this—we need a new way of thinking about our relationship with the living world."[5] Hickel and people like him wish to overthrow our economic system. Yet no political party with such goals has the slightest chance of gaining power. The transformation he desires could only be implemented by a dictatorship, and a global dictatorship at that. No such regime is (happily) in prospect. This is at best unrealistic utopianism. At worst, it is yet another in a long succession of "progressive" calls for tyranny.

Even a true end to economic growth would not solve the problem. Suppose global economic growth did cease and emissions per unit of output continued to decline at the same rate as between 1990 and 2018—that is, at about 1.8 percent a year. Annual global emissions would still have fallen by only 40 percent by 2050. That would not solve the climate problem: it would just mean that it would go on getting worse more slowly. The only ways to achieve zero emissions are either to divorce output from emissions or to eliminate *all* output that depends on inputs of commercial energy. If the former were possible, neither an end to growth nor the far more radical alternative of eliminating all the increase in global output since the industrial revolution would be necessary. The latter is certainly politically impossible. But it is also morally unacceptable. It would require reversal of virtually all increase in economic welfare of the past two centuries, with devastating consequences for individual well-being and political and social stability.

It is essential to grasp what the preindustrial world was like. Two hundred years ago, more than 80 percent of the world's (then much smaller) population lived on the borders of survival. Most people were subsistence farmers. Undernourishment was widespread and starvation a permanent threat. Before COVID-19 the proportion of the world's population in such desperate poverty had already fallen to below 10 percent—still far too high, yet a dramatic improvement from the situation of preindustrial humanity. What is more, nearly half of that decline in the proportion of those living in such destitution occurred in the golden age of globalization after 1980 (see figure 42).

Over these two centuries, the proportion of the world's population living in extreme destitution fell from 80 to 10 percent, *despite a more than sixfold rise in the human population*. That population explosion was also in significant measure due to rising life expectancy: average

FIGURE 42. SHARE OF THE WORLD POPULATION
IN EXTREME POVERTY (PERCENT)
(Source: Bourguignon & Morrison, 2002; World Bank, 2015)

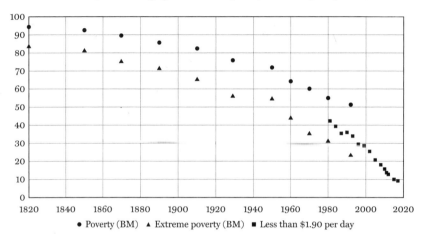

● Poverty (BM)   ▲ Extreme poverty (BM)   ■ Less than $1.90 per day

world life expectancy rose from around thirty years at birth in 1800 to forty-six in 1950, and then seventy-one in 2015, with much of this rising longevity due to falling child mortality.[6] Arguably, this transformation in life expectancy is the most profound improvement of the last two centuries, with revolutionary consequences for the opportunities for women, size of families, investments in education, and the aging of societies, but also for the value we place on human lives and many other valuable aspects of our societies. It is surely a profoundly welcome transformation. How many bewail the fact that children increasingly survive to adulthood? By historical standards, COVID-19 is even a very modest pandemic. The fact that it upset us so much shows how far we now take for granted our ability to control illness and postpone death.[7] Our ancestors took such disasters—indeed, far worse ones—for granted.

In sum, "de-growth"—let alone the far more radical alternative of actually reversing industrialization—is a utopian (or rather dystopian) illusion foisted upon us by people who are more interested in reversing thousands, or at least hundreds, of years of human history than in solving the problems we actually confront.[8] A practical and acceptable solution can come only from a technological transformation that eliminates emissions of greenhouse gases from the economy.[9] What is needed is not de-growth, but rather "de-emissioning" growth.

The value of a dynamic market economy lies not only in the prosperity it has created and the longer lives it has allowed us to live. It lies also in the sort of lives it allows people to lead. Markets allow people to use their imagination, skills, and efforts to better themselves, without approval from a higher authority. They need only find someone interested in paying for what they create. In this respect, markets are egalitarian. They do not have egalitarian outcomes, but the ability to engage in the market is not dependent on social status, though it does depend on inherited abilities and acquired resources. Anybody is allowed to try. Nobody appointed Elon Musk or Bill Gates to their positions in society. In countries with the rule of law and no, or limited, corruption, this opens huge opportunities. That, too, is a value worth cherishing and defending.

Furthermore, markets impart information. Market incentives will influence everybody in the market. The alternative is some form of top-down command and control. Quite apart from the coercion this would require, a central planner will never know all the possibilities, as people operating independently can. They can, above all, never know what is in everybody's head. Even in the age of big data, markets exploit knowledge and adjust incentives in ways no other social mechanism does. Of course this does not mean markets are perfect. On the contrary, the strongest justification for markets is that they encourage independent trial and error in an environment of fundamental uncertainty. They are pluralist. If we enjoyed perfect information about the future, markets would be far less valuable, for we would know so much more about what needs to be done. If they are to work well, both economically and socially, markets need careful design and regulation and must not be dominated by a small number of oligarchs. But they remain an essential social instrument.

Moreover, as Edmund Burke argued in his *Reflections on the Revolution in France*, not only is it impossible to build a new society from first principles, but it is also inhuman even to try.[10] We must always build on what we have and know. The Russian Revolution turned out to be a seventy-four-year journey from a highly unequal and predatory tsarist state, though one with at least some hope of reform, to an even more unequal and predatory state, with even smaller hope of democratic reform. On the way, tens of millions of people were killed in the Soviet Union and tens of millions more, under the same ideology, worldwide.[11] Moreover, so utterly did the utopians smash the possibility of liberating reform that when the chance for that was offered once again, in the 1990s, it was lost. Utopianism is absolutely destructive.

A particularly relevant part of that painful history was the intended creation of "New Communist Man." According to Leon Trotsky, "Man will make it his purpose to master his own feelings, to raise his instincts to the heights of consciousness, to make them transparent, to extend the wires of his will into hidden recesses, and thereby to raise himself to a new plane, to create a higher biologic type, or, if you please, a superman."[12] In practice, the new communist man was an amoral predator. The transformation of actual human beings, with all their faults and virtues, into "ecological" man (and woman) is equally implausible. We must do our best with humans as they are—with their mixture of greed and selflessness. The idea of the perfectly ecological human is quite as much a delusion as Trotsky's communist superman. Just consider the mass extinctions that followed humanity's first arrival in Eurasia and the Americas back in prehistoric times.[13]

In Praise of "Piecemeal Social Engineering"

In brief, we need radical and courageous reform of the capitalist economy, while preserving what is good about it and remedying what is bad, just as was required in the 1930s and 1940s. The reforms we need are not the same as those needed then, because the context and challenges have changed, especially the climate challenge. Moreover, most of what was done then survives today. But the fundamentals are the same: we need to strengthen the economic bonds of citizenship, while deepening international cooperation. We must act radically and yet incrementally, learning from experience as we go. Acting in this way is the only way to make changes likely to work. Karl Popper called this approach "piecemeal social engineering," as opposed to revolutionary transformation of society from top to bottom, stating, "The piecemeal engineer or the piecemeal politician will, accordingly, adopt the method of searching for, and fighting against, the greatest and most urgent evils of society, rather than searching for, and fighting for, its greatest ultimate good."[14]

Social engineering of this kind depends on expertise, but expertise is never enough. We also need public engagement in formulating desired goals and consenting to the outcomes. To deliver the energy transformation we need will require an enormous range of expertise, innovation, planning, and global cooperation, supercharged by incentives. Ultimately, we must rely on an empowered, but socially responsible, technocracy to manage the risk of climate change and achieve the other worthwhile policy goals to be discussed below and in chapter 8. Yet it is also clear that technocrats cannot—and should not be allowed to—bring about the needed radical change in direction on their own. They can only provide the details. A change in the direction of a society requires political leadership. In democracies, words are needed to persuade people to embrace great causes. Franklin Delano Roosevelt and Winston Churchill were masters of this art in the crisis-hit 1930s and 1940s. Comparable leadership is as desperately needed today.

Crucially, Popper recommended focusing on removing evils. One of the best examples of such an approach was the list of the "five giants"—want, disease, ignorance, squalor, and idleness—in the UK's Beveridge Report, written by the liberal William Beveridge and published in 1942.[15] This report was to be the foundation stone of the UK's postwar welfare state.

Some well-intentioned people believe we can achieve something more ambitious: happiness, or "well-being" for all. To my mind, this is an overweening ambition. It is not within the capacity of any government to make a society of free people happy. Nor is it desirable, for reasons explained by Aldous Huxley in his masterpiece, *Brave New World*. Unhappiness is an inescapable part of life. A state of permanent happiness cannot be achieved other than by robbing us of our capacity to feel and experience life to the full. Just as doctors should seek to cure illness, so should governments seek to eliminate miseries. That is a fundamental goal of policy. Indeed, one might argue that the first duty of government is not to *do* harm and the second is to *remove* it. It is right, therefore, to address mental ill health, unquestionably a huge source of misery.[16]

To those who seek a list of positive aims for economic policy, I would propose four: security, opportunity, prosperity, and dignity.[17] People need security because its absence is terrifying. They need opportunity because its absence is crippling. They need prosperity because its absence is oppressive. They need dignity because its absence is corrosive. If human beings lack these things, they become defeated, frightened, or angry. If people want to consider these goals as stepping-stones to "happiness," that is fine.

How, not least, should we measure success? For too long the dominant measurement has been gross domestic product. GDP has value, especially when we are looking at poor societies. In the same way, doubling the material income of a poor person is a big thing. Nevertheless, GDP is defective. It says nothing about security, opportunity, or dignity. It does not say anything about whether prosperity is widely shared or sustainable. It merely measures the total value of domestic (or national) output at market prices in a given period. That has some value. But it omits far too much to be the sole method of evaluation.

So we need measures that focus on these different aspects of reality. Many have been proposed and some are interesting and useful. But it is impossible to construct a single measure. Instead, we must use a family of measures, understanding their value, meaning, and limits. A commission on these issues, under two Nobel laureates in economics, Joseph Stiglitz of Columbia and Harvard's Amartya Sen, in addition to the late Jean-Paul Fitoussi, suggested that proper measurement would cover eight dimensions: material living standards; health; education; personal activities, including work; political voice and governance; social connections and relationships; the environment; and insecurity.[18] We do indeed need measures of all these aspects of our reality. But we have no simple way of adding them up into a single aggregate measure of well-being. We must live with—and accept—the limitations imposed by complexity.

Nevertheless, evidence strongly supports the simple idea that a combination of widely shared prosperity with democracy is crucial to societal well-being. According to the *World Happiness Report 2021*, the ten happiest countries are Finland, Iceland, Denmark, Switzerland, the Netherlands, Sweden, Germany, Norway, New Zealand, and Austria. The next nine are Israel, Australia, the US, Canada, Czech Republic, Belgium, the UK, Taiwan, and France.[19] All these countries are both prosperous and democratic. Many are small, which underlines the point that trade is crucial, since small countries cannot achieve high levels of prosperity without it. Above all, the most successful countries provide opportunity and security to their populations, along with open and democratic government. The discussion in this and the following two chapters fleshes out what this could mean.

Toward a "New" New Deal

The goals of security, opportunity, prosperity, and dignity need to be turned into something more concrete. Franklin Delano Roosevelt spelled out such objectives in words that seem nearly as relevant today as they were in January 1941.[20] Notwithstanding the great war already looming in view for the US, he stated:

Certainly this is no time for any of us to stop thinking about the social and economic problems which are the root cause of the social revolution which is today a supreme factor in the world. For there is nothing mysterious about the foundations of a healthy and strong democracy.

The basic things expected by our people of their political and economic systems are simple. They are:

Equality of opportunity.

Jobs for those who can work.

Security for those who need it.

The ending of special privilege for the few.

The preservation of civil liberties for all.

The enjoyment of the fruits of scientific progress in a wider and constantly rising standard of living.

Roosevelt went on to illustrate some of the things this list implied:

We should bring more citizens under the coverage of old-age pensions and unemployment insurance.

We should widen the opportunities for adequate medical care.

We should plan for a better system by which persons deserving or needing gainful employment may obtain it.

This speech remains, to this day, a convincing statement of the policy objectives of wise democracies, at home and, so far as they are able, abroad. While our times are less fearful for liberal democracy than 1941, similar "social and economic problems" are, as argued in part II, once again the "root cause" of many of today's political upheavals. We have indeed gone back to the future.

Is there anything to alter in Roosevelt's list? Yes. Today, we would stress *equality of status* among citizens more explicitly than he did, given the objective of eliminating discrimination by race, ethnicity, and gender. We would surely qualify "enjoyment of the fruits of scientific progress in a wider and constantly rising standard of living" by insisting that it should be a "a rising, *but sustainable*, standard of living." We would qualify "jobs" by saying they should be "good jobs"—ones that give workers dignity and allow them to participate fully in social life. With these modifications, this remains a superb list.

A few might still make equality of outcomes a separate goal, even after the failure of communism. Yet complex societies are, and always have been, unequal. In a dynamic market economy, some people are going to make a great deal of money. I have no problem at all with this, so long as the money is earned by wealth-creating activities and does not prevent society from achieving the wider goals of a modern democracy. But there must be enough equality to enable everybody to participate in society and ensure a reasonable degree of equality of opportunity.

My revised list, also changed in order (and with civil liberties put to one side until chapter 9), is:

1. A rising, widely shared, and sustainable standard of living
2. Good jobs for those who can work and are prepared to do so
3. Equality of opportunity
4. Security for those who need it
5. Ending special privileges for the few

This list also has implications for the permissible degree of inequality. The most economically successful must not be allowed to control the political system, rig markets, inflict harms (such as environmental damage), establish a hereditary oligarchy, or avoid paying the taxes required to secure all the other objectives. (See chapter 2.) Achieving these goals will require significant taxation. I can also see no reason why the moderate right, center, and moderate left should disagree on these aims even if they disagree over how best to define and deliver them. Success will ultimately depend, as it always does, on getting the right balance between the various elements.

This list covers the economic aspects of the enumerated goals of security, opportunity, prosperity, and dignity. This is not to argue that the economy alone matters. But most social goods also depend on widely shared prosperity. In his critique of meritocracy, Michael Sandel calls for a more equal division of economic goods because these are not only important in themselves, but also signals of social recognition.[21] Again, many are concerned about crime and the health of the family. But both are directly related to economic opportunities and economic status. If people have little hope of earning a decent income, they are more likely to become criminals and less likely to form stable family bonds. The opportunities of their children will be blighted, with further bad economic and social consequences. Mass imprisonment on the US model makes the situation far worse. People want to live in a peaceful world as well. But the best way to ensure this is to spread economic opportunity at home and abroad.

In sum, economics is not everything. But it is the foundation of almost everything. On this, FDR's list of "the basic things expected by our people of their political and economic systems" is the right agenda.

Obstacles to the Economic Relaunch

Before we turn to the detailed policy choices in chapter 8, it will be helpful to consider the general conditions for a successful relaunch of the economies of the high-income countries as foundations for stronger democracies. These conditions cut across the many specific areas of policy to be discussed in the following chapter.

As the British economists John Kay and Mervyn King (a former governor of the Bank of England) note in an important new book, *uncertainty* is a pervasive characteristic of our existence.[22] This does not mean that the world is entirely unpredictable. On the contrary, some events are clearly more likely than others. But the probabilities are themselves usually unknown and unknowable: we cannot rerun history many times and so cannot assess the probability of rare events.

Nevertheless, there are also few true "black swans"—events that nobody had experienced or imagined. There exist instead many known but rare swans—imaginable events that one would still be surprised to see.[23] Since so many of these rare swans clearly exist, one of them must be deemed likely to occur in any given decade. Consider just a few of such (individually, but not collectively) rare swans: intensification of the COVID-19 pandemic; a new and worse pandemic; a huge terrorist attack, maybe with a dirty nuclear bomb, or even a series of such attacks; a stock market collapse; another financial crisis; hyperinflation; coups d'état; collapse of regimes, ideologies, or both; revolutions; counterrevolutions; civil wars; a major regional war (as has happened in Ukraine); nuclear war; a global thermonuclear war; devastating cyber attacks; climate catastrophes; perhaps even asteroid or comet strikes. Any one of these is at least imaginable and one of them at least is surely likely to happen in any decade or so. We may make some rough guesses of the likelihood of some of these events but be unable to do much more than that. Stuff happens and does so unpredictably. *Disruption is normal.*

Closely related to, though distinct from, the challenge of uncertainty is that of thinking *systemically*. The New Approaches to Economic Challenges initiative of the Organization for Economic Co-operation and Development worked hard, with inadequate recognition, to embed this way of thinking inside the Paris-based organization, its members and beyond.[24] Governments should focus on systemic fragility in their internal work. Along with other donors, they should also support the work of international organizations that seek to integrate different aspects of complex realities. The fundamental point is that the world is interconnected in complex ways. People must try to think this way if they are to develop the capacity to respond to events.

Of course, we humans will almost certainly fail to do so adequately: complex systems are, after all, just that—complex. In just the last fifteen years, we have experienced three huge events that demonstrated the fragility of our complex systems: the financial crisis, the

COVID-19 pandemic, and Russia's invasion of Ukraine. These showed how disease, economy, society, government, politics, and warfare are interconnected not just within countries, but globally. Thinking systemically is hard, especially in an age of narrow specialization. But specialists must be forced out of their silos. They must also recognize that thinking systemically is not the same as having a well-specified and empirically validated model of the world. This is naive rationalism, or "scientism," as Friedrich Hayek called it.[25]

In an uncertain world, an essential quality of good systems is *robustness*—the capacity to continue operation throughout unexpected emergencies.[26] We have discovered that some of our primary systems are not robust. This was the biggest shock of the global financial crisis: the financial system not only fragmented but could not put itself back together without support from governments and central banks. COVID-19 has, however, suggested that many of our systems are remarkably robust, notably those for making and distributing vital products—such as food and medical supplies—in a crisis. While there was some disruption of the latter, it was brief, especially if one considers the scale of the initial disruption. The ability to create, produce, and distribute new vaccines was astounding. Nevertheless, the supply constraints that were then revealed in the course of the unexpectedly strong recovery of 2021 showed that robustness was not always present.

One must not take robustness for granted. Robust systems frequently need spare capacity. But spare capacity is costly. In the financial sector, for example, a part of robustness is for intermediaries to be financed by more equity capital and less debt than managers and shareholders would like. In this case, there would in fact be no overall cost of higher equity requirements, but there would be a cost to managers whose pay is linked to equity returns. Such managers make an implicit bet that nothing will go badly wrong while they are in charge. If this odds-on bet wins, they can benefit hugely from raising leverage, even though they are also making the business less robust.

The concern, however, is mostly not about making individual products or services more robust: most people and businesses understand the need to build strong bridges, hold stocks of equipment, and have more capacity than is necessary most of the time, provided it is a matter of their own survival. The problem arises when businesses and countries rely on backup systems that will not work if *everybody needs them at the same time.* This, then, is an "externality"—what makes sense for the individual does not necessarily make sense for everybody. That was a lesson of COVID-19, at least in the early phase of the pandemic, when suddenly everybody wanted masks and so forth. A part of thinking systemically is asking how much one wants to pay for a system to be robust in such circumstances. Moreover, thinking about this should in part be a function of government, because the absence of robustness may make sense for individual businesses, but might impose large costs on society in a crisis.

If important systems are not robust, they need at least to be *resilient*, that is, capable of being reconfigured or rebuilt swiftly after a collapse. Resilience is one of the great virtues of market systems, especially global markets. They usually generate multiple channels of potential production and distribution. After the initial shock of COVID-19, this proved to be true for the medical supplies that were desperately needed. One should never underestimate the capacity of profit-driven business to find a way to bring supplies to the market. But, as with robustness, it is sensible for competent governments to ask how resilient essential systems would be under exceptional pressures and what to do about it if they appear likely to fall short.[27]

A crucial aspect of democratic capitalism is *accountability*. The underlying principles are clear: nobody is above the law; no business is above the market; no politician is above voters; and no person or individual is above public criticism. This is the obverse of the system in autocracies and ought to be one of the great and abiding values and virtues of democratic capitalism. All these systems must be treasured and protected. But that does not mean accountability is easy, even in sophisticated democracies. Nobody wants to be held to account. It is painful. Governments, politicians, businesspeople, and professionals will do whatever they can to avoid this. There are so many ways to obfuscate: unnecessary complexity; deliberate confusion; buck passing; and lack of oversight, clarity, and transparency. Eternal vigilance is the price of accountability.

This is accountability, in the broad. But there is also accountability in specifics. Here are three examples.

First, what is not counted does not count. Accounting, public and private, needs to include as much of what is relevant to decision-making as is measurable. So, for example, public sector cash-flow accounts should be complemented with worked-out public sector balance sheets and accrual accounts, as in New Zealand.[28] The exclusive focus of most systems of public accounts on short-term cash flows and debt stocks relative to gross domestic product is intellectually indefensible. Again, national accounts should include estimates of things beyond market output and expenditure (as discussed earlier). Similarly, corporate accounts should include estimates of the wider aspects of the business in relation to the environment, society, and governance. At the very least, they should estimate the exposure of businesses to these risks.

Second, the preparation and auditing of accounts, public and private, must be independent. In the case of the UK's public sector, the Office for Budget Responsibility, itself an excellent innovation in accountability, should be given the resources to prepare balance sheets. Moreover, a public sector balance sheet would encourage the public sector to manage its assets and liabilities more professionally.[29] In the case of the private sector, the auditing function has long been under a cloud, as a result of two conflicts of interest: within auditing firms, given their other commercial relationships with their clients, and within businesses, given that the auditor is commissioned and paid by the company it is auditing. One solution would be for the cost of the audit to be a part of the listing fee on stock markets. In that case, the stock market would pay for the audit, on behalf of investors, who are the people most interested in the quality of accounts.

Finally, there needs to be accountability for failures. It should be a matter of course to have inquiries into all significant disasters, with a view not so much toward punishing people, but far more toward learning lessons for the future. COVID-19 is already a leading example. Western countries that have failed so signally to manage the disease need to learn what they did wrong and what other countries did right.

Conclusion

There are certain big things we need to get right if our economies and societies are to work better. These have been laid out above. But the fundamental requirement is careful and intelligent reform aimed at bringing substantial improvement to most people's lives. That is the focus of the next chapter.

CHAPTER EIGHT

Toward a "New" New Deal

There's class warfare, all right, but it's my class, the
rich class, that's making war, and we're winning.
                                        —*Warren Buffett*[1]

Taxes are what we pay for civilized society.
                                        —*Oliver Wendell Holmes*[2]

Sometimes simple and bold ideas help us see more
clearly a complex reality that requires nuanced
approaches. I have an "impossibility theorem" for the
global economy that is like that. It says that democracy,
national sovereignty and global economic integration
are mutually incompatible: we can combine any two of
the three, but never have all three simultaneously and
in full.

                                        —*Dani Rodrik*[3]

The previous chapter outlined the approach of this book to reform of contemporary capitalism. This one will explore some of the details of a "new" New Deal. Inevitably, some ideas will be more palatable to some people than to others. But all those to whom this chapter (and book) are addressed will share a commitment to the principles of a law-governed liberal democracy and "social" market economy.

The analysis follows the outline of the updated version of Franklin Delano Roosevelt's aspirations, laid out in the previous chapter. These are:

1. A rising, widely shared, and sustainable standard of living
2. Good jobs for those who can work and are prepared to do so
3. Equality of opportunity
4. Security for those who need it
5. Ending special privileges for the few

Rising, Widely Shared, and Sustainable Standard of Living

As argued in chapter 2, the ideal of universal suffrage democracy was a child of economic advance. It is far easier to share the benefits of rising average prosperity than to share losses from declining prosperity. Indeed, one reason why politics has become so fraught even in countries with what seemed to be robust liberal democracies is that they were sharing losses (at least relative to prior expectations) caused by the financial crisis. The fiscal austerity that characterized the post-crisis period was a particularly important source of such losses. So, too, was the prolonged period of relatively low productivity growth (see chapter 4, figure 19) and the longer-term failure, especially in the US, to respond to adverse shocks caused by trade and technological advance. It is of great importance that the 2020s do not deliver a repeat of this disappointing experience, especially after the damage done by COVID-19 and the upsurge in inflation that followed the recovery. So how are economies to enjoy a rising, sustainable, and widely shared standard of living?

There exist a host of proposals for dramatic actions, many of which seem to suggest we can find magic wands able to deliver an upsurge in sustainable prosperity. This is unlikely. The headwinds discussed in chapter 5 show how difficult this is going to be. Moreover, the simpler reforms—opening economies to trade, for example, or universal secondary education and widespread tertiary education—have largely been done. Also, sadly, we understand only a little about economic growth. It is misleading to suggest that accelerating the growth of economies already at or close to the frontiers of technology is a simple matter. Nevertheless, there are four relatively clear requirements of sustainable prosperity in the 2020s and thereafter: macroeconomic stability; investment and innovation; sustainability; and sensible openness to the world economy.

Macroeconomic stability

COVID-19 came at the end of a long period of what Harvard's Lawrence Summers called "secular stagnation" (an idea discussed more fully in chapter 5) or, more prosaically, structurally weak demand. Rising private indebtedness, itself part of the response to the weak demand, exacerbated the problem, partly because of the financial crisis it triggered, partly because of the depressing effects of debt on new borrowing, and partly because of the vulnerability of an indebted economy to even modest rises in interest rates.

The austerity adopted shortly after the global financial crisis had been a mistaken choice, not a necessity.[4] It was, in some cases, notably the UK's, an attempt to shift the blame for the crisis onto fiscal profligacy from heedless finance.[5] That then justified the politically convenient response of severe fiscal discipline.[6] This policy weakened the recovery, which had damaging consequences for the welfare of the people and even the legitimacy of the democratic system. Among other things, premature austerity led to Brexit and the election of Donald Trump.

Premature, excessive, or badly directed austerity can therefore be a disastrous policy, but so can prolonged, excessive, or badly directed stimulus. It is always a matter of choosing the direction and instruments appropriate to the circumstances.

We relied too heavily on monetary policies (such as quantitative easing), crucial though such policies were in the response to the crisis of 2008–09, then to the eurozone crisis, and more recently to COVID-19.[7] Extreme monetary policies can have dangerous side effects.[8] They rely on incontinent creation of credit and debt and elevation of asset prices. This combination tends to make the financial system more fragile and the economy more unstable. Sometimes sick patients must take such dangerous medicines. But using them for decades can bring damaging side effects. Moreover, monetary instruments, especially low interest rates, may not just be risky: they may also be ineffective. In an era of "secular stagnation" and weak confidence, low interest rates may fail to boost private spending, especially on investment, adequately.[9] That is in line with the "Old Keynesian Economics" of the 1930s, when the phrase "secular stagnation" was first invented.

Even today, many argue that little or nothing should be done to halt depressions on the grounds that, like forest fires, they clear out old growth, so creating room for the new.[10] Sometimes, people even shed crocodile tears over how aggressive monetary policies worsen wealth inequality. But such protestations ignore what would have happened to the jobs of most of the people they pretend to care about in the absence of expansionary policies. Remember, too, that a large proportion of the population has very little wealth. Thus, according to the US Census Bureau, the median net worth of the bottom 20 percent of US households was only $6,030 in 2019, the median net worth of the next 20 percent was just $43,760, and the median net worth of the 20 percent in the middle of the distribution was still only $104,700.[11] A doubling of the wealth of billionaires can have little or no significance to people who own next to nothing.[12] What matters to the latter is how well-off they are, which mostly depends on having a reasonably paid job.[13]

What, then, are the alternative possibilities for dealing with prolonged weakness of demand? One is structural policy, notably, redistribution of incomes toward people who will spend rather than save, along with far stronger incentives for private investment. Another is even more unconventional monetary policies than those we have seen so far. One such option is negative deposit and lending rates. But this is likely to be unpopular and ineffective. Another is "helicopter money"—that is, a direct monetary transfer from the central bank to the public. Yet another is for central banks to lend at negative spreads: they would lend at *below* their deposit rates, which would remain at zero or above, and so they would operate at a loss by transferring income to the private sector.[14]

A further option is even more aggressive fiscal policy—that is, fiscal deficits generated by some combination of tax cuts and higher spending, especially heavy public investment, particularly on the energy transition. Such a fiscal policy could, in turn, be financed in the conventional way, by selling bonds to the public or by direct creation of money. The latter, in turn, might be temporary, as it has been (at least in principle) during the COVID-19 crisis, or permanent. Moreover, monetary financing of fiscal spending might occur relatively transparently via the central bank or via public guarantees for lending by private financial institutions. In the latter case, part of what is notionally private lending will turn out to be fiscal policy after the fact.

So, which of all these alternatives, or what combination, makes sense? The answer is that any of them might do so. They are also all risky. How risky they might be was indicated by the explosion of inflation in 2021 and 2022. The question is which of them would offer the best ratio of effectiveness to risk, those risks being not only economic, but also institutional and political. The answer depends partly on the economic opportunities and the economic and political constraints.

Centralized parliamentary systems, such as those of the UK or

Japan, can use both fiscal and monetary policy freely, with constraints imposed by financial or economic risks. The eurozone, as a union of sovereign states, is at the opposite end of flexibility. A federal system, with the complex balance of powers of the US, falls in between these two cases. It can use fiscal policy. But achieving agreement between the administration and both branches of Congress is onerous and generally results in an ill-considered rummage sale of favors to powerful special interests. Congress was reasonably effective on fiscal policy during COVID-19 and continued to be so under the Biden administration in 2021. But that was a national emergency.

There can be good reasons for using fiscal policy. Quite apart from being relatively effective when interest rates are low, fiscal policy can be targeted in ways that are impossible for normal monetary policy. It can, for example, be aimed at helping specific vulnerable groups or at increasing investment. Moreover, when real interest rates are negative, fiscal deficits carry little risk, provided governments take advantage of the opportunity to borrow on ultra-long maturities, maybe perpetually, as George Soros has suggested.[15] Indeed, it is even possible that fiscal expansion could *improve* long-term fiscal sustainability, provided it is implemented in a depressed economy, by expanding GDP proportionately more than the public debt.[16] Of course, fiscal deficits might generate economic overheating, as Larry Summers warned over the $1.9 trillion stimulus implemented by the Biden administration in early 2021.[17] But this is not an argument against active fiscal policy; rather, it is one against ill-advised fiscal policy.

This brings the discussion to "modern monetary theory" (MMT), an increasingly influential approach to the relationship between fiscal and monetary policy. The idea is straightforward.[18] Governments can create sovereign money—that is, money unbacked by some asset, such as gold—at will. Citizens are required to accept this money in payment for services, under the law. This being so, governments do not need to borrow money in order to pay their bills and can never be forced into default. The only limit is inflation. So governments can and should run money-financed deficits up to the point at which inflation becomes a significant risk.[19]

Critics counter that MMT is neither modern, nor monetary, nor a theory. Instead, they assert, it is old, fiscal, and mostly mere accounting.[20] The MMT view is in fact more dangerous than it is incorrect. We can identify three principal dangers.

The first such danger is the ignorance and wishful thinking of policy makers. The latter, not least elected politicians, do not know when an economy is close to full employment and so to a blast-off into high inflation. Indeed, even the idea that there exists a well-defined and stable output gap for the entire economy is false. That was one of the lessons of the 1970s. The likelihood, underlined by the experience of populist policy making in Latin America over decades, is that an economy driven by the wishful thinking of people with naive hopes about macroeconomics will be forced into high inflation. It may take a while for the economy to arrive there, but it is likely to do so in the end, not because rising inflation is the inevitable result of strong demand, but rather because the underlying recommendation of MMT is one of unlimited money creation so long as the economy is thought to have *any* overall excess capacity. The experience of 2020, 2021, and 2022 suggests such naivete is hardly a remote risk and may be found in central banks as well as in finance ministries.

A second danger is loss of control over the monetary system. Thus, when the central bank creates money to fund the government, it is simultaneously creating reserves for the banking system. Unless reserve requirements are adjusted upward, there is a significant risk that bank lending will also explode in the boom driven by open-ended monetary financing of unlimited fiscal deficits. Suppose, instead, that reserve requirements are increased, with a view to curbing such an inflationary expansion of bank lending. Suppose, too, that interest is not paid by the central bank on these reserves, even though the central bank raises its intervention rate, to curb inflationary pressure. Then the forced holdings of unremunerated loans to the central bank are being taxed. Deposits at banks may not receive interest either. That, too, would be a tax, this time on depositors. These are examples of "financial repression," again a familiar feature of Latin American monetary history.[21]

A third danger is flight from money into goods, services, and assets (including foreign assets), which would generate asset-price bubbles, inflation, or both. If, for example, in such an inflationary environment, bank deposits do not receive interest, such flight from money is nigh on certain. As Sebastian Edwards of UCLA (who has the advantage of Chilean origin) points out, the many Latin American experiments with such monetary policies "led to runaway inflation, huge currency devaluations, and precipitous declines in real wages."[22] What persuades people to hold the government's money is trust, not law. If they lose that trust and so refuse to hold the money, one ends up with an Argentina—a once-prosperous country with a crippled economy and a ruined relationship between citizenry and state.

In managing a modern monetary economy, one must avoid two errors. The first error is to rely excessively on credit-fueled private demand, since that is likely to deliver financial booms and busts. The second is to rely excessively on central-bank-financed government demand, since that is likely to generate inflationary booms and busts. The solution is to delegate the needed discretion to independent central banks and financial regulators. When it makes sense for governments to be financed by the central bank, the decision to do so should rest with the latter, except perhaps when the government is credibly able to declare a national emergency, as in a war, pandemic, or financial crisis. One must avoid fiscal dominance in normal times—that is, a situation in which fiscal policy determines monetary policy.

Yet deficient demand is not the only long-term risk. Demand may also be excessive, perhaps because monetary and fiscal stimulus are overdone, as was the case in 2021.[23] It is right for central banks and governments to support chronically weak demand. But it is also important for them not to overdo it, since that risks a prolonged inflationary overshoot, abrupt monetary and fiscal tightening, and a deep and damaging recession. The situation will become particularly bad if inflationary expectations are destabilized or are shifted semipermanently upward.

Nevertheless, so long as the structural condition of the world economy remains one of weak aggregate demand, and central banks remember their core job, the rise in inflation in 2021 and 2022 may prove temporary and the risks of a return to persistently high inflation may be modest.[24] Against such complacency, the condition of chronically weak demand might change quite soon, for the demographic reasons discussed in chapter 5.[25] In particular, aging will shrink the labor supply and lower savings. The former effect is quite clear. The impact on the balance between savings and investment is less so because an aging population is likely to invest, as well as to save, less. A chronically inflationary future is a possible prospect. But it is far from certain.

A crucial final point includes the urgent need to reduce the fragility of the financial system and especially the fragility created by overhangs of private sector debt. One of the causes of this danger is that debt is favored over equity within almost all current systems of corporate and personal taxation. This increases the fragility of corporate and household balance sheets and so the risks of mass bankruptcy in a slump. That, in turn, forces policy makers, especially central banks, to rescue debt markets in a crisis. A particularly important aspect of this is the growth of private equity, whose business model is to maximize the indebtedness of the companies they own. The incentive to borrow needs to be reduced.[26]

In the long run, some of these problems might be reduced by the development of central bank digital money.[27] Such digital money could even be rather more than a replacement of cash, now an increasingly outdated technology. Central bank digital money could, in theory, replace bank deposits as an unimpeachably safe reserve of purchasing power. This could greatly reduce the fragility of our current financial system, especially its vulnerability to devastating panics—a vulnerability that has forced governments to provide essentially unlimited amounts of insurance, much of it implicit. Instead of benefiting from a government-subsidized license to print money by lending, as they do now, banks would act as intermediaries. With central bank digital money, it would also become simpler to make cash drops, in equal quantities, to every citizen. Yet a shift to central bank digital money would also create challenges, especially those of preserving competition in finance and payments, and managing the possibly destabilizing transition to the new system. Revolutionary change in monetary and payments technology is indeed coming. It should bring big benefits in the long run. But it must also be carefully thought through.[28]

Innovation and investment

Investing more in existing technologies will not be an engine of durable growth, except in a catch-up economy able to adopt technologies already developed elsewhere. For countries at the economic frontier, the fundamental engine of growth is innovation, whose handmaiden is "creative destruction," the phrase invented by the Austrian economist Joseph Schumpeter. Innovators destroy the old and create temporary monopolies, which will then be attacked by new entrants. Competition drives this machine. Its ancillary motors are entrepreneurial vigor, scientific research, and corporate research and development.[29]

These new ideas mostly need to be embodied in physical and intangible capital.[30] A successful economy also needs high-quality infrastructure, from roads to broadband, as well as other capital goods, such as housing, hospitals, and schools. Not least, prosperity depends on the supply of high-quality human capital, which is the outcome of education and training, as well as of the scale and nature of immigration. In sum, a prosperous society requires a high level of high-quality investment.

The private sector does most of this investment. But public policy must play an essential role: it directly supports science and innovation; funds and regulates the supply of infrastructure and use of land; protects and promotes the creation of intellectual property; and finances and governs education. In addition, a range of government policies, including protection of intellectual property, taxation, regulation, and planning both encourage and discourage private investment in innovation and many other forms of valuable capital.

A "dynamic capability theory of growth" gives a revealing explanation of the success of the catch-up growth stories of the past two centuries, from Germany and the US in the nineteenth century to Japan and South Korea in the twentieth century and more recently China.[31] Their success has not come from doing more of the same things, but from development of new capabilities.[32] Private entrepreneurship supported by risk-taking capital markets is the driver of dynamic and innovative market economies. But governments have long played a central role. This realization goes back at least to the mercantilists of the seventeenth and eighteenth centuries. Alexander Hamilton and the German economist Friedrich List argued for infant industry protection in the late eighteenth and nineteenth centuries.[33] List had great influence on nineteenth-century German thinking, while Hamilton was the intellectual force in the US, the most important catch-up economy of the nineteenth century.

DARPA (Defense Advanced Research Projects Agency), created by the US government in 1958, has a particularly significant record as an innovator.[34] Many of the fundamental technologies used by innovative businesses, such as Apple, were developed with government support.[35] Fundamental research in new medical treatments has also frequently been financed, or carried out directly, by government agencies, such as the National Institutes of Health in the US or the UK's Medical Research Council.[36] The state also plays a role as a provider of macroeconomic stability if or when financial manias initially launched by innovation end in financial crises.[37]

Yet, while governments play a positive role in successful economies, they usually play a big—often bigger—role in *unsuccessful* ones. So, what distinguishes successes from failures? In unsuccessful economies, governments fail to provide effective government, legal predictability, and the necessary physical and social infrastructure.[38] They also interfere haphazardly. Governments of successful economies do provide what is necessary and are also careful about how they intervene. In this latter respect, they have broadly four options: leave everything to the market; support the supply of relevant factors of production (especially science and skills); support certain broad industries and technologies; and pick specific firms/technologies/products. Governments should attempt to do the first three of these, albeit cautiously, but not the last. That should be left to banks, venture capitalists, and other investors and lenders. Governments that try to pick the winners usually discover that losers pick them instead.

An important question is how to develop intellectual property law, which has become an important source of rentier profits (see chapter 5). Copyright and especially the tendency for continued copyright extension is highly problematic. There are also difficulties with what may be patented and how patents are used by "patent trolls" as instruments of extortion.[39] More fundamentally, nobody really knows whether the net impact of the system of intellectual property rights is to accelerate innovation in the real world (by rewarding it) or to retard innovation (by slowing its application). A case can be made for funding innovations in different ways—for example, by prizes or other direct rewards to inventors. The use of such mechanisms might even accelerate the application of inventions and innovations. Also, by offering prizes, the government might push innovation in the directions it thinks most important, without having to fund the research itself.[40] Prizes should then be seen as a complement to patents, not a replacement.

In sum, governments need policies aimed at the promotion of

scientific research and innovation, as well as the development of capabilities in new areas. Government spending in such areas provides essential public goods—things that the market will undersupply or fail to provide at all.[41] The question to be asked in the case of such interventions is whether they are likely to generate valuable new capabilities that go well beyond individual businesses.

More broadly, innovation is not just about new products and processes, but also about new *relationships*—particularly between private goods provided competitively and public goods provided cooperatively. Thus, the emergence of modern banking required the evolution of new relationships among banks, as well as the public good of central banking and financial regulation. Similarly, the internet is not just founded on the technical innovation of packet switching and competition among service providers, but also on standards, which are cooperatively governed public goods. Although economists think of public goods as provided by collective institutions, particularly governments, the internet has led to a burgeoning of private provision of public goods. Funding models include for-profit (Google, Facebook, Twitter), philanthropy (Wikipedia), and donations of code to the commons (open-source software). The Australian economist Nicholas Gruen points to potential digital public goods that have yet to be built, because the costs of private development or the obstacles to private coordination prohibit private provision. These would generate large economic and social gains if built as public-private digital partnerships.[42]

Let us now turn to investment. Its relationship with innovation is complex. Yet the two are highly complementary: the higher the level of investment, the faster the newest technologies are embedded in the capital stock; and the higher the investment in research and development and other ideas, the faster innovation should also be. So, raising investment, public and private, is an essential part of raising the rate of growth and also transforming the capital stock to meet environmental needs. Of course, it is also important that investment in labor-saving technologies, an essential part of growth, does not leave workers discarded. That is where active labor market policy comes in. The discussion will return to this issue below.

The role of government as a funder of investment, especially infrastructure, is itself significant for longer-term growth. Fortunately, at the real interest rates of the early 2020s—indeed, the rates in effect after the financial crisis of 2008—markets have been begging government to borrow to invest. Instead, many, notably the UK, chose to cut public investment in order to reduce the deficit. This was penny-wise and pound-foolish. Fortunately, the opportunity was even greater at the low real interest rates on offer in the early 2020s. A big advantage of spending on investment projects, moreover, is that these are not ongoing commitments, other than to maintain and use the capital created. The government can borrow to build the relevant capital, and then need not borrow more after the investment is done.

The government should also try to promote private investment, which is the most significant part of investment. (See figure 43.) Apart from supporting strong demand, government has two other options. One is to improve the incentives to invest. The simplest way to do so would be to allow 100 percent expensing or, better still, a 100 percent tax credit for fixed investment against corporate income. This should be part of a broader reform of taxation. A second (and complementary) option is to change corporate governance. A particularly big issue is the "bonus culture," especially in the US and UK, whereby management is rewarded in direct relation to the share price. This often means using the free cash flow and even borrowing, not for investment but to purchase their own shares—so-called buybacks.[43] This turns a productive business into a financial speculation.

Public investment in fixed capital has been a strikingly low share of gross domestic product in several large high-income countries. (See figure 43.) The average rate of public investment was especially low in Germany, Italy, Spain, and the UK between 2010 and 2018. Germany's low public investment was the price of its obsession with balancing the budget. That of Italy and Spain was the price of the unnecessarily

FIGURE 43. SHARE OF GROSS FIXED CAPITAL FORMATION IN GDP
(2010–18 AVERAGE; PERCENT)
(Source: OECD)

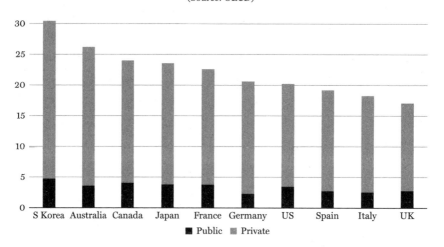

severe eurozone crisis. The UK foolishly decided to cut public investment in response to the financial crisis. Yet private investment is more
important. South Korea's private investment is strikingly high. The
UK's is at the bottom. The low average private investment rates in the
UK and US indicate that these countries' businesses are remarkably
unwilling to invest. This is a significant handicap.

Sustainability

Raising investment and the rate of innovation are necessary and vital
conditions for prosperity. But prosperity must also be sustainable. The
environmental challenge is significant, especially that of climate.

The economic malaise discussed in previous chapters of this book
was due neither to climate change nor to any climate-related action.
The latter has, instead, been a threat growing slowly in the background. The 1990s, 2000s, and 2010s were marked by studies and
conferences that discussed the growing dangers while doing nothing
effective about them. Concentrations of greenhouse gases and average

temperatures rose, roughly in line with the warnings of scientists. In the end, despite substantial debate, almost nothing was done. Trump's withdrawal of the US from the Paris climate agreement of 2015 did not help, but it probably did not make that much difference, especially given the rapid expansion of China's coal-based electrification.

The overwhelming consensus of experts is that these trends must change decisively in the 2020s if there is to be any hope of keeping the increase in average temperatures above the preindustrial average below 2°C, let alone the less dangerous increase of 1.5°C (unless we resort in the end to risky and controversial geoengineering). Moreover, high-income countries must play a leading role, even though these countries will be unable to deliver a solution on their own. (See chapter 5, figure 41.) This is so for four reasons: first, they continue to have relatively high emissions per head (see figure 44); second, their trend rates of economic growth are relatively low and so more easily combined with rapidly falling emissions; third, they have the technological resources necessary to deliver an energy transformation that other countries could follow; and, last but not least, they are responsible for the majority of the historic emissions of greenhouse gases.[44] The election of Joe Biden as US president opened the possibility of faster progress by the US. If the US had continued to be outside the global discussion, it would have been an overwhelming obstacle to progress, not just because the US is a big emitter in its own right, but because other countries would have seen far less point in their own efforts to reduce emissions sharply.

A transformation in technology and cost of renewables over the past decade or so seems to have made achieving zero net emissions globally by 2050 feasible, even at surprisingly modest cost. The International Monetary Fund estimates that achieving this aim might lower world output by a mere 1 percent, relative to its "baseline" (under unchanged policies), once one adds the benefits of damages avoided.[45] But this will still not happen without substantial and swift policy

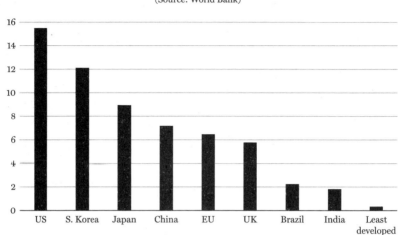

FIGURE 44. EMISSIONS OF CARBON DIOXIDE PER HEAD, 2018 (METRIC TONS)
(Source: World Bank)

changes. If, as is hoped, the high-income democracies are to cut net emissions in half by 2030, a great deal of policy action would be needed very quickly.

In its October 2020 *World Economic Outlook*, the IMF argued that a successful program would require front-loaded green investments, aggressive funding of research and development, and a credible long-term commitment to rising carbon prices. These recommendations are in line with those of other studies.[46] Also important will be complementary regulation, to accelerate needed changes in behavior. Yet, while feasible, this transformation will be enormously politically, socially, and technologically challenging.

In line with views of others, the Energy Transitions Commission argues that the core of the new energy system will be electricity generated by renewables (solar and wind) and nuclear power. This will need to be backed up by a variety of storage systems (batteries, hydroelectricity, hydrogen, and natural gas, with carbon capture and storage). This would clearly be a revolution. A zero-carbon economy (the target of many countries for 2050) would require about four to five times as much electricity as our present one. Hydrogen would also play an essential role in this new economy. As a result, hydrogen consumption might jump elevenfold by 2050.[47]

Wind farms and huge arrays of solar cells are found intrusive and ugly. Still more important, electrification of the world economy will require a huge expansion in battery capacity. With present technologies, this will require a correspondingly large increase in the use of a number of minerals, notably lithium, cobalt, and nickel.[48] Mining is destructive, particularly so when carried out in poor countries, such as the Democratic Republic of the Congo, which supplies about 60 percent of the world's cobalt.[49] It is essential that the people of these countries (not just rapacious elites and mining companies) share in the benefits and the miners themselves and their families are treated with care and respect.

There will be many such difficult environmental and social issues raised by the production and storage of electricity. But replacing fossil fuels with renewables would also improve the quality of local environments as emissions decline. That would make many people's lives better. Yet, the energy transition is essentially a defensive investment, intended to prevent harm—appropriately so—not increase incomes. Many will be made worse off by the shift and many of these adversely affected people will not be particularly well-off. Replacing fossil-fuel boilers with heat pumps, improving insulation of buildings, replacing gasoline-driven cars with electric ones, paying higher prices for air travel, and so on and so forth will be costly (and controversial). We must not pretend otherwise.

One of the big advantages of a tax on carbon is that the revenue it generates can be used to compensate the losers, perhaps via payment of equal lump sum tax dividends to every citizen or taxpayer.[50] Such compensation will be politically essential if these changes are to be accepted. Otherwise, as the gilets jaunes protests in France suggest, the energy transition is likely to generate a deep conflict between progressives and older and less-educated people.[51] Moreover, the compensation cannot just be domestic. It will have to be global since the transition will demand global cooperation.

An important element in making the energy transmission will be internalizing incentives in business decisions. Much of this can be done via carbon pricing. But transparency of the climate risks to which companies are exposed and of the consequences of their practices for the climate will also be important. The Task Force on Climate-Related Financial Disclosures under the Financial Stability Board has made some progress in this regard. The aim is to improve risk assessment, capital allocation, and strategic planning by quantifying and clarifying the situation of each business, for its own benefit and the benefit of investors, regulators, and the wider public.[52]

Raghuram Rajan of the University of Chicago has proposed the idea of a "global carbon reduction incentive."[53] Under this, each country that emits more than today's world average of about five tons a head annually would pay into an incentive fund. The payment would be calculated by multiplying the excess per head by their population and the agreed incentive. Those countries that emit more would contribute and those that emit less would receive. But every country would lose if it increased its emissions per head. So they would all face the same incentive to cut emissions. As global emissions declined, the identity of the laggards would probably change and so would the net payers and recipients.

In addition, countries that commit to imposing a price on domestic emissions should be permitted to put a border tax on emissions-intensive imports from countries that do not. Without this, production might just shift abroad, with limited impact on global emissions. That would make it politically difficult and environmentally ineffective to impose a domestic carbon price. Admittedly, any such border adjustment would be a rough-and-ready mechanism. It would also cause global friction. But a commitment by big, high-income economies to introduce one could ultimately lead to agreement on better policies, including carbon pricing, everywhere.[54]

Finally, we should note an immediate benefit from accelerating the energy transition: it provides a strong justification for a program of public and private investment. As mentioned, this is happening at a time when real interest rates are low. Governments can borrow and then finance investment in this transition on exceptionally favorable terms. A huge part of the challenge and the opportunity lies in developing and emerging countries. It is vital to de-risk such investments, most obviously via guarantees from high-income countries. These opportunities need to be seized.

Globalization

The globalization of the 1980s, 1990s, and 2000s did not happen out of a random whim. On the contrary, it was the result of experience with the success of liberalization of trade and international investment, initially among US allies in the 1940s, 1950s, and 1960s and thereafter across much of the world. The lesson then and since is that countries that opened themselves up to trade and inward direct investment did far better than those that did not. The post–Second World War policy contrasts between West and East Germany, South and North Korea, and mainland China and Taiwan were decisive tests of the argument that economic openness is a handmaiden of prosperity. The poor performance of India, until its reforms in the early 1990s, compared with the more open East Asian economies is another example. Openness does what it has always done: it brings access to new supplies, resources, technologies, ideas, and people.[55]

These are all particularly vital for small countries. The remarkable success of Australia, Ireland, Israel, and the four Nordic countries (Denmark, Finland, Norway, and Sweden), which combine high-quality domestic institutions with an ability to take advantage of opportunities in the world, has been rightly noted.[56] The story of Taiwan is also outstanding. But even the biggest developing countries, such as China and India, could not have achieved their relatively rapid growth of the past few decades if they had not taken advantage of opportunities offered by the world economy. The acceleration of growth in these countries after they embarked on what the Chinese call "reform and opening up" (in 1978 in China's case and 1991 in India's) was re-markable.

It would be a tragedy if the open global economy were to be lost in a rising tide of economic nationalism and superpower rivalry.[57] Yet there is now a backlash against reliance on trade, accelerated by COVID-19. That led to the imposition of export controls, notably on vaccines.[58] But the view that global supply chains turned out to be a problem is the opposite of the truth. Massive and unexpected in-creases in demand for certain products were the predominant prob-lem; supply chains were the solution, because they allowed countries to benefit from output in all the world.[59] Nevertheless, this shock, plus longer-term anxieties about the impact of trade on employment and newer anxieties about the future of international relations and technological competition have undermined confidence in the open world economy and reduced the legitimacy of the international institu-tions and agreements that regulate it, notably the World Trade Orga-nization.[60] Needless to say, the experience of COVID-19 has reminded us of the dangers of disruption of international commerce and travel by disease and other threats (war, terrorism, and other natural disas-ters). Businesses and governments need to take these into account in their planning and operations, as discussed earlier in the sections on resilience and robustness in chapter 7.

Dani Rodrik's quotation at the head of this chapter lays out a broader philosophical framework. He argues that one cannot have all three of deep international integration (given the resulting conver-gence of rules and regulations), full democracy, and national sover-eignty. One can at best have two of them. Thus, deep integration could go with democracy if the people voted to abandon national sovereignty (as in the EU). Again, democracy could go with national sovereignty if the people chose to abandon deep integration. Finally, deep integra-

tion could go with national sovereignty if the people lost their democratic ability to choose.

This supposed trilemma is simplistic. Unbridled discretion is indeed incompatible with deep integration. But unbridled discretion is
a foolish interpretation of sovereignty. Sovereignty concerns the locus
of legitimate coercive power. A wise sovereign not only can, but
does, limit its exercise of discretion, for its own benefit and that of its
people. That is why we have constitutions and the rule of law more
broadly. One way a sovereign may limit its discretion is by reaching
agreements with other sovereigns. These are not a violation of sovereignty, but a constraint on how it is exercised.[61] By agreeing to constrain its discretion, the sovereign creates new opportunities for its
citizens and itself (something Brexiters mostly failed to understand).
Finally, there is no reason to insist only on the extreme options, or
what economists call "corner solutions," as Rodrik does. In real life,
one has agreements that permit a country substantial freedom of action, not a choice between total subordination to international rules
or unlimited sovereign discretion. In practice, neither is sensible or
even feasible.

So the practical question is how best to combine the policy commitments, especially to business, that will make international openness credible and productive, with the discretion needed to make the
economy successful in the areas discussed above (such as innovation)
and below (such as quality of jobs). The best way is through international agreements that can be adjusted to the pressures and needs of
the time. In practice, the WTO already is such an agreement for trade,
though it could and should be updated in some respects. The same
applies to the Basel accords on banking regulation. Here, too, international agreements are needed, to protect against a regulatory race to
the bottom. But they, too, need to be adjusted from time to time.[62]
Again, international agreement is needed on minimum standards
for taxation, labor standards, the environment, and many other aspects
of international economic relations. The idea of absolute sovereign

discretion is absurd, indeed ruinous, in our interconnected world. Wise policy makers have long understood this. Of course, it is also possible to argue that some agreements, notably the EU, override national sovereignty excessively (I would disagree). Thus, the desirable extent of international agreement on regulations and restrictions can be debated. The necessity of some such agreements cannot.

Finally, where should openness be most enthusiastically pursued and where should it be constrained?

Trade and foreign direct investment (FDI) are to be welcomed most: they create important opportunities. But countries also have important interests in regulating both and should do so. To take an obvious example, it is legitimate to regulate trade or investment in support of environmental policies, especially climate policies. It is also legitimate to regulate trade in sectors where domestic capabilities might be needed for strategic reasons or where there is a reasonable chance of promoting domestic innovation. Again, the protection of intellectual property is a form of rent extraction and can obstruct economic development. While such protection may be a part of trade agreements, it should not be an overriding concern, especially when it hinders protection of public health or provision of other vital public goods. Finally, FDI is often essential for the exploitation of natural resources, but contract terms are of great importance. The big point in all this is that trade and FDI are good things, though evidently not at the expense of everything else.

Portfolio equity and debt, bank finance, and short-term capital flows are relatively less desirable (the last being the least desirable) forms of economic openness. While they can all provide useful resources for development in some circumstances, they do not transmit knowledge and create important new opportunities, as FDI and trade do. Moreover, debt—especially short-term debt and, above all, foreign currency debt—may create huge and long-lasting crises. The proximate cause of such crises is frequently a "carry trade," in which speculators exploit the difference between domestic interest rates in high-income countries, especially the US, and the rates on dollar-denominated borrowing in emerging and developing countries.[63] But when dollar rates then rise and the dollar's exchange rate appreciates, money floods out, as the solvency of public and private borrowers comes into question, and so financial crises occur. Such things have happened many times in the past and are likely to do so again. This form of financial openness should be treated with great caution.[64]

Flows of information and data across borders via the internet create huge opportunities, but also novel challenges to social, political, and economic stability. Ideas have always flowed across the world—the spread of the great religions is perhaps the most important example of this. But a completely free flow of commercially driven ideas is perilous; as is now clear, there are too many bad actors able and willing to exploit human weaknesses and undermine national security. It is essential to have controls over this new form of cross-border exchange, as well as defenses against malfeasance. Curbs on what businesses are allowed to do must be a part of the needed approach. It will also be necessary to find ways to block rogue websites, though without bringing in anything comparable to the Great Firewall of China. The technical difficulty of achieving such controls is, alas, very considerable.

Finally, there is the cross-border movement of people, perhaps the most controversial form of openness (see chapter 6). The ability to control who lives in a country is a fundamental aspect of its existence: a country is a geographical space inhabited by people with the right to live, work, and vote there. In a universal suffrage democracy, these adults consist of citizens and permitted foreign residents. Citizenship is a privilege that comes with political rights. Countries should try to implement a policy on the movement of people, especially for permanent residence or citizenship, that is humane yet also acceptable to the great majority of citizens. The latter need to see immigration as fair and under control. If they do not, there is likely to be a backlash, with devastating social and political consequences. This is not an argument against immigration. It is an argument for recognizing that it can never be solely or even mainly about economics. Immigration creates long-term changes in the nature of the population. Immigrants are not just workers; they are people, neighbors, and future citizens. Immigration changes the face of a country and should be managed so far as possible with corresponding attention. There need to be controls on immigration that recognize the potential economic gains while also being politically acceptable and effective.

At today's modest levels of global migration (a little over 3 percent of the world's population lives in a foreign country), the net economic impact on the receiving countries has been modest and mostly positive. Gains for migrants themselves have surely been positive. When someone moves from a low-productivity country to one with high productivity, real income of the migrants will normally rise substantially. For this reason, it is surely the case that if migration were completely free, world economic welfare would also rise substantially. In that sense, the argument is just like that for the free market. But that is, to repeat, not the same as saying that the real incomes of people in the receiving countries would rise. Rising world welfare is perfectly compatible with falling average welfare in many countries. Moreover, one commonly heard argument—that immigration will offset aging—is simply false, because immigrants age, too. The quantity of immigration needed to stabilize the old-age dependency ratio is almost unimaginably large (see chapter 5).

Indeed, this is a broader point. Evidence from the actual, relatively modest levels of migration says nothing about the likely economic (let alone social and political) impacts of unrestricted migration. An obvious starting point for considering that question is the proposition that this would tend to arbitrage away much of the current gaps in real wages across countries, just as it tends to do inside countries today: thus, real wages in rich countries would fall and real wages in poor countries would rise, as people moved from the latter to the former.[65]

Harvard's George Borjas has created a simulation for the case in which real wages for low-skilled workers in rich countries start off four times as high as in poor ones. It concludes that real global output would indeed rise enormously, by $40 trillion (or almost 60 percent).[66] But enormous numbers of workers might also move, perhaps as many as 2.6 billion, he suggests. With dependents, this would imply movement of 5.6 billion people. Just think of the slums we could see around London, Tokyo, or New York in a world with no restrictions on free movement of people. Real wages of workers in the north would, in his simulation, fall by close to 40 percent, while real wages of workers in the south would rise by over 140 percent. This would be a huge gain to the latter and a huge loss to the former. Meanwhile, the income of capitalists would rise by close to 60 percent.

This is a crude analysis. Yet the idea that free movement of people is much like free trade in goods and services is nonsense. We have something very close to free trade today. The impact on the economy and society is vastly smaller than the likely impact of free movement of people. The power of the latter to arbitrage away differences in returns to factors of production, especially to labor, would clearly be orders of magnitude greater and the movement of people would be transformational. One could be reasonably certain that a huge proportion of the prior inhabitants of the receiving countries and their descendants would be worse off, except for a minority of capitalists, who could live in gated communities such as Monte Carlo. World welfare would rise, in a simple sense. But the recipient countries would have ceased to be the countries they were. There is no chance at all that the latter would accept this democratically (or, for that matter, in any other conceivable political setting). The economics reinforces the politics: immigration needs to be controlled in a way that is politically satisfactory and economically advantageous for a substantial majority of existing residents and especially existing citizens. The debate on how best to do this is complex and difficult. But it must be had.

Good Jobs for Those Who Can Work and Are Prepared to Do So

The second big requirement is good jobs. So, how can we define these? In answering, one should distinguish the intrinsic from the extrinsic virtues of a job. The intrinsic value of a job lies in the pleasure of doing it and the sense of purpose and satisfaction it provides. The extrinsic value lies in the income, status, independence, marriageability, and so forth that having a job provides. Both the intrinsic and the extrinsic value of jobs are important. Policy can affect both. But it cannot fully determine either. Policy can shape the economy. It cannot create it, even in the long run. As argued in chapter 5, economies are far too complex to be under anybody's control: they have "minds" of their own.

The pattern of demand and supply, including foreign demand and supply, shapes the economy and so the jobs it generates. Over time these patterns change, as the economy evolves, both domestically and globally. The policies discussed above, notably on innovation and investment, as well as on trade, immigration, capital flows, and so forth, will also alter the economy's structure and the jobs it generates.

The structure of an economy will in turn determine the demand for skills and so the nature and quality of jobs. The proportion of the workforce engaged in manufacturing industries declined universally in the high-income economies in the late twentieth century, for example. The rise in demand for workers with graduate qualifications and skills was similarly universal. These changes were associated with large shifts in relative wages, in favor of those with commercially relevant skills and against the old industrial labor force. Technological change was the most important cause of these changes, with trade far behind. In the nineteenth and early twentieth centuries, in contrast, it was the share of the workforce engaged in agriculture that collapsed, while that in manufacturing rose. In some late-coming, high-income countries (such as Italy, Japan, South Korea, and, more recently, China, which is still at an early stage), this shift away from agriculture continued into the second half of the twentieth century and even into the twenty-first.

Policy finds it hard to affect such broad processes (except by accelerating or halting overall economic development). No doubt, it is possible to influence the skills of the labor force, through education and training, and the stock of capital through investment, through direct support and subsidies. Yet if the skills are not in demand, they will atrophy, and if the capital cannot be productively employed, it will be scrapped. Contemporary science and technology provide an "iron frame" within which an economy develops. It would have been impossible to have a revolution based on chemistry in the early nineteenth century or one based on computing in the early twentieth century. It is similarly impossible to have one based on nuclear fusion today. So, one has to question how far the fundamental characteristics of technology can be influenced by government policies.

Some disagree with this somewhat fatalistic view, arguing that the government can and must guide the direction of innovation by focusing its support on what we want more of—good jobs, better health, and less pollution.[67] This is certainly worth trying, given the urgency of the objectives. In the case of creating good jobs, options include taxing capital more heavily and labor less so, the reverse of today's situation. Governments can also orient the substantially enhanced support for research and development recommended above toward the creation of good jobs. The remarkable progress in developing renewable energy technologies is proof that this can bring fruit, provided the underlying science allows it, as it did with solar and wind energy. Similar efforts, it is suggested, may shift the balance toward more "human-friendly" technologies.[68]

The history of an economy also largely determines the regional distribution of activities and skills. This is just another example of "path-dependency," or how history determines the present. These processes can be very long term: the comparative advantage of the UK in services and the consequent decline of the UK's manufacturing, and so of areas of the country that once specialized in manufacturing, go back over a century.[69] Hitherto at least, it has proved impossible to reverse these trends. Yet these patterns of regional development, decline, or failure to take off at all shape much of the populist revolt we have been seeing. This has been in significant measure a revolt of "the places that don't matter"—that is, places left behind by the structural changes in the economy, such as old manufacturing areas, or in some cases, the failure of certain regions to modernize at all, such as Italy's Mezzogiorno.[70] Unfortunately, it is hard to do much, if anything, about such regional divergences either. Thus, "a combination of misguided investments—frequently pursuing individual interests at the expense of collective ones . . . , income-support transfers, and public employment has often resulted in protected, assisted, and sheltered economies, increasingly incapable of mobilizing their true economic potential."[71]

So, what if anything can turn places that don't matter economically into ones that do? One alternative, suggests Andrés Rodríguez-Pose of the London School of Economics, consists of "policies aimed not at providing transfers or welfare, but at enhancing the opportunities of most territories, regardless of their level of development or economic trajectory and taking into account local context."[72] He is not alone in believing that such place-based and place-specific policies are the answer. Paul Collier of the University of Oxford and Raghuram Rajan of the University of Chicago both suggest that policy must build on local identities, loyalties, and capabilities.[73]

Countries in which local government is highly successful in just this way do indeed exist. Switzerland is probably the world's best example, perhaps because its localism is rooted in strong local identities and loyalties. But elsewhere corruption and incompetence too often get in the way. Even if that were not the case, doing what these economists suggest will often need the transfer of resources to poorer regions from richer ones. With that is likely to come the dead hand of central control. Ideally, local politicians and civic leaders would allocate such funds, but they may lack the competence to do so wisely. In any case, central government may not trust them to do so. A complementary policy would be to create a network of publicly financed local investment banks charged with backing the development of the local economy. Even then, the development of large-scale infrastructure would need to be supported by national or regional governments with the needed resources and skills. In short, regeneration of the places that have fallen behind is a difficult task and one that will involve many players. Not least, it will require the creation (or re-creation) of institutions rooted in deep loyalties. An excellent example of the latter, as well as of regional resurgence itself, is the Basque country in Spain. But those loyalties were already deeply rooted in an ancient culture and language.[74]

An alternative (or complement) to creating more good jobs is to turn ostensibly "bad jobs"—that is, apparently low-skilled, boring, and repetitive jobs—into good ones. A big part of this depends more on management than on government policy. Thus, the former can empower workers, by simultaneously taking advantage of their knowledge and nurturing their commitment. This was what Toyota famously achieved by transforming the operation of its assembly line.[75] If employers treat their employees with dignity and respect, they can also make their jobs more meaningful and productive.

Furthermore, policy in high-income countries can seek to ensure that workers have adequate incomes and are treated with dignity and respect. People should be able to receive an income from work that delivers a standard of living that lets them participate fully in society. The obvious steps are to push minimum wages as high as they can go before their impact on jobs becomes significantly adverse, provide generous employment-related tax credits, and offer decent unemployment compensation. The last should be linked to an active labor market policy, which provides unemployed people with strong support for retraining. Also important are a degree of job security, compensation

for redundancy, paid holidays, and so forth, along with rights to organize and strike. But in the end, the combination of income security
with job flexibility seems to be the best way—what the Danes call
"flexicurity."[76]

Critics will complain that such measures represent an interference
in the market. They are right: it does and properly so since dignity
and security are at stake. We need to recognize the huge imbalance
of power in the contemporary marketplace between footloose corporations and local workers. The success of the minimum wage in the UK
in raising real wages at the bottom, without sacrificing employment
to any noticeable degree, is evidence that monopsony and oligopsony
(or the existence of one or very few employers) are important in the
labor market.[77] Raising minimum wages must be approached with
care. But it can be done without obvious deleterious effects. With the
addition of tax credits, this can provide everybody with an earned
income on which they will be able to participate in society, not just
survive.

Two far more ambitious proposals for turning jobs into good ones
deserve consideration.

The first is for a universal job guarantee. Under such a proposal,
the unemployment benefit would be set at the level of a minimum
wage and be paid to people who do not have a job, in return for their
work. So everybody could work if they chose to do so, at the minimum
wage. The latter would then automatically become the wage floor in
the economy. Unemployment compensation would presumably disappear or be paid only to people who are unable to work, for some
reason (such as disability), or be paid at a lower level.

Pavlina Tcherneva of Bard College describes the proposals as follows: "The Jobs Guarantee has the features of a public option and the
benefits of a price support scheme. As a public option, it guarantees
universal but voluntary access to a basic public service employment
opportunity to anyone who wants one."[78] This idea may be worth
considering, especially if macroeconomic and other policies fail to

generate full employment. But it also creates substantial difficulties. First, creating productive work for an inevitably somewhat random group of unemployed people will demand substantial and valuable resources, notably the capacity to identify useful projects and organize people. Otherwise, the "jobs" will not be jobs at all. Second, if people are working on such projects, it will be more difficult for them to be trained for new jobs or to search for them. Third, the newly employed workers would either compete with (and so undercut) workers already employed in conventional ways, which would damage the latter, or they would not be allowed to compete with them, in which case what they would be allowed to do (and learn from) is likely to be limited, perhaps even soul-destroying.[79] On balance, investment in an aggressive active labor market policy, along with temporary subsidies to employers for new hires, looks like a vastly better approach.

The second option is to raise pay at the bottom and simultaneously compress pay differentials. This, it is argued, could raise productivity and real incomes permanently, thereby creating a Scandinavian economy.[80] This is not completely inconceivable, but the normal assumption would, to the contrary, be that a big rise in real wages at the bottom would lead to the replacement of labor by capital, wherever that is possible, since labor has been made more expensive. It would also lower investment rather than raise it, since higher wages would squeeze profits and corporate savings. In the end, the affected sectors would shrink and so, in all probability, unemployment would rise, not fall.

True, this might not happen if a simultaneous lowering of wages at the middle and the top of firms' pay schedules left the wage bill unchanged or even lowered it. But that would require a high degree of wage coordination and worker solidarity. This might indeed prove possible in small, homogeneous advanced countries with trade unions that encompass the entire labor market and a strong ethic of civic and worker cooperation. I am skeptical that it would work elsewhere, especially in larger countries. Interestingly, even Germany, the most "Scandinavian" of large Western economies, encouraged the creation of low-wage and low-productivity sectors, to create higher employment, with the so-called Hartz reforms implemented between 2003 and 2005.[81] This is not an argument against minimum wages. But it is an argument against the assumption that a high wage floor is a fail-safe way to create more and better employment. This is most unlikely.

A final question concerns the role of trade unions. The argument that they provide countervailing economic and political power seems far more credible today than it was four decades ago. But they clearly work best if they are encompassing organizations able to internalize the conflicts within the labor force and take account of the impact of the bargains they reach on the economy and the sector, as a whole. Frequently, this is impossible to achieve. Yet creation of a high-wage, stably employed "middle" of the income distribution is important. Moreover, trade unions can protect members against arbitrary and unfair treatment by employers. Again, this is an important part of dignity at work and so of being a citizen. On balance, therefore, public policy should support the creation of responsible worker organizations, within the law. To the extent that this cannot happen, it is important that ordinary workers be able to protect their rights against unfair treatment through judicial and quasi-judicial procedures that are affordable and effective.

All this assumes that we will continue to have a reasonably "normal" labor market, notwithstanding COVID-19 and the development of artificial intelligence. The pandemic has accelerated the use of new technologies that allow information workers to be anywhere. This has opened important new opportunities for flexible working and correspondingly new sources of competition in remote places. The pandemic may also durably affect the economics of cities and important business activities such as retail. The advance of AI is likely to be still more radical. It is conceivable that in the not immensely distant future a vast proportion of human beings will become as economically redundant as the horse has already become. Work may cease to be a reliable source of satisfactory incomes for most people. This potentially vital topic will be touched upon in the section after next, in discussing universal basic income. But first let us turn to equality of opportunity.

Equality of Opportunity

Equality of opportunity must be the aspiration of any society that is both democratic and capitalist. As argued in chapter 3, such a society rejects ascribed status. If they are to be legitimate or merely effective, its elite must be open to talent. Otherwise, it will not just appear rigged, but will become ossified. Talent must be allowed to fly. That is a fundamental value in a society founded on democratic principles.

Yet this raises big questions. First, is such equality of opportunity achievable, any more than giving a wonderful job to everybody is achievable? Second, how far should a society go in its attempt to deliver equality of opportunity? Third, does equality of opportunity conflict with other goals and, if so, how might one manage these conflicts? Finally, what are the dimensions over which equality of opportunity should be measured?

The answer to the first question is that absolute equality of opportunity cannot be achieved, certainly not without doing criminal things, such as taking children away from their parents or preventing parents from doing their best for their children. In practice, people's success is determined in large measure by their own natural endowments and the environment in which they grow up. No policy tolerable to a free society could eliminate such advantages and disadvantages altogether.

The answer to the second question is that some things can and should be done to make equality of opportunity more realistic. Clear evidence exists, for example, that the greater the economic inequality among households, the lower the economic mobility of their children (see chapter 4, figure 15). This is partly because parents who suffer from significant poverty find it harder to provide the secure and enriching environment needed by a child. If so, pushing incomes up at the bottom of the income distribution, providing high-quality child-care (also essential if parents are to enjoy the independence and dignity afforded by work), offering the best possible education to all, providing special opportunities for exceptional children to develop, and offering the resources all children now need (computers, broadband, books, and so forth) are both essential and feasible in prosperous countries. Moreover, since talent may emerge later in a young person's life, dividing children into intellectual sheep and goats at an early age is wrong and wasteful. Absolute equality of opportunity is unachievable. But one should try to get closer to that goal and, in the process, ensure a reasonably high quality of education for all. Furthermore, there is no reason why generous fiscal benefits should continue to go to schools and universities that are accessible mainly (or even entirely) by the children of the wealthy and privileged.

Third, how far does the attempt to achieve equality of opportunity conflict with other goals and, if so, what should be done about it? There are three critiques of equality of opportunity.

One is that the more credible the propaganda is that the elite have been selected solely on merit, the angrier and more frustrated everybody else is sure to become.[82] Yet the idea that one should deliberately not choose the best available talent seems absurd and indeed wrong on many dimensions. The answer is instead to attempt to ensure that everybody in a prosperous society enjoys a decent life and is treated with dignity and respect. Moreover, the diversity of valuable talents must also be recognized. In all, equality of opportunity is a desirable social goal, but it is certainly neither a simple one nor can it be the only one.

A second critique is that the promise of equality of opportunity is unachievable. Policy makers should never suggest they can achieve unachievable goals. The response to this is that they can (and should) promise to do what they reasonably can, but also admit the limits on what they can achieve.

A third critique is that the mobility engendered by equality of opportunity would be socially devastating. If individuals born at the bottom are going (relatively) up, then individuals born at the top must be going (relatively) down. This will generate anguish and resistance among successful parents of unsuccessful children. That is no doubt correct. Social mobility certainly works best in economies that generate both upward movement in the real incomes of everybody (so that everybody wins) and a rising proportion of intrinsically satisfactory jobs and lifestyles.[83] This is why economic dynamism and a reasonable degree of equality of earnings are both so important. If jobs that generate incomes close to the median of the distribution are disappearing, genuine equality of opportunity will become particularly fraught.

Finally, what are the relevant dimensions over which equality of opportunity should be measured? The answers given above are essentially in terms of poverty and so class differences. But what, people will ask, about gender, race, or religion? Should we measure success in achieving equality of opportunity not by improvements in the achievements of people from deprived backgrounds, but rather by their sex, race, or religion? It is easy to understand the motivations behind the latter demands. But this focus seems dangerous. First, it tends to generate quotas in employment, which, being transparently zero-sum, are sure to be socially divisive to a high degree. Second, it tends to create arbitrary preferences. Why should a girl or a member of an ethnic minority from an obviously advantaged background be given preference over a boy from the ethnic majority who comes from a highly disadvantaged background? Deprivation is easy to understand as a justification for help, but this sort of favoritism is likely to look very unfair. Third, over time, the structure of preferences will get even more complex, as some minorities become "too successful" and so will need to be penalized, while others fall further behind. Finally, the further society goes toward dividing itself into tribes of "successful" and "unsuccessful" groups, unrelated to differences in the economic positions of individuals within them, the more impossible it will be to generate and sustain the sense of inclusive patriotism on which a functioning democracy must ultimately depend, as will be argued in chapter 9.

Security for Those Who Need It

The state has always been a protector of its subjects against enemies, external and internal. The COVID-19 pandemic has provided us with a powerful contemporary example of this age-old role. Historically, however, states could do rather little even if they wanted. But as societies have become richer, more technologically sophisticated, and more complex, people have demanded yet more protection. The rise of democracy, with its enfranchisement of the "have-nots," has strengthened these demands. In today's high-income democracies, people demand protection against what the UK's Beveridge Report of 1942 famously called the "five giants" of "want, disease, ignorance, squalor and idleness." As argued in chapter 7, eliminating such harms is a core function of a decent government, provided the society is rich enough to do so.

For a democratic state to provide such assistance is both largely inevitable and right. After all, a huge proportion of the population, even in the richest countries, is just one disaster away from ruin: in 2020, the net worth of US households at the 20th percentile from the bottom of the income distribution was only $6,400. It was only $68,000 even at the 40th percentile.[84] Without support, many would find it hard to survive, let alone bring up their children successfully. Private charity will always be inadequate and humiliating.

The state is more than an insurer of last resort. It is also a funder and financier—a sort of "piggy bank."[85] The state can, for example, run a student loan program, with income-contingent repayments, because it can obtain repayment through the tax system. It is also uniquely able to avoid the classic trap of "adverse selection" because it can compel everybody to join the insurance pool. Avoiding adverse selection—that is, ending up with insurance of only the worst risks—is even more important in the case of insurance against ill health and longevity. In private markets, in contrast, insurers seek to avoid being landed with pools of the worst risks. So they end up excluding those with the greatest need, while creating a huge and hostile bureaucracy to do so. This problem—the inability to create wide insurance pools because of the fear of adverse selection—will be made far worse by the advances of genetic science. At the limit, much of what we think of as insurance is likely to turn into state-run income redistribution to the genetically unlucky. In the case of health insurance, this is already happening in almost all high-income countries.

Yet the welfare state remains controversial. Many condemn it as a huge burden on the hardworking, for the benefit of the feckless. To the contrary, a huge part of what a welfare state does, in keeping with its role as a piggy bank, is to redistribute spending over an individual's lifetime and so make almost everybody more secure. An important study of the UK reached four important conclusions, in precisely this vein. First, income is far less unequal over lifetimes than in any given year. This is because a big proportion of inequality is temporary, a result either of changing needs as people age or transitory shocks. Second, largely as a result, more than half of the redistribution achieved by taxes and benefits is over specific individuals' lives rather than among different people. Third, during an adult life, only 7 percent of individuals receive more in benefits than they pay in taxes, even though 36 percent of people receive more in benefits than they pay in taxes in any given year. Finally, in-work benefits are just as good as out-of-work benefits at helping people who remain poor throughout their lives, but they do less damage to incentives to work. Higher rates of income tax, meanwhile, target the "lifetime rich" relatively well because income mobility at the top turns out to be relatively modest: by and large, if people are at the top of the income distribution, they tend to stay there over their lifetimes.[86]

In brief, the welfare state pools a wide range of largely uninsurable risks—risks of being born to poor or inadequate parents or with limited capabilities, risks of becoming a parent, risks of illness and long-term disability, risks from making unlucky choices in education, risks from the inability to diversify one's employment (with just one or at most two jobs at a time), and risks of old age. In some of its aspects the welfare state can be seen as a substitute for incomplete private insurance and in others as a substitute for incomplete capital markets. A universal welfare system is also both an expression and a source of social cohesion.

On the libertarian right, there is a strong desire to eliminate social insurance altogether. But George W. Bush's failure to slash Social Security suggests the political limits of such efforts in a democracy. So, too, does the fact that Donald Trump was unable to eliminate the Affordable Care Act, known also as Obamacare, although that was also because the health sector benefited from this legislation. Even so, the move to the market of the last four decades has also been a move to shift risks onto ordinary people from employers and government. Important examples of the former have been the collapse of defined benefit plans, employer-provided pensions in the US and UK, and the rise of casual or "precarious" work. An important example of the latter has been the virtual disappearance of local authority housing in the UK, tempered by the provision of an (often-inadequate) housing benefit.

So, what needs to be done? The discussion in the rest of this section will look at five aspects: rounding out the welfare state; the delusion of universal basic income; student loans; insuring against old age; and adjusting to import competition.

Rounding out the welfare state

Welfare states differ considerably across the high-income countries. These differences reflect divergent values and history. Some welfare states are predominantly contributory (with benefits tied to a record of contributions), others are not. Some aim principally at stabilizing incomes though the bulk of the income distribution, while others focus on providing a safety net for the poor. Some offer universal benefits, while others target support more narrowly. Some reinforce the patriarchal family, while others support any poor household with children. Some are comprehensive, while others leave large gaps. Not least, their success is about much more than the amount spent. Governments of countries with broadly similar outcomes spend enormously different amounts, relative to gross domestic product, on social protection. The difference between the ratios of public social spending to gross domestic product in the Netherlands, Australia, and Switzerland, at one end, and Denmark and France at the other, is striking. (See figure 45.)[87] Yet all five achieve high levels of social welfare.[88]

FIGURE 45. RATIO OF SOCIAL SPENDING TO GDP, 2017 (PERCENT)
(Source: OECD)

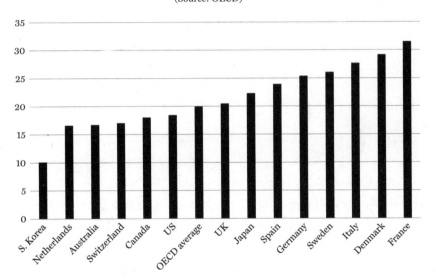

The most damaging remaining lacuna in the welfare states of high-income economies is the US health system, which does not provide universal insurance. It manages to be both staggeringly expensive yet fail to deliver acceptable health outcomes to the population. (See figure 46.) All other high-income countries have universal health coverage. Such systems do, on the evidence, deliver far better health outcomes at far lower overall cost. The US should follow these examples.

FIGURE 46. SPENDING ON HEALTH AND LIFE EXPECTANCY, 2019
(Source: OECD)

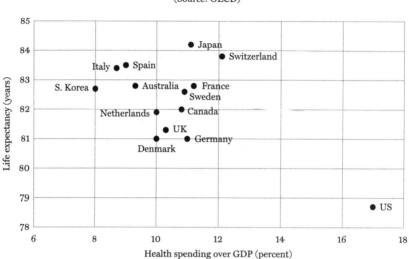

Delusion of universal basic income

Probably the most widely supported addition to (or even partial replacement of) the existing welfare states of high-income countries is the provision of a universal basic income (UBI).[89] The idea is that everybody gets an equal benefit, while the tax raised to finance it is progressive with income. So, UBI is redistributive overall. But the benefits are equal for everybody and so are unrelated to any other characteristics, such as income, age, health, family responsibilities, or work effort.

Philosophically, the idea of UBI attracts people on the left and the right. By giving every adult (with maybe a supplement for each child) an unconditional income, the paternalist aspects of the welfare state might, some hope, be attenuated or even abolished. Thus, if the basic income were large enough, most other anti-poverty and labor-market programs might be unnecessary. Some even hope that government provision of health and education could be abolished. This, some libertarians think, would get us as close to a truly free-market economy as possible. For some on the left, the independence and security that a UBI could provide are also very appealing, provided the basic income were large enough for everybody to be comfortably well-off.

One philosophical issue this raises is whether it would be acceptable to provide everybody with an income, unconditionally. The social contract of Western democracies is based instead on the twin principles of fair contribution and just deserts. The presumption underlying it is that adults able to do so should earn a living, with support provided only in response to identifiable need (such as illness, disability, unemployment, poverty, homelessness, or old age) or via universally available public services (such as education or health).

It is possible to argue, against this, that society is already inconsistent on the link between one's standard of living and individual effort since it allows gifts and bequests. These give a privileged few the opportunity to live well without effort or identifiable need. A rejoinder to this, in turn, might be that this is the result of free disposal of legitimately acquired income and wealth. The ability to do this is also of value in a society of free individuals. A more fundamental argument against an undue stress on the need to earn a living for oneself is that market rewards play only a part in determining people's deserts. Other things also matter, such as the need for a degree of social inclusion. Thus, reasonable people can differ on whether a universal unearned income could be justified philosophically.

Another philosophical issue is: Who should be eligible? Presumably, people would not be allowed to turn up in the country and claim the universal income. The answer would presumably be citizens or long-standing residents. This, then, would be a universal citizens' income. Thus, the idea of a universal basic income further strengthens the argument for the exclusiveness of citizenship. It would further strengthen the case (and the demand) for control over immigration, to ensure that people able to contribute to funding the basic income they would be entitled to receive could enter the country permanently.

Yet UBI also raises quite fundamental practical questions. One is whether a reasonable UBI would be affordable. The second is whether a UBI would be a sensible way to use scarce public resources.

On the former, many analysts have concluded that a worthwhile UBI would simply be unaffordable. Gene Sperling, former economic adviser to Barack Obama, spells this out for the US: "Most UBI plans offer around $12,000 a year for every adult—and sometimes $4,000 for every child."[90] A UBI at this level would in fact have cost $3.4 trillion in 2019, given the US population of 254 million adults and 73 million children.[91] That would have been 16 percent of gross domestic product. Even without children, the UBI would cost 14 percent of GDP. At 16 percent of GDP, the cost of a UBI would amount to around 150 percent of federal spending on Social Security, Medicare, and Medicaid together, about 100 percent of federal tax receipts, and around 75 percent of all federal outlays in the 2019 Fiscal Year.[92] This is obviously unaffordable.

The British economist John Kay provides a more general framework in which he follows the late James Tobin, a Nobel laureate economist.[93] He argues that the governments of modern high-income democracies mostly spend about 25 percent of GDP on the inescapable core public services and obligations of health, education, defense, public administration, police, the judicial system, and debt service. I will assume, in addition, a UBI for the UK set at one third of average incomes of around £11,200 per annum in 2019–20. With some 52 million people over eighteen years old in the country, this would cost the huge sum of £580 billion or just over a quarter of GDP. If this sum were added to existing public spending, it would bring the latter to 65 percent of GDP. Added just to the 25 percent of GDP spent on the core services enumerated by Kay, the share of public spending in GDP would still end up at around 50 percent of GDP. But under the latter somewhat less unaffordable option, the UBI would replace all of today's transfer programs targeted at the poor, infirm, elderly, children, and others with a range of special needs.

While such a shift would make the UBI somewhat less unaffordable, the benefits from introducing it would go to the non-poor, non-infirm, non-minor, non-elderly, and otherwise non-needy, all of whom benefited from the transfer programs eliminated in order to finance the UBI. The biggest beneficiaries of introducing the UBI would then be people who did not receive these now eliminated transfers and especially the nonworking partners of well-off people. In addition, the UBI might well persuade many people, especially second earners who are paid relatively little, to stop working altogether, further shrinking GDP and fiscal revenue, and so making even higher tax rates necessary.[94]

Martin Sandbu of the *Financial Times* offers three responses to these apparently decisive objections.[95] The first is that the UBI could be substantially smaller. He has suggested a UBI of £7,150 per annum for every adult. This sum is a third of average disposable incomes, which might make sense if the UBI is not to be taxable. That would reduce the cost from a little over 25 percent to a still enormous 17 percent of GDP. The second answer is that the UBI—a direct payment to every adult—should replace the current allowance (or exemption) before tax is paid, which is a form of tax expenditure. In the UK, the cost of this allowance before income tax and national insurance contributions are payable amounts to around 7.5 percent of GDP. With the UBI, this allowance could be abolished. That would reduce the cost of the UBI to a little under 10 percent of GDP—still an enormous sum, roughly equal to the annual cost of the National Health Service. The third answer, he suggests, is that the UBI would replace the state pension, which has much the same value (at just over £7,000 per annum). This would save 5 percent of GDP, bringing the cost down to 5 percent of GDP. Yet even this sum, it should be noted, is roughly what the UK spends on education.[96]

The UBI thus structured and financed would amount to a negative income tax payable as a lump sum to every adult, either as cash or as a deduction from tax. It would clearly still be expensive. It would also look even more expensive than it is to the extent that an invisible tax expenditure would be converted into a visible tax offset by a visible universal cash benefit. As designed by Sandbu, the replacement of the zero-rate tax band with a direct payment would indeed give the bulk of the gains to those who earn relatively little, since the value of the present tax exemption is greatest for those with the highest marginal tax rates and least for those who earn less than the threshold at which tax is payable. But many of the people who earn little or even nothing are second earners and so not those living in poor households. His UBI would also bring no benefit to people who live on the basic state pension, which is relatively low in the UK.

The most important question, however, is not whether Sandbu's proposed UBI is affordable (the answer is "yes, albeit with huge political difficulty"), but whether it would represent a good use of scarce public money. My answer would be a definite no. Even Sandbu's relatively modest UBI would require a substantial increase in taxation. If one could raise 5 percent of GDP in additional taxes (about £1,000 billion per annum), as he proposes, would an unconditional payment to everybody, including many who do not need the money, really be a better use of additional fiscal resources than further spending on vulnerable and needy people, health, social services, education, housing, international aid, or the energy transition? Again, under Sandbu's proposal, the current array of special programs for the needy and deserving would continue. Indeed, they would have to do so, given the modest level of his UBI. So, one of the theoretical advantages of the idea—elimination of the investigations associated with conditional assistance and the ultra-high marginal tax rates associated with means-tested assistance—would not be realized. Excluding those who live just on the basic state pension from the benefits of a UBI, as Sandbu suggests, with a view to making UBI less unaffordable, would also be hard to justify, given that pension's currently modest level in the UK.

The fundamental problem is that UBI is *intentionally* ill targeted and so an inescapably wasteful use of scarce fiscal resources. It just involves too much churning of money: robbing Peter to pay Peter. A UBI at a high enough level to render targeted assistance to those who are vulnerable, needy, and deserving would be unaffordable, while a UBI that is affordable would benefit many who do not need the money and fail to benefit important services and people who need more than they now have. In the end, the UBI is too ill targeted to be a good use of the additional tax money that would have to be raised to pay for it. That is, in the last resort, all there is to say about this idea.

Student loans and debt

Among the most controversial issues is how to fund tertiary education. There are three broad options: financing it out of regular taxation; financing out of standard mortgage-type loans (albeit without collateral); and financing out of loans with income-contingent repayment.

The big problem with the first option is that most governments now find funding of high-quality teaching at institutions of higher education has become impossible. The dominant explanation for this is the huge increase in the proportion of young people going into tertiary education. In England, for example, that proportion rose from 4 percent of school leavers in the early 1960s to 50 percent in 2019.[97] Similar expansions have occurred in many other high-income countries. Inevitably, therefore, all systems have become decreasingly well funded. But systems that rely overwhelmingly on taxation tend to be particularly poorly funded and so also mediocre. High-income countries that fall into this latter category include France, Germany, and Italy, which spend relatively little on tertiary education as a share of GDP, despite higher overall tax share in GDP, than Canada, the UK, or the US, where the private share of spending is higher.[98] Moreover, beyond this important practical concern, there is a philosophical one: is it right to offer full taxpayer funding of education that is not a universal right, as primary and secondary education are, but a restricted privilege? The case for full state funding of nursery, primary, and secondary education is clear. It is much less clear for tertiary education.

The second option is also problematic, because these loans are inflexible. Thus, loans remain outstanding whether or not the education turns out to have value. Furthermore, because a young person with no assets can offer no collateral, conventional loans from financial institutions will be offered only if they cannot be discharged in bankruptcy, as is the case in the US. Worse, particularly if the debt cannot be eliminated in bankruptcy, the burden of any given size of loan is heaviest on those who gain very little from their course, perhaps because they fail to complete it, which is a very common problem in the US. Indeed, the family must pay even if the student dies. The size of the US overhang of student debt is also extraordinary: in 2019, more than 40 million Americans owed more than $1.5 trillion (7 percent of GDP) in aggregate. This is the largest source of household debt other than mortgages. Moreover, many of the most burdensome debts are relatively small: borrowers with less than $10,000 in outstanding debt make up over 60 percent of all defaults. In addition, many of these students are people of color. According to a study by the Aspen Institute Financial Security Program, "20 years after enrollment, a typical black student still owes 95 percent of their debt compared with 6 percent for white students."[99] This is a scandal. It is one of the many aspects in which the US has failed to ensure basic equity in such core social arrangements as education (not to mention health).

The income-contingent loan plans of the kind now operated in the UK and Australia are a tolerable halfway house. The university charges a fee that is initially paid by the plan. This becomes a loan that is paid off by students, provided they earn enough. Thus, the plan provides funding to universities that is semi-independent of normal fiscal budgeting and so supports both the finances and the independence of these institutions. Since tax authorities know the income situation of taxpayers, they can make repayments contingent on verified income, at least for those who are resident for tax purposes. Moreover, because the repayment is income-contingent, the debt will not burden those who earn relatively little. In the UK, after thirty years, the residual debt is written off.[100] This system works reasonably effectively, though the details—maximum fees, interest rates, and repayment floors—are open to discussion. Arguably, the fees (currently £9,000 a year in the UK) should be lower. (Maybe that would reduce the ridiculously high salaries of many university administrators.) One could also add an equity element to the loan contracts. The institutions and the government would then receive a part of graduate incomes above a high threshold, thereby benefiting from the success of their most successful students. This would also make the system a bit more like a graduate tax (a special tax on graduates used to pay student fees).

Insuring against old age

UBI is a good example of a utopian idea that does not make sense in practice. The income-contingent loan plan for student fees is an example of a practical idea that does. Another area where countries need practical ideas is pensions. One of the most attractive is collective defined-contribution pension plans, ideally nationwide as in the Netherlands. This idea is particularly relevant in countries with a very low basic state pension, such as the UK. Combined with a high basic contribution rate, automatic enrollment (with opt-outs), and government contributions on behalf of the low paid, this could provide both greater security in old age and develop deeper capital markets, which are the foundation of a dynamic market economy.

Pension systems have developed in different ways. One of these ways was the combination of relatively ungenerous state-run pay-as-you-go systems with defined-benefit (DB) pension plans run by employers (among the latter being different levels of government). The advantage of such systems is that they reduce the fiscal cost. The disadvantage is that private employers are problematic providers of pensions, because a pension is a very long-term and potentially very expensive promise, something most businesses cannot realistically guarantee. The promise of a pension to a twenty-five-year-old might still need to be met seventy-five years later. Many employers will not survive long enough to deliver on their promises. Worse, they have an interest in making promises they will be unable to keep in many states of the world. These conflicts of interest are pervasive in such pension plans.

In the UK, this led to underfunding of many defined-benefit plans, government insurance, and then extremely risk-averse regulation. The result of the latter is that the cost of delivering on the defined-benefit promise has become prohibitively expensive. Private sector defined-benefit plans are duly disappearing. According to the UK's Pension Protection Fund, of the 5,327 defined-benefit pension plans still in existence in 2020 (down from 7,751 in 2006) only 11 percent remained open to new members and only 46 percent remained open to accrual of new benefits by existing members.[101] The defined-benefit pension system is dying, except—unfairly—in the public sector, where the government is able to make use of its power to tax to make good on pension promises. In some respects, this collapse of private sector DB plans is a great pity, not least because the result is a great generational inequity. But it was inevitable, once businesses were forced into meeting their promises in all circumstances and especially as plans became more mature. An open-ended commitment to meeting such long-term and generous promises is too burdensome. That was clear to anybody prepared to investigate these promises with an open mind. Reliance on such private DB plans was foolish.

The replacement for these plans has been the defined-contribution (DC) pension. In this case, the risk rests not with the employer or any other institution, but with the individual. This is one of many examples of the shifting of risks onto the individuals. With a DC plan, the income provided in retirement depends on the amount saved, (often insufficient, given human myopia), the return on investment (unknown), and longevity (also unknown). The return on investment depends on luck and the individual's competence as a manager of investments. As they come closer to retirement, wise investors will also want to reduce the risks they run, since they know they will be less likely to recoup any losses within their shrinking time horizons. But de-risking a portfolio is likely to leave the future pensioner badly off and at current interest rates very badly off. Finally, any risk-averse strategy for managing longevity is likely to mean underspending in retirement, on average, and so result in a surplus upon death. None of this is at all ideal.

An alternative exists: the "collective DC plan," which is a plan with a large number of contributing members, but no external guarantors. Unlike in DB plans, trustees would be allowed to adjust pensions in the light of investment performance. Since those trustees would not be subject to the conflicts of interest inherent in a corporate DB plan, one could expect their decisions to be taken in the interests of all actual and future pensioners. A big advantage of such a plan is that since the pension could be adjusted in the light of performance, there would be no need for investments to be in supposedly "safe" bonds to any significant degree. They could be in real assets instead, which would be vastly better for the long-run performance of the fund and the economy. Locked in their defensive crouch, only 20 percent of UK DB plans under the Pension Protection Fund are now invested in equities, down from 61 percent in 2006. That is disastrous, especially when real interest rates are negative.[102]

Unlike individual DC plans, administrative costs would be very low and investment risk could be pooled across generations. As a result, individuals would not need to make difficult investment decisions and would also not suffer if investment returns were particularly poor at the time they retired. Thus, investment and longevity risks would be shared among all pensioners, rather than be borne by individuals. Creating such plans at the employer level is already under consideration in the UK.[103] But a number of wider plans would be better. They could gain enormous economies of scale and so be very cheap to run. If a government wanted to do something daring to help the disadvantaged young, it could borrow long-term at today's negative real interest rates and invest the money on their behalf into collective DC plans. It could, alternatively or in addition, provide insurance relatively cheaply against big market downturns. In this way, it would be taking some of the risk from citizens. This is of course precisely what governments exist to do.[104]

An issue of comparable significance is insurance of care in old age. Many elderly people never need to go into a nursing home. But those who do may find themselves ruined by paying for it. Again, a plan of compulsory insurance against catastrophic costs is the obvious solution. The plan introduced in the UK in 2021 is, however, a wonderful example of what not to do. Instead of placing the burden on people with the largest assets, it imposes the burden on workers in general, while failing to protect those with modest assets.[105]

Adjusting to import competition

Since 1962, the US has had a special program, Trade Adjustment Assistance, to help workers, businesses, and, more recently, farmers affected by import competition. This program was deemed necessary to alleviate political resistance to trade liberalization. Its existence reflects protectionist attitudes, since disruptions caused by domestic economic changes are likely to be just as hard to cope with. But given that the US has a sketchy welfare safety net, this seemed a sensible way to deal with the protectionist political reality. The program has largely lost support, being considered both ineffective and costly.

Rather than attempting to revive it, the US should create a better system of support for workers, firms, and localities affected by adverse economic changes of any kind.[106]

What is needed in place of such special programs is a reasonably complete system of social protection that can gain and sustain political support, together with an economy that generates high employment with incomes that give people socially acceptable livelihoods. These topics were covered in previous sections on policy for economic growth and opportunity.

Conclusion

A modern democratic state must provide people with protection not just against enemies but against a wider range of perils. The state can do this intelligently or foolishly. A good welfare state will gain legitimacy by allowing people to do things they would otherwise be unable to do and by ensuring them against risks they would otherwise be unable to bear. At the same time, it should not encourage idleness or fecklessness. Striking this balance is at the heart of modern democratic politics.

Ending Special Privileges for the Few

The underlying assumption of a liberal democracy is equality before the law. The opposite of this is a "privilege." Narrowly, a privilege is "a right or immunity granted as a peculiar benefit, advantage, or favor."[107] It comes from the Latin word *privilegium*, which means "a law affecting an individual," itself derived from the words *privus*, meaning "private," and *lex*, meaning "law." Privileges were a salient feature of all premodern societies: the fact that aristocrats were exempt from taxation in prerevolutionary France was a privilege in this sense. In modern societies, there are also privileges, not just in the metaphorical sense used to describe almost any inequality as "privilege," but also in this original sense of a private law. The limited liability enjoyed by shareholders of corporations is such a privilege. The treatment of "carried interest"—the income earned by general partners in private equity or hedge funds—as capital gains rather than as uncertain income serves as another example of a legal privilege: it is obvious that if one is to classify income as a capital gain, it must derive from holding an asset on which one is likely to make a loss. Yet this does not apply to carried interest, which is highly unlikely to be negative.[108] There are many such privileges in contemporary tax codes. These are in turn a reflection of how wealth combines with power to shape contemporary law and justice.

Wealth and power bring many advantages in life. But they also shape more explicit privileges within the political and legal systems. Such privileges threaten democracy, since the latter assumes equality of status as citizens—what the Athenians called "isonomia" (ἰσονομία), or equality of rights.[109] The most obvious threat to a democratic political system is that of "overmighty subjects"—people or institutions able both to make the law and to live above it, by purchasing both politics and justice. They may make themselves above the law by corrupting judges. They may be able to bypass the law by escaping into foreign jurisdictions. At some point, such a polity becomes a blatant plutocracy. All effective power will rest in the hands of the few, not the many. The US is largely there already. Other democracies have plutocratic aspects. Often, as noted in chapter 3, plutocracy leads to autocracy, either because a demagogue attains high office by riding popular rage or because one of the plutocrats attains that position himself. Donald Trump's attempted coup in the election of 2020 should be viewed as a near miss.

The discussion below will focus on five dimensions of privilege (broadly defined): corporate misgovernance; monopoly; the new digital economy; corruption; and tax and the failure to tax.

Corporate misgovernance

As discussed in chapters 3 and 5, corporations are a remarkable institutional innovation and have played a central role in the economic progress of almost two centuries. But their existence poses some big questions. What should they aim at? How should they be governed? These questions about the nature, purposes, and governance of the firm have become increasingly debated.[110] Some now argue, for example, that corporations should have an explicit purpose other than profitability, which should be viewed as a means, not the goal of their activities. The governance of corporations should also be altered, it is argued, to internalize such changes in their goals. A program organized by the British Academy concluded, for example, that "the purpose of business is to solve the problems of people and planet profitably, and not profit from causing problems."[111]

Experimentation in corporate purpose, structure, and governance is desirable. There are indeed problems with the aims of the corporation and the model of corporate governance in which shareholder interests and power are dominant. Indeed, this is now accepted even by the Business Roundtable of the US, a grouping of executives of leading companies, which has come out against shareholder value maximization, in favor of taking the interests of all the stakeholders into account.[112] The approach taken here, in keeping with the aim outlined in chapter 7, is narrower: it focuses on harm reduction. Here are three things that must happen if the harms of corporate irresponsibility are to be contained.

First, *transparency* of what companies do must be improved. To make that possible, excellent accounting standards and accounts audited by genuinely independent auditors are necessary. On the former, some progress is being made in developing environmental, social, and governance (ESG) standards.[113] But agreeing on environmental and social standards for companies, defining these quantitatively, and then measuring them precisely is an enormously problematic task. How does anyone value one set of impacts against others? How far will people agree on those valuations? How far down the chain of downstream and upstream impacts does one need to go? Yet of the three elements in ESG, the last is perhaps the most difficult. Who is entitled to a say in decisions and how? Managers? Shareholders? Workers? Trade unions? Local and national governments? Civil society? And how should this work?

Auditing is a still bigger problem. The practice of letting companies choose and pay their own auditors is corrupt. Listed companies should be paid by the stock markets out of listing fees. But if we are serious about some version of ESG accounting, that still leaves the problem of private companies. After all, the impacts of private companies are also a matter of social concern. It might be better to make auditing a publicly funded function, to be paid out of a tax on all incorporated entities. Alternatively, the choice of auditors could be taken away from companies and handed over to a public body.

Regulators also have a role to play in ensuring relevant corporate transparency. The most important regulators are probably the central banks. These already have a responsibility for ensuring the health of financial institutions, especially since the financial crisis of 2007–09. Now, increasingly and rightly, they are also focusing on issues associated with other risks, notably those related to climate, including exposure to borrowers that are themselves subject to significant climate-related risks, such as those of stranded assets.

Second, *executive remuneration* needs to be reconsidered, not just its scale, but just as much in terms of the incentives it creates. As part of the aim of maximizing shareholder value, it became increasingly common for executives to receive pay linked to returns to shareholders. But shareholders know little about the long-run prospects of the business and enjoy the benefits of limited liability. The simplest way for management to raise the apparent return on equity and the share price is to increase leverage, by repurchasing shares. The funds available to management for net repurchases of shares, apart from borrowing, are net profits plus depreciation. This tempts management to forgo investment (including in research and development), in favor of share buybacks, since the buybacks are likely to have a stronger effect on returns on equity and on share prices, at least in the short run. Such incentive pay should be discouraged, since it motivates executives to make the balance sheets of their companies weaker than they should be, by reducing investment and increasing leverage.[114]

Third, *liability* needs to be strengthened. It is not hard to view corporations as amoral—that is, institutionally incapable of recognizing the distinction between right and wrong or feeling remorse or empathy. This is not just because, being institutions, they are incapable of feeling anything. It is also because incentives encourage such amoral behavior in those who control them. Corporations benefit from limited liability, which protects shareholders, who can only lose their investment. As for the top executives, they can mostly only lose their jobs. Maybe some lower-level flunky will go to prison, as happened in the case of the LIBOR scandal, even though the incentives that drove this misbehavior came from the top.[115] But top executives are most unlikely to be held personally liable for anything.

The executives who drove their banks (and the world economy) into the ground, before the global financial crisis, mostly walked off with large fortunes, while tens of millions of innocent people's lives were ruined and governments were forced to provide huge bailouts.[116] Enormous fines were levied on banks, but these were paid by the mass of shareholders. Only one banker went to prison in the US and none went to prison in the UK, even though these were epicenters of the crisis. Moreover, the one banker in the US to go to prison, Kareem Serageldin, was a minor figure. In Iceland, in contrast, twenty-five bankers were convicted, another eleven in Spain, and seven in Ireland.[117] This degree of impunity in the US and UK undermines the legitimacy of their market systems.

There are solutions. It would, for example, be possible to designate a class of "insiders" who would bear large penalties in the event of corporate failure.[118] Members of the executive board might be liable to a multiple of their accumulated earnings since taking up their positions. Again, large shareholders might be liable for a multiple of the purchase value of their shares in the case of default. Again, in the event of gross malfeasance (such as corporate fraud, manslaughter, or similar crimes), controlling shareholders, the chief executive, and others in the chain of command could be held criminally responsible unless they could prove they did everything anybody could reasonably expect to prevent the crimes in question.

Those who control a company need to have skin in the game. Consider, for example, how many millions of people have been convicted of minor drug crimes in the US: in 2015 alone, 1.3 million people were arrested for possession of illegal drugs, while almost half a million people were in prison for minor drug offenses, according to a report published in 2020.[119] Yet the members of the Sackler family—which bear heavy responsibility for the mass prescriptions of opioids in the US, probably the worst drug-related scandal since the opium wars by the British against China of the nineteenth century—are not going to prison, but are just losing some of their billions of dollars.[120] Such power without accountability is a monstrous privilege, redolent of feudalism more than of a contemporary liberal democracy.

Finally, *corporate political influence* needs to be curbed. As argued in chapter 6, only people can be citizens. Corporations should be subject to what Milton Friedman called the rules of the game, not make the rules. Only citizens should have a place in making such decisions. Corporations' role as lobbyists must also be transparent, as must be their role as political donors (ideally, none). There are questions about the role of money in politics more broadly. At the very least, it should be controlled and made visible.

Monopoly

Monopoly is privilege, too. The evidence of a decline in competition discussed in chapter 5 calls for a more active competition policy, not least in the case of the digital platform monopolies, which exercise extraordinary economic, social, and political influence—overmighty subjects, indeed. The 2019 Furman Review for the UK government addressed the challenges of competition in the digital sector rigorously, detailing both the valuable innovations and the special challenges created by this sector.[121] Lina M. Khan was appointed chair of the Federal Trade Commission by Joe Biden, because of her work on competition in the digital sector, notably on Amazon.[122]

The broad suggestions of these authors are to revitalize competition policy and, above all, to infuse it with far more than a concern for the consumer, though that is indeed essential. The aim should be to ensure that the competitive process itself is vigorous. To do so, general competition policy should shift in three important respects. First, there should be a presumption against mergers or acquisitions between companies that operate in the same market. Those who want to make such mergers or acquisitions need to make compelling arguments in favor, which demonstrate how competition would be strengthened by the merger. Second, attention should be paid to any market in which a very few companies, let alone just one, are dominant, with a view to considering how to engender more competition within it. Finally, countries should try to join forces in seeking more competitive and innovative economies. It should also be noted that liberal trade is one of the best ways of doing so.

On digital enterprises, in particular, the Furman Review recommended the creation of a "digital markets unit." This would develop a code of competitive conduct, which would apply to companies deemed to have "strategic market status." It would also be "charged with enabling data mobility and systems with open standards where these tools will increase competition and consumer choice." Finally, it would tackle "data openness," with a view to promoting the entry of new competitors. In addition, the points made in the previous paragraph need to be applied with force to digital enterprises, especially where network externalities are important.

The new digital economy

The emergence of the new digital and artificial-intelligence-enabled economy raises questions far more profound than those of competition. Moreover, they go far beyond the economy, important though that is. Since these businesses intermediate and indeed create the information ecology of our societies, they are the prime shapers of our economy, society, and polity. It is no accident that language is the defining characteristic of humanity as a social species. Nor is it an accident that the most revolutionary technologies humans have invented are those of communication—writing, printing, telegram, telephone, radio, television, and now the internet. Augmented by machines that can find patterns in almost inconceivably huge quantities of data in unimaginably short periods of time, the new information economy is revolutionary. Yet, as argued in chapter 6, it is not altogether new. Above all, the information economy may be a new set of technologies and institutions, but we humans remain prone to rage, suspicion, tribalism, anxiety, and, above all, to following charismatic frauds who promise to solve all our problems.

So, what are some of the things that need to be considered in bringing the new and emerging digital economy to heel? After all, nobody elected Mark Zuckerberg of Facebook or Sundar Pichai of Alphabet to control the information ecosystems of our societies. If a competitive economy and functioning democracy are to survive, some big issues need to be addressed by policy makers.[123] Here are three such issues.

First, as when we were considering corporate responsibility, *transparency*. Algorithms rule our lives, including our economic lives. They determine where businesses are ranked in search engines and what information of all kinds we see. Inevitably, the data used by these algorithms are themselves defective and biased. Inevitably, too, the algorithms are designed for the interests of their commercial creators, not those of their users or of the societies in which they live. The nationalization of these algorithms by the state, as in China, should surely be unthinkable. But they should be brought under some sort of regulatory control. Food and drugs, for example, are tightly regulated. Why not algorithms designed to spread misinformation and destructive behavior virally? Evidently, regulating all algorithms would be far too intrusive and create the danger of ubiquitous state control. One possibility might be to designate certain technology businesses as "strategic" or "systemic," just as big banks now are. These businesses—not very large in number—should be regulated and any new services they provide or new algorithms they introduce be examined. We have experienced the world of "move fast and break things." Too much has been broken. This needs to stop.

Second, *data*. It is said that, in the case of Facebook and other social media businesses, the users are also the product.[124] This is questionable. What is clear is that the data provided by customers is of great value to the companies they deal with. Is this a fair bargain? Given the monopolistic position of the companies and the fragmented position of the customers, this must be doubtful. One could imagine a world in which companies paid their users a fee every time their data was used. Closely related to this issue is privacy and, above all, the right of users to know what is known about them and the right to ensure that users control what data about them are used. The EU's General Data Protection Regulation may be imperfect—indeed, it must be.[125] But it is surely a move in the right direction. Such restrictions should operate worldwide. That does not necessarily require global agreement. A regime introduced in one of the biggest jurisdictions, especially the US and EU, will inevitably have global reach.

Third, *media*. Real media are not just a matter of venting opinions or encouraging amateur "citizen journalists" to glean whatever information they can, however they can. Real media demand resources and a dedication to the truth (something, alas, neither as popular nor deemed as important as it should be). So, from where are these resources to come? One possibility would be to impose a tax on the social media that have done so much to destroy the business model of real media. The revenue would then go to some sort of trust that would fund relevant media. These resources, to be used for news, current affairs, and documentaries, could go to public service media or, perhaps even more important, to local media, since the latter's business model has been particularly severely devastated.

Finally, *artificial intelligence*. Artificial intelligence may deliver one of the most fundamental transformations in human history. Its implications for our economies, societies, politics, and indeed our sense of what and who we are cannot be left to a small number of businesses focused on how much money they can make out of it. Our politics need to ask some deep questions about how this might work, what needs to be done to ensure that it enhances our humanity rather than destroys it, and how we can ensure it does not create a world in which a small number of organizations (businesses or governments) control the present and the future of our species. That would be "privilege" taken far beyond tolerable limits. Countries should be promoting research and discussion on these themes.

Corruption

Corruption—the abuse of power for private gain—is an eternal feature of organized societies. The more wealth there is to steal, the greater the incentive to do so. Indeed, the distinction between corruption and what is legal can often be quite difficult to draw. For much of human history, wealth and power were two sides of a coin. Power granted access to wealth, and wealth reinforced power. It takes a sophisticated, perhaps somewhat naive, view of society to imagine that power and wealth should or can be separate. An absolute monarch will object if his servant steals what he thinks is his. But he will take for granted that he has a legitimate claim on most or even all the wealth of his domain. Who would dare to say him nay? Only someone with a death wish. This traditional form of government is known as patrimonialism. Vladimir Putin views Russia no differently. He thinks it is his to do with as he pleases, though it is not yet a hereditary estate, as it was under the Romanovs or as North Korea is under the Kim family.

Law-governed liberal democracies (the only sort of regime that deserves to be called democratic) are supposed to be different, and for the most part they are. In Transparency International's ranking of countries in 2020, the least corrupt countries were all such democracies, with the exceptions of Singapore (3rd equal), Hong Kong (11th equal), and the United Arab Emirates (21st equal). These three countries are higher than France (23rd), the US (25th), Spain (32nd), South Korea (33rd), and Italy (ranked 52nd, alas, alongside Saudi Arabia). But at the top are New Zealand and Denmark. No surprise there: small and truly democratic countries, where everybody knows everybody else's business, are the least corrupt, as they are the happiest (see chapter 7).[126]

Nevertheless, all is not well. High-income democracies themselves enable corruption in many ways.[127] This very much includes the UK and US. Furthermore, if a country and its elite are facilitating corruption abroad and tolerating dirty money and the people who have it, then at home, business and politics will inevitably be tainted. Furthermore, there is a great deal of corruption in important high-income democracies and a great deal not generally considered corrupt, which is.[128] The business of campaign finance, for example, is corrupt in the US: a classic example of buying and selling of favors. Cleaning all this up matters for many reasons, not least for the damage it does to people's trust in politics. If voters are cynical, they will conclude that, since all politicians are crooks, why should they not vote for a crook who is at least open and honest about his crookedness?

Fighting corruption is important for the economy since it distorts competition. But it is just as crucial for the protection of democracy. The abuse of power is a step—a large step—toward autocracy. Once theft becomes the purpose of politics, free media, independent courts, the right to protest, and freedom of political organization have to be suppressed. Otherwise, the despot and his dependents will find their position at risk. The democracies should do everything they can to fight corruption both at home and abroad. The idea that power and wealth have to be separated is one of the highest, if most difficult, ideals of democratic capitalism. It must never be forgotten.

Taxation

Taxation, as Justice Oliver Wendell Holmes famously said, is the price of civilization. The ability of an elected legislature to determine what, how, and how much to tax is, correspondingly, the most fundamental feature of a democracy. Unfortunately, there is increasing evidence, especially from the US, that it is not the people who determine tax policy, but a small minority. Indeed, tax policy is supporting the creation of an immensely wealthy and powerful hereditary plutocracy. Members of this plutocracy have also shifted the political debate away from economic inequality by exploiting the identity politics of ethnonationalism. The alliance between the plutocracy and the white working class helped give the US to Trump, who attempted to subvert the electoral process itself in 2020 and since. The issue, then, is not just taxation or even economic policy, but the health of democracy itself. This is what Franklin Roosevelt was concerned about, too, when he called for "the ending of special privilege for the few."[129]

There are several points to be made here: higher taxes will be required in many high-income countries, simply because bills are coming due; but higher taxes can also be introduced without significant economic cost; furthermore, much of the current tax system is unjust, notably, but not solely, in failures to tax capital and tackle tax evasion and avoidance adequately; and so, finally, there need to be radical changes.

. . .

If we look at the longer-term future, in the light of the discussions earlier in this chapter and in part II of the book, it seems clear that the state is going to need more resources in many countries. This is partly because there are things that need to be done to ensure everybody a decent income, support people's ability to work, and provide first-rate education and health care. It is also because the population is aging and will continue to age, which will bring with it costs of higher spending on health and social care. These upward pressures are likely to be strongest in countries with relatively low ratios of government spending to GDP, such as the UK or the US. In the UK, for example, the Office for Budget Responsibility has repeatedly argued that under existing policies and plausible assumptions about growth and interest rates, public debt is on an unsustainable path. In July 2020, for example—admittedly, at the worst of the COVID-19 crisis—its central forecast was for public sector net debt to reach over 400 percent of GDP by 2069–70.[130] A similar exercise by the US Congressional Budget Office published in March 2021 concluded, "By the end of fiscal year 2021, federal debt held by the public is projected to equal 102 percent of GDP. If current laws governing taxes and spending generally remained unchanged, debt would persist near that level through 2028 before rising further. By 2031, debt would equal 107 percent of GDP. . . . Debt would continue to increase thereafter, exceeding 200 percent of GDP by 2051. That amount of debt would be the highest by far in the nation's history, and it would be on track to increase further."[131] Unless one believes there is no limit to how much debt or money a country can create (if you do, please take a look at the history of Argentina), this accumulation of debt cannot continue indefinitely, though with very low real interest rates and continued growth, substantial deficits can be run indefinitely.

Nevertheless, taxes will have to rise to meet current promises, let alone some of the needs for a better future. The question, to be considered further below, is how. Of course, raising revenue is not the only reason for taxation. Taxes can achieve other goals—internalizing negative externalities, for example, notably damage to the environment, as well as reducing inequality. Taxes also need to meet certain criteria, most obviously those of practicality and fairness. But the starting point must be with revenue: there will need to be more of that in many high-income countries.

■ ■ ■

A standard response to the argument that higher taxes will be needed is to argue that they will kill growth and so make the population poorer than it needs to be. This view has superficial plausibility. If one taxes effort, enterprise, and innovation highly, one must expect to get less of it.[132] But the ratio of tax to GDP seems, in practice, to have relatively insignificant effects on prosperity, once other things (such as the quality of institutions and human capital) are equal. It seems instead largely to reflect a social choice over how much insurance the state should provide to households and how big a role the state should play in providing such services as education and health. Furthermore, the spending of the state also provides benefits that matter to people, even if these do not appear in GDP. Not having to worry that an illness would bankrupt one is such a benefit. So is income security, especially for families with children. GDP per head may not be lowered much if the prospects of many children are stunted by poverty, but *their* lives will be stunted. Figure 47 shows the ratio of tax to GDP and GDP per head (relative to the US) of a number of significant high-income countries, including all the members of the Group of Seven leading high-income countries. As the trend line shows, no relationship can be seen. There are prosperous high-tax countries and also prosperous low-tax ones.

FIGURE 47. GOVERNMENT REVENUE AND GDP PER HEAD, 2019 (PERCENT)
(Source: IMF)

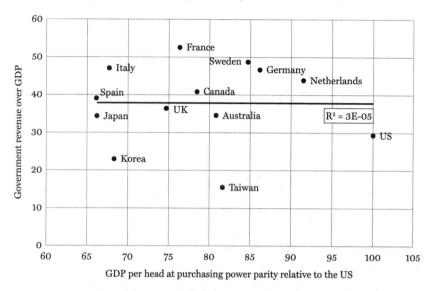

GDP per head at purchasing power parity relative to the US

The US does have the most productive economy in this group of countries. There are many reasons for this, apart from the modest tax burden: size of the market; entrepreneurial culture; quality of higher-education institutions; and, until recently, openness to the world's talent. These qualities offset some of its failures, including a relatively poorly educated domestic labor force. The United Nations Development Program has for a long time published a Human Development Index, which weights together gross national income (GNI) per head, life expectancy, and years of education. On this, the US comes 17th, behind most of the countries in figure 47 (the exceptions being South Korea, Spain, and Italy, in that order, with Taiwan excluded for not being a sovereign country). The US is 10th in GNI per head, behind only a few small countries (including oil-rich ones). It is ranked 38th in life expectancy, which is appalling, given its wealth and resources, and 28th in expected years of schooling, which is remarkably poor, too.[133] A low tax ratio seems a poor bargain if it comes with poor health and education services for a sizable portion of the population, as well as high inequality. True, for most of the world the US remains a paradise. But that says more about the rest of the world than about the relative condition of the US among high-income countries.

■ ■ ■

As discussed in detail in chapter 5, the abuse of tax havens, principally by corporations, has been an open scandal. But this is just one part of a far bigger problem. In *The Triumph of Injustice*, Emmanuel Saez and Gabriel Zucman lay out both the scandal and its main causes, in the case of the US.[134] Saez and Zucman show that "today, each social group funnels between 25 and 30 percent of its income in taxes into the public coffers, except the ultrawealthy who barely pay 20 percent. The US tax system is a giant flat tax—except at the top, where it's regressive."[135] So, "as a group," they note, "the Trumps, the Zuckerbergs, and the Buffetts of this world pay lower tax rates than teachers and secretaries."[136]

The explanation is that the federal income taxes on which US political debate tends to focus generate only a third of total tax revenues (9 percent of national income). Moreover, the income tax legally excludes many forms of income and especially capital income, quite apart from the outright tax evasion. Thus, only 63 percent of US national income is subject to the income tax. Moreover, state income taxes follow the pattern of the federal one: they generate about 2.5 percent of national income. The second-largest source of tax revenue is the Social Security payroll tax, which is a regressive tax on labor income, generating about 8 percent of national income (and so almost as much as the federal income tax). The third-largest source of revenue is consumption taxes, which include excise taxes. They are also regressive, partly because the poor spend a far higher share of their income than the rich and partly because these taxes exclude services (since the US does not have a value-added tax, or VAT). Services are more intensively consumed by the rich. The last and smallest part of tax revenue is taxes on capital. These are very light in the US: the average rate is around 13 percent. Mark Zuckerberg owns 20 percent of Facebook, which paid an effective tax rate of 13 percent on its operational income of $25 billion in 2018. The company's net income was close to $22 billion, of which Zuckerberg's share would have been around $4.4 billion. Zuckerberg paid corporation tax at 13 percent on his share of Facebook's profit, but no income tax.[137] Do not forget that even the generous "philanthropy" of billionaires is tax deductible. So the money they give away is partly at someone else's expense. This surely *is* plutocracy.

Tax evasion is rife, too. Again, evasion is much easier for people with large wealth, since it is easier for ownership to be hidden than income from work. One sophisticated analysis of evasion concludes that "unreported income as a fraction of true income rises from 7 percent in the bottom 50 percent [of the income distribution] to more than 20 percent in the top 1 percent, of which 6 percentage points correspond to undetected sophisticated evasion."[138]

The US is an extreme example, but not all that extreme. One way or the other, rich people do not pay much if any tax. As Leona Helmsley, the late hotel owner, said, "only the little people pay taxes."[139] She was right, most of the time (though she herself was foolish enough to be caught and so went to prison). But why people of immeasurable wealth should fight so hard not to pay taxes is beyond the understanding of any reasonable person.

■ ■ ■

There are innumerable questions about the future of taxation. But here are the three I will consider: the aims; the means; and some specific challenges, especially transparency and global cooperation.

The starting point on aims is with raising enough revenue to deliver the essential purposes of government, as outlined earlier. In some cases, notably the UK and US, this will mean higher revenue as a share of GDP, permanently. In some other cases, it may just mean a temporary increase in revenue, to bring post-pandemic public finances back under control. But, while crucial, this is far from a complete statement of legitimate aims. Tax systems also need to be seen as fair. As indicated above, the US system of today fails to meet this criterion. To some degree, this is true of most other systems. Capital gains, for example, are lightly taxed only upon sale of assets. This allows those with large assets to borrow against their rising value and live tax free, other than whatever they pay in consumption taxes. Yet any reasonable notion of fairness requires that burdens be borne by those best able to do so. Where that is lacking, the result is likely to be pervasive distrust and anger. The tax system should, so far as possible, also promote desirable goals and impose modest economic costs. Finally, the system should also be implemented effectively.

So, what means should be chosen to achieve these broad aims? One obvious rule is to sweat public assets more effectively, by ensuring that they are used productively.[140] Another is to tax "bads," such as pollution. Some form of carbon tax is a no-brainer. Another is to tax rents. Taxing pure rent—the excess of the income earned above what is needed to motivate the supply of something—is efficient, since it should not lower output. When Henry George wrote in the nineteenth century, the dominant source of rent was land.[141] Land rent is still important, which is why it should be heavily taxed, while alleviating the burdens on enterprise, effort, and productive saving. But there are other forms of rent: sustained supernormal corporate profits, for example, as with Apple, or the network benefits of agglomeration (as with successful residents of London or New York). Skilled people do not earn more working in London or New York because they are more competent on average than others but because such cities generate network externalities that make many workers more productive. The far higher incomes earned in high-income countries than elsewhere, even with similar skills, are a form of rent derived from the location in which they live. High taxes can then be viewed as the charge for enjoying the location-specific services that generate such rents.[142]

A crucial question is how best to tax capital. There are various possibilities, each of which goes with somewhat different aims. If the goal is to reduce inherited inequality and so reduce the weight of a hereditary plutocracy, the appropriate means are penal taxes on estates and large gifts among living people. There is no good reason for estates to survive indefinitely. If the goal is to force the wealthy to share in day-to-day fiscal burdens, then the best means would be to tax all forms of income, earned and unearned, at the same rate. In the example of Zuckerberg given above, a simple option would be to tax all corporate income at the top rate of income tax. Alternatively, corporate income could be fully attributed to shareholders and be taxed at their top rate, whatever that is. This would have large adverse effects on investment. So, in measuring corporate income for the purposes of taxation, there should be a 100 percent credit for all investment. The government would then be sharing equally in both the costs of the investment and the returns from it. Finally, the tax deductibility of interest should also be eliminated, to discourage dangerous and unproductive leverage.

Bridgewater has looked at thirty-three cases of annual wealth taxes but concluded that there was no example of one both big enough to make a significant difference to government finances and also longlasting. Of the thirty-three cases, seven were imposed at the time of the world wars and were heavy, but they were either one-off events or abolished quite quickly.[143] Thus, a large wealth tax tends to be an exceptional action justified by exceptional circumstances, such as a war or maybe now a pandemic. It is possible to have an ongoing wealth tax, as both Norway and Switzerland have done for a long time. But the money such wealth taxes raise is modest, with rates of 1 percent or less. Nevertheless, even such a wealth tax could raise about 2 percent of GDP in revenue. That might be worthwhile.

The big challenge when attempting to tax capital is the possibility of flight or other ways of evading the tax. International cooperation is needed to avoid such erosion. The governments of the large countries and especially the US have the capacity to compel other governments to cooperate or, failing that, compel companies to do so. They could turn corporation taxes into destination taxes, instead of taxes on the location of production, which is increasingly difficult to identify for many companies. This would eliminate the relevance of claiming that sales in, say, the UK are made from Luxembourg or intellectual property located in the Bahamas. The tax would be levied in the market. They could also act against countries that have excessively low rates of corporation tax. Again, they could tell companies that they will be unable to do business in their own economies if they persist in making ridiculous claims that they have productive assets, such as intellectual property, located in tax havens. If, for example, the US told its tech companies that the price of locating profits in countries with low corporation tax would be that they could no longer operate in the US market, this nonsense would stop overnight.

The Biden administration at last (and at least) did propose relevant changes for corporation tax, including higher rates at home and a global minimum, in early 2021 and reached agreement on a ground-breaking deal on a global minimum rate of 15 percent among more than 130 countries in October.[144] A global carbon tax could be achieved in much the same way: the major markets would simply impose a countervailing border tax on any country that did not have an adequate tax at home. The EU has already started the necessary move in that direction.

A final issue is the tax treatment of philanthropy, touched on earlier. At present, the tax deductibility of gifts allows very rich people to act in the public realm at least partly at the expense of other taxpayers. It is not at all obvious why their gifts should be tax deductible. An argument in favor is that they will then give more, which suggests that the motivation is not really charity at all. The argument against this is that it deprives the state of revenue that may be needed for equally important purposes. An argument in favor, again, is that in this way philanthropy benefits from the energy of able individuals. The argument against this, again, is that nobody elected Bill Gates to solve the world's health problems. Why should a successful software entrepreneur have such a role in the world? It is reasonable to be of two minds on the advisability of tax deductibility of gifts.

In the end, the obstacle to any of this is the power that corporations and wealthy people have over governments, not the inability of governments to get their way on tax (or other things) if they wanted to do so.

The "New" New Deal

In keeping with the broad agenda of "piecemeal social engineering" laid out in chapter 7, this chapter has laid out realistic reforms designed to deliver a market economy within a democratic polity that seeks to provide welfare to the population at large. It has covered many areas of reform: macroeconomic stability, innovation and investment, sustainability, openness to the world, jobs and the quality of jobs, equality of opportunity, improving the welfare state, and, most important, ending the privileges of the wealthy and powerful, which distort both the market economy and politics. Particularly significant in this last respect are a corporate governance regime that rewards powerful insiders, a competition regime that tolerates powerful monopolies, a regulatory regime that tolerates corruption, and, not least, a tax system that makes paying taxes by the wealthy almost voluntary. What we need are societies that serve everybody, by offering opportunity, security, and prosperity. This is not what many high-income democracies now have.

It is impossible to go into the fine details of all the options, since every section could be a book. But the key requirement is to be prepared to be quite radical, while thinking systematically, rigorously, and realistically. This is piecemeal social engineering in practice. The future must be different from the recent past if our democracies are to be built on firmer foundations. This chapter has tried to spell out an agenda. It is a beginning, not the end. But, it turns out, the agenda of the founding fathers of the post–Second World War states still remains relevant. We should return to it. For that to happen, politics must change, too. That is the subject of the next chapter.

———■———

CHAPTER NINE

Renewing Democracy

As between one form of popular government and another, the advantage in this respect lies with that which most widely diffuses the exercise of public functions; on the one hand, by excluding fewest from the suffrage; on the other, by opening to all classes of private citizens, so far as is consistent with other equally important objects, the widest participation in the details of judicial and administrative business; as by jury-trial, admission to municipal offices, and, above all, by the utmost possible publicity and liberty of discussion.

—John Stuart Mill[1]

Many forms of government have been tried and will be tried in this world of sin and woe. No one pretends that democracy is perfect or all-wise. Indeed, it has been said that democracy is the worst form of Government except for those other forms that have been tried from time to time.

—Winston Churchill[2]

Democracy is the theory that the common people know what they want and deserve to get it good and hard.

—H. L. Mencken[3]

Should universal suffrage liberal democracy survive? If it should, how should it be reformed, if it is to be made more effective, legitimate, and robust? The answers to the first question will be strongly in the affirmative. Just as market capitalism is the least bad economic system, so is liberal democracy the least bad political system. But again, just as market capitalism needs reform, so does liberal democracy.

Historically, we should remember, states in which rulers were selected by and accountable to a significant proportion of the ruled have been rare and tended either to turn into autocracies (as with the Roman Republic) or been swallowed up by them (as Athens was by Macedonia). Elections have played a role in some important countries for centuries. But the UK, which has had an elected House of Commons, was essentially monarchical or aristocratic until well into the nineteenth century. It can be considered very modestly democratic only after the Great Reform Act of 1832. The Constitution of the United States was deliberately constructed to constrain the will of the majority on multiple dimensions. Franchises were also very limited. Only in the early twentieth century did democracies adopt universal adult franchises, without restrictions for women or slaves, as in earlier republics.

Thus, universal suffrage representative democracy is only about a century old (see chapter 3). It is also fragile. It depends above all on the commitment to the system of all those engaged in it and especially of elites. The democratic recession of today might turn into an outright democratic depression, as in Europe in the 1930s, but this time on a global scale.[4] Nevertheless, the aspiration to democracy remains strong. Close to half the world's countries can be deemed democratic, however imperfect many of those democracies are (see chapter 3, figure 5). Events in Hong Kong in 2019 and 2020 and in Belarus in 2020 ended with suppression of democracy, but also reminded us of the profound desire for rulers to be accountable to the people and for the people to speak freely to power. They reminded us, too, how contemptible "strongmen" rulers almost universally are: at best, they are petty tyrants whose abilities fall far short of their pretensions; at worst, they are psychopathic bullies indifferent to anything but their own power.[5]

This chapter focuses on the possibilities for the renewal of liberal democracy in the countries where it has long been considered consolidated. These are "my" societies. Their crisis is personal. Moreover, if democracy cannot sustain itself in these countries, its future must be grim elsewhere. Finally, these are the most powerful democracies. The US and UK were pioneers of modern liberal democracy and ensured democracy's survival through World War I and II and then the Cold War. The success of these democracies, as well as those of western Europe, is essential if the ideal of liberal democracy is to prosper in the twenty-first century.

The discussion will start with the arguments that democracy just does not work very well even in these countries and should be made far more limited. How persuasive are they? It will then look at alternatives to democracy: how attractive might they be to a person who does not expect to become an autocrat, a plutocrat, a high official of the Chinese communist party, or one of their courtiers? This will then lead to a consideration of the aims and some possible means of democratic renewal.

Defending Democracy

Democracy is indeed flawed, as Churchill suggested. The age-old criticism from the rich and educated (historically, much the same people) is that the electorate does not know what it is doing: voters are ill educated, stupid, emotional, and prone to vote for reasons that have nothing to do with the issues. Plato famously thought this. These critiques are helpful even for those who support democracy, not just because we need to understand why it is worth defending, but even more because they raise important questions about how best to do so.

The critique of democracy

The most concise, beautiful, and influential statement of the democratic ideal was in Abraham Lincoln's Gettysburg Address, which described the republic for which the Union's soldiers had died as government "of the people, by the people and for the people." Unfortunately, this idealistic statement of how democracy works is a myth. This is not how it works. Thus argue Christopher Achen and Larry Bartels in their thought-provoking *Democracy for Realists*.[6]

Voters cast votes not in considered response to issues, but on the basis of tribal identities. Thus, "mostly, they identify with ethnic, racial, occupational, religious, or other sorts of groups, and often—whether through group ties or hereditary loyalties—with a political party."[7] Racial identity explains the success of the southern strategy in cementing plutocracy. This was true in the antebellum South and has remained true in that region ever since and increasingly in other parts of the country, too. For many southern whites, the enactment of civil rights definitively turned the Democrats into the party of the "blacks" they despised. Thereupon, they promptly shifted their allegiance to the Republicans, because many Republicans argued that "freedom" should include the right to discriminate and also appealed to (barely disguised) racist tropes on welfare and crime.[8] Donald Trump was a natural end point of this shift, being in some ways the political heir of Governor George Wallace of Alabama.

Given the overwhelming role identity plays, "Issue congruence between parties and their voters, insofar as it exists, is largely a by-product of these other connections, most of them lacking policy content."[9] The absence of any connection between how the majority of voters cast their votes and their interests is no surprise, but rather, an inevitable consequence of how people think about politics, to the extent that they think about it at all.

Joseph Schumpeter was similarly clear on the failings of voters:

Without the initiative that comes from immediate responsibility, ignorance will persist in the face of masses of information however complete and correct. It persists even in the face of the meritorious efforts that are being made to go beyond presenting information and to teach the use of it by means of lectures, classes, discussion groups. Results are not zero. But they are small. People cannot be carried up the ladder.

Thus the typical citizen drops down to a lower level of mental performance as soon as he enters the political field. He argues and analyzes in a way which he would readily recognize as infantile within the sphere of his real interests. He becomes a primitive again. His thinking becomes associative and affective.[10]

The outcome, critics insist, is bad policy and disappointed voters. Since electorates are tribal, politics also tends toward those wars of factions against which Washington warned in his farewell address.[11] So great would be the spirit of faction, he argued, that one side would seek to seize power, probably in support of a charismatic leader. The spirit of rivalry would then overwhelm the commitment to the rules of the game of a democratic republic. Authoritarianism would triumph.

Some thinkers have argued, in response to such persuasive critiques of how democracy actually works, not just that we *will* abandon universal suffrage democracy, but that we *should* do so. Even the protection against the waywardness and ignorance of voters provided by constitutionally entrenched "representative democracy" is not enough. Instead, the franchise should be restricted to the better informed. Such a system is called "epistocracy," or rule by the knowledgeable. The philosopher Jason Brennan of Georgetown University has recently advanced this position.[12]

Brennan divides voters into three categories: Hobbits, who are "low-information citizens with low interest and low levels of participation in politics"; Hooligans are "higher-information citizens who have strong commitments to politics and to their national identity. They are beset by cognitive biases"; and Vulcans are the ideal type: "perfectly rational, high-information thinkers with no inappropriate loyalty to their beliefs."[13] For Brennan, "In modern democracies, rather than having a one-headed incompetent king, we have a many-headed incompetent king."[14] He would like to limit the franchise to the epistocrats. In this, he is channeling Plato. The Athenian philosopher devoted part of his *Republic* to justifying rule by "philosopher kings," who would be selected from a "guardian" (warrior) class. The wisdom of the guardians and philosopher kings would be ensured by selective breeding and appropriate education (from which the fabrications of the poets, notably Homer, the foremost pet of ancient Greece, would be banned) while their impartiality would be guaranteed by ignorance of the identity of their parents or siblings.[15] Karl Popper argued that Plato's ideas on government marked the birth of totalitarianism.[16]

Rebutting the critique

Yes, democracy is highly imperfect and prone to collapse. Plato, Aristotle, the founding fathers of the US, Winston Churchill, and historical experience have all told us so, whatever precise institutional form—direct, representative, proportional voting, first-past-the post voting, parliamentary, presidential, unicameral, bicameral—democracy takes. Individual voters have a low-stakes interest in their vote because it is unlikely to make any difference to the outcome. It does not make sense for them to invest in understanding the issues. Instead, they cast their votes in imitation of what people they identify with and like do. They also tend toward myopia. Given uncertainty about the future, that, too, makes sense. They are "rationally ignorant."

We are morally, intellectually, and emotionally imperfect. The institutions that we have created, to bring a measure of order and predictability into our lives, are also imperfect. Yet we could not exist without them. Robust states and competent governments have been essential institutions since the agrarian revolution. The scale and complexity of modern societies has made such institutions even more important. If we must have government, no better arrangement exists for choosing the people who run them than some form of democracy. Democracy, after all, is political competition, and competition, as we know from our economic history, tends to work in the long run far better than monopoly, however ostensibly benevolent that monopoly may seem.

Even the arch-skeptic Brennan admits that "democracy is positively correlated with a number of important outcomes, and this appears not to be mere correlation, but causation."[17] The best places to live in the world are democratic. One important indicator is their relative lack of corruption, as noted in chapter 8: in 2019, for example, 18 of the 20 least corrupt countries in the world were full democracies.[18] The US was only 24th, which is disappointing. But it was far ahead of Orban's Hungary, the 70th most corrupt; Xi Jinping's China, 81st most corrupt; Erdogan's Turkey, 82nd most corrupt; and Putin's Russia, 144th most corrupt. The world's leading democracies are strikingly rich and honest. This is no accident. It is because liberal democracies have accountable governments and the rule of law. The first thing a would-be autocrat does is try to suppress those who inform the public of his own corruption and that of his coterie. In a democracy, people can and do make a fuss. That embarrasses the government. The political opposition may even turn it into a scandal, halt the misbehavior, or eject those responsible from power.

Even leading skeptics of the efficacy of democracy also admit, "An independent judiciary, freedom of speech and assembly, and other features of democratic institutions and culture are undoubtedly important."[19] They certainly are. And the full range of such freedoms and protections has existed only in societies in which the governed choose who governs. No absolute monarch or despot would allow such freedoms and protections to his subjects. Since the ruler *must* know best, any disagreement is lèse-majesté. In other words, *liberal* democracy protects the individual's right to think and speak as he or she wishes and to do what he or she wishes, subject to social boundaries and the constraints of a law that applies equally to all. This is why the question of whether Donald Trump will be held legally liable for his attempts to engineer the reversal of the results of the presidential election in 2020 matters so much. If he is deemed above the law on so vital a matter as honest counting in elections, a central pillar of democracy will lie broken.[20]

These wider benefits of democracy are of huge importance. But what is the value of voting itself? Among other benefits, "elections generally provide authoritative, widely accepted agreement about who shall rule. In the United States, for example, even the bitterly contested 2000 presidential election—which turned on a few votes in a single state and a much-criticized five-to-four Supreme Court decision—was widely accepted as legitimate."[21] Legitimate authority is a hugely important benefit. The only other way it has been achieved is by inheritance of some kind, which is far more arbitrary. What does one do if a Caligula is the inheritor? The answer was assassination—a terrible way to decide who rules. Moreover, since the wheel is likely to turn in a democracy, losers can expect to win again another day and so are more willing to tolerate defeat than if it were to be forever. Not least, "electoral competition also provides some incentives for rulers at any given moment to tolerate opposition. The notion that citizens can oppose the incumbent rulers and organize to replace them, yet remain loyal to the nation, is fundamental both to real democracy and to social harmony."[22]

There are other benefits of liberal democracy that depend on voting. Autocracies have no eject button, unlike democracies. The autocrat might be competent, balanced, and far-seeing. But he (historically almost always a "he") is at least as likely to be incompetent or even psychopathic. In countries with regular free elections, the latter types will be removed from office. Of course, such a person might be elected freely, once. That has happened, as in Germany in 1933 or Russia in 2000. But there will then not be another free election, unless or until the tyrant is removed by force. "One person, one vote, once" is, of course, not liberal democracy.

These are cumulatively powerful arguments for free elections. But they are not arguments for universal suffrage. Some indeed think the right to vote should be limited to the well informed (the epistocrats), as mentioned earlier, or to people with specific economic, gender, or ethnic characteristics, as once was the case everywhere. There are, however, overwhelming arguments against such restrictions.

First, there exists no characteristic that clearly separates those worthy to vote from those who are not. Why men, but not better-educated women? Why white people, but not people of color? Why people with a certain wealth or income, but not those with less? These distinctions are all arbitrary. It is a gross error even to believe that the more educated will cast their vote more intelligently than others. As the great eighteenth-century Scottish philosopher David Hume wrote, "Reason is and ought only to be the slave of the passions, and can never pretend to any other office than to serve and obey them."[23] One can debate the view that this *ought to be* the case. But it unquestionably *is* the case. Emotions drive our choices. The more sophisticated the intellect, the more elaborate the cloak over loyalties, prejudice, or self-interest. Thus, "the historical record leaves little doubt that the educated, including the highly educated, have gone astray in their moral and political judgments just as often as anyone else."[24] Many highly educated Germans, including some of the country's greatest intellectuals and most successful businessmen, supported the Nazis. Plenty of highly educated Europeans were communists. Plenty of highly trained experts have been wrong: the failure of economists, policy makers, and financiers to foresee and prevent the global financial crisis is a salient example. The only nonarbitrary criterion for whether people should have the vote is one that divides adults from the immature. A credible diagnosis of dementia might also serve as such a characteristic. Moreover, any attempt to limit the franchise beyond that is not just arbitrary but must lead to repression. While

China may or may not have an epistocracy, it certainly has plenty of repression.

Second, even if it is true, as critics of universal suffrage argue, that most voters are unclear about how politics and policy interact with their interests or even their views, the failures of effective voice in decision-making will be greatly worsened by eliminating some people, usually the poorer and more economically and socially marginal, from the register of voters.[25] So long as people can vote, their interests and views cannot be ignored. The black South Africans and African Americans who fought so hard for the right to vote were not wrong in believing that the vote would make a difference to how they were treated. It did, just not as much as it should have done. Disenfranchising the less educated and poor would certainly ensure less attention to their interests. The Black Act of 1723 in the UK specified more than two hundred offenses, most of them against property, as capital crimes.[26] A parliament that represented a wider cross section of the public could never have enacted such a monstrous piece of legislation. The well-off people who kept the franchise narrow in the nineteenth century understood the benefits to themselves of doing so, as did the whites in the post–Civil War South. The thesis of the Nobel laureate Amartya Sen, that famines are less likely to occur in democracies with a free press, makes the same point: people with political rights matter more politically and so socially.[27] For this reason, he argues, political and liberal rights, including the right to vote, play "an instrumental role in enhancing the hearing that people get in expressing and supporting their claims to political attention (including the claims of economic need)."[28]

Finally, the right to vote shows that people are full members of the political community. They have the right to take part in public life, and those who manage public life are, in turn, accountable to them. It is a statement of membership in the political community as a citizen. Human beings have to act collectively, but how we do so makes a great difference. In the Platonic vision of the state (or that of the contemporary Chinese party-state), most people are subjects: they exist to be told what to do. In democracies, they are citizens. The rulers are servants. The question is how to make this work, not perfectly, but better. To this we now turn.

Democracy is not just good in itself, though it is that. Democracies are not just the world's most prosperous and freest societies, though they are that, too. There also exist no decent alternatives in today's world. One alternative is demagogic authoritarianism, in which would-be autocrats and their enablers erode liberal democracy from within. This is the strategy of a depressingly long list of contemporary politicians. The second is bureaucratic authoritarianism, in which a self-selecting mandarin elite controls all power. This is the strategy of China. Liberal democracies can, alas, be transformed into autocracies or narrow oligarchies. But the resulting regimes will be oppressive, divisive, dehumanizing, and incompetent, as we know from historical experience. Liberal democracies cannot be transformed into bureaucratic authoritarianism without first suffering collapse and revolution. Such regimes may be a success, as China has shown for a few decades, though only after first suffering the unchecked calamities of Mao's tyranny. On one side, then, are failures that the modern West could copy but must not. On the other is a fragile success it cannot (thank heavens) copy at all. This makes life simpler. There is no credible alternative to making the system we have—the combination of liberal democracy with market capitalism—work better, because they need each other.

Restoring Democracy

There have been many proposals for improving the institutions of the West's democracies.[29] This discussion seeks instead to focus on a few fundamentals. Democracies need to combine fair voting with professional politics, disinterested expertise, independent institutions, and, above all, universal civil rights. Crucially, since liberal democracy is not the same as tyranny of the majority, it cannot work without robust safeguards. The most important safeguard is not the precise words of a constitution or body of law, which can be politicized and subverted. What matters are the hearts and minds of the people and especially of elites. A free and democratic society rests ultimately on the links among citizens and between them and the public sphere. As Fernando Henrique Cardoso, former president of Brazil, argues of our contemporary crisis of democracy, "Our challenge is to bridge the gap between *demos* and *res publica*, between people and the institutions of public interest, reweaving the thread that may reconnect the political system with the demands of society."[30]

Necessity of citizenship

Democracy creates, but also demands, citizens. If the wider public and elites are not bound together in the shared endeavor of a democratic republic, it will founder. In all democracies that have endured, this mutual commitment is expressed as patriotism, which has, in turn, included the willingness to fight and die for one's country. But what is patriotism? In 1945, George Orwell famously explained: "By 'patriotism' I mean devotion to a particular place and a particular way of life, which one believes to be the best in the world but has no wish to force upon other people. Patriotism is of its nature defensive, both militarily and culturally. Nationalism, on the other hand, is inseparable from the desire for power. The abiding purpose of every nationalist is to secure more power and more prestige, *not* for himself but for the nation or other unit in which he has chosen to sink his own individuality."[31] To be a citizen of a country, one does not even need to believe its way of life is "the best in the world," any more than a spouse needs to believe their spouse is the best in the world. They need only know they love them, despite their faults, as they are loved in return.

Why is patriotism important?[32] The answer is that liberal democracy means *rule by consent*. One must be willing to accept as legitimate rule by people one despises with ideas one detests. If this combination of consent with dissent is to work, people must place their loyalty to the institutions of the democratic republic—elections, parliaments, the government, and the law—above their attachment to any party, faction, or region. If that deeper loyalty perishes, the democratic republic risks breakdown, perhaps civil war. Moreover, people are rarely devoted to institutions per se, however essential these may be. The loyalty to institutions must in turn be founded upon belief in the norms of equal civil and political rights for all citizens, regardless of their status, gender, ethnicity, or religion, as well as in the right of the winners of a fair election to constitute the government one is obliged to obey, provided it acts in accordance with the law. The great majority of people must accept these fundamental democratic norms.[33] Yet even adherence to such norms may fail to carry the weight of democratic life through all strains. Patriotism works because a shared love of one's country, as a place, a history, an idea, a reality, and a promise of a better tomorrow makes toleration of differences in opinions and values easier and may be all that makes it possible.

This perspective is captured in the remarkable notion of a *"loyal opposition."* It is explained more colorfully in Winston Churchill's defense to a local Tory member of parliament of the Labour leader Clement Attlee, who played a huge role in making him prime minister in 1940 but defeated him in the general election of 1945: "Mr. Attlee is a great patriot. Don't dare call him 'silly old Attlee' at Chartwell or you won't be invited again."[34]

Patriotism is one side of a coin. The other is civic virtue: the understanding that citizens have obligations to one another. This idea is captured in a line from the second century BC Latin poet Ennius: "Moribus antiquis res stat romana virisque." ("The Roman state stands on its ancient traditions and its men.")[35] This again is about much more than obedience to the law. The daily life of people depends on how they behave toward one another, in small things and big ones. COVID-19 was an acid test of civic virtue. Did people believe that they had a duty of consideration and care for one another? In some cases, the answer has been no. A society that lacks such virtues risks becoming feral and disordered.

A big mistake of the Brahmin left has been its contempt for patriotism, particularly working-class patriotism. For the vast majority of ordinary people, citizenship is a source of pride, security, and identity. Attlee, the most successful of Labour prime ministers, was a patriot. So was Ernest Bevin, his most powerful minister. The desire of parts of the contemporary left to excoriate all that their country has done and stood for in the past is destructive of their hopes for winning power and even for democracy itself.

Yet something more concrete is also needed if patriotism is to work in a modern universal suffrage democracy. The cornerstone of contemporary Western democracy is a contract of reciprocity among citizens. Thus, "The benefits of reciprocity within a community were scaled up as the community became the nation."[36] The modern state is not least a mechanism through which citizens can protect themselves against the otherwise uninsurable risks of life: ill health, longevity, unemployment, and destitution.

A seminal event for welfare states was the decision of Otto von Bismarck, the conservative Iron Chancellor, to introduce health insurance in Germany in 1883.[37] He did so in order to neutralize the political appeal of Germany's Sozialdemokratische Partei Deutschlands (Social Democratic Party of Germany). He recognized that the organized working class was sure to demand a measure of security: if the conservatives did not offer it, they would elect socialists who would. Since then, some form of welfare state bargain has become a defining characteristic of all Western high-income, universal suffrage democracies.[38] It is striking, in this context, that the National Health Service was taken as the symbol of British patriotism at the opening ceremonies of the 2012 Olympic Games.

Citizenship necessarily means privileged access to the opportunities afforded by the economy and the insurance provided by the state. Handing such benefits over to "outsiders" who are not part of the reciprocal bargain of citizenship is widely viewed as unfair. Thus, according to one recent paper, "Research on population diversity in the United States suggests that ethnic and racial diversity undermine social trust and solidarity . . . , which in turn negatively influence attitudes toward redistribution."[39] This is a part of the tragedy over race that continues to bedevil the US. The same paper, coauthored by the late Alberto Alesina of Harvard, argues that in Europe, too, "native workers lower their support for redistribution if the share of immigrants in their country is high."[40] Illegal immigrants are likely to be viewed as particularly undeserving, however understandable their desperate desire to achieve safety and enjoy opportunity in a new country. That is why it was a big mistake not to try to control the employment of undocumented workers in the US more strenuously.[41]

Renewing democratic citizenship also requires countries to give people, especially the young, an ethical education, including on what democracy means, how it works, and what the responsibilities of citizens must be. There is also a case for some form of national service aimed at bringing young people of all backgrounds together in shared endeavors. A particularly deep education in civic values and norms is needed for people who aspire to elite positions in society. If history offers one lesson it is that if elites come to be viewed as avaricious, corrupt, lying, and indifferent to the fate of ordinary people, a republic is likely to fall. The story of David Cameron's egregiously rewarded role in lobbying government on behalf of the subsequently bankrupt Greensill Capital is one such example.[42] Without ethical elites, democracy becomes a demagogic spectacle hiding a plutocratic reality. That also is its death.[43]

Dangers of identity politics

Strong ethnic, religious, or other identities may prevent the emergence of an overarching patriotic loyalty. If one wishes to see the consequences in extreme conditions, one need only look at Northern Ireland. Lebanon is an even worse example because there is no outside state able to impose order, as the UK can in Northern Ireland. Where the narrower identities are geographically concentrated, physical separation is feasible, as may soon happen between Scotland and England and did happen between Czechs and Slovaks and between Slovenia and the rest of the former Yugoslavia. But where the different groups live side by side, as in Bosnia or Lebanon, the outcomes may include the horrors of ethnic cleansing or ghettoization.

Even if things do not go this far, narrow and exclusive identities are a problematic basis for democratic politics. One reason for this is that people cannot be defined by just one attribute of ethnicity, race, sex, or gender. They have many and generally overlapping identities. Worse, if we embrace the politics of identity, we are returning to the old politics of ascribed or inherited status, from which our democratic world struggled to escape. That would reverse one of the greatest achievements of the modern era. Yet another reason why identity is a problematic basis for politics is that it leads naturally to the notion of group, rather than individual, rights. Thus, it is believed, members of a given identity group should be granted certain positions in certain proportions as of right. But this risks turning politics into a zero-sum civil war among identity groups.

If this happens, the identity politics of minorities are almost certain to stimulate the identity politics of majorities. Such majoritarian identity politics of culture, religion or race can now be seen all over the world. These are the politics of Recep Tayyip Erdogan in Turkey, Jaroslaw Kaczynski in Poland, and Viktor Orban in Hungary. They are the politics of Donald Trump and the contemporary Republican Party, who increasingly define their identity as white, Christian, and conservative. This is also what is happening in Modi's India, with the appeal to Hindu identity. Majoritarian identity politics is also likely to fuse with an exclusive form of nationalism. The greatest danger of all is that majoritarian identity politics will turn into ethnic domination, in which notions of equal rights for all and of a shared national identity are lost.[44] Such outcomes must be avoided at all cost. The political debate should focus instead on widely shared and measurable predicaments, such as poverty, unemployment, disability, age, sickness, or family responsibilities, none of which is tied to cultural, religious, or ethnic identities.

Yet problems unavoidably arise when certain groups have been treated as if they were a separate "caste," with an ascribed lower status. The most widespread and historically entrenched example of such a caste division has been the status of women. Race has played such a role, too, above all in the US, where the legacy of slavery created a caste of disadvantaged people defined by the color of their skin. India's caste system creates some even bigger challenges. The solution must be to focus on opening opportunities for *all* those in disadvantaged classes, while paying particular attention to those who have suffered from such entrenched discrimination.[45]

Managing immigration

The big question about migration is *how* to control it, not *whether* it should be controlled. The democratic state belongs to its citizens, who are bound by ties of loyalty and trust in one another. It is inevitable that who becomes a member of this community and on what terms is at least as much a political as an economic question.

Immigrants could conceivably be viewed as "metics"—people with rights of residence, but with no obligations or rights as citizens. In many countries, people may live like that indefinitely, subject to deportation if they behave inappropriately. Switzerland seems to be one. Even so, mass deportation is, quite rightly, impossible in a civilized country. In practice, one must assume that immigrants and their children will be present forever. Their potentially permanent presence makes migrants obviously entirely different from trade in goods. If you do not want to continue to buy goods from, say, China, you just stop. You cannot escape from your neighbors. Thus, migration is, even in this shallow sense of belonging, quite different.

In many countries, however, migrants and so their children are entitled, after a time, to become citizens, and rightly so. This is particularly true in "creedal" democracies, which are bound together more by shared ideals than by ethnicity. The basic creeds of modern democracies—individual liberty, equality of legal and political status, fair elections, rule of law, and so forth—are quite similar. But citizens are bound by loyalty to what Benedict Anderson called an "imagined community." The people of a successful country are bound by a shared story of who they are, where they came from, and how it is appropriate to behave. Where this national story has not been fully shared, the outcome has been entrenched social and political division.

Countries that allow immigrants to become citizens assume that they will become a full part of the national community. This process of absorption has been successful in many countries. But scale matters. Turning immigrants into citizens, accepted fully, and participating enthusiastically, is a task of years and of generations. It will go better if immigrants interact substantially with people from other backgrounds, including those born and brought up in the country. Again, for these reasons, quite apart from the economic ones discussed in chapter 8, it is perfectly right and proper to manage immigration and acquisition of citizenship.

The mistake of the far right is to insist that only "kith and kin" can become devoted citizens. But the more sensible right is correct in believing that immigration needs to be controlled. Citizenship of a democracy is exclusive, not inclusive of all of humanity. The mistake of the left is to argue that there must be minimal inequality among people who happen to live in a country, yet no reason to control who these people are. Either one's fellow citizens matter far more to us than foreigners, which is why we are committed to looking after them, or they are of little or no greater significance than foreigners, in which case there is no reason to be particularly concerned about inequality among them. We should then focus on global inequality instead. Citizenship cannot simultaneously matter decisively and hardly matter at all. In fact, citizenship must matter a great deal if one believes in funding a specifically national welfare state, as people of the left do, since it is a system of solidarity with people who live in one's own country.

Immigration can bring huge benefits, not least because immigrants tend to be exceptionally energetic, ambitious, and determined. But it also needs to be controlled. It is necessary to agree on an acceptable compromise on immigration, one that takes account of the obligations of humanitarian relief, economic benefit, and a harmonious society. This will be hard, but it is inescapable.

Limits of meritocracy

It is far better morally and practically for the elite of a society to be selected by merit than by privileges of birth and wealth, as Adrian Wooldridge argues. Yet danger also lies in an unquestioning belief that the competition is a fair one, in unalloyed admiration for intellectual qualities, and contempt for those without them.[46] Decency, reliability, honesty, self-respect, diligence, kindness, and respect for fellow citizens and the law must also be admired and valued. Indeed, such virtues are essential to the health of a liberal democracy. Should the mass of the people become convinced that elites look down upon them, they are likely to feel humiliated, enraged, vengeful, and even willing to pull down the structure of power, even if it falls on their own heads. Moreover, members of the meritocratic elite should not confuse their merits with deserts. We do not create ourselves. Our personal attributes are given to us by birth and environment. While meritocracy is desirable and inescapable, it cannot be the dominant value system of a stable democracy.

Reforming government

A shared identity as citizens and internalization of the fundamental democratic norms are the most important conditions for a successful democracy. But competent governance is also required. Experience with COVID-19 should serve as an alarm bell for Western democracies. Countries in the Chinese cultural sphere have long understood the need for a high-class bureaucracy. The meritocratic bureaucracies of Confucian political systems were invented almost two millennia before comparable systems anywhere else.[47] Effective bureaucracies arrived in Western countries only in the eighteenth and nineteenth centuries. But these remain essential if a modern society is to function. Some modern Western governments seem to have fallen behind the best contemporary standards in this respect. Some of these difficulties are no doubt the result of the obstacles to reaching legislative decisions in some polities, notably the US.[48] But some of the difficulties seem to lie in administrative systems themselves: many find it disturbingly hard to get things done effectively.

The scale and significance of state functions make high-quality administration essential. In the large high-income countries, the share of government spending in gross domestic product prior to COVID-19 ranged from 36 percent in the US to 56 percent in France. (See chapter 3, table 1, and figure 48.) The massive expansion in the share of government spending in GDP is a signal outcome of our democratic age. These figures are larger than the direct government contribution to GDP, because they include transfers, such as unemployment benefits, pension contributions, and similar forms of support. But they also understate the government's actual impact on society and the economy, since they exclude the role of the state in supplying the physical, financial, and regulatory framework governing life in complex modern societies. The range of essential services expected from the state—provision of legal services; supply of infrastructure and housing; protection against enemies, pandemics, natural disasters, crime, and other threats; insurance against penury, unemployment, old age, ill health, and similar misfortunes; regulation of competition, finance, money, and the environment; support for education, scientific research, culture, the arts, and public service news organizations; and, not least, management of the economy and the public finances that pay for much of all this—is enormous. The efficient operation of all this is a sine qua non for civilized life. The only reason this is not universally understood is that, like fish in the sea, many do not recognize the medium in which we live and breathe.

FIGURE 48. GENERAL GOVERNMENT SPENDING IN LARGE HIGH-INCOME COUNTRIES, 2018 (AS A SHARE OF GDP) (PERCENT)
(Source: IMF)

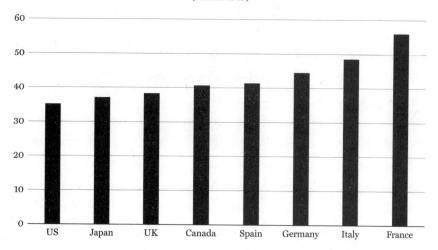

Just as democracy depends on the values of a patriotic citizenship, so does effective administration depend on the values of a meritocratic "eunuch" bureaucracy. What makes it eunuch is that the individuals working in the system must owe loyalty to the state more than to their families or to any individual, notably including the head of government.[49] This is what makes a bureaucracy distinct from a court.

Governments led by demagogues tend to value loyalty far higher than competence.

A central requirement of good government, then, is respect for— and the determination to possess—expertise. Experts can be wrong, particularly if they are tunnel-visioned and isolated from experts in other relevant fields. The failure of economists to recognize the risks of a financial crisis before it happened between 2007 and 2009 offers an example.[50] Most important, only representatives of the people may make the fundamental value judgments: these cannot be left to the experts. The response to COVID-19 has provided an important example. While experts could advise governments on the costs of alternative policies for health or the economy (and even then had to admit vast and unavoidable uncertainty), only governments could decide among options. When governments say they are "following the science," they are talking confusing (and confused) nonsense. The science was not certain enough to follow. More important, science cannot deliver value judgments.[51] Of course, it is also important that the politicians themselves be competent and sensible. Evidence suggests that the performance politics of populist demagogues, such as Jair Bolsonaro, Boris Johnson, Narendra Modi, and Donald Trump, failed to manage the pandemic as well as the competence politics of more sober leaders.[52]

The internet- and social-media-induced plague of conspiracy theories and fraudulent claims to knowledge is poison to good government and the reasoned debate on which democracy depends. We now see increasing contempt for the notion of expertise and a corresponding admiration for those who despise it.[53] If hostility to experts becomes a characteristic of a government, one ends up with disaster. More broadly, as Minouche Shafik, director of the London School of Economics, has said, "The application of knowledge and the cumulation of that through education and dissemination through various media and institutions are integral to human progress. The question then is not how to manage without experts, but how to ensure that there are mechanisms in place to ensure they are trustworthy."[54]

Many democratic governments need substantial renewal of their administrative systems. This is true in terms of both personnel and functions. So far as personnel is concerned, it is essential to identify, attract, and keep the highest possible quality of people, with diverse intellectual and personal backgrounds. This means paying competitively. Moreover, having four thousand political appointees in top administrative jobs, all of whom are thinking about their next job, as in the US, can hardly be conducive to informed or even disinterested government.[55] Singapore provides an alternative model: it offers extremely high pay to top officials but selects them carefully and demands superlatively competent and devoted public service in return. It is important to have a spine of long-serving and dedicated public servants, as well as the ability to attract and use high-quality people on a temporary basis. Diverse intellectual backgrounds should also be valuable. Most difficult policy issues have multiple facets and cannot be decided by people with one dominant professional background or, for that matter, just a high-quality general education. Finally, it is important to respect the independence of the public service and its dedication to the public weal. If government is treated with contempt, it is rather likely to become contemptible.

The more the functions of the state are commercialized, the more difficult preservation of a public service ethos becomes. This is partly because the further this goes, the greater the likelihood that public functions will be subverted for private gain, including the private gain of public servants, if not directly, at least in terms of aspirations for future careers. A deeper reason is that making money comes to be seen as the aim of the exercise and so profit-seeking as the principal virtue, with other goals and the values that serve them reduced to second place. The deepest reason of all is that governments set the rule of the game: they must be and be seen to be *independent, impartial,* and *competent* when doing so.[56] As the late Jane Jacobs taught us, the "guardian" ethos of public service and the law must be kept distinct from the "commercial" ethos of business.[57]

For good reason, governments have delegated powers to independent agencies. The list of such regulatory bodies is very long. In the case of the UK, for example, there are at least twenty regulatory bodies in the health sector alone.[58] Delegation of regulatory powers can (and often does) improve the quality of governance and the people's understanding of what agencies are trying to do. But independent agencies also have enormous influence upon the lives of the people. How, then, are such institutions to be managed? A crucial part of the answer is that they must have first-class staff. Delegation should be to competent and disinterested people and the terms should be as clearly set out and circumscribed and as transparent as possible.[59]

Another issue is devolution of power to local levels. There are many reasons for substantial devolution, in particular the benefits of exploiting local knowledge and (as will be argued in the succeeding section) of ensuring local accountability. Experience supports this. Many of the most successful countries have small populations. Consider Denmark, Finland, Ireland, Israel, New Zealand, Norway, Singapore, Sweden, Switzerland, or, on a slightly bigger scale, Australia, the Netherlands, or Taiwan.[60] These countries are rich, stable, and democratic. Given open world markets and modern communications, they can combine the benefits of *global scale* in business operations with those of *small scale* in politics. This suggests that large countries should be subdivided, with power and responsibility decentralized to the lowest level at which it can be effectively exercised. This idea is known as "subsidiarity." Even many of the successful small countries are themselves highly decentralized. With such decentralization must go decentralization of administrative competence. The success of the federal model in Germany and the capacity for decentralized experimentation in the US supports this idea.[61]

Finally, governance also needs to be transferred upward if states are to serve the interests of their peoples. This is why the post–World War II period saw the creation of the United Nations, a host of important international organizations, such as the International Monetary Fund, the

World Bank, and the General Agreement on Tariffs and Trade, and the European Economic Community. But these are just a small part of the web of treaty arrangements that bind states. The UK, for example, has signed over fourteen thousand treaties.[62] Such institutions and agreements do not undermine sovereignty, but make it more effective: by working together, states can achieve what their citizens need better than they can on their own. In some cases they can *only* achieve what their citizens need in this way. Management of the global commons is the most important example. So is providing predictability in international transactions. Membership in the World Trade Organization allows a country to give more predictable behavior by foreign governments to its citizens, something it cannot give on its own.

Sovereignty may end at the border, but national interests do not. The UK was always sovereign, as its decision to leave the EU showed, but as a member of the EU. It was able to provide its citizens with a degree of opportunity, security, and prosperity they have now lost with Brexit. It is tragic that resurgent nationalism is consuming this compelling idea of sharing power in the common interest.

Ensuring democratic accountability

A further challenge is to make political power accountable to those who depend on it. Representative democracy was a wonderful invention. It allowed the creation of accountable political systems across large geographic areas, even areas as big as the US. It made government accountable to a wide electorate. It encouraged the emergence of a class of professional politicians who act as necessary intermediaries between the electorate and the government.

It is essential to have universal, safe, and secure voting. A situation in which a candidate for office casts doubt on voting itself, as Donald Trump did during the US presidential election of 2020 and the aftermath of his decisive defeat, including the attempted coup at the Capitol on January 6, 2021, was a huge and possibly decisive step toward the death of representative democracy.[63] The electoral system should preclude gerrymandering. Independent commissions should create constituency boundaries. Voting itself should be as secure as technology permits. Ideally, the system of voting and counting should be managed by entirely nonpartisan officials.

An important defect of representation is that children and the unborn cannot vote, while old people can and do. Maybe adults should have more votes the younger they are. Alternatively (or in addition), parents could be given extra votes for their minor children, up to some numerical limit.

A complex issue is that of voting systems. First-past-the-post is a defective system, since it encourages government by the most concentrated minority, not by a majority. After the general election of 2019, for example, Boris Johnson could push through the most extreme form of Brexit with the support of just 43.6 percent of the electorate. Even with the votes of the Brexit party, he had the votes only of 45.6 percent of the electorate. The majority of votes went to parties against Brexit or committed to a second vote. Yet the Tories won a majority of eighty. Such an unrepresentative outcome is questionably democratic. Because the idea of a constituency member of a legislature is desirable and that of party lists undesirable, since it puts individual members under the thumb of party leaders, the best system seems to be the transferable vote, as in Ireland. The basic idea is that second and third (and further) preferences also count, unless first choices deliver an overall majority.[64] Such a system tends to force politics toward the middle, where the bulk of the electorate lies, and to make unrepresentative majorities less likely. The broader consent thus achieved could lead to better, more considered, government.

Another question is whether voting should be compulsory, as in Australia. The argument against this is that participation in politics ought to be a free choice. A further argument is that there is little point in adding further low-information voters. Against this, if voting is obligatory, the state must ensure that it is possible, rather than tolerating (or even sometimes encouraging) suppression of votes. As important, one should not escape so fundamental a duty of citizenship. The arguments for compulsion are strong: everybody should vote.

A crucial issue is the role of political parties. The American founding fathers loathed them, thinking them, in Washington's words, "potent engines, by which cunning, ambitious, and unprincipled men will be enabled to subvert the power of the people and to usurp for themselves the reins of government."[65] Nevertheless, they are an essential means of organizing policy and politics in representative democracies. They play an essential role as bridges between the electorate and power. Yet there are difficult questions about how they should be run, given their essential political function. One is who should choose party leaders or candidates. It is highly desirable that people with a central role in the party and so an interest in reaching out to voters play a leading role. Members of parliament should play the decisive role in choosing the leader in a parliamentary system and party officials should play a leading role in choosing candidates in a presidential system. The aim should be to seek majorities in the population, not satisfy an activist minority. The dominant role of primaries in the US has proved particularly vulnerable to capture.[66] The least bad outcome would be for informed insiders to have a big role in choosing candidates for the presidency. That was the original rationale for the Electoral College. Unfortunately, it no longer performs any independent role in vetting the quality of presidential candidates.[67]

A further issue is party funding. Parties should not be entirely dependent on private money. They need access to public funding. This should not only increase their independence from powerful lobbies but also give them the resources needed to develop good policy. One way of doing this might be to allow taxpayers to donate a certain amount of their tax payment to the political party of their choice in their tax return. This must be seen in terms of the still bigger question of the role of private money in politics. At the very least, there should be complete transparency on all political donations, to causes as well as to parties. Dark money must be eliminated from politics.[68] Ideally, limits on the size of donations should also be imposed.

Direct political donations by corporations and foreigners should be banned. Corporations are not citizens. They have been granted legal personality solely for commercial reasons. That fiction should not extend to politics. On the contrary, it is the job of politics, which represents citizens, to set the framework of laws and regulations within which these powerful and legally privileged entities work. Corporate lobbying should also be subject to control or at the least be made entirely transparent. This is the only way to ensure politics can control their behavior, not the other way around.[69] Equally, foreigners must not be allowed to interfere in elections, including by donating money.[70] These limits on the role of money in politics and on who is entitled to contribute are essential preconditions for the survival of a democracy that not only does belong to its citizens, but is seen to do so.

Beyond this lies the question of strengthening the political system itself. One issue is the role of people of exceptional quality within the legislature. While the government should indeed be selected by the house elected by the people, a "house of representatives," there would be substantial value in also having a "house of merit," to improve and delay legislation and develop studies of important policy issues. I approve of the idea of the UK's House of Lords, though not the current system of appointment, since the House has been packed with political cronies and donors. The value of an appointed house of merit, with limited terms for members (say, ten years, with a tenth replaced every year) selected independently of the government, is substantial. The idea would be to make up the house with people of exceptional achievement in a wide range of civic activities—the law, national and local politics, public service, business, trade unions, media, academia, education, social work, the arts, literature, sports, and so forth. There can be great value in unelected senates, properly constructed and run. A second elected house seems far less useful.

There is also the possibility of building upon the idea of the jury.

I have served on a jury twice. On both occasions, I was impressed by the devotion to duty of the twelve people randomly chosen. The jury is also a way for people to act as responsible citizens, a point made by to Alexis de Tocqueville in his study of American democracy.[71] The Australian economist Nicholas Gruen has been particularly insistent on the idea of introducing selection by lots (sortition), a core practice of Athenian democracy, into contemporary democratic politics.[72] He refers, in this context, to the ancient Greek idea of "isegoria" (ἰσηγορία), or equality of speech. We have lost such equality, with the young and less educated the obvious victims.

There are two fundamental arguments for choosing people by lot: first, the result will be genuinely representative; second, it gets us away from the often ambitious, unprincipled, fanatical, unbalanced, and, not least, *unrepresentative* people who fill representative elected bodies, as well as their manipulative campaigns, made more damaging by contemporary information technology.

Here are three possible ways in which sortition might be introduced into democratic politics.

One would be to create deliberative assemblies to investigate specific contentious issues. These citizen juries would exist for a time-limited period. Their members would be appropriately compensated for lost time and earnings. They would be advised by officials, as jurors are by judges, and be allowed to call witnesses. They would seek to reach an agreed position, or at least one backed by a strong majority of participants. This notion has been successfully operated in Ireland on several issues, including the highly contentious one of abortion. A deliberative assembly of one hundred people, made up of one appointed chairperson and ninety-nine ordinary people chosen by lot, was established in 2016. It advised the Irish parliament on abortion (coming out in favor of "repeal and replace" of the ban then in force) and on the question to be put to the people in a referendum.[73] This deliberative assembly broke the deadlock on the issue. It might have been invaluable if something similar had been done before the Brexit campaign.

Another possibility would be to create a "house of the people," chosen by lottery, alongside the house of representatives and the house of merit. This could be a permanent body of, say, five hundred people, with a chairperson and advisers. Members might be selected to serve for a year, with half replaced every six months. This house of the people could be allowed to halt or delay approval of proposed legislation from the house of representatives. A similar structure could be used, on a smaller scale, in local government, just as similar efforts could be made at local deliberation. A sensible approach might be to start this innovation off at the local government level, learn from experience, and build the idea up to the national level.

A third possibility could be to institutionalize referendums, but subject them to the oversight of the house of the people and the house of merit. Only the house of the people would be allowed to decide whether a petition for a referendum would be granted. The house of the people might also decide, perhaps in conjunction with the house of merit, the precise questions to be asked in a referendum and whether the issue was of constitutional importance. If it was not a constitutional issue, a majority of voters would be sufficient. If it was a constitutional issue, the needed votes in favor might be set as 50 percent of eligible voters or 60 percent of votes. This would satisfy the requirement that constitutions should be entrenched. Such a normalization of referendums would bring ordinary people into the political process, but in a more disciplined way than is now happening in countries like the UK. Switzerland has demonstrated that referendums may make democracy more vital. But they also need to be made part of a disciplined and well-understood constitutional system.

The house of representatives, house of merit, and house of the people should be viewed as complementary. The first would consist of professional politicians, elected by the people, from whom the government would be chosen. It would be where legislation would originate. The second would consist of people of substantial merit who are independent of government. Their job would be to keep the government in check and amend and delay legislation. They would not have an absolute veto. Finally, the third would consist of ordinary people. It, too, could delay legislation. But its more important role would be to consider controversial questions, particularly those likely to go before referendums. The representative principle would remain dominant. But it would not be the only one at work in the constitution.

Revitalizing media

As the late Daniel Patrick Moynihan said almost four decades ago, "Everyone is entitled to his own opinion, but not his own facts."[74] Democracy cannot operate without high-quality media that speak to an agreed set of facts. Nowadays, however, there is no such agreement on facts. This is partly because of the grotesque irresponsibility of some parts of the old media, partly because of politicians who think they can say whatever seems useful today, however false, and partly because of the click-driven advertising model of powerful social media. (See figure 49.)

FIGURE 49. LEADING SOCIAL MEDIA PLATFORMS BY AVERAGE
MONTHLY USERS (MILLIONS)
(Source: Our World in Data)

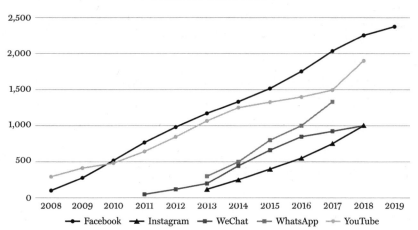

Two decades ago, "cyber-optimists" thought the internet might liberate humanity from government oppression. Instead, we live increasingly in an age of autocrats. Many also thought the internet would make us better informed and more united. Instead, we are drowning in divisive lies. As has been the case with previous transformations in communication technology—writing, printing, cable, radio, and television—the one thing we know is that this new revolution is changing our world permanently, for both good and ill, and doing so very quickly. At present, it looks as though the democracies that emerged with the old media are being destroyed by the new ones.

What might be done to preserve decent media in the hope that this will help us get through the storm? Here are five ideas.

First, countries that are lucky enough to have inherited high-quality public service broadcasters, such as the British Broadcasting Corporation, from a better past should defend them to the death. There is a reasonable question about the range of output of such institutions: news and current affairs are more central to their task than popular entertainment. There is also a reasonable question about how best to fund them. Yet these institutions are still among the most important sources of a body of facts, national sensibility, and national conversation. Without them, we risk ending up with the splintering of the national debate into echo chambers. That almost all politicians think the BBC is biased against them shows it is doing what it needs to do. Moreover, what it provides are classic public goods. We all benefit from the existence of such a national conversation, even if we do not contribute to it. The license fee is understandably controversial, especially now that there are so many other sources of entertainment. One option could be to fund public service broadcasting from a tax on the digital media.

Second, the restrictions the UK has imposed on political advertising on radio and television and the requirements on all broadcasters to be impartial have proved hugely valuable and should be copied. They have prevented the emergence of the hyper-partisan media that are killing democracy in the US, led by Fox "News," that poisonous creation of Murdoch and Roger Ailes. Once people feel their opponents are not just wrong but treacherous, the possibility of maintaining a culture in which the opposition is viewed as "loyal" dies and stealing elections becomes a duty, not a disgrace. Requirements for balance in broadcasting must be maintained if democracy is to endure. Print media have also been capable of generating deep divisions by disseminating lies. With the move of print online, the BBC is again able to help as a balancing factor. Finally, there is a case for extending bans on political advertising to social media, especially bans on advertisements targeted at vulnerable parts of the population.

Third, there is a desperate need for a variety of high-quality news sources, especially at the local level. The loss of advertising revenue has killed most of them. They clearly need public support. Private philanthropy is not enough. Again, the tax on digital media I propose could be used to fund a public trust that supports news-gathering operations, especially local ones. There cannot be a revived local democracy, as is so very desirable, without a revived local media.

Fourth, we must eliminate the most destructive feature of the new media landscape: anonymous comments and posts. We insist that banks know their customers, for good reason. This is aimed at suppressing money laundering and other forms of criminal behavior. Anonymous commenting is similarly noxious. It destroys the possibility of a civil realm for public deliberation. Comments on women seem to be disproportionately vicious. Every organization that posts comments or blogs must, by law, know who the commenter or blogger is. The comment or post may itself be anonymous. But the person concerned must be identifiable and must know that he or she can be identified. There should also be clear legal limits on what can be posted, apart from what is already defined as libel or slander. We have hate-crime laws for good reason. They are a way to allow diverse communities of people to live among one another in a degree of psychological safety. These laws should be enforced online. Moreover, and most important, if we know who posters are, we can identify and cut out the criminal enterprises, many sponsored by foreign governments, that are polluting cyberspaces. This is a war we must fight with all possible means.

Finally, the media are far too socially and politically important to be left to the unmediated whims of private businesses. Facebook is the most important media business in the history of the world. There is a public interest in how the algorithms of Facebook and similar companies work. There should be a public regulator with a high-quality staff checking the implications of these algorithms for the quality of public debate and information. More broadly, Facebook and all other such companies should be recognized for being what they so obviously are: publishers. They must be held responsible for what they publish. That is what being a publisher means. It is that simple. Where what is published is illegal in some jurisdictions, fines must be imposed—if necessary, very extreme ones.

Above all, perhaps, there is a need to mount a major investigation into the impact of the new media on the health of all aspects of our democracy. The US has gone down a rabbit hole of destructive, money-fueled "freedom." The emergence of a leader with fascistic attitudes to the truth and elections has shown that this freedom eats itself. That is unacceptable.

Conclusion

Liberal democracy is a morally better and more successful regime than authoritarianism has ever been. That does not make it perfect. But it does make it worth fighting for and so worth renewing. We need to make our democracies stronger, by reinforcing civic patriotism, improving governance, decentralizing government, and diminishing the role of money in politics. We must make government more accountable. We must have a media that supports democracy rather than destroying it. Only with such reforms is there any hope of restoring vigorous life to that delicate flower, democratic capitalism.

Part IV

—— ■ ——

A HINGE OF HISTORY

Prologue to Part IV

Three enormous transformations are under way. The first, on which this book has focused, is the corrosion of democratic capitalism and the rise of demagogic, autocratic, and totalitarian capitalism as rival ways of organizing politics and economics. The second is the rise of China as a superpower. The last is the need to manage the challenges created by humanity's emergence as the cuckoo in the planetary nest.[1] We should want to preserve freedom, peace, and cooperation. It is going to be a difficult task to do so, given our remarkable capacity for destruction and the authoritarianism, tribalism, and shortsightedness characteristic of our species.

What do these challenges mean for us now? That is the subject of the fourth part of the book. It is perhaps the most important.

CHAPTER TEN

Democratic Capitalism in the World

Let China sleep, for when she wakes, she will shake the world.
— *Attributed to Napoleon Bonaparte*[1]

What do democratic capitalism, the global order, and the global environment have in common? The answer is "fragility." They need to be strengthened. But the complexity and scale of each challenge makes this ever more difficult.

The biggest threats to the survival of liberal democracy are domestic: they come from poor political and policy responses to economic and technological changes. This makes the restoration of democratic capitalism primarily a domestic challenge. But it cannot only be domestic. A country may be an island, but it cannot be isolated. The history of the world over the past five centuries has repeatedly demonstrated that. Managing global relations has always been important. But it has never been as important as in the twenty-first century. Humanity faces many shared challenges: sustaining prosperity; managing pandemics; delivering cybersecurity; containing nuclear proliferation; avoiding war among great powers; and preserving the global commons. In sum, liberal democracies need to preserve the vitality of their own system, while managing their relationships with the rest of the world, in order to preserve peace, prosperity, and planet.

This discussion in this chapter will consider five aspects of these interlocking challenges: defending democratic capitalism in the world; managing global cooperation; avoiding a destructive conflict with China; appreciating Western strengths and China's weaknesses; and managing cooperation, confrontation, and competition with China.

Defending Democratic Capitalism

Liberal democracy is under growing external pressure. The most important sources of such pressure are today's autocratic states, especially China, but also a revanchist Russia (as shown dramatically by its invasion of Ukraine), North Korea, and Iran. It is essential, in response, to strengthen alliances among liberal democracies across the world.

These alliances have always been crucial. Victories in the two world wars and the Cold War would not have been achieved without them. The US was the most potent democratic power, but it could not have achieved its aims without cooperation with other countries. What is more, it was economic success, rather than military power, that proved decisive in destroying the legitimacy of the Soviet system, abroad and at home. Military alliances, especially NATO, were crucial in stabilizing postwar Europe and protecting fragile democracies. But the alliance of democracies was far more than just a military one.

Central in promoting prosperity for themselves and the world have been the combined efforts of the liberal democracies in economics. They created the International Monetary Fund, the World Bank, the regional development banks, and the Organization for Economic Cooperation and Development. They also promoted the rules-based and market-driven multilateral trading system, which culminated in the birth of the World Trade Organization in the mid-1990s. These institutions and arrangements brought forth unprecedented prosperity to the liberal democracies and much of the wider world, including Deng Xiaoping's China.

In many other areas, too, the development of the capitalist market economy has depended on close cooperation among liberal democracies. Such an economy cannot be restricted to just one country, however big that country may be, because there are such huge opportunities in cross-border flows of trade, investment, people, and ideas. Yet, if activity goes across borders, so must at least some regulation. One important example is finance. The need for deep cooperation in financial regulation was demonstrated by the global financial crisis of 2007–09. Indeed, one can argue that finance has never been regulated enough. Another area is tax. For market-oriented states whose economies are also open to the world, cooperation is a condition for effective taxation and regulation of their businesses.

Institutionalized cooperation has been regional as well as global. The most important example is the EU. The cooperation brought about by the integration of the European economy helped generate post–World War II prosperity. This attractive force ultimately pulled the Soviet satellites in central and eastern Europe into the Western orbit. It also made the conflicts that had been a familiar part of European history almost unthinkable. To many English people, living on an island that has not felt enemy boots for centuries, this notion appears to be ridiculous. At least to the older generation of Europeans, it is not. The EU can also go too far in its impulse toward integration. In the case of the monetary union, it arguably did just that. More broadly, the relationship between policy making, often European, and democratic political legitimacy, still largely national, is fraught. Nevertheless, the underlying ideal of a European union was wise and powerful. National sovereignty cannot and should not be viewed as absolute.

Democracies find it relatively easy to form such close and supportive alliances: they are necessarily built on law and have active civil societies, which frequently demand international cooperation. A law-governed democracy should be compelled by its own judiciary to abide by a treaty's terms. Even where agreements are not binding, the fact that a democracy has free media and a free public opinion means that rulers who ignore their external obligations are likely to pay a domestic price. The situation is different in the case of an agreement between, say, Vladimir Putin and Xi Jinping. The constraint on them is only what the other could do. They are subject to no significant domestic constraints. That is what being an autocrat means.

In sum, an alliance of stable liberal democracies is a crucial requirement for the health of democracy in the twenty-first century. This alliance should aim at mutual support—ideological, economic, technological, and military—in a world in which many countries are illiberal democracies, autocracies, or even absolute dictatorships. Democracies will need their mutual alliance and the web of laws, regulations, and institutions it creates to underpin their own security and prosperity and to help manage their dealings with the rest of the world. But if the global public goods of prosperity, peace, and protection of the commons are to be achieved, a degree of cooperation with non-democracies, notably China and even Russia, after its invasion of Ukraine is resolved, will also be essential.[2] We may be unable ever to cooperate with Putin. But Putin will not be forever.

Liberal Democracies in the World

The high-income democracy countries accounted for a mere 16 percent of the world's population in 2019, though they still accounted for 41 percent of global output at purchasing power parity and 57 percent at market prices.[3] So, despite a small share of the world's population, they still possess a huge amount of economic power and influence. Moreover, the high-income countries have many other sources of influence: their companies remain technologically and economically dominant; they contain the great majority of the world's leading universities and research institutes; their ideas and ideals still carry great weight; their currencies are the world's reserve assets; their financial markets dominate those of the world; and they have decisive influence in the world's most significant international institutions. This hegemony is eroding as China rises. But it has not yet gone.

What, then, are the principles on which the relations of the high-income democracies with the rest of the world should be organized? Let us start with economics. During the post–Cold War era of globalization, the answer to this question was to include as many countries as possible in the liberal international order created by the US and its allies after the Second World War. One of the most significant outcomes was the agreement to establish the WTO in 1995, at the end of the Uruguay Round of multilateral trade negotiations. Yet the creation of the WTO turned out to be the high-water mark of institutionalized economic integration. Nothing equivalent has ever been agreed on movement of capital or people, both of which are at least equally important. In those domains, countries are still able to make up their own minds, though how they do so depends on the balance of political forces, with owners of capital particularly potent nowadays. Ideas flow relatively easily, though China is always trying hard to control them.

In today's world, the rules on trade may need to be made more flexible. One argument for doing so is that countries need more "policy space."[4] A simple case for loosening the constraints is that there is now a political backlash against the liberal trade rules of the WTO in many countries, notably the US, even though this backlash is largely because countries failed to develop the policies needed to help their people adjust to shocks. Another is that governments need room to experiment with growth-promoting sectoral policies, free from global constraints. But such loosening of the rules comes at a cost, in the form of greater uncertainty for the traders and especially the exporters from smaller and weaker countries dependent on foreign markets yet lacking the power to defend themselves unaided.

A naive belief persists that moving away from tight rules will be of great benefit to small and poorer countries. The opposite will in fact be the case. In a world without rules that have some moral and practical authority, rich and powerful countries will always be able to protect themselves—or at least the rich and powerful within them—and so force others to bend to their will. Yet even they, and even more their businesses, would benefit from credible rules. It is, to take an important example, easier for a conflict among superpowers to be resolved peacefully and productively if both sides can present necessary compromises not as a humiliating defeat but as the mutually beneficial outcome of a shared commitment to higher principles of trade relations.

Another policy area of importance is development assistance. This remains a moral obligation upon the wealthy and powerful, but there is also a more practical aspect to this. If the world does not mostly contain reasonably prosperous and stable societies, it will remain politically fragile and afflicted by civil wars and pressures for mass migration. In addition to the moral obligations the wealthy and fortunate have toward those less so, they should also recognize their practical interest in a less unequal world, at home and abroad. There needs to be innovations in development assistance, too. A recent example was the Millennium Challenge Corporation, established in 2004, during the administration of George W. Bush, which links lending to policy and institutional reform.[5] One of the most important current opportunities is to encourage the flow of more private capital to developing countries, including by some form of risk-sharing insurance, especially to finance climate mitigation and adaptation. Especially in an era of secular stagnation, it makes sense to encourage the flow of excess savings from high-income countries to poorer ones, perhaps through insurance of tail risks.

It is also appropriate to provide relatively more assistance and economic opportunity to countries struggling to create the foundations of liberal democracy. Indeed, liberal democracies should be interested in the fate of liberal democracies everywhere. As freedom is dwindling or being snuffed out in many countries, including important places like Russia, the alliance of liberal democracies needs to be more active in support of countries that aspire to be or remain democratic.

Nevertheless, we should also remember that direct intervention in the domestic affairs of emerging and developing countries has repeatedly failed. One needs only think of the Vietnam war, the war in Afghanistan, the second Iraq war, and the war in Libya, to realize just how much damage reliance on force has done. It is not that outside intervention never works. It can, but only when the means at the disposal of the so-called international community and the will to use those means are adequate to the task. That was the case in post–Second World War Japan and Germany and subsequently in South Korea and Taiwan. In these cases, both the right circumstances and the will were present. Too often they have not been. In Germany and Japan, the culture of an advanced economy and society also already existed. This made democratization relatively simple. Even in South Korea, which has been a stunning success, the emergence of an advanced economy and democracy took more than a generation.

No wonder the twenty years in Afghanistan were not enough, particularly given the doubts over how long the foreigners would stay. It might have taken a century. Who is prepared to engage anywhere for so long? The answer is that the EU and NATO have been prepared to do so, but only inside Europe, partly because the EU is of necessity already in Europe but also because the US has recognized a long-term strategic interest in European stability and prosperity. This is why the countries of the former Yugoslavia look quite promising today. Before this, Portugal, Spain, and Greece were remarkable successes of democratization. Despite their recent backsliding, countries of central and eastern Europe have also made substantial progress.

A radical possibility for intervention in other parts of the world might be to create mandates under the United Nations. A UN foreign legion might also be established, under the control of the Security

Council. The aim would be to depoliticize interventions and make them as long-lasting as needed where the state has collapsed. A country could be governed in this way until stability returned. One must doubt, however, whether such a radical idea could be accepted in our divided world.

Two decades ago, many hoped that economic openness and rising prosperity would transform China into a country noticeably more democratic and liberal. This was naive, at least on the assumed timetable. Yet it is also hard to believe that China can indefinitely combine a sophisticated information economy and educated population with today's political system. The idea that a bureaucracy dominated by one man will control everything in such a vast and sophisticated country forever seems implausible. A reasonable guess is that the pressure to give the Chinese people a greater say in how they are governed will have to be released at some point. If not, the system might explode. In the meantime, which may be many decades, high-income liberal democracies need to strengthen their relations with one another and with like-minded developing countries.

Russia's invasion of Ukraine has brutally reminded us that hard power remains a frightening reality. The alliance of liberal democracies will have to be effectively armed and both able and willing to defend its vital security interests on land and on sea and in the air and in space. Victory in the Cold War depended on the shield of the NATO alliance in Europe, which provided the peaceful environment in which the burgeoning prosperity of the western European nations could be built.

Many other geopolitical issues arise. These include managing relations with hostile autocracies, such as Iran, Russia, and North Korea, as well as our many shared global challenges. Dealing with all this also will need a core alliance of liberal democracies, ideally one that includes a democratic India, although, unfortunately, the future of Indian democracy is open to doubt under the Hindu nationalism of Narendra Modi and the BJP (Bharatiya Janata Party).

The Delusion of Another "Cold War" with China

Relations with China will be central for liberal democracies. Even in the case of Russia's war on Ukraine, it is hard to believe that Putin would have started without a green light from Xi Jinping. A great number of people in the West and especially in the US are seeing this emerging relationship with China as another Cold War, similar to that with the Soviet Union. This is an unhelpful way of thinking about this relationship. Indeed, in many ways, it will be far more difficult. Given the rising risk of war, as well as the many other dimensions of the relationship, it is likely to prove even more important. Yet it will not be the same.[6]

The underlying Cold War perspective is that this is a zero-sum relationship. Such a view of the US-China relationship is contained in *The World Turned Upside Down* by Clyde Prestowitz. He insists: "There is no contest between the Chinese people and those of the United States."[7] His objection is rather to the communist party. A similar view infuses *The Longer Telegram: Toward a New American China Strategy*, written by an anonymous "former senior government official" (in reference to George Kennan's celebrated long telegram of February 1946, which proposed containment of the Soviet Union).[8] This also states: "The single most important challenge facing the United States in the twenty-first century is the rise of an increasingly authoritarian China under President . . . Xi Jinping."[9] The challenge, it argues, is not China but its despotic state.

The anxiety that infuses these publications is comprehensible: China is not just a rising economic superpower. It has developed what has been, at least hitherto, a stunningly effective blend of a dynamic market economy with a totalitarian state. Its actions in Xinjiang and Hong Kong underline its contempt for human rights and international agreements.[10] It threatens Taiwan's de facto autonomy and is expanding its sway over the South China Sea.[11]

The Longer Telegram argues that the threat from China's attempt to achieve global dominance must be met by defending a long list of vital US interests: retaining collective economic and technological superiority; protecting the global status of the US dollar; maintaining overwhelming military deterrence; preventing Chinese territorial expansion, especially forcible reunification with Taiwan; consolidating and expanding alliances and partnerships; and defending (and, as necessary, reforming) the rules-based liberal international order. Yet, simultaneously, the paper calls for addressing shared global threats, notably climate change.

A great deal of this may seem desirable. But is it feasible? I doubt it. Above all, China is *not* the Soviet Union, and the US is not what it was in the mid-twentieth century.

First, China is a far more potent adversary than the Soviet Union. Graham Allison of Harvard, an authoritative analyst, writes, "The time has come to recognize China as a full-spectrum peer competitor of the United States."[12] China has made enormous economic and technological progress. Its pragmatic strategy of "reform and opening up" allowed it to exploit foreign markets and know-how on a gigantic scale. The strategy was accompanied by forced savings, the highest investment rates in history, especially in infrastructure, rapid upgrading of the skills of the labor force, and mass urbanization. This was much the same approach as those of post–Second World War Japan, South Korea, and Taiwan, but on a far larger scale. By 2019, just before the pandemic, China's output at purchasing power parity had risen to 17 percent of the world's, from a negligible share twenty years earlier. This was still only 42 percent of the aggregate size of the economies of the high-income liberal democracies. Yet China's GDP at purchasing power parity was already 9 percent larger than that of the US, though its GDP remained 33 percent smaller. Crucially, China's population is two-thirds bigger than those of the US, EU, and UK combined.

If its GDP per head at purchasing power parity were to rise from about a third of US levels in 2020 to roughly half over the next few decades, its economy would be roughly as big as those of the US, EU, and UK combined. With a far more successful economy, a more dynamic technology sector, a far larger population, a more cohesive polity, and a more competent government than the Soviets ever had, China is on its way to becoming a comprehensive power at least the equal of the US.

Second, while China is a great power by any standards, it is not an ideological proselytizer in the way the old Soviet Union was. China wishes to limit the ability of its own citizens to criticize their government. It also wishes to limit other countries' ability to criticize, let alone threaten, it. It wishes control in its own neighborhood. It is seeking influence and power, as other great powers have done, including the UK in the nineteenth century and the US in the twentieth and early twenty-first. But it is not trying to turn foreign countries into little images of itself. This is surely because China is far more nationalist than communist and believes it is impossible for foreigners to replicate what only the Chinese could do. China is trying, instead, to make trade, commerce, and investment the foundation of a Chinese-led global order.[13] Viewing China in this light makes more sense than viewing it as an ideological force in the twentieth century mode. It is behaving as other great global powers have done before it but can hope to do so on a larger scale than ever before.[14]

Third, China's economy, unlike that of the Soviet Union, is highly internationally integrated. Although this is a source of vulnerability for China, it is also a source of influence. The Chinese market exerts a magnetic pull on a host of countries across the globe and especially in the Asian region. Most countries want good relations with the US *and* China and not all that many, even some close US allies, will willingly choose the US *against* China.[15]

Fourth, China has gained greatly in international influence and prestige, especially among emerging and developing countries.[16] Many who have lived under Western power and influence for centuries enjoy watching a rising power challenge Western hegemony, even though many do also fear China's power.

Finally, the US has declined since the Cold War, not just in terms of its relative economic power, but also in terms of its reputation for morality, good sense, decency, reliability, and adherence to democratic norms. Whether or not people around the world liked the US, they used to think it knew what it was doing. Thereupon, "three strikes and it was out." First came the global financial crisis, in fact a trans-atlantic financial crisis originating in the US-led financial system, then Donald Trump won the presidency, and finally came the failure to manage COVID-19 competently partly because of the huge political fissures in the population. Above all, "the world cannot unsee the Trump presidency."[17] This is especially true of its end, in the refusal to accept the outcome of the election and the subsequent transformation of the Republican Party into an antidemocratic cult. US policy makers used to talk about the need for China to be a "responsible stakeholder."[18] After the hubris of the "unipolar moment," the Iraq war, the financial crisis, Trump's presidency, and the shambolic management of COVID-19, is the US a responsible stakeholder? Not obviously.

Western strengths and China's weaknesses

Fortunately, the West does have significant assets in a contest for influence with China's form of despotic capitalism. In aggregate, the economies of the US and its allies still exceed that of China by well over two to one. They continue to be at or near the technological frontier in most industries. People around the world may like to see a counterweight to Western hegemony, but they do not for the most part appreciate the Chinese system. The move toward an Orwellian "big brother" society, in which surveillance technology is employed by the party-state to control society down to the very last individual, may work. But it is terrifying, threatening to crush the human desire for autonomy and self-expression.

Democracy is also a self-correcting system, in the obvious sense that a failing government need not be violently overthrown but can be voted out of office instead. Change is far more difficult, delayed, and bloodier under autocracy. It took the deaths of many tens of millions as well as that of Mao Zedong, the man who caused these fatalities, before Deng Xiaoping could alter the system's direction.[19] How many mistakes might dictator-for-life Xi Jinping make before he loses power or dies in office? His persistence with his zero-COVID policy into 2022 indicates how far such foolish policies can go in a totalitarian system. In the long run, absolute rulers almost always become the prisoners of their past, their isolation, and the sycophants who end up surrounding them. Xi now enjoys an extraordinary degree of absolute power. But, as Lord Acton said, "Power tends to corrupt and absolute power corrupts absolutely. Great men are almost always bad men."[20]

China relies on its economic performance for legitimacy, albeit mixed with nationalism. China's real output per head is still less than a third of that of the US, which gives it room to grow quickly. But it is easier to catch up on the economic leaders than to forge ahead of everybody else. It is possible that performance will deteriorate sharply, well before it gets much closer to the productivity levels of high-income democracies. Its economy is already burdened by high debt. This reflects an unbalanced economy, with suppressed consumption, excessive savings, and so an overriding need for high and often wasteful investment. Without radical reform, it may be impossible to sustain high growth without resorting to further rapid increases in indebtedness.[21]

More profoundly, China's economic system confronts a profound strategic dilemma. Xi Jinping's anticorruption campaign should be viewed as a reaction against the corruption attendant upon the economic liberalization of his predecessors, Deng Xiaoping, Jiang Zemin, and Hu Jintao. But his repressive reaction, especially his war on entrepreneurs and the corrupt officials that allowed them to operate, risks stifling the economy. In the absence of clear definition and protection of legitimate action—in simpler terms, in the absence of anything close to a rule of law—the natural response of entrepreneurs in both private and public sectors to Xi's crackdown must be both to risk less and to do less. For a regime whose legitimacy depends on rising prosperity, this creates a painful dilemma between unacceptable stagnation and runaway corruption. That dilemma is, moreover, a necessary feature of markets under bureaucratic absolutism, not a bug.

Cooperating, Confronting, and Competing with China

The relationship with China must be one of cooperation, competition, coexistence, and confrontation, but not, we must hope, of open conflict, let alone of armed conflict. That would be a catastrophe.

So, how might the complex relationship between liberal democracies and China work? Here are five essential elements of what needs to be done.

First, the West needs to appreciate its core strengths and protect its core assets. These include individual freedom and democracy, which remain beacons to a vast number of people around the world, including many Chinese people; maintenance (or perhaps revival) of the historic alliance of the liberal democracies; autonomy in strategic technologies; security in the most important aspects of the economy, notably energy and health; and preservation of a rules-based and cooperative international system. It is necessary that all of these are protected by common action, if necessary. It is essential not least that the US continues to be actively engaged and committed to this alliance.

Second, it is essential for both sides to avoid what Graham Allison calls the "Thucydides trap"—the tendency for mutual suspicion and fear to drive established and rising powers into conflict.[22] This needs to be done via a range of measures aimed at enhancing mutual confidence, protecting core interests, and sustaining a credible balance of power. There will need to be agreement on what those core interests are and how friction over them is to be managed. Above all, it must be understood by both sides that nobody can "win" from a head-on confrontation. War must remain unthinkable, which makes Russia's war in Ukraine so dangerous for all, including China.

Third, it is necessary to promote mutually beneficial interdependence. While both sides want to preserve a degree of strategic autonomy, it is also essential to preserve interdependence, notably in trade and capital flows, but also in other areas. It is good for young Chinese people to study in Western institutions. It is good, too, for both sides to trade with—and invest in—each other. We know that commercial exchange and culture interchange are no panacea: the collapse of pre–First World War Europe into ruinous war demonstrates that economic interdependence may be a far smaller deterrent against suicidal folly than one might hope. Yet it still accounts for something, though only if the interdependence is complemented by measures aimed at ensuring the widest possible sharing of the gains.[23] Meanwhile, there will also be a need to deepen trading relationships with friendly nations.

Fourth, it is necessary to cooperate on common global tasks. We share a small and fragile planet, a complex and interdependent economic system, and a moral imperative to help vulnerable human beings everywhere. In all areas one can imagine—climate, the biosphere, disease, economic development, international debt, financial stability, technological development, peace, and security—a degree of cooperation or, at the least, of mutual understanding will be needed. This is going to be very hard to achieve. But these relationships must be designed to promote mutual confidence.

Finally, it is necessary to make use of carefully designed carrots and sticks. Thus, it is essential to reward China for cooperation, but also to impose penalties on failure to cooperate. This must apply in all areas of concern—security, human rights, the world economy, development, the global environment, and operation of global institutions. Again, none of this will work without carefully considered and coordinated policy on the part of the liberal democracies. The US may coerce allies in certain limited respects. But without wholehearted support of allies, the alliance itself will fail and the US will then end up confronting a rising China on its own.

All this creates challenges. Consider some of those raised by the issues listed above.

First, *security*. It is reasonable for countries to seek to preserve control of technologies fundamental to national security. This is not an argument for total self-sufficiency since that would impose excessive costs. But it is reasonable for liberal democracies to define technologies in which they intend to remain individually or collectively self-sufficient and remove them from the normal rules of international trade. Yet this should, ideally at least, be based on open discussion and explanation of the reasons for such exceptions to the rules.

Security also concerns the ability of countries to protect their core interests in the world. One way of achieving this is via a rough balance of power. It is reasonable for liberal democracies to create alliances that limit China's ability to get its own way. But such alliances must also avoid creating a dangerous ratcheting up of tensions over intrinsically insignificant issues. The Cuban missile crisis of 1962 brought the world to the brink of nuclear war.[24] This was grotesque folly. Humanity cannot afford a repeat of such events. Confidence-building measures are essential. The balance of power must be complemented by the maximum feasible degree of openness and transparency between the leaderships and militaries of the great powers. Ambiguities in such areas invite trouble. An additional risk is misbehavior by junior partners. In the First World War, for example, Austria and Serbia dragged everybody else into war. The war might have happened anyway. But this is a risk that needs to be curtailed, especially in multinational alliances.

A vital aspect of security nowadays is cybersecurity, on many different dimensions: operation of the media, freedom of expression, cyberespionage, and so forth. Liberal democracies need to reduce their huge vulnerabilities in such areas. Most of this has little to do with China or any other external actor. Domestic forces are also dangerous. Yet, whatever the source of the threat, it needs to be contained. Whether this is now technically possible is a big question. Unfortunately, conformity with an international agreement on cybersecurity may at present be impossible to verify. A likely outcome is progressive splintering of the internet—a "splinternet."

Second, *human rights*. Liberal democracy has a core value: the right of people to act freely. This value needs to be defended domestically. But China can use its rising economic clout to influence what people are allowed to say about it. This pressure applies quite obviously to governments.[25] But it also applies to people in business and to scholars and students, especially Chinese students. Liberal democracies should treat Chinese attacks on freedom of opinion and expression on one of them as an attack upon all of them. Sanctions, including sanctions on trade, should if necessary be considered in response, because core values need to be protected at home. But the effectiveness of any such sanctions may be limited.

Third, the *world economy*. Trade is perhaps the most visible dimension of global economic cooperation. Unfortunately, the WTO is failing to manage relations between the US and China. The US has argued that China has failed to live up to its WTO agreement.[26] China argues, in response, the same thing about US behavior and, in the case of Trump's trade war, is right to do so.[27] China's alleged failures were the justification for Trump's assault. The US under Trump also responded to what it saw as the WTO's unacceptable rule making, by rendering the Appellate Body in the dispute settlement process inquorate, thereby making the policing function of the organization ineffective.[28]

The question is how to re-create a legitimate and predictable regime and so avoid collapse into trade anarchy. This is in the interests of the superpowers, too, since it would help take the heat out of their trading relationship. Ideally, what is needed is an ambitious renegotiation of rules and disciplines. The most fundamental difficulty is that the WTO rests on the assumption that its most important member countries are market-oriented, in the traditional Western sense: businesses are privately owned and free to operate, subject to overarching laws that are administered by independent judiciaries. China's economy, with its complex blend of private enterprise, state-owned nonfinancial enterprises, state-dominated banking, and state guidance, subject to the sovereignty of the Chinese Communist Party, is different. Moreover, under Xi Jinping, China is moving backward toward a still more state-dominated model.[29] In view of all this, there may exist no reform of the trading system that will command assent from all sides; certainly there will be none so long as China insists on being treated as a developing country. Yet let us try, not least because China is going to be the world's most important trading power and a pole of magnetic attraction for all other trading countries. Freezing it out of world trade is impossible. Meanwhile, there is a strong case for creating a free trade arrangement open to all liberal democracies.

Trade is not the only economic area where cooperation among major powers is needed. That is also true of exchange rate management, financial regulation, and management of international debt. The bigger the Chinese economic impact becomes, the more important it will be to reach mutually beneficial agreement in such areas. China's rise as a creditor country is particularly important. It is crucial, for example, to ensure that the management of excessive external debt of vulnerable countries is cooperative and the burden of any restructuring or write-downs borne equally. Otherwise, there may be great reluctance to restructure or write-down loans, because of the fear that other creditors will gain rather than the borrowers in difficulty. Huge efforts must be made to cooperate with China in this area, however difficult it will be.

Fourth, *economic development*. There already exists a shared commitment to promoting development. That is why international development agencies exist. It is both a moral and a practical obligation: a less unequally prosperous world would be a better one. There is also no doubt that China has the know-how and the resources needed to help developing countries massively. At the same time, there are concerns about the value developing countries gain from close engagement with China, notably via the Belt and Road Initiative, especially over terms of debt. Close engagement with China on ensuring that this ambitious program works to the benefit of developing countries is vital.[30] Beyond this, liberal democracies interested in promoting economic development will need to cooperate with China and vice versa, if shared development goals are to be achieved. Remember, too, that Western powers have a long history of using it as an excuse for political control. Just consider the history of the Suez or Panama canals. Finally, the democracies could combine their surplus savings with a view to creating a rival to the Belt and Road Initiative for developing countries. Competition in promoting investment in development would even be desirable.

Fifth, *sustainability*. The atmosphere is the heart of this, though biodiversity is also a challenge.[31] This will require an ambitious package of globally implemented measures. It will also require high-income countries to take the lead, because they have the capacity to act relatively quickly and because they remain heavy emitters per head. But the emerging and developing countries and especially China, far and away the largest emitter in the world, will have to play a huge part, too, if the global temperature increase is to be kept below 1.5°C. Again, the question is how to achieve a radical shift onto less emissions-intensive growth paths. High-income countries will have to provide substantial technical and financial assistance to emerging and developing countries. If they can agree on suitably radical commitments of their own, they can also use their powerful collective leverage, especially border taxes, to force China to accelerate the planned decarbonization of its economy, which is currently far too slow. Again, avoid hypocrisy: if the high-income democracies want China to accelerate decarbonization, they must do the same.

If, as one would hope, high-income democracies make carbon pricing part of their answer, they would also need to adopt an offsetting tariff on imports of emissions-intensive goods from countries without equivalent carbon pricing. This would be technically difficult.[32] But it would have three important advantages: it would eliminate at least some of the political resistance to introducing carbon pricing; it would shift global production away from more emissions-intensive technologies and activities; and, finally, it would provide an incentive to other countries, including China, to introduce carbon pricing of their own. This, then, would be an important and justifiable "stick," to ensure that the world implements the needed climate policies.[33]

China must not only play a dominant role in protecting the world climate. It must also play a major role in meeting other environmental challenges, such as protecting biodiversity. It is, for example, the world's third-largest market for fish and fishery products, after the EU and US.[34] It is also believed to be the world's largest importer of endangered wildlife and wildlife products, such as ivory, rhinoceros horn, tiger bones, and so forth.[35] A huge effort needs to be made to change this. China must be made to understand its global responsibility.

Finally, *global governance*. Like it or not, we have created a world in which human beings interact with one another, with the biosphere, the atmosphere, and even space beyond the atmosphere, on an unprecedented scale. If the pandemic has taught us anything, it is this. We are doomed to interact peacefully and cooperatively if anything good is to survive. This takes global governance of just about every imaginable kind. Indeed, it is rather clear we need far more of it, not less of it if we are to manage the challenges that confront us. We need enlightened and close cooperation on, at least, disease, climate, biodiversity, cybersecurity, nuclear proliferation, economic development, trade, macroeconomic stability, and development and use of intellectual property. Achievements in such areas are not impossible. Consider, for example, the Montreal Protocol on Substances That Deplete the Ozone Layer of 1987 and the United Nations Convention on the Law of the Sea of 1994. But while the former has been universally ratified, the US and a number of other countries have still not ratified the latter.[36]

Global governance can no longer be the plaything of the high-income democracies alone. It must be shared with other powers, China above all, but also increasingly India. It is essential to adjust votes and other sources of influence in the global institutions. In 2021, for example, China's share in the total vote in the IMF was still only 6.08 percent, against 16.51 percent for the US, 6.15 percent for Japan, 5.32 percent for Germany, and 4.03 percent for France and the UK.[37] If these voting shares are not adjusted to reflect China's growing power, it is inevitable that China will create international institutions of its own, so dividing the world further. Indeed, it has already started to do so, with the creation of the Asian Infrastructure Investment Bank and the New Development Bank.[38] Equally, the Security Council should be reformed. France should surrender its permanent seat to the EU and the UK should surrender its seat to India. This would at once create a far more representative council.

At the same time, the liberal democracies do have concerns, priorities, and values of their own to defend. Thus, alongside the global institutions that are important in many domains, notably in overseeing management of the global commons, they need also to create and protect informal and formal institutions of their own. Thus, while informal discussions in economics are conducted at the global level in the cumbersome group of twenty (G20), it continues to be valuable for the leading liberal democracies to preserve the group of seven (G7), in which they can develop their positions in concert with countries that are most similar to them, and they trust most. Again, in many areas of regulation—of finance, cyberspace, cybersecurity, media, and so forth—they need to develop systems that work best for them and consequently to accept a substantial degree of fragmentation of the world order.

The Future of Democratic Capitalism in the World

How, then, should stable liberal democracies seek to conduct themselves within this complex and changing world? The argument above can be separated into three fundamental points. First, liberal democracies have their own values and interests. They should defend these, partly by cooperating closely with one another. Second, liberal democracies have many significant interests in the wider world. Again, they should nurture these, by acting together to preserve global order and defend and promote liberal democracy, but they should do so as peacefully as possible. Third, they confront a new superpower with different values and a different system of governance. But they cannot contain China in the way they contained the Soviet Union. China is far too big and globally engaged for that. It is also a country with which deep cooperation is essential in many domains. Thus, a complex web of relations will need to be created with China that protect our core values while sustaining global stability and making global progress. It will be necessary to compete, cooperate, and coexist peacefully on a daily basis. Occasionally, there will be confrontation. But there must not be military conflict. It will be difficult, but it will also be essential, in the interests of all of humanity.

Conclusion:
Restoring Citizenship

It is rather for us to be here dedicated to the great task remaining before us—that from these honored dead we take increased devotion to that cause for which they gave the last full measure of devotion—that we here highly resolve that these dead shall not have died in vain—that this nation, under God, shall have a new birth of freedom—and that government of the people, by the people, for the people, shall not perish from the earth.

—Abraham Lincoln[1]

Romae omnia venalia sunt.
(Everything is for sale in Rome.)

—Sallust[2]

Democracy and competitive capitalism make a difficult, but precious, marriage of complementary opposites. A market economy that operates under trustworthy rules, rather than the whims of the powerful, underpins prosperity and lowers the stakes of politics. In turn, a competitive democracy induces politicians to offer policies that will improve the performance of the economy and so the welfare of the people. Beyond these practical reasons for the marriage of liberal democracy and market economy, there is also a moral one: both are founded on a belief in the value of human agency—people have a right to do the best they can for themselves; people have a similar right to exercise a voice in public decisions. At bottom, both are complementary aspects of human freedom and dignity.

This is not just an abstract and theoretical notion, let alone a utopian one. The world's stable liberal democracies have prosperous market economies, while the prosperous market economies are almost all liberal democracies. There are no exceptions to the former rule. Hong Kong and Singapore may be viewed as exceptions to the latter (though the former, alas, not for much longer). Yet both benefited from an exceptional phenomenon—a benevolent pro-capitalist autocracy. The template for Hong Kong was, however, created by colonial outsiders and is now disappearing under Xi's heavy-handed rule. The rulers of Singapore not only inherited a colonial system, but also must give foreign capitalists, on whose knowledge and connections they rely, the security and openness they need. This is a vital constraint on what they may safely do: if voice is relatively impotent in Singapore, exit is not. China might ultimately become a far more significant exception to the rule that rich market economies are also liberal democracies. But its gross domestic product per head (at purchasing power parity) was still eightieth in the world in 2019, between Suriname and Turkmenistan.[3] For all its progress, it is a very long way from being a high-income country. It is also quite likely to flounder under Xi's increasingly heavy-handed rule.

Prosperity is far from all that this is about, important though it is. On almost any measure one could imagine—life expectancy, educational standards, and the progressive push for equal rights—the high-income democracies are the most successful societies in human history. The freedom they grant, together with their opposition to ascribed status, opens opportunities for improvement of both individuals and society. And what is the alternative? It is either unaccountable rule by thugs and bureaucrats or the iron cage of custom. Both are recipes for stagnation and oppression. They are death to the human spirit and social progress.

For all its faults, democratic capitalism is worth defending. But it is in grave peril. Remember what makes a working democracy: elections must be seen to be free and fair, and victors must be accepted as politically legitimate. For this to happen, the ties that bind participants to one another must be as strong as those that bind people to factions. In chapter 9, I argued that patriotism—a shared attachment to place, history, values, and culture—is the most powerful source of the needed sense of a common identity. Such patriotism may also be called civic nationalism. It may be based in part on myths. But myths are a universal attribute of human communities.

There exist other sources of democratic political legitimacy. An essential one is widely shared prosperity. Another is a shared trust in rules of the game viewed as fair by all. Yet another is confidence that, whoever may (temporarily) be in power, the government will be competent, the law will be impartially applied, and the rights of all people to live their lives freely will be protected. Expressing the foundations of a stable democracy in this way makes clear how fragile it is. Democracy is peaceful civil war. The divisions that emerge in democratic politics may, in the wrong circumstances and with the wrong people, become sources of insurrection, civil war, or creeping authoritarianism in the name of the people. The latter has been happening recently all over the world. It has definitely been happening in the US, the heartland of contemporary democracy, with Donald Trump's insurrection against the presidential election. Democracy is not yet a lost cause. But it is highly endangered.

Elite failures and malfeasance, along with the economic, social, and technological developments discussed earlier in this book, have broken the confidence of many people in the institutions and values of democracy. This has facilitated the rise of the demagogues against whom Plato warned. In the US, above all, the Republican Party has ceased to abide by core democratic norms. It resembles movements in which the Leader's word defined what was true and right more than it does a normal democratic political party. The most notorious example was the Führerprinzip of the Nazis: if the Leader said jump, the question was just "how high."[4] So, too, it now seems to be with Trump. Yet, amazingly and depressingly, the subservience of Republican elites is the product not so much of fear, as it was for many in the Germany of the 1930s, as of personal ambition and moral collapse.

The danger Donald Trump posed to liberal democracy was clear when he was elected on a platform that was part nationalism, part xenophobia, and part cult of personality. As president, he rejected alliances, multilateralism, international rules, science, truth, and the reality of climate change. Yet in 2020, even after the disastrous experience with the pandemic, he won 46.8 percent of the vote. More important, the majority of Republicans agreed with him that the election had been rigged against him by the Democrats.[5] This loyalty continued even after the invasion of the Capitol on January 6, 2021, which he fomented. Indeed, believing in his "big lie" about the stolen election became a litmus test for recognition as a true Republican. The Republicans had moved from being a normal political party in the world's most influential liberal democracy to embracing the view that not only was losing an election ipso facto illegitimate, but riot and murder were acceptable responses. The implications of this for democracy in the US and, given that country's historic role in defending democracy, for liberal democracy worldwide are disturbingly clear.

How did this happen, particularly after the euphoria of the collapse of Soviet communism? The Trump-led Republican Party, or for that matter the Johnson-led Conservative Party, did not come from nowhere. They came from forty years of elite failure. The fragile marriage of liberal democracy with capitalism requires maintaining difficult balances between individual and community, between private and public, between freedom and responsibility, between economics and politics, between money and ethics, between elites and people, between citizen and noncitizen, and between the national and global. This is why MHΔEN AΓAN (Nothing in excess) has been this book's motto. When these balances work, the marriage of liberal democracy with market capitalism is the most successful system in the history of the world. But liberal democracy is vulnerable to the selfishness of elites and ambitions of would-be despots. Historically, democratic republics have been exceptions. The normal human political patterns have been plutocracy or tyranny. The latter always waits in the wings. In today's world, tyrannies—demagogic and bureaucratic—are not just in the wings, but on the march.

Parts III and IV of the book set out an agenda for restoring a balance in both democratic politics and market economics. It takes into account both the internal weaknesses and global responsibilities of liberal democracies. The proposals are pragmatic, but also idealistic. They are based not on revolutionary transformation, but on reform of democratic institutions and economic policies. But we must recognize, too, the scale of the task: the combination of new technology with laissez-faire ideology has accelerated the emergence of a plutocracy dedicated to increasing its wealth and power and of new technologies with extraordinarily destructive potential.

We do indeed need to build on the foundations we have. But we cannot go back to the past. The world of the mid-twentieth century is, for both good and bad, gone forever. We need to "build back better." The path forward is to adapt the goals of the reformers of the past to the needs of the present. The most important reformer of the twentieth century was Franklin Delano Roosevelt. In his speech on January 1941 on the "four freedoms," he laid out a role for the US in the world, predicated upon a domestic transformation. Building on this outline, chapters 7 and 8 set out the following goals for reform of the capitalist economy:

1. A rising, widely shared, and sustainable standard of living
2. Good jobs for those who can work and are prepared to do so
3. Equality of opportunity
4. Security for those who need it
5. Ending special privileges for the few

Removing harms, not universal happiness, is the objective. The approach to reform is that of "piecemeal social engineering," as recommended by Karl Popper, not the revolutionary overreach that has so often brought calamity.[6]

Behind these specific proposals is a wider perspective. A universal suffrage democracy will insist on a citizenship that is both economic and political. This means that business cannot be free to do whatever it wishes. It means that taxes must be paid, including by the economically powerful. It means that the state must be competent and active, yet also law-governed and accountable. All of this was the clear lesson of the twentieth century.

There are, it is true, alternative ways to seek power under democratic capitalism. All will fail. One extreme is to offer a fully socialized economy. But the economy will founder, and the rulers will be forced out of power or seize it undemocratically, as happened most recently in Venezuela. An opposite extreme is to marry laissez-faire economics to a populism founded on anti-intellectualism, racism, and cultural conservatism. Such pluto-populism is also likely to end in an autocracy in which even plutocrats are insecure. A still faster route to autocracy is via a blending of the two extremes in nationalist socialism (or national socialism). This combines a welfare state with arbitrary rule by demagogues. This, too, will ultimately ruin both the economy and democracy, as the unaccountable gangster in charge rewards cronies and punishes opponents.

Interwar Europe, the history of Latin America, and the more recent experience of many emerging and developing economies, including some of the former communist countries of central and eastern Europe, offer copious warnings. The greater the inequality, insecurity, feeling of abandonment, fear of unmanageable change, and sense of injustice, the more vulnerable to collapse the fragile balance that makes democratic capitalism work will become.

If the needed reforms are to happen, elites must play a central role.

A complex society without elites is inconceivable. Alas, one dominated by predatory, shortsighted, and amoral elites is all too plausible. If such elites emerge in a democratic republic, it will collapse. That happened to the late Roman Republic. Anne Applebaum has described brilliantly how it has been happening in Hungary, Poland, and even the UK and US.[7] Liberal democracy is a complex system of restraints, some of them in law, but many tacit. It depends ultimately on truthfulness and trustworthiness in those in positions of responsibility. The corruption, injustice, and lies of elites are powerful solvents of bonds that tie citizens together, inevitably replacing patriotism with deepening cynicism. As the great journalist Hunter S. Thompson declared, "In a closed society where everybody's guilty, the only crime is getting caught. In a world of thieves, the only final sin is stupidity."[8] Only a corrupt oligarchy or autocracy is then possible. Democracy will perish.

Adrian Wooldridge of *The Economist* has rightly argued that members of the elite need to be competent.[9] This is one of the reasons why equality of opportunity is a founding value of a liberal democracy. There is no alternative to some form of meritocracy. All societies have mechanisms for training such elites. But it is not enough for members of elites to be clever, well trained, and ambitious if they are also self-satisfied, narrowly educated, and selfish, possibly even amoral. Members of a functioning elite, which includes the business elite, need wisdom as well as knowledge. Above all, they need to feel responsible for the welfare of their republic and its citizens. Indeed, if there are to be citizens at all, members of the elite must be exemplars. It is not hard: instead of lies, honesty; instead of greed, restraint; instead of fear and hatred, appeals to what Abraham Lincoln called "the better angels of our nature."

Elite failings are pervasive in today's story of the democratic recession in the high-income democracies and elsewhere. This is true on both left and right. It is a failing of the Brahmin elites of the left to downplay the distinction between citizens and noncitizens fundamental to any functioning democracy. It is a failing of that self-same elite to despise the conservative and patriotic values of less-educated fellow citizens. It is a failing, again, to rail against the patriotism on which any liberal democracy must depend.

Yet it is an even greater failing of economically successful elites to push for policies that generate enormous wealth for themselves and insecurity for everybody else. It is a great failing to encourage the emergence of a rigged capitalism, which destroys the legitimacy of the market economy and of the state that protects and promotes it. It is a great failing, above all, to cement power by creating a pluto-populist coalition based on self-seeking at the top and rage at the middle and bottom. It is all too easy to motivate people by hatred and fear and so by a tribalism that divides the world into the "good people" like us, and everybody else. But as society becomes more plutocratic, the sinews that bind citizens together snap. Then comes the false reformer and, worse, the faux populist—the ambitious demagogue who pretends "to drain the swamp" as he makes it wider and deeper.

In his *Republic*, Plato, a fierce critic of democracy, pointed to the likely rise of the sort of demagogue we see all around us today. Instead of democracy, he proposed the selection of "guardians," or philosopher rulers. These guardians would not only be philosophers. They would also be freed from temptation by being without possessions or family. Their children would be raised together. These guardians then would be not just a meritocracy but a monastic one.

The logic is clear. The danger with any elite is that it will subordinate the fulfillment of its vital social role to its personal interests. It can be almost impossible to avoid this. A long time ago, I was told why corruption was rife in the bureaucracy of a certain large developing country. The mechanism was simple and effective. A young, able, and idealistic recruit would be offered a large bribe early in his career. He would refuse it. This would happen a few times. Then, in a private meeting, he would be told by a superior that if he did not take the bribe, he would never be promoted. He thinks of his wife and hopes for a family. And so, next time, he would accept the bribe.

This is blatant. Yet there are so many more subtle ways of corrupting people whose roles in society are those of guardians: lawyers whose only interest is in winning cases; business executives whose only interest is in creating a dynastic fortune; creators whose only interest is in getting the money they need to make their creations a reality; politicians whose only interest is in winning elections; and so forth. As professional standards erode, it becomes ever more difficult to be the exception. Honor and decency come to seem old-fashioned, even ridiculous. And so, when a corrupt thug accuses the elite of being corrupt, not to mention incompetent, it is easy for a great mass of the people to agree, because it is seen to be true. Without decent and competent elites, democracy will perish.

Alas, as I write these last paragraphs in the winter of 2022, I find myself doubting whether the US will still be a functioning democracy by the end of the decade. If US democracy collapses, what future can there be for the grand idea of "government of the people, by the people, for the people"?

We must *not* be complacent about this danger. Democracy is very recent: even a broad male franchise is less than two centuries old anywhere; universal adult suffrage representative democracy is only a little over a century old. For the first time in history, this system recognized the political rights of *all* adult citizens. It was a great achievement. It has already had to confront powerful enemies in World War II and the Cold War.

Yet the enemy today is not without. Even China is not that potent. The enemy is within. Democracy will survive only if it gives opportunity, security, and dignity to the great majority of its people. As Aristotle told us, it depends on a large, contented, and independent middle class. If, in contrast, the system benefits only the most successful, the most cynical, and the greediest, it will founder. If elites are only in it for themselves, a dark age of autocracy will return.

The renewal of capitalism and democracy must be animated by a simple, but powerful, idea: that of citizenship. We cannot just think as consumers, workers, business owners, savers, or investors. We must think as citizens. This is the tie that binds people together in a free and democratic society.[10] It is by thinking and acting as citizens that a democratic political community survives and thrives. If that tie is dissolved, the democratic polity will founder. Its replacement will be some combination of oligarchy, autocracy, or outright dictatorship.

Citizenship must have three aspects: concern for the ability of fellow citizens to have a fulfilled life; the desire to create an economy that allows citizens to flourish in this way; and, above all, loyalty to democratic political and legal institutions and the values of open debate and mutual tolerance that underpin them.

So, what might such a revival of the idea of citizenship mean, in today's challenging global environment?

Here are things this does not mean.

It does not mean that democratic states should have no concern for the welfare of noncitizens. Nor does it mean that it sees the success of its own citizens as a mirror image of the failures of others. On the contrary, it must seek mutually beneficial relations with other states.

It does not mean that states should cut themselves off from free and fruitful exchange with outsiders. Trade, movement of ideas, movement of people, and movement of capital, properly regulated, can be highly beneficial.

It does not mean that states should avoid cooperating closely with one another to achieve shared goals. This applies above all to actions designed to protect the global environment.

Yet there are things it clearly does mean.

It means that the first concern of democratic states is the welfare of their citizens. If this is to be real, certain things must follow.

Every citizen should have the reasonable possibility of acquiring an education that would allow them to participate as fully as possible in the life of a high-skilled modern economy.

Every citizen should also have the security needed to thrive, even if burdened by the ill luck of illness, disability, and other misfortunes.

Every citizen should have the protections needed to be free from abuse, physical and mental.

Every citizen should be able to cooperate with other workers in order to protect their collective rights.

Every citizen, and especially successful ones, should expect to pay taxes sufficient to sustain such a society.

Those who manage corporations should understand that they have obligations to the societies that make their existence possible.

Citizens are entitled to decide who is allowed to come and work in their countries and who is entitled to share the obligations and rights of citizenship with them.

Politics must be susceptible to the influence of all citizens, not just the wealthiest.

Policy should seek to create and sustain a vigorous middle class, while ensuring a safety net for everybody.

All citizens, whatever their race, ethnicity, religion, or gender are entitled to equality of treatment by the state and the law.

The West cannot go back to the 1960s. It cannot go back to a world of mass industrialization, where most educated women did not work, where there were clear ethnic and racial hierarchies, and where the Western countries still dominated the globe.

Moreover, we face today, with climate change, the rise of China and the transformation of work by information technology—very different challenges. The world has changed too profoundly for nostalgia to be a sane response.

Yet some things remain the same. Human beings must act collectively as well as individually. Acting together, within a democracy, means acting and thinking as citizens.

If we do not do so, democracy will fail, and our freedoms will evaporate.

It is our generation's duty to ensure it does not. It took too long to see the danger. Now it is right there in front of us.

This is a moment of great fear and faint hope. We must recognize the danger and fight now if we are to turn the hope into reality. If we fail, the light of political and personal freedom might once again disappear from the world.

Acknowledgments

I submitted the proposal for this book to my agent, Andrew Wylie, in August 2016. I planned to write it over two summers, as I had done with my previous books, and submit it at the end of 2018. As it transpired, I submitted a completed draft in the early summer of 2021, almost three years late. I completed a final version, after two rounds of editorial comments, in June 2022.

Self-evidently, this project has proved far more time-consuming than I had hoped. The main explanation is that it proved far more ambitious than I had imagined. It required me to keep up with what turned out to be significant further developments, notably the career of Donald Trump, the ramifications of Brexit, and COVID. It required me to venture beyond economics into a huge literature on politics, especially on the rise of populism. It required me to think more deeply on the relationship between politics and economics in general, and democracy and capitalism more specifically. Only the reader can judge whether this effort was worthwhile. But it surely was an effort, not just intellectually but also morally, since it required me to reconsider and in some cases reject many prior beliefs.

Since completing the book proved so much more difficult and took so much longer than I had expected, my thanks, too, must be more effusive than those offered after completion of my previous three books, *Why Globalization Works*, *Fixing Global Finance*, and *The Shifts and the Shocks*.[1]

I must start, as before, with my remarkable agent, Andrew Wylie, whose belief in me proved immensely heartening from the very beginning of this project. I also want to thank Stuart Proffitt and Scott Moyers of Penguin Press for taking on the book and sticking with it despite the delays. Even more important were the detailed editorial comments they (and their colleague Helen Rouner) provided on successive versions of the book. The book is, as a result, substantially shorter, better focused, and clearer than it would otherwise have been. Good editors drive authors mad. They also make the difference between a turgid and ill-focused book and one that is at least somewhat better written and constructed. I am grateful to them all.

I owe enormous thanks to four people who have read and commented on the entire book. One is Nicholas Gruen, an Australian economist, who is also among the most original thinkers I have known. As an independent consultant, he is superbly unconstrained by conventional ways of thinking. He has influenced this book in many ways, but especially in the discussion of political reform. Another is Mervyn King, former governor of the Bank of England, who has been a friend for some three decades. I have always admired his intelligence and integrity. I am hugely grateful to him for giving me once again so many helpful and supportive comments. Yet another is Robert Johnson, founding president of INET (the Institute of New Economic Thinking). His comments and, above all, his vast erudition made a huge contribution to the book. The fourth is Daniel Wolf, my brother and only sibling. No other person I know shares so completely my sense of the perils of our time. This anxiety is rooted in our inherited awareness of the great catastrophe of interwar Europe, which made our parents homeless and led to the slaughter of almost every member of their wider families. No other person could help me frame so precisely what I have to say.

I would also like to thank Lionel Barber, editor of the *Financial Times* when I began this task, and Roula Khalaf, his successor, for their support and patience. I have taken off a huge amount of time to write the book, indeed very much more than I had hoped. I appreciate how generously the *FT* has accommodated the effort. I would also like to thank colleagues whose ideas have helped me gain greater clarity. These include Jonathan Derbyshire, for frequent conversations on politics and philosophy; Gideon Rachman, for many discussions, especially on the rise of the "strongmen"; Alec Russell, for reading one crucial chapter at an early stage; Edward Luce, for educating me on US politics; Martin Sandbu, for the many ideas in his writings for the *FT* and especially his book, *Economics of Belonging*;[2] and John Thornhill, particularly for his thoughts on the impact of technology, notably in media.

Inevitably, countless others have influenced my ideas in many ways over the years. It would be impossible to list them all. But I am particularly grateful for the friendship and guidance of Larry Summers. In the last decade his resurrection of the idea of "secular stagnation" and his critique of the fiscal policies of the Biden administration have been particularly helpful. Others who have been particularly important to me as friends and sources of ideas are Andy Haldane, formerly at the Bank of England, and Paul Collier and John Kay, both of whom I have known since we were at Nuffield College, Oxford, together more than half a century ago. I would also like to thank Eric Lonergan for many stimulating conversations over the years.

Finally, I must, as always, give my thanks to my family.

My children, Jonathan, Benjamin, and Rachel, and my grandchildren, Zach, Rebecca, Alex, Anna, Abigail, and Eden, are the delight of my life and in the most profound sense also its purpose. They make me care about the future because it is *their* future.

Far above all others, I thank Alison, my wife and companion of more decades than she would care to admit. I thank her for her encouragement and support in writing this book. Without her, I am sure it would have been abandoned. Alison is the best editor I have ever had. I thank her for reading all the drafts and giving me, as she has always done, comments that were sensible, perceptive, and to the point: I thank her for forcing me to explain what I mean to a highly intelligent reader not directly involved in these debates. The value of such a reader is beyond measure. In the Book of Proverbs, it asks: "A woman of valor who can find? For her value is far beyond jewels." In Alison, I found such a woman, and I thank her for giving me everything that could make a man's life happy. My gratitude and love are far beyond anything I can hope to convey. She has been the miracle of my life.

Needless to say, none of these people bear responsibility for the many failings of this book.

NOTES

Preface: Why I Wrote This Book
1. This seems never to have been said by Mark Twain. See "History does not repeat itself, but it rhymes," *Quote Investigator*, https://quoteinvestigator.com/2014/01/12/history-rhymes/.
2. "Martin Wolf Accepts the Gerald Loeb Lifetime Achievement Award," *Financial Times*, July 3, 2019, https://www.ft.com/content/5e828d50-9d86-11e9-b8ce-8b459ed04726.
3. Martin Wolf, *Why Globalization Works* (London and New Haven: Yale University Press, 2004).
4. Martin Wolf, *Fixing Global Finance* (Baltimore and London: Johns Hopkins University Press and Yale University Press, 2008 and 2010) and *The Shifts and the Shocks: What We've Learned—and Have Still to Learn—from the Financial Crisis* (London and New York: Penguin, 2014 and 2015).
5. See Sergei Guriev and Daniel Treisman, *Spin Dictators: The Changing Face of Tyranny in the 21st Century* (Princeton, NJ, and Oxford: Princeton University Press, 2022).
6. See Masha Gessen, *Surviving Autocracy* (London: Granta, 2020).
7. See Anne Applebaum, *Twilight of Democracy: The Seductive Lure of Authoritarianism* (London: Allen Lane, 2020).
8. Edmund Burke, "Reflections on the Revolution in France," 1790, in *The Works of the Right Honorable Edmund Burke*, vol. 3 (London, 1899), 359, https://www.bartleby.com/73/1715.html.
9. New World Encyclopedia, "Golden Mean (Philosophy)," https://www.newworldencyclopedia.org/.
10. See Friedrich A. Hayek, *The Road to Serfdom* (London: Routledge, 1944), and Karl Polanyi, *The Great Transformation: The Political and Economic Origins of Our Time* (Boston: Beacon Press, 1957; first published 1944).

Chapter One: The Fire This Time
1. The title of this chapter is in homage to *The Fire Next Time*, by James Baldwin, published in 1963.
2. Francis Fukuyama, "The End of History?" *National Interest* 16 (Summer 1989): 3–18, https://www.jstor.org/stable/24027184.
3. On the nature of Polish populism, in particular, see an excellent article by Slawomir Sierakowski, director of the Institute for Advanced Study in Warsaw: "The Five Lessons of Populist Rule," January 2, 2017, *Project Syndicate*, https://www.project-syndicate.org/commentary/lesson-of-populist-rule-in-poland-by-slawomir-sierakowski-2017-01.
4. On Trump's admiration for strongmen, see Domenico Montanaro, "6 Strongmen Trump Has Praised—and the Conflicts It Presents," May 2, 2017, http://www.npr.org/2017/05/02/526520042/6-strongmen-trumps-praised-and-the-conflicts-it-presents. On his view of the Western alliance, see Gideon Rachman, "Atlantic Era under Threat with Donald Trump in White House," *Financial Times*, January 19, 2017, https://www.ft.com/content/73cc16e8-de36-11e6-86ac-f253db7791c6. On his support for trade protection, see "The Inaugural Address," January 20, 2017, https://trumpwhitehouse.archives.gov/briefings-statements/the-inaugural-address. On his day-to-day interventionism, see Greg Robb, "Nobel Prize Winner Likens Trump 'Bullying' of Companies to Fascist Italy, Germany," MarketWatch, January 6, 2017, http://www.marketwatch.com/story/nobel-prize-winner-likens-trump-bullying-of-companies-to-fascist-italy-germany-2017-01-06?mg=prod/accounts-mw, which cites remarks by Edmund (Ned) Phelps, Nobel laureate in economics.
5. From somewhat different starting points, books by Barry Eichengreen and Robert Kuttner agree that economic forces have played a significant role in the erosion of domestic support for the

Western political and economic systems. See Eichengreen, *The Populist Temptation: Economic Grievance and Political Reaction in the Modern Era* (New York: Oxford University Press, 2018), and Kuttner, *Can Democracy Survive Global Capitalism?* (New York: W. W. Norton, 2018). John B. Judis, *The Populist Explosion: How the Great Recession Transformed American and European Politics* (New York: Columbia Global Reports, 2016), makes the point especially well.

6. This idea is hardly novel. Among many other discussions, the works of the German sociologist Wolfgang Streeck stand out. See *Buying Time: The Delayed Crisis of Democratic Capitalism*, trans. Patrick Camiller (London and New York: Verso, 2013), and *How Will Capitalism End? Essays on a Failing System* (London and New York: Verso, 2016). See also Timothy Besley, "Is Cohesive Capitalism under Threat?" in Paul Collier, Diane Coyle, Colin Mayer, and Martin Wolf, eds. "Capitalism: What Has Gone Wrong, What Needs to Change, and How It Can Be Fixed," *Oxford Review of Economic Policy* 37, no. 4 (Winter 2021): 720–33. Besley's term "cohesive capitalism" seems to be quite close to my term "democratic capitalism." See also Besley and Torsten Persson, *Pillars of Prosperity: The Political Economics of Development Clusters* (Princeton, NJ: Princeton University Press, 2011).

7. When writing about the nineteenth century, one can either say that there were no democracies or—given the need to distinguish, say, the late-nineteenth-century UK from czarist Russia—one can talk of a country being a form of "democracy" if there were elections on a wide, albeit limited, franchise, particularly one that continued to exclude women.

8. See "The Universal Value," in Larry Diamond, *The Spirit of Democracy: The Struggle to Build Free Societies throughout the World* (New York: Henry Holt, 2009), chapter 1.

9. John Stuart Mill, *Considerations on Representative Government*, 1861, Project Gutenberg, https://www.gutenberg.org/files/5669/5669-h/5669-h.htm.

10. Isaiah Berlin, "Two Concepts of Liberty" in *Four Essays on Liberty* (Oxford: Oxford University Press, 1969), 118–72, https://cactus.dixie.edu/green/B_Readings/I_Berlin%20Two%20Concepts%20of%20Liberty.pdf.

11. See William A. Galston, *Anti-Pluralism: The Populist Threat to Liberal Democracy* (London and New Haven: Yale University Press, 2018).

12. On illiberal democracy, see Fareed Zakaria, *The Future of Freedom: Illiberal Democracy at Home and Abroad* (London and New York: W. W. Norton, 2007).

13. I discussed globalization at length in *Why Globalization Works* (London and New Haven, CT: Yale University Press, 2004).

14. Tom Bingham, *The Rule of Law* (London: Penguin, 2011), 8.

15. Martin Wolf, *The Shifts and the Shocks: What We've Learned—and Have Still to Learn—from the Financial Crisis* (London and New York: Penguin, 2014), "Conclusion."

16. Ibid., 352–53.

Chapter Two: Symbiotic Twins: Politics and Economics in Human History

1. Aristotle, *Politics*, trans. T. A. Sinclair, revised and re-presented by Trevor J. Saunders (London: Penguin Classics, 1981), Book I, 13.

2. See Eric D. Beinhocker, *The Origin of Wealth: The Radical Remaking of Economics and What It Means for Business and Society* (Cambridge, MA: Harvard University Press, 2006), 8–9.

3. "Energy capture" is a direct measure of the ability of a society to exploit energy sources. By "western," Professor Morris refers to western Eurasia, North Africa, and the Americas. By "eastern," he refers to eastern Eurasia. The logic of this distinction is that the former not only interacted with one another very closely over the millennia, but descended economically from shared cultural ancestors who lived in Mesopotamia. Similarly, the latter also interacted with one another closely, but in this case descended economically from shared cultural ancestors who lived between the Yellow and Yangzi rivers. See Ian Morris, "Social Development," Stanford University, October 2010, http://ianmorris.org/docs/social-development.pdf, 12.

4. Maya Wei-Haas, "Controversial New Study Pinpoints Where All Modern Humans Arose," *National Geographic*, October 28, 2019, https://www.nationalgeographic.com/science/article/controversial-study-pinpoints-birthplace-modern-humans.

5. *World Atlas*, "List of Primates by Population," https://www.worldatlas.com/articles/list-of-primates-by-population.html.

6. See Martin Wolf, "Humanity Is a Cuckoo in the Planetary Nest," *Financial Times*, March 9, 2021, https://www.ft.com/content/a3285adf-6c5f-4ce4-b055-e85f39ff2988. See also Partha Dasgupta, *The Economics of Biodiversity: The Dasgupta Review—Full Report*, April 23, 2021, https://www.gov.uk/government/publications/final-report-the-economics-of-biodiversity-the-dasgupta-review.

7. See Richard Leakey and Roger Lewin, *The Sixth Extinction: Biodiversity and Its Survival* (London: Weidenfeld and Nicolson, 1996).

8. Although the human population has risen substantially, so has real output per head. It follows that the proposition of Thomas Malthus that population increase would always outstrip output growth, bringing incomes per head back to subsistence, has proved definitively false, on two dimensions: First, it has been possible to generate exponential increases in real output over two centuries; and, second, it has been possible to curb population growth via deliberate control over fertility. See Malthus, *An Essay on the Principle of Population*, 1798, http://www.esp.org/books /malthus/population/malthus.pdf.

9. Angus Maddison, http://www.ggdc.net/maddison/oriindex.htm.

10. Conference Board, "Total Economy Database," May 2017, https://www.conference-board.org/data /economydatabase/

11. Yuval Harari, *Sapiens: A Brief History of Humankind* (London: Vintage Books, 2014).

12. On the emergence of tribes, Francis Fukuyama, *Political Order and Political Decay: From the Industrial Revolution to the Globalization of Democracy* (London: Profile Books, 2014).

13. Benedict Anderson, *Imagined Communities: Reflections on the Origin and Spread of Nationalism* (London and New York: Verso, 1983).

14. The late Mancur Olsen called these rulers "stationary bandits," arguing that they at least had some interest in increasing prosperity of the state, because that would also make the ruler richer and more powerful. See *Power and Prosperity: Outgrowing Communist and Capitalist Dictatorships* (New York: Basic Books, 2000).

15. S. E. Finer, *The History of Government: Ancient Monarchies and Empires*, vol. 1, *Ancient Monarchies and Empires* (Oxford: Oxford University Press, 1997 and 1999), "The Conceptual Prologue," 196.

16. The great German sociologist Max Weber invented this nomenclature. See Francis Fukuyama, *Political Order and Political Decay: From the Industrial Revolution to the Globalization of Democracy* (London: Profile Books, 2014).

17. Walter Scheidel, *The Great Leveler: Violence and the History of Inequality from the Stone Age to the Twenty-first Century* (Princeton, NJ, and Oxford: Princeton University Press, 2017), 43.

18. Branko Milanovic, Peter H. Lindert, and Jeffrey G. Williamson, "Measuring Ancient Inequality," National Bureau of Economic Research Working Paper 13550, October 2007, especially figure 2, http://www.nber.org/papers/w13550.pdf.

19. On the importance of the failure to re-create anything similar to the Roman Empire in western Europe, see Walter Scheidel, *Escape from Rome: The Failure of Empire and the Road to Prosperity* (Princeton, NJ: Princeton University Press, 2019).

20. UK Parliament, "Simon de Montfort's Parliament," https://www.parliament.uk/about/living-heritage /evolutionofparliament/originsofparliament/birthofparliament/overview/simondemontfort/.

21. See, on creative destruction in the market economy, Philippe Aghion, Céline Antonin, and Simon Bunel, *The Power of Creative Destruction: Economic Upheaval and the Wealth of Nations*, trans. Jodie Cohen-Tanugi (Cambridge, MA: Belknap Press of Harvard University Press, 2021). See also Martin Wolf, "How 'Creative Destruction' Drives Innovation and Prosperity," *Financial Times*, June 11, 2021, https://www.ft.com/content/3a0aa7cb-d10e-4352-b845-a50df70272b8.

22. See Jan De Vries, "The Industrial Revolution and the Industrious Revolution," *Journal of Economic History* 54, no. 2 (1994): 249–70, http://www.jstor.org/stable/2123912.

23. Karl Polanyi made this last point in his classic book *The Great Transformation: The Political and Economic Origins of Our Time* (Boston: Beacon Press, 1957; first published 1944).

24. Kenneth Pomeranz ascribes the success of western Europe and the failure of China to launch the industrial revolution to environmental factors, particularly the location of coal in western Europe and its easy access to resources from the New World. See Pomeranz, *The Great Divergence: China, Europe, and the Making of the Modern World Economy* (Princeton, NJ: Princeton University Press, 2000).

25. Daron Acemoglu and James A. Robinson, *Why Nations Fail: The Origins of Power, Prosperity, and Poverty* (New York: Crown Business, 2012), argue that institutions explain development.

26. See Deirdre McCloskey, *Bourgeois Equality: How Ideas, Not Capital or Institutions, Enriched the World* (Chicago: University of Chicago Press, 2016). Joel Mokyr, *The Enlightened Economy: An Economic History of Britain 1700–1850* (New Haven, CT, and London: Yale University Press, 2009), also provides a superb account of how Enlightenment ideas animated economic progress.

27. Robert C. Allen, "The British Industrial Revolution in Global Perspective: How Commerce Created the Industrial Revolution and Modern Economic Growth," 2006, https://www.nuffield.ox .ac.uk/media/2162/allen-industrev-global.pdf.

28. The classic study of Indian industrial and trade policies after independence was Jagdish N. Bhagwati and Padma Desai, *India: Planning for Industrialization* (Oxford: Oxford University Press, for the Development Center of the Organization for Economic Co-operation and Development, 1970).

29. Adrian Wooldridge points to the revolutionary consequences of the meritocratic idea in *The Aristocracy of Talent: How Meritocracy Made the Modern World* (London: Allen Lane, 2021).

30. Larry Siedentop, *Inventing the Individual: The Origins of Western Liberalism* (London: Allen Lane, 2014), 349. Dierdre McCloskey of the University of Illinois makes much the same argument, this time with a focus on the economy, in *Bourgeois Equality*.

31. It may be argued that contemporary China is seeking to operate a form of market economy, without equal political rights. It would be accurate to declare that nobody has political rights in China. This, too, is a form of political equality. Only the communist party has rights. People merely have obligations, from the highest to the lowest. Even Xi Jinping has no rights, as an individual. He has rights only as chairman of the party. This is why some argue that the party's sovereignty has replaced that of the emperor. Whether this is a sustainable political form is a great question of our era—to be explored further in later chapters.

32. In republics that continued to have ascribed status, other ways of constraining the political power of the upper classes have been employed, such as the "tribunes of the people" of the ancient Roman Republic. See "Tribune (Roman Official)," *Britannica*, https://www.britannica.com/topic/tribune-Roman-official.

33. Benjamin Friedman, *The Moral Consequences of Economic Growth* (New York: First Vintage Books Edition, 2006), 327.

34. On the role of a strong middle class in creating democracy, see among many others the classic work by J. Barrington Moore, *Social Origins of Dictatorship and Democracy: Lord and Peasant in the Making of the Modern World* (Boston: Beacon Press, 1966). It is important to distinguish its role in the nineteenth century from its subsequent role. Once representative democracies had been created, they could also be imitated.

35. Carnegie Corporation of New York, "Voting Rights: A Short History," https://www.carnegie.org/our-work/article/voting-rights-timeline/.

36. In *The Anxious Triumph: A Global History of Capitalism 1860–1914* (London and New York: Allen Lane, 2019), David Sassoon argues that the global spread of capitalism and the ceaseless change it brought about demanded and created a political response, including linked demands for democratic political rights and radical reforms.

37. Robert Lowe, Lord Sherbrooke 1811–1892, British Liberal politician, in *Oxford Essential Quotations*, 5th ed., https://www.oxfordreference.com/view/10.1093/acref/9780191843730.001.0001/q-oro-ed5-00006834.

38. Daniel Ziblatt, *Conservative Parties and the Birth of Democracy* (Cambridge: Cambridge University Press, 2017), 363.

39. This is a theme of Olsen, *Power and Prosperity*.

40. Albert O. Hirschman made this distinction in his classic *Exit, Voice, and Loyalty: Responses to Decline in Firms, Organizations, and States* (Cambridge, MA: Harvard University Press, 1972).

41. See Daron Acemoglu and James A. Robinson, *The Narrow Corridor: States, Societies, and the Fate of Liberty* (London and New York: Viking and Penguin Press, 2019).

42. Martin Wolf, "The Narrow Corridor—the Fine Line between Despotism and Anarchy," *Financial Times*, September 26, 2019, https://www.ft.com/content/d8eaaaba-deee-11e9-b112-9624ec9edc59.

43. Anders Aslund, *Russia's Crony Capitalism: The Path from Market Economy to Kleptocracy* (New Haven, CT: Yale University Press, 2019). See also Catherine Belton, *Putin's People* (London: William Collins, 2020).

44. See "UK treaties," https://www.gov.uk/guidance/uk-treaties.

45. Plato, *The Republic*, trans. Benjamin Jowett, http://classics.mit.edu/Plato/republic.html. Karl Popper attacked Plato's political views as totalitarian in *The Open Society and Its Enemies*, vol. 1, *The Age of Plato* (London: Routledge, 1945).

46. Martin Wolf, "Donald Trump Embodies How Great Republics Meet Their End," *Financial Times*, March 1, 2016, https://www.ft.com/content/743d91b8-df8d-11e5-b67f-a61732c1d025; Wolf, "A Republican Tax Plan Built for Plutocrats," *Financial Times*, November 21, 2017, https://www.ft.com/content/e494f47e-ce1a-11e7-9dbb-291a884dd8c6; and Wolf, "How We Lost America to Greed and Envy," *Financial Times*, July 17, 2018, https://www.ft.com/content/3aea8668-88e2-11e8-bf9e-8771d5404543.

47. Plato, *Republic*, Book VIII, http://classics.mit.edu/Plato/republic.9.viii.html.

48. That was the argument of John O'Sullivan, the conservative blogger, in an influential article on Trump published in May 2016. See "Democracies End When They Become Too Democratic," *New York*, May 1, 2016, http://nymag.com/daily/intelligencer/2016/04/america-tyranny-donald -trump.html.

49. In a compelling book, *Disordered Minds: How Dangerous Personalities Are Destroying Democracy* (Hampshire: Zero Books, 2018), the Irish writer Ian Hughes suggests such men tend to be narcissists or psychopaths. He argues that democracy is a vital defense against such people. But Plato rightly suggests that the defense may fail. See also Martin Wolf, "The Age of the Elected Despot Is Here," *Financial Times*, April 23, 2019, https://www.ft.com/content/9198533e-6521-11e9-a79d -04f350474d62.

50. Samuel E. Finer, *The Man on Horseback: The Role of the Military in Politics* (Abingdon and New York: Routledge, 1962 and 2017).

51. Martin Wolf, "A New Gilded Age," *Financial Times*, April 25, 2006, https://www.ft.com/content /76def9b0-d481-11da-a357-0000779e2340. See also Wolf, "How We Lost America to Greed and Envy," *Financial Times*, July 17, 2018, https://www.ft.com/content/3aea8668-88e2-11e8-bf9e-87 71d5404543.

52. Aristotle, *Politics*, trans. T. A. Sinclair, revised and re-presented by Trevor J. Saunders (London: Penguin Classics, 1981), especially Books IV and V.

53. Julian Baggini, "Aristotle's Thinking on Democracy Has More Relevance Than Ever," *Prospect*, May 23, 2018, https://www.prospectmagazine.co.uk/philosophy/aristotles-thinking-on-democracy -has-more-relevance-than-ever.

Chapter Three: The Evolution of Democratic Capitalism

1. Thucydides, *History of the Peloponnesian War*; epigraph text from "Thucydides, Pericles' Funeral Oration," http://hrlibrary.umn.edu/education/thucydides.html.

2. For an interesting history of democracy, see David Stasavage, *The Decline and Rise of Democracy: A Global History from Antiquity to Today* (Princeton, NJ, and Oxford: Princeton University Press, 2020).

3. See Adam Przeworski, "Conquered or Granted? A History of Suffrage Extensions," *British Journal of Political Science* 39, no. 2 (April 2009): 291–321, and "Universal Suffrage," https://en.wikipedia .org/wiki/Universal_suffrage.

4. See Larry Diamond, "Facing Up to the Democratic Recession," *Journal of Democracy* 26, no. 1 (January 2015): 143, http://www.journalofdemocracy.org/sites/default/files/Diamond-26-1_0.pdf.

5. "Global Trends in Governance, 1800–2018," Center for Systemic Peace, http://www.systemicpeace .org/polityproject.html.

6. See "U.S. Voting Rights Timeline," https://a.s.kqed.net/pdf/education/digitalmedia/us-voting-rights -timeline.pdf.

7. See Diamond, "Facing Up," 144.

8. Ibid.

9. Freedom House, "Democracy Under Siege," *Freedom in the World 2021*, 1, https://freedomhouse .org/sites/default/files/2021-02/FIW2021_World_02252021_FINAL-web-upload.pdf.

10. Martin Wolf, "The American Republic's Near-Death Experience," *Financial Times*, January 19, 2021, https://www.ft.com/content/c085e962-f27c-4c34-a0f1-5cf2bd813fbc; and "The Struggle for the Survival of US Democracy," *Financial Times*, May 11, 2021, https://www.ft.com/content /aebe3b15-0d55-4d99-b415-cd7b109e64f8.

11. Roberto Stefan Foa and Yascha Mounk, "The Danger of Deconsolidation: The Democratic Disconnect," *Journal of Democracy* 27, no. 3 (July 2016): 6.

12. Ibid., 8.

13. R. S. Foa, A. Klassen, M. Slade, A. Rand, and R. Collins, "The Global Satisfaction with Democracy Report 2020" (Cambridge, UK: Centre for the Future of Democracy, 2020), 12, https://www .cam.ac.uk/system/files/report2020_003.pdf.

14. Larry Diamond, *Ill Winds: Saving Democracy from Russian Rage, Chinese Ambition, and American Complacency* (New York: Penguin Press, 2019), 4.

15. This section draws from Martin Wolf, *Why Globalization Works* (London and New Haven, CT: Yale University Press, 2004), chapters 7 and 8.

16. See David Sassoon, *The Anxious Triumph: A Global History of Capitalism 1860–1914* (London and New York: Allen Lane, 2019).

17. On the evolution of the company, see John Micklethwait and Adrian Wooldridge, *The Company: A Short History of a Revolutionary Idea* (London: Phoenix, 2003), and Colin Mayer, *Prosperity: Better Business Makes the Greater Good* (Oxford: Oxford University Press, 2018), part 2.

18. See FRED Economic Data, table 1.14, https://fred.stlouisfed.org/release/tables?rid=53&eid=17676&od=2021-01-01#, and Gross Domestic Product, https://fred.stlouisfed.org/series/GDP.

19. This conception goes back to a classic article by the late Ronald Coase. See "The Nature of the Firm," *Economica* 4, no. 16 (1937): 386–405, https://onlinelibrary.wiley.com/doi/full/10.1111/j.1468-0335.1937.tb00002.x.

20. The seminal figure on the role of management in the modern corporation was Peter Drucker.

21. See William J. Baumol, *The Free-Market Innovation Machine: Analyzing the Growth Miracle of Capitalism* (Princeton, NJ: Princeton University Press, 2004).

22. "Monopsony" and "oligopsony" refer to the role of businesses as buyers in the marketplace.

23. See Thom Hartmann, *Unequal Protection: How Corporations Became "People"—and How You Can Fight Back* (San Francisco: Berrett-Koehler, 2010); and Colin Mayer, *Firm Commitment: Why the Corporation Is Failing Us and How to Restore Trust in It* (Oxford: Oxford University Press, 2013).

24. See Emmanuel Saez and Gabriel Zucman, *The Triumph of Injustice: How the Rich Dodge Taxes and How to Make Them Pay* (New York: W. W. Norton, 2019).

25. See Luigi Zingales, Jana Kasperkevic, and Asher Schechter, *Milton Friedman 50 Years Later, Pro-Market*, 2020. Stigler Center for the Study of the Economy and the State, https://promarket.org/wp-content/uploads/2020/11/Milton-Friedman-50-years-later-ebook.pdf/.

26. Luca Pacioli, known as the "Father of Accounting," lived between 1447 and 1517 in Italy. On the creation of chartered accountants in the nineteenth century, see Richard Brown, *A History of Accounting and Accountants* (London: Routledge, 1905).

27. James K. Galbraith wrote the seminal work on countervailing power in the early 1950s. See Galbraith, *American Capitalism: The Concept of Countervailing Power* (New York: Houghton Mifflin, 1952), especially chapter 9.

28. John Kenneth Galbraith introduced the concept of countervailing power in his classic book *American Capitalism*.

29. See Alec Nove, *An Economic History of the USSR, 1917–1991* (London: Penguin Economics, 1993).

30. See, for an excellent discussion of the conference that created the postwar global economic order, Benn Steil, *The Battle of Bretton Woods: John Maynard Keynes, Harry Dexter White, and the Making of a New World Order* (Princeton, NJ: Princeton University Press, 2013).

31. Saez and Zucman, *Triumph and Injustice*, xvi.

32. "History of Taxation in the United Kingdom," https://en.wikipedia.org/wiki/History_of_taxation_in_the_United_Kingdom.

33. On the correct use and pervasive abuse of the phrase "Washington Consensus," which he himself invented in 1989, see the late John Williamson's "The Washington Consensus as Policy Prescription for Development," January 2004, https://www.piie.com/publications/papers/williamson0204.pdf. Williamson listed a set of ten modest reforms as reflecting that consensus. He did not mean what is now frequently called the "neoliberal" agenda. But the belief that "Washington Consensus" and "neoliberalism" are virtually synonyms has become almost universal.

34. See Business Roundtable, "Statement on the Purpose of a Corporation," August 19, 2019, https://opportunity.businessroundtable.org/ourcommitment/.

35. Karl Marx and Frederick Engels, *The Communist Manifesto*, 1848, 16.

36. Ronald Findlay and Kevin H. O'Rourke, "Commodity Market Integration, 1500–2000," from Michael D. Bordo, Alan M. Taylor, and Jeffrey G. Williamson, eds., *Globalization in Historical Perspective* (Chicago: University of Chicago Press, 2003), 14, http://www.nber.org/chapters/c9585.pdf.

37. For a brief discussion, see Joshua J. Mark, "Silk Road," World History Encyclopedia, http://www.ancient.eu/Silk_Road/. For a remarkable historical study, see Peter Frankopan, *The Silk Roads: A New History of the World* (London: Bloomsbury, 2015), especially chapter 1.

38. By far the best account of the role of trade in the world economy over the last millennium is in Ronald Findlay and Kevin H. O'Rourke, *Power and Plenty: Trade, War, and the World Economy in the Second Millennium* (Princeton, NJ: Princeton University Press, 2009).

39. Adam Smith, *An Inquiry into the Nature and Causes of the Wealth of Nations*, 5th ed. (London: Methuen, 1904; first published 1776), http://www.econlib.org/library/Smith/smWN.html.

40. Ronald Findlay and Kevin O'Rourke, "Commodity Market Integration, 1500–2000," 25, https://www.tcd.ie/Economics/TEP/2001_papers/TEPNo13KO21.pdf.

41. See "Trade and Globalization," Our World in Data, https://ourworldindata.org/trade-and-global
ization. Trade ratios are computed using GDP at purchasing power parity. The long-run data this
source uses are reported in Antoni Estevadeordal, Brian Frantz, and Alan M. Taylor, "The Rise
and Fall of World Trade, 1870–1939," National Bureau of Economic Research Paper No. 9318,
November 2002, figure 1, http://www.nber.org/papers/w9318. The data for 1870 to 1949 are from
Mariko J. Klasing and Petros Milionis, "Quantifying the Evolution of World Trade, 1870–1949,"
March 29, 2014. The data for 1950 to 2011 are from Penn World Tables 8.1, https://rdrr.io/cran
/pwt8/man/pwt8.1.html; https://papers.ssrn.com/sol3/papers.cfm?abstract_id=2087678.

42. Prometheus was the mythical titan who brought fire to humanity, thus earning the anger of Zeus,
king of the Greek gods. Thus, the growth brought about by the taming of fire can rightly be
termed "Promethean." See Deepak Lal, *Unintended Consequences: The Impact of Endowments,
Culture, and Politics on Long-Run Economic Performance* (Cambridge, MA, and London: MIT Press,
2001).

43. Marx and Engels, *The Communist Manifesto*, 16.

44. On the history of Britain's role as a promoter of free trade, see Frank Trentmann, *Free Trade Nation: Commerce, Consumption, and Civil Society in Modern Britain* (Oxford: Oxford University
Press, 2009).

45. Findlay and O'Rourke, "Commodity Market Integration, 1500–2000," 40, https://www.tcd.ie
/Economics/TEP/2001_papers/TEPNo13KO21.pdf.

46. Ibid., 42.

47. Ibid.

48. This is the title of an important book by Kenneth Pomeranz: *The Great Divergence: China, Europe,
and the Making of the Modern World Economy* (Princeton, NJ: Princeton University Press, 2000).

49. Karl Polanyi famously recognized this "double movement," by which he meant the movement
toward laissez-faire followed by the reaction against it, in the form of regulation. He argued that
the latter was spontaneous and nonideological, while the former was deliberate and intensely
ideological. There is some truth in this. But the anti-liberal reaction clearly had important (albeit
diverse) ideological elements, which became increasingly important as the nineteenth century
turned into the twentieth. See Polanyi, *The Great Transformation: The Political and Economic Origins of Our Time* (Boston: Beacon Press, 1957), 141–43.

50. On bilateralism, see Douglas Irwin, "Multilateral and Bilateral Trade Policies in the World Trading System: An Historical Perspective," in *New Dimensions in Regional Integration*, ed. J. de Melo
and A. Panagariya (Cambridge: Cambridge University Press, 1993), 90–127.

51. Tom Friedman of *The New York Times* was an influential protagonist of globalization. See Thomas
L. Friedman, *The World Is Flat: The Globalized World in the Twenty-first Century* (London and
New York: Penguin, 2005). See also Martin Wolf, *Why Globalization Works* (London and New
Haven, CT: Yale University Press, 2004).

52. Martin Wolf, "The US-China Conflict Challenges the World," *Financial Times*, May 21, 2019,
https://www.ft.com/content/870c895c-7b11-11e9-81d2-f785092ab560.

53. See World Bank, "World Development Indicators," http://data.worldbank.org/data-catalog/world
-development-indicators.

54. See International Monetary Fund, "Global Trade: What's Behind the Slowdown," *World Economic
Outlook*, October 2016, chapter 2, 63. See also Gary Clyde Hufbauer and Euijin Jung, "Why Has
Trade Stopped Growing? Not Much Liberalizaton and Lots of Micro-protection," Peterson Institute for International Economics, March 2016, https://piie.com/blogs/trade-investment-policy
-watch/why-has-trade-stopped-growing-not-much-liberalization-and-lots.

55. IMF, "Global Trade: What's Behind the Slowdown," figure 2.1, 64, and IMF, *World Economic
Outlook* database, October 2019, https://www.imf.org/external/pubs/ft/weo/2019/02/weodata
/index.aspx.

56. See Martin Wolf, "The Tide of Globalization Is Turning," *Financial Times*, September 6, 2016,
https://www.ft.com/content/87bb0eda-7364-11e6-bf48-b372cdb1043a; and "Sluggish Global
Trade Growth Is Here to Stay," *Financial Times*, October 25, 2016, https://www.ft.com/content
/4efcd174-99d3-11e6-b8c6-568a43813464.

57. On the "Doha Development Round," launched in 2001, see World Trade Organization, "Doha
Development Agenda," https://www.wto.org/english/thewto_e/whatis_e/tif_e/doha1_e.htm. On
the TPP, an agreement among Australia, Brunei Darussalam, Canada, Chile, Malaysia, Mexico,
New Zealand, Peru, Singapore, and the US, negotiated under President Barack Obama and repu-
diated by Donald Trump on January 23, 2017, see James McBride, Andrew Chatzky, and Anshu

Siripurapu, "What Next for the Trans-Pacific Partnership (TPP)?" Council on Foreign Relations, September 20, 2021, https://www.cfr.org/backgrounder/what-trans-pacific-partnership-tpp. On TTIP, see "Making Trade Policy," http://ec.europa.eu/trade/policy/in-focus/ttip/.

58. Donald Trump, "Inaugural Address," January 20, 2017, https://www.whitehouse.gov/inaugural -address.

59. Martin Wolf, "Donald Trump Creates Chaos with His Tariffs Trade War," *Financial Times*, July 10, 2018, https://www.ft.com/content/ba65ac98-8364-11e8-a29d-73e3d454535d. See also "21st Global Trade Alert Report: Will Awe Trump Rules?" (London, Center for Economic Policy Research, 2017), https://www.globaltradealert.org/.

60. Aime Williams, "Persistence of Donald Trump's China Tariffs Frustrates US Business," *Financial Times*, June 3, 2021, https://www.ft.com/content/fb775a22-eaa5-44b4-8643-16c3f40a5d02.

61. On the CPTPP, see Dominic Webb and Matt Ward, *The Comprehensive and Progressive Agreement for Trans-Pacific Partnership*, House of Commons Library, June 22, 2021, https://researchbriefings .files.parliament.uk/documents/CBP-9121/CBP-9121.pdf. The UK has applied to join the CPTPP.

62. On RCEP, see Robin Harding and John Reed, "Asia-Pacific Countries Sign One of the Largest Free Trade Deals in History," *Financial Times*, November 15, 2020, https://www.ft.com/content /2dff91bd-ceeb-4567-9f9f-c50b7876adce; and Robin Harding, Amy Kazmin, and Christian Shepherd, "Asian Trade Deal Set to Be Signed after Years of Negotiations," *Financial Times*, November 11, 2020, https://www.ft.com/content/ddaa403a-099c-423c-a273-6a2ed6ef45f2.

63. Chris Giles, "Brexit Is an Example of Deglobalisation, Says Carney," *Financial Times*, September 18, 2017, https://www.ft.com/content/9b37cf6e-9c82-11e7-9a86-4d5a475ba4c5.

64. See Full Fact, "Everything You Might Want to Know about the UK's Trade with the EU," November 22, 2017, https://fullfact.org/europe/uk-eu-trade/.

65. Peter Nolan, *Is China Buying the World?* (Cambridge and Malden: Polity, 2012). Professor Nolan demonstrates the extraordinary domination of important global industries by a small number of predominantly western companies that he calls "systems integrators." See also Martin Wolf, "Why China Will Not Buy the World," *Financial Times*, July 9, 2013, https://www.ft.com/content /28d1a4a8-e7ba-11e2-babb-00144feabdc0.

66. Richard Baldwin, *The Great Convergence: Information Technology and the New Globalization* (Cambridge, MA: Belknap Press of Harvard University Press, 2016).

67. See Martin Wolf, "Donald Trump Faces the Reality of World Trade," *Financial Times*, November 22, 2016, https://www.ft.com/content/064d51b0-aff4-11e6-9c37-5787335499a0.

68. Baldwin, *The Great Convergence*.

69. Robert Kuttner stresses these political consequences of trade in an era of unprecedentedly mobile trade. See *Can Democracy Survive Global Capitalism?* (New York: W. W. Norton, 2018), especially chapter 8.

70. Data are from the IMF's *World Economic Database*, April 2021. Data for 2019, rather than 2020, are used in order to avoid the distortions created by COVID-19 in the latter year.

71. These data are from World Trade Organization, *World Trade Statistical Review 2020*, table A7, 83, https://www.wto.org/english/res_e/statis_e/wts2020_e/wts2020chapter06_e.pdf.

72. Daron Acemoglu, David Autor, David Dorn, Gordon H. Hanson, and Brendan Price, "Import Competition and the Great US Employment Sag of the 2000s," *Journal of Labor Economics* 34, no. 1 (part 2, January 2016): 141–98, http://www.journals.uchicago.edu/doi/pdfplus/10.1086 /682384.

73. David H. Autor, David Dorn, and Gordon H. Hanson, "The China Shock: Learning from Labor Market Adjustment to Large Changes in Trade," National Bureau of Economic Research Working Paper Number 21906, January 2016, http://www.nber.org/papers/w21906.

74. On the reversal of globalization, see Martin Wolf, "The Tide of Globalization Is Turning," *Financial Times*, September 6, 2016, https://www.ft.com/content/87bb0eda-7364-11e6-bf48-b372cdb1043a.

75. On the adoption of exchange controls by the UK during World War II, see "The U.K. Exchange Control: A Short History," *Bank of England Quarterly Bulletin*, 1967, Third Quarter, https://www .bankofengland.co.uk/-/media/boe/files/quarterly-bulletin/1967/the-uk-exchange-control -a-short-history.pdf. See also Forrest Capie, *Capital Controls: A 'Cure' Worse Than the Problem?* (London, Institute of Economic Affairs, 2002), http://www.iea.org.uk/sites/default/files/publica tions/files/upldbook135pdf.pdf.

76. On the post–2007 financial crises, see Martin Wolf, *The Shifts and the Shocks: What We've Learned—and Have Still to Learn—from the Financial Crisis* (London and New York: Penguin, 2014 and 2015).

77. The data for the years before the Second World War come from Nicholas Crafts, *Globalization*

and Growth in the Twentieth Century, IMF Working Paper WP/00/44 (Washington, DC, International Monetary Fund, 2000), https://www.imf.org/external/pubs/ft/wp/2000/wp0044.pdf. The data for the postwar era, up to 2000), come from Maurice Obstfeld and Alan M. Taylor, "Globalization and Capital Markets," in Michael D. Bordo, Alan M. Taylor, and Jeffrey G. Williamson, eds., *Globalization in Historical Perspective* (Chicago: University of Chicago Press, 2003), 143, figure 3.3, http://www.nber.org/chapters/c9587pdf. After 2000, the data come from McKinsey Global Institute, *The New Dynamics of Financial Globalization,* August 2017, 7, exhibit E4. See also Philip R. Lane and Gian M. Milesi-Ferretti, "The External Wealth of Nations Mark II, Revised and Extended Estimates of Foreign Assets and Liabilities 1970–2004," *Journal of International Economics* 73, no. 2 (2007): 223–50; and Stephen D. King, *Grave New World: The End of Globalization and the Return of History* (London and New Haven, CT: Yale University Press, 2017), 72.

78. Alan M. Taylor, "International Capital Mobility in History: The Saving-Investment Relationship," National Bureau of Economic Research Working Paper Number 5743, September 1996, http://www.nber.org/papers/w5743.pdf.

79. Michael Bordo, Barry Eichengreen, and Jongwoo Kim, "Was There Really an Earlier Period of International Financial Integration Comparable to Today's?" National Bureau of Economic Research Working Paper 6738, September 1998, 4. On British net assets, see Forrest Capie, *Capital Controls: A "Cure" Worse Than the Problem?* (London: Institute of Economic Affairs, 2002), 33.

80. Data are from the IMF, *World Economic Database,* April 2018.

81. The way in which the policies of Asian emerging economies shifted the global pattern of current account imbalances, the role of self-insurance and the impact that had on the financial system were the focus of the analysis in Martin Wolf, *Fixing Global Finance* (Baltimore and London: Johns Hopkins University Press and Yale University Press, 2008 and 2010), and Martin Wolf, *The Shifts and the Shocks: What We've Learned—and Have Still to Learn—from the Financial Crisis* (London and New York: Penguin, 2014 and 2015). On the development of global imbalances, see also Pierre-Olivier Gourinchas and Hélène Rey, "From World Banker to World Venture Capitalist: U.S. External Adjustment and the Exorbitant Privilege," in Richard H. Clarida, ed., *Current Account Imbalances: Sustainability and Adjustment* (Chicago: University of Chicago Press, 2007), 11–66, https://www.nber.org/chapters/c0121.pdf.

82. Martin Wolf, "Dealing with America's Trade Follies," *Financial Times,* April 18, 2017, https://www.ft.com/content/fca7e9a4-2366-11e7-a34a-538b4cb30025.

83. IMF, *World Economic Database,* April 2018.

84. D'Vera Cohn, "How U.S. Immigration Laws and Rules Have Changed throughout History," Pew Research Center, September 30, 2015, https://www.pewresearch.org/fact-tank/2015/09/30/how-u-s-immigration-laws-and-rules-have-changed-through-history/.

85. On the history of migration regimes, see Jeffrey G. Williamson, "The Evolution of Global Labor Markets Since 1830: Background Evidence and Hypotheses," *Explorations in Economic History* 32, no. 2 (April 1995): 141–96. On the economic impact of restrictions on migration, see Michael A. Clemens, "Economics and Emigration: Trillion-Dollar Bills on the Sidewalk?" *Journal of Economic Perspectives* 25, no. 3 (Summer 2011): 83–106.

86. Peter H. Lindert and Jeffrey G. Williamson, "Globalization and Inequality: A Long History," April 2001, paper prepared for the World Bank Annual Conference on Development Economics—Europe, Barcelona, June 25–27, 2001. See also Paul Hirst and Grahame Thompson, *Globalization in Question: The International Economy and the Possibilities of Governance,* 2nd ed. (Cambridge: Polity, 1999), 23. "Convergence" here refers to reductions in the size of differences among countries in their real wages, GDP per worker, and GDP per head.

87. Kevin H. O'Rourke, "Europe and the Causes of Globalization, 1790 to 2000," in Henryk Kierzkowski, ed., *From Europeanization of the Globe to the Globalization of Europe* (London: Palgrave, 2002), 73, http://www.tcd.ie/Economics/TEP/2002_papers/TEPNo1KO22.pdf.

88. See, for example, David Goodhart, *The Road to Somewhere* (London: Hurst, 2017), 122–27.

89. For a strongly positive review of the economics of migration, see Jonathan Portes, "The Economics of Migration," June 2019, https://journals.sagepub.com/doi/pdf/10.1177/1536504219854712.

90. James Gwartney, Joshua Hall, and Robert Lawson, *Economic Freedom of the World 2016 Annual Report,* Washington, DC, Cato Institute, 2016, https://www.cato.org/economic-freedom-world, and Freedom House, Freedom in the World 2020, https://freedomhouse.org/report/freedom-world/2020/leaderless-struggle-democracy.

91. For an excellent discussion of the long and tortuous road to democracy in Europe and its contemporary fragility, see Sheri Berman, *Democracy and Dictatorship in Europe: From the Ancien Régime to the Present Day* (New York: Oxford University Press, 2019).

92. A classic history of financial crises is Robert Z. Aliber and Charles P. Kindleberger, *Manias, Panics, and Crashes: A History of Financial Crises*, 7th ed. (London and New York: Palgrave Macmillan, 2015).

Chapter Four: It's the Economy, Stupid

1. Aristotle, *Politics*, trans. T. A. Sinclair, revised and re-presented by Trevor J. Saunders (London: Penguin Classics, 1981), Book IV, xi, 1295b13–34.
2. Aristotle's argument is close to that of Michael J. Sandel's in *The Tyranny of Merit: What's Become of the Common Good?* (London: Penguin, 2020). Sandel emphasizes the need for a broad "equality of condition" if democracy is to thrive.
3. On November 24, 1992, Queen Elizabeth II referred to 1992 as an "annus horribilis" in a speech at Guildhall commemorating the fortieth year of her reign. See https://www.royal.uk/annus-horribilis-speech.
4. Barry Eichengreen, *The Populist Temptation: Economic Grievance and Political Reaction in the Modern Era* (New York: Oxford University Press, 2018), 163.
5. See Noam Gidron and Peter A. Hall, "The Politics of Social Status: Economic and Cultural Roots of the Populist Right," *British Journal of Sociology* 68, no. S1 (November 2017): 59, https://onlinelibrary.wiley.com/doi/epdf/10.1111/1468-4446.12319. See also Richard Wilkinson and Kate Pickett, *The Inner Level: How More Equal Societies Reduce Stress, Restore Sanity and Improve Wellbeing* (London: Penguin, 2019).
6. Gidron and Hall, "Politics of Social Status," 10.
7. John Kay and Mervyn King, *Radical Uncertainty: Decision-making for an Unknowable Future* (London: Bridge Street Press, 2020), 122–24.
8. Tim Haughton, "It's the Slogan, Stupid: The Brexit Referendum," https://www.birmingham.ac.uk/research/perspective/eu-ref-haughton.aspx.
9. Gidron and Hall, "Politics of Social Status," 59.
10. Anne Case and Angus Deaton, "Mortality and Morbidity in the 21st Century," *Brookings Papers on Economic Activity* (Spring 2017): 397, https://www.brookings.edu/wp-content/uploads/2017/08/casetextsp17bpea.pdf. See also, for greater detail, Case and Deaton, *Deaths of Despair and the Future of Capitalism* (Princeton, NJ: Princeton University Press, 2020).
11. See Patrick Radden Keefe, *Empire of Pain: The Secret History of the Sackler Dynasty* (New York: Doubleday, 2021).
12. Émile Durkheim, *Le Suicide: Étude de Sociologie* (Bar-le-Duc, France: Imprimerie Contant-Laguerre, 1897).
13. James Truslow Adams coined the phrase "The American Dream" in *The Epic of America* (New Brunswick and London: Transaction Publishers, 1931 and 2012). But his idea was broader than the merely material: "Life should be better and richer and fuller for everyone, with opportunity for each according to ability or achievement."
14. See, on this, Robert D. Putnam, *Bowling Alone: The Collapse and Revival of American Community* (New York and London: Simon & Schuster, 2000), and Theda Skocpol, *Diminished Democracy: From Membership to Management in American Civic Life* (Norman: University of Oklahoma Press, 2003).
15. Mayhill Fowler, "Obama: No Surprise That Hard-Pressed Pennsylvanians Turn Bitter," *Huffington Post*, November 17, 2008, updated May 25, 2011, https://www.huffingtonpost.com/mayhill-fowler/obama-no-surprise-that-ha_b_96188.html.
16. Wendy Brown, *In the Ruins of Neoliberalism: The Rise of Antidemocratic Politics in the West* (New York: Columbia University Press, 2019), especially chapter 5, "No Future for White Men," for a perspective on the resentment of "white men" in the modern world.
17. Thomas Piketty, *Capital in the Twenty-first Century*, trans. Arthur Goldhammer (Cambridge, MA: Harvard University Press, 2013), is now a classic reference. Other important books on inequality are Anthony B. Atkinson, *Inequality: What Can Be Done* (Cambridge, MA, and London: Harvard University Press, 2015); Branko Milanovic, *Global Inequality: A New Approach for the Age of Globalization* (Cambridge, MA: Harvard University Press, 2016); and Roger Brown, *The Inequality Crisis: The Facts and What We Can Do about It* (Bristol and Chicago: Policy Press, 2017). The book by the late Tony Atkinson, doyen of scholars on inequality, focuses on the high-income countries. Milanovic's book provides a global perspective. Brown provides an excellent overview of research, with particular reference to the UK.
18. See "Inequality and Poverty," http://www.oecd.org/social/inequality.htm.

19. The Gini coefficient is zero for a country with perfect equality of household incomes, and it is one for a country in which all income accrued to just one household.

20. Deborah Hargreaves, *Are Chief Executives Overpaid?* (Cambridge: Polity, 2019), 6.

21. Ibid.

22. Ibid., 7.

23. Andrew Smithers, *Productivity and the Bonus Culture* (Oxford: Oxford University Press, 2019).

24. On stock buybacks, see William Lazonick, "Profits Without Prosperity," *Harvard Business Review*, September 2014, https://hbr.org/2014/09/profits-without-prosperity; and Mustafa Lazonick, Erdem Sakinç, and Matt Hopkins, "Why Stock Buybacks Are Dangerous for the Economy," *Harvard Business Review*, January 2020, https://hbr.org/2020/01/why-stock-buybacks-are-dangerous -for-the-economy.

25. Emmanuel Saez, "Striking It Richer: The Evolution of Top Incomes in the United States (Updated with 2015 Preliminary Estimates)," June 30, 2016, https://eml.berkeley.edu/~saez/saez-UStopin comes-2015.pdf.

26. See, for example, Jane Mayer, *Dark Money: The Hidden History of the Billionaires behind the Rise of the Radical Right* (New York: Anchor Books, 2016).

27. Federico Cingano, "Trends in Income Inequality and Its Impact on Economic Growth," OECD Social, Employment and Migration Working Papers No. 163, 2014, 28, http://dx.doi.org/10.1787 /5jxrjncwxv6j-en. Very similar results emerge from a global study by Jonathan D. Ostry, Andrew Berg, and Charalambos G. Tsangarides, "Redistribution, Inequality and Growth," IMF Staff Discussion Note SDN/14/02, February 2014, https://www.imf.org/external/pubs/ft/sdn/2014/sdn1402 .pdf.

28. On the many adverse consequences of high and rising inequality, see Richard Wilkinson and Kate Pickett, *The Spirit Level: Why Greater Equality Makes Societies Stronger* (New York: Bloomsbury, 2009), and Joseph Stiglitz, *The Price of Inequality: How Today's Divided Society Endangers Our Future* (New York: W. W. Norton, 2012).

29. *An Overview of Growing Income Inequalities in OECD Countries: Main Findings* (Paris: Organization for Economic Co-operation and Development, 2011), figure 1.

30. More recent work by economists suggests that some of the data on rising inequality reported here are open to question. See "Economists Are Rethinking the Numbers on Inequality," *Economist*, November 28, 2019, https://www.economist.com/briefing/2019/11/28/economists-are-rethinking -the-numbers-on-inequality. But this work does not deny that inequality in the US is relatively high.

31. Income inequality is measured as the Gini coefficient of household disposable incomes. Intergenerational economic mobility is measured as the elasticity between the father's relative earnings and his son's relative adult earnings. For the economic mobility measure, Corak used data on a cohort of children born, roughly speaking, during the early to mid-1960s and measuring their adult outcomes in the mid- to late 1990s. For the inequality measure, Corak used the Gini coefficients for about 1985. Thus, this is a measure of how far inequality during a child's upbringing affected his subsequent earnings mobility. See Miles Corak, "Income Inequality, Equality of Opportunity, and Intergenerational Mobility," IZA Discussion Paper No. 7520, July 2013, 3, figure 1, http://ftp.iza.org/dp7520.pdf.

32. Alan Krueger, "The Rise and Consequences of Inequality in the United States of America," Center for American Progress, January 12, 2012, https://cdn.americanprogress.org/wp-content /uploads/events/2012/01/pdf/krueger.pdf. The name comes from *The Great Gatsby*, the classic novel on the Gilded Age of the 1920s by F. Scott Fitzgerald.

33. An obvious problem is that in relatively equal societies, the difference between positions on the distribution is, on average, small. So relatively modest absolute shifts in position will lead to relatively large changes in relative positions across generations. In this case, the discovery of low immobility is essentially just another aspect of low inequality and vice versa for the high-inequality countries.

34. Martin Wolf, "Hypocrisy and Confusion Distort the Debate on Social Mobility," *Financial Times*, May 2, 2019, https://www.ft.com/content/577a0abe-6c04-11e9-a9a5-351eeaef6d84. See also John Goldthorpe, "Social Class Mobility in Modern Britain: Changing Structure, Constant Process," Lecture in Sociology, The British Academy, read March 15, 2016, posted July 18, 2016, *Journal of the British Academy* 4 (July 18, 2016): 89–111, https://www.thebritishacademy.ac.uk /sites/default/files/05%20Goldthorpe%201825.pdf.

35. See Federica Cocco, "Most US Manufacturing Jobs Lost to Technology, Not Trade," *Financial Times*, December 2, 2016, https://www.ft.com/content/dec677c0-b7e6-11e6-ba85-95d1533d9a62.

36. On the "gig economy," see Sarah Kessler, *Gigged: The Gig Economy, the End of the Job and the Future of Work* (New York: Random House Business, 2019).

37. On the Precariat, see Guy Standing, *The Precariat: The New Dangerous Class* (London: Bloomsbury, 2011 and 2014), 41.

38. In economics, rent is the return to an activity over and above the cost of the factors of production needed to produce its output in competitive markets. The existence of rent reflects a temporary or permanent monopoly position of some kind.

39. Raghuram Rajan made this argument in his book *Fault Lines: How Hidden Fractures Still Threaten the World Economy* (Princeton, NJ, and Oxford: Princeton University Press, 2011). Among more recent authors, one of those who emphasizes most powerfully the role of unsustainable accumulations of debt in keeping the entire capitalist show on the road is the German left-wing sociologist Walter Streeck. See Streeck, *How Will Capitalism End? Essays on a Failing System* (London: Verso, 2016). See also Martin Wolf, "The Case against the Collapse of Capitalism," *Financial Times*, November 2, 2016, https://www.ft.com/content/7496e08a-9f7a-11e6-891e-abe238dee8e2.

40. See Martin Wolf, *The Shifts and the Shocks: What We've Learned—and Still Have to Learn—from the Financial Crisis* (London and New York: Penguin, 2014 and 2015); Tamim Bayoumi, *Unfinished Business: The Unexplored Causes of the Financial Crisis and the Lessons Yet to Be Learned* (New Haven, CT: Yale University Press, 2017); and Robert Kuttner, *Can Democracy Survive Global Capitalism?* (New York: W. W. Norton, 2018).

41. GDPs per head were not necessarily on the fitted 1990–2007 exponential trend line in 2007, which is why the starting point is not at deviations of zero. Germany's GDP per head was 2.2 percent above the 1990–2007 fitted trend in 2007, while Spain's was 1.6 percent below it. These were the two extreme deviations.

42. McKinsey Global Institute, *Poorer Than Their Parents? Flat or Falling Incomes in Advanced Countries*, July 2016, https://www.mckinsey.com/featured-insights/employment-and-growth/poorer-than-their-parents-a-new-perspective-on-income-inequality.

43. "Banks Paid $321 Billion in Fines Since Financial Crisis: BCG," Reuters, January 19, 2017, https://www.reuters.com/article/us-banks-fines/banks-paid-321-billion-in-fines-since-financial-crisis-bcg-idUSKBN1692Y2.

44. Ronald Reagan Presidential Foundation & Institute, "Reagan Quotes and Speeches," https://www.reaganfoundation.org/ronald-reagan/reagan-quotes-speeches/news-conference-1/.

45. Martin Wolf, "Ten Ways Coronavirus Will Shape World in Long Term," *Financial Times*, November 3, 2020, https://www.ft.com/content/9b0318d3-8e5b-4293-ad50-c5250e894b07; Wolf, "Martin Wolf Looks Back at the Pandemic One Year Later," *Financial Times*, March 11, 2021, https://www.ft.com/content/e02ec5cb-f08b-4bc9-a5ba-2978b680103c; Wolf, "Economic Recovery Masks the Dangers of a Divided World," *Financial Times*, April 20, 2020, https://www.ft.com/content/0be32ec5-8a75-48f2-99f3-eb5bcd055287; Wolf, "We Can End the COVID Pandemic in the Next Year," *Financial Times*, May 25, 2021, https://www.ft.com/content/12fc9f47-7fd3-4690-93c5-f641688fca36; and Wolf, "The G20 Has Failed to Meet Its Challenges," *Financial Times*, July 13, 2021, https://www.ft.com/content/c9448d15-8410-47d3-8f41-cd7ed41d8116.

46. See Adam Tooze, *Shutdown: How Covid Shook the World's Economy* (London: Penguin, 2021).

47. Ernest Hemingway, *The Sun Also Rises* (New York: Charles Scribner's Sons, 1926), 8, 157.

48. See, on this anger, Eric Lonergan and Mark Blyth, *Angrynomics* (Newcastle upon Tyne, UK: Agenda, 2020).

49. On the need for social cohesion if democracy is to function, see Sandel, *Tyranny of Merit*.

50. Ronald F. Inglehart and Pippa Norris, "Trump, Brexit, and the Rise of Populism: Economic Have-nots and Cultural Backlash," RWP16-026, August 2016, 29, https://www.hks.harvard.edu/publications/trump-brexit-and-rise-populism-economic-have-nots-and-cultural-backlash.

51. Eric Kaufmann, *Whiteshift: Populism, Immigration, and the Future of White Majorities* (London and New York: Allen Lane, 2018), 516.

52. See, on this, Martin Sandbu, "Is Culture or Economics at the Root of Our Strange Politics?," *Financial Times*, September 11, 2017, https://www.ft.com/content/c841a8d4-96d5-11e7-a652-cde3f882dd7b; and *The Economics of Belonging: A Radical Plan to Win Back the Left Behind and Achieve Prosperity for All* (Princeton, NJ, and Oxford: Princeton University Press, 2020), chapter 3, "Culture Versus Economics."

53. Manuel Funke, Moritz Schularik, and Christoph Trebesch, "Going to Extremes: Politics after Financial Crises, 1870–2014," *European Economic Review* 88 (2016): 228, http://www.macrohistory.net/wp-content/uploads/2015/10/Going-to-extremes.pdf.

54. See Stuart Jeffries, "Britain's Most Racist Election: The Story of Smethwick, 50 Years On," *Guardian*, October 15, 2014, https://www.theguardian.com/world/2014/oct/15/britains-most-racist-election-smethwick-50-years-on, and "Enoch Powell's 'Rivers of Blood' Speech," https://anth1001.files.wordpress.com/2014/04/enoch-powell_speech.pdf.

55. Adam Tooze, *Crashed: How a Decade of Financial Crises Changed the World* (London: Allen Lane, 2018), especially part IV, "Aftershocks."

56. Ibid., chapter 9, "Europe's Forgotten Crisis: Eastern Europe."

57. "The Great Depression," Alpha History, https://alphahistory.com/nazigermany/the-great-depression/.

58. Dick Geary, "Who Voted for the Nazis?" *History Today* 48, no. 10 (October 1948), https://www.historytoday.com/archive/who-voted-nazis; and Christopher H. Achen and Larry M. Bartels, *Democracy for Realists: Why Elections Do Not Produce Responsive Government* (Princeton, NJ, and Oxford: Princeton University Press, 2016), 204.

59. Wiener Holocaust Library, "How Did the Nazis Consolidate Their Power?" The Holocaust Explained, https://www.theholocaustexplained.org/the-nazi-rise-to-power/how-did-the-nazi-gain-power/1933-elections/.

60. Achen and Bartels, *Democracy for Realists*, 315.

61. Sebastian Doerr, Stefan Gissler, José-Luis Peydró, and Hans-Joachim Voth, "Financial Crises and Political Radicalization: How Failing Banks Paved Hitler's Path to Power," BIS World Papers, No. 978, November 22, 2021, https://www.bis.org/publ/work978.htm.

62. Achen and Bartels, *Democracy for Realists*, 316.

63. Martin Wolf, "Italy's New Rulers Could Shake the Euro," *Financial Times*, May 22, 2018, https://www.ft.com/content/eb82fdfe-5ce4-11e8-9334-2218e7146b04. Also, Josef Janning, "Crisis and Cohesion in the EU: A Ten-Year Review," European Council on Foreign Relations Policy Brief, February 2018, https://www.ecfr.eu/page/-/ECFR-_245_-_Crisis_and_Cohesion_-_A_10_Year_Review_Janning_WEB.pdf.

64. Arjun Jayadev and Robert Johnson, "Tides and Prejudice: Racial Attitudes during Downturns in the United States, 1979–2014," *Review of Black Political Economy* 44 (2017): 370–92, https://journals.sagepub.com/doi/full/10.1007/s12114-017-9264-y.

65. Ibid., 390.

66. Thiemo Fetzer, "Austerity Caused Brexit," *VoxEU*, April 8, 2019, https://voxeu.org/article/austerity-caused-brexit, and "Did Austerity Cause Brexit?" Warwick University Working Paper Series, no. 381, revised June 2019, https://warwick.ac.uk/fac/soc/economics/research/centers/cage/manage/publications/381-2018_fetzer.pdf. See also Sandbu, "Sweden's Far-Right and the Left-Behind," *Financial Times*, July 4, 2019, https://www.ft.com/content/ec4adebc-99bc-11e9-8cfb-30c211dcd229.

67. Fetzer, "Did Austerity Cause Brexit?"

68. Pippa Norris, "It's Not Just Trump. Authoritarian Populism Is Rising Across the West. Here's Why," *Washington Post*, March 11, 2016, https://www.washingtonpost.com/news/monkey-cage/wp/2016/03/11/its-not-just-trump-authoritarian-populism-is-rising-across-the-west-heres-why/.

69. Ernesto Dal Bó, Federico Finan, Olle Folke, Torsten Persson, and Johanna Rickne, "Economic Losers and Political Winners: Sweden's Radical Right," February 2019, 1, http://perseus.iies.su.se/~tpers/papers/CompleteDraft190301.pdf.

70. Ibid., 2.

71. Ibid.

72. Ibid., 3.

73. Ibid.

74. Sandbu, "Sweden's Far-Right and the Left-Behind."

75. Gregori Galofré-Vilà, Martin McKee, María Gómez-León, and David Stuckler, "The 1918 Influenza Pandemic and the Rise of Italian Fascism: A Cross-City Quantitative and Historical Text Qualitative Analysis," *American Journal of Public Health* 112, no. 2 (February 2022): 242–47.

76. In "Populism and Trust in Europe," *VoxEU*, August 23, 2017, https://voxeu.org/article/populism-and-trust-europe, Christian Dustmann, Barry Eichengreen, Sebastian Otten, André Sapir, Guido Tabellini, and Gylfi Zoega state that "our main finding is that older birth cohorts and less-educated individuals are less trusting of national parliaments and the European Parliament, are less supportive of the EU, and are more likely to vote for populist parties." This is consistent with the idea that people are responding to the threat or actuality of declining status, economic and also social. Their response, inevitably, has a strong element of nostalgia.

77. Michael Beschloss, "The Ad That Helped Reagan Sell Good Times to an Uncertain Nation," *New*

York Times, May 7, 2016, https://www.nytimes.com/2016/05/08/business/the-ad-that-helped
-reagan-sell-good-times-to-an-uncertain-nation.html.

78. Donald Trump, "The Inaugural Address," January 20, 2017, https://trumpwhitehouse.archives
.gov/briefings-statements/the-inaugural-address.

79. See Anne Applebaum, *Twilight of Democracy: The Seductive Lure of Authoritarianism* (London:
Allen Lane, 2020).

80. See the opening quotation for this chapter.

81. This remark is widely attributed to Chesterton, but first recorded in Emile Cammaerts, *Chesterton: The Laughing Prophet* (1937). See Susan Ratcliffe, ed., *Oxford Essential Quotations* (Oxford:
Oxford University Press, 2016).

Chapter Five: Rise of Rentier Capitalism

1. "Remarks by President Trump in a Meeting with Republican Members of Congress on the United
States Reciprocal Trade Act," January 24, 2019, https://trumpwhitehouse.archives.gov/briefings
-statements/remarks-president-trump-meeting-republican-members-congress-united-states-re
ciprocal-trade-act.

2. Robert Kuttner makes this argument powerfully in *Can Democracy Survive Global Capitalism?*
(New York: W. W. Norton, 2018).

3. Alvin H. Hansen, "Economic Progress and Declining Population Growth," *American Economic
Review* 29, no. 1, part 1 (March 1939), http://digamo.free.fr/hansen39.pdf. Hansen defined secular stagnation as "sick recoveries which die in their infancy and depressions which feed on
themselves and leave a hard and seemingly immovable core of unemployment."

4. The idea of such a statistical relationship was proposed by the New Zealand economist William
Phillips in 1958. This was an immensely influential idea in the 1960s and early 1970s. See Tejvan
Pettinger, "Phillips Curve," March 1, 2019, *Economics Help*, https://www.economicshelp.org/blog
/1364/economics/phillips-curve-explained/.

5. See, on the dangers of such nostalgia, Martin Wolf, "The US Should Spurn the False Promise of
Protectionism," *Financial Times*, June 15, 2021, https://www.ft.com/content/4edc2c5a-298f-4edd
-81b7-5b94b7b23b93; Adam Posen, "The Price of Nostalgia: America's Self-Defeating Economic
Retreat," *Foreign Affairs*, May/June 2021, https://www.foreignaffairs.com/articles/united-states
/2021-04-20/america-price-nostalgia; and Anne O. Krueger, *International Trade: What Everyone
Needs to Know* (New York: Oxford University Press, 2020).

6. See, on this, Paul Collier, *The Future of Capitalism: Facing the New Anxieties* (London: Allen Lane,
2018), chapter 7, "The Geographic Divide: Booming Metropolis, Broken Cities."

7. Ibid., 125.

8. See Peterson-KFF, "Health System Tracker," https://www.healthsystemtracker.org/.

9. Robert J. Gordon, *The Rise and Fall of American Growth: The U.S. Standard of Living Since the
Civil War* (Princeton, NJ, and Woodstock, England: Princeton University Press, 2016), paraphras-
ing Evsey Domar, "On the Measurement of Technological Change," *Economic Journal* 71, no. 284
(December 1961): 712.

10. See Tyler Cowen, *The Great Stagnation: How America Ate All the Low-Hanging Fruit of Modern
History, Got Sick, and Will (Eventually) Feel Better* (New York: Dutton, 2011).

11. These data are for the UK. See Office of Health Economics, "Infant and Child Health," December 1975, https://www.ohe.org/publications/infant-and-child-health, and United Nations, Department of Economic and Social Affairs, Population Dynamics, *World Population Prospects 2019*,
https://population.un.org/wpp/Download/.

12. Martin Wolf, "Is Unlimited Growth a Thing of the Past?" *Financial Times*, October 2, 2012,
https://www.ft.com/content/78e883fa-0bef-11e2-8032-00144feabdc0.

13. David Noble draws this parallel between religion and the enchantment of technology in *The
Religion of Technology: The Divinity of Man and the Spirit of Invention* (New York: Alfred A. Knopf,
1997).

14. See Ian Goldin, Pantelis Koutroumpis, François Lafond, Nils Rochowicz, and Julian Winkler, *The
Productivity Paradox: Reconciling Rapid Technological Change and Stagnating Productivity*, Oxford
Martin School, April 2019, 8–14, https://www.oxfordmartin.ox.ac.uk/downloads/reports/Pro
ductivity_Paradox.pdf. It turns out to be difficult to identify the causes of the weak productivity
performance, though many are listed. The most plausible, in the view of this report, is "lack of
competition." The more plausible, in my view, is that innovation is, as Gordon argues, just not
what it used to be.

15. Dan Andrews, Chiara Criscuolo, and Peter Gal, *The Global Productivity Slowdown, Technology*

Divergence and Public Policy: A Firm Level Perspective, OECD, Paris, 2016, https://www.oecd.org /global-forum-productivity/events/GP_Slowdown_Technology_Divergence_and_Public_Policy _Final_after_conference_26_July.pdf.

16. Ibid., 5.

17. See Dietrich Vollrath, *Fully Grown: Why a Stagnant Economy Is a Sign of Success* (Chicago and London: University of Chicago Press, 2020), especially 207, table 17.1.

18. Gordon, *Rise and Fall of American Growth.*

19. See Guy Standing, *The Precariat: The New Dangerous Class* (London: Bloomsbury, 2011 and 2014).

20. For more optimistic views than Gordon's on the impact of the ICT revolution, including artificial intelligence, on productivity, present or future, see Erik Brynjolfsson and Andrew McAfee, *Race against the Machine: How the Digital Revolution Is Accelerating Innovation, Driving Productivity, and Irreversibly Transforming Employment and the Economy* (Lexington, MA: Digital Frontier Press, 2011); Brynjolfsson and McAfee, *The Second Machine Age: Work, Progress, and Prosperity in a Time of Brilliant Technologies* (New York: W. W. Norton, 2014); and McAfee and Brynjolfsson, *Machine, Platform, Crowd: Harnessing the Digital Revolution* (New York: W. W. Norton, 2017).

21. On the impact of technology and especially automation on employment, real wages, and the distribution of income, see Daron Acemoglu, "Written Testimony" at a virtual hearing on "Machines, Artificial Intelligence, & the Workforce: Recovering & Readying Our Economy for the Future," House Committee on the Budget, September 10, 2021, https://www.congress.gov/116 /meeting/house/111002/witnesses/HHRG-116-BU00-Wstate-AcemogluD-20200910.pdf.

22. On the wider economic impacts of aging, see Charles Goodhart and Manoj Pradhan, *The Great Demographic Reversal: Aging Societies, Waning Inequality, and an Inflation Reversal* (London: Palgrave Macmillan, 2020).

23. United Nations Population Division, *Replacement Migration: Is It a Solution to Declining and Aging Populations?* 2000, https://www.un.org/en/development/desa/population/publications/aging/re placement-migration.asp.

24. See, on this shift in the US, Thomas Ferguson and Joel Rogers, *Right Turn: The Decline of the Democrats and the Future of American Politics* (New York: Farrar, Straus and Giroux, 1987).

25. In the parlance of the old General Agreement on Tariffs and Trade (GATT) and now the World Trade Organization, tariffs are "bound" in the process of reaching a negotiated trade agreement. For most high-income countries (and many others, too), bound and applied tariffs are the same. But countries are allowed to *apply* a tariff lower than the bound rate. The advantage is that it allows a country to raise the applied level without legal questions. India, for example, has much higher bound than applied rates. This gives it substantial legal room to raise the applied tariffs when it wants to do so. It is also possible to raise tariffs above bound levels. But dutiful members need justifications for doing so, though under Donald Trump the US had more or less ceased to offer plausible justifications. From the economic point of view, the applied rate matters most, except to the extent that the greater ease of raising it when it is well below the bound rate makes it more likely that it will in fact be raised. That would increase trade policy uncertainty, which is costly.

26. The chart stops in 2019, because of the distorting effects of the COVID-19 pandemic.

27. Christoph Lakner and Branko Milanovic, "Global Income Distribution from the Fall of the Berlin Wall to the Great Recession," World Bank Policy Research Working Paper 6719, December 2013, 31, figure 1(a), http://documents.worldbank.org/curated/en/914431468162277879/pdf/WPS 6719.pdf.

28. Facundo Alvaredo et al., *World Inequality Report 2018* (Paris: World Economic Lab, 2018) 13, figure E4, "The Elephant Curve of Global Inequality and Growth, 1980–2016," https://wir2018 .wid.world/.

29. Ibid.

30. Data on GDP at market prices and purchasing power parity are from the *World Economic Outlook Database*, https://www.imf.org/external/pubs/ft/weo/2019/01/weodata/index.aspx.

31. Holly Ellyatt, "Who Are 'Davos Man' and 'Davos Woman'?" CNBC, January 19, 2018, https:// www.cnbc.com/2018/01/19/who-are-davos-man-and-davos-woman.html.

32. Robert Shrimsley, "Boris Johnson's Brexit Explosion Ruins Tory Business Credentials," *Financial Times*, June 25, 2018, https://www.ft.com/content/8075e68c-7857-11e8-8e67-1e1a0846c475.

33. See Maurice Obstfeld, "The Global Capital Market Reconsidered," in Paul Collier, Diane Coyle, Colin Mayer, and Martin Wolf, eds., "Capitalism: What Has Gone Wrong, What Needs to Change, and How It Can Be Fixed," *Oxford Review of Economic Policy* 37, no. 4 (Winter 2021): 690–706.

34. See Max Roser, "Employment in Agriculture," in Our World in Data, https://ourworldindata.org /employment-in-agriculture.

35. Institut National d'Études Démographiques, "Migration Worldwide," https://www.ined.fr/en /everything_about_population/demographic-facts-sheets/focus-on/migration-worldwide/.

36. See Sari Pekkala Kerr and William R. Kerr, "Economic Impacts of Immigration: A Survey," National Bureau of Economic Research Working Paper 16736, January 2011, 14–15, https://www .nber.org/papers/w16736.

37. Ibid., 18–21.

38. Martin Wolf, "The Fight to Halt the Theft of Ideas Is Hopeless," *Financial Times*, November 12, 2019, https://www.ft.com/content/d592af00-0a29-11ea-b2d6-9bf4d1957a67.

39. Elhanan Helpman, *Globalization and Inequality* (Cambridge, MA, and London: Harvard University Press, 2018), 170–71.

40. Daron Acemoglu, David Autor, David Dorn, Gordon H. Hanson, and Brendan Price, "Import Competition and the Great US Employment Sag of the 2000s," *Journal of Labor Economics* 34, no. 1 (part 2, January 2016): 141–98, http://www.journals.uchicago.edu/doi/pdfplus/10.1086 /682384.

41. Helpman, *Globalization and Inequality*, 174.

42. David H. Autor, David Dorn, and Gordon H. Hanson, "The China Shock: Learning from Labor Market Adjustment to Large Changes in Trade," National Bureau of Economic Research Working Paper Number 21906, January 2016, http://www.nber.org/papers/w21906.

43. See Lawrence H. Summers, "The Threat of Secular Stagnation Has Not Gone Away," *Financial Times*, May 6, 2018, https://www.ft.com/content/aa76e2a8-4ef2-11e8-9471-a083af05aea7; Lukasz Rachel and Lawrence H. Summers, "On Falling Neutral Real Rates, Fiscal Policy, and the Risk of Secular Stagnation," BPEA Conference Drafts, March 7–8, 2019, *Brookings Papers on Economic Activity*, https://www.brookings.edu/wp-content/uploads/2019/03/On-Falling-Neutral -Real-Rates-Fiscal-Policy-and-the-Risk-of-Secular-Stagnation.pdf; Martin Wolf, "Monetary Policy Has Run Its Course," *Financial Times*, March 12, 2019, https://www.ft.com/content/08c4eb8c -442c-11e9-a965-23d669740bfb; and Ben S. Bernanke, "The Global Savings Glut and the U.S. Current Account Deficit," March 10, 2005, Federal Reserve Board, https://www.federalreserve .gov/boarddocs/speeches/2005/200503102/.

44. I use UK data, because the UK Treasury has issued index-linked bonds for a relatively long time.

45. Atif Mian, Ludwig Straub, and Amir Sufi, "The Saving Glut of the Rich and the Rise in Household Debt," March 2020, https://scholar.harvard.edu/files/straub/files/mss_richsavingglut.pdf. See also Martin Wolf, "How to Escape the Trap of Excessive Debt," *Financial Times*, May 5, 2020, https://www.ft.com/content/2c5ddbd0-8e09-11ea-9e12-0d4655dbd44f.

46. Matthew Klein and Michael Pettis, *Trade Wars Are Class Wars* (New Haven, CT: Yale University Press, 2020), and Martin Wolf, "What Trade Wars Tell Us," *Financial Times*, June 18, 2020, https://www.ft.com/content/f3ee37e0-b086-11ea-a4b6-31f1eedf762e.

47. Charles Dumas quite rightly emphasizes these macroeconomic causes of economic instability and the consequent rise of populism in *Populism and Economics* (London: Profile Books, 2018). See also Martin Wolf, "The Price of Populism," *Financial Times*, October 24, 2018, https://www .ft.com/content/06181c56-d13b-11e8-a9f2-7574db66bcd5.

48. Klein and Pettis, *Trade Wars Are Class Wars*.

49. Atif Mian, Ludwig Straub, and Amir Sufi, "Indebted Demand," March 26, 2020, https://scholar .harvard.edu/files/straub/files/mss_indebteddemand.pdf.

50. Martin Wolf, "The Folly of Donald Trump's Bilateralism in Global Trade," *Financial Times*, March 14, 2017, https://www.ft.com/content/ce92ae28-058e-11e7-ace0-1ce02ef0def9; and Howard S. Ellis, "Bilateralism and the Future of International Trade," *Essays in International Finance*, No. 5, International Finance Section, Department of Economics and Social Institutions (Princeton: Princeton University, Summer 1945), https://ies.princeton.edu/pdf/E5.pdf.

51. See Martin Wolf, "Why Rigged Capitalism Is Damaging Liberal Democracy," *Financial Times*, September 18, 2019, https://www.ft.com/content/5a8ab27e-d470-11e9-8367-807ebd53ab77; and Wolf, "How to Reform Today's Rigged Capitalism," *Financial Times*, December 3, 2019, https:// www.ft.com/content/4cf2d6ee-14f5-11ea-8d73-6303645ac406.

52. For a thought-provoking critique of the development of finance over the past four decades, from a Marxist perspective, see Cédric Durand, *Fictitious Capital: How Finance Is Appropriating Our Future* (London and New York: Verso, 2017).

53. I discussed this explosion in financial sector leverage in *The Shifts and the Shocks: What We've Learned—and Have Still to Learn—from the Financial Crisis* (London and New York: Penguin, 2014 and 2015).

54. Susan Lund et al., *The New Dynamics of Financial Globalization*, McKinsey Global Institute, August 2017, https://www.mckinsey.com/industries/financial-services/our-insights/the-new-dynamics-of-financial-globalization.

55. See Bank for International Settlements, "Global OTC Derivatives Market," table D5.1, https://stats.bis.org/statx/srs/table/d5.1.

56. See Michael McLeay, Amar Radia, and Ryland Thomas, "Money Creation in the Modern Economy," *Bank of England Quarterly Bulletin*, 2014, Quarter One, 14–27, https://www.bankofengland.co.uk/-/media/boe/files/quarterly-bulletin/2014/money-creation-in-the-modern-economy.

57. Thomas Philippon and Ariell Reshef, "Wages and Human Capital in the U.S. Financial Industry 1909–2006," National Bureau of Economic Research Working Paper 14644, January 2009, especially figure 6, https://www.nber.org/papers/w14644.

58. On the hedge fund industry, for example, see Martin Wolf, "Why Today's Hedge Fund Industry May Not Survive," *Financial Times*, March 18, 2008, https://www.ft.com/content/c8941ad4-f503-11dc-a21b-000077b07658. See also Simon Lack, *The Hedge Fund Mirage: The Illusion of Big Money and Why It's Too Good to Be True* (Hoboken, NJ: John Wiley & Sons, 2012).

59. See Angela Monaghan, "City Is Too Big and Socially Useless, Says Lord Turner," *Telegraph*, August 26, 2009, https://www.telegraph.co.uk/finance/newsbysector/banksandfinance/6096546/City-is-too-big-and-socially-useless-says-Lord-Turner.html; https://www.pauljorion.com/stewardship-of-finance/wp-content/uploads/2015/04/College-09-03-2015_-Turner-useful-and-useless-financial-activities.pdf; and Adair Turner, *Between Debt and the Devil: Money, Credit, and Fixing Global Finance* (Princeton, NJ, and Oxford: Princeton University Press, 2016).

60. John Kay, *Other People's Money: The Real Business of Finance* (London: Profile Books, 2016); Joseph Stiglitz, "Inequality and Economic Growth," in Michael Jacobs and Mariana Mazzucato, eds., *Rethinking Capitalism: Economics and Policy for Sustainable and Inclusive Growth* (Chichester, UK: Wiley-Blackwell, 2016), 134–55, chapter 8; and https://www8.gsb.columbia.edu/faculty/jstiglitz/sites/jstiglitz/files/Inequality%20and%20Economic%20Growth.pdf.

61. Stephen G. Cecchetti and Enisse Kharroubi, "Why Does Financial Sector Growth Crowd Out Real Economic Growth?" BIS Working Papers 490, February 2015, https://www.bis.org/publ/work490.pdf. See also Cecchetti and Kharroubi, "Reassessing the Impact of Finance on Growth," BIS Working Papers 381, July 2012, https://www.bis.org/publ/work381.pdf.

62. See Fred Hirsch, *The Social Limits to Growth* (London: Routledge, 1995).

63. Michael Lewis, *Flash Boys: Cracking the Money Code* (London: Penguin, 2014).

64. For a discussion of the impact of "financialization" on the firm, see Anat Admati, "Capitalism, Laws, and the Need for Trustworthy Institutions," in Paul Collier, Diane Coyle, Colin Mayer, and Martin Wolf, eds., "Capitalism: What Has Gone Wrong, What Needs to Change, and How It Can Be Fixed," *Oxford Review of Economic Policy* 37, no. 4 (Winter 2021): 678–89. See also Martin Hellwig, "'Capitalism: What Has Gone Wrong?': Who Went Wrong? Capitalism? The Market Economy? Governments? 'Neoliberal' Economics?" in Paul Collier et al., "Capitalism," 664–77.

65. Milton Friedman, "The Social Responsibility of Business Is to Increase Its Profits," *New York Times Magazine*, September 13, 1970, https://web.archive.org/web/20060207060807/https://www.colorado.edu/studentgroups/libertarians/issues/friedman-soc-resp-business.html.

66. For a thoughtful discussion of what this means, see Michael C. Jensen, "Value Maximization, Stakeholder Theory, and the Corporate Objective Function," *European Financial Management* 7, no. 3 (2001): 297–317, https://efmaefm.org/bharat/jensen_efm2001.pdf.

67. H. L. Mencken, *Prejudices: Second Series*, 1920, https://www.goodreads.com/author/quotes/7805.

68. Ronald Coase, "The Nature of the Firm," *Economica* 4, no. 16 (1937): 386–405, https://onlinelibrary.wiley.com/doi/full/10.1111/j.1468-0335.1937.tb00002.x.

69. On these issues, see Colin Mayer, *Firm Commitment: Why the Corporation Is Failing Us and How to Restore Trust in It* (Oxford: Oxford University Press, 2013), and *Prosperity: Better Business Makes the Greater Good* (Oxford: Oxford University Press, 2018). See also Martin Wolf, "Opportunist Shareholders Must Embrace Commitment," *Financial Times*, August 26, 2014, https://www.ft.com/content/6aa87b9a-2d05-11e4-911b-00144feabdc0, and "We Must Rethink the Purpose of the Corporation," *Financial Times*, December 11, 2018, https://www.ft.com/content/786144bc-fc93-11e8-ac00-57a2a826423e.

70. Adam Smith, *An Inquiry into the Nature and Causes of the Wealth of Nations*, Book V, chapter I, part III, 1776, http://media.bloomsbury.com/rep/files/primary-source-93-adam-smith-the-wealth-of-nations-on-joint-stock-companies.pdf.

71. John Stuart Mill, *Principles of Political Economy*, 9th ed. (London: Longmans, Green, 1885), 140.

72. See Andrew Smithers, *Productivity and the Bonus Culture* (Oxford: Oxford University Press, 2019), especially chapter 14. See also Roland Bénabou and Jean Tirole, "Bonus Culture: Competitive Pay, Screening, and Multitasking," *Journal of Political Economy* 124, no. 2 (2016): 305–70.

73. On the empirically supported tendency of capital markets to generate short-term decision-making and so also underinvestment, see Andrew G. Haldane, "The Costs of Short-termism," chapter 4 in Jacobs and Mazzucato, *Rethinking Capitalism*, 66–76.

74. On the lack of a link between pay and performance, see Stiglitz, "Inequality and Economic Growth," 141. See also Lucian Bebchuk and Jesse Fried, *Pay without Performance: The Unfulfilled Promise of Executive Compensation* (Cambridge, MA: Harvard University Press, 2004); Lucian Bebchuk and Yaniv Grinstein, "The Growth of Executive Pay," National Bureau of Economic Research Working Paper No. 11443, June 2005, https://www.nber.org/papers/w11443; and Lawrence Mishel and Josh Bivens, "The Pay of Corporate Executives and Financial Professionals as Evidence of Rents in Top 1 Percent Incomes," Economic Policy Institute Working Paper No. 296, June 20, 2013, https://www.epi.org/publication/pay-corporate-executives-financial-professionals/.

75. See David Card and Alan B. Krueger, *Myth and Measurement: The New Economics of the Minimum Wage*, Twentieth-Anniversary Edition (Princeton, NJ: Princeton University Press, 2015), and Arindrajit Dube, "Guest Post: Minimum Wage Laws and the Labor Market: What Have We Learned Since Card and Krueger's Book *Myth and Measurement?*" September 1, 2011, https://rortybomb.wordpress.com/2011/09/01/guest-post-minimum-wage-laws-and-the-labor-market-what-have-we-learned-since-card-and-krueger%E2%80%99s-book-myth-and-measurement/.

76. See Cardozo Law, "Disney's Influence on U.S. Copyright Law," August 26, 2021, https://online.yu.edu/cardozo/blog/disney-influence-copyright-law.

77. This is the central point of Mancur Olson's masterpiece, *The Logic of Collective Action: Public Goods and the Theory of Groups* (Cambridge, MA: Harvard University Press, 1965 and 1971).

78. Robert H. Frank and Philip J. Cook, *The Winner-Take-All Society: Why the Few at the Top Get So Much More Than the Rest of Us* (New York and London: Penguin, 1996).

79. Patrick Barwise, "Nine Reasons Why Tech Markets Are Winner-Take-All," London Business School, July 10, 2018, https://www.london.edu/lbsr/nine-reasons-why-tech-markets-are-winner-take-all.

80. Martin Wolf, "Taming the Masters of the Tech Universe," *Financial Times*, November 14, 2017, https://www.ft.com/content/45092c5c-c872-11e7-aa33-c63fdc9b8c6c.

81. Bob Bryan, "One Quote from Warren Buffett Is the Perfect Advice for Investing in the Age of Uber and Netflix," *Business Insider*, May 4, 2019, https://www.businessinsider.com/buffett-on-moats-2016-4?IR=T.

82. Paul Collier, *The Future of Capitalism: Facing the New Anxieties* (London: Allen Lane, 2018), chapter 7.

83. On the role of the world's great cities, see Martin Wolf, "Cities Must Be Open to the World When Nations Are Not," *Financial Times*, June 7, 2017, https://www.ft.com/content/fea537f8-34d6-11e7-99bd-13beb0903fa3.

84. Noah J. Toly and Sam Tabory, "100 Top Economies: Urban Influence and the Position of Cities in an Evolving World Order," October 13, 2016, Chicago Council on Global Affairs, https://www.thechicagocouncil.org/publication/100-top-economies-urban-influence-and-position-cities-evolving-world-order.

85. *OECD Regional Outlook 2016: Productive Regions for Inclusive Societies* (Paris: OECD, 2016), 19.

86. Jane Jacobs, *The Economy of Cities* (New York: Vintage Books, 1969).

87. Henry George, *Progress and Poverty: An Inquiry into the Cause of Industrial Depressions and of Increase of Want with Increase of Wealth: The Remedy* (Vega Publishing, 2019; first published 1879).

88. Collier, *The Future of Capitalism*, chapter 7.

89. See Jonathan Tepper, with Denise Hearn, *The Myth of Capitalism: Monopolies and the Death of Competition* (Hoboken, NJ: Wiley, 2018), and Tim Wu, *The Curse of Bigness: Antitrust in the New Gilded Age* (New York: Columbia Global Reports, 2018).

90. Robert H. Bork, *The Antitrust Paradox: A Policy at War with Itself*, 2nd ed. (New York: Free Press, 1993).

91. See, on these arguments, Jason Furman, "Beyond Antitrust: The Role of Competition Policy in Promoting Inclusive Growth," Searle Center Conference on Antitrust Economics and Competition Policy, September 16, 2016, https://obamawhitehouse.archives.gov/sites/default/files/page/files/20160916_searle_conference_competition_furman_cea.pdf.

92. "Introduction from the Expert Panel," in Jason Furman et al., *Unlocking Digital Competition: Report on the Digital Competition Expert Panel*, March 2019, https://assets.publishing.service.gov.uk/gov ernment/uploads/system/uploads/attachment_data/file/785547/unlocking_digital_competition _furman_review_web.pdf.

93. Thomas Philippon, *The Great Reversal: How America Gave Up on Free Markets* (Cambridge, MA: Belknap Press of Harvard University Press, 2019), 205.

94. Ibid., part 4.

95. Hannah Murphy and Patrick McGee, "Apple Makes Unexpected Concession on 30% App Store Fees," *Financial Times*, September 25, 2020, https://www.ft.com/content/fbabedb0-3ed2-4c47 -94f2-f165bd15edb3.

96. Philippon, *The Great Reversal*, 100.

97. Ibid., 108, figure 6.5.

98. Ibid., 126.

99. Ibid., chapter 8.

100. Ibid., 147–48.

101. See Organization for Economic Co-operation and Development, "BEPS: Inclusive Framework on Base Erosion and Profit Shifting," https://www.oecd.org/tax/beps/.

102. Chris Giles, Emma Agyemang, and Aime Williams, "136 Nations Agree to Biggest Corporate Tax Deal in a Century," *Financial Times*, October 8, 2021, https://www.ft.com/content/5dc4e2d5-d7bd -4000-bf94-088f17e21936.

103. "Tax on Corporate Profits," Organization for Economic Co-operation and Development, https:// data.oecd.org/tax/tax-on-corporate-profits.htm#indicator-chart.

104. Ernesto Crivelli, Ruud De Mooij, and Michael Keen, "Base Erosion, Profit Shifting and Develop-ing Countries," WP/15/118, May 2015, figure 3 and table 6, https://www.imf.org/en/Publications /WP/Issues/2016/12/31/Base-Erosion-Profit-Shifting-and-Developing-Countries-42973. On rates, see also https://www.imf.org/external/np/exr/consult/2018/corptaxation/pdf/2018commentscorp taxation.pdf.

105. Crivelli et al., "Base Erosion, Profit Shifting," figures 1 and 2.

106. Tax Justice Network, "Corporate Tax Haven Index 2019," citing *The New York Times*, https:// corporatetaxhavenindex.org/.

107. Thomas Wright and Gabriel Zucman, "The Exorbitant Tax Privilege," National Bureau of Economic Research Working Paper 24983, September 2018: 1, https://www.nber.org/papers/w24983.

108. Annette Alstadsæter, Niels Johannesen, and Gabriel Zucman, "Who Owns the Wealth in Tax Havens? Macro Evidence and Implications for Global Inequality," National Bureau of Economic Research Working Paper 23805, September 2017, especially figures, 5, 8, and 9, https://www .nber.org/papers/w23805.pdf.

109. "The Tax Policy Center's Briefing Book," https://www.taxpolicycenter.org/briefing-book/what -carried-interest-and-should-it-be-taxed-capital-gain.

110. Martin Gilens and Benjamin I. Page, "Testing Theories of American Politics: Elites, Interest Groups, and Average Citizens," *Perspectives on Politics*, September 18, 2014: 564–81, https://www .cambridge.org/core/journals/perspectives-on-politics/issue/32534CA34A6B58E6E4420 B56764850E1.

111. Gilens and Page replied to objections to their thesis in "Critics Argued with Our Analysis of U.S. Political Inequality. Here Are 5 Ways They're Wrong," *Washington Post*, May 23, 2016, https:// www.washingtonpost.com/news/monkey-cage/wp/2016/05/23/critics-challenge-our-portrait -of-americas-political-inequality-heres-5-ways-they-are-wrong/.

112. Philippon, *The Great Reversal*, 189.

113. Ibid., part III.

114. This is the theme of Paul Collier and John Kay, *Greed Is Dead: Politics after Individualism* (London: Allen Lane, 2020).

115. Joris Luyendijk, *Swimming with Sharks: My Journey into the World of the Bankers* (London: Guardian Faber Publishing, 2015).

116. On this, see Joseph Stiglitz, "Ten Years Later," Keynote Address, Roosevelt Institute Work-ing Paper, September 2018, https://www8.gsb.columbia.edu/faculty/jstiglitz/sites/jstiglitz/files /Roosevelt%2010-Years-After-the-Financial-Crisis.pdf. See also the Independent Commission on Banking, chaired by Sir John Vickers, *Final Report: Recommendations*, September 2011, https:// bankingcommission.s3.amazonaws.com/wp-content/uploads/2010/07/ICB-Final-Report.pdf.

117. See Anat Admati and Martin Hellwig, *The Banker's New Clothes: What's Wrong with Banking and What to Do about It*, updated ed. (Princeton, NJ: Princeton University Press, 2014). On pro-cyclical

regulation and persistently high leverage, see Martin Wolf, "Why Further Financial Crises Are Inevitable," *Financial Times*, March 19, 2019, https://www.ft.com/content/d9d94f4a-4884-11e9 -bbc9-6917dce3dc62.

118. See Martin Wolf, "COP26 Is the Real Thing and Not a Drill," *Financial Times*, October 19, 2021, https://www.ft.com/content/799b7b93-9ec5-4318-9ac1-1c82cb81f96d; and "What Is the Least We Need from COP26?" *Financial Times*, October 26, 2021, https://www.ft.com/content/f859d515 -f1d0-405f-9aee-c609951f4254.

119. See Lewis Carroll, "The Hunting of the Snark," https://www.poetryfoundation.org/poems/43909 /the-hunting-of-the-snark.

120. Martin Wolf, "Dancing on the Edge of Climate Disaster," *Financial Times*, November 23, 2021, https://www.ft.com/content/6e2b366f-e139-4d69-bd4f-9254333bf316.

121. The phrase "workers by hand and by brain" appeared in Clause IV of the Labour Party, adopted in 1918 and amended in 1995, under the leadership of Tony Blair.

122. See Carl Benedikt Frey, *The Technology Trap: Capital, Labor, and Power in the Age of Automation* (Princeton, NJ, and Oxford: Princeton University Press, 2019), especially part V, "The Future," for a more benign view, and Daniel Susskind, *A World without Work: Technology, Automation and How We Should Respond* (London: Allen Lane, 2020), especially part II, "The Threat," for a darker perspective.

123. For an early assessment of the impact of COVID-19 on an unprepared world, see Adam Tooze, *Shutdown: How Covid Shook the World's Economy* (London: Penguin, 2021).

124. James Politi, Colby Smith, and Brendan Greeley, "Donald Trump Raises Tariffs on Chinese Goods after Stocks Tumble," *Financial Times*, August 24, 2019, https://www.ft.com/content/2db9c1ec -c5b9-11e9-a8e9-296ca66511c9.

Chapter Six: Perils of Populism

1. "Washington's Farewell Address 1796," https://avalon.law.yale.edu/18th_century/washing.asp.

2. Foundation for Economic Education, "H. L. Mencken Quotes on Government, Democracy, and Politicians," https://fee.org/articles/12-hl-mencken-quotes-on-government-democracy-and -politicians/.

3. Masha Gessen, *Surviving Autocracy* (London: Granta, 2020), 16.

4. Erica Frantz, *Authoritarianism: What Everyone Needs to Know* (Oxford: Oxford University Press, 2018). See also Martin Wolf, "The Rise of the Populist Authoritarians," *Financial Times*, January 22, 2019, https://www.ft.com/content/4faf6c4e-1d84-11e9-b2f7-97e4dbd3580d.

5. See, on this process, especially in Hungary and Poland, Anne Applebaum, *Twilight of Democracy: The Seductive Lure of Authoritarianism* (London: Allen Lane, 2020).

6. Ibid., 17.

7. See S. E. Finer, *The History of Government*, vol. 1, *Ancient Monarchies and Empires* (Oxford: Oxford University Press, 1997 and 1999), 1–96, "The Conceptual Prologue."

8. Applebaum, *Twilight of Democracy*, and also Martin Wolf, "Alarm Signals of Our Authoritarian Age," *Financial Times*, July 21, 2020, https://www.ft.com/content/5eb5d26d-0abe-434e-be12 -5068bd6d7f06.

9. See Martin Sandbu, "Populists and Kleptocrats Are a Perfect Match," *Financial Times*, September 22, 2020, https://www.ft.com/content/ef4111a6-8ac8-419e-8747-8ce1b887cb61.

10. Ivan Krastev and Stephen Holmes, *The Light That Failed: A Reckoning* (London: Penguin, 2019).

11. Roberto Stefan Foa and Jonathan Wilmot, "The West Has a Resentment Epidemic: Across the West, the Main Trigger of Populism Has Been the Growing Inequality—and Hostility—Between Urban and Rural Regions," *Foreign Policy*, September 18, 2019, https://foreignpolicy.com/2019 /09/18/the-west-has-a-resentment-epidemic-populism/.

12. Michael J. Sandel, *The Tyranny of Merit: What's Become of the Common Good?* (London: Penguin, 2020).

13. A lively account of this history is in Simon Schama, "Who Speaks for the People? Liberal Institutions Are Under Attack from Leaders Who Claim to Embody the Popular Will," *Financial Times*, October 4, 2019, https://www.ft.com/content/9e8f70b8-e5eb-11e9-b112-9624ec9edc59.

14. Anne Applebaum describes how disappointed careerism plays a role in driving people (especially ambitious and mediocre people) toward supporting would-be tyrants. See Applebaum, *Twilight of Democracy*. See also Martin Wolf, "Alarm Signals of Our Authoritarian Age," *Financial Times*, July 21, 2020.

15. Jan-Werner Müller, *What Is Populism?* (Philadelphia: University of Pennsylvania Press, 2016), 3.

16. Ibid., 21.

17. Ibid., 22.
18. Ibid., 27.
19. This is a play on *"L'état, c'est moi,"* a sentence commonly (but probably erroneously) attributed to Louis XIV of France. See *Oxford Reference*, https://www.oxfordreference.com.
20. Steven Levitsky and Daniel Ziblatt, *How Democracies Die: What History Reveals about Our Future* (New York: Crown, 2018), 23–24.
21. Ibid., 72–96, chapter 4.
22. See Barry Eichengreen, *The Populist Temptation: Economic Grievance and Political Reaction in the Modern Era* (New York: Oxford University Press, 2018), chapter 1 and especially page 4.
23. Our Documents: The Second New Deal, "Franklin Delano Roosevelt's Address Announcing the Second New Deal," October 31, 1936, http://docs.fdrlibrary.marist.edu/od2ndst.html.
24. John B. Judis, *The Populist Explosion: How the Great Recession Transformed American and European Politics* (New York: Columbia Global Reports, 2016), 14.
25. Miles Johnson, "Will Italy's New Coalition Flourish or Succumb to Resurgent Salvini?" *Financial Times*, September 5, 2019, https://www.ft.com/content/84431938-cf45-11e9-b018-ca4456540ea6. It is worth noting, however, that the PD partly has roots in the old Italian communist party.
26. Judis, *The Populist Explosion*, 14–15.
27. "George Wallace: American Politician," *Britannica*, https://www.britannica.com/biography/George-C-Wallace; and David Leonhardt and Prasad Philbrick, "Donald Trump's Racism: The Definitive List, Updated," *New York Times*, January 15, 2018, https://www.nytimes.com/interactive/2018/01/15/opinion/leonhardt-trump-racist.html.
28. Martin Wolf, "A Republican Tax Plan Built for Plutocrats," *Financial Times*, November 21, 2017, https://www.ft.com/content/e494f47e-ce1a-11e7-9dbb-291a884dd8c6.
29. "Jarosław Kaczyński: Prime Minister of Poland," *Britannica*, https://www.britannica.com/biography/Jaroslaw-Kaczynski. On the characteristics of the PiS government, see Slawomir Sierakowski, "The Five Lessons of Populist Rule," *Project Syndicate*, January 2, 2017, https://www.project-syndicate.org/commentary/lesson-of-populist-rule-in-poland-by-slawomir-sierakowski-2017-01?barrier=accesspaylog.
30. Brett Meyer, "Pandemic Populism: An Analysis of Populists Leaders' Responses to Covid-19," Tony Blair Institute for Global Change, August 17, 2020, https://institute.global/policy/pandemic-populism-analysis-populist-leaders-responses-covid-19.
31. Thus, the Centre for the Future of Democracy's *The Great Reset: Public Opinion, Populism, and the Pandemic*, published in January 2022, concludes from opinion surveys in twenty-seven countries that "we find strong evidence that the pandemic has reversed the rise of populism, whether measured using support for populist parties, approval of populist leaders, or agreements with populist attitudes." However, it also finds that "we find a disturbing erosion of support for core democratic beliefs and principles." See page 1 in Roberto S. Foa, Xavier Romero-Vidal, Andrew J. Klassen, Joaquin Fuenzalida Concha, Marian Quednau, and Lisa Sophie Fenner, *The Great Reset: Public Opinion, Populism, and the Pandemic*, Centre for the Future of Democracy, University of Cambridge, January 2022.
32. See Martin Baxter, "Three-D Politics and the Seven Tribes," *Electoral Calculus*, April 20, 2019, https://www.electoralcalculus.co.uk/pol3d_main.html. The data used come from British Election Study, a long-running series of polls run by academics at the universities of Manchester, Nottingham, and Oxford.
33. New Labour's introduction of the minimum wage and greater protection of worker rights were important symbols of this orientation.
34. This definition of the more nationalist and socially conservative members of the traditional working class as "Somewheres" is taken from David Goodhart's seminal book *The Road to Somewhere: The Populist Revolt and the Future of Politics* (London: C. Hurst & Co, 2017). In Goodhart's view, "Somewheres" are people who are strongly attached to a particular place and can be opposed to the normally university-educated "Anywheres." Somewheres are not just attached to a place, but also tend to be socially conservative and patriotic. Goodhart attributes to Somewheres the decisive support for right-wing populism in the US, the UK, and continental Europe.
35. Polly Curtis, "Gordon Brown Calls Labour Supporter a 'Bigoted Woman,'" *Guardian*, April 28, 2010, https://www.theguardian.com/politics/2010/apr/28/gordon-brown-bigoted-woman.
36. Martin Baxter, "Voter Migration by Group 2017–2019," *Electoral Calculus*, January 21, 2020, https://www.electoralcalculus.co.uk/pseph_group_migration_2019.html.
37. Francis Fukuyama, *Identity: The Demand for Dignity and the Politics of Resentment* (New York: Farrar, Straus and Giroux, 2018), 6.

38. Thomas Piketty, "Brahmin Left vs Merchant Right: Rising Inequality & the Changing Structure of Political Conflict (Evidence from France, Britain and the US, 1948–2017)," March 2018, WID .world Working Paper Series No 2018/7, http://piketty.pse.ens.fr/files/Piketty2019.pdf. This argument is elaborated further in Thomas Piketty, *Capital and Ideology* (Cambridge, MA, and London: Belknap Press of Harvard University Press, 2020), 807–61, chapter 15; and Amory Gethin, Clara Martínez-Toledano, and Thomas Piketty, "Brahmin Left vs Merchant Right: Changing Political Cleavages in 21 Western Democracies 1948–2020," *Quarterly Journal of Economics* 137, no. 1 (2022).

39. Piketty, "Brahmin Left vs Merchant Right," abstract.

40. Piketty, *Capital and Ideology*, 833.

41. Gethin, Martinez-Toledano, and Piketty, "Brahmin Left Versus Merchant Right," 3.

42. Piketty, *Capital and Ideology*, 859, figure 15.18.

43. Thomas B. Edsall, "We Aren't Seeing White Support for Trump for What It Is," *New York Times*, August 28, 2019, https://www.nytimes.com/2019/08/28/opinion/trump-white-voters.html?action =click&module=Opinion&pgtype=Homepage.

44. Demetri Sevastopulo, "Trump Sees Clearer Path to Republican Nomination," *Financial Times*, February 24, 2016, https://www.ft.com/content/8bf2aeb0-db1e-11e5-a72f-1e7744c66818.

45. OECD, "Intergenerational Mobility in Education," OECD.Stat, stats.oecd.org.

46. See Global Security.org, "'Führerprinzip' (Leader Principle)," https://www.globalsecurity.org /military/world/europe/de-fuhrerprinzip.htm.

47. Joseph A. Schumpeter, *Capitalism, Socialism and Democracy*, 3rd ed. (New York: Harper & Row, 1950).

48. Thomas E. Mann and Norman J. Ornstein, "Let's Just Say It: The Republicans Are the Problem," *Washington Post*, April 27, 2012, https://www.washingtonpost.com/opinions/lets-just-say-it-the -republicans-are-the-problem/2012/04/27/gIQAxCVUlT_story.html. See also Mann and Ornstein, *It's Even Worse Than It Looks: How the American Constitutional System Collided with the New Politics of Extremism* (New York: Basic Books, 2012).

49. Katherine Stewart, "Why Trump Reigns as King Cyrus," *New York Times*, December 31, 2018, https://www.nytimes.com/2018/12/31/opinion/trump-evangelicals-cyrus-king.html?action =click&module=MoreInSection&pgtype=Article&region=Footer&contentCollection=Opinion.

50. Jonathan Portes, "The Economics of Migration," June 5, 2019, https://journals.sagepub.com/doi /10.1177/1536504219854712.

51. Yascha Mounk, *The Great Experiment: How to Make Diverse Democracies Work* (London: Bloomsbury, 2022); and Martin Wolf, "A Call to Arms for Diverse Democracies and Their 'Decent Middle,'" *Financial Times*, May 5, 2022, https://www.ft.com/content/83ba0474-70ea-4759-81f1 -e14f6ea269fa

52. Yascha Mounk, "Illiberal Democracy or Undemocratic Liberalism?" *Project Syndicate*, June 9, 2016, https://www.project-syndicate.org/commentary/trump-european-populism-technocracy-by -yascha-mounk-1-2016-06.

53. Martin Wolf, "Counter-revolution by Jan Zielonka—Project Backlash," *Financial Times*, February 1, 2018, https://www.ft.com/content/e4290c10-069f-11e8-9650-9c0ad2d7c5b5; and Zielonka, *Counter-revolution: Liberal Europe in Retreat* (Oxford: Oxford University Press, 2018).

54. Martin Wolf, "A Republican Tax Plan Built for Plutocrats," *Financial Times*, November 21, 2017, https://www.ft.com/content/e494f47e-ce1a-11e7-9dbb-291a884dd8c6.

55. Martin Wolf, "A New Gilded Age," *Financial Times*, April 25, 2006, https://www.ft.com/content /76def9b0-d481-11da-a357-0000779e2340.

56. Ibid.

57. See, for example, Arthur Laffer, "Trump's Tax Cut Will Put America Back on a Path to Growth," *Financial Times*, October 29, 2017, https://www.ft.com/content/50c5a34c-b8d0-11e7-bff8-f994 6607a6ba. Laffer was one of the principal proponents of supply-side economics under Ronald Reagan.

58. In an outstanding book, *The Vanishing Middle Class: Prejudice and Power in a Dual Economy* (Cambridge, MA: MIT Press, 2017), Peter Temin of the Massachusetts Institute of Technology provides an account of the role of racial prejudice in cementing the political power of the American economic elite. Note, in particular, what he terms "racecraft," the politically convenient division of the bottom 80 percent of American workers into the "whites" and people of color. See, for example, chapter 5 and page 154. See also Heather Cox Richardson, *How the South Won the Civil War: Oligarchy, Democracy, and the Continuing Fight for the Soul of America* (New York: Oxford University Press, 2020).

59. This is not to argue that there is no value in the idea of "trickle down" in economics. There is no doubt that almost everybody has benefited from the vast improvements in economic know-how and productivity of the past two centuries. In an obvious sense, this is a "trickle down" from a process of development in which capitalist economics played a huge part. But that is quite different from arguing that manipulations of the tax system aimed at benefiting the most successful and richest are sure to benefit everybody.

60. Between 1933 and 1995, the Democrats held a majority in the House of Representatives in all Congresses, bar two (1947 and 1953). Since 1995, the Republicans have held a majority in the House in all Congresses, bar four (2007, 2009, 2019, and 2021).

61. "Jim Crow Law: United States [1877–1954]," *Britannica*, https://www.britannica.com/event/Jim -Crow-law.

62. The most important decisions were *Brown v. Board of Education of Topeka* (1954), which ruled against segregation in public education; *Heart of Atlanta Motel, Inc. v. United States* (1964), which challenged the constitutionality of the Civil Rights Act of 1964; and *Loving v. Virginia* (1967), which ruled the bans on interracial marriage unconstitutional. See "Ten Important Supreme Court Decisions in Black History," February 28, 2017, https://www.infoplease.com/us/government/ju dicial-branch/ten-important-supreme-court-decisions-in-black-history.

63. On the role of the southern system and its Western offshoots in contemporary American conservatism, see Richardson, *How the South Won the Civil War*.

64. Peter H. Lindert and Jeffrey G. Williamson, "American Incomes 1774–1860," National Bureau of Economic Research Working Paper No. 18396, September 15, 2012, https://www.nber.org/papers /w18396.

65. See James W. Loween, "5 Myths about Why the South Seceded," *Washington Post*, January 11, 2011, https://www.washingtonpost.com/wp-dyn/content/article/2011/01/07/AR2011010706547.html.

66. "Civil War Casualties: Casualty Numbers and Battle Death Statistics for the American Civil War," https://www.historynet.com/civil-war-casualties. See also Guy Gugliotta, "New Estimate Raises Civil War Death Toll," *New York Times*, April 2, 2012, https://www.nytimes.com/2012/04/03 /science/civil-war-toll-up-by-20-percent-in-new-estimate.html.

67. National Park Service, "The Civil War," https://www.nps.gov/civilwar/facts.htm.

68. See Gordon Rhea, "Why Non-Slaveholding Southerners Fought," American Battlefield Trust, January 25, 2011, https://www.battlefields.org/learn/articles/why-non-slaveholding-southerners -fought.

69. Elaine Kamarck, "How Many Undocumented Immigrants Are in the United States and Who Are They?" November 12, 2019, https://www.brookings.edu/policy2020/votervital/how-many -undocumented-immigrants-are-in-the-united-states-and-who-are-they/.

70. William H. Frey, "The US Will Become 'Minority White' in 2045, Census Projects: Youthful Minorities Are the Engine of Future Growth," Brookings, March 14, 2018, https://www.brookings .edu/blog/the-avenue/2018/03/14/the-us-will-become-minority-white-in-2045-census-projects/.

71. In an important judgment in 2013, the Supreme Court struck down central elements in the Voting Rights Act of 1965, thereby allowing nine states, mostly in the South, to free themselves of federal surveillance of the bad behavior. See Adam Liptak, "Supreme Court Invalidates Key Part of Voting Rights Act," *New York Times*, June 25, 2013, https://www.nytimes.com/2013/06/26 /us/supreme-court-ruling.html.

72. Steven Levitsky and Daniel Ziblatt, "Why Republicans Play Dirty," *New York Times*, September 20, 2019, https://www.nytimes.com/2019/09/20/opinion/republicans-democracy-play-dirty.html ?action=click&module=Opinion&pgtype=Homepage.

73. See Matthew Wills, "How Antebellum Christians Justified Slavery," *JSTOR Daily*, June 27, 2018, https://daily.jstor.org/how-antebellum-christians-justified-slavery/.

74. As of December 10, 2019, Donald Trump had made 15,413 false claims since he took office. See Glenn Kessler, Salvador Rizzo, and Meg Kelly, "President Trump Has Made 15,413 False or Misleading Claims over 1,055 Days," *Washington Post*, December 16, 2019, https://www.washington post.com/politics/2019/12/16/president-trump-has-made-false-or-misleading-claims-over-days/.

75. Philip Schwadel and Gregory A. Smith, "Evangelical Approval of Trump Remains High, but Other Religious Groups Are Less Supportive," Pew Research Center, March 18, 2019, https://www .pewresearch.org/fact-tank/2019/03/18/evangelical-approval-of-trump-remains-high-but-other -religious-groups-are-less-supportive/.

76. Matthew Yglesias, "Fox News's Propaganda Isn't Just Unethical—Research Shows It's Enormously Influential: Without the 'Fox Effect,' Neither Bush nor Trump Could Have Won," *Vox*, March 4, 2019, https://www.vox.com/2019/3/4/18249847/fox-news-effect-swing-elections.

77. Clyde Haberman, "Roger Ailes," *New York Times*, May 18, 2017, https://www.nytimes.com/2017/05/18/business/media/roger-ailes-dead.html.

78. David Mikkelson, "Rush Limbaugh 'Racist Quotes' List," Snopes, https://www.snopes.com/fact-check/bone-voyage/.

79. Robert D. McFadden and Michael M. Grynbaum, "Rush Limbaugh," *New York Times*, February 18, 2021, https://www.nytimes.com/2021/02/17/business/media/rush-limbaugh-dead.html.

80. Thomas Philippon, *The Great Reversal: How America Gave Up on Free Markets* (Cambridge, MA: Belknap Press of Harvard University Press, 2019), chapter 10, especially pages 178–89 and figures 10.2a and 10.2b on page 189. See also Martin Wolf, "Why the US Economy Isn't as Competitive or Free as You Think," *Financial Times*, November 14, 2019, https://www.ft.com/content/97be3f2c-00b1-11ea-b7bc-f3fa4e77dd47.

81. "Joseph McCarthy: United States Senator," *Britannica*, https://www.britannica.com/biography/Joseph-McCarthy; and "John Birch Society," *Britannica*, https://www.britannica.com/topic/John-Birch-Society.

82. Social Capital Project, "The Class Divide in Marriage," SCP brief, November 2017, https://www.jec.senate.gov/public/_cache/files/aba9b359-7457-4704-b0f1-93232f54b650/class-divide-in-marriage.pdf.

83. "You know, to just be grossly generalistic, you could put half of Trump's supporters into what I call the basket of deplorables. Right? The racist, sexist, homophobic, xenophobic, Islamaphobic— you name it. And unfortunately there are people like that, and he has lifted them up." See Katie Reilly, "Read Hillary Clinton's 'Basket of Deplorables' Remarks about Donald Trump Supporters," *Time*, September 10, 2016, https://time.com/4486502/hillary-clinton-basket-of-deplorables-transcript/.

84. Stuart Stevens, "Wake Up, Republicans. Your Party Stands for All the Wrong Things Now," *Washington Post*, January 1, 2020, https://www.washingtonpost.com/opinions/wake-up-republicans-your-party-stands-for-all-the-wrong-things-now/2019/12/31/c8347b32-2be8-11ea-9b60-817cc18cf173_story.html?utm_campaign=opinions&utm_medium=E-mail&utm_source=Newsletter&wpisrc=nl_opinions&wpmm=1.

85. See Jon Riley and Robert Chote, "Crisis and Consolidation in the Public Finances," Office for Budget Responsibility Working Paper No. 7, September 2014, https://obr.uk/docs/dlm_uploads/WorkingPaper7a.pdf.

86. See Ch. Wiburski, *Libertas as a Political Idea at Rome during the Late Republic and Early Principate* (Cambridge: Cambridge University Press, 1950), published online by Cambridge University Press 2009, https://www.cambridge.org/core/books/abs/libertas-as-a-political-idea-at-rome-during-the-late-republic-and-early-principate/general-characteristics-of-libertas/9A3E2748D31B349194E1CC439A280911.

87. "Blackshirt: Italian History," *Britannica*, https://www.britannica.com/topic/Blackshirt; and "SA: Nazi Organization," *Britannica*, https://www.britannica.com/topic/SA-Nazi-organization.

88. Michael Barthel, "5 Key Takeaways about the State of the News Media in 2018," Pew Research Center, July 23, 2019, https://www.pewresearch.org/fact-tank/2019/07/23/key-takeaways-state-of-the-news-media-2018/.

89. Yascha Mounk, *The People vs. Democracy: Why Our Freedom Is in Danger and How to Save It* (Cambridge, MA: Harvard University Press, 2018), 149–50.

90. Jonathan Haidt and Tobias Rose-Stockwell, "The Dark Psychology of Social Networks: Why It Feels Like Everything Is Going Haywire," *Atlantic*, December 2019, https://www.theatlantic.com/magazine/archive/2019/12/social-media-democracy/600763/.

91. Martin Gurri, *The Revolt of the Public and the Crisis of Authority in the New Millennium* (San Francisco: Stripe Press, 2018), 395.

92. See Marietje Schaake, "Greater Online Transparency Is the Key to Defending Democracy," *Financial Times*, January 10, 2022, https://www.ft.com/content/0e1d1cd8-73af-4a63-b426-e0ee5a7bf834.

93. Marshall McLuhan, *Understanding Media: The Extensions of Man* (Cambridge, MA: MIT Press, 1964 and 1994).

94. Roberto S. Foa et al., *The Great Reset*.

95. Shawn W. Rosenberg, "Democracy Devouring Itself: The Rise of the Incompetent Citizen and the Appeal of Right Wing Populism," 2019, in Domenico Uhng Hur and José Manuel Sabucedo, eds., *Psychology of Political and Everyday Extremisms*, forthcoming, https://escholarship.org/content/qt8806z01m/qt8806z01m_noSplash_eef039c0e7aa9b1263a0d0b757d3d886.pdf.

96. Ibid.

97. Martin Wolf, "Democrats, Demagogues and Despots," *Financial Times*, December 21, 2016, https://www.ft.com/content/9310dcea-c5d2-11e6-8f29-9445cac8966f.

Prologue to Part III

1. Branko Milanovic, *Capitalism Alone: The Future of the System That Rules the World* (Cambridge, MA, and London: Belknap Press of Harvard University Press, 2019).
2. Ibid., 20711.
3. See Torben Iversen and David Soskice, *Democracy and Prosperity: Reinventing Capitalism through a Turbulent Century* (Princeton, NJ, and Oxford: Princeton University Press, 2019).
4. Martin Wolf, "The Case for Capitalism," *Financial Times*, March 28, 2019, https://www.ft.com/content/d8b903d0-4bfe-11e9-bbc9-6917dce3dc62.

Chapter Seven: Renewing Capitalism

1. *The Independent*, September 16, 1998, https://www.oxfordreference.com/view/10.1093/acref/978 0191843730.001.0001/q-oro-ed5-00012411.
2. Cited in D. E. Moggridge, *Maynard Keynes: An Economist's Biography* (London and New York: Routledge, 1992), 695. The words come from a letter from Keynes to Frederick Pethick-Lawrence (1st Baron Pethick-Lawrence) on June 21, 1942. A facsimile of the letter is available online at Trinity College Cambridge, "Letter from J. M. Keynes to F. W. Pethick-Lawrence," https://archives.trin.cam.ac.uk/index.php/letter-from-j-m-keynes-to-f-w-pethick-lawrence-23.
3. Karl Popper, *The Open Society and Its Enemies*, vol. 1, *The Spell of Plato* (London: Routledge, 1945).
4. Jason Hickel argues that we should embrace "degrowth" (that is, give up the aim of economic growth), that capitalism is a five-hundred-year-old moral and practical catastrophe, and that human beings should stop thinking they are masters of nature in *Less Is More: How Degrowth Will Save the World* (London: William Heinemann, 2020).
5. Ibid., 287.
6. Our World in Data, "Life Expectancy," https://ourworldindata.org/life-expectancy.
7. Martin Wolf, "What the World Can Learn from the COVID-19 Pandemic," *Financial Times*, November 24, 2020, https://www.ft.com/content/7fb55fa2-4aea-41a0-b4ea-ad1a51cb415f.
8. See Martin Wolf, "Last Chance for the Climate Transition," *Financial Times*, February 18, 2020, https://www.ft.com/content/3090b1fe-51a6-11ea-8841-482eed0038b1.
9. On the required technological revolution, see Bill Gates, *How to Avoid a Climate Disaster: The Solutions We Have and the Breakthroughs We Need* (London: Allen Lane, 2021), as well as various publications of the Energy Transitions Commission, notably *Making Mission Possible: Delivering a Net-zero Economy*, September 2020, https://www.energy-transitions.org/publications/making-mission-possible/; *Keeping 1.5°C Alive: Closing the Gap in the 2020s*, September 2021, https://www.energy-transitions.org/publications/keeping-1-5-alive/; and International Energy Agency, *Net Zero by 2050: A Roadmap for the Global Energy Sector*, October 2021, https://iea.blob.core.windows.net/assets/deebef5d-0c34-4539-9d0c-10b13d840027/NetZeroby2050-ARoadmapfortheGlobalEnergySector_CORR.pdf.
10. Edmund Burke, *Reflections on the Revolution in France and on the Proceedings in Certain Societies in London Relative to That Event* (London: Dodsley, 1790), https://gallica.bnf.fr/ark:/12148/bpt6k111218p.r=.langEN.
11. See Stéphane Courtois Nicolas Werth, Jean-Louis Panné, Andrzej Paczkowski, Karel Bartosek, and Jean-Louise Margolin, *The Black Book of Communism: Crimes, Terror, Repression*, trans. Jonathan Murphy and Mark Kramer (Cambridge, MA: Harvard University Press, 1999).
12. Leon Trotsky, "Revolutionary and Socialist Art," *Literature and Revolution*, chapter 8, https://www.marxists.org/archive/trotsky/1924/lit_revo/ch08.htm.
13. See Christopher Sandom, Soren Faurby, Brody Sandel, and Jens-Christian Svenning, "Global Late Quaternary Megafauna Extinctions Linked to Humans, Not Climate Change," *Proceedings of the Royal Society, Biological Sciences*, July 22, 2014, https://royalsocietypublishing.org/doi/10.1098/rspb.2013.3254.
14. Jeremy Shearmur and Piers Norris Turner, eds., "Ideal and Reality in Society" in *Popper: After the Open Society: Selected Social and Political Writings* (London and New York: Routledge, 2008), 55.
15. See "The Beveridge Report and the Foundations of the Welfare State," National Archives, December 7, 2017, https://blog.nationalarchives.gov.uk/beveridge-report-foundations-welfare-state/.
16. Richard Layard, *Can We Be Happier? Evidence and Ethics* (London: Pelican Books, 2020), and Andrew E. Clark, Sarah Flèche, Richard Layard, Nattavudh Powdthavee, and George Ward, *The Origins of Happiness: The Science of Well-being over the Life Course* (Princeton, NJ: Princeton

University Press, 2018). See also Martin Wolf, "The Case for Making Wellbeing the Goal of Public Policy," *Financial Times*, May 30, 2019, https://www.ft.com/content/d4bb3e42-823b-11e9 -9935-ad75bb96c849.

17. Gene Sperling, former economic adviser to Barack Obama, has written an outstanding book built on the idea of economic dignity. This is a useful way of framing the approach to reform. See *Economic Dignity* (New York: Penguin, 2020).

18. Joseph Stiglitz, Amartya Sen, and Jean-Paul Fitoussi, *Report by the Commission on the Measurement of Economic Performance and Social Progress* (Paris: Organisation for Economic Co-operation and Development, 2009), 14–15, https://web.archive.org/web/20160806043140/http://www.com munityindicators.net/system/publication_pdfs/9/original/Stiglitz_Sen_Fitoussi_2009.pdf? 1323961027. One of the first official efforts to go beyond conventional GDP accounting was the *Human Development Index*, launched in the *Human Development Report 1990*, which was produced by the United Nations Development Program under the direction of the late Mahbub ul Haq, with the advice of the Indian Nobel laureate, Amartya Sen. See "Human Development Index," http://hdr.undp.org/en/content/human-development-index-hdi.

19. See John F. Helliwell, Richard Layard, Jeffrey D. Sachs, Jan-Emmanuel De Neve, Lara B. Akin, and Shun Wang, *World Happiness Report 2021*, table 2.1, https://happiness-report.s3.amazonaws .com/2021/WHR+21.pdf. See also Our World in Data, "Self-Reported Life Satisfaction vs GDP per capita, 2020," https://ourworldindata.org/grapher/gdp-vs-happiness.

20. Franklin Delano Roosevelt, "The Four Freedoms," speech, January 6, 1941, https://www.ameri canrhetoric.com/speeches/fdrthefourfreedoms.htm. This speech is known even more for the goals Roosevelt set out for the world. In it he introduced the idea of the "four freedoms"—freedom of speech, freedom of worship, freedom from want, and freedom from fear. These freedoms might be viewed as the global corollary of his domestic objectives. The US was, he insisted, bound up in the fate of the world. It could not, argued Roosevelt, be an island of democratic freedom in an ocean of despotism. Thus, as he asserted, "those who would give up essential liberty to purchase a little temporary safety deserve neither liberty nor safety."

21. Michael Sandel, *The Tyranny of Merit: What's Become of the Common Good?* (London: Penguin, 2020).

22. John Kay and Mervyn King, *Radical Uncertainty: Decision-making for an Unknowable Future* (London: Bridge Street Press, 2020).

23. On black swans, Nicholas Taleb, *The Black Swan: The Impact of the Highly Improbable* (London and New York: Penguin, 2007.

24. See Organization for Economic Co-operation and Development, "New Approaches to Economic Challenges," https://www.oecd.org/naec/. See also Martin Wolf, "Coronavirus Crisis Lays Bare the Risks of Financial Leverage, Again," *Financial Times*, April 28, 2020, https://www.ft.com /content/098dcd60-8880-11ea-a01c-a28a3e3fbd33.

25. See Friedrich A. Hayek, "Scientism and the Study of Society, Part I," *Economica* 9, no. 35 (August 1942): 267–91, https://www.jstor.org/stable/2549540?origin=crossref.

26. See Sébastien Miroudot, "Resilience Versus Robustness in Global Value Chains: Some Policy Implications," *VoxEU*, June 18, 2020, https://cepr.org/voxeu/columns/resilience-versus-robustness -global-value-chains-some-policy-implications.

27. On resilience, see Markus Brunnermeier, *The Resilient Society* (Colorado Springs: Endeavor, 2021).

28. See International Federation of Accountants, Public Sector Committee, *Implementing Accrual Accounting in Government: The New Zealand Experience*, October 1994, https://www.ifac.org /system/files/publications/files/no-1-implementation-accr.pdf.

29. See Dag Detter and Stefan Fölster, *The Public Wealth of Nations: How Management of Public Assets Can Boost or Bust Economic Growth* (Basingstoke, UK: Palgrave Macmillan, 2015).

Chapter Eight: Toward a "New" New Deal

1. Warren Buffett, https://www.goodreads.com/author/quotes/756.Warren_Buffett.

2. This was written by Supreme Court Justice Oliver Wendell Holmes in a dissenting opinion in 1927. See "Taxes Are What We Pay for Civilized Society," https://quoteinvestigator.com/2012 /04/13/taxes-civilize/.

3. Dani Rodrik, *The Inescapable Trilemma of the World Economy*, Dani Rodrik's blog, June 27, 2007, https://rodrik.typepad.com/dani_rodriks_weblog/2007/06/the-inescapable.html.

4. See Mark Thomas, *99%: Mass Impoverishment and How We Can End It* (London: Apollo, 2019).

5. On the dangers of excessive private debt and consequent crises, see Richard Vague, *A Brief History of Doom: Two Hundred Years of Financial Crises* (Philadelphia: University of Pennsylvania Press, 2019).
6. On the "blame game" played by politicians, see Simon Wren-Lewis, *The Lies We Were Told: Politics, Economics, Austerity and Brexit* (Bristol: Bristol University Press, 2018).
7. See, in particular, Martin Wolf, *The Shifts and the Shocks: What We've Learned—and Have Still to Learn—from the Financial Crisis* (London and New York: Penguin, 2014 and 2015), chapter 6.
8. Jason Furman and Lawrence H. Summers, "A Reconsideration of Fiscal Policy in the Era of Low Interest Rates," November 30, 2020, Discussion Draft, Brookings Institution, https://www .brookings.edu/wp-content/uploads/2020/11/furman-summers-fiscal-reconsideration -discussion-draft.pdf.
9. See Lawrence H. Summers and Anna Stansbury, "The End of the Golden Age of Central Banking?: Secular Stagnation Is about More Than the Zero Lower Bound," November 2020, preliminary and incomplete.
10. I condemned what I called "liquidationism" in *The Shifts and the Shocks*.
11. See Kimberly Amadeo, "Average American Middle-Class Net Worth?" *The Balance*, updated December 30, 2021, https://www.thebalance.com/american-middle-class-net-worth-3973493.
12. On these arguments, see Martin Wolf, "What Central Banks Ought to Target," *Financial Times*, March 2, 2021, https://www.ft.com/content/160db526-5e8d-4152-b711-21501a7fbd01.
13. See on these issues Martin Wolf, "A Matter of Interest—the Battle over Monetary Policy," *Financial Times*, July 27, 2022, https://www.ft.com/content/e7cc3c01-08e3-47fc-9442-d45378b34bb8, which discusses Ben S. Bernanke, *21st Century Monetary Policy: The Federal Reserve from the Great Inflation to Covid-19* (London and New York: W. W. Norton, 2022), and Edward Chancellor, *The Price of Time: The Real Story of Interest* (London: Allen Lane, 2022).
14. See Eric Lonergan, "Reply to Larry Summers," August 26, 2019, https://www.philosophyofmoney .net/a-reply-to-larry-summers/.
15. George Soros, "The EU Should Issue Perpetual Bonds," *Project Syndicate*, April 20, 2020, https:// www.project-syndicate.org/commentary/finance-european-union-recovery-with-perpetual -bonds-by-george-soros-2020-04.
16. See Martin Wolf, "Restoring UK Growth Is More Urgent Than Cutting Public Debt," *Financial Times*, December 13, 2020, https://www.ft.com/content/50394d54-1b2e-417b-ba6d-2204a4b 05f24.
17. See Lawrence H. Summers, "The Biden Stimulus Is Admirably Bold and Ambitious. But It Brings Some Big Risks, Too," *Washington Post*, February 4, 2021, https://www.washingtonpost.com /opinions/2021/02/04/larry-summers-biden-covid-stimulus/.
18. See L. Randall Wray, *Modern Money Theory: A Primer on Macroeconomics for Sovereign Monetary Systems* (New York: Palgrave Macmillan, 2012). On the history of these ideas, see Warren Mosler, *Soft Currency Economics II: What Everyone Thinks They Know about Monetary Policy Is Wrong* (US Virgin Islands: Valance, 1996 and 2013), and Stephanie Kelton, *The Deficit Myth: Modern Monetary Theory and How to Build a Better Economy* (London: John Murray, 2020).
19. These ideas go back to Abba Lerner, one of the most significant disciples of John Maynard Keynes. See Lerner, "Money as a Creature of the State," *Papers and Proceedings of the Fifty-ninth Annual Meeting of the American Economic Association, American Economic Review* 37, no. 2 (May 1947): 312–17.
20. On modern monetary theory, see Martin Wolf, "States Create Useful Money, but Abuse It," *Financial Times*, May 28, 2019, https://www.ft.com/content/fcc1274a-8073-11e9-9935-ad75bb 96c849.
21. Edward Shaw and Ronald McKinnon, both then at Stanford University, introduced the idea of "financial repression" in 1973. See Edward S. Shaw, *Financial Deepening in Economic Development* (New York: Oxford University Press, 1973), and Ronald McKinnon, *Money and Capital in Economic Development* (Washington, DC: Brookings Institution, 1973).
22. Sebastian Edwards, "Modern Monetary Disasters," *Project Syndicate*, May 16, 2019, https://www .project-syndicate.org/commentary/modern-monetary-theory-latin-america-by-sebastian -edwards-2019-05.
23. Martin Wolf, "Larry Summers: I'm Concerned That What Is Being Done Is Substantially Excessive," *Financial Times*, April 12, 2021, https://www.ft.com/content/380ea811-e927-4fe1-aa5b -d213816e9073.

24. See, on this, Martin Wolf, "The Return of the Inflation Specter," *Financial Times*, March 26, 2021, https://www.ft.com/content/6cfb36ca-d3ce-4dd3-b70d-eecc332ba1df.

25. See Charles Goodhart and Manoj Pradhan, *The Great Demographic Reversal: Aging Societies, Waning Inequality, and an Inflation Reversal* (London: Palgrave Macmillan, 2020), and Martin Wolf, "Why Inflation Could Be on the Way Back," *Financial Times*, November 17, 2020, https://www.ft.com/content/dea66630-d054-401a-ad1c-65ebd0d10b38.

26. See, on this, Martin Wolf, "The World Needs to Change the Way It Taxes Companies," *Financial Times*, March 7, 2019, https://www.ft.com/content/9a22b722-40c0-11e9-b896-fe36ec32aece. See also Alan Auerbach, Michael Devereux, Michael Keen, and John Vell, "Destination-Based Cash Flow Taxation," Oxford Legal Studies Research Paper No. 14/2017, Said Business School WP 2017-09, Oxford University Center for Business Taxation WP 17/01, https://papers.ssrn.com/sol3/papers.cfm?abstract_id=2908158.

27. See Martin Wolf, "The Threat and the Promise of Digital Money," *Financial Times*, October 22, 2019, https://www.ft.com/content/fc079a6a-f4ad-11e9-a79c-bc9acae3b654.

28. See, on digital currencies, Bank for International Settlements, "CBDCs: An Opportunity for the Monetary System," *Annual Economic Report 2021*, June 2021, chapter III, https://www.bis.org/publ/arpdf/ar2021e3.pdf; House of Lords Economic Affairs Committee, *Central Bank Digital Currencies: A Solution in Search of a Problem?*, HL Paper 131, January 13, 2022; and Markus Brunnermeier and Jean-Pierre Landau, *The Digital Euro: Policy Implications and Perspectives*, January 2022, Directorate-General for Internal Policies.

29. See Philippe Aghion, Céline Antonin, and Simon Bunel, trans. Jodie Cohen-Tanugi, *The Power of Creative Destruction: Economic Upheaval and the Wealth of Nations* (Cambridge, MA: Belknap Press of Harvard University Press, 2021). See also Martin Wolf, "How 'Creative Destruction' Drives Innovation and Prosperity," *Financial Times*, June 11, 2021, https://www.ft.com/content/3a0aa7cb-d10e-4352-b845-a50df70272b8.

30. See Jonathan Haskell and Stian Westlake, *Capitalism without Capital: The Rise of the Intangible Economy* (Oxford and Princeton, NJ: Princeton University Press, 2018).

31. See David Sainsbury, *Windows of Opportunity: How Nations Create Wealth* (London: Profile Books, 2020).

32. Ibid., chapter 2. For empirical support of this important idea, see Ricardo Hausmann, César A. Hidalgo, Sebastián Bustos, Michele Coscia, Alexander Simoes, and Muhammed A. Yildrim, *The Atlas of Economic Complexity: Mapping Paths to Prosperity* (Cambridge, MA: MIT Press, 2014).

33. See Alexander Hamilton, *Report on the Subject of Manufactures*, December 1791, and Friedrich List, *Das nationale System der politischen Oekonomie*, 1841.

34. See DARPA, "Innovation at DARPA," July 2016, https://www.darpa.mil/attachments/DARPA_Innovation_2016.pdf.

35. Mariana Mazzucato, *The Entrepreneurial State: Debunking Public vs Private Myths* (London: Penguin, 2018). See also Martin Wolf, "A Much-Maligned Engine of Innovation," *Financial Times*, August 4, 2013, https://www.ft.com/content/32ba9b92-efd4-11e2-a237-00144feabdc0. Mazzucato has proposed something rather more ambitious in her *Mission Economy: A Moonshot Guide to Changing Capitalism* (London: Allen Lane, 2021). John Kay provided a riposte in "*Mission Economy* by Mariana Mazzucato—Could Moonshot Thinking Help Fix the Planet?" *Financial Times*, January 13, 2021, https://www.ft.com/content/86475b94-3636-49ec-9b3f-7d7756350b30.

36. See "National Institutes of Health," https://www.nih.gov/, and "Medical Research Council (MRC)," https://mrc.ukri.org/about/institutes-units-centers/.

37. William H. Janeway, *Doing Capitalism in the Innovation Economy* (Cambridge: Cambridge University Press, 2012 and 2018).

38. Sainsbury, *Windows of Opportunity*, 226–27.

39. See Electronic Frontier Foundation, "Patent Trolls," https://www.eff.org/issues/resources-patent-troll-victims.

40. The Nobel Prize–winning economist Joseph Stiglitz has proposed greater reliance on prizes for promoting innovation. See "Prizes, Not Patents," *Project Syndicate*, March 6, 2007, https://www.project-syndicate.org/commentary/prizes—not-patents.

41. See Tejvan Pettinger, "Definition of Public Goods," *Economics Help: Helping to Simplify Economics*, July 28, 2019, https://www.economicshelp.org/micro-economic-essays/marketfailure/public-goods/.

42. Nicholas Gruen, "Government as Impresario," NESTA, October 20, 2014, https://www.nesta.org.uk/report/government-as-impresario/.

43. See William Lazonick, "Profits without Prosperity," *Harvard Business Review*, September 2014, https://hbr.org/2014/09/profits-without-prosperity; William Lazonick, Mustafa Erdem Sakinç, and Matt Hopkins, "Why Stock Buybacks Are Dangerous for the Economy," *Harvard Business Review*, January 2020, https://hbr.org/2020/01/why-stock-buybacks-are-dangerous-for-the-economy; and Andrew Smithers, *Productivity and the Bonus Culture* (Oxford: Oxford University Press, 2019).

44. In 2018, Europe and North America were responsible for 63 percent of cumulative emissions of carbon dioxide. According to Our World in Data, https://ourworldindata.org/grapher/cumulative -co2-emissions-region?time=earliest.latest.

45. International Monetary Fund, "Mitigating Climate Change," *World Economic Outlook October 2020*, chapter 3, https://www.imf.org/en/Publications/WEO/Issues/2020/09/30/world-economic -outlook-october-2020#Chapter%203.

46. Energy Transitions Commission, *Making Mission Possible: Delivering a Net-Zero Economy*, September 2020, https://www.energy-transitions.org/publications/making-mission-possible/; and Bill Gates, *How to Avoid a Climate Disaster: The Solutions We Have and the Breakthroughs We Need* (London: Allen Lane, 2021).

47. Martin Wolf, "Last Chance for the Climate Transition," *Financial Times*, February 18, 2020, https://www.ft.com/content/3090b1fe-51a6-11ea-8841-482eed0038b1.

48. See Earthworks, "FACT SHEET: Battery Minerals for the Clean Energy Transition," https://earthworks.org/fact-sheet-battery-minerals-for-the-the-clean-energy-transition/.

49. M. Garside, "Major Countries in Worldwide Cobalt Mine Production from 2010 to 2020," Statista, https://www.statista.com/statistics/264928/cobalt-mine-production-by-country/.

50. See, for example, "Economists' Statement on Carbon Dividends," January 17, 2019, https://clcouncil.org/economists-statement/; and James K. Boyce, *The Case for Carbon Dividends* (Cambridge, MA: Polity, 2019).

51. See Victor Mallet and David Keohane, "Year of 'Gilets Jaunes' Leaves Angry Mark on France, November 14, 2019, https://www.ft.com/content/9627c8be-0623-11ea-9afa-d9e2401fa7ca.

52. See Task Force on Climate-Related Financial Disclosures, "Climate Change Presents Financial Risk to the Global Economy," https://www.fsb-tcfd.org.

53. See Raghuram Rajan, "A Fair and Simple Way to Tax Carbon Emissions," *Financial Times*, December 17, 2019, https://www.ft.com/content/96782e84-2028-11ea-b8a1-584213ee7b2b.

54. See Martin Wolf, "Action Must Replace Talk on Climate Change," *Financial Times*, May 4, 2021, https://www.ft.com/content/3fa154f3-84e7-4964-9a21-d3dbd41e1470.

55. John Kay, *Culture and Prosperity: The Truth about Markets: Why Some Nations Are Rich and Most Remain Poor* (New York: Harper Business, 2004).

56. See R. James Breiding, *Too Small to Fail: Why Some Small Nations Outperform Larger Ones and How They Are Reshaping the World* (Uttar Pradesh, India: HarperCollins 2019).

57. See on the virtues of trade the outstanding book by Anne O. Krueger, former first deputy managing director of the International Monetary Fund, *International Trade: What Everyone Needs to Know* (New York: Oxford University Press, 2020), especially 294–97.

58. See Michael Peel, Sam Fleming, and Guy Chazan, "EU Clamps Down on Covid Vaccine Exports," *Financial Times*, January 29, 2021, https://www.ft.com/content/24867d39-4507-4c48-be27-c34b 581220b0.

59. See Martin Wolf, "The Big Mistakes of the Anti-Globalisers," *Financial Times*, June 21, 2022, https://www.ft.com/content/fa1f3a82-99c5-4fb2-8bff-a7e8d3f65849, and Martin Wolf, "In an Era of Disorder, Open Trade Is at Risk," *Financial Times*, June 28, 2022, https://www.ft.com /content/df62d58c-e864-4e3b-9aa6-5587e8ef1667.

60. On the US, in particular, see Adam Posen, "The Price of Nostalgia: America's Self-Defeating Economic Retreat," *Foreign Affairs*, May/June 2021, https://www.foreignaffairs.com/articles/united -states/2021-04-20/america-price-nostalgia.

61. On the distinction between sovereignty and discretion, see Martin Wolf, "Brexit: Sovereignty Is Not the Same as Power," *Financial Times*, May 3, 2016, https://www.ft.com/content/fece7238 -1071-11e6-91da-096d89bd2173.

62. See Bank for International Settlements, "Basel III: International Regulatory Framework for Banks," https://www.bis.org/bcbs/basel3.htm.

63. See Valentina Bruno and Hyun Song Shin, "Global Dollar Credit and Carry Trades: A Firm-Level Analysis," BIS Working Papers 510, Bank for International Settlements, August 2015, https://www .bis.org/publ/work510.pdf. The costs of currency mismatches were a theme of Martin Wolf, *Fixing Global Finance* (Baltimore and London: Johns Hopkins University Press, 2008 and 2010).

64. See Maurice Obstfeld, "The Global Capital Market Reconsidered," in Paul Collier, Diane Coyle, Colin Mayer, and Martin Wolf, eds., "Capitalism: What Has Gone Wrong, What Needs to Change, and How It Can Be Fixed," *Oxford Review of Economic Policy* 37, no. 4 (Winter 2021): 690–706.

65. It is worth noting that China controls internal migration precisely because of its concern over the social and demographic effects of such arbitrage, within a vast country with huge regional inequalities.

66. George J. Borjas, "Immigration and Globalization: A Review Essay," *Journal of Economic Literature* 53, no. 4 (2015): 961–74, https://sites.hks.harvard.edu/fs/gborjas/publications/journal/JEL 2015.pdf.

67. On the idea of guiding innovation, see Dani Rodrik and Stefanie Stantcheva, "Fixing Capitalism's Good Jobs Problem," in Paul Collier et al., eds., *Oxford Review of Economic Policy* 37, no. 4 (Winter 2021): 824–37.

68. See Daron Acemoglu, "Written Testimony," at a "Hearing on Machines, Artificial Intelligence, & the Workforce: Recovering & Readying Our Economy for the Future," House Committee on the Budget, September 10, 2021, https://www.congress.gov/116/meeting/house/111002/witnesses /HHRG 116 BU00 Wstate AcemogluD 20200910.pdf.

69. See Peter Scott, *Triumph of the South: A Regional Economic History of Early Twentieth Century Britain* (London and New York: Routledge, 2007 and 2018).

70. See Andrés Rodriguez-Pose, "The Revenge of the Places That Don't Matter (and What to Do about It)," *Cambridge Journal of Regions, Economy and Society* 11, no. 1 (March 2018): 189–209, title page, https://eprints.lse.ac.uk/85888/1/Rodriguez-Pose_Revenge%20of%20Places.pdf.

71. Ibid., 30.

72. Ibid., 32.

73. Paul Collier, *The Future of Capitalism: Facing the New Anxieties* (London: Allen Lane, 2018); and Raghuram Rajan, *Third Pillar: The Revival of Community in a Polarized World* (London: William Collins, 2019).

74. Martin Wolf, "Lessons in 'Leveling Up' from the Basque Country," *Financial Times*, November 30, 2021, https://www.ft.com/content/bb2c627f-1baa-4230-9cb8-3876c216b8f7.

75. See Nicholas Gruen, "The Evaluator General," Club Troppo, May 29, 2020, https://clubtroppo .com.au/2020/05/29/the-evaluator-general/.

76. EurWORK: European Observatory of Working Life, "Flexicurity," May 7, 2013, https://www .eurofound.europa.eu/observatories/eurwork/industrial-relations-dictionary/flexicurity,

77. David Card and Alan B. Krueger, *Myth and Measurement: The New Economics of the Minimum Wage*, Twentieth-Anniversary Edition (Princeton, NJ: Princeton University Press, 2015).

78. Pavlina R. Tcherneva, *The Case for a Jobs Guarantee* (Cambridge, UK, and Medford, MA: Polity, 2020), 46–47.

79. Michael Hiscox, "The Job Guarantee—Weakening Worker Power?" *Challenge Magazine*, August 22, 2020, https://www.challengemag.org/post/the-job-guarantee-weakening-worker-power.

80. Martin Sandbu, *The Economics of Belonging: A Radical Plan to Win Back the Left Behind and Achieve Prosperity for All* (Princeton, NJ, and Oxford: Princeton University Press, 2020), chapter 6.

81. See Johanna Hop, "The Hartz Employment Reforms in Germany," Center for Public Impact, September 2, 2019, https://www.centreforpublicimpact.org/case-study/hartz-employment-reforms -germany/.

82. Michael Sandel, *The Tyranny of Merit: What's Become of the Common Good?* (London: Penguin, 2020).

83. See Martin Wolf, "Hypocrisy and Confusion Distort the Debate on Social Mobility," *Financial Times*, May 2, 2019, https://www.ft.com/content/577a0abe-6c04-11e9-a9a5-351eeaef6d84.

84. Personal Finance Data, "Net Worth Percentile Comparison Calculator by Age," https://personal financedata.com/networth-percentile-calculator/.

85. On the role of the welfare state, see Nicholas Barr, *The Welfare State as Piggy Bank: Information, Risk, Uncertainty, and the Role of the State* (Oxford: Oxford University Press, 2001).

86. See Martin Wolf, "The Welfare State Is a Piggy Bank for Life," *Financial Times*, March 31, 2016, https://www.ft.com/content/b7ae7e52-f69a-11e5-96db-fc683b5e52db; and Peter Levell, Barra Roantree, and Jonathan Shaw, "Redistribution from a Lifetime Perspective," Institute for Fiscal Studies, September 22, 2015, https://www.ifs.org.uk/publications/7986.

87. According to the OECD, "Social expenditure comprises cash benefits, direct in-kind provision of goods and services, and tax breaks with social purposes. Benefits may be targeted at low-income households, the elderly, disabled, sick, unemployed, or young persons. To be considered 'social,'

programs have to involve either redistribution of resources across households or compulsory participation." See "Social Spending," https://data.oecd.org/socialexp/social-spending.htm.

88. Denmark, the Netherlands, and Switzerland are among the top ten countries in human development, according to the Human Development Index of the United Nations Development Program. See United Nations Development Program, Human Development Reports, "Human Development Index," http://hdr.undp.org/en/composite/HDI. France is substantially lower, at twenty-sixth.

89. See Philippe Van Parijs and Yannick Vanderborght, *Basic Income: A Radical Proposal for a Free Society and a Sane Economy* (Cambridge, MA, and London: Harvard University Press, 2017).

90. Gene Sperling, *Economic Dignity* (New York, Penguin, 2020), 185. A full discussion of UBI is contained in ibid., 184–89.

91. Annie E. Casey Foundation, Kids Count Data Center, Demographics, "Total Population by Child and Adult Populations in the United States," https://datacenter.kidscount.org/.

92. On federal receipts and outlays, see Congressional Budget Office, "Monthly Budget Review: Summary for Fiscal Year 2019," November 7, 2019, https://www.cbo.gov/. On gross domestic product, see Bureau of Economic Analysis, US Department of Commerce, https://www.bea.gov/. On Social Security spending, see American Association of Retired Persons, "How Much Social Security Will I Get?" https://www.aarp.org/retirement/social-security/questions-answers/how-much-social-security-will-i-get.html. On Medicare, see Kaiser Family Foundation, "State Health Facts: Medicare Spending per Enrollee 2018," https://www.kff.org/medicare/state-indicator/per-enrollee-spending-by-residence. On Medicaid, see Robin Rudowitz, Rachel Garfield, and Elizabeth Hinton, "10 Things to Know about Medicaid: Setting the Facts Straight," Kaiser Family Foundation, March 6, 2019, https://www.kff.org/medicaid/issue-brief/10-things-to-know-about-medicaid-setting-the-facts-straight/.

93. John Kay, "The Basics of Basic Income," https://www.johnkay.com/2017/04/05/basics-basic-income/. Following the late Nobel laureate James Tobin, he starts with the fundamental equation of basic income as $t = x + 25$, where t is the average tax rate of the country, x is basic income as a percent of average incomes per head, and 25 (percent) is the proportion of national income needed by high-income countries to pay for health, education, defense, public administration, police, the judicial system, and debt service. Evidently, if every resident gets a basic income equal to x percent of national income per head, the program's fiscal cost will be x percent of aggregate national income.

94. In the jargon of economists, the "income effect" of the UBI would more than offset the "substitution effect" of lower marginal tax rates.

95. Martin Sandbu, "The Case for the Affordability of Universal Basic Income," *Financial Times*, December 23, 2021, https://www.ft.com/content/3788b99e-7b8c-4641-8250-6f6823f1a7f6.

96. "Government Expenditure on Education, Total (% of GDP)—United Kingdom," The World Bank, https://data.worldbank.org/indicator/SE.XPD.TOTL.GD.ZS?locations=GB.

97. Liz Lightfoot, "The Student Experience—Then and Now," *Guardian*, June 24, 2016, https://www.theguardian.com/education/2016/jun/24/has-university-life-changed-student-experience-past-present-parents-vox-pops#:~:text=In%20the%20early%201960s%2C%20only,back%20over%20their%20working%20lives; and Sean Coughlan, "The Symbolic Target of 50% at University Reached," BBC News, September 26, 2019, https://www.bbc.com/news/education-49841620.

98. See Ron Diris and Erwin Ooghe, "The Economics of Financing Higher Education," *Economic Policy*, April 2018, 272, figure 2, https://ideas.repec.org/a/oup/ecpoli/v33y2018i94p265-314.html.

99. See Kiese Hansen and Time Shaw, "Solving the Student Debt Crisis," Aspen Institute Financial Security Program, February 2020, https://assets.aspeninstitute.org/wp-content/uploads/2020/03/SolvingStudentDebtCrisis.pdf.

100. On the details, see Money Advice Service, "Repaying Your Undergraduate Student Loan," https://www.moneyadviceservice.org.uk/en/articles/repaying-student-loans.

101. Pension Protection Fund, *The Purple Book 2020: DB Pensions Universe Risk Profile*, https://www.ppf.co.uk/sites/default/files/2020-12/PPF_Purple_Book_20.pdf.

102. On the economics of pensions, see Martin Wolf, "Radical Reform of British Pension Provision Is Urgent," *Financial Times*, June 13, 2021, https://www.ft.com/content/791876ae-7ce2-4c0b-9f7a-c12b4f39f6d5; Wolf, "It Is Folly to Make Pensions Safe by Making Them Unaffordable," *Financial Times*, June 27, 2021, https://www.ft.com/content/138974df-5dc0-47e4-acb8-e2eb048fe8bd; and Wolf, "Equities Are the Only Sensible Foundation for Private Pensions," *Financial Times*, July 11, 2021, https://www.ft.com/content/e3a621d3-5cfc-4410-bd3c-0fde3535582b.

103. See Nick Green, "UK Steps Closer to Introducing CDC Pension Schemes," December 3, 2020,

https://www.unbiased.co.uk/news/financial-adviser/uk-steps-closer-to-introducing-cdc-pension-schemes.

104. See, on this idea, Nicholas Gruen, "Superannuation Again," Club Troppo, May 31, 2005, https://clubtroppo.com.au/2005/05/31/superannuation-again/.

105. Martin Wolf, "We Must Accept Higher Taxes to Fund Health and Social Care," *Financial Times*, November 29, 2021, https://www.ft.com/content/efc67bb9-cff4-49e5-9101-67d2382ece09.

106. See US Department of Labor, "Trade Act Programs," https://www.dol.gov/general/topic/training/tradeact#:~:text=The%20Trade%20Adjustment%20Assistance%20(TAA,a%20result%20of%20increased%20imports.

107. See "Privilege," https://www.merriam-webster.com/dictionary/privilege.

108. Matthew Johnston, "Carried Interest: A Loophole in America's Tax Code," Investopedia, March 31, 2021, https://www.investopedia.com/articles/investing/102515/carried-interest-loophole-americas-tax-code.asp.

109. ἰσονομία was one of two conceptual foundations of democracy. The other was ἰσηγορία ("isegoria," or the equal right to speak in debate).

110. See, for example, Luigi Zingales, Jana Kasperkevic, and Asher Schechter, *Milton Friedman 50 Years Later. ProMarket*, 2020, Stigler Center for the Study of the Economy and the State, https://promarket.org/wp-content/uploads/2020/11/Milton-Friedman-50-years-later-ebook.pdf; and British Academy, *Principles for Purposeful Business: How to Deliver the Framework for the Future of the Corporation*, 2019, https://www.thebritishacademy.ac.uk/publications/future-of-the-corporation-principles-for-purposeful-business/.

111. British Academy, *Principles for Purposeful Business*, 8.

112. Business Roundtable, "Statement on the Purpose of a Corporation," August 19, 2019, https://system.businessroundtable.org/app/uploads/sites/5/2021/02/BRT-Statement-on-the-Purpose-of-a-Corporation-Feburary-2021-compressed.pdf.

113. See Richard Barker, Robert G. Eccles, and George Serafeim, "The Future of ESG Is . . . Accounting?" *Harvard Business Review*, December 3, 2020, https://hbr.org/2020/12/the-future-of-esg-is-accounting.

114. Smithers, *Productivity and the Bonus Culture*.

115. Jane Croft, "Ex-Barclays Libor Traders Receive Jail Sentences," *Financial Times*, July 7, 2016, https://www.ft.com/content/16215d97-971f-3209-87da-55d0a1f08c5f.

116. On the costs of this financial crisis, see chapter 6, and Andrew G. Haldane, "The $100 Billion Question," speech delivered March 30, 2010, Bank for International Settlements, https://www.bis.org/review/r100406d.pdf. At that time, Haldane was executive director, Financial Stability, Bank of England.

117. See Laura Noonan, Cale Tilford, Richard Milne, Ian Mount, and Peter Wise, "Who Went to Jail for Their Role in the Financial Crisis?" *Financial Times*, September 20, 2018, https://ig.ft.com/jailed-bankers/#:~:text=Forty%2Dseven%20bankers%20were%20sentenced,the%20financial%20sector's%20catastrophic%20failures.

118. See Goodhart and Pradhan, *The Great Demographic Reversal*, 243–45.

119. Wendy Sawyer and Peter Wagner, "Mass Incarceration: The Whole Pie 2020," Prison Policy Initiative, March 24, 2020, https://www.prisonpolicy.org/reports/pie2020.html.

120. See Patrick Radden Keefe, "How Did the Sacklers Pull This Off?" *New York Times*, July 14, 2021, https://www.nytimes.com/2021/07/14/opinion/sackler-family-opioids-settlement.html; and, on the entire dreadful story, see the same author's *Empire of Pain: The Secret History of the Sackler Dynasty* (New York: Doubleday, 2021). See also Centers for Disease Control and Prevention, "Opioid Overdose Deaths," https://www.cdc.gov/drugoverdose/epidemic/index.html. On the opium wars, see "Opium Wars," *Britannica*, https://www.britannica.com/topic/Opium-Wars.

121. Jason Furman et al., *Unlocking Digital Competition: Report on the Digital Competition Expert Panel*, March 2019, https://assets.publishing.service.gov.uk/government/uploads/system/uploads/attachment_data/file/785547/unlocking_digital_competition_furman_review_web.pdf.

122. Lina M. Khan, "Amazon's Antitrust Paradox," *Yale Law Journal* 126, no. 3 (January 2017), https://www.yalelawjournal.org/note/amazons-antitrust-paradox.

123. On the political implications of the new technologies, see Anne Applebaum and Peter Pomerantsev, "How to Put Out Democracy's Dumpster Fire," *Atlantic*, April 2021, https://www.theatlantic.com/magazine/archive/2021/04/the-internet-doesnt-have-to-be-awful/618079/. See also Luohan Academy, "Understanding Big Data: Data Calculus in the Digital Era 2021," February 5, 2021, https://www.luohanacademy.com/research/reports/2bcc5a5e3074df15.

124. Will Oremus, "Are You Really the Product? The History of a Dangerous Idea," *Slate*, April 27, 2018, https://slate.com/technology/2018/04/are-you-really-facebooks-product-the-history-of-a-dangerous-idea.html.

125. See GDPR.EU, "What Is GDPR, the EU's New Data Protection Law?" https://gdpr.eu/what-is-gdpr/#:~:text=The%20General%20Data%20Protection%20Regulation,to%20people%20in%20the%20EU.

126. Transparency International, *Corruption Perceptions Index*, https://www.transparency.org/en/cpi. On happiness, see John F. Helliwell, Richard Layard, Jeffrey D. Sachs, Jan-Emmanuel De Neve, Lara B. Akin, and Shun Wang, eds., *World Happiness Report 2021* (New York: NY: Sustainable Development Solutions Network, 2022), https://happiness-report.s3.amazonaws.com/2021/WHR+21.pdf.

127. See Tom Burgis, *Kleptopia: How Dirty Money Is Conquering the World* (London: William Collins, 2020); and Frank Vogl, *The Enablers: How the West Supports Kleptocrats and Corruption—Endangering Our Democracy* (Lanham, MD: Rowman & Littlefield, 2021).

128. On the uneasy borderline between legality and illegality and the role of well-paid professionals in converting the latter into the former, see Chuck Collins, *The Wealth Hoarders: How Billionaires Pay Millions to Hide Trillions* (Cambridge: Polity, 2021).

129. Franklin Delano Roosevelt, "The Four Freedoms," speech, January 6, 1941, https://www.americanrhetoric.com/speeches/fdrthefourfreedoms.htm.

130. Office for Budget Responsibility, "Fiscal Sustainability Report, July 2020," 15, chart 5, https://cdn.obr.uk/OBR_FSR_July_2020.pdf.

131. Congressional Budget Office, "The 2021 Long-Term Budget Outlook, March 2021," 5, https://www.cbo.gov/system/files/2021-03/56977-LTBO-2021.pdf.

132. For a somewhat dated survey of issues and evidence, see Willi Leibfritz, John Thornton, and Alexandra Bibbee, "Taxation and Economic Performance," OECD, Economics Department Working Paper No. 176, OCDE/GD(97)107, Paris, https://econpapers.repec.org/paper/oececoaaa/176-en.htm, which concluded, "It is clear from the literature review and from the additional results presented here that the effects of taxes on economic performance are ambiguous in some areas and unsettled and controversial in others."

133. See United Nations Development Program, "Human Development Reports," http://hdr.undp.org/en/content/human-development-index-hdi.

134. Emmanuel Saez and Gabriel Zucman, *The Triumph of Injustice: How the Rich Dodge Taxes and How to Make Them Pay* (New York: W. W. Norton, 2019).

135. Ibid., 14.

136. Ibid.

137. Ibid., 19, and Facebook Investor Relations, "Facebook Reports Fourth Quarter and Full Year 2018 Results," https://investor.fb.com/investor-news/press-release-details/2019/Facebook-Reports-Fourth-Quarter-and-Full-Year-2018-Results/default.aspx.

138. John Guyton, Patrick Langetieg, Daniel Reck, Max Risch, and Gabriel Zucman, "Tax Evasion at the Top of the Income Distribution: Theory and Evidence," National Bureau of Economic Research Working Paper 28542, March 2021, http://www.nber.org/papers/w28542.

139. Enid Nemy, "Leona Helmsley, Hotel Queen, Dies at 87," *New York Times*, August 20, 2007, https://www.nytimes.com/2007/08/20/nyregion/20cnd-helmsley.html.

140. See Dag Detter and Stefan Fölster, *The Public Wealth of Nations: How Management of Public Assets Can Boost or Bust Economic Growth* (Basingstoke, UK: Palgrave Macmillan, 2015).

141. See Henry George, *Progress and Poverty: An Inquiry into the Cause of Industrial Depressions and of Increase of Want with Increase of Wealth: The Remedy* (Vega Publishing, 2019, first published 1879).

142. This is one way to understand the core argument of Torben Iversen and David Soskice, *Democracy and Prosperity: Reinventing Capitalism through a Turbulent Century* (Princeton, NJ, and Oxford: Princeton University Press, 2019).

143. Ray Dalio, Jordan Nick, Steven Kryger, and Bill Longfield, "Wealth Taxes," March 22, 2021, Bridgewater, unpublished.

144. James Politi, Aime Williams, and Chris Giles, "US Offers New Plan in Global Corporate Tax Talks," *Financial Times*, April 8, 2021, https://www.ft.com/content/847c5f77-f0af-4787-8c8e-070ac6a7c74f; and Chris Giles, Emma Agyemang, and Aime Williams, "136 Nations Agree to Biggest Corporate Tax Deal in a Century," *Financial Times*, October 8, 2021, https://www.ft.com/content/5dc4e2d5-d7bd-4000-bf94-088f17e21936.

Chapter Nine: Renewing Democracy

1. John Stuart Mill, *Considerations on Representative Government*, 1861, Project Gutenberg, https://www.gutenberg.org/files/5669/5669-h/5669-h.htm.
2. "The Worst Form of Government," International Churchill Society, https://winstonchurchill.org/resources/quotes/the-worst-form-of-government/.
3. Foundation for Economic Education, "H. L. Mencken Quotes on Government, Democracy, and Politicians," https://fee.org/articles/12-hl-mencken-quotes-on-government-democracy-and-politicians/.
4. See, on this, Anna Lührmann and Staffan I. Lindberg, "A Third Wave of Autocratization Is Here: What Is New about It?" *Democratization* 26, no. 7 (2019): 1095–1113, https://www.tandfonline.com/doi/full/10.1080/13510347.2019.1582029. In the 1930s, a large proportion of humanity was still subject to the inherently autocratic rule of empires.
5. See Ian Hughes, *Disordered Minds: How Dangerous Personalities Are Destroying Democracy* (Hampshire: Zero Books, 2018).
6. See Christopher H. Achen and Larry M. Bartels, *Democracy for Realists: Why Elections Do Not Produce Responsive Government* (Princeton, NJ, and Oxford: Princeton University Press, 2016).
7. Ibid., 299.
8. See, for example, references by Ronald Reagan to "welfare queens" and by George H. W. Bush to the murderer Willie Horton in his presidential election campaign in 1988. See National Public Radio, "The Original 'Welfare Queen,'" *Code Switch*, June 5, 2019, https://www.npr.org/transcripts/729294210?t=1654518358287; and Peter Baker, "Bush Made Willie Horton an Issue in 1988 and the Racial Scars Are Still Fresh," *New York Times*, December 3, 2018, https://www.nytimes.com/2018/12/03/us/politics/bush-willie-horton.html.
9. Ibid., 301.
10. Joseph A. Schumpeter, *Capitalism, Socialism and Democracy* (London: George Allen & Unwin, 1994, first published in the UK in 1943), 262.
11. "Washington's Farewell Address 1796," https://avalon.law.yale.edu/18th_century/washing.asp.
12. Jason Brennan, *Against Democracy* (Princeton, NJ, and Oxford: Princeton University Press, 2017).
13. Ibid., Preface to the 2017 paperback edition.
14. Ibid., 243.
15. On Plato's view of poetry, see Stanford Encyclopedia of Philosophy, "Plato on Rhetoric and Poetry," February 12, 2020, https://plato.stanford.edu/entries/plato-rhetoric/.
16. Karl Popper, *The Open Society and Its Enemies*, vol. 1, *The Age of Plato* (London: Routledge, 1945).
17. Brennan, *Against Democracy* (2017 ed.), Preface.
18. "Corruption Perception Index, 2019," Transparency International, https://www.transparency.org/en/cpi.
19. Achen and Bartels, *Democracy for Realists*, 317.
20. See Edward Luce, "A Sea of Troubles Surrounds the Question of Whether to Prosecute Trump," *Financial Times*, July 29, 2022, https://www.ft.com/content/8263e5c9-d886-4c81-807b-f9eb0d92508f.
21. Achen and Bartels, *Democracy for Realists*.
22. Ibid.
23. David Hume, *A Treatise of Human Nature*, book III, part III, section III, "Of the Influencing Motives of the Will," 3, https://www.pitt.edu/~mthompso/readings/hume.influencing.pdf.
24. Achen and Bartels, *Democracy for Realists*, 310.
25. See, on this, Nicholas Gruen, "Beyond Vox Pop Democracy: Democratic Deliberation and Leadership in the Age of the Internet," *More or Less: Democracy and the New Media*, 2012, http://www.futureleaders.com.au/book_chapters/pdf/More-or-Less/Nicholas_Gruen.pdf#zoom=80.
26. "Black Act 1723," Google Arts and Culture, https://artsandculture.google.com/entity/black-act-1723/m02sc6n?hl=en; and The Statutes Project, "1723: 9 George 1 c.22: The Black Act," https://statutes.org.uk/site/the-statutes/eighteenth-century/9-geo-i-c-22-the-black-act-1723/.
27. Michael Massing, "Does Democracy Avert Famine?" *New York Times*, March 1, 2003; and Amartya Sen, *Development as Freedom* (Oxford: Oxford University Press, 1999), chapter 6, "The Importance of Democracy."
28. Sen, *Development as Freedom*, 148.
29. See Nathan Gardels and Nicholas Berggruen, *Renovating Democracy: Governing in the Age of Globalization and Digital Capitalism* (Oakland, CA: University of California Press for the Berggruen Institute, 2019); Commission on the Practice of Democratic Citizenship, *Our Common Purpose: Reinventing American Democracy for the 21st Century* (Cambridge, MA: American

Academy of Arts and Sciences, 2020); and Andrew Gamble and Tony Wright, eds., *Rethinking Democracy* (Newark, NJ: John Wiley for Political Quarterly Publishing, 2019).

30. Fernando Henrique Cardoso, "Brazil's Crisis Reflects Demise of Representative Democracy across the West," *Huffington Post*, September 5, 2016, https://www.huffpost.com/entry/brazils-crisis-reflects-demise-of-democracy_b_11867368.

31. George Orwell, "Notes on Nationalism," *Polemic*, October 1945 (New York: Penguin Modern Classics, 2018).

32. A valuable and thought-provoking discussion of the role of patriotism in an established democracy is contained in Tim Soutphommasane, *The Virtuous Citizen: Patriotism in a Multicultural Society* (Cambridge: Cambridge University Press, 2012).

33. See Martin Wolf, "When Multiculturalism Is a Nonsense," *Financial Times*, August 30, 2005, https://www.ft.com/content/ff41a586-197f-11da-804e-00000e2511c8.

34. "McKinstry's Churchill and Attlee: A Vanished Age of Political Respect," Richard M. Langworth, December 4, 2019, https://richardlangworth.com/mckenstry-attlee.

35. Ennius, *Annales*, https://www.loebclassics.com/view/ennius-annals/2018/pb_LCL294.193.xml.

36. Paul Collier, *The Future of Capitalism: Facing the New Anxieties* (London: Allen Lane, 2018), 8.

37. Lorraine Boissoneault, "Bismarck Tried to End Socialism's Grip—by Offering Government Healthcare," *Smithsonian Magazine*, July 14, 2017, https://www.smithsonianmag.com/.

38. The role of the welfare system and especially high-quality education in creating contemporary democratic high-income countries is a theme of Torben Iversen and David Soskice, *Democracy and Prosperity: Reinventing Capitalism Through a Turbulent Century* (Princeton, NJ, and Oxford: Princeton University Press, 2019). See also Martin Wolf, "The Case for Capitalism," *Financial Times*, March 28, 2019, https://www.ft.com/content/d8b903d0-4bfe-11e9-bbc9-6917dce3dc62.

39. See Alberto Alesina, Johann Harnoss, and Hillel Rapoport, "Immigration and the Future of the Welfare State in Europe," December 2014 (updated February 2018), Working Paper 2018-04, 2, Paris School of Economics, https://halshs.archives-ouvertes.fr/halshs-01707760/document.

40. Ibid., 1.

41. Martin Wolf, "Disputed Fruit of Unskilled Immigration," *Financial Times*, April 4, 2006, https://www.ft.com/content/ba686d9a-c407-11da-bc52-0000779e2340.

42. Robert Smith and Jim Pickard, "Greensill Capital Paid Cameron Salary of More Than $1M a Year," *Financial Times*, July 12, 2021, https://www.ft.com/content/536867f4-2dd3-42a1-9b29-54ed92693635.

43. Dierdre McCloskey provides a fascinating account of the role of the "seven virtues" in a good life and a good society. These virtues are the "pagan four"—courage, justice, temperance, and prudence—and the "theological three"—faith, hope, and love. See McCloskey, "Life's Primary Colours: How Humanity Forgot the Seven Principal Virtues," ABC News Australia, July 2, 2019, https://www.abc.net.au/religion/primary-colors-how-humanity-forgot-the-seven-principal-virtues/11272726.

44. On the challenge of maintaining democracy in heterogeneous societies, see Yascha Mounk, *The Great Experiment: How to Make Diverse Democracies Work* (London: Bloomsbury, 2022), and Martin Wolf, "A Call to Arms for Diverse Democracies and Their 'Decent Middle,'" *Financial Times*, May 5, 2022, https://www.ft.com/content/83ba0474-70ea-4759-81f1-e14f6ea269fa. Mounk argues that diverse societies go wrong in three ways: anarchy, domination, and fragmentation. Majority identity politics generates the second, and minority identity politics the third. Anarchy happens if neither domination nor a *modus vivendi* among groups is reached. All these are real and worrying dangers.

45. See, on this issue, Isabel Wilkerson, *Caste: The Origins of Our Discontents* (New York: Random House, 2020).

46. See Adrian Wooldridge, *The Aristocracy of Talent: How Meritocracy Made the Modern World* (London: Allen Lane, 2021); David Goodhart, *Head Hand Heart: The Struggle for Dignity and Status in the 21st Century* (London: Penguin, 2021); and Michael Sandel, *The Tyranny of Merit: What's Become of the Common Good?* (London: Penguin, 2020).

47. For the early Chinese administrative system, see S. E. Finer, *The History of Government: Ancient Monarchies and Empires*, vol. 1, *Ancient Monarchies and Empires* (Oxford: Oxford University Press, 1997 and 1999), book II, chapters 5 and 6; Francis Fukuyama, *The Origins of Political Order: From Prehuman Times to the French Revolution* (London: Profile Books, 2011), chapters 7 and 8; and Adrian Wooldridge, *The Aristocracy of Talent: How Meritocracy Made the Modern World* (London: Allen Lane, 2021).

48. See Francis Fukuyama, *Political Order and Political Decay: From the Industrial Revolution to the Globalization of Democracy* (London: Profile Books, 2014), chapter 34, "America the Vetocracy."

49. This idea of "eunuch" values in a modern bureaucracy applies just as much in corporate bureaucracies. The loyalty of the employee is similarly to the company, not to its chief executive. The important underlying idea was proposed by Ernest Gellner in his classic work *Nations and Nationalism* (Oxford: Blackwell Press, 1983 and 2006).

50. On the limits of economics as a source of expertise, see Martin Wolf, "How Economists Failed as 'Experts'—and How to Make Them Matter Again," Institute for New Economic Thinking, March 12, 2019, https://www.ineteconomics.org/perspectives/blog/why-economists-failed-as-experts-and-how-to-make-them-matter-again.

51. Anjana Ahuja, "UK's Confused Claim to 'Follow the Science' Eroded Public Trust," *Financial Times*, May 19, 2020, https://www.ft.com/content/66413e62-98e7-11ea-871b-edeb99a20c6e.

52. On the lessons from the handling of the pandemic for the quality of the required leadership and especially the disadvantages of leadership by populist demagogues, see Adecco Group, "Comparing the Outcome of Government Responses to COVID-19," January 2022, https://www.adeccogroup.com/en-ch/future-of-work/insights/government-response-2022/.

53. Tim Nichols, *The Death of Expertise: The Campaign against Established Knowledge and Why It Matters* (New York: Oxford University Press, 2017).

54. Minouche Shafik, "In Experts We Trust?" Bank of England, February 22, 2017, 12, https://www.bankofengland.co.uk/-/media/boe/files/speech/2017/in-experts-we-trust.pdf?la=en&hash=51801143BE9C2BAA60EF3F56F04D7A2E2C694952.

55. See Center for Presidential Transition, "Unconfirmed: Why Reducing the Number of Senate-Confirmed Positions Can Make Government More Effective," August 9, 2021, https://presidentialtransition.org/publications/unconfirmed-reducing-number-senate-confirmed-positions/.

56. On this, see Nicholas Gruen, "Trust and the Competition Delusion: A New Frontier for Political and Economic Reform," Griffith Review, https://www.griffithreview.com/articles/trust-competition-delusion-gruen/.

57. See Jane Jacobs, *Systems of Survival: A Dialogue on the Moral Foundations of Commerce and Politics* (New York: Random House, 1994).

58. "List of regulators in the United Kingdom," Wikipedia, https://en.wikipedia.org/wiki/List_of_regulators_in_the_United_Kingdom.

59. Paul Tucker, *Unelected Power: The Quest for Legitimacy in Central Banking and the Regulatory State* (Princeton, NJ, and Oxford: Princeton University Press, 2018).

60. R. James Breiding, *Too Small to Fail: Why Some Small Nations Outperform Larger Ones and How They Are Reshaping the World* (Uttar Pradesh, India: HarperCollins, 2019).

61. Raghuram Rajan, *The Third Pillar: The Revival of Community in a Polarized World* (London: William Collins, 2019), especially part III; and Collier, *The Future of Capitalism*, chapter 7.

62. "UK Treaties," https://www.gov.uk/guidance/uk-treaties.

63. Michael Crowley, "Trump Won't Commit to 'Peaceful' Post-Election Transfer of Power," *New York Times*, September 23, 2020, https://www.nytimes.com/2020/09/23/us/politics/trump-power-transfer-2020-election.html.

64. Electoral Reform Society, "Single Transferable Vote," https://www.electoral-reform.org.uk/voting-systems/types-of-voting-system/single-transferable-vote/.

65. George Washington, "Farewell Address," https://www.ourdocuments.gov/doc.php?flash=false&doc=15&page=transcript.

66. The extreme extent of popular involvement in choosing party nominees in the US and its untoward consequences is the theme of an excellent article by Stephen Gardbaum and Richard H. Pildes, "Populism and Institutional Design: Methods of Selecting Candidates for Chief Executive," *New York University Law Review* 93 (2018): 647–708, https://www.nyulawreview.org/wp-content/uploads/2018/10/NYULawReview-93-4-Gardbaum-Pildes.pdf. See also Jonah Goldberg, "The Hollowing Out of American Parties," American Enterprise Institute, November 7, 2018, https://www.aei.org/articles/the-hollowing-out-of-american-political-parties/.

67. Alexander Hamilton wrote of the Electoral College that "the process of election affords a moral certainty, that the office of President will never fall to the lot of any man who is not in an eminent degree endowed with the requisite qualifications." (See Alexander Hamilton, "The Mode of Electing the President," *Federalist Papers* No. 68, March 14, 1788, https://avalon.law.yale.edu/18th_century/fed68.asp.) It may be debated whether this has ever been the case. But the elimination of independent judgment from the College has guaranteed that it could not now be so, while also

delivering several presidents who, in addition to lacking qualifications, did not even receive the majority of votes.

68. See Anne Applebaum, "The U.S. Shouldn't Be a 'Sleazy Offshore Principality," *Atlantic*, October 14, 2020, https://www.theatlantic.com/ideas/archive/2020/10/us-shouldnt-be-sleazy-offshore -principality/616717/.

69. See, on the role of corporations in politics, Thom Hartmann, *Unequal Protection: How Corporations Became "People"—and How You Can Fight Back* (San Francisco: Berrett-Koehler, 2010), and Martin Wolf, "There Is a Direct Line from Milton Friedman to Donald Trump's Assault on Democracy," *ProMarket*, October 4, 2020, https://promarket.org/2020/10/04/milton-friedman-donald -trump-assault-on-democracy-corporations/.

70. On the impact of foreign (predominantly Russian) interference in American elections, see David Shimer, *Rigged: America, Russia, and One Hundred Years of Covert Electoral Interference* (New York: Alfred A. Knopf, 2020).

71. In his *Democracy in America* (1835 and 1840), Alexis de Tocqueville made frequent references to the institution of the jury.

72. See John Bernheim and Nicholas Gruen, "Bernheim and Gruen on the Path toward Sortition," *Equality by Lot*, August 6, 2020, https://equalitybylot.com/2020/08/06/burnheim-and-gruen -on-the-path-toward-sortition/; and Nicholas Gruen, "An Unpublished Column on Sortition and Brexit," *Equality by Lot*, April 17, 2019, https://equalitybylot.com/2019/04/17/an-unpublished -column-on-sortition-and-brexit/.

73. See Michela Palese, "The Irish Abortion Referendum: How a Citizens' Assembly Helped to Break Years of Political Deadlock," Electoral Reform Society, May 29, 2018, https://www.electoral -reform.org.uk/the-irish-abortion-referendum-how-a-citizens-assembly-helped-to-break -years-of-political-deadlock/.

74. "Daniel Patrick Moynihan," https://www.brainyquote.com/quotes/daniel_patrick_moynihan _182347.

Prologue to Part IV

1. Martin Wolf, "Humanity Is a Cuckoo in the Planetary Nest," *Financial Times*, March 9, 2021, https://www.ft.com/content/a3285adf-6c5f-4ce4-b055-e85f39ff2988.

Chapter Ten: Democratic Capitalism in the World

1. No verified source exists for this quotation.

2. See Martin Wolf, "How We Can Share Our Divided World," *Financial Times*, November 2, 2021, https://www.ft.com/content/b371e181-eac3-41ef-88c5-ca2bb20edd99.

3. Population and GDP data are from https://data.worldbank.org/ and https://www.imf.org/en/Pub lications/WEO/weo-database/2021/April. The World Bank's list of high-income countries includes eight non-democracies: Bahrain, Brunei, Hong Kong, Kuwait, Oman, Qatar, Saudi Arabia, and the UAE. The population and GDP of these non-democracies are excluded from the totals for high-income countries. Together, they had a population of 65.6 million and a share in world GDP of 2.6 percent at PPP and 2.3 percent at market prices in 2019. Apart from Hong Kong, they are all oil producers.

4. See, on this issue, Dani Rodrik, *The Globalization Paradox: Democracy and the Future of the World Economy* (New York and London: W. W. Norton, 2011), and Rodrik, *Straight Talk on Trade: Ideas for a Sane World Economy* (Princeton, NJ: Princeton University Press, 2017).

5. Millennium Challenge Corporation, "Our Impact," https://www.mcc.gov/our-impact.

6. See Martin Wolf, "Containing China Is Not a Feasible Option," *Financial Times*, February 2, 2021, https://www.ft.com/content/83a521c0-6abb-4efa-be48-89ecb52c8d01; and Richard Haass, "A Cold War with China Would Be a Mistake," Council on Foreign Relations, May 11, 2020, https:// www.cfr.org/article/cold-war-china-would-be-mistake.

7. Clyde Prestowitz, *The World Turned Upside Down: America, China, and the Struggle for Global Leadership* (New Haven, CT: Yale University Press, 2021), 223.

8. Anonymous, *The Longer Telegram: Toward a New American China Strategy*, Atlantic Council, Scowcroft Center for Strategy and Security, 2021, https://www.atlanticcouncil.org/content-series /atlantic-council-strategy-paper-series/the-longer-telegram/.

9. Ibid., 6.

10. Demetri Sevastopulo, "US Accuses China of Operating 'Open-Air Prison' in Xinjiang," *Financial Times*, May 12, 2021, https://www.ft.com/content/1f9f5f30-dc6e-4228-8b43-5faf522f223a; and

Tom Mitchell, "Business Worries Intensify Over China's Tightening Grip on Hong Kong," *Financial Times*, March 16, 2021, https://www.ft.com/content/098017c2-1c83-4da3-ac2a-53e7ed 7fac81.

11. Demetri Sevastopulo and Kathrin Hille, "US Fears China Is Flirting with Seizing Control of Taiwan," *Financial Times*, March 27, 2021, https://www.ft.com/content/3ed169b8-3f47-4f66-a914 -58b6e2215f7d.

12. Graham Allison, "The Geopolitical Olympics: Could China Win Gold?" *National Interest*, July 29, 2021, https://nationalinterest.org/feature/geopolitical-olympics-could-china-win-gold-190761.

13. See Martin Jacques, *When China Rules the World: The End of the Western World and the Birth of a New Global Order* (London: Penguin, 2009).

14. See Sean Golden, "A 'China Model' for the 'New Era,'" Barcelona Center for International Affairs, 2017, https://www.cidob.org/en/publications/publication_series/opinion/asia/a_china_model_for_ the_new_era.

15. Kishore Mahbubani, "Biden and China: Friends or Foes," *Alumnus*, issue 124, January–March 2021, National University of Singapore, https://www.nus.edu.sg/alumnet/thealumnus/issue-124 /perspectives/panorama/biden-and-china-friends-or-foes.

16. On the failures of the West, see the jeremiad by the Singaporean scholar and former diplomat Kishore Mahbubani, *Has the West Lost It? A Provocation* (London: Allen Lane, 2018).

17. Jonathan Kirshner, "Gone but Not Forgotten: Trump's Long Shadow and the End of American Credibility," *Foreign Affairs*, March/April 2021, https://www.foreignaffairs.com/articles/united -states/2021-01-29/trump-gone-not-forgotten.

18. This phrase was coined by Robert Zoellick as deputy secretary of state, in "Whither China: From Membership to Responsibility?" September 21, 2015, US Department of State Archive, https:// 2001-2009.state.gov/s/d/former/zoellick/rem/53682.htm.

19. Branko Milanovic, *Capitalism Alone* (Cambridge, MA: Harvard University Press, 2019), 208.

20. John Emerich Edward Dalberg Acton (1st Baron Acton), Phrase Finder, https://www.phrases.org .uk/meanings/absolute-power-corrupts-absolutely.html.

21. See Martin Wolf, "The Economic Threats from China's Real Estate Bubble," *Financial Times*, October 5, 2021, and Matthew Klein and Michael Pettis, *Trade Wars Are Class Wars* (New Haven, CT: Yale University Press, 2020).

22. See Graham Allison, *Destined for War: Can America and China Escape Thucydides's Trap?* (Boston and New York: Houghton Mifflin Harcourt, 2017), and Graham Allison, "China's Geopolitics Are Pumped Up by Its Economic Success," *Financial Times*, October 4, 2020, https://www.ft.com /content/e2902988-ca56-4d21-ab2a-b416c9006c7b.

23. Famously, the British Liberal Norman Angell argued that war would turn out to be ruinous, in his book *The Great Illusion: A Study of the Relation of Military Power in Nations to Their Economic and Social Advantage*, initially published as *Europe's Optical Illusion* in 1909 and republished as *The Great Illusion*. The thesis proved all too true. But this did not prevent imbeciles from starting the war.

24. "Cuban Missile Crisis," *Britannica*, https://www.britannica.com/event/Cuban-missile-crisis.

25. Jamie Smyth, "Chinese Tensions Put Australian Businesses under Pressure," *Financial Times*, November 11, 2020, https://www.ft.com/content/b764e4c9-cc38-43b6-848c-dba0cbc6475a.

26. On the US view of China's trade policy practices, see Office of the United States Trade Representative, Executive Office of the President, *Findings of the Investigation into China's Acts, Policies, and Practices Related to Technology Transfer, Intellectual Property, and Innovation under Sector 301 of the Trade Act of 1974*, March 22, 2018, https://ustr.gov/sites/default/files/Section%20301 %20FINAL.PDF. See also Martin Wolf, "Donald Trump Declares Trade War on China," *Financial Times*, May 8, 2018, https://www.ft.com/content/dd2af6b0-4fc1-11e8-9471-a083af05aea7.

27. On the illegality of the US trade policy actions, notably against China, under the WTO, see Martin Wolf, "Donald Trump Creates Chaos with His Tariffs Trade War," *Financial Times*, July 10, 2018, https://www.ft.com/content/ba65ac98-8364-11e8-a29d-73e3d454535d.

28. Alan Beattie, "WTO to Suffer Heavy Blow as US Stymies Appeals Body," *Financial Times*, December 8, 2019, https://www.ft.com/content/f0f992b8-19c4-11ea-97df-cc63de1d73f4.

29. See Nicholas Lardy, *The State Strikes Back: The End of Economic Reform in China?* (Washington, DC: Peterson Institute for International Economics, 2019).

30. John Hurley, Scott Morris, and Gailyn Portelance, "Examining the Debt Implications of the Belt and Road Initiative from a Policy Perspective," Center for Global Development, CGD Policy Paper 121, March 2018, https://www.cgdev.org/sites/default/files/examining-debt-implications-belt-and -road-initiative-policy-perspective.pdf.

31. Martin Wolf, "Humanity Is a Cuckoo in the Planetary Nest," *Financial Times*, March 9, 2021, https://www.ft.com/content/a3285adf-6c5f-4ce4-b055-e85f39ff2988.

32. Alan Beattie lays out the daunting difficulties in "Carbon Border Taxes Cannot Fix the Damage of Trump's Climate Move," *Financial Times*, June 8, 2017, https://www.ft.com/content/1d5e54ca-4b86-11e7-919a-1e14ce4af89b. In practice, this would have to be a rough-and-ready adjustment.

33. See Martin Wolf, "Action Must Replace Talk on Climate Change," *Financial Times*, May 4, 2021, https://www.ft.com/content/3fa154f3-84e7-4964-9a21-d3dbd41e1470, which discusses a package of policies, including the border tax on emissions-intensive products, aimed at achieving a shift to global net zero emissions by 2050.

34. See Statista, "Leading Importers of Fish and Fishery Products Worldwide in 2019 (in billion U.S. dollars)," https://www.statista.com/statistics/268266/top-importers-of-fish-and-fishery-products/.

35. World Atlas, "Countries Where Illegal Wildlife Trade Is a Major Threat to Wildlife," https://www.worldatlas.com/articles/10-countries-most-infamous-for-illegal-wildlife-trade.html.

36. See US Department of State, "The Montreal Protocol on Substances That Deplete the Ozone Layer," https://www.state.gov/key-topics-office-of-environmental-quality-and-transboundary-issues/the-montreal-protocol-on-substances-that-deplete-the-ozone-layer/; and US Department of State, "Law of the Sea Convention," https://www.state.gov/law-of-the-sea-convention/.

37. International Monetary Fund, "IMF Members' Quotas and Voting Power, and IMF Board of Governors," May 23, 2021, https://www.imf.org/external/np/sec/memdir/members.aspx.

38. See Asian Infrastructure Investment Bank, https://www.aiib.org/en/index.html, and New Development Bank, https://www.ndb.int/.

Conclusion: Restoring Citizenship

1. "Gettysburg Address," *Britannica*, https://www.britannica.com/event/Gettysburg-Address.

2. Sallus, *Bellum jugurthinum*, https://penelope.uchicago.edu/Thayer/E/Roman/Texts/Sallust/Bellum_Jugurthinum/1*.html.

3. These data are from the International Monetary Fund, World Economic Outlook database April 2021, https://www.imf.org/en/Publications/SPROLLs/world-economic-outlook-databases#sort=%40imfdate%20descending.

4. Global Security.org, "'Führerprinzip' (Leader Principle)," https://www.globalsecurity.org/military/world/europe/de-fuhrerprinzip.htm.

5. James M. Lindsay, "The 2020 Election by the Numbers," Council on Foreign Relations, December 15, 2020, https://www.cfr.org/blog/2020-election-numbers; and Martin Wolf, "The American Republic's Near-Death Experience," *Financial Times*, January 19, 2021, https://www.ft.com/content/c085e962-f27c-4c34-a0f1-5cf2bd813fbc.

6. Karl Popper, *The Open Society and Its Enemies*, vol. 1, *The Spell of Plato* (London: Routledge, 1945).

7. Anne Applebaum, *Twilight of Democracy: The Seductive Lure of Authoritarianism* (London: Allen Lane, 2020).

8. Steve Alexis, "Quotes by Hunter S. Thompson," April 13, 2020, Inspiring Alley, https://www.inspiringalley.com/hunter-s-thompson-quotes/.

9. Adrian Wooldridge, *The Aristocracy of Talent: How Meritocracy Made the Modern World* (London: Allen Lane, 2021).

10. This section draws extensively from Martin Wolf, "Democracy Will Fail If We Don't Think as Citizens," *Financial Times*, July 6, 2020, https://www.ft.com/content/36abf9a6-b838-4ca2-ba35-2836bd0b62e2.

Acknowledgments

1. Martin Wolf, *Why Globalization Works* (London and New Haven, CT: Yale University Press, 2004), Wolf, *Fixing Global Finance* (Baltimore and London: Johns Hopkins University Press and Yale University Press, 2008 and 2010), and Wolf, *The Shifts and the Shocks: What We've Learned—and Have Still to Learn—from the Financial Crisis* (London and New York: Penguin, 2014 and 2015).

2. Martin Sandbu, *The Economics of Belonging: A Radical Plan to Win Back the Left Behind and Achieve Prosperity for All* (Princeton, NJ, and Oxford: Princeton University Press, 2020).

BIBLIOGRAPHY

Acemoglu, Daron. "Written Testimony." At a virtual hearing on "Machines, Artificial Intelligence, & the Workforce: Recovering & Readying Our Economy for the Future." House Committee on the Budget, September 10, 2021. https://www.congress.gov/116/meeting/house/111002/witnesses /HHRG-116-BU00-Wstate-AcemogluD-20200910.pdf.

Acemoglu, Daron, and James A. Robinson. *The Narrow Corridor: States, Societies, and the Fate of Liberty.* London and New York: Penguin Press, 2019.

Acemoglu, Daron, and James A. Robinson. *Why Nations Fail: The Origins of Power, Prosperity, and Poverty.* New York: Crown Business, 2012.

Acemoglu, Daron, David Autor, David Dorn, Gordon H. Hanson, and Brendan Price. "Import Competition and the Great US Employment Sag of the 2000s." *Journal of Labor Economics* 34, no. 1 (part 2, January 2016): 141–98. http://www.journals.uchicago.edu/doi/pdfplus/10.1086/682384.

Achen, Christopher H., and Larry M. Bartels. *Democracy for Realists: Why Elections Do Not Produce Responsive Government.* Princeton, NJ, and Oxford: Princeton University Press, 2016.

Adams, James Truslow. *The Epic of America.* New Brunswick and London: Transaction Publishers, 1931 and 2012.

Adecco Group. "Comparing the Outcome of Government Responses to COVID-19." January 2022. https://www.adeccogroup.com/en-ch/future-of-work/insights/government-response-2022/.

Admati, Anat. "Capitalism, Laws, and the Need for Trustworthy Institutions." In Paul Collier, Diane Coyle, Colin Mayer, and Martin Wolf, eds. "Capitalism: What Has Gone Wrong, What Needs to Change, and How It Can Be Fixed." *Oxford Review of Economic Policy* 37, no. 4 (Winter 2021): 678–89.

Admati, Anat, and Martin Hellwig. *The Banker's New Clothes: What's Wrong with Banking and What to Do about It.* Updated edition. Princeton, NJ: Princeton University Press, 2014.

Aghion, Philippe, Céline Antonin, and Simon Bunel. *The Power of Creative Destruction: Economic Upheaval and the Wealth of Nations.* Translated by Jodie Cohen-Tanugi. Cambridge, MA: Belknap Press of Harvard University Press, 2021.

Ahluwalia, Montek Singh. *Backstage: The Story Behind India's High Growth Years.* New Delhi: Rupa Publications, 2020.

Ahuja, Anjana. "UK's Confused Claim to 'Follow the Science' Eroded Public Trust." *Financial Times,* May 19, 2020. https://www.ft.com/content/66413e62-98e7-11ea-871b-edeb99a20c6e.

Alesina, Alberto, Johann Harnoss, and Hillel Rapoport. "Immigration and the Future of the Welfare State in Europe." December 2014 (updated February 2018). Working Paper 2018-04, Paris School of Economics. https://halshs.archives-ouvertes.fr/halshs-01707760/document.

Alexis, Steve. "Quotes by Hunter S. Thompson." Inspiring Alley, April 13, 2020. https://www.inspir ingalley.com/hunter-s-thompson-quotes/.

Aliber, Robert Z., and Charles P. Kindleberger. *Manias, Panics, and Crashes: A History of Financial Crises.* 7th ed. London and New York: Palgrave Macmillan, 2015.

Allen, Robert C. "The British Industrial Revolution in Global Perspective: How Commerce Created the Industrial Revolution and Modern Economic Growth." 2006. https://users.nber.org/~confer /2006/SEGs06/allen.pdf.

Allison, Graham. "China's Geopolitics Are Pumped Up by Its Economic Success." *Financial Times,* October 4, 2020. https://www.ft.com/content/e2902988-ca56-4d21-ab2a-b416c9006c7b.

Allison, Graham. *Destined for War: Can America and China Escape Thucydides's Trap?* Boston and New York: Houghton Mifflin Harcourt, 2017.

Allison, Graham. "The Geopolitical Olympics: Could China Win Gold?" *National Interest*, July 29, 2021. https://nationalinterest.org/feature/geopolitical-olympics-could-china-win-gold-190761.

Alpha History. "The Great Depression." https://alphahistory.com/nazigermany/the-great-depression/.

Amadeo, Kimberly. "What Is the Average American Net Worth?" *The Balance.* Updated December 30, 2021, https://www.thebalance.com/american-middle-class-net-worth-3973493.

American Association of Retired Persons. "How Much Social Security Will I Get?" https://www.aarp .org/retirement/social-security/questions-answers/how-much-social-security-will-i-get.html.

Anderson, Benedict. *Imagined Communities: Reflections on the Origin and Spread of Nationalism.* London and New York: Verso, 1983.

Andreau, Jean. "Personal Endebtment and Forgiveness in the Roman Empire." CADTM, December 17, 2012. http://www.cadtm.org/Personal-endebtment-and-debt (translated from the French).

Andrews, Dan, Chiara Criscuolo, and Peter Gal. *The Global Productivity Slowdown, Technology Divergence and Public Policy: A Firm Level Perspective.* OECD, Paris, 2016. https://www.oecd.org/global -forum-productivity/events/GP_Slowdown_Technology_Divergence_and_Public_Policy_Final _after_conference_26_July.pdf.

Angell, Norman. *The Great Illusion: A Study of the Relation of Military Power in Nations to Their Economic and Social Advantage.* 3rd ed. New York and London: G. P. Putnam's Sons, 1911.

Annie E. Casey Foundation. Kids Count Data Center, Demographics. "Total Population by Child and Adult Populations in the United States," 2020. https://datacenter.kidscount.org/.

Anonymous. *The Longer Telegram: Toward a New American China Strategy.* Atlantic Council, Scowcroft Center for Strategy and Security, 2021. https://www.atlanticcouncil.org/content-series/atlantic -council-strategy-paper-series/the-longer-telegram/.

Applebaum, Anne. *Twilight of Democracy: The Seductive Lure of Authoritarianism.* London: Allen Lane, 2020.

Applebaum, Anne. "The U.S. Shouldn't Be a 'Sleazy Offshore Principality.'" *Atlantic*, October 14, 2020. https://www.theatlantic.com/ideas/archive/2020/10/us-shouldnt-be-sleazy-offshore-principality /616717/.

Applebaum, Anne, and Peter Pomerantsev. "How to Put Out Democracy's Dumpster Fire." *Atlantic*, March 8, 2021. https://www.theatlantic.com/magazine/archive/2021/04/the-internet-doesnt-have -to-be-awful/618079/.

Aristotle. *Politics.* Translated by T. A. Sinclair. Revised and re-presented by Trevor J. Saunders. London: Penguin Classics, 1981.

Asian Infrastructure Investment Bank. https://www.aiib.org/cn/index.html.

Aslund, Anders. *Russia's Crony Capitalism: The Path from Market Economy to Kleptocracy.* New Haven: Yale University Press, 2019.

Atkinson, Anthony B. *Inequality: What Can Be Done.* Cambridge, MA, and London: Harvard University Press, 2015.

Auerbach, Alan, Michael Devereux, Michael Keen, and John Vell. "Destination-Based Cash Flow Taxation." Oxford Legal Studies Research Paper No. 14/2017. Said Business School WP 2017-09. Oxford University Center for Business Taxation WP 17/01. https://papers.ssrn.com/sol3/papers .cfm?abstract_id=2908158.

Autor, David H., David Dorn, and Gordon H. Hanson. "The China Shock: Learning from Labor Market Adjustment to Large Changes in Trade." National Bureau of Economic Research Working Paper Number 21906. January 2016. http://www.nber.org/papers/w21906.

Baggini, Julian. "Aristotle's Thinking on Democracy Has More Relevance Than Ever." *Prospect*, May 23, 2018. https://www.prospectmagazine.co.uk/philosophy/aristotles-thinking-on-democracy-has -more-relevance-than-ever.

Baker, Peter. "Bush Made Willie Horton an Issue in 1988 and the Racial Scars Are Still Fresh." *New York Times*, December 3, 2018. https://www.nytimes.com/2018/12/03/us/politics/bush-willie -horton.html.

Baldwin, James. *The Fire Next Time.* New York: Dial, 1963.

Baldwin, Richard E. *The Globotics Upheaval: Globalization, Robotics, and the Future of Work.* London: Weidenfeld & Nicolson, 2019.

Baldwin, Richard E. *The Great Convergence: Information Technology and the New Globalization.* Cambridge, MA: Belknap Press of Harvard University Press, 2016.

Baldwin, Richard E., and Philippe Martin. "Two Waves of Globalization: Superficial Similarities,

Fundamental Differences." National Bureau of Economic Research. Working Paper Number 6904, January 1999. http://www.nber.org/papers/w6904.pdf.

Baldwin, Richard E., and Simon J. Evenett. *COVID-19 and Trade Policy: Why Turning Inward Won't Work*. A CEPR Press VoxEU.org eBook, 2020. https://voxeu.org/content/covid-19-and-trade-policy -why-turning-inward-won-t-work.

Baldwin, Tom. *Ctrl Alt Delete: How Politics and the Media Crashed Our Democracy*. London: Hurst and Company, 2018.

Bank of England. "Further Details about Sectoral Deposits and Divisia Money Data." https:// www.bankofengland.co.uk/statistics/details/further-details-sectoral-deposits-and-divisia-money -data.

Bank of England. "The U.K. Exchange Control: A Short History." *Bank of England Quarterly Bulletin*, 1967, Third Quarter. https://www.bankofengland.co.uk/-/media/boe/files/quarterly-bulletin/1967 /the-uk-exchange-control-a-short-history.pdf.

Bank for International Settlements. *Annual Economic Report*. June 2020. https://www.bis.org/publ /arpdf/ar2020e.pdf.

Bank for International Settlements. "Basel III: International Regulatory Framework for Banks." https:// www.bis.org/bcbs/basel3.htm.

Bank for International Settlements. "Global OTC Derivatives Market." Table D5.1. https://stats.bis .org/statx/srs/table/d5.1.

Barker, Richard, Robert G. Eccles, and George Serafeim. "The Future of ESG Is . . . Accounting?" *Harvard Business Review*, December 3, 2020. https://hbr.org/2020/12/the-future-of-esg-is-accounting.

Barr, Nicholas. *The Welfare State as Piggy Bank: Information, Risk, Uncertainty, and the Role of the State*. Oxford: Oxford University Press, 2001.

Barthel, Michael. "5 Key Takeaways about the State of the News Media in 2018." Pew Research Center, July 23, 2019. https://www.pewresearch.org/fact-tank/2019/07/23/key-takeaways-state-of-the-news -media-2018/.

Barwise, Patrick. "Nine Reasons Why Tech Markets Are Winner-Take-All." London Business School, July 10, 2018. https://www.london.edu/lbsr/nine-reasons-why-tech-markets-are-winner-take-all.

Baumol, William J. *The Free-Market Innovation Machine: Analyzing the Growth Miracle of Capitalism*. Princeton, NJ: Princeton University Press, 2004.

Baxter, Martin. "Three-D Politics and the Seven Tribes." *Electoral Calculus*, April 20, 2019. https:// www.electoralcalculus.co.uk/pol3d_main.html.

Baxter, Martin. "Voter Migration by Group 2017–2019." *Electoral Calculus*, January 21, 2020. https:// www.electoralcalculus.co.uk/pseph_group_migration_2019.html.

Beattie, Alan. "Carbon Border Taxes Cannot Fix the Damage of Trump's Climate Move." *Financial Times*, June 8, 2017. https://www.ft.com/content/1d5e54ca-4b86-11e7-919a-1e14ce4af89b.

Beattie, Alan. "WTO to Suffer Heavy Blow as US Stymies Appeals Body." *Financial Times*, December 8, 2019. https://www.ft.com/content/f0f992b8-19c4-11ea-97df-cc63de1d73f4.

Bebchuk, Lucian, and Jesse Fried. "The Growth of Executive Pay." National Bureau of Economic Research Working Paper No. 11443, June 2005. https://www.nber.org/papers/w11443.

Bebchuk, Lucian, and Jesse Fried. *Pay without Performance: The Unfulfilled Promise of Executive Compensation*. Cambridge, MA: Harvard University Press, 2004.

Beinhocker, Eric D. *The Origin of Wealth: The Radical Remaking of Economics and What It Means for Business and Society*. Cambridge, MA: Harvard University Press, 2006.

Belton, Catherine. *Putin's People*. London: William Collins, 2020.

Bénabou, Roland, and Jean Tirole. "Bonus Culture: Competitive Pay, Screening, and Multitasking." *Journal of Political Economy* 124, no. 2 (2016): 305–70.

Berlin, Isaiah. "Two Concepts of Liberty." In Isaiah Berlin, *Four Essays on Liberty*. Oxford: Oxford University Press, 1969, 118–72. https://cactus.dixie.edu/green/B_Readings/I_Berlin%20Two%20 Concpets%20of%20Liberty.pdf.

Berman, Sheri. *Democracy and Dictatorship in Europe: From the Ancien Régime to the Present Day*. New York: Oxford University Press, 2019.

Bernanke, Ben S. "The Global Saving Glut and the U.S. Current Account Deficit." Remarks, March 10, 2005. Federal Reserve Board. https://www.federalreserve.gov/boarddocs/speeches/2005/2005 03102/.

Bernanke, Ben S. *21st Century Monetary Policy: The Federal Reserve from the Great Inflation to Covid-19*. New York and London: W. W. Norton, 2022.

Bernheim, John, and Nicholas Gruen. "Bernheim and Gruen on the Path toward Sortition." *Equality by Lot*, August 6, 2020. https://equalitybylot.com/2020/08/06/burnheim-and-gruen-on-the-path-toward-sortition/.

Beschloss, Michael. "The Ad That Helped Reagan Sell Good Times to an Uncertain Nation." *New York Times*, May 7, 2016. https://www.nytimes.com/2016/05/08/business/the-ad-that-helped-reagan-sell-good-times-to-an-uncertain-nation.html.

Besley, Timothy. "Is Cohesive Capitalism Under Threat?" In Paul Collier, Diane Coyle, Colin Mayer, and Martin Wolf, eds. "Capitalism: What Has Gone Wrong, What Needs to Change, and How It Can Be Fixed." *Oxford Review of Economic Policy* 37, no. 4 (Winter 2021): 720–33.

Besley, Timothy, and Torsten Persson. *Pillars of Prosperity: The Political Economics of Development Clusters*. Princeton, NJ: Princeton University Press, 2011.

Bhagwati, Jagdish N., and Padma Desai. *India: Planning for Industrialization*. Oxford: Oxford University Press, for the Development Center of the Organization for Economic Co-operation and Development, 1970.

Bingham, Tom. *The Rule of Law*. London: Penguin, 2011.

Boissoneault, Lorraine. "Bismarck Tried to End Socialism's Grip—by Offering Government Healthcare." *Smithsonian Magazine*, July 14, 2017. https://www.smithsonianmag.com/.

Bordo, Michael D., Alan M. Taylor, and Jeffrey G. Williamson, eds. *Globalization in Historical Perspective*. Chicago: University of Chicago Press, 2003.

Bordo, Michael D., Barry Eichengreen, and Jongwoo Kim. "Was There Really an Earlier Period of International Financial Integration Comparable to Today's?" National Bureau of Economic Research Working Paper 6738, September 1998. www.nber.org.

Borjas, George J. "Immigration and Globalization: A Review Essay." *Journal of Economic Literature* 53, no. 4 (2015): 961–74. https://sites.hks.harvard.edu/fs/gborjas/publications/journal/JEL2015.pdf.

Bork, Robert H. *The Antitrust Paradox: A Policy at War with Itself*. 2nd ed. New York: Free Press, 1993.

Boyce, James K. *The Case for Carbon Dividends*. Cambridge, MA: Polity, 2019.

Breiding, R. James. *Too Small to Fail: Why Some Small Nations Outperform Larger Ones and How They Are Reshaping the World*. Uttar Pradesh, India: Harper Business, 2019.

The British Academy. *Principles for Purposeful Business: How to Deliver the Framework for the Future of the Corporation*, 2019. https://www.thebritishacademy.ac.uk/publications/future-of-the-corporation-principles-for-purposeful-business.

Brown, Chad P., and Melina Kolb. "Trump's Trade War Timeline: An Up-to-Date Guide." Peterson Institute for International Economics, August 6, 2020. https://www.piie.com/sites/default/files/documents/trump-trade-war-timeline.pdf.

Brown, Richard. *A History of Accounting and Accountants*. London: Routledge, 1905.

Brown, Roger. *The Inequality Crisis: The Facts and What We Can Do about It*. Bristol, UK, and Chicago: Policy Press, 2017.

Brown, Wendy. *In the Ruins of Neoliberalism: The Rise of Antidemocratic Politics in the West*. New York: Columbia University Press, 2019.

Brunnermeier, Markus. *The Resilient Society*. Colorado Springs, CO: Endeavor, 2021.

Brunnermeier, Markus, and Jean-Pierre Landau. *The Digital Euro: Policy Implications and Perspectives*, January 21, 2022. Directorate-General for Internal Policies.

Bruno, Valentina, and Hyun Song Shin. "Global Dollar Credit and Carry Trades: A Firm-Level Analysis." BIS Working Papers 510, August 2015, Bank for International Settlements. https://www.bis.org/publ/work510.pdf.

Brunsden, Jim, Sam Fleming, and Mehreen Khan. "EU Recovery Fund: How the Plan Will Work." *Financial Times*, July 21, 2020. https://www.ft.com/content/2b69c9c4-2ea4-4635-9d8a-1b67852c0322.

Bryan, Bob. "One Quote from Warren Buffett Is the Perfect Advice for Investing in the Age of Uber and Netflix." *Business Insider*, May 4, 2019. https://www.businessinsider.com/buffett-on-moats-2016-4?IR=T.

Brynjolfsson, Erik, and Andrew McAfee. *Race against the Machine: How the Digital Revolution Is Accelerating Innovation, Driving Productivity, and Irreversibly Transforming Employment and the Economy*. Lexington, MA: Digital Frontier Press, 2011.

Brynjolfsson, Erik, and Andrew McAfee. *The Second Machine Age: Work, Progress, and Prosperity in a Time of Brilliant Technologies*. New York: W. W. Norton, 2014.

Bureau of Economic Analysis. US Department of Commerce. https://www.bea.gov/.

Burgis, Tom. *Kleptopia: How Dirty Money Is Conquering the World*. London: William Collins, 2020.

Burke, Edmund. *Reflections on the Revolution in France and on the Proceedings in Certain Societies in London Relative to That Event*. London: Dodsley, 1790.

Burn-Murdoch, John, Valentina Romei, and Chris Giles. "UK Economic Recovery Tracker: What the Latest Data on Activity Are Signaling." *Financial Times*, August 5, 2020. https://www.ft.com/uk-econ-tracker.

Business Roundtable. "Statement on the Purpose of a Corporation." August 19, 2019. https://system.businessroundtable.org/app/uploads/sites/5/2021/02/BRT-Statement-on-the-Purpose-of-a-Corporation-Feburary-2021-compressed.pdf.

Callaghan, James. "Leader's Speech, Blackpool 1976." http://www.britishpoliticalspeech.org/speech-archive.htm?speech=174.

Capie, Forrest. *Capital Controls: A "Cure" Worse Than the Problem*. London: Institute of Economic Affairs, 2002.

Card, David, and Alan B. Krueger. *Myth and Measurement: The New Economics of the Minimum Wage*. Twentieth-Anniversary Edition. Princeton, NJ: Princeton University Press, 2015.

Cardoso, Fernando Henrique. "Brazil's Crisis Reflects Demise of Representative Democracy across the West." *Huffington Post*, September 5, 2016. https://www.huffpost.com/entry/brazils-crisis-reflects-demise-of-democracy_b_11867368.

Cardozo Law. "Disney's Influence on U.S. Copyright Law." August 26, 2021. https://online.yu.edu/cardozo/blog/disney-influence-copyright-law.

Carnegie Corporation of New York. "Voting Rights: A Short History," November 18, 2019. https://www.carnegie.org/our-work/article/voting-rights-timeline/.

Carroll, Lewis. "The Hunting of the Snark." https://www.poetryfoundation.org/poems/43909/the-hunting-of-the-snark.

Case, Anne, and Angus Deaton. *Deaths of Despair and the Future of Capitalism*. Princeton, NJ: Princeton University Press, 2020.

Case, Anne, and Angus Deaton. "Mortality and Morbidity in the 21st Century." *Brookings Papers on Economic Activity*. Spring 2017. https://www.brookings.edu/wp-content/uploads/2017/08/casetextsp17bpea.pdf.

Casleton, Scott. "It's Time for Liberals to Get Over Citizens United." *Vox*, May 7, 2018. https://www.vox.com/the-big-idea/2018/5/7/17325486/citizens-united-money-politics-dark-money-vouchers-primaries.

Cecchetti, Stephen G., and Enisse Kharroubi. "Reassessing the Impact of Finance on Growth." BIS Working Papers 381, July 2012. https://www.bis.org/publ/work381.pdf.

Cecchetti, Stephen G., and Enisse Kharroubi. "Why Does Financial Sector Growth Crowd Out Real Economic Growth?" BIS Working Papers 490, February 2015. https://www.bis.org/publ/work490.pdf.

Center for Financial Stability. "Advances in Monetary and Financial Measurement," 2021. http://www.centerforfinancialstability.org/amfm_data.php?startc=1984&startt=2000#methods.

Center for Presidential Transition. "Unconfirmed: Why Reducing the Number of Senate-Confirmed Positions Can Make Government More Effective." August 9, 2021. https://presidentialtransition.org/publications/unconfirmed-reducing-number-senate-confirmed-positions/.

Centers for Disease Control and Prevention. "Opioid Overdose Deaths." https://www.cdc.gov/drugoverdose/epidemic/index.html.

Chancellor, Edward. *The Price of Time: The Real Story of Interest*. London: Allen Lane, 2022.

Cingano, Federico. "Trends in Income Inequality and Its Impact on Economic Growth." OECD Social, Employment and Migration Working Papers No. 163, Paris, 2014. http://dx.doi.org/10.1787/5jxrjncwxv6j-en.

Clark, Andrew E., Sarah Flèche, Richard Layard, Nattavudh Powdthavee, and George Ward. *The Origins of Happiness: The Science of Well-Being over the Life Course*. Princeton, NJ: Princeton University Press, 2018.

Clemens, Michael A. "Economics and Emigration: Trillion-Dollar Bills on the Sidewalk?" *Journal of Economic Perspectives* 25, no. 3 (Summer 2011): 83–106.

Coase, Ronald H. "The Nature of the Firm." *Economica* 4, no. 16 (1937): 386–405. https://onlinelibrary.wiley.com/doi/full/10.1111/j.1468-0335.1937.tb00002.x.

Coggan, Philip. *More: The 10,000-Year Rise of the World Economy*. London: Economist Books, 2020.

Cohn, D'Vera. "How U.S. Immigration Laws and Rules Have Changed throughout History." Pew Research Center, September 30, 2015. https://www.pewresearch.org/fact-tank/2015/09/30/how-u-s-immigration-laws-and-rules-have-changed-through-history/.

Collier, Paul. *The Future of Capitalism: Facing the New Anxieties*. London: Allen Lane, 2018.

Collier, Paul, and John Kay. *Greed Is Dead: Politics after Individualism*. London: Allen Lane 2020.

Collins, Chuck. *The Wealth Hoarders: How Billionaires Pay Millions to Hide Trillions.* Cambridge, UK: Polity, 2021.

Commission on the Practice of Democratic Citizenship. *Our Common Purpose: Reinventing American Democracy for the 21st Century.* Cambridge, MA: American Academy of Arts and Sciences, 2020.

Conference Board. "Total Economy Database," 2021. https://www.conference-board.org/data/econo mydatabase/total-economy-database-productivity. Consensus Economics. https://www.consen suseconomics.com/.

Congressional Budget Office. *The 2021 Long-term Budget Outlook.* March 2021. https://www.cbo.gov /system/files/2021-03/56977-LTBO-2021.pdf.

Congressional Budget Office. "Monthly Budget Review: Summary for Fiscal Year 2019." November 7, 2019. https://www.cbo.gov/.

Cooper, Andrew F., and Colin I. Bradford Jr. *The G20 and the Post-Crisis Economic Order.* Center for International Governance Innovation G20 Papers No 3, June 2020. https://www.cigionline.org /sites/default/files/g20_no_3_0.pdf.

Corak, Miles. "Income Inequality, Equality of Opportunity, and Intergenerational Mobility." IZA Discussion Paper No. 7520. July 2013. http://ftp.iza.org/dp7520.pdf.

Coughlan, Sean. "The Symbolic Target of 50% at University Reached." BBC News. September 26, 2019. https://www.bbc.com/news/education-49841620.

Courtois, Stéphane, Nicolas Werth, Jean-Louis Panné, Andrzej Paczkowski, Karel Bartosek, and Jean-Louise Margolin. *The Black Book of Communism: Crimes, Terror, Repression.* Translated by Jonathan Murphy and Mark Kramer. Cambridge, MA: Harvard University Press, 1999.

Cowen, Tyler. *The Great Stagnation: How America Ate All the Low-Hanging Fruit of Modern History, Got Sick, and Will (Eventually) Feel Better.* New York: Dutton, 2011.

Coyle, Diane. "Building Back Better Requires Systemic Shifts." *Financial Times,* July 30, 2020. https:// www.ft.com/content/72b1fbd7-6059-4cb9-835d-c608acc3e603.

Crafts, Nicholas. *Globalization and Growth in the Twentieth Century.* IMF Working Paper WP/00/44. Washington, DC, International Monetary Fund, 2000. https://www.imf.org/external/pubs/ft/wp /2000/wp0044.pdf.

Crivelli, Ernesto, Ruud De Mooij, and Michael Keen. "Base Erosion, Profit Shifting and Developing Countries." IMF Working Paper WP/15/118. May 2015. https://www.imf.org/en/Publications /WP/Issues/2016/12/31/Base-Erosion-Profit-Shifting-and-Developing-Countries-42973.

Croft, Jane. "Ex-Barclays Libor Traders Receive Jail Sentences." *Financial Times,* July 7, 2016. https:// www.ft.com/content/16215d97-971f-3209-87da-55d0a1f08c5f.

Crowley, Michael. "Trump Won't Commit to 'Peaceful' Post-Election Transfer of Power." *New York Times,* September 23, 2020. https://www.nytimes.com/2020/09/23/us/politics/trump-power-trans fer-2020-election.html.

Curtis, Polly. "Gordon Brown Calls Labor Supporter a 'Bigoted Woman.'" *Guardian,* April 28, 2010. https://www.theguardian.com/politics/2010/apr/28/gordon-brown-bigoted-woman.

Dal Bó, Ernesto, Federico Finan, Olle Folke, Torsten Persson, and Johanna Rickne. "Economic Losers and Political Winners: Sweden's Radical Right." February 2019. http://perseus.iies.su.se/~tpers /papers/CompleteDraft190301.pdf.

Dalio, Ray, Jordan Nick, Steven Kryger, and Bill Longfield. "Wealth Taxes." March 22, 2021. Bridgewater, unpublished.

DARPA. "Innovation at DARPA." July 2016. https://www.darpa.mil/attachments/DARPA_Innovation _2016.pdf.

Dasgupta, Partha. *The Economics of Biodiversity: The Dasgupta Review—Full Report.* April 23, 2021. https://www.gov.uk/government/publications/final-report-the-economics-of-biodiversity-the -dasgupta-review.

Day, Chris. *The Beveridge Report and the Foundations of the Welfare State.* National Archives, blog, December 7, 2017. https://blog.nationalarchives.gov.uk/beveridge-report-foundations-welfare-state/.

De Vries, Jan. "The Industrial Revolution and the Industrious Revolution." *Journal of Economic History* 54, no. 2 (1994): 249–70. http://www.jstor.org/stable/2123912.

Dervis, Kemal, and Caroline Conroy. "Nationalists of the World, Unite?" Brookings, November 26, 2018. https://www.brookings.edu/opinions/nationalists-of-the-world-unite/.

Detter, Dag, and Stefan Fölster. *The Public Wealth of Nations: How Management of Public Assets Can Boost or Bust Economic Growth.* Basingstoke: Palgrave Macmillan, 2015.

Diamond, Jared M. *Guns, Germs and Steel: A Short History of Everybody for the Last 13,000 Years.* London: Vintage, 1998.

Diamond, Jared M. "Jared Diamond: Lessons from a Pandemic." *Financial Times*, May 28, 2020. https://www.ft.com/content/71ed9f88-9f5b-11ea-b65d-489c67b0d85d.

Diamond, Larry. "Facing Up to the Democratic Recession." *Journal of Democracy* 26, no. 1 (January 2015). http://www.journalofdemocracy.org/sites/default/files/Diamond-26-1_0.pdf.

Diamond, Larry. *Ill Winds: Saving Democracy from Russian Rage, Chinese Ambition, and American Complacency*. New York: Penguin Press, 2019.

Diamond, Larry. *The Spirit of Democracy: The Struggle to Build Free Societies throughout the World*. New York: Henry Holt, 2009.

Diewert, W. Erwin. "Decompositions of Productivity Growth into Sectoral Effects." Paper Prepared for the IARIW-UNSW Conference on Productivity: Measurement, Drivers and Trends, November 2013. http://www.iariw.org/papers/2013/Diewert_Paper2.pdf.

Diris, Ron, and Erwin Ooghe. "The Economics of Financing Higher Education." *Economic Policy*, April 2018. https://ideas.repec.org/a/oup/ecpoli/v33y2018i94p265-314.html.

Doerr, Sebastian, Stefan Gissler, José-Luis Peydró, and Hans-Joachim Voth. "Financial Crises and Political Radicalization: How Failing Banks Paved Hitler's Path to Power." BIS World Papers, No. 978. November 22, 2021. https://www.bis.org/publ/work978.htm.

Domar, Evsey. "On the Measurement of Technological Change," *Economic Journal* 71, no. 284 (December 1961): 709–29.

Draghi, Mario. "Verbatim of the Remarks Made by Mario Draghi." July 26, 2012. European Central Bank. https://www.ecb.europa.eu/press/key/date/2012/html/sp120726.en.html.

Dube, Arindrajit. "Guest Post: Minimum Wage Laws and the Labor Market: What Have We Learned Since Card and Krueger's Book *Myth and Measurement?*" September 1, 2011. https://rortybomb.wordpress.com/2011/09/01/guest-post-minimum-wage-laws-and-the-labor-market-what-have-we-learned-since-card-and-krueger%E2%80%99s-book-myth-and-measurement/.

Dumas, Charles. *Populism and Economics*. London: Profile Books, 2018.

Durand, Cédric. *Fictitious Capital: How Finance Is Appropriating Our Future*. London and New York: Verso, 2017.

Durkheim, Émile. *Le Suicide: Étude de Sociologie*. Bar-le-Duc, France: Imprimerie Contant-Laguerre, 1897.

Dustmann, Christian, Baerry Eichengreen, Sebastian Otten, André Sapir, Guido Tabellini, and Gylfi Zoega. "Populism and Trust in Europe." *VoxEU*, August 2017. https://voxeu.org/article/populism-and-trust-europe.

Earthworks. "FACT SHEET: Battery Minerals for the Clean Energy Transition," April 17, 2019. https://earthworks.org/fact-sheet-battery-minerals-for-the-clean-energy-transition/.

"Economists Are Rethinking the Numbers on Inequality." *Economist*, November 28, 2019. https://www.economist.com/briefing/2019/11/28/economists-are-rethinking-the-numbers-on-inequality.

"Economists' Statement on Carbon Dividends." Climate Leadership Council, January 17, 2019. https://clcouncil.org/economists-statement/.

Editorial Board. "New Issuance of SDRs Is Vital to Help Poorer Countries." *Financial Times*, April 12, 2020. https://www.ft.com/content/2691bfa2-799e-11ea-af44-daa3def9ae03.

Edsall, Thomas B. "Trump Says Jump. His Supporters Ask How High?" *New York Times*, September 14, 2017. https://www.nytimes.com/2017/09/14/opinion/trump-republicans.html?action=click&pgtype=Homepage&clickSource=story-heading&module=opinion-c-col-right-region&region=opinion-c-col-right-region&WT.nav=opinion-c-col-right-region&_r=0.

Edsall, Thomas B. "We Aren't Seeing White Support for Trump for What It Is." *New York Times*, August 28, 2019. https://www.nytimes.com/2019/08/28/opinion/trump-white-voters.html?action=click&module=Opinion&pgtype=Homepage.

Edwards, Sebastian. "Modern Monetary Disasters." *Project Syndicate*, May 16, 2019. https://www.project-syndicate.org/commentary/modern-monetary-theory-latin-america-by-sebastian-edwards-2019-05.

Edwards, Sebastian. "On Latin American Populism, and Its Echoes around the World." National Bureau of Economic Research Working Paper No. 26333. October 2019. https://www.nber.org/papers/w26333.

Eichengreen, Barry. *The Populist Temptation: Economic Grievance and Political Reaction in the Modern Era*. New York: Oxford University Press, 2018.

Electoral Reform Society. "Single Transferable Vote," 2017. https://www.electoral-reform.org.uk/voting-systems/types-of-voting-system/single-transferable-vote/.

Electronic Frontier Foundation. "Patent Trolls." https://www.eff.org/issues/resources-patent-troll-victims.

Ellis, Howard S. "Bilateralism and the Future of International Trade." *Essays in International Finance* No. 5, Summer 1945. International Finance Section, Department of Economics and Social Institutions, Princeton University, Princeton, New Jersey. https://ies.princeton.edu/pdf/E5.pdf.

Ellyatt, Holly. "Who Are 'Davos Man' and 'Davos Woman'?" CNBC, January 19, 2018. https://www.cnbc.com/2018/01/19/who-are-davos-man-and-davos-woman.html.

Encyclopedia Britannica, https://www.britannica.com.

Energy Transitions Commission. *Keeping 1.5°C Alive: Closing the Gap in the 2020s*. September 2021. https://www.energy-transitions.org/publications/keeping-1-5-alive/.

Energy Transitions Commission. *Making Mission Possible: Delivering a Net-Zero Economy*. September 2020. https://www.energy-transitions.org/publications/making-mission-possible/.

"Enoch Powell's 'Rivers of Blood' speech." https://anth1001.files.wordpress.com/2014/04/enoch-powell_speech.pdf.

Estevadeordal, Antoni, Brian Ftrantz, and Alan M. Taylor. "The Rise and Fall of World Trade, 1870–1939." National Bureau of Economic Research Paper No. 9318. November 2002. http://www.nber.org/papers/w9318.

European Council on Foreign Relations. *Crisis and Cohesion in the EU: A Ten-Year Review*. February 5, 2018. https://www.ecfr.eu/page/-/ECFR-_245_-_Crisis_and_Cohesion_-_A_10_Year_Review_Janning_WEB.pdf.

EurWORK: European Observatory of Working Life. "Flexicurity." May 7, 2013. https://www.eurofound.europa.eu/observatories/eurwork/industrial-relations-dictionary/flexicurity.

Evans, Geoff, and Florian Schaffner. "Brexit Identities: How Leave Versus Remain Replaced Conservative Versus Labor Affiliations of British Voters." January 23, 2019. https://ukandeu.ac.uk/brexit-identities-how-leave-versus-remain-replaced-conservative-versus-labor-affiliations-of-british-voters/.

Facebook Investor Relations. "Facebook Reports Fourth Quarter and Full Year 2018 Results." https://investor.fb.com/investor-news/press-release-details/2019/Facebook-Reports-Fourth-Quarter-and-Full-Year-2018-Results/default.aspx.

Federal Reserve. "Federal Reserve Announces the Establishment of Temporary U.S. Dollar Liquidity Arrangements with Other Central Banks." March 19, 2020. https://www.federalreserve.gov/newsevents/pressreleases/monetary20200319b.htm.

Ferguson, Thomas, and Joel Rogers. *Right Turn: The Decline of the Democrats and the Future of American Politics*. New York: Farrar, Straus and Giroux, 1987.

Fetzer, Thiemo. "Austerity Caused Brexit." *VoxEU*, April 8, 2019. https://voxeu.org/article/austerity-caused-brexit.

Fetzer, Thiemo. "Did Austerity Cause Brexit?" Warwick University Working Paper Series No. 381. Revised June 2019. https://warwick.ac.uk/fac/soc/economics/research/centers/cage/manage/publications/381-2018_fetzer.pdf.

Financial Times. "Coronavirus Tracked: See How Your Country Compares." https://www.ft.com/content/a2901ce8-5eb7-4633-b89c-cbdf5b386938.

Findlay, Ronald, and Kevin H. O'Rourke. "Commodity Market Integration, 1500–2000." In Michael D. Bordo, Alan M. Taylor, and Jeffrey G. Williamson, eds. *Globalization in Historical Perspective*. Chicago: University of Chicago Press, 2003. http://www.nber.org/chapters/c9585.pdf.

Findlay, Ronald, and Kevin H. O'Rourke. *Power and Plenty: Trade, War, and the World Economy in the Second Millennium*. Princeton, NJ: Princeton University Press, 2009.

Finer, S. E. *The History of Government: Ancient Monarchies and Empires*. Vol. 1, *Ancient Monarchies and Empires*. Oxford: Oxford University Press, 1997 and 1999.

Finer, S. E. *The Man on Horseback: The Role of the Military in Politics*. Abingdon and New York: Routledge, 1962 and 2017.

Fleming, Sam, Miles Johnson, and Ian Mount. "EU Rescue Package: Borrowing to Prevent a North-South Split." *Financial Times*, July 24, 2020. https://www.ft.com/content/1fd5785b-5f6f-4175-bae4-214b43a55804.

Fleming, Sam, Mehreen Khan, and Jim Brunsden. "EU Leaders Strike Deal on €750bn Recovery Fund after Marathon Summit." *Financial Times*, July 21, 2020. https://www.ft.com/content/713be467-ed19-4663-95ff-66f775af55cc.

Foa, R. S., A. Klassen, M. Slade, A. Rand, and R. Collins. "The Global Satisfaction with Democracy Report 2020." Cambridge, UK: Centre for the Future of Democracy, 2020. https://www.cam.ac.uk/system/files/report2020_003.pdf.

Foa, Roberto S., Xavier Romero-Vidal, Andrew J. Klassen, Joaquin Fuenzalida Concha, Marian Quednau, and Lisa Sophie Fenner. *The Great Reset: Public Opinion, Populism, and the Pandemic*. Centre for the Future of Democracy, University of Cambridge, January 14, 2022.

Foa, Roberto Stefan, and Yascha Mounk. "The Danger of Deconsolidation: The Democratic Disconnect." *Journal of Democracy* 27, no. 3 (July 2016): 5–17.

Foundation for Economic Education. "H. L. Mencken Quotes on Government, Democracy, and Politicians." https://fee.org/articles/12-hl-mencken-quotes-on-government-democracy-and-politicians/.

Fowler, Mayhill. "Obama: No Surprise That Hard-Pressed Pennsylvanians Turn Bitter." *Huffington Post*, November 17, 2008, updated May 25, 2011. https://www.huffingtonpost.com/mayhill-fowler/obama-no-surprise-that-ha_b_96188.html.

Frank, Robert H., and Philip J. Cook. *The Winner-Take-All Society: Why the Few at the Top Get So Much More Than the Rest of Us*. New York and London: Penguin, 1996.

Frankopan, Peter. *The Silk Roads: A New History of the World*. London: Bloomsbury, 2015. Especially chapter 1.

Frantz, Erica. *Authoritarianism: What Everyone Needs to Know*. Oxford: Oxford University Press, 2018.

Freedom House. "Democracy in Crisis." *Freedom in the World 2018*. https://freedomhouse.org/sites/default/files/2020-02/FH_FIW_Report_2018_Final.pdf .

Freedom House. "Democracy under Siege." *Freedom in the World 2021*. https://freedomhouse.org/sites/default/files/2021-02/FIW2021_World_02252021_FINAL-web-upload.pdf.

Frey, Carl Benedikt. *The Technology Trap: Capital, Labor, and Power in the Age of Automation*. Princeton, NJ, and Oxford: Princeton University Press, 2019.

Frey, William H. "The US Will Become 'Minority White' in 2045, Census Projects: Youthful Minorities Are the Engine of Future Growth." Brookings, March 14, 2018. https://www.brookings.edu/blog/the-avenue/2018/03/14/the-us-will-become-minority-white-in-2045-census-projects/.

Friedman, Benjamin. *The Moral Consequences of Economic Growth*. New York: First Vintage Books Edition, 2006.

Friedman, Milton. "The Social Responsibility of Business Is to Increase Its Profits." *New York Times Magazine*, September 13, 1970. https://web.archive.org/web/20060207060807/https://www.colorado.edu/studentgroups/libertarians/issues/friedman-soc-resp-business.html.

Friedman, Thomas L. *The World Is Flat: The Globalized World in the Twenty-first Century*. London and New York: Penguin, 2005.

Fukuyama, Francis. "The End of History?" *National Interest* 16 (Summer 1989): 3–18. https://www.jstor.org/stable/24027184.

Fukuyama, Francis. *Identity: The Demand for Dignity and the Politics of Resentment*. New York: Farrar, Straus and Giroux, 2018.

Fukuyama, Francis. *The Origins of Political Order: From Prehuman Times to the French Revolution*. London: Profile Books, 2011.

Fukuyama, Francis. *Political Order and Political Decay: From the Industrial Revolution to the Globalization of Democracy*. London: Profile Books, 2014.

Full Fact. "Everything You Might Want to Know about the UK's Trade with the EU." November 22, 2017. https://fullfact.org/europe/uk-eu-trade/.

Funke, Manuel, Moritz Schularik, and Christoph Trebesch. "Going to Extremes: Politics after Financial Crises, 1870–2014." *European Economic Review* 88 (2016): 227–60. http://www.macrohistory.net/wp-content/uploads/2015/10/Going-to-extremes.pdf.

Furman, Jason. "Beyond Antitrust: The Role of Competition Policy in Promoting Inclusive Growth." Searle Center Conference on Antitrust Economics and Competition Policy. September 16, 2016. https://obamawhitehouse.archives.gov/sites/default/files/page/files/20160916_searle_conference_competition_furman_cea.pdf.

Furman, Jason, and Lawrence H. Summers. "A Reconsideration of Fiscal Policy in the Era of Low Interest Rates." Brookings, November 30, 2020. https://www.brookings.edu/wp-content/uploads/2020/11/furman-summers-fiscal-reconsideration-discussion-draft.pdf.

Furman, Jason, et al. *Unlocking Digital Competition: Report on the Digital Competition Expert Panel*. March 2019. https://assets.publishing.service.gov.uk/government/uploads/system/uploads/attachment_data/file/785547/unlocking_digital_competition_furman_review_web.pdf.

Galbraith, John Kenneth. *American Capitalism: The Concept of Countervailing Power*. New York: Houghton Mifflin, 1952.

Galofré-Vilà, Gregori, Martin McKee, María Gómez-León, and David Stuckler. "The 1918 Influenza Pandemic and the Rise of Italian Fascism: A Cross-City Quantitative and Historical Text Qualitative Analysis." *American Journal of Public Health* 112, no. 2 (February 2022): 242–47.

Galston, William A. *Anti-Pluralism: The Populist Threat to Liberal Democracy*. New Haven and London: Yale University Press, 2018.

Gamble, Andrew, and Tony Wright, eds. *Rethinking Democracy*. Chichester: John Wiley for Political Quarterly Publishing, 2019.

Gardbaum, Stephen, and Richard H. Pildes. "Populism and Institutional Design: Methods of Selecting Candidates for Chief Executive." *New York University Law Review* 93 (2018): 647–708. https://www.nyulawreview.org/wp-content/uploads/2018/10/NYULawReview-93-4-Gardbaum-Pildes.pdf.

Gardels, Nathan, and Nicholas Berggruen. *Renovating Democracy: Governing in the Age of Globalization and Digital Capitalism*. Oakland, CA: University of California Press for the Berggruen Institute, 2019.

Garside, M. "Major Countries in Worldwide Cobalt Mine Production from 2010 to 2020." Statista. https://www.statista.com/statistics/264928/cobalt-mine-production-by-country/.

Gates, Bill. *How to Avoid a Climate Disaster: The Solutions We Have and the Breakthroughs We Need*. London: Allen Lane, 2021.

GDPR.EU. "What Is GDPR, the EU's New Data Protection Law?" https://gdpr.eu/what-is-gdpr/#:~:text=The%20General%20Data%20Protection%20Regulation,to%20people%20in%20the%20EU.

Geary, Dick. "Who Voted for the Nazis?" *History Today* 48, no. 10 (October 1948), https://www.historytoday.com/archive/who-voted-nazis.

Gellner, Ernest. *Nations and Nationalism*. Oxford: Blackwell Press, 1983 and 2006.

George, Henry. *Progress and Poverty: An Inquiry into the Cause of Industrial Depressions and of Increase of Want with Increase of Wealth: The Remedy*. Vega Publishing, 2019. First published 1879.

Gessen, Masha. *Surviving Autocracy*. London: Granta, 2020.

Gethin, Amory, Clara Martínez-Toledano, and Thomas Piketty. "Brahmin Left Versus Merchant Right: Changing Political Cleavages in 21 Western Democracies 1948–2020." *Quarterly Journal of Economics* 137, no. 1 (2022).

Gidron, Noam, and Peter A. Hall. "The Politics of Social Status: Economic and Cultural Roots of the Populist Right." *British Journal of Sociology* 68, no. S1 (November 2017). https://onlinelibrary.wiley.com/doi/epdf/10.1111/1468-4446.12319.

Gilens, Martin, and Benjamin I. Page. "Critics Argued with Our Analysis of U.S. Political Inequality. Here Are 5 Ways They're Wrong." *Washington Post*, May 23, 2016. https://www.washingtonpost.com/news/monkey-cage/wp/2016/05/23/critics-challenge-our-portrait-of-americas-political-inequality-heres-5-ways-they-are-wrong/.

Gilens, Martin, and Benjamin I. Page. "Testing Theories of American Politics: Elites, Interest Groups, and Average Citizens." *Perspectives on Politics* 12, no. 3 (September 18, 2014): 564–81. https://www.cambridge.org/core/journals/perspectives-on-politics/issue/32534CA34A6B58E6E4420B56764850E1.

Giles, Chris. "Brexit Is an Example of Deglobalisation, Says Carney." *Financial Times*, September 18, 2017. https://www.ft.com/content/9b37cf6e-9c82-11e7-9a86-4d5a475ba4c5.

Giles, Chris, Emma Agyemang, and Aime Williams. "136 Nations Agree to Biggest Corporate Tax Deal in a Century." *Financial Times*, October 8, 2021. https://www.ft.com/content/5dc4e2d5-d7bd-4000-bf94-088f17e21936.

Global Security.org. "'Führerprinzip' Leader Principle." https://www.globalsecurity.org/military/world/europe/de-fuhrerprinzip.htm.

Global Trade Alert. *Going Spare: Steel, Excess Capacity, and Protectionism*. 22nd Global Trade Alert Report. London: Center for Economic Policy Research, 2018. https://www.globaltradealert.org/.

Global Trade Alert. *Will Awe Trump Rules?* 21st Global Trade Alert Report. London: Center for Economic Policy Research, 2017. https://www.globaltradealert.org/.

Goebbels, Joseph. "On National-Socialist Germany and Her Contribution toward Peace." Speech to the representatives of the international press at Geneva on September 28, 1933. German League of Nations Union News Service, PRO, FO 371/16728. Included within *Völkerbund: Journal for International Politics*, Ausgaben 1–103 (1933): 16. https://en.wikiquote.org/wiki/Joseph_Goebbels.

Goldberg, Michelle. "Trumpism Is a Racket, and Steve Bannon Knew It." *New York Times*, August 20, 2020. https://www.nytimes.com/2020/08/20/opinion/sunday/trump-steve-bannon-fraud.html.

Golden, Sean. "A 'China Model' for the 'New Era.'" Barcelona Center for International Affairs. 2017. https://www.cidob.org/en/publications/publication_series/opinion/asia/a_china_model_for_the_new_era.

Goldin, Ian, Pantelis Koutroumpis, François Lafond, Nils Rochowicz, and Julian Winkler. *The Productivity Paradox: Reconciling Rapid Technological Change and Stagnating Productivity*. Oxford Martin School, April 2019. https://www.oxfordmartin.ox.ac.uk/downloads/reports/Productivity_Paradox.pdf.

Goldthorpe, John H. "Social Class Mobility in Modern Britain: Changing Structure, Constant Process." Lecture in Sociology. The British Academy, read March 15, 2016. *Journal of the British Academy*

4 (July 18, 2016): 89–111. https://www.thebritishacademy.ac.uk/sites/default/files/05%20Gold thorpe%201825.pdf.

Goodhart, Charles, and Manoj Pradhan. *The Great Demographic Reversal: Aging Societies, Waning Inequality, and an Inflation Reversal.* London: Palgrave Macmillan, 2020.

Goodhart, David. *Head Hand Heart: The Struggle for Dignity and Status in the 21st Century.* London: Penguin, 2021.

Goodhart, David. *The Road to Somewhere: The Populist Revolt and the Future of Politics.* London: C. Hurst & Co, 2017.

Gordon, Robert J. *The Rise and Fall of American Growth: The U.S. Standard of Living Since the Civil War.* Princeton, NJ, and Woodstock, England: Princeton University Press, 2016.

Gourinchas, Pierre-Olivier, and Hélène Rey. "From World Banker to World Venture Capitalist: U.S. External Adjustment and the Exorbitant Privilege." In Richard H. Clarida, ed. *Current Account Imbalances: Sustainability and Adjustment.* Chicago: University of Chicago Press, 2007, 11–66. https://www.nber.org/chapters/c0121.pdf.

Groningen Growth and Development Centre, University of Groningen. Maddison Project. http://www.ggdc.net/maddison/maddison-project/data.htm.

Gruen, Nicholas. "Beyond Vox Pop Democracy: Democratic Deliberation and Leadership in the Age of the Internet." *More or Less: Democracy and the New Media,* 2012. http://www.futureleaders.com.au/book_chapters/pdf/More-or-Less/Nicholas_Gruen.pdf#zoom=80.

Gruen, Nicholas. "The Evaluator General." Club Troppo, May 29, 2020. https://clubtroppo.com.au/2020/05/29/the-evaluator-general/.

Gruen, Nicholas. "Government as Impresario." NESTA, October 20, 2014. https://www.nesta.org.uk/report/government-as-impresario/.

Gruen, Nicholas. "Superannuation Again." Club Troppo, May 31, 2005. https://clubtroppo.com.au/2005/05/31/superannuation-again/.

Gruen, Nicholas. "An Unpublished Column on Sortition and Brexit." *Equality by Lot,* April 17, 2019. https://equalitybylot.com/2019/04/17/an-unpublished-column-on-sortition-and-brexit/.

Guriev, Sergei, and Daniel Treisman. *Spin Dictators: The Changing Face of Tyranny in the 21st Century.* Princeton, NJ, and Oxford: Princeton University Press, 2022.

Gurri, Martin. *The Revolt of the Public and the Crisis of Authority in the New Millennium.* San Francisco: Stripe Press, 2018.

Guyton, John, Patrick Langetieg, Daniel Reck, Max Risch, and Gabriel Zucman. "Tax Evasion at the Top of the Income Distribution: Theory and Evidence." National Bureau of Economic Research Working Paper 28542. March 2021. http://www.nber.org/papers/w28542 .

Gwartney, James, Joshua Hall, and Robert Lawson. *Economic Freedom of the World 2016 Annual Report.* Washington, DC: Cato Institute. https://store.cato.org/book/economic-freedom-world-2016-annual-report.

Haass, Richard. "A Cold War with China Would Be a Mistake." Council on Foreign Relations, May 11, 2020. https://www.cfr.org/article/cold-war-china-would-be-mistake.

Haidt, Jonathan, and Tobias Rose-Stockwell. "The Dark Psychology of Social Networks: Why It Feels Like Everything Is Going Haywire." *Atlantic,* December 2019. https://www.theatlantic.com/magazine/archive/2019/12/social-media-democracy/600763/.

Haldane, Andrew G. "The $100 Billion Question." Speech delivered March 30, 2010. Bank for International Settlements. https://www.bis.org/review/r100406d.pdf.

Haldane, Andrew G. "The Costs of Short-termism." In Michael Jacobs and Mariana Mazzucato, eds. *Rethinking Capitalism: Economics and Policy for Sustainable and Inclusive Growth.* Chichester: Wiley-Blackwell, 2016. Chapter 4, 66–76.

Hamilton, Alexander. "The Mode of Electing the President." *Federalist Papers* No. 68. March 14, 1788. https://avalon.law.yale.edu/18th_century/fed68.asp.

Hamilton, Alexander. *Report on the Subject of Manufactures.* December 1791.

Hansen, Alvin H. "Economic Progress and Declining Population Growth." *American Economic Review* 29, no.1, part 1 (March 1939). http://digamo.free.fr/hansen39.pdf.

Hansen, Kiese, and Time Shaw. "Solving the Student Debt Crisis." February 2020. Aspen Institute Financial Security Program. https://assets.aspeninstitute.org/wp-content/uploads/2020/03/SolvingStudentDebtCrisis.pdf.

Harari, Yuval. *Sapiens: A Brief History of Humankind.* London: Vintage Books, 2014.

Harding, Robin, Amy Kazmin, and Christian Shepherd. "Asian Trade Deal Set to Be Signed after Years of Negotiations." *Financial Times,* November 11, 2020. https://www.ft.com/content/ddaa403a-099c-423c-a273-6a2ed6ef45f2.

Harding, Robin, and John Reed. "Asia-Pacific Countries Sign One of the Largest Free Trade Deals in History." *Financial Times*, November 15, 2020. https://www.ft.com/content/2dff91bd-ceeb-4567 -9f9f-c50b7876adce.

Hargreaves, Deborah. *Are Chief Executives Overpaid?* Cambridge: Polity, 2019.

Hartmann, Thom. *Unequal Protection: How Corporations Became "People"—and How You Can Fight Back.* San Francisco: Berrett-Koehler, 2010.

Haskell, Jonathan, and Stian Westlake. *Capitalism without Capital: The Rise of the Intangible Economy.* Oxford, England, and Princeton, NJ: Princeton University Press, 2018.

Haughton, Tim. "It's the Slogan, Stupid: The Brexit Referendum." University of Birmingham, no date. https://www.birmingham.ac.uk/research/perspective/eu-ref-haughton.aspx.

Hausmann, Ricardo, César A. Hidalgo, Sebastián Bustos, Michele Coscia, Alexander Simoes, and Muhammed A. Yildrim. *The Atlas of Economic Complexity: Mapping Paths to Prosperity.* Cambridge, MA: MIT Press, 2014.

Hayek, Friedrich A. *The Road to Serfdom.* London: Routledge, 1944.

Hayek, Friedrich A. "Scientism and the Study of Society, Part I." *Economica* 9, no. 35 (August 1942): 267 91. https://www.jstor.org/stable/2549540?origin=crossref.

Helliwell, John F., Richard Layard, Jeffrey D. Sachs, Jan-Emmanuel De Neve, Lara B. Akin, and Shun Wang. *World Happiness Report 2021.* https://happiness-report.s3.amazonaws.com/2021/WHR+ 21.pdf.

Hellwig, Martin. "'Capitalism: What Has Gone Wrong?': Who Went Wrong? Capitalism? The Market Economy? Governments? 'Neoliberal' Economics?" In Paul Collier, Diane Coyle, Colin Mayer, and Martin Wolf, eds. "Capitalism: What Has Gone Wrong, What Needs to Change, and How It Can Be Fixed." *Oxford Review of Economic Policy* 37, no. 4 (Winter 2021): 664–77.

Helpman, Elhanan. *Globalization and Inequality.* Cambridge, MA, and London: Harvard University Press, 2018.

Henderson, Richard, and Eric Platt. "'K-shaped' Stock Recovery Widens Gap between Winners and Losers." *Financial Times*, August 21, 2020. https://www.ft.com/content/680d9605-f112-4ea5-a5af -3b9138b5bf07.

Hickel, Jason. *Less Is More: How Degrowth Will Save the World.* London: William Heinemann, 2020.

Hirsch, Fred. *The Social Limits to Growth.* London: Routledge, 1995.

Hirschman, Albert O. *Exit, Voice, and Loyalty: Responses to Decline in Firms, Organizations, and States.* Cambridge, MA: Harvard University Press, 1972.

Hirst, Paul, and Grahame Thompson. *Globalization in Question: The International Economy and the Possibilities of Governance.* 2nd ed. Cambridge: Polity Press, 1999.

Hiscox, Michael. "The Job Guarantee—Weakening Worker Power?" *Challenge Magazine*, August 22, 2020. https://www.challengemag.org/post/the-job-guarantee-weakening-worker-power.

Hop, Johanna. "The Hartz Employment Reforms in Germany." Center for Public Impact. September 2, 2019. https://www.centreforpublicimpact.org/case-study/hartz-employment-reforms-germany/.

Horn, Sebastian, Carmen M. Reinhart, and Christoph Trebesch. "China's Overseas Lending." NBER Working Paper No. 26050. July 2019. Revised May 2020. National Bureau of Economic Research. http://papers.nber.org/tmp/36603-w26050.pdf.

House of Lords Economic Affairs Committee. *Central Bank Digital Currencies: A Solution in Search of a Problem?* HL Paper 131. January 13, 2022.

Hudson, Michael. *And Forgive Them Their Debts: Lending, Foreclosure and Redemption from Bronze Age Finance to the Jubilee Year.* Dresden: Islet-Verlag, 2018.

Hufbauer, Gary Clyde, and Euijin Jung. *Why Has Trade Stopped Growing? Not Much Liberalization and Lots of Micro-protection.* Peterson Institute for International Economics, March 23, 2016. https:// piie.com/blogs/trade-investment-policy-watch/why-has-trade-stopped-growing-not-much -liberalization-and-lots.

Hughes, Ian. *Disordered Minds: How Dangerous Personalities Are Destroying Democracy.* Hampshire: Zero Books, 2018.

Hume, David. *A Treatise of Human Nature.* Book III. Part III. Section III. "Of the Influencing Motives of the Will." https://www.pitt.edu/~mthompso/readings/hume.influencing.pdf.

Hurley, John, Scott Morris, and Gailyn Portelance. "Examining the Debt Implications of the Belt and Road Initiative from a Policy Perspective." CGD Policy Paper 121. March 2018, Center for Global Development. https://www.cgdev.org/sites/default/files/examining-debt-implications-belt-and-road -initiative-policy-perspective.pdf.

Imperial College COVID-19 Response Team. "Report 9: Impact of Non-pharmaceutical (NPIs) to Reduced COVID-19 Mortality and Healthcare Demand." March 16, 2020. https://www.imperial

.ac.uk/media/imperial-college/medicine/sph/ide/gida-fellowships/Imperial-College-COVID19
-NPI-modelling-16-03-2020.pdf.

Independent Commission on Banking. Chair: Sir John Vickers. *Final Report: Recommendations.* September 2011. https://bankingcommission.s3.amazonaws.com/wp-content/uploads/2010/07/ICB
-Final-Report.pdf.

Inglehart, Ronald F., and Pippa Norris. "Trump, Brexit, and the Rise of Populism: Economic Have-Nots and Cultural Backlash." RWP16-026, August 2016. https://www.hks.harvard.edu/publications
/trump-brexit-and-rise-populism-economic-have-nots-and-cultural-backlash.

Institut National d'Études Démographiques. "Migration Worldwide." https://www.ined.fr/en/every
thing_about_population/demographic-facts-sheets/focus-on-migration-worldwide/.

International Civil Aviation Organization. "The World of Air Transport in 2018." https://www.icao
.int/annual-report-2018/Pages/the-world-of-air-transport-in-2018.aspx.

International Energy Agency. *Net Zero by 2050: A Roadmap for the Global Energy Sector.* October 2021.
https://iea.blob.core.windows.net/assets/deebef5d-0c34-4539-9d0c-10b13d840027/NetZeroby
2050-ARoadmapfortheGlobalEnergySector_CORR.pdf.

International Federation of Accountants. Public Sector Committee. *Implementing Accrual Accounting in Government: The New Zealand Experience.* October 1994. https://www.ifac.org/system/files
/publications/files/no-1-implementation-accr.pdf.

International Monetary Fund. *Global Financial Stability Report, April 2020.* https://www.imf.org/en
/Publications/GFSR/Issues/2020/04/14/global-financial-stability-report-april-2020.

International Monetary Fund. "IMF Datamapper: Population." https://www.imf.org/external/datamap
per/LP@WEO/OEMDC/ADVEC/WEOWORLD.

International Monetary Fund. "IMF Members' Quotas and Voting Power, and IMF Board of Governors."
May 23, 2021. https://www.imf.org/external/np/sec/memdir/members.aspx.

International Monetary Fund. "The IMF's Response to COVID-19." June 29, 2020. https://www.imf
.org/en/About/FAQ/imf-response-to-covid-19#Q1.

International Monetary Fund. "Where the IMF Gets Its Money." March 31, 2020. https://www.imf
.org/en/About/Factsheets/Where-the-IMF-Gets-Its-Money.

International Monetary Fund. *World Economic Outlook, April 2020: The Great Lockdown.* Washington,
DC: International Monetary Fund, 2020.

International Monetary Fund. *World Economic Outlook Database.* October 2020. https://www.imf.org
/en/Publications/WEO/weo-database/2020/October.

International Monetary Fund. *World Economic Outlook Databases.* https://www.imf.org/en/Publications
/SPROLLs/world-economic-outlook-databases#sort=%40imfdate%20descending.

International Monetary Fund. *World Economic Outlook, October 2016: Subdued Demand: Symptoms and Remedies.* Chapter 2, "Global Trade: What's behind the Slowdown."

International Monetary Fund. *World Economic Outlook, October 2020: A Long and Difficult Assent.*
Chapter 3, "Mitigating Climate Change." https://www.imf.org/en/Publications/WEO/Issues/2020
/09/30/world-economic-outlook-october-2020#Chapter%203.

Irwin, Douglas. "Multilateral and Bilateral Trade Policies in the World Trading System: An Historical Perspective." In Jaime de Melo and Arvind Panagariya, eds. *New Dimensions in Regional Integration.*
Cambridge: Cambridge University Press, 1993.

Iversen, Torben, and David Soskice. *Democracy and Prosperity: Reinventing Capitalism through a Turbulent Century.* Princeton, NJ, and Oxford: Princeton University Press, 2019.

Jacobs, Jane. *The Economy of Cities.* New York: Vintage Books, 1969.

Jacobs, Jane. *Systems of Survival: A Dialogue on the Moral Foundations of Commerce and Politics.* New York: Random House, 1994.

Jacobs, Michael, and Mariana Mazzucato, eds. *Rethinking Capitalism: Economics and Policy for Sustainable and Inclusive Growth.* Chichester: Wiley-Blackwell, 2016.

Jacques, Martin. *When China Rules the World: The End of the Western World and the Birth of a New Global Order.* London: Penguin, 2009.

Janeway, William H. *Doing Capitalism in the Innovation Economy.* Cambridge: Cambridge University Press, 2012 and 2018.

Jaspers, Karl. *The Origin and Goal of History.* New Haven, CT, and London: Yale University Press,
1953. http://www.collegiumphaenomenologicum.org/wp-content/uploads/2010/06/Jaspers-The-Or
igin-and-Goal-of-History.pdf.

Jeffries, Stuart. "Britain's Most Racist Election: The Story of Smethwick, 50 Years On." *Guardian,*
October 15, 2014. https://www.theguardian.com/world/2014/oct/15/britains-most-racist-election
-smethwick-50-years-on.

Jensen, Michael C. "Value Maximization, Stakeholder Theory, and the Corporate Objective Function." *European Financial Management* 7, no. 3 (2001): 297–317. https://efmaefm.org/bharat/jensen_efm2001.pdf.

Johnston, Matthew. "Carried Interest: A Loophole in America's Tax Code." Investopedia, March 31, 2021. https://www.investopedia.com/articles/investing/102515/carried-interest-loophole-americas-tax-code.asp.

Judis, John B. *The Populist Explosion: How the Great Recession Transformed American and European Politics.* New York: Columbia Global Reports, 2016.

Kagan, Robert. *The Jungle Grows Back.* New York: Alfred A. Knopf, 2018.

Kagan, Robert. "The World America Made—and Trump Wants to Unmake." Brookings, September 28, 2018. https://www.brookings.edu/opinions/the-world-america-made-and-trump-wants-to-unmake/.

Kaiser Family Foundation. "State Health Facts: Medicare Spending per Enrollee 2018." https://www.kff.org/medicare/state-indicator/per-enrollee-spending-by-residence.

Kaufmann, Eric. *Whiteshift: Populism, Immigration, and the Future of White Majorities.* London and New York: Allen Lane, 2018.

Kay, John. "The Basics of Basic Income." https://www.johnkay.com/2017/04/05/basics-basic-income/.

Kay, John. *Culture and Prosperity: The Truth about Markets: Why Some Nations Are Rich and Most Remain Poor.* New York: Harper Business, 2004.

Kay, John. "*Mission Economy* by Mariana Mazzucato—Could Moonshot Thinking Help Fix the Planet?" *Financial Times*, January 13, 2021. https://www.ft.com/content/86475b94-3636-49ec-9b3f-7d7756350b30.

Kay, John. *Other People's Money: The Real Business of Finance.* London: Profile Books, 2016.

Kay, John, and Mervyn King. *Radical Uncertainty: Decision-Making for an Unknowable Future.* London: Bridge Street Press, 2020.

Keefe, Patrick Radden. *Empire of Pain: The Secret History of the Sackler Dynasty.* New York: Doubleday, 2021.

Keefe, Patrick Radden. "How Did the Sacklers Pull This Off?" *New York Times*, July 14, 2021. https://www.nytimes.com/2021/07/14/opinion/sackler-family-opioids-settlement.html.

Kelton, Stephanie. *The Deficit Myth: Modern Monetary Theory and How to Build a Better Economy.* London: John Murray, 2020.

Kessler, Glenn, Salvador Rizzo, and Meg Kelly. "President Trump Has Made 15,413 False or Misleading Claims over 1,055 Days." *Washington Post*, December 16, 2019. https://www.washingtonpost.com/politics/2019/12/16/president-trump-has-made-false-or-misleading-claims-over-days/.

Kessler, Sarah. *Gigged: The Gig Economy, the End of the Job and the Future of Work.* New York: Random House Business, 2019.

Khan, Lina M. "Amazon's Antitrust Paradox." *Yale Law Journal* 126, no. 3 (January 2017). https://www.yalelawjournal.org/note/amazons-antitrust-paradox.

Kierzkowski, Henryk, ed. *From Europeanization of the Globe to the Globalization of Europe.* London: Palgrave, 2002.

King, Stephen D. *Grave New World: The End of Globalization and the Return of History.* London and New Haven: Yale University Press, 2017.

Kirshner, Jonathan. "Gone but Not Forgotten: Trump's Long Shadow and the End of American Credibility." *Foreign Affairs*, March/April 2021. https://www.foreignaffairs.com/articles/united-states/2021-01-29/trump-gone-not-forgotten.

Klasing, Mariko J., and Petros Milionis. "Quantifying the Evolution of World Trade, 1870–1949." March 29, 2014. https://papers.ssrn.com/sol3/papers.cfm?abstract_id=2087678.

Klein, Matthew, and Michael Pettis. *Trade Wars Are Class Wars.* New Haven, CT: Yale University Press, 2020.

Kochhar, Rakesh. "Hispanic Women, Immigrants, Young Adults, Those with Less Education Hit Hardest by COVID-19 Job Losses." Pew Research Center, June 9, 2020. https://www.pewresearch.org/.

Krastev, Ivan, and Stephen Holmes. *The Light That Failed: A Reckoning.* New York and London: Penguin, 2019.

Krueger, Alan. "The Rise and Consequences of Inequality in the United States of America." Center for American Progress, January 12, 2012. https://cdn.americanprogress.org/wp-content/uploads/events/2012/01/pdf/krueger.pdf.

Krueger, Anne O. *International Trade: What Everyone Needs to Know.* New York: Oxford University Press, 2020.

Kuttner, Robert. *Can Democracy Survive Global Capitalism?* New York: W. W. Norton, 2018.

Lack, Simon. *The Hedge Fund Mirage: The Illusion of Big Money and Why It's Too Good to Be True.* Hoboken, NJ: John Wiley & Sons, 2012.

Lakner, Christoph, and Branko Milanovic. "Global Income Distribution from the Fall of the Berlin Wall to the Great Recession." World Bank Policy Research Working Paper 6719. December 2013. http://documents.worldbank.org/curated/en/914431468162277879/pdf/WPS6719.pdf.

Lal, Deepak. *Unintended Consequences: The Impact of Endowments, Culture, and Politics on Long-Run Economic Performance.* Cambridge, MA, and London: MIT Press, 2001.

Lane, Philip R., and Gian M. Milesi-Ferretti. "The External Wealth of Nations Mark II: Revised and Extended Estimates of Foreign Assets and Liabilities, 1970–2004." *Journal of International Economics* 73, no. 2 (2007).

Lardy, Nicholas. *The State Strikes Back: The End of Economic Reform in China?* Washington, DC: Peterson Institute for International Economics, 2019.

Layard, Richard. *Can We Be Happier? Evidence and Ethics.* London: Pelican Books, 2020.

Lazonick, William. "Profits without Prosperity." *Harvard Business Review*, September 2014. https://hbr.org/2014/09/profits-without-prosperity.

Lazonick, William, Mustafa Erdem Sakinç, and Matt Hopkins. "Why Stock Buybacks Are Dangerous for the Economy." *Harvard Business Review*, January 2020. https://hbr.org/2020/01/why-stock-buybacks-are-dangerous-for-the-economy.

Leakey, Richard, and Roger Lewin. *The Sixth Extinction: Biodiversity and Its Survival.* London: Weidenfeld and Nicolson, 1996.

Leibfritz, Willi, John Thornton, and Alexandra Bibbee. "Taxation and Economic Performance." OECD, Economics Department Working Papers no. 176. OCDE/GD(97)107. OECD. Paris, 1997. https://econpapers.repec.org/paper/oececoaaa/176-en.htm.

Leonhardt, David, and Prasad Philbrick. "Donald Trump's Racism: The Definitive List, Updated." *New York Times*, January 15, 2018. https://www.nytimes.com/interactive/2018/01/15/opinion/leonhardt-trump-racist.html.

LePan, Nicholas. "History of Pandemics." March 14, 2020. https://www.visualcapitalist.com/history-of-pandemics-deadliest/.

Lerner, Abba. "Money as a Creature of the State." *Papers and Proceedings of the Fifty-ninth Annual Meeting of the American Economic Association. American Economic Review* 37, no. 2 (May 1947): 312–17.

Levell, Peter, Barra Roantree, and Jonathan Shaw. "Redistribution from a Lifetime Perspective." Institute for Fiscal Studies, September 22, 2015. https://www.ifs.org.uk/publications/7986.

Levitsky, Steven, and Daniel Ziblatt. *How Democracies Die: What History Reveals about Our Future.* New York: Crown, 2018.

Levitsky, Steven, and Daniel Ziblatt, "Why Republicans Play Dirty." *New York Times*, September 20, 2019. https://www.nytimes.com/2019/09/20/opinion/republicans-democracy-play-dirty.html?action=click&module=Opinion&pgtype=Homepage.

Lewis, Michael. *Flash Boys: Cracking the Money Code.* London: Penguin, 2014.

Lightfoot, Liz. "The Student Experience—Then and Now." *Guardian*, June 24, 2016. https://www.theguardian.com/education/2016/jun/24/has-university-life-changed-student-experience-past-present-parents-vox-pops#:~:text=In%20the%20early%201960s%2C%20only,back%20over%20their%20working%20lives.

Lindert, Peter H., and Jeffrey G. Williamson. "American Incomes 1774–1860." National Bureau of Economic Research Working Paper No. 18396. September 15, 2012. https://www.nber.org/papers/w18396.

Lindert, Peter H., and Jeffrey G. Williamson. "Globalization and Inequality: A Long History," Paper prepared for the World Bank Annual Conference on Development Economics—Europe, Barcelona, June 25–27, 2001.

Lindsay, James M. "The 2020 Election by the Numbers." Council on Foreign Relations, December 15, 2020. https://www.cfr.org/blog/2020-election-numbers.

Liptak, Adam. "Supreme Court Invalidates Key Part of Voting Rights Act." *New York Times*, June 25, 2013. https://www.nytimes.com/2013/06/26/us/supreme-court-ruling.html.

List, Friedrich. *Das nationale System der politischen Oekonomie.* 1841.

Little, I. M. D., Tibor Scitovsky, and Maurice Scott. *Industry and Trade in Some Developing Countries.* Paris: Development Center of the Organization for Economic Co-operation and Development, 1970.

Liu, Nicolle, Yuan Yang, Demetri Sevastopulo, Jamie Smyth, and Michael Peel. "China Draws Condemnation for New Hong Kong Security Law." *Financial Times*, July 1, 2020. https://www.ft.com/content/052989fc-2748-4f8e-a2b0-539c32e1ad72.

Lonergan, Eric. "Reply to Larry Summers." August 26, 2019. https://www.philosophyofmoney.net/a-reply-to-larry-summers/.

Lonergan, Eric, and Mark Blyth. *Angrynomics*. New York: Columbia University Press, 2020.

Loween, James W. "5 Myths about Why the South Seceded." *Washington Post*, January 11, 2011. https://www.washingtonpost.com/wp-dyn/content/article/2011/01/07/AR20110706547.html.

Lubin, David. "IMF Needs New Thinking to Deal with Coronavirus." Chatham House, April 27, 2020. https://www.chathamhouse.org/expert/comment/imf-needs-new-thinking-deal-coronavirus.

Luce, Edward. "A Sea of Troubles Surrounds the Question of Whether to Prosecute Trump." *Financial Times*, July 29, 2022. https://www.ft.com/content/8263e5c9-d886-4c81-807b-f9eb0d92508f.

Lührmann, Anna, and Staffan I. Lindberg. "A Third Wave of Autocratization Is Here: What Is New about It?" *Democratization* 26, no. 7 (2019): 1095–1113. https://www.tandfonline.com/doi/full/10.1080/13510347.2019.1582029.

Lund, Susan, et al. *The New Dynamics of Financial Globalization*. McKinsey Global Institute, August 2017. https://www.mckinsey.com/industries/financial-services/our-insights/the-new-dynamics-of-financial-globalization.

Luohan Academy. "Understanding Big Data: Data Calculus in the Digital Era 2021." February 5, 2021. https://www.luohanacademy.com/research/reports/2bcc5a5e3074df15.

Luyendijk, Joris. *Swimming with Sharks: My Journey into the World of the Bankers*. London: Guardian Faber Publishing, 2015.

Maddison, Angus. Database. http://www.ggdc.net/maddison/oriindex.htm.

"Maddison Project." http://www.ggdc.net/maddison/maddison-project/home.htm.

Mahbubani, Kishore. "Biden and China: Friends or Foes." *Alumnus*, issue 124, January–March 2021. National University of Singapore. https://www.nus.edu.sg/alumnet/thealumnus/issue-124/perspectives/panorama/biden-and-china-friends-or-foes.

Mahbubani, Kishore. *Has the West Lost It? A Provocation*. London: Allen Lane, 2018.

Mahler, Daniel Gerszon, Christoph Lakner, R. Andres Castaneda Aguilar, and Haoyu Wu. "Updated Estimates of the Impact of COVID-19 on Global Poverty." June 8, 2020. https://blogs.worldbank.org/opendata/updated-estimates-impact-covid-19-global-poverty.

Mallet, Victor, and David Keohane. "Year of 'Gilets Jaunes' Leaves Angry Mark on France." *Financial Times*, November 14, 2019. https://www.ft.com/content/9627c8be-0623-11ea-9afa-d9e2401fa7ca.

Malthus, Thomas. *An Essay on the Principle of Population*. 1798. http://www.esp.org/books/malthus/population/malthus.pdf.

Mann, Thomas E., and Norman J. Ornstein. *It's Even Worse Than It Looks: How the American Constitutional System Collided with the New Politics of Extremism*. New York: Basic Books, 2012.

Mann, Thomas E., and Norman J. Ornstein. "Let's Just Say It: The Republicans Are the Problem." *Washington Post*, April 27, 2012. https://www.washingtonpost.com/opinions/lets-just-say-it-the-republicans-are-the-problem/2012/04/27/gIQAxCVUlT_story.html.

Mark, Joshua J. "Silk Road." Ancient History Encyclopedia. http://www.ancient.eu/Silk_Road/.

Martin, Katie. "Fearful Consumers Power an Uneven Rally." *Financial Times*, August 25, 2020. https://www.ft.com/content/9678c481-52e0-45e0-8610-a49b33aeec45.

"Martin Wolf Accepts the Gerald Loeb Lifetime Achievement Award." *Financial Times*, July 3, 2019, https://www.ft.com/content/5e828d50-9d86-11e9-b8ce-8b459ed04726.

Massing, Michael. "Does Democracy Avert Famine?" *New York Times*, March 1, 2003. https://www.nytimes.com/2003/03/01/arts/does-democracy-avert-famine.html.

Mayell, Hillary. "Human 'Footprint' Seen on 83 Percent of Earth's Land." *National Geographic News*, October 25, 2002. http://news.nationalgeographic.com/news/2002/10/1025_021025_HumanFootprint.html.

Mayer, Colin. *Firm Commitment: Why the Corporation Is Failing Us and How to Restore Trust in It*. Oxford: Oxford University Press, 2013.

Mayer, Colin. *Prosperity: Better Business Makes the Greater Good*. Oxford: Oxford University Press, 2018.

Mayer, Jane. *Dark Money: The Hidden History of the Billionaires behind the Rise of the Radical Right*. New York: Anchor Books, 2017 and 2018.

Mazzucato, Mariana. *The Entrepreneurial State: Debunking Public vs Private Myths*. London: Penguin, 2018.

Mazzucato, Mariana. *Mission Economy: A Moonshot Guide to Changing Capitalism*. London: Allen Lane, 2021.

McAfee, Andrew, and Erik Brynjolfsson. *Machine, Platform, Crowd: Harnessing the Digital Revolution*. New York: W. W. Norton, 2017.

McCloskey, Dierdre. *Bourgeois Equality: How Ideas, Not Capital or Institutions, Enriched the World.* Chicago: University of Chicago Press, 2016.

McCloskey, Dierdre. "Life's Primary Colors: How Humanity Forgot the Seven Principal Virtues." July 2, 2019. https://www.abc.net.au/religion/primary-colors-how-humanity-forgot-the-seven-principal-virtues/11272726.

McKinnon, Ronald. *Money and Capital in Economic Development.* Washington, DC: Brookings Institution, 1973.

McLeay, Michael, Amar Radia, and Ryland Thomas. "Money Creation in the Modern Economy." *Bank of England Quarterly Bulletin,* 2014, First Quarter, 14–27. https://www.bankofengland.co.uk/-/media/boe/files/quarterly-bulletin/2014/money-creation-in-the-modern-economy.

McLuhan, Marshall. *Understanding Media: The Extensions of Man.* Cambridge, MA: MIT Press, 1964 and 1994.

McTernan, John. "The Left Must Decide Which Green New Deal They Want." *Financial Times,* February 15, 2020. https://www.ft.com/content/63c78642-4e8b-11ea-95a0-43d18ec715f5.

Medical Research Council (MRC). https://www.ukri.org/councils/mrc/.

Menon, Anand, ed. *Brexit and Public Opinion 2019: The UK in a Changing Europe.* https://ukandeu.ac.uk/wp-content/uploads/2019/01/Public-Opinion-2019-report.pdf.

Meyer, Brett. "Pandemic Populism: An Analysis of Populist Leaders' Responses to COVID-19." Tony Blair Institute for Global Change, August 17, 2020. https://institute.global/policy/pandemic-populism-analysis-populist-leaders-responses-covid-19.

Mian, Atif, Ludwig Straub, and Amir Sufi. "Indebted Demand." March 26, 2020. https://scholar.harvard.edu/files/straub/files/mss_indebteddemand.pdf.

Mian, Atif, Ludwig Straub, and Amir Sufi. "The Saving Glut of the Rich and the Rise in Household Debt." March 2020. https://scholar.harvard.edu/files/straub/files/mss_richsavingglut.pdf.

Michels, Robert. *Political Parties: A Sociological Study of the Oligarchical Tendencies of Modern Democracy.* Translated by Eden Paul and Cedar Paul. New York: Free Press, 1915.

Micklethwait, John, and Adrian Wooldridge. *The Company: A Short History of a Revolutionary Idea.* London: Phoenix, 2003.

Mikkelson, David. "Rush Limbaugh 'Racist Quotes' List." https://www.snopes.com/fact-check/bone-voyage/.

Milanovic, Branko. *Capitalism Alone: The Future of the System That Rules the World.* Cambridge, MA, and London: Belknap Press of Harvard University Press, 2019.

Milanovic, Branko. *Global Inequality: A New Approach for the Age of Globalization.* Cambridge, MA: Harvard University Press, 2016.

Milanovic, Branko, Peter H. Lindert, and Jeffrey G. Williamson. "Measuring Ancient Inequality." National Bureau of Economic Research. Working Paper 13550. October 2007. http://www.nber.org/papers/w13550.pdf.

Mill, John Stuart. *Considerations on Representative Government.* 1861. Project Gutenberg. https://www.gutenberg.org/files/5669/5669-h/5669-h.htm.

Mill, John Stuart. *Principles of Political Economy.* 9th ed. London: Longmans, Green and Co., 1885.

Millennium Challenge Corporation. "Our Impact." https://www.mcc.gov/our-impact.

Minsky, Hyman. *Stabilizing an Unstable Economy.* New York: McGraw Hill, 2008.

Miroudot, Sébastien. "Resilience Versus Robustness in Global Value Chains: Some Policy Implications." *VoxEU.* June 18, 2020. https://voxeu.org/article/resilience-versus-robustness-global-value-chains#:~:text=Resilience%20can%20be%20defined%20as,2014).

Mishel, Lawrence, and Josh Bivens. "The Pay of Corporate Executives and Financial Professionals as Evidence of Rents in Top 1 Percent Incomes." Working Paper No. 296. June 20, 2013. Economic Policy Institute. https://www.epi.org/publication/pay-corporate-executives-financial-professionals/.

Mitchell, Tom. "Business Worries Intensify over China's Tightening Grip on Hong Kong." *Financial Times,* March 16, 2021. https://www.ft.com/content/098017c2-1c83-4da3-ac2a-53e7ed7fac81.

Moggridge, D. E. *Maynard Keynes: An Economist's Biography.* London and New York: Routledge, 1992.

Mokyr, Joel. *The Enlightened Economy: An Economic History of Britain 1700–1850.* New Haven, CT, and London: Yale University Press, 2009.

Money Advice Service. "Repaying Your Undergraduate Student Loan." https://www.moneyadviceservice.org.uk/en/articles/repaying-student-loans.

Montanaro, Domenico. "6 Strongmen Trump Has Praised—and the Conflicts It Presents." May 2, 2017. http://www.npr.org/2017/05/02/526520042/6-strongmen-trumps-praised-and-the-conflicts-it-presents.

Morris, Ian. "Social Development." Stanford University, October 2010. http://ianmorris.org/docs/so cial-development.pdf.

Mosler, Warren. *Soft Currency Economics II: What Everyone Thinks They Know about Monetary Policy Is Wrong.* US Virgin Islands: Valance, 1996 and 2013.

Mounk, Yascha. *The Great Experiment: How to Make Diverse Democracies Work.* London: Bloomsbury, 2022.

Mounk, Yascha. "Illiberal Democracy or Undemocratic Liberalism?" *Project Syndicate,* June 9, 2016. https://www.project-syndicate.org/commentary/trump-european-populism-technocracy -by-yascha-mounk-1-2016-06.

Mounk, Yascha. *The People Vs. Democracy: Why Our Freedom Is in Danger and How to Save It.* Cambridge, MA: Harvard University Press, 2018.

Müller, Jan-Werner. *What Is Populism?* Philadelphia: University of Pennsylvania Press, 2016.

Murphy, Hannah, and Patrick McGee. "Apple Makes Unexpected Concession on 30% App Store Fees." *Financial Times,* September 25, 2020. https://www.ft.com/content/fbabedb0-3ed2-4c47-94f2 -f165bd15edb3.

National Institutes of Health. https://www.nih.gov/.

National Park Service. "The Civil War." https://www.nps.gov/civilwar/facts.htm.

National Public Radio. "The Original 'Welfare Queen.'" *Code Switch,* June 5, 2019. https://www.npr .org/transcripts/729294210?t=1654518358287.

Nelson, Brett. "Fear, Not Government Shutdowns, Chilled the Economy." August 4, 2020. https:// review.chicagobooth.edu/economics/2020/article/fear-not-government-shutdowns-chilled -economy.

Nemy, Enid. "Leona Helmsley, Hotel Queen, Dies at 87." *New York Times,* August 20, 2007. https:// www.nytimes.com/2007/08/20/nyregion/20cnd-helmsley.html.

New Development Bank. https://www.ndb.int/.

New World Encyclopedia. https://www.newworldencyclopedia.org/.

Nichols, Tim. *The Death of Expertise: The Campaign against Established Knowledge and Why It Matters.* New York: Oxford University Press, 2017.

Noble, David F. *The Religion of Technology: The Divinity of Man and the Spirit of Invention.* New York: Alfred A. Knopf, 1997.

Nolan, Peter. *Is China Buying the World?* Cambridge and Malden: Polity, 2012.

Noonan, Laura, Cale Tilford, Richard Milne, Ian Mount, and Peter Wise. "Who Went to Jail for Their Role in the Financial Crisis?" *Financial Times,* September 20, 2018. https://ig.ft.com/jailed -bankers/#:~:text=Forty%2Dseven%20bankers%20were%20sentenced,the%20financial%20sector's %20catastrophic%20failures.

Norris, Pippa. "It's Not Just Trump. Authoritarian Populism Is Rising across the West. Here's Why." *Washington Post,* March 11, 2016. https://www.washingtonpost.com/news/monkey-cage/wp/2016 /03/11/its-not-just-trump-authoritarian-populism-is-rising-across-the-west-heres-why/.

Nove, Alec. *An Economic History of the USSR, 1917–1991.* London: Penguin Economics, 1993.

Obstfeld, Maurice. "The Global Capital Market Reconsidered." In Paul Collier, Diane Coyle, Colin Mayer, and Martin Wolf, eds. "Capitalism: What Has Gone Wrong, What Needs to Change, and How It Can Be Fixed." *Oxford Review of Economic Policy* 37, no. 4 (Winter 2021): 690–706.

Obstfeld, Maurice, and Alan M. Taylor. "Globalization and Capital Markets." In Michael D. Bordo, Alan M. Taylor, and Jeffrey G. Williamson, eds. *Globalization in Historical Perspective.* Chicago: University of Chicago Press, 2003. http://www.nber.org/chapters/c9587.

Office for Budget Responsibility. *Fiscal Sustainability Report.* July 2020. https://cdn.obr.uk/OBR_FSR _July_2020.pdf.

Office of Health Economics. "Infant and Child Health." December 1975. https://www.ohe.org/publica tions/infant-and-child-health.

Office for National Statistics. "Deaths Involving COVID-19, England and Wales: Deaths Occurring in June 2020." July 17, 2020. https://www.ons.gov.uk.

Office of the United States Trade Representative. Executive Office of the President. Findings of the Investigation into China's Acts, Policies, and Practices Related to Technology Transfer, Intellectual Property, and Innovation under Sector 301 of the Trade Act of 1974. March 22, 2018. https://ustr .gov/sites/default/files/Section%20301%20FINAL.PDF.

Olson, Mancur. *The Logic of Collective Action: Public Goods and the Theory of Groups.* Cambridge, MA: Harvard University Press, 1965 and 1971.

Olson, Mancur. *Power and Prosperity: Outgrowing Communist and Capitalist Dictatorships.* New York: Basic Books, 2000.

Oremus, Will. "Are You Really the Product? The History of a Dangerous Idea." *Slate*, April 27, 2018. https://slate.com/technology/2018/04/are-you-really-facebooks-product-the-history-of -a-dangerous-idea.html.

O'Rourke, Kevin H. "Europe and the Causes of Globalization, 1790 to 2000." In Henryk Kierzkowski, ed. *From Europeanization of the Globe to the Globalization of Europe*. London: Palgrave, 2002. http:// www.tcd.ie/Economics/TEP/2002_papers/TEPNo1KO22.pdf.

Orwell, George. "Notes on Nationalism." *Polemic*, October 1945. Penguin Modern, 2018.

Opportunity Insights. Economic Tracker. "Percent Change in Employment." https://tracktherecovery .org/.

Organization for Economic Co-operation and Development. "BEPS: Inclusive Framework on Base Erosion and Profit Shifting." https://www.oecd.org/tax/beps/.

Organization for Economic Co-operation and Development. "COVID-19 and Global Capital Flows." *OECD Policy Responses to Coronavirus (COVID-19)*. July 3, 2020. http://www.oecd.org/coronavirus/policy-responses/covid-19-and-global-capital-flows-2dc69002/.

Organization for Economic Co-operation and Development. "COVID-19 and International Trade: Issues and Actions." *OECD Policy Responses to Coronavirus (COVID-19)*. June 12, 2020. http://www.oecd.org/coronavirus/policy-responses/covid-19-and-international-trade-issues-and-actions -494da2fa/.

Organization for Economic Co-operation and Development. "Inequality." https://www.oecd.org/social /inequality.htm.

Organization for Economic Co-operation and Development. "New Approaches to Economic Challenges." https://www.oecd.org/naec/.

Organization for Economic Co-operation and Development. *OECD Regional Outlook 2016: Productive Regions for Inclusive Societies*. Paris: OECD, 2016.

Organization for Economic Co-operation and Development. *An Overview of Growing Income Inequalities in OECD Countries: Main Findings*. Paris: OECD, 2011.

Organization for Economic Co-operation and Development. "Social Spending." https://data.oecd.org /socialexp/social-spending.htm.

Organization for Economic Co-operation and Development. "Tackling Coronavirus (COVID-19): Contributing to a Global Effort." 2020. https://www.oecd.org/coronavirus/country-policy-tracker/.

Ostry, Jonathan D., Andrew Berg, and Charalambos G. Tsangarides. "Redistribution, Inequality and Growth." IMF Staff Discussion Note SDN/14/02, February 2014. https://www.imf.org/external /pubs/ft/sdn/2014/sdn1402.pdf.

O'Sullivan, John. "Democracies End When They Become Too Democratic." *New York*, May 1, 2016. http://nymag.com/daily/intelligencer/2016/04/america-tyranny-donald-trump.html.

Our Documents: The Second New Deal. "Franklin Delano Roosevelt's Address Announcing the Second New Deal." October 31, 1936. http://docs.fdrlibrary.marist.edu/od2ndst.html.

Our World in Data. "Life Expectancy." https://ourworldindata.org/life-expectancy.

Our World in Data. "Self-Reported Life Satisfaction vs GDP per Capita, 2020." https://ourworldindata .org/grapher/gdp-vs-happiness.

Oxford Essential Quotations 2022. https://www.oxfordreference.com/view/10.1093/acref/978019184 3730.001.0001/q-oro-ed5-00006834.

Oxford Reference. https://www.oxfordreference.com.

Palese, Michela. "The Irish Abortion Referendum: How a Citizens' Assembly Helped to Break Years of Political Deadlock." Electoral Reform Society, May 29, 2018. https://www.electoral-reform.org .uk/the-irish-abortion-referendum-how-a-citizens-assembly-helped-to-break-years-of-political -deadlock/.

Peel, Michael, Anna Gross, and Clive Cookson. "WHO Struggles to Prove Itself in the Face of COVID-19." *Financial Times*, July 12, 2012. https://www.ft.com/content/c2809c99-594f-4649 -968a-0560966c11e0.

Peel, Michael, Sam Fleming, and Guy Chazan. "EU Clamps Down on Covid Vaccine Exports." *Financial Times*, January 29, 2021. https://www.ft.com/content/24867d39-4507-4c48-be27-c34b581220b0.

Pei, Minxin. *China's Crony Capitalism: The Dynamics of Regime Decay*. Cambridge, MA: Harvard University Press, 2016.

Pellegrini, Bruno, and Luigi Zingales. "Diagnosing the Italian Disease." September 2014. http://faculty .chicagobooth.edu/luigi.zingales/papers/research/Diagnosing.pdf.

Penn World Tables 8.1. https://rdrr.io/cran/pwt8/man/pwt8.1.html.

Pension Protection Fund. *The Purple Book 2020: DB Pensions Universe Risk Profile*. https://www.ppf .co.uk/sites/default/files/2020-12/PPF_Purple_Book_20.pdf.

Personal Finance Data. "Net Worth Percentile Comparison Calculator by Age." https://personalfinance
    data.com/networth-percentile-calculator/.
Peterson-KFF. "Health System Tracker." https://www.healthsystemtracker.org/.
Pettinger, Tejvan. "Definition of Public Goods." *Economics Help*, July 28, 2019. https://www.econom
    icshelp.org/micro-economic-essays/marketfailure/public-goods/.
Pettinger, Tejvan. "Phillips Curve." *Economics Help*, March 1, 2019. https://www.economicshelp.org
    /blog/1364/economics/phillips-curve-explained/
Philippon, Thomas. *The Great Reversal: How America Gave Up on Free Markets*. Cambridge, MA:
    Belknap Press of Harvard University Press, 2019.
Philippon, Thomas, and Ariell Reshef. "Wages and Human Capital in the U.S. Financial Industry
    1909–2006." National Bureau of Economic Research Working Paper 14644. January 2009. https://
    www.nber.org/papers/w14644.
Piketty, Thomas. "Brahmin Left vs Merchant Right: Rising Inequality & the Changing Structure of
    Political Conflict (Evidence from France, Britain and the US, 1948–2017)." WID.world Working
    Paper Series No. 2018/7. March 2018. http://piketty.pse.ens.fr/files/Piketty2018.pdf.
Piketty, Thomas. *Capital and Ideology*. Cambridge, MA, and London: Belknap Press of Harvard Uni-
    versity Press, 2020.
Piketty, Thomas. *Capital in the Twenty-First Century*. Translated by Arthur Goldhammer. Cambridge,
    MA: Harvard University Press, 2013.
Plato. *The Republic*. Translated by Benjamin Jowett. http://classics.mit.edu/Plato/republic.html.
Polanyi, Karl. *The Great Transformation: The Political and Economic Origins of Our Time*. Boston: Beacon
    Press, 1957. First published 1944.
Politi, James. "Migration Opens the Door to Italy's Populists." *Financial Times*, August 1, 2017. https://
    www.ft.com/content/b964453a-72b1-11e7-aca6-c6bd07df1a3c.
Politi, James, Aime Williams, and Chris Giles. "US Offers New Plan in Global Corporate Tax Talks."
    Financial Times, April 8, 2021. https://www.ft.com/content/847c5f77-f0af-4787-8c8e-070ac6a7c74f.
Politi, James, Colby Smith, and Brendan Greeley. "Donald Trump Raises Tariffs on Chinese Goods
    after Stocks Tumble." *Financial Times*, August 24, 2019. https://www.ft.com/content/2db9c1ec
    -c5b9-11e9-a8e9-296ca66511c9.
Pomeranz, Kenneth. *The Great Divergence: China, Europe, and the Making of the Modern World Economy*.
    Princeton, NJ: Princeton University Press, 2000.
Popper, Karl. *The Open Society and Its Enemies*. Vol. 1, *The Age of Plato*. London: Routledge, 1945.
Portes, Jonathan. "The Economics of Migration." June 2019. https://journals.sagepub.com/doi/pdf/10
    .1177/1536504219854712.
Posen, Adam. "The Price of Nostalgia: America's Self-Defeating Economic Retreat." *Foreign Affairs*,
    May/June 2021. https://www.foreignaffairs.com/articles/united-states/2021-04-20/america-price
    -nostalgia.
Powell, Jerome H. "New Economic Challenges and the Fed's Monetary Policy Review." Federal Reserve,
    August 27, 2020. https://www.federalreserve.gov/newsevents/speech/powell20200827a.htm.
Prestowitz, Clyde. *The World Turned Upside Down: America, China, and the Struggle for Global Leader-
    ship*. New Haven, CT: Yale University Press, 2021.
Przeworski, Adam. "Conquered or Granted? A History of Suffrage Extensions." *British Journal of Po-
    litical Science* 39, no. 2 (April 2009): 291–321.
Putnam, Robert D. *Bowling Alone: The Collapse and Revival of American Community*. New York and
    London: Simon & Schuster, 2000.
Rachel, Lukasz, and Lawrence H. Summers. "On Falling Neutral Real Rates, Fiscal Policy, and the Risk
    of Secular Stagnation." BPEA Conference Drafts. *Brookings Papers on Economic Activity*, March 7
    and 8, 2019. https://www.brookings.edu/wp-content/uploads/2019/03/On-Falling-Neutral-Real
    -Rates-Fiscal-Policy-and-the-Risk-of-Secular-Stagnation.pdf.
Rachman, Gideon. "Atlantic Era under Threat with Donald Trump in White House." *Financial Times*,
    January 19, 2017. https://www.ft.com/content/73cc16e8-de36-11e6-86ac-f253db7791c6.
Rachman, Gideon. "The US and China's Dangerous Blame Game Will Do No Good." *Financial Times*,
    May 4, 2020. https://www.ft.com/content/ffc6ac00-8de0-11ea-9e12-0d4655dbd44f.
Rajan, Raghuram G. "A Fair and Simple Way to Tax Carbon Emissions." *Financial Times*, December
    17, 2019. https://www.ft.com/content/96782e84-2028-11ea-b8a1-584213ee7b2b.
Rajan, Raghuram G. *Fault Lines: How Hidden Fractures Still Threaten the World Economy*. Princeton,
    NJ, and Oxford: Princeton University Press, 2011.
Rajan, Raghuram G. *Third Pillar: The Revival of Community in a Polarized World*. London: William
    Collins, 2019.

Ratcliffe, Susan, ed. *Oxford Essential Quotations*. Oxford: Oxford University Press, 2016.

Reilly, Katie. "Read Hillary Clinton's 'Basket of Deplorables' Remarks about Donald Trump Supporters." *Time*, September 10, 2016. https://time.com/4486502/hillary-clinton-basket-of-deplorables -transcript/.

Rhea, Gordon. "Why Non-Slaveholding Southerners Fought." American Battlefield Trust, January 25, 2011. https://www.battlefields.org/learn/articles/why-non-slaveholding-southerners-fought.

Richardson, Heather Cox. *How the South Won the Civil War: Oligarchy, Democracy, and the Continuing Fight for the Soul of America*. New York: Oxford University Press, 2020.

Riley, Jon, and Robert Chote. "Crisis and Consolidation in the Public Finances." Office for Budget Responsibility Working Paper No. 7. September 2014. https://obr.uk/docs/dlm_uploads/Working Paper7a.pdf.

Riordan, Primrose, and Sue-Lin Wong. "WHO Expert Says China Too Slow to Report Coronavirus Cases." *Financial Times*, February 5, 2020. https://www.ft.com/content/8ede7e92-4749-11ea-aeb3 -955839e06441.

Robb, Greg. "Nobel Prize Winner Likens Trump 'Bullying' of Companies to Fascist Italy, Germany." *Market Watch*, January 6, 2017. http://www.marketwatch.com/story/nobel-prize-winner-likens -trump-bullying-of-companies-to-fascist-italy-germany-2017-01-06?mg=prod/accounts-mw.

Rodan, Garry. "Consultative Authoritarianism and Regime Change Analysis: Implications of the Singapore Case." In Richard Robison, ed. *Routledge Handbook of Southeast Asian Politics*. London and New York: Routledge, 2012, 120–34.

Rodriguez-Pose, Andrés. "The Revenge of the Places That Don't Matter (and What to Do about It)." *Cambridge Journal of Regions, Economy and Society* 11, no. 1 (March 2018): 189–209. https:// eprints.lse.ac.uk/85888/1/Rodriguez-Pose_Revenge%20of%20Places.pdf.

Rodrik, Dani. *The Globalization Paradox: Democracy and the Future of the World Economy*. New York and London: W. W. Norton, 2011.

Rodrik, Dani. "The Inescapable Trilemma of the World Economy." Dani Rodrik's blog, June 27, 2007. https://rodrik.typepad.com/dani_rodriks_weblog/2007/06/the-inescapable.html.

Rodrik, Dani. *Straight Talk on Trade: Ideas for a Sane World Economy*. Princeton, NJ: Princeton University Press, 2017.

Rodrik, Dani, and Stefanie Stantcheva. "Fixing Capitalism's Good Jobs Problem." In Paul Collier, Diane Coyle, Colin Mayer, and Martin Wolf, eds. "Capitalism: What Has Gone Wrong, What Needs to Change, and How It Can Be Fixed." *Oxford Review of Economic Policy* 37, no. 4 (Winter 2021): 824–37.

Ronald Reagan Presidential Foundation & Institute. "Reagan Quotes and Speeches." https://www .reaganfoundation.org/ronald-reagan/reagan-quotes-speeches/news-conference-1/.

Roosevelt, Franklin Delano. "The Four Freedoms." January 6, 1941. https://www.americanrhetoric .com/speeches/fdrthefourfreedoms.htm.

Rudowitz, Robin, Rachel Garfield, and Elizabeth Hinton. "10 Things to Know about Medicaid: Setting the Facts Straight." Kaiser Family Foundation, March 6, 2019. https://www.kff.org/medicaid /issue-brief/10-things-to-know-about-medicaid-setting-the-facts-straight/.

Saez, Emmanuel. "Striking It Richer: The Evolution of Top Incomes in the United States (Updated with 2015 Preliminary Estimates)." June 30, 2016. https://eml.berkeley.edu/~saez/saez-UStopin comes-2015.pdf.

Saez, Emmanuel, and Gabriel Zucman. *The Triumph of Injustice: How the Rich Dodge Taxes and How to Make Them Pay*. New York: W. W. Norton, 2019.

Sainsbury, David. *Windows of Opportunity: How Nations Create Wealth*. London: Profile Books, 2020.

Sandbu, Martin. "The Case for the Affordability of Universal Basic Income." *Financial Times*, December 23, 2021. https://www.ft.com/content/3788b99e-7b8c-4641-8250-6f6823f1a7f6.

Sandbu, Martin. *The Economics of Belonging: A Radical Plan to Win Back the Left Behind and Achieve Prosperity for All*. Princeton, NJ, and Oxford: Princeton University Press, 2020.

Sandbu, Martin. "Is Culture or Economics at the Root of Our Strange Politics?" *Financial Times*, September 11, 2017. https://www.ft.com/content/c841a8d4-96d5-11e7-a652-cde3f882dd7b.

Sandbu, Martin. "Populists and Kleptocrats Are a Perfect Match." *Financial Times*, September 22, 2020. https://www.ft.com/content/ef4111a6-8ac8-419e-8747-8ce1b887cb61.

Sandbu, Martin. "Restructuring after COVID Will Matter Even More Than Recovery." *Financial Times*, October 15, 2020. https://www.ft.com/free-lunch.

Sandbu, Martin. "Sweden's Far-Right and the Left-Behind." *Financial Times*, July 4, 2019. https://www .ft.com/content/ec4adebc-99bc-11e9-8cfb-30c211dcd229.

Sandel, Michael J. *The Tyranny of Merit: What's Become of the Common Good?* London: Penguin, 2020.

Sandom, Christopher, Soren Faurby, Brody Sandel, and Jens-Christian Svenning. "Global Late Quaternary Megafauna Extinctions Linked to Humans, Not Climate Change." *Proceedings of the Royal Society, Biological Sciences*, July 22, 2014. https://royalsocietypublishing.org/doi/10.1098/rspb .2013.3254.

Sassoon, David. *The Anxious Triumph: A Global History of Capitalism 1860–1914*. London and New York: Allen Lane, 2019.

Sawyer, Wendy, and Peter Wagner. "Mass Incarceration: The Whole Pie 2020." Prison Policy Initiative, March 24, 2020. https://www.prisonpolicy.org/reports/pie2020.html.

Schaake, Marietje. "Greater Online Transparency Is the Key to Defending Democracy." *Financial Times*, January 10, 2022. https://www.ft.com/content/0e1d1cd8-73af-4a63-b426-e0ee5a7bf834.

Schama, Simon. "Who Speaks for the People? Liberal Institutions Are Under Attack from Leaders Who Claim to Embody the Popular Will." *Financial Times*, October 4, 2019. https://www.ft.com/con tent/9e8f70b8-e5eb-11e9-b112-9624ec9edc59.

Schechter, Asher. "Raghuram Rajan: Populist Nationalism Is 'the First Step toward Crony Capitalism.'" *ProMarket*, August 30, 2017. Stigler Center at the University of Chicago Booth School of Business. https://promarket.org/raghuram-rajan-populist-outcry-cry-help/.

Scheidel, Walter. *Escape from Rome: The Failure of Empire and the Road to Prosperity*. Princeton, NJ: Princeton University Press, 2019.

Scheidel, Walter. *The Great Leveler: Violence and the History of Inequality from the Stone Age to the Twenty-first Century*. Princeton, NJ, and Oxford: Princeton University Press, 2017.

Schlesinger, Arthur. *The Imperial Presidency*. Boston and New York: Mariner Books, Houghton Mifflin, 1973 and 2004.

Schrimpf, Andreas, Hyun Song Shin, and Vladyslav Sushko. "Leverage and Margin Spirals in Fixed Income Markets during the COVID-19 Crisis." *BIS Bulletin* No. 2, April 2, 2020. Bank for International Settlements. https://www.bis.org/publ/bisbull02.pdf.

Schumpeter, Joseph A. *Capitalism, Socialism and Democracy*. London: George Allen & Unwin, 1994. First published in the UK in 1943.

Schwadel, Philip, and Gregory A. Smith. "Evangelical Approval of Trump Remains High, but Other Religious Groups Are Less Supportive." Pew Research Center, March 18, 2019. https://www.pe wresearch.org/fact-tank/2019/03/18/evangelical-approval-of-trump-remains-high-but-other -religious-groups-are-less-supportive/.

Scott, Peter. *Triumph of the South: A Regional Economic History of Early Twentieth Century Britain*. London and New York: Routledge, 2007 and 2018.

Seabright, Paul. *The Company of Strangers: A Natural History of Economic Life*. Princeton, NJ: Princeton University Press, 2010.

Sen, Amartya. *Development as Freedom*. Oxford: Oxford University Press, 1999.

Sevastopulo, Demetri. "Trump Sees Clearer Path to Republican Nomination." *Financial Times*, February 24, 2016. https://www.ft.com/content/8bf2aeb0-db1e-11e5-a72f-1e7744c66818.

Sevastopulo, Demetri. "US Accuses China of Operating 'Open-Air Prison' in Xinjiang." *Financial Times*, May 12, 2021. https://www.ft.com/content/1f9f5f30-dc6e-4228-8b43-5faf522f223a.

Sevastopulo, Demetri, and Kathrin Hille. "US Fears China Is Flirting with Seizing Control of Taiwan." *Financial Times*, March 27, 2021. https://www.ft.com/content/3ed169b8-3f47-4f66-a914-58b6e 2215f7d.

Sevastopulo, Demetri, and Katrina Manson. "Trump Says He Is Confident COVID-19 Came from Wuhan Lab." *Financial Times*, May 1, 2020. https://www.ft.com/content/84935e17-b50e-4a66 -9c37-e2799365b783.

Shafik, Minouche. "In Experts We Trust?" Bank of England, February 22, 2017. https://www.bankofeng land.co.uk/-/media/boe/files/speech/2017/in-experts-we-trust.pdf?la=en&hash=51801143 BE9C2BAA60EF3F56F04D7A2E2C694952.

Shaw, Edward S. *Financial Deepening in Economic Development*. New York: Oxford University Press, 1973.

Shearmur, Jeremy, and Piers Norris Turner, eds. "Ideal and Reality in Society." In *Popper: After the Open Society: Selected Social and Political Writings*. London and New York: Routledge, 2008.

Shepherd, Christian. "Fear and Oppression in Xinjiang: China's War on Uighur Culture." *Financial Times*, September 12, 2019. https://www.ft.com/content/48508182-d426-11e9-8367-807ebd53ab77.

Shimer, David. *Rigged: America, Russia, and One Hundred Years of Covert Electoral Interference*. New York: Alfred A. Knopf, 2020.

Shrimsley, Robert. "Boris Johnson's Brexit Explosion Ruins Tory Business Credentials." *Financial Times*, June 25, 2018. https://www.ft.com/content/8075e68c-7857-11e8-8e67-1e1a0846c475.

Siedentop, Larry. *Inventing the Individual: The Origins of Western Liberalism*. London: Allen Lane, 2014.

Sierakowski, Slawomir. "The Five Lessons of Populist Rule." *Project Syndicate*, January 2, 2017. https://www.project-syndicate.org/commentary/lesson-of-populist-rule-in-poland-by-slawomir-sierakowski-2017-01?barrier=accesspaylog.

Skocpol, Theda. *Diminished Democracy: From Membership to Management in American Civic Life*. Norman: University of Oklahoma Press, 2003.

Slack, James. "Enemies of the People: Fury over 'Out of Touch' Judges Who 'Declared War on Democracy' by Defying 17.4M Brexit Voters and Who Could Trigger Constitutional Crisis." *Daily Mail*, November 4, 2016. https://www.dailymail.co.uk/news/article-3903436/Enemies-people-Fury-touch-judges-defied-17-4m-Brexit-voters-trigger-constitutional-crisis.html.

Smith, Adam. *An Inquiry into the Nature and Causes of the Wealth of Nations*. 5th ed. London: Methuen, 1904. First published 1776. http://www.econlib.org/library/Smith/smWN.html.

Smith, Robert, and Jim Pickard. "Greensill Capital Paid Cameron Salary of More Than $1M a Year." *Financial Times*, July 12, 2021. https://www.ft.com/content/536867f4-2dd3-42a1-9b29-54ed92693635.

Smithers, Andrew. *Productivity and the Bonus Culture*. Oxford: Oxford University Press, 2019.

Smyth, Jamie. "Chinese Tensions Put Australian Businesses under Pressure." *Financial Times*, November 11, 2020. https://www.ft.com/content/b764e4c9-cc38-43b6-848c-dba0cbc6475a.

Social Capital Project. "The Class Divide in Marriage." SCP brief, November 2017. https://www.jec.senate.gov/public/_cache/files/aba9b359-7457-4704-b0f1-93232f54b650/class-divide-in-marriage.pdf.

Soros, George. "The EU Should Issue Perpetual Bonds." *Project Syndicate*, April 20, 2020. https://www.project-syndicate.org/commentary/finance-european-union-recovery-with-perpetual-bonds-by-george-soros-2020-04.

Soutphommasane, Tim. *The Virtuous Citizen: Patriotism in a Multicultural Society*. Cambridge: Cambridge University Press, 2012.

Sperling, Gene. *Economic Dignity*. New York: Penguin, 2020.

Standing, Guy. *The Precariat: The New Dangerous Class*. London: Bloomsbury, 2011 and 2014.

Stanford Encyclopedia of Philosophy. "Plato on Rhetoric and Poetry." February 12, 2020. https://plato.stanford.edu/entries/plato-rhetoric/.

Stasavage, David. *The Decline and Rise of Democracy: A Global History from Antiquity to Today*. Princeton, NJ, and Oxford: Princeton University Press, 2020.

The Statutes Project. "1723: 9 George 1 c.22: The Black Act." https://statutes.org.uk/site/the-statutes/eighteenth-century/9-geo-i-c-22-the-black-act-1723/.

Steil, Benn. *The Battle of Bretton Woods: John Maynard Keynes, Harry Dexter White, and the Making of a New World Order*. Princeton, NJ: Princeton University Press, 2013.

Stevens, Stuart. "Wake Up, Republicans. Your Party Stands for All the Wrong Things Now." *Washington Post*, January 1, 2020. https://www.washingtonpost.com/opinions/wake-up-republicans-your-party-stands-for-all-the-wrong-things-now/2019/12/31/c8347b32-2be8-11ea-9b60-817cc18cf173_story.html?utm_campaign=opinions&utm_medium=E-mail&utm_source=Newsletter&wpisrc=nl_opinions&wpmm=1.

Stewart, Katherine. "Why Trump Reigns as King Cyrus." *New York Times*, December 31, 2018. https://www.nytimes.com/2018/12/31/opinion/trump-evangelicals-cyrus-king.html?action=click&module=MoreInSection&pgtype=Article&region=Footer&contentCollection=Opinion.

Stiglitz, Joseph. "Inequality and Economic Growth." In Michael Jacobs and Mariana Mazzucato, eds. *Rethinking Capitalism: Economics and Policy for Sustainable and Inclusive Growth*. Chichester: Wiley-Blackwell, 2016. Chapter 8: 134–55.

Stiglitz, Joseph. *The Price of Inequality: How Today's Divided Society Endangers Our Future*. New York: W. W. Norton, 2012. https://www8.gsb.columbia.edu/faculty/jstiglitz/sites/jstiglitz/files/Inequality%20and%20Economic%20Growth.pdf.

Stiglitz, Joseph. "Prizes, Not Patents." *Project Syndicate*, March 6, 2007. https://www.project-syndicate.org/commentary/prizes—not-patents.

Stiglitz, Joseph, Amartya Sen, and Jean-Paul Fitoussi. *Report by the Commission on the Measurement of Economic Performance and Social Progress*. 2009. https://web.archive.org/web/20160806043140/. http://www.communityindicators.net/system/publication_pdfs/9/original/Stiglitz_Sen_Fitoussi_2009.pdf?1323961027.

Stiglitz, Joseph E., and Hamid Rashid. "How to Prevent the Looming Sovereign-Debt Crisis." *Project Syndicate*, July 31, 2020. https://www.project-syndicate.org/commentary/how-to-prevent-looming-debt-crisis-developing-countries-by-joseph-e-stiglitz-and-hamid-rashid-2020-07.

Streeck, Wolfgang. *Buying Time: The Delayed Crisis of Democratic Capitalism.* Translated by Patrick Camiller. London and New York: Verso, 2013.

Streeck, Wolfgang. *How Will Capitalism End? Essays on a Failing System.* London and New York: Verso, 2016.

Summers, Lawrence H. "The Biden Stimulus Is Admirably Bold and Ambitious. But It Brings Some Big Risks, Too." *Washington Post,* February 4, 2021. https://www.washingtonpost.com/opinions /2021/02/04/larry-summers-biden-covid-stimulus/.

Summers, Lawrence H. "The Threat of Secular Stagnation Has Not Gone Away." *Financial Times,* May 6, 2018. https://www.ft.com/content/aa76e2a8-4ef2-11e8-9471-a083af05aea7.

Summers, Lawrence H., and Anna Stansbury. "The End of the Golden Age of Central Banking?: Secular Stagnation Is about More Than the Zero Lower Bound." November 2020. Preliminary and incomplete.

Susskind, Daniel. *A World without Work: Technology, Automation, and How We Should Respond.* London: Allen Lane, 2020.

Taleb, Nicholas. *The Black Swan: The Impact of the Highly Improbable.* London and New York: Penguin, 2007.

Task Force on Climate-Related Financial Disclosures. "Climate Change Presents Financial Risk to the Global Economy." https://www.fsb-tcfd.org.

Tax Justice Network. "Corporate Tax Haven Index 2019." Citing *New York Times.* https://corporatetax havenindex.org/.

"Tax Policy Center's Briefing Book." https://www.taxpolicycenter.org/briefing-book/what-carried -interest-and-should-it-be-taxed-capital-gain.

Taylor, Alan M. "International Capital Mobility in History: The Saving-Investment Relationship." National Bureau of Economic Research Working Paper Number 5743. September 1996. http://www .nber.org/papers/w5743.pdf.

Temin, Peter. *The Vanishing Middle Class: Prejudice and Power in a Dual Economy.* Cambridge, MA: MIT Press, 2017.

"Ten Important Supreme Court Decisions in Black History." Infoplease, February 28, 2017 (updated January 11, 2021). https://www.infoplease.com/us/government/judicial-branch/ten-important-su preme-court-decisions-in-black-history.

Tepper, Jonathan, with Denise Hearn. *The Myth of Capitalism: Monopolies and the Death of Competition.* Hoboken, NJ: Wiley, 2018.

Thomas, Mark E. *99%: Mass Impoverishment and How We Can End It.* London: Apollo: 2019.

Thurley, Djuna, and James Mirza Davies. "Collective Defined Contribution Schemes." House of Commons Briefing Paper Number CBP 8674. July 2, 2020. file: https://researchbriefings.files.parlia ment.uk/documents/CBP-8674/CBP-8674.pdf.

Tocqueville, Alexis de. *Democracy in America.* Parts I and II. 1835 and 1840.

Toly, Noah J., and Sam Tabory. "100 Top Economies: Urban Influence and the Position of Cities in an Evolving World Order." October 13, 2016. Chicago Council on Global Affairs. https://www .thechicagocouncil.org/publication/100-top-economies-urban-influence-and-position-cities -evolving-world-order.

Tooze, Adam. *Crashed: How a Decade of Financial Crises Changed the World.* London: Allen Lane, 2018.

Tooze, Adam. *Shutdown: How Covid Shook the World's Economy.* London: Penguin, 2021.

Transparency International. *Corruption Perceptions Index.* https://www.transparency.org/en/cpi.

Trentmann, Frank. *Free Trade Nation: Commerce, Consumption, and Civil Society in Modern Britain.* Oxford: Oxford University Press, 2009.

Trinity College Cambridge. "Letter from J. M. Keynes to F. W. Pethick-Lawrence." https://archives .trin.cam.ac.uk/index.php/letter-from-j-m-keynes-to-f-w-pethick-lawrence-23.

Trotsky, Leon. "Revolutionary and Socialist Art." *Literature and Revolution.* https://www.marxists.org /archive/trotsky/1924/lit_revo/ch08.htm.

Trump, Donald. "Inaugural Address." January 20, 2017. https://www.whitehouse.gov/inaugural-address.

Trump, Donald. "Remarks by President Trump in a Meeting with Republican Members of Congress on the United States Reciprocal Trade Act." January 24, 2019. https://www.whitehouse.gov/briefings -statements/remarks-president-trump-meeting-republican-members-congress-united-states -reciprocal-trade-act/.

Tucker, Paul. *Unelected Power: The Quest for Legitimacy in Central Banking and the Regulatory State.* Princeton, NJ, and Oxford: Princeton University Press, 2018.

Turner, Adair. *Between Debt and the Devil: Money, Credit, and Fixing Global Finance.* Princeton, NJ, and Oxford: Princeton University Press, 2016.

UK Parliament. "Simon de Montfort's Parliament." https://www.parliament.uk/about/living-heritage/evolutionofparliament/originsofparliament/birthofparliament/overview/simondemontfort/.

"UK Treaties." https://www.gov.uk/guidance/uk-treaties.

UNHCR. *Central Mediterranean Route Situation, Supplementary Appeal*, January–December 2018. http://www.unhcr.org/5aa78775c.pdf.

United Nations. Department of Economic and Social Affairs, Population Dynamics. *World Population Prospects 2019*. https://population.un.org/wpp/Download/.

United Nations Development Program. "Human Development Index." http://hdr.undp.org/en/content/human-development-index-hdi.

United Nations Population Division. *Replacement Migration: Is It a Solution to Declining and Aging Populations?* 2000. https://www.un.org/en/development/desa/population/publications/aging/replacement-migration.asp.

US Department of Labor. "Trade Act Programs." https://www.dol.gov/general/topic/training/tradeact#:~:text=The%20Trade%20Adjustment%20Assistance%20(TAA,a%20result%20of%20increased%20imports.

US Department of State. "Law of the Sea Convention." https://www.state.gov/law-of-the-sea-convention/.

US Department of State. "The Montreal Protocol on Substances That Deplete the Ozone Layer." https://www.state.gov/key-topics-office-of-environmental-quality-and-transboundary-issues/the-montreal-protocol-on-substances-that-deplete-the-ozone-layer/.

"U.S. Voting Rights Timeline." https://a.s.kqed.net/pdf/education/digitalmedia/us-voting-rights-timeline.pdf.

Vague, Richard. *A Brief History of Doom: Two Hundred Years of Financial Crises*. Philadelphia: University of Pennsylvania Press, 2019.

Van Parijs, Philippe, and Yannick Vanderborght. *Basic Income: A Radical Proposal for a Free Society and a Sane Economy*. Cambridge, MA, and London: Harvard University Press, 2017.

Vogl, Frank. *The Enablers: How the West Supports Kleptocrats and Corruption—Endangering Our Democracy*. Lanham, MD: Rowman & Littlefield, 2021.

Vollrath, Dietrich. *Fully Grown: Why a Stagnant Economy Is a Sign of Success*. Chicago: University of Chicago Press, 2020.

Wallace-Stevens, Fabian, and Emma Morgante. *Who Is at Risk? Work and Automation in the Time of Covid-19*. Royal Society of Arts, October 2020. https://www.thersa.org/globalassets/_foundation/new-site-blocks-and-images/reports/2020/10/work_and_automation_in_time_of_covid_report.pdf.

Washington, George. "Farewell Address." https://www.ourdocuments.gov/doc.php?flash=false&doc=15&page=transcript.

Webb, Dominic, and Matt Ward. *The Comprehensive and Progressive Agreement for Trans-Pacific Partnership*. House of Commons Library, June 22, 2021. https://researchbriefings.files.parliament.uk/documents/CBP-9121/CBP-9121.pdf.

Wei-Haas, Maya. "Controversial New Study Pinpoints Where All Modern Humans Arose." *National Geographic*, October 28, 2019. https://www.nationalgeographic.com/.

White House. "Remarks by President Trump, Vice President Pence, and Members of the Coronavirus Task Force in Press Briefing." April 2, 2020. https://www.whitehouse.gov/briefings-statements/remarks-president-trump-vice-president-pence-members-coronavirus-task-force-press-briefing-17/.

Wiener Holocaust Library. "How Did the Nazis Consolidate Their Power?" The Holocaust Explained. https://www.theholocaustexplained.org/the-nazi-rise-to-power/how-did-the-nazi-gain-power/1933-elections/.

Wilkerson, Isabel. *Caste: The Origins of Our Discontents*. New York: Random House, 2020.

Wilkinson, Richard, and Kate Pickett. *The Inner Level: How More Equal Societies Reduce Stress, Restore Sanity and Improve Well-Being*. London: Penguin, 2019.

Wilkinson, Richard, and Kate Pickett. *The Spirit Level: Why Greater Equality Makes Societies Stronger*. New York: Bloomsbury, 2009.

Williams, Aime. "Persistence of Donald Trump's China Tariffs Frustrates US Business." *Financial Times*, June 3, 2021. https://www.ft.com/content/fb775a22-eaa5-44b4-8643-16c3f40a5d02.

Williamson, Jeffrey G. "The Evolution of Global Labor Markets Since 1830: Background Evidence and Hypotheses." *Explorations in Economic History* 32, no. 2 (April 1995): 141–96.

Williamson, John. "The Washington Consensus as Policy Prescription for Development." January 2004. https://www.piie.com/publications/papers/williamson0204.pdf.

Wills, Matthew. "How Antebellum Christians Justified Slavery." *JSTOR Daily*, June 27, 2018. https://daily.jstor.org/how-antebellum-christians-justified-slavery/.

Wolf, Martin. *Fixing Global Finance*. Baltimore and London: Johns Hopkins University Press and Yale University Press, 2008 and 2010.

Wolf, Martin. *India's Exports*. Washington, DC: Oxford University Press for the World Bank, 1982.

Wolf, Martin. *The Shifts and the Shocks: What We've Learned—and Have Still to Learn—from the Financial Crisis*. London and New York: Penguin, 2014 and 2015.

Wolf, Martin. *Why Globalization Works*. London and New Haven, CT: Yale University Press, 2004.

Wolf, Martin. "When Multiculturalism Is a Nonsense." *Financial Times*, August 30, 2005. https://www.ft.com/content/ff41a586-197f-11da-804e-00000e2511c8.

Wolf, Martin. "Disputed Fruit of Unskilled Immigration." *Financial Times*, April 4, 2006. https://www.ft.com/content/ba686d9a-c407-11da-bc52-0000779e2340.

Wolf, Martin. "Why Today's Hedge Fund Industry May Not Survive." *Financial Times*, March 18, 2008. https://www.ft.com/content/c8941ad4-f503-11dc-a21b-000077b07658.

Wolf, Martin. "Is Unlimited Growth a Thing of the Past?" *Financial Times*, October 2, 2012. https://www.ft.com/content/78e883fa-0bef-11e2-8032-00144feabdc0.

Wolf, Martin. "Why China Will Not Buy the World." *Financial Times*, July 9, 2013. https://www.ft.com/content/28d1a4a8-e7ba-11e2-babb-00144feabdc0.

Wolf, Martin. "A Much-Maligned Engine of Innovation." *Financial Times*, August 4, 2013. https://www.ft.com/content/32ba9b92-efd4-11e2-a237-00144feabdc0.

Wolf, Martin. "Opportunist Shareholders Must Embrace Commitment." *Financial Times*, August 26, 2014. https://www.ft.com/content/6aa87b9a-2d05-11e4-911b-00144feabdc0.

Wolf, Martin. "Donald Trump Embodies How Great Republics Meet Their End." *Financial Times*, March 1, 2016. https://www.ft.com/content/743d91b8-df8d-11e5-b67f-a61732c1d025.

Wolf, Martin. "The Welfare State Is a Piggy Bank for Life." *Financial Times*, March 31, 2016. https://www.ft.com/content/b7ae7e52-f69a-11e5-96db-fc683b5e52db.

Wolf, Martin. "Brexit: Sovereignty Is Not the Same as Power." *Financial Times*, May 3, 2016. https://www.ft.com/content/fece7238-1071-11e6-91da-096d89bd2173.

Wolf, Martin. "The Tide of Globalization Is Turning." *Financial Times*, September 6, 2016. https://www.ft.com/content/87bb0eda-7364-11e6-bf48-b372cdb1043a.

Wolf, Martin. "Sluggish Global Trade Growth Is Here to Stay." *Financial Times*, October 25, 2016. https://www.ft.com/content/4efcd174-99d3-11e6-b8c6-568a43813464.

Wolf, Martin. "The Case against the Collapse of Capitalism." *Financial Times*, November 2, 2016. https://www.ft.com/content/7496e08a-9f7a-11e6-891e-abe238dee8e2.

Wolf, Martin. "Donald Trump Faces the Reality of World Trade." *Financial Times*, November 22, 2016. https://www.ft.com/content/064d51b0-aff4-11e6-9c37-5787335499a0.

Wolf, Martin. "Too Big, Too Leninist—a Chain Crisis Is a Matter of Time." *Financial Times*, December 13, 2016. https://www.ft.com/content/6a1b4010-be4c-11e6-8b45-b8b81dd5d080.

Wolf, Martin. "Democrats, Demagogues and Despots," *Financial Times*, December 21, 2016. https://www.ft.com/content/9310dcea-c5d2-11e6-8f29-9445cac8966f.

Wolf, Martin. "The Long and Painful Journey to World Disorder." *Financial Times*, January 5, 2017. https://www.ft.com/content/ef13e61a-ccec-11e6-b8ce-b9c03770f8b1.

Wolf, Martin. "The Folly of Donald Trump's Bilateralism in Global Trade." *Financial Times*, March 14, 2017. https://www.ft.com/content/ce92ae28-058e-11e7-ace0-1ce02ef0def9.

Wolf, Martin. "Dealing with America's Trade Follies." *Financial Times*, April 18, 2017. https://www.ft.com/content/fca7e9a4-2366-11e7-a34a-538b4cb30025.

Wolf, Martin. "Cities Must Be Open to the World When Nations Are Not." *Financial Times*, June 7, 2017. https://www.ft.com/content/fea537f8-34d6-11e7-99bd-13beb0903fa3.

Wolf, Martin. "Taming the Masters of the Tech Universe." *Financial Times*, November 14, 2017. https://www.ft.com/content/45092c5c-c872-11e7-aa33-c63fdc9b8c6c.

Wolf, Martin. "A Republican Tax Plan Built for Plutocrats." *Financial Times*, November 21, 2017. https://www.ft.com/content/e494f47e-ce1a-11e7-9dbb-291a884dd8c6.

Wolf, Martin. "*Counter-Revolution* by Jan Zielonka—Project Backlash." *Financial Times*, February 1, 2018. https://www.ft.com/content/e4290c10-069f-11e8-9650-9c0ad2d7c5b5

Wolf, Martin. "Donald Trump Declares Trade War on China." *Financial Times*, May 8, 2018. https://www.ft.com/content/dd2af6b0-4fc1-11e8-9471-a083af05aea7.

Wolf, Martin. "Italy's New Rulers Could Shake the Euro." *Financial Times*, May 22, 2018. https://www.ft.com/content/eb82fdfe-5ce4-11e8-9334-2218e7146b04.

Wolf, Martin. "Donald Trump Creates Chaos with His Tariffs Trade War." *Financial Times*, July 10, 2018. https://www.ft.com/content/ba65ac98-8364-11e8-a29d-73e3d454535d.

Wolf, Martin. "How We Lost America to Greed and Envy." *Financial Times*, July 17, 2018. https://www.ft.com/content/3aea8668-88e2-11e8-bf9e-8771d5404543.

Wolf, Martin. "The Price of Populism." *Financial Times*, October 24, 2018. https://www.ft.com/content/06181c56-d13b-11e8-a9f2-7574db66bcd5.

Wolf, Martin. "We Must Rethink the Purpose of the Corporation." *Financial Times*, December 11, 2018. https://www.ft.com/content/786144bc-fc93-11e8-ac00-57a2a826423e.

Wolf, Martin. "The Rise of the Populist Authoritarians." *Financial Times*, January 22, 2019. https://www.ft.com/content/4faf6c4e-1d84-11e9-b2f7-97e4dbd3580d.

Wolf, Martin. "The World Needs to Change the Way It Taxes Companies." *Financial Times*, March 7, 2019. https://www.ft.com/content/9a22b722-40c0-11e9-b896-fe36ec32aece.

Wolf, Martin. "Monetary Policy Has Run Its Course." *Financial Times*, March 12, 2019. https://www.ft.com/content/08c4eb8c-442c-11e9-a965-23d669740bfb.

Wolf, Martin. "How Economists Failed as 'Experts'—and How to Make Them Matter Again." March 12, 2019. Institute for New Economic Thinking. https://www.ineteconomics.org/perspectives/blog/why-economists-failed-as-experts-and-how-to-make-them-matter-again.

Wolf, Martin. "Why Further Financial Crises Are Inevitable." *Financial Times*, March 19, 2019. https://www.ft.com/content/d9d94f4a-4884-11e9-bbc9-6917dce3dc62.

Wolf, Martin. "The Case for Capitalism." *Financial Times*, March 28, 2019. https://www.ft.com/content/d8b903d0-4bfe-11e9-bbc9-6917dce3dc62.

Wolf, Martin. "The Age of the Elected Despot Is Here." *Financial Times*, April 23, 2019. https://www.ft.com/content/9198533e-6521-11e9-a79d-04f350474d62.

Wolf, Martin. "Hypocrisy and Confusion Distort the Debate on Social Mobility." *Financial Times*, May 2, 2019. https://www.ft.com/content/577a0abe-6c04-11e9-a9a5-351eeaef6d84.

Wolf, Martin. "Greek Economy Shows Promising Signs of Growth." *Financial Times*, May 20, 2019. https://www.ft.com/content/b42ee1ac-4a27-11e9-bde6-79eaea5acb64.

Wolf, Martin. "The US-China Conflict Challenges the World." *Financial Times*, May 21, 2019. https://www.ft.com/content/870c895c-7b11-11e9-81d2-f785092ab560.

Wolf, Martin. "States Create Useful Money, but Abuse It." *Financial Times*, May 28, 2019. https://www.ft.com/content/fcc1274a-8073-11e9-9935-ad75bb96c849.

Wolf, Martin. "The Case for Making Wellbeing the Goal of Public Policy." *Financial Times*, May 30, 2019. https://www.ft.com/content/d4bb3e42-823b-11e9-9935-ad75bb96c849.

Wolf, Martin. "Martin Wolf: Why Rigged Capitalism Is Damaging Liberal Democracy." *Financial Times*, September 18, 2019. https://www.ft.com/content/5a8ab27e-d470-11e9-8367-807ebd53ab77.

Wolf, Martin. "The Narrow Corridor—the Fine Line between Despotism and Anarchy." *Financial Times*, September 26, 2019. https://www.ft.com/content/d8eaaaba-deee-11e9-b112-9624ec9edc59.

Wolf, Martin. "The Threat and the Promise of Digital Money." *Financial Times*, October 22, 2019. https://www.ft.com/content/fc079a6a-f4ad-11e9-a79c-bc9acae3b654.

Wolf, Martin. "The Fight to Halt the Theft of Ideas Is Hopeless." *Financial Times*, November 12, 2019, https://www.ft.com/content/d592af00-0a29-11ea-b2d6-9bf4d1957a67.

Wolf, Martin. "Why the US Economy Isn't as Competitive or Free as You Think." *Financial Times*, November 14, 2019. https://www.ft.com/content/97be3f2c-00b1-11ea-b7bc-f3fa4e77dd47.

Wolf, Martin. "How to Reform Today's Rigged Capitalism." *Financial Times*, December 3, 2019. https://www.ft.com/content/4cf2d6ee-14f5-11ea-8d73-6303645ac406.

Wolf, Martin. "A Partial and Ineffective US-China Trade Truce." *Financial Times*, January 21, 2020. https://www.ft.com/content/65557ec4-3851-11ea-a6d3-9a26f8c3cba4.

Wolf, Martin. "Last Chance for the Climate Transition." *Financial Times*, February 18, 2020. https://www.ft.com/content/3090b1fe-51a6-11ea-8841-482eed0038b1.

Wolf, Martin. "Britain Needs to Be Crystal Clear about Belated Virus Strategy." *Financial Times*, March 27, 2020. https://www.ft.com/content/f1871f34-6f46-11ea-89df-41bea055720b.

Wolf, Martin. "Coronavirus Crisis Lays Bare the Risks of Financial Leverage, Again." *Financial Times*, April 28, 2020. https://www.ft.com/content/098dcd60-8880-11ea-a01c-a28a3e3fbd33.

Wolf, Martin. "How to Escape the Trap of Excessive Debt." *Financial Times*, May 5, 2020. https://www.ft.com/content/2c5ddbd0-8e09-11ea-9e12-0d4655dbd44f.

Wolf, Martin. "Covid-19 Will Hit Developing Countries Hard." *Financial Times*, June 9, 2020. https://www.ft.com/content/31eb2686-a982-11ea-a766-7c300513fe47.

Wolf, Martin. "What Trade Wars Tell Us." *Financial Times*, June 18, 2020. https://www.ft.com/content/f3ee37e0-b086-11ea-a4b6-31f1eedf762e.

Wolf, Martin. "The Dangerous War on Supply Chains." *Financial Times*, June 23, 2020. https://www
.ft.com/content/e27b0c0c-1893-479b-9ea3-27a81c2506c9.

Wolf, Martin. "Democracy Will Fail If We Don't Think as Citizens." *Financial Times*, July 6, 2020.
https://www.ft.com/content/36abf9a6-b838-4ca2-ba35-2836bd0b62e2.

Wolf, Martin. "Covid-19 Aggravates Adverse Underlying Trends." *Financial Times*, July 16, 2020.
https://www.ft.com/content/d9c02dd2-81d8-4ee9-9552-034a599e1c79.

Wolf, Martin. "Alarm Signals of Our Authoritarian Age." *Financial Times*, July 21, 2020. https://www
.ft.com/content/5eb5d26d-0abe-434e-be12-5068bd6d7f06.

Wolf, Martin. "Martin Wolf—Will Covid-19 Kill Off Populism?" *Financial Times*, August 13, 2020.
https://www.ft.com/video/1d5916ab-66b9-44ef-8528-804f518837f0.

Wolf, Martin. "There Is a Direct Line from Milton Friedman to Donald Trump's Assault on Democracy." *ProMarket*, October 4, 2020. https://promarket.org/2020/10/04/milton-friedman-donald
-trump-assault-on-democracy-corporations/.

Wolf, Martin. "Ten Ways Coronavirus Will Shape World in Long Term." *Financial Times*, November 3,
2020. https://www.ft.com/content/9b0318d3-8e5b-4293-ad50-c5250e894b07.

Wolf, Martin. "Why Inflation Could Be on the Way Back." *Financial Times*, November 17, 2020. https://
www.ft.com/content/dea66630-d054-401a-ad1c-65ebd0d10b38.

Wolf, Martin. "What the World Can Learn from the Covid-19 Pandemic." *Financial Times*, November
24, 2020. https://www.ft.com/content/7fb55fa2-4aea-41a0-b4ea-ad1a51cb415f.

Wolf, Martin. "Restoring UK Growth Is More Urgent Than Cutting Public Debt." *Financial Times*,
December 13, 2020. https://www.ft.com/content/50394d54-1b2e-417b-ba6d-2204a4b05f24.

Wolf, Martin. "The American Republic's Near-Death Experience." *Financial Times*, January 19, 2021.
https://www.ft.com/content/c085e962-f27c-4c34-a0f1-5cf2bd813fbc.

Wolf, Martin. "Containing China Is Not a Feasible Option." *Financial Times*, February 2, 2021. https://
www.ft.com/content/83a521c0-6abb-4efa-be48-89ecb52c8d1.

Wolf, Martin. "Why Once Successful Countries Like the UK Fall Behind." *Financial Times*, February
21, 2021. https://www.ft.com/content/217f6d28-5a3e-48e0-bf6e-c2618da8f34b.

Wolf, Martin. "What Central Banks Ought to Target." *Financial Times*, March 2, 2021. https://www
.ft.com/content/160db526-5e8d-4152-b711-21501a7fbd01.

Wolf, Martin. "Humanity Is a Cuckoo in the Planetary Nest." *Financial Times*, March 9, 2021. https://
www.ft.com/content/a3285adf-6c5f-4ce4-b055-e85f39ff2988.

Wolf, Martin. "Martin Wolf Looks Back at the Pandemic One Year Later." *Financial Times*, March 11,
2021. https://www.ft.com/content/e02ec5cb-f08b-4bc9-a5ba-2978b680103c.

Wolf, Martin. "The Return of the Inflation Specter." *Financial Times*, March 26, 2021. https://www
.ft.com/content/6cfb36ca-d3ce-4dd3-b70d-eecc332ba1df.

Wolf, Martin. "Larry Summers: I'm Concerned That What Is Being Done Is Substantially Excessive."
Financial Times, April 12, 2021. https://www.ft.com/content/380ea811-e927-4fe1-aa5b-d213816
e9073.

Wolf, Martin. "Economic Recovery Masks the Dangers of a Divided World." *Financial Times*, April 20,
2021. https://www.ft.com/content/0be32ec5-8a75-48f2-99f3-eb5bcd055287.

Wolf, Martin. "Action Must Replace Talk on Climate Change." *Financial Times*, May 4, 2021. https://
www.ft.com/content/3fa154f3-84e7-4964-9a21-d3dbd41e1470 https://www.ft.com/content/3fa
154f3-84e7-4964-9a21-d3dbd41e1470,

Wolf, Martin. "The Struggle for the Survival of US Democracy." *Financial Times*, May 11, 2021. https://
www.ft.com/content/aebe3b15-0d55-4d99-b415-cd7b109e64f8.

Wolf, Martin. "We Can End the Covid Pandemic in the Next Year." *Financial Times*, May 25, 2021.
https://www.ft.com/content/12fc9f47-7fd3-4690-93c5-f641688fca36.

Wolf, Martin. "How 'Creative Destruction' Drives Innovation and Prosperity." *Financial Times*, June
11, 2021. https://www.ft.com/content/3a0aa7cb-d10e-4352-b845-a50df70272b8.

Wolf, Martin. "Radical Reform of British Pension Provision Is Urgent." *Financial Times*, June 13, 2021.
https://www.ft.com/content/791876ae-7ce2-4c0b-9f7a-c12b4f39f6d5.

Wolf, Martin. "The US Should Spurn the False Promise of Protectionism." *Financial Times*, June 15,
2021. https://www.ft.com/content/4edc2c5a-298f-4edd-81b7-5b94b7b23b93.

Wolf, Martin. "It Is Folly to Make Pensions Safe by Making Them Unaffordable." *Financial Times*, June
27, 2021. https://www.ft.com/content/138974df-5dc0-47e4-acb8-e2eb048fe8bd.

Wolf, Martin. "Equities Are the Only Sensible Foundation for Private Pensions." *Financial Times*, July
11, 2021. https://www.ft.com/content/e3a621d3-5cfc-4410-bd3c-0fde3535582b.

Wolf, Martin. "The G20 Has Failed to Meet Its Challenges." *Financial Times*, July 13, 2021. https://
www.ft.com/content/c9448d15-8410-47d3-8f41-cd7ed41d8116.

Wolf, Martin. "COP26 Is the Real Thing and Not a Drill." *Financial Times*, October 19, 2021. https://www.ft.com/content/799b7b93-9ec5-4318-9ac1-1c82cb81f96d.

Wolf, Martin. "What Is the Least We Need from COP26?" *Financial Times*, October 26, 2021. https://www.ft.com/content/f859d515-f1d0-405f-9aee-c609951f4254.

Wolf, Martin. "How We Can Share Our Divided World." *Financial Times*, November 2, 2021. https://www.ft.com/content/b371e181-eac3-41ef-88c5-ca2bb20edd99.

Wolf, Martin. "Dancing on the Edge of Climate Disaster." *Financial Times*, November 23, 2021. https://www.ft.com/content/6e2b366f-e139-4d69-bd4f-9254333bf316.

Wolf, Martin. "We Must Accept Higher Taxes to Fund Health and Social Care." *Financial Times*, November 29, 2021. https://www.ft.com/content/efc67bb9-cff4-49e5-9101-67d2382ece09.

Wolf, Martin. "Lessons in 'Leveling Up' from the Basque Country." *Financial Times*, November 30, 2021. https://www.ft.com/content/bb2c627f-1baa-4230-9cb8-3876c216b8f7.

Wolf, Martin. "A Call to Arms for Diverse Democracies and Their 'Decent Middle.'" *Financial Times*, May 5, 2022. https://www.ft.com/content/83ba0474-70ea-4759-81f1-e14f6ea269fa.

Wolf, Martin. "The Big Mistakes of the Anti-globalisers." *Financial Times*, June 21, 2022. https://www.ft.com/content/fa1f3a82-99c5-4fb2-8bff-a7e8d3f65849.

Wolf, Martin "In an Era of Disorder, Open Trade Is at Risk." *Financial Times*, June 28, 2022. https://www.ft.com/content/df62d58c-e864-4e3b-9aa6-5587e8cf1667.

Wolf, Martin. "A Matter of Interest—the Battle Over Monetary Policy." *Financial Times*, July 27, 2022. https://www.ft.com/content/e7cc3c01-08e3-47fc-9442-d45378b34bb8.

Wolff, Alan. "Trade, Global Cooperation Can Best Deliver Adequate Medical Supplies." September 4, 2020. World Trade Organization. https://www.wto.org/english/news_e/news20_e/ddgaw_04sep20_e.htm.

Woodhouse, Alice, and James Politi. "Populist Five Star Movement Secures 32 Percent of Vote in Italian Election. *Financial Times*, March 5, 2018. https://www.ft.com/content/ecd89a82-2045-11e8-a895-1ba1f72c2c11.

Wooldridge, Adrian. *The Aristocracy of Talent: How Meritocracy Made the Modern World*. London: Allen Lane, 2021.

World Atlas. https://www.worldatlas.com.

World Bank. "COVID-19: Debt Service Suspension Initiative." June 19, 2020. https://www.worldbank.org/en/topic/debt/brief/covid-19-debt-service-suspension-initiative.

World Bank. *Global Economic Prospects June 2020*. Washington, DC: World Bank, 2020.

World Bank. "International Migrant Stock, Total." http://data.worldbank.org/indicator/SM.POP.TOTL.

World Bank. *World Development Indicators*. http://data.worldbank.org/data-catalog/world-development-indicators.

World Inequality Report 2018. https://wir2018.wid.world/.

World Trade Organization. "Trade Falls Steeply in First Half of 2020." June 22, 2020. https://www.wto.org/english/news_e/pres20_e/pr858_e.htm.

World Trade Organization. *World Trade Statistical Review 2017*. https://www.wto.org/english/res_e/statis_e/wts2017_e/wts17_toc_e.htm.

Wray, L. Randall. *Modern Money Theory: A Primer on Macroeconomics for Sovereign Monetary Systems*. New York: Palgrave Macmillan, 2012.

Wren Lewis, Simon. *The Lies We Were Told: Politics, Economics, Austerity and Brexit*. Bristol: Bristol University Press, 2018.

Wright, Thomas, and Gabriel Zucman. "The Exorbitant Tax Privilege." National Bureau of Economic Research Working Paper 24983. September 2018. https://www.nber.org/papers/w24983.

Wu, Tim. *The Curse of Bigness: Antitrust in the New Gilded Age*. New York: Columbia Global Reports. 2018.

Yglesias, Matthew. "Fox News's Propaganda Isn't Just Unethical—Research Shows It's Enormously Influential: Without the 'Fox Effect,' Neither Bush Nor Trump Could Have Won." *Vox*, March 4, 2019. https://www.vox.com/2019/3/4/18249847/fox-news-effect-swing-elections.

Yglesias, Matthew. "Justin Trudeau, Unlike Trump, Is Taking NAFTA Renegotiation Really Seriously." *Vox*, August 23, 2017. https://www.vox.com/policy-and-politics/2017/8/23/16178914/trump-nafta-trudeau.

Zakaria, Fareed. *The Future of Freedom: Illiberal Democracy at Home and Abroad*. London and New York: W. W. Norton, 2007.

Ziblatt, Daniel. *Conservative Parties and the Birth of Democracy*. Cambridge: Cambridge University Press, 2017.

Zielonka, Jan. *Counter-Revolution: Liberal Europe in Retreat*. Oxford: Oxford University Press, 2018.

Zingales, Luigi, Jana Kasperkevic, and Asher Schechter. *Milton Friedman 50 Years Later. ProMarket*, 2020. Stigler Center for the Study of the Economy and the State. https://promarket.org/wp -content/uploads/2020/11/Milton-Friedman-50-years-later-ebook.pdf/.

Zoellick, Robert. "Whither China: From Membership to Responsibility?" September 21, 2015. US Department of State Archive. https://2001-2009.state.gov/s/d/former/zoellick/rem/53682.htm.

Zuboff, Shoshana. *The Age of Surveillance Capitalism: The Fight for a Human Future and the New Frontier of Power*. New York: Public Affairs, 2019.

INDEX

Italicized page numbers indicate material in tables or illustrations.

CW00970332

Handbook of Water Economics

20175

Handbook of Water Economics

Principles and Practice

Colin Green

University of Middlesex

NERA (LONDON) LIBRARY

WILEY

Copyright © 2003   John Wiley & Sons Ltd, The Atrium, Southern Gate, Chichester,
West Sussex PO19 8SQ, England

Telephone (+44) 1243 779777

Email (for orders and customer service enquiries): cs-books@wiley.co.uk
Visit our Home Page on www.wileyeurope.com or www.wiley.com

All Rights Reserved. No part of this publication may be reproduced, stored in a retrieval system or
transmitted in any form or by any means, electronic, mechanical, photocopying, recording,
scanning or otherwise, except under the terms of the Copyright, Designs and Patents Act 1988 or
under the terms of a licence issued by the Copyright Licensing Agency Ltd, 90 Tottenham Court
Road, London W1T 4LP, UK, without the permission in writing of the Publisher. Requests to the
Publisher should be addressed to the Permissions Department, John Wiley & Sons Ltd, The
Atrium, Southern Gate, Chichester, West Sussex PO19 8SQ, England, or emailed to
permreq@wiley.co.uk, or faxed to (+44) 1243 770620.

This publication is designed to provide accurate and authoritative information in regard to the
subject matter covered. It is sold on the understanding that the Publisher is not engaged in
rendering professional services. If professional advice or other expert assistance is required, the
services of a competent professional should be sought.

Other Wiley Editorial Offices

John Wiley & Sons Inc., 111 River Street, Hoboken, NJ 07030, USA

Jossey-Bass, 989 Market Street, San Francisco, CA 94103-1741, USA

Wiley-VCH Verlag GmbH, Boschstr. 12, D-69469 Weinheim, Germany

John Wiley & Sons Australia Ltd, 33 Park Road, Milton, Queensland 4064, Australia

John Wiley & Sons (Asia) Pte Ltd, 2 Clementi Loop #02-01, Jin Xing Distripark, Singapore 129809

John Wiley & Sons Canada Ltd, 22 Worcester Road, Etobicoke, Ontario, Canada M9W 1L1

Wiley also publishes its books in a variety of electronic formats. Some content that appears
in print may not be available in electronic books.

Library of Congress Cataloging-in-Publication Data

Green, Colin H.
   Handbook of water economics: principles and practice / Colin Green.
     p. cm.
   Includes bibliographical references and index.
   ISBN 0-471-98571-6 (alk. paper)
    1. Water resource development. I. Title.

HD1691 .G74 2003
333.91–dc21

                                    2002191057

British Library Cataloguing in Publication Data

A catalogue record for this book is available from the British Library

ISBN 0-471-98571-6

Typeset in 10/12pt Times by Laserwords Private Limited, Chennai, India
Printed and bound in Great Britain by Antony Rowe Ltd, Chippenham, Wiltshire
This book is printed on acid-free paper responsibly manufactured from sustainable forestry
in which at least two trees are planted for each one used for paper production.

Contents

1

Introduction

The relationship of the economy to the environment is as the leaf to the tree. Therefore, the decisions we take concerning the environment, and the effectiveness of the implementation of those decisions, will determine whether or not we achieve sustainable development. Economics, the application to choice, offers a means of understanding the nature of the choices we must make and, through this understanding, of making better choices.

Nowhere is this dependence of society and the economy upon the environment seen more clearly than in relation to water. Traditionally, the start of civilisation is ascribed to the settlements in the valleys of the Euphrates/Tigris, where the combination of fertile river-deposited sediment and readily available water enabled secure food supplies. The same pattern of settlement can be seen in other parts of the world from the Americas (Williams 1997) to Asia (Mendis 1999). That each society depends on water meant that we began very early on to try to modify the water environment for our purposes; the Shaopi reservoir was built around 590 BC, a navigation canal in Guangxi in 219 BC, and Dujiangyan dam in around 200 BC (Xhang 1999). In turn, the inability to manage water successfully, particularly under prolonged drought conditions, has resulted in the death of cultures in the Americas (Williams 1997) and Asia (Postel 1992).

One result of the dependence of society on successful water management is that until very recently water engineers saw their purpose as being to determine what the public need, to determine the best means of satisfying that need, and then to construct the required works. By defining the issue as one of necessity rather than desirability, the question of whether or not the project was desirable was finessed; it was instead inevitable. In turn, the task in water resource planning became one of predicting by how much demand for water would inevitably increase in the future and then providing for this increase. The assumption was that all growth is good as well as inevitable, and that economic and social development will necessarily require a proportionate growth in all inputs, including water.

That the identification of the possible options and the decision as to which is the best option were defined as being part of the engineer's job, led inevitably to both a focus on engineering approaches and to the identification of the best in terms of engineering issues. After all, engineers became engineers in order to build

Handbook of Water Economics: Principles and Practice.   C. Green
© 2003 John Wiley & Sons, Ltd   ISBN: 0-471-98571-6

things and after all the socially construed role of engineers is to build things. That something could be done became to imply that something should be done. Whilst the result was a number of major engineering triumphs, there were a number of significant failures as well (Adams 1992); a number of expensive projects that had been built to match a predicted growth in demand that did not occur (USACE 1995); a growing recognition of the environmental and human consequences of some projects (Acreman *et al.* 1999); and an increasing questioning of whether some projects were really necessary (Bowers 1983; Reisner 1993). A significant number of projects have also never delivered successfully; in India, only some 70% of hand pumps are estimated to be working at any one time (South East Region 1999) and some 30% of the public latrines in Bombay are out of service (Operations Evaluation Department 1996).

Today, this dependence of development upon water management is even more pronounced. The availability and management of water is increasingly seen as perhaps the defining constraint upon development (World Water Council 2000), with an increasing number of countries reaching conditions of water scarcity. By 2025, IWMI (2000) estimates that 78% of the world's population will live in areas facing some degree of water scarcity. To release this constraint on development will involve major investments: the World Water Council (2000) estimates that annual investment in water management will have to rise to US$180 billion from the current US$70–80 billion in order to reduce the number of people lacking basic water or sanitation and to increase average calorific intake to a minimum of 2750 calories per day. Increasing food production to meet this target and to accommodate population growth is a critical problem. An oft-quoted figure is that it takes 1000 tonnes of water to produce 1 tonne of wheat, although the actual requirement depends upon amongst other things the potential evapotranspiration rate in the region (Rockstrom *et al.* 1999). In turn, whilst each person uses 7 to 100 tonnes of water in their home for drinking, cooking, washing and other purposes, another 1000 to 2000 tonnes of water is required to grow the food that they eat. It does not matter whether this water is delivered directly as rainfall, indirectly by concentrating the runoff from a wider area through rainfall harvesting, or through irrigation. Thus, whilst the average European uses twice their body weight of water in their home each day, the food that they eat has consumed roughly three tonnes of water. Growth in population and a shift toward higher meat consumption translate directly into a demand for more water.

However, it is not just water that is scarce; so, too, over much of the world is arable land, and most of the rest of the land is already in use as forests, wetlands and grasslands. In China, there is approximately 0.10 hectares of arable land per person so that roughly 2.5 square metres of land must supply enough food to feed one person for a day. A major benefit of irrigation is that more than one crop can be harvested in a year; consequently, irrigation in conjunction with high yield varieties and high inputs can yield 8000 kg/ha (Seckler 2000). Thus, 40% of the world's food is currently produced from the 17% of land that is irrigated.

About 50% of the world's population live partly or wholly in arid or semi-arid lands where not only is average rainfall less than 30 cm but there is wide variability in the amounts from year to year. Consequently, the IWMI (2000) estimates that meeting projected food requirements will require an expansion of 29% in the irrigated area together with an increase in irrigated crop yields from a global average of 3.3 to 4.7 tonnes per hectare. Or, alternatively, irrigated cereal yields will need to increase to 5.8 tonnes per hectare if the irrigated area is not to be expanded. Achieving either will require substantial investment. On a more parochial basis, of the £197 billion modern asset equivalent value of the water and wastewater system in England and Wales, £109 billion is the network of sewers (OFWAT 2002a). This is roughly equivalent to £7000 per household. If climate change results in an increase in the intensity of rainfall from the frequent events, as it is reported to have done in the USA (Hurd *et al.* 1996), then the costs of upgrading the network to cope with increased runoff will amount to a significant fraction of the current asset value.

At the same time, almost any intervention in managing water affects the environment either intentionally or incidentally. Globally, an estimated 20% of freshwater fish species became extinct, threatened or endangered in recent decades (Wood *et al.* 2000). We have, however, only recently realised the dependence of the economy on the environment; notably the functional value of the environment (de Groot 1987), and particularly the importance of wetlands (Pearce and Turner 1990). Constanza *et al.* (1997) sought to estimate the global value of the services provided by the environment on the basis of previously published studies. Whilst not too much attention should be given to the resulting values, since the leaf cannot value the tree, their paper further emphasises the dependency of the economy on the environment. Rivers conveniently transport runoff from those usually inhospitable places where there is high precipitation to those areas where it is most useful for human purposes. In addition, for centuries, rivers provided the best transport routes. Similarly, lakes and groundwater store water until we need it.

In the developed world, much of the current investment is going into undoing the damage caused by past intentional or accidental damage to the environment. The modification of the river Rhine for navigation and other reasons (the Upper Rhine has been shortened by 82 km and the Lower Rhine by 23 km) and the reclamation of the natural flood plains for agricultural purposes have created a number of flood problems. The results of the various works on the Rhine have cut the time taken for the flood peak to travel from Basle to Karlsruhe from 2 days to 1 day and from Basle to Maxau from 64 hours to 23 hours. This has tended to increase the risk that the flood peak on the main stem will coincide with that on the downstream tributaries. The discharge for the 200-year return period flood has also increased from 5000 m^3/sec in 1955 to 5700 m^3/sec in 1977 (Bosenius and Rechenberg 1996).

Much of flood management in Germany today is consequently concerned with removing some of these past modifications to the catchments, the river corridors and the river channel itself and to reducing runoff, recreating storage in the flood plain and in restoring the natural form of the river (Bismuth *et al.* 1998). The Flood Action Plan (International Rhine Commission n.d.) is the archetype of this approach. The same principles are being applied to other rivers in Germany: for example, the planned recreation of some 28 wetlands on the Elbe (BMBF 1995). Similarly, in the Netherlands, both the plans for the river Meuse (de Bruin *et al.* 1987) and for the Rhine (Ministry of Transport, Public Works and Water Management 1996) involve the recreation of wetlands and a degree of river restoration. On smaller scales, river restoration, or 'daylighting' (Pinkham *et al.* 1999), is increasingly common in other countries (Brouwer *et al.* 2001; Riley 1998). In the USA, a number of dams have now been demolished (Pritchard 2001) and the discharge regimes of others are being modified to provide a more natural variation in the flow regime of the river downstream (Acreman *et al.* 1999).

Already in the UK, the costs of collecting and treating wastewater exceed the costs of providing potable water, and the Water Framework Directive (European Parliament 1999) will further increase these costs in Europe. The salts leached from irrigated soils have caused severe problems (Postel 1993), whilst pesticide and fertiliser residues, along with animal manure, are a widespread problem (Nixon 2000; USEPA 2000). Over-abstraction of groundwater has caused major problems in cities as diverse as Mexico City and Bangkok (Briscoe 1993), and some rivers, of which the Yellow River is simply the best known, also run dry because of over-abstraction (English Nature and the Environment Agency 1999).

In short:

- water is critical to social and economic development,
- over much of the world, both arable land and water are scarce,
- managing water is highly capital-intensive, and capital is also scarce; and
- there are environmental consequences to almost any intervention in the water cycle whilst the economy depends upon the environment.

In turn, water management is about seeking to change risks, to alter either the probability of some event or the consequence of that event whether that event be a drought, a flood, or a pulse of pollution. The individual risks may be vanishing close to zero or to one, but in principle the decisions are always about choosing risks. However, since choices are always about the future, we are seeking to choose the future but the one thing that the rational person can be absolutely certain about is that the future is inherently uncertain. So, we are seeking to make choices about risks under conditions of uncertainty. Indeed, I shall argue later that uncertainty is a precondition for a choice to exist.

Achieving sustainable development therefore requires us to make 'better' decisions: to be more successful at avoiding mistakes; to make more efficient use of available resources including water; and to maintain the environment as the necessary support for the economy. But, 'better' decisions are not simply technically better; they have to be socially better as well. We need to be more successful in resolving the multiple and frequently conflicting objectives that we bring to decisions; in particular in regard to equity considerations. These objectives explicitly include a regard to gender equality, not least because women are often the principal sufferers from existing water problems (Mehta n.d.). Moreover their position has often been made worse by past projects (Rathgeber 1996) because they were seen as not having separate interests of their own but simply as part of a household production unit (Haddad *et al.* 1997). The adequate resettlement of those who, given the population density across much of the world, will be displaced by a project is now recognised as a question of justice and as necessarily involving that they will have a voice in the decision process (WCD 2000).

From the Dublin Declaration (ACC/ISGWR 1992) onwards, it has been accepted that public involvement in all levels of decision making is both an objective in itself and also essential if management plans are to be successful. Thus, the Government of New South Wales's (n.d.) guidelines on preparing River, Groundwater and Water Management Plans state that 'Community involvement is critical in identifying potential issues, differing values, opportunities and constraints, and available alternatives at a catchment level.' Similarly, in the UK, the DETR (2000) stated that: 'Public participation in making decisions is vital. It brings benefits in making an individual decision and also for democracy more generally. ... It is also a moral duty. Public authorities work for the public. To do so in a way that the public want and to ensure that they know what the public needs, they must involve the public when they make decisions.'

Adding new objectives and recognising the complexities has made decision making and identification of appropriate options more difficult where the options themselves are more complex. Twenty years ago, designing a flood alleviation scheme was easy: the engineer simply drew a straight line from A to B, built a concrete trapezoidal channel and called it a 'river improvement' scheme. Today, environmentally sensitive solutions can involve sewing together into one integrated system a myriad of small-scale local works.

However, we are of limited intellectual capacity and the decisions that face us threaten to be too complex for us to adequately understand the nature of the choice we must make. In his classic paper, G.A. Miller (1956) reported that experimental studies showed that we could handle no more than seven, plus or minus two, factors at a time. A raft of studies by Tversky and Kahneman (1973, 1981) and others (e.g. Slovic *et al.* 1976) have also shown that our cognitions are affected by all sorts of biases. The purposes of economic analysis are therefore three-fold:

- To simplify the nature of the choice to a level that we can comprehend;
- To enable us to understand the key elements of that choice; and
- To communicate that understanding to all of the stakeholders so as to form a framework in which they can debate, argue and negotiate their concerns.

At the same time, better decisions depend upon better options being created. In the past, there has been a tendency to propose that whatever approach had been adopted in the Netherlands, or for the Mississippi, or for London, should immediately be adopted in Zambia, on the Yangtze and in Buenos Aires. The result has been that the latter countries have been supplied with expensive, inappropriate technologies that fail to work in the local conditions or, in some cases, have created a worse problem than that they were intended to solve. Akuoke-Asibey (1996) describes a rural water supply programme where the investment had effectively to be made three times before a sustainable system emerged; this experience has not been atypical. Many of those heroic projects also had significant, negative consequences, particularly in terms of the environment; the Aral Sea disaster is simply the best known of many failures. So, we have accumulated a history in which there were many projects that failed to deliver what was promised and, when they did, the other unintended or unanticipated impacts of the projects were significant.

However, this past can be painted too bleakly as if the whole history of water management was one of unmitigated failure which self-evidently it has not been. Moreover, we need to remind ourselves that development is not possible without failures; if we only repeat that which has worked in the past, there can be no improvements. If we seek to innovate, there will inevitably be some failures; indeed, we must legitimate failure as a way of learning if we want to innovate. The condition is that the failure should teach us something new and not simply repeat a past lesson. Clare Johnson (2001) paraphrased Al Capone by suggesting that once is a lesson, twice is a failure and thrice is incompetence.

One negative consequence of the history of only partial success has been that some people have sought to preclude some options, particularly dams, from ever being considered. At the same time, the myth of magic bullets has been updated with a new set of bullets, or several sets of bullets. Some of the more promising new options are in danger of being treated uncritically, as if they are always more appropriate than any of the options that have been used in the past. This is precisely the mistake we made in the past. As the World Commission on Dams (WCD 2000) emphasised, we need better ways of making decisions as well as better options.

Better options depend upon the creativity, imagination, experience and skills of designers; here economic analysis cannot help directly. But better options also depend upon the designers' understanding of the nature of the problem and here economics can help because it seeks to clarify what the decision all about, what is the problem and what are our objectives. Better answers often emerge as a result of better questions being asked.

The first and fundamental question that economics keeps asking is: why are we doing this? Again, experience suggests that after a project has been under design and construction for 10–15 years, the primary objective of all involved is to complete it. Again, once it is operational, the project is frequently operated in a particular way because that is what the manual says should be done. The second fundamental question economics asks is: what are the alternatives? There is no point in being against some option unless there exists an option that is in some sense 'better'. Thirdly, it asks: what sacrifices do we have to make for this option? It is a presumption of economics that no choice is painless, that any choice involves a real sacrifice so that if a choice appears painless, it is only because the implications have not been examined. Fourthly, it asks: does it work? Many of the new options proposed as magic bullets turn out only to work in some conditions and to have significant problems. Thus, source control looked superficially to be an attractive way of resolving an urban flooding problem in one city; unfortunately, the city turned out to be so densely developed that implementing source control would involve massive resettlement.

2

What is Economics?

The popular definition of economics is that it is the study of the economy but few dictionaries of economics define the term 'economy' although definitions of subcategories such as market and planned economies usually are given. This absence of a definition shows both that economists do not define economics as the study of the economy and the apparent irrelevance of the economy to economics.

But, if economics is not the study of the economy, then it may be asked what it actually is. John Stuart Mill's (1844) definition of political economy actually came close to defining it in terms of the study of the economy: 'The science which traces the laws of such of the phenomena of society as arise from the combined operations of mankind for the production of wealth, in so far as those phenomena are not modified by the pursuit of any other object.' But later definitions of economics focus on the relationship between means and ends. Thus, Robbins (1935) defined economics as being: 'The science which studies human behaviour as a relationship between ends and scarce means which have alternative uses.' Similarly, Samuelson's (1970) definition is: 'Economics is the study of how men and society end up *choosing*, with or without the use of money, to employ *scarce* productive resources which could have alternative uses, to produce various commodities and distribute them for consumption, now or in the future, among various people and groups in society' (emphases in the original). On the basis of the definitions of Robbins and Samuelson, then the pithiest definition of economics and that which will be used here is: 'The application of reason to choice' (Green and Newsome 1992).

There is a further definition that ought to be mentioned and that is the one given by Hausman (1992): 'Economic phenomena are the consequences of rational choices that are governed by some variant of consumerism and profit maximization. In other words, *economics studies the consequences of rational greed*' (emphasis in the original). This is a somewhat aberrant definition in that the claim that economics is solely concerned with greed was explicitly rejected by Alfred Marshall, perhaps the key figure in the development of the dominant paradigm of economic analysis, neoclassical economics. Marshall (1920) wrote: '... the splendid teachings of Carlyle and Ruskin as to the right aims of human endeavour and wealth would not have been marred by bitter attacks on economics, based upon

Handbook of Water Economics: Principles and Practice. C. Green
© 2003 John Wiley & Sons, Ltd ISBN: 0-471-98571-6

the mistaken belief that science (economics) had no concern with any motive except the selfish desire for wealth, or even that it inculcated a policy of sordid selfishness.'

2.1 Why Do We Have to Choose?

If economics is defined as the application of reason to choice, this simply shifts the burden to defining choice and reason. Conventionally, reason is essentially regarded as a rigorous, logical framework of argument, whether the argument is internal to the individual or made within a group of individuals seeking to determine what common course of action should be adopted. Conventionally, economics follows Russell (1954) in arguing that the application of reason leads to the choice of the best means of achieving some predetermined objectives: '"Reason" has a perfectly clear and precise meaning. It signifies the choice of the right means to an end that you wish to achieve. It has nothing whatever to do with the choice of ends.' Thus, in neoclassical economics it is assumed that the objectives are givens and choices do not involve a choice of objectives. But, the difficulty of some choices lies precisely in that we have to choose between objectives. However, Kant (1785) argued that we should apply reason to determining what our objectives should be, and concluded that reason dictated that our objective should be duty. It seems reasonable therefore to assume that we may use reason to argue as to the objectives that we should seek to achieve. Furthermore although as Simon (1986) observed '... in economics, rationality is viewed in terms of the choices it produces: in the other social sciences, it is viewed in terms of the processes it employs', here I will refer to rationality purely in terms of a logical, rigorous process of argument. The outcomes of that process will only be consistent with each other if nothing changes in the interim: we neither gain new information nor learn anything.

The neoclassical economic model then asserts that choice is necessary because of the scarcity of resources: this is too narrow a definition of conditions that make choice necessary. For example, I have to make a choice to decide which part of a newspaper to read first and parents have to choose what name to give to a baby. Thus, a choice is necessary whenever the alternatives are mutually exclusive; a choice exists when there are two or more options and only one can be chosen. Conversely, if there is only one course of action, then there is no choice to be made. Equally, even if there are alternatives but one option is clearly to be preferred to all the others then effectively the choice has already been made. For a choice to still exist, the alternatives must compete in some way; it must be possible to argue that at least two options should be preferred to all the others but for a decision not yet to have been reached between the two options. For a choice to still exist, there need to be competing reasons that lead to different conclusions as to which option should be preferred. Once the logical argument leads to the conclusion that one option should be preferred to all others, then the choice is made.

The second condition for a choice to exist is that we cannot decide between the alternatives; we are uncertain as to which option should be preferred where we can define uncertainty as 'an inability to differentiate': in this case, in terms of the order of preference across the alternatives. Once we are reasonably confident that one option should be preferred to all others, then the choice is made.

Therefore, the simplest definition of the conditions under which we have to make a choice is:

$$\text{Choice} = \text{Conflict} + \text{Uncertainty}$$

Thus, we only have to make a choice when the available alternatives are mutually exclusive, the adoption of one precluding the adoption of the others, and it is not self-evident which is the best option to adopt. If all the stakeholders in the decisions are both certain and agreed as to which is the best option then only in the most trivial sense is there a choice to make. So choice is a process through which we seek to resolve the conflict and achieve a level of confidence that one option should be preferred to all other available alternatives. It is a rational process in that a rigorous, logical framework of argument is used to decide which option should be adopted.

If this definition of choice is adopted then a number of results follow:

- We may be falsely confident that one option should be preferred to all others;
- Conversely, we may be falsely uncertain as to which option should be preferred to all others; and
- Some choices may be truly marginal in that the reasons for choosing one option over another are exactly counterbalanced by reasons for making the opposite choice. It may, in short, be impossible to resolve the conflict even if we had perfect information.

However, the neoclassical economic model starts with the assumption of perfect information and then relaxes the conditions to allow choice under imperfect information. But, under the definition of choice just given, if there is perfect information there is no choice to make unless the options are all equally attractive. Consequently, to start with the assumption of perfect information is the least appropriate place to begin an analysis of choice. It is extremely unlikely that we will ever have perfect information and the logical starting point is one of uncertainty and how we may seek to reach a state where we can say with some confidence that one option is to be preferred to all others.

Finally, choices are necessarily always prospective: the choice and its consequences lie in the future. In short, we are always trying to choose a future and choices are between hypothetical futures or expectations of the future. We must make choices on the basis of what we expect will be the consequences of those choices and choices are always about what we 'ought' to do in one or both of the two senses of 'ought': that course of action that logically follows from the argument and that which morally should be done (Beyleveld and Brownsword 1994).

In turn, what I chose yesterday has no force in determining what I should choose today; 'is' does not determine 'ought' in either of the two senses of 'ought'. The choices we have made are no more than history and it cannot be argued that what we choose next should be consistent with what we have chosen before. Indeed, to the extent that we learn from the outcomes of the choices we have made in the past, our choices now and in the future will be different. In consequence, past purchasing decisions are ephemera of only historical significance. Whilst choices should logically be influenced by the lessons learnt from past choices, each choice is a new choice that, in principle, must be made anew rather than be dictated by the past. However, routine and habit, simple unthinking repetition of previous choices, are convenient ways of minimising the effort that must be put into making choices although they are treated with some contempt simply because they do not involve any thought, any rational process of choosing.

2.1.1 Conflict

The available alternatives can be mutually exclusive because of a number of reasons and often a combination of these different reasons (Figure 2.1).

2.1.1.1 Functional equivalence

If I am thirsty then I may choose between a cup of coffee or tea; I would be thought somewhat strange if I took a cup of each and even more so if I choose a cup of mixed tea and coffee. In this case, tea and coffee are functional substitutes although I may have a taste preference for one rather than the other

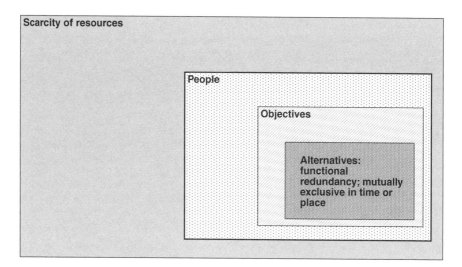

Figure 2.1   *The conflicts that make choice necessary*

at a particular point in time – and a preference that may also depend upon where I am. Similarly, faced with three possible sites from which to pump a given quantity of groundwater, it would be a waste of resources to develop all three.

If the extent to which two or more options are near perfect substitutes for each other is one reason why we can be forced to choose, it is easy then to become confused between different types of substitution. If I ask for a drink and am offered a pair of shoes, I would be surprised. We can distinguish between at least three different possible forms of substitution:

- functional substitutes;
- utility substitutes (the pleasure gained from one is equivalent to the pleasure gained from the other so that having one compensates for the other);
- exchange substitutes (one can be bought or sold for the other).

Thus, whilst I gain utility from both cups of coffee and pairs of shoes and I can sell a pair of shoes to buy a cup of coffee, a pair of shoes is of no use to me when I am thirsty. The danger is, as occurs in some economic analyses, that what starts as an assumption of one form of substitution then subtly glissades into another. In particular, collective choices are typically about functional equivalence, they are specific, e.g. the choice is about whether and how to provide a potable water supply rather than simply about increasing the sum of utility.

The concept of utility substitution is fundamental to neoclassical economic analysis but should not be confused with a lack of differentiation. One pair of shoes quite obviously can provide greater utility than another; Lancaster (1966) argues that a good, such as a pair of shoes, is a bundle of attributes each of which attributes is more or less desirable. In turn, there can be no constraints of the functional form of either the utility function with respect to an attribute, nor on the functional relationship of the utilities for the different attributes, nor as to the rate at which one good can be substituted for another. There is by now a very large literature covering utility theory and its measurement (e.g. Hull *et al.* 1987).

In fact, in making individual choices we can readily accommodate both a lack of functional equivalence for individual goods (e.g. someone will not regard someone else's wedding photographs as being in any way a substitute for photographs of their own wedding) and quite complex utility functions. It is only necessary to make the wider assumptions of universal utility substitution when economists seek to argue that individual choices and markets achieve the optimum.

2.1.1.2 *Space*

One fundamental reason why two options are mutually exclusive is that they cannot exist in the same space; a reservoir and climax forest cannot occupy the same space. Nor can two people sit on the same chair with any comfort. Similarly, I cannot go on holiday to two different places nor can a meadow be used for pasture and planted with a crop of wheat. Again, it is not possible to have a 60 cm diameter and 90 cm diameter water main in the same trench since to place both pipes would be equivalent to having the capacity of a 108 cm diameter pipe.

2.1.1.3 Time

Similarly, the need to choose is often because of the constraints of time; we may be able to afford to rent two videos but cannot watch both of them tonight. Consumption is thus time constrained (Soule 1955) and the extent to which resources can be sacrificed to gain time is extremely limited. Indeed, in Western societies, we might argue that consumption is ultimately constrained more by the availability of time than by income. That there are more things we could do, and would like to do, than there is time to do them. The need to choose whether to visit the National Gallery or Hampstead Heath, for example, arises not because we cannot afford to do both but because we do not have the time to do both.

Most goods are time rivals: the time required for the consumption of one cannot simultaneously be used to consume another. Thus, it is not possible to watch television and weed the garden at the same time. Others are not time-rival goods and may be consumed simultaneously: most activities are apparently compatible with simultaneously listening to music. Equally, some goods are joint-time goods: drinking beer, reading a book and lying on the beach being one possible example.

Goods differ in their time availability. Some, like newspapers and many foods, are ephemeral: these only have a utility if they are consumed within a relatively short timespan. Others are only available for short periods of time; examples include television programmes and hot, sunny days. Yet others, such as landscapes are essentially permanently available although their utility will often vary over time depending upon other variables, notably the weather, the time of day and the mood of the children.

Moreover, only a few goods can be consumed in discontinuous time segments; most require a discrete segment of time. Thus, whilst a newspaper or book can be put down and picked up later, a meal or holiday requires one continuous period of time.

Consequently, one of the major problems faced by the consumer is the time scheduling of consumption. The availability of the good and the time to consume it must be matched: the individual must maximise utility by choosing that good which has the highest value from those available in that time period. Consequently, the opportunity cost of consumption is the utility that would have been gained from the next most desirable consumption within that time period.

Furthermore, the individual's time is already subject to a schedule which is relatively fixed before consumption can be considered. Patterns of sleep cannot be easily changed into amounts or timings in order to take advantage of consumption opportunities. Similarly, the timing of consumption must conventionally be arranged around the timing of work, or school, or in families. Thus, one possible reason for the popularity of video-recorders is that these enable goods which are only available at a single point in time, television programmes and films, to be stored until either time, or the most appropriate time, is available for their consumption.

Few economists have paid any attention to this question although geographers (Carlstein 1982) have been concerned. But as Soule (1955) noted, it is arguable that increasing consumption is constrained primarily by the time available, and by the problems of time-scheduling consumption, rather than by resources. Local recreation is perhaps particularly constrained by time, the decision being which visits to undertake in the time available rather than by income since parks, coasts and rivers typically involve no entrance charge and the resource costs of travel on foot are negligible. Similarly, the resource costs of reading a book, watching the television or listening to the radio or hi-fi are also negligible once the book, television or radio has been bought. The decision of which of these activities to undertake is thus likely to be governed by consideration of what other activity could be undertaken in the same period of time rather than by comparing the resource costs. As Table 2.1 shows, a considerable proportion of a household's time is spent in such activities and on the input side of a household's life, one set of decisions that must be made is between committing the time to the activity (e.g. DIY, cooking) or buying in the service.

Table 2.1 *Household time and expenditure allocation*

| Category of expenditure | Amount per week (£) | | | Time per week (hrs) | |
| | | | | Full-time working | |
	Total	Durables	Flows	Woman	Man
Work				32.50	36.95
Travel to work				4.83	8.23
Breaks				2.90	3.60
Total work				40.23	48.78
Sleep				56.33	56.48
Motoring and bicycles		23.80			
Motoring: spares and accessories		1.70			
Motoring: insurance and taxation, repairs		12.70			
Fuel etc.			17.60		
Fares and other travel costs			9.50		
Total travel		38.20	27.10		
Housing, gross rent		24.90	12.80		
Water			4.20		
Repairs, maintenance and decoration		8.90			
Professional fees		2.20			

(*continued overleaf*)

Table 2.1   *(continued)*

Category of expenditure	Amount per week (£)			Time per week (hrs)	
				Full-time working	
	Total	Durables	Flows	Woman	Man
Other services			3.70		
Fuel, light, power			11.90		
Telephone			8.40		
Total housing services		36.00	41.00		
Meal preparation				5.00	2.15
Food for home consumption			41.40		
Washing up				1.63	2.15
Laundry				2.88	0.13
Tidying				0.98	0.38
Laundry, shoe repairs and dry cleaning			0.70		
Cleaning				2.20	0.20
Total housework		0.00	42.10	12.69	5.01
Clothing			22.00		
Furniture and fittings		26.00			
Operating, maintenance, repairs		3.60			
Kitchen/garden equipment		5.00			
Leather and travel goods, jewellery, watches etc.		2.10			
Shopping				4.90	4.03
Other household/garden				0.83	2.10
Total household durables and consumables		36.70	22.00	5.73	6.13
Eating in the home				5.40	5.13
Personal care			9.40	7.25	5.08
General childcare			2.60	0.95	0.58
Playing/teaching				0.40	0.28
Total personal and childcare		0.00	12.00	14.00	11.07
Greetings cards, stationery, paper goods			2.30		
Leisure goods		19.70			
Watching TV				11.23	18.38
Reading				3.48	1.65
Relaxing				6.83	2.60
Alcohol			15.00		
Tobacco			6.10		
Crafts and knitting/sewing				1.60	1.65
Pets			3.00		
Total home leisure		19.70	26.40	23.14	24.28

Table 2.1 *(continued)*

Category of expenditure	Amount per week (£)			Time per week (hrs)	
				Full-time working	
	Total	Durables	Flows	Woman	Man
Subscriptions			1.10		
Seeing family/friends				9.00	8.00
Sports			0.60	0.48	1.65
Clubs/societies			2.70	3.23	3.58
Pubs				0.23	0.95
Meals out/cinema			20.50	0.58	0.53
Other leisure services including holidays			46.10		
Miscellaneous			7.60		
Other			2.00	2.53	1.95
Total outside leisure		0.00	80.60	16.05	16.66
EXPENDITURE TOTAL	385.70	130.60	251.20		
Savings and defensive expenditures	23.50				
Structural insurance	3.90				
Medicines, prescriptions etc.	4.70				
Total	32.10				
Council tax, domestic rates	11.30				
Income tax	70.40				
National Insurance	18.40				
Savings and investments	10.40				
Repayment of debts	3.10				
TOTAL TAX	113.60				
TOTAL	531.40				

Sources: Anderson *et al.* (1994); National Statistics (n.d.).

Time is equally crucial in production although it was left to operations research rather than economics to identify its importance. Thus, the origin of linear programming lies in time scheduling different tasks between machines so as to maximise profitability (Williams 1967). Time allocation is similarly a critical issue in irrigation management; for a given quantity of water in a reservoir, the varying needs of the crops for water as a function both of the time in their growing cycle and the predicted weather, how much water should be released at what point in time, given that once released it will no longer be available? A similar problem confronts managers of potable water reservoirs; at what time should restrictions on releases and hence cutbacks in supply be announced?

The time and space constraints are linked; the mutual exclusivity in space constraint can be relaxed if we allow the same space to be occupied at different times or we can occupy different spaces at different times. Whilst famously we cannot be in two places at the same time, we can be in two places at different times: I can go on holiday to two different places at different times. This is, however, to assume that the two different times are perfect substitutes for each other. Frequently they are not: next year's labour is often no substitute for the same quantity of labour now unless, for example, it does not matter whether the scheme is constructed this year or next year. Equally obviously, time is not reversible.

Hence, an issue is the extent to which there is path dependency over time in the occupation of space; who occupies a chair at this moment in time has no necessary effect on who can occupy that chair in a subsequent moment in time. Similarly, the use of a field for pasture this year does not affect its potential use for growing wheat next year; conversely, the conversion of the meadow from pasture to wheat means that it will take longer to convert that field back to pasture and particularly to a meadow. Equally, maintaining an area as a climax forest does not prevent its conversion to a reservoir at some future date; conversely, once the area is converted to a reservoir, it will take between 100 and 1000 years before it can be re-established as a climax forest, depending upon the predominant species of trees.

If there can be a question as to the extent to which one future time is substitutable for another, the degree to which one point or area of space is substitutable by another can also be important. The extent to which they are substitutable depends in part on the activity concerned; a mountainside at 6000 metres is not realistically a substitute for a flood plain for growing arable crops. Soil, topography, microclimate and the availability of water are all characteristics that can determine the suitability of an area or point of land for a particular purpose. Moreover, location, the relationship of that area of land to other activities is also usually important; estate agents often claim that location is the primary determinant of house prices. These are self-evident points but it is not unknown for policies to be proposed that implicitly assume that there are near perfect substitutes for particular areas of land. For example, that habitats could be re-established elsewhere or that development should not be allowed on flood plain land but forced to take place elsewhere. Similarly, in the case of the climax forest and the reservoir, there may be nowhere else a climax forest could develop, even given sufficient time to elapse. Again, the assumption that in response to climate change, ecosystems can simply move or be moved uphill and towards the polar regions assumes that the soil and other conditions are similar there to those in the areas where the ecosystem is currently established.

A key characteristic of the precautionary principle (O'Riordan and Cameron 1994) is then to keep open as many futures as possible to avoid making choices that create path dependency.

2.1.1.4 Objectives

Russell's (1954) assertion that the use of reason is limited to the choice of means to some ends assumes that our objectives are givens, perhaps through religious authority, or have been determined before and outside of any choice as to ends. Thus, that there can be a complete separation of the discussions of means and of ends: that we can determine what we should do prior to and in the absence of any knowledge of what we can do. Moreover, either that there are no possible conflicts between the choice of action that each of our objectives should cause us to adopt, or that any such conflicts have already been resolved prior to any choice actually being confronted.

However, sometimes the objectives we bring to a choice are mutually exclusive; achievement of any one objective necessarily means that we have to sacrifice the achievement of another. Thus, Sen (1992) has argued that the problem with equality is that one form of equality can only be achieved by sacrificing another form of equality. Alternatively, there may simply be no available option that is superior to all others against all of our objectives although in principle there could be such an option. Choices that self-evidently involve a conflict of objectives are the most difficult which we face: the agony of the judges asked to decide in the case of conjoined twins was self-evident, given the choice between an operation to separate the twins that would necessarily result in the death of one and not operating and the strong probability that both would die.

2.1.1.5 People

Once more than one person is involved or affected by a decision then potentially there is a conflict between those people as to which option should be chosen. At the simplest level, the balance of gains and losses to each person is unlikely to be identical for each person; we differ in our preferences not least as a function of age, physical, cultural (Schwartz and Thompson 1990) and psychological differences (Seligman *et al*. 1994). Since choices are about the future then a key question is: how is the future created, how does the world work? The diagram adopted by cultural theorists (Schwartz and Thompson 1990) is insightful: differences in the views as to how to choose the future between groups are described as a reflection of their fundamental views as to whether the world is inherently stable, inherently unstable, or locally stable. At the one extreme lie the 'contrarians' who believe that it will always turn out all right in the end and hence there is no need to worry since if technology creates problems, technology will then solve those problems.

People may equally disagree as to the likelihoods of the potential outcomes of each option and differ in the degree to which they are risk averse or risk seeking; what is an acceptable risk to one person may be quite unacceptable to another. Hull *et al*. (1987), for example, observed that managers from the oil industry found 50–50 gambles implausible because they never experienced as good odds as those. Conversely, managers from other industries considered that the odds that oil industry managers face every day were quite unacceptable.

Nor is there likely to be an option that is a Pareto optimum (Pearce and Turner 1990) in that it leaves all people at least as well off as they were before and nobody worse off. But more importantly, we may disagree as to the objectives that we ought to pursue in making the choice. Since choices are always about the future, we always have to decide what we ought to do, and the logical 'ought' and the moral 'ought' are frequently bound together. Collective choices are then seldom solely between different means to an agreed end but involve arguments about what ought to be the ends we seek to achieve. However, choices are usually between different means and it has been observed that what is important is to decide upon the means. Thus, it is possible for agreement to be reached on the means even when we continue to disagree on the ends to be pursued. Spending too much time debating the ends can be counter-productive, simply establishing that we disagree about these, when it may be possible to reach agreement as to what to do.

2.1.1.6 Resources

Mutual exclusivity in time or place and conflicting objectives are internal constraints to choices in project appraisal. They force the choice between the available options; even if infinite resources were available, it will not be possible for a reservoir and a climax forest to occupy the same space. Similarly, even if I had an infinite income, I still could not go to the theatre and the cinema at the same time. In collective decisions in particular, resource scarcity is an external constraint: it may be possible to determine the best option in each of a number of different choices but resource scarcities preclude us from adopting all of those best options. For example, if there were to be universal agreement both that education policy A is preferable to education policy B and also that health care policy M is preferable to health care policy N, resource constraints might still limit us to choosing between the combinations of A plus N or B plus M. However, the choice between A or B and M or N is almost certainly about conflicts between the objectives we want to achieve and disagreements between people as to what importance should be attached to achieving each objective. Thus, these choices would remain even if we had infinite resources.

In choices about project prioritisation, programmes or policies, it is this resource scarcity which forces the choice; nothing precludes the provision, for example, of potable water supplies to all villages in an area except the scarcity of some resource where that resource might be money or the availability of skilled technicians.

2.1.1.7 The nature of value

In everyday language, if we ask someone what are their values, there is usually a long pause and then they say something about justice, democracy or religion:

in common parlance, values refer to ends (Boulding and Lundstedt 1988). But economics uses value in different senses and it is possible to distinguish between two different bases for value:

1. Value in itself, and
2. Instrumental value.

Adam Smith, for example, adopted the first approach by using a cost of production theory of value and Ricardo, as did Marx, developed a labour theory of value: the value of a good is given by the cost of producing that good. On the other hand, neoclassical economics is associated with the instrumental theory of value: the value of something is its contribution to the achievement of some objective. In the case of neoclassical economics, this objective is the maximisation of the individual's utility so economic value is subjective and, importantly, a good can have a value without having a price. Indeed, in economic analysis money is simply used as a yardstick or numeraire by which to assess the relative values of different actions.

The neoclassical economics definition of value in instrumental terms has two major implications:

• It is actions rather than things that have value; and
• An action necessarily has as many values as objectives are brought to that choice of action.

First of all, it is implied that it is actions that have value rather than the thing involved in the action itself. Thus, wearing a hat has values relating to keeping off the rain, keeping my head warm, keeping my bald patch from being sunburnt, and so forth. Similarly, eating food assuages hunger and gives pleasure; and it is watching television that has a value: the value of a television is given by the expectations of the programmes it will then be possible to watch. The value of things, such as hats, food and a television, is then an imputed value based on the expectation of the actions that can be undertaken with it in the future. It is a function of the likelihood of different actions being undertaken and the contribution of each action to the achievement of each objective. The thing itself has no value outside of expectations of future actions in which it can be used.

These actions are all necessarily in the future although the relevant future may be very short-term; an ice cream is usually bought with the expectation of eating it immediately whereas a bottle of wine may be bought to lay down for many years. Thus, it is possible to talk about the value of a 'thing' only in terms of the potentiality for action associated with that thing, a form of expected value.

Secondly, since value is defined in instrumental terms, an action has as many instrumental values as are the objectives engaged by that choice of action. Hence it is not possible to argue that an action only has an economic value unless economic value is defined so widely as to cover all possible objectives. Even then, only once those objectives are completely ordered hierarchically can an action be taken as having a single value. The neoclassical economics definition of economic value, as the contribution of some action to maximising the individual's utility, is then either one possible value, or utility must be expanded to include all of the individual's objectives. In addition, the neoclassical economic definition of value obviously means that value is subjective: value lies in the eye of the beholder. The neoclassical model also requires the assumption to be made that an individual has developed a utility function which defines how all possible acts of consumption will contribute to this overarching objective of utility and has done so in advance of making any actual choice.

Because the value of a thing is imputed by the individual's expectations of the actions that can be undertaken with it or for which it is necessary, quite clearly the imputed value of that thing can vary markedly between individuals and the market in turn may be highly segmented. Thus, to a vegetarian a beefburger will have no value at all except in so far, for example, in that it can be used to keep a fractious niece happy.

If an action has as many values as objectives are brought to a decision, then a critical question is: which objectives are engaged by the decision? In neoclassical economics, it is assumed that the individual and individuals define the objectives and, conveniently, each have predefined a completely ordered utility function. In turn, in neoclassical economic analysis, in collective choices, the only objective considered is some aggregate of individual utilities where the potential Pareto improvement, or Hicks–Kaldor compensation principle, is conventionally taken to be the appropriate aggregation function. It is usual to make some reference to equity (in the relatively trivial sense of income distribution) but equity is not considered to be an objective to be considered in making the collective choice. But the problem even with recognising equity is that it raises the question: where does this objective come from? In neoclassical economics it is assumed that value is given solely by the individual, it measures individual preference, the contribution of that action to the individual's utility function. For equity to be accepted as an objective in collective choices, it is then necessary to ask why the individual should bring equity to a choice outside of his or her utility function. By treating equity as a separate objective, it has been assumed that it does not form part of the individual's utility function, that the individual's utility function does not include some form of altruism, nor that the individual experiences a duty with respect to other people. If the individual's utility function does include altruism or normative components, then neoclassical economic theory dictates that such elements should be considered in collective choices except in so far as to do so would involve double-counting.

In practice, two different issues are involved. Firstly, the assumption that values are solely given by individual preference is itself a moral claim that can be disputed and which cannot be treated as axiomatic. In particular, Islam (Khalid and O'Brien 1992) is centred around duties to other people and other species and so the economic question is what ought we to do rather than what do we want to do? Again, deep ecologists (e.g. Naess 1993) argued that other species have an inherent value by right of existence. More widely, deep ecologists are asserting that some thing can have a value in itself; they only differ from the classical economists in their conclusion as to the basis through which that value is derived. It would also seem that some other things may have a value in themselves: some people collect the teeth of their children or their first shoe, whilst many people build up collections of photographs. Whilst the act of collecting the tooth or shoe or of taking a photograph may be argued to have an instrumental value, once acquired, that tooth, shoe or photograph would seem to have a value in itself. So, similarly does a grave. The potential problem with things that have a value in themselves is that they are not then substitutable by anything else either in functional terms or in utility terms.

Secondly, whilst the individual can have objectives in isolation, in any community a second set of objectives has to be created that refers to relations between individuals. Thus, children are commonly taught not to be greedy, to share their toys, not to fight, to be polite and other principles that define relationships between individuals. So, for example, equity is explicitly about the relationships between individuals; it refers either to what ought to be the relationships between individuals or to what relationships are necessary if the community is to be maintained. In general, these objectives concerning relationships between individuals can have very little scope for expression in individual choices concerning the consumption of priced goods, except in so far, for example, as the individual has a choice to buy Fair Trade coffee or tea as opposed to coffee or tea produced through conventional trading channels. But in collective choices, these objectives can be central, as can the argument as to the trade-off that ought to be made between these objectives and also between these objectives and individual preference. Collective choice is inherently about what ought to be the weight we give to different objectives, including those with regard to the relationships between individuals, in the choice in question.

This conflict can exist even when these objectives and the relationships between them are taken to be predefined prior to any actual choice (Section 2.1.1.4). In turn, neoclassical economics seeks to avoid discussion of these issues by implicitly assuming that there are natural laws (Beyleveld and Brownsword 1994) that govern these relationships. Thus, it is conventional to refer to property rights instead of relationships between individuals, assuming that some entitlements and obligations necessarily follow from the possession or use of some property. However, if public involvement in decision making is a principle accepted as a defining basis for the sustainable management of water (ACC/ISGWR 1992), then the objectives we bring to a decision and the trade-offs we make between them, are necessarily socially constructed out of the dialogue, argument and negotiation that makes up that process of public involvement.

Where does this leave economics and the way in which economic analysis can usefully be undertaken? To sum up, I have argued here and earlier that:

- It is actions that have value and that goods have only imputed values except for a probably limited class of goods that have a value in themselves.
- Because actions can contribute to the achievement of multiple objectives, any action can consequently have multiple values.
- The achievement of an objective can have resource implications without that objective being a component of economic efficiency (Section 2.1.1.6).
- Equity is relative rather than absolute (Section 2.1.1.7).
- Two important reasons why choices have to be made are that our objectives are in conflict or because we disagree about what weight should be given to those objectives (Section 2.1.1.4).
- In turn, choices often are about what we ought to do rather than simply about what individuals want to do.
- Thus, values in collective choices emerge from the process of social negotiation rather than being predefined.

These arguments should not be seen as destroying the basis of economics since to make such a claim would be to argue that reason has nothing to contribute to choice. What they do imply is about the nature and purpose of economics. The rationale for economics is then to inform the social dialogue and to provide a framework for that dialogue; economics cannot be mechanistic and optimising but must instead provide a transparent and rigorous framework of analysis that focuses upon the reasons why we must make any particular choice and the implications of adopting each of the different courses of action open to us. The emphasis must be upon creating an understanding of the nature of the choice.

Nor does it mean that we should abandon numbers where they are useful; they are a useful means of simplifying that which would otherwise be too complex to comprehend. In turn, it is the understanding about the nature of the choice that gives meaning to numbers: what was too complex should be reduced to the self-evident, it being the process of analysis rather than the number which is important. At present, too often, the derivation of a number seems to result instead in the end of thought. The test of economics is thus what we learn about the nature of the particular choice we must make.

2.1.2 Uncertainty

Water management is about changing risks (Section 2.1.3), where we commonly have a great deal of uncertainty concerning the magnitude of those risks. In turn, risk and uncertainty are two different concepts. Uncertainty is an inability to differentiate between a range, continuous or discrete, of different possibilities. Although risk and uncertainty appear similar in nature, uncertainty is fundamentally different from risk; the opposite of uncertainty is information which is formally defined as that which destroys uncertainty (MacKay 1969).

The simplest example of uncertainty is when we are asked to call 'heads' or 'tails' when a coin is tossed. We can define the risks when tossing a fair coin exactly; the probabilities of a head or tails are both equal to 0.50. In consequence, a fair coin is defined as one where there is uncertainty as to what course of action to adopt: there is no rational basis for calling heads or tails. Thus, the coin is fair precisely because there is no rational basis for calling heads or tails. We are and should be uncertain what to do precisely because the risks are known exactly: we should be rationally uncertain. The only uncertainty about the risk is then whether the coin is fair. If we can be confident that the coin is biased, then we can eliminate the uncertainty as to whether to call heads or tails: as soon as we can be confident that the probability of throwing a head is at least 0.5001, we know what to do. Similarly, if the outcome of throwing heads is to lose £100 000 and the outcome of throwing tails is to lose £1, we should also always call tails even if the coin is fair. If we can remove uncertainty either as to the probability or the outcome, we remove uncertainty about what to do. Therefore, the crucial issue is whether the decision maker should rationally be uncertain rather than whether the world is uncertain.

We can define a decision maker who is uncertain, after Green, Nicholls and Johnson (2000), as being in 'a state of doubt as to what to do'. When they are in such a state, we can call this 'decision uncertainty'; the decision maker is unable to differentiate between the options in terms of a preference between those options. In turn, a decision maker can be rationally uncertain for two different reasons:

- They don't know, or
- They cannot decide.

We may be uncertain because we are uncertain about the state of the world now and in the future, or because we cannot resolve the conflict that is the reason that the choice has to be made. This 'uncertainty in the world' is inherent, only a god being able to have perfect information. Because uncertainty in the world is a universal problem when taking decisions, it is decision uncertainty that is more important.

However, even perfect information about the future would not mean that the decision maker would necessarily cease to be uncertain. When someone says that they can't decide between ordering the steak or the salmon, it is because they cannot decide what they would like most rather than a lack of knowledge about the steak and the salmon. Similarly, it is rational to be uncertain when the arguments for each of two options are equally balanced. Clearly, whilst uncertainty about the state of the world now and in the future can be a cause of decision uncertainty, the fundamental question is whether the decision maker ought to be uncertain which course of action to adopt. Not infrequently we can be very uncertain about the world without this uncertainty implying that we ought to be uncertain as to what to do.

2.1.2.1 Uncertainty in the world

Choices are always about selecting a future; the only difference between choices is how immediate is this future. When I am deciding whether or not to watch a particular television programme, I am dealing with an immediate future although that choice may also have implications for a longer term future. For example, I have now watched the penultimate episode of one television series in three different countries but seen the final episode in none. Had I known that this would happen, it might have influenced my decision as to whether to start watching the series.

To predict the future, we need to know both the relevant state of the world now and also the causal processes that are operating. However, often we are uncertain about the state of the world now. There are usually measurement errors, or parametric uncertainty (Blockley 1980); what Penning-Rowsell *et al.* (1992) described as 'what we know we don't know'. In addition, there is the possibility that the model which we are using to measure the state of the world now is itself either incomplete or simply wrong. Blockley (1980) termed this 'systemic' uncertainty and in Penning-Rowsell *et al.* (1992) is described as 'what we don't know that we don't know'.

Thus, typically, the length of a streamflow gauging record for a stretch of water course will be much shorter than the return period of the drought or flood whose severity it is intended to predict. Estimates of the flood or drought flows are then estimated by applying some statistical distribution to the data. If the distribution function is inappropriate, then so will the estimate of the magnitude of the flow for that return period. Thus, as described in Chapter 22, the original estimate of the probable maximum flood (PMF) for the Macchu II dam was out by a factor of five. Similarly, Moench *et al.* (2001) sought to establish whether groundwater levels were declining on a worldwide basis but discovered that there is inadequate data on present and past levels of groundwater to be able to draw any conclusions.

Nor are we likely to be certain that we understand all of the processes and interactions involved in the system; for this reason, Holling (1978) argued for the adoption of an adaptive management approach. Given that there is uncertainty about the present and also about the processes, it follows that we have to be uncertain about the future state of the world. As Lord Keynes remarked: 'all prediction is difficult, predicting the future is particularly difficult.' In turn, if predicting the future is difficult then the approach developed by Holling and others (Gunderson 1999; Walters 1986) is to argue that we should instead recognise that the one thing about which the rational individual can be certain is that the future is uncertain. This being so, then the issues are then:

- How should we choose when we know that we are uncertain? And
- Knowing that we are uncertain, what options should we choose?

2.1.2.2 Change

Because water management is capital intensive, and hence adaptation is slow, water resource projects have to be based on expectations about the medium-term future. Our expectations about that future then depend both upon our incomplete knowledge of the present and our equally incomplete understanding of the causal processes that create change. The greater the rate at which change is occurring and will occur, the more critical the understanding of the causal processes involved.

If change is occurring or is predicted to occur, then there are three questions:

- Do we understand the causal processes involved that both create the change and determine responses to that change?
- Does understanding necessarily imply the ability to predict change? And
- Does that understanding imply only quantitative changes will occur?

Typically, the future is simply predicted to be the same as yesterday only bigger: for example, when a trend series analysis of water demand is used to predict the demand for water in 20 years' time. The basic assumption is that change is continuous but well-behaved so that, in principle, we could be pretty certain about the future. But, these methods are not based on any causal model of the nature of the change; they are strictly descriptive models of the present extended into the future (Section 14.5). Hence, a causal model should be expected to perform better. But, the background to the development of the concept of adaptive management in ecology (Holling 1978) is that we do not understand the causal mechanisms in some instances and if we do not understand them, we cannot predict the outcome with any reliability.

Secondly, a change may necessarily mean that the future must be different from the past and equally, in some cases, these changes will be very large indeed. For example, in an economy growing at 7% per annum, a rate that has been typical of the tiger economies of Asia, the economy will be seven times as large as it is now in 30 years' time. Since it is impossible to scale up the inputs to the economy by a factor of seven, the structure and nature of the future economy in those countries will necessarily be radically different to that which exists now. Rather than quantitative change, a qualitative change will necessarily have to occur.

It is qualitative changes that are the most important. The driver for the development of adaptive management in ecology was the recognition that ecological systems may have more than one stability zone and a change may cause a leap from one zone to another (Gunderson 1999). At the extreme, the term 'surprise' has been introduced (Brooks 1986; Gunderson *et al.* 1995) to refer to that which was not or could not be foreseen in advance so that when such an event does occur, the initial response is incredulity. It is the nature of surprises that as soon as an example can be worded, then that example is foreseen and it ceases to be a surprise. So a surprise is not a low probability event, it is one for which there was no prior probability at all since it was not foreseen because our models are incomplete or false. The ozone hole was such a surprise and therefore it was necessarily discovered by accident.

Finally, the very purpose of choice is to choose the future and thus to take action to change the future. So, for example, a reason for introducing charges for wastewater is to induce technological innovation that will result in lower treatment costs. In turn, other people's attempts also to choose the future increase the uncertainties and affect the likelihood that we will be successful in our attempt to choose the future. By our collective actions, we change the future and so to predict the future reliably, we need to know both what everyone else is doing now and what they will do in the future. In turn, the only rational conclusion that can be drawn is that the future is inherently uncertain: we do not and cannot know the future.

2.1.2.3 *Uncertainty in the mind*

Uncertainty and risk are two different things; when we toss a coin, we can define the probabilities of a heads and a tails being thrown, but, as already noted, it is because there is no rational reason for expecting one outcome rather than the other that defines the coin as being fair.

Decision uncertainty exists to the extent to which it is not possible to have a preference between the different courses of action that are open to the decision makers. Since it is only possible to adopt a single course of action, decision uncertainty only exists to the extent to which it is not possible to clearly determine a rank order of preference across the two best options. We can be very uncertain about the order of preference across the remaining options but if we are able to be confident that the two best options are preferable to all other options, our uncertainty between the remaining options is irrelevant.

What is important is whether or not the decision makers ought to be uncertain as to which course of action to adopt out of those known to them. The decision makers may rationally be uncertain if all of the alternatives are equally attractive or unattractive, or if the 'best' alternative depends upon the very uncertain state of the future world. Conversely, they may be irrationally certain, often because they have arbitrarily excluded some options or some objectives from consideration. They may also be irrationally uncertain: they are unable to make up their minds as to which is the best option, often because the choice is so complex that it is difficult to see through the complexity to the core of the decision. One of the primary purposes of economic analysis is then to reduce this irrational uncertainty.

Choices are always about the future and there are two quite different paradigms in an uncertain future (Box 2.1). The first, the car journey analogy, treats uncertainty as essentially degenerate risk; uncertainty can then be reduced to risk through collecting further information and undertaking further research. Uncertainty is treated as if it solely derives from parametric uncertainty, and the means

---

Box 2.1 Managing under Uncertainty: Two World Views

There are two models of decision making under risk and uncertainties. Each defines the problem in entirely different ways of thinking and recommends different strategies for dealing with the risks and uncertainties.

The first model is analogous to a car journey to a known destination using a good, detailed map. Firstly, you plan the journey from beginning to end. After you set out, you keep track of your position on the map and use the road signs to confirm which turnings to make as each junction is reached. If you take a wrong turning, the map and road signs will sooner or later indicate this to you, and you can plan a new route to reach your destination. In other words, the journey can only follow a finite number of predetermined choices.

The second model takes a sea voyage of discovery (e.g. Magellan or Captain Cook) as the parallel. There are no maps because the oceans have neither been mapped nor have any features to be mapped and the final destination is vague and uncertain. Instead, a clock and sights are used to determine the ship's present location and from that the course is plotted. The helmsman is then ordered to follow a particular compass heading, and makes constant small adjustments as currents, waves and wind force the ship off course. At fixed intervals, the actual position of the ship is recalculated from sun and stars, and a new course plotted allowing for the actual position. Head winds will mean that it is sometimes impossible to sail directly in the intended direction and discoveries of land will result in the intended direction being changed in order to investigate that land and to restock with water. A lookout is required to watch out for land, rocks and other dangers, and a leaded line is used when it is thought that the ship is entering shallow waters.

Source: Green et al. *2000.*

---

recommended (Greeley-Polhemus Group 1992) to take account in decision making of that uncertainty that cannot be removed through more information and further research is based upon Monte Carlo simulations. Probability distributions are assumed for the key variables, and ideally the interdependencies of the key variables are taken in account. In the case of benefit–cost analysis, the result of the Monte Carlo simulation is to generate a probability density function for the benefit–cost ratio. The drawbacks of this approach are firstly that it treats decision uncertainty as arising solely from uncertainty in the world. Secondly, that it is necessary to make assumptions about the nature of the probability density functions (Haas 1997) and the interdependencies between the uncertainties associated with each parameter. However, if I am uncertain about the expected value of a parameter, I am even more uncertain about the functional form of the probability density function and the standard deviation of that function. Thirdly, it excludes systemic uncertainty. The results of applying this approach are usually two-fold; most importantly the analyst can be left with an irrational state of certainty about uncertainty. In addition, the outcome is likely to be that the benefit–cost ratio lies somewhere between a small number and a large number which is pretty much what we knew in the first place.

The alternative paradigm, that developed by Holling (1978) and others (Walters 1986), asks what do we do when we know that we are uncertain, that uncertainty is inherent to decision making and the largest uncertainties are in terms of systemic uncertainties? This is the Captain Cook analogy (Box 2.1). Adaptive management (Holling 1978) closely parallels the Captain Cook analogy by working on the basis that we should keep track of where we want to go but the most important objective is to avoid being wrecked upon an uncharted shoal or reef. Equally, we can expect to be blown off course at different times.

These two visions of uncertainty are part of wider different paradigms. In one world view, the future is knowable but with confidence limits; and systems are regarded as generally linear, homeostatic and optimising, the world is seen as a clock. Neoclassical economics clearly has this view of the world but then so too do many other disciplines. In many ways it is equivalent to the view of physicists prior to the development of quantum theory. The second view tends to view systems are complex, nonlinear and chaotic in nature, neither having a single stability domain nor being homeostatic. As a nonlinear system, they are liable to make sudden transitions from one stability zone to another, a behaviour sometimes characterised in terms of catastrophe theory (Woodcock and Davis 1978), and now usually known as chaos theory (Stewart 1990). Chaos theory in turn can be seen as simply one aspect of discovery of the necessary indeterminacy of the world of which other manifestations are Gödel's theorem as to necessary incompleteness of axiomatic systems (Hofstadter 1980), and Heisenberg's uncertainty principle in quantum physics (Barrow 1999). Smithson (1985) delightfully labels the overarching concept that includes uncertainty as 'ignorance'. All this is well away from the clockwork world of conventional economics (Ormerod 1994) where optimisation and homeostasis, and hence stability, are assumed to be natural.

Adopting the Captain Cook model, then there are a number of implications for both the way in which we logically should make choice and as to the nature of the options that we should then adopt. The emphasis is on decision uncertainty and not uncertainty in the world since the latter is part of the very stuff of decision making. It directs attention to managing the entire range of possible events.

The implications for the way in which we make decisions are:

- To forget optimality: optimality requires that we know everything important and know it both accurately and precisely; since we know neither, pursuing optimality is illogical.
- Instead, we need to consider how the different options will fail and the consequences of failure.
- We need to undertake sensitivity analyses at the beginning of what should be an iterative, learning process of design and decision making. The purpose of the sensitivity analysis is to identify the critical variables that influence which options should be adopted. It is these variables upon which we should

concentrate our efforts to refine the remainder of the design and decision process. In general, the critical parameters are those concerning high frequency events that occur early in the life of the project. For example, the duration of the construction period can be more important than the capital cost because no benefits will come on-stream until the project is substantially completed.

- At the end of the project, we should carry out a robustness analysis (Penning-Rowsell *et al.* 1992); to determine whether the values of the critical parameters influence the rank order of preference across the options. Does our necessary uncertainty about the world mean that we should be uncertain as to what to do?
- The precautionary principle should be applied in the sense that we should be adverse to creating path-dependent futures, when the possible rate of adaptation will necessarily be slower than the rate of change or where the change will be catastrophic.
- Interventions have to be treated as experiments (Holling 1978) through which we hope to learn more about the systems in which we are intervening. In turn, this means that the making of mistakes by institutions has to be legitimated; if nothing new is tried then we will not learn anything. But if we try new things, some will inevitably not be successful. Equally, the only way in which we could avoid making mistakes is if we had perfect information about the future and this is precisely what we do not have and cannot have. Thus, mistakes must be accepted provided that they teach us something new rather than the action being a repeat of an error that we had made previously.

In turn, the options that we should choose will often be characterised by one or more of the following features:

- When they fail, they will do so slowly and relatively benignly without failure occurring either suddenly or being catastrophic when it occurs.
- The option will be either robust, that is, it can cope with conditions outside of its designed range, or resilient (Gunderson 1999; Holling 1973; Ludwig *et al.* 1997) where resilience involves the capacity to be adjusted to changes in conditions. Concrete is, for example, robust whilst rubber is resilient. What we cannot have is an option that is both robust and resilient; this is equivalent to asking for rubber concrete. Equally, we cannot guarantee that there will be any option that is either robust or resilient.

2.1.3 Risk

'Risk' is commonly used in a number of different meanings: as a synonym for probability, as one for expected value (probability times outcome), or to refer to potentially harmful events of different kinds. Since a risk is always a 'risk of', this mixed usage is almost inevitable, although 'risk' is only used in relation to undesirable events. Thus, whilst we may refer to a risk that it will rain, we do not talk of a risk that it will be sunny.

The purpose of almost all water projects is to change either the probabilities of some events or the consequences of those events. For example, a benefit–cost analysis of two maintenance regimes for sewers or water mains is likely to include one involving replacement or renovation prior to failure and an alternative of replacement on failure, the costs of each regime being compared to the risks of failure. A wastewater treatment programme will reduce the probability that an event will occur which will have temporary or long-term impacts on the receiving water. These probabilities will seldom if ever change from one to zero, so the analysis will necessarily require a basic understanding of probability theory in the form of reliability engineering (Kaufmann 1972) including the concepts of event and fault trees (Watson 1989; Clark and Tyrer 1987). Moreover, these probabilities are likely to change over time as existing structures decay or conditions change: for example, as the catchment is developed or climate changes occurs.

In many cases, however, the only source of the estimated probabilities of the different outcomes will be engineering judgement; statistical data is often not available. For example, whilst there are several hundred thousand kilometres of flood embankments worldwide, and theoretically (Wolff 1997) it is quite straightforward to predict the likelihood that a dike will fail before it is overtopped as a function of ground and foundation conditions, together with the structure of the dike itself, there is virtually no data with which to estimate the probability that any particular dike will fail. Similarly, when a tunnel is being proposed as part of a project, a critical parameter in determining the costs can be the probabilities that the works will overrun either or both time and budget. Again, whilst the theory is not complex (Isaksson 1998), there is an absence of statistical data with which to apply that theory (Isaksson 2001). In general, water management has traditionally been undertaken with the minimum amount of data; estimates of leakage from water mains are often given as the difference between what it is guessed is put into supply less the amount that it is guessed is consumed. Similarly, flows in sewers and particularly estimates of the surface water runoff are seldom available. What data that is available is often inaccurate; for example, water meters are prone to underestimate water usage and meters measuring flows in water mains may be accurate to $\pm 10\%$. Again whilst an appraisal of the benefits of replacing or renovating a sewer system or water mains will require an assessment of the likelihood and consequences of the failure of both the existing system and the proposed system, methods of assessing the probability of failure (Green *et al.* 1989a) give qualitative rather than quantitative results. In turn, collecting data is expensive so that a question that may need to be addressed is: what is the value of collecting data? (Chapter 22).

The situation is usually somewhat better with regards to hydrology; there is usually some data as to rainfall or streamflows or regional models (NERC 1975) that can be applied to the river in question. However, when predicting future flows, the conventional approach has been to assume that the future is an extension of the past. Thus, the usual method of predicting the flow with a probability of occurrence of 0.01 per year is to take the available length of record of stream-flow gauging, fit one or another probability function to that frequency count and use that probability function to estimate the magnitude of the flow with a probability of 0.01. Two obvious potential problems are then as to which probability function should be fitted to the data and the length of record that is available. However, more especially this approach involves assuming that there have been no changes over time and hence the complete historical record can be used to estimate the risk now and in the future. In addition, it involves estimating the probability of the flow rather than of the events that could give rise to that flow. For example, floods are the result of a combination of the precipitation event and the antecedent conditions, and the consequences of the precipitation event may themselves depend upon the pattern of movement of the precipitation event. Thus, the consequences of a rain front moving down a river can be different from those of a front that moves up the catchment: movement in one direction or the other is likely to increase the risk that the flood peaks from the tributaries and main stem coincide.

In the case of floods, dynamic simulation methods of calculating the probabilities of flooding are being developed that take account of antecedent conditions (Calver 2001): if the soil is already saturated as a result of previous rainfall, a greater proportion of rainfall will run off than if the soil is relatively dry. More generally, even if it cannot be applied in detail, a dynamic approach should be adopted where it is sought explicitly to identify changes over time in probabilities. Rather than the natural state being one of stasis, it is preferable to assume that the natural state is one of change and rather than talking in terms of 'risk' it may be more helpful to speak of managing 'variability', change over time. We can then identify three different patterns of change over time:

- Cyclical: the seasonal cycle is an obvious one but other longer period cycles may also be present (e.g. as a result of El Niño).
- Trend: changes in precipitation, runoff or flows may be occurring either because of climate change or changes to the catchment.
- Random: the problem with apparently random changes is that such changes can be generated through the operation of causal but nonlinear systems. Systems exhibiting chaotic behaviour are often defined by quite simple functional forms but their behaviour at least superficially appears to be random (Gleick 1987).

The obvious difficulty is that if the length of record is insufficient to enable good predictions to be made assuming no changes over time, it is unlikely to be adequate to identify any changes over time. It is likely therefore to be necessary to see whether there are any indications that critical parameters have changed or to ask local residents whether they believe that there have been such changes.

Not only is most of water management about changing the probabilities or outcomes of events, it is also generally about buffering systems of concern to humans from perturbations arising from climatic or other factors. The whole purpose of water resource management is thus generally to reduce the risk that seasonal and other variations in rainfall seriously reduce the availability of water for human use: to reduce the degree of variability in supply. Beck (1996) then argues that it is necessary to consider both the whole spectrum of perturbations to the system and the effect of human intervention on those initial perturbations. Thus, for wastewater and surface water management, he argued that it is necessary to consider the way in which management changes the frequency and severity of perturbations in the water quality as a result of surface water runoff. This can then be taken as a general model and applied to water quantity (Figure 2.2). The function of all water management is to cope with *all* the natural perturbations in the system so as to maintain the state of the environment and/or the economy within some limits. Beck's approach can then be extended to apply to the quantity side of water management (Chapter 14).

Taken together, the adoption of a conceptualisation of the systems to be managed in dynamic terms and Beck's approach mean that we should stop thinking exclusively in terms of probabilities. It reinforces the need to adopt the approaches outlined in Section 2.1.2.3. Conventionally, in the case of floods, some design standard of protection is determined either by fiat, as in the case of the Netherlands (Huisman *et al.* 1998) or on the basis of a benefit–cost analysis (DEFRA 1999). What will happen if a more severe flood then occurs is ignored. This approach is exemplified by the drawing of lines on maps to represent the extent

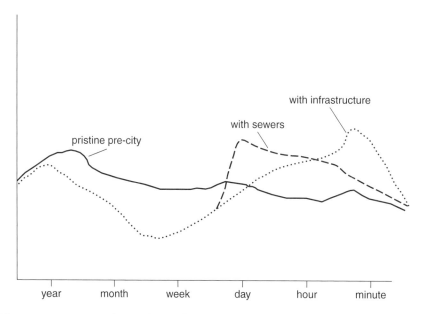

Figure 2.2 *Water quality and perturbations. Source: Beck 1996*

of the flood either with a specified return period or the largest known historical flood. In reality, there is neither a significant difference in the risk and consequences of a flood on either side of that line nor can that line be located with any degree of certainty; it becomes a line for the sake of having a line. Similarly, water resource planning is typically based upon some design standard drought.

Instead, the necessary uncertainty approach is concerned with managing all events. In an ideal world, we would filter out all the extreme perturbations rather than the small magnitude, high frequency events. This is seldom possible so instead the focus of attention should be on what will happen when an extreme perturbation occurs or the core management strategy fails for another reason. So, in following droughts the lesson is learnt that it is necessary to have a drought management plan (AWWA 1992; Environment Agency 2000a; National Drought Mitigation Center 1996); in the case of California, this requires the utility planning for a 50% drop in water resources (California Urban Water Conservation Council 1994). Similarly, where there is a significant population of risk, dams are designed to be able to pass the probable maximum flood (National Research Council 1985).

3

The Nature of the Economy

The popular view of economics is probably that it is the study of the economy. However, this is not what economics is about to economists; indeed, if you look at dictionaries of economics, you will not usually find the term 'the economy' defined at all. Curiously, terms such as 'market economy' and 'planned economy' typically are defined even though these are particular instances of the general term economy. Equally, this omission is odd given the enthusiasm for economists to make recommendations as to how a national or the global economy should be run.

One possible definition of the economy is then: '*The social organisation whereby resources are converted to intermediate products, capital stock and final consumption.*' This definition is sufficiently wide as to embrace the specific cases of market and planned economies. For the neoclassical economist it has the profound disadvantage of placing social relations at the centre of the economy but it does contain the neoclassical concern with the conversion of resources into consumption. An economy is then a relationship in the form of the conversion of some stocks and flows into other stocks and flows.

In abstract terms, we can then express the nature of the flows that relate the economy to consumption and the environment (Figure 3.1). A fraction of the output of the economy is reinvested in the form of production durables (e.g. machine tools, roads); a second fraction is reinvested to increase the skills of the workforce; and a further fraction is reinvested into technological innovation. The balance of the output is in the form of direct consumption (e.g. cans of beer) and of consumption durables (e.g. houses, televisions); notably, whilst the former are effectively priced at the point of consumption, the latter are not.

The economy is conditional upon the environment, the natural endowment, both drawing all the raw materials and energy from the environment and depending upon the natural endowment for food stuffs and water. A proportion of human consumption in the widest sense is taken directly from the environment in the form of, for example, walks by the river or sunbathing on the beach. In turn, the natural endowment can be categorised as shown in Table 3.1.

In each case, the stock yields a flow and using Hicks' (1946) definition of income in terms of a flow that does not deplete capital, in Table 3.1, the two

Handbook of Water Economics: Principles and Practice. C. Green
© 2003 John Wiley & Sons, Ltd ISBN: 0-471-98571-6

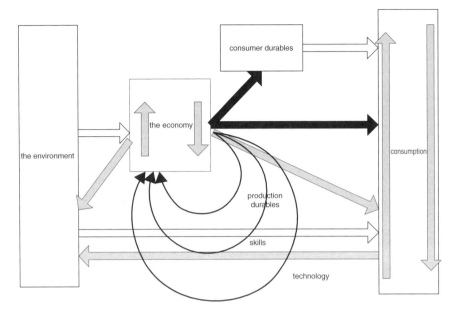

Figure 3.1   *The economy and the environment*

Table 3.1   *Resources*

	Depletable	Nondepletable
Self-renewing	Forestry, soil, fisheries, aquifer, crops (stock)	Solar energy, water (in long term), wind energy and other forms of energy that ultimately are driven by solar energy (flow)
Nonself-renewable	Fossil fuels, minerals, fossil aquifer (stock)	Land (stock)

cells on the main diagonal represent capital. Thus, capital can be defined as that which generates indefinitely some level of income by which it is not depleted. However, in the case of depletable resources, the rate at which they are harvested can exceed the rate of self-renewal.

In formulae terms, the total output that the economy can achieve can then be expressed as:

$$O = f(NE \times H \times X)$$

where:

O is the total output.
NE is the natural endowment.

H   is human inputs in the form of labour and reinvestment (e.g. in production durables).

X   is skills, social capital, technology.

The relationship is multiplicative, no output is possible unless there are some natural resources. The function in this equation is the economy; it represents how well these inputs can be put together. Thus, economists usually argue that a market economy is more efficient than a centrally planned economy: the same combination of technology, skills, the natural endowment and labour yields a higher value output. We can further refine the definition of the economy given earlier; the economy is composed of and defined by the formal institutional structures and informal social structures, the latter usually being termed 'social capital' (Woolcock 1998).

Inverting Hick's definition of income in this way to define capital, it follows that production durables are not capital: they naturally wear out, not only through use but also through natural processes such as rust, degradation through ultra-violet action and other forms of chemical and physical decay. To describe roads, machine tools and computers, for example, as 'human capital' is thus strictly incorrect and in Hicksian terms, the only true parallel to money capital is these two components of the natural endowment. Consequently, if 'soft' sustainability (Pezzey 1989) is couched in terms of substitution of trees by computers, it is strictly incorrect because the capital base is being reduced.

However, if sustainable development is defined not in terms of maintaining a constant level of capital but instead of being able to at least maintain a given level of consumption indefinitely, equivalent to maintaining a Hicksian income, then a reduction in the capital base of the economy can potentially be substituted by enhancements in the state of technology and/or improvements in the level of skill. In each case, this will be achieved to the extent to which we can do more with less. A basic condition for sustainable development is therefore the output–input ratios for depletable resources and the efficiency of energy conversion in particular. The rate of conversion to the use of nondepletable resources then needs to match the rate of draw down of depletable nonrenewable resources.

3.1 What is Output?

We can then define *technical efficiency* as the ratio of output or consumption relative to use of resources; to maximise $O/(NE \times H)|X$ whilst *efficiency* is defined as the ratio of the achievement of our objectives relative to all of the resources consumed. The problem is that we have good measures only of the divisors but not of either output and consumption nor of the objectives we seek to achieve. Instead, measures of gross domestic product (GDP) or net domestic product are usually used instead. Unfortunately, the GDP family of measures are no more than a form of double entry book-keeping for national economics, an accountancy rather than an economic measure that measures only money flows within the economy. As a system of double entry book-keeping, where resource use and output are equal it is necessarily impossible to assess the technical efficiency of an economy either over time or relative to other economies. Equally, since it only includes priced consumption and the use of priced resources, unknown proportions of resource use and consumption are excluded at any given point in time. Both the labour inputs and outputs of subsistence agriculture are thus necessarily excluded, along with housework and DIY activities on the resource side. On the consumption side, over time the real value of goods may change: the performance of household durables has increased over time whilst the real price has fallen (Mishan 1993). Similarly, only a proportion of consumption is priced at the point of consumption and a significant proportion of people's time is taken up with unpriced consumption (Section 2.1.1.3). Thus, playing with one's children is excluded from the consumption side of the analysis; similarly, whilst visits to brothels will notionally at least be included in the GDP figures, sex which is not accompanied with a monetary payment is not.

The GDP family of indicators is subject to a range of other well-known problems (Mishan 1993); for example, the inclusion of defensive expenditures, those incurred in order to reduce or avoid damage, such as national defence, police and fire services, and sanitation services. In addition, the depletion of capital enters the GDP as a positive amount rather than being subtracted from it: the unsustainable harvesting of forests appears as a positive item rather than being subtracted from it (Daly and Cobb 1990). Thus, various efforts are being made to provide an adjusted index of economic output and attempts are being made to extend the GDP family of measures to provide a more comprehensive accounting system (Bartelmus 1994).

However, the fundamental problem is that we do not have a comprehensive measure of output or consumption but only a measure of priced inputs and consumption. In addition, when considering output and efficiency, there are three further problems to be considered:

- frictional losses,
- externalities, and
- changes in capital.

3.1.1 Frictional losses

In the ideal world of the economist, supply and demand would automatically match each other without either party incurring any costs in achieving this match. In the real world, there is a lot of frictional resistance to be overcome in achieving this match: transaction costs are significant. Anything which does not have a value itself as a form of consumption is then a frictional cost. Thus, in the ideal world, transport costs would be zero. The products of government are more complex and depend upon what responsibilities have been given to government. A significant part of government spending is often in subsidies to different sectors of the economy with agriculture almost invariably being subsidised. Governments typically also invest heavily in the 'X' factor, bearing all or most of the costs of education and a high proportion of the costs of research. Whatever the outputs of government, the objective is to maximise their output relative to the resource costs involved; consequently, simply reducing the costs of government need not increase efficiency. These two cost elements can make up a significant proportion of GDP. Overall, in the USA, between 14% (Rhode Island) and 31% (Wyoming) of the GDP of the individual states is composed of transport and government costs.

Similarly, in so far as retailing does not generate consumption in itself (e.g. the act of shopping rather than the goods brought gives pleasure), retailing and distribution are a frictional cost. Again, in the ideal economic world, retailing costs would be zero. The financial sector provides some consumption goods (e.g. pensions, insurances) and also carries out some rather more problematic activities (e.g. speculative foreign exchange dealing).

The problem in each case is that the technical efficiency of the economy is higher than if the sector or activity did not exist, but the sector itself is not necessarily efficient and ideally the resources required for the sector, outside for any pure consumption provided by the sector, would be zero. Thus, the difference between the actuarially expected cost of insurance and the retail price of insurance is a measure of inefficiency, as is the difference between the cost of borrowing and the interest payable on savings. In each case, only the value of the consumption provided should be included in the measure of output; everything else is a frictional cost.

3.1.2 Externalities

We have already seen that a significant problem in assessing the efficiency of an economy is the existence of unpriced resource use and unpriced consumption. Another and special case of unpriced flows is then externalities: the positive or negative impact of one person's actions on another so as to either change the amount or value of resources available to that person or to change the enjoyment they gain from consumption. As shown in Figure 3.1, there are a multitude of possible externality relationships between the environment, the economy and consumption. Pollution is the obvious example of an externality and water management is riddled with externalities of one kind or another. In turn, there have been a large number of studies of the magnitude of these externalities. These range from estimates of the total loss to the nation (Table 3.2) from water pollution through the damages resulting from a particular incident, by way of estimates of specific categories of losses or benefits, to estimates of the benefits of improvement resulting from a specific scheme. Estimates of the losses from particular events, such as the Amoco Cadiz disaster, have also been calculated (Bonnieux and Rainelli 1991). Many studies in several countries have been undertaken

Table 3.2   *Estimates of national water pollution costs*

Country		Loss per year
Germany	potable water	780 DM million
(1991)	groundwater	4.1 to 6.9 DM billion
(1986)	measurable damage to rivers and lakes	greater than 17.6 DM billion
Italy	coastal waters	6.0 billion lire
(1974)	inland waters	19.0 billion lire
France (1978)		10 150 FF million
The Netherlands (1990)		300–930 Dfl million

Sources: Court 1987; Kuik *et al.* 1991; Muraro 1974; Wicke 1986; Winje *et al.* 1991.

which assess one of the streams of benefits resulting from pollution abatement, particularly the recreational benefits (e.g. Bonnieux and Rainelli 1991; Smith and Desvouges 1986). Overall, these analyses indicate that out of stream recreational uses contribute, on average, the largest component of the benefits of water quality improvements where a reduction in water quality can be seen as the consequence of the externalities associated with discharging untreated or poorly treated wastewater, runoff from agricultural land, and other actions.

The standard response of economists is then to argue that these externalities should be internalised to the individual who created them through the imposition, in the case of a negative externality, of some charge and a subsidy being given in the case of positive externalities. This charge or subsidy should be exactly equal to the economic value of the externality: a Pigovian tax (Pearce and Turner 1990) should be adopted. Theoretically, it can be shown that such taxes would be more efficient than other means of controlling externalities, notably regulations (Baumol and Oates 1988). However, there are then a number of problems with applying the Pigovian tax approach and these are discussed in Sections 11.2 and 15.5.

3.2 What is 'X'?

In different forms, the nature of the 'X' factor has been of pervasive concern for at least 100 years when the UK in the nineteenth century became concerned to identify and remedy the reasons why the UK economy was being outpaced by first the German and then the US economies (Hobsbawn 1969). Thus, the 'X' factor is seen as critical both in terms of identifying what this magic factor actually is and more importantly, how to engineer it into a society, or a firm, or another form of institution.

What it does is to provide some capacity to change both in terms of changing itself and to adapt to changes in conditions. It is the capacity to create change and to adapt to change that is crucial. In terms of the definition given earlier, this capacity would seem to be the economy itself: the differences in the efficiency of economies and their capacity to expand and adapt being given by the nature of the individual economies, the social organisation. This at least is consistent with the tendency of economics to provide tautological explanations.

This 'X' factor may also be said to correspond to Homer-Dixon's 'ingenuity' (Homer-Dixon 2001) and there are also a range of other partial explanations including technology, institutional arrangements and different forms of social capital. The 'X' factor is then multidimensional in character and three different characteristics have been put forward as partial or complete explanations of the 'X' factor:

- technology,
- institutions, and
- social capital.

There can be some questions about classification, for example, is joint stock banking (Kemp 1978) a technology or an institution? But semantics are not what is important here; either the 'X' factor is one or several of these factors in combination or it is the way that they are put together.

3.2.1 Technology and skills

Technology is the obvious candidate. For example, in 1788, it took 7 tons of coal to make 1 ton of pig iron; in 1810, 5 tons; and in 1840, 3.5 tons; similarly, the amount of pig iron required to make a long bar reduced from 30–35 cwt at the beginning of the nineteenth century to 26–27 cwt in the 1840s (Deane 1979). Similarly, in 1900, it took 1 tonne of water to produce 1 kg of paper in Europe; by 1990, this had fallen to 64 kg per kg and more recently it has fallen further to 20–30 kg, with 1.5 kg per kg being achieved in some instances (von Weizsacker *et al.* 1997). Crop breeding (Figure 3.2) is consequently a technology (Heiser 1990); since 1910, yields of wheat in the UK have increased by 250% to 8 tonnes per hectare and in the USA yields have increased by nearly 200% to 3 tonnes per hectare.

Pohoryles (n.d.) concluded that in its first 20 years, growth in agricultural productivity was equally the result of changes in the factors of production and of the 'X' factor. However, in the last 20 years, changes in the tangible factors accounted for only 4% of the improvement in agricultural productivity and intangible factors for the remainder. Further he concludes that over the last 18 years, whilst agricultural water use has remained basically static, the real value of agricultural output has increased by a factor of 2.9. Therefore, in the Negev, he concludes that a 10% reduction in water availability could result in a reduction of only 1.1% in agricultural incomes.

If technology is so important, then a critical question is whether we can decide what to invent and innovate or whether invention occurs randomly, the nature of

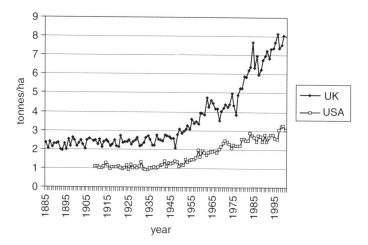

Figure 3.2   *Increase in wheat yields. Source: USDA/NASS 2001*

the inventions that occur being essentially outside of human control. Endogenous growth theory (Romer 1990, 1994) argues that we can, to a greater or lesser extent, influence the areas and direction of technological innovation rather than technological change being something that appears out of the blue. Thus, we can both choose those areas in which technological change is required and influence the rate of progress of technological change. Equally importantly, it implies that we choose where technological change will not occur by directing effort in other directions. In a way endogenous growth theory is a self-evident truth in that the two world wars saw very rapid technological innovation in weapons design, notably in aircraft technologies. At the start of the First World War, an aeroplane was barely capable of flying the English Channel; four years later, aircraft technologies had developed to the point where flying the Atlantic was possible.

One consequence of endogenous growth theory is that policy changes cause technological change and indeed perhaps this should be their main intent. For example, pollution regulation creates a market for pollution abatement technologies, induces technological change, and creates economies of scale in the production of pollution abatement equipment. The performance of a policy measure is then given partly by its effectiveness in inducing technological change and the adoption of that technological change. One consequence is that the costs of pollution abatement have frequently proved to be substantially below the costs initially estimated (Putnam, Hayes and Bartlett Inc. 1980).

Invention and innovation are created by people so the reinvestment in skills and technological innovation is potentially a virtuous circle; more skills not only enable the available technologies to be utilised effectively but also result in the development of new technologies. Using best available knowledge appropriate to the area in question can significantly improve efficiency. Jacobs and Asokan

(2000) report that whilst average output per hectare in the USA and India varies between 1.7 and 5 for different crops, the productivity on some trial farms in India was approximately doubled simply by providing the local farmers with the knowledge available to US farmers.

3.2.2 Social capital

> *'... norms and networks that enable people to act collectively'* (Woolcock and Narayan 2000).

Social capital is variously defined in two different but interlinked ways: as social norms such as trust, the absence of corruption (e.g. Inglehart 1997) that reduce both the frictional costs of exchanges and the risks involved in entering into those exchanges. Secondly, in terms of informal networks (Woolcock and Narayan 2000) that promote the sense of community out of which social norms are established and enforced. The first definition refers effectively to the nature of the social norms that are established. The second in part sees informal networks as in themselves ways of establishing support networks that create claims on resources of others and can prevent access by other groups to particular resources. Such informal networks have been found in many poor communities.

The shift back to farmer-managed irrigation systems and to community-based water and sanitation systems is then both an attempt to exploit social capital and also an attempt to create social capital which can then be mobilised for other purposes.

3.2.3 Institutions

Institutions are argued to be critical to effective water management. Turton and Ohlsson (1999) argued that when demand is small relative to the natural endowment, institutions do not matter. However, once a country utilised more than 15–20% of its annual renewable water, Falkenmark and Lundqvist (1998) argued that complex institutional arrangements are required. Therefore, two important questions are: what institutional structures are most effective? And how can we implement such structures?

The problem is then how to design institutions that can actually deliver such integrated management; Ostrom (1990) and others (Gibbs and Bromley 1989) have been investigating how institutions work. However, the problem with institutions is that their actions must be governed by a set of rules; indeed, this rule structure defines an institution. Thus, Scott (1995) gives the following definition: *'Institutions consist of cognitive, normative, regulative structures that provide stability and meaning to social behaviour.'*

Institutions are defined by formal or informal rules not least to provide accountability and predictability. For these reasons, it is as important to define what they cannot do as much as what they can do. For accountability, it must be clearly established what an institution may do and what it may not do, and also how it is to go about deciding and implementing those actions. Predictability is related to accountability but it is quite important that institutions behave in a predictable way, that when a farmer is thinking of applying for an abstraction licence, the farmer can make a reasonable prediction of whether or not a licence is likely to be issued.

That they are rule-defined in turn makes it difficult for an institution to change; it can change its internal rules but the external rules are fixed. Moreover, if an institution is defined by its rules then it is difficult for an institution to learn because learning means changing its rules. In turn, these external rules can be very difficult to change, particularly where they are defined by the national constitution. Secondly, amongst those rules are those that define the geographical boundaries of the institution and also its functional boundaries. Those geographical boundaries are typically also fixed by historical, cultural and political factors; and catchment boundaries are only incidentally consistent with the boundaries defined in those terms or those likely to promote efficiency in the delivery of other services such as education, policing or health. Hence, it is unlikely that there will be one set of institutional boundaries that are ideal for all purposes. As will be argued in Chapter 23, integrated catchment management is not enough; it has to be integrated into a whole series of other national and regional policies. We have, in short, to create holistic catchment management through boundaried institutions.

In turn, in assessing the performance of institutions, it would be helpful to have some measure of the difficulties of water management in that country; if Turton and Ohlsson are right, institutional structure only becomes important when management becomes difficult. Two obvious measures of the pressures are then population density and arable land per capita (Green, Parker and Tunstall 2000), with the ratio of potential evapo-transpiration requirement to precipitation (Chapter 14) being the most important water constraint. On the output side, in the absence of any economic measure of consumption or efficiency, GDP/km^2 is a rough measure of how hard the natural endowment is being worked, and the extent of that natural endowment (Green, Parker and Tunstall 2000). As it stands, it is not possible to make comparisons between countries as to the institutional effectiveness of each. In consequence, recommendations as to the best form of catchment management (Section 10.1) and of service delivery (Section 10.2) have to be tentative.

3.2.3.1 Markets

The core claim is that competition will act in the public interest, Adam Smith (1986) famously arguing that when co-operation would be against the public interest, then the answer was to force the producers to compete through the introduction of a competitive market. Conversely, self-interest drives producers towards seeking to cooperate since if a producer cannot achieve a monopoly, to be part of a cartel is then the next best means of reducing risk and increasing profitability. In turn, markets are a means to an end and not an end in themselves, nor are markets a means of establishing what our ends, our objectives, should be. When competition is desirable in order to achieve our ends, then a competitive market can be structured so as to achieve these ends; it needs to be structured since our objectives and those of the individual producers will generally be different.

This then is the negative reason for ensuring competition. There are two positive reasons. Firstly, in a stable environment, some producers will be more efficient than others and hence produce at a lower cost. These producers will force the higher cost or low quality producers out of business because they can undercut them. A question, therefore, is; what proportion of producers should, in any year, be exiting a product market if efficiency is to be achieved? Clearly, if no companies are going bankrupt or being taken over then there is an insufficient degree of competition. A proper market is thus a brutal place of Darwinian survival and unless some firms are being killed off, then there is necessarily inefficiency and excess profits. Therefore, a necessary condition when considering privatisation is to consider how services will be maintained if a firm fails (Green 2001b).

Secondly, in a more realistic dynamic environment, the advantage is one of diversity; whatever the nature of the change, one or more producers will be better equipped than the others to adapt successfully to that change and so it will survive whilst the other firms collapse. It will survive because it has more appropriate technology or better ideas. These two models are, obviously, in contradiction to each other: in the stable situation, survival of the fittest tends to lead towards uniformity in terms of technologies and approaches. Conversely, in a changing environment, diversity increases the likelihood that one or another producer will be equipped to take advantage of the change whilst others die out. The two concepts are only consistent if there exists more than one combination of technology and output that are equally efficient.

Finally, the purposes of analysis, a perfectly competitive market has a significant advantage: the market price falls out of the market at the point where marginal cost and marginal value are exactly equal and efficiency is automatically achieved (Lipsey 1971). Moreover, it is assumed such markets will be both homeostatic, adjusting to any disturbance, and optimising. It is possible to criticise this model on theoretical grounds since the performance of a market is either a consequence of the decision rules used by individual producers and consumers, or is the result of the interactions between producers and consumers. Since the same people perform other activities, it must be either the approach that they take to making production or consumption decisions in a market, or the interactions between producers that are important. Thus the critical question is how the producers decide by how much to increase or decrease production, whether they can do so, and how long it takes for the change in output to be achieved. Deciding how much to produce in the next time period becomes an even more difficult task if the world is not stable but subject to both external perturbations and trends. In turn, if relatively simple decision rules are used to explain how an individual producer decides how much to produce in the next period (Smith 1990), then the result is chaos rather than homeostasis. The practical problems with water are that where there is a market it is far from perfect and that prices prove to be relatively ineffective inducing optimal responses (Section 15.3).

4

How Do We Choose?

The force of economics lies in the extent to which it provides prescriptions for collective choice, to the degree to which it provides a rational argument for adopting one option rather than another.

4.1 Individual Choice

Neoclassical economic theory has been derived as a theory of how individuals make choices amongst priced goods. This model of choice is then used to provide a basis for arguing how collective choices should be made; it is treated as a general theory of choice so that it can be used to make normative recommendations about the provision of goods through collective action. Thus, two presumptions are made:

- That the individual approaches choices about the provision of goods through collective action as if the choice was about purchase of a priced good; and
- The individual believes that society should base the decision on this premise.

These are two very sweeping presumptions for which we have absolutely no evidence and I will return to them later. But, first it is necessary to examine the economic theory of individual choice between priced goods since there are a number of problems with this approach. Firstly, as a theory built on the demand for priced goods it is a matter of some embarrassment for economics that the very area where economic theory should be the most relevant, the decisions of firms as to what goods to market at what prices, it is least used. If a Sony, for example, has invented a new consumer good then it does not ask an economist how many it can sell at what price. Instead, companies use market research techniques (e.g. Assael 1992) and these are based upon theory from psychology and sociology rather than upon economic theory. When economists (Samuelson 1954) argue that only behaviour is real and asking people what they would do in a hypothetical choice is unreliable, the manufacturer's reply would be that it may be theoretically impossible but that it is necessary to do it. Moreover, if Samuelson's argument is accepted, micro-economics is essentially redefined as a branch of history.

Handbook of Water Economics: Principles and Practice. C. Green
© 2003 John Wiley & Sons, Ltd   ISBN: 0-471-98571-6

Secondly, it is essentially a trivial theory; the individual is assumed to made all the really important decisions, those involved in constructing a completely ordered utility function, before they approach any decision. What individual choice theory then covers is simply the mechanical process of applying these pre-existing utility functions to the particular choice.

Thirdly, the third axiom (Robbins 1935) of neoclassical economics is that the individual is rational but rational in a number of specific senses. In particular, it is assumed that the individual never makes mistakes when buying goods in the market. This assumption is simply implausible; there is a wealth of material on the error rate for all kinds of other tasks including car driving (Quimby and Watts 1981) so that we know that we are fallible and prone to make both random and systematic errors when performing tasks. Indeed, an entire science, ergonomics, has developed so as to define the task, and the environment of that task, in order to reduce the risk of human failure. Thus, Watson (1989) reports that human error rates vary from 1 in 1 to 1 in 100 for knowledge-based tasks down to 1 in 10 000 for skill-based tasks. For economists to claim that there is, for example, a small but finite risk of the pilot making an error when flying but that same person never makes an error when buying a toothbrush would simply bring the profession into disrepute. We cannot claim that purchasing decisions are different to other choices without specifying why they are different, nor, equally, without arguing what it is about the individual's performance of such tasks that makes them different. We cannot argue that purchasing choices are more important than other choices; it would be absurd to argue that making the right choice of toothbrush is more important than, for example, deciding when to turn right across traffic or in making the right choice of a partner. If we argue that it is something that the individual brings to the task, then we are necessarily forced to admit that we are more likely to be successful in some purchasing decisions than in others. If it is experience that makes us good at making particular types of choices then, unless it is experience in making purchases in general, we will be better at making some purchases than others; better, for example, at buying toothbrushes than at buying homes or cars. Moreover, if it is experience, then this is to explicitly admit to learning and change; once change is let into the model then it is difficult to claim that once we have learnt how to purchase, we never learn or change any more. Conversely, if it is the attention we give to the decision, where the more important the choice the greater the attention we give to the decision, so that we are good for that reason at buying houses, then it is implied that we will not be so good at routine, habitual choices like buying a cup of coffee. It is further assumed that we make consistent choices; strictly, this rules out learning and learning is a necessary characteristic of a person. In turn, this implies that consistency is a highly undesirable characteristic of choice.

Fourthly, economists have been fond of using the story of Robinson Crusoe as a way of explaining economic theory (Bergmann 1995). The Robinson Crusoe model has been criticised as being both sexist and racist (Grapard 1995). But, the problem with taking Robinson Crusoe as an example is that he would today be expected to have been severely damaged by the experience and to require a long period of therapy and recovery before he was able to re-adapt to normal life. Indeed, living in isolation is usually taken as a particularly severe form of punishment, or as a high form of sacrifice for religious reasons. It is not, therefore, encouraging that the story of a damaged individual living in an alien context is uscd as a metaphor to explain the basic principles of economics.

Since we grow up in households and spend most of life in some sort of household, I shall argue in Section 4.2 that the logical place to start in constructing a general theory of choice is with choice in households. Thus, in turn, that individual choice constitutes the trivial case of the household choice model. Secondly, it is not possible to simply assume that the individual has already determined their preferences and constructed their utility function before they make any choice. It is necessary instead to consider how this learning may come about since this learning process itself has implications for how we choose.

4.1.1 Learning to choose

The neoclassical economic theory of choice is essentially trivial; it is merely a matter of the individual mechanically applying knowledge that they already have. Before they make a choice, the individual is assumed to be aware of all of the consumption options and to have decided what is the marginal value of each and every consumption option. In turn, neoclassical economics is predominantly a static view of the world. In part this is a result of the assumption of perfect information: in a world of omniscience, we know not only what is but also what could be and can choose between them in perfect certainty. If we know everything, then the future has no surprises and time is dissolved.

Thus, it fails to address either of the two fundamental problems: how do we discover what is available and how do we decide what we want? We begin in the real world as babies with limited knowledge and even more limited preferences. We grow up into a world of rapid change where we are necessarily ignorant about the future. We have to learn to have preferences for goods which we did not know existed, or which have just been invented. Thus, knowing how our preferences are formed is of greater interest than knowing what these may be at any single moment in time.

One fundamental human trait is learning; as we learn more of the world, we also learn what are our preferences. Whilst some preferences may be innate, quite clearly other preferences are learnt or developed. It is, for example, unlikely that we were born with a utility schedule for camcorders or karaoke machines. Neoclassical economics, by assuming perfect information, limits itself to a description of the instantaneous present. Without describing how that state has arisen, it cannot predict the future.

If we have to discover our preferences, then we also have to find out what goods are on offer. Bayesian analysis identifies the value of the potential information gain to a decision (Enis and Broome 1971); essentially, the economic concept of 'quasi-option' value (Henry 1974) is equivalent to this information gain.

Finally, by defining rationality as little more than consistency, rather than as a process of decision making (Arrow 1987; Sen 1987), neoclassical economics made itself better at describing repetitive behaviour than first purchases. But consistency in choice can only occur if we are not learning; consequently, consistency in choices is not necessarily desirable.

4.2 Household Choice

Therefore, it is not unreasonable to argue that we have to learn how to choose as well as learn what we want. Choices in households are then crucial because we grow up in households and it is in this context that most of us learn both what we want and how we should choose. Moreover, in practice, most choices are made in the contexts of households, either the atomistic Western household, or in extended kinship groups. Hence, it is reasonable to take choices by households as the basic model of choice. We might expect, therefore, that the way in which we approach choices in a household influences the way in which we approach choices in other contexts, including formal groups such as at work, informal groups such as friends or clubs, and perhaps even when voting.

In addition, it is necessary to look at exactly what resource and consumption decisions are made by households; in particular, to link the use of unpriced resources to both priced and unpriced consumption. One of the results is that economic value may diverge markedly from willingness to pay and, of course, in an entirely subsistence economy, willingness to pay is a meaningless concept whilst economic value will remain.

There are significant problems in defining a 'household' (Gershuny 1998; Hart 1992; Roberts 1991) because there is such a wide variety around the world, particularly where households are woven into kinship or other linkages. This variety is reflected in the roles within the household, but we might characterise a household as involving some pooling of resources and some sharing or abrogation of decision making amongst its members. Within such households, children have no access to any income of their own; their choices are limited to the allocation of their time and often vociferous attempts to influence the consumption choices made by others in the household.

4.2.1 The household's resources

The basic resources available to the household are the combination of time and energy; the household has to allocate both to the provision and also to the consumption of different goods and services (Figure 4.1). Thus, cash income is purely an intermediary on the way to consumption. In a purely subsistence economy in which each household provides its own household durables (e.g. a

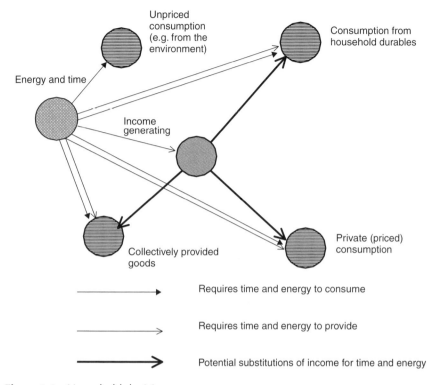

Energy and time

Unpriced consumption (e.g. from the environment)

Consumption from household durables

Income generating

Collectively provided goods

Private (priced) consumption

———————→ Requires time and energy to consume

———————⇀ Requires time and energy to provide

━━━━━━━⟶ Potential substitutions of income for time and energy

Figure 4.1 *Household decisions*

home, furnishing, cooking utensils) and private consumption (e.g. food, drink, clothing), the only other decision they have to make is as to how much time and energy should be allocated to the provision of collective goods (e.g. hunting large animals, irrigation works). However, once either bartering or a cash economy is introduced, then the household can allocate some time and energy to the genera-tion of bartering goods or a cash income. In a cash economy, the household must decide whether it is better to provide some household durables directly through the investment of their time and energy (e.g. DIY) or indirectly by paying some-one else to undertake those works. Similarly, they can either provide some private consumption directly through the use of their own energy and time (e.g. making jam or clothes) or indirectly by buying those goods. Again, collectively provided works (e.g. irrigation schemes) can either be provided directly through the con-tribution of the time and energy of the household, or indirectly through a cash payment. A critical question is consequently as to the relative rates at which time and energy can be converted directly into the desired consumption versus via the indirect route of first generating income. Which route is more efficient clearly depends critically upon the availability of income producing opportunities; where these are sparse, the direct route will be more efficient.

In turn, many goods require the simultaneous availability of time for their consumption. Indeed, unpriced goods, such as a walk by the river or playing with the children, require only the availability of time for their consumption. Some household durables require time (and energy) for their consumption (e.g. watching television, canoeing) whilst others do not (e.g. a refrigerator, washing machine). A benefit of some durables is then that they reduce the time required for the activity which can then be reallocated to other uses (e.g. electric drills, washing machines, vacuum cleaners).

Whether collective goods require time for consumption depends upon the nature of the good provided; in the case of leisure centres and art galleries, time is required although it is not for other collective goods such as defence or law and order. Private goods usually require the joint availability of income and time. Hence, the household has to allocate time and energy between both production and consumption, with some forms of consumption also being income constrained. We have seen from time budget studies (Table 2.1) that a relatively small proportion of the day is spent on the consumption of immediate consumption priced goods.

On the resource side of the equation, even in households in the UK, a significant proportion of labour inputs are unpriced. Attributing activities to work and necessary support activities is somewhat problematic. Housework is generally regarded as a pure input whose output is consumption in the form of cooked food, clean clothes and so forth. But, like DIY, some forms of housework, such as gourmet cooking, may yield pleasure, consumption as an activity rather than consumption being solely an output of the time expended on the activity. Time expenditure, to some extent, therefore gives a misleading picture of the unpriced inputs to the household. Pahl's (1989) study of households in Sheppey found that nearly 90% of house painting was performed by members of the household, and roughly the same percentage for cake making, vegetable growing and clothing repairs. About 10% of households would undertake major house modifications such as putting in a steel joist or double glazing or a bathroom. Significant proportions of households also made jam, beer, bread and clothes, as well as knitting. Consequently, there are some unpriced resource inputs to the household (e.g. vegetables) but most of the unpriced inputs are in the form of labour. In developing countries, the proportion of unpriced labour inputs in rural communities is often much higher (Table 4.1): the greater labour inputs from women is typical (Brismar 1997). So, too, is a high proportion of resource inputs often unpriced; thus in rural India, some 20% of the resource inputs, such as firewood, water and fodder, have been found to be unpriced (Jodha 1992). In the extreme of subsistence farming, the proportion of inputs to the household and outputs from the household which are priced approaches zero.

Thus, the fundamental problem for the household is the allocation of time and energy between different forms of production, income generation and consumption

Table 4.1   *Time use in the dry zone, Sri Lanka, during the peak season*

	Males		Females	
	Hours/month	%	Hours/month	%
Agricultural production	298	41	299	42
Household tasks	90	13	199	28
Fetching water and firewood	30	4	50	7
Social and religious duties	8	1	12	2
Leisure/sleep	294	41	160	22

Source: Momsen 1991.

whilst at the same time a significant proportion of household consumption is unpriced at the point of consumption.

4.2.2 Decision making by households

If the task of a household is to use its available resources to maximise the consumption of the household, how then does it determine how to allocate its resources? The early economic theory of households (Becker 1991) was essentially that of a benevolent dictator. It has been criticised by development theorists as having little practical relevance in planning interventions with the aim of promoting development (Alderman *et al.* 1995). It also seems to bear little relationship to what has been observed by sociologists and anthropologists (Hart 1992; Jelin 1991).

The second household model is divisive: resources and decisions are shared out between the members of the household. Pahl (1983, 1989), and later Anderson *et al.* (1994), have sought to explore both how decisions are made about the allocation of resources with households and the variations in access to financial resources by gender and income level. There are a wide variety of approaches adopted ranging from the 'female whole wage' system, in which the husband hands over the whole wage packet, minus personal spending money, to the wife through to the 'male whole wage' system in which the male has sole responsibility for managing all of the household finances.

Anderson *et al.* (1994) make the distinction between strategic and executive control over the household's finances, executive control for day-to-day responsibility for organising the household's finances and day-to-day payment of bills. They define strategic control in terms of which allocative system should be used, the proportions of income which should be allocated to personal spending money and who has the final say in big financial decisions. Overall, 70% of their respondents indicated that there was joint strategic decision making; as is logical, this proportion varied with the type of executive decision making, falling to 50% in households in which the executive financial management was via a 'housekeeping allowance'.

Applied consumer theory (market research) has relied on a third model: an interactive model coming out of sociology, particularly on the work of Sprey (1969) who developed a model of household decision making as a system of 'co-operative conflict', a model which was independently proposed by Sen (1990). In this model co-operation, or collusion, can yield a better set of outcomes than individual actions, variously labelled as the 'breakdown position' or the 'status quo'. However, unless there is only one possible collusive outcome which is better than that which results from individual actions then a choice must be made between the two or more collusive actions. The different members of the household may well have entirely different preferences between these outcomes; for example, as to which television programme is to be watched on which television, or where to go on holiday. This choice is, Sen points out, one of pure adversity. Since any of the outcomes is better than the breakdown position, who wins in such choices is dependent upon their bargaining power. Sen argues that 'winners' in one round achieve a better bargaining position in future rounds, particularly as such victories relate to access to household and external resources. There is now quite a large literature that examines the different strategies that the different household members use in order to try to influence household choices (e.g. Kirchler 1993). US market research studies have logically focused upon differences in terms of influence between specific consumer goods (e.g. Munsinger *et al.* 1975) in order to determine the most effective marketing strategy.

The key characteristic of this model of household decision making is thus interaction between the members of the household. Such interactions are completely absent from the neoclassical economic model which Chattoe (1995) describes as consumer theory without people. Tannen (1991) further claimed that: 'Many women feel it is natural to consult with their partners at every turn, while many men automatically make more decisions without consulting their partners. This may reflect a broad difference in conceptions of decision making. Women expect decisions to be discussed first and by consensus.' Thus, she claims that women expected decisions to be discussed and agreed; Wilson (1991) found in a study of women in North London that the dominant ideology of marriage held by a majority of women was 'sharing', although she noted that the reality was less than equal shares. Thus, the two key messages from work on households are:

- There is both interaction between partners and an expectation by many that decisions will be discussed first; and
- A wide variety of strategies are used to influence the outcome of the decision whether or not it is formally discussed.

If people first learn how to make choices in this context and then use this in their everyday life to discuss and negotiate the allocation of household resources then we might anticipate that they will bring the same expectations to group or social choices. If they expect major financial decisions to be made jointly, and a significant proportion pool their household resources, then this form of enculturation might be expected to spill over into the way that they expect larger groups to take resource decisions.

4.2.3 Problems for assessing economic values

The household model shown in Figure 4.1 also illuminates the question of economic value and in particular the extent to which preparedness to pay can be equated to economic value. Economic value is both subjective, measuring how much someone wants something, and is assessed by the sacrifice they are prepared to make to get that something. Hence, economic value exists in a purely subsistence economy where money values do not exist; in such economies, people still both want things and have to make sacrifices in order to obtain them. We cannot, however, in such an economy measure the economic value of something by asking people how much they would be prepared to pay in order to obtain that something. Only if either there is some priced good or some income that they could sacrifice will preparedness to pay be a meaningful measure of economic value.

Since substantial proportions of household inputs and consumption are unpriced, it follows that the prices of priced inputs and consumption are distorted away from those that would prevail if all inputs and consumption were priced. If all housework had to be brought in from, say, a supplier of robotic labour, or we had to pay to see sunsets, then the household would have less money to spend on other things and both the quantities and prices paid for those goods would necessarily fall.

More generally, there are a number of problems for economic evaluation, particularly when undertaking expressed preference studies (Section 12.2.3) either of unpriced consumption or of collective goods. Firstly, the combined rate at which time and energy can be translated first into income and then into priced consumption may be below the rate at which time and energy can be translated into unpriced consumption. In this case, using preparedness to pay will yield a value below the economic value, properly measured as the most valuable sacrifice the household is prepared to make to obtain that which we want to value. Indeed, there may be more efficient ways for the household to translate time and energy into consumption than going through the intermediary step of first generating an income; this is characteristic of poor communities. Thus, importantly, the most successful means of providing water and sanitation in such areas has been through community self-help (Black 1998) where time and energy is directly translated into consumption in the form of water and sanitation services. In turn, this means that preparedness to pay is a poor metric for measuring the value of these services since the compound rate at which time and energy can be translated into income and then into consumption is less than the rate at which time and energy can be directly translated into consumption. In turn, this has implications for the best means of providing those services (Sections 10.2, 14.6.1 and 16.1.1). In particular, for the provision of water and sewerage service by a private company to be viable (Section 10.2.3), it is necessary for the rate at which time and energy can be converted into income to exceed the rate at which they can be converted into the community provision of a water and sewerage service.

Generally, respondents in expressed preference studies are asked how much they are prepared to pay for the good in question rather than what they are prepared to sacrifice. This amount can then only be made available by reducing private consumption, investment in household durables, or by sacrificing further time and energy to produce income. A consequence of this approach is that the proportion of a household's incomes that are committed to the provision of collective goods funded through taxes can only increase as there is no scope with this technique for respondents to either reduce as a whole the proportion of their income taken through taxation, or to reallocate that amount between services. This leaves an asymmetrical approach where individual households can agree to increase taxation to serve a particular purpose but only the political process can decide to reduce tax either as a whole or for the provision of specific goods and services. In general, there is a lacuna in the neoclassical economic approach which argues that the goods supplied should reflect individual preferences but that both the level of taxation and the use of that revenue should be based upon macro-economic theories about the economy and, in particular, as to the appropriate level of public expenditure.

The further problem with a significant fraction of consumption not being priced at the time of use is to evaluate changes in non-priced consumption. The obvious problem is that if we ask for the individual's preparedness to pay then this amount can only be freed up by reducing expenditure on priced goods. The only sacrifice that can be considered is of priced consumption. If the change is nontrivial then the effect will be to reduce demand for priced goods; across demand as a whole, then the effect will be to reduce the demand for different priced goods and in turn, the prices at which those goods can be sold. If we try to value all of the consumption that is not priced, then the new equilibria for priced goods will be at lower levels; in addition, the individual will be at a lower utility level. The change is equivalent to a reduction in real income.

4.3 Societal Choice

Neoclassical economics takes its theory of individual choices for priced goods and treats it as a general theory of choice. So, societal choices are simply individual choices writ large. It is therefore assumed both that individuals approach all choices as if they were about the purchase of a priced good and also that individuals believe that society ought to make choices on that basis although without any evidence for these claims. Nor is the model consistent with how collective choices are made in practice. Both Margolis (1982) and Sagoff (1988) have suggested alternative bases upon which individuals might approach choices involving public goods.

There are six reasons to question whether the assumption that individual choice for priced goods constitutes a general theory of choice:

- It is only a partial theory of choice.
- There are fundamental differences in the nature of different goods which the public might be expected to recognise and take into account in the way in which they approach choices.
- Individuals do not exist in isolation but are subject to social norms and peer pressure which influence their understanding of how they ought to behave in particular circumstances.
- The basis and extent of the provision of goods through a society is intimately connected to our understanding of our relations with each other.
- Moral, ethical and religious issues are typically much sharper in regard to societal decisions.
- It predicts behaviours that are inconsistent with the results of experimental studies.

Any general theory of choice has to encompass all choices and not just some. There are some choices that have no resource implications of any kind such as what colour to paint the front door, what name to give to the baby, or whether to believe in the existence of a deity. A theory of choice about priced goods is not the obvious place to start in providing a theory that can cover all choices.

Secondly, the one distinction that is drawn in neoclassical economics is between 'private goods', those that are readily produced and sold in a market, and 'public goods' (Table 4.2), as well as two other classes of good. Public goods cannot be produced in a market although a charge can be levied for the use or access to them. A public good is distinguished from a private good by reason that:

- once the good is provided for by one individual, it is necessarily available for other individuals; and
- its use by any one individual does not reduce the amount available to other individuals or the value to them of making use of the public good.

Conventionally, the only real implications of the difference are:

- the demand curve is based upon horizon aggregation rather than vertical aggregation of individual preferences; and

Table 4.2 *Public and private goods*

Subtractability	Excludability	
	High	Low
High	Priced goods	Open access
Low	Toll goods	Public goods

Source: Easter, Becker and Tsur 1997.

- to charge for access to a public good can be shown to result in inefficiency so the costs of the provision of public goods are best recovered by a means other than a price or fee for use.

Now, this difference is defined on the demand side of the equation and it may be asked whether there is any similar difference on the supply side of the equation. I have previously argued (Green 1997) that a distinction can be drawn between goods where the individual can make private arrangements, such as purchase, for the provision of the good and those goods that can only be provided by collective action. In addition, that there exist some goods that can be provided by either means but for which economies of scale make their provision cheaper through collective provision (Section 7.2).

This gives a four-way categorisation of goods (Table 4.3). National defence can only be provided collectively: because of the cost of modern weaponry, no individual can afford to construct and maintain a fleet of nuclear submarines or aircraft carriers. Nor, similarly, can any individual afford to send a crew of astronauts on a mission to Mars. Again, no individual can decide to preserve blue whales as it requires agreement of all nations that blue whales will not be hunted.

Conversely, where there is groundwater, the individual can choose to supply himself with water by digging or drilling a well; alternatively, they may buy water from a water vendor. Similarly, they may dispose of sanitary waste by digging a cesspit and paying for the solids to be collected. Again, they can reduce the potential losses from floods by building their home on stilts or flood-proofing it. What is typically true is that it is cheaper to access these services through collective provision but that this will only occur if there is collective agreement that the service shall be provided. A water distribution system cannot be constructed without it crossing some people's land; the construction of a canal irrigation system requires the agreement of the farmers concerned to the construction of the off-take works, the distribution and drainage systems. So, too does the building of a flood embankment require the agreement of the farmers whose land will be taken up by its construction.

The conditions which constrain some provisions to being collective are partly resource constraints; unless individuals club together, insufficient resources are

Table 4.3 *Supply and demand conditions*

Supply	Demand	
	Private	Public
Individual	Cup of coffee, well, cesspit, flood-proofing	Lighthouse, breakwater, wastewater treatment works
Collective	Piped water supply and sanitation, flood warnings, canal irrigation	Conserving blue whales, national defence, flood embankment

Source: Green 1997.

available. In other cases, what is possible depends upon the way in which the relations between individuals are constructed; what system of entitlements and obligations is established. Thus, the individual provision of piped sanitation and water is possible but only if the individual, usually the company, is given rights of eminent domain to enter into private land. In the case of piped sewerage, a purely private solution is only possible if the individual company is either given the right to levy a tax or it is paid through the collective because it is not practical to meter discharges from private properties. In addition, it is usually necessary to establish an obligation on individual households to connect to the sewerage system.

To assume that a theory of choice for the consumption of private, individually supplied goods can be generalised to the other three possibilities is to imply that we cannot tell or there is no real difference between the four categories of good. We assume that for the purposes of economic analysis, blue whales can be treated as being no more than very, very large cups of coffee. This is not a particularly plausible assumption to make.

Thirdly, neoclassical economics takes individuals as the nexus of choice; the opposite extreme is Duesenberry's (1960) remark: 'Economics is all about how people make choices. Sociology is all about why they don't have any choices to make.' That is, that the cultural and social context of the individual will determine the choices made by the individual. Cultural theorists in particular have claimed (Schwartz and Thompson 1990) that different groups have radically different perspectives which will influence, amongst other things, how they believe that goods ought to be provided.

The Duesenberry model treats individuals as little more than ants in an ant nest; the neoclassical economic model simply treats society as being no more than the collective noun for individuals. Clearly, both are gross oversimplifications. Children are socialised, the whole basis for the argument about single-parent families, for example, being about the nature of this socialisation process. Part of this socialisation process is to establish internal norms as to the behaviour to adopt in particular circumstances (e.g. 'let your sister play with your car'), and another part is to inculcate social norms: the behaviour expected of individuals by society (e.g. 'you mustn't steal'). Between cultures, differences should be expected to be greater than the differences between groups within a single culture. If this socialisation process has been successful at all, then we should expect the consequences to be particularly apparent when choices concern the provision of public, collective goods.

Fourthly, the way that decisions are to be taken is clearly associated with expectations about the nature of relations between us. These expectations affect both the way in which a decision is taken and how the individual should respond in the social context of such a decision. Women, Tannen argued, expect decisions to be taken by agreement and after discussion. Moreover, there are a whole series of objectives and values that relate to relations between people

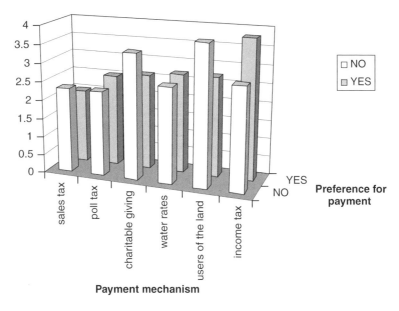

Figure 4.2   *Preferences between cost recovery methods*

(Section 2.1.1.7). However narrowly or widely we define it, equity is about the nature of the relationships between individuals and groups; so too are beliefs in justice and democracy.

Two obvious consequences of this relationship dependence is that, firstly, in social survey studies, such as contingent valuation, people have a clear preference for the means by which the costs of projects are to be recovered and that this preference is associated with whether or not they are prepared to pay (Figure 4.2). Those who are not prepared to pay, in this case for reducing coastal erosion, are more likely to favour payment mechanisms that allow others to pay but do not force the individual respondent to pay towards the cost. Those prepared to pay tend to prefer payment via income tax over the other possible methods of recovering the costs since the tax model forces others to comply with the decision.

The second consequence is in terms of the means of provision that they would prefer. For example, the costs of a wastewater treatment programme may be raised locally, regionally or on a national basis. Respondents may favour one form of programme over another; in a study of river restoration, Tapsell *et al.* (1995) found a slightly higher percentage of local residents were definitely prepared to pay for a project to restore the local river (59%) than for a national programme (52%). Conversely, when asked about programmes to improve river water quality, respondents both in the qualitative studies (Tunstall 1995) and in a contingent valuation method (CVM) study preferred a national programme (80% in the CVM study).

These relationships between us are different to personal moralities. The debate about altruism, its nature (Sen 1977) and whether it can be included in economic analyses (Milgrom 1992), is about personal moralities. I can choose whether to give to beggars; I cannot choose whether or not to pay towards the costs of social security. Moreover, in many countries, a refusal to serve in the armed forces is a punishable offence as it is understood that citizens have a duty to fight to protect their fellow citizens. So, the issue here is not whether I would feel better if I contribute towards the well-being of my fellows but whether I interpret the situation as being that I have duty to contribute, in this instance, to the well-being of my fellow citizens.

Similarly, public involvement in all levels of decision making has been accepted as a necessary condition for sustainable development (ACC/ISGWR 1992). But the whole point of public involvement is to influence each other, to persuade others that our viewpoint should be adopted, or to negotiate a compromise. One of the drivers for adopting public involvement is that the public expect to be involved and such involvement is regarded as a precondition for the legitimisation of the institution with central responsibility for the decision and its implementation (Lawrence *et al.* 1997).

Studies on procedural justice or equity have shown that the perceived legitimacy of the decision-making body is important. This legitimacy is enhanced when people believe that the authorities are honest and competent, people's willingness to voluntarily accept the authority's decisions, and people's feelings of obligation to follow the rules implemented (Tyler and Degoey 1995). Where individuals are personally involved in a dispute, individuals are likely to believe that they were treated fairly if they have an opportunity to have an input to the decision (Thibaut and Walker 1975). It has been suggested (Stroessner and Heuer 1996) that this is less an issue of self-interest than whether group members were treated in a manner implying respect for the group and its rights.

Fifthly, choices about the provision of public goods give more opportunity to express moral values, be these internal or the reflection of understood social norms than do purchases of private goods. In practice, the market research evidence is that understood social norms also influence the purchase of even quite mundane private goods (Ryan and Bonfield 1975).

In psychology, as in everyday speech, an individual's core beliefs are termed their values, Rokeach (1973) defining them as follows: 'A value is an enduring belief that a specific mode of conduct or end-state of existence is personally or socially preferable to an opposite or converse mode of conduct or end-state of existence.'

Rokeach argues that an individual's values function as standards in order to make evaluations and judgements and so as to enable us to heap praise and fix blame on ourselves and others. A second function of values he suggests is motivational; they serve as the objectives which individuals seek to satisfy through their behaviours. Thus, in Rokeach's view, values serve both as Kant's moral values, those which carry a sense of absolute obligation, or 'ought', and those which carry only a sense of desirability, of I 'want' or I 'like'. Furthermore, Rokeach proposes that such values are all or nothing in form; one either believes in freedom or one does not; it cannot be said that an individual believes in a little freedom or a small amount of democracy. Kelly (1955) argued that beliefs are structured hierarchically, lower-level beliefs tending to be narrow in scope or range and specific in form. The highest-level beliefs are more abstract and are, he argued, difficult to change. Again, such high-level abstract beliefs may be labelled as 'values'. Indeed, such beliefs are so central that they may be argued to define the core of the individual's personality.

If the individual uses these abstract values as the basis of making choices, then these moral principles must be turned into criteria for action. Consequently, Rokeach goes on to differentiate between terminal values and instrumental values as parts of this cognitive structure. Kelly (1955) goes further to propose a complete form of cognitive organisation in which simple descriptive beliefs, such as 'sweet–salty', are integrated into a framework which can also include a belief in democracy.

There is a significant body of experimental evidence that social value orientations do significantly influence (e.g. Seligman *et al.* 1994; van Liere and Dunlap 1981) people's beliefs and attitudes. An attempt to explore the nature of the motivations which determined respondents' preparedness to pay for improvements in river water quality (Green *et al.* 1990) found very strong support for the statement 'it is a moral issue; we ought not to pollute'. In subsequent studies, a series of 42 statements were developed to explore the nature of the motivations that motivated people to be prepared to pay for the supply of public, collective goods

Table 4.4   *Optimistic utilitarianism*

Statement	Mean	Standard deviation
If we kept on worrying about the future, nothing would ever get done	2.8	1.9
You learn more about plants and animals from watching them on television than from seeing them yourself	2.9	2.1
I am fascinated by machines and technology	3.4	2.0
Scientists are the only people who know the facts	3.6	1.9
Change is nearly always for the better	3.6	1.6
Life in this country is improving all the time	3.7	1.7
Scientists will always be able to find a solution to a problem	3.7	1.6
Politicians can be trusted to take care of the environment	4.6	1.7
There is nothing to do in the country	4.8	1.6
Cronbach's alpha = 0.63	$n = 542$	
Scale mean	39.3	9.1

Scale: 0 = strongly agree; 6 = strongly disagree.
Source: Green and Tunstall 1996.

Table 4.5 *General environmental value*

Statement	Mean	Standard deviation
I like to be in the open air	0.7	1.2
We owe a duty to our children and grandchildren to take care of the environment	0.8	1.6
I love the peace and quiet of the countryside	0.8	1.4
I want my children and grandchildren to see and enjoy those things I enjoyed as a child	0.8	1.2
We owe a duty to animals and nature, they don't exist just for our enjoyment	0.9	1.4
The Earth and Nature are fragile, and we can easily cause irreversible damage	1.1	1.6
We have a duty to other people as well as to our families	1.1	1.4
We have no choice: we have to protect the environment or we will destroy the human race	1.1	1.5
The countryside is important for recreation	1.2	1.5
It is important to understand the past	1.3	1.5
We should live in harmony with nature even if it means sacrifices on our part	1.4	1.5
Cronbach's alpha = 0.89	$n = 542$	
Scale mean	13.0	11.9

Scale: 0 = strongly agree; 6 = strongly disagree.
Source: Green and Tunstall 1996.

(Green *et al.* 1992). Cluster analysis yielded three groups of statements which were readily identified as:

- optimistic utilitarianism (Table 4.4);
- general environmental value (Table 4.5);
- moral pessimism.

The statements that cluster on the general environmental scale notably include statements that refer to duties and not simply to wants: 'We owe a duty to our children and grandchildren to take care of the environment', 'We owe a duty to animals and nature, they don't exist just for our enjoyment', and 'We have a duty to other people as well as to our families'.

We have found that there are significant associations between scores on these dimensions and the memberships of societies and pressure groups, the features desired of a river corridor and the choice of leisure visits (Green and Tunstall 1996). Table 4.6 illustrates that there are significant differences in the importance given to features of nature reserves when considering whether they should be protected from coastal erosion.

Finally, Hardin's (1968) provocative paper generated two lines of research; the first to establish why a Commons regime did not collapse in the way he appeared

Table 4.6 *Beliefs about the relative importance which should be given to different factors in determining which nature reserves should be protected from loss through coastal erosion (Pearson's product moment)*

	GE	Mean score	OU
It contains wildlife or plants that are disappearing in the UK	+	4.6	
It includes a very rare species of wildlife or plant		4.3	
It includes a natural landscape rather than a manmade landscape	+	4.1	
The wildlife or plants it contains have always been rare in Britain		4.1	
The variety of wildlife and plants it contains		4.0	
The wildlife and plants it contains are typical of the countryside as it used to be	+	3.9	
There are no other sites like it locally		3.8	
The reserve contains a large proportion of the plants and animals of that kind in the UK		3.8	
It contains wildlife or plants that are attractive to look at	+	3.5	
The amount that there is to see when visiting		3.2	+
The number of visitors to the site		2.7	+

Scale: 1 = strongly disagree; 5 = strongly agree.
Key: GE: general environmental scale score;
      OU: optimistic utilitarian scale score.

to predict (Cox 1985; Feeny *et al.* 1990), and secondly experimental studies by psychologists. The latter work, social dilemmas theory (Dawes 1980; Kopelman *et al.* 2000), has explored the extent to which people are prepared to cooperate in groups and the allocation rules adopted by individuals in such groups. This work has shown that individuals consistently allocate a substantial proportion of resources to the group rather to themselves as individuals (Batson *et al.* 1995); co-operative action seems to be the expected norm, with individuals contributing 40–60% of their endowment in the game to the common good. This is too much for neoclassical economic theory but it is also too little to maximise the gains to the experimental group as a whole. Sally (1995) found that allowing face-to-face communication increases co-operation by 45% – in the majority of the social dilemmas studies, individuals are only allowed limited written communication with each other. A similar effect has been found when the individuals in the experimental group are told that they have been selected from a wider group with whom they share some identity or interest.

Thus, choices involving the provision of public, collective goods could be expected to involve a rich mixture of:

- What we personally would like.
- What we believe ought to be and what society therefore ought to choose.
- How we believe that a society should choose.

- What we believe should be the relationships between individuals and groups.
- What we believe that other people will expect that we will do.

In turn, we lack a grounded economic theory of collective choice. This can be seen as one aspect of the lack of any economic explanation for the existence of societies, a rather profound omission given the resources that have been committed to the establishment and maintenance of societies.

In carrying out economic analyses, this omission is less disastrous than it might appear. It does mean that in carrying out such analyses the emphasis must be upon exploring how people are approaching the choice, and how they believe it ought to be made, rather than fitting the study into textbook economic theory. Such studies will almost inevitably be based upon the use of expressed preference evaluation techniques, those based on social survey methods (Section 12.2.3), and consequently it is possible to build up the necessary understanding through the use of both qualitative (Krueger 1988) and quantitative methods. Whittington (Lauria *et al.* 1999; MacRae and Whittington 1988; Whittington 1996) has undertaken a number of such studies which illustrate the richness of the material that can be generated if we listen to what people are saying. Similarly, when Burgess (Burgess *et al.* 1997) interviewed people who had recently participated in a CVM study, they reacted with horror when told that the amounts they said that they would be prepared to pay would form the basis of the decision as to whether to preserve the area.

What is necessary to ensure in such studies is that people are prepared to pay real money and put in the context of making a real choice; providing that those conditions are met, it is less important why they are prepared to pay. What I suspect is happening is that people first consider whether they have a responsibility in regard to the issue in question as only then should they be prepared to consider paying at all. Secondly, they consider whether the proposed change is desirable both in social and individual terms. Then, thirdly, if they consider that they have a responsibility and that the change is desirable, then they will decide how much they are prepared to pay. In turn, this means that whether or not someone is prepared to pay is considerably more important than the amount they are prepared to pay, and a refusal to pay is quite different from a preparedness to pay a zero amount. Thus, if a vegan were asked how much s/he would be prepared to pay in order that each school child should receive a free glass of milk each day, the vegan will refuse to pay and object strongly to the proposed programme on principle.

The more difficult problem is that of interaction; if Tannen is right even in part that there are some people of either gender who expect decisions to be taken after discussion, then either discussion needs to be included as part of the process of determining whether or not people are prepared to pay and how much they are prepared to pay, or the results of such discussions need to be used as feedback to those taking part in the expressed preference study.

5

Dimensions of Choice

Although it is said that we cannot compare apples and oranges, choice is the one thing at which we are good. Offered an apple or orange, few people are unable to make the choice between them. Choices necessarily are comparative because we must choose between alternatives. In turn, this means that it always the differences that are important where the differences are between the performance of the different options against the different objectives, or more simply in their consequences, or between the stakeholders in terms of their preferences between the options.

Choices, to a greater or lesser extent, involve comparing alternative options that differ in terms of who experiences what type of consequence and when that consequence is experienced. 'Who', 'what' and 'when' are then the basic dimensions of choices and in choosing between the different courses of action open to us, we have somehow to compare those options across these three dimensions. To make this comparison, we can adopt formal strategies and these have the advantage of being explicit and open to argument. Alternatively, an implicit comparative strategy may be used in making the choice even if that strategy is to ignore the differences.

Not only is choice comparative, it is also relative: differences between the options must be estimated from some baseline. The two basic options are to take the situation now as the baseline or to seek some zero point as a baseline. What is fundamental is that the analysis informs the choice; in turn, this means it must be directed to the nature of conflicts that require the choice to be made.

5.1 How

To compare the perhaps widely different impacts from the different options, some implicit or explicit numeraire or yardstick is necessary. In conventional economic analyses, this yardstick is money. Because money fulfils many roles in economic analysis, there is a danger of confusion. In benefit–cost analysis, money is used solely as a yardstick, by which to compare the value of different things to different people. In using it in this restricted sense, nothing is being

Handbook of Water Economics: Principles and Practice.   C. Green
© 2003 John Wiley & Sons, Ltd   ISBN: 0-471-98571-6

said or implied about money as a medium of exchange or as capital. In addition, value is conceptually distinct from both cost and price; using some quick intellectual footwork or perhaps sleight of hand, it is possible, as discussed earlier (Section 3.2.3.1), to define conditions under which they will all coincide. But, conceptually, value is not the same as either the cost or the price of something: how much I want something, how it contributes to the achievement of one of my objectives is quite different from how much it costs me or its price. Indeed, it may not even have a price.

Money is used as a numeraire instead of the thing that economists would ideally like to measure, utility, because it is held that the utility that one individual gains from a good cannot be compared to what another individual will gain from the same amount of that good. In addition, money has had the advantage that when economics was effectively limited to the study of exchanges in the market, money transactions could be easily observed whilst estimating utilities would have required doing some work.

Using money as a numeraire has two obvious disadvantages: different people have different amounts of money available to them and it is assumed that the marginal utility of money also decreases. Thus, measuring value using money is rather like measuring length with a spring. To get around the first problem, the assumption is made that the existing income distribution is optimal. Irrespective of the merits of this claim in general, in many parts of the world, women have only limited access to a household's cash resources (Haddad *et al.* 1997). Given that water and sanitation often provide more benefits to women than to men, and women often lack access to the cash resources of the household, the values ascribed by men for water and sanitation are likely to be distorted and the benefits of water and sanitation underestimated.

As a yardstick, money is also limited in its range of application. As a surrogate for utility, difficulties arise when one or more objectives are involved that do not relate to utility. Achieving either personal moral objectives or those objectives relating to interpersonal relationships does not contribute to utility but their achievement does usually require the commitment of resources. Similarly, where the choice is necessary because of a conflict of objectives or because we disagree as to the importance that should be given to different objectives, then money ceases to be useful. In the latter case, we will necessarily need to argue, negotiate and debate our objectives. In these cases, multi-criteria analysis (von Winterfeldt and Edwards 1986) can be used (Chapter 13).

5.1.1 Values

The three critical characteristics of value are:

- It measures the contribution of some proposed action towards the achievement of an objective, or, rarely, the value in itself of some resource or good;

- It is, therefore, necessarily a desirable consequence of undertaking that action; and
- It is measured by the difference from the baseline case.

As we have seen, an action has as many values as there are independent objectives brought to the particular choice. Conventional economic analysis can, however, only compare the alternatives against the single objective of economic efficiency and multi-criteria analysis whenever multiple objectives are involved in a choice. Whilst the above three points also apply to the assessment of values in multi-criteria analysis, the following discussion is specific to economic analyses.

5.1.1.1 Use value

Conventionally, economic value is held to have a number of different possible components. Use value, the value of the action of accessing, consuming or otherwise using a good, is the most obvious component of value. Where a good is priced then the price can be used as the basis for assessing value although almost invariably (Belli *et al*. 1997) the observed prices need some correction before they equal those that would be found in a hypothetical perfectly competitive market.

Where goods are not priced, such as recreation, then things become more difficult and the possible methods of inferring or deriving the value of such goods are summarised in Chapter 12. With all goods, the question that the economist is asking is: what other good would you sacrifice for this good? The essence of economic value is what is the most valuable thing that you would give up in order to get this good? But we have seen that not everything that has a value also has a price and hence the most valuable thing that someone would be prepared to sacrifice for a good may not have a price. For example, in a fire, faced with the choice of whether to save your child or a Rembrandt painting, only the socially deviant will save the Rembrandt. Whilst the Rembrandt has a price as well as a value, the value of the child exceeds that of the Rembrandt although it does not have a price. In this instance, the price of the object that must be sacrificed is irrelevant to the choice since by definition the value of a child exceeds that of any object. We cannot then infer anything about the value of the child from the price of a Rembrandt.

Similarly, we have seen that there are four different streams of consumption contributing to the utility of a household: from consumer durables that are unpriced at the point of consumption, consumption priced at the point of consumption, unpriced consumption from the natural endowment, and from collective services paid for through taxation or other means. It is consequently quite possible that the most valuable form of consumption that the individual would be prepared to sacrifice for one unpriced good is another unpriced good. Secondly, if we were to introduce a charge for a good that is currently unpriced then the utility level of the household would necessarily have to fall; the quantities of priced goods consumed would also have to fall. In turn, if enough households were involved, the consequent fall in demand for priced goods would mean that their prices should also fall (provided that there are diseconomies of scale).

In turn, this means that great care must be taken in seeking to derive monetary values for goods that are currently unpriced. We cannot, for example, derive a value for walks by a river by asking people how much they would be prepared to pay for the walks they take at the moment.

5.1.1.2 Option value

An option value is defined as the value of holding open the opportunity to make use of a good at some future point in time although the individual makes no current use of that good. For example, in developed countries, some agricultural land would almost certainly presently be more valuable in other uses than agriculture, particularly environmental uses. However, given the uncertainties about the impacts of climate change and the future in general, there is likely to be an option value associated with avoiding the conversion of agricultural land to uses that preclude its use as agricultural land in the future, or its reconversion to agricultural land only at high cost. Similarly, I might attach an option value to the maintenance of a specialist cancer unit against the possibility that I may develop cancer at a later date.

5.1.1.3 Quasi-option value

Effectively, quasi-option value (Henry 1974) is the value of the information gained by not taking action now but spending time assessing in more detail the consequences of taking the action.

5.1.1.4 Functional value

The environment provides a number of obvious resources to the environment and other equally obvious forms of consumption, notably recreation. All are unpriced although the acquisition of those resources may incur a resource cost: thus, wild fisheries are free but there are costs attached to catching the fish. Some of the environmental resources are less obvious: common land traditionally provided a wide variety of resources including fuel wood, construction materials, materials for weaving, fish and game as well as water. Equally, some parts of the environment are necessary to support other parts of the environment which produce resources that are directly useful; the areas where fish breed are not necessarily where those fish are caught. Thus, to yield a resource that is useful to humans, a functional ecological web may need to be maintained where the loss of one part of that web results in breakdown of the system as a whole. Thus, Weston (n.d.) argues that the trees of the Canadian forests depend for supplies of trace minerals on the migration of salmon which are then eaten by bears who then excrete the trace minerals.

Table 5.1   *The functional value of saltings*

Width of saltings (metres)	Height of seawall (metres)	Cost of seawall (per kilometre)
80	3	400 000
60	4	500 000
30	5	800 000
6	6	1 500 000
0	12	5 000 000

Source: Dixon, Lagget and Weight 1998.

De Groot (1987) introduced the term 'functional value' to refer particularly to these indirect functional values but more widely to cover the whole range of unpriced support services provided by the environment. The problem for the analyst is then to identify the nature of the support services provided in particular circumstances. For example, Table 5.1 summarises how the cost of providing a seawall to protect the land behind from coastal erosion and flooding varies according to the width of saltmarsh in front of the wall. Similarly, if an aquifer were to be polluted, then alternative means of collecting and storing rainwater for human use would be required. For wetlands in particular, a great deal is now known about the services provided by them (Maltby 1986).

5.1.2 Nonuse value

In Section 4.3, I argued that we have a lack of grounded economic theory as to how we both approach societal choices concerning the provision of collective goods and we lack an understanding as to how people believe that such choices should be made. This problem becomes sharpest when we have to analyse choices involving environmental resources. It is clear that we value the environment for other reasons in addition to any current or future use that we may make of it. This value and the associated preparedness to pay towards the cost of preserving these resources extends to quite remote areas. In the entrance to the Centre of the Forest Park Friendship in eastern Finland, there is a row of transparent collection boxes for visitors' contributions; Figure 5.1 shows the amounts collected over one period. The Saimaa seal is an indigenous species that is under threat, which probably accounts for the greatest amount being donated towards its preservation, but conserving the Amazonian rainforest attracted a nontrivial amount, although Kuhmo is several thousand kilometres away and the centre of an important old growth forest.

This additional value has variously been termed 'passive use', 'existence' or 'nonuse' value. Of these labels, the latter is to be preferred because the only thing that we can be confident about is that it is not use value. From Krutilla (1967) onwards, economists have speculated as to the nature of the motivations that create this value; for example, that we value the environment because we

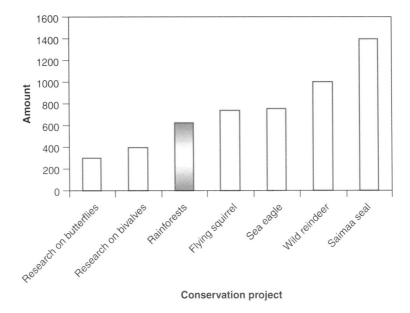

Figure 5.1   *Donations at the Centre of the Forest Park Friendship, Kuhmo. Source: Mantymaa 1996*

want to bequeath it to our descendants. But the motives that have been put forward are strictly speculative and not based upon any empirical evidence. We know that people do value the environment but we do not know why. Although we have a number of hypotheses, there is very little empirical evidence (Croke *et al.* 1994; Green and Tunstall 1996; Spash 1997) as to why people value these environmental resources.

If we do not know why people place such a value on environmental resources, we do not know what it is they value. In turn, if we do not know what and why people value something, it is difficult to claim and more especially to demonstrate that we have derived a valid and reliable measure of that value. This obviously leaves us with a major problem. The practical way forward is then to derive a preparedness to pay for the environmental good, and to assume that this is made up of two components: use plus nonuse value. If we derive preparedness to pay values (Section 12.2.3) for users and nonusers, then the difference in the two values should be the use value, nonusers only offering an amount equal to the nonuse value. This, of course, assumes both that preparedness to pay is given by the sum of use and nonuse value and that those who do not use the resource have the same nonuse value as those who use the resource.

It is, however, more important to try to discover what it is that people value and why they value it. In practice, the values people place upon environmental resources seem to involve three different factors:

- response to public, collective goods is different to that for individual, private goods;
- choices about environmental resources frequently involve moral issues; and
- there are cognitive issues relating to the nature of the good in question.

5.1.2.1 Public, collective goods

I discussed earlier why people might both approach choices about the provision of public, collective goods in a different way to that in which they approach choices about private goods, and also believe that society should make choices in a different way. There is suggestive evidence that they do approach such choices in a different way.

House *et al.* (1994) undertook a contingent valuation study of the value of alleviating low flows in a number of rivers. After being asked whether or not they were prepared to pay to alleviate the existing low flow problem, and then how much they were prepared to pay, respondents were asked which of a number of factors were important in these decisions. Table 5.2 shows the principal components factor analysis of the results. What is significant here is that the statement 'Your household's fair share of the costs' loads on to the affordability dimension and not on the value dimension where neoclassical economic theory would imply that it ought to be: that is, what it is fair for me to pay is its value to me. In turn, the statement about what would be fair was included because when the respondents in the studies by Marwell and Ames (1981) were asked how they decided how much they were prepared to pay, the common response was that they tried to decide what it would be fair to pay. This tends to suggest that people offer what they see as a fair contribution towards the cost of providing such collective goods if they believe that they have both a responsibility to do so and its provision is desirable.

Table 5.2 *Factor analysis of importance of reasons respondents gave as to why and how much they were prepared to pay*

Reason why people were or were not prepared to pay and how much they were prepared to pay	Factor 1 (affordability)	Factor 2 (value)
The other things upon which you would like to spend more money	4.1	
What your household could afford to pay	4.5	
Your household's fair share of the costs	4.3	
The value to you of the improvements to rivers as a place to visit		4.1
The value to wildlife of improvements in water quality		4.6
Explained variance	45.8	24.9

Source: House *et al.* 1994.
Key: 1 = not important; 8 = very important.

5.1.2.2 Moral issues

Choices about environmental conservation and other issues seem not infrequently to be understood in terms of tests of how good we are. How good we are is one aspect of who we are and how we relate to one another. Suppose that a very large oil reserve was discovered in the UK that would increase its GDP by 20% for the next 20 years. Unfortunately, for geological reasons, the only possible location for the oil well head is the area currently occupied by Westminster Abbey. The construction of the Abbey was started some 1000 years ago, and it is the traditional site of the coronation of British monarchs and other similar national occasions. Some 20 monarchs are also buried there along with major writers. So, too, is the Unknown Warrior, who honours those who died fighting for the country in the two World Wars.

It would be quite easy to calculate the use value of the Abbey in terms of tourism (e.g. Willis *et al.* 1993) and many economists would also be prepared to estimate the nonuse value. It would therefore be possible to determine whether, in economic efficiency terms, the Abbey should be demolished and the oil extracted; and, equally, whether it would be worth reconstructing the Abbey on another site.

However, I doubt whether any government or the board of any oil company would wish such an economic analysis to be done because of the way in which the public would then understand the government or oil company. The Abbey symbolises the country's history, culture and identity; how we then treat the Abbey is a message about how much we respect that culture and identity, and by extension, each other. In particular, those who died in war may have had many motivations, from simple patriotism to a desire to protect democracy and freedom; the one motivation that none will have had is to enable future generations to be somewhat richer. To contemplate such an analysis would then convey a clear message that achievement, or to die for one's country, is as nothing to being richer.

The above examples are all apparently quite clear-cut; the complications set in when the choice is as a moral aspect or some people see it in moral terms. The problem is then to recognise when for some people at least the question is one of moral principle and not one of economic efficiency. When this occurs, we are faced with a disagreement about objectives and other techniques, such as multi-criteria analysis, will be more helpful in the debate than applying economic analysis.

5.1.2.3 Cognitive issues

When considering nonuse value, the good in question is frequently very abstract and certainly complicated, involves a complex relationship between the whole and the part, and not infrequently involves a good that has a high symbolic value, most obviously the giant panda and, for the USA, the bald eagle. In the UK, salmon and otters have the same symbolic importance as the Saimaa seal has in Finland. In part, their presence defines the degree to which the environment is unspoilt but their presence or absence also tells us how good we are. In turn, before the question was raised, it may be that we had not heard of the good at all.

We can construct our preferences in one of two ways: working from the part to the whole, or from the whole to the part, from the general to the particular. We can wish to preserve the giant panda because we are in favour of preserving giant pandas and in turn we become in favour of preserving some or all species. Alternatively, we can be in favour of preserving the giant panda because we are in favour of preserving nature. In either case, a critical question is: what is the relationship between the part and the whole? It should not be assumed that we construct our preferences from parts and that the whole is simply the sum of these parts (Green and Tunstall 1997). Indeed, the evidence from studies of cognition suggests that this is not how we work at all (Lakoff 1987; Rosser 1994). Nor would it be a very efficient way of operating in a world of very imperfect information. Finally, the world itself is often complex so that, for example, preserving the giant panda necessarily requires preserving the entire habitat upon which it depends. These issues are then crucial when we ask people to put a value on some good using expressed preference techniques (Section 12.2.3). If we do not understand how people understand the world, how they structure it, there is a risk that we will ask an entirely meaningless question.

5.2 Who

However widely or narrowly across the species the boundary is drawn, any course of action can be expected to result in some gainers and some losers as compared to the present situation. Since neoclassical economics is concerned solely with the net effect on the nation, it has nothing to say about how these gains and losses are shared out. The only issue of concern is whether the total of gains exceeds the total of losses. The basis for the adoption of the benefit–cost ratio and net present value criteria in economic analysis is that those who gain make sufficiently large gains that in theory they could fully compensate those who lose and still make a net gain if the project goes ahead. This is the 'potential Pareto improvement principle', or the 'Hicks–Kaldor compensation principle'.

In turn, this means that an option that results in gains to those are already wealthy and losses to the poor will be preferred to another option where the distribution consequences are the opposite if the net gains of the first option exceed the net gains from the second option. Applying distributional weights has therefore been proposed (Howe 1971); two difficulties are then in deciding what those weights should be and who should determine them. Conversely, economists have routinely argued against using projects to bring about desirable redistributions of income on the grounds that tax and benefit systems are more efficient ways of achieving that end. Equally, in the neoclassical economic model, it does not matter who pays for the project and most projects involve transfers of funds from

Table 5.3   *Possible distributional outcomes*

National net benefits	Local net benefits	
	Positive	Negative
Positive	Win-win situation	Transfer sufficient of national gain to local area to make local net benefits positive
Negative	Project may be justified in terms of social/economic development of the area. Alternatively, the project should be locally funded	

Source: after Green, Parker and Tunstall 2000.

central government to the regional or local area. Those transfers themselves may be negative as, for example, if the revenue from a regressive form of taxation is used to finance a project whose primary beneficiaries are already relatively wealthy by national standards. There is, therefore, a need to examine who gains and loses through a project with attention obviously being given to the effects of the project on those who are already disadvantaged. In turn, there are three possible outcomes of a project (Table 5.3) where 'local' applies to the local area and also to specific groups within the area affected by the project's construction and operation. The obvious proposal for outcomes that fall into the top-right cell is to ensure that local benefits now balance local costs (WCD 2000).

5.3 When

All decisions involve consequences that occur at different points in time and, therefore, implicitly or explicitly some basis for comparison is made. A virtue of benefit–cost analysis is that a formal, explicit approach is adopted. Where there is no such formal approach there is an obvious risk that an inconsistent approach will be adopted; one which involves errors simply as a result of human error. It is difficult to establish such a formal logic in multi-criteria analysis.

5.3.1 Discounting

The rationale for adopting discounting in benefit–cost analysis is two-fold. Firstly, it is assumed that we prefer consumption now rather than later and equally that we would prefer to put off making expenditures. Secondly, since the investment required for the project precludes those resources being invested elsewhere in the economy, it is obviously desirable not to undertake the project if those resources could generate a higher return if invested elsewhere in the economy. Unfortunately, the first argument does not lead to the adoption of discounting and there are major problems in applying the latter approach. Both arguments use money capital and income as a metaphor but with the danger of confusing the metaphor with the reality.

5.3.1.1 Time preference

The first rationale for discounting is the assumption that we have a preference for consumption now rather than later: a time preference. Economists frequently attempt to demonstrate that we have such a time preference by use of a technically incorrect argument; by asking whether someone would prefer £100 today or next year. However, the argument for time preference is about a preference for consumption in time and £100 is both capital, and hence can generate an income, and also potential consumption which can be taken at any time in the future. The concern instead is strictly with consumption. Thus, for example, a technically correct offer is one of £100 of additional consumption to be taken over the next year, or £100 of additional consumption to be taken over the year starting in one year's time. As it is consumption, it is a 'Brewster's millions' offer: it can only be spent on consumption and cannot be used to acquire any durable that would provide consumption after the end of the year, nor held as money capital to provide an income after the end of the year.

The distribution of potential consumption over time is given by plotting the net benefits from the project against time over the life expectancy of the project. Discounting then gives a weighed measure of the area underneath the curve. Moreover, for any one discount rate, there is an infinite number of curves beneath each of which the weighed area will be the same. Therefore, if we assume that we have preferences only for the area beneath the curve and none about the shape of the curve, does discounting provide a basis for preferring one curve to another (CNS 1992)? The arguments concerning intergenerational equity (Goodin 1982) are then simply a specific instance where it is proposed that we ought to have preferences for curves of one shape over other shapes. It follows that if we do have any preferences as to the shape of the curve, then these cannot be taken into account by the adoption of any discount rate.

Thus Figure 5.2 (DEFRA 1999a) shows three project options. If we rely on the discounting rule, the choice between the options is dictated by the discount rate applied (Table 5.4).

Given the discount rate adopted in the UK at the time of writing, then we should adopt option 1. In practice, most people asked prefer option 2 although some engineers have a preference for option 3 on the grounds that the need for substantial further investments at different points in the project's life gives the option of abandoning or at least rethinking the project at those times. Since discounting does not address the issue of our preferences for the distribution of benefits and costs over time, all that can be done is prepare plots of the form shown and then prepare a reasoned argument for the adoption of one option over another where the option preferred may have a lower net present value (NPV) than the other options (DEFRA 1999). Because this is an issue of preferences,

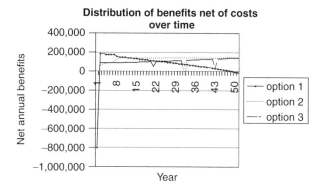

Figure 5.2   *Net benefits over time*

Table 5.4   *Option to be preferred at different discount rates*

SUM	Option 1	Option 2	Option 3
	3 899 505	5 990 465	5 033 415
NPV (2%)	2 634 504	3 393 392	2 973 244
NPV (6%)	1 319 490	1 237 902	1 308 474
NPV (10%)	694 597	458 903	720 156

or value judgements, there is no technical rule that can be provided to determine what this choice ought to be.

5.3.1.2 Opportunity cost of capital

Using the analogy of money, the argument for applying a discount rate that reflects the opportunity cost of capital is quite straightforward. The two practical problems in applying the opportunity cost of capital approach are:

- What is capital, and
- What is the economic return on capital in other uses?

If we think solely in terms of money, then the logic of the approach is obvious; given two savings accounts offering different interest rates, but otherwise identical in all respects, then we will choose the savings account offering the higher rate of interest. However, money capital and income can be seamlessly substituted for each other; the income from the savings account can be reinvested or spent on consumption, or the capital can be drawn at any time for consumption. What is important is that at the end of the period, we still have the capital.

What is capital?   It was argued in Chapter 3 that the only forms of Hicksian capital that exist in physical terms are elements of the natural endowment;

Table 5.5   *Potential substitutions between resources*

	Loss		Gain	
	Now	Future	Now	Future
Priced consumption	●	●	●	●
Nonpriced consumption	●	●	●	●
Production durable	●	●	●	●
Depletable, nonrenewable resource	●	●	●	●
Depletable, renewable resource	●	●	●	●
Nondepletable, nonrenewable resource	By definition, cannot occur			
Nondepletable, renewable resource	By definition, cannot occur			

specifically, that production durables are not capital. Secondly, the advantage of money capital is that it can be converted into income which can be taken as consumption and money income can be converted into capital. No such seamless substitution between capital, income and consumption is possible for all capital resources. Instead, there is a wide range of substitutions that may be implied by an action (Table 5.5). Thus, for instance, we may need to compare a reduction in a depletable, nonrenewable resource now against a gain in non-priced consumption in the future. It is not a self-evident truth that the rate of return on money capital has anything to do with the rate at which we should be prepared to make the trade-off between the capital resource and non-priced consumption, or indeed that the rates of substitution between any pair of gains and losses should be identical with any other.

What is the opportunity cost of money capital?   The obvious place to look is at the rates levied on borrowing capital in commercial markets, or at the return on capital that can be earned by legitimate commercial activities. Taxes on profits have to be taken out so that the after-tax return is used. Equally, it has been argued that governments have a large enough investment portfolio that the risk-free rate should be used (Arrow and Lind 1970). Thus, in the USA, the rate at which the government can borrow money is used as a measure of the opportunity cost of capital (US Water Resources Council 1983). However, this rate depends upon what that capital could earn if put to commercial purposes and the financial rates of return in commercial investments require similar adjustments to those that have been proposed for the gross domestic product (Section 3.1). If investments in the commercial sector can export externalities to consumers then the commercial return is above the true economic return. The exact distribution of externalities is, however, unknown but it does not seem unrealistic to conclude that the flow of negative externalities is predominantly to the consumer, or to the consumer in their other role as a tax payer. Therefore, we cannot simply use the after-tax rate of return on commercial investments as the appropriate discount rate.

If those investments can export externalities abroad then from the narrow national perspective, the return on capital need not be adjusted downwards. It may be immoral and may cause international friction but unless the result is to require an increase in defence expenditure, no adjustment need be made to the opportunity cost of capital. It can be argued that externalities imposed upon other commercial sectors will tend to cancel each other out but the rate we require is the marginal cost of capital; the investment that will be displaced by the proposed investment. However, we might expect that the lowest returns on capital are earned in those commercial sectors where other commercial activities have been most successful as treating as a sink for externalities and which are least successful themselves at imposing externalities on other companies.

The next problem is that we have to assume that the current allocation of capital is optimal between public investment and private investment before we can determine what that allocation ought to be. We are seeking, for example, to determine what is the opportunity cost of capital to be employed in constructing a hydroelectric plant by looking at the return from companies manufacturing air-conditioning equipment and televisions. A similar problem arises if we seek to determine the opportunity cost of capital to be used to improve navigation from the return on capital from transport firms. In general, government investment is in the upstream side of the economy: in transport and other infrastructure, R&D, education and skills provision. The returns to the commercial sector depend heavily on the prices charged to them for these provisions.

If the commercial side of the economy is not being charged the full cost of these provisions then the return on capital in the commercial side of the economy is artificially inflated. Similarly, if parts of the commercial economy are subsidised, as is typically the case for agriculture, then the returns on capital in those areas are also artificially inflated. In the case of agriculture, the returns on capital in associated industries such as seed, pesticide and fertiliser producers, as well as by food processors and retailers, will also tend to be artificially inflated.

Finally, the analogy is with money capital; so, at the end of the period assessed, we require either to have the capital intact or to have generated a sufficient excess return to replace the money capital. For example, a dam will eventually fill with sediment and cease to have the capacity to store useful amounts of water. Similarly, a water main will require replacement at some future date. We can approach this issue in one of two ways: we can extend the time horizon so as to include replacements of physical plant, or adopt a time horizon at the end of which all of the capital is recovered and include an annual payment into a sinking fund to accumulate the necessary replacement capital at the end of the project's effective lifetime.

Consequently, estimating the economic opportunity cost of capital is fraught with difficulties. Given that the three drivers of growth, other than drawing down on capital, are reinvestment in production durables, R&D and education, it is not unreasonable to expect the economic opportunity cost of capital to be related to the growth rate in the economy.

In turn, the argument sometimes proposed that since the regional growth rate is higher than that for the nation as a whole, then growth factors should be applied to the streams of benefits is the obverse of the correct argument. Where regional growth rates are higher than for the nation as a whole then the regional opportunity cost of capital is higher than the national average and so a higher discount rate should be used for projects in that region. In general, it is more conservative to assume constant real prices over the lifetime of the project but where a growth factor is used for one stream of benefits or costs, then growth factors must be applied to all streams of benefits and costs. In addition, since an expectation of growth is built into the discount rate, all growth factors are relative to this assumption and it follows that for some streams of benefits or costs, the correct growth factor is negative.

In practice, the discount rate is more realistically set as a capital rationing device and by being set in this way, creates its own truth. If a project is not viable at the designated discount rate, then almost certainly there is some other project that is viable.

6

Choosing What?

Whilst choices must be made between alternatives, the economist is primarily concerned with three areas of choice:

- between different forms of consumption;
- between different patterns of production and resource usage; and
- between consumption and investment.

6.1 Starting or Stopping

There are two quite different potential rules for decision making:

- Where to start; what should we do first?
- Where to stop; what should we do last?

Neoclassical economics is centred on the idea of optimality: a 'stopping' rule. However, in practice, the issue is usually one of where to start: what should we do first? In the case of project prioritisation and policy evaluation; is this the best use of resources this year? It is thus a question of priorities. It is also a question of prioritisation over time since next year there will be another tranche of resources available; whilst we have to make the best use of the labour available this year, next year there will be more labour available. Unfortunately, we cannot, of course, use any of next year's labour this year although our decisions this year may involve resource commitments in future years.

What we decide are the priorities this year equally have no force for next year; our priorities may have changed and we will, in any case, have undertaken the highest priority projects this year so that next year the available resources can be allocated amongst the remaining lower-priority projects.

The economic approach is to determine priorities on the basis of the benefits and costs associated with each of the options being considered. Individual consumers are presumed to choose their consumption by comparing the marginal value and cost of each of the available consumption options. Values and thus willingness to pay determine priorities. Similarly, in benefit–cost analysis, for a single project, the benefits from the options are compared to the costs of those options, and the option with

Handbook of Water Economics: Principles and Practice. C. Green
© 2003 John Wiley & Sons, Ltd ISBN: 0-471-98571-6

the highest ratio or net present value is chosen as is appropriate (Section 13.4.7.1). For a programme of works, that combination of individual projects which yields the highest benefit–cost ratio for the available resources is selected.

Starting and stopping rules converge to the extent to which the overall economy is close to efficiency at present and there is free movement of resources between sectors. In an inefficient economy, and one where resource allocation to public investment is constrained by macroeconomic concerns, then the resources available may restrict the projects which can be undertaken to those high on the priority list. More generally, for the efficient level of public investment to be achieved, the tax taken from private investment and consumption must be equal to the efficient level of public investment. Taxation levels are unlikely to be set either in this manner or with this effect; thus, less or more resources are likely to be available for investment than are appropriate for efficiency to be achieved.

There are a number of problems with the optimality approach and it probably should be dropped altogether. Firstly, where we should stop is a moving target: what we want is liable to change over time, as are the relative costs of the different options. Not only may the value of pollution abatement increase next year but so too might the marginal cost of pollution abatement. Given that programmes of capital expenditure for water management often take 20 years, it is very unlikely that what is optimum now will still be the optimum in 20 years' time.

Secondly, it also requires that we know all values and know them precisely; that we do not is the one thing about which we are certain. We have seen that economic value refers to only one objective and hence is only one value amongst a number. Furthermore, we cannot be precise even about the present and seeking optimality is precisely the wrong approach to making choices when we know that we are uncertain.

Thirdly, the concept of optimality also leads us into problematic concepts such as that of an optimal level of pollution. Douglas (1966) has argued that the label of 'pollution' is one that defines an activity as a moral wrong and consequently we can no more talk of an optimal level of pollution than of child abuse or murder. However, defining an issue in moral terms does not release the resource constraint; we lack sufficient resources to remove all moral ills even if some issues did not involve fundamental conflicts between moral values. But faced with a series of moral wrongs, it is reasonable to ask which should we tackle first. Thus, for example, in assessing the Greater Cairo Wastewater Project rather than seeking to determine what was the optimum level of pollution of the agricultural drains, and hence whether the investment in secondary and tertiary treatment was justified, it was possible to ask whether the pollution of the agricultural drains was the most urgent pollution problem facing the country (Surr *et al.* 1993).

Usually, the fundamental question we face is: how to make a better decision about where to start. At the same time, we need to determine both policies, at a national or regional level as well as at a catchment level, and to determine the best option for implementing that policy in a specific cases.

7

Costs

Costs can be defined in two overlapping but not equivalent ways: as the inputs to an activity and as the undesirable consequences of undertaking that decision. The two definitions are not equivalent because some of the consequences of an activity, the outputs, can be undesirable (e.g. negative externalities).

The four key characteristics of costs are:

- The cost of using a resource for some purpose is given by the value of that resource if used for the best alternative use ('opportunity cost');
- Costs are measured as the difference from the baseline ('marginal costs'), if there is no difference, there is no cost;
- Costs are always in the future; those costs that were incurred in the past and will not be changed by the proposed action are lost and gone ('sunk costs'); and
- Costs are the undesirable consequences of the proposed action, notably the resource costs involved but also any other undesirable consequences including externalities (e.g. the noise generated during construction should be treated as a cost and not as a negative benefit).

Thus, in Figure 7.1, the solid line represents the costs of using the available water for irrigation. To these costs must be added the negative externalities of this use. Water should then be allocated to irrigation if the value of the water to irrigation both exceeds these costs and also the value of that water to alternative uses, such as for industry. In some of the literature on water management (Rogers *et al.* 1998) some confusion has arisen as to the nature of opportunity costs and the question is dealt in more detail in Section 15.5.

The general methods of evaluating costs are discussed in Section 12.2. However, in analysing water-related projects, two convenient assumptions adopted in most economic textbooks do not apply:

- the marginal costs of production can fall as quantities rise as a result of economies of scale or of scope; and
- in a perfectly competitive market, change is costless and instantaneous; in the real world, many costs occur because change is expensive and takes time to happen. So-called transaction costs are often high and information is expensive

Handbook of Water Economics: Principles and Practice. C. Green
© 2003 John Wiley & Sons, Ltd ISBN: 0-471-98571-6

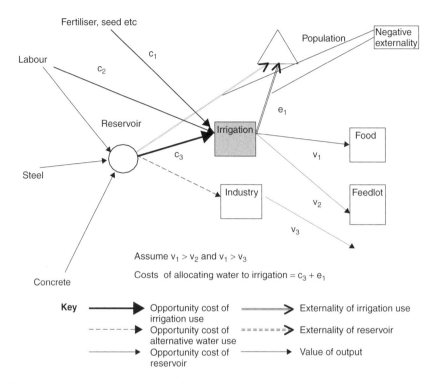

Figure 7.1   Opportunities costs and values

to obtain. Similarly, as economies become more concentrated and specialised, so called 'indirect' costs can be significant.

7.1 General Issues of Costs

Costs are apparently much more straightforward than values. Clearly, they include the capital costs such as land acquisition, resettlement, and operational and maintenance (O&M) costs. Often in analyses, construction costs are left as financial costs, those given in the bill of quantities, rather than adjusted to give economic costs. Strictly, it is necessary to correct these costs by taking out so-called transfer payments – notably revenue taxes – where a transfer payment is any transfer of money not accompanied by an equal transfer of resources or goods in the opposite direction. A movement of money alone is purely a financial or fiscal action, in national terms, it is no more than the transfer of money from one pocket to another. It can be necessary to apply shadow pricing (Squire and van der Tak 1975), particularly where there is a high level of structural unemployment or the national currency is artificially pegged to a specified exchange rate. Too much attention is often paid to potential cost overruns: given all the inevitable uncertainties about predicting benefits and costs for perhaps 50 years into the future, an inability to predict construction costs to within plus or minus 20% is a very minor issue.

The costs of the adequate resettlement (WCD 2000) of those displaced by a project are also a necessary part of the capital costs of construction. Care needs to be taken to avoid confusing things (e.g. dams) with resettlement issues whereas the magnitude of the resettlement problem is determined by the spatial extensivity of the project and the population density. When countries have a high population density, then virtually any action involves some displacement of people and this is may be the case for even apparently benign strategies. For example, implementing source control (Balanovski *et al.* 1997) in Buenos Aires as a way of alleviating the major storm water flooding problem would probably involve resettling around 20% of the population. At present, the area responds as if it is 100% impermeable, being very densely developed with very little public or private open space. A significant number of buildings would probably need to be demolished in order to create the space necessary for source control measures. Similarly, on the Yangtze, whilst the Three Gorges Dam is expected to involve the resettlement of around 1 million people, there are 4.2 million already living in the areas designated as emergency flood storage areas on the flood plain, and around 10 times that number living on the flood plain as a whole.

At the same time, population growth creates additional needs for land and work and the Brundtland definition of sustainable development (World Commission on Environment and Development 1987) requires us to take account of these needs of coming generations. When considering the acceptability or otherwise of resettlement then it is appropriate to take account of these future needs unless we are to condemn those future generations to occupy the most marginal and hazardous areas, as these are typically the only land areas left available for new settlement.

Attention should generally be focused upon two other areas rather than uncertainties about capital costs: delays in construction and O&M costs. At high discount rates, the problem with delays in construction is that the benefits are also delayed. For example, in one project, assuming that construction would take four years instead of three resulted in the net present value of the project falling by 22%. In turn, construction delays are commonplace and the risk should be foreseeable; for example, the Greater Cairo Wastewater project (Section 16.5) was expected during the years it was being built to (and it did) require more than the annual Egyptian production of engineering bricks to line the tunnel. In consequence, the project overran by several years as the work was held up by the scarcity of bricks.

Secondly, O&M costs are often not assessed in anything like the same detail as the construction costs where the resources required are usually broken down into fine detail with a unit cost for each. This is frequently not the case for O&M costs and it is not unusual for the organisation who will be responsible for operating and maintaining the works to be different from the organisation responsible for the design and construction of the works. Where the same organisation is responsible for both, the responsibilities frequently lie with different parts of the organisation with often limited communication. But a significant number of projects fail in the long run because they are inadequately maintained, often because the resources are not available to maintain them. Therefore, part of the design process ought to be a priced schedule of O&M activities and a choice may need to be made between a high capital cost, low O&M cost option versus a low first cost, high O&M cost option. Equally, attention must be given to the realism of the funding mechanism assumed to cover O&M costs. These considerations of O&M costs apply equally to projects or programmes that involve institutional changes but perhaps with even more force since concrete tends to stand up to neglect better than institutions.

7.1.1 Critical and constant natural assets

The loss or damage to sites of environmental, heritage or archaeological significance is a particular problem. In countries that have long been densely populated, most of the environment is at least partly a product of human activity; one consequence can be that a project necessarily involves an environment–environment trade-off; doing nothing involving some environmental loss and all of the do-something options also involving damage (Green and Penning-Rowsell 1999). In turn, the different interests of the environment are themselves in conflict: geomorphologists generally would like to preserve change as it is development over time that is their primary concern. Where those habitats of concern have resulted from past human interventions, then it may require considerable human intervention to maintain the current conditions that those habitats require. For example, in a study of the benefits of renovating weir structures on a heavily modified river in the east of England, a considerable part of the benefits was generated by maintaining the water levels in the series of habitats that had developed along the river since it was first modified several hundred years ago (Balfour Maunsell 1995).

Ecologists, however, are usually risk averse; although something of ecological significance may result from geomorphological or other change, the ecologists would typically like to preserve what is there now. Archaeologists clearly do not want any change that damages an unexcavated site and since the process of excavation destroys the archaeological value of a site, they frequently want to leave sites alone until archaeological techniques have improved.

Now, it is usually comparatively easy to determine the use and functional values yielded by a site; the problem lies with the remaining values. Many environmental economists will then go on to derive a nonuse value for the site but for the reasons given in Section 5.1.2, thought needs to be given as to whether this will help make the decision. In particular, given that such a value will reflect what people are prepared to pay to preserve the site, but a decision is necessarily about what we ought to do, it is open to environmental advocates to argue that people say they are prepared to sacrifice to preserve the site but that they have got it wrong.

An alternative approach is then given by the concepts of 'constant natural assets' and 'critical natural capital' (Countryside Commission *et al.* 1993).

Constant natural assets are those where, provided we maintain the current stock at the present level or above, we can lose some sites, with the obvious provision that it is then necessary to replace what is lost by creating new sites. This approach can necessarily only be applied to those habitats and sites which can be recreated in some reasonable period of time. The 'no net loss' policy (Heimlich 1991) and wetland banking policies (Reppert 1992) of the USA are an example of the use of a 'constant natural asset' approach. Three virtues of this approach are firstly that replacement need not be on a one-to-one basis; it would be quite reasonable to require that the loss of one hectare of wetland must be replaced by two elsewhere in order to allow for the risk that recreation will be unsuccessful. Secondly, it is likely to take pressure off sites that are part of critical natural capital, those that must be preserved and are irreplaceable. Given the choice between trying to develop in an area that forms part of critical natural capital and in one that is part of constant natural assets, most developers are likely to choose the latter since they can gain environmental cookie points by exceeding the minimum requirements and they can avoid the legal and political problems of trying to develop in an area of critical natural capital. Thirdly, in developed countries, important habitats are simply the bits left over after past developments, the individual sites may be too small and, in addition, climate change will mean that some will lose the most important species on those sites. Adopting a wetland banking and no net loss approach then gives the resources which could be used to expand some present sites and acquire others that will increase the capacity of the system to adapt to climate change. Clearly, the recreated sites need to be established well in advance of the loss.

The critical natural capital approach is exemplified by the European Union's Birds and Habitats Directives. In the latter, a brilliant piece of drafting requires that governments may only allow damage to, or loss of, sites designated under these directives if there is both no alternative and there are overwhelming socio-economic reasons for allowing this damage or loss. Whilst economic analysis may be a useful support when framing a law, economic analysis cannot be used to determine whether there should be compliance with a law.

In applying this approach, what is then important is to determine what habitats can be treated as part of constant natural assets; unless it is possible to recreate over a reasonable period of time and with a reasonable degree of success such a habitat, it must either be included under the category of critical natural capital or is only of local or regional interest. DEFRA (1999) provides a flow chart for determining how an individual site would appropriately be treated.

7.2 Economies of Scale

Economies of scale are both pervasive and critical in water management. Econo-mies of scale arise as a function of size, a single large plant, at least up to some point, having lower unit costs than many small plants providing the same throughput. For example many construction activities also have a high fixed cost irrespective of the size of the plant which is then installed; this also results in economies of scale in construction. Some economies of scale arise as a function of geometry: a large pipe is cheaper to construct and run than several small pipes of equivalent total capacity because the perimeter increases as a function of the radius but the cross-sectional area increases as a function of the square of the radius. For example, Brown and Schueler (1997) give the costs of stormwater retention basins as US$1 per ft^3 for a 10 000 ft^3 basin, falling to US$0.50 per ft^3 for a 5 million ft^3 basin. Similar economies of scale are reported for wastewater treatment (Bradley and Isaac 1969, Knapp 1978, Water Research Centre 1985).

That there are such economies of scale in regard to so many water management functions has a number of important implications:

- It is one reason why so many services have been collectively provided rather than each individual making his or her arrangements;
- The marginal costs of building to a higher standard of service or ahead of future demand are low; and
- They restrict the degree to which it is possible to introduce competition into the provision of water functions.

As will be described later in more detail, historically irrigation and land drainage in particular have been provided by landowners banding together and forming an organisation to construct and maintain irrigation, land drainage or flood alleviation works. It is generally considerably cheaper to overprovide in the first instance than to go back later and provide additional capacity, hence historically conservative engineers tended to build in a large allowance for future growth in demand. In general, the total cost of individuals making their own provision rises as a linear function of the number of people who make that provision. Conversely, the costs of collective provision are much less dependent upon the number of people served (Figure 7.2). For example, individuals might choose to flood-proof their own homes or build separate flood alleviation works around each small community. Penning-Rowsell *et al.* (1987) examined some local protection options for Maidenhead in the Thames Valley. Updated to 1997 prices, the costs of flood-proofing each individual property were calculated as £15 843. Constructing bunds or walls around each neighbourhood was estimated as resulting in an average cost per property of £2986. Finally, the costs of providing bunds around each of the main built-up areas was estimated to cost £2222 per property. The individual protection option requires the construction of some 140 kilometres of walling; the neighbourhood option, some 42 kilometres of bunding or wall; and the community option, the building of 26 kilometres of bunding. These figures relate to post-development flood protection and the costs of building flood protection into the initial construction of a development might be expected to be lower.

The third implication follows from the first; in urban areas, it is generally cheaper, for example, to provide piped water supply and sewerage than to sell

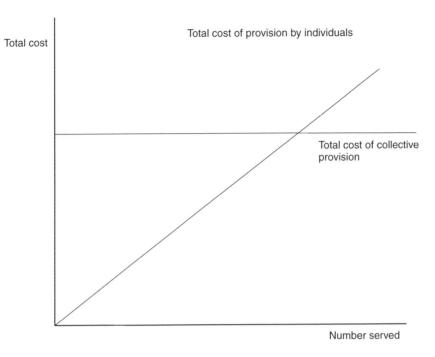

Figure 7.2 *Economies of scale. Source: Green, Parker and Tunstall 2000*

water from trucks (Briscoe 1993) and to remove wastewater from cesspools (Chapter 16) although the latter two solutions are perfect examples of the scope for introducing competition. In principle, the greater the fragmentation of provision in a market, the greater the competition and hence the potential gain in efficiency. Indeed, a key part of the definition of the perfectly competitive market which economic theory asserts will result in efficiency is that there are so many small producers that the entry or exit of any firm will have no effect (Lipsey 1971). So, for the maximum gains from privatisation through competition, we would like to fragment the system as far as possible. If, however, there are significant economies of scale in terms particularly of bulk servicing and treatment then it will not be possible to introduce a significant degree of competition and a local monopoly covering possibly a large geographic area is necessarily the result of privatisation. Economic analyses consequently must explore the extent to which there are, in the particular instance, economies or diseconomies of scale.

7.3 Economies of Scope

The case for integrated catchment management is partly based on the expectation that there are economies of scope associated with water management. That is, managing all aspects of water management will result in a lower cost strategy than trying to manage each separately and in isolation. The second rationale for integrated catchment management is that purely local solutions will be suboptimal from the perspective of the catchment as a whole, so increasing total costs. This is not a claim that there are economies of scale but that local solutions will often simply shift the problem on to another place.

As with economies of scale, the extent to which there are economies of scope has important implications for the institutional form of water management. In particular, the greater these economies of scope then the more likely it is that a monopoly will control a multiplicity of functions. If, for example, there are inherently economies of scope from managing bulk water resources, processing and distribution then even if the three functions are privatised as separate units, the consequence even in the relatively short term is likely to be one company taking over the other two companies. A further economy of scope being explored in the UK in particular is the potential economy of scope of a multi-utility company, one that provides two or more of the major utility services: water, sewerage, electricity, gas and telecommunications.

Taken together, the extent to which there exist economies of scale and of scope will determine whether an integrated organisation covering a large area will have lower costs than single purpose organisations covering small areas where the latter arrangement would make competition possible. In the former case, there is necessarily local or perhaps regional monopoly and introducing efficiency through competition and privatisation is much more problematic.

7.4 Market Imperfections

In the hypothetical perfectly competitive market, everyone has perfect information, there are numerous small and identical producers, and change is instantaneous and costless. None of these assumptions can be expected necessarily to approximate to reality when considering water management.

7.4.1 The costs of data and information

Water is a bulk, low unit-value product and hence it has not generally been considered to be worth spending very much money on collecting very much data since the cost of that data collection, processing and archiving could rapidly approach the value of the water itself. Thus, determining how much data to collect is itself an important economic question in water management (Chapter 22) and when analysing other water management issues, it should be expected that the available data will be sparse and possibly unreliable.

7.4.2 Transaction costs

Again because water is a bulk, low unit-value product, the costs of charging for water or otherwise raising the revenue necessary to pay for the costs of water management can be a significant proportion of the revenue raised. Although economists in principle favour adopting marginal cost pricing, the additional costs of applying this approach can outweigh any efficiency gain that would in theory result from the use of the approach. It may thus be better to find a simple, easy to administer, low cost method of charging than to seek to apply some sophisticated marginal cost pricing approach that is expensive to administer. Indeed, there may be a lower cost means of achieving the same effect than marginal cost pricing is intended to produce. For example, in principle, charging for irrigation water in Egypt by volume should be expected to induce more efficient use of that water. However, in practice, since farmers use human, animal or motor power to lift that water, a simple marginal cost pricing mechanism is already in place. In turn, the cost of metering small fields would be significant and Perry (1996) has shown that other cost recovery methods are more efficient. As Abernethy (n.d.) has pointed out, the ability to pay for irrigation water depends on the farmer producing cash crops rather than being a subsistence farmer. Similarly, the cost of installing meters in dwellings in England and Wales amounts to an increase of around 15%, as compared to the present property-based charge, in the average household (OFWAT 2002). Again, as treatment standards for wastewater increase, so the greater proportion of the domestic water and wastewater bill becomes for wastewater collection and treatment. Logically, therefore, it is outflows rather than inflows that should be metered but such metering is impractical. Hence, the usual practice is simply to multiply the charge for water by some factor to cover the cost of wastewater collection and treatment on the assumption that most of the water that goes in is returned. As households switch to rainwater collection and greywater reuse, this simple relationship will start to break down.

Thus, when considering methods of recovering the costs of water management, it is necessary to consider the practicality of the different methods of recovering these costs and the costs involved. The question of metering water supplies is covered in more detail in Section 15.1.2.

7.4.3 Indirect costs

In a perfectly competitive market, all changes are costless: if one plant ceases to produce, the consumers can immediately buy the same good from another factory at exactly the same cost. However, real economies are becoming increasingly concentrated and specialised; instead of many plants producing near identical goods, there are often only one or two plants in a country or even in the world that can produce a particular product. Thus, for example, the Kobe earthquake stopped production at the one plant in the world that produced a particular component for personal computers. Similarly, one plant in the UK produces 60% of bakers' yeast for the country (Parker *et al.* 1987). Consequently, the effects of a water shortage or flood can disrupt an entire economy rather than the lost production being seamlessly and costlessly taken up elsewhere in that economy.

8

Social Relations

An economy is made up of a system of exchanges of goods and services, each of which exchanges consists of two parties who are linked through the exchange. In turn, the nature of the exchange defines and is defined by the relationship between the two parties making the exchange. In part, those relationships are formalised into law which also defines what exchanges are permitted. Neoclassical economics, however, focuses exclusively on the content of the exchange to the exclusion of the nature of the relationship and assumes that the nature of the relationship is irrelevant to the content of the exchange. But, in Section 2.1.1.7, I argued that some objectives or values derive specifically from relations between people. In consequence, when we believe that we are asking about the value of something, it may be that the respondents understand the question in terms of relationships defined by the nature of the exchange. Equally, the way in which costs are recovered may then define the nature of the relationship that is understood to exist. Therefore, when considering possible institutional structures, such as privatisation, to manage water, or possible means of cost recovery, it is reasonable to consider what such arrangements say about our relationships with each other and the consequences that flow from those understood relationships.

Secondly, neoclassical economics is largely based upon the assumption that the system of entitlements and obligations derives from Anglo-Saxon law, with its stress on private entitlements and derivation of those entitlements from land. In turn, this is to assume either that Anglo-Saxon law is superior to all other systems of law in terms of its performance, or that Anglo-Saxon law represents 'natural law' (Beyleveld and Brownsword 1994). Notably, it is also usual to talk about 'property rights' as defining individual rights and obligations. This links property and a right, and conjoins the questions of 'what is right' with 'who has a right' and associates both with the possession of property. The term 'entitlement' will be used here as being a less confused and confusing term. Thus Bohannan (1960) points out that tenure is a relationship between people and 'rights' are attributes of people against other people; in Anglo-Saxon law, some of these rights then become attributes of the land. But, as Wood *et al.* (1990) note, there are many rights that are created from other bases than the ownership of land.

Handbook of Water Economics: Principles and Practice. C. Green
© 2003 John Wiley & Sons, Ltd ISBN: 0-471-98571-6

Two questions then arise from the presumption in neoclassical economics of Anglo-Saxon law:

- Does neoclassical economics then have anything of value to contribute in countries where there is a different legal structure, notably in those countries where the legal system is based upon Islamic law (Caponera 1992)?
- If we derive a set of criteria by which to define the most effective system of water law, is Anglo-Saxon law the best?

To answer these questions means considering the nature of entitlements and obligations, and how they are derived.

8.1 Entitlements and Obligations

Schlager and Ostrom (1992) defined a series of hierarchy of entitlements (Table 8.1) that give progressively wider entitlements in terms of the actions to which the holder of the entitlement is empowered. In turn, these entitlements translate into management regimes. Usufructory entitlements are entitlements to withdrawal, whilst alienation entitlements are the classic Anglo-Saxon property ownership entitlements. The two categories in between, management and exclusion entitlements, are then those associated with common property management (Section 10.2.1). There is no natural or universal tendency to ascribe alienation entitlements to land or to water. Thus, famously it was remarked: 'Our land is more valuable than your money. It will last forever. It will not even perish by the flames of fire. As long as the sun shines and the waters flow, this land will be here to give life to men and animals. We cannot sell the lives of men and animals; therefore, we cannot sell this land. It was put here for us by the Great Spirit and we cannot sell it because it does not belong to us. ... As a present to you, we will give you anything we have that you can take with you; but the land, never' (quoted in McLuhan (ed.) 1971).

It is also possible to categorise possible entitlements as shown in Figure 8.1. Some entitlements are associated to the individual; of these, some are tradable, notably the use of labour, and others are not: such as the pursuit of life, liberty

Table 8.1   *Hierarchy of entitlements*

Entitlement	Power
Access	To enter a defined physical property
Withdrawal	To gain benefits from that property
Management	To define withdrawal entitlements
Exclusion	To define who will have an entitlement to access
Alienation	To sell or lease withdrawal entitlements

Source: Schlager and Ostrom 1992.

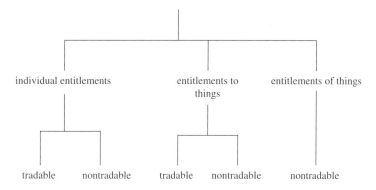

Figure 8.1   *Categories of entitlement*

and happiness. Surrogate motherhood, wherein women rent out their bodies for pregnancy, arouses concern because it is on the fringes of what is a tradable entitlement and what is not. The abortion debate is fought out entirely in the framework of nontradable entitlements; of the right of women to choose versus the right to life. It is unlikely that any suggestion that any woman who was prepared to pay enough could buy a right to choose would be felt to enrich the moral debate. Equally, whilst the problem of partner bashing could be cast in efficiency terms so as to determine the frequency and severity of battering where the gain to the batterer just equals the suffering to the battered, such an approach would be unlikely to be seen to reflect any understanding as to what the choice is about. What has been described above as 'individual' entitlements is a reductionist view; organisations, institutions and groups all have entitlements and can hold entitlements. Limited companies have entitlements, and recognised churches in many countries have an entitlement to tax exemption.

Other entitlements are associated with things; where an entitlement is tradable, then an individual can acquire entitlements to that thing, and those entitlements can be bought and sold in a market. As Common (1934) pointed out, what is bought and sold in a market is not the thing but some defined entitlements to that thing. Thus, an entitlement to buy a gun does not now carry with it the entitlement to kill someone with that gun. In any particular culture, there are entitlements associated with things which are not tradable: for example, it is not possible in the United Kingdom to acquire an entitlement to mistreat an animal, indeed, entitlements to kill animals are tightly controlled. The pattern or distribution of entitlements varies between cultures; for example, there are wide differences in the extent to which it is possible for an individual to have any tradable entitlement to land rather than, for example, some specified rights to use that land for a particular purpose. Where such entitlements to a tradable entitlement exist, there are wide differences in the limits of such entitlements. For example, whilst land has tradable entitlements in Scandinavia, this does not restrict others from having coterminous entitlements to the use of that land. Anyone may, for example, pick berries or camp on that land, subject to some understood but incompletely formalised practices: thus, for instance, one should not pick berries within 200 metres of someone's house or camp on that land for more than a day (Swedish Environmental Protection Agency 1996).

In particular, there are wide differences between countries and cultures with regard to entitlements with respect to water and especially in whether an entitlement to land defines the entitlements to the use of water on or about that land. Similarly, the pattern is dynamic over time within a culture; thus, until comparatively recently, there were many societies in which it was possible to hold a tradable entitlement over another human being: in addition to slavery, wives or children could be sold. Traditionally, in most cultures, women have been treated as having fewer entitlements than men both in terms of individual entitlements and in their ability to claim 'things' entitlements, or to those things over which it was possible for them to have entitlements. Such an arbitrary distinction in entitlements is now becoming increasingly untenable. The emphasis both upon countries and dynamic change indicates that entitlements are derived as the outcome of a social process rather than being in any sense 'natural'. Consequently, what is a tradable entitlement and what is an untradable entitlement are in the longer term socially negotiable, and attempts are being made to introduce into Western society a new category of entitlements: entitlements which things have to themselves. Hence, the fifth branch in Figure 8.1; some cultural traditions have long recognised that some things have their own entitlements as opposed to individuals having entitlements in relation to those things. Thus, under Islam, other species have entitlements; indeed, since the universe is part of God's creation, people have obligations towards all parts of that creation and it is within this context that humans have subsidiary entitlements to those things which are part of God's creation.

There are those who object to the application of economics to environmental issues, arguing that this results in the 'commodisation' of the environment. In part, what they are arguing is that what they regard as nontradable entitlements in the environmental good, or what cannot in practical terms be tradable entitlements, are being treated as if they were tradable entitlements. Libertarians indeed commonly argue that what are now in practical terms nontradable entitlements should be converted to tradable entitlements, and argue that such a conversion is the best way of safeguarding those resources. Such an argument embodies what are effectively ideological claims both as to the superiority of one form of allocation of entitlements over all others, and as to the process by which entitlements may be reallocated. Thus, those who argue against the 'commodisation' of environmental goods may fear a slippery slope where once the concept of applying monetary evaluation to environmental goods is accepted, the slide follows as this necessarily then implies that entitlements in such goods are or should be tradable.

The most important societal decisions may be those about conflicts in entitlements; for example, that over abortion. Those who object to the commodisation of the environment may argue that a debate over entitlements is being trivialised to one about the allocation of resources. Thus, the story is told that George Bernard Shaw, at a dinner party, asked the woman next to him whether she would sleep with him for £100 000. When she answered yes, he then asked whether she would do so for £5. Her reply was: 'What do you take me for?'; Shaw's response was: 'We have established what you are; now we are negotiating a price.' The more money involved, the greater the temptation but the issue may not be changed. Conversely; the neoclassical economist can sometimes give the impression that Judas's only failing was that he did not hold out for the market rate, that there would have been some qualitative difference if he had obtained 300 or 3000 pieces of silver instead of 30.

The linkage between technology and institutions is also close (Kohler 2000); unless something is technologically possible, there is no need to have any law that covers the issue. Thus, in many if not most countries, the invention of tube-well technology coupled to relatively cheap diesel or electric pumps has created a groundwater crisis with overabstraction rapidly and drastically lowering levels in the aquifer. The Ogallala aquifer (Postel 1993) is perhaps the best known instance of such a crisis but similar problems have occurred in many other countries, including the Yemen (Kohler 2000). In the absence of any effective means of making use of underground water, it was been unnecessary to have any law controlling abstraction of groundwater and groundwater has typically been left as an open access resource or it has been assumed that the landowner has a right to the waters beneath their land. Law has been left to try to catch up with the technology.

This example illustrates a second issue; to be real, an entitlement has to define some actions in regard to something that is also specific; an abstract principle must be translated into some concrete and relevant entitlements and obligations. Conversely, only when action is possible is it necessary to define the principle that will define the relevant entitlements and obligations.

The different legal frameworks vary in the relationship which is defined between individual rights and the rights of the community, which may be formalised as those of the State. There are two main conceptual pathways that have commonly been argued by which a property right can emerge: all land is originally held by the Crown or the State or the community; alternatively, property rights are initially created by individual use or annexation out of waste land. In the former case, any private property right is granted by and held at the pleasure of the State; the latter approach, at least, in part was adopted by some philosophers (e.g. Locke 1960) in order to avoid formally resting ultimate ownership in the State. Interestingly, these are two extreme versions of an individualistic model; the pole extremes of the divine 'I' and individual 'I'. Depending upon how property rights are defined to originate, then the nature of the entitlements and obligations of individuals versus the community are then argued to largely follow from that initial allocation. Thus, Locke (1960) argued that once individuals combined together to form a commonwealth governed by consent, entitlements and obligations derive from that commonwealth: 'Whosoever, therefore, out of a state of nature unite into a community, must be understood to give up all the power necessary to the ends for which they unite into society to the majority of the community . . .'.

Again, the neoclassical model rests centrally upon the assumption of an inherent individual property right as justification for the individual behaving so as to maximise his/her self-interest. If property rights flow in the opposite direction, the appropriate question would instead be how to allocate labour and other resources so as to maximise some State or community objective.

Within Europe and the countries formerly colonised by European traditions, there are two legal traditions: Anglo-Saxon law and Roman law. The Roman law tradition articulated the conflict between the individual and the community, seeking to define the relationship between each. The third great legal tradition is that of Islam (Bagader *et al.* 1994). This is the only one of the three traditions which has an explicitly ethical or religious basis and it is one in which individuals, through duties to their god, have duties to other people and other species.

In turn, there continues to be a debate in jurisprudence between those who argue that there is natural law and the legal positivists (Beyleveld and Brownsword 1994; Dworkin 1971; Hart 1961; Lloyd 1991; Lyons 1984; Morawetz 1980).

8.1.1 Criteria for a legal framework for water

Given the variety of alternative systems of water law which exist around the world, it is appropriate to look for some criteria with which to assess the relative advantages of these different systems. South Africa, for example, has determined that the predemocracy system of a combination of Anglo-Saxon and Romano–Dutch law needs to be replaced because it institutionalises the inequitable distribution of resources of the apartheid era (DWAF 1996).

Since the supply of the resource is exogeneously and dynamically determined, a necessary criterion is that:

- the system can adjust to changes in the availability of the quantity and quality of water over time as a result of climatic or other factors; that it is resilient.

This also means that it should be able to recover relatively easily and quickly from what are discovered in hindsight to have been errors; if yesterday's allocations bind us for ever, then the scope for adjusting to future changes is progressively diminished.

The principles of sustainable development require that:

- the environmental consequences of the use of the resource are factored into the decisions that are taken as to its use;
- the use of the resource does not exceed supply; thus that use equals the sustainable yield of the resource; and
- the efficient use of water both by the individual user and in terms of the allocation of water between users is promoted.

The economist will further argue that:

- the available resource should be allocated to the highest and best use;
- the externalities of those uses are internalised into the users' decisions;
- the system can adjust readily to changes in the patterns of demand, and to changes over time in the relative values of the different possible uses;
- the system does not encourage the creation of monopolies; and
- it does not give undue weight to mere geography or time – for example, that the use of land above an unconstrained aquifer does not give unnecessary entitlements.

The process of adjusting the claims to the available resource must also satisfy some criteria:

- it must be transparent and promote accountability;
- it must be seen to be fair both in outcome and in process;
- all interested parties must have equal access to the decision process in real terms;
- it must be cheap and simple to administer, and decisions must not take an undue length of time;
- where time and costs reflect any bureaucracy involved and also any legal proceedings.

Beyond this common base, a society will want to take account of its own cultural, religious or moral traditions as these reflect its beliefs about the common character of water resources; beliefs about the rights and entitlements associated with ownership or use of some resources; and those of the individual *qua* individual; the duties and obligations of individuals to both other individuals and to society; and those of society to its citizens.

In developing a system of water law to match these criteria, it is also logical to start with systems of law (Caponera 1992) that have performed well over several hundred years in the context of an arid climate where irrigation is required. The Anglo-Saxon model, whilst ideal in a colonial system of apparently infinite resources and empty spaces, or at least of lands in which the interests of the indigenous peoples could be ignored, would seem now almost universally to create problems in those countries which have adopted it of overabstraction, inflexibility and inequity. Again, the principle of *sic utere tuo alienum non laedas* – one must so use his own as not to do injury to others – depends both on a relatively large supply relative to demand and nonconsumptive uses. If water is scarce, and water is required for irrigation, it is not a practical rule to apply. Consequently, when human interventions became large compared to natural variations, they had to be replaced by administrative law (e.g. Brubaker 1995; Gustard *et al.* 1987).

Whilst the eastern United States was able to continue with English riparian law, in the western states, irrigation was a requirement for effective farming. Since the use by one person of water from a river necessarily reduces its availability for those downstream, the riparian doctrine could not be applied. The prior appropriation doctrine developed instead (Wright 1990). If the presence and interests of the indigenous populations were ignored, then the west could be treated as empty. If there is nobody living there and using water, then the principle of 'first in time, first in right' has obvious advantages in a process of colonisation where government and law follow after the settlement of the land. In turn, this doctrine has run into trouble when the available water has been fully appropriated and is used inefficiently for low-value uses, leaving no available water for incoming and higher-valued uses. This is a general problem in countries with an Anglo-Saxon legal philosophy: more resources have been converted into private property than actually exist so that rights to abstract water may exceed the drought flows.

Conversely, in arid climates, viable systems of law had to be developed and both Islamic (Caponera 1992) and Spanish colonial law (Stevens 1988) have been successful in managing surface water for several hundred years. Hence, when seeking to reform water law, these two models are the logical place to start. But, as noted earlier, law has generally yet to catch up with the technological advances that opened groundwater to exploitation.

8.1.2 Different systems and categories of resource management

The pattern of entitlements and obligations translates into systems of resource management; these are two sides of the same coin. It is possible to distinguish between five main classes of entitlements in relation to land (Table 8.2). Of these approaches, common property management is particularly important because it has both been historically important in the management of water and because it is a model that is being rediscovered.

In 1968, Hardin wrote an important and influential paper in which he effectively argued that the only way that common property resources, such as environmental resources, could be preserved was if they were converted into private property. A self-evident problem with his paper was he explicitly referred to the English Commons, a system that had survived for several hundred years without the consequences he predicted occurring (Clapham 1963). Rather than demonstrating that a Commons inevitably resulted in disaster, he indirectly drew attention to what was a neglected but apparently rather successful way of sustainable management.

Hardin's paper provoked two forms of response. Ciriacy-Wantrup and Bishop (1973) made the distinction between 'common property' (*res communes*) and 'open access' (*res nullius*) resources and pointed out that Hardin confused the two. Whereas his analysis holds true for open access resources, those to which there is no control over who may use them and for what purposes, common property resources, like the English Commons itself, has historically proved to be an effective and sustainable form of resource management. Some common property resource systems have survived successfully over centuries. The best known of these is Netting's (1981) analysis of common property management in

Table 8.2 *Categories of entitlements*

Category of entitlement	Description
Open access	Open to all uses by anyone without control; for example, wasteland or wilderness in a society where there is an excess of land over demand
Common property	Management by a group who controls the uses which may be made of the resource and who make such uses. Those who, by membership of the group, acquire such entitlements are not able to trade these entitlements
State property	Resources which are owned by the state and which are 'farmed' either by state bodies or by individuals under usufructory entitlements
Limited individual ownership entitlements	Entitlements which are granted by the state but within the boundaries of those entitlements, and the obligations to others, the individual may do what so ever s/he pleases. The owner of such an entitlement can pass this entitlement on to their children or to whomsoever they think fit. The United Kingdom model of Anglo-Saxon property rights
Unrestricted individual entitlements	Derived from the assertion that entitlements to land in particular are the 'natural law' and the highest form of liberty. Claimed that any restriction or limitation of the use that may be made by the individual of that which s/he has an entitlement is an infringement of their rights and liberty. The US libertarian view of property rights

the Swiss Alps, where common property management dates from the thirteenth century. Historical analyses of the English Commons were also available (see Cox 1985 for sources), which refuted Hardin's claim that private property ownership was the only way of preserving environmental resources.

There is then an expanding body of research covering the extent of common property resource management. These studies have shown that common property resources form a large part of available resources and contribute a significant fraction of household income in less developed societies (e.g. Jodha 1992). Common property is markedly different from an open access resource; there are typically strong controls over who may use it and for what purposes, as, indeed, there were with the traditional English Commons. The difference compared to private property is that it is owned and managed collectively by those who use it. The rights to the use of the property are often inheritable and may or may not be saleable.

In agrarian societies, resources such as forests and woods, lands providing fodder or grazing, game for hunting, fisheries and sources of running water, along with 'rights of way', were all often managed as common property. Whilst some writers have argued that it is low intensity and somewhat marginal resources that are usually managed as common property, many irrigation works (and land drainage schemes (Wagret 1967)) have been constructed as common property resources. Therefore, the explanation does not appear to be wholly adequate.

The characteristics of other successful common property resource management bodies such as the Watershappen in the Netherlands (Wagret 1967) are similar: a highly democratic decision-making process; both law and tax-making power; and a means of enforcing those laws and of collecting those taxes. Effectively, they are a state in miniature. What is particularly notable is the democratic structure; the Watershappen have been said to be the oldest democratic institutions in the Netherlands and to date back to the first polders. Similarly, the Huerta system in Valencia dates back to the fourteenth century (Glick 1970). But it appears that some common property resource management bodies were democratic well before the host country as a whole was democratic.

Most recently, given that the evidence is that common property resource management has proved historically to be a highly effective means of managing some resources over centuries, the question has turned to defining under what conditions is common property resource management successful. The World Bank (1993) is now promoting the use of the strategy, in terms of Water User Associations, to manage irrigation, water supply and local sanitation.

8.2 Social Exchanges

Neoclassical economics entirely excludes the relationships between people and treats these as being wholly irrelevant to the relations of an individual to things. Indeed, it seeks to construe the relationships between individuals and between groups in terms of the relationship between an individual and objects and services. However, in reality, our relations to things are set in social contexts and decisions are commonly taken as part of a social group, be this a household, community or a company. Even when we take decisions as individuals, socialisation is likely to affect the way we take decisions. In turn, relationships between individuals and things need to be understood and interpreted in terms of the relationships between individuals and individuals to groups. For example, the roles of 'consumer' and 'owner' are both social constructs. Similarly, a 'price', a 'charge' and a 'tax' all define different forms of social relations. Again, as both Marx and Common (1934) pointed out, the economists' 'property rights' are actually not relations between people and property but about relations between people.

The gender role of women is also intimately linked to the relationships and roles that constitute households. A number of irrigation projects in West Africa, for example, have failed because it was assumed that women's labour would be available for working on cash crops; something which has traditionally been a male's task (Zwarteveen 1997).

One specific articulation of a relationship is exchange; this is of particular interest to economics since a focus of economics is the exchange of resources for consumption. Many societies have complex systems of exchange (Davis 1992) of goods which are completely different to, and outside of, the concept of market exchange. As Davis notes, even in Western societies, a significant proportion of exchange is semi-ritualistic exchange outside of the money economy (e.g. Christmas and birthday presents, lift giving, buying rounds of drinks etc.). Davis (1992) described a partial repertoire of exchanges in British society and showed that these varied highly.

If we look at this repertory, it is found (Green 2000b) that each exchange can be characterised in terms of the roles of the two sides involved and the social legitimacy of the transaction. The difference between a 'tip' and a 'bribe' is largely socially defined: some inferiors may be tipped (e.g. taxi drivers, waiters) but equals and superiors may not be (e.g. doctors), nor may other classes of inferiors (e.g. water meter readers). In addition, a 'tip' is given after a service whereas a bribe is given in order to induce a service. Similarly, a 'gift' may only be given to socially appropriate others and be of limited forms; small children are, for example, warned never to accept gifts from strangers. Other gifts, such as the exchange of Christmas cards, are socially expected. This table also excludes all purely personal exchanges such as handshakes, kissing, hugging and embracing.

There is an equally high variety of labels given to transfers of money in British society (Table 8.3), and the labels again distinguish between the roles of the giver

Table 8.3 *Different forms of monetary transfer*

Definition	Definition
Alimony	Housekeeping
Bequest	Incentive
Blackmail payment	Inheritance
Bonus	Loan
Bribe	Pay
Capital gains	Payment
Charge	Payoff
Child support	Pension
Christmas box	Performance pay
Compensation	Pocket money
Covenant	Profit share
Damages	Prize
Donation	Repayment
Embezzlement	Salary
Extortion	Smuggling
Fee	Surcharge
Fine	Tax
Fringe benefit	Theft
Gift/present	Tithe
Golden handshake	Tip
Holdup	Winnings

Source: Green 2000.

and recipient, the nature of the transfer, and the moral/legal basis of the transfer. There seem to be rather fewer labels applied to the giver and recipient, illustrating that between two people in the same relationship, transfers can differ both in their nature and basis.

These labels very clearly define both the relationship between the two parties, and its legitimacy, as well as the roles of the two parties; the same transfer can then have different labels depending on the relationship and roles. Payment transforms the nature of a relationship; for example, payment for sex transforms the nature of the exchange: what was potentially an exchange of pleasure becomes merely a transaction wherein pleasure is exchanged for money. What was of mutual benefit now becomes a one-way transfer that can only be brought back into balance by a cash transfer. The introduction of a transfer of money in this instance at least signifies the nature of the relationship and perhaps even transforms it.

Thus, the form of payment for water and sewage denotes the relationship involved; attempts to change the form of payment imply an attempt to change the nature of the relationship and the roles of the parties involved. Were a water company to demand a tithe of my income, then I would find this a very strange and wholly illegitimate demand because a tithe is a religious duty and the water company is not a religious organisation to which I have chosen to belong. In the long run, water metering is therefore almost a prerequisite for a privatised water supply system because a charge per property is effectively a tax. Prices are set by suppliers and the consumer can choose whether or not to buy at that price. However, taxes are set by accountable forms of government; a private company accountable only to its shareholders cannot be allowed to set a tax. Therefore, if costs are to be recovered through charges, rather than metered prices, then price regulation is almost inevitable.

Against this richness of forms of relationship and roles, the standard economic approach seems trite and barren. Thus, the problem with standard economics is not that it introduces money but that it treats all of the variety of exchanges as equivalent to that of buying and selling, and all roles as being those solely of a consumer and producer. Therefore, when considering how to recover the costs of water and the management strategies to be adopted, we need to consider the nature of the relationship, the behaviours consequently appropriate to that relationship, and the desirability of those behaviours. For example, in the 1976 drought in England, when water supply was run through public institutions, the government appointed a minister to be responsible for managing responses to the drought. In 1993, after the water industry had been privatised, in another drought, the minister called in the chief executives of the water companies in order to issue a press statement announcing that he found their performance unacceptable. Finally, whereas in 1976, some water suppliers that had no water resource problems called for voluntary cuts and banned some uses out of solidarity with neighbouring water suppliers who had real problems; this did not happen in 1993.

9

What is a Better Decision?

The entire force of economics lies in the extent to which it enables us to make 'better' societal decisions: what we mean by 'better' is therefore critical. By 'better' we certainly mean that today's decisions should be an improvement on past decisions and we also want to perform consistently better in making the 'right' decisions. By 'right', we are concerned to make decisions that are right in both senses of the word: they are correct and they are equitable or just. At a minimum, we want to get closer to achieving these two aims than we have in the past.

In turn, a decision is to make a choice and a decision thus has three elements: objectives, alternative means to achieving those objectives, and a procedure for making the choice. Whilst the objectives are abstract, the means is concrete, literally so in many cases, and it is the means selected that determines who therefore bears the costs of the decision: who pays and who bears the adverse consequences of the choice.

9.1 Making Correct Decisions

By 'correct', we mean that if we could look back at today's decisions with the advantage of, say, 200 years' hindsight of each of the possible alternative futures that would result from adopting each of the possible options open to us, then it would prove that we had adopted the best course of action, that which came closest to achieving our objectives. Since it is impossible to carry out this test, we have to use the characteristics of the decision process as a test of the likelihood that we have made the correct decision. How rigorous and complete was the framework of analysis that was used to inform the decision, and was the decision based upon this analysis?

In other words, as a species, we take it as an article of faith that using reason will result in making better decisions than the use of other methods of informing decisions. A simple and cheap method of determining which option to adopt would instead be to toss a coin; as argued above, it is difficult to determine whether using reason is more likely to result in the right choice being made. In short, we cannot prove conclusively that using reason results in better decisions than any other process but the use of reasoning has a number of advantages:

Handbook of Water Economics: Principles and Practice. C. Green
© 2003 John Wiley & Sons, Ltd ISBN: 0-471-98571-6

- It promotes transparency and accountability because the chain of logic can be seen and tested.
- It provides a basis for argument, debate and discussion, because we can identify where we disagree.
- It reduces the risk of errors being made in the analysis and increases the likelihood that they will be identified during the course of the decision.
- It promotes consistency of approach between different projects and hence equality of treatment to the gainers and losers from different projects.

9.2 What is the Equitable or Just Decision?

Dictionary definitions of equity include: 'that which is fair or right; impartiality; the recourse to the principles of justice; the quality of being equal or fair' (*Shorter OED* 3rd edition). Again, in early English law, 'equity' was that part of the legal system built around the principles of natural justice and fair conduct and it was specifically designed to deal with those cases where formal law would result in an unfair outcome in the case in question (Lloyd 1991). Thus, equity has two components: a moral principle as what ought to happen coupled with the fair or equal application of that principle to different decisions. Notably, equity is a far richer and more diverse and complex subject than its treatment in neoclassical economics as equality of income. In particular, equity relates both to the outcome of the decision and the procedure by which that decision is reached. Thus, we seek to make the right choice by the right procedure, and distinctions can thus be drawn between outcome and procedural equity (Mitchell *et al.* 1993).

If equity is composed of a moral principle plus its fair application, then a distinction must be drawn between economic efficiency as technical efficiency and economic efficiency as an objective in its own right (Section 3.1). As soon as economic efficiency is treated as an objective in its own right, it becomes merely one possible interpretation of equity, one moral claim as to what ought to be an objective of collective decisions. Hence, to claim that there is a conflict between equity and economic efficiency is false, the argument is between moral claims as to what is equitable. Therefore, a distinction must be drawn between 'technical efficiency', the maximisation of the achievement of some set of objectives within some set of constraints, and 'economic efficiency', the maximisation of some aggregation of consumption within some set of the constraints. The former is a technical question; the latter relies upon a moral claim.

However, there is a distinction between law and decision making; legal decisions are zero-sum games: what one party gains from the decision, the other party loses. Conversely, societal decisions are multi-party and the objective is generally to achieve an outcome where the gains outweigh the losses except where the intention is deliberately only redistributive.

What objectives should be pursued is a moral, ethical, religious and political question. Different countries place different emphasis on different objectives or make different trade-offs between them. Thus, over much of western Europe, 'national solidarity' or 'communal solidarity' is given as a basis for taking decisions. For example, the French constitution asserts that there will be national solidarity in the face of natural disasters. Traditionally, in Britain, the basis for societal decisions was taken to be the 'national interest'; something that both existed over and above individual interests and which could be objectively identified. Other countries place an emphasis on following the laws of the deity or seeking to maintain social stability. Libertarians assert that individual rights must have primacy and that individual property is the highest form of liberty; in turn, this implies that libertarians should neither contribute towards nor gain from collectively provided goods. In some other countries, such as the Netherlands, the objective is primarily about the process by which decisions should be taken; that decisions should ideally be made through a process of establishing a consensus. Most countries now also include sustainable development amongst the objectives brought to a decision.

9.2.1 Outcome equity

Depending upon the nature of the choice, the outcome may result in some surplus that is to be allocated across the collective; there will certainly be some costs, monetary and/or otherwise, to be shared. These costs need not always be monetary; for example, if there is inadequate water available to meet existing demand, for which and to whose demands should supply be cut back?

In terms of distributional equity, Pettit (1980) categorises the various bases of theories of justice into three, in order of historical development:

- Proprietary; the natural law model (e.g. Noznick 1974).
- Utilitarian; welfare models following from Bentham (1948).
- Contractual; distributions which the individual would choose if s/he did not know their initial starting position (Rawls 1971).

Pettit (1980) also notes that what is equitable can be defined either as a principle that can be used to determine the appropriate outcome or as being a characteristic, or property, of the individual. Sen (1992) shows that these models can further be defined as models of equality of one form or another; all embody some belief in equality, but they differ widely in what is to be allocated equally. Whilst the debate on equality is often defined in terms of income, Sen shows that the libertarian claims about the primacy of individual rights and liberties and utilitarian theory are essentially arguments about equality. Thus, although Bentham described the natural right model as 'nonsense on stilts' and sought instead to derive a principle to select the outcome of a choice, rather than basing choice upon the basis of some property of the individual, the maximisation of welfare assumes that the utilities of all individuals are to be treated equally. Consequently, Sen (1992) points out that the central question in discussing equality is 'equality of what?' whilst almost all approaches to the ethics of societal arrangements are based upon some assertion of the requirement of equality of something. There is, however, wide debate and conflict as to in what respect individuals are to be treated or regarded equally. Moreover, Sen (1992) argues that ascribing one characteristic as the centre of a claim to equality typically implies that consequentially individuals cannot be treated equally in terms of another property.

The problems for economic appraisal of considering equality as an objective are then two-fold: firstly, equality is relative rather than absolute, and, secondly, which equality is appropriate? The advantage of restricting the analysis to economic efficiency is that more economic efficiency is always better and in consequence different decisions can be made entirely independently of each other. But equality is by definition a balancing act; often then the appropriate outcome depends upon what other actions are also being taken that will in turn impact on equity. If, for example, eight decisions are taking place simultaneously, and in each case the benefits are distributed according to the relative need of individuals or groups then the result may be to radically alter their standing, and hence need, so that now another group of individuals stand out as being in need. Thus, Mitchell *et al.* (1993) similarly remark that: 'Justice is not a stable, well-defined ideal end-state toward which people purposefully move; rather it is a dynamic, ever-shifting equilibrium between the excesses of too little regulation on the one hand and too much on the other.'

The moral principles that have been proposed as the basis of decisions regarding the provision and allocation of goods, and the allocation of the costs of provision, include:

- The benefits should be distributed on the basis of the contribution of the individual to the provision of the good or of their wider contribution or importance to the group;
- The benefits should be distributed according to the relative need of the individual or group (Farmer and Tiefenthaler 1995);
- The benefits should be shared equally between individuals;
- The costs should be borne according to the value of the resource to the individual or group ('user-pays principle');
- The costs should be borne according to ability of the individual or group to pay; or
- That the polluter ought to pay according to their contribution to the problem ('polluter-pays principle').

These principles in turn may and often do conflict, with quite different outcomes. In the case of flood alleviation, the application of the user-pays principle may be argued to require that those who are protected against flooding should bear the costs of providing that protection. However, flooding may equally be treated as an externality of other people's land use in so far as the way in which they have developed that land has changed the pattern of runoff. In this case, the polluter-pays principle should be applied and those upstream land users should bear the costs of the downstream flood alleviation scheme. We have in short to argue and determine the moral principle, or principles since one principle may not result in a unique outcome, to be applied in a societal decision before we can take that decision. Moreover, of the above six principles, only the first and fourth result in the same distribution of benefits and costs.

In addition, projects often involve significant transfers from national or provincial funds towards a local area or groups within that area. In many cases, the reason for these transfers is an objective other than economic efficiency: for example, national solidarity or to promote socio-economic regeneration, or development, in a relatively poor region. To then apply the user-pays principle would be to vitiate the entire purpose of the project. Thus, the EU's Water Framework Directive excludes projects intended for these purposes from the general requirement that there should not be subsidies towards water management activities. In general, other than a concern for 'pork barrelling', the tendency to promote projects for local political reasons where those projects are subsidised from national funds, transfers from the nation to particular groups are not very problematic. That people should agree to give to others is clearly their right although if the gainers were relatively wealthy and the tax system is regressive, then there are obvious questions.

Conversely, projects where a small group lose a lot but a much larger group gains, usually a relatively small amount, are much more problematic. Historically, the displacement of the population to make way for a large-scale project has been the most extreme example of such redistributions. In particular, those lacking power are most likely to be displaced, and, in turn, those with least power are usually minority groups. Nor can any nation claim an unblemished reputation with regard to its treatment of minority groups. More than adequate compensation and resettlement, the primary concern should be to involve the groups affected in the decision (WCD 2000). Where the area concerned holds graves or religious sites, then compensation for those losses is impossible in principle; the issue is one of whether the overall good generated by the project, and the lack of good alternatives, is sufficient to outweigh the losses.

Absent from the list of principles that might be used to determine the distribution of benefits and costs from a project is the potential Pareto improvement principle applied in benefit–cost analysis. In turn, this does not seem to be commonly used in practice: for example, the Huerta in Spain use different principles to determine how water should be allocated when water is scarce (Maas and Anderson 1978).

9.2.2 Procedural equity

One aspect of procedural equity is equality of treatment: 'all those in the same category shall be treated as equal' (Lloyd 1991); that is, in accordance with the categories laid down by law and not in either an arbitrary or biased manner.

Lloyd also differentiates between formal and substantial or concrete justice where formal justice involves treating in a like way so that:

- there are rules setting out how people are to be treated in given cases;
- these rules shall be general in character; and
- these rules are impartially applied.

Conversely, substantial justice then refers back to outcome equity so that each shall be treated according to their just deserts.

A rather limited amount of research has been undertaken on aspects of procedural equity in regard to water management. That work which has been done (Tyler and Degoey 1995; Syme and Nancarrow 1997) suggests that principles similar to those given by Lloyd are important to promote compliance with the decision that has been reached (Lawrence *et al.* 1997).

Possible tests for the adequacy of the decision process are then:

- Were all key stakeholders engaged in the decision process?
- Were the key objectives that the different stakeholders bring to the choice considered?
- Was an adequate range of options considered, including those favoured by particular stakeholders?
- Were all the most probable and most important consequences of adopting each option considered?
- Was the process of analysis rigorous and logical?
- Was the best available data (not incurring excessive cost) used in the analysis?

Two quite specific requirements for procedural equity are then the consideration of gender and other issues of power, and stakeholder involvement. In the case of gender and parallel issues, these are necessarily also an issue in outcome equity.

9.2.2.1 Gender/power issues

One of the Dublin Principles (ACC/ISGWR 1992) for the sustainable management of water is to recognise the importance of the role of women in the management of water. It is now more common to speak of the need to recognise gender issues where gender is: 'a social construct through which all human beings organise their work, rights, responsibilities and relationships' (Thomas-Slayter and Rocheleau 1995). Equally, a gender approach looks at women and men, and not women in isolation (Maharaj *et al.* 1999). The gender approach is further extended to cover the wider issues of inequalities of access to resources, to power, to education and to money within communities as a result of caste, ethnicity, religion and other factors (Mehta n.d.). Thus, Maharaj *et al.* (1999) point out that: 'A community is not a collection of equal people living in a particular geographic region. It is usually made up of individuals and groups who command different levels of power, wealth, influence and ability to express their needs, concerns and rights.'

Within this wider framework of inequalities, there continues to be a wide range of gender differences and these differences are not limited to the developing countries. For example:

- A significant proportion of households in many countries are female headed as a result of death, divorce, or the migration of the male partner to find work in urban areas. In Sri Lanka, for example, one in five households is now female headed (Maharaj *et al.* 1999).
- In many countries, women have traditionally had responsibility for finding and collecting water (Table 9.1) and carrying water may consume one-third of a woman's daily calorific intake (Tahseen n.d.). In Nepal, 94% of women alone are solely responsible for fetching water (84 litres/day).
- Collecting and carrying water exposes women to more risks than men – and not just from water-related disease vectors (White *et al.* 1972).
- At the same time, collecting water and washing may be an important opportunity for women to socialise with other women and so water collection and use plays a social role as well as having a utilitarian purpose (Brismar 1997; van Wijk-Sijbesma 1985).
- Because finding and collecting water is women's work, water management may consequently be regarded as of no importance (Katko 1992).
- Because of their greater workload than men, women may have no time to attend meetings or participate in organisations. Again, girls are often too busy with household work to go to school. For example, one respondent in an Egyptian village is quoted by El-Katsha *et al.* (1989): 'By nightfall I feel as if somebody is banging at my head as a result of carrying water back and forth during the day. I have no energy to do anything but sleep. Do you expect me to worry about bad conditions in the village?'
- Women are typically the main producers of staple crops, producing 60–80% of the food in developing countries (FAO 1997); in Tanzania they produce 60–70% of all food consumed whilst they provide 90% of the labour for rice cultivation in southeast Asia and 53% of agricultural labour in Egypt (FAO 1997). As men have to move to the cities to find work, agriculture is being

Table 9.1 *Time spent collecting and carrying water*

Place	Hours per week spent drawing and carrying water
Botswana	5.5
Mozambique – dry season	15.3
Mozambique – wet season	2.9
India, Baroda	4.0

Source: Brismar 1997.

feminised. It is usually men who plough fields and drive draught animals (and similarly grow cash crops) but women who sow, weed, apply fertiliser and pesticides, harvest and thresh. In turn, irrigation schemes can result in an increase in women's workload (Hart 1992).

- Women have the primary responsibility for childcare and dealing with illness in the household and hence the burden of water-related diseases falls on them. Sen (1990) points out that if a rural woman were to be asked about her personal welfare, she would find this a meaningless question, being only able to conceptualise welfare in terms of her family.
- Women are often responsible for re-establishing a household after a disaster such as a flood.
- Women commonly have less access to cash than men, and also other household resources, including food. They also have less time available to earn income; in developing countries, men spend 76% of the time earning income, women 34% (UNDP 1995).
- Whilst women generally have less entitlements to land and other property than men, it cannot be assumed that the household holds such rights in common and that the male members of the household control such rights (Meinzen-Dick *et al*. 1997). In parts of Africa in particular, women have traditionally held separate and distinct rights to land to men. But when projects have involved redistributing land or resettlement, women's rights have been ignored in the past (Zwarteveen 1997).

In turn, the implications for the design and appraisal of projects are:

- To take account of the differences between genders and other groups in their work, experience and behaviour with participatory studies being essential to discover these differences and the interactions between the groups (Mehta n.d.). If these differences are ignored then projects often fail or are only partially successful.
- Equity: it is clearly necessary to avoid exacerbating existing inequalities, whilst it is desirable to achieve a reduction in inequalities.
- Finally, since more than 50% of a country's population is female, no country can afford not to make the best use of this resource.

9.2.2.2 Stakeholder involvement

The maximum involvement of the public in all levels of decision making is one of the Dublin Principles (ACC/ISGWR 1992) and one of the clear requirements for procedural equity. There is a wide range of arguments in support of increasing stakeholder involvement:

- 'It is also a moral duty. Public authorities work for the public' (DETR 2000a).
- The experience of projects is that they do not succeed unless the different stakeholders are committed to them. For this to happen, they have to be involved

in the decisions that resulted in the particular option being adopted (Garn 1997). In rural areas, the doctrine is that community involvement is essential if rural water supply systems are to be sustainable (Black 1998) in the long run, particularly with respect to the operations and maintenance of the system, and perhaps especially with regard to funding the latter function (Breslin 1999). Indeed, it is currently argued that demand responsive service provision is essential (Cernea 1992).

- The local population will have more knowledge about some aspects of local conditions than any outside specialists.
- One or more of the options may only work if the community changes its behaviour; the community therefore first has to decide that such a change in behaviour is desirable.
- To strength democracy and the community.
- Participation increases the perceived legitimacy of the decision that is the outcome of the process.
- The constitutional structures are such that the only way to make the system work is by bringing together the different stakeholders; there is no way of creating an institutional structure that can otherwise implement the plan.
- It is in any case inevitable as a result of an ageing population: retirement now leaves a large number of physical and mentally active people with high levels of skills, knowledge and experience – often more in total than that of the design team who are developing the project.

There is now a very large literature on stakeholder involvement in decision making (e.g. Creighton *et al.* 1991; World Bank 1996a); what it is understood to mean varies almost as much as do definitions of sustainable development. Birkeland (1999) set out a useful comparative analysis (Table 9.2) which emphasises that its meaning derives from the wider paradigm that is adopted. This table is perhaps more useful for defining the first three paradigmatic approaches than that which is labelled as ecofeminist and bioregional, not least because others, such as green ecologists, would lay claim to some or all of that conceptualisation.

Stakeholder involvement is necessarily about the degree of power transferred to those engaged in the process; at one extreme, power is wholly vested in the stakeholders involved. In terms of single-function organisations, relatively common examples are farmer-managed irrigation schemes (e.g. Sutawan 1989) and the provision and management of water supply systems by the local community (e.g. Garn 1997). The most developed example of such multi-functional, stakeholder-based organisations is probably the Watershed Councils that are being established in Australia (Comino 2001).

At the other extreme, the views of the different stakeholders are simply sought in order to inform the decision process. In between lie different forms of dialogue with more or less control over the final decision being reserved. Goss (1999) (Table 9.3) has provided a useful structure of the different levels of involvement and the tools that may be used to support this involvement.

Table 9.2   Participatory planning models

	Technocratic/comprehensive	Liberal/incremental	Radical/advocacy	Ecofeminist/bioregional
Objective	Public or national interest	Reconcile the conflicting individual interests	Redistribution to the marginalised communities	Sustainable development
Concept of community	Public interest as determined by experts	Individual interests and preferences	Under-represented groups threatened by development	Interdependence; systems model of society and ecosystems
Form of participation	Public consultation by experts	Consumer choice	Development of counter-plans and offers	Discourse based
Planner's role	Determine optimal solutions	Determine public preferences	Ensure equal access to decision making	Facilitate bioregional/global perspective
Concept of planning	Comprehensive	Incremental	Advocacy	Debate and negotiation
Process	Scientific evaluation	Democratic representation	Law-based, adversarial	Self-help and empowerment
Favoured methods	Benefit–cost analysis, SEA, social impact analysis	Voting analogies e.g. surveys, participation	Educational and adversarial strategies	Self-help and empowerment
Ethical basis	Utilitarianism	Liberalism	Critical theory	Ethic of care
Key role of community	Input into the scientific process	Input into pluralist process	Counter-plans, protest, obstruction	Self-determination
Government's ideal role	Weigh expertise and other policies	Balance competing interests	Distribute wealth, arbitrate	Meet basic needs, facilitate
Project initiator	Private or public developer	Private or public developer	Private or public developer	Community self-reliance
Philosophical aim	Rationality	Procedural justice	Distributive justice	Justice, well-being
Competing values	Majority wins	Balance of interests, trade-offs	Equal opportunity, fair game rules	Consensus
Preferred reforms	Transparency of decision making	Deregulation and less government	More community power and autonomy	Systems change

Based on Birkeland 1999. SEA = Strategic Environmental Assessment.

Table 9.3 *Local authorities and public involvement*

Giving information	Consultation/ listening	Exploring/innovating/ visioning	Judging/deciding together	Delegating/supporting/ decision making
Sign-posting	Surveys	Consultative workshops	Deliberative polls	Neighbourhood committees
Leaflets/newsletters	Focus groups, priority search	Visioning workshops	Citizens' juries	Town/estates
Community profiles	Interactive community profiles	Simulations; open-space events	Negotiation workshops	Tenant-managed organisations
Feedback on surveys and consultation	Public meetings, forums		Community issue workshops	
Annual performance reports			Community workshops	Community development
Support/advice	Panels	Planning for real community discovery	Consensus conferences	Partnership with communities
Video/internet communication	Video boxes	Use of theatre, arts/media		Referendum tele-voting

Source: Goss 1999.

However, stakeholder involvement does not change the nature of the choice; it only changes who makes the choice. In terms of the choice that must be made, it changes nothing; its virtue lies in procedural equity rather than there being any necessary improvement in the quality of the decision that will emerge from the process. As Birkeland (1999) noted, there is an assumption that if the process is right, then the outcomes will take care of themselves. Indeed, there is a danger that elected representatives will shift the most difficult and contentious decisions onto a stakeholder involvement process simply because they are difficult and contentious. Thus, those who are presumably best prepared and are being paid to make such decisions will shift the burden onto the public without necessarily providing the time and resources that we need to take those decisions.

Similarly, a fully participatory approach cannot be assumed to inevitably result in the best choice being made and equally there are likely to be more or less successful approaches to participation. In practice, the literature about the performance of small groups is not particularly encouraging (Brown 1965); a great deal of care is necessary if the outcome is not simply to be the result of the original composition of the group and the dynamics within the group (Sunstein 1999). Simply creating a deliberative group neither necessarily results in a consensus nor in a decision that is better than the decisions the individuals would have taken on their own. Sackman (1975) has stressed the dangers of the pressure within the group towards compliance with apparent social norms.

Trial juries are the direct inspiration for one participatory technique, variously known either as 'citizen juries' or *plannungszelle* (Dienel 1978; Dienel and Renn 1995). Examining how well trial juries perform and the conditions that either promote or inhibit the success of trial juries should therefore be expected to provide useful lessons for citizen juries and other forms of stakeholder involvement. Trial juries do have a relatively simple task to perform in that there are generally only two possible verdicts on each charge in a criminal trial, although the task in a civil trial may be more complicated. In the UK, research into juries has been forbidden, in part perhaps to protect the mystique of the jury. What research is available provides mixed messages; juries do take their duty very seriously (Young *et al.* 1999) and will seek to uphold the interests of justice when the law seems to them to violate justice (Krivoshey 1994).

However, the jury foreperson is, as might be expected, likely to be a white, male professional (Wrightsman 1978) and the procedure adopted by the foreperson influences the final verdict – those who bring a coherent structure to the deliberations increase the likelihood that the verdict will be based on the evidence. Whether the jurors are asked, immediately after they have retired to consider their verdict, by the foreperson to give an initial verdict, or, alternatively, to outline what they see as the critical issues, influences the final verdict (Young *et al.* 1999). Moreover, in a majority of trials in the New Zealand study, the jury misunderstood the law in fairly fundamental ways (Young *et al.* 1999). The overall lessons from the New Zealand study are:

- Oral evidence is poorly assimilated.
- A route map, such as a flow chart, helps the jury to make sense of the evidence.
- Evidence is best presented in the form of a story line; juries can then set up a narrative story and fit the evidence they hear into this picture.
- Juries find it difficult to assess credibility.
- Transcripts of evidence should be provided.
- Jury members should be encouraged to take notes.
- Expert witnesses are needed who can communicate.

Whether the majority pressures a minority to accept the majority decision or whether the minority can persuade the majority or whether the jury seeks a compromise (Young *et al.* 1999), such as a finding of guilt on a lesser charge, is also a function of the personal dynamics of the particular jury (Law Commission 1999).

So, it is necessary to provide support so as to enable stakeholder groups to reach better decisions. Goodin (1999) points out that 'deliberative' is defined as studied rather than rash or hasty, as reasoned (Pettit 1980), and as involving a consideration of the reasons for and against the alternatives whilst 'governance' is taken to mean equal respect for all deliberators. The first part of this definition is precisely what has been found to be so difficult in taking any complex decision. Expanding and opening out the group who have to make the decision, with limited time, increases the need for supportive project appraisal techniques and ones that meet the needs of these users.

There are three developing strands in terms of decision aids; the first supports the definition of the problem, supporting debate on the nature of the problem and dialogue on the key issues. Much of this work derives from Checkland's (Checkland and Scholes 1990) 'soft systems theory'. One example of this approach being applied to catchment management is the 'IdeaMap' (Gill and Wolfenden 1998). A second strand is information support; effective stakeholder involvement requires the democratisation of information and a means whereby participants can extract useful information from what may be an overwhelming mass of data. GIS systems are starting to be employed for this purpose (Correia *et al.* 1994). The third strand is of tools to support the discovery and arguing of preferences between the options. This strand is typically composed of variants of multi-criteria analysis (Section 13.3).

Since shifting to stakeholder-based decision processes does not change the nature of the choice that must be made, it does not eliminate the conflicts that are at the heart of the choice. There are three possible outcomes from each round of participation: consensus on one option being the best option; a compromise to adopt one option; or out and out disagreement as to which is the best option. It cannot be expected that either of the first two outcomes will necessarily occur: indeed, it is possible that the process will simply make the nature of the disagreement sharper. In both the USA (Priscoli 1996) and Australia (Handmer *et al.* 1991), techniques of conflict mediation have been quite widely used. But, equally, it is necessary to have a formal structure through which conflicts are finally resolved. In this sense, it is not necessarily a failure if a conflict has finally to be resolved in the courts; in some cases, there may be no middle ground for a compromise.

Increasing public involvement creates a series of new problems or perhaps exposes issues that have not previously been considered:

- Who has a right to participate?
- How to include the excluded?
- How to include the interests of outsiders?
- How representative are those involved?
- Groups will frequently be spending other people's money; how can these others be confident that their money is wisely spent?

Do I have a right to participate in decisions as to the future management of the Mississippi and on what grounds can I claim this right? Or, equivalently, by what right can, say, a developed country-based NGO claim a right to participate in decisions about the Mekong or Ganga, or the population of Vietnam to participate in decisions about US or European energy policy? We each may claim that we have an interest in the best management strategy being adopted for each of the three rivers but does that establish a right to be involved? In particular, it is obviously easier for those in the developed world to involve ourselves in decisions in the developing world: we are richer, and we have more time and greater access to information and to influence. There is consequently a risk of a new form of neocolonialism where we deny people in these other countries the right to take their own decisions simply because we don't like the decisions they take. When it is someone from a country with an average per capita annual income of US$25 000 who claims the right to overrule the decisions of people in a country with an average income of US$500, the moral legitimacy of such a claim is not self-evident.

We can define three possible levels of involvement:

- the right to inform, to advise;
- the right to argue or advocate; and
- the right to decide.

It is only the third and highest level where the question of the legitimacy of the interest becomes evident. Maximum involvement in informing and in advocacy can only enrich the debate but the extent of the right to decide is more restrictive. Two possible basic conditions for a legitimate claim to have a right to involvement in deciding are then a willingness to negotiate and to compromise, and to be bound by the conclusions of the group. Refusal to accept these conditions is to claim a right to determine the decision unilaterally. In turn, it is not necessarily the case that all groups should seek involvement in decision making. I would prefer that, for example, Greenpeace stays outside of decisions and acts as an advocate for the environment. If they formally take part in decisions and become involved in reaching decisions that balance environmental and other considerations, then they will inevitably have to make compromises. A further condition for a right to involvement in the decision is that the individual or group must either commit resources to the decision or potentially experience a material benefit or loss as a result of the decision. Van Koppen (n.d.) therefore defines a stakeholder as someone who links resources and people. Neither that I don't think a decision is right, nor that I don't like the decision that has been made, are sufficient reasons to claim a right to override the decisions of those directly affected.

There are obvious risks that those who have power and influence at present will use the involvement process to reinforce their power and influence, and those who are currently excluded will be further excluded. Women, as already noted, often do not have the time to participate and in general participation costs time and also money. Since both are differentially distributed across society, some people are more likely to participate than others. Pastoralists may be excluded by neglect so that land owners, particularly arable farmers, use the process against the interests of the pastoralists. Hence, it is necessary to identify all those who have an interest and then to seek to ensure that all those interests are represented.

One risk is that public involvement is then simply a way of reinforcing NIMBY ('not in my back yard'); that a local community puts its own interests over all others. It has been argued, for example, that environmental impact assessments provide a useful weapon for local communities to keep out low-income groups by raising the cost of development and hence thereby excluding low-cost housing. At the same time, resources are often passed to local areas from central or regional government. Thus, stakeholders will often be spending other people's money and with that goes a responsibility to ensure that money is spent wisely. There thus needs to be some formal mechanism to justify the spending of that money. Equally, integrated catchment management, by definition, involves a coherent strategy rather than piecemeal local plans.

Stakeholder involvement raises questions of how representative are the participants of any wide group, and of the legitimacy of the process versus the legitimacy given by election, and hence of the views of elected politicians. The latter concern is raised whenever those involved and those elected reach different conclusions. Again, with decisions shifted to local stakeholders, those stakeholders may reach conclusions that are inconsistent with wider policies; the EU Water Framework Directive both sets mandatory standards for rivers and promotes public involvement. The two principles are contradictory in that the decisions are already mandated.

9.2.3 Means and ends

If we can have concerns both about the outcome of a decision and the process by which that decision was reached, it is also true that there need be no clean

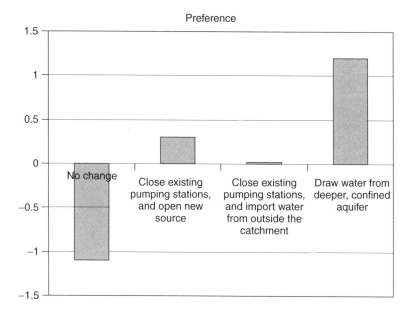

Figure 9.1   *Preferences between options for alleviating low flows. Source: House et al. 1994*

separation of ends and means. Actions are made by coupling means and ends, and earlier I argued that it is actions that have values and not things, that, by definition, instrumental value is associated with an action. However, it is relatively easy to fall into the trap of presuming that people are only concerned with the ends and not at all with the means. Thus, for example, it would be a mistake to assume that whilst people may want river pollution to be reduced, they are entirely indifferent either to the means to be adopted to achieve that reduction or the means by which the costs will be recovered from them.

Not surprisingly, not only do people have preferences between alternative methods of cost recovery (Figure 4.2), they can have strong preferences between the three different options that could be adopted in order to alleviate the low flows in the river (Figure 9.1). Such preferences ought not to be surprising and must be taken into account.

9.3 Better Options

The decision can be no better than the quality of the options considered; if only a poor set of options are considered, then the choice will be poor. Therefore, we need better sets of options to be considered but unfortunately there can be no set of rules that will necessarily result in the 'best' option being amongst those considered. This is because options need to be invented so the quality of the options is ultimately down to the quality of the imagination, creativity and expertise of the team responsible for developing possible options. What we can do is to adopt rules that reduce the risk that the solution space will not be narrowed prematurely. DEFRA (1999) includes a set of such rules for flood and coastal defence projects and a wider set of such possible rules are to:

- adopt an appraisal-led design process;
- use the public participation process;
- look at variations in the standard of service offered by the project;
- consider whether now is the best time to do this project;
- look at what approaches have been adopted or proposed elsewhere;
- consider the options that others will expect to be considered;
- assess what courses of action would be best for the environment and for the local communities.

Adopting an appraisal-led design process can contribute to the identification of the best options both by creating an understanding of what the decision involves and by keeping attention focused on what we are trying to achieve. In two of the case studies, those for Cairo and for Grootvlei, I shall claim that one outcome of the appraisal process was a suggestion of some additional options that could be examined. Moreover, inventing a new option can be a way of resolving conflicts between objectives and between people.

Small variations in the standard of service offered by the project are obvious options to consider; a small reduction could make possible either a drastic reduction in cost or be achieved by a radically different alternative. Conversely, a small increase in the standard of service may offer a larger increase in the benefits of the project in comparison to the increase in costs.

Equally, an obvious question is whether now is the best time to undertake the project; delay may enable additional information to be collected. Again, where there is some existing provision, it may be more efficient to continue to use that provision until rising costs and/or the increased risk of failure of that existing system show that replacement would be more efficient.

It clearly makes sense to look at the options that have been adopted elsewhere. However, merely because an option was adopted elsewhere does not mean that it is the best option to be adopted in the country or region in question. What is the best option for charging for water is likely to be different in a city where current domestic consumption is nearly 1000 litres per person per day (Winnipeg, Canada) than in a city where supply is both intermittent and averages 70 litres per person per day (Taiyuan, China). Similarly, the appropriate water management strategy for food production is likely to be different in a country where there is 0.10 hectares of arable land per capita (China) to that in a country where there is nearly 0.90 hectares of arable land (USA). The appropriate water resource strategy in an arid climate (e.g. Australia) is likely to be different to that in a temperate climate (e.g. Germany). There has probably been far too much export of the solutions appropriate to one country to another in the past and there is a danger that this will continue in the future only in a different form. In the past, the export was of capital-intensive, technologically complex solutions; the risk is now that these will be replaced by the export of the environmental needs of the developed countries.

Similarly, it should be self-evident that those options that stakeholders propose ought to be considered both as potential options and to show respect for those stakeholders. Not to consider such an option or to dismiss it summarily sends a very clear message that those stakeholders are not going to be heard, let alone their concerns become incorporated into the appraisal.

Looking for the best options for the environment and the local community serve to bring these issues into focus. There may not be a clear-cut environmental best option; this is often true in coastal erosion projects where continued erosion may result in the loss of an important freshwater wetland whilst preventing erosion results in coastal squeeze and the loss of mudflats (Green and Penning-Rowsell 1999). As the World Commission on Dams (2000) has reported, as have many others before, the interests of the local communities most affected by a project are often the least considered. In each case, even if the best environmental and community options are not finally adopted, their consideration will make it clearer what are the concerns.

9.4 Criteria for Project Appraisal Tools

Decision aids, methods of helping us make choices, have themselves to be chosen. Several sets of criteria have, therefore, been proposed as the basis upon which to make this selection (Green, Tunstall and House 1989; Lichfield 1964; Nash, Pearce and Stanley 1975). One possible set of criteria (Penning-Rowsell *et al.* 1992) is:

- **Elucidation of the issues.** As a result of the analysis, all those interested in the decision should be left with a clearer understanding of the issues and the trade-offs involved than they had before the analysis was undertaken. This is the most basic criterion. As the emphasis in decision making shifts to stakeholder involvement, it becomes increasingly critical that project appraisal performs in a communications role, enabling the different stakeholders to understand the nature of the choice that must be made, including the differences between stakeholders in their definition and interpretation of the choice.
- **To simplify the issues.** Decisions are difficult not least because of their complexity; the project appraisal method must structure and organise the data and issues so that the decision is comprehensible.
- **Value basis.** The values and trade-offs in the analysis should be those of the public rather than those of some expert or specialist.

- **Completeness.** The method should be able to encompass all of the significant differences in the consequences of the different options and thus to cover all those objectives which should be considered in making the choice.
- **Rigour.** The analysis should be transparent and logical; the results should not depend upon who undertakes the analysis. In particular, rigour is essential to accountability, to the establishment of a clear audit trail.
- **Feasibility.** The methodology must be capable of application both within the time and resources which are available and within those which are appropriate to the importance of the decision.
- **Reliability.** Since decisions are about the future, a project appraisal method involves predicting the future. A method is reliable to the extent that the predictions embodied in it and consequently the prediction made as to the best option subsequently are borne out in the future.

If those interested in the decision are not left with a better understanding as to what the decision involves, then there are no advantages over tossing a coin. Thus, the most important test of a project appraisal is: do we have a better understanding of what the choice involves than we did before? Glyde (1992), reflecting on the lessons of probably the most important contingent valuation study yet undertaken (Imber *et al.* 1991), points out that when the results of a study are rejected, then it must be held to have failed.

Equally, decisions increasingly involve more data, in increasingly specialised forms, than can be assimilated and we bring more objectives and constraints to choices. It has been found that we cannot, on average, juggle more than seven considerations at once (Miller 1956), and a function of an appraisal method is thus to reduce complexity to a manageable level. However, it should not oversimplify reducing the problem below the level of complexity that we can handle since simplification can only be achieved by imposing a structure on the problem. So, elucidation and simplification are themselves conflicting criteria.

At the same time, there are too many decisions to make in a developed society; I neither wish nor have the time to participate in every collective decision that must be made. Hence, most decisions are left to institutions and I want those institutions to take those decisions that I would take had I the time and energy to be involved. Essentially, an important role of project appraisal is thus to routinise the trivial decisions so as to leave time for the important decisions. For those routine decisions, rigour, feasibility and their value basis of the project appraisal technique adopted are important considerations, with rigour being particularly important in that it promotes transparency and the establishment of an audit trail. Whilst the secrecy of a jury deliberation may be important in a trial, in other decisions, transparency is critical.

None of the available project appraisal techniques are clearly superior to all others against all of these criteria. The choice of the appraisal technique, or techniques, therefore needs to be made by considering the nature of the conflicts that make the choice necessary in the first place. Where it is conflicting objectives or differences between groups that are the central concerns, multi-criteria analysis is likely to be most appropriate. Conversely, the greater rigour of benefit–cost analysis (Section 13.2) is more appropriate to routine decisions which are left to different institutions to take.

10

Institutions for Managing Resources

Institutions matter: it is institutions, and the interaction between institutions, that largely both take decisions and implement those decisions as to water policy and water projects. Secondly, the form of the institutions makes a difference to the effectiveness of catchment management. In terms of improving the efficiency with which we use water, there are two concerns:

- Delivering integrated catchment management; and
- Delivering specific functional services within the context of that overall management strategy.

If we want integrated catchment management then there needs to be some mechanism to provide the coordination between the different functions. This mechanism can then be separate from the institutions that deliver the services and provide the functions. Even if we use market mechanisms to provide the services, the market must be structured so that it acts to achieve the wider objectives as well as controlled so that competitive pressures are maintained.

There are then two alternative mechanisms for service delivery: cooperation or competition. In turn, competition is necessary when cooperation would be against the public interest, but traditionally water services have been provided through cooperative structures in the form of common property management or through government, notably local government, or special-purpose bodies such as the levee districts (Harrison and Mooney 1993) or special-purpose water districts (California Department of Water Resources 1998) in the USA.

10.1 Catchment Management

Mostert *et al.* (1999) identify three possible models for catchment management:

- The administrative model, where water management is the responsibility of the provinces and municipalities whose boundaries are not based on hydrological boundaries.

Handbook of Water Economics: Principles and Practice. C. Green
© 2003 John Wiley & Sons, Ltd   ISBN: 0-471-98571-6

- The hydrological model, an organisational structure based on hydrological boundaries.
- The coordination model of a river basin commission which is charged with coordinating the activities of the provinces, municipalities and other bodies.

The differences in these models lie in their boundaries and in the mechanisms used to promote coordinated service delivery. The available mechanisms are: coercion, where the catchment administration orders other groups to adopt particular courses of action; narrow self-interest, where the catchment administration offers incentives to other groups to adopt particular courses of action; and cooperation, where the different bodies agree a plan and then take action to implement it. Money is the obvious example of a mechanism that uses narrow self-interest to promote the adoption of particular courses of action. In the first two cases, the catchment administration decides on a plan and then seeks to ensure that others act according to that plan. But in the last case, the plan is essentially a widely shared vision of the future.

All three models have been tried, the most famous example of the hydrological model being the Tennessee Valley Authority (Miller and Reidinger 1998) which has, with varying degrees of success, been exported to China and Africa (Adams 1992; Barrow 1998). However, the coordination model will often be the forced solution when constitutionally the powers necessary to achieve integrated catchment management are reserved to provincial or municipal government but the catchment crosses several or many administrative areas. The Ruhrverband (Kneese and Bower 1968), although limited both functionally and geographically, is the best known example of administrative areas recognising that they had to coordinate their activities within an agreed plan if water management was to be successful. ORSANCO in the USA (Vicory 2001) and the Murray–Darling Basin Commission (Pigram 1999) in Australia are notable examples of this approach, both in countries with weak federal systems and constitutionally reserved powers to the provincial governments. Only through the provinces agreeing to form a compact to coordinate their activities could a catchment-based approach be implemented. On the other hand, in another weak federal system, that of Germany where water management is constitutionally reserved to the provincial governments, achieving catchment management is a problem. Again, in the USA, for smaller scale catchments, the cooperative approach is necessarily being developed (e.g. Center for Watershed Protection 1996; Personett 2001). In the case of international rivers, a cooperative approach is the only option; of these, the International Rhine Commission (Academie de l'eau 1998) appears to be the most successful. In turn, the best place to learn lessons about the cooperative model is then in those situations where there is no other possible option.

On the other hand, France chose a cooperative approach in the form of the Agence Bassin (Barraque *et al*. 1994; Barraque 1999). In many ways, this has resulted in one of the most successful catchment management systems but one that has had to fight off political challenges from other branches of government, notably the Finance Ministry (Commissariat General du Plan 1997). Similar approaches are being adopted elsewhere, notably in Mexico (Wester *et al.* n.d.) and Chile (Academie de l'eau n.d.). Again, as part of the COAG water reforms, the states in Australia are developing innovative forms of stakeholder-driven cooperative catchment management (Comino 2001; New South Wales Government 1986), as they are in, for example, India (Turton and Farrington 1998) and elsewhere by NGOs in particular, although Marshall (2000) argues that our desire for stakeholder-driven integrated catchment management has outrun our ability to deliver it.

Because of the necessary boundary problem in institutions, the number of policy and management areas that overlap with catchment management, and the number of different policy tools and instruments necessary to implement integrated catchment management, the cooperative model looks like the best approach. In this model, the involvement of the stakeholders should then result in a plan that is a widely shared vision of the future, one to which the stakeholders commit themselves. How that plan is then implemented, and how the behaviour of individuals and organisations is to be changed so that they act in accordance with the plan, is discussed in Chapter 11. What is, however, certain is that they need some power to raise the monies necessary to implement those actions; who provides the money, has the power. A strength of the Agence Bassin is that they have powers to levy charges on abstraction and wastewater discharges which revenue can then be used in the form of grants and soft loans to finance works that are agreed in accordance with the plan (Barraque *et al.* 1994).

Ostrom's (1990) eight rules for effective common property management provide a core for the delivery for integrated, participative catchment management but the reviews of such systems in the USA argue that it is too soon to tell what works and what does not (Adler and Straube 2000; Imperial and Hennessey 2000).

10.2 Service Delivery

The choice is between cooperatives or competition whilst the issue is which will provide the greatest efficiency in the particular circumstances. To the economist, privatisation is no more than a means to create, if possible, competition, since a monopoly is expected to be inefficient whether it is a private or public monopoly. The only difference between a private and a public monopoly is that they are expected to be inefficient in different ways: the first, to extract an excessive profit and the latter to provide a poor service to the consumers. There are then three basic models for service delivery:

- in the form of special-purpose common property bodies;
- various forms of privatisation; and
- municipal companies.

The first is sometimes misleadingly included within the privatisation category but it is quite distinct from a private company in that the owners are the consumers so that there is an identity of interest. Conversely, under the private company model, there is usually little or no, and only an incidental, overlap between the owners, the shareholders and the consumers. The interest of the owners is then to maximise long-term profits and the latter to maximise the ratio of service quality to cost, and the only ways to bring the two sets of interest into alignment are competition or regulation.

The third approach is a specialised company wholly owned by one or more municipalities or other elected local governments. This was the traditional form of delivery of water and sewerage services and continues to be particularly strong in the Netherlands (Blokland *et al.* 1999) and in other parts of Europe, notably Germany and Austria.

10.2.1 Common property management

The model was developed in societies that were labour rich and cash poor and, in the past, this was probably the predominant form of water management, especially for agriculture (Wagret 1967). The benefits of economies of scale promoted collective action in irrigation (e.g. Tardieu n.d.), land drainage (e.g. Huisman 2000) and flood control (e.g. Zorkoczy 1993). Amongst the advantages of the model is that the owner and consumers are the same people and consequently there is pressure both to maximise performance and to reduce costs whether these costs be in the form of contributed labour or cash. That the system belongs to all and is managed by all creates strong normative social pressures on individuals, although those who are already powerful maintain their power to influence the group decisions (Mehta n.d.). Finally, it is clearly this approach which achieves the maximum of public involvement.

As an approach, it has been rediscovered in recent years; irrigation schemes are increasingly being turned over to the farmers who serve the system with Water User Associations being established to operate the schemes (e.g. Bruns and Atmanto 1992). There are, however, a whole range of other forms of service in which a common property management approach has been tried including condominial sewerage systems (Otis and Mara 1985), rural water supplies (Evans and Appleton 1993) and projects such as that in Orangi (Zaidi 2000). In developed countries, there are an increasing number of community-based projects (e.g. Pinkham *et al.* 1999) that approximate to a common property management approach.

However, the common property management approach presupposes that either there is an existing community or that one can be created. Thus, White (1997) argues that the success of farmer-managed irrigation services in Haiti are a consequence of the strong tradition of collective action, the strong role of social norms favouring collective action, and the recognition within the society of the importance of banking favours. Agarwal (n.d.) argues that when seeking to establish communal water harvesting systems, the first two years of any programme must be spent on social mobilisation. Moreover, this presupposes that there is at least a latent community to which an appropriate project form can be mapped, it being important to map the project to the community rather than attempting to create a community than matches the project (Schoeffel 1995).

Ostrom (1990) proposes eight principles as being necessary for common property resource management to be a success:

- the user group and the resource both have well-defined boundaries;
- the use rules are appropriate to local conditions;
- the users can participate in rule modification;
- the users themselves monitor compliance;
- the users themselves enforce compliance through graduated sanctions;
- there are low-cost methods of conflict resolution;
- user groups have quasi-independence from higher forms of government; and
- in complex cases, the regime is organised in a federal, hierarchical form.

The problem for catchment management is then one of seeking to coordinate the actions of an almost feudal system of geographical small-scale, single-purpose organisations into one holistic approach to the management of the catchment. That the organisations are usually single functional also tends to mean that their locus of concern may exclude wider concerns; thus, the waterschappen in the Netherlands have been called 'farmer republics' because they were elected largely by farmers and tended to exclude any other interest other than that of the farmers when they made decisions.

10.2.2 Municipal management

In urban areas, the development of water supply and sanitation in the nineteenth and twentieth centuries was almost exclusively undertaken by the municipalities (Hassan 1998; Hietala 1987). Particularly in those countries where local governments have constitutionally protected powers and entitlements to tax revenues, notably Germany and France, the municipal model continues to be important. In particular, it continues to be the primary mode of provision in the Netherlands (Blokland *et al.* 1999) and also Sweden (Gustafsson 2001), and one which after the initial somewhat dogmatic enthusiasm for privatisation is being considered more closely (Hall 2001).

There appear to have been many reasons for the importance of municipal provision. The first is externalities of provision: water and sanitation works were partly undertaken as a response to the outbreaks of cholera and typhoid which spread to those who had their own drinking water and sanitation from those who had not. The second is philosophical; John Stuart Mill (1848) was in favour of provision of services by voluntary associations and municipalities, and was almost as acerbic about the capabilities of joint stock companies as he was about central government. He was opposed to the provision of water services through private companies (Schwartz 1966), and indeed the granting of a monopoly to any private company (Mill 1848); and he was caustic about their performance: '... the gas and water companies, among which, though perfect freedom is allowed to competition, none really takes place, and practically they are found to be even more irresponsible, and unapproachable by individual complaints, than the government' (Mill 1848). But, perhaps surprisingly in this period of liberal economics there was a strong reluctance to allow private companies to profit from the supply of water and *laissez-faire* principles were seen as limited in their application (Taylor 1972). In turn, as Mill concluded, it proved extremely difficult to introduce competition into water supply and sanitation and where it occurred, the result was inefficiencies (e.g. two companies' pipes down the same street) rather than efficiency (Hassan 1998).

Thirdly, the only practical means of charging for sanitation is effectively through a tax whether this tax is levied on a per property basis or as an addition to a charge for water supply. It has been commonly asserted that only governments have the right to levy a tax, with the public demanding accountability of that government. Fourthly, municipalities had access to cheap money in the form of long-term loans at much better rates of interest and periods than any private company could obtain and certainly lower than the rates of return demanded on share capital (Alexander and Mayer 1997; NERA 1999).

Most of these advantages remain true and the municipal model is still the default model for water and sewerage provision because they can be very efficient (Shirley *et al.* 2000); they provide accountability to the consumer; they avoid the problems of trying to introduce competition in what is generally a natural monopoly; and municipal companies can generally borrow money at better rates than can private companies. In turn, because water and sewerage services are so capital intensive, the cost of capital either borrowed or equity effectively determines the cost of provision.

Conversely, these comparative advantages can be offset by other problems that may suggest instead that privatisation of the services is the only way to improve the standards of service. These problems tend to be macro-economic and political rather than concerned with service provision per se. If the country has a poor credit rating then it may no longer be true that the cost of public borrowing is less than the cost of private capital. Again, corruption may be so endemic that only a radical change is seen as a way to reduce if not eliminate it; there are a number of well-known water supply systems where as soon as chlorine goes in the front door, it is sold out of the back door, or where your water bill depends upon how much you bribe the meter reader. Equally, since each contract requires a pay-off, the costs of constructing works may be higher in the public sector than in the private sector. Public services may also be largely politically controlled as a way of rewarding voters or other client groups. Again, the public sector is often a way of soaking up graduate employment so that public agencies are overstaffed, although pay levels will also be low. A consequent problem may then be that any attempt to provide training and institutional support simply serves to enable those trained to find higher paid jobs in the private sector or abroad. It may consequently be reasonable to consider public agencies as a training agency as well as a service provider.

10.2.3 Competition

The economist's mantra of 'why are you doing this, what is the problem and what are the alternatives?' is perhaps particularly important in this context because it is often not clear exactly why privatisation is on the agenda. From a purely economic standpoint, the critical issue is the extent to which it is possible to introduce competition: in turn, this depends upon the extent to which there are economies of scale and/or scope. The greater these are then the more quickly will the market collapse into monopoly if it does not start as one.

Secondly, there is an apparent conflict between the Dublin criterion of increasing public involvement in water management and the introduction of privatisation which reduces citizens to consumers. From the Dublin principles it necessarily follows that any change in the institutional structure of water and sanitation must be undertaken through a process of discussion and negotiation with all of the principal stakeholders, most notably the consumers. This is particularly true in developing countries where the consumers and communities have commonly already invested in some form of water supply and sanitation and where the most effective means of extending water and wastewater services is likely to involve working with those communities (Sections 14.6.1 and 16.1.1). The most dramatic failures of attempts to introduce privatisation have been those where it was attempted to introduce privatisation by fiat (Hasan 2001; Lobina 2000) and where it was forgotten that privatisation is no more than a potential means of improving the quality of service and cost of that service to the consumer.

From a wider perspective, there are a variety of reasons why privatisation may be an appropriate option (Green 2001b). Of these, the institutional problems of the existing utility are often an important driver. In some cases, the levels of corruption or sclerosis within the existing organisation may be such that only the most radical change has a chance of introducing efficiency to the organisation. Or, it may simply seem easier to pass the problems off to someone else rather than to try to solve them. For politicians, this has the great advantage of giving them someone else to blame for any subsequent problems and failures.

A second reason is that the requirements for capital investment to expand and upgrade services may be very high. This inevitably means that prices will have to rise. The dominant school of macro-economists has held that who is responsible for the debt, whether this is a governmental or quasi-governmental organisation or a private firm, is more important than the cost of raising and servicing that debt. In this case, privatisation has the virtue of shifting debt out of the public sector and into the private sector.

In addition to the institutional issues, there is typically a range of service problems as well. In the developed world, the problem facing a wastewater or water supplier is likely to be the requirement for heavy investment to improve treatment standards. In less developed countries, the problems facing the suppliers are likely to be:

- expanding connections to all urban customers; and
- expanding supply to customers (e.g. to c. 100 litres/person/day).

There are also likely to be all sorts of operational and other problems including high levels of leakage. There are some general rules concerning privatisation that seem to emerge from world experience (Green 2001b):

- Don't sell the infrastructure with the aim of raising money for the government.
- Don't follow the model of England and Wales: adopt the concession approach.
- In so far as there are not significant economies of scale and scope, let the concession be in separate parts and functions.
- The contract must be let on a competitive tender basis.
- True competition must be promoted and certainly not discouraged.
- The contract must be a public document.
- The relations between the concessionaire and the parent company must be clearly defined.
- There must be a sophisticated system of regulation in place to ensure that the supplier complies with the contract in terms of service standards and to control prices.
- In developing countries, a major problem is often that the coverage of the services is well below 100% of the population and expanding the service to reach 100% will involve major capital expenditure. It is necessary to decide how this expansion will be funded.
- There must be an exit strategy in place so that wastewater and water services will continue if the supplier goes bankrupt, the contract is terminated because of a failure in compliance by the company, or the company decides that the contract is no longer profitable.
- There must be a requirement that the supplier shall let all major engineering and construction works through competitive tender.
- The structure of the contract and the pricing mechanisms must be such as to promote sustainable water management; options such as rainwater harvesting, source control, demand management and reuse/recycling are to be encouraged rather than forbidden.
- The contract must specify how particular risks are to be shared between the concessionaire and the government.
- Finally, privatisation is only one option amongst several with regard to the institutional arrangements for supplying wastewater and water services. A comparative assessment needs to be made as to the advantages and disadvantages

of each before one form of privatisation is adopted; in turn, such a comparison implies that a privatisation option will not always be the best option.

10.2.4 Comparative advantages

It is difficult to compare the relative efficiency of different service providers, particularly between countries, since efficiency is the ratio of output to inputs. It is particularly difficult to do so between countries where the relative costs of labour and capital can be very different, especially where some services are contracted out. Contracting out services to private companies can then give a superficial appearance that, for example, the ratio of supply points to employees is higher in one area than another. Equally, lower charges for water may simply reflect lower qualities of service, or economies of scale, or simply different conditions (e.g. ample groundwater may be available in one area whereas another must rely on long-distance transfer and pumping), or that the capital costs were incurred many years ago so that loan repayments have been much reduced through inflation. The different systems of performance indicators (OFWAT 2000a; VEWIN 2001; World Bank 1999a) should therefore be used with care. For example, Hall and Lanz (2001) report that in France, charges are 14% higher where the service is provided by private water and sewerage companies than when it is provided by a public body. This is interesting rather than decisive evidence. More generally, it is not unreasonable to expect that the communes let a concession when the capital costs of provision will be high. For example, the extent of municipal provision of water services in Germany is probably associated with the reliance on groundwater for water supply in Germany.

Table 10.1 gives a number of criteria that might be used to make this comparison between different strategies of provision. There are arguments that private companies are inherently more efficient than public bodies (Shirley and Walsh 2000). This is an 'on average' argument: it clearly cannot be claimed that all private companies are always more efficient than all public bodies, not least because we all have had experience of some incompetent private companies. At times, where private companies have performed badly, the blame at least partly lies with the structure in which they operate. Bakker and Hemson (2000) partly blame the structure in which 'build–operate–train and transfer' was introduced in South Africa, as well as the structure of the concessionaire, for the poor performance of the system.

But, at the same time, equity finance is generally more expensive than debt finance (Alexander and Mayer 1997; Haarmeyer and Mody 1998; NERA 1999) where the cost of debt depends upon the creditworthiness of the country where the debt is incurred rather than of the particular company (Haarmeyer and Mody 1998).

Finally, two sets of social relationships will change through privatisation. Firstly, a primary benefit for politicians of privatisation is that they will have someone to blame; and they will blame the concessionaire for all problems of

Table 10.1 *Performance of privatisation compared to some form of ownership by the public*

Criterion	Relative performance of privatisation
Cost of capital	Higher: equity capital is more expensive than debt financing
Efficiency	Higher ? – the workforce will be reduced but reductions in labour costs do not necessarily result in a reduction in total costs, nor does a reduction in cost necessarily translate into lower prices
Technological transfer	Higher: multinational companies will usually be involved and they will be more aware of technological advances
Government bad	Essentially an ideological argument
Accountability	Lower: to shareholders rather than to the public
Public involvement	Lower
Regulatory burden	Higher and expensive: this is probably desirable in itself but the country may have a scarcity of expertise in precisely those areas required for effective regulation
Environmental performance	Higher but because of forced separation of gamekeeper and poacher roles; this separation is desirable in itself but does not require privatisation to be achieved
Reduction in public debt	There is a dangerous tendency for privatisations being undertaken in a form that maximises the price the government gets for the utility rather than the long-term least cost solution
Reduction in government expenditure	Yes, but since the public will now pay as consumers instead of as tax payers, the economic question is whether this cost will be lower or more equitably distributed?

whatever form. Secondly, the consumer–company relationship is quite different from those of voter–government and citizen–society. Consumers expect to get what they have paid for; any problems are then ones for the supplier and not for the consumer. This change has particularly important implications for drought management plans as calls for voluntary reductions in demand are likely to be much less effective in a privatised regime than when water supply is owned directly or indirectly by the consumers. Since calls for voluntary reductions typically result in a 25% cut in demand (USACE 1994), this is potentially a significant problem. On the same basis, it might also be expected that compliance with mandatory demand cuts will also be lower under privatisation.

In the longer term, it may be questioned whether models of privatisation other than the concessionaire approach have a future. There are two reasons why it is not self-evident that approaches to privatisation on the English and Welsh model are sustainable in the long run. Firstly, mutuals owned by their customers or municipalities can be financed through debt at a lower cost than through equity capital. The 'Glas' model in Wales is a possible model of this development where the operation of the facilities has been let out on a competitive tender basis (OFWAT 2000c). Potentially, this gives the advantages of competition without creating a monopoly.

Secondly, the expertise of the multinational companies is in designing, building and operating plants. It does not make very good sense for them to tie up very large amounts of capital in then owning that plant when inevitably the return on capital will be driven down to realistic rates. Nor is an industry where demand will eventually fall whilst the costs of quality increase one that looks a particularly good industry in which to invest. One model for the development of the companies is then to increasingly act as operators of public facilities, owned by mutuals, and to sell package services to large consumers (Ernst & Young 1999).

11

Implementing Decisions: Inducing Change

A policy or plan without a means of implementing that policy or plan is an empty gesture; it may make the originators feel good, which may be the main purpose of the policy or plan, but it will have no practical effect. Equally, part of the review of options that went into the decision process should have included a comparison of alternative strategies for implementing that policy or plan. This is obviously particularly important when it is the actions of other stakeholders that will need to change. However, the plan itself should have been developed with the stakeholders as a widely shared vision of the future so that the stakeholders take ownership of the plan.

The actions that it is desired that the different actors adopt may be to use water more efficiently, reduce demand, reduce abstraction, adopt source control, treat wastewater before discharging it, and so forth. The two options are to use a carrot and/or a stick; to encourage change or force change. At the same time, it is also necessary to identify the barriers to adopting the actions we hope to promote and specifically to address those barriers either by removing them or by providing a sufficient incentive to overcome them. However, conventionally, economics assumes that only economic incentives have any real effect and that they are always effective. In practice, prices do not seem a very effective way of inducing change in the behaviour of the different actors. In consequence, a wider range of possible carrots and sticks needs to be considered.

11.1 Barriers

A lack of knowledge is one obvious barrier to change; people cannot change their behaviour until they are aware that an alternative behaviour is possible. One of the roles of waste minimisation clubs (Johnston 1994) is to reduce the 'costs' of access to information and to provide the individual actor with a comparative assessment of his or her performance. Unless it is possible to change, then no change is possible; in the absence of a suitable technology, we cannot expect

Handbook of Water Economics: Principles and Practice. C. Green
© 2003 John Wiley & Sons, Ltd ISBN: 0-471-98571-6

change to occur. For example, permeable pavements as means of source control are only considered to be suitable for lightly trafficked roads (Office of Water 1999) otherwise they would be a convenient strategy for handling the increases in rainfall intensity that appear to be occurring in some areas as a result of climate change (Hurd *et al.* 1996). However, the very purpose of signalling that the change is desirable may be to promote the development of the technologies that will make the change possible. Similarly, it is concluded in Section 14.5.1 that domestic water demand is to a large extent determined by technological factors so that unless low flow shower heads, low flush toilet cisterns and front-loading washing machines are available, there is comparatively little scope for the consumer to make significant reductions in internal water use.

If people do not have the resources, defined in the widest sense of skills, time and money, to make the change then no change can be expected. The poor will typically have limited access to capital and that at a very high cost; changes which involve the investment of capital will then be particularly difficult to promote. Reducing the cost of capital through micro-credit facilities (Saywell 1999) may then be necessary if the change is to be encouraged. The success of systems like condominial sewerage systems (Otis and Mara 1985) thus are the result of redirecting the burden away from a resource that is scarce: capital, to a resource that it is relatively plentiful: voluntary labour.

A weakness of the use of charges to change behaviour is that it reduces the money resources available to the actor to make that change. A way around this problem is to hypothecate the income from the charge to provide soft loans and grants for the purposes of undertaking works that will result in the change that is desired. The comparative success of the charging systems for wastewater adopted in the Netherlands and France is ascribed to the hypothecation of the revenue in this way (Andersen 1994).

Legal barriers are relatively commonplace; government agencies and departments cannot act except in regard to the powers that they have, including the restrictions upon the purposes for which they can spend money. It may, therefore, be necessary to change the boundaries of the relevant institution and one of the unanswered questions concerning catchment management is whether it is possible to have multifunctional management whilst having functional budgets (Green, Johnson and Penning-Rowsell *et al.* 2001).

Tenants may be expected to be reluctant to make investments where they cannot recover the costs when and if they leave that property. The legal definition of a 'sewer' has also been argued to have a chilling effect on the willingness of developers to construct source control measures in new developments (Howarth 1992).

Social/cultural barriers may restrict the adoption of a particular technology; for example, treadle pumps for irrigation can greatly increase agricultural productivity but women may feel too exposed when using them (IPTRID 2000). Making unrealistic assumptions about gender roles or assuming that women would be prepared to sacrifice their resources for the gain of male members of the household have been common problems in projects in the past (Zwarteveen 1997).

Given the obsessive concern with the cleanliness of WCs in the UK and the USA, and the related heavy proportion of products that claim to kill all known germs, there may be problems of cultural adaptation to low flush toilet cisterns or waterless toilets. A number of religions require washing at particular times or occasions and those behaviours will be particularly resistant to change.

There are in addition purely practical barriers; source control tends to take up significant amounts of land and this limits the possible density of development. In turn, high density development may be desirable for planning or community reasons, or simply be the consequence of high land prices.

11.2 Prices/Charges/Subsidies

Economists usually assume that prices always work but that nothing else does. This leaves us with a very restricted range of policy tools. In practice, prices do not seem to work particularly well in water management as a means of changing behaviour, and other tools can be more effective. It needs also to be noted that prices themselves do not change behaviour, they only provide an incentive and a signal for people to change their behaviour. Thus, water metering does not reduce demand for water but people may respond to the signal provided by metering and incentive given by charging by volume to change their behaviours in ways that result in a reduction in water demand. In turn, prices can only work to the extent to which there are the means to change behaviour, and people know what these means are, or can find out at a relatively low cost.

Although conventionally economists believe that only prices, or market-like instruments, are effective in changing behaviour, in practice prices often seem relatively ineffective at changing behaviour. The results from waste minimisation studies around the world consistently show that industrial firms are using 15–25% more water than the amount that would maximise their profitability (e.g. ETBPP 1997; Porter and van der Linde 1995). In part, such reductions are possible because reducing water intake can often save money in four ways: through the reduction in the consumption of water, reduced wastewater charges, reduction in energy usage and a reduction in the raw materials lost.

Secondly, short-term price elasticities are typically low, in the order of −0.1 to −0.2 (Herrington 1987), so that doubling water prices is necessary in order to induce, respectively, a 10% or 20% reduction in demand. There are obvious political problems with doubling prices to achieve a relatively small change in demand. Equally, for the water supplier, metering is a high risk strategy as it means that revenue falls if demand falls (Section 15.1.2). That companies who pay for water on a metered basis still use more water than would maximise their profitability suggests that price elasticities may measure no more than the extent of market failure; that technical elasticity is considerably higher than revealed elasticities. This increases the revenue risks to the water supplier as the response to a price rise may be a considerably greater fall in demand and hence revenue than was predicted. On the other hand, a somewhat cynical view is that farmers perform very closely to the hypothetical economic person: provided that they are given a large enough subsidy, they will produce whatever you want, be this wheat or butterflies.

In addition, in water management, there are:

- strong economies of scale; and
- a high degree of interdependencies between the actions of individuals.

So, we often should seek to promote cooperative, collective action rather than action by the individual if we are to achieve the efficient solution. For example, it will often result in an inefficient outcome if individuals all construct their own cesspits, or flood-proof their properties, or construct on-site detention basins. In each case, economies of scale will often, and especially in urban areas, make collective provision a more efficient solution.

Secondly, a catchment is a system and one with pronounced spatial differentiation. As a result, the consequences of the action of one individual depend upon what actions other individuals undertake. Externalities are simple interdependencies, with the effect flowing in one direction, but in a catchment the interactions can be two-way with actions of one individual affecting another whose actions in turn affect the first (Falkenmark and Lundqvist 1999). In some cases, the result can be positive feedback making things worse rather than better. For example, suppose that everyone on a catchment installs source control to hold the 10-year return period rainfall event, after which storage is released. When, say, the 20-year return period rainstorm occurs, not only will the storage capacity be full so that the peak rainfall intensity is unattenuated, but the storage from the earlier part of the rainstorm may also be released. The result may be flooding that is more severe than if nobody had installed source control. To create a pricing system that reflects these differences adequately is likely to be expensive and imposing a low variety system through regulations may be much simpler to manage.

Next, we are seldom so lucky as to be in a 'second-best' situation (Lipsey and Lancaster 1956–7); if we impose a charge on a negative externality, the effect may be to make things worse if it shifts actions towards those that impose larger but different externalities. When land use imposes multiple externalities, the logic is to examine the relative importance of the different externalities and decide where to begin to introduce charges in a way that reduces the total magnitude of the externalities from all sources.

The other risk with introducing charges on externalities is that they will be captured by the finance ministry. Finance ministries operate on only two principles: to maximise revenue and to stop government spending any of that revenue. Introducing charges on environmental externalities have two great advantages to a finance ministry. Firstly, they are taxes on sin and hence difficult for anyone to object to; secondly, they are relatively invisible as compared to taxes on income, sales or property. In turn, rather than be set at the level which will change behaviours, the likelihood is that the finance ministry will seek to ensure that they are set at a level that maximises tax revenue. Hypothetication of the revenue, reserving it to a specific purpose, as is the case with charges on water pollution in France and the Netherlands (Andersen 1994) avoids this problem. However, it does introduce other risks notably that the revenue will be spent simply because it exists and the creation of a very complex system of hypothecated charges, which is resistant to reform.

Finally, as discussed in Section 8.2, exchanges define or are defined by social relations. A complaint that has been made by industry about charges on pollution is that it creates a right to pollute; legally it does not, socially it does as a price buys a right to consume. Similarly, Thomas and Syme (1988), in a contingent valuation study of the price elasticity of domestic water demand found that high income groups were quite prepared to pay large sums to use water for external purposes. The way they framed the issue was in terms of buying a right to use water for these purposes in all circumstances rather than as a payment for the water they used.

11.3 Motivations and Changing Behaviour

That people are motivated wholly by narrow self-interest does not seem to be true; the evidence concerning behaviour related to sustainable behaviours suggests that life is more complicated and that social or environmental value orientations are a determinant of such behaviours (e.g. Aragon-Correa and Llorens-Montes 1997).

11.4 Social Norms

Social norms are a significant influence on very mundane consumer behaviour (Ryan and Bonfield 1975). Hence, mobilising social norms to change behaviours with regard to collective goods is quite effective; people do what they think other people do and groups also impose sanctions on deviants. Thus, the USACE (1994) report that calls for voluntary reductions in water use can result in falls of 25% in demand. In Indonesia, the government has established a system of rating the pollution performance of industrial concerns from world leaders down to very poor; the rate of improvement in the worst performers is impressive (Wheeler *et al.* 2000). Again, voluntary approaches to pollution control in Japan are reported to have been successful (Imura 1999). More generally, if there is not a social norm that consumers will pay for a good or service, or that social norm breaks down, then the market model will collapse.

For this to work, it is necessary to have a community and some clear social norms that are established by that community (Cleaver 2000). Creating stakeholder organisations then creates a forum in which strong social pressures can be put upon deviant members to comply with group decisions. At a crude level, one reason for the success of the Agence Bassin (Barraque 1999) is that executives of companies that resist complying with the plan suspect that they will be black-balled from the golf club they want to join. Thus, Alan Vicory (2001), the Exec-utive Director of Ohio River Valley Water Sanitation Commission (ORSANCO), has argued that the critical issue in catchment management is to resolve the rela-tionships between the stakeholders and that for this to occur, there needs to be a forum for the stakeholders. A governor of an upper stream state comes under con-siderable pressure from the members of other states, including those not directly effected, to change the policies of that state. Again, Crichton (2001) reports that in flood management groups in Scotland, similar pressures are exerted on mem-bers to comply with the group's policy. Equally, the literature on juries shows that jurors feel under strong pressure to either agree with the majority verdict or to reach a compromise (Young *et al.* 1999). Indeed, sometimes the force of the social norms established are quite scary; in Switzerland, one group of spies were caught because they were making a noise after 10 p.m. on a Sunday and a neighbour reported them to the police.

This example illustrates one advantage of the social norms approach; it multi-plies the number of enforcers. Equally, it can be argued that social norms underlie all of the approaches; unless there is a social norm to comply with regulations or to pay charges, then compliance will be so low as to cause the regulatory or charge approach to be ineffective. If the majority of water connections are illegal then introducing metering is meaningless, as it is if the consumer can simply bribe the meter reader to record whatever amount of water the consumer chooses to pay for.

11.5 Regulations

Two very desirable characteristics of any system of control are that there is pre-dictability and transparency; that it is immediately obvious what it is desired that people should do. The great virtue of regulations can then be that they are simple, transparent and clearly define the behaviour that is desired. The disad-vantage of economic instruments is that those whose behaviour it is sought to influence have to decide what they should do. It costs them time and money to determine what to do. Regulations can then offer economies of scale to those whose behaviour it is intended to influence; it is likely to be considerably cheaper to require that toilet cisterns have a maximum flush capacity than for several mil-lion households to each determine the relative economics of installing cisterns of different sizes.

The transaction costs of regulation can also be low and will usually be lower than for economic instruments. A regulation that no chimney shall emit visible black smoke is easy to apply and to check, including by neighbours. Conversely, if a charge is applied based upon the weight of particles emitted above a certain size, then measuring equipment has to be installed on all relevant chimneys. This equipment then has to be checked and the records audited. If tradable permits for emissions are issued then, in addition, public available records have to be maintained and a system for trading permits also has to be established.

This is an example of the advantages of reducing variety; the virtue of pricing and competition is that it will generate innovations. But some of those innovations will simply be ways of avoiding the charges without satisfying the intent of the charging mechanism in the same way that taxation generates tax specialists who seek ways of avoiding taxation by finding loopholes in the tax law. In turn, governments then spend time seeking to close those loopholes. Neither activity contributes anything to economic efficiency. In principle, therefore, any pricing mechanism needs to cover all possible ways of responding to those price incentives. Conversely, regulation can either restrict allowable responses to a given range or exclude some behaviours altogether. A combination of regulations to define the boundaries of permissible behaviour and prices within that range is then the traditional model of a market – laws covering weights and measures were introduced very early into markets.

Where behaviour is determined by technology then it will be considerably cheaper to mandate the use of a particular standard of performance that can be achieved by that technology than to start by instituting a pricing mechanism with incentives such that people will then adopt that technology. For example, domestic water demand is markedly determined by technological factors (Section 14.4.1); therefore, establishing regulations that define the maximum water usage of a washing machine can save everyone a great deal of time and effort. Conversely, a virtue of adopting a price mechanism is then that it may spur the development of a new technology that will achieve the desired end at a lower cost than existing technologies. In addition, it will tend to increase demand for such technologies which may in turn drive down costs.

Regulation is more efficient in practice when it defines the ends rather than the means; when it mandates the maximum flush volume of a toilet cistern than when it specifies the technology to be used to achieve that flush volume (e.g. flapper valve or siphonic action). If we define the ends then we can hope that competitive pressures will result in innovations that can deliver these ends at lower costs. The weakness of regulation is when it freezes technology at a particular state rather than promoting change.

11.6 Comparative Advantages and Disadvantages

The economist's perpetual cry is: what are the alternatives? It should not then be assumed that there is only one way of changing people's behaviour and the whole range of possible ways of both signalling a change is desired and of providing an incentive to that change need to be examined on a case-by-case basis. In this comparison, the transaction costs and the costs of information to all parties need to be considered and may indeed form a large part of the total costs. One way of reducing those costs is then to reduce the variety of possible actions that each individual must consider.

Equally, since the purpose is to change the world, the actions should promote further change where that change will further the intent of the intervention. We want to encourage better and cheaper means of achieving our ends; the ends therefore need to be clearly signalled.

There will also be some behaviours that are not economically practical to change, or are not feasible to change. For example, in the UK, gardens are being converted to hard standings for car parking; the effect is to increase the proportion of rainfall that is converted to runoff and to increase urban flood problems. It is unlikely that either regulations or charges for runoff would be effective means of controlling this problem; the regulatory approach would require that households knew that there is a restriction and the costs of instituting a charge could well exceed the revenue generated.

Some general criteria that might then be used to appraise alternative means of inducing changes in behaviour:

- *Theoretical efficiency*: performance compared to the theoretical position where the required or optimal reduction in pollution is achieved at the lowest possible cost.
- *Administrative cost*: the costs to regulators of monitoring pollution, maintaining records, undertaking inspections and, in the case of tradable permits, creating and maintaining a market.
- *Science base required*: the level of knowledge required as to the physical, chemical and biological processes involved together with the data on the particular media in the specific location. This has a cost but there is also a limit at any point in time; for example, new pesticides may be introduced ahead of any technical means of detecting residues of those pesticides in water, food or animals. The requirement is that the intervention strategy can work successfully with very imperfect information.
- *Adaptability to changes in supply and demand*: adaptability to both exogenously determined changes in the receiving media (e.g. as a result of climate change) and to new entrants who will pollute.
- *Compliance cost to the polluter*: the costs to polluters of monitoring, maintaining records, applying for necessary licences or permits tradable or otherwise.
- *Probability of effect*: how certain it is possible to be in advance that the expected change in pollution will actually be achieved.
- *Transparency to the polluter*: the certainty which the polluter has as to how to respond to the stimulus in the best manner and, indeed, what change in behaviour is required.
- *Risk of regulatory capture*: the likelihood that the regulator will only require what the polluters claim that they can afford to deliver.

- *Revenue raised*: the 'tax' revenue raised; finance ministries are attracted to new ways of raising tax revenue and 'green taxes' are particularly attractive as they are hidden and have a moral connotation.
- *Dependency upon the approximation to a perfect, competitive market*: the extent to which the intervention to work in the predicted way and to achieve what is expected the strategy relies upon the assumption of a perfect competitive market. Conversely, the extent to which imperfections in the market will result in either failure to achieve the desired end, undesirable effects or unexpected effects.
- *Incentive effect to technological innovation*: the extent to which the measure induces technological innovation or otherwise drives down costs, or, conversely, tends to freeze technology in its current state.
- *Maintains res commune*: it should not require the creation of new private entitlements at the expense of common property rights (or those of other individuals) unless the ideological argument for such a shift has been first accepted.
- *Degree to which short-run efficiency promotes long-run efficiency*: if the demand for pollution abatement is income elastic then in the long run the optimum level of pollution is likely to shift downwards. Any such effect will be amplified by technological innovations which drive down the marginal cost of pollution abatement. If pollution abatement is capital intensive, then these changes should not necessarily require the complete replacement of existing capital stocks. For example, the UK was in the process of building long sea outfalls to discharge raw sewage, relying upon dispersal and dilution, when a policy shift to a requiring treatment before discharge occurred. In effect, something like £800 million was wasted on constructing such long sea outfalls.
- *Dependency upon other externalities being taken into account*: it is unlikely that the externalities of any individual or company are limited to a single form of externality. That there may be multiple externalities is, for example, recognised by the multimedia approach which the Environment Agency was set up to achieve. In such circumstances, a reduction in one form of externality may simply result in an increase in other externalities; the result might then be a decrease in economic efficiency.

Absent from this list is the effect on international competitiveness. This is because there are no clear-cut answers. There is usually a concern that Pigovian taxes will affect international competitiveness, particularly on imports since taxes on goods going for export could be rebated. This is more generally an argument that requiring tougher environmental standards will affect the home country's industry competitiveness as compared to industry based in countries with lower environmental standards. For a given environmental standard, Pigovian taxes or tradable permits ought, theoretically, to have less effect upon international competitiveness than the other two alternatives. Very high Pigovian taxes are calculated from studies of price elasticity needed in order to have a required effect and these would damage competitiveness. But, as I have argued earlier, price inelasticity is often no more than a sign of market failure, firms failing to respond in the optimum manner to market signals.

Also missing from this list is public accountability, an essential requirement of any regulatory system. The test of public accountability is taken to be that the regulatory agency is achieving what the public requires that agency to achieve and is doing so fairly. It is assumed that the criteria defined above, together with the avoidance of arbitrary or wholly subjective judgements and fair and equal treatment of all parties, constitute the overriding criterion of public accountability.

Comparison across these criteria suggests that there is no clear-cut winner (Table 11.1). Performance-based regulation is generally preferable to technology-based regulation except when the science base is thin and administrative costs

Table 11.1   *Comparative performance of different intervention strategies*

Criteria	Command and control		Tradable permit	Pigovian tax
	Emission standards or receiving media standard	Technology standards		
Theoretical efficiency	●●	●	●●●	●●●
Administrative cost	●●	●●●	●	●
Science base required	●●	●●●	●	●
Adaptability to changes in supply/demand	●●●	●	●●	●●●
Compliance cost to polluter	●●	●	●●●	●●●
Probability of effect	●●●	●●●	very uncertain	uncertain
Transparency to polluter	●●	●●●	●	●●
Risk of regulator capture by polluter	●	●	●●●	●●
Revenue raised	●	●	●	●●●
Dependency upon approximation to perfect market	●●●	●●●	●	●●
Incentive effect to technological innovation	●	●	●●	●●●
Maintains res commune	●●●	●●●	●	●●●
Degree to which short-run efficiency promotes long-run efficiency	●	●	●●	●●●
Independence of extent to which other externalities are being taken into account	●●●	●●●	●●	●

Scores: ● = poor; ●● = moderate; ●●● = good.

must be minimised. Pigovian taxes are similarly generally preferable to tradable permits when the externalities problem is marked or there is a high risk of regulatory capture. More generally, a society which is highly developed and so has an advanced science base, for a good where the situation approximates to a perfect competitive market with clearly established private property rights, is likely to favour Pigovian taxes or tradable permits. Conversely, a developing country with a thin scientific base, few administrative resources and thin markets, is likely to start by favouring command and control mechanisms. Unfortunately, those are precisely the situations in which the risk of regulatory capture is greatest, in some cases by corrupt means.

12

Turning Theory into Practice

Achieving the sustainable management of water is accepted as requiring the integrated management of land and water across the catchment as a whole (Global Water Partnership Technical Advisory Committee 2000). Figure 12.1 outlines a simple model of the intentional and accidental interactions between the economy and the water environment.

Water management is concerned with managing both the natural (e.g. seasonal variations in flows) and unnatural (e.g. climate change) perturbations in water quantity, water quality and the erosion and deposition of sediment. These three systems are themselves quite closely coupled. Moreover, for human uses, we seek stability from systems that are naturally dynamic. So, in the case of water resource management, we seek to bring variations in the supply of water into line with the variations in the demand for water where the variations in demand over time are typically less than the variations in supply. In particular, a main reason for intervention is to manage the perturbations in the perturbations, floods and droughts being extreme cases of normal variations in the flows over the year. At the same time, human activities induce shifts in the water quantity, quality and the processes of erosion and deposition where these changes both directly impact on other human activities and on ecosystems. Indirectly, human activities are further impacted by the latter effects. It is these changes, both intentional and consequential, in the dynamics of the different systems that determine the benefits and costs of any project or policy.

Thus, abstracting water for irrigation and potable water use have direct benefits to the socio-economic system; similarly, so does the collection of wastewater and surface water runoff, not least because a significant benefit of collecting wastewater is that it enables people to use more water. Similarly, drainage is often a necessary part of irrigation if salinisation of the soil is to be avoided. But both abstraction and the discharge of drainage water will typically have negative effects upon the flow regime and quality of the riparian environment.

Some economic products such as recreation and fisheries are a function of the state of the watercourse, defined by its water quality and flow regime (and hence also its geomorphology); others such as hydropower and navigation require

Handbook of Water Economics: Principles and Practice. C. Green
© 2003 John Wiley & Sons, Ltd ISBN: 0-471-98571-6

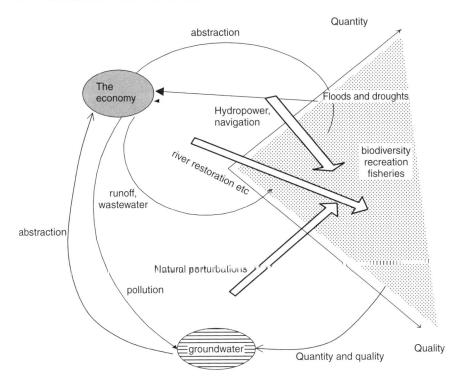

Figure 12.1   *Interactions between the economy and the water environment*

changing the flow regime, and consequently have a series of knock-on effects on the riparian environment. The magnitude and value of changes in these products depend upon the extent of the change in water quality or quantity and not upon the reason why such a change has occurred. The economic justification for constructing a wastewater treatment works, undertaking low flow alleviation works, or river restoration works all arise from these benefits. Conversely, navigation works, dams, water abstractions and improvements in land drainage are all likely to negatively impact on these economic products. Some forms of flood alleviation works, such as channel deepening, are also likely to impact negatively upon these economic products but other forms of works, such as engineered wetlands, are likely to have positive effects.

Integrated catchment requires that the economic analyses undertaken must be based upon the analysis of the impacts of the proposed scheme upon the catchment as a whole and in terms of each of the three systems. However, historically, projects have been developed on a functional approach and one that treats specific perceived problems. For example, the objective will have been to provide an irrigation system, a wastewater treatment works or a flood alleviation scheme and economic analyses have been undertaken in these primarily functional terms.

Such a simple functional approach would have made it possible for the reader to identify a single section of this text as being relevant to the project although with considerable overlaps between sections. Conversely, an integrated approach is likely to result in more projects being undertaken that are multifunctional; an engineered wetland, for instance, that provides wastewater treatment, flood storage, groundwater recharge and recreational benefits. Or, similarly, methods of source control that also provide water for flushing toilets or providing amenities (Pinkham 2000). Therefore, the sections that are relevant depend in part on the options being considered in a particular project.

Moreover, a key stage in an economic analysis is to identify each of the different positive and negative consequences, both those intended and also those that are side-effects, of the proposed project. We seek therefore to undertake a holistic analysis through a piecemeal approach and adopt this approach precisely in order to reduce the complexity to a manageable and comprehensible level. In turn, each of these separate impacts is generally evaluated in terms of a unit value multiplied by the size of the population, be this households or fields, that is affected. In this way, we reduce the risks of missing out specific impacts but at the cost of increasing the risk that we will miss out synergistic effects of the different consequences (SACTRA 2000).

Furthermore, the economy is itself a system and needs to be treated as such. For example, the locus of concern in development is 'sustainable rural livelihoods' (Ashley and Carney 1999). One aspect of the failure to consider the economy as a system has been the failure to differentiate between gender roles (Hart 1992), to omit the inputs of unpriced resources (Jodha 1992), and the failure of many irrigation schemes to take account of the complex farming patterns in parts of Africa have been well documented (Adams 1992; Marchand 1987).

12.1 Evaluating Impacts

The basic approach to the economic evaluation of the consequences of some action is:

- Identify all the disparate consequences of that action.

This is easy to say but difficult to do: significant consequences have been omitted in the past because we did not notice them and because it is difficult to predict the behaviour of complex systems of which we have incomplete knowledge. Seeking advice from as wide a range as possible of specialists and particularly the people who live in the area offers the best chance of identifying the significant consequences of the alternative courses of action being considered.

Then, for each consequence, it is necessary to:

- Quantify the nature of the change.
- Specify the change in terms which can be related to a value.

- Relate this change to parameters that can be predicted.
- Estimate size of the population of people, households, or others who will gain or lose by that change.
- Estimate the unit value of a change.
- Estimate the benefit or cost of that change by multiplying the unit value by the number within the affected population.

This does not involve a simple linear process of analysis because there are a number of interdependencies between the components. In particular, the nature of the population who benefit from a given change depends upon what it is that people value about the river and whether that will be changed by the proposed project.

12.1.1 Quantifying impacts

The second stage is usually undertaken by water quality scientists, epidemiologists or other appropriate specialists. For example, the estimation of the change in the nitrates or suspended solids (SS) in a river as a result of works on a combined sewer overflow (CSO) and the distance downstream that these works will have an impact is a task to be carried out by water quality specialists. Similarly, estimates of the response of crops to changes in the availability of water is a task for agronomists rather than economists. In general, developing such 'dose response' models (Hanley and Spash 1993) requires expertise that economists lack. However, the economist does need to understand what the specialist is saying and jointly they must build the bridge so that the change is defined in way that is related to the value of the good.

12.1.2 Determine what it is that people value

Since value is no more than a reflection of what people want, we must first determine what it is that people want. If economic value is subjective, so necessarily are the characteristics of the good that determine that value. In turn, knowledge of who wants what determines the population who will benefit or lose by a specified change. A valued change in river water quality is one that people will want for the particular purpose they have in view. If we seek to value the benefits for informal recreation of an improvement in river water quality, then it is necessary to start by understanding what makes a river desirable and valuable as a place to visit. In turn, the critical parameters that define river water quality are then those that affect the desirability of the river as a place to visit. Fortunately, in this instance, quite a lot is now known about the characteristics of a river that make it valuable and hence what changes would increase or decrease this value (e.g. Ditton and Goodale 1973; Tunstall *et al.* 1997).

Again, if consumers are to be asked how much they would be prepared to pay for an improvement in the taste of tapwater, then it is first necessary to determine the characteristics of tapwater that are important to the consumer (Guirkinger 1988). Similarly, in evaluating a potential improvement in a recreational fishery, it is first necessary to determine what it is about the fishing venue that anglers value (Section 21.2.2.1).

Therefore, it is necessary to start by discovering what is that people value. Where there is a distinction between what it is that people value currently and what would maximise their best interests, then the two need to be brought into line. If they cannot, then there is no point in providing what would be in their best interests if they knew what those were. Hygiene, sanitation and water supplies can all be instances where there is a distinction between traditional practices and behaviours (Water and Sanitation Program n.d.), and consequently the characteristics that are used to define the value of a water source, for example, and best practices as based on current health science.

In many cases, what determines economic value depends upon perceptual evidence but it is what people understand the relevant concept, such as river water quality, to mean and imply that determines which perceptual cues they seek. Simultaneously, perceptual data is being interpreted in cognitive terms. In turn, people may then either have different cognitions of the good of issue or use the wrong signals: for example, turbid water is commonly interpreted as meaning that the water is polluted (Burrows and House 1989; Green *et al.* 1989b).

The 'market' for a particular activity may be segmented; in turn, the preferences of different groups, and more particularly those seeking different activities can conflict (Daubert and Young 1981).

12.1.3 Relate change to parameters that can be predicted

Whilst economic value is subjective, since what people want is subjective, we need to be able to predict how much of a change will result from the alternative actions being considered. These predictions will be based in turn on mathematical or physical models whose outputs will be given in physical, chemical or biological units. It is therefore necessary to establish a link between that which can be predicted and what people want.

For example, part of a methodology to evaluate the benefits of river water quality improvements (WRc/OXERA/FHRC 1996) involved angling benefits. In turn, it was necessary to determine what different types of anglers wanted from a fishing visit. The necessary next step was then to tie these classes to both the water classes used for reporting river water quality (WRc/OXERA/FHRC 1996) and the parameters that can be predicted by water quality models (Russell *et al.* 2001). This is a critical step since that which can predicted may be meaningless in cognitive and perceptual terms. Equally, the signs that people use to determine the state of some good may be extremely difficult to relate to some biological, physical or chemical parameters than can be measured and predicted. Moreover, people may only distinguish between quite wide classes.

12.1.4 Estimating the number of beneficiaries

Typically, the benefits of a change are estimated by multiplying the estimate of the number of people or others who will benefit by a unit value. The former number is often very large and the latter number can be very small. Consequently the effect on the estimate of the project benefits of errors in the definition of the population who benefit can be larger than from errors in the estimates of the unit value. In consequence, it is at least as important to define the population who benefit as to estimate the unit value accurately. It is, however, a question which is often neglected in economic analyses or dealt with by making quite arbitrary assumptions.

The questions of what someone wants and the definition of the population who benefit are clearly linked: if someone wants the change then they benefit from that change. It may be obvious who benefits from a change; for example, all those who live or have property within an area protected by a flood defence scheme, or anglers who will benefit from improvements in the ecological status of a stretch of river. In the former case, the current population who benefit is already enumerated by the action of definition. More often, as is the case for the anglers, we can define the class who will potentially benefit but then need to calculate the number of people in that population. It is rare for there to be data available on the number of visits made by anglers to the site at present, or indeed for any class of visitor to a river. Moreover, an improvement to the river should be expected to attract more visits to that river either as a result of those who already visit the river visiting more often or because people are attracted away from other sites. In either case, those visits will be made at the cost of sacrificing some other activity, in the latter case by making fewer visits to a comparable site.

In practice, even in those cases where the population who benefit is well defined, the estimates of the size of the population who are affected are frequently very imprecise. For example, in the Grootvlei case study (Section 21.7), three different estimates of the water withdrawn for irrigation were obtained and these varied by a factor of five. Similarly, whilst flood extent maps have an appearance of precision, both the flood outline itself and the estimates of the number of properties within the flood plain are often subject to large margins of error.

Nor should such changes in behaviour be expected to occur instantaneously; the rate of take-up will be important to the accurate estimation of the present value of benefits. Thus, following the completion of an irrigation scheme, it should not be expected that all farmers will immediately change their existing pattern of cropping.

If the rather nebulous concept of 'nonuse' value (Section 5.1.2) is considered, then the definition of the population who benefit becomes even more ill-defined. The conventional assumption is that to hold a nonuse value for a resource does not depend upon the individual currently using that resource. Consequently, who should be expected to have a nonuse value for a river improvement? Those who live near to it, those who know of it, those people who live in the administrative unit which will bear the costs of the improvement, those people who in principle would wish to see such an improvement made? There is no logical way of predetermining what are the boundaries of the population who benefit and, as was shown in Section 5.1.2, in some cases people very remote from an environmental resource are prepared to pay towards the cost of its conservation or enhancement. The conventional approach assumes that people hold nonuse values that are specific to particular cases so that, in principle, to determine what is the nonuse value of improving the one million or so kilometres of river in the USA (US EPA 2000), it is necessary to ask some populations about each kilometre of river or to generalise from questions about some specific lengths of river to all rivers (Section 5.1.2.3).

12.1.4.1 Counting visitors

For recreational activities, the number of adult visitors to a site at present is seldom known but may be very large. A number of different techniques (Scottish Natural Heritage 1993; Tourism and Recreation Research Unit 1983) can be used to estimate the number of visits made to that site. Ideally, a reliable count is made of those visits using infra-red or similar people counters. However, those counters require calibration since a bicycle may register as several passages past the counter and some visitors will pass several counters. In addition, some counters will fail to record on some days so that estimates of the number of people who passed the counter on those days must be estimated on the basis of regression equations using the measured numbers on other counters. Consequently, estimating the number of visitors on the basis of recorded counts can be both complex and time consuming (Garner *et al.* 1994).

Often, inferential methods will have to be used; counts of visits made to one area of the site, such as a visitor centre or car park, being used to estimate the total number of visits made to the site. Frequently, such data or infra-red counter data will only be available for part of the year and it will be necessary to use a growth curve, similar to those used to convert short period traffic counts to estimates of annual traffic flows, to generate an estimate of the total number of visits made by adults over the whole year. However, the pattern of visitors to different types of sites shows significant variations (Table 12.1) and so it is necessary to decide to which kind of site the one under study is most similar.

Moreover, even apparently similar sites, such as the selection of forests shown in Figure 12.2, can show very marked differences between sites with those that attract predominantly local visitors showing the least variation in numbers over the year. Moreover, even given a year's data of visit numbers, it is possible that it could be an abnormal year; the weather in particular may have been unusually good or bad. In principle, it is possible to go further and adjust the estimate of visit numbers for these abnormal conditions.

If we can determine how many visits are made to a site at present, then the next problem is to predict how that number will change in consequence to some

Table 12.1 Variations in visitor numbers over the year

	January	February	March	April	May	June	July	August	September	October	November	December
Total tourism trips by UK residents to England	0.46	0.54	0.66	0.80	0.79	0.73	0.85	1.00	0.77	0.75	0.52	0.75
National Trust properties	0.14	0.00	0.00	0.50	0.64	0.55	0.68	1.00	0.45	0.36	0.23	0.00
RSPB reserves	0.73	0.45	0.45	0.82	1.36	1.18	0.91	1.00	0.64	0.73	0.55	0.45
The Wallace Collection	0.00	0.00	0.00	0.91	1.00	1.03	0.96	1.00	0.85	1.01	1.12	0.92
Imperial War Museum	0.71	0.95	1.01	0.85	0.73	0.71	0.88	1.00	0.64	0.88	0.71	0.50
Cabinet War Rooms	0.39	0.44	0.69	0.60	0.68	0.77	0.89	1.00	0.74	0.73	0.51	0.38
HMS Belfast	0.33	0.48	0.57	0.77	0.51	0.51	0.75	1.00	0.44	0.64	0.30	0.25
Duxford	0.39	0.44	0.69	0.60	0.67	0.77	0.89	1.00	0.74	0.73	0.51	0.38
English Heritage – mean	0.06	0.11	0.28	0.39	0.50	0.83	0.72	1.00	1.06	0.39	0.22	0.06
Dinton Pastures Country Park	0.00	0.00	0.00	0.00	0.94	0.65	0.74	1.00	0.72	0.76	0.47	0.42
Wat Tyler country park	0.04	0.15	0.12	0.42	0.38	0.35	0.50	1.00	0.54	0.23	0.08	0.04

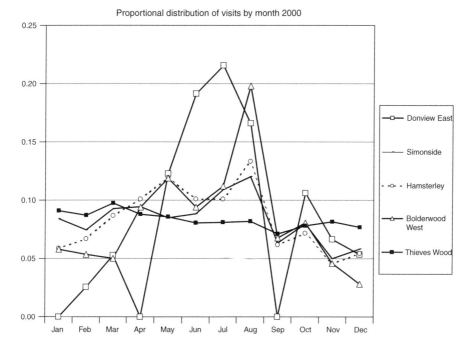

Proportional distribution of visits by month 2000

Figure 12.2   *Variations in growth curves for forests*

change to that site. If the site is improved, then either those who visit now may make additional visits or other visitors will be attracted away from alternative sites. Conversely, if the site degrades then some of those visits that are now made should be deflected to other sites or into other activities.

12.1.4.2 Predicting the number of visitors

The alternative to working from the visits actually made to a site is to predict the number of visits that will be made to the site from different residential areas. It is obviously necessary to use this approach when a site is improved and anticipated to attract more visitors, or when a new site is created. Although the travel cost method (Clawson 1959) was intended to be used for estimating the recreational value of a site, it can also be used simply to predict the number of visits (Bateman *et al.* 1996). In seeking to predict the number of visits made to a site, we are necessarily invoking a model of recreational choice, and the process through which people decide to visit a particular site.

The travel cost method is itself a reinvention by economists of the gravity model originally developed by geographers in order to predict the number of journeys that will be made between different urban areas (Haggett 1965), or to particular types of facilities such as shops and health care facilities (Smith 1979). It is an attractor model: it is assumed that a site pulls visitors from different residential areas against the friction of travelling: the more attractive the site and the fewer the competing sites, the greater the number of visitors attracted to the site and the further they will travel to the site.

Thus, the number of visitors received at a particular recreation site should be as follows:

$$V = \Sigma \times A \cdot P^y / c^z$$

where:

V is the number of visits made to the site
A is the attraction of the site
P is the relevant population at each population centre
c is the cost of travel from home to the recreation site
and x, y and z are coefficients.

As given, cost and time are assumed to be perfect substitutes; if the journey was slower but cost less than the current journey time, this change would have no effect on the number of visits made. But, as argued earlier (Section 4.2), it would be more realistic to treat time as a separate constraint to income. Thus, in making a visit, the constraint faced by the potential visitor is that the total travel time plus the time required for the visit must be less than the available time. In turn, time is lumpy, there being a difference between two one-day trips and a two-day trip. It has been found in the context of visits to the coast by local residents that a significant proportion of visits are apparently constrained by time (Garner *et al.* 1994).

Not surprisingly, therefore, the journey, in whole or part, is often part of the enjoyment of the trip: 'Recreational travel is unique in that the actual journey itself is frequently a part of the total recreation experience, rather than just a means to an end' (Patmore 1983). People may choose the destination, therefore, in part because of the anticipated pleasure from the journey, or choose the route because of the pleasure from that route rather than others. As much attention may be paid to the choice of the route as to the destination: 'It is clear from such work that the direct route to a destination is not necessarily the most preferred route, nor do outward and return journeys, even to a single destination, necessarily coincide' (Patmore 1983). Indeed, there is often a desire to minimise the proportion of the inward and outward routes which are duplicated. As with other forms of consumption, declining marginal utility applies: the more frequently the journey is made, at some point, the pleasure wears off and the journey becomes a cost.

However, in this model, the proportion of the population and the number of visits they make is solely determined by the attractiveness and distance to the sites. If, however, not all of the population want to undertake the activity or the number of days in which they can undertake the activity is restricted, then P should be adjusted to be this saturation figure.

The alternative model, developed in geography to explain migration patterns (Hagerstrand 1957), is the diffusion model. This is a push model; it assumes that people first want to make a recreational visit and the numbers who visit different sites depends on the number of intervening competitive sites and how strongly is the intention to make a recreational visit. In terms of recreational behaviour, the first approach is based on the assumption that someone thinks 'I want to go to xxxx' and the diffusion model assumes that the basis for recreational behaviour is: 'let's go out this Saturday, where shall we go?'

The number of visits made to a particular site is then explicable as follows:

$$M_x = kX^{-1}e^{-ax}$$

where M_x is the percentage of in-migration to a centre from a zone at distance (or cost) X, k is a constant and a is the absorption coefficient (Haggett 1965) which here depends upon the attractiveness of the site.

In practical terms, the two models are quite similar in effect but conceptually they are quite different in emphasis. In the diffusion model, a central concern would be what is the pressure which drives the population to undertake this behaviour? The diffusion model also provides an explanation of Patman's (1983) demonstration that people in large cities travel further for recreational visits than people living in smaller urban areas. Put simply, they have to because the recreational sites are further away. Conversely, the gravity model would suggest uniform distance-decay functions with residents of large urban areas making fewer visits to recreational sites than those in smaller urban areas because the costs of making a visit are higher. In practice, recreational behaviour seems to be complex with a mixture of pull factors (e.g. unique attractors such as relatives and major theme parks) and push factors: a significant proportion of visits to some sites were only made on the way to somewhere else or were not planned when the journey was started (Cheshire and Stabler 1976).

Whether or not visitors are pulled to a site or are absorbed by it, a critical question is: what is the latent demand for that form of recreation? What proportion of the population, for example, wishes to go angling? How many days a year will they fish, or how much time do they have to go angling? For example, the number of visits that will be made to an angling site depends upon:

- what proportion of the population wishes to go angling;
- how many days a year anglers can go fishing, or how much time they have to do so;
- how they choose the places to go angling.

Whilst there may be a link between the second and third questions, there is no obvious link between them and the first question. Thus, if a new or improved angling site is created next to a population centre, it does not follow that the entire population will take up angling. Indeed, in some parts of Europe participation rates in angling have dropped significantly in recent years; thus, the number of anglers in France fell from 2.8 million to 1.4 million (Breton 2000). Clearly, those who would in the past have gone fishing are now doing something else, so there are issues both as to the degree of substitution between sites and between the leisure activities.

Nor, unless ease of access is the sole determinant of the choice of place to go angling, does it follow that the new site will be the preferred place to go angling or that local anglers will now make more angling trips. Only those for whom the number of angling visits they can make has been limited by the cost or difficulty of visiting a desirable angling site should be expected to make more angling visits in total or to visit this site preferentially. In then determining how that potential demand is distributed between alternative sites, a further question is: to what extent are different sites, and different forms of recreational activity, substitutes for each other? If we assume that all individuals have fully allocated their available time, then any visit must be a substitute for some other activity that would otherwise be undertaken in that time. Therefore, an increase in the number of visits to one site necessarily involves less time spent on some other activity either in the home or at some other recreational site.

Ideally, we would start with the individual's basic problem of maximising utility, given the constraints of time, income and other factors such as life-cycle stage. The individual then has to decide either jointly or separately which activities to undertake when and where. Whether this decision is taken jointly or separately is itself an important issue; for example, in the UK, many anglers belong to clubs and their fishing is largely restricted to club-owned waters. At the same time, preferences can change; notably the proportion of the population who wish to go fishing appears to be falling in many countries whilst both income, and to a lesser extent, time constraints (e.g. changes in the working week, retirement) are changing over time. There are equally large differences between countries; Walsh (1986) cites data showing that in 1979, 53% of the US population participated in fishing whereas in 1995, in England and Wales, only one household in nine contained at least one person who had been fishing for pleasure in the last two years (National Rivers Authority 1995a).

For the informal recreation that makes up the bulk of recreational use of rivers and lakes, a critical question is whether a river or lake site is a potential substitute for all other recreational sites, and equally potentially substitutable by those sites. Will an improved river corridor simply attract visitors away from other rivers or also from forests?

Figure 12.3 shows the results of cluster analysis of the responses to a question that asked visitors how much enjoyment they would expect to get from a visit to each of a variety of different leisure and recreational sites. The closer to the left the sites are linked together, the more similar were the amounts of enjoyment that respondents expected to get from visits to those sites. Thus, lakes and rivers

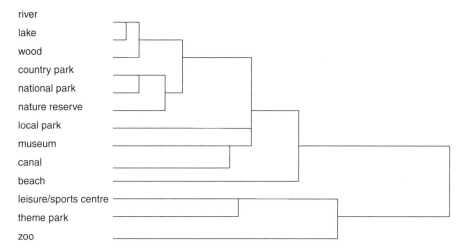

river
lake
wood
country park
national park
nature reserve
local park
museum
canal
beach
leisure/sports centre
theme park
zoo

Figure 12.3   *Similarities between different recreational sites as a place to visit*

were seen as offering very similar amounts of enjoyment, whilst theme parks, leisure facilities and zoos were seen as being quite different to the other types of site. Intriguingly, canals are seen as offering similar amounts of enjoyment as museums, and so seem to be interpreted as historical sites, rather than being seen as similar to rivers. This cluster analysis implies that a canal is not a good substitute for a river as a place to visit, and that a leisure centre is no substitute at all.

In short, we need better models of recreational choice (Vickerman 1975) if we are to make reliable predictions of the number of visits that will be made to a particular site.

12.2 Methods of Evaluation

There are three general strategies for deriving values, and hence also opportunity costs:

- market prices;
- inferential methods;
- expressed preference methods.

12.2.1 Market prices

It can readily be shown for a priced good sold in a perfectly competitive market – one where there are so many small producers, all producing identical products, and consumers that none can affect the price; with entry as well as exit from the market being costless – then the prevailing price in such a market would equal both the marginal value and the marginal cost (Lipsey 1971). As a conceptual model the concept of a perfectly competitive market provides a useful starting point for estimating the value or cost of a priced good. In the real world, markets are commonly imperfect or distorted in some way. It is then usually necessary to make some corrections to the observed market price in order to estimate the economic value or opportunity cost, its shadow price, of the good or service in question.

For example, in assessing the benefits of flood alleviation schemes, one important correction is that for second-hand goods. It is argued that imperfect information on the part of the consumer means that the prices of second-hand goods are depressed below their true value (Akerlof 1970). Therefore, in evaluating the loss of, say, a five-year-old television the economic value is greater than the market price of an apparently identical second-hand television. Consequently, the values used for the losses of the contents of dwellings are based upon the use of straight-line depreciation.

It is also necessary to remove direct and indirect subsidies on both inputs and outputs of production. For example, in much of the world, irrigation water is heavily subsidised either directly or indirectly (Garrido 1999). If an irrigated crop is lost as a result of the flood, the real loss is given by calculating the market value of the crop less the real costs of all inputs; that is, by subtracting the real rather than the subsidised costs of providing the irrigation water. Again, agricultural outputs are commonly either subsidised or supported; here, too, the value of a lost crop needs to be adjusted downwards by removing the subsidy or price support element. In turn, where inputs or outputs are subsidised in this way, the capital value of the asset that produces the outputs is also artificially inflated. Thus, when assessing the value of agricultural land, the market price of that land must also be corrected downwards to that level which would exist were there no subsidies on inputs or outputs. It is generally safe to assume that agriculture is always subsidised, the only question being how cleverly the subsidies have been hidden.

There is an exception to the general rule that subsidies shall be removed and this is where a subsidy is intended to represent a positive externality. Some agricultural subsidies are in this form; those intended, for example, to promote environmentally friendly farming. For example, the bare moors of the Lake District in England are a product of sheep grazing but sheep farming in these areas is now only viable because of the upland sheep farming subsidies.

Indirect taxes must also be removed as they are simply a tax intended to generate revenue rather than a real opportunity cost. However, 'green taxes', those that are intended to reflect the externalities caused by the use of a particular good, are real economic costs for that reason and should not be removed. For example, any tax on pesticides intended to reflect the damage caused to the environment, or the cost of removing pesticide residues from potable water, is a real economic cost. The practical problem in analysis is then that it is necessary to determine whether any indirect tax is solely for revenue raising purposes or is designed to incorporate the costs of externalities into the cost of using the product. Where a resource would be put to no other use if it were not applied to the project then its opportunity cost is zero whatever the price actually paid for it. This situation is most likely to be found when looking at labour inputs. Where there is a high level of unemployment or underemployment, the wage rates paid to those building the project will overstate the opportunity costs of that labour and a shadow wage rate needs to be estimated (Squire and van der Tak 1975).

At times, where the good in question is not priced there may exist a near perfect substitute that is priced and this can then be used to set an upper bound on the value of the good it is intended to evaluate. The value of the good in question can be no greater than the cost of this least cost alternative.

One limitation of this approach is that the alternative must either not yet have been undertaken or all the costs can be recovered if it has already been adopted. Any irreversible expenditure, a sunk cost, must not be included.

12.2.2 Inferential methods

The use of market prices is often referred to as revealed preference techniques but, as can be seen from the above discussion, it is often necessary to make quite a large number of corrections to the observed prices in order to calculate the economic values and costs. The second group of techniques may be termed inferential methods and these use statistical techniques to infer the value of the variable of interest which does not have an observable price. They differ fundamentally from the revealed preference in that it is necessary to draw statistical inferences as to the reasons why individuals are behaving as they are from aggregate data. We have to fit the data to the theory, and consequently it is impossible to test the theory, and the theory is also underspecified.

The travel cost method, attributed to Clawson (1959), is a variant of the gravity model discussed in Section 12.1.4.2. It is a way of putting a value on a recreational resource by determining the distances that different visitors have travelled to a site and the costs they have incurred in doing so. By regression analysis, a relationship between the distance travelled and the probability of making a visit is deduced and the resulting function used to estimate the value of a visit to the site. It has been extensively used in the USA (e.g. Smith and Desvouges 1986) and quite widely used in the UK in the late 1960s and early 1970s (e.g. Smith and Kavanagh 1969). However, following some critical reviews of the adequacy of the method in the UK context, including Vickerman (1975) arguing that 'The assumptions of the approach are, however, very suspect on a number of grounds and whilst previous authors have expressed reservations the ease of use has been felt to outweigh any disadvantages', it fell into disuse in the UK, only to be subsequently revived. A problem is that any function can be fitted more or less badly to any set of data and we have no theoretical reason for expecting one functional relationship rather than another. Depending upon what relationship is actually applied, the values derived may then vary by a factor of about 10 (Common 1973). Nor do the assumptions about recreational choices made in the model actually seem to be consistent with recreational behaviour (Green *et al.* 1990).

The hedonic price technique (Rosen 1974) is intended to determine the influence of the land characteristic in question, such as a sea view, on the market price of the land or more usually houses. A number of studies have been undertaken on the effects of flood risks on house prices (e.g. Donnelly 1989) as well as other environmental attributes (e.g. Kirschner and Moore 1989). The reasonable assumption is made that the market price of a particular house is a function of a series of attributes, including the variable of interest, which make that house more or less desirable. Given enough data on the values of each such parameter for the houses sold in an homogeneous market, together with knowledge of the functional relationship between those parameters and the market price of each property, then we could determine how the market price varied as the parameter of interest varies. In practice, we do not know exactly which are the parameters that influence house prices, we cannot measure all of these parameters but have to use surrogate variables in some cases. Thus, in 1979, Freeman observed that: '... the selection of explanatory variables seems to be almost haphazard.... Convenience and data availability appear to be major determinants of this part of model specification.'

Overall, it is also inconsistent with models of residential mobility (e.g. Clark and Onaka 1985). In addition, we do not know what is the functional relationship between these variables and have to infer this relationship in order to undertake the statistical analysis. It appears that the actual functional forms are complex: Timmermans and Veldhuisen (1981) derived utility functions for a wide range of physical and locational attributes. However, Phipps (1983) reported finding two different subsamples, differentiated by their personal household characteristics, who used different utility functions; the first used variants of a multiplicative utility function; the second variants of a disjunctive utility function. Moreover, these different subgroups may use different attributes in making their assessments (Hourihan 1984).

In consequence, Ducci (quoted in Ardila *et al.* 1998) refers rather despairingly to the practical problems of obtaining results of any real value from this method referring to the time spent on 'torturing the data to provide a decent coefficient' and the hedonic price method being as '... more unreliable (than the contingent valuation method) with respect to whether you will be able to get a usable result.' More generally, both methods seek to explain the aggregate of behaviour that is individually determined.

12.2.3 Expressed preference methods

Neoclassical economists long resisted the use of the remaining approach, express-ed preference techniques, which employ social survey techniques because these involving asking people what choices they would make. The basis of the criticism is that what people say they will do in a situation is necessarily not as reliable as observing what they do in such situations were we able to observe their behaviour, and that people are being asked to respond to hypothetical circumstances. The weakness of this criticism is that all choices that are important are hypothetical: everything else is history.

In particular, companies need to be able to predict how much of a new product they can sell at what price. Market research (e.g. Assael 1992) was therefore invented to fill the gap left by economics and one of the two techniques, conjoint analysis, was developed in market research (Huber 1987) where it has been extensively used (Wittink *et al.* 1994). There has been a comparatively small but an increasing number of applications around water management (Adamowicz *et al.* 1997).

In conjoint analysis, respondents are asked to make a series of choices between different combinations of different levels of what are understood to be the most important characteristics, including the one in which we are interested, of the good in question. For example, if we were interested in how proximity to a lake affected house prices, we would first determine what are the critical parame-ters that determine the amounts individual households are prepared to pay for dwellings. One of the characteristics then included in the study is price and another proximity to a lake. The respondents are asked to choose between pairs of houses having different combinations of levels of the different attributes. Then, by statistical analysis it is then hoped to determine how changes in the quantity of the characteristic of interest affect the amounts people are prepared to pay for the good (Orme 2001; Williams and Kilroy 2000). Conjoint analysis is thus the expressed preference equivalent of the hedonic price method and subject to some of the same problems but with the additional ones associated with the use of a social survey method. Firstly, the 'magic number seven' (Miller 1956) issue arises: there may be more attributes than can be used in making comparisons, in which case choices using samples of the different attributes must be used. Secondly, actually making the choices is difficult, particularly trying to make the choices in a consistent way. In turn, it is likely that in the first choices respon-dents make they are learning what are their preferences whilst in the last choices, those respondents have become tired or bored.

Contingent valuation method (CVM) is a rather simpler technique, originally proposed by Ciricacy-Wintrup, in that respondents to the interview survey are asked directly how much they are prepared to pay for a change in the availability of the good in question. In using either technique, it is essential to treat the approach as primarily one of social survey rather than economic analysis, following good social survey practice in terms of question design, sampling and fieldwork (Mitchell and Carson 1989).

Both techniques have a number of virtues. The first is that they are experimental techniques: we can therefore test whether or not there is a particular relationship rather than being forced to assume it. A second is that they involve listening to the public both through the qualitative research studies (e.g. Krueger 1988) that invariably should precede the quantitative interview survey, and in the quantitative study itself. Since the primary aim of benefit–cost analysis is to better understand what the choice involves, this is a significant virtue. Thus, the use of social survey techniques is potentially a good way of learning how members of the public, or of more specialised groups, interpret the choice and the issues it raises.

A set of criticisms levelled by psychologists and others (Fischhoff 1991; Burgess *et al.* 1997) is centred upon the task which respondents are set in a CV study. These criticisms centred upon the issues which social scientists raise as to the nature of preferences and how these are learnt (Section 4.1.1). Thus, three groups of question are raised:

- Can respondents answer such questions?
- How do they answer such questions?
- What do their answers mean?

Fischhoff (1991) argues that CV questions set respondents a very difficult task; some cannot be answered from memory or by instinct but respondents must construct an answer to them using some logical framework of analysis. Moreover, that the task involved may be one to which respondents neither know the appropriate form of analysis by which to construct an answer nor have the information available with which to calibrate such an analysis. Analogously, respondents asked what is two times two will generally know the answer from memory; failing that, they can count on their fingers. Asked what is the cube root of 512, some may know the answer from memory, others may know the formal procedure for deriving an answer and others may develop a heuristic by which means to develop an answer. Rather fewer people are likely to be able to give a correct answer than to the question on two times two and developing an answer is likely to take longer. Asking someone how much they are prepared to pay for some good may thus be closer in terms of task difficulty to asking them what is the cube root of 512 than to the sum of two times two. If respondents have to construct an answer then the questions of how they go about constructing an answer and what they need to know in order to construct an answer become important.

Thus, contingent valuation (CV) studies should be approached from an ergonomic perspective (Green and Tunstall 1997); as a task where the respondent has to decide how much s/he is prepared to pay, often for a good about which they have not previously considered or perhaps even heard. The issue then is to determine those conditions under which respondents can most accurately and reliably undertake this task. From this perspective, any format that involves a single question, including both the 'referendum' format promoted by the NOAA Panel (1993) and the single open-ended question, should be avoided.

Conversely, in general, economists have assumed that respondents know in advance of the CVM survey how much they would be prepared to pay for the good, and think in the same terms as the economist. In turn, economists have been concerned to minimise the ability of respondents to lie, in the form of 'free-riding' (Samuelson 1954); such a strong systematic bias has in fact only been found in samples of economics students (e.g. Marwell and Ames 1981). More generally, the experimental work on the Commons dilemma (Kopelman *et al.* 2000) has found that people's behaviour is more complex and more interesting than economic theory would lead us to expect.

What is critical is to differentiate between the proportion of the sample who are prepared to pay and the amounts that those prepared to pay then offer. There is a very significant difference between the situation where 80% of the sample are prepared to pay an average of £5 each and that where 8% of the sample are prepared to pay an average of £50.

The jury is still out on the validity of the results obtained from expressed preference approaches. It appears probable that the estimates of the proportion of the sample who are prepared to pay something are quite reliable. It is much less certain that the amounts offered by those who are prepared to pay are valid and reliable; computing a sample mean preparedness to pay gives a misleading picture by combining the two statistics together.

Table 12.2 summarises the results from a number of CVM studies carried out at the Flood Hazard Research Centre across a number of different goods. Essentially the same methodology was used in each case: a filter question that asked whether or not they would be prepared to pay at all for the good; then a bidding game followed by an open-ended question. Consequently, there can be some confidence that the differences are not simply the result of methodological differences. The bidding game format is known to suffer from an anchoring effect, but anchoring effects are a universal problem in social survey design (Poulton 1979). As compared to other CVM formats, the advantage of the bidding game is that we know the nature of this anchoring effect whereas with other formats the nature and extent of anchoring are unknown. Again, unlike the referendum format, the sample means do not have to be inferred by fitting a statistical function to the data.

That the proportions of respondents in each sample who were prepared to pay varied from 4% to 81% is encouraging; that the annual amounts that those prepared to pay offered varied between £3.80 and £35.56 is less encouraging. Since the distributions of preparedness to pay are always highly skewed, the logarithmic mean is a better indicator of the central tendency than the arithmetic mean.

Table 12.2   Variations in the proportions prepared to pay and mean amount between different goods

Study	Good	Those prepared to pay			
Social costs of sewerage		% prepared to pay	Mean (£/yr)	Log mean	Sample size
Visitors	River water quality – specific site	55	15.80	1.06	839
Remote sites	Water quality improvements to all rivers	49	18.65	1.16	319
Amenity	Water quality in neighbouring watercourse	40	14.40	1.05	303
Clacton – visitors	Prevention of loss of beach	64	5.13	0.18	146
Dunwich – visitors	Prevention of loss of beach	65	11.22	0.46	147
Filey – visitors	Prevention of loss of beach	81	5.62	0.45	152
Frinton	Prevention of loss of beach	58	4.11	0.32	150
Those living inland from the coast	Prevention of coastal erosion	66	12.35	0.39	412
Herne Bay – visitors	Prevention of loss of beach	56	3.80	0.35	143
Herne Bay – residents	Prevention of loss of beach	73	10.72	0.46	189
Hurst Spit	Prevention of breach in spit	74	24.49	0.69	550
St Mildreds Bay	Prevention of loss of beach and promenade	61	31.44	0.96	462
Cliftonville	Prevention of erosion of cliffs and loss of low level walkway	62	19.47	0.80	524
OFWAT	Reduced risk of supply interruption	4	30.66	1.28	997
OFWAT	Reduction in the risk of sewage flooding	30	28.77	1.17	997
OFWAT	Improvement in the taste of tapwater	26	35.56	1.3	997
OFWAT	All three services	43	39.25		997
Misbourne	Alleviation of low flows in river	63	26.11	1.18	412
Wey	Alleviation of low flows in river	39	24.32	1.09	351
Skerne	River restoration	43	22.45	1.02	121
Dtp	Reduction in traffic nuisance	59	10.57	0.77	620
GEV	Programmes of improvement in national river water quality				
	1st priority programme	54	29.63	0.42	542
	2nd priority	46	21.81	0.40	542
	3rd priority	40	20.46	0.39	542
	4th priority	26	21.32	0.41	542

In particular, in the OFWAT study in which respondents were asked about three water and sewerage services, the proportion of respondents who were prepared to pay for improvements in at least one of those services varied between 4% and 30%. However, those who were prepared to pay for an improvement in at least one of those services offered amounts which are not really different. Meta-analyses of the results of CVM studies (e.g. Brouwer *et al.* 1997) often result in the depressing conclusions that the majority of the variance that can be explained is accounted for by methodological differences between the studies.

In only a relatively few instances are these different techniques for estimating values alternatives. The travel cost method and hedonic price methods have very limited ranges of application, and both the inferential and expressed preference approaches were invented for those situations where market prices do not exist. Some judgements can be made as to the likely accuracy of the different techniques (Table 12.3).

For any stream of benefits or costs, the overall accuracy then also depends on the accuracy of the estimate of the number of beneficiaries. Clearly, we are unable to claim that the estimates of benefits and costs are highly accurate, certainly not so precise that it is sensible to seek to find an optimal level of provision of the good in question. This precludes the adoption of Pigovian taxes from being a sensible strategy – which would, in any case, require that all values were considered and not just economic values.

However, as discussed in Section 13.4.8.1, we often do not need highly accurate estimates of the different streams of benefits and costs when undertaking a benefit–cost analysis.

12.2.4 Benefit transfer

All benefit–cost analyses use benefit or cost transfers in some form: the cost of the project is predicted on the basis of unit costs derived for similar work

Table 12.3   *Comparative accuracy of different evaluation techniques*

Technique	Accuracy
Market prices	Within 15–25%? (given market failures to greater or lesser extent)
Shadow prices	As good as market prices?
Hedonic price method	Can we even get the right sign?
Travel cost method	Within a factor of 10?
Contingent valuation	Within a factor of three?
Conjoint analysis	Insufficient evidence to make a judgement

Source: Green 2000a.

tasks in similar construction projects. Similarly, it is rare for all benefit streams to be estimated specifically for the particular project. Thus, in estimating the benefits of an irrigation project, the predicted yields will be based on actual yields in supposedly comparable conditions. Similarly, the hydrological analysis will typically be based on data transfer: the use of data from another catchment or the use of equations calibrated from other catchments (e.g. IOH 1999). Hence the use of benefit transfer is simply the adoption of a well-established approach in other disciplines from which useful lessons may be learnt.

There are two basic methods of benefit transfer (Navrud and Bergland 2001): one method transfers data and the other transfers equations. In turn, there are three forms of data transfer:

- the use of standard data;
- the use of average values;
- the use of sparse point values.

Frequently, standard data values are derived specifically for use in benefit–cost analyses; in countries that routinely apply benefit–cost analysis to flood alleviation projects, it is routine to develop standard depth-damage curves that give flood losses for particular building types as a function of depth (e.g. Penning-Rowsell and Chatterton 1977). So, similarly, in the benefit–cost analyses of transport options is it normal practice to use standard values for the value of reduction of journey times (DTLR 2000). These values are specifically constructed for such purposes and in such a way that what are believed to be the principal factors resulting in differences in values are taken into account. Alternatively, in the absence of any tested hypotheses as to the factors that will create differences in values, the average value of some sample of values may be taken.

The third case occurs when there are no standard values but there are a limited number of different values for apparently similar changes in somewhat different contexts, or somewhat different changes in somewhat similar contexts. In this case, it is necessary for the analyst to reach a reasoned judgement as to which value in which context is likely to be closest to that which would pertain to the change that s/he is trying to evaluate. In the prefeasibility stage of a benefit–cost analysis, it is often necessary to use this approach. Only if it seems likely that the project is justified can a case be made for undertaking the survey work necessary to derive the specific values appropriate in the context of the specific project.

Given a sufficiently large sample of data, it is possible to move from such point estimates to a regression approach. This seeks to derive a general equation that explains differences in values by differences in the nature of the change and its context and so by the use of the appropriate local values for the explanatory variables, a specific value for the particular case in question can be derived. Once again, such general equations are routinely used in hydrological analyses where, for example, local stream flow gauging records are not available (IOH 1999).

In economics, such meta-analyses have been used to derive economic values for specific changes (e.g. Smith *et al.* 2000): by comparing across individual analyses, it should be possible to explain some real differences in the values derived in each analysis. Meta-analyses, in principle, offer a way to establish convergent and divergent validity: different techniques should yield the same value for the same change in the same good but each technique should give different values when either the change or the good are different. When there is not such a pattern of similarities and differences (Campbell and Fiske 1959), then some or all of the results must be suspect.

Thus, that meta-analysis potentially offers a means of testing convergent and divergent validity is probably more important than the chance of transferring values. The ideal test of techniques is then Campbell and Fiske's (1959) 'multitrait-multimethod' analysis where different measurement techniques are applied in a consistent way to different goods, and retests are also included. Unfortunately, the details of the measurement techniques adopted typically vary from good to good. In turn, apparently real differences in values may simply be the result of methodological differences (Brouwer *et al.* 1997) rather than real differences.

A second danger is that of falling into the ecological fallacy (Langbein and Lichtman 1978): of assuming that the relationships found between the means for different samples also hold within those samples, and to draw such a causal inference. The classic example of the ecological fallacy is to compare the cancer rates for the US states with their mean altitudes; it is found that the higher the altitude, the lower the cancer rate. This is the result of mis-specifying the equation because other known and suspected causes of cancer were omitted from the equation. Since meta-analysis works with sample means, there is an obvious risk of falling into ecological fallacy.

13

Project Appraisal

Project appraisal techniques are means of informing decisions; they can be applied to all decisions and not simply those where the options are for capital works. Project appraisal techniques are then equally applicable to what are conventionally called maintenance works, and to institutional or other strategies in addition to those that involve physical works on or in the ground. In each case, the different options will change the risk of some outcomes whether the outcome is a flood, drought restrictions, unacceptable taste to tapwater, the collapse of a sewer, or the failure to deliver a flood warning.

13.1 The Nature of the Appraisal Process

Earlier (Section 2.1), decisions were defined as being choices where:

$$\text{Choice} = \text{Conflict} + \text{Uncertainty}$$

Thus, a decision is a process through which we try to resolve the different conflicts between the available options so as to attain some degree of confidence that one option should be preferred to the others. Decision making is, or should be, a learning process; at the end of the process we should have a better understanding of the nature of the choice we must make than we had at the beginning. As a learning process, it is an iterative process as indeed is the process of design of which decision making is a part. It is also necessarily a process during which change will occur, since to learn is to change. Figure 13.1 is a generic model of such a decision process, starting with the definition of the problem that brings us to the decision in the first place, and of the objectives we bring to that choice. It differs in a number of ways to the usual diagrams of project appraisal techniques by being explicitly a model that assumes the entire purpose of appraisal is to learn which option should be adopted.

Unfortunately, the possible options do not simply sit there but have to be invented or discovered. The improved understanding as to the nature of the choice generated by the project appraisal may enable a better option to be created

---

Handbook of Water Economics: Principles and Practice. C. Green
© 2003 John Wiley & Sons, Ltd ISBN: 0-471-98571-6

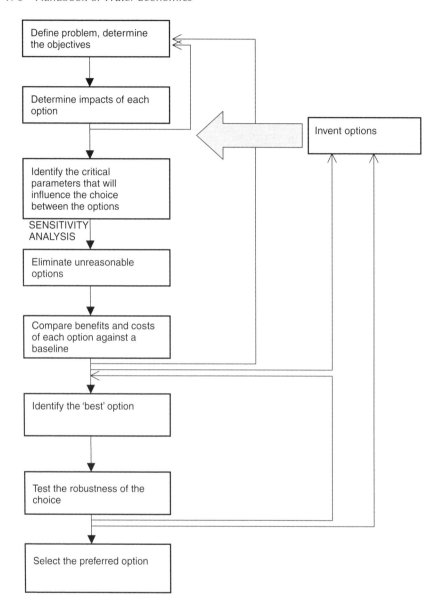

Figure 13.1   Project appraisal flow chart

or discovered. Thus, although the aim is to narrow down the option space to a single option, it is desirable to start by widening the option space, and the decision process may involve an iterative process of widening and narrowing the option space.

Nor do the options exist in fully detailed form, a rather important part of the design process being to determine what data to collect (e.g. hydrological data, soil samples, rapid rural appraisals) in order to develop the design options through an iterative process. In turn, the appraisal process must match the design process, beginning with strategic assessments when catchment plans are being developed. The techniques adopted at this level must necessarily be workable with sparse and coarse data. At the project level, prefeasibility or reconnaissance studies for individual projects must also be practical using existing data. In both cases, project appraisals should identify what data is necessary in order to refine the analysis; too often, those responsible for designing the strategy or project either collect every conceivable item of data in the hope that some of it will be relevant, or select only some data for collection and not necessarily that which is most important to the decision. Generally, the analyst will find themselves in one of two situations: too much data but not enough information, or too little data and too little information.

Reconnaissance level studies are more difficult to undertake than detailed benefit–cost analyses because they rely quite heavily upon experience gained from assessing similar schemes. They rely heavily upon experiential knowledge of what are acceptable simplifications and as to the key factors which determine the magnitude of the benefits and costs. The problems of undertaking broad scale appraisals of policies and programmes are similar.

In turn, it is important to undertake a sensitivity analysis early in the appraisal cycle. We need to know early on what are the critical parameters that will affect the choice of the 'best' option; it is on refining our estimates of the values of these parameters upon which attention should be focused during the remainder of the appraisal process. In turn, if one parameter does not differentiate between the options, there is no point in collecting data on that parameter. If we only discover these at the end of the analysis, it is far too late to do anything about them. With experience, the analyst will generally have learnt which are these parameters for particular types of project, but as a general rule it will be those which affect impacts that occur early in the project life; those that have the highest probability of occurrence; and those that affect the largest number of people or involve very large impacts on a few people.

Ideally, there will be too many options to examine in detail, given the costs likely to be incurred in collecting more data about each option. If one or more options is clearly inferior to another option against all of the objectives we bring to the decision then the inferior options can be rejected at this point. We may decide in the next iteration that we wish to reconsider our objectives, the process of comparing real options enabling us to learn more about our objectives, or what we really consider the problem to be. This may in turn mean that one or more of the options that we have just excluded now turns out to have virtues that were previously obscure.

Appraisal is by its nature comparative and relative, all the impacts being measured against some baseline. The choice of the baseline is consequently important.

The process of identifying the 'best' option can be more or less mechanical because the critical step is the next one: testing how confident we can be, given all the necessary uncertainties, that one option should be preferred to all others. This stage of testing the robustness of our choice is the core of the decision and takes place at the point in the appraisal process usually given over to sensitivity analysis. However, sensitivity analysis and robustness analysis are fundamentally different, performing different functions. Sensitivity analysis tells us which are the critical parameters whose values we should try to refine and so deals with uncertainty about the world; robustness analysis explores whether we should be uncertain as to which option to adopt.

13.2 Making 'Better' Choices?

The purpose of project appraisal techniques is then to help make better choices through learning about the nature of the choice that must be made. Two essential requirements of a project appraisal technique are that it addresses the conflicts that make the choice necessary in the first place, and that it does enable us to learn about the nature of the choice that must be made. In addition, the involvement of the public and other stakeholders in decision making means that project appraisal techniques are increasingly required to support the communication between the different interested parties, to share common understanding on the one hand and to highlight differences on the other. Hence, the four most important criteria for a project appraisal technique out of those given in Section 9.4 are:

- It aids understanding.
- It is comprehensive, encompassing all of the conflicts that make the choice necessary.
- It simplifies the elements of the choice to a level that is comprehensible as we cannot understand that we which cannot comprehend.
- It is feasible.

In addition, we want rigour but not to the point where it inhibits understanding and comprehension. Unfortunately, neither of the two available project appraisal techniques is superior to the other against all of these criteria (Table 13.1).

Table 13.1   *Criteria for project appraisal techniques*

Criterion	Benefit–cost analysis	Multi-criteria analysis
Elucidation	●	●●●
Comprehensive	●	●●
Simplification	●●●	●
Feasibility	●●	●●●
Rigour	●●●	●

● Poor; ●● moderate; ●●● good.

Benefit–cost analysis provides the greater understanding to the economist, but unfortunately this understanding is not usually shared by any noneconomist. There are ways of improving the degree to which a benefit–cost analysis can communicate with the nonspecialist, and, for that matter, make it easier for the analyst to both identify the crucial points and check for errors when the analysis is being prepared (Section 13.4.7.1). Multi-criteria analysis potentially performs much better against this criterion, provided that some rigour is sacrificed for the sake of transparency.

Benefit–cost analysis considers a single objective, economic efficiency, and hence is of limited value when the primary reason why a choice is necessary is because of conflicts between objectives, or because we cannot agree as to the relative importance that should be given to each objective. In addition, whilst some economists are optimistic as to the extent to which economic analysis can be extended to include all unpriced resources, it was argued earlier (Section 2.1.1.6) that this is a reckless claim when we do not know what it is people value and why they value it. Therefore, it is weak in terms of the nature of the conflict involved in the choice, not being comprehensive. Multi-criteria analysis is ideally suited to choices involving a conflict of objectives and some writers argue that it can also be used to promote a consensus between stakeholders (von Winterfeldt and Edwards 1986). Unfortunately, although it was argued previously that resource scarcity is typically an external constraint upon societal choices, it is none the less a real constraint. Even if we decide to make choices on the basis of moral or religious principles, we will still be limited in what decisions we can actually make by the scarcity of resources. One limitation of multi-criteria analysis, as we shall see later, is the difficulty in incorporating resource constraints in a meaningful way. Whilst the definitions of value and cost in a conventional economic analysis, and the equation of the two, elegantly resolves the problem of relating the two, multi-criteria analysis provides a way of valuing the achievement on noneconomic efficiency objectives but only at the penalty of breaking the linkage between value and cost.

Benefit–cost analysis certainly simplifies the choice, to a benefit–cost ratio or net present value, but in doing so, it oversimplifies the problem beyond the level necessary. Simplification necessarily involves imposing a structure and the loss of some of the detail and richness of the problem. If then we can cope with seven factors plus or minus two (Miller 1956), there is no need to simplify the problem beyond this point. Conversely, multi-criteria analysis starts with so much detail so that one cannot see the wood for the trees. It is quite common then to do some simple arithmetic which yields a single number in the same way as benefit–cost analysis. The same criticism then applies: simplification beyond the level necessary for us to be able to comprehend throws away information by imposing a structure. In addition, the procedures for obtaining a single number from multi-criteria analysis lack rigour.

Both techniques are feasible for most scales of decision but for decisions involving small amounts of money, MCA is generally cheaper and quicker to do.

Too much should not be made of the former virtue. Although engineers typically complain about the cost of undertaking project appraisals, the critical question is: how much is it worth spending to reduce the risk of wasting several million or hundreds of millions of public money? The probability of making such an error need only be relatively small to justify spending a significant amount of money, although one which is almost invariably considerably less than the amount spent on design.

Benefit–cost analysis is based upon a rigorous framework of analysis whereas it is, for example, difficult to apply a consistent approach to discounting in multi-criteria analysis. Almost paradoxically, the lack of rigour of multi-criteria analysis is a strength as a learning tool; it is easy to experiment to see how the choice would be changed if other values are used. But, the lack of rigour means that it is difficult to maintain consistency in treatment both between decisions and between options and criteria.

13.3 Benefit–Cost Analysis and Multi-Criteria Analysis

Benefit–cost analysis is now in widespread use for decisions involving water and the environment both by national government (e.g. US EPA (United States Environmental Protection Agency) 2000) and international agencies (e.g. Asian Development Bank 1997; Belli *et al.* 1997). Specialised methodologies have also been developed for such purposes as the evaluation of benefits of river water quality improvements (WRc/OXERA/FHRC 1996) or of flood alleviation schemes (DEFRA 1999). In general, such methodologies are based upon the use of standard data which has been derived in a variety of ways; this procedure is now often termed 'benefit transfer' (Section 12.2.4). In other instances, it is necessary to derive specific estimates of some of the streams of benefits and costs for particular options and sites under consideration using the techniques described in Section 12.2. Transfer payments, subsidies and other distortions also need to be removed (Squire and van der Tak 1975).

Consequently, it is almost invariably necessary to adjust market prices to obtain economic values and costs (Belli *et al.* 1997), to calculate the appropriate shadow prices. In the past, developing countries maintained artificial exchange rates and trade barriers, both of which mean that adjustments are necessary in carrying out a benefit–cost analysis. Finally, shadow wage rates are often used in developing countries where market wage rates often overestimate the opportunity cost of unskilled labour and, in the public sector, may underestimate the opportunity cost of skilled labour (Squire and van der Tak 1975). A convenient test of the likely quality of a benefit–cost analysis is whether unadjusted market prices have been used; if so, it is probable that the analysis is deficient and closer examination will reveal other problems.

Multi-criteria analysis covers a variety of methods that involve the use of what are commonly referred to as 'scoring and weighting', although the different methods available vary considerably in how this is undertaken. The technique has multiple roots: the concept of a matrix for assessing impacts has been adopted in a whole range of fields including the goal achievement matrix in planning (Hill 1966), and environmental impact assessment (Leopold *et al.* 1971). Again, under the name of multi-attribute decision making, it was incorporated into the market research literature relatively early (Green and Wind 1973) and into policy appraisal (von Winterfeldt and Edwards 1986). The method has not been used (e.g. Environment Agency 1999; Goeller *et al.* 1977) to anything like the same extent in water management as has benefit–cost analysis. But, importantly, the World Commission on Dams (2000) argued that multi-criteria analysis should be adopted; because of the nature of the panel and of the sponsors, the implications of the Commission's report extend beyond projects involving dams.

The essence of the procedure is to define a set of criteria against which the performance of the different alternative options can be tested. These criteria are in turn either explicitly derived from some set of objectives or imply those objectives, though it can often be easier to define criteria than objectives. The different criteria are then given weights in terms of the relative importance of satisfying each criterion. The different options are in turn scored in terms of their performance against each criterion.

Important decisions have to be taken in deciding how the score against each criterion should vary as the performance against that criterion; is, for example, a capital cost of 1 million euros twice as good as one of 500 000 million euros? The function of the score against the performance may have one of a multiplicity of functions, the most important being a lexicographic function, where the criterion is failed if the option's performance does not pass a particular threshold (Timmermans 1984).

13.4 Generic Problems of Benefit–Cost Analysis and Multi-Criteria Analysis

The two approaches differ substantially in detail but are faced with the same problems. First, each must confront the problem of comparing the unlikely consequences of each option across the three dimensions of choice: who, what and when (Chapter 5). Either explicitly or implicitly, widely different effects of different options must be brought together so that a choice can be made between the different options; we can change the way we do this, but we have to do it. The advantage of having an explicit procedure to cover each dimension of choice is consistency both within and between decisions. In principle, that there is an explicit procedure increases the transparency of the analysis.

13.4.1 Defining spatial and temporal boundaries

All analyses must have boundaries in time and space; how far into the future the analysis of the consequences of each option should be extended. The explicit use of discounting can be argued to enforce a form of myopia onto benefit–cost analysis but uncertainty necessarily increases rapidly as the future is extended. To the geomorphologist, 500 years may be a moment in time but no economist should hazard a guess as to the nature of the economy in 500 years' time. Any analysis should cover the engineering life of the longest lasting option but it is likely to be more important to examine the distribution of benefits and costs over time (Section 5.3).

The question of the boundary of the analysis also occurs for the geographical scope of the project. If the world was homeostatic then at some point many of the effects of a project would be offset by countervailing effects caused by the initial change. Thus, if one factory is closed by a shortage of water, some other factory would increase production so as to make up the lost production. Since economics developed at the time when the nation state seemed self-evident, it seemed logical to define the boundaries of the analysis by the national boundaries and hence the focus is on national economic efficiency. So, if the factory that is closed is in Spain and the factory that makes up the production is in Portugal, a real economic loss to Spain occurs. The naturalness of national boundaries is becoming less self-evident when on the one hand there is a movement towards greater cooperation between countries and on the other, towards a greater degree of devolution down from the nation state. Thus, if the factory that is shut is in Catalunya and the factory that makes up the loss is in Valencia, it could be argued that the analysis should be based on the boundaries of Catalunya and not Spain, or in the case of Spain and Portugal, on the boundaries of the European Union. If the analysis instead were to involve the benefits of wastewater treatment for an area of Germany on the Rhine, bordering the Netherlands, then using the national boundary would probably conclude that there were few benefits since the effects of the pollution were experienced in the Netherlands. That projects may then be partly or wholly funded by multinational bodies, such as the European Union, or through overseas aid simply makes the picture more cloudy. Furthermore, since the purpose is to implement an integrated catchment management approach, the boundaries of the catchment imply yet another set of boundaries. There is no self-evident answer to this question; it is one to worry about in each individual analysis.

13.4.2 Defining the baseline for measurement

All comparison is relative and all measurement made from some baseline. The choice of the baseline then matters, not least because it affects the level of measurement achieved and consequently the mathematical operations that can be performed on the resulting measurements (e.g. Galtung 1967). Only if the zero point given by the baseline is absolute, that it is entirely impossible for there to be any other, are multiplication and division valid operations (Galtung 1967). The zero in the Kelvin scale of temperature is such an absolute zero that it is meaningful to say that 200 K is twice as hot as 100 K. On the other hand, the zeros on the Centigrade and Fahrenheit scales are arbitrary. There is a debate as to whether in psychological or social measurement, as opposed to the physical sciences, it is possible to achieve as high a level of measurement as the ratio scale (Stevens 1975; Poulton 1989). In economic analysis, it is intended that money provides a more demanding scale of measurement than is achieved by the ratio scale; an absolute scale where not only is the zero point absolute but so too is the unit of measurement.

What points are adopted as baselines from which to make the comparison between the options then depends on what level of measurement can be achieved but that choice also creates some specific problems.

- absolute zero;
- arbitrary zero;
- current situation;
- worst-present case for each criterion/objective.

In benefit–cost analysis, the present situation is taken as the baseline. This baseline option is usually the 'do nothing' option, make no changes to the present situation at all. Thus, the present situation is not formally compared to the alternatives but all the alternatives are compared to the present situation. However, where the question is whether to renovate, enhance or repair some existing system, the appropriate baseline option is the 'walk away' option: abandon all maintenance and repairs to the present system other than those to make it safe before abandoning it. Therefore, one of the options to be considered is maintaining and repairing the current system.

That all of the changes that would result from adopting each of the 'do something' options are measured against the 'do nothing' baseline means that what is being measured is the changes, some of which are desirable and some are undesirable. It is then important to define what is a benefit and what is a cost because, unfortunately, their treatment makes a difference to the benefit–cost ratio (Table 13.2). For example, the loss of a valued view as the result of building a

Table 13.2 *Defining benefits and costs*

Present values	Benefits		Costs	
	Negative benefits	Gains	Negative costs	Losses
Capital			1000	1000
O&M			200	200
Loss of view	−100			100
Water supply benefits	3000	3000		
Sale of soil		80	−80	
Totals	2900	3080	1120	1300
NPV	1780	1780		
Benefit–cost ratio	2.59	2.37		

water tower could be regarded as a cost of the water tower or treated as a negative benefit and subtracted from the benefits. Similarly, if the soil excavated in order to construct a storage reservoir can be sold, then the income from the sales can be treated as a benefit of the project or as a negative cost, and subtracted from the estimate of project costs. Treating all desirable changes, such as the sale of soil, as benefits and all undesirable changes as costs results in the least distortion in the benefit–cost ratio – otherwise, for example, if enough soil could be sold then the costs net of negative costs could fall to zero.

Exactly the same problem occurs in multi-criteria analysis if the current situation is taken as the baseline. However, it may be desirable to include the current situation explicitly rather than to include it implicitly as the baseline. Since using the worst case on each criterion as the baseline means that potentially that baseline changes every time another option is added, the choice lies between an arbitrary zero and an absolute zero. In practice, an arbitrary zero point is usually used so that the scoring scale is an interval scale at best but probably only achieves an ordinal scale of measurement.

13.4.3 Identifying the options

Since the option identified as the best option can be no better than the best of those considered, defining a good set of options is critical to the exercise (Howe 1971). In the end, better decisions depend upon having better options. However, the definition of these options is usually a matter for engineers and others rather than for economists. The economist can help by ensuring that the problem or aims are defined in a way that does not artificially narrow the solution space: the nature of the question classically determining the answer that will be found (Rittel and Weber 1974).

Thus, the aim of a water supply system could be defined in two alternative ways:

- 'To meet predicted per capita water consumption requirements in 2050'; or
- 'To ensure that the probability of water restrictions being applied does not exceed 0.05 per annum in 2050'.

The former definition implies first determining predicted water demand in 2050, then defining some design standard drought year, and finally designing some water resource strategy that will meet the predicted water demand, given those drought conditions. The second definition would allow demand management options to be considered as well as resource reinforcement. So, the goal for the Melbourne water resource plan has been set as a 1 in 20 chance of water restrictions, lasting not more than 12 months and requiring a level three response within the Drought Response Plan (Government of Victoria 2001).

Feasible options vary between different types of project as well as from location to location. It is consequently not possible to define any rule that will ensure that the best of all possible options will always be included amongst those considered. However, it is possible to set out some guidelines to avoid options being prematurely discarded or not considered in the first place (Section 9.3): some if not all of these options should normally be expected to be amongst the options considered. More generally, widening involvement in the decision process should result in widening the option space and, in turn, options proposed by those involved in the decision process should obviously be considered.

Some of the past criticism of 'big bang' engineering approaches may be unfair in that in practical terms engineering analysis was limited in capacity to fairly simple approaches. Faced with a flooding problem from a combined sewer, one approach is to consider a number of different alignments and sizes for a new trunk sewer. Alternatively, it is possible to think in terms of some source control here, some underground storage there, and a flow constrictor somewhere else. Given a large enough network, the possible number of combinations of source control, storage and flow constrictors will rapidly approach the infinite. The same is true of using many small tanks or reservoirs to provide irrigation as compared to one large one.

Many of these combinations will perform poorly and at a high cost. Armed with only a slide rule and book of log tables, the chance of the engineer in the past hitting on a combination that was anywhere near optimal would be low; indeed, so too was the likelihood that they would even be able to assess whether the system would operate at all. Computers help but an infinite number of possible solutions to test still requires infinite computing time. To find a good solution from this universe of possible solutions, one promising approach being tried is the use of genetic algorithms to identify feasible solutions (Gill *et al.* 2001).

13.4.4 Identifying the consequences of the different options

At the initial stage, the net should be drawn too widely rather than too narrowly and the problems of measurement and evaluation ignored for the moment. It is necessary to identify the significant differences in the consequences of each option relative to the baseline option and between each of the options. At this stage, all the significant consequences should be identified. The only differences that may be omitted are those which are insignificant; however, at this stage, the only guide to the 'significance' of each will be experience, which can be a misleading guide.

There are some consequences which can be excluded;

- those which would occur irrespective of which option is selected; unfortunately, the greater the variety of options considered, the greater the variety of consequences which are likely to have to be considered; and
- those consequences which have an equal and opposite reaction. For example, if drivers along an existing road visit one petrol station and a new road will direct that traffic, and those visits, to a different existing petrol station. In this case,

the loss of business to the petrol station will be counterbalanced by the gain to the other. An equal and opposite reaction only takes place if the consumers gain exactly the same benefits at exactly the same costs; therefore, that a transfer of consumption occurs as a result of one option does not necessarily mean that no economic gain or loss take place. The same principle applies to the transfer of production; there is no economic loss unless the costs of production and supply increase or the value to the consumer falls, unless production is transferred abroad, it being convention to define the boundaries of the analysis as national boundaries.

Not all of these consequences will be certain and it is often also necessary to estimate the probabilities of each occurring. For example, in assessing the benefits of rehabilitating systems or undertaking preventative maintenance, the benefits of such works are the reduction in the probability of system failure and the costs of such a failure (Section 16.1.3). Similarly, the benefits of flood alleviation works arise as the change in the expected value of flood losses, the difference in the probability of a flood times the losses resulting from such a flood (Chapter 18).

The quantification of the different streams of consequences from each of the options is commonly not an economic problem but rather one which can be resolved as part of a concurrent environmental assessment (e.g. European Commission 2001; World Bank 1991), or as part of the engineering studies associated with the project development. Thus, for an irrigation project, the increase in yield, shift to higher valued crops or the reductions in losses as a result of the project are questions which the analyst will either rely on the predictions of agricultural engineers or can only resolve with the help of agricultural engineers. Similarly, the analyst will depend upon hydrologists and water engineers for estimates of the volumes of water which the irrigation system will yield.

The analyst will consequently need to have enough technical understanding of the other disciplines involved in the project to both ask sensible questions and to understand what the answers mean; and, more especially, to interpret the critical assumptions that are being made in making those predictions. What the economist needs to know and what the specialist is used to providing are often different, so that establishing a common dialogue can take some time.

The value of such consequences will not necessarily be a linear function of the magnitude of the effects and it is also necessary to identify when a consequence will occur. Moreover, some consequences will themselves take time to occur. For example, if a new irrigation scheme is constructed, then it will take a number of years for farmers to change their cropping patterns in response to the increased availability of water. The accurate assessment of the benefits from a scheme is often critically dependent upon the assumptions made about the rate of take-up of the benefits (Morris and Hess 1986; Morris *et al.* 1984).

In multi-criteria analysis, double-counting is almost inevitable but this is not a problem to which excessive attention should be given in the establishment of the criteria. Instead, it is more important to cover the domain of interest. In turn, that the consequences included are those that affect one or more criteria means that the identification of the consequences and the identification of the criteria are two sides of the same coin.

Double-counting is, however, a problem to be avoided in benefit–cost analyses; in particular, care needs to be taken to avoid including the same impact as a flow change and a stock change, given that the value of a stock is the present value of the flows it generates. Thus, for example, the value of agricultural land is given by the profits it produces. In general, that which is included is whichever it is easiest to calculate; for example, it is generally easier to calculate the change in the value of a dwelling than the change in the stream of utility provided by that dwelling.

In addition, benefit–cost analysis is effectively limited to the assessment of only those consequences that affect economic efficiency. For example, a change in the number of people employed is generally not included in a benefit–cost analysis since in the absence of the project those jobs would be maintained elsewhere. This then limits the analysis of projects that are specifically intended to provide employment or to result in socio-economic regeneration or development of an area to cost-effectiveness analysis: it is possible to determine which is the cheapest way of achieving such goals, and how this compares to other similar projects, but not whether the project is worthwhile.

13.4.5 Changes over time

All benefit–cost analyses are undertaken using real prices; that is, the rate of over-all inflation in the economy is ignored. Generally, analyses are also undertaken using constant relative prices, demand and supply. However, in theory, changes in the relative prices, as well as the quantities, of the different forms of resources and consumption which make up the different streams of benefits and costs should be considered (Section 5.3.1.2). The use of a discount rate itself assumes some growth in overall wealth so that it is only differences relative to base assumption incorporated in the discount rate with which we need to be concerned.

Where changes over time are incorporated into the analysis, it is most commonly in the form of predictions of growth in future demand; for example, for increases in water or energy demand over time. Because of the long lead time between initiating a project and the project coming on-stream, often in the case of water projects 10–15 years, it is usually necessary to make such predictions. Moreover, the returns to scale for water projects also mean that building to meet anticipated expansion in demand can result in a more efficient future than a succession of small-scale projects to chase current demand. However, predictions of future demand are difficult and often markedly erroneous in retrospect, and have often been based upon the extrapolation of past trends, or on descriptive analyses, rather than upon causal models (Section 14.5). Thus, for example, demand may be predicted to grow without limit or satiation. Similarly, whilst demand is usually considered to be exogenous to supply, there may instead be feedback loops between supply and demand: it is found that new roads generate new traffic (SACTRA 1994).

Faced with a decision where it is appropriate to include predictions of future growth in demand, then response by the analyst should include the comparison of two alternative sets of options:

- Demand management: comparing an option which has the effect of reducing that projected growth in demand to zero by, for example, making more efficient use of the resource in question. For instance, if the project is a new reservoir to meet a projected demand for irrigation water, then an option to be considered might be promoting a shift to more efficient forms of irrigation.
- Alternative timings for the construction of works to satisfy the projected demand. Given the necessary uncertainty about levels of demand in the future, constructing a series of small-scale plant over time allows readjustment of capacity over time to actual levels of demand.

Incorporating changes in relative real prices over time is even more problematic. Two clear rules are that if a growth factor is applied to one stream of benefits or costs, then growth factors should be applied to all of the streams of benefits and costs. Secondly, since we are concerned with relative changes in real values and prices, an assumption about the general trend being embodied in the discount rate, of the different streams of benefits and costs, some streams will have negative growth rates. Consequently, the greater the number of streams of benefits and costs included in the analysis, the more complex the problem of assessing the likely trends in relative real prices and values.

The relative real prices and values of different forms of resource and consumption may change over time for a number of reasons:

- Differences in the income elasticity of demand for different goods; although the discount rate implies an overall growth in real income, the income elasticities of demand for different goods are different. Consequently, there should be a shift in demand towards goods for which demand is income elastic. There is normally an assumption that demand for environmental goods is income elastic.
- Increased scarcity of supply, notably for environmental goods which are non-renewable stock goods, should bid up willingness to pay for access to the remaining stock of such goods.
- Historically, technological improvements have led to real reductions in the prices of many manufactured goods, notably electrical goods.
- Overall, there has tended to be a shift towards capital investment in fixed assets, be these houses or factories. Thus, Kosmin (1988) argued that the real value of houses in the UK has increased by some 2% per annum over the post-war period. In part at least this is likely to be due to the increased investment in the performance of such properties in the form of fitted kitchens, central heating and other performance enhancements.

- For imported and exported goods, long-term changes in the exchange rate, reflecting a country's economic performance relative to the rest of the world, will have a significant effect. For example, in the evaluation of the Soar Valley land drainage scheme (Rayner *et al.* 1984), a major anticipated benefit was the shift from dairy farming to wheat cultivation where wheat production was evaluated against the price of Canadian Red Wheat in US dollars as the wheat produced would substitute for imports. In the 18 years since the scheme was evaluated, the pound to US dollar exchange rate has fallen significantly so increasing the scheme's economic efficiency. Again, such shifts are to an extent incorporated in the 'true' discount rate which should be used since an economy with a low growth rate in global terms, and hence a falling exchange rate, should imply a low discount rate.
- People's preferences may simply change over time in ways unrelated to changes in real income. For example, in the nineteenth century, a preference for neo-classical architecture was replaced by one for gothic revival; thus, the relative values of renaissance and medieval buildings will have changed at that time.
- Finally, new technologies will also change the values attached to existing products; thus, the development of cassette tape recorders and CDs radically reduced the value of, and demand for, record players.

Overall, it is appropriate to be reluctant to apply growth factors in the basic analysis; it is more likely to be appropriate to test the effects of the consequences in terms of choices between the options if growth factors are applied to the different streams of benefits and costs. Where a growth factor is applied to one stream of benefits or costs, growth factors should be applied to all. Since an allowance for growth is built into the discount rate, it follows that some of these growth factors must be negative.

The same general principles also apply to multi-criteria analysis but such changes are often only included in a subjective way with the consequent risk of inconsistency.

13.4.6 Evaluating the significant consequences

In a benefit–cost analysis, the consequences can then be evaluated by the methods described in Section 12.2 in each case specifying the year in which they occur and, where necessary, by their probability of occurrence or rate of take-up. A spreadsheet is the logical procedure to adopt for setting out these streams of benefits and costs over time; one column can then be allocated to each stream of benefits and costs. A second advantage of such a procedure is that it makes documentation of the analyses easier and retrieval of the analysis easier; most analyses generate vast quantities of material as the analysis is progressively refined. It is also almost inevitable that at some date some years after an analysis has been undertaken a reanalysis will be required which either embodies new information or is based upon a new option which has been identified, or is simply a post-project appraisal. If the analyses are not adequately documented and archived then the result is a nightmare.

There are at least two conventions as to how the years of the project life are to be defined. Brent (1990) suggests defining the base date for the analysis, the reference point for calculating the present values of the different streams of benefits and costs, as being the last day of year zero. The benefits and costs then start accruing through year 1 onwards; in the absence of more detailed knowledge as to the distribution of these costs occurring at the end of that year; the end of the year being taken for all subsequent benefits and costs. In the UK, common practice instead (DEFRA 1999) is to take the base date of analysis as mid-year 0 and all of the benefits and costs as accruing in mid-year, starting in mid-year 0. The convention which has been adopted locally should be followed.

In multi-criteria analysis, the distribution of the consequences is not usually formally considered; instead, scores are assigned to consequences according to the equivalent of their present values. Importance weights have also to be given to the different criteria and then these are standardised in some way, commonly by the proportion of each weight to the sum of the weights across all of the criteria.

13.4.7 Identifying the 'best option'

13.4.7.1 Benefit–cost analysis

The two normal tests for selecting the best option are the benefit–cost ratio, the present value of the benefits divided by the present value of the costs, and net present value, the present value of the benefits minus the present value of the costs. Both rules are forms of the Hicks–Kaldor compensation principle, or potential Pareto improvement. A third test which is sometimes applied is the internal rate of return (IRR); this establishes the maximum discount rate at which the present value of the benefits exactly equals the present value of the costs. This is sometimes also termed the 'switching value'.

The IRR has often been used but is both complex to calculate and a rather unsatisfactory test. It is usually calculated by iterative trial and error but Gittinger (1982) suggests a method to calculate it with the least effort. Unfortunately, there need not be a single IRR at which the present value of the benefits exactly equals the present value of the costs; indeed, the number of solutions is related to the number of times the sign changes of the annual net benefit (Brent 1990).

The three different rules do not necessarily give the same ranking for projects. The IRR rule should not generally be used, the decision lying between selecting the option which has the maximum benefit–cost ratio and that which has the greatest net present value.

When the projects are mutually exclusive in terms of benefits, then the net present value should be used to select the project to be undertaken. Where there is a budget constraint in the first year, depending upon the format used, year 0 or year 1 in the analysis, then the project with the highest benefit–cost ratio should be used. Indeed, when there are many different projects competing for the rationed capital, selecting those projects whose total costs sum to the capital constraint and which have the highest benefit–cost ratios will ensure that the programme of projects as a whole has the highest possible net present value (Brent 1990). If there are expenditure constraints for all years then operational research techniques are required to select the optimum programme of projects (Baumol 1972).

Since economic efficiency is not the only objective which the decision makers may want to consider, the choice of the option does not rest on the benefit–cost ratio alone but on the performance of the options against other objectives. Equally, almost all benefit–cost analyses are incomplete; some benefits and costs will have been omitted as being insignificant; more importantly, some benefits and costs will have been left as 'intangibles' because it is either not possible or too difficult to evaluate them. That they are left as intangibles does not mean that they should not be considered in taking the decision. How important they are depends upon whether the intangible impacts are common to all of the 'do something' options or whether there are significant differences between the options as to occurrence of intangible impacts. How easy it is to take account of the intangibles depends upon the extent to which it has been possible to measure them if not to evaluate them. For example, it is possible to make some predictions in quantitative terms about the health benefits of providing piped water and sewerage services (Esrey *et al.* 1998), and of reducing the risk from flooding (Green and Penning-Rowsell 1986).

Diagnostic analyses should also be undertaken both to check for possible errors and to identify the main contributors to the benefits and costs. For example, Figure 13.2 shows the incremental present value of flood alleviation benefits for different design standards of protection according to the land use classes

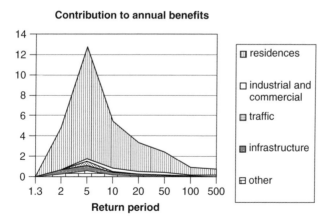

Figure 13.2   *Strategic urban drainage plan for Buenos Aires: components of flood alleviation benefits*

affected by flooding. It shows quite clearly that reducing the risks of flooding to dwellings produces most of the benefits and also the incremental benefits of increasing the design standard of protection is markedly peaked for the increase from a two-year design standard to a five-year design standard of protection, and then falls away rapidly thereafter. Pie diagrams are also useful for examining the relative contributions of the different streams of costs and benefits, and plots of the different streams over time should usually also be prepared (Section 5.3.1.1).

13.4.7.2 Multi-criteria analysis

The potential Pareto improvement offers an apparently simple rule by which to identify the 'best' option in benefit–cost analysis: no such simple rule exists in multi-criteria analysis. An apparently simple rule is to simply multiply each score (s_j) by the relevant weight (w_i) and choose the option with the highest score:

$$\Sigma w_i \cdot s_j$$

However, this procedure should be avoided for a number of reasons. The most important is that it destroys the main strength of multi-criteria analysis, that it enables a number of different criteria to be considered simultaneously. If the use of benefit–cost analysis runs the risk of trivialising the choice, this is even more true of the use of a such a crude device in multi-criteria analysis.

Technically, there are a number of other reasons for avoiding this approach:

- It is unlikely that the scores achieve higher than an interval level of measurement and hence multiplication is a mathematically illegitimate operation.
- It assumes that the choice should be made on the basis of an additive utility model (Moore and Thomas 1988); one of the most important things that we should seek to discover in the analysis is whether we are adopting an additive utility model or some other form.
- It unnecessarily destroys information; given that we can cope with between five and nine factors (Section 9.4), imposing an additive utility function reduces the complexity of the choice below the necessary level. However, a potential strength of multi-criteria analysis is that it can avoid unnecessary simplification. Moreover, it can be used to enable us to learn what we prefer.

Rather than reach a conclusion as to which option should be preferred, the best use of multi-criteria analysis is to move directly to the next phase.

13.4.8 Testing the robustness of the choice

13.4.8.1 Benefit–cost analysis

It is usual to recommend that the results of a benefit–cost analysis be subject to a sensitivity analysis; the values for key streams of benefits and costs and other factors being varied and the effects upon the benefit–cost ratio and net present values of each option determined. This is not a very useful exercise since it does not usually tell the analyst any more than they already know; if the results of analysis are not sensitive to the values of a particular variable then it is not very helpful to include that variable. What it is important to determine at this point is whether the rank order of preference across the different options is robust to the various inherent uncertainties.

We know, from the earlier sensitivity analysis, to which parameters the rank order of preference across the options is most sensitive. The issue is whether the uncertainties are sufficient to lead us to choose an option other than that with the highest NPV or benefit–cost ratio as appropriate. One approach is to associate probabilities with values of the different critical parameters and to undertake a Monte Carlo analysis but this, it was argued, cannot handle systemic uncertainty (Section 2.1.2.1).

An obvious guide to the robustness of the decision is the benefit–cost ratio; this shows by how much the benefits or costs need to change before the benefit–cost ratio falls below unity. Thus a benefit–cost ratio of 2.5 shows that the present value of the costs would have to overrun by a factor of 150% before the project ceases to be worthwhile. In turn, the larger the benefit–cost ratio, then the greater can be the errors in the predictions before the outcome would be a project which is inefficient. To test the robustness of the choice to outcome uncertainty, the appropriate procedure is to hit the choice with as large a hammer as possible until it breaks. Thus, to take a variable to which it is known that the outcomes are highly sensitive and to see how extreme a value may be adopted before the benefit–cost ratio falls below one. What variable constitutes an appropriate hammer depends upon the type of project being appraised and specific tests of robustness can be developed for specific types of project; Case Study 18.1 illustrates an example of such a specific analysis.

In fact, the benefit–cost ratio should not be treated as a 'pass-failure' criterion but as an indicator of the confidence we have that the 'do something' option can be preferred to the baseline option. A benefit–cost ratio of one is then the point of maximum decision uncertainty; the decision between the 'do something' and the baseline option is marginal. Conversely, if the benefit–cost ratio is well below one, then the smaller it is, the more confident we can be that the baseline option is the best option. Where the benefit–cost ratio is well above one we can be confident that the 'do something' option is preferable to the baseline option. However, if the benefit–cost ratio is very high then we should start to expect that some fundamental error has been made in the analysis such as failing to discount the benefits and costs (Figure 13.3).

This approach works well when all the 'do something' options are sensitive to the same parameters. If the decision is simply to identify the design standard or to identify to which parts of a system priority should be given for additional works, then generally each of the 'do something' options will be sensitive to the

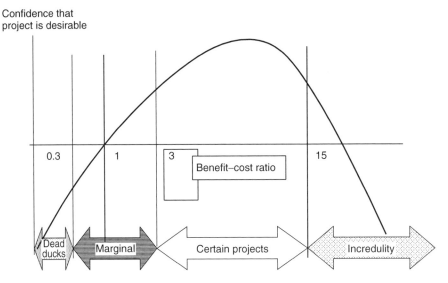

Figure 13.3   *The benefit–cost ratio and confidence that the 'do something' option is to be preferred to the baseline option*

same parameters. In other cases, the performance of each of the different options will depend upon different parameters. For example, two options to meet the objective set out for water supplies to Melbourne (Section 13.4.3) might be:

- Retrofitting all properties with water-efficient fittings and requiring all new construction to adopt rainwater harvesting for toilet flushing and external uses.
- Construct a new reservoir.

It may then be found that the performance of each of the two options depends upon different critical parameters and hence the order of preference across the two options (Table 13.3).

Such decisions are more complex than when the same parameters are critical for all the options. Without being able to attach probabilities to the likelihood that the different variables for each option will in reality differ from the baseline predictions or estimates, the decision makers may nevertheless have some preferences as to the risks which they would prefer to run and may want to modify

Table 13.3   *Critical parameters for two options for a hypothetical water supply study*

	Capital costs	O&M costs	Rate of take-up	Environmental impact
Demand management		•	•	
Reservoir	•			•

their preferences between the options to take their risk preferences into account. For instance, if an option is highly sensitive to the predicted growth in demand, then the decision makers may prefer options which instead are highly sensitive to capital cost. Whilst precautions can be taken to control variations in the out-turn cost compared to the predicted cost, it is more difficult to influence future growth in demand. What is of importance to the decision is not then the sensitivity of the outcome as such but the cause of the uncertainty and the degree to which actions can be taken to manage that uncertainty.

When, as is often the case, all of the do something options are sensitive to the same set of variables, then the order of preference between the do something options will not change significantly. What will change is the order of preference relative to the do nothing option; what the decision maker needs to know is how wrong can the analysis be and will the best option still be to do something rather than to do nothing? How robust is the decision to 'do something' to outcome uncertainty?

13.4.8.2 Multi-criteria analysis

Multi-criteria analysis leaves us with too much data to handle: a matrix of options against criteria. Table 13.4 presents analysis of the options for a hypothetical flood alleviation project; neither plotting the scores nor using an additive utility function show dramatic differences between the options. In addition, although scores have been given to each option against each criterion, and the criteria have been weighted in terms of their relative importance, neither scores nor weights should be considered to be definite. Equally, we do not know how to combine the different scores. The great strength of multi-criteria analysis is that it can be used to learn, argue or negotiate which option we actually do prefer. Moreover, it is easy to use graphical techniques to support this learning or negotiating process. A useful technique is then to rank the options against each criterion and then to plot the mean rank of each option against the standard deviation of the rank (Figure 13.4).

In the unlikely event that the rank order of the options against every criterion were to be identical, this plot would result in all of the options lying along the *x*-axis. In practice, we might hope that some options are clearly separated from the rest by lying close to the zero point whilst others lie close to the *x*-axis but off to the right. The former are then those which, on average, perform better against the criteria whilst the latter tend to perform poorly against all of the criteria. This latter group can be discarded. What this approach is doing is testing the extent to which the choice of the option depends upon the weights given to each criterion. In this case, flood storage and flood warning stand out from the remainder of the options.

The same technique can be used when seeking to prioritise different projects for inclusion of an overall programme of works. For example, the government of Hungary wanted to determine which of 151 flood basins were those upon which the limited available resources for maintenance and repairs should be

Table 13.4   Hypothetical multi-criteria analysis of flood alleviation options

5 = desirable
0 = undesirable

	CRITERION population vulnerability															
	Risk to life in consequence	Capacity to respond to flood	Capacity to recover from flood	Critical systems affected	Number of properties involved	Failure mode	Reliability	Local socio-economic impact	Flood risk changing	Positive environmental impacts	Negative environmental impacts	Flood losses	Other benefits	Capital costs	O&M costs	B/C ratio
	6 = low	6 = low	6 = low	6 = major, national systems	absolute numbers	6 = reduces the impacts of all floods	6 = probability of failure on demand is zero	6 = strongly positive	6 = increasing	6 = significant	6 = none	absolute number (present value)	6 = significant	1/absolute number (present value)	1/absolute number (present value)	1 + absolute value
	1 = high	1 = high	1 = high	1 = no		1 = rapid transition to failure and dangerous	1 = probability of failure on demand is high or uncertain	1 = critical negative	1 = decreasing	1 = none	1 = significant		1 = none			
Weights																
Importance	10	0	0	0	0	9	7	4	0	6	7	6	5	5	5	5
stdised	0.14	0.00	0.00	0.00	0.00	0.13	0.10	0.06	0.00	0.09	0.10	0.09	0.07	0.07	0.07	0.07
Baseline	2	6	6	4	1	4	2	1	1	6	5	5	1	2	6	1
Maintain and repair	3	6	6	4	1	4	1	2	1	6	4	4	2	5	5	5.8
Source control	4	6	6	4	1	4	6	2	3	6	5	6	3	5	1	1
Options Storage	3	6	6	4	1	4	5	6	5	6	3	3	6	6	5	1.5
Lower standard of protection	2	6	6	4	1	4	1	4	1	6	4	6	2	2	5	6.2
Conveyancing	5	6	6	4	1	4	3	6	2	6	1	2	5	4	3	1
Separate floods and land uses	4	6	6	4	1	4	6	5	2	6	1	3	3	5	3	2.4
Flood proofing	3	6	6	4	1	4	5	4	4	6	1	4	3	3	1	2.5
Flood warning	6	6	6	4	1	4	5	3	4	6	1	6	5	2	6	1.9
std dev	1.3	0.0	0.0	0.0	0.0	0.0	2.0	1.8	1.5	0.0	1.8	1.5	1.7	1.6	2.1	2.0

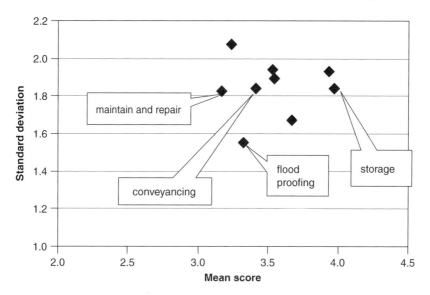

Figure 13.4 *Standard deviation of rank against mean rank against each criterion*

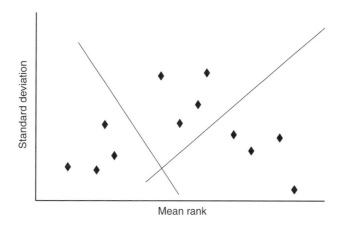

Figure 13.5 *Hungary: prioritising flood basins for maintenance and investment. Source: Green, Parker and Tunstall 2000*

concentrated (Evans *et al.* 2000). A number of different criteria were developed, including the risk to life if the embankments were to fail and whether the flood basin protected a critical national asset such as an oil field. However, they were unwilling to attach importance weights to the risk to life and the other criterion. Figure 13.5 then illustrates the pattern of results that was found when the ranking and plotting technique was applied to the 151 flood basins. One group of flood basins scores heavily on each of the criteria and clearly should therefore be treated as priorities; a second group scores badly against all of the criteria and equally clearly can be excluded from further consideration. It is then the middle group of flood basins that need further examination to determine whether the criteria on which they score highly are sufficiently important to outbalance those against which they score poorly.

The same procedure can be used when the different stakeholders each assign weights to the different criteria. In this case, the plot shows about which criteria there is relative agreement and those where there is marked disagreement.

A second plot is given if the total scores of the individual options using an additive utility function are plotted (Figure 13.6) against those using a multiplicative utility function ($\Pi w_i \cdot s_j$). In this case, flood warning and storage again stand out from the other options but the order of preference across the two options depends upon whether an additive or multiplicative utility function is adopted.

Janssen (2001) suggests another technique; setting each criteria in turn to an arbitrarily large proportion of the total weights and comparing the resulting weighted scores for the different options. All of these tests leave storage and flood warning showing up as the two options between which a final choice must be made in this case. In turn, we might then think of combining the two options and adopting this combined approach if affordable.

It is important to recognise that none of these techniques can reveal order where there is none; if Figure 13.4 simply showed a circle of points closely clustered about the middle of the x-axis and with very similar standard deviations of the ranks, then the choice of the option depends critically upon the weights given to the different criteria. In this event, it can be worthwhile to carry out a cluster

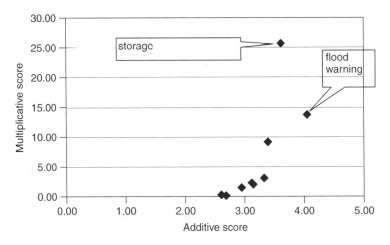

Figure 13.6   *Multi-criteria analysis: robustness analysis*

analysis on the criteria to determine whether the different options perform very similarly on several different criteria; if this is the case, then it suggests that there may be double-counting and in any case that there is some degree of redundancy amongst the criteria. A similar cluster analysis carried out on the options will show whether any of the options perform so similarly against the different criteria that it is possible to decide between those two options. Setting some of the criteria to be lexicographic – so that an option fails altogether if it does not score at least a minimum score on that criterion – is a further way of thinning down the number of options to be considered. But, sometimes the choice will clearly be a marginal choice with not much to choose between the options when all factors are considered.

14

Capturing Water for Human Use: General Issues

Beck (1996) has argued that the problem in wastewater management is to manage the entire time frequency distribution of perturbations in the quality of runoff, operating wastewater treatment plants so as to maintain the quality of the receiving waters within desired limits. Human actions change perturbations: suppressing or removing disturbances, transforming pulse events into persistent or chronic stress, or introducing new disturbances.

So, similarly, on the quantity side the problem is to bring the variations in supply and demand into alignment (Figure 14.1). Hence water resource management is about matching the variation in supply to the variation in demand where demand, especially for crops, is usually highest at the times when rainfall is least. Consequently, the greater the variation in water availability over the year and between years, the greater is the problem. Moreover, the necessity is to manage as a whole the variations in water availability rather than to treat separately some part as 'droughts', other parts as 'water resources' and the remainder as 'floods'. In arid climates, floods are the water resource and since a key quality characteristic is the reliability of supply, it is inappropriate to differentiate between water resource management and drought management, these areas often experiencing both drought and flood problems. Therefore, any water resource management plan should consider how to respond when the resources are unusually low and a critical question is: how much storage to provide in order to reduce the risk that supplies will have to be rationed (Section 14.2).

The basic choice in water resources management is between:

- enhancing the supply; or
- reducing demand by making more efficient use of the existing resources.

The appropriate strategy or combination of strategies depends upon the local circumstances, but, in developed countries in particular, the latter strategy will often be appropriate. Any enhancement strategy involves a combination of three components:

Handbook of Water Economics: Principles and Practice.   C. Green
© 2003 John Wiley & Sons, Ltd   ISBN: 0-471-98571-6

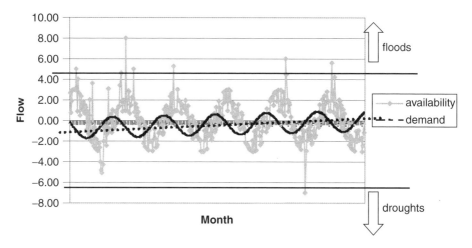

Figure 14.1   *Managing perturbations in water quantity*

- Capturing the water (as runoff or in the form of groundwater).
- Storing the water (surface or groundwater).
- Conveying it to the point of use.

In the simplest situation, the rainfall is captured on a field through infiltration, and stored for a few days as soil moisture where it is immediately available to the plants. Similarly, for urban uses, the simplest traditional approach is to collect rainwater runoff from roofs, store it in an underground cistern and raise that water with a bucket when it is needed.

In turn, there are major differences between agricultural and urban or industrial uses (Table 14.1). Crops are a consumptive use of water, the water being lost through evaporation and transpiration with 99% of crop water use being required by the crop for cooling. Moreover, plants are very heavy consumers of water, with hundreds and often thousands of tonnes of water being required to produce one tonne of a crop (Figure 14.2). Consequently, in every country, agriculture is

Table 14.1   *Significant differences between agricultural and urban water uses*

Agricultural	Urban/industrial uses
Consumer of water; most water used is necessarily lost through evapotranspiration	Most water used is available for reuse or recycling
The volume required is largely fixed through the needs of plant and climatic conditions	In large part, use is technologically determined
Very high water requirement	Relatively low water requirement

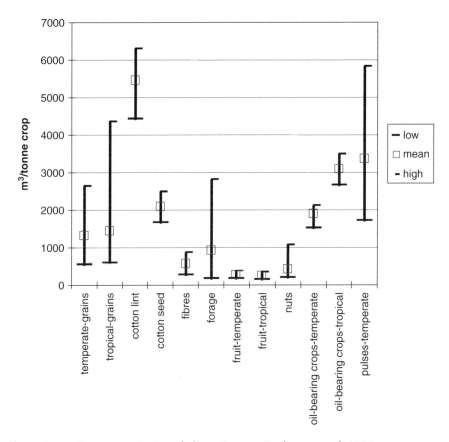

Figure 14.2 *Evapotranspiration of plants. Source: Rockstrom et al. 1999*

the largest consumer of water whether that water is directly provided by rainfall or indirectly by irrigation.

Turning to the availability of water, the first two questions then are:

- Is there enough rainfall locally?
- What is the variability of that rainfall?

For agriculture, if rainfall exceeds the crop evapotranspiration requirement then rainfed crop production is in principle possible. Thus, the ratio of precipitation to evapotranspiration for East Anglia in eastern England is 1.1 (Morris *et al.* 1997). However, a crude comparison of precipitation (P) to evapotranspiration (PET) is somewhat misleading because water can only be stored in the soil for a matter of days. If then on a monthly basis, evapotranspiration exceeds precipitation, then relying on local rainfall will not be enough. Thus, in the Taihu Basin (Figure 14.3), traditionally the grain basket of China, irrigation is

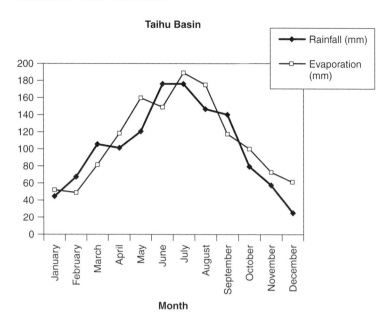

Figure 14.3 *Precipitation and evapotranspiration in the Taihu Basin, China*

necessary to raise output from one to two or three crops a year. Arid regions (P/PET ratio of between 0.03 to 0.20) are characterised by a concatenation of water management problems:

- Rainfall is concentrated into relatively short periods in the year.
- There is high variability in rainfall from year to year.
- Poor groundwater recharge occurs because the soil is seldom already saturated when rain occurs.
- Locally rainfall can be very intense (e.g. over 500 mm in one day in some areas of Spain when the average annual rainfall varies from 200 mm to 1315 mm – Estrela *et al.* 1996).
- In turn, the locally intense rainfall results in soil erosion.

If variability is high but overall average precipitation exceeds potential evapotranspiration, we can get by with local storage. If we are lucky, then storage will be available naturally either in the form of groundwater or as lakes. However, if potential evapotranspiration exceeds local precipitation, then we are forced to one of several options:

- rainwater harvesting;
- groundwater;
- importing water.

If rainfed agriculture is not possible, or additional water would increase the number of crops that can be harvested in a year, then rainwater harvesting is an option.

Cities are in practice very efficient systems for rainwater harvesting and when water is used for urban purposes, we get most of it back, significant losses occurring from transpiration and evaporation only when it is used for outdoor uses such as garden watering. So, for example, the output of water from Manchester in northern England is seven times as great as the potable water supplied to it (Green 1998a). Even in Melbourne, a much less dense and hence less impermeable city than Manchester, and one that is also located in an arid climate, the output of water from the city is over twice the amount of water supplied to it (Government of Victoria 2001). In principle, therefore, for urban purposes, there is generally sufficient rainfall on the city itself to support urban uses. The obvious problem is that the runoff water is polluted, as, in general, most uses of land by humans mean that runoff requires treatment before it can be put to use. The second problem is that water management has historically been about energy use: because water is heavy and incompressible, the use of potential energy, gravity, has been preferred to kinetic energy. Thus, the problem with using rainwater harvesting in cities has been the energy cost associated with pumping and historically cities have been supplied from higher areas, with the water being distributed by gravity.

The collection of the runoff from roofs for domestic usage has been traditional in some arid climates (Maalel *et al.* 1987) and is now being increasingly considered in developed countries, particularly for arid areas, to provide for external uses (Texas Water Development Board 1997). In urban areas, rainwater harvesting can save money twice since capturing rainfall also reduces the amount of runoff that must be disposed of through the drainage network. Requirements for new dwellings to capture rainwater from the roof are increasingly common: in Waterloo, Canada, 20% of lots in new subdivisions are required to have 5000–8000 litre cisterns to capture rainwater for garden watering (Cook 1994).

The primary resource is groundwater: assessments of global water availability (e.g. Shiklomanov 1998) suggest that the quantity of water stored as groundwater is of the order of 7 to 10 million cubic kilometres, roughly equivalent to 70 times the total annual precipitation on land. Given the quantity of water stored as groundwater, around 170 times the flow in all the world's rivers, groundwater is critical to water management. Unfortunately, knowledge of groundwater resources, and of the relationships between precipitation, runoff, groundwater resources and surface waters is often limited (Moench *et al.* 2001; Shah *et al.* 2000); Figure 14.4 gives the overall water balance for Spain.

The great advantage of groundwater is that its storage is free. Of those 7–10 million cubic kilometres, what is accessible depends upon the depth at which it occurs since there are limits in terms of the depth to which different forms of wells can be dug, drilled or bored; as are the limits over the depths to

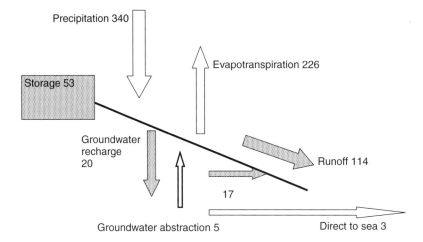

Figure 14.4 *Water balance for Spain. Sources: Estrela et al.; Mendiluce and del Rio n.d.*

which different forms of pumps can usefully raise water; and both the capital and O&M costs of raising water increase with increasing depths (Caballer and Guadalajara 1998). US AID (1982) gives a range of practical depths according to the means of constructing the well. In general, only high valued uses can justify abstracting from a depth of greater than 100 metres. Similarly, pumping requires electrical or mechanical power if substantial quantities are to be raised since the outputs respectively of hand, animal and wind power pumps are $3-5\,m^3$/day, $10-15\,m^3$/day and $50\,m^3$/day (Eberhard *et al.* 2000). The consequence is to greatly increase the demand for energy: thus, centre pivot sprinklers require 14 GJ/ha (Simmons 1989); 20% of Jordan's electricity supply and 12% of Israel's is used for pumping water (Brooks 1996).

It is necessary to differentiate between confined and unconfined aquifers, where the former have some form of outlet to surface waters. Fossil aquifers are those where the water has accumulated as a result of rainfall in the past, usually thousands of years ago, and where there is effectively no recharge as a result of current rainfall because that rainfall is too low. Thus fossil aquifers are a non-renewable, depletable resource and the question, as with any such resource, is when to deplete that resource and at what rate (Chapter 3); equally, as the aquifer is depleted, the costs of pumping will increase.

For non-fossil aquifers, the externalities of abstracting water from the aquifer depend in part upon whether the aquifer is confined or unconfined. If abstraction consistently exceeds the rate of recharge then in both cases, abstraction may result in subsidence; it may also result in saline intrusion from the sea or from linked aquifers of brine water. Where the aquifer is unconfined, abstraction will reduce flows to surface waters, reducing the availability of those waters for other uses. In England, the resulting low flows in rivers and reductions in the water supply to wetlands have created a number of major environmental problems with some rivers ceasing to have any continuous flow (English Nature and the Environment Agency 1999). Again, if abstraction consistently exceeds the rate of recharge, then the water level will fall increasing the costs of pumping and also eventually requiring the construction of deeper wells. In addition, major problems of arsenic and fluoride levels in groundwater, first identified in India and Bangladesh (Pearce 1998), now are, in the case of arsenic, being found to be quite widespread (Smedley and Kinniburgh 2002). Similarly, if groundwater levels drop, any naturally occurring sulphides in the soil will oxidise and the resulting acid will both damage the soil and when discharged to watercourses cause environmental damage (White *et al.* 1999).

The final option is to capture the rainfall at some distance from the point of demand and then transport the water to the demand centre. The most obvious and convenient way of doing this has been via rivers that carry away the runoff and snow melt from the areas where there is high precipitation but little use for that water, notably mountain areas, to those areas where human needs are high. Typically, these are the lowlands and flood plains that can be intensively used for agriculture. Estimates of the availability of water in this form are widely available and per capita availabilities of water of <500, <1000 and $1700 \, m^3$/capita/year have been used (Falkenmark 1989) to classify areas as being 'beyond the water barrier', 'water scarce' and 'water stressed' respectively. However, on their own, these figures can be dangerous. For example, in East Anglia, the per capita availability of water is very low at $691 \, m^3$/person/year (Environment Agency 2001a). This is not much more than the per capita availability of water in Jordan and Algeria but whereas Jordan and Algeria are confronted by major water management problems, there is no critical problem in East Anglia. In Jordan and Algeria, irrigation is required to ensure crop production whereas East Anglia is one of the richest crop producing areas in England and only supplementary irrigation is required, largely to ensure crop quality and the date at which at the crop can be harvested (Weatherhead *et al.* 1994). The critical measure of water availability is the ratio of precipitation (P) to the potential evapotranspiration (PET), or the moisture index I_h (UNESCO 1979). If agriculture can be supported through rainfed agriculture, then only relatively small quantities of water are necessary to support domestic and industrial uses, and substantially less than $500 \, m^3$/capita/year.

Often rain occurs in the wrong place as well as at the wrong time. In India, whilst the average annual rainfall is 1.2 m a year, it varies between 200 mm in the Thar Desert to 11.4 m in Cherrapungi in Meghalaya state (Agarwal and Narain

1997). Whilst rivers have offered convenient ways of transporting the water to the places where it is required, the flood plains of the rivers offering the most fertile soils, these may have to be supplemented by canals, tunnels or aqueducts to transfer water between catchments. Equally, it is frequently necessary to distribute the water across the fertile area by canals.

Variability in supply is generally a greater problem than the overall quantity. Climate is a determining factor in water resource management. In arid climates, for example, the problem is not so much the low amounts of rainfall as the concentration of rainfall in short periods of the year and the variation of the rainfall from year to year. Smith (1998) notes that the variability of annual precipitation is inversely related to annual precipitation, whilst McMahon *et al.* (1992) showed that this relationship varies between continents, the coefficient being greatest for Australia where it is roughly twice that of Europe. The net result is that, depending upon the size of the catchment, four to eight times as large a volume of storage is needed in Australia as in Europe to give the same security of supply. So, for example, per capita storage for Sydney is $600\,\mathrm{m}^3$ (Deen 2000). Again, whereas London has 90 days of storage capacity (de Garis 2001), Melbourne has storage for rather more than three years' demand (Melbourne Water 2001): however, it is experiencing a five-year drought (Haby and Fisher 2001). Overall, in Australia, with one of the most arid climates in the world, there are $5000\,\mathrm{m}^3$ of water storage capacity per person (World Bank 2001).

Similarly, rainfall in India is also concentrated into four months of the year in the form of heavy rainstorms: Delhi's rainfall of 800 mm occurs in 80 hours during the year (Agarwal and Narain 1997). In turn, rainfall variability affects the variability of flows so that in the eastern USA, reliable flow (that available 9 years out of 10) is 60–80% of the long-term average, whilst this falls to 30% in the western USA and to 10% in the Middle East (Brooks 1996).

In turn, matching time-varying demand and supply means that the basic question in water resource management is one of how much storage needs to be provided and how? There are a number of options for storing water so as to bring demand and supply into alignment (Keller *et al.* 2000) but storage is inevitably required whenever the peaks of supply and demand do not coincide – unless the ratio of supply to demand is very large, even at the times of highest demand and lowest supply. The options are surface storage in lakes, reservoirs ranging from the very small to the very large, or wetlands is one option; underground storage, ideally in groundwater but also in cisterns, is another option; and combinations in the form of groundwater recharge and conjunctive use being the third option. There are typically strong economies of scale in water storage so that large bulk storage is cheaper than multiple small stores, and losses through evaporation and leakage also tend to be lower.

How water is to be stored has become a matter of major controversy, with large dams being viewed by some as inherently evil. However, this is somewhat to miss the point; the real problem is that all land and water is already being used in one way or another either by people or by ecosystems (Wood *et al.* 2000). Whatever we do will consequently impact on either people or ecosystems or both, and the choice in surface water storage is between the spatially extensive or intensive. A major determinant of whether it is people or the environment that is then affected is the density of population. Thus, in North America where population densities are incredibly low, it is possible to find areas in which very few people live but that these will be true wilderness areas. Over most of the rest of world, all useful land is already heavily populated and the remaining environment is often an artefact of several thousand years of human settlement. Here it is likely that it is people who will have to be resettled. The crunch in countries where populations are still increasing, especially where population densities are already high, is that there is seldom any available land or water available to accommodate them.

In addition, ecosystems develop around the prevailing water regime, the variations in water flows over time. Since it is those variations in water availability over time that we seek to change, water management can scarcely avoid having some environmental impact. Whilst it is the changes in flow regimes that result from dams that are most widely recognised (Acreman *et al.* 1999), meeting the demand from an unconfined aquifer, one with an outlet to surface water, will similarly impact on the environment (English Nature and the Environment Agency 1999). The only source of stored water whose use will not generally have an impact on the environment is then a confined aquifer.

14.1 Catchment Efficiency

It is necessary to consider the water balance over the catchment as a whole because so much water is reused after use rather than consumed, the only actual losses of water occurring when water is evaporated or transpired, or reaches a sink such as the sea (Seckler 1996; Merrett 1997). On a global basis all water is recycled; within a catchment, an issue is how much water can be reused or recycled, and how many times, before the remaining water is discharged to the sea or to another sink. Where the catchment is 'open' (Seckler 1996), where there is water which is not allocated to any apparent use, then the least cost option is typically as to the best means of capturing some of that water. Once the catchment is 'closed' then the choice is one of reallocating water between competing uses, reducing the losses from some uses, or increasing the degree to which water is reused (used for another purpose) or recycled (reused for the same purpose, commonly after treatment).

Apparent gains in the efficiency of water use may merely change the patterns of flows and stocks within the catchment rather than 'save' water: Seckler (1996) differentiates between 'wet' and 'dry' water savings, where the latter has no real effect on the total amount of water available within the catchment. During the last drought in California, the same distinction was drawn between 'real' and 'paper' water savings (California Department of Water Resources 1993); thus, if the losses from an irrigation canal are reduced by lining the canal, this loss will be a 'dry' or 'paper' saving if the only effect is to reduce the recharge flows to accessible groundwater. Similarly, low flush toilet cisterns do not increase the efficiency of use of water within a catchment if the wastewater is available for reuse.

'Wet' water savings occur when (Seckler 1996):

- Output is increased per unit of water that is lost through evaporation, transpiration or to a sink;
- Reducing water pollution and hence the availability of water for reuse or recycling;
- Reallocating water to higher valued uses.

14.2 Managing Extremes

Rainfall and runoff vary from year to year apparently randomly. In addition, there are cyclical patterns in rainfall and runoff of which the most obvious is the cycle associated with Niňo. There are also trends in both demand and supply over time with climate change potentially affecting both future demand and supply. The critical question is then what should be the reliability of supply and hence how much storage should be provided? What risk of what extent of a shortfall in water is acceptable?

But, however low the probability of that drought, which is the worst with which the system is designed to cope, it is inevitable that in one place or another, a more extreme event will occur sooner or later. It is therefore necessary to consider from the beginning how such an event will be managed. Thus, in 1991, California adopted legislation which required any supplier of more than 3000 customers to prepare a water shortage contingency plan. Each such plan must (Department of Water Resources 1991):

- estimate the minimum water supply availability at the end of the next 12, 24 and 36 months assuming worst-case shortages;
- determine increasing stages of action to be taken in response to water supply shortages of up to 50%;
- outline specific water supply conditions which will trigger each stage;
- establish consumption limits;
- adopt mandatory no-waste regulations; and
- provide a method to overcome the revenue impacts.

In particular, it must outline how demand will be managed downwards to match the reduced availability of water. There are a number of ways of rationing supply:

- voluntary calls for restraint;
- bans on less important uses e.g. bans on garden watering, car washing;

- rationing through price;
- rationing by volume e.g. the fitting of flow constrictors, reductions in pressure;
- rationing by energy e.g. installing standpipes so that consumers must carry water;
- rationing through time e.g. cutting off the supply for part of the day.

These different strategies vary in terms of their effectiveness; for example, Husain (1978) reports that calls for voluntary constraint reduced demand by 25% during the 1976 drought. However, 60% of respondents in the Green *et al.* (1993) study in one of the two areas affected by a current hosepipe ban were not aware of such a ban. The different strategies also differ in terms of equity, and in costs. During the major droughts from 1991 to 1993, amongst the methods tried to reduce demand in the city of Bulawayo (Ndubiwa 1996) were rota cuts; supplies being cut off between 8.30 a.m. and 16.30 p.m. This method was abandoned after a week for three reasons:

- the heavy demand on labour to open and close valves;
- a significant increase in the number of mains bursts as a result of the pressure transients; and
- the hoarding of water by consumers.

Since the overall effect was an increase in water demand, the method was abandoned in favour of supply restrictions and rationing.

Moreover, the city of Bulawayo reports that when consumption was cut by two-thirds, the frequency of blockages and other problems with sewers significantly increased as flows were now no longer sufficient for the system to be self-clearing. The costs of running wastewater treatment works might also change but whilst flows will be less, the concentration of pollutant loads can be expected to be higher and the assimilative capacity of the receiving waters will be lower because of lower flows.

Systems that are wholly or partly reliant on groundwater have the advantage in that it is usually possible to overdraft groundwater on a short-term basis; equally, a common response to a drought is a switch either by the supplier or by the consumers to using groundwater. Thus, in the California drought of 1987 to 1992, farmers replaced some of the irrigation water that they had previously received by drilling wells (Frederick 1993). Whereas before the drought, groundwater provided 37% of the state's water supply, during the drought, this increased to an average of 60% and up to 90% in some areas. In turn, a number of aquifers were overdrafted: the cumulative change in storage in Fresno County being some 2 million acre-feet whilst the number of wells drilled rose from around 15 000 in 1987 to 25 000 in 1990 (Department of Water Resources 1993).

In general, analyses of past droughts (Russell *et al.* 1970; Schlemmer *et al.* 1989; USACE 1995; Wheaton and Arthur 1989) have found that the costs to urban consumers of water of managing down demand are very small, provided that demand is managed down rather than supplies being suddenly cut with little or no warning. The costs are instead borne by the environment and by farming, available water being switched away from agriculture to urban uses (Department of Water Resources 1993). The degree of advanced warning that can be given of a potential shortfall in supply then depends upon the pattern of rainfall. In the same way that in arid climates, a large amount of storage is required to bridge between the rainy seasons, the failure of one set of rains provides a long lead time before storage is expended. Thus, in Bulawayo, Zimbabwe, the city plans for potential droughts 21 months in advance (Ndubiwa 1996). At the end of the rains in April, the test applied is whether there is enough water in the reservoirs to last 21 months through a 10% low flow year to the beginning of the following rainy season. If the answer is no, then rationing is put in place such that the water will last the 21 months. A series of measures are adopted in the following sequence:

- publicity campaign;
- hosepipe bans between 6 a.m. and 6 p.m.;
- rationing based on occupancy per unit or a percentage of the last six-month period of unrestricted supply;
- penalties are levied for excess consumption with supplies being cut off for persistent excessive consumption; and
- flow restrictors also being installed.

In the 1991–93 drought, these measures were used to manage a reduction in consumption from 150 000 m^3/day in October 1990 to 57 000 m^3 in December 1992, at which time households of up to 15 people would be managing upon 300 litres per day. Whilst, at the time, there were grave concerns about the possible threats to health of such a minimal water availability, there were no epidemics.

Varying the pressure in the mains is thus another option; the pressure in the mains in the UK being higher than in some others, the network in Japan operating at pressures of 15–20 m compared with what is thought to be somewhere between 40–50 m in the UK (National Rivers Authority 1995b). Reducing the pressure at an outlet from 100 psi to 50 psi can reduce water flow by about one-third; a comparison of dwellings in high and low pressure zones in Denver, Colorado found consumption to be 6% lower in the latter (US EPA 1995).

One reason why the costs of droughts to urban consumers has been found in the past to be low, however, is that there has always been scope for consumers to reduce inefficiencies in the use of water. When average domestic per capita consumption is 280 litres/person/day, it is considerably easier to reduce demand by 50% and less pain is caused to the consumer than when the per capita consumption is 70 litres/person/day. Concern has consequently been expressed about whether the costs of responding to drought periods will increase as urban water use becomes more efficient.

Secondly, it is not clear how a switch to greater reliance on rainwater harvesting will affect the capacity of the system to respond to droughts. Because of the economies of scale, the capacity of on-site storage of rainwater is likely to be relatively low and perhaps only sufficient to bridge between the average wet and dry seasons in a year. The consumer will then rely upon storage by the water supplier to maintain supplies during droughts. This will increase the problems for the supplier, because the consumer will only want water at those times when it is most expensive to make that water available.

Similarly, where water is metered or the charge otherwise reflects the amount of water used, then a major problem for the water supplier is that a fall in the amount of water supplied as a result of a drought will result in reduced revenues (Braver n.d.). Since a large part of the supplier's costs are, however, fixed, revenue will fall to a greater extent than costs and so revenue may fall below costs. Thus to the supplier, metering increases risks. In turn, the supplier needs to consider how to balance costs and revenue when demand must be forced down to cope with reduced resources.

14.3 Water Sources

There is not necessarily a choice between using groundwater, rainwater harvesting or surface water since groundwater is only accessible in some areas. Where there is a choice, then in large measure the choice is between capital costs versus O&M costs; using groundwater, when available, tends to involve lower capital costs than abstracting surface water, not least because the storage capacity is inherent in the aquifer, but higher O&M costs because of the need to pump the water over a significant height. Economies of scale are, as ever, important; the costs of storage falling as a function of the capacity of the storage.

There are generally advantages in using a combination of ground- and surface water as a means of increasing reliability and redundancy. Typically, the time lag between precipitation and water availability will differ between surface and groundwater and hence it may be possible to reduce year to year variability in supply. In turn, the likelihood that the supply will fall below a threshold level will tend to be lower. Thus, conjunctive use, using surface water to recharge groundwater when demand is low, and drawing down groundwater in periods of high demand can be an attractive option.

Reliance on a single point of abstraction, of conveyance (e.g. an aqueduct), or of treatment exposes the system to risks such as transient pollution pulses and floods. The analysis should take account of the risks of such events, including those of common mode failure.

14.4 Understanding Demand

To predict or to manage demand, we must first know where we are now: we need to know how much water is used for what purposes by whom. But generally in water management, this is poorly known. Because water is a low unit-cost bulk product, it has not been worthwhile to invest heavily in monitoring flows within the system; equally, mechanical meters have not generally proved to be very reliable or accurate. So, estimates of leakage within potable water distribution systems are frequently derived as the difference between the guess about how much water is put into the system and the guess about how much water is delivered. Except for the Netherlands, it is only in the last five years or so that good data have been available about how water is actually used in the home. As Figure 14.5 shows, the largest component of potable water use in England and Wales is domestic demand; if we ignore cooling water, use in hotels is the next highest use after industry.

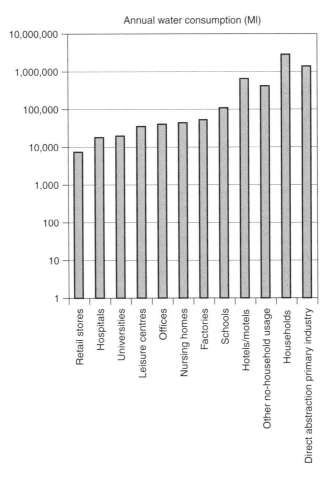

Figure 14.5   *Components of water demand in England and Wales. Source: Surendran 2001*

The need to predict future demand is, perhaps, sharper in water resource management than in any other area of water management; the time lapse between deciding to expand water resource capacity and the new capacity coming on-stream can be 15 years. Hence, it is necessary to assess what will be the balance of supply and demand at least 15 years in the future. Since the majority of potable water is then discharged to the sewers, the expected demand for water also predicts the demand for sewers and for wastewater treatment.

14.4.1 Domestic demand

What is most noticeable is the extremely large differences between countries (Figure 14.6) both in the total per capita daily usage and the individual components of usage. For example, it is not immediately obvious why in Perth, Australia, toilet flushing takes 41 litres/person/day whilst in New York City, 136 litres

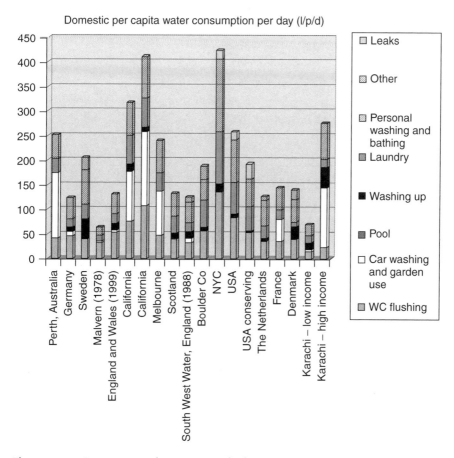

Figure 14.6 *Components of water use in the home*

Table 14.2   *Frequency of use of water fittings and applications in the home*

	Scotland 1991	England and Wales 1991	The Netherlands 1992	USA 1998
Bath				
Bath – households with shower	0.22	0.3		
Bath – households with no shower	0.47			
Bath – all households	0.33		0.62	0.05
Bath – power shower		0.52		
Shower	0.52	0.29		0.7
WC	4.84	4.01	5.94	5.05
Use of tap			0.92	
Kitchen sink			2	
Wash basin			4.2	
Washing machine			0.24	0.37
Automatic	0.34		0.155	
Nonautomatic	0.26			
Hand clothes wash				
Dishwasher	0.26		0.24	0.1
Bowls of dishes washed by hand			0.78	
Households with a dishwasher	0.51			
Households with no dishwasher	1.64			
All households	1.47		0.03	
Leaks				0.46

are required for this purpose, and 108 litres in California, whilst in the Netherlands, in 1998, domestic usage was only 128 litres per person per day for all purposes. There are apparently very large differences in the amount of water used by an appliance or fitting each time it is used in different countries (Table 14.2). For example, washing machines in the USA have traditionally been top-loaders as opposed to the front-loading machines standard in Europe. Top-loading washing machines are inherently less water-efficient than front-loading machines (Pugh and Tomlinson 1999). At the same time, the water used for washing machines in Europe fell from nearly 180 litres per cycle in 1970 to 70–80 litres per cycle in 1998; the consumption of water in dishwashers fell over the same period from nearly 60 litres per cycle to 20–30 litres per cycle (Lallana *et al.* 2001). Conversely, in the USA, the average consumption of vertical axis washing machines is 150 litres per wash and 98 litres per wash with high-efficiency horizontal machines (Tomlinson and Rizy 1998). On the other hand, it is not apparent why there should be such a difference in the consumption of dishwashing machines between France and Germany – as is frequently the case with statistics about water, the accuracy of the statistics is perhaps doubtful. Nor are the differences in the volumes used for flushing toilets accountable solely by differences in the capacities of the cisterns.

There are estimates of how often one person flushes a toilet each day (generally, the estimates are about four times a day) but not about how often a person uses a toilet during the day: the US figures imply that toilets are flushed more frequently. But, we do not know the likelihood that a toilet is flushed after each of the different purposes for which it is used. Consequently, the reductions in the water used anticipated by installing dual flush toilet cisterns will be less than expected if the probability that a toilet is flushed after urination is less than one.

Again, the frequency of the use of a shower in Germany and the USA averages out at about 0.7 per person per day; higher than in Scotland or England and Wales although there is anecdotal evidence that frequency of use is increasing in the UK. To explain the differences in the quantities of water used in a shower between England and Wales and the USA requires both differences in flow rates (USA, 9.5 litres/minute; UK 3.5–4.0 litres/minute) and the assumption that people take longer showers in the USA. The average volume used in a shower in each of the two countries implies that the average shower in the USA takes just over 14 minutes whilst one in England takes just under 9 minutes. What these figures do illustrate is the extent to which domestic water consumption is determined by the technologies adopted.

14.4.2 Industrial and commercial demand

Water is used in industry for heat transfer (cooling and heating), steam production, plant and vessel washing, product washing, air pollution control, vacuum systems, effluent dilution, domestic uses, housekeeping and it is also incorporated in some products. Table 14.3 gives some figures for the industrial uses in the USA and UK. Water usage per unit output shows very marked differences

Table 14.3 *Water use per unit output by different industrial sectors*

		USA			UK	Unit
		Range			Range	
		from	to	median		
Food and beverages						
Beer		8	13		6.1	m³/tonne
Poultry dressing – chicken				38	8 to 15	per bird
Poultry dressing – turkey				87	40 to 60	per bird
Building materials	hydraulic cement			3	0.74	m³/tonne
Metals	steel			159	28–62	m³/tonne
Textiles	dyeing	25	49		17–98	m³/tonne

Sources: ETBPP 1997, 1998b, 2000a; Gleick 1993; Mathieson *et al.* 1998; North Carolina Department of Environment and Natural Resources 1998.

Table 14.4   *Water use in industrial food processing*

	Min.	Mean	Max.
Asparagus	1.9	8.5	29
Snap beans	1.3	4.2	11.2
Broccoli	4.1	9.2	21
Carrot	1.2	3.3	7.1
Cauliflower	12	17	24
Pea	1.9	5.4	14
Pickle	1.4	3.5	11
Sweet potato	0.4	2.2	9.7
White potato	1.9	3.6	6.6
Spinach	3.2	8.8	23
Squash	1.1	6	22
Tomato – peeled	1.3	2.2	3.7
Tomato – product	1.1	1.6	2.4
Apple	0.2	2.4	13
Apricot	2.5	5.6	14
Berry	1.8	3.5	9.1
Cherry	1.2	3.9	14
Citrus	0.3	3	9.3
Peach	1.4	3	6.3
Pear	1.6	3.6	7.7
Pineapple	2.6	2.7	3.8
Pumpkin	0.4	2.9	11

Source: North Carolina Department of Environment and Natural Resources 1998.

within what would appear to be a homogeneous sector (Table 14.4). Unfortunately, the available figures are also largely in terms of water use per tonne output rather than for water use per unit value of output but the ratio of water to gross value added in the UK chemical industry varies between $0.008 \, m^3/\text{£gva}$ and $0.11 \, m^3/\text{£gva}$ (ETBPP 2000).

14.4.3 Agricultural demand

Agriculture is both so large a consumer of water and so important that the discussion of the determinants of agricultural water demand, the prediction of those requirements and the whole question of water management for agriculture is covered in Chapter 17.

14.5 Predicting Demand

Traditionally, water engineers sought to predict future demand for water in order to construct the necessary infrastructure to supply the required amount of water. This will continue to be true in those countries where supplies of potable water in adequate amounts are not yet available to all of the population. Now, increasingly in developed countries, estimates of forecasts of demand are required in order to determine the effect of demand management strategies, coupled with some degree of resource reinforcement.

14.5.1 Domestic demand

Herrington (1987) has identified a range of decisions which require consideration of demand responsiveness:

- Long-term strategic planning over a time horizon of 30–50 years to identify potential gaps between supply and demand, as a basis for prioritising the different options for bridging those gaps.
- Investment appraisal; the capital intensive nature of the industry requires building supply ahead of demand and hence is based upon predictions of the future demand–supply balance.
- Operations planning; to enable the minimisation of the costs of operating the system where that system typically includes storage, which will be drawn down, and may include multi-purpose storage facilities such as dams which act as hydroelectric stations as well as for flood control or water storage.
- Appraisal of demand management strategies.
- Medium to short-term crisis management ranging from a drought to a failure of an aqueduct or mains.

To predict demand, a time-dependent measure of demand also has to be defined: average daily demand or peak demand, for example. Demand varies over the day, the week and the month and it is variations in each of these that we will be interested in forecasting. These variations also imply that water has many marginal costs. Peaks in the day and in the week are mainly of importance in designing the distribution system; average daily demand and peak demand for determining how much storage to provide. Peak daily domestic consumption has been found to be 180% of mean hourly flow in one study in Scotland (Wilson *et al.* 1993), an effect buffered there by the requirement of in-house storage. Peak seasonal demands are commonly in the range of 1.4 to 1.8 times mean daily demand but in Melbourne, peak demand is 2.5 times average demand (Government of Victoria 2001). In general, the greater the proportion of demand that is for external domestic uses, the higher the ratio of peak to average demand.

A number of methods for predicting future water consumption have been conventionally used to predict the demand for water:

- trend forecasting;
- micro-component analysis (Environment Agency 2001b);
- input–output analysis (Tate and Scharf 1985; Tate 1986);
- price elasticity (Herrington 1987);
- scenarios (Environment Agency 2001a; Pinkham n.d.).

The first four techniques essentially assume that the future will be like the past, only bigger; change will be positive but quantitative rather than qualitative. Estimates in the past have generally proved to be gross overestimates of actual future demand. For example, in 1975, when consumption in the USA was about 350 billion gallons/day; predictions of demand in 2000 varied from 330 to 1128 billion gallons a day: actual consumption in 2000 was down on 1975 levels (USACE 1995). The more recent scenario approach (Environment Agency 2001a) is based upon a different conceptual approach and asks why could the future be different from the present and how will those differences affect the variable which we seek to predict?

The forecasting technique adopted should also be able to explain the past; why, for example, when per capita domestic water use in England and Wales rose from 98 litres per day in 1978 (Thackrey *et al.* 1978a, 1978b) to 160 litres per day in the most recent figures (Edward 1996), did the quantity of water used for toilet flushing increase from 32 litres per day to 53 litres a day and the amount used for personal washing and bathing more than double from 17 to 40 litres per day? Compared to the techniques used in other industries (Bright 1972), it will be recognised that demand forecasting in the water industry is somewhat unsophisticated – though not necessarily any more inaccurate.

The limitation of the techniques described for predicting demand is that change is not treated in a causal manner, but as either innate and constant (e.g. trend series analysis) or as a result of behavioural response (e.g. price elasticity). None of the techniques just discussed can really account for the increase in water consumption in England and Wales between 1978 and the present. In practice, there would seem in fact to be three drivers of changes in water consumption: technology, demographic factors and social/cultural reasons. Moreover, as others have argued, the really important elasticity is not price elasticity, but income elasticity, particularly at times when real incomes are rising and real prices are falling. This gives the matrix shown in Table 14.5.

Rising real incomes should be expected to result in increased water usage whilst increases in real prices will reduce the rate of increase in demand or yield a decrease in demand. Thus, it is the combination of change in income and price that will affect overall demand. For California, Renwick *et al.* (1998) estimated the price elasticity of residential water demand as -0.16 whilst the income elasticity was estimated as 0.25. In developing countries with rates of economic growth of 7–10% per annum, the latter figure would imply significant

Table 14.5   *Determinants of domestic water use*

	Income elasticity	Price elasticity
Technology	high	low
Demographic	moderate	very low
Social/cultural	high	moderate

increases in the demand for water when frequently the existing demand is not adequately met, with water often only available to part of the urban populations, or only for a few hours a day. Thus, Webb and Iskandarani (1998) report income elasticities of demand of 0.37 (Egypt), 1.2 for Sub-Saharan Africa, 1.0 for India, 0.8 for China, between 0.4 and 0.8 for different countries in Southeast Asia, and 0.6 for Latin and Central America.

There have now been a large number of studies of the price elasticity of domestic demand; summaries of these studies being given in Gibbons (1986), Herrington (1987), Winpenny (1994) and Young (1996). Typically, these show a short-term (2 to 5 years) price elasticity for internal uses in the range of −0.1 to −0.2, with long-term price elasticity (5 to 10 years) generally being in the range of −0.2 to −0.35. So, for example, an increase in the price of water in Bogor, Indonesia, from US$0.15 to US$0.42 resulted in a reduction in demand of 30% (Bhatia and Falkenmark 1993).

In comparing studies between different countries and different contexts, we should expect (Martin and Thomas 1986) that:

- the greater the current level of consumption, the more likely demand is to be price elastic or the greater the price elasticity;
- long-term elasticity will be greater than short-term elasticity as capital and durable goods are progressively replaced by more water-efficient equipment;
- for a given price and consumption level, price elasticity will be less where incomes are higher; and elasticity is likely to be greater where the tariff adopted is a rising block tariff rather than a flat rate tariff.

Consequently, we should expect differences between studies, rather than a single measure of price elasticity to emerge from each and every study. Whereas the majority of price-elasticity studies have used recorded data, such as meter readings and associated bills, Thomas and Syme (1988) undertook a contingent valuation study and were able, therefore, to test the extent to which most of these predictions were found in the responses. Thus, for example, price elasticity rose from 0 for households consuming less than 151 kl/year to −0.31 for those consuming more than 600 kl/year. Similarly, it fell from −0.19kl/year for households earning less than $A12 000 per annum to 0.13 for those earning more than $A26 000/year. Since the design was a social survey, they were also able to test price elasticity against some attitude questions; price elasticity for those who answered yes to the question 'Is water important to your lifestyle' was −0.14 whilst it was −0.52 for those who answered no. Where they can be compared to the results from econometric studies, the different sets point in the same direction. When Thomas and Syme's methodology was applied in South Africa, the overall price elasticity for indoor water use was −0.13 and −0.38 for external uses (Veck and Bill 1998).

Technologies have a marked and direct effect on consumption. A significant part of the differences between the USA and the UK in per capita domestic consumption for different purposes is explicable by technological differences (Section 14.1.1). Similarly, the difference in consumption between the AWWA's (2001) conventional and water-efficient dwelling is almost entirely determined by technical factors. So, changes in technology are, on the one hand, very strong drivers of water consumption but on the other, the most effective means of controlling demand is by influencing the technologies adapted.

Thus, consumption is being driven up by such factors as the 40% of homes in the USA which have whirlpool baths that consume between 75 and 200 litres per use (Vickers 2001). Similarly, hot tubs are available in a variety of sizes with capacities of between around 550 litres and 2100 litres, the average capacity being around 850–900 litres. Although hot tubs do not require emptying after every use, the recommended frequency of refilling implies an average weekly consumption of 90 to 350 litres per week (Johnson 2002). Again, the evaporative loss from a swimming pool in Arizona is 250 litres per day (Gelt 1995), roughly sufficient to supply all the daily household needs of two people in Denmark.

Demand for all of these high water using household durables is likely to be income elastic. Since water usage by equipment and fittings can only be significantly reduced by replacing them with more water-efficient appliance and fittings, technologically driven demand is likely to be price inelastic.

An ageing population has a direct effect on household water demand in that two age-related diseases, diabetes and, in men, prostate problems, result in an increased frequency of micturition: a frequency of urination of once an hour being a diagnostic test for prostate problems. For example, the percentage of males with diabetes mellitus rises from 1.7% in males aged 45 to 6.9% in males aged 75 (Malmesten *et al.* 1997). Garraway *et al.* (1991) report that the proportion of males with benign prostatic enlargement increases from 13% at age 45 to 43% at age 60–90 with higher rates being found in post-mortem studies. Since a number of studies have reported that the frequency of toilet flushing per person per day is in the range of 4–5 (Wilson *et al.* 1993), and assuming that a toilet is flushed every time it is used (something about which we have no data), the implication is for a substantial rise in the amount of water used for toilet flushing as the population ages.

Secondly, urinary incontinence also increases with age; the proportion of males reporting urinary incontinence rose from 3.6% at age 45 to 28% at age 90 (Malmsten *et al.* 1997). This in turn should be expected to result in an increase in the frequency of clothes washing and also in personal washing. Dutch data does show daily toilet flush volumes rising from 33 litres/person for ages under 24 to 49 litres for the over-65s. The quantity of water used in showering, on the other hand, is highest for those under 24 (54 litres/day), falls to 13 litres/day for the age band 55–64, and rises again to 29 litres for the over 65s. The quantity of water used for clothes washing falls significantly on retirement and but data is truncated to the over-65s.

Overall, single or two-person households have a higher per capita use of water than the per capita usage in larger households (Edward 1996): the existing data does not make it possible to determine the extent to which this is an age-related difference. It is notable that people in higher income groups tend to have a longer life expectancy than do poorer people.

Now, water usage is not purely functional, but carries with it strong cultural, psychological and social symbolic meanings. Thus, for example, the following quote about a Friday night bath is taken from one of a series of focus group studies undertaken by Odeyemi (1998): 'Yessss it is, I do enjoy it once a week ... to get rid of the tension, ... stress. It like washing away all your ... getting ready for the weekend ... it's a mental thing. Some people don't do that, it's my way of washing away the preceding week.' For this person, a bath is much more than a way of getting clean, a function fulfilled by their daily shower. Odeyemi also found that being brought up in a water-scarce country tended to leave people more cautious in their use of water than those who had been brought up in a country, such as the UK, where there is no apparent scarcity of water. Moral and social norms then appear to influence water use and more especially the likelihood that consumers will adopt sustainable water management practices (Government of Victoria 2001). Finally, some uses of water are required for religious reasons; Hengeveld and De Vocht (1982) estimate that in Islamic countries, ablutions before prayer require between 1–20 l/p/day and anal cleansing a further 2–5 l/p/day. For these reasons, it is not surprising that the price elasticity of internal domestic uses of water is very low (e.g. Herrington 1987), it being necessary on this basis to double the price of water in order to achieve a 10–20% reduction in demand.

There are three ways of determining existing patterns of usage. The first is to meter individual properties or groups of properties, determining the ownership and use of the appliances and fitting through interview surveys and asking the consumers to keep diaries of water use, and to undertake regression analysis to determine the contribution of each use to total demand. Diary recording does result in an under-recording of facility and appliance use but not as much as might be expected; 7–10% under-recording being reported (Wilson *et al.* 1993). The second is to fit data loggers to each and every water delivery point in a sample of properties so as to record the frequency of use and the amount consumed in each use. The final option is to fit data loggers at the meter which record and capture flow rate every few seconds (DeOreo *et al.* 1996). Once the time traces resulting from the use of each of the appliances and fittings in the property have been established, it is then possible to detect from the specific patterns of changes in flow over time which appliances have been used.

14.5.2 Industrial and commercial demand

In practice, in the developed countries, potable water use has stabilised or tended to decline in recent years. On the industrial side, key determinants are:

- The rate of growth in output and hence the rate of increase in production durables, with the new production durables being more efficient in their use of water (e.g. the predicted demand for ICI's ammonia plant was largely responsible for the Kielder reservoir being built – but the manufacturing process changed and the demand for water was dramatically reduced). Equally, the greater the growth rate, so will the average age of the capital stock tend to be younger, the rate at which existing stocks are replaced also tending to be greater than in slow growing or stable economies.
- The structure of the economy; the shifts away from the older 'metal bashing' industries towards service and financial sectors are a major cause of water demands falling well below earlier demand forecasts. The apparent current shift towards hyperclean industries such as microelectronics, pharmaceuticals and then to nanotechnologies may either reverse this trend or reinforce it. That the water used has to be extensively treated before it is sufficiently pure to be usable in these processes probably implies that recycling or reuse will be more efficient than disposal of the water once used.
- The rate at which technological innovation that improves the efficiency of water use is called forth.

Forecasting industrial demand, as with all aspects of demand, has always been hampered by the inadequacies of data on the nature of existing use. There is relatively little information on the nature of the demand for water in different industrial sectors (Table 14.3) or on the proportion of water that is reused or recycled in industry. A number of studies have also sought to determine the price elasticity of demand for water for industrial purposes (Rees 1969). The largest of these studies (Tate *et al.* 1992) shows the difficulties of these studies given the different uses for which water is required in industry, the differences in requirements for water as a factor of production, and the variations between companies in the structure of water costs. Nevertheless price elasticities between −0.50 and −1.20 were obtained. As discussed below, however, there is a great deal of evidence that industrial usage of water continues to be inefficient.

14.5.3 Climate change

Climate change means that it is necessary to predict the change in the resource as well as the change in demand. Overlaying the consequences of climate change on top of these other changes implies that changes in the concentration of rainfall in time and space, and in the variability of rainfall, are more important than changes in the absolute amount of rainfall. Changes in the concentration of rainfall over time and any increase in the variability of rainfall are likely to require increases in storage capacity, whilst changes in the geographic distribution of rainfall mean either moving the water or the human activities. Karl and Knight (1998) have shown that there has been an increase in overall precipitation in the USA of 10% since 1910 and that this has largely been in the form of high intensity events.

At the same time, relatively small changes in climate variables can have disproportionate effects on water availability. Thus, Nemec and Schaake (1982) show that small changes in inflows could result in large changes in the reliability of yields of reservoirs. Again, Gleick (2000) concludes that small changes in precipitation and temperature can, in some regions, result in significant changes in runoff and Sandstrom (1995) has shown that a 15% reduction in rainfall could result in a 45% reduction in groundwater recharge in parts of Africa.

14.5.4 Deciding the reliability of supply

Once demand has been predicted, then the required level of supply can be determined; however, a decision has to be reached on what level of security of supply to provide. For example, whether to ensure that supply, and, particularly water storage, will be sufficient to cope with the 1 in 50-year drought year or 1 in 100-drought year or the 1 in 200-year drought week, where specifying the period of the drought is itself a difficult question. What is the appropriate form of the target depends in part upon the form of the water resource, whether this is by direct abstraction of groundwater, or of river water, or by way of storage reservoirs. Traditionally, urban water supplies have been designed to very high standards of service, in the order of the 1 in 200- to 1 in 500-year drought. But, as water is used increasingly for less valuable purposes, and so, in a drought, demand can be more easily managed down to available supplies, the standard of service is also decreasing. When the average domestic consumer, for example, normally receives 50 l/day, a 50% reduction in supplies has more serious consequences than when the normal supply provides 400 l/day.

The same risk-based approach needs also to be considered in regard to other risks: of the failure of an aqueduct, a plug of pollution or a flood affecting a water treatment works, the failure of a dam, or a major pipe burst. The question is then one of evaluating the cost of reducing the expected value of the costs incurred by an interruption or reduction in water availability with a given lead time before that interruption or reduction occurs. Thus, for example, in the UK, the historical standard for a ban on garden watering and car washing has been 1 in 10 years (OFWAT 1998). It is possible to determine how much consumers would be prepared to pay for a lower risk of such a ban, or of other forms of supply variations (Green *et al.* 1993).

14.6 Value of First Time Supply

Since water is essential to life, we are always considering an improvement over the existing provision. The three dimensions of such an improvement are then:

- Reductions in the real resource cost – the time and energy required to obtain water, the cost of buying water, or the running costs of the existing system.

- Improvements in the quantity of water available where this is constrained by the real resource cost of use; essentially, where the resource costs are very high, a purpose of the improvement is to increase consumption to provide for basic needs for drinking, cooking, washing and other hygiene requirements.
- Improvements in the quality of the water available, notably in terms of health risk posed by using that water, but also in terms of other characteristics such as taste, colour, reliability of supply and pressure.

The relative importance of these improvements then vary with the characteristics of the existing supply. Thus, in rural areas, a primary benefit of installing a tube well or piped system is the reduction in the time and energy costs of collecting water. As shown in Section 9.2.2.1, this burden is predominantly borne by women and the time freed by making available a secure local supply can be used by women for better purposes, including making time available for girls to go to school. So, too, can the energy currently consumed by carrying that water be put to better purposes: Cairncross (1987) cites a figure of 14 hours per week in one case and Lewis (1994) reports that in some regions of East Africa women spend 27% of their caloric intake in fetching water. El Katsha *et al.* (1989) quote one woman's reasons for washing clothes in a canal rather than using water from a public standpipe: 'I prefer to wash in the canal because it is less strenuous. If I wash at home, I'll have to walk back and forth at least four times carrying clean and dirty water, especially since I have no water at home.' However, collecting water and washing may be one of the future social occasions open to women (Rathgeber 1996) and it should not be assumed that energy minimisation is the only criterion that women use to select a water point.

Because of the economies of scale, distributing water by pipes is typically lower in cost than carrying it on animals or vehicles. It is characteristic of urban areas that the higher income groups are supplied with piped water supplies whereas the poor have to buy water from water vendors, from neighbours or from other sources. The poor thus pay higher prices for water and also spend a higher proportion of their income on buying water, water being expensive (Briscoe 1993). Moreover, when the water is of poor quality, the household needs to boil the water before use. Briscoe (1993) cites a figure of 11% of income for households in the lowest income quartile in Bangladesh being required for this purpose and 29% for squatter settlements in Peru.

White *et al.* (1972) estimated the quantities of water that are used as these vary according to access and to the ease of disposing of wastewater (Table 14.6): at some point of consumption, the quantity of water used is constrained by the problems of disposing of that water after use (Chapter 16). Thus, Cairncross (1987) reports that the installation of a village standpipe or pump increases water usage four-fold because it reduces the time required to obtain water.

When the real resource costs of water are high, then use is constrained so that only the most essential needs are met: drinking and cooking. Only when the real resource costs of water are reduced are the less urgent, except where there are

Table 14.6 *Variation in water use by conditions*

Conditions	Likely range of usage (l/c/d)
Water carried from distant or low quality sources	4 to 20
Water carried from easily accessible abundant sources of good quality	10 to 40
Piped water with single taps and no indoor waste disposal	16 to 90
Piped water with multiple indoor taps and indoor waste disposal	25 to 600

Source: White *et al.* 1972.

religious or cultural prescriptions, needs of personal washing, washing cooking utensils, clothes washing and other uses supplied. Equally, where there are several sources of water, the apparently least important needs are satisfied by the apparently lowest quality water. The obvious potential improvement in water quality relates to health improvements. Cairncross (1999) estimates that 90% of the health benefits of improved water and sanitation result from a reduction in diarrhoeal illnesses. In turn, the direct economic effects of water-related disease can be significant. Thus, the 1991 cholera outbreak in Peru resulted in costs estimated to be around 1.5% of Peru's GDP (Idelovitch and Ringskog 1997). More generally, ill-health will reduce the amount of labour that individuals can employ in both productive and also leisure activities. However, evaluating that loss of labour capacity has proved extremely difficult (e.g. Mills 1994).

Lane (1996) differentiates between four different categories of health risks associated with water:

- **Water-borne:** transmitted through drinking water containing pathogens as a result of contamination with human faecal waste.
- **Water-washed:** diseases whose transmission is reduced by use of water for personal hygiene. These include diarrhoeal diseases transmitted by a faecal-oral route, bacteria and fungal skin and eye diseases (e.g. scabies, trachoma) as well as infections carried by lice and mites.
- **Water-based:** worm infections in which the pathogen spends part of its time in an aquatic host organism; for example, schistosomiasis, flukes and guinea worm.
- **Water-related:** diseases transmitted by insects that breed or bite near water such as malaria, Rift Valley fever, western equine encephalitis (Lane 1996) and onchocerciasis (Cairncross and Feachem 1993). Different species of insect have different preferences for water; thus, *Culex Pipiens* mosquitoes breed in sewage and sullage and are one vector of *Bancroftian filiasis*, the cause of elephantitis, although this nematode worm is transmitted by different mosquitoes in different parts of the world. *Anopheles* mosquitoes breed in fairly clean water (e.g. flood or irrigation water) and carry malaria whilst *Aedes Aegypti* carry yellow

fever and dengue fever and prefer clean water, especially that stored in pots and cisterns.

In turn, there are four different vectors involved (Feachem *et al.* 1983):

- viruses (e.g. poliomyelitis, hepatitis A, rotaviruses);
- bacteria (e.g. typhoid, paratyphoid, cholera, Weil's disease);
- protozoa (e.g. giardia);
- helminths, or parasitic worms (e.g. hookworm, whipworm, roundworm).

Women are at a higher risk of disease partly because of the gender division of labour (Lewis 1994), such as washing clothes (El Katsha and White 1989) and they are also exposed to other hazards in the course of collecting water (White *et al.* 1972).

The provision of clean water in adequate amounts then can potentially reduce the first two water-related health risks; clean water in adequate amounts forming a barrier to the transmission of water-borne vectors (Figure 14.7). However, to do so, the different elements of water provision must all be such as to reduce the risk of contamination. Thus, the source of the water, the means of transporting that water and storage at the point of use must all be appropriate. So, when wells are the source, both the means of carrying that water and its storage in the home are points of potential contamination (e.g. Brismar 1997). Similarly, in piped supply systems of the developed economies, we have discovered rather to our

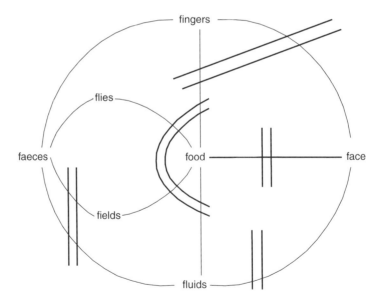

Figure 14.7   *Disease transmission routes*

surprise that Legionnaire's disease can occur as a result of the storage of warm water. The contamination of the water with heavy metals may similarly occur at the source, during transport (i.e. from the pipework) or during storage (El Katsha *et al.* 1989). Much of that contamination is natural but human activities also create additional risks from metal contamination but also from other sources such as pesticides, industrial chemicals, fertilisers and the like.

There is, however, no simple relationship between the provision of adequate water and sanitation and health improvements (Cairncross 1999). The consensus now is that education in the nature of disease and in the principles of hygiene are necessary if there is to be such an improvement in health status (e.g. Cairncross and Kochar 1994). Secondly, rather than the provision of an adequate supply being a technical problem, it is now seen very much more as an institutional problem. Table 14.7 summarises the interventions in one area in Ghana as the donor sought to achieve the anticipated benefits from the provision of a clean water supply (Akuoke-Asibey 1996). This pattern of learning is not untypical of many similar programmes of that period in what was seen to be the apparently simple problem of providing access to good quality water proved to be much more complicated.

In developed economies, there is a presumption that there are no health risks associated with piped water, and thus the problems recently recognised with giardia and cryptosporidum have been something of a shock. However, the water supply has other characteristics that influence its value and consequently those improvements for which consumers may be prepared to pay. These other characteristics of the water itself include taste, colour and odour. In addition, the characteristics of the service itself may also be improved; for example, the pressure at which the water is supplied, the quantity supplied, the reliability of supply and the likelihood that the service will be interrupted. When systems other

Table 14.7 *CIDA support for rural water sector in the Upper East Region of Ghana*

Date	Budget (millions)	Activities
1973–1981	$C17.00	Construction of 1648 boreholes; operation and maintenance system organised
1978–1983	$C2.00	Pump maintenance and site development; introduction of water caretakers and water user committees
1981–1987	$C8.05	Rehabilitation of hand pumps
1984–1990	$C8.60	Health/hygiene education programme; training of water organisers

Source: Akuoko-Asibey 1996.

than a piped connection to every home are being considered, privacy, ease of operation and maintenance can be important aspects (van Wijk-Sijbesma 1985).

14.6.1 Economic assessment

The standard condition applies of identifying the baseline condition and then evaluating the benefits and costs of a series of alternative 'do something' options (Figure 14.8). These 'do something' options obviously vary from place to place; the Asian Development Bank (Asian Development Bank 1998) has set out the basic economic principles involved and WELL (DFID 1999a) discusses the wider issues in appraising water and sanitation projects.

The easiest part of the valuation is to calculate the reductions in the costs of buying water and of boiling it to make it safe. Beyond that, the benefits lie in the increase in consumption and health benefits; further still beyond that limit, the concern is to evaluate the benefits of further increases in quantity and improvements in quality although reliability is an important requirement of water supply at almost any level of supply (Littlefair 1998). In turn, it is possible to make some estimate of the costs incurred as a result of interruptions in supply. Thus, Tate (1968), summarised in Herrington (1977), undertook a detailed assessment of the benefits of improving the reliability of supply to a rural area. The area was currently served directly from an aqueduct which had

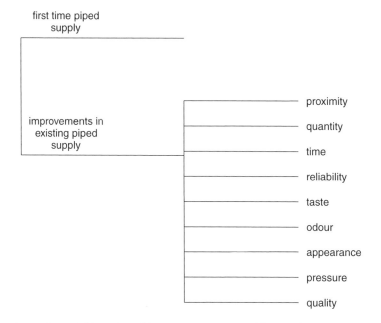

Figure 14.8   *Potential benefits of improvements in potable supply*

to be shut down and dewatered three or four times a year; several farms also suffered from low water pressure. Tate surveyed the consumers to determine what costs they incurred in transporting and storing water in preparation for these preplanned shutdowns and the losses of production, notably of milk, that were experienced.

Although in principle the health benefits may be evaluated, this is difficult for the reasons discussed in Section 14.6. Instead, the most common approach to evaluating the benefits of improvements in water supplies has been the use of contingent valuation. This has been extensively used both in developing countries (e.g. Altaf *et al.* 1997; Briscoe *et al.* 1990) and also to appraise the benefits of improvements in piped systems (Howe and Smith 1994; Carpentier and Vermersch 1997). The hedonic price method has been used in a few studies (e.g. Coeillie *et al.* 1991; North and Griffin 1993).

A very early contingent valuation study of the value of improvements in the quality of water supply was that conducted by the Central Water Planning Unit (CWPU 1978) during the 1976 drought in England. At this time, per capita domestic water consumption was 120 litres/day (compared to about 150–160 litres/day now). The respondents, 75 civil servants, were asked how much they were prepared to pay to avoid restrictions of varying intensities, up to 50% of normal supply, for periods of one month. The crude results were that the respondents were not prepared to pay anything to avoid a reduction of up to 12% per day and above that point, willingness to pay increased linearly at the rate of £1.35/m^3. Budge (1980) carried out a similar explorative study using Thames Water Authority personnel, followed by a small-scale survey of domestic users.

The three major differences between developed and developing countries are firstly that in the former there is an established institutional delivery system as well as a physical delivery system. Secondly, the former are, in relative terms, cash rich whilst the latter, in relative terms, are time rich. Thirdly, in developing countries, much land settlement takes place in the absence of any clear legal entitlement to the use of that land.

Where the issue is one of the value to the beneficiaries of first time supply, the institutional and physical systems cannot be separated, nor can means and value. One question is then whether to provide water kiosks, standpipes or individual house connections, and the second is how this system is to be initially funded and maintained. It is not clear that the two questions can or should be separated and, rather than simply seeking to determine how much people are prepared to pay, the more useful approach is to determine what system the community wants and can sustain (Black 1998).

It was argued (Section 4.2) that in poor communities the rate at which time and energy can be converted into firstly a cash income and then into priced consumption may be lower than the rate at which time and energy can be translated directly into consumption. In turn, estimating willingness to pay will then be a poor method of establishing the value of that consumption, and community-based provision (McPherson and McGarry 1987) will be more efficient. In particular, such systems often involve contributions of labour rather than cash. In this case, the decision is participatory; the only time the economic question of the value of the service then arises is when a government or international body is approached for a grant or loan, and it then is sharpest when part or all of the capital costs are to be subsidised for explicitly redistributive reasons. Conversely, in developed countries, the basis for priced provision is that the rate at which time and energy can be directly turned into consumption is less than the rate at which they can be turned first into income and then into consumption.

In poor urban communities, the problem is compounded by the informal nature of much settlement and the consequent lack of any clear legal title to the occupation of that land. Whilst the individuals typically make equally informal linkups to water and electricity where they can, the lack of a secure title will inhibit both the households and others (e.g. McPhail 1993) from committing investments to the area. A prerequisite to improving the standard of provision of water and sanitation in those areas may then be the creation of a clear legal entitlement to the occupation of those lands.

Case Study 14.1 Preparedness to Pay for Improvements in Water and Sewerage Services

The Office of Water Services (OFWAT) is the price and quality regulator for the water and wastewater industry in England and Wales. In large part, the price increases allowed to the companies is a function of their anticipated needs for investment; in turn, their profitability has been strongly influenced by the companies' success in then delivering that improvement in quality at a lower capital cost than they had predicted (Green 2001b). The price formula agreed at the time of privatisation, $rpi + k - x$, where rpi is inflation, k is the investment requirement and x is the predicted efficiency gain, gives the companies an incentive to increase investment and reduce O&M costs.

In large part, those investment requirements have been required to satisfy the standards of the different European Union directives on water and wastewater that had in turn been agreed by successive UK governments. At the same time, the Environment Agency and its predecessor, the National Rivers Authority, seek investment to reduce the environmental impact of water abstractions and discharges. In addition, there are a number of very powerful environmental NGOs in England and Wales, including the Royal Society for the Protection of Birds which has a membership far larger than that of any political party. Those NGOs also seek increased investment to reduce the environmental impact of the industry. Thus, all of the main players would like to see increases in investment. OFWAT then has the twin task of balancing the interests of the consumer in terms of the trade-off between increases in prices and improvements in service delivery whilst also ensuring that efficient firms in the industry generate sufficient revenue to continue to be commercially viable.

Continued on page 235

__ *Continued from page 234* _____

The initial determinations of the *k* and *x* factors were made by the then Thatcher government on privatisation. The first quinquennial review of prices took place in 1994 and OFWAT commissioned FHRC to carry out a demonstration CVM study to illustrate to the water and wastewater companies the scope of the technique in determining customer requirements.

Three different areas of service were selected: the taste of tapwater, the risk of supply interruptions in the form of restrictions on the use of hosepipes, and the risk of sewage flooding. As an exploratory study, the sample size was limited to 1000 and four water company areas were selected (Green *et al.* 1993) on the basis of (a) the current and future levels of charges, and (b) the existing level of service in different areas (in terms of whether or not there was currently a hosepipe ban in force). Within each water company area, high and low income census enumeration districts (EDs) were selected for sampling. Random samples of addresses within each of the selected EDs were then drawn; a total of 1955 addresses in 85 EDs. Fieldwork was then undertaken by a fieldwork company selected by competitive tender on a specification set out in accordance with FHRC's quality assurance guidelines. A total of 997 interviews were conducted.

For each area of service, a theoretical model was developed to explain preparedness to pay for service improvements which worked from beliefs through attitudes to the behaviours (Fishbein and Ajzen 1975), notably preparedness to pay, that it was desired to predict. Since it was assumed that it is the individual's core beliefs or values that ultimately determine their preferences (Kelly 1955), the interview schedule contained a set of statements intended to tap the individual's core beliefs, measures of that individual's social value orientation (e.g. Stern *et al.* 1999) or environmental value orientation (Green and Tunstall 1991a; Spash 2000). A subset of the statements developed in an earlier study to measure environmental value orientations (Green and Tunstall 1996) were used. Then for each of the three areas of service, a series of questions specific to that service area were used. In the interviews, the order in which the three service areas were introduced was rotated to check for any order or context effects. For each area of service, respondents were asked whether or not they were satisfied with the present standard of service; 21% were satisfied with the then standard of service for sewerage flooding (no property should be flooded more often than twice in 10 years), 74% were satisfied with the taste of tapwater, and 86% with the risk of a hosepipe ban (once in 10 years).

Following a suggestion from Michael Jones-Lee (1993), a double bidding ladder format was used: each respondent being offered the opportunity to work from both starting points. The use of the bidding ladder format was introduced to the respondents as a way of helping them to decide how much they were prepared to pay: 'I am now going to ask you how much you would be prepared to pay. You probably will not have thought about this before and may want some time to think about it. Some people have found it helpful to start by deciding whether or not they would be prepared to pay particular amounts.'

During the pilot studies, the wording of the contingent valuation question was changing from 'willing to pay' to 'prepared to pay' after one respondent remarked that she was willing to pay but could not afford to do so. Having completed both bidding ladders, if they so wished, respondents were asked an open-ended question as to the amount they would be prepared to pay. The usual questions concerning the reasons by which they had made this decision were then asked.

In the final section of the interview schedule, respondents were asked to rate the importance that should be given to improvements in eight areas of service, including

__ *Continued on page 236* __

— Continued from page 235 —

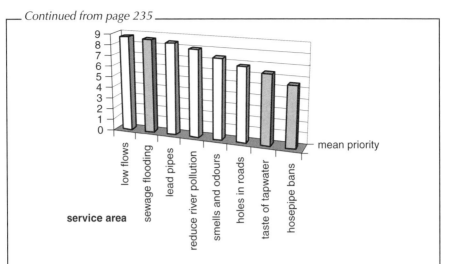

Figure 14.9   *Priority that should be given to improvements in different areas of service*

the three areas for preparedness to pay that had just been asked (Figure 14.9). Immediately afterwards, respondents were reminded of the amounts they had offered for improvements in each of the three areas of service that had been the focus of the study, and the total increase in annual payment they offered. They were then asked if they wanted to change any the amounts that they had offered. The proportions who wish to change the amount that they had originally stated varied between 19% (reduction in the risk of a hosepipe ban and a reduction in the risk of sewage flooding) to 29% in the case of an improvement in the taste of tapwater.

Detailed analyses are given by Green *et al.* (1993), including the results of the tests of construct validity (Carmines and Zeller 1979), but there were marked differences in the proportions of respondents prepared to pay for improvements in each level of service (Table 14.8). Thus, Figure 14.10 illustrates that the proportion of the respondents who would be prepared to pay for improvements in the taste of tapwater falls with the respondent's assessment of the acceptability of the taste of tapwater at present. Figure 14.11 highlights the differences in the importance that

Table 14.8   *Preparedness to pay for improvements in water and sewerage services*

	% prepared to pay	Of those, mean amount prepared to pay (£/year)
Reducing the risk of sewage flooding to the homes most at risk	30	30.34
A noticeable improvement in the taste of tapwater	26	37.50
Reducing the risk of restrictions on the use of water such as hosepipe bans	4	32.34

— Continued on page 237 —

— *Continued from page 236* —

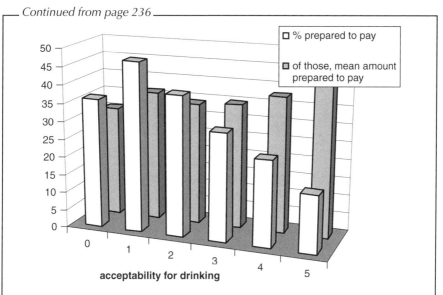

Figure 14.10 *Consumer assessment of the taste of tapwater and the proportion prepared to pay for improvements in the taste*

respondents gave to the different reasons why they were or were not prepared to pay for improvements in each service area. In particular, the importance given to the value to other people of reductions in the risk of flooding from sewers is notable; 30% of the sample were prepared to pay for a reduction in this risk whereas only 12% believed that their home or garden had ever been flooded by rainwater or sewage. It is only possible to speculate whether this 30% are being altruistic, accept sewage flooding as an externality of their own actions, include an option price, or simply find flooding from sewers as morally unacceptable.

There are a number of lessons to be drawn from the study. Firstly, that up to 29% of respondents, when offered the opportunity after considering all three levels of service and having prioritised a total of eight service areas for improvement, changed the amounts that they were prepared to pay shows the importance of setting CVM questions in context. Although neoclassical economic theory assumes that we have defined a complete set of trade-offs between different goods before we make any choice, this is an implausible assumption. In subsequent studies, we asked respondents to prioritise different policy areas for improvement before we asked about preparedness to pay for a single area (Section 21.6). Secondly, there are marked and significant differences between the proportions of respondents prepared to pay (Table 14.8), but those who are prepared to pay do not seem to differentiate between amounts that they are prepared to pay for improvements in each area of service. We should probably place more trust in whether or not people say that they would be prepared to pay than in how much they say they would be prepared to pay.

— *Continued on page 238* —

___ *Continued from page 237* ___

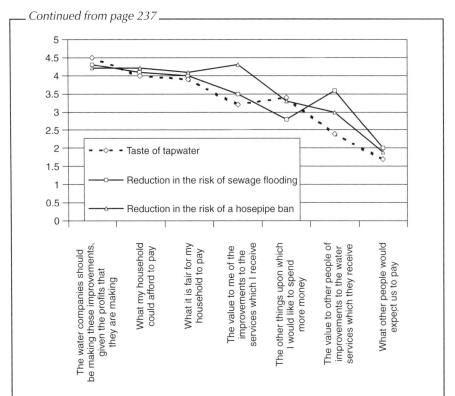

Figure 14.11   *Respondents' reasons for being prepared to pay for improvements*

Thirdly, at the time this study was undertaken, public attitudes towards the companies was markedly unfavourable, many respondents believing that they had already paid for high standards of service but that the companies were simply using that revenue to make excessive profits rather than delivering the standards of service for which respondents had paid. In other studies (e.g. House *et al.* 1994), a similar negative attitude towards the companies has been found either as to their trustworthiness or competence. Such attitudes create problems in contingent valuation studies, not least because it is difficult to ascertain whether those who refuse to pay do so because of their negative attitudes towards the service provider, or mask their refusal to pay by a claim that they will not get what they are paying for. One of the early questions in the study explored in more detail respondents' beliefs and attitudes towards water and its management: in addition to negative beliefs about the companies, on average the respondents also underestimated the problems of making water available although they also held a conservationist view, believing that we can reduce the amount of water we use.

15

Demand Management

The point at which it becomes more efficient to shift from water resource rein-forcement to demand management depends upon the levels of water consumption and of water availability (Chapter 14). The levels of domestic water use show very pronounced variations around the world (Section 14.4.1); for example, from an average of 140 l/c/d in Belgium to a peak of 700 l/c/d in Winnipeg. Once domestic demand has reached the 50 to 100 l/c/d range, then water is an almost pure private good. The needs of drinking, cooking, personal hygiene and sani-tation have been satisfied and water is increasingly being used for 'luxury' uses including garden watering. Once water is a pure private good, then the emphasis switches from meeting needs to managing the demand.

Demand management is taken to cover both interventions which reduce the amount of water used by consumers and also the leakage from the distribution system; in effect, therefore the demand which is being managed is the demand placed upon the environment. Commonly, even ignoring the environmental costs of increasing abstractions or reservoir construction, the costs of demand man-agement have proved to be lower than those of supply reinforcement (National Rivers Authority 1995). When the rate at which building stocks are replaced by new buildings is low (e.g. in England, less than 0.1% of housing is replaced each year (DETR 2001), then any significant gains in water efficiency will require retrofitting existing buildings. The rate of replacement for consumer durables will be higher but to the extent to which poorer households acquire second-hand or low first cost household durables, they will be differentially penalised by attempts to use price to control demand.

In economic terms, there are two different contexts to be considered:

- where demand is outgrowing the available resource; and
- where the available resource is capable of supplying the forecast demand.

In the first case, the primary economic justification for demand management is to defer or eliminate the high capital costs of resource reinforcement, together with the variable costs of putting that additional quantity into supply. The objec-tive is typically, therefore, to stabilise demand at the present level. Actually

Handbook of Water Economics: Principles and Practice. C. Green
© 2003 John Wiley & Sons, Ltd ISBN: 0-471-98571-6

cutting demand below the present level may cause revenue problems because of high fixed costs of supply. In assessing the benefits of deferring resource reinforcement measures such as the construction of reservoirs, increasing abstractions from rivers, conjunctive use schemes, water transfer or increased groundwater abstraction, the environmental costs of those options should also be taken into account. In the case of reservoir construction, there may be some environmental gains and there are often recreational benefits to be had (e.g. Shucksmith 1979) that may offset or outweigh the environmental losses caused by the conversion of the land to the reservoir and also from the change in the water regime downstream (Acreman *et al.* 1999). A reservoir may provide angling (Section 21.2.2) and boating opportunities as well as for informal recreation (Section 21.2.1). In assessing the environmental costs of the necessary increase in abstractions and works, the principles of critical natural capital and constant natural assets (Section 7.1.1) require to be applied.

In the second case, demand management may be justified as a way of reducing the environmental opportunity costs of abstracting water from the environment or to reduce demand to the sustainable yield of the resource. In many parts of the world, most famously the Ogallala aquifer in the United States, the level of a contained aquifer is falling because the rate of abstraction is greater than the rate of replenishment (US Congress, Office of Technology Assessment 1993). Again, abstraction from uncontained aquifers, or from rivers, is resulting in the destruction of wetlands or rivers fed by groundwater (English Nature 1996). There may be functional benefits as well as purely environmental benefits from allowing the recovery of these wetlands and rivers. In addition, there may be significant recreational benefits (Section 21.2).

15.1 Domestic Demand

Unfortunately, but not surprisingly, most work on demand management (e.g. US EPA 1998; California Urban Water Conservation Council 1994) has been carried out in North America where they start from a very high base of consumption and very inefficient water-using equipment (Surendran 2001). The relevance and effectiveness of some of those practices in countries where per capita domestic water consumption is in the order of 120–180 litres per day needs therefore to be considered when thinking of transferring some of the North American practices. The potential for reduction in domestic demand is also considered to be substantial; Gates (1994) argues that, in Canada, a 10% reduction is possible through low or no cost retrofits through to 40% for an aggressive whole house approach and up to 60–75% for those with a strong environmental ethic. Potential reductions will be less in those countries where domestic consumption is already lower.

The three strategies that need to be evaluated when considering demand management both against each other and against resource reinforcement are:

- information campaigns;
- the use of prices;
- retrofitting properties.

15.1.1 Information measures

Calls for voluntary constraint in times of drought are the normal first step and can result in reductions of 25% in demand (Husain 1978; USACE 1995) although Higueras and Lop (2001) report that whilst a public awareness campaign reduced water consumption in Madrid by 22%, consumption subsequently returned to pre-campaign levels. But, individual consumers will not be able to reduce their water consumption unless they are aware of the ways in which it can be done. Continuing publicity, information and advice are necessary parts of any demand management strategy; particularly vigorous campaigns have been mounted in South Africa. A baseline survey including consumer attitudes towards water conservation is likely to be a necessary baseline.

In addition to leaflets and educational packages, a number of water utilities, including Vancouver and East Bay Utility District now have web sites which include hints on how to save water. The United Water Company in New York State distributed kits and videos on garden watering, together with establishing a scheme whereby consumers could call to hear a recorded telephone message advising how much water gardens needed. However, it is not thought to have been very effective. Some utilities have also sponsored demonstration projects, such as xeriscape gardens. If water charges are to be effective in reducing consumption, then the consumer must be able to use the bills as a guide to how effective is their control over water use, particularly if the meters themselves are not installed in positions where the consumer can easily read them on a daily basis. Monthly or quarterly bills are required if this is to happen. The bill might also record whether the user's consumption was rising or falling compared to the same period in previous years. More problematically, the amount of water consumed might be shown in comparison to the average amount consumed by similar consumers.

In Germany, an 'eco-labelling' programme has been introduced; this is a necessary step if consumers are to have the chance to purchase water-efficient appliances and fittings. Commonly, building or plumbing codes are also modified to reduce the maximum allowable usage of water fittings, or, in the case of equipment such as washing machines and dishwashers, the appropriate standards are also modified accordingly.

Some utilities have offered domestic consumers free water audits (Clough and Ridgewell n.d.) and free, or subsidised, repairs of leaks on the consumer's property are also increasingly being offered. Utilities or governments have sponsored water audits of public, commercial or industrial buildings. The experience of energy audits, however, is that they are barely cost-effective, because frequently there is a low take-up of the audit recommendations (Judd 1993).

15.1.2 Prices

The case for metering in a particular case needs careful examination as there are a number of major problems with metering:

- It is expensive.
- In itself, metering does not save any water; it simply sends a signal and provides an incentive to save water: the cost of metering is a transaction cost.
- It assumes that demand is behaviourally controlled (Section 14.5.1).
- It assumes that without metering demand will otherwise rise.
- It is risky.
- The costs are likely to fall heaviest upon low income groups.

Metering is expensive; meters require replacement and renovation of about a seven-year cycle (OFWAT 2000a) if they are to be reasonably accurate. Reading meters, preparing bills, sending out bills and so forth is expensive; in England and Wales, OFWAT (2000a) calculated the additional costs of metering domestic consumers as £29.60 per year as compared to an average bill for water of £112 per year and £236 for water and sewerage combined (OFWAT 2002b). Therefore, whether or not metering is economically justified depends primarily upon the consumption figures, the marginal cost of water, and the reduction in demand expected to occur as a result of metering. A secondary benefit of fitting meters is that their installation helps to detect existing leaks and also since it is now possible to estimate how much water is being taken out of supply, to more accurately estimate losses through leakage.

In general, it will never be efficient to meter everyone because some households cannot reduce demand sufficiently to pay for the costs of installing, maintaining and reading the meter (Figure 15.1). Here, the x-axis is the quantity of water consumed by households, which varies in practice as some function of the number of people in the household, with the vertical lines representing households of different sizes. The y-axis is the reduction in water consumption per day. The different diagonal lines then represent the reductions in water consumption that will actually result from the adoption of metering. Of the two horizontal lines, the lower one is the additional cost of charging by meter over the existing charging system, represented by the reduction in daily water consumption necessary in order to recover those costs. Adding the costs to the households of reducing demand, either by investing in water-efficient appliances, or by the loss of utility from reducing demand, then the upper horizontal line is obtained. In turn, the darker shaded area then represents the households where it is economically efficient to meter once the costs of metering and reducing demand are taken into account. Therefore, two factors are crucial: the equivalent water cost of metering together with the cost of reducing demand, and the effectiveness of metering in inducing a reduction in demand. If the cost of water is high, if the alternative to metering is to construct an expensive new water resource system, then the

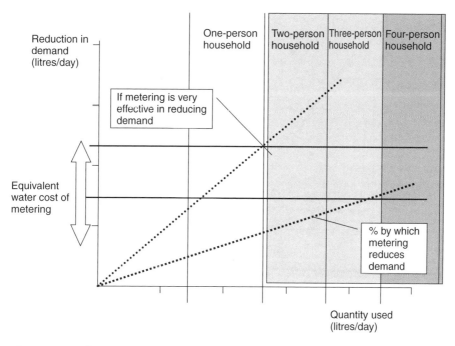

Figure 15.1   *The economics of metering. Source: Green 1998a*

horizontal line will be relatively near to the origin and in turn it will be economically efficient to meter more households. Conversely, if water resources are ample and the only saving resulting from a reduction in demand will be a reduction in treatment and pumping costs, then it will only be efficient to meter the very heavy users. For European consumption figures of 110–170 litres/person/day, it is extremely unlikely that a single person living in an apartment could reduce demand sufficiently to equal the additional cost of metering.

Thus, Yepes (1999) notes that in Guayaquil, it costs US$1 per month connection to collect charges, more than the income generated from each of the households that receive subsidised water. In turn, the utility therefore has no incentive to expand the service to the households that are currently unconnected because it would simply lose more money. But, unfortunately we cannot meter individuals but only the household and in turn this implies that it will be more efficient to meter large households who may tend also to be the poorer households. But metering targeted at high users is likely to be more effective, both because the reduction in demand is more likely to be sufficient to recover the costs of metering and because the price elasticity of demand is higher.

A further implicit assumption in the argument for metering is that otherwise consumption will grow unchecked. So, the rationale for incurring the additional costs of metering hangs on the likelihood that consumption will otherwise rise.

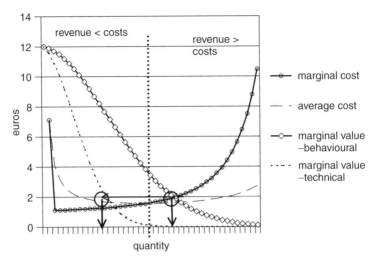

Figure 15.2   *Behavioural and technical price elasticities*

In turn, the possibility that demand may be falling, or even that metering will result in a real fall in demand, makes metering a risky business for the water supplier. Figure 15.2 shows how marginal and average cost vary with demand; if revenue is less than average cost times demand, revenue is below costs. The problem for the water supplier is then two-fold: firstly, to ensure that revenue exceeds costs. If marginal cost pricing is adopted, then this will occur throughout the region where marginal cost exceeds average cost. Secondly, from an economic theory point of view, to set the price so that at that point marginal value and cost both equal the price.

There is then a potential problem (Figure 15.2) if the predicted price elasticity is in error. Moreover, short-term and long-term price elasticities typically differ (Section 14.5.1). In Figure 15.2, the curve labelled as the marginal behavioural value represents the predicted price elasticity of demand on the basis of statistical analysis of the form discussed in Section 14.5.1. The other line, labelled as the marginal technical value, represents the potential to reduce demand as a function of the costs of investing in water-efficient appliances and fittings. Thus, the figure assumes that consumers, even when metered, are behaving inefficiently; this is certainly true for industrial users (Section 15.3).

The risk is that instituting marginal cost pricing or other factors will squeeze out the present inefficiency and demand will jump to the technical marginal value curve. For example, Brooks *et al.* (1990) report that in some cases the simple announcement that metering will be introduced is followed by a fall in demand. Any such fall is not an economic effect since that depends upon the price structure adopted. If demand jumps to the technical marginal value curve but price is set according to the behavioural marginal value curve, then the reduction in revenue will exceed the savings in costs. In turn, prices will then have to be raised to increase revenue to match costs; it will then be difficult to explain to consumers why reductions in demand are accompanied by rising prices. Conversely, to the utility, a charge per property guarantees the revenue stream. In turn, it is sensible when looking at price elasticities to consider the technical value curve as well as any predictions based on behavioural price elasticity.

Equity issues are also an important question; except in so far as there are differences in external uses, household size is perhaps the most important indicator of differences in per capita water consumption. Hence one of the targets of metering will be larger households but these are typically the poorer households. One option is then to provide a 'lifeline' allowance but unless this is specifically attached to large but poor households, it is a crude and inefficient way of targeting the poor. The alternative is forms of means-tested allowances such as have been used in Chile (Yepes 1999). More generally, when considering any system of charging for water and wastewater, it is appropriate to assess the distributional impacts of the proposals (Gomez-Lobo *et al.* n.d.; Komives n.d.; Maxwell Stamp 1998).

In developing countries, a simple alternative to metering is to charge by the diameter of the connecting pipe, an approach developed in South Africa (CSIR n.d.). There charges are fixed according to the size of the pipe and the associated storage tank. The maximum daily consumption of the household cannot then exceed the volume that can flow through the pipe; the practical maximum daily consumption is then influenced by the size of the storage tank.

15.1.3 Retrofitting

Since building and equipment standards and codes are a major determinant of water usage, if demand is to be managed downwards, then these standards must be modified to allow and require the adoption of available best practice for water efficiency. The great advantage of retrofitting the existing stock is that the anticipated reduction in demand necessarily occurs. Whereas metering may have the effect of encouraging consumers to install more efficient fitments, a retrofitting programme ensures that they do. For internal uses, the economic advantage of a metering programme compared to a retrofitting programme is consequently problematic since metering must result in more savings compared to a retrofitting programme in order to pay for the additional cost of a meter on top of the costs of replacing fitments. In addition, some utilities that have metering have gone to institute retrofitting programmes which implies that metering is relatively ineffective at inducing such replacements.

The fittings which are generally targeted for replacement are: toilet cisterns by low flush toilet cisterns; conventional taps by aerated taps; and the adoption of low flow showerheads. Table 14.2 summarised the water usage of a number of water fitments and water using appliances; there remain marked differences in the performance achieved in different countries. Moreover, these examples do not represent the state of the art; Denmark and Singapore require toilets that flush with 4.5 litres and Australia has adopted a dual flush (3/6 litres) toilet (Baynes 2002).

The majority of these retrofitting programmes have started with replacing toilet cisterns (US EPA 1995), as, for example, in the programme in Santa Monica. The retrofitting programme in Phoenix, Arizona has been calculated to have yielded US$88 million for US$15 million in costs (Dziegielewski and Baumann 1992). The Massachusetts Water Resources Authority spent £22 million on a programme which yielded benefits of £89–396 million whilst in New York City, the cost of replacing 1.5 million high volume toilet cisterns with 6-litre cisterns is estimated as £0.6–0.7 million per Ml/d compared to £1.9–2.8 million per Ml/d for resource expansion (Amy Vickers 1996). Again, for the City of Rohnert Park's toilet replacement programme, the benefit–cost ratios of the different programmes varied between 1.7 to 2.7 (John Olaf Nelson Water Resources Management 1998). In England and Wales, devices for reducing the effective flush of an existing cistern have been given away by a number of water companies.

Most of the retrofitting programmes in the USA include low flow shower-heads. For other fitments, self-closing spray taps are considered to offer up to a 50% reduction in water consumption compared to the conventional screw type (National Rivers Authority 1995b). Similarly, compared to a flow rate of 40 l/min for the standard domestic tap, flow regulators can be fitted which limit this to between 6 l/min and 17 l/min (Anon 1997).

These retrofitting programmes have been relatively successful and achieved demand reductions of 6–23% (Amy Vickers 1996) but these have been in the USA where, given the initial high consumption of water, these reductions have been very valuable but have still left per capita domestic water consumption much higher than is found, for example, in Europe. Braver (n.d.) also warns that it is possible that customers who volunteer to participate in retrofitting pro-grammes may have lower than average uses. However, there is experience outside of the USA and Canada, most notably in Mexico City (National Research Council 1995) and a number of small-scale programmes in Germany (Rees *et al.* 1993). In the UK, the National Rivers Authority Demand Management Centre (National Rivers Authority 1995b) compared a range of demand management against some indicative costs for resource reinforcement. The estimates of the costs of resource reinforcements were taken from the lower range of costs for such reinforcement, £0.75 M/Ml/day which generally relates to direct ground or surface water abstraction up to £1.50 M/Ml/day which would include some indirect effluent reuse and reservoir schemes. Compared over a 40-year time horizon at a discount rate of 6%, efficient washing machines, controllers for urinals, leakage control to reduce losses to an average of 6 l/property/hour as compared to the current industry average of 11.9, either conversion of pre-1981 WCs with 7.5 litre flush or with a 9/5 dual flush, were all more efficient than demand expansion. These results were national averages and for the regions with the narrowest margin between available resources and demand (National Rivers Authority 1995b), resource reinforcements might require inter-regional transfer schemes which have costs of more like £2–5 M/ML/day (Cryer 1995).

Different strategies to encourage and promote retrofitting have been tried ranging from cutting water bills if consumers agree to adopt such fittings, subsidising the purchase of such fittings, giving them away or actually installing them. In addition, the utility may carry out free water audits of properties and repair leakages. Since the new equipment will not last forever, continuing maintenance is likely to be necessary. In some cases, the costs of retrofitting programmes have been recovered by special charges on developers (Braver n.d.).

Where, as is generally the case, a single meter serves an entire apartment building, there is scope for a market solution in the form of a contracted water service company as is to be found both in France and the USA (Judd 1993). The building owner contracts such a firm on a fee for service basis or a shared savings basis; the water service company and the building owner share the savings made on the existing water bill. The water service company typically then undertakes some retrofitting as well as repair and maintenance. Judd reports that two US water service companies report savings ranging up to 70% with one company reporting an average saving of 29%.

A number of cities have gone on to develop long-term water management plans in which demand management plays a key role; for example, Seattle (Seattle Public Utilities 1998) and Melbourne (Government of Victoria 2001). Melbourne's plan includes the expectation of a 50% take-up of low flow showerheads, saving 12 000 ML/year; a reduction in garden watering from every day to twice a week during dry periods (8000 ML/Year); a 5% take-up of the use of greywater for toilet flushing and garden watering (6000 ML at an equivalent cost of A$ 1700/ML); and a 10% take-up of rainwater tanks to provide water for garden watering, car washing and toilet flushing (12 000 ML at A$2100/ML).

15.2 Reuse, Recycling and Rainwater Capture

The emphasis in the domestic sector has been upon increasing the efficiency with which water is used; using less water to achieve the same ends: reuse rather than recycling. However, as the price of water and wastewater collection and treatment increase, then economics of recycling will improve.

Depending upon the country, two different directions have been taken. In North America, where garden watering consumes a substantial proportion of domestic water demand, the emphasis has been upon the reuse of greywater for garden watering. Thus, in California the use of greywater for subsoil drip irrigation via a 50–100 gallon surge tank or directly through a minileach field has been legalised. However, the sodium salts from soap and detergents can build up and destroy soil structure, especially in clay (Grant *et al.* 1996). In those countries where external uses constitute a lower proportion of domestic water use, attention has been on recycling greywater for use in toilet flushing. For example, a condition of the construction of the Oasis Holiday Village in Kent, England was that greywater should be collected and treated for use in toilet flushing (Guy and Martin 1996). Hills (1995) reports that in Tokyo in buildings over eight storeys water must be collected for recycling, and Tokyo also reuses a significant proportion of wastewater for industrial purposes (Asano *et al.* 1996; Tokyo Metropolitan Government n.d.). Studies of greywater reuse for toilet flushing (Surendran 2001) have not yet shown these to be viable for the individual domestic consumer. The advantage of greywater recycling is that the water may then be returned via a wastewater treatment facility to the water environment for further abstraction and use whereas greywater used for garden watering is essentially lost through evaporespiration.

Reuse of wastewater after treatment for irrigating parks and similar purposes is also increasingly commonplace (e.g. Sala and Millet 1997), whilst Windhoek has pioneered the reuse of wastewater for direct potable use (van der Merwe 1999). Booker *et al.* (2000) compared costs of a conventional water/wastewater system to three alternatives – including local treatment plants for grey- and blackwater for reuse in dwellings. There were no significant differences in costs but the benefits of reuse included a 45% reduction in phosphorus and 10% in total nitrogen to the environment.

A third way of reducing potable water consumption is rainwater capture by collection from roof and other hard surfaces (Texas Water Development Board 1997). In Germany, this is increasingly widespread (Hermann 2002). A second advantage of these techniques is that such a form of source control (Section 16.2) thereby reduces the problems caused by surface water runoff. In some rural areas, consumers traditionally had no choice but to be self-reliant in terms of water collection, treatment and wastewater disposal. The great advantage to consumers is the availability of land so that rainwater collection and cistern storage together with wastewater treatment in lagoons or by reedbeds can be undertaken (UNEP 2000), which will make the water available for reuse. Whilst systems to recycle a significant proportion of the influent water have been tried in urban areas, the costs and land requirements are high.

15.3 Industrial Demand

It is almost invariably found in waste minimisation studies (e.g. Porter and van der Linde 1995; Johnston 1994) that industrial users should cut water use by 15–25% if they are to maximise profitability, where those waste minimisation studies include only actions with a payback time of less than two years. The three options available are: reduce demand, reuse water and recycle water. The possible potential for water recycling in industry and the resulting reduction in the intake of water was reported by Tate (1989) as varying between 44% for beet sugar refining to 90% for organic chemicals. Similarly, van der Merwe (1999) reports on a brewery that requires 4 litres of water per litre of beer produced as compared to an average of 5–7 litres in Europe. The ETBPP has published a whole range of guidance on means of improving water efficiency in different areas of industry, coupled with data to tonne per tonne consumption figures (e.g. ETBPP 1997).

In the Aire and Calder project in England, a study of 11 companies identified savings in the use of inputs such as water, energy and raw materials (Johnston 1994). Water savings of £512 000 and effluent savings of £462 000 a year, with a three-fold reduction of the amount of water discharged to the sewers, were achieved out of total savings of £3 350 000 per annum. Seventy per cent of these savings had a payback period of less than one year and only 10% a payback period of more than two years. Whilst there may be an element of self-selection by the companies choosing to take part in waste minimisation studies, the implication is that water prices fail to induce companies to perform efficiently. Rees *et al.* (1993) argued that this might be because water costs are generally so low a proportion of total manufacturing costs that companies do not consider them. The problem with that argument is that it implies that companies will seldom maximise their profits since there will usually be one input whose total cost is too small for the company to consider it. The potential benefits of demand management in industry are so large because it is potentially possible to save money four times: a reduction in metered water use, a reduction in the energy required for heating or cooling, a reduction in the charges for wastewater treatment, and through the recovery of materials from the wastewater. Nevertheless, the evidence is persuasive that prices are ineffective in optimising consumption.

The different waste minimisation studies have shown major differences between companies in the same industrial sector in the efficiency of use with which they use water (e.g. ETBPP 1997, 1998a, 1998b, 1998c, 1999a, 1999b, 2000a, 2000b). Similar differences exist between countries; Table 15.1 gives figures for the proportion of water that is reused in different countries. The high figures for water reuse for Shanxi Province in China reflect the critical water problem in that Province (Yang 2001).

Table 15.1 *Proportion of water that is reused (%)*

	USA 1983	Canada 1991– sample survey	China 1996
Metal mining	77	78	
All manufacturing industries	70	48	83
Paper and allied products	74	48	
Chemicals and allied products	65	67	76
Petroleum and coal products	87		
Primary metal industries	60	0	72

Source: Gleick 1993; Tate and Scharf 1995; World Bank 1997.

15.4 Leakage Reduction

It is possible to calculate the economic rate of leakage but one of the main reasons for seeking to control leakage is often to promote the message that water should be conserved and hence to promote demand management by the consumer. Unless the water utility is seen to be pursuing a rigorous programme of leakage control, any message to the consumers to control their demand is likely to be undermined. A series of distinctions need to be drawn: 'unaccounted for water' is the difference between the amount of water put into the supply and the amount of water received by the consumers. A 'leak' involves the escape of water from a joint or from a crack in a pipe. However, the structural integrity of the pipe continues and the loss of water through that particular leak is small relative to the flow along the pipe. 'Leakage' is usually taken to refer to losses in the distribution system between the treatment works and the consumer and 'wastage' to refer to losses within the consumer's property. When the structural integrity of the pipe is lost and all or most of the water is lost through the breakage point, a 'burst' has occurred. The effects and consequences of 30% of the water put into supply being lost through leakage and through bursts can be quite different, as can the costs of reducing that loss. Unaccounted for water then also includes losses through leakage or theft, measurement error and also water used for fire fighting. Yepes (1995) notes that 50–65% of unaccounted for water is actually the result of meter errors or straight theft; and in a sample of zonal meters (covering 200 to 500 properties), only two-thirds had a systematic error of less than 10% (Wilson *et al.* 1993).

The amount of unaccounted for water varies markedly between countries and cities and there are controversies about how to measure leakage (Lambert 2002). For example, utilities serving low-density areas where the ratio of the length of supply mains to consumer is high will be penalised by a measure of leakage in terms of loss per consumer. The 4% figure for Singapore is generally considered to be the world's lowest whilst figures for Spain of 24–34%, France of 30%, the Czech Republic of 20–30%, Croatia of 30–60% and Albania of up to 75% are given in Lallana *et al.* (2001). The rate for Cairo of more than 60% (Coville (1996) and Bardarska (2002)) gives figures of 70% for large towns in Bulgaria, 60% for Estonia, 39% for Romania and 25% for Latvia. In 1993, in Malta, a water-critical island heavily dependent upon desalination for water supplies, unaccounted for water was estimated to be 65% of the quantity put into supply (Water Services Corporation 1994). Of this, leakage and theft was considered to take 29% whilst under-recording by water meters was found to account for 20% of the calculated difference between the water put into supply and that recorded as being delivered.

The total percentage of water lost is a function of the number and size of individual leaks. So, whilst the total costs of leakage reduction can be balanced against the costs of supply reinforcements, or reductions in service to the consumer, the total costs of leakage reduction depend upon how leaks occur. A total loss of 30% in a year through leakage might, for example, be the result of millions of small leaks through joints or a few major leaks. Similarly, different parts of the network are likely to have different leakage rates and associated loss figures; therefore, it may be efficient to concentrate upon leakage reduction in some areas of the network, and a uniform leakage rate across the entire network may be inefficient. A 'burst', where the pipe completely fails, is likely to justify a rapid repair where a major pipe is involved since in addition to the loss of water, there will be a loss of service, as well as the costs of flooding and other disruption: these are likely to massively outweigh the costs of decreasing the response time. Even here, there is the possibility of identifying the optimum response time as a function of the costs of a burst so that the response time is designed to vary as a function of the size and criticality of the pipe.

Consequently, one decision is which leaks is it efficient to reduce and by what means; another is how quickly should the response time be to identify major bursts; taken together, this will determine what is the optimum leakage rate. Where leakage rates tend to increase as some function of the age and material of the pipe, soil type and location (UKWIR 2001), the same concerns can be used to guide the decision as when to replace or rehabilitate a pipeline; or whether preventative maintenance is more efficient than waiting for a major leak to occur. Such decisions are analysed in relation to failures in sewers in Section 16.1.3. Operationally, since the loss rate is partly a function of the pressure in the network, varying as a function of pressure to the power 1.5 (Lambert 2002), the leakage rate is one consideration which should be taken into account in deciding what pressure to maintain in the network. Another decision is what is the leakage rate which should be sought for new pipelines, assuming that higher capital costs are counterbalanced by lower losses.

An economic analysis will focus upon the comparison of alternative programmes of leakage control. The same economic approach to leakage control can be adopted as for other demand management strategies: does the value of the water saved as a result of the anticipated reductions in leakage, together with the economic losses resulting from any leak, exceed the cost of the proposed leakage control? The economic losses from a burst of a mains can include flooding, the disruption of traffic, damage to other services and distribution to commerce and industry (Section 16.1.3), in addition to the value of the water lost. Moreover, the costs of an emergency repair are usually greater than the cost of precautionary maintenance or rehabilitation. Since precautionary maintenance and rehabilitation can also often be undertaken by 'no-dig' techniques, the costs of traffic disruption caused by open cut working (Read and Vickridge 1990) will also be lower. Therefore, the benefits of a leakage detection and response programme are:

$$(Q_w - Q_p)V_w + (P_w - P_p)L_b$$

where:

Q_w is the loss of water now;
Q_p is the loss of water with the programme;

V_w is the resource and environmental cost of the water;
P_w is the probability of a burst now;
P_p is the probability of a burst with the programme;
L_b is the cost of a burst.

This equation can, in principle, be used to determine how much it is worth spending on a leakage control strategy. The practical difficulties are in assessing the relative probabilities of bursts and the likely losses under the different alternative programmes. However the issue is addressed, a range of leakage control strategies should be compared including:

- responding only to complaints from the public, other utilities or highway authorities thus effectively responding largely to bursts;
- reducing pressure in parts of the distribution system;
- district or local gauging of the distribution network to detect flow anomalies (in New York City, some sewers have also been gauged to detect such unexpected flows which then trigger searches for leaks);
- leakage detection either on some predetermined cycle or as part of other activities; and preventative maintenance, rehabilitation or renewal of parts of the distribution system so as to reduce the probability of a leak occurring. This strategy may be based upon a risk analysis which identifies those parts of the system where the expected gains from such a strategy will result.

Such an approach is likely to be targeted at the critical parts of the system where failure would cause either major disruption or temporary loss of supply. For example, a burst in a 42-inch main in Leeds in 1985 left some 140 000 consumers experiencing water restrictions for several days (Jeffrey *et al.* 1986) Mains rehabilitation strategies may result in other benefits which also need to be included in the assessment of the benefits of this strategy. These include a reduction in the discoloration of water caused by corrosion, bacteriological problems, and nodular deposits on cast iron pipes restricting flow and pressure.

15.5 Charges for Abstraction

Neoclassical economic theory assumes that a perfectly competitive market will determine how a good is allocated between alternative users, and also that the market will both automatically determine the quantity provided and the price charged for the good. Thus, it provides very little help in determining how a fixed quantity of water should be allocated between competing uses when there are externalities associated with each. Rogers *et al.* (1998) sought to address this question. Figure 15.3 is a redrawing of part of Rogers *et al.*'s Figure 1 as applied to two alternative uses of some given quantity of water; the order of the elements has been changed for clarity of exposition. What they describe as 'environmental

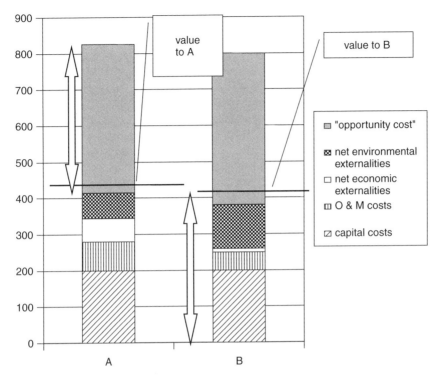

Figure 15.3 *Pricing water: the Rogers methodology. Note: 'opportunity cost' follows Rogers' terminology rather than conventional usage in economics*

externalities' can be expanded to include the effects of water use on all of the other objectives brought to the choice.

However, Rogers *et al.* then wish to add what they describe as 'the opportunity cost of water' in alternative uses, which they describe as the 'value' of the water in those alternative uses, to these costs in order to determine the appropriate price for each use. The use of the term 'opportunity cost' to describe this value in another use differs from standard economic usage which restricts the term to inputs to a particular activity. It would be more appropriate to call this value of water in an alternative use, its 'opportunity value'. This term does not appear in conventional economic theory because the perfectly competitive market is presumed to ensure that each product is allocated to the highest value use.

Nor is it quite clear what Rogers *et al.* mean by value. In Figure 15.3, it has been assumed that the value of the available quantity of water for use A is 420 and for use B it is 410: thus, that these are the maximum prices at which each user would be prepared to buy the water if it were to be offered. This is the standard economic use of the term 'value'. If the value to B of the water (410)

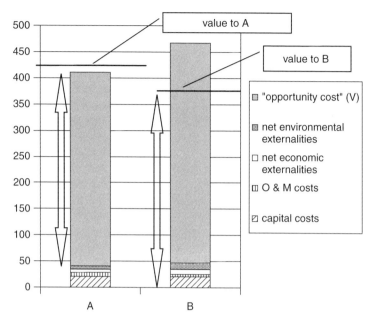

Figure 15.4   *Pricing water: values*

is then added to the other costs for use A, the resulting price that the Rogers' model would apply exceeds the value to A of that water. The same is also true for B. However, there is an economic gain from putting that water to use B where the difference between the itemised costs and the value of water in that use is 30. So, under the Rogers' model, for the available water to be allocated to any use, it is necessary that the value of the water in each use is high relative to all of the costs; Figure 15.4 illustrates such a case where the value to use A of the available water would exceed a price that includes the value to B of that same water.

   Such a massive difference between the costs, including the externalities, and the benefits is unlikely and will only exist where there is no real allocation problem, when the basin is still 'open' (Seckler 1996). Moreover, economic theory defines the optimal level as being that where marginal cost and marginal value are equated: it is at this point of equivalence where the price should be set. Up to that point, we want to maximise the difference between benefits and costs. So, it is more usual to consider not just how a single unit quantity of water should be allocated but how much water in total should be made available. In particular, it is usual and generally reasonable to assume that as the quantity of water available for some use increases, its incremental value in that use falls. Equally, it is also assumed that the incremental cost of supplying an additional unit quantity increases as the total quantity supplied increases.

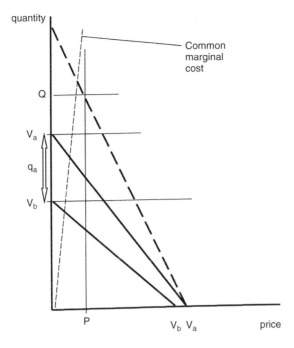

Figure 15.5 *Net marginal value of water*

The standard economic analysis assumes that the marginal cost of supply is identical for all possible uses and ignores externalities. However, the basic question that Rogers *et al.* (1998) sought to address was precisely that of how to allocate a fixed quantity of water when the marginal costs of supplying different uses and the externalities associated with each use differ. In these circumstances, even just considering two possible uses, the conventional 'scissors' diagram becomes essentially unusable; fortunately, it is easy to simplify it.

If, in the standard scissors diagram (Figure 15.5), the marginal costs are subtracted from marginal value, then the new line cuts the y- and x-axes at points which are the optimum combination of quantity and price. Similarly, in the more complex case of charging for water, we can also net out externalities as well as the marginal costs of the two uses, to give the net value of each use. However, it can be helpful to net out only the differences between the potential uses in terms of externalities and marginal costs, maintaining a marginal cost curve that covers the common costs.

In this diagram, the two lines $v_A - v_A$ and $v_B - v_B$ represent the net value curves for the two uses. Because the constraint on allocation is the quantity available rather than the common cost of provision, the allocation strategy is determined by the point where the demand curve cuts the quantity curve. Hence, we should charge price P in order to fully allocate the quantity Q of water available. To allocate this water between the two uses, q_A should clearly be allocated to use A since this is the amount for which use A has a net value greater than its net value to use B. The remainder, $Q - q_A$ should then be allocated between uses A and B in accordance with the ratio of net values of the two uses at Q. If the cost of provision is the dominant constraint, so that it is not efficient to allocate all of the water available, then the procedure is similar but the prices and quantities are determined by the point where the common marginal cost curve cuts the demand curve.

Like a lot of economic analyses, this appears more helpful than it actually is; given n potential uses, we need to know the marginal costs of supply, the externalities and marginal values for each and to be able to do so accurately. In reality, we are unlikely to be able to determine all of these precisely and, in particular, to be able to put a money value on some of the externalities (Chapter 21) nor, importantly, to be able to precisely assess the differences in externalities in different uses. In this case, it will not be possible to either set the correct price or to determine what the best allocation of water between the uses should be. If we recognise that we do not and cannot have such precise knowledge, the question becomes: what should we do?

An alternative is to auction fixed-term entitlements to abstraction. In this case, because the curves shown in Figure 15.5 are net benefit curves rather than demand curves, the users will bid more than the amounts implied in the diagram. The problem that remains is to determine by how much the bids should be corrected – the highest bids should not be simply accepted since the difference between these bids and the next highest bids may not be sufficient to take account of the differences in externalities and marginal costs. Therefore, we need to set some charges that reflect the relative magnitude of externalities without being able to be precise as to what these charges should be.

The approach adopted in Germany (Imhoff 1992) of a ratcheting system of charges for wastewater may be the most sensible strategy to adopt. This recognises the capital-intense nature of investment in water and hence the need to set price signals well in advance. At the same time, since the efficiency or 'optimum' level of pollution is unknown and probably unknowable, the charge can be adjusted upwards or downwards depending on the results. Moreover, as was argued in Section 2.1.2.2, in capital-intensive industry, by the time the investments have been made to achieve what was the optimum level, both the marginal costs and marginal values are likely to have changed so that the optimum has also changed. In short, optimality is probably a moving target which we can never catch. Secondly, Andersen (1994) has ascribed the success of the wastewater charging systems in the Netherlands and France to the institutional structure: recycling the monies raised in the form of soft loans and grants. So, it seems to matter less what are the prices than how the decisions are made, coupled to the hypothecation of the revenue.

There is a further question of whether such pricing will actually have any incentive effect. Given a monopoly supplier of water, if that supplier can pass the cost directly on to the consumer, there is no incentive for the supplier to reduce the demand for water either directly through cutting leakage or indirectly by promoting demand management by the consumers. For there to be any effect, then the consumer must be both metered and able to take action. Therefore, the logic is that if such a pricing system is introduced then its purpose should be to raise funds for investment in demand management (Green 1998b).

16

Sanitation

It is necessary to differentiate between faecal waste and other streams of wastewater. It is also necessary to distinguish between the problems of removing waste streams and the treatment of that waste once removed. Removal typically enables the producer to externalise the costs of that waste by depositing that waste on other people or in the environment. For faecal waste, the purpose of sanitation is to reduce the risk of faecal contamination of potable water, and disease transmission through other routes (Figure 14.7). In rural areas, this is the primary if not the only problem as far as domestic sanitation is concerned. In urban areas, sanitation is necessary in order to dispose of the other streams of wastewater left over after cooking, washing and other uses. In urban areas, the quantity of water that can be used for these purposes is effectively constrained by the ability to dispose of the wastewater produced, along with the resource costs, either monetary or energy, of disposing of that water. With wastewater, as with all water management, gravity is the ideal way of moving water.

In principle, therefore, it is useful to differentiate between the water used to move faecal waste, 'blackwater', and the other waste streams, 'greywater' or sullage. The amounts of human waste produced are relatively trivial: some 400–500 litres of urine and 50–100 kg (wet weight) of faeces per person per year (Esrey *et al.* 1998). In turn, the safe collection and disposal of this material is in principle relatively straightforward (Grant *et al.* 1996), the use of water to flush away and transport this material significantly increasing the problems. The urine stream contains reasonable amounts (Pickford 1995) of nitrogen (8.5 gm/day and of phosphorus (2 gm/day) which are either potentially recoverable or a problem to treat whilst the solids are only useful as a soil conditioner. The various disease vectors are predominantly concentrated in the faecal material although some specific vectors are transmitted via the urine. Hence, in principle, it can also be useful to differentiate between the urine and faecal waste as well as from sullage water. The fourth stream is then surface water runoff which generally is by far the largest in quantity; and in the 'first flush' contains significant polluting loads in the form of animal waste, organic material (e.g. leaves) and deposited material from vehicles. Industrial wastes are then to be distinguished from these other waste streams because of the wider variety of pollutants they

Handbook of Water Economics: Principles and Practice.   C. Green
© 2003 John Wiley & Sons, Ltd   ISBN: 0-471-98571-6

contain (Gleick 1993). In principle, these four streams may be separated although the commonest notional separation is between foul and surface water systems. Such separated systems have perhaps been a better idea in theory than in practice, with high levels of misconnections being reported. In Sacramento, 50% of the water discharged from notional surface water sewers was in fact foul sewage (US EPA 2000): this level of misconnection is not uncommon in developed countries, with similar rates being reported in London. A further problem in developing countries is that surface water sewers are often also treated as convenient ways of disposing solid waste, and missing manhole covers pose a significant safety hazard.

In rural areas, the baseline option is typically defecation in the fields whilst wastewater is simply thrown out the door. There are a variety of options for the collection and disposal of human waste (Pickford 1995; Reed 1995). In urban areas, some sort of underground tank that leaks to groundwater, overflows on occasion, and needs to be emptied of accumulated solids is the common baseline option. Here, piped systems are necessary although the conventional large bore piped system is but one option (Cotton *et al.* 1995). Some of those systems are also based upon community involvement, such as the condominial system (Otis and Mara 1985; Wilson 1995) and that adopted in the Orangi study (Hasan 1990).

16.1 Economic Evaluation

The two main options are to evaluate the benefits in terms of the reduced costs to the community or to undertake a contingent valuation study to determine how much the community is prepared to pay for an improved system. There are problems with implementing both approaches: the former seeking to build up a model of what a hypothetical consumer who is fully informed and takes account of all externalities would be prepared to pay.

16.1.1 The benefits of first time sewerage

Firstly, in urban areas, the costs of the existing system of disposal will be avoided: emptying the tanks can be expensive. Foley *et al.* (n.d.) cite a figure of about US$9/household/year for tank emptying as compared to annual maintenance costs of US$1.20 for a community-based sewer system in Malang, Indonesia. Secondly, there will be expected health benefits. The assessment of the health benefits of sanitation are complex; it is improvements in hygiene behaviours that result in the improvements whilst adequate water supplies and means of disposing of faecal material are necessary but not sufficient preconditions for improvements in hygiene to be possible (e.g. Cairncross and Kochar 1994; Esrey *et al.* 1990). Thirdly, the leaking tanks will contaminate groundwater and hence where groundwater is used for drinking purposes, there is a second-order health effect.

One of the consequences of first- and second-order health effects is that those affected will be able to translate time and energy less effectively into income and consumption and, as a result, will experience lower levels of both than they would if a sewerage system were to be provided. One option for evaluating the second-order health benefits is to use the cost of providing an equivalent quantity of safe water by other means but this is likely to provide only an upper bound to these benefits.

Fourthly, piped collection systems for sullage water typically allow for increased water use and involve lower costs in using water. For example: 'Thank God I have a water connection in the home. Nevertheless, I prefer to wash in the canal so as not to dirty my house, since the septic tank we have is small. Therefore, I don't want it overflowing at short intervals' (El Katsha *et al.* 1989). Overall, it is difficult to assess all of these benefits in a reliable way.

The alternative approach is to undertake a contingent valuation study to determine how much the community is prepared to pay for an improved sanitation system and the nature of the particular system that they want (e.g. Altaf and Hughes 1994; Lauria *et al.* 1999). This is subject to the same problems described in Section 4.3. Moreover, part of the rationale for providing sanitation is that ill-health is a contributing cause to poverty, by reducing the potential effectiveness of translating time into income, as well as an outcome of poverty. Hence, potentially the provision of sanitation may result in an increase in income rather than, as the preparedness to pay format implies, resulting in a reduction in real income. Secondly, there is a problem in establishing the informed consumer: the rationale for hygiene programmes is that the connection between clean water, sanitation and health is not a self-evident truth, nor are recommended hygiene practices necessarily consistent with cultural traditions (Water and Sanitation Program n.d.). Hence, households may underestimate the true benefits of sanitation for their community and preparedness to pay will understate the perceived value to those households. Thirdly, piped sanitation in particular involves externalities: it is usually possible to arrange that when tanks overflow, they do not overflow into the household's home but into the street or into other people's homes. Similarly, the problem with diseases is that they may then be transmitted to the rest of community. This is even more true of piped systems where overflows are shifted either to watercourses or to areas downhill of the households contributing the load. Fourthly, piped sewerage is perhaps the archetypal collective good and there is an apparent contradiction between asking individual households how much each is prepared to pay for a system where it requires collective agreement and action to provide it. This is even more true with the shift to condominial systems (Otis and Mara 1985), and other low-cost systems (e.g. Pickford 1995), some of which also require households to contribute labour to the construction of the system (Watson 1995).

These points suggest that we reframe the question or rather questions. The two questions that are of concern are: is it the most desirable means of using available resources? And is it sustainable? There may be other problems that to the affected community are more pressing and to which any available resources, by whomsoever they are made available, the community would wish to allocate those resources. It does not matter whether those resources are contributed by the affected community or by a wider community, they should still be put to the highest use for the affected community. Secondly, the pragmatic approach is that inadequate O&M causes many water projects to fail in the medium- to long-term and hence a commitment to fund or undertake adequate levels of O&M is a prerequisite for a project to be sustainable. Therefore, a commitment by the affected community to resource O&M requirements is essential since the community is the most reliable source of such resources.

If then the community is prepared to commit sufficient resources, including money resources, to a viable system then there is no further economic question to answer. The only times when the economic question bites is when they cannot contribute at present sufficient resources to support a project and the issue is then one as to whether a wider community should contribute towards the cost of the project. This continues to be a difficult question to answer and one that is not measured by preparedness to pay.

16.1.2 Improvements in service

Generally, it is appropriate to analyse the choice in terms of a reduction in the probability of different forms of failure, including flooding, blockage or collapse (Figure 16.1). Simple look-up tables to enable the evaluation of the reduction of flooding and road closures are given in Green *et al.* (1989a).

16.1.3 Maintenance issues

Although some Roman sewers are still functioning after nearly 2000 years, sewers are prone to failure, structural failure resulting in collapse or, in the case of pressurised systems, to bursting. In addition, the sewer network comprises the greater part of the assets of water and wastewater systems – for England and Wales, the sewer network comprises 70% of the total value of the assets (OFWAT 2002a). Consequently, a critical issue for wastewater management utilities is: what is the most efficient maintenance regime to adopt?

The baseline option is to do no routine maintenance but simply to replace sewer lengths as and when they fail. But, failure will result in costs, possibly including disruption to other utilities, flooding and disruption of traffic, including access to adjacent properties. Undertaking works on sewers also causes disruption, notably to traffic (Read and Vickridge 1990) and operating on a replace on failure basis precludes the adoption of 'no-dig' technologies which would reduce that disruption.

Alternative do-something options then include renovation or rehabilitation using 'no-dig' technologies (e.g. Read and Vickridge 1990) or replacement using

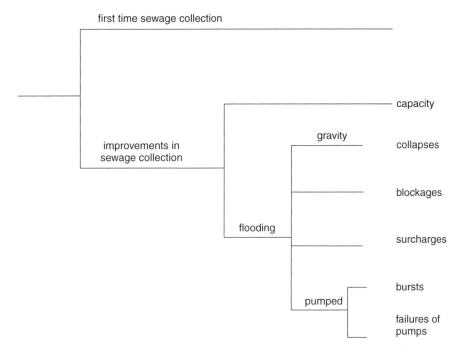

Figure 16.1   *Improvements in sewerage service*

open-cut techniques. The purpose of these 'do-something' options is to reduce the probability of collapse. The problem therefore is to determine whether the discounted present value of $P_1(F + R_1) - P_2(F + R_2)$ is less than $C_2 + D_2$ where:

P_1 is the annual probability of failure by the sewer now;

F is the costs of disruption and damages associated with the failure of the existing sewer – assuming that these costs are dependent upon the location of the failure rather than the construction of the sewer;

R_1 is the cost of repairing the existing sewer on failure including the disruption costs associated with these works;

P_2 is the annual probability of failure by the sewer when renovated, rehabilitated or replaced;

R_2 is the cost of repairing the renovated, rehabilitated or renewed sewer;

C_2 is the cost of renovating, rehabilitating or renewing the sewer;

D_2 is the cost of disruption associated with renovating, rehabilitating or renewing the sewer.

Table 16.1 *Structural performance grades and the estimated probability of sewer collapse*

Structural performance grade	1	2	3	4	5
Probability of collapse/manhole length/year (P_I)	5×10^{-5}	2×10^4	7×10^{-4}	3×10^{-3}	1×10^{-2}

Source: Green *et al*. 1989a.

Table 16.1 gives some indicative failure probabilities for sewers of different assessed conditions in England and Wales. However, in any given year P_I, the probability that the sewer will fail in that year depends upon what has happened before: given a long enough time horizon, the sewer will have already failed and have been replaced once. Hence, the probability of failure in a given year needs to take into account the probability that it has already failed and been replaced.

The probability that in year n, a sewer has collapsed and been replaced is:

$$(1 - (1 - P_i)^{n-1})$$

The probability of collapse in nth year is:

$$(1 - (1 - P_I)^{n-1})P_2 + (1 - P_1)^{n-1}P_1$$

This equation can be simplified to:

$$P_2 + (1 - P_1)^{n-1}(P_1 - P_2)$$

This formula is easily applied in a spreadsheet.

The disruption costs associated with failure, repair or other works include the costs of traffic disruption and damage to other utility systems. The disruption to business will typically be only a financial cost rather than an economic cost since the loss of business will simply be displaced to other areas and other firms. However, if the utility has a legal liability for these costs, then it will wish to include them when evaluating alternative maintenance strategies. Thus, the largest component of the disruption costs is generally traffic disruption. These costs of traffic disruption can be readily estimated using conventional traffic models and approximate values calculated per hour of disruption in different types of roads in the network (Green *et al*. 1989a). The expected costs of flooding can also be calculated relatively simply.

This same general procedure can also be applied to the evaluation of alternative maintenance strategies for water mains, although here it is necessary to include the cost of loss of service. It is also applicable to other elements in water management such as pumping stations. Where failure probabilities are expected to change over time, applying the approach becomes more problematic. Such changes should be expected when the engineering life of the component is relatively short or where conditions are changing.

16.2 Surface Water Runoff

The first effect of urbanisation is typically to increase both the quantity and the speed of runoff. The second effect is to change the pattern of pollution loads over time on the receiving waters (Beck 1996). The benefits of providing surface water drainage through either separate or combined sewerage systems are reducing local flooding, and perhaps also enhancing slope stability; the potential costs are increasing the flood risk downstream and the impacts on receiving waters. It will usually be the case that only a relatively low design standard of protection against flooding can be justified. For surface water drainage, commonly the effect is to reduce the extent of all flooding, 'above design standard' benefits forming a significant proportion of total benefits (Chapter 18).

Increasingly, attention is being given to source control approaches to managing surface water runoff (Maskell and Sheriff 1992; Sydney Water Board n.d.). There are two main forms of source control: those that reduce or delay the amount of runoff that will eventually be released to the watercourse; and those that reuse some of the rainfall for potable water purposes. The former may affect both the runoff from ground surfaces and from roofs; the latter rely upon rainwater harvesting from the roof. The benefits of the former are then restricted to the reduction of local flooding and the impacts on watercourses, and any resulting downstream flooding; when rainwater is harvested from roofs, a second potential benefit is given by the potential value of the water harvested (Section 15.2). These latter benefits will obviously only arise when water for potable use is scarce. The major cost disadvantage of source control is that it is spatially extensive so that more land is required for development than might otherwise be the case. In turn, this tends to make source control most viable when development takes place at the very low densities characteristic of North America (Center for Watershed Protection 1996) or where the harvested rainwater is of high value (Asano *et al.* 1996).

16.3 The Reuse of Wastewater

All wastewater is reused in one way or another; a widely cited figure is that the water drunk in London has already been through six pairs of kidneys. In turn, there are eight possible options for the reuse of wastewater:

- environment (quantity and quality);
- groundwater recharge;
- golf courses (Sala and Millet 1997);
- agricultural irrigation (Shevah 2000);
- fish farms (Rose 1999);
- industrial water (Asano *et al.* 1996);

- potable water (van der Merwe 1999);
- completely closed systems.

The last three systems were discussed earlier (Section 15.2). The standard of treatment varies according to the form of reuse intended; in general, there is a trade-off in treatment between the spatially extensive forms of treatment, reed beds (Cooper *et al.* 1996) and waste stabilisation ponds (WHO 1987), and the spatially and energy intensive forms of conventional treatment. Thus, Rose (1999) quotes a land requirement of $0.5-1\,m^2$/person equivalent for conventional treatment versus $5-10\,m^2$/person equivalent for natural treatment systems. In addition, each form of treatment yields at least one other waste stream, in addition to wastewater, which requires safe disposal (i.e. the product from screening, grit, sludge or dredged material from the ponds or reed beds).

Using the environment for treating wastewater incurs costs as discussed in Chapter 21; improving the treatment standard so that wastewater can be directly reused then generates the benefits associated with that use. In urban areas, the high value uses for wastewater often turn out to be for golf courses (Sala and Millet 1997) or green urban areas. Thus, roughly 25% of the wastewater that is reused in Mexico City is used for irrigating parks/green areas, with the remainder of untreated water being used for the Tula irrigation district (Scott *et al.* 2000). The reuse of wastewater for irrigation has long been practised, being almost routine in mid-nineteenth century Britain (Shuval *et al.* 1986). As the pressure on water resources is felt more clearly, attention is increasingly being given to using treated domestic sewage for irrigation after various levels of treatment. There is an obvious potential risk to health (Edwards 1992; Feachem *et al.* 1983) but this can largely be ameliorated by the appropriate wastewater treatment method and the appropriate combination of crop and application method (Shuval *et al.* 1990). In some water-scarce areas, a large proportion of wastewater is already reused for irrigation; in Israel, 275 mcm, or 65% of generated wastewater, goes towards Israel's total irrigation demand of 1200 mcm (Shevah 2000).

The benefits of treating and reusing wastewater for irrigation depend necessarily upon what is the alternative. If there is no system for collecting sewage at present then the benefits of treating and using the wastewater are to be compared with the costs and negative benefits of otherwise disposing of the effluent, be this to a river or to the sea. To the conventional benefits of irrigation should be added in the case of wastewater reuse the savings in fertilisers which the farmers can obtain from applying wastewater.

If there is some existing system of collecting sewage, then it is highly likely that if the resulting effluent discharges are in any way accessible to farmers then some of that effluent is already being used for irrigation. In this case the benefits of wastewater treatment are the improvements in health to both farmers and consumers as a result of the reduction of pathogens from the effluent and also the possible benefit to the waters which would otherwise receive the effluent. Typically, the critical determinant as to whether a project to reuse wastewater is economically viable is the difference in height between the area which may be irrigated and the wastewater treatment plant. If the wastewater has to be pumped up to farmers then the costs of pumping rapidly wipe out the potential benefits of irrigation.

The reuse of wastewater to provide food for fish is also a traditional practice (Rose 1999), where the ponds required to treat the wastewater (WHO 1987) can also produce fish, the effluent from the ponds then being available for other forms of reuse (Rose 1999).

Finally, where raw water is very scarce, then treatment to the standards required for immediate reuse may be justified (van der Merwe 1999; Tokyo Metropolitan Government n.d.)

16.4 Charging for Sanitation and Surface Water Runoff Collection

Effectively the only two ways of charging for sanitation are by a flat rate or property tax, or as a multiplier on the cost of water supply where water supplies are metered. The former method is effectively a tax and hence must be set by a government body and not a private profit-seeking company. In turn, historically, sewers have been provided by municipal or other levels of government (Hietala 1987), probably in part because otherwise a private company could have no guarantee of a return on investment, it being impossible to stop people illicitly connecting to a sewer where one is provided.

Using a multiplier to the charge for water supply is convenient when the wastewater collected for treatment is equal to or less than the volume of water supplied, and where the costs of wastewater collection and treatment are roughly equivalent to those of supplying the water. When the consumer engages in rain-water harvesting then the volume of wastewater to be collected and treated will exceed the quantity of water supplied, and the simple multiplier approach will result in such consumers being cross-subsidised by other consumers.

Hence for domestic consumers, charging for sanitation is always something of a crude instrument and two advantages of a tax approach are that a property tax can be relatively cheap and simple to collect. Secondly, the public good nature of sanitation means that individuals should be encouraged to connect to a system once it has been provided. Moreover, in such circumstances imposing a charge simply increases the likelihood that illegal connections will be made. Lump sum 'connection charges' are more logical when incomes are higher and dwellings are provided through a market rather than being constructed by the occupants themselves. In principle, those connection charges should represent the marginal cost of extending the sewerage network to serve the property in question and hence should vary by location. As the balance of the costs shift from water supply to wastewater collection and treatment, the purely theoretical argument for adopting this approach becomes stronger. However, unless charges for every one of the externalities associated with development are imposed, the risk is of distorting development, resulting in higher total external costs. Where a land use planning and control system is effective, then it is more logical to include the impacts on the water and wastewater systems into the planning considerations rather than seek to develop a sophisticated system of varying connection charges. Where no such system of land use control is practical then the likelihood is of illegal connections being made, so that a subtle system of charging will be pointless.

However, for industry and other large users, charging according to the volume of water discharged to the sewers and the quantity of pollutants in that water is logical, the 'Mogden' formula being an early example of such a system (Ingold and Stonebridge 1987). Here, the polluter has three costs to compare: the cost of discharging to a sewer, the cost of treatment on site, and the cost of discharging directly to a water body. For many pollutants, there should be economies of scale and so the cost of treating the wastewater via a treatment works connected to the sewer network should be expected to be less than the costs of treatment on site except in so far as on-site treatment allows a reduction in water demand, as well as allowing the recovery of waste materials and heat. Nor does it particularly matter which of the two strategies the polluter adopts. But care may be needed to avoid giving the polluters a perverse incentive to discharge directly to a water body. Equally, when a monopoly supplier is charging for wastewater, there is an obvious danger that the charges levied will be determined by what the market will bear rather than the true costs of wastewater treatment. Price and quality regulation will be essential to avoid monopoly profits from being extorted in this way.

In principle, the charge for collecting and treating surface water runoff should vary according to the quantity and rate of discharge of runoff. It is only with the development of GIS systems that it has realistically become affordable to introduce such charging structures. Such charges have, for example, been introduced in Los Angeles, Palo Alto, Santa Cruz and San Jose in California (Null n.d.). In Santa Cruz, areas are estimated from aerial photographs with the 'basic assessment unit' being a single family residence on a plot of 7723 ft^2; as this attracts a charge of roughly US$1/month (Null n.d.), this charging system probably costs more to administer than is collected.

Fort Collins in Colorado sets a charge based on the estimated runoff, adjusted for on-site runoff controls, that varies between basins with the rate taking account of both O&M costs and capital works. Of the average monthly charge for a single family residential plot, about US$3.42 is levied for O&M costs and US$6.41 for capital works (Center for Urban Policy and the Environment n.d.). In addition, developers are required to provide stormwater facilities for new parcels and a development fee is levied on all such parcels where the fee per parcel varies between basins from US$2175 to US$10 000.

Case Study 16.1 The Greater Cairo Wastewater Project

Cairo has negligible rainfall and consequently essentially all of the water entering the sewerage system has already been put into supply. At the same time, the water table is very near the surface and connected to the River Nile. That high water table in turn means that the old sewerage system was a pumped, pressurised system rather than relying on gravity. The sewerage system was already inadequate when it was completed in the 1930s and, following the massive growth in population over the next 40 years (Shorter 1989), was failing badly by the 1970s. By that time, almost 100 failures were occurring each day causing flooding; in addition, large parts of the city were not served by a piped sewerage system (Coville 1996). Following the Camp David agreement, substantial aid monies were made available to fund the implementation of the sewerage master plan that had been drawn up in 1977 (Taylor Binnie and Partners 1977). In implementing that master plan, the USA focused on the West Bank of the city and the UK on the East. On the West Bank, the initial works concentrated on extending piped sewerage (FAR projects) to areas previously unsewered whilst the main focus on the east bank was on building a new deep spine tunnel up to 5 m in diameter (Surr *et al.* 1993). The Overseas Development Administration carried out an interim evaluation of the project in late 1992 (Surr *et al.* 1993), by which time total investment was £1.5 billion; one of the objectives of that study was to define the data requirements for a full economic analysis to be undertaken on completion.

Cairo has experienced rapid urbanisation (Shorter 1989), much of it informal so that around 46% of the population now lives in such settlements (Coville 1996), with 50% of new construction in 1992 being unlicensed (Surr *et al.* 1993). One typical development pattern for informal developments has been for, first, the construction of vaults under the buildings: an estimated 73% in the case of Abou Qetada. These vaults are concrete boxes that leak, retaining solids whilst allowing much of the water to escape. The second stage is the construction of tube wells. Thirdly, through community self-help an unofficial water main is laid connected to a trunk mains so that by 1996, there were 500 000 legal connections and an estimated 200 000 illegal connections (Coville 1996).

The benefits of extending piped sewerage are thus:

- since the capacity of a vault limits the water which can be consumed, a piped collection system allows for an increased consumption of potable water;
- overflows from vaults and the disposal of sullage water to the streets result in flooding and health hazards;
- the costs of cleaning and emptying the vault are significant; and
- vaults, with the uncontrolled leaching, result in a build-up of waste material in the soil, the contamination of groundwater and a possible increase in groundwater levels.

The cost of constructing a vault depends upon its size – it is usually shared between several households and may be up to 20 m long. Based on five to six families sharing, the likely cost of construction is of the order of LE500:LE15–16 per capita. Once constructed, this cost is a sunk cost which cannot be counted against the costs of the subsequent provision of a piped collection system.

The capacity of the vaults is limited and it is reported that sullage water is thrown on the streets and, in other areas, children are encouraged to use waste land for a

Continued on page 270

__ *Continued from page 269* __

toilet (El-Katsha *et al.* 1989). Since water supplies are limited, it is not clear which is the greatest constraint: the availability of potable water or the capacity of the vaults. However, it is clear that the higher consumption levels in some parts of Cairo (average domestic per capita consumption equals 159 l/c/d) could not be sustained in areas served by vaults. The probable resulting restrictions on hygiene are a possible explanation of health problems. Thus, that it is not sewage spillages on the streets which are the cause of disease but the inability, either because of shortages of water or because water consumption is limited by difficulty of disposing of wastewater, to wash hands, food and surfaces so as to avoid cross-contamination.

Furthermore, flooding of streets as a result of overflows from vaults is quite common, as are backflows from latrines into ground floor apartments. One test of the effectiveness of the project is then to determine whether per capita water consumption increases in newly sewered property. Widely varying estimates of the frequency with which vaults needed to be emptied and the costs of so doing were obtained. Both are likely to vary from locality to locality: in areas where the clay layer is near the surface, the rate of water loss from the vaults will be relatively low, and hence the required rate of emptying higher. If no water leached away from the vault, then the cost of donkey trailer collection per individual per year in a low consumption area (49 litres/day) would be LE41 – over LE220 for the average family. The low estimates of the costs of emptying were in the range of LE12 per year; say, LE0.33 per capita per year. However, in the Abou Qetada area, a study by ES Parsons reported that a significant number of vaults require emptying every three days or less. The reported cost is 50 pt per load of 200–300 litres; LE1.70–20.00 per capita/year, depending upon the number of residents served by the vault. This cost is also equivalent to LE1.50–2.50/ m^3 of material removed.

One of the project reports for the FAR works compared the cost of a range of different options based around the use of the existing vaults or modified systems. The range of computed cost varied from LE1.35/m^3 to LE3.55/m^3; the amortised cost of a donkey trailer being, for example, LE2.27/m^3. On this basis, the cost of a piped collection system will be considerably less than the cost of collection from vaults even at present low consumption levels, unless at least 90% leaching rates are both possible and acceptable. Assuming a 90% leaching rate, then the marginal cost of collection associated with increasing water consumption to the average domestic consumption in Cairo is LE9 per capita per year, or about LE50 per family. In their sample survey, Hoehn and Krieger (1996) report that the mean cost of vault cleaning reported in the four weeks prior to the interview was some LE14. Moreover, those without piped water and sanitation incurred costs of LE18 a month, plus 28 hours labour, as compared to LE5.5 a month for those connected to both water and sanitation networks. The waste collected from the vaults is then disposed of in a number of ways: some is reported to be sold as fertiliser; the balance to be simply dumped into the nearest watercourse, sewer manhole or piece of waste ground.

In turn, it was reported that in Zenein land values had increased following the FAR schemes by a factor of approximately 10: from about LE30–40/m^2 to LE300–400/m^2. This gives an increase in the value per hectare of, say, 2.6 million LE which, given the land densities, comes to a gain of c. LE1300 per capita. Because of rent controls, this gain is reported to be captured by the resident population rather than leading to their displacement. However, the existing informal potable water supply network is replaced in the course of the FAR works, and, as it would be reasonable to assume that the replacement work is of a higher standard, so that some part of this

__ *Continued on page 271* __

__ *Continued from page 270* __

gain should be attributed to improvements in the water supply. The implication is that the economic benefits of first time sewerage, coupled with adequate supplies of potable water, are substantial.

On the East Bank, the purpose of the spine tunnel and associated pumping stations is to reduce the frequency of failure of the existing local sewer networks and to allow the expansion of the network. Thus, one project report stated that 225 000 out of a population of 650 000 lived in areas subject to fairly regular flooding. In approaching the economic evaluation of the works, it was not clear what were the causes of these failures of the existing sewerage system. Breakdowns of the pumps and ejectors were common, but the proportions of failures caused by blockages, under capacity, and bursts are not uncertain. In 1993, after rehabilitation of the pumps and ejectors, the reported rate of failures for the ejectors was an average of three per day: a failure rate of 1 in 13 per day. Another report estimated that 35% of flooding incidents were attributable to blockages caused by some 800 small industrial plants scattered throughout the city. Certainly, a significant proportion of 'floods' were concentrated in the leather working district, suggestive of blockages being caused by the discharges from tanneries. The latter cause of failure might be effectively and rapidly reduced through a Trade Waste management programme. Rather mixed views were expressed on the frequency of sewer collapse in Cairo, varying from that these pose only an infrequent problem at present to that these were a frequent occurrence – one which could be identified by the presence of bypass pumping. One example given was the Cairo Tower in Zamalek which is reported to have taken six months to repair; a not unreasonable figure. Other recent incidents reported were near the Wimpy in Mohandiseen, and another in Ein Shams. Hence, for a full economic analysis, rather better data is required on both the causes of the failures in the existing system and the frequencies and consequences of the different forms of failure.

Wherever there is flooding, then people take action to minimise the losses which occur. This should be expected particularly where flooding is frequent. In turn, the losses from floods should be expected to be small but the costs of taking action and the inconvenience caused by those actions should be expected to be high. A usual adaptation is to construct mini-walls to protect property or to install flood boards to close entrance ways. Such mini-walls may be seen in parts of Maadi although they may alternatively be simply ways of demarcating private space in front of property. But a survey by ES Parsons reported the construction of brick barricades in the Athar el Nabi area specifically for the purposes of flood protection. In economic terms, any such existing mini-walls are potentially 'sunk' costs; the labour used to construct them cannot be 'recaptured' if the risk of flooding is reduced although the materials could be reused. A further loss is incurred by occupiers of the areas that are flooded; since the entire flow in the sewers is returned potable water, flooding is minimised by cutting off the water supply to the areas affected.

Flooding also causes serious damage to road surfaces. As a result of poor quality control during construction, road surfaces are slightly crazed and the high axle pressures force flood water down these cracks under very high pressure into the subsurface. As a result, large areas of surface break up, as can be seen in the underpasses below the railway lines. The Roda subway leading from Old Cairo to El Roda and the Giza Bridge has been rebuilt three or four times in the last 25 years; the most recent rebuilding cost LE3 million. The normal expectation would be that a road will only need rehabilitating after 10 years: that is, levelling and resurfacing. The life expectancy of roads is estimated to be reduced by at least 50%. Flooding

__ *Continued on page 272* __

___ *Continued from page 271* ___

causes major disruption to traffic in Cairo partly because local drivers do not like driving on wet streets and proceed extremely carefully: tyres are often bald and the risk of a skid is high. The last time there was flooding outside the National Institute for Transport, three accidents were counted over a distance of 300 m. The evaluation of traffic disruption is relatively straightforward (Parker *et al.* 1987) but no traffic count was available at the time of the interim evaluation.

A second reason for taking care when driving through flooding is that the standard way of relieving flooding is to remove manhole covers. Therefore, vehicles drive in single file through flood waters to avoid falling into an open manhole. In the flood near the Corniche, rocks were observed to have been placed in one carriageway, apparently to warn of some underwater danger, and in the remaining carriageway, used by traffic, there was either a serious pothole or other depression.

In addition to flooding or surcharging, and bursts, a third potential problem was the exfiltration of water leading to contamination of groundwater. Exfiltration from the sewers and surcharging sewers may both raise the level of groundwater and add pollutants, notably sulphates and chlorides, to that water which may attack structures. Faecal contaminants may also spread to wells for potable water. There is a widely held view that the level of groundwater has been rising in Cairo in recent years: this was the focus of a proposed study by the Academy of Sciences. This rise may have occurred through a number of reasons including exfiltration from the sewerage system or from the water supply system. The view was also expressed that water levels have risen in the Islamic quarter following the construction of the Metro system. The predominant pattern of groundwater movement is towards the north-west and it was argued that the Metro acted as an underground dam to retain groundwater on the 'downstream' side. Insufficient data was available to determine to what extent the present state of the sewerage system was responsible for changes in the level of groundwater, not least because very little data on groundwater levels was available. From the limited data available, the groundwater level is very near the surface in a number of areas.

Damage may be caused to existing buildings, antiquities being a particular concern, and additional protection may be required for new buildings to reduce the risk of damage. The two potential damage mechanisms are:

- rises in the groundwater level; and
- salts in the water.

Osmosis will lift water to varying heights above ground level and sulphates and chlorides will attack materials, particularly steel and carbonate materials (e.g. concrete and calcareous stone–limestones). The accepted limit values for sulphates are chlorides are 300 ppm. A limited amount of data was obtained on groundwater levels and the concentration of salts.

The benefits of improvements in the sewerage system are thus the degree to which this would result in changes in the combination of the groundwater levels and salt concentrations that would reduce the risk of damage. Therefore, it is necessary to be able to compare the 'with' scheme levels to the 'without' scheme levels. Estimation of the 'with' scheme levels might be estimated as the background levels; given the gypsum outcrops in the Cairo area, some nonzero level of sulphate salts in groundwater is to be anticipated. Equally, the groundwater level in Cairo is associated with the Nile; and the effect of leakage from the water system also requires to be estimated. Furthermore, there are significant variations in ground conditions

___ *Continued on page 273* ___

___ *Continued from page 272* ___

within Cairo, particularly between the East and West Bank. No longitudinal data could be obtained (although it was reported that 40 years ago the water level could not be found in Heliopolis by conventional boring but is now found at around 4 m); such data is clearly desirable not only to enable the economic evaluation of the project.

For existing buildings, the effect of heightened groundwater and salts is to shorten the life of those buildings by damaging the foundations and fabric of those buildings. The economic impact of this life shortening depends upon the reduced life expectancy versus the actual life expectancy: many buildings are demolished before their theoretical life expectancy of 50–60 years because of obsolescence. The damage will, however, increase the maintenance costs in the interim. This loss could, in principle, be evaluated provided that groundwater conditions were mapped.

More critically, inspection of the Islamic Quarter, a World Heritage site, showed the marks of rising damp to heights in many cases of 2–3 m, coupled with major spalding of the limestone surface. At the entrance to the Madrassa and Khanqah of Sultan Barquq, a slap on the surface of the external wall resulted in spalling from the surface.

The cost of repairing the damage which has already been done to the some 550 Islamic monuments in Cairo and to other antiquities is a sunk cost. Improvements in sewerage will only reduce the potential of further damage to these monuments; it will not undo the damage that has already been done. Whilst there is major above-ground damage to these monuments, the real concern is the damage to the foundations and the consequent risk of collapse of these buildings. Many of these buildings are constructed on fill up to 10 m deep, including organic matter, and water saturation is affecting the bearing strength of the soil. Indeed, a few experts expressed the fear that some buildings would collapse before the long-term improvements resulting from the Greater Sewerage Project were achieved. For this reason, the Department of Antiquities has undertaken some sewerage works of its own to deal with critical problems.

In this case, the 'do nothing' alternatives are either to allow the destruction of the monuments to continue, which is unacceptable, or to adopt the least-cost alternative to reduce the risk of further damage. This alternative would involve dewatering; this was carried out by the Department for the Mosque of al-Hakim at a cost of some LE500 000. Hence an approximate order of magnitude of the benefits of preserving the Islamic monuments through an adequate sewerage system is LE275 million. In a full benefit–cost analysis, these benefits would, as would the costs, have to be phased in over time as the extension of the sewerage system protected individual monuments. Additional benefits would also arise through the protection of other categories of monument, such as the Coptic area where standing water can be observed in the Hanging Church and at the Babylon Roman western gates.

Overall, the study brought out a number of general lessons. First, in Cairo, essentially all of the water entering the sewerage system has already been put into supply. In turn, reducing leakage and wastage saves money twice, leakage from mains pipes under high pressure being likely to infiltrate the sewers which operated under a lower pressure. It proved difficult to get good data on the rates of leakage and wastage, but infiltration was estimated to contribute 30% of the total load on the sewers, some of which was from natural groundwater. Wastage rates were clearly high, one study concluding that in the apartment buildings monitored it reached 35% and one World Bank report claiming that night-time water consumption in the Mugamma office

___ *Continued on page 274* ___

__ *Continued from page 273* __

building reached 95% of daytime usage. Estimates of the overall rate of leakage and wastage thus reached 60%. In turn, one way of improving the effectiveness of a sewage system could be to reduce leakage and wastage (Surr *et al.* 1993).

Secondly, in Cairo, 40% of sewer connections were estimated to be illegal. In areas undergoing rapid rates of informal development, such illicit connections to piped sewers and to mains water supply should be expected. Indeed, given the health and other benefits associated with such services, they should be welcomed. The institutional question is then how such informal connections are to be encouraged, an adequate standard of construction and service is to be promoted, and the necessary trunk sewer capacity is to be funded.

Thirdly, because of the septicity of sewage, the main collector tunnels had to be lined with blue engineering bricks. The analyses undertaken as part of the development of the master plan recognised that the requirement exceeded the then capacity of the Egyptian brick industry; it was not surprising therefore that shortages of bricks delayed the completion of the project. It is therefore important to consider the availability of resources in such projects, not least to avoid imports being sucked in by the project.

Fourthly, as is fairly common, construction and operation, together with maintenance, were the responsibility of different organisations. In turn, O&M requirements were somewhat neglected in the design phase; the preparation of priced O&M schedules should be regarded as an essential element of design.

Fifthly, one of the main functions of public bodies in Egypt has been to provide work, particularly for graduates. Since wages are low, employees then seek to move into the private sector and their mobility is improved if they are trained. In turn, those who are given training then tend to leave the public organisation. One approach, therefore, is to treat public organisations explicitly as part of the technical education system and to give them a continuing and funded training role.

Sixthly, there are logical hierarchies in the provision of sewerage services. Downstream provision of sewers logically precedes upstream provision; equally, separation of industrial waste loads from domestic sewage logically precedes the provision of high standards of wastewater treatment. Not only does industrial waste contain heavy metals and other pollutants that are difficult to treat, but those pollutants can also threaten the integrity of the sewer system.

17

Water for Food

Growing crops is by far the greatest consumer of water in the world: what is called the 'water crisis' is actually a 'food crisis'. Since land is also scarce, it is essential to manage water and land effectively if the world is to be fed. At the same time, most of the world's farms are very small, less than 5 hectares in size, and farm policies are as much about rural development and poverty relief as about food production. Again, across much of the world, agricultural production contributes a substantial production of GDP, the cost of food consumes a substantial fraction of the income of most people, the largest part of the population lives in rural areas, and agricultural development is both essential to development and to prevent an uncontrolled migration from the rural areas to the urban areas of the world. Conversely, in the developed world, agriculture contributes a negligible proportion of GDP, employs an equally small proportion of the workforce, food is cheap and agriculture is very heavily subsidised. So, it is a world of two parts and any economic analysis must reflect the local realities.

Arable production is a far more efficient way of producing food value than livestock (Table 17.1). In turn, crops provide 77% of the world's food, with livestock another 16%, and fisheries the remaining 7% (Global Vision on Water, Life and the Environment 2000), with aquaculture producing an increasing proportion of the output of fisheries. Thus, agriculture provides 93% of the protein and 99% of the calories consumed by people (Wood *et al.* 2000). But, in 18 countries in Africa and Asia, fisheries provide at least 40% of the animal protein in the diet (Edwards 2000) and generally provide trace elements and vitamins that are otherwise absent in diets. In addition, aquaculture can provide synergies with arable land, particularly when that land is irrigated (Moehl 2000).

But arable production requires the joint availability of water and land where both are scarce. Only a limited proportion of land is suitable for arable usage – for instance, only 5–6% of Canada is suitable for arable use. Much of the land that is suitable is subject to constraints that limit its productivity (Wood *et al.* 2000). To these soil constraints must be added those of topography, that of the slope of the land. Much of the land is also becoming degraded after centuries of use: some 70% of the 5.2 billion hectares of drylands used for agriculture is degraded.

Handbook of Water Economics: Principles and Practice. C. Green
© 2003 John Wiley & Sons, Ltd ISBN: 0-471-98571-6

Table 17.1   *Protein and energy output by foodstuff*

		Protein kh/ha/year	Energy MJ/ha/yr
Crops	Dry grass	1100	180 000
	Cabbage	1100	33 500
	Corn	430	83 700
	Wheat	350	58 600
	Rice	320	87 900
	Potatoes	420	100 460
Livestock	Rabbits	180	7 400
	Chickens	92	4 600
	Lamb	43	4 800
	Beef	43	7 900
	Milk	115	10 460

Source: King n.d.

In addition, around 10 million hectares are lost each year through desertification (Sweet 1999). Some of these problems are a result of the interaction of water and soil: salinisation becomes a problem if the soil contains salts and the water table becomes too high either as a result of excessive irrigation, or a reduction in demand allows the water table to rise. In Australia, salinisation of dryland farming is becoming a major problem because of the removal of trees and shrubs which previously lowered the water table (Land and Water Resources Research and Development Corporation 1998). Conversely, in acid sulphate soils, if the water table falls, the soil oxidises to form sulphuric acid, in turn the acid destroys the productivity of the soil and the acid drainage water damages the ecosystems in the river, estuary and coastal fringe (White *et al.* 1999).

Traditionally, the poorer quality soils and conditions were used for extensive livestock use, particularly in arid climates. In turn, whilst on a global basis meat does not contribute a significant proportion of food needs, it is considerably more important in arid regions. Moreover, some cultures and societies are woven around livestock production and the effects of droughts are then particularly devastating in such cultures (Hazell *et al.* 2001), and the poorest suffer most (von Braun *et al.* 1999).

Arable land is scarce because it is only made available by converting land from other uses, notably from wetlands, forests and grasslands, areas that are also already scarce and environmentally valuable. Thus, around 30% of the potential area of temperate, subtropical and tropical forests has already been converted to agriculture and agriculture takes up nearly 70% of land area in Europe and more than 70% in southeast Asia (Wood *et al.* 2000). Of the remaining 1.8 billion hectares of land with rain-fed crop potential, most is in Sub-Saharan Africa (44%) and Latin America and Caribbean (48%) whilst there is virtually none in South Asia, Near East and North Africa; the majority of this land is currently under forest and is subject to soil and terrain constraints (FAO 1996).

Some 800 million people currently receive inadequate amounts of food and Seckler, Molden and Barker (1999) estimate that cereal production will have to increase by 38% to meet future food needs. But increases in wealth also increase food consumption and shift the pattern of demand away from grains and legumes towards meat. Per capita demand for meat is projected to double between 1995 and 2020: poultry by 85%, beef by 50%, and pigmeat by 45% (Pinstrup-Andersen *et al.* 1999). In turn, livestock production is supported by grain production and so the net effect of an increase in meat eating is an increase in the demand for grain, the grain requirements to produce 1 kg of beef, pork and poultry being 7, 4 and 2 kg respectively (World Water Council 2000). Moreover, the shift in diet to meat consumption drastically increases the requirement for water. Thus, in California, wheat requires 1.3 m^3 of water per kg, poultry takes 5.8 m^3/kg and beef 16 m^3/kg. Consequently, the typical Californian diet requires about 2200 m^3 of water per year, of which 64% is used in meat production. Conversely, in Tunisia, the dietary water requirement is 1100 m^3/year of which 27% is for meat (FAO 1996). This pressure on land will only increase as the demand for industrial crops (e.g. for pharmaceuticals, raw materials for plastics, fuel etc.) expands to replace reliance on fossil fuels.

Thus, the two basic options are either to convert more land to arable use or to increase the productivity of the land that is currently in arable use. Whilst regional food demands may be partly met by 'virtual water', importing food (Allen 1994), globally the problem of expanding food and the resulting demand for water remains.

Whilst countries typically seek to prohibit the conversion of high-value agricultural land to urban uses, urban pressures are almost invariably so great that agricultural land adjacent to existing urban centres is converted to allow the expansion of those areas. Therefore, part of the benefits of, say, converting rainfed agriculture to irrigated agriculture could be the avoidance of the conversion of that equivalent area of forest to arable uses which would otherwise be required to achieve the same increase in production. In so far as improvements in agricultural productivity in one area would prevent other land being converted to agricultural use then there are potential environmental benefits associated with that improvement. Conversely, in other instances, a benefit of such an improvement in the agricultural productivity of one area may be to release some land that is currently under arable management for other uses. Equally, an improvement in the efficiency in the use of water may release some of that water for other uses. Finally, in some instances, it may be desirable to allow some agricultural land to revert to its natural state. For example, in England and Wales, it is a requirement that in assessing the benefits of renovating an existing agricultural drainage system, the environmental benefits of allowing that area to revert to a wetland be considered (DEFRA 1999). In England and Wales, some land is worth more in environmental use than in its current agricultural use, after subsidies are removed.

Therefore, making efficient use of arable land is a critical issue and maximising crop production involves providing water to the plant during the growing period. Too much water and there is a drainage problem and the risk, in some soils, of salinisation of the soil; too little water and the crop will be poor or fail altogether. Therefore, it is necessary to consider water provision and drainage together; the relative importance of the two aspects of agricultural water management vary from place to place. In some instances, both problems occur: for example, in Bangladesh, crop production has been inhibited by scarcity of water at some periods of the year and flooding at others (Rogers *et al.* 1989).

Moreover, over large parts of potential arable land, there is either insufficient rainfall to support crop production, or the rainfall is highly concentrated, sometimes even in the form of floods, in parts of the year and not when needed for crop growth, or is so variable that farmers have to be very risk-averse in their practices. The Sahel region is characterised by a climate in which 20% of annual rainfall may fall in a single day, and the Tropics by rainfall being concentrated into a single period of around three months. In turn, the growing season is limited to less than 100 days. The high variability of rainfall in arid regions (Chapter 14) means that many Sub-Saharan African countries experience complete crop failure every four years; for Ghana and other more humid countries, it is every five years.

Conversely, farming results in significant negative externalities (Figure 17.1): pesticide runoff can destroy fisheries and the ecological value of receiving waters, as can nitrates produced both from livestock and by the use of fertilisers. Thus, of the rivers assessed in the USA, in 59% of cases, agriculture is regarded as the leading source of pollutants (USEPA 2000b). Diffuse agricultural pollution is increasingly the primary cause of poor water quality in rivers and estuaries (Nixon

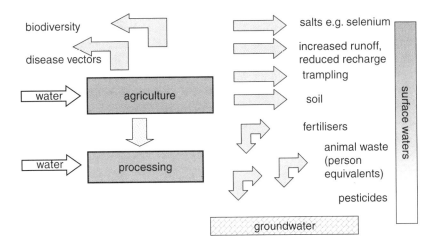

Figure 17.1   *Negative externalities associated with agriculture*

2000). Pollution by both pesticides and nitrates also results in significant increases in the cost of treating water before it can be put into potable supply (Water UK 2001). Drainage water from irrigation use often contains high concentrations of salts and minerals such as selenium which have adverse effects on wildlife (Postel 1992). In turn, agricultural products are processed and both the water demands of and pollution loads discharged from agribusinesses such as dairies, tanneries and meat processing plants are substantial (Gleick 1993).

Water management for agriculture is complicated by a series of factors:

- There are a great variety of different agricultural systems across the world, many of which have resulted from adaptation to local conditions over the centuries.
- Crop production is often only one part of the web of activities that provide sustainable livelihoods (Ashley and Carney 1999).
- Agricultural systems are intimately linked to local social systems and institutions.
- The agricultural policies of different governments are seldom primarily about agricultural production.

At the same time, the demands for water for crop production are both enormous (Figure 14.2) and consumptive, with the majority of the water supplied to a field being lost through evaporation and transpiration. Because by far the largest proportion of water use is agricultural, it is commonplace to call for a reallocation of water away from agriculture towards the 'higher' valued urban uses, particularly as urban demands for water grow.

17.1 Agricultural Systems

The large monocultural arable farms of North America and Western Europe are a recent development. Traditionally, agricultural systems are complex systems of crops, livestock, game, fisheries and trees (e.g. Zhu *et al.* 1991), typically including common property resources (Shackleton *et al.* 2000). Complex laying systems of multicropping have also been frequent; for example, coffee has traditionally been grown in the shade of other crops such as bananas. Similarly, the *montadas* and *dehesas* in Portugal and Spain are both vertically and horizontally layered systems combining trees, shrubs, arable crops and livestock (Goncalves 2000). Such multicropping systems perhaps reached their peak in the agroforests of Tanzania (the 'Chagga') and in the Pekaranga of Java (Fernandes n.d.). The integrated pest management approaches (e.g. DFID 1999b) increasingly being adapted involve a shift away from the monocultural approach.

Livestock and arable farming have typically been symbiotic and complementary; for example, the traditional rice–fish farming in parts of China where the fish both manure the rice and eat pests (MacKay 1995). In Africa, the interactions between both the ways in which different areas of land are used (Brummett and

Chikafumbwa 2000) and between arable farmers and pastoralists (e.g. Drijver and Marchand 1987) have been particularly complex, especially the ways in which the uses of wetlands (e.g. the fadama of Nigeria and dambos of southern Africa) fit into this broader system (Marchand 1987). In the past, some interventions to increase arable production have failed because they assumed a much simpler pattern of use and ignored these interactions (Adams 1992).

Critically, farmers have to be risk managers; each planting is a gamble in which the farmer commits substantial resources in the form of seeds, labour, fertiliser and other inputs against an expected return some time in the future, where that future varies from a few months for some crops to many years in the case of trees. Between the planting and the harvest, the household then has to live off the surplus, if any, from the previous harvest plus any other income or resources to which they may have access. For the subsistence farmer in particular, it is a gamble where the penalty for losing can be starvation or the loss of their land and permanent impoverishment. The risks of partial or complete crop loss from drought, pests and diseases, frost or flooding may then be substantial. Average global losses to wheat from pests are 33% but would rise to 52% without the use of control measures; those to rice would rise to 83% without controls from the current 52% (Wood *et al.* 2000). Complete crop loss from drought occurs every four to five years in parts of Africa. In addition, for cash crops, there is no guarantee as to the price that will be achieved; if everyone has a good harvest, prices will be low and may not be sufficient to recover the initial investment. Farmers have therefore been described as people who lose either way: from a poor harvest or from a good harvest. In these circumstances, it is rational to plant crops that are resistant to the different threats so that although the average yield is relatively poor, year-to-year variance is minimised. In addition, there is logic in diversifying the crops so as to reduce the risk of total crop failure.

Irrigation then reduces the risks that water will not be available when needed in the growth cycle of the crop; average year-to-year yields will consequently increase and hence, in the case of cash crops, will increase capital availability. In turn, the farmer may then be prepared to risk increasing other inputs, such as fertiliser and pesticides, so as to increase the yield further whilst paddy irrigation can reduce the requirement for labour inputs and also counter-balances some soil problems which would otherwise limit productivity. However, the farmer must also be concerned with the productivity of labour as a scarce, and perhaps the scarce, resource; in turn, planning their cropping pattern, the farmer will be concerned to maximise the return to labour rather than to land (Stomal and Weigel n.d.).

Given good access to markets then the farmer may then be prepared to switch to the production of higher valued cash crops. However, these higher valued crops are, in most countries, vegetables and fruit which spoil considerably more rapidly than grain and legumes so the risks of these crops are higher. Conversely, if there are other constraints on the farmer that are left unchanged, then irrigation alone will often not yield the predicted benefits. In turn, those constraints vary by the type of farmer and the nature of their holding. Over much of the world, subsistence farmers with what are in world terms very small holdings, often less than 1 hectare, dominate the picture. Their responses are different to those of farmers in the developed world who have much greater access to capital and much larger farms. It is also necessary to adopt a whole livelihood approach so that, for example, irrigation may not result in higher agricultural outputs but free up resources for the household to use in other ways (Johnson 1999).

In subsistence-based agriculture, farming, social organisation and institutional structures are also necessarily interwoven. The open fields that characterised Anglo-Saxon farms and the Commons have, for example, been argued to be a consequence of the use of the heavy plough drawn by up to eight oxen (White 1982). The subak in Bali are also as much a social and institutional system as an irrigation system (Bali-plus n.d.); so too are the Huerta of Valencia (Glick 1970) and the acqueias of New Mexico (Brown and Rivera 2000). Changing farming practices by, for example, introducing irrigation consequently has implications for both the social organisation and for the institutional structures; in particular of gender roles. In such changes, women not unfrequently lose out (Zwarteveen 1997), having been disadvantaged to start with (IFPRI n.d.).

17.2 Rural Economies

In developing countries, a large part of the population still depends upon agriculture and the associated industries, and in turn these industries provide a large part of those countries' GDP. The obverse is the case for developed countries. So, agriculture accounts for 40–60% of the GDP of the Philippines, with agribusinesses adding a further 21%, whilst for Argentina the 11% of GDP contributed by agriculture becomes 39% when the contribution of agribusinesses is taken into account (Bathrick 1998). In developed countries, the proportion of GDP contributed by agriculture and the proportion of the population engaged in agriculture is about 4%. In turn, droughts can have a devastating effect on the economies of developing countries, the 1990s' drought in Zimbabwe causing a 60% decline in GDP (World Bank 2001). Whilst the effect of droughts in developed countries on agriculture and the environment is also severe, the effects on urban uses are generally relatively small and so the overall effect of droughts on the national or regional economy is considerably less (USACE 1995).

In developing countries, agriculture is a net contributor to national revenue; whilst there generally are some subsidies, these are outweighed by the tax revenue produced by the agricultural sector. In the developed world, agricultural practices are almost invariably subsidised. Only rarely are the full costs of irrigation borne by the farmers (Garrido 1999); for example, the US General Accounting Office (1994) has analysed to what extent the costs of the water provided to cities, as a result of tradable entitlements being sold by farmers, will need to continue to

Table 17.2 *Forms of subsidy for agriculture*

electricity
fuel
fertiliser
transportation (e.g. subsidies for the construction and/or operation of navigation)
land drainage works
irrigation (capital works and operation/maintenance costs subsidised or
    cross-subsidised)
export subsidies
production quotas
import quotas/tariffs
crop insurance
payment for fallowing fields
crop price supports
flood alleviation works (i.e. subsidised construction and operation)
low-cost credit including for buildings/roads
soil erosion/desalination and similar works (i.e. subsidies towards the costs of reducing)
agricultural extension services
livestock feed subsidies
tax relief (e.g. exclusion from property taxes)

be subsidised in order for farmers to be prepared to trade abstraction rights. In economic analyses, these subsidy elements need to be stripped out; Table 17.2 lists the forms of direct and indirect subsidies most commonly found in agriculture. In total, these subsidies are very large indeed; 70% of the value of agricultural products in the UK, Germany and Ireland is made up of one form of subsidy or another (Goncalves 2000). The value of irrigation subsidies alone in the USA was estimated by Repetto (1986) as around US$1 billion and a Democratic staff report (1994) analyses seven projects where the cost recovery for irrigation was found to range from 0.1% to 39% so that in turn, the subsidy per m^3 ranged up to US$0.20/$m^3$. A US General Accounting Office study (1996) reveals a similar picture across a larger number of irrigation schemes.

One reason for the extent of these subsidies is that the schemes are inefficient: the value of crops produced is insufficient for the farmers to be able to pay the full economic cost of the irrigation water. In turn, it is likely that in some parts of the world, including much of California, agriculture would cease in the absence of subsidised irrigation. On a global scale, the consequence is that the terms of trade for agricultural products are severely distorted against the developing countries.

In turn, it should be recognised that agricultural policy is rarely about food; instead, it is usually about achieving other objectives. It may be about securing the land through settlement, as arguably was agricultural policy in the USA in the nineteenth century (Howe 1971); it may be about alleviating rural poverty and in turn slowing migration to the cities; it may be about creating and maintaining a class of small-scale yeomen farmers, who are often seen as the backbone of the nation. It may be about achieving a cheap food supply for the urban population, or it may be about creating or rewarding political support. Moreover, few countries are comfortable about relying upon imports to feed their population, any more than they are happy to rely upon imports to meet any other critical requirement such as energy.

Increasingly, a key element of agricultural policy is environmental policy; to preserve those landscapes that have been created by past agricultural activity. For example, in the UK, upland sheep farming is subsidised because such iconic landscapes as the Lake District were created by sheep farming. If sheep farming were to be abandoned, then the open moor lands would naturally revert to shrub and then to forest. Again, the oak cork forests of Portugal are very important habitats, but cork production is threatened by the introduction of plastic 'corks' for wine bottles (Goncalves 2000). In order to protect the positive environmental externalities of oak cork production, either a subsidy to cork production or a charge on plastic corks may be appropriate. Again, in the long run, rice production from the famous tiered rice paddies of Indonesia is unlikely to be able to compete with production in other areas; again, a subsidy of production in such areas may be appropriate to preserve a World Heritage site. Analysing agricultural practices solely in terms of economic efficiency may therefore be to entirely miss the point.

This is particularly the case when considering the reallocation of water away from agricultural uses; it is increasingly commonplace to call for water to be reallocated from agricultural purposes, where its economic value is low, to high value, that is urban, uses. Thus, that water should be reallocated away from wheat production to such higher valued uses as toilet flushing and domestic swimming pools. However, it is necessary to be clear what this proposal actually means: this is that too much food is being produced at too low a price. The effects will then be three-fold: on rural economies, on food prices and national economies.

If water is switched out of agriculture into other uses then some farms will cease to be viable. Villarejo (1996) analysed the effect of the 1987–92 drought in California on an agricultural community. Contrary to expectations, the production of high valued crops fell – probably because the risk of planting such crops in the face of uncertainties about water availability was too high. Some 70% of small family farms closed; in turn, three out of seven wholesale vegetable packing houses closed, total county payroll fell by 14%, retail sales fell by 11% as compared to a countywide average increase of 5%, and the official unemployment rate rose to 41%.

Similarly, Wolfenden *et al.* (2001) analysed the effects of a reduction in irrigation from 342 000 ML to 308 000 ML in a cotton-growing area of Australia. They anticipate a loss of 300 jobs out of the 3000 directly and indirectly associated with cotton with a resulting increase in regional unemployment of 3%. The total impact in the regional economy was estimated as A$15 million with returns on investment falling from 4.7% to 4.4% per annum with a consequent risk that some businesses would fail, with further knock-on effects on employment and income.

As farming is abandoned, the former farmers will seek work elsewhere, typically in towns and cities (Howe *et al.* 1990). This will increase the rate at which urbanisation is occurring in those countries that have not already been urbanised.

It will add to the pressures to create work in urban areas where many countries already find it difficult to achieve a sufficient rate of economic growth to create jobs at the rate at which the population is growing. Such migration also means that existing infrastructure is abandoned and replacement schools, hospitals and roads must be built in the areas to which the population has migrated. This is clearly a much more significant problem for the developing countries which are still starting on the path to urbanisation than in the developed world where rural populations are already low.

For the value of water in agricultural and in urban uses to coincide, agricultural uses and hence agricultural production would have to fall, with lower valued agricultural uses being squeezed out. Therefore, agricultural production would necessarily fall and the prices of agricultural crops would rise (Rosegrant and Ringler 1998). The critical questions then are by how much agricultural water use and production would have to fall, and agricultural prices rise, before a new price equilibrium is established. Rosegrant and Ringler (1998) modelled the effects of a global switch of water away agricultural use into urban and industrial uses of 10–35% by 2020, the percentage varying from country to country. The predicted result is a 68% rise in the price of rice over the period 1993 to 2020, and a 50% rise in the price of wheat. For a switch from low efficiency irrigation systems to high efficiency systems to occur, the same falls in production and increase in market prices are required. How agricultural prices will change as supply falls, the price elasticity of supply, is important. If small changes in supply result in large changes in prices, then there are obvious political implications. This volatility seems to be uncomfortably high. Adam Smith (1986) gives figures for the market price of the best quality wheat for the period from 1595 to 1764, with the exception of the period of the English Civil War. Prices of wheat fluctuated markedly from year to year over that period (Figure 17.2): the maximum year-on-year price rise is 93% and the maximum fall is to 59%. Without attempting to determine the extent to which these variations are the result of political factors, such as the Glorious Revolution and the Jacobite rebellions, or weather conditions, such year-to-year variations in the basic food staple, one that made up the bulk of the population's diet (Braudel 1974), would not now be politically acceptable to any government. Even the five-year rolling mean shows variations of plus 26% to minus 19%. As an example of the hidden hand of the market in operation, it is not encouraging: given an essentially fixed demand, prices varied dramatically in the short-term as a result of changes in supply.

The obvious solution to stabilising prices, given annual variations in supply, is storage, a practice that is currently adopted in many countries with regard to wheat; currently storage capacity is about 25% of annual production and demand. Even so, prices remain quite volatile, notably for rice where the entire rice-growing region is subject to the same climatic and meteorological variation from year to year (Jayne 1993). Essentially there is an asymmetry to society in the

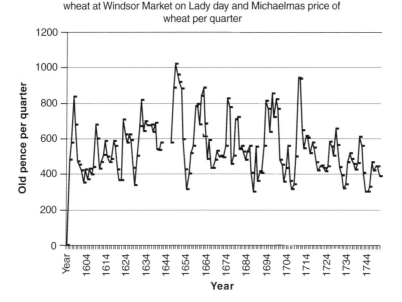

Prices of the quarter of nine bushels of the best or highest priced wheat at Windsor Market on Lady day and Michaelmas price of wheat per quarter

Figure 17.2 *Variations in wheat prices*

payoffs from over- and under-production; it is markedly preferable to have a situation where there is some degree of excess production, even over a long period, than experience a situation where there is under-production, let alone a famine. When the other reasons behind agricultural policies are taken into account, an efficient agricultural policy starts to look singularly unattractive. Given that those people in Asia who live below the poverty line spend around 60% of their total income on cereals which in turn provide over 70% of their total nutrients (Seckler *et al.* 1999), governments in those countries will understandably be highly adverse to volatility in grain prices and concerned to hold down these prices.

So, in agriculture, a competitive market would produce outcomes that are unacceptable and essentially we want market failure; the question is how far it is desirable to move towards another state of market failure than that currently prevailing.

17.3 Agricultural Water Management

In all countries, agriculture takes up the greatest proportion of water demand be this directly in the form of rainfall or indirectly from runoff or groundwater. Essentially, there are three water regimes for agriculture, depending upon whether or not rainfall is sufficient to support crops in terms of quantity, reliability and

Table 17.3 *Precipitation versus potential evapotranspiration requirement*

P/PET ratio	Classification	Implications for agriculture	Rainfall requirements
0.5–0.75	sub-humid zones	humid – rainfed agriculture	>300 mm year in Israel
0.2–0.5 some possible rainfall harvesting – semi-arid 0.03–0.2 rainfall harvesting – arid	semi-arid zones	arid and semi-arid – rainwater harvesting	
<0.03	hyper-arid		<70 mm/year in Israel

Source: Bruins *et al.* 1986.

compatibility with the crop growing cycle (Table 17.3) and, if not, the extent to which the concentration of water in time and space is necessary to support agriculture. In turn, the economic issues in evaluating a shift from one regime to another are fundamentally similar (Section 17.3.4).

Of these three regimes, irrigated agriculture is the most productive, 40% of the world's food being produced from the 17% of arable land that is irrigated. Potentially, irrigated cropland is 3.6 times more productive than non-irrigated cropland and about 36 times more productive than range land (Sundquist 2000).

17.3.1 Rainfed agriculture and supplementary irrigation

Rainfed agriculture requires rainfall that matches or exceeds the crop needs at the different points in the cropping cycle, the soil itself acting as a short-term store for water (Droogers *et al.* 2001). However, rainfall may fail at critical points in the cropping cycle and the timing of the rainfall is obviously uncertain. Supplementary irrigation – defined as the application of a limited amount of water to the crop when rainfall fails to provide sufficient water to increase and stabilise yields (Oweis *et al.* 1999) – may then be used, particularly for high value crops. In England and Wales, in the dry eastern side of the country, supplementary irrigation is used particularly on potatoes and other horticultural crops partly to guarantee the quality of the crop. In addition, the supermarkets and food processors require tight delivery dates for the crops to be met by the farmers. The marginal value of water for these purposes is so high that it can be economic for some farmers to use potable water for irrigation and some do (Rees *et al.* 1993). Weatherhead *et al.* (1994), for example, estimate the crop response to irrigation as varying between £0.21/m^3 for spring field beans and £5.37/m^3 for runner beans in the United Kingdom. Weatherhead *et al.* (1994) calculated crop responses as varying between £3.50/m^3 for raspberries down to £0.10/m^3 for grass for grazing. To these crop response benefits must be added a quality price differential which Morris *et al.* calculated as £1/m^3. Similarly, in Syria, supplementary irrigation increased average rainfed wheat yield from 2.25 tons/ha to 5.9 tons/ha; with increases in dry years from 0.74 tons/ha to 3.83 tons/ha (Oweis *et al.* 1999).

17.3.2 Rainwater harvesting

Water harvesting is defined as the process of concentrating rainfall as runoff from a larger area for use in a neighbouring and smaller area, with the water usually stored in the soil profile of the target area (Oweis *et al.* 1999). Frequently, some storage is added and the system is then one of supplementary irrigation. Rainwater harvesting is most likely to be appropriate where rainfall is reasonably distributed in time (e.g. at least 100 mm in winter rains and 250 mm in summer rains) but inadequate to balance evapotranspiration. Marginal lands with rainfall less than 30 cm a year can be cultivated if controlled but limited additional water is available (Oweis *et al.* 1999); however, the absence of storage complicates the risk analysis (Cohen *et al.* 1995). Some 50% of the world's population live in arid or semi-arid areas and Gilbertson (1986) estimates that 3–5% of these areas may be brought under cultivation by runoff farming.

There are two variants of rainwater harvesting for agriculture; some systems, such as terracing and contour lines of stones (Critchley *et al.* 1991), largely increase the proportion of local rainwater that is captured by reducing the proportion of rainwater that is lost through runoff. If this would still not capture sufficient water then the runoff from a relatively large area can be gathered and used to support a smaller and adjacent area of crops (e.g. Gilbertson 1986). Historically, rainwater harvesting has been a very important method of supplying water for agricultural uses (Lavee *et al.* 1997; Yapa 2001): the Shruj system developed in the Yemen around 6000 years ago (Brunner 2000) and Albarradas of Ecuador are believed to date from at least 4000 years ago (Yapa 2001).

Methods of rainwater harvesting can also conserve soil (Hudson 1987) and there has been a renewed interest in these traditional methods (Agarwal and Narain 1997). However, labour requirements both for construction and maintenance are often high; for example, 1 ha of contour terrace in Kenya is estimated to take 300 person-days to construct and 320 person-hours a year to maintain. Rainwater harvesting has also been a common method of providing for livestock watering. For example, in England, dew ponds were a traditional method of collecting water for these purposes and similar methods are quite widespread in other countries (van Wesemael *et al.* 1998).

For rainwater harvesting to be feasible:

- landscape surfaces must be such that runoff is relatively easily generated by rainfall;
- there must be differences in topography so that runoff can be concentrated; and
- soils in receiving parts must be able to retain and store water.

Increases in yield by a factor of three to four have been demonstrated by experiments in Burkina Faso, Kenya and the Sudan (FAO 1996).

17.3.3   Irrigation

Irrigation works, often on very large scales, characterise these early civilisations on most of the continents and most famously those of Mesopotamia, Egypt and the Indus basin (Postel 1992). The Marib dam in Yemen was constructed around *c*. 600 BC and had a length of 500 metres: effectively this was a very large weir which diverted spate flows into two canals (Hehmeyer 2000). The Dujiangyan project in Sichuan Province in China was constructed around 256 BC as both a flood control and irrigation measure: some 160 000 ha were brought under irrigation by its construction. In Sri Lanka, the kantalai tank, some 16 metres high, was constructed around 280 AD, and King Dhatusena constructed the kalawena tank towards the end of the fifth century AD. With a length of nearly 5 kilometres, and a height of up to 18 metres, this created a reservoir with an area of nearly 20 square kilometres (Mendis 1999). Large-scale dams were similarly being constructed in Iran at least 1300 years ago; for example, the Bahman weir in Fars province. Significant dams were also constructed in North Africa prior to the Roman period (Shaw 1984) and also in South America (Yapa 2001).

The construction of irrigation canals began even earlier and is extremely widespread through the world. Qanats, underground canals running in tunnels that connect to a high point in the water table, are believed to have originated in Persia around 1000 BC. Some 60 000 qanats are still in use in Iran (Lightfoot 2000), as are 11 000 Aflaj in Oman, each irrigating an area of up to 5 square kilometres. The Islamic conquest spread their use across the Middle East (Lightfoot 1997) into North Africa into Spain and from there to Latin America (Beckman *et al.* 1999). The same approach was adopted by the Nasca in Peru from around 600 BC (Yapa 2001). The enormous human effort to construct and to maintain these systems testifies to the gain in productivity that resulted. Droughts, earthquakes, wars, rivers changing course and salinisation of the soil brought down some of these systems (Postel 1992; Williams 1997). However, some irrigation systems have survived for hundreds and in some cases thousands of years, most famously the Huerta of Valencia (Glick 1970) but also the Acequias de Comun of New Mexico (Brown and Rivera 2000) and the water management systems in the Yemen (Hehmeyer 2000).

17.3.4   The benefits of shifting from one regime to another

Provided that the soil is adequate and other inputs are appropriate, then the availability of the required quantities of water at the appropriate times in the growing cycle will increase agricultural productivity in one or more of the following ways:

- increased average yield;
- reduction in year-to-year variability in crop yield;
- reductions in other inputs (e.g. labour for weeding);
- an increase in cropping intensity to more than one crop a year;
- a shift to higher valued crops (e.g. to vegetables or soft fruit);

- an improvement in the quality of the crop;
- greater precision in the time at which the crop can be harvested.

When evaluating the benefits and costs of a potential shift of one regime to another, it is essential to consider the other constraints affecting the decisions of farmers. For example, soil conditions are a major constraint on the crops that can be growth and the potential yield. Thus, Niemi *et al.* (2001) calculate the value of 1 acre foot of water in Oregon as varying from US$9 to US$44 for class V and class 1 soils, respectively.

Whilst the same basic principles apply when evaluating a possible shift from rainfed to supplementary irrigation as from rainfed to rainwater harvesting, and in all other possible shifts, the secondary benefits and costs associated with each shift can be different. In each case, these also need to be considered. For example, rainwater harvesting can reduce soil erosion and reduce the risk of flooding (Yapa 2001); irrigation will make water available for household purposes and may promote groundwater recharge (IWMI-TATA 2002), as may some forms of rainwater harvesting (Agarwal 2001). Conversely, water is often a breeding ground for the insects and other species that carry diseases (Section 14.6).

17.3.4.1 Increases in yield

The increase in yield as a result of irrigation can be significant; in Namibia, the yield of irrigated maize is three times that of rainfed maize; and across Africa as a whole, on average, 1 ha of irrigated land produces 2.2 times the yield of rainfed land (FAO 1996). Across Sub-Saharan Africa, the ratio of the yield from irrigated land to unirrigated land for different crops varies between 1.4 to 5.5 (Figure 17.3). Sanmuganathan *et al.* (2000) give figures of increases in yields through irrigation in India as a factor of between 1.3 and 4.6, and for China of between 1.8 and 6.4. Moreover, the 'green revolution' has in many senses been a water revolution; whilst yields have risen from 2–3 tonnes/ha to 5–6 tonnes/ha (Guerra *et al.* 1998), water productivity has increased by a factor of 3.3 because once the field is adequately irrigated and the crop canopy is closed, evaporation is constant so that improvements in crop yield are not accompanied by an increase in water demand (Seckler 1999).

17.3.4.2 Reduction in year-to-year variability in yields

Whilst the reduction in the probability of partial or complete crop failure is a benefit, the primary benefit from such a reduction is usually the increase in inputs or the switch to a higher valued crop.

17.3.4.3 Reduction in other inputs

Irrigation can have a number of other benefits in addition to adjusting the soil moisture in the root zone of plants. It can have effects on the physical and chemical properties of the soil; reduce soil temperature; substitute for mechanical or

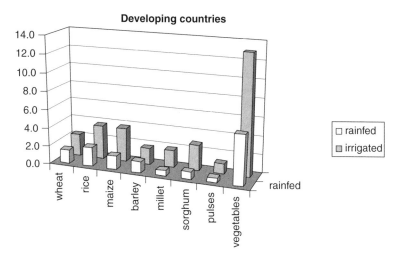

Figure 17.3   *Yields of irrigated and rainfed agriculture. Source: Rosegrant and Perez n.d.*

chemical means of weed control; and substitute for mechanical land preparation before seeding (Smith 1992). These other benefits are particularly true for paddy rice but in turn water is required for these other purposes: 150–250 mm water for land preparation, 50 mm for growing seedlings, plus an ET requirements of 500–1200 mm over 100 days after allowing for losses from seepage and percolation (Guerra *et al*. 1998). Of the water required for land preparation, a high proportion is drained off and during the growing season outflows of water can be 50–80% of the total water input. The paddies themselves provide important local storage that can buffer variations in the availability of irrigation water. Indeed, paddy rice and dryland irrigation are markedly different forms of irrigation. In addition, if water is available for irrigation, it is also available for other purposes, notably household use.

17.3.4.4 Increases in cropping intensity

Given the right temperature conditions, more than one crop a year can be grown given adequate water; in some cases, three crops can be achieved – and rather more in the case of vegetables. However, whilst feasibility studies of irrigation schemes have commonly expected cropping intensities in Asia of 1.8 to 2, the actual achievement has averaged only 1.2 (FAO 1996).

17.3.4.5 Shift to high valued crops

The benefits of irrigation are greatest when conditions allow a shift towards cash crops particularly luxury foods such as soft fruit and vegetables, although potatoes also typically give a high return. This pattern is relatively consistent between countries. Such a switch clearly requires good access to a market in the widest sense; that is, in institutional terms as well as physical access. There is also a gain in output per unit input of water; for example, the water requirement per kg yield varies between 418 kg for citrus fruits through to 1383 kg for bananas and to 2352 kg for wheat in parts of the Middle East (Pohoryles 2000). Yields are also higher for soft fruit and vegetables than for grains and legumes.

17.3.5 Stages in evaluation of changes in regime

The three main stages in evaluating the benefits of a proposed regime change are consequently:

- What is the anticipated cropping pattern with regime as compared to the present pattern?
- How much water will be required for the proposed cropping pattern?
- What is the increased gross margin; the difference between the value of the crop grown and the inputs required?

The first two stages will normally be undertaken by agronomists and social scientists with the economist being involved in the third stage. The first stage is partly a technical and partly a social question; it is usually fairly straightforward to predict what would be the most profitable crops in theory to grow in the particular soil and climate conditions. However, what crops will actually be grown depends upon a range of social and other factors; what might notionally be the most profitable will not be so if it is impossible to get that crop to market. Similarly, a massive expansion in production of what is currently a highly profitable crop will drive the market price downwards. In the second stage, the FAO Penman–Monteith approach (Smith *et al.* 1990) is now typically used to estimate crop water requirements using the crop coefficients given in, for example, Allen *et al.* (1996).

The increase in the gross margin per unit area is the difference in yield times price per unit quantity minus the change in variable costs per unit area plus any changes in fixed costs. Variable costs may increase under the new regime if the anticipated new crop requires additional fertiliser or pesticides; it will almost invariably require an increase in labour costs. Fixed costs may also increase and for this reason it is necessary to consider the effects of irrigation on individual farm holdings.

The analyst is, once an agronomist has assessed what is potentially the changed pattern of agricultural activity in the area, faced with three problems:

- considering whole-farm effects;
- estimating the rate of take-up; and
- evaluating changes in output.

However, because both irrigation and drainage are about changing risks, an important first step is to consider the pattern of water availability that will result from the proposed scheme; the right amount of water at the wrong times in the cropping season will have scant benefits. Hence, a key issue is how will water availability be allocated both spatially and over time? This refers not just to an ordinary year but also to drought years when there will not be enough water for all farmers to satisfy all of their crop requirements. In turn, the obvious questions are how and by whom will these decisions be made? In particular, cropping patterns should be expected to change over time, or cropping patterns would change except that they are constrained by the existing pattern of water allocation.

17.3.5.1 Considering whole-farm effects

A farm is an integrated system which the farmer manages as a whole; however, the area of that farm which may benefit from the changed water management regime may be only a small part of the total farm. A farmer may adopt crop rotations, or there may be interdependencies in the use made of land in different areas; for example, the use of grass for silage for winter feed of animals which are in the summer grazed on higher land. Similarly, fixed costs such as barns and equipment have to be spread over the entire farm and it is unlikely to be worth incurring a high fixed cost if this can only be spread over a small area. A farmer will consequently only make a change to the cropping pattern for land that would benefit from the new water management regime if doing so will result in a higher return from the farm as a whole. In addition, farmers will have adapted to the existing pattern of water management regime and farming may be one of a multiple number of activities which the farmers undertake as part of their adaptation strategy.

Consequently, the focus must be upon the whole-farm effect. Again, in some countries, the two different genders differ in the agricultural activities they undertake. If regime change results in gains to one of those activities which is gender-specific, it may or may not result in benefits to the household as a whole but it will probably have differential effects in terms both of labour and of income on men and women (Rathgeber 1996). Finally, households exist within and are dependent upon a wider community and the effects of the proposed scheme must be assessed in terms of the effects on the wider community.

17.3.5.2 Estimating the rate of take-up

The benefits of the regime change or of land drainage will only occur to the extent that individual farmers adopt new practices or otherwise respond in an efficient manner to the change in the water management regime. Not all farmers will respond at once or indeed at all, so the rate of adaptation or take-up must be estimated. Consequently, it is necessary to assess the rate at which the shift to the predicted new pattern of cropping will take place. As with most forms of innovation it is usual to anticipate an 'S' shaped curve; a slow initial take-up (Bright 1972), followed by a steady rate of take-up, with the last farmers only adapting after a long period, if ever (Morris and Hess 1986). If the rate of take-up is anticipated to be slow then the scheme is less likely to be efficient. Assessing who will take up the predicted change is then critical in assessing the rate of take-up: are some farmers more likely than others to change their farm management practices, and which groups of farmers? Changeover between generations is often a time when the young farmer is prepared to make changes in farm practices which the elder generation did or would not consider (Morris and Hess 1986). At the same time, it is necessary to examine what are the potential barriers to farmers taking up a new cropping pattern. These barriers can include a lack of knowledge, a lack of access to affordable credit, or no access to the market for the crops which are to be produced. The possible responses by the farmers to the proposed change in the water management regime are best understood by talking with the farmers themselves.

The proportion of farmers who are prepared to change will depend in part on the change that they perceive in the risk schedule that they face. In the UK, with relatively large-scale farms, a reduction in the risk of flooding from 1 in 5 to 1 in 10 is usually adjudged to be sufficient for a wide-scale shift in farming practices to occur (Morris and Hess 1986), in part because the other risks of drought, disease, pests and so forth are either low or controlled through pesticides, coupled to a subsidy regime that reduces risks. Thus, land drainage provides a relatively large reduction in the total risk schedule that they face. Other farmers in other countries may be considerably more risk averse or the change brought about by drainage or irrigation may be considerably less in the total risk that they face.

17.3.5.3 Evaluating changes in output

In evaluating the changes in output resulting from the regime change, or land drainage, it is necessary to first correct for own nation distortions in farm gate prices by netting out the effective national subsidies. Where the basis of evaluating the increased yield or change in cropping is to be world prices, it is then necessary to correct for distortions in world prices (Black and Bowers 1984); unfortunately, world prices in many agricultural commodities are thin and world prices are in any case distorted by other countries' subsidisation of their own agriculture. It is also necessary to correct the exchange rate (Squire and van der Tak 1975). One consequence is that the prediction of future movements in the real exchange rate can become critical in assessing the economic efficiency of the scheme (Rayner *et al.* 1984). If the realistic expectation is of a worsening exchange rate against the reference currency, then any project which either results in import substitution or increases exports is more likely to be efficient than if the likelihood in the medium term is of a rising exchange rate.

17.3.6 Externalities of irrigation

The necessary starting point in the evaluation of any new irrigation scheme is: how will the water be collected and transported? The disbenefits of any requirement for a new storage reservoir will require to be evaluated. These disbenefits include possible environmental losses and the displacement of population to make way for the reservoir (WCD 2000). Abstraction from any contained aquifer may also have disbenefits in the form of subsidence of the land above. Pumping in excess of the rate at which that groundwater is renewed is obviously only possible for a limited length of time and raises the question of what will happen to the irrigated area when the groundwater is exhausted. Pumping from unconfined aquifers will usually have environmental consequences as the rivers and wetlands fed from the aquifer dry up. Diverting water may reduce wetlands which typically have a high environmental value.

The transfer of water may have a number of consequences which will depend on the distance over which the water is transferred and whether the water is then mixed with local waters; waters may differ by their temperature, hardness and other factors and the receiving ecosystem may be damaged by the change in the physical-chemical characteristics of the water as well as by the change in flow regime. The linkage of previously unconnected waters may also allow species to move too; there are increasing problems with introduced species and transfer canals, tunnels or pipes may allow these to spread further. Static water is also a good breeding ground for some forms of insects, notably malarial mosquitoes and in Africa, canals and drains serve as breeding grounds for the bilharzia-bearing snails. The canals or pipes will also obstruct both human movement and animal movement including migratory travel.

In developing countries, the use of lands proposed for irrigation is often complex both in socio-economic and environmental terms, and in ways which are not necessarily immediately apparent. Wetlands are often of both high environmental and functional value (e.g. Seyam *et al.* 2001) providing fisheries that are an essential contributor to the local diet. The drainage water from the irrigated areas will often have an enhanced content of salts which may damage the ecosystem of downstream areas, particularly if the drainage water also carries away excess nitrates from fertiliser applications and pesticide runoff.

17.3.6.1 Improvements in the efficiency of an existing irrigation scheme

What is efficiency? Discussions of the efficiency of irrigation combine two elements: loss and productivity. Only some of the water withdrawn actually reaches the plant with the rest being lost through leakage, evaporation and as drainage water. Assessments of the productivity of irrigation water are conditional on the quantity and temporal distribution of all other inputs. In turn, it may thus be better to change the distribution and quantity of other inputs rather than the irrigation regime. Thus, discussions of the efficiency of irrigation are complex

(Kloezen and Garces-Restrepo 1998) and to be useful, multiple measures are necessary, with different decisions requiring different performance indicators. Consequently, various methods of measuring the efficiency of use of water for irrigation have been proposed (e.g. Bos and Nugteren 1990). The proportion of water supplied which is converted into either enhanced crop or a reduction in other inputs can generally be increased but at the cost of increases in capital intensity or in other inputs.

Three possible techniques for improving the efficiency of a scheme are then:

- reducing losses during transfer by, for example, canal lining;
- improving management of irrigation waters by, for example, a shift in application technology; or
- improved water management and cropping by the farmer as the result of an information or educational programme (timing and amounts).

But some of the leakage during transfer may serve to recharge groundwater which is then used for other purposes and the drainage water may be reused by other abstractors or the natural systems downstream. Therefore, a whole catchment approach must be adopted to assessing losses (Chapter 14); what is apparently an inefficient leaky canal may in effect be a very effective way of recharging groundwater (Seckler 1999), as may paddy fields (Seckler *et al.* 1999). In India, Seckler (1999) notes that approximately half of the recharge of the aquifers is from the outflow of irrigation systems.

Sprinkler and drip irrigation are usually argued to be more efficient than the different forms of flood irrigation (Postel 1992). However, the real efficiency measure here is what is lost in evaporation before reaching the plants since runoff flows will be captured by the drainage system and are available for use downstream. It is therefore undesirable to reduce apparent losses through runoff at the cost of increasing evaporation losses. In addition, drip irrigation is not suitable for all crops (Brooks 1996).

Of the water that reaches the plant, some of it is delivered at the wrong times in the wrong amounts to the wrong crops so the productivity of the water may be low as compared to the optimum. That groundwater irrigation is generally found to be twice as efficient as surface water irrigation (Chambers 1988; Estrela *et al.* 1996) is probably a reflection of the greater ability to control when and how much water is delivered through groundwater irrigation: irrigation from groundwater has increased rapidly as real energy costs have fallen so that now 50% of irrigation in India is from tube wells (Crosson and Anderson 1992). Conversely, the travel time for water released from storage is typically about 3 km/hr so that, for example, water released from the High Aswan Dam takes 10 days to reach the delta areas (Keller *et al.* 2000). Better control over the timing of deliveries and application of water can reduce water usage by up to 50%. Where there is uncertainty, farmers may apply more water than necessary to provide a buffer against the next delivery being either late or too small in volume.

This ability to match supply to demand can to some extent to be mirrored by local small-scale reservoirs where these reservoirs are either fed from a main large remote reservoir (Keller *et al*. 2000) or where they collect local rainfall, notably the traditional tank systems of India (Agarwal and Narain 1997) and Sri Lanka (Mendis 1999). Moreover, a major benefit of some large-scale canal irrigation systems is now seen to be the recharge of groundwater through leakage from canals (IWMI-TATA 2002).

Moreover, unless the other inputs to the growing process are also optimised, then the productivity of the water will also be less than could be achieved. Just improving farm management skills via farmers' organisations can improve irrigation efficiency by 10–15% overall and productivity by up to 30% (Xie *et al*. 1993). Opinions differ as to whether it is sensible to make comparisons between areas in terms of the efficiency of water use rather than to compare different irrigation options for one area of land. In general, in developed countries a more efficient outcome is likely to result when capital is substituted for operating costs because capital is relatively cheap and labour and other inputs are relatively expensive. Conversely, in developing countries because capital is expensive, high inputs are usually more efficient than increasing capital intensity. Equally, high capital intensity is associated with high inputs of skilled labour which are also likely to be scarce in the developing countries.

Scale   Across the world, the majority of farms are small, especially subsistence farms. However, such farms produce the majority of food in the world; thus, for example, one million small farmers produce 80% of the food production in Africa. In turn, both irrigation systems and possible methods of improving irrigation efficiency must meet the needs of these small farmers; a small farm translating into both a scarcity of capital and systems suitable for small areas of land.

Low-cost groundwater pumps are particularly useful in raising the incomes of near-subsistence farmers. Although treadle operated pumps were reported in China in 1210 AD (Braudel 1974), these were first introduced in the modern period in Bangladesh and are able to irrigate an area of up to 0.24 ha. In Zambia, farmers' incomes increased from US$125 with bucket irrigation to US$850–1700 with treadle pumps; cropping intensities rose by up to 300%. Similarly, in the Niger, where treadle pumps replaced hand pumps, the average irrigated area per farm rose from 0.17 ha to 0.24 ha, and incomes from US$109 to US$312. In Kenya, where irrigation with a bucket was replaced by a treadle pressure pump, cropping intensities rose to 2.7 per year, irrigated areas per farm from 0.1 ha to 0.27 ha and farm income rose from US$80 to US$690 (IPTRID 2000).

Distribution systems are faced with the same problems; traditional flood irrigation requiring little capital investment. There have been attempts to develop small-scale irrigation systems that are affordable (Polak *et al*. 1998) or institutional systems such as co-operatives may enable small-scale farmers to buy and use more efficient equipment.

17.3.7 Agricultural drainage

Both natural rainfall and excessive irrigation can cause crop losses through water logging, as well as possibly other problems such as salinisation (Postel 1992). Some 500 million hectares of arable land are not adequately drained for optimal production (FAO 2000), largely because of the expense: subsurface drainage in the form of tile drains is particularly expensive with figures of US$1500–3000 per hectare being given for Australia.

In most cases, the purpose of agricultural drainage and its benefits are the same as for irrigation and the economic evaluation of these benefits follows the same procedures. Whether irrigation, irrigation and drainage or drainage alone is required depends partly upon the climate and partly upon cropping. Thus, for example, the Fens of eastern England were first reclaimed from the sea and drained (Purseglove 1988) and are now increasingly being irrigated as well. As Table 17.4 shows, the response of crops to drainage shows a very similar pattern to that found for irrigation: the greatest gains are when cropping can switch to horticulture.

17.3.7.1 Flood losses

Flood and recession irrigation is a traditional form of irrigation (e.g. Shaw 1984), and one that is still quite widely practised in some parts of the world (Marchand 1987). Thus, for example, Paul (1984) points out that in Bangladesh rice paddy farming depends upon some flooding, and varieties of rice that are adapted to relatively deep water flooding are used. Hence, it is only the extreme floods that cause problems. Floods may bring other benefits; for example, the addition of silt or blue-green nitrogen-fixing algae which will improve soil fertility (Brammer 1990). In turn, this means that it is necessary to look across several years of

Table 17.4 *Economic benefits of land drainage in the UK*

Land use type	Economic net return (£/ha drainage status – 1997/98 prices)		
	good	bad	very bad
Extensive grass	−73	−81	−103
Intensive grass	320	245	131
Grass/arable rotation	283	215	115
All cereal rotation	280	217	109
Cereal/oil seed rotation	329	263	165
Cereal/root crop rotation	280	217	109
Horticulture	1500	750	109

Source: Dunderdale 1998.

crop figures in order to assess flood losses to crops as yields may increase in the following year as a result of these flood-induced improvements in fertility. Conversely, floods may also deposit sand, as did the 1993 Mississippi flood (Galloway Report 1994), with a consequent reduction in soil fertility.

In addition, crop losses are usually reported as financial losses (Galloway Report 1994) and hence markedly overstate the economic costs of losses; what is lost is the economic value of the crop minus the variable costs that would have been committed even if the flood did not occur. In turn, under subsidy regimes, the real economic value of the crop can be markedly less than the financial value. Equally, it may sometimes be possible for the farmer to plant a different crop after the flood which will give a return that makes up some of the losses to the standing crop during the flood. However, irrespective of the loss to crops, the loss of livestock and particularly of draught animals in floods can still have severe consequences. Equally, to poor farmers, the loss of one crop may be sufficient to destroy their capacity to plant in a subsequent year, particularly if they have had to go into debt to buy the seeds and other inputs for the crop that was lost in the flood. To the farming family who are now destitute it is of little compensation that from a national economic perspective those who take over their land will get a bumper crop next year.

Hess and Morris (1986) provide the following equation to estimate the losses caused by flooding to arable crops:

$$L = Y + (P_r \times RC) - (P_h \times HC) + REM$$

where:

Y is the loss of output (reduction in yield times price);
P_r is the annual probability of the need to reseed;
RC is the cost of reseeding;
P_h is the annual probability of complete harvest loss;
HC is the cost of harvest and inputs avoided because of flooding;
REM are the post-flood clean-up costs.

For the flooding of grassland and other animal feedstuffs, Hess and Morris (1986) then give the following equation:

$$D = GMJ \times RF + C$$

where:

GMJ is the energy from grass lost due to flooding (MJ/ha);
RF is the cost of replacement feed (£/MJ); and
C refers to the other costs incurred.

Care is also needed to distinguish between losses that are the result of poor drainage and flood losses; rises in groundwater levels into the root zone, or

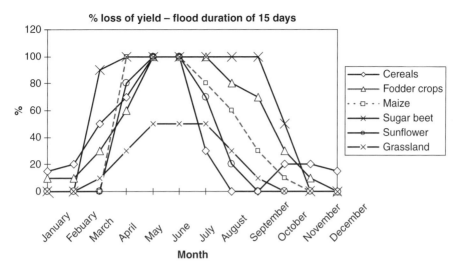

Figure 17.4 *Agricultural losses from flooding in Hungary. Source: Podmaniczky 1999*

standing local rainfall, have often damaged or destroyed most of the value of the standing crop before the land is flooded from the nearby river (Hong and Zhang-Yu 1999). For example, the drainage system, and particularly the pumping system, of a polder will not usually be designed to cope with a rainfall greater than that with a 10- to 20-year return period whilst the polder dikes may be designed to contain river flows with a return period of 50 to 100 years. If local rainfall accompanies high flows in the river, then the crops will have been damaged before the dike fails. A significant fraction of the crop losses in the 1993 Mississippi flood appear to have been losses from local rainfall and drainage problems rather than flood losses (Galloway Report 1994).

The extent of the crop losses due to flooding then depend upon the point in the growing season at which the flood occurs and the duration of the flooding, and to a lesser extent on the depth of flooding. In turn, the critical months for flooding differ between the northern and southern hemispheres (Figures 17.4 and 17.5).

17.4 Charging for Irrigation Water

Having determined what is the cost of the water supplied for irrigation (Chapter 7), the question is then how to recover that cost. The general rule is that the cost of controlling access to a resource and recovering the costs should not exceed the benefits of doing so. Applying marginal cost pricing will be easiest and most likely to be viable when water is supplied by pipeline, by elevated canals or from boreholes and in developed economies where the capital and maintenance costs of water meters are relatively low. Furthermore, transaction

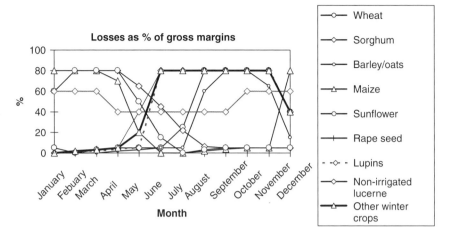

Figure 17.5   *Agricultural losses from flooding in Australia. Source: Higgin 1981*

costs as a function of revenue show economies of scale: the costs of charging a few big users are considerably less than charging many small users for the same total amount of water.

Secondly, it does not follow that excessive use is simply the result of too low a price: salinisation of soil as a result of over-irrigation is an observable problem with a high associated cost; the implication is that the farmers do not know what is the marginal value of water since they are applying water beyond the point where it has a negative marginal value.

In systems when water is simply available in open channels from which it is then moved on to the land which is to be irrigated, it is difficult to measure how much water is being abstracted, the necessary first step to applying marginal cost pricing. In some cases, a marginal cost mechanism is in place in that the water must be physically lifted from the supply canal on to the land using human, animal or mechanical power. Thus, for example, in Egypt, the farmer has an incentive to minimise the use of irrigation water because the labour or other costs of lifting water are significant. In principle, where mechanical or electrical power is used for lifting, taxation on the lifting cost could be used as a surrogate for marginal cost pricing of water, but such a tax would spill over in other, possibly undesirable, directions. Even where volumetric charging is feasible in theory, it will require meters which must be maintained by scarce skilled labour and possibly the import of the meters themselves.

Alternative cost recovery mechanisms are charges per unit area of the farm or taxes based upon the notional value of the improvement in land value or on the notional crops produced (Johansson n.d.). These mechanisms may provide an incentive to the farmer to change the cropping pattern; they do not provide any incentive for the farmer to make the best use of available water.

One way round the problem is the conversion of state-run systems to farmer-run organisations (e.g. Bruns and Atmanto 1992). If farmers as a group are required to pay $x for a bulk quantity y of water then they have some incentive to spread that cost over a group until the size of that group z is such that the marginal value of the water to the individual farmer is equal to x/z. The group then has an incentive to ensure that water is properly allocated since one farmer can only increase his or her allocation at the cost of the other farmers. The individual farmer also in theory has an incentive to make the best use of the quantity of water for which she or he has paid both in terms of cropping and in application of that water. However, it is not yet entirely clear that water is used more efficiently in water user associations than in conventional state-run irrigation systems (Vermillon 1997).

A possible way of introducing an incentive for farmers to use water efficiently is to require them to provide on-site storage of water. Since this will take up land which could otherwise be used to grow crops, they are then provided with an incentive to make the most efficient use of water and so minimise the land requirement for storage. In England, in recent years, new licences for irrigation have often been limited to winter abstraction, when the rivers are in flood, so farmers have been effectively compelled to build on-farm reservoirs.

17.5 Tradable Entitlements to Abstraction

Tradable entitlements have proved to be a very successful way of reducing the costs of air pollution abatement (Opschoor and Vos 1989). Consequently, it is not surprising that their application to water abstraction has been recommended (e.g. Howe *et al.* 1986), or that they have been tried in some countries (e.g. Pigram *et al.* 1992).

Tradable entitlements to abstraction have been proposed for a number of reasons:

- The existing allocation of entitlements to abstract water is inflexible and incapable of responding to changes in uses and to the relative values of those uses (this is particularly the case where agricultural uses have established an entitlement to abstract and consequently consume the majority of water available, but where the value of this water is relatively low compared to expanding urban uses).
- The theoretical efficiency gain from their use relative to administrative methods.

Whilst some reallocation between agricultural uses is foreseen to result from the introduction of tradable abstraction permits, generally the main reason for proposing their introduction is so that water is transferred from agricultural to urban uses.

The extent to which the first problem has been created depends upon the system of water law that exists; the Prior Appropriation doctrine in the western United

States (Wright 1990) was a remarkably successful means of bringing water into use. However, most of the 'First in Time, First in Right' entitlements created under the doctrine were for agricultural uses and the only way that existed to reallocate water to other uses was to buy the land to which the water entitlement was attached. Hence, some urban areas have been buying farms in order to acquire the entitlement to use the water (Chang and Griffin 1992). Equally, overallocation of water has resulted in environmental damage. So Landry (1998) has made the rather bizarre suggestion that those who believe that rivers should support trout, should buy water entitlements from the farmers who are abstracting unsustainable amounts of water that render the rivers unable to support trout. In countries where other systems of law exist, notably Islamic or Spanish colonial law (Section 8.1.1), effective legal mechanisms exist to reallocate water and the only reason for creating tradable entitlements to abstraction is then the possibility of efficiency gains.

A distinction must also be made between the nature of the resource that supports the abstraction. Groundwater is treated as an open access resource in most countries so, whilst active markets exist in a number of countries for the sale of abstracted groundwater (Shah 1993), these are not examples of a system of tradable entitlements to abstraction. The two other systems of resource are then entitlements to abstract from the run of the river, and abstractions that are supported by reservoirs and distribution systems. In the latter case, the obvious first step is to eliminate subsidies to irrigation; in turn, this should both free up some water for other uses and drive up the efficiency of use. Hence, the key test of tradable entitlements in unsupported abstractions.

17.5.1 Experience with tradable entitlements to abstraction

The country with greatest experience in the use of tradable entitlements is Australia and it is also the country where they seem to have been most successful. Pigram (1999) reports that in the four states involved, trades have involved 5–10% of total water use. However, most of the trades involve a temporary leasing: in the Goulburn-Murray Irrigation district in 1997/98, some 250 000 ML were leased (8% of total water use) and only about 25 000 ML were permanently traded, 1.1% of the total entitlement (Earl and Turner 2000); by 1996, some 20% of irrigators had been involved in some sort of trading. Similarly, the majority of transfers in New South Wales have also been on a temporary basis; for example, in the Macquaries valley, cotton planters drove up the price from A$80 to A$120 for the last watering (Department of Land and Water Conservation 1999). Consequently, in Australia as a whole, the majority of transfers were temporary: over 800 000 ML in 1994/95. Trading is very largely restricted to supported catchments in New South Wales but trading has increased by over thirteen-fold since the 1993–94 season (Department of Land and Water Conservation 1999). As the Department goes on to observe, since government policy is to adjust entitlements downwards to match available resources, the price will rise: consequently, it makes sense to hold on to any entitlements or to lease them rather than to sell them now.

On the down side, only 40% of volumes traded in Victoria resulted in increased or reduced water use so the remainder were of unused entitlements (Earl and Turner 2000). Bjornlund and McKay (2000) also report that a significant proportion of the trades involved sleeper or 'dozer entitlements': ones not currently being used by the seller. In turn, Smith (1998) reports that the effect of such trades was to increase total abstraction in a single year. However, for some time previously, the pattern of development of water use had been one of the activation of sleeper permits (Department of Land and Water Conservation 1998). In turn, the Murray–Darling Basin Ministerial Council announced a cap on diversions from the Basin in order to protect downstream rights and also to reduce the stress on the aquatic environment. This cap was then set at the level for the 1993/94 season for each valley.

However, Bjornlund and McKay (2000) also report that there was a shift of water towards efficient irrigators although this was within existing farming practices. The Department of Land and Water Conservation (1999) reports that 49.3% of water sales in South Australia were from lucerne and grain, with another 13.3% from dairy pastures whilst 26.9% of buyers were vineyards and 38.1% were engaged in horticulture. Thus, water was being traded away from low valued agricultural uses towards high valued uses. A similar pattern was found in Victoria although the trades were largely within the livestock industry but away from meat towards dairy production. In addition, tax provisions are thought to influence the pattern of sales/leases: leasing water on an annual basis can be offset against income tax but the purchase of a permanent entitlement is not tax deductible, whilst the leasing out of water can be offset against expenses for tax purposes whereas a sale might attract capital gains tax. Australian irrigation is also supported by reservoirs and effectively an entitlement is then a share of capacity sharing versus release sharing (Pigram 1999). Although charges for irrigation have been increased, the level of charges does not yet cover the full costs of providing for the storage and the distribution of irrigation water (Musgrave 2000).

The other major experiment in tradable entitlements to abstraction has been in Chile. Quite different views are held about the relative success of this experiment (e.g. Bauer 1998; Briscoe *et al.* 1998). But, in the upper Maipo and Elqui, there have been relatively few transactions, with sales in the Elqui being sales out of agriculture of water not previously used – sleeper rights (Hearne and Easter 1995). Although in 1992, 85% of sales were from agriculture to urban areas, these accounted for only 3% of sales by volume and only provided sufficient water to supply 10 000 customers (Brehm and Castro 1995). As in Australia, the majority of trades were leasing rather than sales (Brehm and Castro 1995). Transactions of the Limari river were relatively frequent but here irrigation is supported by a reservoir and there is a publicly provided infrastructure by which the water can be transferred (Hearne and Easter 1995). Davis and Lund (2000) argue that in the other, short and steep valleys, it is difficult to transfer water. Sales of water entitlements to mining companies are reported to have resulted in increased usage (Bauer 1998).

Two significant failures in the strategy to create tradable entitlements in Chile are, firstly, that there was a failure to establish a clear record of who held what entitlements and the way in which these entitlements were initially distributed (Brehm and Quiroz 1995). Secondly, there is no cost associated with holding an unused entitlement, so there is a tendency to hold on to such entitlements rather than to sell them (Solanes 1999).

Rather more limited experiments have been conducted in the USA (Howe *et al.* 1986) although the Colorado studies may be said to have started the interest in the approach. Outside of Colorado, on the Lower Rio Grande in Texas, sales of sleeper permits away from agriculture are reported (Chang and Griffin 1992). 'Water banks' then offer a way of lubricating the sale or leasing of water entitlements. The Texas Water Development Board water bank, established in 1993, allows the holders of water entitlements to deposit up to half of their allocation to the bank for others to buy or lease; rights placed in bank are protected from cancellation for nonuse for an initial 10 years. In Idaho farmers with surplus entitlements lease more than 100 000 acre-feet annually through water banks (Bowman n.d.).

During the drought of 1991 to 1992, a Drought Water Bank was established in California and this actively sought for purchases, offering a price of US$125 per acre-foot: 369 water transfers were made through the bank, totalling just over 1 million acre-feet of water. Of that amount, some 414 000 acre-feet of water were released from fallowing but 420 000 acre-feet were from groundwater (Department of Water Resources 1993). The experience of that bank illustrates some of the problems in ensuring that what is sold or leased is 'real water' rather than 'paper water' (Seckler 1996), and it was found that each deal had to be evaluated separately in order to ensure that only 'real' water made available by reducing losses or flow to unusable water bodies was actually being purchased. Paper water then included return flows that would otherwise have been used by downstream appropriators, which also revealed an additional problem in that irrigators can measure how much they put on to the fields but have to guess what they lose through evapotranspiration or, alternatively, the quantity of drainage water. The California Department of Water Resources reported that the bank and potential sellers often had different views of these hydrological realities (Department of Water Resources 1993). The problem of paper water transfers is a major one: there must be a suspicion that the transfer of some water entitlements from the Imperial Valley irrigation district in exchange for the lining of some irrigation canals (Postel 1992) was something in the nature of a paper transaction with the real losers being those who were using the groundwater recharged by leakage from the canals.

17.5.2 Transfers out of agriculture

If towns can buy farms in order to acquire that farm's water entitlement, then is there an advantage to separating the water entitlement from the land? In the case of arid land, effectively the entire value of the land for agricultural purposes will be determined by its access to water. More generally, for the farmers to be prepared to sell some or all of their entitlement to water, then, unless they are not currently using all of their entitlement, they have to reduce their use of water. The possibilities are:

1. Fallowing the land.
2. Switching to dryland farming.
3. Shifting to crops that require less water.
4. Increasing the efficiency of irrigation.
5. Retiring from agriculture and converting the land to other uses.
6. Constructing on-site storage so as to shift demand to high flow periods when abstraction entitlements can be more cheaply acquired.
7. Using groundwater instead of surface water if controls, possibly including tradable entitlements, are not also imposed on the use of groundwater.

For the outcome of a system of tradable entitlements to be advantageous, then the circumstances under which farmers sell some or all of their entitlements need to result in a desirable outcome. The conventional assumption would seem to be that the farmer will adopt strategy 2, 3 or 4. But the farmer has other options, some of which are undesirable from the wider perspective. If the farmer is contemplating retiring from farming then attractiveness to the farmer of selling the water entitlement and land separately will depend upon the relative states of the two markets. If prices of agricultural land with or without water are low, but the market for water for urban uses is strong, then it is logical to seek to sell the two separately, provided that the premium for urban uses exceeds the difference in the price of agricultural land with and without an attached water entitlement. If the difference in the value of agricultural land with and without a water entitlement is large, then it should be expected that there will now be strong pressure to convert that land to another use. So, we should expect farms on urban fringes to sell the water and develop the land.

To avoid perverse incentives, then it would be logical to require all developers of land to purchase a water entitlement sufficient to provide the water needs of that development. If this is not done, then it would be open for a farmer to sell the water entitlement, develop the land for urban purposes and then require the municipality to supply that development with water. Under some circumstances, the municipality would be left worse off under this arrangement than before; if the farmer had an entitlement to 50 cm per square metre but the development had a density of 60 people per hectare, each of whom uses 250 l/p/d, the water requirement per hectare of land increases after development.

Finally, the farmer may switch from surface water irrigation to abstracting groundwater. This is what seems to have been the basis of a proportion of the transactions with the water bank set up in California during the 1987–1992 drought (Department of Water Resources 1993). Such a switch is clearly a danger particularly where groundwater is an open access resource and especially when the aquifer is unconfined.

More generally, as Davis and Lund (2000) have pointed out, agricultural and urban supplies are associated with very different levels of risk; the risk of unavailability of supply that is acceptable to a farmer is quite unacceptable for urban uses. Even when irrigation is supported by a reservoir, the design drought for that reservoir is typically a much lower standard than would be required for urban uses.

17.5.3 Tradable entitlements?

For a market approach to be effective, there are a series of conditions that must be satisfied:

- There must be many different and relatively small potential purchasers and sellers of water if there is to be effective competition.
- There must be heterogeneity of demand particularly over time – if the entire demand is from potato growers then there are unlikely to be any gains from trade since all the farmers require water at exactly the same time and all have a very similar scope for using water more efficiently.

The hidden element in the standard definition of the conditions for the perfect competitive market is that whilst the pool of sellers and the pool of buyers are both individually homogeneous, the two populations are different. The primary assumed difference is that one produces and the other consumes. But a market for water abstraction is a market between consumers; by analogy, it is as if loaves of bread were first to be shared out between consumers and then consumers were to be left to trade bread with each other.

In such a market for tradable entitlements, there have to be sufficient differences within the common pool of potential sellers and buyers so that some are prepared to sell in order for others to buy. If the pool is completely uniform, there will be no one prepared to sell and hence nothing to be bought. Unless there is a reason to believe that the pool is heterogeneous, then there is no purpose in introducing a system of tradable entitlements. These are the conditions necessary to create an approximation to a perfectly competitive market and they are likely to limit potential use of tradable entitlements to relatively large rivers, or where there are marked differences in the quality of the soils in different areas, or differences in access to markets. In the latter case, there are likely to be sales of water away from farmers on poor soils and with limited access to markets towards those who can, for example, plant vines or engage in horticulture. Thus, in New South

Wales, the gross margin on water use is A$25/ML for wheat in the Macquarie Valley versus A$1289 for avocados, A$2456 for macadamias and A$2917 for Murcott mandarins, and A$2917 for vines in the Hunter valley (Department of Land and Water Conservation 1999). But critically the higher gross margins are associated with permanent plantings and the demand is for high security water rather than the low security water which is acceptable for wheat farming.

If these conditions are met and a tradable entitlement approach is feasible, then a further series of decisions must be made:

- At any point in the catchment, the individual demand must be low relative to supply in the river at that point otherwise location effects will be significant – for example, if the demand is shifted upstream by a trade then the impacts will be different to that same demand being shifted downstream.
- It has been found necessary to ensure that there is a cost to holding a water right (Solanes 1999) otherwise holding rights is an effective way of blocking the entry of competitors into the market. If water is currently subsidised, then it is more logical to eliminate those subsidies rather than to try a band-aid approach of introducing tradable entitlements.
- If a private property right to water abstraction does not already exist then a decision has to be made as to how tradable entitlements are to be allocated initially. In Chile, when the state monopoly hydroelectric power company was privatised, it was allowed to take with it all its existing water rights. As a result, it is able to exploit its monopoly position (Solanes 1999). A tradable entitlement where there is an active market will necessarily be of a higher value than an existing right. Therefore, those with existing rights can be offered the choice of either keeping their existing fixed right or exchanging it for an entitlement for a lower but tradable amount. Alternatively, the entitlements could be auctioned with the sums raised being used to extinguish existing rights; this option also allows scope for cutting down the total permitted volume of abstraction to what is either realistically available or sustainable. It also avoids giving a further subsidy to agriculture as is the case if farmers are simply awarded a tradable entitlement equal to their current right to abstract.
- Whether environmental requirements are to be top-sliced from the available sustainable flows or environmental requirements are to be met through purchase in the market (Department of Land and Water Conservation 1999; Landry 1998). In the latter case, there is then the question of how such purchases are to be funded and the sum that is to be made available to fund such purchases (Morris *et al.* 1997).
- A decision has to be made as to what a right is to consist of; whether it is to a proportion of the flow at particular times in the year, or whether there are to be layered rights to particular quantities of water if that water is available. Since there will usually be more water available at one time of the year than another, rights will also need to be specified in terms of a quantity in a given month or perhaps season; furthermore, whether this right is as to the amount

that can be abstracted or as to the amount that can be consumed (e.g. net of return flows).

• These rights have to take account of possible changes in the amount of water available either because of changes elsewhere on the catchment that will change runoff, as a result of climate change, or because flows were miscalculated in the first place. Solanes (1999) reports that present applications for water amount to four times total exploitable resources available in Chile.

• A system for both enabling trades to take place and to monitor compliance also has to be established, along with an enforcement regime. This is unlikely to be less costly than a conventional licensing regime, particularly if rights are to the amounts consumed rather than to the amounts abstracted.

Transfer of an entitlement to abstract water from one basin to another is unlikely to be practical and transferring water from one basin to another will tend to create additional externalities. In addition, unless the flows in the river or canal are large then there are practical limits to the amounts that can be transferred up or downstream. A hypothetical irrigation system is shown in Figure 17.6.

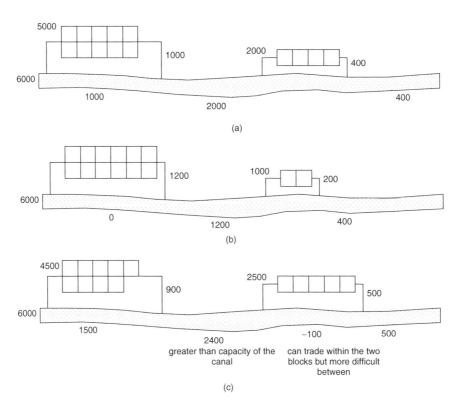

Figure 17.6   *Hypothetical catchment and irrigation*

There are 10 farmers in the upstream irrigation district and four farmers in the downstream district; each farmer abstracts 500 units of water and returns 100 units as drainage water to the irrigation canal. Consequently, out of the 6000 units of water available in the system, total utilisation is 7000 units of water. In Figure 17.6b, two of the farmers in the downstream irrigation area have sold their total entitlement to farmers in the upstream irrigation district. This is the maximum it is possible to sell because only 6000 units of water enter the main irrigation canal. As Figure 17.6c shows, it is not physically possible for a sale to occur from the upstream to downstream block; a cut of 500 units of abstraction to the upstream block only increases the flow to the downstream block by 400 units. Moreover, if the main irrigation canal was only designed to have a capacity of 2000 units then it would be impossible to transfer the additional amount to the downstream area.

If instead of a canal, the main irrigation water distributor is a river, then in the baseline condition it is already very badly degraded; if water entitlements are traded from the downstream area to the upstream area, then further damage is done to the ecosystems dependent upon the flow, with one section of river running completely dry. Since the geomorphological form of a river is a function of its flow, the river channel would be expected to degrade and narrow as a consequence of the lower flows in this section so that the natural capacity of the channel is decreased. In turn, this might result in an increased flood risk in the areas neighbouring those stretches of the river. Either effect might be sufficiently large to overwhelm any apparent gains from trade.

In this hypothetical example, there is limited scope for reallocating water between the two irrigation districts. Transaction costs would be expected to be quite high since it will be necessary to determine whether the transfer involves real and not paper water, to assess the environmental externalities associated with any change, and any side effects such as an increase in flood risk. The marketplace will not be able to take care of these effects because the farmers cannot be expected to have knowledge of the hydrological functioning of the canal or river as a whole. This example illustrates that there can be a conflict between the principle of holistic catchment management so as to maximise the efficiency of use of the catchment as a whole and the approach of piecemeal local optimisation that forms the basis of the tradable permits approach. As the basin approaches closure, the impacts on the functioning of the basin as a whole from one small change will tend to increase. However, it is precisely when the basin is either closed or approaching closure that we need to make improvements in managing it.

These problems do not exist or not to the same extent for trades within the two irrigation districts and so more trades are likely to be possible between the farmers in each of those two districts. Hence this example does provide some clues as to the extent and nature of trades that are likely to take place in the real world.

Case Study 17.1 Tradable Abstraction Entitlements in East Anglia

The Water Resources Act 1963 brought abstractions in England and Wales under a coherent system of control. However, it created two classes of abstractors; those who could demonstrate that they have been abstracting a given quantity of water in the five years prior to 1965 gained a licence of right in perpetuity. There was no provision that the licence would be lost if there was no use made of that abstraction right; however, those licences tied the use of the water to particular parcels of land in the case of licences for irrigation. Licences granted to those who applied to abstract water after 1965 are time limited and a number of conditions may also be applied to those licences. Thus, an inequitable system was created of two different classes of abstractors. Moreover, for some rivers, the abstraction licences allow abstraction of more water than was available (Drake and Sherriff 1987), whilst at the same time, the amounts abstracted are, on average, far less than the amounts licensed. Where those unused abstraction licences, 'sleeper' licences, are licences of right then there would be major problems if the holders of these licences sought to abstract that water.

The Water Resources Act 1991 allows the Environment Agency to introduce restrictions on abstractions during drought years. It also allows the Agency to charge for abstractions; to a base charge rate constant for all forms of abstraction, a series of multipliers are applied that cover the time of year when abstraction occurs, the nature of the source, and the proportion of the abstraction amount that will not be returned to the river. In 1995/96, the basic charge rate in the Anglian region of the Environment Agency was £13.94 per 1000 cubic metres.

Agriculture is not a major user of water in England and Wales, with only supplementary irrigation via spray irrigation being useful in some parts of the country, notably East Anglia – other forms of irrigation (drip, trickle and subirrigation) do not require a licence.

In 1995, the Flood Hazard Research Centre and Silsoe College were commissioned by the Royal Society for the Protection of Birds, an NGO, to conduct a study of the potential impacts of the introduction of tradable abstraction licences. A number of the RSPB's most important reserves are wetlands which could be severely damaged by a reduction in water availability. The Society, whilst broadly favouring the extension of the use of economic instruments, was concerned that the adoption of tradable permits would not result in the activation of some of the sleeper licences.

The area study was in East Anglia and covered *c.* 300 ha RSPB nature reserve at the Nene Washes and 11 861 ha of agricultural land within the Middle Level Commissioners Internal Drainage Board – drainage being essential in the area if the low-lying land is to be put to arable use. The Nene Washes nature reserve is designated a Special Protected Area in accordance with the European Union's Birds Directive; in consequence, the UK is required under European law to ensure that no damage occurs to that site. The agricultural area is one of the richest in the country; the crop pattern at the time of the study being: cereals 54%; sugar beet 22%; potatoes 11%; and grassland 10%. The mean rainfall is 536 mm compared to a PET of 487 mm so supplementary irrigation can be required; this is focused on potatoes, vegetables and soft fruit. The water is taken directly from the river and there is no storage reservoir to maintain flows on that river. The marginal value of that water is very high; for example, £10.20 ha/mm for early potatoes and £42 ha/mm for strawberries (Weatherhead *et al.* 1994). However, of the amount of water licensed for abstraction, only 26 to 57% of that amount is actually abstracted.

Continued on page 311

___ *Continued from page 310* ___

The research plan was first to carry out a series of focus groups with the farmers in the area in order to develop a system of tradable permits that would meet their needs. The intention was then to carry out with the farmers a simulation of a number of annual rounds of trading using that system of tradable permits and individual farm models. However, the results of the focus groups showed that the farmers did not have the knowledge of the current costs and benefits of irrigation for the simulation exercise to be useful. Equally, those focus groups suggested that farmers would only sell tradable rights if they intended to leave agriculture altogether. Box 17.1 lists the issues that were discussed in the focus groups; Box 17.2 summarises the main points that emerged in regard to agriculture and water whilst Box 17.3 outlines the main points made by the farmers concerning tradable abstraction licences.

Box 17.1 *Issues addressed in the focus groups*

- Should the allowance for the environment be 'top-sliced' or should water for the environment be bid for?
- How should the initial allocation of tradable permits be determined?
- What should the entitlement be under a permit (e.g. amount per month, share of resource)?
- How should the system adapt to future increases or decreases in available supply (e.g. as a result of climate change)?
- Who should administer the scheme?
- Over what area should the permits be tradable?
- Between which classes of abstractors should the permits be tradable?
- Should there be different classes of permit with different guarantees of reliability of supply?
- How should the system be policed?
- Should there also be charges for abstraction?

Box 17.2 *Farmers' general views on water and farming*

- The existing system is inefficient because abstraction points are tied to particular parcels of land; therefore, farmers often require larger licensed quantities than they actually need.
- The existing system of licensing is difficult to understand, cumbersome, expensive and slow.
- The Navigation Acts dating back to the 1760s impose significant constraints on water abstraction.
- Winter runoff from their land is their water and they ought to be able to keep it for themselves for summer use.
- They see agriculture as being given the lowest priority for water use.

___ *Continued on page 312* ___

___ *Continued from page 311* ___

- The cost of water itself used in irrigation does not feature strongly in financial appraisals of irrigation and is not considered in assessing alternative methods of irrigation: the main costs are pumping and labour.
- An abstraction license adds value to the land.
- Because the farmers are all growing the same crop, they all want water at the same time, especially July and August.

Box 17.3 Farmers' views on tradable abstraction licences

- Tradable permits would mean that water ran out earlier and hence cessation orders would be issued earlier in the season. The threat of cessation makes the value of a tradable permit more difficult to assess.
- Other potential buyers (e.g. the water companies, environmental groups) have more spending power with which farmers would find it difficult to compete. They would not therefore want any trading to be extended outside of the agricultural market.
- Because irrigation is capital intensive, 10 years of certainty is needed to justify investment in irrigation so short-term (annual or seasonal) water leasing is not very helpful.
- The idea of a banded priority system of permits is extremely unattractive because of lack of certainty that water will be available when needed.
- Environmental requirements should be set first by the Environment Agency with water being 'top-sliced' for the environment.
- Permits, like licences, would need to set both daily and annual abstraction limits.
- The cost of water is likely to rise under a tradable permit system.
- Selling water would mean changing the cropping pattern.
- No one will be willing to give up water and therefore tradable permits will not work. Moreover, since water was anticipated to become scarcer in the longer term, they would hold their licences in order to keep their options open for the future.
- Those who would be prepared to sell water would be farmers retiring or leaving the industry and those who invested in on-farm storage and would be prepared to sell any surplus – tradable permits would encourage investment in on-farm storage.
- Any tradable permit system would need policing.

The end conclusion was that freeing up the existing licensing system would achieve most of the potential gains from a tradable permits system. The proposed improvements were to cease to specify the parcel of land to which the water could be applied; to encourage farmers to construct on-farm reservoirs for winter filling; and to allow farmers who had constructed an on-farm storage reservoir to sell water

___ *Continued on page 313* ___

___ Continued from page 312 ___

to their neighbours. A subsequent, wider study also concluded that there would be few economic benefits from introducing a system of tradable abstraction licences in England and Wales (RPA 2000). Equally, the farmers placed great stress on the need for certainty, whereas the potential gain from a system of tradable permits is that of flexibility and adaptability.

As compared to other countries where tradable permits have been introduced, the notable differences here were:

- Irrigation has not been subsidised nor supported by major infrastructural works and abstraction from rivers instead attracts a significant charge.
- Only supplementary irrigation is necessary and the marginal value of water for that purpose is high compared to its value for domestic or industrial purposes.
- Irrigation is a small proportion of the total demand for water, and in the event of a drought, the first use for which the use of water is restricted.
- The rivers are very small as are the areas across which water could be traded.

The general lesson is that there are no general lessons about the applicability of tradable permits; the solution needs to be tailored to local circumstances and the starting point must be to discuss with the current and potential abstractors what are their needs and requirements.

A review by the government of the system of abstraction licensing resulted in a decision to phase out licences of right, without compensation, so as to bring all licences within a single system of time limited licences with associated conditions (DETR 2000b) and the introduction of strategic abstraction plans for catchments (Environment Agency 2000b).

17.6 Aquaculture

One-fifth of the total value of fish production is from freshwater (Winpenny n.d.) and as wild sea fisheries decline through over-fishing, fish farming is increasing, growth averaging nearly 10% a year since 1984 (Rana 1997). In some areas, freshwater fisheries contribute a significant proportion of the total intake of protein (Brummett and Chikafumbwa 2000) although globally fish provide only a small part of the diet (FAO 1996). The negative impacts of different projects, notably dams, channelisation of rivers, and particularly either the draining or reduction of water supply to wetlands on wild fisheries can be significant. The expansion of shrimp production also frequently involves the conversion of mangroves which in turn play an important role is sustaining wild fisheries. Alternative, the expansion of aquaculture through either combined paddies/fisheries can yield significant economic benefits (MacKay 1995; Halwart 1998), as may the construction or use of ponds or tanks for fisheries, as part of a sustainable livelihood approach (Edwards 2000). The FAO (1997) sets out the framework for the economic appraisal of aquacultural projects.

It is reported that for carp ponds in Germany, discharges of phosphorus and nitrogen are reduced below the levels in the inflow water (Knosche *et al.* 1998), however, intensive fish production systems release quite large amounts of nutrients (European Inland Fisheries Advisory Commission 1998) and the overall inter-relationships between aquaculture and the environment are complex (Barg and Phillip n.d.). However, aquaculture can be more water intensive than irrigation (Boyd and Gross 1998).

Thus fisheries may be proposed as part of an integrated system with arable and other uses, or as a separate and distinct project. In either case, however, the analysis should be undertaken of the change in the system as a whole.

18

Flood Management

In Chapter 14, the importance of treating floods as part of managing variations in river flows was pointed out: in arid regions, the floods are the water resource. Since ecosystems are dependent on the water regime, ideally what we want to do is to maintain the high frequency variations in flows (e.g. 1 to 10 years) but to filter out the extreme flows (Figure 18.1). In practice, this is difficult to do and typically flood alleviation schemes filter out the high and medium frequency events without necessarily having much effect on the extreme events.

The general issues and principles in flood management have been discussed elsewhere (Green, Parker and Tunstall 2000; Green *et al.* 2001). The two most important of these principles are that the objective in flood management is to increase the efficiency of the use of the catchment and not to minimise flood losses; annual flood losses are a misleading indicator of performance (Green, Parker and Tunstall 2000). Secondly, it is necessary to consider how to manage all floods and not just some; it has become common in recent years to design a flood alleviation scheme to some design standard of performance, such as a flood with a predicted return period of 200 years. Instead, it is important to assess what will happen when an extreme flood occurs and how that flood will be managed: in short, to design for failure (Green *et al.* 1993; Green 2002). In the time before formal engineering design, such an approach was generally adopted; in the Netherlands, 'terps', raised mounds of earth, were constructed as places of refuge within the polders. Similarly, in Japan, traditionally dikes have included low points for planned spill areas, *Eturyutei*, and discontinuous sections, *Kasumitei* (Iwasada *et al.* 2000). More recently in such countries as Hungary, dikes have been constructed with demolition chambers in place: in the event of an extreme flood, it will be necessary to deliberately allow some areas to flood in order to protect more important areas. The concept of a design standard of protection is an idea that ought to be abandoned (Green 2002).

The application of benefit–cost analysis is well established in many countries with guidance being given as to the detailed procedures to adopt (e.g. DEFRA 1999; Ministry of Water Resources 1998; River Planning Division 1990; US Water Resources Council 1983). However, the quality of that guidance varies;

Handbook of Water Economics: Principles and Practice. C. Green
© 2003 John Wiley & Sons, Ltd ISBN: 0-471-98571-6

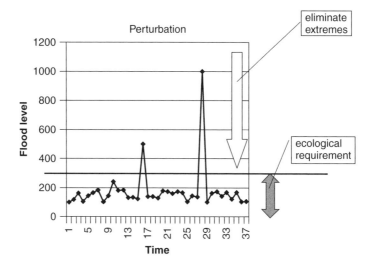

Figure 18.1   *Floods and ecosystem requirements*

for example, that for the USA is very dated and does not require agricultural prices to have the subsidy element removed.

Flood alleviation benefits are the expected value of the reduction in future flood losses; the core of the method is to plot the loss-probability curves under the baseline and do-something options (Figure 18.2): on the *x*-axis, the exceedance probability of the flood is plotted and the loss from each such flood is plotted against the *y*-axis. The area between the curves is then the reduction in the expected value of flood losses in the average year at some point in time and this reduction in expected value is then simply discounted back to give the present value. The derivation of the loss-probability curves is thus central to flood alleviation benefit cost analyses.

If neither the probability of the loss nor the size of the loss changes over time, it is only necessary to do this once. However, flood management is about changing risks and hence the actual analysis will often be more complex; indeed, once some standard data on flood losses has been compiled, the critical part of the analysis is handling the changes in probabilities over time and the differences in probabilities between the baseline and the do-something option. For example, where an existing dike is in a poor state either because of poor initial construction, unsuitable ground conditions or poor maintenance, it is possible that it will fail catastrophically before it is overtopped, this probability of failure in turn depending upon the height of the flood and hence the exceedance probability of that flood. Enlarging and widening that dike will then reduce the probability of failure before overtopping as well as lowering the exceedance probability of the event which will overtop the dike. In general it is necessary to apply a

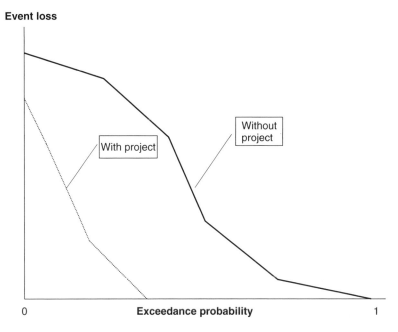

Figure 18.2 *Loss–probability curves*

reliability engineering approach (Kaufmann 1972) to identify the ways in which the intervention strategy may fail and the likelihood that such a failure will occur.

Again, where runoff in the catchment is changing as a result of changes in land use or climate change, then the probability of a flood of a given magnitude and flood loss will change over time. A question in the circumstances is whether a flood alleviation scheme should be undertaken now or later.

The construction of the loss–probability curves is a sampling problem: how many and which flood events will give the best representation of the true curves? Fortunately, we can always define the upper and lower bounds about the curve, and for any section of that curve (DEFRA 1999); the area under each curve being calculated by the trapezium approximation (that is, the area under each curve is the integral of the curve but the functional form of that curve is unknown and indeterminate). In practice, it is losses from the most frequent events that contribute the greatest proportion of the benefits. Figure 18.3 shows the loss–probability curve for a hypothetical project broken down by the type of property affected; but as Figure 18.4 illustrates, it is the losses from the five-year return period event that contribute the largest proportion of the benefits.

Since we need to consider how to manage all floods and not just those up to the design standard of protection, we need also to examine how the proposed scheme will affect the losses from all events. Depending upon the nature of the scheme,

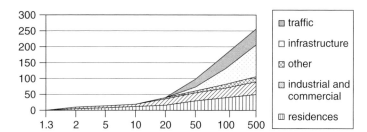

Figure 18.3   *Contributions to event losses*

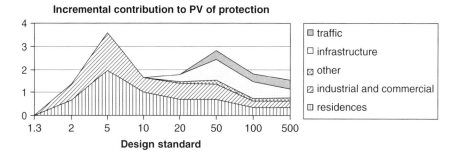

Figure 18.4   *Contributions to present value of benefits*

the losses from these events may also be reduced: for example, if a bypass channel is constructed then the losses from all flood events will be less than they would otherwise be because there will always be less water out of bank. Conversely, it is possible if a dike is constructed that losses when that dike fails will be greater than they would otherwise have been because of the increased velocity of the flood flow (Green, Parker and Tunstall 2000). These above design standard benefits (DEFRA 1999) should be included in the benefit–cost analysis.

   The magnitude of the flood losses from a particular event are partly determined by its characteristics; the depth, duration, velocity and loads carried and deposited by the flood (Green *et al.* 1994). In general, the most important determinants of flood losses are the depth of flooding and the duration of the flood; however, this may be a response to the limitations of hydraulic models which in the past did not predict velocities. Standard depth-damage curves are available in a number of countries (Table 18.1) and the methods of deriving such curves are discussed in Green *et al.* (1994). In some countries where data is available as to the value of assets at risk, these curves are expressed as losses as a proportion of the value at risk. For instance, the US and Japanese curves have been developed in this way. The practical problem with such curves is that the geographical and administrative

Table 18.1 Depth-damage curves (loss as proportion of loss at 1 metre depth)

Contents	Depth (metres)											
	−0.3	0	0.3	0.5	0.6	0.9	1.2	1.5	1.8	2.1	2.4	2.7
UK – FLAIR	0.00	0.00	0.77	0.92	1	1.16	1.24	1.27	1.29	1.29	1.29	1.29
UK – survey	0.00	0.31	0.86	0.95	1	1.21	1.39	1.55	1.69			
USA	0.00	0.00	0.55	0.85	1	1.55	2.00	2.55	3.00	3.45	4.00	4.55
USA – one storey, no basement (as % of structural value)	0.13	0.45	0.74	0.91	1	1.23	1.44	1.61	1.76	1.89	1.99	2.08
USA – 2 or more storeys, no basement (as % of structural value)	0.08	0.41	0.71	0.90	1	1.27	1.52	1.75	1.96	2.16	2.33	2.48
USA – split level, no basement (as % structural value)	0.29	0.39	0.63	0.88	1	1.48	2.04	2.68	3.36	4.07	4.76	5.45
Japan	−0.53	0.00	0.51	0.84	1	1.46	1.90	2.30	2.67	3.01	3.31	3.58
Bangladesh			0.61	0.87	1	1.32	1.62	1.88	2.14	2.38	2.62	
Australia			0.55	0.86	1	1.41	1.81	2.19	2.56	2.91	3.27	3.61
Taihu Basin, China	−0.10	0.26	0.63	0.88	1	1.37	1.74	2.10	2.47	2.84	3.21	3.58
Germany	0.31	0.46	0.68	0.88	1	1.47	2.16	3.18	4.68	6.88	10.13	14.89

areas for which data as to value of assets exists rarely coincide with the areas that are flooded. Moreover, a proportion of that value will be above any plausible flood depth and adjustments will need to be made for multistorey buildings.

Alternatively, the curves express losses per building or per unit area of a particular building type. In this case, it is necessary to determine the number or area of buildings of each type that are at risk. Satellite data and GIS systems are increasingly being used in flood alleviation benefit–cost analyses but land use data in such forms (e.g. CORINNE) distinguishes much more clearly between rural land uses than amongst urban ones. For example, the ground floors of buildings in central urban areas often include mixtures of residential, commercial and other uses, including small industrial uses; the satellite data is likely simply to classify large areas as dense urban usage. Nor in central urban areas is data likely to differentiate between, for example, department stores and offices or such critical installations as major electricity substations.

An issue in either case is to identify uses below ground level: the most obvious example is underground car parks which, if occupied, result in a very high loss. Department stores and shopping centres may include shopping and related areas below ground level; Les Halles in Paris is the most obvious example. More importantly, underground spaces pose a very severe threat to life; for example, in Hong Kong, there are cinemas in which the auditorium is below ground level.

The depth of flooding in a building is then the difference between the level of the flood and the ground level. How important it is to be accurate in assessing the depth of flooding then depends upon the depth of flooding anticipated: for large areas currently protected by a dike which would flood to a depth of 3 or 4 m if that dike were to fail, there is little point in being precise to more than the nearest metre. Conversely, where flooding is only expected to a depth of around 60 cm, particularly when a project protecting a relatively small area is being assessed, then differences of 10 cm can make a considerable difference to the estimate of the project's benefits. Ground levels can now be measured quite accurately and relatively cheaply by GPS and other techniques such as LIDAR. However, the floor levels of buildings are seldom actually those of the ground outside and either the floor levels of individual properties need to be assessed or some general adjustment factor incorporated (e.g. assuming that the floor level is the ground level plus 20 cm). This leaves the flood level to be estimated; simple hydraulic models predict only the flood level in the river itself in which case the analysts will find themselves constructing what is in effect an overland flow model in order to predict the depth of flooding in particular locations. Increasingly hydraulic models also include predictions of overland flow, the movement and depth of water outside of the main river channel. In either case, it is necessary to groundtruth the data as far as possible, particularly for the most frequent events.

The duration of the flood is particularly important when considering indirect losses, such as the loss of industrial production, when flooding lasts for several weeks or months. In principle, since the chemical and physical mechanisms that cause damage to buildings and their contents are time dependent, direct damages should also depend upon the duration of the flood. However, understanding of the relationship between the duration of flooding and physical damages is somewhat limited; but in the case of crop losses, the losses are dependent upon both the duration of flooding as well as the time of the year when flooding occurs (Figure 17.4). Commonly, crops will have been damaged by local waterlogging before they are flooded (Section 17.3.7); therefore, only any additional losses caused by flooding should be counted when assessing the benefits of a flood alleviation scheme as opposed to a drainage scheme.

High velocity flows pose a very significant threat to life, particularly when the local combination of velocity and depth is sufficient to cause buildings to collapse. Data on these conditions is somewhat limited (Table 18.2) and there are problems with scour around columns, the 'rough' nature of urban areas (e.g. buildings) which will create variations in water velocity, and the rocks, trees and other loads carried by the flood water. Where it is considered that velocities may be high, the focus must be on reducing the risk to life rather than estimating more accurately the additional damages that will occur to buildings.

In some areas, the load of sediment carried and deposited by the flood waters can be significant; the Japanese depth-damage curves (Dutta 2002) include an allowance for the additional losses caused by this material. Commonly, the flood waters will also be contaminated with sewage, oil and petrol that have escaped from underground storage tanks, and other materials.

The scale of flooding is an important consideration in the analysis; at either end of the scale, data will be sparse and collecting more detailed data is expensive. For very large areas (e.g. the Netherlands or the Yangtze), it is necessary to make some approximations in order to match the availability of the data. A number of different computer models have been developed to carry out such broad-scale assessments (Klaus *et al.* 1994). Similarly, at very small scales, such as assessing the benefits of alleviating a local problem caused by surcharging from a sewer, relatively small-scale details (e.g. the height of the curbs) influence

Table 18.2 *Conditions for serious risk to life*

	Damage parameter D $\times$ v (m²/ sec)		
	Low	Medium	High
Children	<0.1	0.1–0.25	>0.25
Adults	<0.3	0.3–0.70	>0.70
Personal cars	<0.9	0.9–1.50	>1.50
Lightly constructed houses	1.3	1.3–2.50	>2.50
Well-constructed wooden houses	<2.0; v > 2.0 m/s	2.0–5.0; v > 2.0 m/s	>5.00
Brick houses	<3.0; v > 2.0 m/s	3.0–7.0; v > 2.0 m/s	>7.00

Source: Reiter 2000.

the amount of local ponding that can occur before properties are flooded, and the capacity of the road to carry the surcharged volumes away. Measurement of all the necessary details to build an accurate overland flow model would be excessively expensive and simplifications are again necessary; for example, Green *et al.* (1989a) prepared simple look-up tables of the benefits of reducing the risk of sewage flooding to different types of property.

In reality, flood alleviation schemes are constructed primarily in order to reduce the suffering caused to people rather than to reduce the damages to property. It has been found that to those who suffer them, the stress, health damage, disruption and other 'intangible' impacts of floods can be far more serious than the losses they experience in terms of damages to their home and its contents (Green and Penning-Rowsell 1986, 1989). Attempts have been made to evaluate those losses in economic terms (Allee *et al.* 1980) but to do so means first being able to predict how the severity of these losses vary according to the population affected and the characteristics of the flood, with the nature of their home itself being a possible mediating factor. So far, it has not been possible to establish clear relationships between these different factors in a way that would enable reliable and valid predictions to be made (Green *et al.* 1994).

Again, floods can cause significant loss of life but the conditional probability of death in a flood varies from some small chance, probably around 1 in 10 000, up to a high risk of the order of 1 in 5 (Graham 1999). It is undesirable to seek to put a 'value on life' in the economic assessment of a flood alleviation scheme but it is necessary to try to estimate, at least in relative terms, what is the relative risk to life. There are a number of ways in which people die in floods (New South Wales Government 1986), the most common in the USA being attempting to travel by foot or in a vehicle through flood water (Center for Communicable Diseases 2000). The three conditions likely to pose the greatest conditional risk of death should a flood occur are:

- underground areas (including metro systems and underground car parks);
- small, steep and consequently flashy catchments; and
- behind natural or artificial defence lines and below natural or artificial dams if those structures then fail.

18.1 The Likelihood of Failure

If we are to manage all floods, it is critical to assess how likely is each intervention strategy to fail and what are the consequences of such a failure. The first question is how likely is it to work in the first place; second, how will it perform in 'above design' standard situations, what does this section of the loss–probability curve look like?

It is commonplace, if rather misleading, to distinguish between 'structural' and 'non-structural' options; it is misleading because the latter category includes actions, like flood-proofing and house raising, that are structural in nature. The purpose of the original terminology was to introduce new intervention strategies in addition to those commonly adopted by engineers. A more general classification is then between physical and institutional changes and as to the point of intervention in the flood sequence: before, during and after the flood. The principles of reliability engineering need to be applied not just to physical interventions (e.g. KGS Group 1999) but also to institutional interventions. The cynic might claim that in the past it has proved easier to undertake physical interventions that have worked rather than institutions that are effective; equally, that concrete has proved rather more robust when inadequately maintained than have institutions.

18.1.1 Flood warnings

Flood warnings may be provided in order to:

- reduce the risk to life;
- support the management of the hydraulic system so as to reduce the extent of flooding; or
- enable the population to reduce their losses.

The benefits of flood warnings vary according to the purpose of the warnings and the appropriate purpose of flood warnings will often differ between catchments. The 'do something' option may, for example, include improvements in flood modelling, in dissemination systems, telemetering rain gauges or installing weather radar. The gain over the existing system may then lie in one or more of the following improvements: in lead time (the length of time between the receipt of the warning and the arrival of the flood); reliability (the likelihood that a warning is issued prior to a flood and that a warning is followed by a flood); precision (the characterisation of the flood in terms of depth, extent and other characteristics); and accuracy (how closely the flood characteristics are predicted).

18.1.1.1 Risk to life

The fundamental reason for providing flood warnings is to reduce the risk to life if a flood occurs. The conditional risk to life given a flood varies markedly from context to context (Graham 1999). The primary problem is then to calculate the conditional risk of death or injury without and with the proposed flood warning system. In then deciding whether or not to enhance the flood warning system, it is more helpful to consider what to say at a disaster inquiry than to rely upon a 'value of life': to be able to say that all reasonable options were considered after the risk was assessed.

18.1.1.2 Improvements in the performance of structures

Flood forecasts are important to operating storage and flow controls so as to maximise their effect on reducing the extent of flooding. They also give time for emergency crews to be called out and emergency works to be undertaken to strengthen or raise dikes. The benefit of the flood forecast is then given by the difference between the performance of the system with warnings and the performance of the system without warnings. This can be calculated in the usual way from the loss-probability curve and might be expected to be substantial in some cases.

18.1.1.3 Enabling the population to reduce their losses

People can reduce their losses in one of three ways:

- moving animals and property either out of the flood risk area; or
- moving upwards (uphill or upstairs); or
- flood-proofing their property.

Which behaviour will be most effective depends upon the nature of the catchment; where flooding will be several metres deep, then evacuation will be necessary and the reductions in losses will depend upon what can be removed from the area. Where flooding will less than 2 m, and buildings will not collapse during the flood, then losses can be reduced by carrying possessions upstairs or lifting them above the anticipated depth of flooding. In shallow flooding, less than a metre deep, then it may be possible to flood-proof the property preventing any water entering the building. The reductions in losses then depend upon the means adopted and the success of the method adopted.

18.1.1.4 Assessing reliability

CNS (1991) presented a simple model for estimating the likely benefits of flood warnings in terms of likely damage reducing action taken:

$$P_f P_d P_i P_a P_c$$

where:

P_f is the probability that an accurate forecast is made and converted into a warning;

P_d is the probability that the warning is disseminated;

P_i is the probability that a member of the individual household will be available to be warned;

P_a is the probability that the individual household is physically able to respond to the warning; and

P_c is the probability that the individual knows how to respond effectively.

The benefits of the proposed system are given by the product of the above equation for the existing system minus the product of the equation for the proposed system, times the reduction in flood losses through the action adopted on warning. Where taking action on a warning which is not followed by a flood incurs costs (C_n) then the change in the expected value of these losses must be added to the above results:

$$[(P_{f0}P_{d0}P_{i0}P_{a0}P_{c0}) - (P_{f1}P_{d1}P_{i1}P_{a1}P_{c1})]L_r + (P_{0n} - P_{1n})C_n$$

where P_{0n} and P_{1n} are the probabilities that the warning will not be followed by a flood with the present system and the proposed system, and L_r are the losses expected from a flood. The results of this equation are then aggregated over the properties at risk.

Household time budgets can be used to estimate the P_i coefficient (e.g. Anderson *et al.* 1994); a warning issued when there is no one there to receive it will be ineffective and it is difficult to give an effective warning during the sleeping hours. The P_a coefficient can be approximated from national statistics on disability and chronic ill health. In the UK, 18% of the population have been assessed as having a moderate or serious disability, with 4% of men and 5% of women having a serious disability (Department of Health 1997). Of those aged over 85, more than 70% of both men and women have a disability. The relevant coefficient depends in part on the nature of the action that it is intended those warned will undertake on warning; a higher proportion of the population will be able to evacuate unaided than will be able to lift household goods above expected flood levels. In addition, the likelihood of a person suffering a disability is related to their socio-economic conditions. Together, the P_i and P_a coefficients set the upper limit on the potential effectiveness of a flood warning system but only the P_a coefficient is fixed.

Coefficients P_f, P_d and P_i should be expected to vary as a function of the time available. Sorensen (1988) has estimated, for example, the proportions of the population who had evacuated an area against the elapse of time. The standard techniques of redundancy and diversity of communication channels ought, in principle, to increase P_d. However, the empirical evidence is that since this largely depends upon institutional factors, this probability falls over time if the system is not rehearsed; warning systems work best when they are most often used. Overall, the reliability of a flood warning system is likely to be low; a result found in practice (Parker 1999; Penning-Rowsell *et al.* 2000, Smith 1986, Torterotot 1992). A similar approach needs to be applied when considering other intervention strategies.

Economies of scale are very marked in flood management hence flood-proofing (DTLR 2002; USACE 1998) is only more efficient than the traditional structural solutions when the intensity of development is low. For example, in the UK the cost of flood-proofing a property is estimated to be around £2000 per room or £10 000 per dwelling (Johnson 2002) whereas when the author analysed the results of 35 flood alleviation benefit–cost analyses across the UK, the average benefit per property was £8000.

Case Study 18.1 Yangtze Dike Strengthening and Raising Project

The Yangtze is one of the two main rivers in China. It is has a very flat gradient, the base of the Three Gorges Dam being only 75 m above datum. Although the average fall is 4 cm/km, maximum depths can exceed 40 m and 100 000-tonne ships can navigate up to Wuhan. It drains an area of 1 000 000 km^2, a peak flow of 110 000 m^3/sec being recorded in 1870. The Yangtze has been characterised as being a series of linked lakes rather than being a river; these lakes have been important for flood storage in the past but their capacity has been reduced by reclamation in response to the pressure for land (Green 2001a).

The flood season is from July to September and floods are the result of rainfall, the rain fronts moving from east to west. Whilst it follows that the coincidence of flooding from the tributaries has a significant effect on the flood peak on the main river, flood flows are dominated in the middle section by flows from the main stem. Floods are, however, characterised by multiple peaks; eight in the 1998 flood (Daoxi and Siping 1999).

China is very short of arable land (an average of 0.10 ha per capita compared to a world average of 0.24), and the potential of irrigated land to produce multiple crops has long been important. So, between the ninth and thirteenth centuries, the balance of the population shifted from rainfed agriculture in the north to irrigated, multicropping agriculture in the south. Consequently, the Yangtze valley is densely populated with 42 million people living on the flood plain of the Yangtze. Rural population densities are high and small-scale industrial enterprises are widespread in those areas. In turn, whilst retreating the line of flood defences and allowing part of the flood plain to revert to wetlands is an option that is often appropriate in developed countries (Zockler 2000), this is clearly inappropriate in China's current circumstances.

Administratively, central government takes a very low proportion (12%) of GDP in tax revenue, and the undertaking of public works relies significantly upon specific Provincial and County hypothecated taxes.

Yangtze Flood Management Plan

A comprehensive flood management policy for the Yangtze (Green, Parker and Tunstall 2000) has been prepared, including afforestation, flood warnings, flood refuges, detention basins and live storage in the meanders (for example, there is a 50 km meander on the Yangtze in which the live storage is approximately 2 billion cubic metres), main and secondary dikes, and flood fighting. The first detention basins were designated in 1954 and the operation rules for the existing hydroelectric dams on the tributaries are being altered to include flood storage. The Three Gorges Project (TGP) will add a further 22 billion m^3 of storage (Hong Qingyu and Luo Zhang-Yu 1999) to take off the peak of most floods (the 60-day flow in Hankou in 1998 was 188 billion m^3). The main dikes along the river are, however, of a low defence standard (generally providing protection against only the 10–15 year return period flood). The construction standard is also poor and the dikes are likely to fail through seepage or leakage or for other reasons before they are overtopped. As part of that much larger flood management plan, the Government of China is strengthening and raising the main dikes, notably in Hubei and Hunan provinces.

The strategy for responding to a flood is also complex. At present, the dikes will cope with a relatively small flood but as a flood develops progressively more

Continued on page 327

___ *Continued from page 326* ___

resources are mobilised for flood fighting, there being a highly developed system for flood fighting, including stockpiles of materials on the landside berm of the dikes. Initially, these resources are required to support emergency reinforcement of weak points in the dikes, such as sand boils, and to close any breaches that occur. If the flood then threatens to exceed the height of the dike then emergency measures are taken to raise the height of the dike. At this point, the designated detention basins will be utilised; these provide 47 billion m³ of storage. The reluctance to use these basins is because of the costs of using them; 4.2 million people live in these basins and the costs of evacuating and rehousing this population, together with the economic losses to agriculture and industry within the basins would be substantial (fixed asset values in the basins in Hubei were estimated as 30 billion RMB). But the low design standard of protection offered by the existing dikes means that the use of the detention basins must be contemplated even in the event of relatively frequent floods.

With the completion of the Three Gorges Project, this strategy will change; the dikes in conjunction with the Three Gorges Project will provide protection up to the 100–200-year return period flood and the use of the detention basins will take the standard of protection beyond the 500-year return period event.

Analysis

Because a major component of the project is dike strengthening, it was necessary to use estimates of the probability of the existing and new dikes failing before they were overtopped. Thus, the probability of a dike failing from a flood of a given return period is a combination of the probability that it will fail or be overtopped. As there is remarkably little information world wide on the probabilities of dike failure (Wolff 1997), the engineers had to use engineering judgements for these failure probabilities. These probabilities were then used as the thresholds at which progressively greater efforts at flood fighting would begin and then the use of the detention basins would be initiated. In addition, two separate analyses had to be undertaken: one covering the early years before Three Gorges is operational and the second covering the latter period when the availability of Three Gorges will substantially reduce the benefits of the dike raising and strengthening. For example, for one dike section, the present value of the benefits for the period prior to the commissioning of TGP is 1.9 billion RMB; the present value of the benefits of the dike works over the remaining period of their life is 0.35 billion RMB.

It is a requirement of the National Codes (Ministry of Water Resources 1998), that sample surveys of flood losses for different land uses be undertaken after every flood. This data is then used to calculate losses per mu (c.0.06 hectares) in rural areas and loss per capita in urban areas. Depth-damage curves have not been calculated but across much of the flood plain, either there is a flood to 3–4 metres or there is not; once a breach occurs, neither the extent nor the depth of flooding varies markedly with the return period of the flood. These estimates of loss per mu and loss per capita were used to calculate the event losses, having been cross-checked against other available data such as the levels of compensation set out in the Resettlement Action Plan, a summary of flood losses in China in the 1980s, and the losses as a proportion of the assets at risk found in other countries that have good loss data.

A second potential benefit is that a reduction in operating and maintenance costs should be expected for the renovated and new dikes over the existing dikes. This

___ *Continued on page 328* ___

__ Continued from page 327 __

benefit could not be estimated for a number of reasons. Firstly, the National Code covering O&M expenditure (Ministry of Water Resources 1995) requires that the allowance for O&M be taken as 5% of the capital cost; this itself is problematic. Detailed, costed O&M schedules had not been prepared but rather an allowance based on this Code requirement had been used instead as the estimate of the O&M costs for the new dikes. Current O&M expenditure is also inadequate to maintain the present standards offered by the existing dikes, the maintenance engineer in one county estimating that he had only 50% of the budget he needed. Since neither figure was reliable, the benefits of reduced O&M expenditure had to be left as an intangible. Whilst changes in O&M expenditure are expected to be an economic benefit, funding adequate levels of maintenance in the future may be a real problem.

The requirements for bank protection caused some concern. At one bend, an estimated 133 m³ of rip rap have been placed over the last 50 years per linear metre of embankment. Therefore, the time interval at which bank protection will need to be renewed was a major uncertainty.

Robustness Analysis

The high proportion of capital costs taken up by bank protection, and the uncertainty concerning the life expectancy of those works, means that reducing the life expectancy of those works was an obvious candidate for the robustness analysis. More generally, the results of an economic analysis are known to be sensitive to those streams of benefits and costs that either occur early in the project's life or events that occur frequently. In this case, the large reduction in benefits following the completion of the TGP means that the benefits should be very sensitive to delays in completion of the project. The results of the robustness analysis (Table 18.3) showed that the conclusion that the project is to be preferred to the baseline option is robust to uncertainties. At a 12% discount rate, the uncertainties concerning the life expectancy of the bank protection works proved not to have that great an effect on the benefit–cost ratio, even in the area where they constituted a large part of the capital costs – in part because resettlement and other works contributed a significant fraction of total project costs.

Table 18.3   *Results of the main robustness tests for Hubei and Hunan Provinces: variations in the benefit–cost ratio*

Case	Hubei			Hunan
	Jianan section	Wuhan section	Babu section	
Base	11.0	4.9	10.2	2.7
Delay benefits by 2 years	8.4	3.0	5.9	1.8
Probability of failure by existing dikes is lower	1.7	2.3	6.3	1.5
New dikes are not properly maintained	9.1	5.0	9.4	2.3
Bank protection works required every 5 years	8.0	4.9	10.1	1.2

19

Hydropower

Utilising the potential energy in a river is one of the oldest energy conversion strategies known, traditionally having been used for hulling rice, grinding wheat and cutting wood, and then the early large industrial plants. With the invention of electricity, hydropower was then an obvious extension of these uses. Now, in 65 countries, hydropower produces more than 50% of total electricity production, whilst in 24 countries more than 90% of electricity is produced by hydropower; over 18.4% of the world's electricity is produced by hydropower (IEA 2000).

Electricity, however, does not provide a large part of the world's energy requirements and much of that electricity is generated using fossil fuels. It is more useful therefore to frame choices involving hydropower in the context of a matrix of energy source (e.g. fossil fuels, hydropower) versus the components of consumption. The pattern shown by this matrix varies markedly between countries. Thus, in rural areas in developing countries, households consume 90% of total energy consumption, almost all of that for cooking for which they rely upon fuel wood and dung (World Bank 1996b). Conversely, in developed countries, a significant fraction of total energy demand is taken up by transport, almost all of which is dependent on oil. In the UK, in 1998, the largest fraction of energy demand was from transport (34%), as opposed to domestic uses (29%), industrial (22%) and commercial/public services (13%) (Royal Commission on Environmental Pollution 2000). Thus, there are marked variations between countries in the per capita use of energy, the source of that energy, and use of that energy. The conversion efficiencies also differ markedly between countries (Jochem 2000).

There are two main forms of hydropower:

- run of river projects (e.g. Niagara Falls) where there is little or no storage; and
- reservoir based systems.

Since the former is wholly reliant on the momentary stream flow they rely upon relatively constant river flows, those found in temperate climates. In arid climates, storage is necessary if the supply of electricity is to be reliable. However, reservoirs are very contentious both in terms of their environmental impact (Acreman *et al.* 1999) and the issues of resettlement. In turn, in developed countries, two

Handbook of Water Economics: Principles and Practice. C. Green
© 2003 John Wiley & Sons, Ltd ISBN: 0-471-98571-6

further issues that can require economic analysis are (a) changes in the operating rules and hence the patterns of discharges from the reservoir, and (b) the decommissioning of dams. In the USA, some 587 dams have been removed since 1990 (Pritchard 2001).

19.1 Economic Issues

Conceptually, the assessment of enhancements in electricity supply is very similar to water supply (Section 14.6):

- the benefits of first time electricity; and then
- the incremental benefits of enhancements in the quality, including the quantity, of the service provided.

The former need to be assessed in the broader context of development policy, particularly of rural development policy. In the analysis of the latter, it is essential to consider the electricity supply system as a whole, particularly the interactions between different forms of generation.

Secondly, as with water management, the problem is to match variations in supply and demand but as compared to water, supply can be adjusted through changes in generation capacity. However, demand varies over much shorter time periods as compared to water and whilst there can be considerable inertia in the water distribution system that buffers changes in demand, for electricity, supply must respond instantaneously.

Again, as with water, demand forecasting is a critical issue in energy management. Thus, the potential importance of hydropower depends upon the current and possible future form of the supply–demand matrix. In particular, whilst the Kyoto Agreement calls for some real cuts in greenhouse gas emissions, much greater cuts are necessary to stabilise the climate (Royal Commission on Environmental Pollution 2000), a switch to a hydrogen economy for vehicles or to directly electrically powered vehicles being two options. The former requires electricity to split water into oxygen and hydrogen, so the effect is an increase in the demand for electricity whilst avoiding an increase in greenhouse gas emissions from generating that electricity.

In developing countries, with large areas of the country, especially rural areas, lacking any electricity supply at all, the benefits of first time electricity supply are a major issue. At present, 3% of the population of Nepal are connected to an electricity supply and it is estimated that it will be another 30 years before the whole of Nepal is provided with electricity supply (Eberhard *et al*. 2000). Thus, the problem is likely to be whether to provide a local electricity supply and by what means. Electricity supply systems are likely to be local, lacking the geographical large-scale distribution grids that characterise the developed countries where large-scale plants supply demand centres hundreds of kilometres away.

Hence, another issue is whether to provide an electricity supply by extending the existing grid systems or to provide local, separate sources of generation and distribution. The first offers potential economies of scale but those economies occur through large installations; the latter offers more scope for community involvement and control. Those areas that are served are likely to suffer blackouts and brownouts, fluctuations in voltage and other problems in the quality of the service provided, the question then being whether and which improvements in service can be justified.

In developed countries, service is usually near universal, with high levels of consumption, and the issue is commonly one of whether to expand generation capacity to meet predicted increases in demand and, if so, by what mix of generation capacity. Here, there is a clear question of whether supply expansion is likely to be more efficient than demand management. Where supply expansion is appropriate, then existing grids allow a wide range of generating options to be considered including those located at a long distance from the sources of demand. In addition, these grids increase redundancy and diversity and so enhance the reliability of the system as well as allowing some economies of scale. Issues such as the most efficient means of supplying base load and peak load generating capacity then become important, with high standards of security of supply also being expected in developed countries. In developing countries, a sudden increase in demand is likely to result in a brownout, a response that will not be acceptable in a developed country. Ensuring the quality of supply then requires analysis of the interactions between the different forms of generation capacity, of the dynamic response of the system. In this regard, hydropower has a number of advantages in terms of the control of voltage and frequency, and to maintain a spinning reserve capable of very rapid response to increases in demand.

19.2 The Benefits of First Time Electricity Supply

As with water, women are the primary direct and indirect beneficiaries of the provision of first time electricity supply and some two billion people currently have no access to electricity (Eberhard *et al.* 2000). The benefits then lie in the substitution of electricity for other energy sources (e.g. kerosene and candles for lighting) where the alternatives often have significant health risks associated with them, as well as possibly higher costs. The economic evaluation of these benefits may then be undertaken by assessing the reductions in the costs of buying existing energy supplies, together with an estimate of a reduction in the health risks associated with those existing energy supplies. However, a significant fraction of the demand is for new uses, e.g. watching television (World Bank 1996b) and a willingness to pay study, subject to the usual reservation that women may have, at best, only limited access to the household's cash resources, is necessary to evaluate such benefits.

Although women may spend one-fifth of their working day collecting fuel wood for cooking (Eberhard *et al.* 2000), electricity will not normally be a viable alternative at least initially because of the high power requirements for cooking. Improvements in the utilisation of biomass are likely to be a better option for cooking in the short term although the combustion of wood and other biomass can produce carcinogens and other pollutants.

Small-scale hydropower is an option that can be appropriate in rural communities. For example, in Ethiopia, the lack of wind rules out wind power whilst solar power is prohibitively expensive (Shewarega 1999); it also requires a high level of technology and skills, a problem that also rules it out in rural areas in Pakistan (LEAD – Pakistan n.d.). For example, 1 m drops and very simple technology have been used to provide 50 W power supplies in Laos (ourworld n.d.).

19.3 Enhancing the Standard of Service

Where there is some basic electricity supply, then the choice is between improvements in the quantity, or quality, of the service (e.g. improved reliability, reduction in interruptions etc.) and demand management. Where an increase in the resource is justified then the choice lies between alternative generation options. The higher the current level of consumption, the more likely it is that demand management will be more efficient than increasing generation capacity, and one problem reported with market reforms of electricity services is a serious reduction in the incentives to electricity suppliers to support demand management (World Bank 1996b). However, in the economic analysis, the demand management option should be considered even when current institutional arrangements do not permit its use: the achievement of efficiency then requires those institutional arrangements to be changed.

Amongst the demand management options to be considered may be reductions in losses in the transmission and distribution system: for example, in India, 35% of electricity is lost in this way (Eberhard *et al.* 2000). As with water usage, demand is to a large part determined by technology (e.g. the replacement of tungsten light bulbs by high efficiency fluorescent bulbs).

The quality of service, including reliability, is a function of the characteristics of the system as a whole, and both redundancy and diversity may be important. The characteristics of the system are then partially determined by the mix of generation options adopted; different generation options may be appropriate to provide base load and peak load capacity. Therefore, decisions concerning increases in generating capacity need to be taken in the context of system performance. An important quality criterion is the reliability of supply and a decision must be made as to what reliability of supply is appropriate for each category of consumer. Reliability is in part a function of the degree of redundancy in the distribution network but is also a function of the relationship between generating capacity and demand. A number of studies have therefore been undertaken to determine the economic losses associated with interruptions in electricity supply (Primen 2001; Eto *et al.* 2001) in order to try to determine the optimum levels of reliability for different consumers.

In turn, when considering increasing generation capacity the issue is really one of the reliability of supply; what margin of supply over anticipated demand to provide in order to take account of plants being out of action because of unscheduled maintenance, sudden extreme peaks in demand, and other issues. The problem becomes more complex when different generating sources are themselves subject to variations in their availability (e.g. droughts reduce the availability of hydropower, lack of wind reduces the output from wind farms and so forth). It is the performance of the system rather than its parts that is important.

An advantage therefore of regional grids is the potential to increase reliability or reduce the margin of supply: the excess of generating capacity over anticipated demand. Thus, providing a higher degree of interconnectivity can be an alternative to increasing generating capacity, particularly where demand peaks are out of synchronisation in the different areas. The obvious limitation of a local network reliant upon a single generating source is that the standard of service is wholly reliant upon that single source. Interconnectivity also allows for advantage to be taken of economies of scale.

As with water, a capital intensive industry, demand forecasting is critical and the same techniques discussed in Section 14.5 can be used. However, an important issue here is the possibilities of substitution between energy sources and normally the environmentally preferred option will be away from other energy sources towards electricity. Thus, in the long term, at one level a switch from a reliance on fuel wood or kerosene for cooking to electricity is likely to be desirable whilst a switch away from petrol or diesel powered vehicles is also likely to be necessary if climate change is not to run out of control. In energy management, rather than simply chasing the future, it is likely to be necessary to choose the future and then set out to achieve that future.

20

Navigation

Transport is a frictional cost in an economy: transport consumes resources which could otherwise be put to productive purposes and in the ideal economy, transport costs would be zero. The proportion of economic output that is wasted in transport is obviously largely determined by location, population density and topography: thus, whilst 15% of the GDP of Wyoming is taken up by transport and 14% of that of Montana, for New York state only 8% of the state's GDP is wasted in transport costs. Reducing the costs of transport where possible frees up resources, especially energy, for productive uses. Equally, resources and consumption goods in transit are not being put to any productive use; again, reducing time spent in transit and in store increases overall economic efficiency.

Historically, inland waterways were the primary means of transport in many countries literally because frictional losses and hence energy consumption were lower than transport along the ground. Where the natural watercourses were unsuitable for transport, canals were constructed in early periods or the natural watercourses 'improved' by the construction of locks or the widening or deepening of the channel. Thus, the Grand Canal in China was constructed more than 1000 years ago to transport grain from the Yangtze delta to the north and Beijing. Up to 200 metres wide and approximately 1000 kilometres long, it remains a key transport link, as inland waterways continue to be in many countries. Thus, 47% tonne/kilometres of freight in China are transported by water as is 54% in the Netherlands, 20% in Germany and 15% in the USA. In other countries such as Bangladesh, the proportion of freight moved by water is probably even higher.

Compared to other modes such as trains and road transport, water-borne traffic is slower and primarily suited to bulk freight movements of low unit-value goods. In terms of energy efficiency, it is markedly superior to trucks and only somewhat inferior to rail, water-borne traffic averaging 411 btu/ton/mile as compared to 371 btu/ton/mile for rail and 4359 btu/ton/mile for trucks (Department of Transportation 2001). In cost terms, there are very marked economies of scale with increasing ship size (Table 20.1). The size of the vessel also influences the maximum traffic density per unit length of watercourse and hence the capacity of the navigation route.

Handbook of Water Economics: Principles and Practice. C. Green
© 2003 John Wiley & Sons, Ltd ISBN: 0-471-98571-6

Table 20.1   *Economies of scale in navigation costs*

Vessel size (dwt)	Vessel operating cost (US cent/ton-km)		
	Low	Base	High
50	10.78	13.54	16.25
100	7.91	9.31	10.43
300	4.35	5.12	5.74
500	2.38	2.89	3.14
1000	1.23	1.46	1.62
3000	1.00	1.17	1.31

Source: World Bank n.d.

There are two types of project that may require assessment:

- new canals; or
- improvements to existing routes (e.g. deepening or widening the channel, enlarging locks or increasing the reliability of water supply, reducing transhipment times).

As usual, it is necessary to predict both the number of beneficiaries and to calculate the unit benefit. Here the number of beneficiaries is given by the quantity of freight moved and predicting the future volume of traffic is crucial. This has four elements:

- the existing volume of freight;
- shifts of freight from (or to) other transport modes and routes;
- induced traffic: lower costs generating additional volumes of traffic;
- that generated through economic growth.

The primary benefit is likely to arise from freight either being attracted away from other transport modes, particularly from road transport, or retained for water transport when otherwise it would be shifted to another transport mode. As noted later, relative costs are not the only determinant of the choice of transport mode.

Improvements in transport should be expected to induce a growth in traffic; for example, farmers are restricted to subsistence farming unless adequate transport links connect them to the markets in urban areas. In such cases, it may be preferable to make an overall assessment in terms of rural development rather than to focus narrowly on transport improvements.

Economic growth should be expected to result in increased demand for transport and indeed economic growth is itself partially dependent upon adequate transport linkages. However, economic growth is likely to result in changes in the proportion of total freight movements made up of different resources and goods. In particular, a fall in the proportion of low unit-value goods and an increase in the proportion of high unit-value goods in the total volume of freight transported is likely. The result is probably a growth in demand for other transport modes relative to waterways in the future. In addition, the movement of bulk foodstuffs, notably grain, is a major source of traffic for waterways. In most developed countries in particular, grain production is heavily subsidised directly and indirectly through, for example, irrigation being provided at below cost (Section 17.2). When considering the transport of grain, the real economic value of grain should be used since otherwise the result is subsidised navigation being used to transport subsidised grain. But in addition, the extension of WTO rules to agricultural production and consequently a rise in the prices of grain as subsidies are eliminated is likely to result in a fall in demand and hence a reduction in demand for transport in developed countries and especially in North America and Europe. Equally, in principle, the WTO rules will affect the subsidies provided to the construction and operation of waterways and ports to transport grain. For example, the predictions of demand used in the assessment of the Upper Mississippi–Illinois river navigation project (Berry *et al.* 2000; Sweeney 2000) appear to have taken no account of the possible changes in world trade rules and the resulting fall in US grain production for export.

There are significant negative externalities associated with all forms of transport most obviously with the energy consumed and the resultant greenhouse gas emissions. The nature and extent of other externalities then varies according to the mode of transport. Hence in assessing possible navigation improvements, it is more than usually important to consider the alternative: what mode of transport will otherwise be adopted and the resulting externalities. Navigation improvements to an existing watercourse are likely to result in a major reduction in its ecological value; the wash from vessels results in bank erosion which in turn leads to hard bank protection measures being constructed and the effective conversion of a natural river into a canal. Deepening, widening and straightening the channel necessarily results in loss of shallow water habitats. These effects are obviously more severe when the river is currently in a nearly natural condition (Dembek 2000). Spillage of fuel and the discharge of sewerage from vessels may significantly degrade water quality. Particularly where navigation improvements result in intercontinental ship movements, there is a significant problem with introduced species (Carlton 2001). Nevertheless, the externalities associated with water-borne traffic may be less in a particular instance than those associated with the alternatives.

The potential benefits of navigation improvements are:

- savings in transport resource costs;
- reductions in transfer times and waiting times;
- reductions in travel time including reductions in congestion;
- reductions in packaging costs;
- reductions in losses in transit;
- increase in reliability of delivery.

In evaluating these benefits it is necessary to consider complete journeys and not simply that part of the freight movement that could be undertaken on the proposed navigation improvement. Trans-shipment costs can be substantial and additional costs may outweigh any reductions in movement costs. In turn, there can consequently be significant benefits in completing a route to avoid trans-shipment being necessary. In addition, with the exception of pipelines, movements on all transport modes require an outward and inward journey with the costs largely being fixed irrespective of whether the vessel, train or vehicle is fully loaded.

Enlarging or deepening the channel so that larger vessels can be used is the most likely means whereby transport costs can be reduced both relative to those of existing water transport and compared to those of alternative modes. In most countries, no mode of transport bears the full economic cost: the income from tolls or vehicle taxes is not usually sufficient to pay for the full cost and O&M costs of road construction; railways are commonly subsidised and construction costs borne by government; and in each case, the charges or taxes levied are commonly insufficient to cover the full externalities associated with that mode of transport. Similarly, the extent of cost recovery is usually low for waterways, rates of 20% in the USA and 2% in the Netherlands being two major examples. Therefore, it is important to compare the real resource costs of the different modes of transport and also, for economic sustainability, to compare the fiscal costs to government of alternative transport modes.

Loading and unloading can be both expensive in terms of the delays in moving goods, in the idle time of the vessels, and also as an activity itself. There can be economies of scale in loading and unloading costs as a function of the size of the load. The daily cost of resources or goods in transit should also be calculated and included in the comparison of transport costs across the different modes. Water-borne transport will generally be slower than road or rail movements and water-borne transport is most usually competitive for bulk, low unit-cost goods where the value of the load does not justify the use of a higher-cost, faster mode of transport. At the same time, goods in transit provide a degree of mobile storage and a reduction in transport time may then result in requirements for increased storage capacity at one or both ends of the journey. Locks are a notable cause of delays in transport and either improvements in lock handling or increases in lock size so that a larger number of vessels can be raised or lowered in one lock cycle may therefore yield significant benefits. One of the results of queuing theory (Hillier and Lieberman 1967) is that queues can increase exponentially, being infinite in the limit. Hence delays at locks may set the limiting capacity of the navigation. But there may be relatively cheap methods of increasing the throughput of a lock system rather than enlarging the lock (Sweeney 2000).

Economies of scale can also apply to packaging whilst there are typically some losses to goods being transported both during transport and also in trans-shipment. For some resources, notably food stuffs, the rate of loss through natural deterioration is partly a function of the elapsed time. In all forms of transport, the reliability of delivery dates can be a significant determinant of the choice of transport mode: a lower transport cost may not be sufficient to induce the use of water-borne transport if the time taken to transfer the goods varies over time: for example, low flows during droughts may halt all shipping movements. Variability in journey time requires that goods are dispatched earlier so as to increase the probability that they arrive on time and in turn this requires that storage is provided at the destination in order to buffer variations in deliveries. The vessels themselves will be utilised for a lower proportion of the time and this in turn increases unit costs.

The primary benefit is likely to arise in the second way with freight either being attracted away from other transport modes, particularly from road transport, or retained for water transport when otherwise it would be shifted to another transport mode. As noted, relative costs are not the only determinant of the choice of transport mode.

21

Environment

The state of the river environment and the connected river corridor is a function of the flow regime, and with that regime, the process of erosion, transportation and deposition of sediment, together with the quality of the water. In summary, the environment is then a joint product of the flow regime, channel form and water quality as well as the wider environmental context of the river. It follows that it does not matter what is the reason that a change occurs, the benefits of achieving a preferable environmental state are the same whether that state will be achieved by a shift to a more desirable flow regime, a reduction in pollution or conversion to a more natural river form. In short, the nature of the benefits and the means of evaluating those benefits are the same whether the project under consideration is the alleviation of low flows, a reduction in the pollution load from point or non-point sources, or through river restoration. Equally, it can turn out that the real problem is not that which was originally believed; this is one of the lessons from the Groovtlei case study (Case Study 21.2).

Equally, almost any intervention to support other functions, such as navigation, hydropower generation, flood management or abstraction will have as part of its cost one or more impacts on the environment as these change the flow regime, the quality regime or the form of the river. So, too, can attempts to improve the river by, for example, augmenting the flow from groundwater at a lower ambient temperature (Cowx 1998).

Ecosystems and the linkages between them form very complex systems. Moreover, whilst rivers are dynamic systems, ecosystems are only able to cope with specific dynamic ranges of conditions. For example, Figure 21.1 summarises the factors and the interconnections between them that affect the life cycle of the brown trout. In turn, this complexity makes assessing the impact of a change difficult. For example, climate change will affect the runoff and the flow regime which in turn will affect the channel structure as well the depth and velocity of flow (Arnell *et al.* 1994). Temperature will also change and this in turn will affect the level of dissolved oxygen.

Hence, short-term changes, such as a pollution pulse, flood or period of low flow may cause damage from which the river does not naturally recover for a long period of time. Therefore, as has been seen earlier (Chapter 14), the problem is to

Handbook of Water Economics: Principles and Practice. C. Green
© 2003 John Wiley & Sons, Ltd ISBN: 0-471-98571-6

Factors affecting the brown trout (Salmo trutta) life cycle

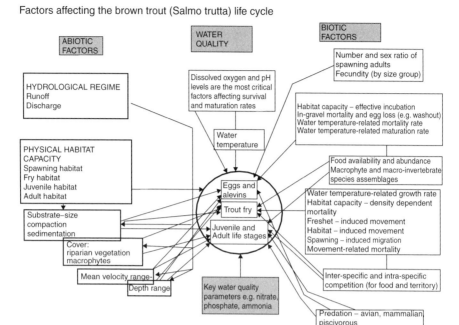

Figure 21.1   *Factors influencing the success of a trout fishery. Source: Burrows 2001*

manage the frequency distribution of perturbations. Some of these perturbations are deliberate (e.g. overflows from sewerage networks during thunderstorms); others are accidental (e.g. escape of slurry from a farm, the misconnection of pipe during the cleaning of a factory, or a fire at a chemical storage warehouse). It is therefore necessary to carry out a full risk assessment before undertaking any specific works otherwise the works may have little real effect. If the state of the river environment is controlled by the runoff of pesticides and fertilisers from agricultural land, then the benefits of improving sewage treatment are likely to be marginal. Equally, it is important to consider whether these changes will extend into the coastal zone. For example, the canalisation of river channels in Spain has resulted in sediment being carried out to sea; in turn, this is considered to have damaged the offshore beds of sea-grass (Fos 1997). Conversely, the flash floods in the Sinai desert carry off heavy loads of sediment which are deposited on the offshore coral reefs, damaging those reefs (Ras Gharib *et al.* 1997).

Figure 21.2 summarises the main benefits, in the case of an improvement, and costs where the river environment will be harmed. Those that are applicable in a particular case depend upon the nature of the river; if the river is small, then there is unlikely to be any scope for commercial fisheries or boating for pleasure. The standard rule applies: since the benefits (or costs) are given by a unit value times the number of beneficiaries, the starting point is to make

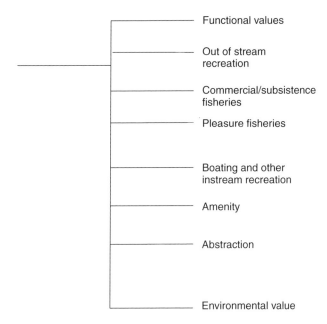

Figure 21.2   *Benefits/costs related to environmental changes*

some assessment of the likely number of beneficiaries and then to concentrate on refining the estimates for those with the largest number of potential beneficiaries. The number of beneficiaries in each category will generally vary to a much greater extent than the unit value; it is not unusual to find, for example, that whilst there are only 2500 canoe trips each year on the stretch of river, there are 500 000 visits by people walking along or picnicking on the river banks. With the exception of commercial and subsistence fisheries which were discussed in Section 17.6, the problems of evaluating these different streams of benefits or costs are outlined below.

An early methodology, together with standard data, to evaluate the benefits of sewerage schemes was produced by Green *et al.* (1989a). More recently, general discussions of the appropriate methodology have also been prepared by van Beukering *et al.* (1998) and Russell *et al.* (2001). The UK appears to be unusual in that benefit–cost analyses are required for all improvement projects and that a standard methodology, together with standard data, has been produced for that purpose (WRc/OXERA/FHRC 1996).

21.1 Functional Value

De Groot (1987) pointed out the general importance of functional value and the functional values of wetlands in particular are well established (e.g. Maltby

1986). The functional values in a particular case need, however, to be established; for example, W S Atkins (1992) identified a benefit of watercourses as being to form barriers for livestock, and their use as a source of water for livestock is self-evident. However, the emphasis needs to be upon exploring the particular functional importance in the particular circumstances. Especially in partially subsistence economies, functional relationships may not be self-evident and require careful investigation before they can be identified. In general, the evaluation technique that is then most appropriate to their evaluation is the least-cost alternative approach (Section 12.2.1).

21.2 Recreational Uses

The basic theory to evaluating all recreational uses is the same; if a site is improved then there will be two streams of benefit:

- Those who visit that site already will gain more enjoyment from that visit.
- In turn, unless a charge is introduced that is exactly equal to that increase in enjoyment, then they will tend to visit more often. In addition, some new visitors will be attracted to the site and away from some existing activity, such as visiting some other site.

Clearly, in the extreme situation, there may be no visits made at all to the site at present, and all visits will be new. Hence, to put a value on the recreational gain to the site, it is necessary to estimate:

- the increase in enjoyment;
- the number of additional visits by existing visitors and the net gain per visit; and
- the number of visits by new visitors and the net gain per visit.

These three values can be different. It also needs to be recognised that it is possible to be spectacularly wrong in the assessments of the number of visits that will be made to the site. For example, when Euro Disney opened outside Paris, the number of visitors and the resulting revenue were far below projections, so much so that it had to be refinanced.

21.2.1 Out-of-stream recreation

Out-of-stream recreation, such as walking or picnicking, in developed countries is important simply because so many visits are made to river corridors; in some cases, the number of visits can exceed 500 000 a year. A relatively low value per individual visit thus generates a substantial annual benefit and a correspondingly large present value.

21.2.1.1 What do people want?

The value of a visit to a river corridor and the effect of some proposed change clearly depends upon what people would like to experience when visiting that river corridor and how the river matches up to those desires both now and after the change. Hence it is necessary to discover what are the attributes that make rivers desirable as a place to visit. For the UK, we now know a great deal (e.g. Tunstall *et al.* 1997) but those characteristics that are important are likely to be very much influenced by the size of the rivers in the UK. It should not therefore be assumed that the same attributes are important in other countries. Overall, what people want of rivers in the UK (Green and Tunstall 1996) is something that looks like what they believe is a natural river, but they also want easy access, including dry paths and car parking, and toilets. At the same time, most people do not want many other people to be there. However, there is a significant degree of market segmentation, those with children wanting attributes that others do not want – things for children to do.

As a result of this market segmentation, the preferences of the different groups of informal recreaters are in conflict; as similarly are those of anglers and boaters (European Inland Fisheries Advisory Commission 1998; O'Riordan and Paget 1978). Equally, those who simply want to go for a walk or a picnic by a river do not want anglers to be there. The results shown in Figure 21.3 are quite typical: making provision for angling would reduce rather than enhance the enjoyment of the majority of those who visit the river, as would pubs and cafes. However, there is no conflict between the desires of those seeking informal recreation and the ecological value of the river corridor. What people want is precisely what they believe constitutes a rich and diverse ecosystem. But this will not always be the case. Figure 21.3 also illustrates the nature of the river environment as a joint product; the respondents want fish, they want to see many water insects, and they want to see more water plants: in this particular river, which is small and suffering from low flows, the only way that these species will be able to colonise the river is if flows are allowed to increase. In addition to the kind of overall studies just described, there are many more specific studies on water quality (e.g. Burrows and House 1989; Ditton and Goodale 1973; Tunstall *et al.* 1997), and sewage debris (House and Herring 1995; Smith *et al.* 1995). Similar studies are required before seeking to evaluate changes to lakes or reservoirs, or to canals.

21.2.1.2 Valuing a recreational visit

There have been a great many studies that have sought to put an economic value on informal recreation by rivers and canals, mainly through the travel cost method (e.g. Harrison and Stabler 1981) and contingent valuation (e.g. Green and Tunstall 1991b; Stabler and Ash 1978). More complete listings of what is now a very large body of work are given in two databases available on the web www.evri.ec.gc.ca/evri/ and http://www2.epa.nsw.gov.au/envalue/StudyCnt.asp, as well as in texts such as

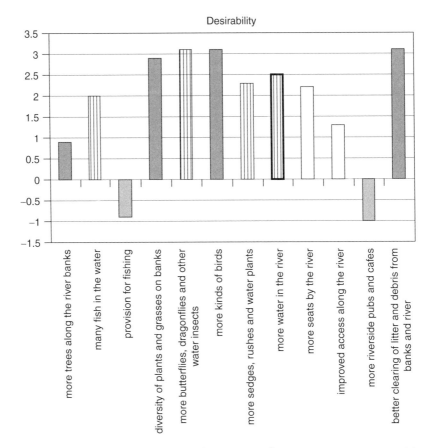

Figure 21.3   *Desired improvements to the river as a place to visit – River Wey residents' survey*

Russell *et al.* (2001), Navrud (1992) and van Beukering *et al.* (1998). Meta-analyses of this work have been undertaken by Walsh *et al.* (1989).

In many places, access to the river corridor is free and, in addition, in Europe in particular, a significant fraction of visits are made on foot. The latter condition means that the travel cost method is not applicable because no resource costs are incurred in making the visit. One approach to valuing the recreational enjoyment given by the site would be to ask visitors what entry charge they would be prepared to pay to use the site now and after the change in conditions.

There are four problems with this approach:

- Since there is no charge for entry at present, respondents have no experience in placing a monetary value on the enjoyment given by a visit. Valuing enjoyment and differentiating this value from the values of other leisure activities is not a task that is necessarily easy – not least because so many leisure activities are not priced.

- An entry charge ought to reduce the frequency with which visits are made to the site (Stabler and Ash 1978). In practice, the reductions in the frequency with which visits are made can be substantial. For example, Savage (2001) reports that the Sydney Museum of Contemporary Art more than doubled visitor numbers when it dropped entry charges. Conversely, when the Australian Museum, the Powerhouse Museum and the Museum of Victoria introduced charges, visitor numbers dropped 50–80%, whilst visitor numbers at the Science Museum fell by 55% and 35% at the Victoria and Albert Museum in London when charges were introduced.
- Introducing an entry charge redefines social relations, and the respondents may regard the changes in social relations as being more important than the monetary value. For example, in one study, respondents said that they choose an amount which would keep undesirables out of the site (Simmonds 1976). More generally, it has not been established that the identity assumed by economists between value and willingness to pay is widely shared by the population as a whole.
- The entry charge is generally in any case hypothetical and only intended as a way of deriving an economic value. It is difficult to explain to respondents that there is no intention of introducing an entry charge, and that it is being used solely as a way of deriving an economic value, without it sounding both silly and contrived. Where there is an entry charge at present – for example, a day licence for angling – this argument no longer holds. But, if an entry charge is used to elicit values, then the methodology developed by Stabler and Ash (1978) must be used: this requires the respondents to state both an entry charge and the frequency of visiting at this charge, and also that entry charge at which the frequency of visiting would fall to zero.

An alternative approach that was developed to get around these problems is the 'value of enjoyment' method (Penning-Rowsell *et al.* 1992). This attacks the first problem by asking people to identify an activity that gives the same subjective amount of enjoyment as a visit to the site in question. For example, a visit to a river may give them the same enjoyment as a visit to a local park or to museum. If this alternative involves costs then this gives the respondents a basis upon which to anchor their estimate of the value of the visit to the river.

The obvious criticism of this approach is that there is no explicit income constraint. However, when the values placed upon the enjoyment per visit are small, so should be any distortion that occurs by not imposing an income constraint. In addition, there are two checks that can be made, one external and one internal. The external check is that the value of any visit must at least equal the value of the time spent at the site where values of time have been calculated for use in transport studies (e.g. DTLR 2000). On this basis, the values obtained by the value of enjoyment method might be considered to be low. Secondly, in each study, respondents were also asked to rate the enjoyment that they obtained from the visit on a 0–10 scale; the relationship between the mean values obtained. When the two are compared across the 21 river and coastal sites for which we have data, the results are not discouraging but more data is required before a meta-analysis can be undertaken.

21.2.2 Instream recreation

The same principles that apply to valuing outstream recreation can be used to value instream recreation such as swimming and boating. However, there are two added complications. Firstly, instream uses tend to conflict with ecological values and also to conflict with outstream uses for small-scale watercourses. Secondly, when considering water quality improvement, different parameters determine the suitability for swimming and water contact activities than determine its capacity to support a diverse ecosystem. Whereas for the latter purposes, it is the removal of nutrients and the reduction of the oxygen demand of the waste stream that is important, for water contact activities, the problem is usually to reduce the quantities of disease vectors (viruses, bacteria, protozoa and helminths). This is a more difficult and expensive task, and where conditions are suitable, maturation ponds are likely to be more effective than conventional treatment (WHO 1987). Even then runoff from naturally occurring animal waste or the presence of leptospirosis may still limit the suitability of the waters for contact activities.

Probably more economic evaluations have been carried out of recreational fisheries than of any benefit dependent upon the environment, particularly in North America. Many of these evaluations have been carried out using the travel cost method (Loomis *et al.* 1986) but a significant number have also been undertaken by the contingent valuation method (e.g. Loomis *et al.* 1986). At least one meta-analysis has also been undertaken (Sturtevant *et al.* 1995).

21.2.2.1 What do anglers want?

Quite marked market segmentation often exists between anglers (Holland and Ditton 1992) with preferences for the fishing experience being different between the different market segments (Hudgins 1984). Similarly, there appear to be some differences between countries in the nature of the fishing experience and also as to who goes fishing.

This segmentation has two consequences:

- There can be differences between the segments in terms of what improvements will increase their enjoyment when angling, and hence their choice of sites.
- It restricts the degree to which any one site is a substitute for any other. In turn, the nature of the fishing experience that can be offered at a site is defined by the characteristics of that site; the most radical change that is made to change what can be offered at a site is introducing alien species.

In the UK, the simplest differentiation is between salmonid and coarse fisheries, the obvious difference between the two being that coarse fisheries are take and return fisheries. In coarse fisheries it is also necessary to differentiate between still and flowing water fisheries. Very few still water anglers wish to fish in flowing waters; and there are also only a relatively few number of anglers who would like to change between coarse and salmonid fishing or vice versa (Figure 21.4). In addition, there are very marked differences between those who prefer still waters and those who prefer running waters in terms of what features they look for in a fishing site (Green, Newsome and Stephen 2000). In turn, there are differences in terms of what still water, other coarse anglers, and game anglers want from a fishing day (Table 21.1), what they therefore look for in a site, and how far they are prepared to travel in order to reach a site (Table 21.2). These results are taken from an interview survey of anglers taken in order to generate the data given in the FWR manual (WRc/OXERA/FHRC 1996). In part these differences are simply a reflection of reality; it is easier to provide good footpaths beside the lowland rivers that support coarse angling as opposed to

| species caught | % | species would like to catch | | | | | | | | | | |
		bream	carp	perch	roach	rudd	tench	brown trout	rainbow trout	salmon	sea trout	Number of cases
bream		28	36	14	27	7	22	8	9	4	2	258
carp		19	48	12	20	5	20	8	9	4	1	277
perch		23	34	17	26	7	23	9	10	4	2	273
roach		24	34	14	27	6	23	8	9	4	2	309
rudd		22	34	16	28	8	24	8	8	5	3	195
tench		22	37	12	23	5	27	6	7	3	2	264
brown trout		6	13	7	9	3	7	35	30	23	10	221
rainbow trout		8	13	9	9	3	8	33	39	21	11	194
salmon		1	8	0	4	0	1	26	21	38	24	78
sea trout		4	8	1	3	0	1	27	22	45	29	73
Number of cases		157	266	103	176	43	156	168	163	152	85	

Figure 21.4 *Preferred species*

Table 21.1 *Importance of factors in making a day's fishing enjoyable: game v. coarse anglers*

	Game	Coarse
Freedom	8.7	8.4
Peace and quiet	8.7	8.5
Relaxation	8.6	8.5
Wildlife	8.2	7.8
Challenge	8.3	7.9
Achievement	6.5	7.1
Meeting other anglers	5.5	5.7
Quantity	4.0	5.4
Size	4.6	5.2
Competition	2.9	4.0

Note: Shaded cells show differences that are statistically significant at the 5% level.

Table 21.2   *Travel to usual site*

	Distance to usual site (miles)	Time to usual site (minutes)	Travel cost to usual site (£)	Number of days
Coarse	16.9	28	3.10	27
Still water	13.5	22	3.36	30
Running water	21.2	33	2.94	25
Trout	24.2	29	5.17	46
Salmon	41.0	41	9.45	39

Note: excludes travel times over 270 minutes.

Table 21.3   *Coarse fishing: quality of fishery*

Quality class	Assumed average biomass of coarse fish	Description
C1	$>2000\,g/100\,m^2$	Large number of fish, some of them specimen, from a wide variety of species
C2	600 to 2000 $g/100\,m^2$	Moderate number of fish, but no specimen fish, from quite a wide variety of species
C3	$<600\,g/100\,m^2$	Few, small fish from a limited range of species

Table 21.4   *Salmon and sea trout: quality of fishery*

Quality class	Migratory	Non-migratory
S1	1 in 10 chance of catching a salmon for each day's fishing by an average angler	1 in 2 chance of catching a sea trout for each day's fishing by an average angler
S2	1 in 40 chance of catching a salmon for each day's fishing by an average angler	1 in 5 chance of catching a sea trout for each day's fishing by an average angler

the upper land rivers that provide the fast flowing rivers necessary to support salmonid angling.

The most obvious difference between coarse and salmonid anglers is in what constitutes a good site in terms of the fish there to be caught. To derive such measures of the quality of fishing provided by rivers, different angling groups were consulted. In the UK, coarse anglers expect to catch one or more fish during any visit; what is important is the size and species present (Table 21.3). Trout anglers look for wild fish of a good size but for salmon anglers, a good site is one where the chance of catching a fish is as high as 1 in 10 (Table 21.4).

In valuing both a new site and an improvement to an existing site, market segmentation must be taken into account but where anglers are used to paying for a one-day ticket, this provides a straightforward way of determining the value

Table 21.5   *Benefits of angling*

	Amount (£ 1993)	Days would fish per year
River Ver – House *et al.* (1994)	5.10	10.5
River Misbourne – House *et al.* (1994)	8.18	9.2
Stabler and Ash (1978)	6.10	n/a
Smith and Kavanagh (1969)	13.90	n/a

placed on the site. There are some complications when anglers pay for an annual fishing licence which includes access to the existing site, or where that site is owned by an angling club and access is limited to club members. However, the major problem is in predicting the change in the number of visits that will be made, particularly when, as seems to be the case in Europe, the participation rate for angling is falling.

Table 21.5 summarises the results from the study by House *et al.* (1994), where alleviating the low flows in two separate rivers would allow the river to return to being a fishery, together with the results of two earlier UK studies. For comparison, the then price of a one-day ticket for coarse fishing was in the range of £2 to £6, and that for trout fishing between £15 to £25 so the values appear to be plausible.

21.3 Amenity

Living near a body of water may increase the enjoyment of those living there; in turn, that increase in enjoyment should be reflected in an increase in the value of those properties. Thus, the Office of Water (1995) cites figures showing that such proximity to water can increase the price of housing by up to 28%. Green and Tunstall (1992) found strong correlations between the attractiveness of a road or estate as a place to live, and the surrounding environment, particularly the presence of an attractive river. A number of studies have been undertaken to estimate the resulting increase in value (e.g. Feitelson 1991). The danger here is of double-counting since proximity to the water should be expected to increase the number of visits made to that water which may be included separately.

Similarly, pubs and leisure facilities situated near water may also attract more customers; again, this increase in custom and revenue should in turn be reflected in an increase in the value of those properties. In a different way, proximity to water may also generate a higher rent or sales price, and improvements to waterways have been undertaken as a way of stimulating economic regeneration (Button and Pearce 1989).

21.4 Abstraction

In principle, improving the quality or quantity of flow in a river may result either in allowing that water to be abstracted for some purpose, or reduce the cost of treating that water so that it can be used for that purpose. In the first case, the benefit is given by the least cost alternative for providing an equivalent quantity of water and in the latter, the cost of the treatment that is avoided. In some cases, the critical parameter for industry can be the reliability of characteristics of supply; Husain (1978) reports that a dyeing company experienced problems during a drought not because of the quality of the water but because the water's characteristics had changed and so in turn did the colours of the dyed cloth.

21.5 Environmental Value

Part of the value of biodiversity is given by the functional value of that asset. A second component is given by what is loosely labelled as 'nonuse' value. Deep ecologists (e.g. Naess 1993) argue that in addition, species have an inherent right by reason of existence. It is necessary to consider the two cases: valuing a loss caused by our actions or avoiding a loss, and achieving an improvement.

There are both pragmatic and theoretical reasons for avoiding putting a money value on a loss caused by our actions. The pragmatic reason is that doing so is unlikely to enhance a common understanding between the different stakeholders (Section 13.2). Putting a monetary value on, for example, the avoidance of the loss of a breeding pair of a Red List species may in one instance mean that this loss is avoided. But in another project, this additional cost will be insufficient to justify not doing the action that results in the loss. In this case, a significant proportion of the stakeholders are likely to conclude that the analyst is mad, bad or simply does not understand what the choice involves. The theoretical reason is that 'is' cannot imply 'ought' so that even if we could put a value on the loss of a breeding pair of a Red List species, it is open to anyone to argue that this is not the value that we ought to put on their preservation. Moreover, there may be no option that does not involve some environmental loss, a critical part of the choice being to decide which is the least worst option (Green and Penning-Rowsell 1999).

Hence, when action would result in an environmental loss, the adoption of the critical natural capital/constant natural asset approach (Section 7.1.1) is recommended. The same approach is recommended when the decision involves avoiding a loss that would otherwise occur. For example, in an assessment of the benefits of renewing the weirs and other structures on the River Nene in East Anglia, it was found that a large number of important nature reserves had developed as a result of the extensive modification of the river over hundreds of years. These were deemed by the local authorities as being critical natural capital; hence the benefits of reconstructing the weirs could be estimated as the costs of maintaining the existing water regimes of those reserves by other means (Balfour Maunsell 1995).

This approach is not possible when an investment to improve environmental quality is considered. Here, we are forced to consider explicitly how much we are prepared to sacrifice now to gain an improvement. Unfortunately, we are confronted with all of the difficult and unresolved problems surrounding that which is loosely labelled as 'nonuse' value (Section 5.1.2). What is important here is whether the action is one of the first actions we should take; if we deem pollution to be morally wrong, is this action one of the first we should do?

Case Study 21.1 General Environmental Value of River Water Quality Improvements

The form of this study was designed to address four problems:

- We knew from previous studies (Green *et al.* 1990; Green and Tunstall 1991b), and the focus groups confirmed, the finding that people value clean rivers and are prepared to pay towards the achievement of such improvements in river water quality. However, whilst such 'nonuse' motivations appear to be important, economic theory regarding preparedness to pay for such goods was highly speculative (Section 4.3).
- Those earlier studies and the focus group studies indicated that for some people at least, there is a moral component to such a desire for clean rivers. For example, in one focus group when one respondent said (correctly) that untreated raw sewage was being discharged into estuaries, the general reaction from other respondents was that this sort of thing should not happen in this day and age.
- We were asking respondents to state a preparedness to pay for a change about which they were unlikely to have thought about until they were asked the question.
- Given some 35 000 km of river in England and Wales, it is not possible to ask people to value improvements in each and every kilometre. On the other hand, such specific values are necessary for use in the benefit–cost analyses of proposed new treatment works.

Conventionally, experiments are intended to test hypotheses (Blaug 1992) but the purpose of this study was to obtain real values rather than to test whether conventional economic theory is an adequate or appropriate description of the way in which people approach choices for collective goods. For the purpose of the study, what was important was that the amounts offered represented real money, a preparedness to make a real sacrifice, and not the reasons why they were prepared to make that sacrifice.

If something is a moral wrong there can be no optimum level of 'wrongness', however, there are resource constraints which will influence the rate at which we can correct those moral wrongs. In addition, it will take time to make even initial improvements. Hence, the study was framed to determine where we should start: at what point we should stop seeking to improve water quality can be left to the future.

Thirdly, rather than assuming respondents simply had to recall whether or not they were prepared to pay, and how much they were prepared to pay, the preparedness

Continued on page 354

__ *Continued from page 353* __

to pay question was designed so as to help respondents decide how much they were prepared to pay.

Both the possibility that some respondents would see the choice in terms of a moral wrong and the implausibility of assuming that they could differentiate between improvements to each of some 35 000 kilometres of river, led to the study being developed as a choice between different programmes of improvements, a choice of where we should start work on improving river water quality. The initial intention had been to undertake a conjoint analysis in which different packages of improvements at different cost levels were offered. However, the focus groups did not identify any attributes, other than the existing water quality, by which people wished to prioritise improvements.

To define such a programme, it was necessary to develop a simple means of defining different standards of water quality. It was not possible to use the water quality ladder that Mitchell and Carson (1981) developed for their study in the USA because of the difference in the scale of rivers in the two countries. The USA scale differentiates between boatable, fishable and swimmable water quality. In the UK, the 95% exceedance flow for more than 75% of UK gauging stations is less than 1 m^3/sec (CNS 1991); hence, most rivers will never be boatable, or fishable for any practical purpose. Moreover, with such low flows, and thus the small capacity to dilute runoff discharges or naturally occurring loads of bacteria (for some UK rivers, 70% of the flow is treated wastewater), few of those rivers can be expected to achieve swimmable water quality. In addition, the US water quality ladder is strictly use orientated whereas the studies of preferences for river corridors in the UK (Tunstall *et al.* 1997) have found that what people want is a river that looks like a natural river that supports a wide range of flora and fauna. Hence, an appropriate water quality ladder had to be developed that related to people's preferences for river corridors to recognisable species that are in turn truly indicative of water quality. Thus, although the kingfisher is an iconic species for rivers, its presence or absence depends more upon the physical form of the river than on water quality, and hence it could not be included as an indicator. On the other hand, the indicator species used in biological water quality indicators (WRc/OXERA/FHRC 1996) could not be used because these are obtained through grab-netting. After consultation with specialists from the Natural History Museum, English Nature, the Royal Society for the Protection of Birds and the National Rivers Authority, three descriptions of water quality were agreed which could also be matched against the formal criteria used to define water quality in the UK (WRc/OXERA/FHRC 1996) and to the output of water quality models.

Four possible programmes (A, B, C and D) of improvements in river water quality (Table 21.6) were also developed; these programmes were designed in such a way that given a preparedness to pay for each programme it was possible statistically to derive a value of improving one kilometre of river from one class to the next. Each programme was described as taking 10 years to implement.

An interview schedule was then developed from the theoretical model shown in Figure 21.5 and a framework developed covering four regions on two dimensions: high–low water quality, high–low charges. A random, preselected address sample was drawn in two stages in each of the four regions. First, eight census enumeration districts (EDs) were drawn for each region, where the probability of drawing each ED was proportional to its population size. Secondly, 27 addresses from each ED were drawn from the postcode address file, 27 being used to cover reserves, the target being to complete 500 interviews. The fieldwork was contracted to a

__ *Continued on page 355* __

__ Continued from page 354 __

Table 21.6   *Programmes for river water quality improvements*
'Improving the standard of the moderate and poor quality waters would be both expensive and take several years to achieve. So we have to decide what our priorities are: where to start and how much it is worth spending.'

Water quality	At present	Improvement programmes – proportion of rivers in each category after completion of 10-year programme			
		A	B	C	D
Good There are abundant fish, birds and plants: fish like trout or dace and grayling which are sensitive to pollution will form a breeding population; rarer species of birds, crayfish, dragonflies and other insects will be found, many plants growing in the water	53%	53%	87%	70%	87%
Moderate Some species such as roach can live in the water but not species sensitive to pollution; some species of birds and some insects will visit the river; some plants will grow in and near the water	34%	47%	0%	23%	13%
Poor This supports very few if any fish and plants; water visited by swans and common types of duck which do not depend on the water for food. There are often many midges and, in really bad cases, the water may be discoloured, covered in foam and smell badly. There may be obvious signs of pollution by sewage or oil	13%	0%	13%	7%	0%
Mean rank (1 = best programme)		2.7	2.9	2.4	1.9
% prepared to pay		39.3	29.7	44.1	46.5
mean amount prepared to pay (£)		8.24	6.32	9.29	13.18

professional fieldwork company who complied with the UK quality and ethical codes of practice.

The interview schedule itself was long, taking an average of 38 minutes to complete. Amongst the questions preceding the preparedness to pay questions were three in which respondents were asked to rank eight different national problems (e.g. healthcare, law and order, the environment) in terms of priorities, then to rank eight environmental problems (e.g. noise pollution, sea pollution), and finally the nine different water and wastewater services in terms of importance. This last set had been used in earlier studies (Green *et al.* 1993; Green 1997). The discharge of sewage to rivers was one of the service aspects included in the third level.

__ Continued on page 356 __

___ Continued from page 355 ___

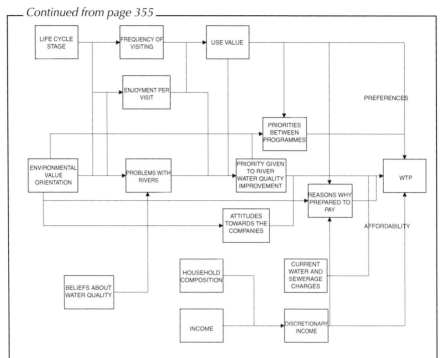

Figure 21.5 *Conceptual model of preparedness to pay for river water quality improvements*

Respondents were first asked to rank order the four programmes; as logically it should, D was generally rated the best programme, whilst B was rated the worst programme, with very mixed views being held about A. When they were asked an open-ended question why they ranked that particular programme as the best, by far the commonest reason given for their preference was that it improved the poor-quality rivers. Next, they were asked whether or not they would be prepared to pay towards the cost of each programme. All those except those who said that they were definitely not prepared to pay towards the cost of a programme were then asked about how much they were prepared to pay. The format was used as described in Section 14.7. Thus, each respondent was started at one bidding level, completed that ladder, and was then offered the opportunity of starting at the other starting point on the same ladder. At the end, the respondent was asked an open-ended question as to the amount that they would be prepared to pay (Table 21.7). When Guy Garrod and Ken Willis at the University of Newcastle-upon-Tyne analysed the data, the implied value of improving one kilometre of river from one class to another is as shown in Table 21.8.

The proportions of respondents who were prepared to pay fell away from 57% (visitors to rivers) and 44% (non-visitors) for the most preferred option to 29% (visitors) and 19% (non-visitors) for their least preferred option. The usual question was asked as to what were the reasons for their decision as to whether or not

___ Continued on page 357 ___

___ Continued from page 356 ___

Table 21.7   *Reasons why prepared to pay: visitors v. non-visitors*

	Non-visitor	Visitor
What your household could afford to pay	4.9	4.4
Your household's fair share of the cost	4.6	4.1
The other things upon which you would like to spend more money	4.5	3.9
The value to wildlife of improvements in water quality	4.4	4.7
The value to you of the improvements to rivers as a place to visit	3.7	4.3

Note: All differences significant at 5%. Scale: 1 = not important; 5 = very important.

Table 21.8   *Value of river water quality: general environmental value*

From	To	Value (£)
Poor: Supports few fish and plants; water visited only by swans and common types of duck that do not depend on water for food; many midges; water may be discoloured, covered in foam, and may smell bad; may be obvious signs of pollution by sewage or oil	**Medium:** Some fish such as roach survive but not species sensitive to pollution; some species of birds and insects will visit the river; some plants will grow in and near the water	0.00541 /household /year
Medium: Some fish such as roach survive but not species sensitive to pollution; some species of birds and insects will visit the river; some plants will grow in and near the water	**Good:** Abundant fish, birds and plants; fish like trout, dace or grayling which are sensitive to pollution will form a breeding population; rarer species of birds, crayfish, dragonflies and other insects will be found; many plants growing in the water	0.00201 /household /year

they were prepared to pay for their preferred programme. There were significant differences in the importance the respondents attached to the different reasons between those who visit river corridors and those who do not, although, as usual, a principal components analysis found two factors which could be readily identified as 'value' and 'affordability', with fairness cross-loading on the two factors. In addition, over 80% of respondents, with no difference by gender, said that they would expect to discuss such a commitment with their partner before making it.

Case Study 21.2 Grootvlei, South Africa

The Problem

The remaining gold mines of East Rand Basin, east of Johannesburg, are marginally profitable. Gold mines are also deep and require extensive pumping in order to remain workable. Since the mines are interconnected for safety reasons, it is possible to use one pumping station to drain the entire basin. This pumping station is, logically, located below the deepest level of the deepest working mine. Minewater is commonly loaded with heavy metals, is acidic and may be saline.

With the closure of the then deepest mine, pumping was shifted to No. 3 shaft of the Grootvlei mine after the appropriate environmental assessment and granting of the necessary permit; pumping commenced in November 1995. Unfortunately, both the volume and quality of the water pumped were worse than predicted and breached the permitted limits. The discharge point for the untreated water is immediately adjacent to the Blesbokspruit, a Ramsar designated wetland. The immediate result was a red plume of water spreading downstream through the wetland as iron and manganese oxidised and were then deposited on the bed of the wetlands. This particularly affected bottom-feeding fish and the death of these fish reduced the food supply for some bird species and hence the number of those species using the wetlands. The discharge permit was therefore withdrawn and pumping stopped.

As an immediate but interim response, a lagoon system for aeration, liming and clarification was constructed whilst permanent works were designed and constructed. An interim permit was issued and pumping recommenced. However, whilst both the temporary and permanent works would remove the iron and manganese, the effluent would still be very saline which could cause a number of negative effects. But the only way to reduce this salinity is through partial or complete desalination, with the Grootvlei discharge contributing 30% of the total salt load entering the Vaal Barrage (Water Research Commission 2000). However, desalination is a process which is both expensive in capital and operating costs, and leaves the problem of disposing of the saline wastes captured through the process.

All of the possible options that the government of South Africa could adopt were markedly unattractive. Since the Blesbokspruit is a Ramsar site, it was argued that should the South African government allow such damage to occur, it would reduce the credibility of South Africa's commitment to the environment, a right guaranteed by the Constitution, and reduce the confidence of foreign investors where foreign investment is in turn essential if the economy is to be expanded. Again, if the government were seen to violate one constitutional right then its credibility with respect to protecting all constitutional rights would be reduced.

Equally the objective of the government had to be to improve the living standards of the majority of the population by expanding employment and also in providing basic water and sanitation. The government's emergency water and sanitation programme had an initial objective of providing a water point within 200 m of every household in the 12 000 to 15 000 communities currently lacking such facilities (Department of Water Affairs and Forestry 1994). Any government-financed treatment of the minewater could be at the expense of the progress of the emergency water and sanitation programme. At the same time, the East Rand Basin directly employs 6000 people in an area where unemployment was already 30%.

Continued on page 359

___ *Continued from page 358* ___

The government therefore set up an interdepartmental committee, the Grootvlei Joint Venture Committee, to commission research on the issues and to undertake a cost–benefit analysis relating to mining in the East Rand Basin (Grootvlei Joint Venture Committee 1996). As part of this process, the Water Research Commission asked the Foundation for Water Research to apply the UK methodology to the assessment of the options (Foundation for Water Research 1996) and a longer discussion of the FWR study is given in Green (1999).

The options

The baseline was taken to be the permanent aeration, liming and clarification works. The two main alternative immediate 'do something' options were then to stop pumping and close the mines, or to install a form of desalination plant, either putting the treated water into the potable supply or discharging it to the Blesbokspruit. However, sooner or later the mine will close and a decision will then have to be taken as to what to do then; either to continue pumping but from a higher level in another mine or to allow the water level to rebound to its natural level and to decant downstream. Identifying what would happen under the baseline option and its consequences proved to be important in assessing the do-something option.

The benefits

In turn, a wide range of impacts from one or another option were identified; obtaining sufficient information to be able to evaluate each was more difficult. For example, wetlands are well known to yield benefits in terms of removing polluting loads (e.g. Maltby 1986). However, there was insufficient water quality sampling data to determine what pollution load is removed by the wetlands at present. So, this benefit could not be evaluated. Other categories of benefit which were evaluated, such as the recreation value of the wetlands, proved to have trivial benefits. Therefore, analysis focused upon the five most important categories of benefit to the decision: mining, potable water, irrigation, critical and constant natural capital, and the dolomitic layer.

Mining

The very high unemployment rate indicated that the opportunity costs of the labour employed in the mine were well below the financial costs of wages. Methods of estimating the opportunity cost, or shadow wage, of labour are well established (Squire and van der Tak 1975) if difficult to apply in practice. Using available data, two different estimates of this opportunity cost were made. The estimates of the yield from mining were further adjusted to take account of the remittance of wages and profits overseas. The net effect was to show that the economic value of the mines was significant, a present value of around R580 million.

As export earners, the contributions of the mines to the South African economy depend critically upon both the level of gold prices and the dollar–rand exchange rate in the future. Analyses of projects involving exports or import substitution typically depend critically upon projected future exchange rates. The higher the

___ *Continued on page 360* ___

— *Continued from page 359* —

dollar gold price, the greater the proportions of gold reserves which it will be financially viable to extract in the future, the greater the contribution of the mines to the economy, the longer the viable life of the mines and the lower the grade of ore which it will be viable to mine. The assumption was made that neither the exchange rate nor the world price for gold would change in real terms in the future. Therefore, whilst the mine has significant reserves of low-grade ore, it was assumed that it would be uneconomic to mine these and that the economic life of the mine would be a minimum of 12 years and a maximum of 30 years at current output levels. In this particular instance, the final conclusion did not depend upon future movements in the world price of gold and the dollar–rand exchange rate, both of which have moved since the analysis.

Critical natural capital or constant natural asset

The Blesbokspruit wetlands are designated under the Ramsar Convention. Thus, two critical questions were: the extent to which discharges would damage the wetlands; and how to incorporate that damage potential into the cost–benefit analysis in a way which would both work and help the decision process. The approach adopted was the use of the concepts of constant natural assets and critical natural capital (Countryside Commission *et al.* 1993). Consequently, if the Blesbokspruit reserve, a designated Ramsar site, is part of critical natural capital then there can be no question of allowing any discharge which would result in damage to that site. Conversely, if it is better classed as part of constant natural assets then any damage would be acceptable providing that equivalent sites were created or provided. Strictly, such sites should have been created prior to the loss occurring but this could, in this instance, be counterbalanced by requiring a greater area to be provided in compensation for the area lost.

The evidence indicated that the existing wetlands were themselves created by relatively recent human activity; the road, rail and pipeline embankments partly damning the river corridor and resulting in permanent wetlands. The peat samples taken in the wetlands (Breen *et al.* 1996) were all, except one at the very top of the wetlands, dated after the start of nuclear testing, giving the date of earliest peat deposition to be slightly over 50 years ago.

Moreover, it was also found that some 50% of the water flow in the river originates from the discharges of the wastewater plants upstream; given that the potable water supplies are pumped up from the Vaal Barrage rather than originating in the catchment, the seasonal stability of the flow in the wetlands and a large part of the total flow may also be argued to result from human intervention. On these grounds, it was concluded that it would be appropriate to treat the wetlands as a constant natural asset rather than as part of critical natural capital.

The deposition of metal salts undoubtedly caused major damage to the wetlands but this deposition stopped with the completion of the aeration, liming and clarification works. The wetlands will, however, continue to be subject to both a high salt load and also to increased water flows. We did not find an ecologist who was prepared to argue that the saline load would damage the value of the wetlands; indeed, some argued that the increased salinity would make the wetlands more attractive to some Red List species. In the end, it was concluded that the main problem would be the increased flow of water, which would double current flows, and it was claimed that the wetland is already suffering from overwatering.

— *Continued on page 361* —

— *Continued from page 360*

However, the policy of extending basic potable water and sewerage provision to the population necessarily means that wastewater flows to rivers will increase and the major proportion of the current flow comes from the upstream treatment works. Therefore, the local sewerage utility was asked to provide estimates of the growth to be expected in those discharges; their estimate was that growth in those discharges over the next 12 years would equal the current flow in the river. Thus, if there were to be no minewater discharges then flows through the wetlands will double and if minewater is discharged then they will treble. Hence water flows would seem to potentially pose a major threat to the wetlands, irrespective of whether pumping continues. Therefore, it was recommended that a management plan be developed for the wetlands, including a water management plan, and that the ecological health of the wetlands should be monitored. As a result of that monitoring, it may become necessary either to provide a bypass channel for the main flow through the wetlands or to construct an equivalent site.

Irrigation

Without desalination, the high salinity of the discharges will make the river waters unsuitable for irrigation use and hence those farms downstream which currently use irrigation will have to abandon its use. As discussed in Section 17.3.4, irrigation yields benefits in a number of ways. On the other hand, water which is used for irrigation is largely lost through evaporespiration. Therefore, water which is freed from irrigation use is available for other uses which may have higher values than its use for irrigation and which, like most potable water uses, return a far higher fraction of the water used than do irrigation uses.

In order to evaluate the value of the water currently used for irrigation, and to compare it to its value in other uses, estimates were required of:

- how much land is being irrigated;
- how much water is used;
- for what crops;
- what cropping pattern would be followed if irrigation water were not to be available; and
- the relative profitability of the farming under the cropping pattern with irrigation water compared to without water.

The estimates of the area under irrigation varied between 640 ha and 1000 ha. The amounts of water that the farmers abstract is not metered and three widely differing estimates of the amounts of water abstracted were also found:

- 16 557 ml/annum based upon an assumed rate of application of irrigation water;
- 3020 ml/annum based upon the amount of water which disappears from the system; and
- 4808 ml/annum (Breen *et al.* 1996).

Breen *et al.* (1996) estimated the loss if all land were converted to dryland maize growing as R2 486 000/year, very small relative to the cost of desalination.

Continued on page 362

— *Continued from page 361* —

Potable water supplies

Thus, the economic justification for any desalination had largely to lie in the benefits from increasing the local water resource. Discharge of minewater will increase the salinisation problem which is already affecting the Vaal Barrage, the principal water resource for the province. Conversely, desalination could yield an additional resource close to the centre of demand. However, the new resource would equal a maximum of 2% of current output whilst demand is growing at approximately 3.5% annually in Gauteng Province.

The local water utility, Rand Water, estimates the marginal value of potable water available in the Springs area as being around $55 \, c/m^3$, this being the saving in pumping treated water up to the area from their existing works. Thus, the benefit of desalination would be in the order of R11.7 million/year. That water which was not lost through leakage and evapotranspiration and so was returned to the river after wastewater treatment would be available for reuse but no value was put on this water. These benefits were considerably below the estimated capital and operating costs of a desalination plant, which had a present value of R3000 million, the other benefits resulting from desalination being insufficient to justify desalination.

The dolomitic resource

An outstanding question at the beginning of the Joint Venture Committee study was the consequences of ceasing pumping and allowing water in the basin to rise until it naturally discharged downstream. The basin is overlain by a layer of dolomite. Scott (1995) estimated that the total inflow to the dolomite layer from rainfall might be of the order of 51 Ml/day. This is a potential water resource, with the 51 Ml/day being the upper bound of the potential yield from the aquifer and it could be evaluated in the same way as above. Since this water is currently a significant part of the flows which require to be pumped from the mines, such use would reduce the pumping costs, where again this reduction can be evaluated both in terms of the savings of pumping and treatment costs and also in terms of the downstream consequences of discharging the water from Grootvlei.

In addition, the Scott (1995) report concluded that, if the water level were to be allowed to rebound to its natural level, then there would be a risk of polluted water breaking through the surface as springs so spreading pollution. Thus, there would be a risk of dispersed and diffuse pollution. Furthermore, it is likely that additional sinkholes might be formed. Neither loss can be evaluated without more data but the potential consequences are such to make the acceptability of this option appear very problematic. One consequence is that pumping from some depth will have to continue after the mines have closed.

Lessons

The final conclusion of the analysis was that neither closing the mines nor the use of desalination was economically justified, and that the existing approach of aeration, liming and clarification was the best option. A further study by the Water Research Commission (2000) concluded that when compared to a number of desalination options, the best option was the construction of a 130 Ml/d channel around the

— *Continued on page 363* —

— *Continued from page 362* —

Bleksbrokspruit, on the assumption that 50% of the water entering the Grootvlei workings originates from the Bleksbrokspruit.

Two almost equally important findings were, firstly, that the wetlands were probably under threat irrespective of the decision about the minewater discharges because of the anticipated doubling of flows through the wetlands from the waste-water plants upstream. Secondly, the conclusion was that the uncertainties as to the consequences of allowing the water in the basin to rebound to its natural level were too great for this to be an acceptable option. In turn, this implies that pumping and treatment will have to be continued after the mines have closed.

22

Information

In water management, data is sparse, unreliable and it is expensive to collect and process. River water quality changes over both time and distance yet water quality sampling is usually collected at a limited number of points, typically where access is convenient, and with a limited frequency. Similarly, flows in rivers are generally measured at only a few points. In turn, even estimates of probable maximum flows, critical for the safe design of dams, can be very inaccurate. The Macchu II dam in Gujarat was built with a spillway capacity of $5415\,m^3/sec$; overtopping and dam failure caused a 8–10 metre flood wave to sweep down the valley, killing at least 2000 people. The dam was redesigned on the basis of a PMF (probable maximum flood) of $20\,925\,m^3/sec$ but before it was rebuilt on this basis, a cyclonic rainstorm produced 700 mm of rainfall in the catchment in a single day. The PMF was reassessed upward to $26\,420\,m^3/sec$ (Herschy 1998). Again, a major problem in the Colorado River Compact is that the original allocation of 7.5 million acre-feet (maf) per year to the lower basin states was based on estimates of an annual flow of 16.4 maf whereas subsequently the best estimate of mean annual flow was revised to 13.5 maf but ranging from 4.4 to 22 maf (Gelt 1997).

Again, the accuracy of bulk water supply meters is normally only within plus or minus 10%, and often estimates of the flows of wastewater are no more than guesses. Thus, the legal prospectuses for the water and sewerage companies in England and Wales gave details about the quantity of water each supplied but were entirely silent, since no accurate data existed, on the quantities of wastewater that were treated. Generally, data on the state of distribution and collection networks is similarly sparse; one problem in a major water mains burst in Leeds (Jeffrey 1986) was that the location of the stop valve for that mains was not known with any precision. One of the tasks that the privatised water companies in England and Wales have therefore undertaken is simply one of finding out what networks they have acquired and where those pipes and sewers are actually located. The physical state of those networks is also generally largely unknown and, as discussed in Section 2.1.3, judgements as to the probability that an embankment will fail have to be made qualitatively. Similarly, we have seen (Section 14.4) how little is generally known about how much water households

Handbook of Water Economics: Principles and Practice.   C. Green
© 2003 John Wiley & Sons, Ltd   ISBN: 0-471-98571-6

and industries use for what purposes. Thus, it is as well for the economist to work on the basis that although engineers may produce estimates to the nearest millimetre, they will be wrong to the nearest metre.

In addition, it is necessary to distinguish between data and information: information is a structure imposed on a set of data so that the data can be interpreted to reduce uncertainty as to the answer to one question. Therefore, economists will usually find themselves either in a situation where both data and information are sparse, or, sometimes, where there is an abundance of data and a scarcity of information. In turn, an important question in water management is whether it is worth collecting any more data, or whether it is worth improving the accuracy or reliability of data collection. For example, whether it is worth undertaking CCTV surveys of sewers in order to assess their condition, or installing district meters in a water supply network in order to monitor patterns of demand and improve leak detection.

The appropriate theoretical approach to undertaking such analyses is the use of Bayesian analysis (e.g. Hadley 1967),

$$p(f_I \mid e_k) = \frac{p(e_k \mid f_I)p(f_I)}{\sum_{(u=1 \text{ to } s)}^{s} p(e_k \mid f_u)p(f_u)}$$

where $p(f_j \mid e_k)$ is the *a posteriori* probability that f_j is true given that event e_k occurs, and $p(f_j)$ is the *a priori* probability that f_j is true.

Enis and Broome (1971) give a simple example of how this equation can be used. Their example refers to a decision as to whether or not to expand a franchise but the approach can equally apply to one concerning enhancements to water resources and other decisions in water management. As shown in Table 22.1, there are three possible courses of action and the outcome of each depends upon the state of nature which the decision maker assesses as having the probabilities of occurrence of 0.5, 0.3 and 0.2 respectively. Thus, the expected value of A1 is 1070, that of A2 is 790 and for A3 the expected value is −250. Hence, we should choose action A1. Alternatively, the regret matrix (Table 22.2) can be calculated; the loss that is incurred by adopting each course of action if we were certain as to the state of nature. Using the original probabilities, the expected opportunity loss can then be calculated as the probability of each outcome times the opportunity

Table 22.1   *Payoff matrix*

Course of action	State of nature		
	S1 0.5	S2 0.3	S3 0.2
A1	1000	1100	1200
A2	−500	2000	2200
A3	−2000	500	3000

Table 22.2 *Regret matrix*

Course of action	State of nature		
	S1	S2	S3
A1	0	900	1800
A2	1500	0	800
A3	3000	1500	0

loss. So, for example, the expected opportunity loss for A3 is 1950. The maximum value of perfect information is therefore given by the minimum of the three expected opportunity losses for A1, A2 and A3; here, this is 630 for A1. The question is then what is it worth paying for imperfect information?

Ennis and Broome give the example of a survey which would have a reliability, a conditional probability, of 0.70: that is, the likelihood that it will assert that S_j is true when S_j is actually true is 0.70. The conditional probabilities that it will assert that S1 is true when the true state of nature is S2 or S3 is 0.15 in each case.

In this case, the Bayes formula can be simplified to:

$$P(S_j \mid R_k) = \frac{P(R_k \mid S_j)P(S_j)}{P(R_k)}$$

Table 22.3 shows the process of calculating the *a posteriori* probabilities. When the values in the payoff matrix are multiplied by the appropriate values of $P(S_1 \mid R_k)$, a revised set of expected values is given. The value of the information given by the survey is then given by the sum of maximum value for each survey result times the probability of that outcome, $P(R_k)$; in this case, a value of 1244.23. The value of the information gained from the survey is 1244.23 minus 1070, and so it would be worth spending 174.3 to acquire this information. The same approach can be applied when the states of nature are not discrete and where there is a probability distribution associated with different states of nature (Hadley 1967).

This Bayesian approach is equally applicable on the supply side of the equation, to the estimation of water availability, as to the demand side of the equation. For

Table 22.3 *Calculation of* a posteriori *probabilities*

Survey result	$P(R_k \mid S_j)$ State of nature			$P(R_k)$	$P(S_1 \mid R_k)$	$P(S_2 \mid R_k)$	$P(S_1 \mid R_k)$
	P(S1) 0.5	P(S2) 0.3	P(S3) 0.3				
R1	0.70	0.15	0.15	0.425	0.823	0.106	0.071
R2	0.15	0.70	0.15	0.315	0.238	0.667	0.095
R3	0.15	0.15	0.70	0.260	0.289	0.173	0.538

example, in principle, it could be applied to predictions of future water demand as well as the estimation of sustainable river flows. However, it is more difficult to see what information we could acquire that would reduce our uncertainty about the future.

The practical problems of applying this theoretical approach are that we need a great deal of information: it is necessary to be able to specify both the prior probabilities and also the reliability of the information that will be obtained. Where the states of nature are not discrete, it is necessary to be able to define the probability distribution. In practice, whilst Bayesian approaches have been tried to assess the value of the data to be gained from hydrometric gauging (e.g. Attanesi and Karlinger 1977), few hydrologists or others have been prepared to venture guesses as to the prior probability distributions or the reliability of the proposed method of obtaining further data. For example, the engineers who were asked to assess the probability that dikes would fail (Section 18.2) before they were overtopped were extremely reluctant to venture even point estimates. So, similarly, were those engineers who were asked to estimate the probabilities that sewers would collapse (Section 16.1.3).

A further limitation of the Bayesian model as a method of valuing data is that it assumes that we collect data simply to refine our estimates of that which we already know. But an important reason to collect data is to find out things that we did not know in advance: to uncover 'surprises' (Brooks 1986). For example, the ozone hole was discovered by accident. It would not have been possible in advance to estimate a prior probability of discovering the ozone hole, or equally of the payoffs from discovering an ozone hole, given that the existence of such a hole was not predicted or anticipated. So, one reason for monitoring is to detect surprises, particularly unanticipated changes. Moreover, generally we cannot go back in time to collect data that now turns out to be useful. It would, for example, be extremely interesting to compare Adam Smith's time series data on wheat prices (Section 17.2) for climatic data for that period but the time series of rainfall data was not started until after the end of the wheat price series. There are sometimes surrogate data sets, such as tree ring series or core samples, that can be used to reconstruct past time series but this is limited; for example, tree ring data cannot tell us the variations in daily stream flows.

22.1 Streamflow Gauging

The two types of decisions that use streamflow data are operational decisions and those concerning capital investments. The former require real-time information whereas the latter typically require estimates of extreme or average values of hydrometric parameters, whose estimation can be improved by increasing the length of record. An additional purpose of gauging is to comply with international law; whilst it can be possible to assess the benefits of introducing a law, it is not legitimate to attempt to assess the benefits of complying with an existing law.

For capital investment, the requirement is to be able to estimate flows, usually extreme flows, in the future. Hence, the length of record is an important factor: Herschy (1980) calculated that in order to achieve a precision of 10% around estimates of the mean monthly discharge of UK rivers, 50 years of record were required (the average length of record in the UK is now 30 years). There are therefore two decisions: whether it is worth installing a local gauging station rather than rely upon the use of regional growth curves; and what is the value of each additional year's data? For operational use, it is accuracy and immediacy of the flows now that are important in so far as these can then be used to predict flows some distance downstream.

The data yielded by a particular gauge must usually also be applied to another, or other, locations and other points in time. Therefore, marginal changes in the information yielded by a hydrometric network can be made in seven ways:

- a change in the accuracy of the gauge reading;
- a change in the reliability of the operation of the gauges, a reduction in the proportion of the time when the gauge is not working;
- changes in the accuracy of transferring data from gauged sites to ungauged sites by proximity, modelling or other methods;
- changes in the density of gauging;
- changes in the speed and reliability with which data is transmitted to the decision maker;
- changes in the speed, accuracy and reliability of methods of analysing and integrating that data; and
- increases in the length of record.

In each case, a different baseline option is defined. In addition, the comparison may involve different technologies, e.g. the assessment of the benefits of installing weather radar against a current reliance on telemetered rainfall and streamflow gauging.

The most detailed formal approach of the value of data in capital decisions is that of Mawdsley *et al.* (1988); they concluded that the value of local streamflow data for the design of three hypothetical impounding direct supply reservoirs varied between 0.4% of the construction cost and 3.8% for four years and 50 years of records respectively. The optimum length of record was then highly dependent on the coefficient of variation of the flow but in their example, the optimum length of record was 50 years.

CNS (1991) undertook a benefit–cost analysis for the UK's streamflow gauging network and the associated data archive. Now the existence or otherwise of the network as a whole is a non-marginal decision and in turn different baselines had to be used in order to get some estimate of the marginal value of the data provided for different purposes. In turn, in order to put a value on the information to a decision, the decision itself must be capable of economic analysis. In short, if those decisions are not themselves based on an economic analysis, or the means are not available to calculate the opportunity losses associated with making incorrect decisions, then the value of information to those decisions cannot be calculated. At the time of the CNS study, economic analysis was only being applied to some decisions in water management and approximations had to be made in other cases. Thus, for example, potentially it is possible to set effluent adjustable discharge consents (e.g. Eheart 1988) so that treatment standards vary according to the assimilative capacity of the river, which in turn is dependent upon the flow and the temperature of the water (Boner and Furland 1982). However, whilst seasonal discharge consents were widely used in the USA (Lamb and Hull 1985), they were little used in the UK (Mathews 1986); indeed, as the study was undertaken, consents were set essentially at a level at which each individual plant could achieve (Green 2001b). But in principle, setting seasonal discharge consents on the basis of flows can significantly reduce costs (Eheart *et al.* 1987), as can adjusting the discharge point according to flow conditions (Kuchenrither *et al.* 1983).

The payoff from over- or underestimating river flows is then as shown in Figure 22.1. It is likely to be asymmetrical as the ecosystem may take a significant time to recover from the effect of a pollution pulse. Moreover, the costs of underestimating the flow are considerably easier to evaluate than those of overestimating the flow which requires calculating the probability of different pollution pulses affecting different stretches of river for different periods of time, taking into account the time taken for the ecosystem to fully recover from the pulse.

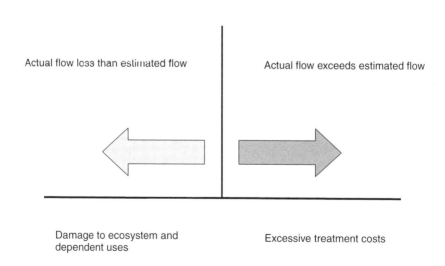

Estimated flow level

Actual flow less than estimated flow

Actual flow exceeds estimated flow

Damage to ecosystem and dependent uses

Excessive treatment costs

Figure 22.1 *Asymmetries of the costs of incorrect estimates of river water quantity*

A similar pattern as shown in Figure 22.1 should also be expected for water abstractions, with the penalty for incorrectly estimating flows depending upon the nature of the consent given for abstraction. If unrestricted private entitlements to abstraction are created then the penalty is borne by the environment, and the uses dependent upon the environment. Conversely, if as in the UK, major abstractions are limited so that a minimum flow must be maintained at some designated control point, then the costs fall either on the abstractor or the consumer. In this UK context, if flows are greatly overestimated then the decision to abstract the water and the investment made may have been wrong, and another alternative may offer a better return; indeed, it may be necessary to undertake further capital works to create the capacity that it was believed the original source offered.

The CNS study looked at three major abstractions. For example, the flow on the Severn at Bewdley, which is supported by discharges from the Clywedog Reservoir, must equal some $9 \, m^3 s^{-1}$ before any abstractions are permitted. In turn, errors in gauging at Bewdley would result in unnecessary releases from the reservoir. Replacing the existing gauge by an ultrasonic gauge was estimated to reduce unnecessary releases by up to 5 million m^3 a year. Scaling this figure up by the ratio of total surface water abstractions to the total volume from the three abstractions, and using a value of $1.5 \, p/m^3$, the result is an annual benefit of approximately £10 million.

Irrigation in the UK is unsupported and limited to supplementary irrigation. In the absence of streamflow gauging, the assumption was made that licences would be restricted to winter abstraction with the farmers having to construct on-farm reservoirs to store that water for the summer months. Morris (n.d.) estimated the relative costs of constructing such storage being in the range of £1.1 to £5.1/mm/ha/year, giving an estimate of the benefit of streamflow gauging in the range of £7.7 to £35.7 million/year.

Mawdsley *et al.* (1988) calculated the benefits of streamflow gauging to the design of flood alleviation schemes as equalling 4–5% of the cost of these schemes. Given an annual capital spend of some £58 million a year, and the proportion of schemes undertaken on rivers for which gauging data is likely to be available (50%), this gives a value of around £1 million per year.

In the UK, we have got into the habit of believing that floods are relatively benign and hence flood warnings are intended to enable people to protect their property from flooding rather than to reduce the risk to life by moving above the anticipated flood level. Bussell *et al.* (1978) estimated that the annual benefits of flood warnings to domestic properties would amount to £3.2 million (1989 prices); however, this assumed that all of the coefficients in the equation given in Section 18.1.1 are one. Using more realistic coefficients reduced this figure to £0.53 million/year with a practical upper bound of £1.97 million/year. In practice, both these figures are likely to be too high because for small, flashy catchments, reliance on streamflow gauging gives too short a lead time for an effective flood warning system to be practical. Equally, three of the coefficients in that equation should be expected to vary with the warning lead time. The Working Group on National Weather Radar Coverage (1983) assessed the benefits of flooding to industrial and commercial organisations as being small. Hence, given the low reliability of flood warnings, no value was allowed for this stream of benefits. However, Neal and Parker (1988) had found in a post-flood audit of the performance of flood warnings in the Severn–Trent region that warnings had reduced flood losses by £90 000 to farms, largely by allowing farmers to move stock. Scaling the benefits up from these figures to the UK gave a best estimate of £1.5 million a year with an upper bound of £4.5 million a year.

But a major reason for all forms of environmental monitoring is to detect change if it occurs and to discover the unexpected. Thus, there is a quasi-option value associated with streamflow gauging and option value with the network itself. In turn, if significant change were to be discovered then methods of analysis based upon previously collected data would cease to be reliable. Hence, there is a risk that if the streamflow gauging network were to be closed down, then it would have to be reinstated in part at a later date. But since we cannot know in advance the probability that an unanticipated change will occur, it is only possible to make a crude estimate of this option value. Since much of the network is made up of

Table 22.4   Benefits of the UK streamflow gauging network (1991 £ million)

Purpose		Best estimate	Lower bound	Upper bound
Abstraction	Potable – capital investment	0.3	0.2	1.5
	Potable – operating	10.0	2.5	17.0
	Irrigation	8.0	8.0	35.0
Effluent discharges	Consents – seasonal	Not currently estimated; potentially significant		
	Consents – other			
	Consents – capital			
Floods	Flood allevia-tion – capital works	0.8	0.2	1.0
	Flood warnings	1.7	0.5	5.2
Structures (bridges, culverts, weirs etc.)	Capital			Not estimated
Risk of climatic or other change	Current	Cannot be evaluated but a main reason for gauging		
	Reinstating network if closed	7.6	2.4	46.0
Total annual benefits		20.8	11.4	59.7
Total annual costs		9.0		

physical structures in the form of velocity–area structures, crump and other forms of weirs, and flumes, abandonment of the existing network would not mean that these structures would require complete reconstruction if they were needed again after having been abandoned. Equally, the change that had been discovered by other means would not necessarily require reinstatement of the entire network. Hence, in determining the best estimate, it was assumed that only 40% of the network would require reinstatement and that the existing structures decayed at 3.3% per annum. In turn, the risk of requiring such partial reinstatement was assumed to be 0.01 in the first year, rising to 0.1 in year 50. A further series of analyses were then undertaken to calculate upper and lower bounds on the present value (Table 22.4).

The value of a formal data archive is then the increase in the probability that the data will actually be found when needed, coupled to the reduction in cost in accessing that data. Adams (1992) has reported on the problems in actually finding any data in the absence of a formal archiving system.

23

Implementing Integrated Catchment Management

Integrated catchment management is easier to define as an ideal rather than perform as a task, and the integration of the management of land as well as water is perhaps the most difficult part of the task. Land–water interactions present formidable problems of management. Runoff, as we have seen, is both the water resource and the problem where runoff is a function of the use of the land. Land use also generates pollution and influences sediment loads whilst runoff affects soil erosion. At the same time, water management is necessary to support those land uses. In terms of institutional structures to support the management of these interactions, France is probably the country with the most advanced approach in theory with the use of SAGE and related plans (Barraque *et al.* 1994). At the smaller scale, good practice is also developing in the USA (Center for Watershed Protection 1996; Schueler 1995). But, economic analysis should also help in managing the different land–water interactions.

23.1 Erosion Control

Newson (1997) pointed out that rivers are conveyors of sediment as much as of water, sometimes in very large quantities. The Yellow River in China carries some 1.6 billion tonnes of sediment each year, of which 1.2 billion tonnes is carried to sea, down from the loess plateau at its head (Leung 1996). On a smaller scale, 900 000 tonnes of sand arrive in the Netherlands as erosional material from the river bed of the Rhine where the greatest loads are carried and deposited by floods; over 300 000 tonnes in the January 1995 flood. A further 2.5 million tonnes of silt are carried by the Rhine into the Netherlands, the silt originating from soil erosion and urban sewer systems (Silva *et al.* 2001).

The original source of that material is from erosion of the land, much of it being from the natural processes of erosion but some also the result of human uses of that land. It is dangerous to focus exclusively on the problems of deforestation as to do so may result in the real causes being overlooked (Calder 1999).

Handbook of Water Economics: Principles and Practice. C. Green
© 2003 John Wiley & Sons, Ltd ISBN: 0-471-98571-6

Moreover, forests are not permanent but a process, the natural processes of fire and regeneration having significant effects both on the yield of water and of sediment. Thus, in the forested catchments that supply Melbourne with water, it is estimated that after a bush fire, during the regeneration of mountain ash, runoff is reduced by up to 50% of that from the current mature forest, with full regeneration taking up to 150 years (Melbourne Water 2001). On small catchments in particular, the consequences of road construction and building activity (Calder 1999) or animal grazing can be a primary source of the problem. Moreover, only some of the material from soil erosion reaches the river and is deposited downstream, the proportion of upland soil erosion that is deposited in dams or deltas varying from 0.03 to 0.90 (de Graff 2000).

Works to control soil erosion as well as to control runoff were traditional in arid climates (Yapa 2001) and economic analysis can then be applied to assess the benefits of soil erosion control (e.g. Brooks *et al.* 1982). An assessment of the benefits of reducing the erosion from the loess plateau feeding the Yellow River was undertaken for a World Bank project (World Bank 1999b); parts of the plateau, covering some $430\,000\,\text{km}^2$ of arid land, have been eroding at a rate of 1000 tonnes/km^2/year (Leung 1996). As a result of deposition, the Yellow River is now perched several metres above the surrounding flood plain. Reducing the rate of erosion through check dams and other means will reduce the rate at which the bed of the river is rising, and hence the rate at which the flood embankments have to be raised to match the rise in the level of the river bed. In addition, the rate of siltation of irrigation canals will also be reduced (World Bank 1999b).

23.2 Alien Species

Introduced species, both land- and water-based, are a significant problem in many parts of the world (Revenga *et al.* 2000); some of these introductions are deliberate but others are accidental such as the flat worms from Australia and New Zealand introduced in the UK with imported plants. Ballast water has also been a major route through which accidental introduction has taken place (Carlton 2001).

Alien plant species in South Africa are both forcing out native species and, in turn, the insect and bird species that depend upon those plants. But, in addition, they have increased the demand for water and hence reduced the flows in rivers. In turn, eliminating these species from the river corridors is a cost-effective alternative to water resource reinforcement (Water Research Commission 2001).

23.3 Agricultural Runoff and Infiltration

Over both the USA and Europe, the majority of river water quality problems are the result of agricultural runoff (US EPA 2000; Nixon 2000). But without the use of pesticides or other control measures such as integrated pest management (DFID 1999), the current global rate of loss of wheat would rise from 33% to

52%; that for rice, from 52% to 83% (Wood *et al.* 2000) with Schmitz (2001) calculating that a drop of 75% in pesticide usage in Germany would result in a drop in wheat production by 25% and a drop in farm incomes of 32–45%.

However, a significant part of the problem results from pesticide usage associated with urban usages, including on railway lines and the verges of roads (USGS n.d.). Some 800 different pesticides are now in use in Europe (Nixon 2000) and the cost of adopting activated carbon treatment of ground and surface water abstracted for potable supply has involved a capital spend of £1 billion with annual costs of a further £120 million in England and Wales alone (Water UK 2001). Not surprisingly, therefore, the option of adopting a Pigovian tax on pesticides has looked attractive (Rayment *et al.* 1998) but the problems of avoiding perverse incentives, given the number of pesticides available, have proved to be difficult to overcome (ECOTEC 1999).

Nitrates and phosphorus in runoff are equally a major problem in much of the world: Nixon (2000) reports that the surplus of nitrates applied in the Netherlands amounts to 200 kg/ha/year and that the agricultural surplus of phosphorus amounts to 13 kg/ha/year. Part of these loads are from fertiliser but animal wastes can also be a major problem: for example, the Delaware basin is badly affected by the wastes produced by factory chicken farming. Eutrophication then causes damage both in rivers and lakes. Nitrate concentrations in groundwater are also a problem; in Europe, 85% of groundwater below agricultural land now exceeds the EU guidelines for nitrate concentration (Stanners and Bourdeau 1995); again, the cost of treating water with high nitrate concentrations before it can be put into potable supply is non-trivial (Bhumbla n.d.).

The options to manage these externalities depend upon whether the water that is affected is groundwater or surface water; in the latter case, buffer strips (Applied Research Systems 1999; Eastern Canada Soil and Water Conservation Centre n.d.) can be an effective means of reducing pollution loads. The five general strategies are then:

- Education and training of farmers in good practice.
- Taxing inputs.
- Regulation; for example, groundwater protection zones (Cartwright *et al.* 1991).
- Subsidising changes in farming practices.
- Tradable permit systems.

It should not be a surprise that it has proved politically more feasible to subsidise farmers not to pollute than to tax or otherwise control these externalities associated with farming. In Germany, the water utilities pay farmers to avoid or reduce pesticide or fertiliser usage whereas in the UK, central government pays the costs of a number of different programmes which are either intended to reduce nitrate usage (ENTEC 1998) or have the indirect consequences of reducing nitrate and pesticide usage although the announced purpose is to protect traditional landscapes, for environmental conservation or other reasons (MAFF 2000).

On a more limited scale, buffer strips can significantly reduce the loads of nitrogen, phosphorus and suspended solids from agriculture to water courses. In the USA, a large-scale programme to pay farmers to introduce buffer strips has been introduced (Applied Research Systems 1999). The advantage of such programmes is that their economic cost is low, farmers being subsidised to produce environmental goods rather than crops that can only be dumped into overseas markets.

In the USA, a number of schemes for tradable pollution systems have been established in which urban areas can 'buy' the pollution from farms: instead of the urban area treating urban water runoff, the municipality can seek to reduce the pollution load from agricultural areas by an equivalent amount. However, at least as yet, there seems to be very little activity in these schemes (e.g. Environomics 1999). Equally, they raise the question of why agriculture should be further subsidised.

23.4 Integrating Integrated Catchment Management into National Policies

Integrated catchment management is not enough; indeed, it could become a snare. Water and land management need to be integrated with other local, regional, national and international policies (Figure 23.1). Thus, it is conventional wisdom

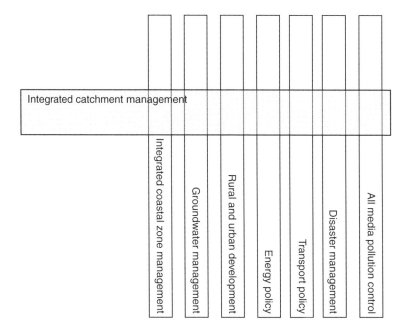

Figure 23.1   *Integrating catchment management into the wider context*

that there should be an 'all hazards' approach to emergency planning (UNDR 1984) and that the system will follow the existing institutional structure of local government. Again, most rivers also reach the sea and there is general agreement that integrated coastal zone management (OECD 1993) is as important as integrated catchment management, where the coastal zone certainly includes the estuary but also a substantial hinterland.

Groundwater is a critical element in water management, and land–groundwater interactions are similarly important. But aquifers and catchments do not necessarily coincide, a catchment therefore not being a logical geographic area over which to manage an aquifer. That there should be a national energy policy seems to be an almost self-evident truth; similarly, a coherent national policy for transport is also logically necessary not least because transport has in the past resulted in significant problems with introduced species (Carlton 2001).

Particularly in countries that are still largely rural societies, a national policy to cover urban and rural development is also a necessity and in developed economies, as the importance of agriculture to the national economy declines, a rural policy becomes more important. Decisions about the use of water for agriculture will impact on food prices, as well as on rural unemployment and migration to urban areas, and to ignore these linkages might outweigh the gains from an integrated catchment management approach. Similarly, the adoption of 'best environmental option' approaches to pollution management results in an 'all media' approach being adopted, as opposed to one that considers only water pollution. In turn, a catchment based approach is not appropriate when considering air or soil pollution.

All these different areas both impact on water management and are impacted by water management. We have therefore to integrate across a whole series of policy areas and not simply land and water management within catchments. It would be fair to describe this as a challenge.

References

Abernethy, C.L. n.d. 'Financing river-basin organisations', paper given at an IWMI workshop, Colombo.

Academie de l'eau (1998) *Deliberation on the Management of Shared Water Resources*, Paris: Academie de l'eau.

Academie de l'eau n.d. *Etude Comparative de la Gestion par Bassin*, Paris: Academie de l'eau.

ACC/ISGWR (1992) *The Dublin Statement and the Report of the Conference*, Geneva: World Meteorological Organisation.

Acreman, M., Barbier, E., Birley, M. *et al.* (1999) *Managed Flood Releases from Reservoirs – a Review of Current Problems and Future Prospects*, Project R7344, report to DFID, Wallingford: Institute of Hydrology.

Adamowicz, W., Swait, J., Boxall, P., Louviere, J. and Williams, M. (1997) 'Perceptions versus objective measures of environmental quality in combined revealed and stated preference models of environmental valuation', *Journal of Environmental Economics and Management* 32, 65–84.

Adams, W.M. (1992) *Wasting the Rain: Rivers, People and Planning in Africa*, London: Earthscan.

Adler, R. and Straube, M. (2000) 'Lessons from large watershed programs' in National Academy of Public Administration, *Learning from Innovations in Environmental Protection*, Washington, DC: National Academy of Public Administration.

Agarwal, A. (2001) *Drought? Try Capturing the Rain*, New Delhi: Centre for Science and Environment.

Agarwal, A. and Narain, S. (eds) (1997) *Dying Wisdom*, New Delhi: Centre for Science and the Environment.

Akerlof, G.A. (1970) 'The market for lemons: qualitative uncertainty and the market mechanism', *Journal of Economics* 84(4), 488–500.

Akuoke-Asibey, A. (1996) 'A summative evaluation of a rural water supply programme in Ghana', *Applied Geography* 16(3), 243–56.

Alderman, H., Chiappori, P.-A., Haddad, L., Hoddinott, J. and Kanbur, R. (1995) 'Models of the household: is it time to shift the burden of proof?', *The World Bank Observer* 10(1), 1–19.

Handbook of Water Economics: Principles and Practice.   C. Green
© 2003 John Wiley & Sons, Ltd   ISBN: 0-471-98571-6

Alexander, I. and Mayer, C. (1997) *Incentives on Private Infrastructure Companies*, Washington, DC: World Bank.

Allee, D.J., Osgood, B.T., Antle, L.G., Simpkins, C.E., Motz, A.B., Van der Slice, A. and Westbrook, W.F. (1980) *Human Costs of Flooding and Implementability of Non-Structural Damage Reduction in the Tug Fork Valley of West U.S.*, Fort Belvoir, VA: US Army Corps of Engineers, Institute for Water Resources.

Allen, R.G., Smith, M., Pruitt, W.O. and Pereira, L.S. (1996) 'Modifications to the FAO crop coefficient approach', *Proceedings of the ASAE International Conference on Evatranspiration and Irrigation Scheduling*, San Antonio, Texas.

Allen, T. (1994) *Water: A Substitutable Resource?* Department of Geography, School of Oriental and African Studies, University of London.

Altaf, M.A. and Hughes, J.A. (1994) 'Measuring the demand for improved urban sanitation services: results of a contingent valuation study in Ouagadougou, Birkina Faso', *Urban Studies* **31**, 1763–76.

Altaf, M.A., Jamal, H., Liu, J.L., Smith, V.K. and Whittington, D. (1997) *Measuring the Private Benefits from Connections to Public Water Systems in Developing Countries: A Case Study of the Punjab, Pakistan*, Duke Economics Working Paper #97–24 (http://www.econ.duke.edu/papers/abstracts97).

Amy Vickers & Associates Inc. (1996) *Water Conservation Planning: USA Case Studies Project*, report to the Demand Management Centre, Environment Agency, Amherst, MA: Amy Vickers & Associates.

Andersen, M.S. (1994) *Governance by Green Taxes: Making Pollution Prevention Pay*, Manchester: Manchester University Press.

Anderson, M., Bechhofer, F. and Gershuny, J. (eds) (1994) *The Political Economy of the Household*, Oxford: Oxford University Press.

Anon (1997) 'Dramatic saving in water usage', *WET NEWS* **3**(14), 3.

Applied Research Systems (1999) *The National Conservation Buffer Initiative: A Qualitative Evaluation*, Washington, DC: US Department of Agriculture.

Aragon-Correa, J.A. and Llorens-Montes, F.J. (1997) 'Ecological concern and environmental behaviour towards sustainable development: a model applied to potential change in the recycling systems of Spanish beverage companies', *Sustainable Development* **5**, 43–9.

Ardilla, S., Quiroga, R. and Vaughan, W.J. (1998) *A Review of the Use of Contingent Valuation Methods in Project Analysis at the Inter-American Development Bank*, ENV-126, Washington, DC: Inter-American Development Bank.

Arnell, N.W., Jenkins, A. and George, D.O. (1994) *The Implications of Climate Change for the National Rivers Authority*, R&D Report 12, London: HMSO.

Arrow, K.J. (1987) 'Rationality of self and others in an economic system' in Hogarth, R.M. and Reder, M.W. (eds) *Rational Choice: The Contrast between Economics and Psychology*, Chicago: Chicago University Press.

Arrow, K.J. and Lind, R.C. (1970) 'Uncertainty and the evaluation of public investment decisions', *American Economic Review* **60**, 364–78.

Asano, T., Maeda, M. and Takaki, M. (1996) 'Wastewater reclamation and reuse in Japan: overview and implementation examples', *Water, Science and Technology* **34**(11), 219–26.

Ashley, C. and Carney, D. (1999) *Sustainable Livelihoods: Lessons from Early Experience*, London: Department for International Development.

Asian Development Bank (1997) *Guidelines for the Economic Analysis of Projects*, Manila: Asian Development Bank.

Asian Development Bank (1998) *Handbook for the Economic Analysis of Water Supply Projects*, Manila: Asian Development Bank.

Assael, H. (1992) *Consumer Behavior and Marketing Action*, Boston: PWS-Kent.

Atkins, W.S. (1992) *Evaluation of the Costs and Benefits of Low Flow Alleviation*, R&D B3-401, Bristol: National Rivers Authority.

Attanesi, E.D. and Karlinger, M.R. (1977) 'The economic basis of resource information systems: the case of streamflow data network design', *Water Resources Research* **13**(2), 273–80.

AWWA (American Water Works Association) (1992) *Drought Management Planning*, Denver, CO: American Water Works Association.

AWWA (American Water Works Association) (2001) *Residential Water Use – Potential Savings by End Use*, Denver CO: American Water Works Association.

Bagader, A.A., El-Sabbagh, A.T.E.-C., Al-Glayand, M.A.-S., Samarrai, M.Y.I.-D. and Llewellyn, O.A.-A.-R. (1994) *Environmental Protection in Islam*, 2nd edition, Gland: IUCN.

Bakker, K. and Hemson, D. (2000) 'Privatising water: BoTT and hydropolitics in the New South Africa', *South Africa Geographical Journal* **82**(1), 3–12.

Balanovski, V., Redín, M.E. and Poggiese, H. (1999) *PERCEPCION SOCIAL DEL RIESGO: Inundaciones en el arroyo maldonado: mapa de riesgo elaborado con participación comunitaria*, Buenos Aires: GAO.

Balfour Maunsell (1995) *River Nene Structures – Benefit Assessment*, report to Anglian Region, National Rivers Authority.

Bardarska, G. (2002) 'Water problems in some EU pre-accession countries', paper given at the 3rd WATERSAVE Network Meeting, London.

Barg, U. and Phillip, M.J. 'Environment and sustainability' *FAO Fisheries Department Review of Aquaculture and Sustainability*, Rome: FAO.

Barraque, B. (1999) 'Assessing the efficiency of economic instruments: the case of the French Agences de l'eau', Paris: CRNS LATTS-ENPC.

Barraque, B., Berland, J.-M. and Cambon, S. (1994) *EUROWATER – Vertical Report on France*, Noisy-le-Grand: LATTS-ENPC.

Barrow, C.J. (1998) 'River basin development planning and management: a critical review', *World Development* **26**(1), 171–186.

Barrow, J.D. (1999) *Impossibility, the Limits of Science and the Science of Limits*, London: Vintage.

Bartelmus, P. (1994) *Environment, Growth and Development*, London: Routledge.

Bateman, I.J., Lovett, A.A. and Brainard, J.S. (1996) *Evaluating Recreation Demand for Natural Areas: A GIS/Benefit Transfers Approach*, Norwich: CSERGE, University of East Anglia.

Bathrick, D. (1998) *Fostering Global Well-Being: A New Paradigm to Revitalise Agriculture and Rural Development*, Washington, DC: IFPRI.

Batson, C.D., Batson, J.G., Todd, R.M., Brumett, B.H., Shaw, L.L. and Aldeguer, C.M.R. (1995) 'Empathy and the collective good: caring for one of the others in a social dilemma', *Journal of Personality and Social Psychology* **68**(4), 619–31.

Bauer, C. (1998) *Against the Current: Privatization, Water Markets and the State in Chile*, Boston: Kluwer.

Baumol, W. and Oates, W. (1988) *The Theory of Environmental Policy*, Cambridge: Cambridge University Press.

Baumol, W.J. (1972) *Economic Theory and Operations Analysis*, 3rd edition, London: Prentice-Hall.

Baynes, S. (2002) 'Water-efficient toilets: a Canadian perspective', paper given at the 3rd Meeting of the WATERSAVE Network, London.

Beck, M.B. (1996) 'Transient pollution events: acute risks to the aquatic environment', *Water Science and Technology* **33**(2), 1–15.

Becker, G.S. (1991) *A Treatise on the Family*, Cambridge: Harvard University Press.

Beckman, C.S., Weigand, P.C. and Pint, J.J. (1999) 'Old world irrigation technology in a new world context: qanats in Spanish Colonial Western Mexico', *Antiquity* **73**(279), 440–6.

Belli, P., Anderson, J., Barnum, H., Dixon, J. and Tan, J.-P. (1997) *Handbook on Economic Analysis of Investment Decisions*, Operations Policy Department, Learning and Leadership Center, Washington, DC: World Bank.

Bentham, J. (1948) *Principles of Morals and Legislation*, Oxford: Oxford University Press.

Bergmann, B.R. (1995) 'Becker's theory of the family: preposterous conclusions', *Feminist Economics* **1**(1), 141–50.

Berry, S., Hewings, G. and Leven, C. (2000) *Adequacy of Research on Upper Mississippi–Illinois River Navigation Project*, Washington, DC: Northeast Midwest Institute.

Beyleveld, D. and Brownsword, R. (1994) *Law as a Moral Judgment*, Sheffield: Sheffield Academic Press.

Bhatia, R. and Falkenmark, M. (1993) *Water Resource Policies and the Urban Poor: Innovative Approaches and Policy Imperatives*, Washington, DC: World Bank.

Bhumbla, D.K. n.d. *Agriculture Practices and Nitrate Pollution of Water*, Extension Service, West Virginia University.

Birkeland, J. (1999) '"Community participation" in urban project assessment (an ecofeminist analysis)', in Martin, B. (ed.) *Technology and Public Participation*, Wollongong: University of Wollongong.

Bismuth, C. *et al.* (1998) *Causes of Flooding and Anthropogenic Influences on their Occurrence – Proposed Measures*, Texte 48/98, Berlin: Umweltbundesamt (Federal Environment Agency).

Bjornlund, H. and McKay, J. (2000) 'Are water markets achieving a more sustainable water use?' paper given at Water 2000, Melbourne.

Black, C.J. and Bowers, J.K. (1984) 'The level of protection of UK agriculture', *Oxford Bulletin of Economics and Statistics* **46**(4), 291–310.

Black, M. (1998) *1978–1998 Learning What Works: A 20-Year Retrospective View on the International Water and Sanitation Cooperation*, Washington, DC: UNDP–World Bank Water and Sanitation Program.

Blaug, M. (1992) *The Methodology of Economics*, Cambridge: Cambridge University Press.

Blockley, D. (1980) *The Nature of Structural Design and Safety*, Chichester: Ellis Horwood.

Blokland, M., Braadbaart, O. and Schwartz, K. (eds) (1999) *Private Business, Public Owners: Government Shareholdings in Water Enterprises*, Nieuwegein: The Ministry of Housing, Spatial Planning, and the Environment.

BMBF (Bundesministerium für Bildung, Wissenschaft, Forschung und Technology) (1995) *Ecological Research in the Elbe Catchment Area (Elbe Ecology)*, Bonn: BMBF.

Bohannan, P. (1960) 'Africa's land', *The Centennial Review* IV (4), 439–49.

Boner, M.C. and Furland, L.P. (1982) 'Seasonal treatment and variable effluent quality based on assimilative capacity', *Journal of the Water Pollution Control Federation* **54**(10), 1408–16.

Bonnieux, F. and Rainelli, P. (1991) *Catastrophe Ecologique et Dommages Economiques: Problemes d'evaluation à Partir de l'Amoco-Cadiz*, Paris: INRA-Economica.

Booker, N., Gray, S., Mitchell, G., Priestley, A., Shipton, R., Speers, A., Young, M. and Syme, G.J. (2000) 'Sustainable alternatives in the provision of urban water services – an Australian approach', paper given at Water 2000, Melbourne.

Bos, M.G. and Nugteren, J. (1990) *On Irrigation Efficiencies*, Wageningen: International Institute for Land Reclamation and Improvement.

Bosenius, U. and Rechenberg, J. (1996) *Water Resources Management in Germany*, Bonn: Federal Ministry for the Environment, Nature Conservation and Nuclear Safety.

Boulding, K.E. and Lundstedt, S.B. (1988) 'Value concepts and justifications' in Peterson, G.L., Driver, B.L. and Gregory, R. (eds) *Amenity Resource Evaluation: Integrating Economics with other Disciplines*, State College: Venture.

Bowers, J.K. (1983) 'Cost–benefit analysis of wetland drainage', *Environment and Planning A*(15), 227–35.

Bowman, J.A. n.d. *Reallocating Texas' Water: Slicing up the Leftover Pie*, College Station TX: Texas Water Resources Institute, Texas A&M University.

Boyd, C.E. and Gross, A. (1998) 'Water use and conservation for inland aquaculture ponds' in European Inland Fisheries Advisory Commission, *Report of the Symposium on Water for Sustainable Inland Fisheries and Aquaculture*, Rome: FAO.

Bradley, R.M. and Isaac, P.C.G. (1969) *Capital and Operating Costs of Sewage Treatment*, Newcastle-upon-Tyne: Oriel.

Brammer, H. (1990) 'Floods in Bangladesh 2, flood mitigation and environmental aspects', *Geographical Journal* **156**, 158–65.

Braudel, F. (1974) *Capitalism and Material Life 1400–1800*, translated by M. Kochan, London: Fontana.

Braver, D. n.d. *Demand Offset Programs – Guidelines to make them Work*, Sacramento: California Department of Water Resources.

Breen *et al.* (1996) *The Costs to the Environment of Pumping Minewater into the Blesbokspruit*, report to the Department of Environmental Affairs and Tourism.

Brehm, M. and Castro, J.Q. (1995) *Market of Water Rights in Chile: Major Issues*, Washington, DC: World Bank.

Brehm, M.R. and Quiroz, J. (1995) *The Market for Water Rights in Chile*, World Bank Technical Paper Number 285, Washington, DC: World Bank.

Brent, R.J. (1990) *Project Appraisal for Developing Countries*, New York: Harvester Wheatsheaf.

Breslin, E.D.D. (1999) 'Lessons from the field: rethinking community management for sustainability', paper given at Conference on *Rural and Peri-Urban Water Supply and Sanitation in South Africa – Appropriate Practice Conference*.

Breton, B. (2000) 'Urban fisheries in France, or the difficulty of transferring know-how (fishing schools)', in European Inland Fisheries Advisory Commission *Symposium on Fisheries and Society*, Rome: FAO.

Bright, J.R. (1972) *A Brief Introduction to Technology Forecasting: Concepts and Exercises*, Austin TX: The Permaquid Press.

Briscoe, J. (1993) 'When the cup is half full', *Environment* **35**(4), 7–37.

Briscoe, J., Furtado de Castro, P., Griffin, C., North, J. and Olsen, O. (1990) 'Toward equitable and sustainable rural water supplies: a contingent valuation study in Brazil', *The World Bank Economic Review* **4**, 115–34.

Briscoe, J., Salas, P.A. and Pena, H. (1998) *Managing Water as an Economic Resource: Reflections on the Chilean Experience*, Environment Department Papers 62, Washington, DC: World Bank.

Brismar, A. (1997) *Freshwater and Gender, a Policy Assessment*, Background Paper 5, Stockholm: Stockholm Environment Institute.

Brooks, D. (1996) 'Between the great rivers: water in the heart of the Middle East' in Rached, E., Rathgeber, E. and Brooks, D.B. (1996) *Water Management in Africa and the Middle East*, Ottawa: IDRC.

Brooks, D., Rogers, P. and Robillard, P. (1990) 'Pricing: a neglected tool for managing water demand', *Alternatives* **17**(3).

Brooks, H. (1986) 'The typology of surprises in technology, institutions and development' in Clark, W.C. and Munn, R.E. (eds) *Sustainable Development of the Biosphere*, Cambridge: Cambridge University Press.

Brouwer, R., Langford, I.H., Bateman, I.J., Crowards, T.C. and Turner, R.K. (1997) *A Meta-analysis of Wetland Contingent Valuation Studies*, Working Paper GEC 97-20, Norwich: Centre for Social and Economic Research on the Global Environment.

Brouwer, R., van Ek, R., Boeters, R. and Bouma, J. (2001) *Living with Floods: An Integrated Assessment of Land Use Changes and Floodplain Restoration as Alternative Flood Protection Measures in the Netherlands*, Lelystad: RIZA.

Brown, J.R. and Rivera, J.A. (2000) 'Acequias de Comun: the tension between collective action and private property rights', paper given at IASCP2000.

Brown and Schueler (1997) quoted in US EPA *Costs and Benefits of Storm Water BMPs*, Washington, DC: Office of Water.

Brown, R. (1965) *Social Psychology*, New York: Macmillan.

Brubaker, E. (1995) *Property Rights in Defence of Nature*, Toronto: Environment Probe.

Bruins, H.J., Evenari, M. and Nessler, U. (1986) 'Rainwater-harvesting agriculture for food production in arid zones: the challenge of the African famine', *Applied Geography* **6**, 13–32.

Brummett, R.E. and Chikafumbwa, F.J.K. (2000) 'An incremental, farmer-participatory approach to the development of aquaculture technology in Malawi', *FAO Aquaculture Newsletter* **23**, 26–31.

Bruns, B. and Atmanto, S.D. (1992) *How to Turn Over Irrigation Systems to Farmers? Questions and Decisions in Indonesia*, Irrigation Management Network Paper 10, London: Overseas Development Institute.

Budge, A.L. (1980) *Sewer Flooding, Supply Failures and Restrictions: Results of Three Delphi Studies into Levels of Service*, Development Advisory Group, Reading: Thames Water Authority.

Burgess, J., Clark, J. and Harrison, C.M. (1997) '"I struggled with this money business": respondents to the wildlife enhancement scheme CV survey discuss the validity of their WTP figures', London: School of Geography, University College, London.

Burrows, A. (2001) personal communication.

Burrows, A. and House, M.A. (1989) 'Public perception of water quality and the use of rivers for recreation' in Laikari, H. (ed.) *River Basin Management – V*, Oxford: Pergamon.

Bussell, R.B., Cole, J.A. and Collier, C.G. (1978) *The Potential Benefit from a National Network of Precipitation Radars and Short Period Forecasting*, Reading: Central Water Planning Unit.

Button, J.J. and Pearce, D.W. (1989) 'Infrastructure restoration as a tool for stimulating urban renewal – the Glasgow canal', *Urban Studies* **26**(6), 559–71.

Caballer, V. and Guadalajara, N. (1998) *Valoración Económica del Agua de Riego*, Madrid: Ediciones Mundi-Prensa.

Cairncross, S. (1987) 'Water, women and children: the benefits of water supply' in Pickford, J. and Leedham, B. (eds) *Developing World Water II*, London: Grosvenor.

Cairncross, S. (1999) *Measuring the Health Impact of Water and Sanitation*, WELL Technical Brief 10, London: WELL.

Cairncross, S. and Feachem, R. (1999) *Environmental Health Engineering in the Tropics*, Chichester: Wiley.

Cairncross, S. and Kochar, V.J. (1994) *Studying Hygiene Behaviour: Methods, Issues and Experiences*, London: Sage.

Calder, I.R. (1999) *The Blue Revolution: Land Use & Integrated Water Resources Management*, London: Earthscan.

California Department of Water Resources (1991) *Guidelines for Water Shortage Contingency Plans*, Sacramento, CA: Department of Water Resources.

California Department of Water Resources (1993) *Water Transfers in California: Translating Concept into Reality*, Sacramento, CA: Department of Water Resources.

California Department of Water Resources (1998) *The Reclamation Board General Manager's Report – 1998 Annual Report*, Sacramento, CA: Department of Water Resources.

California Urban Water Conservation Council (1994) *Memorandum of Understanding regarding Urban Water Conservation in California*, Sacramento, CA: California Urban Water Conservation Council.

Calver, A. (2001) 'Generalised river flood frequency estimation using continuous simulation', paper given at the 36th DEFRA Conference of River and Coastal Engineers, Keele.

Campbell, D.T. and Fiske, D.W. (1959) 'Convergent and discriminant validation by the multitrait-multimethod matrix', *Psychological Bulletin* **56**, 85–105.

Caponera, D.A. (1992) *Principles of Water Law and Administration*, Rotterdam: Balkema.

Carlstein, T. (1982) *Time, Resources, Ecology and Society*, London: Allen and Unwin.

Carlton, J.T. (2001) *Introduced Species in US Coastal Waters*, Arlington VA: Pew Oceans Commission.

Carmines, E.G. and Zeller, R.A. (1979) *Reliability and Validity Assessment*, Reston VA: Reston.

Carpentier, A. and Vermersch, D. (1997) *Measuring Willingness to Pay for Drinking Water Quality using the Econometrics of Equivalence Scales*, Rennes: INRA.

Center for Communicable Diseases (2000) 'Morbidity and mortality associated with Hurricane Floyd – North Carolina, September–October 1999', *MMWR Weekly* **49**(17), October 5, 369–72.

Center for Urban Policy and the Environment n.d. 'Stormwater management financing case study: Fort Collins, Colorado'.

Center for Watershed Protection (1996) *Recommended Model Development Principles for Frederick County, MD*, Ellicott City, MD: Center for Watershed Protection.

Cernea, M.M. (1992) *The Building Blocks of Participation, Testing Bottom-up Planning*, World Bank Discussion Paper 166, Washington, DC: World Bank.

Chambers, R. (1988) *Managing Canal Irrigation*, Oxford: Oxford University Press.

Chang, C. and Griffin, R.V. (1992) 'Water marketing as a reallocative institution in Texas', *Water Resources Research* **28**(3), 879–90.

Chattoe, E. (1995) *Can Sociologists and Economists Communicate? The Problem of Grounding and the Theory of Consumer Behaviour*, ESRC Economic Beliefs and Behaviour Programme Discussion Paper 4, Guildford: University of Surrey.

Checkland, P. and Scholes, J. (1990) *Soft Systems Methodology in Action*, Chichester: Wiley.

Cheshire, P.C. and Stabler, M.J. (1976) 'Joint consumption benefits in recreational site surplus: an empirical estimate', *Regional Studies* **10**, 343–51.

Ciriacy-Wantrup, S.V. and Bishop, R.C. (1973) '"Common property" as a concept in natural resources policy', *Natural Resources Journal* **15**, 713–27.

Clapham, J. (1963) *A Concise Economic History of Britain*, Cambridge: Cambridge University Press.

Clark, P.B. and Tyrer, M.J. (1987) *A Probabilistic Risk Assessment of an Earth Embankment Dam*, HS/RANN/2/29/WP1, Warrington: Safety and Reliability Directorate, United Kingdom Atomic Energy Authority.

Clark, W.A.V. and Onaka, J.L. (1985) 'An empirical test of a joint model of residential mobility and housing choice', *Environment and Planning A* **17**, 915–30.

Clawson, M. (1959) *Methods of Measuring the Demand for Outdoor Recreation*, Reprint No 10, Washington, DC: Resources for the Future.

Cleaver, F. (2000) 'Moral ecological rationality, institutions and the management of common property resources', *Development and Change* **31**, 361–83.

Clough, J. and Ridgewell, C. n.d. *Watersmart Working with Essex & Suffolk Water: Executive Summary*.

CNS Scientific and Engineering Services 1991 *Benefit–Cost Analysis of Hydrometric Data – River Flow Gauging*, for the Department of the Environment, Marlow: Foundation for Water Research.

CNS Scientific and Engineering Sevices (1992) *Economic Value of Changes to the Water Environment*, R&D Note 37, Bristol: National Rivers Authority.

Coelli, T., Lloyd-Smith, J., Mossison, D. and Thomas, J. (1991) 'Hedonic pricing for cost–benefit analysis of a public water supply system', *The Australian Journal of Agricultural Economics* **35**(1), 1–20.

Cohen, I.S., Lopes, V.L., Slack, D.C. and Yanez, C.H. (1995) 'Assessing risk for water harvesting systems in arid environments', *Journal of Soil and Water Conservation* **50**(5), 446–9.

Comino, M.P. (2001) 'Democratising down under: the role of the community in water resource decision making in Australia', paper given at the AWRA/ IWLRI – University of Dundee International Speciality Conference, Dundee.

Commissariat Général du Plan (1997) *Évaluation du Dispositif des Agences de l'eau*, Paris: La Documentation française.

Common, J.R. (1934) *Institutional Economics*, New York: Macmillan.

Common, M.S. (1973) 'A note on the use of the Clawson method for the evaluation of recreation site benefits', *Regional studies* **7**, 401–6.

Constanza, R., d'Arge, R., de Groot, R., Farber, S., Grasso, M., Hannon, B., Limburg, K., Naeem, S., O'Neill, R.V., Paruelo, J., Raskin, R.G., Sutton, P. and van den Belt, M. (1997) 'The value of the world's ecosystem services and natural capital', *Nature* **387**, 15 May, 253–60.

Cook, I. (1994) 'Water conservation: the builder's perspective' in Shrubsole, D. and Tate, D. (eds) *Every Drop Counts*, Ontario: Canadian Water Resources Association.

Cooper, P.M., Job, G.D., Green, M.B. and Shutes, R.B. (1996) *Reed Beds and Constructed Wetlands for Wastewater Treatment*, Swindon: Water Research Centre.

Correia, F.N., da Graca Saraiva, M., Rocha, J., Fordham, M., Bernardo, F., Ramos, I., Margquwa, Z. and Soczka, L. (1994) 'The planning of flood alleviation measures: interface with the public' in Penning-Rowsell, E. and Fordham, M. (eds) *Floods across Europe: Flood Hazard Assessment, Modelling and Management*, London: Middlesex University Press.

Cotton, A. *et al.* (1995) *Onplot Sanitation in Low Income Communities: A Review of Literature*, Water, Engineering and Development Centre (WEDC), Loughborough: University of Loughborough.

Countryside Commission/English Heritage/English Nature (1993) *Conservation Issues in Strategic Plans*, Northampton: Countryside Commission.

Court, L. (1987) *Le Cout Economique et Social de la Pollution de l'eau*, vol. 2, Paris: Association Française pour l'etude des Eaux.

Coville, J. (1996) *Cairo*, Paris: Academie de l'eau.

Cowx, I.G. (1998) 'Potential impact of groundwater augmentation of river flows on fisheries: a case study from the River Ouse, Yorkshire' in European Inland Fisheries Advisory Commission *Report of the Symposium on Water for Sustainable Inland Fisheries and Aquaculture*, Rome: FAO.

Cox, S.J.B. (1985) 'No tragedy on the commons', *Environmental Ethics* **7**, 49–61.

Creighton, J.L., Dunning, C.M., Priscoli, J.D. and Ayres, D.B. (1991) *Public Involvement and Dispute Resolution: A Reader on the Second Decade of Experience at the Institute for Water Resources*, Alexandria, VA: Institute for Water Resources, US Army Corps of Engineers.

Crichton, D. (2001) personal communication.

Critchley, W., Siegert, K., Chapman, C. and Finkel, M. (1991) *Water Harvesting* AGL/MISC/17/91, Rome: FAO.

Croke, K.G., Swartzman, D. and Freeniman, G.R. (1984) 'The relationship between perceived motivation for water pollution abatement programs and preferred methods of financing such programs', *Journal of Environmental Systems* **14**(4), 395–404.

Crosson, P. and Anderson, J.R. (1992) *Resources and Global Food Prospects*, Technical Paper No. 184, Washington, DC: World Bank.

Cryer, R. (1995) 'Changing responses to water resource problems', *Geography* **86**(1), 45–57.

CSIR n.d. *The Water Regulator*, Development Services and Technology Programme, Pretoria: CSIR.

CWPU (Central Water Planning Unit) (1978) *Implications of Consumer Preferences for Water Supply Reliability*, Reading: CWPU.

Daly, H. and Cobb, J. (1990) *For the Common Good*, London: Merlin.

Daoxi, W. and Siping, H. (1999) 'Role of reservoirs in 1998 heavy flood fighting on the Yangtze River', paper given at the *Workshop on Benefits of and Concerns about Dams*, Anatalya.

Daubert, J.T. and Young, R.A. (1981) 'Recreational demands for maintaining instream flows: a contingent valuation approach', *American Journal of Agricultural Economics* **63**(4), 666–76.

Davis, J. (1992) *Exchange*, Buckingham: Open University Press.

Davis, M.D. and Lund, J.R. (2000) 'Reconciling economic, environmental, and social objectives in Chilean water resources management', paper given at Water 2000, Melbourne.

Dawes, R.M. (1980) 'Social dilemmas', *Annual Review of Psychology* **31**, 169–93.

De Bruin, D., Hamhuis, D., van Nieuwnhuijze, L., Overmars, W., Sijmons, D. and Vera, F. (1987) *Ooievaar. De toekomst van het rivierengebied*, Arnhem: Stichting Gelderse Milieufederatie.

De Garis (2001) personal communication.

De Graff, J. (2000) *Downstream Effects of Land Degradation and Soil and Water Conservation*, Rome: FAO.

de Groot, R.S. (1987) 'Environmental function as a unifying concept for ecology and economics', *Environmentalist* **7**(2), 105–9.

Deane, P. (1979) *The First Industrial Revolution*, Cambridge: Cambridge University Press.

Deen, A.R. (2000) 'Drought assessment and management in Sydney during 1992–98', paper given at Water 2000, Melbourne.

DEFRA (Department of the Environment, Food and Rural Affairs) (1999) *Project Appraisal Guidance 3: Economic Appraisal*, London: Department of the Environment, Food and Rural Affairs.

Dembek, W. (2000) *Preliminary Assessment of the Proposed East–West Waterway Scheme in Poland*, Copenhagen: WWF International.

Democratic Staff Report, Subcommittee on Oversight and Investigations Committee on Natural Resources (1994) *Taking from the Taxpayer: Public Subsidies for Natural Resource Development*, US House of Representatives, 103rd Congress 2nd Session, 8/94.

DeOreo, W. Bm, Heaney, J.P. and Mayer, P.W. (1996) 'Flow trace analysis to assess water use', *Journal of the American Water Works Association*, 79–90.

Department of Health (1997) *Health Survey for England 1995*, London: The Stationery Office.

Department of Land and Water Conservation (1998) *Water Sharing the Way Forward 5 The Cap – A Basis for the Evolution of Water Management*, Sydney: Government of New South Wales.

Department of Land and Water Conservation (1999) *Water Trading Development and Monitoring*, Sydney: Government of New South Wales.

Department of Water Resources (1991) *California's Continuing Drought 1987–1991*, Sacramento: Department of Water Resources.

Department of Water Resources (1993) *California's 1987–92 Drought*, Sacramento: Department of Water Resources.

DETR (Department of the Environment, Transport and Regions) (2000a) *Public Participation in Making Local Environmental Decisions: The Aarhus Convention Newcastle Workshop*, London: DETR.

DETR (Department of the Environment, Transport and Regions) (2000b) *Economic Instruments in Relation to Water Abstraction: A Consultation Paper*, London: Department of the Environment, Transport and Regions.

DFID (Department for International Development) (1999a) *DFID Guidance Manual on Water Supply and Sanitation Projects*, Loughborough: WELL.

DFID (Department for International Development) (1999b) *Integrated Pest Management*, London: Department for International Development.

Dienel, P. (1978) *Planningszelle*, Opladen: Westdeutscher Verlag.

Dienel, P. and Renn, O. (1995) 'Planning cells: a gate to "fractal" mediation' in Renn, O., Webler, T. and Wiedemann, P. (eds) *Fairness and Competence in Citizen Participation*, Dordrecht: Kluwer.

Ditton, R.B. and Goodale, T.L. (1973) 'Water quality perception and the recreational uses of Green Bay, East Michigan', *Water Resources Research* **9**, 569–79.

Dixon, A.M., Leggett, D.J. and Weight, R.C. (1998) 'Habitat creation opportunities for landward coastal re-alignment: Essex case studies', *JCIWEM* **12**, April, 107–12.

Donnelly, W.A. (1989) 'Hedonic price analysis of the effect of a floodplain on property values', *Water Resources Bulletin* **25**, 581–6.

Douglas, M. (1966) *Purity and Danger*, London: Routledge.

Drake, P.J. and Sherriff, J.D.F. (1987) 'A method for managing river abstractions and protecting the environment', *Journal of the Institute of Water and Environmental Management* **1**, Part 1, 27–38.

Drijver, A. and Marchand, M. (1985) *Taming the Floods: Environmental Aspects of Floodplain Development in Africa*, Leiden: Centre for Environmental Studies, University of Leiden.

Droogers, P., Seckler, D. and Makin, I. (2001) *Estimating the Potential of Rainfed Agriculture*, Working Paper 20, Colombo: IWMI.

DTLR (Department of Transport, Local Government and the Regions) (2000) *Highways Economics Note*, London: DTLR.

DTLR (Department of Transport, Local Government and the Regions) (2002) *Preparing for Floods*, London: DTRL.

Duesenberry, J.S. (1960) 'Comment' in *Demographic and Economic Change in Developed Countries*, Princeton: Princeton University Press.

Dunderdale, J.A.L. (1998) *Evaluation of FDMM and Guidelines for the Justification of River Maintenance*, unpublished MPhil thesis, Silsoe: Silsoe College, Cranfield University.

Dutta, D. (2002) personal communication.

DWAF (Department of Water Affairs and Forestry) (1994) *Water Supply and Sanitation Policy: Water – An Indivisible National Asset*, White Paper WP-1, Cape Town: Republic of South Africa.

DWAF (Department of Water Affairs and Forestry) (1996) *Water Law Principles*, Pretoria: Department of Water Affairs and Forestry.

Dworkin, R. (1971) 'Philosophy and the critique of law' in Wolff, R.P. (ed.) *The Rule of Law*, New York: Simon and Schuster.

Dziegielewski, B. and Baumann, D.D. (1992) 'The benefits of managing urban water demands', *Environment* **34**(9), 6–11, 35–41.

Dziegielewski, B., Opitz, E.M., Kiefer, J.C. and Baumann, D.D. (1993) *Evaluation of Urban Water Conservation Programs: A Procedures Manual*, Denver CO: American Water Works Association.

Earl, G.C. and Turner, G.K. (2000) 'Planning for a competitive future – resource allocation and water markets in Victoria', paper given at Water 2000, Melbourne.

Easter, K.W., Becker, N. and Tsur, Y. (1997) 'Economic mechanisms for managing water resources: pricing, permits and markets' in Biswas, A.K. (ed.)

Water Resources: Environmental Planning, Management and Development, New York: McGraw-Hill.

Eastern Canada Soil and Water Conservation Centre n.d. *Buffer Strips and Water Quality: A review of the literature*, New Brunswick: Eastern Canada Soil and Water Conservation Centre.

Eberhard, A., Lazarus, M., Bernow, S., Rajan, C., Lefevre, T., Cabrera, M., O'Leary, D., Peters, R., Svensson, B. and Wilkinson, R. (2000) *Electricity Supply and Demand Side Management Options*, Thematic Review IV.1, Cape Town: World Commission on Dams.

ECOTEC (1999) *Design of a Tax or Charge Scheme for Pesticides*, London: DETR.

Edward, K. (1996) 'Methods of estimating water usage in unmeasured households', paper given at the Minimising Leakage in Water Supply and Distribution Systems conference, London.

Edwards, P. (1992) *Reuse of Human Wastes in Aquaculture: A Technical Review*, Washington, DC: World Bank.

Edwards, P. (2000) 'Aquaculture, poverty impacts and livelihoods', *Natural Resource Perspectives 56*, London: Overseas Development Institute.

Eheart, J.W. (1988) 'Effects of streamflow variation on critical water quality from multiple discharges of decaying pollutants', *Water Resources Research* **19**(6), 1–8.

Eheart, J.W., Brill, E.D., Lence, B.J., Kilgore, J.D. and Uber, J.G. (1987) 'Cost-efficiency of time-varying discharge permit programs for water quality management', *Water Resources Research* **23**(2), 245–51.

El Katsha, S. and White, A.U. (1989) 'Women, water and sanitation: household behavioral patterns in two Egyptian villages', *Water International* **14**, 103–11.

El-Katsha, S., Younis, A., El-Sebaie, O. and Hussein, A. (1989) *Women, Water and Sanitation: Household Water Use in Two Egyptian Villages*, Cairo Papers in Social Science 12(2), Cairo: The American University in Cairo.

English Nature (1996) *Impact of Water Abstraction on Wetland SSSIs*, Peterborough: English Nature.

English Nature and the Environment Agency (1999) *Water Abstraction and Sites of Special Scientific Interest in England*, Peterborough: English Nature.

Enis, B.M. and Broome, C.L. (1971) *Marketing Decisions: A Bayesian Approach*, Scranton: Intext.

ENTEC (1998) *Economic Evaluation of the Nitrate Sensitive Areas Scheme*, London: DEFRA.

Environment Agency (1999) *MAT Scoring and Weighting System*, Bristol: Environment Agency.

Environment Agency (2000a) *The Environment Agency's Review of Water Company's Drought Plans*, Bristol: The Environment Agency.

Environment Agency (2000b) *Managing Water Abstraction: Towards a Shared Strategy*, Bristol: Environment Agency.

Environment Agency (2001a) *A Scenario Approach to Water Demand Forecasting*, Worthing: National Water Demand Management Centre, Environment Agency.

Environment Agency (2001b) *Water Resources for the Future*, Bristol: Environment Agency.

Environomics (1999) *A Summary of U.S. Effluent Trading and Offset Projects*, Washington, DC: US Environmental Protection Agency.

Ernst & Young (1999) *Beyond Monopoly: Future Histories of Competition in the Water Industry*, London: Ernst & Young.

Esrey, S.A., Gough, J., Rapaport, D., Sawyer, R., Simpson-Hebert, M., Vargas, J. and Winblad, U. (1998) *Ecological Sanitation*, Stockholm: SIDA.

Estrela, T., Marcuello, C. and Iglesias, A. (1996) *Water Resources Problems in Southern Europe: An Overview Report*, Copenhagen: European Environment Agency.

ETBPP (Environmental Technology Best Practice Programme) (1997) *Water Use in Textile Dyeing and Finishing*, EG98 (http://www.etsu.com/etbpp/).

ETBPP (Environmental Technology Best Practice Programme) (1998a) *Practical Water Management in Paper and Board Mills*, GG111 (http://www.etsu.com/etbpp/).

ETBPP (Environmental Technology Best Practice Programme) (1998b) *Reducing Water and Effluent Costs in Breweries*, GG 135 (http://www.etsu.com/etbpp/).

ETBPP (Environmental Technology Best Practice Programme) (1998c) *Water Use in the Soft Drinks Industry*, EG126, (http://www.etsu.com/etbpp/).

ETBPP (Environmental Technology Best Practice Programme) (1999a) *Minimising Chemical and Water Waste in the Metal Finishing Industry*, GG160 (http://www.etsu.com/etbpp/).

ETBPP (Environmental Technology Best Practice Programme) (1999b) *Reducing Waste for Profit in the Dairy Industry*, GG242 (http://www.etsu.com/etbpp/).

ETBPP (Environmental Technology Best Practice Programme) (2000a) *Reducing Water and Effluent Costs in Red Meat Abattoirs*, GG234 (http://www.etsu.com/etbpp/).

ETBPP (Environmental Technology Best Practice Programme) (2000b) *Benchmarking Environmental Performance in the Chemical Industry*, ES269, Harwell: ETBPP.

Eto, J., Koomey, J., Lehman, B., Martin, N., Mills, E., Webber, C. and Worrell, E. (2001) *Scoping Study on Trends in the Economic Value of Electricity Reliability to the US Economy*, Palo Alto: Electric Power Research Institute.

European Commission (2001) *Guidance on EIA – Screening*, Luxembourg: Office for Official Publications of the European Communities.

European Inland Fisheries Advisory Commission (1998) *Report of the Symposium on Water for Sustainable Inland Fisheries and Aquaculture*, Rome: FAO.

European Parliament (1999) *Proposal and Amended Proposals for a Council Directive Establishing a Framework for Community Action in the Field of Water Policy (COM(97)0049-C4-0192/97, COM(97)0614-C4-0120/98 and COM(98)0076-97/0067(SYN))* (http://www2.europarl.eu.int/oml/).

Evans, E.P., Johnson, P., Green, C. and Varsa, E. (2000) 'Risk assessment and programme prioritisation: the Hungary flood study', paper given at the 35th MAFF conference for flood and coastal defence engineers, Keele.

Evans, P. and Appleton, B. (eds) (1993) *Community Management Today: The Role of Communities in the Management of Improved Water Supply Systems*, Occasional Paper No. 20, Delft: IRC.

Falkenmark, M. (1989) 'The massive water scarcity now threatening Africa, why isn't it being addressed', *Ambio* **18**(2).

Falkenmark, M. and Lundquist, J. (1998) 'Towards water security: political determination and human adaptation crucial', *Natural Resources Forum* **21**(1), 37–51.

FAO (Food and Agriculture Organisation) (1996) *Food Production: The Critical Role of Water*, Rome: FAO.

FAO (Food and Agriculture Organisation) (1997) *Aquaculture Economics in Developing Countries: Regional Assessments and an Annotated Bibliography*, Rome: FAO.

FAO (Food and Agriculture Organisation) (2000) *Crops and Drops: Making the Best Use of Water for Agriculture*, Rome: FAO.

Farmer, A. and Tiefenthaler, J. (1995) 'Fairness concepts and intrahousehold allocation of resources', *Journal of Developmental Economics* **47**(2), 179–89.

Feachem, R.G., Bradley, D.J., Garelick, H. and Mara, D. (1983) *Sanitation and Disease – Health Aspects of Execreta and Wastewater Management*, World Bank Studies in Water Supply and Sanitation, Chichester: Wiley.

Feeny, D., Berkes, F., McCay, B.J. and Acheson, D.M. (1990) 'The tragedy of the commons: twenty-two years later', *Human Ecology* **18**(1), 1–19.

Feitelson, E. (1991) 'Consumer preferences and willingness-to-pay for water-related residences in non-urban settings: a vignette analysis', *Regional Studies* **26**, 49–68.

Fernandes, E.C.M. n.d. 'Agroforestry homegardens' (http://wwwscas.cit.cornell.edu/ecf3).

Fischhoff, B. (1991) 'Value elicitation: is there anything in there?' *American Psychologist* **46**(8), 835–47.

Fishbein, M. and Ajzen, I. (1975) *Belief, Attitude, Intention and Behavior*, Reading MA: Addison-Wesley.

Foley, S., Soedjarwo, A. and Pollard, R. n.d. *Of the People, by the People, for the People: Community-Based Sewer Systems in Malang, Indonesia*, Washington, DC: World Bank.

Fos, J. (1997) 'Some ecological concepts that one should never forget when thinking on coastal vulnerability', paper given at *Coastal Vulnerability: Natural and Human Dimensions*, Barcelona.

Foundation for Water Research (1996) *Grootvlei Socio-Economic and Environmental Cost Benefit Analysis*, Report to the Water Research Commission, South Africa, Marlow: Foundation for Water Research.

Freeman, A.W. (1979) 'Hedonic prices, property values and measuring environmental benefits: a survey of the issues', *Scandinavian Journal of Economics* **81**(2), 154–73.

Galloway Report (the Interagency Floodplain Management Review Committee) (1994) *Sharing the Challenge: Floodplain Management into the 21st Century*, Washington, DC: US Government Printing Office.

Galtung, J. (1967) *Theory and Methods of Social Research*, London: Allen and Unwin.

Garn, H.A. (1997) *Lessons from Large-Scale Rural Water and Sanitation Projects: Transition and Innovation*, Washington, DC: World Bank.

Garner, J.L., Tunstall, S.M. and Green, C.H. (1994) *Cliftonville: An Assessment of Coast Protection Benefits*, report to Thanet District Council, Enfield: Flood Hazard Research Centre.

Garraway, W.M., Collins, G.N. and Lee, R.J. (1991) 'High prevalence of benign prostatic hypertrophy in the community', *The Lancet* **338**, August 24, 469–71.

Garrido, A. (1999) *Agricultural Water Pricing in OECD Countries*, ENV/EPOC/GEEI(98)11/Final, Paris: OECD.

Gates, C. (1994) 'The potential for improving water efficiency in existing housing: implications for municipal DSM programming' in Shrubsole, D. and Tate, D. (eds) *Every Drop Counts*, Ontario: Canadian Water Resources Association.

Gelt, J. (1995) 'Water recreation makes big splash in Arizona', *Arroyo* **8**(3).

Gelt, J. (1997) 'Sharing Colorado river water: history, public policy and the Colorado River Compact', *Arroyo* **10**(1).

Gershuny, J. (1998) *Households and Family Structure: Issues for the Future*, London: Foresight.

Gibbons, D.C. (1986) *The Economic Value of Water*, Washington, DC: Resources for the Future.

Gibbs, C.J.N. and Bromley, D.W. (1989) 'Institutional arrangements for management of rural resources: common-property regimes' in Berkes, F. (ed.) *Common Property Resources: Ecology and Community-Based Sustainable Development*, London: Belhaven.

Gilbertson, D.D. (1986) 'Runoff (floodwater) farming and rural water supply in arid lands', *Applied Geography* **6**, 5–11.

Gill, E., Parker, M., Savic, D. and Walters, G. (2001) 'Cougar: a genetic algorithm and rapid integrated catchment modelling application for optimising capital investment in combined sewer systems', paper given at the ASCE conference, Miami.

Gill, R.A. and Wolfenden, J.A.J. (1998) *Participative Environmental Planning and Decision Making: A Purposeful Approach*, Center for Water Policy Research, University of New England.

Gittinger, J.P. (1982) *Economic Analysis of Agricultural Products*, Baltimore: John Hopkins.

Gleick, J. (1987) *Chaos*, Harmondsworth: Penguin.

Gleick, P.H. (ed.) (1993) *Water in Crisis: A Guide to the World's Fresh Water Resources*, Oxford: Oxford University Press.

Gleick, P.H. (ed.) (2000) *Water: The Potential Consequences of Climate Variability and Change for the Water Resources of the United States*, Oakland, CA: Pacific Institute for Studies in Development, Environment and Security.

Glick, T.F. (1970) *Irrigation and Society in Medieval Valencia*, Cambridge, MA: Belkamp.

Global Vision on Water, Life and the Environment (2000) *A Vision of Water for Food and Rural Development*.

Global Water Partnership Technical Advisory Committee (2000) *Integrated Water Resources Management*, TAC Background Paper 4, Stockholm: Global Water Partnership.

Glyde, P. (1992) 'Difficulties of integrating contingent valuation results into decision-making processes' in Lockwood, M. and DeLacy, T. (eds) *Valuing Natural Areas: Applications and Problems of the Contingent Valuation Method*, Albury: Johnstone Centre of Parks, Recreation & Heritage, Charles Sturt University.

Goeller, B.F., Abrahamse, A.F., Bigelow, J.H., Bolten, J.G., De Ferrantu, D.M., DeHaven, J.C., Kirkwood, T.F. and Petruschell, R.L. (1977) *Protecting an Estuary from Floods – A Policy Analysis of the Oosterschelde – Summary Report*, R-2121/1-NETH, Rand Corporation.

Gomez-Lobo, A., Foster, V. and Halpern, J. n.d. *Information and Modelling Issues in Designing Water and Sanitation Subsidy Schemes*, Washington, DC: World Bank.

Goncalves, E. (2000) *The Cork Report: A Study on the Economics of Cork*, Sandy: Royal Society for the Protection of Birds.

Goodin, R. (1982) 'Discounting discounting', *Journal of Public Policy* **2**, 53–72.

Goodin, R.E. (1999) 'Democractic deliberation within', paper presented to *Deliberating about Deliberative Democracy*, Austin, Texas.

Goss, S. (1999) *Managing Working with the Public*, London: Kogan Page.

Government of New South Wales n.d. *Water Sharing – The Way Forward: Community/Government Partnership in Water Management – A Reciprocal Agreement*.

Government of Victoria (2001) *Planning for the Future of our Water Resources: Discussion Starter*, East Melbourne: Natural Resources and Environment.

Graham, W.J. (1999) *A Procedure for Estimating Loss of Life Caused by Dam Failure*, DSO-99-06, Denver CO: Bureau of Reclamation, Dam Safety Office.

Grant, N., Moodie, M. and Weedon, C. (1996) *Sewage Solutions: Answering the Call of Nature*, Machynlleth: The Centre for Alternative Technology.

Grapard, U. (1995) 'Robinson Crusoe: the quintessential economic man?', *Feminist Economics* **1**(1), 33–52.

Greeley-Polhemus Group (1992) *Guidelines for Risk and Uncertainty Analysis in Water Resources Planning*, IWR Report 92-R-1, Fort Belvoir, VA: US Army Corps of Engineers, Institute for Water Resources.

Green, C.H. (1997) 'Are blue whales really simply very large cups of coffee?', paper given at the 7th Stockholm Water Symposium.

Green, C.H. (1998a) 'Charging for water and wastewater: issues and options', opening address conference on The Future of Charging for Water and Wastewater, London.

Green, C.H. (1998b) *Economic Instruments for Water Pollution: A Response to the DETR Consultation Paper*, Enfield: Flood Hazard Research Centre.

Green, C.H. (1999) 'The economics of pollution abatement: a case study' in Trudgill, S.T., Walling, D.E. and Webb, B.W. (eds) *Water Quality: Processes and Policy*, Chichester: Wiley.

Green, C.H. (2000a) 'If only life were that simple: optimism and pessimism in economics', *Physics and Chemistry of the Earth (B)* **25**(3), 205–12.

Green, C.H. (2000b) *The Social Relations of Water*, paper given at the International Seminar 'Water, town-and-country planning, and sustainable development', Paris.

Green, C.H. (2001a) 'Flood management of the Yangtze River: the lessons of economic appraisal', paper given at the 36th DEFRA conference for flood and coastal defence engineers, Keele.

Green, C.H. (2001b) 'The lessons from the privatisation of the wastewater and water industry in England and Wales' in Holzwarth, F. and Kraemer, R.A. (eds) *Umweltaspekte einer Privatisierung der Wasserwirtschaft in Deutschland*, Berlin: Ecoscript.

Green, C.H. (2002) 'Design standards of protection: a snare and a delusion', paper given at the 37th DEFRA conference for flood and coastal defence engineers, Keele.

Green, C.H., Johnson, C. and Penning-Rowsell, E. (2001) *Flood Management in the Context of Integrated River Basin Management*, report to the World Meteorological Organisation/Global Water Partnership, Enfield: Flood Hazard Research Centre.

Green, C.H. and Newsome, D. (1992) 'Ethics and the calculi of choice', *A Holistic Approach to Water Quality Management – Proceedings of the Stockholm Water Symposium*, Stockholm: Stockholm Vatten.

Green, C.H., Newsome, D.H. and Stephen, C.D. (2000) 'Can and *ought* rivers to be valued?', paper given at Water 2000, Melbourne.

Green, C.H., Nicholls, R. and Johnson, C. (2000) *Climate Change Adaptation: An Analysis of Decision-Making in the Face of Risk and Uncertainty*, Report No. 28, London: National Centre for Risk Assessment and Options Appraisal, Environment Agency.

Green, C.H., Parker, D.J. and Penning-Rowsell, E.C. (1993) 'Designing for failure' in Merriman, P.A. and Browitt, C.W.A. (eds) *Natural Disasters: Protecting Vulnerable Communities*, London: Thomas Telford.

Green, C.H., Parker, D.J. and Tunstall, S.M. (2000) *Assessment of Flood Control and Management Options*, Cape Town: World Commission on Dams (http://www.dams.org).

Green, C.H. and Penning-Rowsell, E.C. (1986) 'Evaluating the intangible benefits and costs of a flood alleviation proposal', *Journal of the Institution of Water Engineers and Scientists* **40**(3), 229–48.

Green, C.H. and Penning-Rowsell, E.C. (1999) 'Inherent conflicts at the coast', *Journal of Coastal Conservation* **5**, 153–62.

Green, C.H. and Tunstall, S.M. (1991a) 'Is the economic evaluation of environmental resources possible?' *Journal of Environmental Management* **33**, 123–41.

Green, C.H. and Tunstall, S.M. (1991b) 'The benefits of river water quality improvements', *Applied Economics* **23**(7), 1135–46.

Green, C.H. and Tunstall, S.M. (1992) 'The recreational and amenity value of river corridors' in Boon, P.J., Calow, P. and Petts, G.E. (eds) *River Conservation and Management*, Chichester: Wiley.

Green, C.H. and Tunstall, S.M. (1996) 'The environmental value and attractiveness of river corridors', in Bravard, J.-P., Laurent, A.-M., Davallon, J. and Bethemont, J. (eds) *Les Paysages de l'eau aux Portes de la Ville*, Lyon: Centre Jacques Cartier.

Green, C.H. and Tunstall, S.M. (1997) 'Contingent valuation: a psychological perspective' in Bateman, I. and Willis, K.G. (eds) *Contingent Valuation*, Oxford: Oxford University Press.

Green, C.H., Tunstall, S.M., Herring, M. and Sawyer, J. (1992) *Customer Preferences and Willingness to Pay for Selected Water and Sewerage Services*, Report to the Office of Water Services, Birmingham: OFWAT.

Green, C.H., Tunstall, S. and House, M. (1989b) 'Evaluating the benefits of river water quality improvement' in van der Staal and van Vught, F.A. (eds) *Impact Forecasting and Assessment*, Delft: Delft University Press.

Green, C.H., Tunstall, S.M., N'Jai, A. and Rogers, A. (1990) 'The economic evaluation of environmental goods', *Project Appraisal* **5**(2), 70–82.

Green, C.H., Tunstall, S.M., Suleman, M., Wood, J.R. and Noriega, N.C. (1989a) *Investment Appraisal for Sewerage Schemes – The Assessment of Social Costs – The User Manual*, Swindon: Water Research Centre.

Green, C.H., van der Veen, A., Wierstra, E. and Penning-Rowsell, E. (1994) 'Vulnerability refined: analysing full flood impacts' in Penning-Rowsell, E. and Fordham, M. (eds) *Floods across Europe: Flood Hazard Assessment, Modelling and Management*, London: Middlesex University Press.

Green, P.E. and Wind, Y. (1973) *Multiattribute Decisions in Marketing: A Measurement Approach*, Hinsdale IL: Dryden.

Grootvlei Joint Venture Committee (1996) *Report of the Grootvlei Joint Venture Committee in Respect of a Preliminary Cost–Benefit Analysis should the Pumping of Mine Water into the Blesbokspruit Continue*, Johannesburg.

Guerra, L.C., Bhuiyan, S.I., Tuong, T.P. and Barker, R. (1998) *Producing More Rice with Less Water from Irrigated Systems*, SWIM Paper 5, Colombo: International Water Management Institute.

Guirkinger, B. (1988) 'Le cout d'une politique de qualitie gouts et odours', paper given at *Cout et Prix de l'eau en Ville*, Paris: Presses de L'Ecole Nationale des Ponts et Chaussees.

Gunderson, L. (1999) 'Resilience, flexibility and adaptive management – antidotes for spurious certitude?' *Conservation Ecology* 3(1) (http://www.consecol.org).

Gunderson, L.H., Holling, C.S. and Light, S. (1995) *Barriers and Bridges to Renewal of Ecosystems and Institutions*, New York: Columbia University Press.

Gustafsson, J.-E. (2001) 'Public water utilities and privatisation in Sweden', paper given at the EPSU Public Service Conference, Brussels.

Gustard, A., Cole, G., Marshall, D. and Bayliss, A. (1987) *A Study of Compensation Flows in the UK*, Report 99, Wallingford: Institute of Hydrology.

Guy, S. and Martin, S. (1996) 'Managing water stress: the logic of demand side infrastructure planning', *Journal of Environmental Planning and Management* **39**(1), 123–8.

Haarmeyer, D. and Mody, A. (1998) *Financing Water and Sanitation Projects – The Unique Risks*, Public Policy for the Private Sector, Washington, DC: World Bank.

Haas, C.N. (1997) 'Importance of distributional form in characterizing inputs to Monte Carlo risk assessments', *Risk Analysis* **17**(1), 107–13.

Haby, D. and Fisher, T. (2001) *Planning for the Future of our Water Resources*, Fitzroy: Australian Conservation Foundation.

Haddad, L., Hoddinott, J. and Alderman, H. (1997) *Intrahousehold Resource Allocation in Developing Countries*, Washington, DC: International Food Policy Research Institute.

Hadley, G. (1967) *Introduction to Probability and Statistical Decision Theory*, San Francisco: Holden-Day.

Hagerstrand, T. (1957) 'Migration and area: survey of a sample of Swedish migration fields and hypothetical considerations on their genesis', *Land Studies in Geography, Series B* **13**, 27–158.

Haggett, P. (1965) *Locational Analysis in Human Geography*, London: Edward Arnold.

Hall, D. (2001) *The Public Sector Water Undertaking – A Necessary Option*, London: Public Services International Research Unit, University of Greenwich.

Hall, D. and Lanz, W. (2001) *A Critique of the 2001 PricewaterhouseCoopers Report on Water Services in Austria*, London: PSIRU.

Halwart, M. (1998) 'Trends in rice–fish farming', *FAO Aquaculture Newsletter* **18**, 3–11.

Handmer, J.W., Dorcey, A.H.J. and Smith, D.I. (1991) *Negotiating Water: Conflict Resolution in Australian Water Management*, Canberra: Centre for Resource and Environmental Studies, Australian National University.

Hanley, N. and Spash, C.L. (1993) *Cost–Benefit Analysis and the Environment*, Aldershot: Edward Elgar.

Hardin, G. (1968) 'Tragedy of the Commons', *Science* **162**, 1243–8.

Harrison, R.W. and Mooney, J.F. (1993) *Flood Control and Water Management in Yazoo-Mississippi Delta*, Social Science Centre, Mississippi State University.

Harrison, A.J.M. and Stabler, M.J. (1981) 'An analysis of journeys for canal-based recreation', *Regional Studies* **15**(5), 345–58.

Hart, G. (1992) 'Household production reconsidered: gender, labor conflict, and technological change in Malaysia's Muda region', *World Development* **20**(6), 809–23.

Hart, H.L.A. (1961) *The Concept of Law*, Oxford: Clarendon Press.

Hasan, A. (1990) 'Community groups and NGOs in the urban field in Pakistan', *Environment and Urbanization* **2**, 74–86.

Hasan, S. (2001) *The Privatisation Process of Water and Sewerage Services in an Asian Metropolis: Global Politics, Citizens' Organisations and Local Poor: A Case Study of Karachi*, Occasional Paper No. 34, London: SOAS.

Hassan, J. (1998) *A History of Water in Modern England and Wales*, Manchester: Manchester University Press.

Hausman, D.M. (1992) *The Inexact and Separate Science of Economics*, Cambridge: Cambridge University Press.

Hazell, P., Oram, P. and Chaherli, N. (2001) *Managing Droughts in the Low-Rainfall Areas of the Middle East and North Africa*, EPTD Discussion Paper No. 78, Washington, DC: International Food Policy Research Institute.

Hearne, R.R. and Easter, K.W. (1995) *Water Allocation and Water Markets: An Analysis of Gains-From-Trade in Chile*, Technical Paper 315, Washington, DC: World Bank.

Hehmeyer, I. (2000) 'The spirit of cooperation in Yemeni agricultural practices – successful cases from the past, and their applicability for the present', paper given at The Place of Ancient Agricultural Practices and Techniques in Yemen Today: Problems and Perspectives, Sanaa.

Heimlich, R.E. (1991) *National Policy of 'No Net Loss' of Wetlands: What Do Agricultural Economists Have to Contribute?* Washington, DC: Resources and Technology Division, US Department of Agriculture.

Heiser, C.B. (1990) *Seed to Civilisation: The Story of Food*, Cambridge, MA: Harvard University Press.

Hengeveld, H. and De Vocht, C. (1982) *Role of Water in Urban Ecology*, Amsterdam: Elsevier.

Henry, C. (1974) 'Investment decisions under uncertainty: the irreversibility effect', *The American Economic Review* **63**(6), 1006–12.

Hermann, T. (2002) 'German experience in rainwater recycling', paper given at the 3rd Meeting of the WATERSAVE Network, London.

Herrington, P.R. (1987) *Pricing of Water Services*, Paris: OECD.

Herschy, R.W. (1980) 'An examination of the variation of mean monthly discharge of British rivers from a short period record to assess the need of planning and design', *Proceedings of the Institution of Civil Engineers Part 1*, **68**, 477–88.

Herschy, R.W. (1998) 'Dam failure' in Herschy, R.W. (ed.) *Encyclopedia of Hydrology and Water Resources*, London: Kluwer.

Hess, T.M. and Morris, J. (1986) *The Estimation of Flood Damage Costs for Arable Crops*, Silsoe: Silsoe College.

Hicks, J.R. (1946) *Value and Capital*, Oxford: Oxford University Press.

Hietala, M. (1987) *Services and Urbanization at the Turn of the century*, Studia Historica 23, Helsinki: Finnish Historical Society.

Higgin, R.J. (1981) *An Economic Comparison of Different Flood Mitigation Strategies in Australia*, unpublished PhD thesis, School of Civil Engineering, University of New South Wales.

Higueras, M.A. and Lop, A.F. (2001) *Alcobendas, City of Water for the 21st Century*, Madrid: WWF/Adena.

Hill, M. (1966) *A Method for Evaluating Alternative Plans: the Goal Achievement Matrix Applied to Transport Plans*, PhD thesis, University of Pennsylvania.

Hillier, F.S. and Lieberman, G.J. (1967) *Introduction to Operations Research*, San Francisco: Holden Day.

Hills, J.S. (1995) *Cutting Water and Effluent Costs*, London: Institute of Chemical Engineers.

Hobsbawm, E.J. (1969) *Industry and Empire: Volume 3 of the Penguin Economic History of Britain*, Harmondsworth: Penguin.

Hoehn, J.P. and Krieger, D.J. (1996) *Valuing Water in a Desert Metropolis: An Economic Analysis of Infrastructure Investments in Cairo, Egypt*, East Lancing, MI: Michigan State University.

Hofstadter, D.R. (1980) *Gödel, Escher, Bach: An Eternal Golden Braid*, Harmondsworth: Penguin.

Holland, S.M. and Ditton, R.B. (1992) 'Fishing trip satisfaction: a typology of anglers', *North American Journal of Fisheries Management* **12**, 28–33.

Holling, C.S. (1973) 'Resilience and stability of ecological systems', *Annual Review of Ecology and Systematics* **4**, 1–23.

Holling, C.S. (1978) *Adaptive Environmental Assessment and Management*, Chichester: Wiley.

Homer-Dixon, T. (2001) *The Ingenuity Gap*, London: Vintage.

Hong, Qingyu and Luo, Zhang-Yu (eds) (1999) *Flood Control and 1998 Flood of the Yangtze River* (in Chinese).

Hourihan, K. (1984) 'Context-dependent models of residential satisfaction: an analysis of housing groups in Cork, Ireland', *Environment and Behavior* **16**(3), 369–93.

House, M.A. and Herring, M. (1995) *Aesthetic Pollution: Public Perception Survey*, Marlow: Foundation for Water Research.

House, M., Tunstall, S., Green, C., Portou, J. and Clarke, L. (1994) *Evaluation of Use Values from Alleviating Low Flows*, R&D Note 258, Bristol: National Rivers Authority.

Howarth, W. (1992) *Wisdom's Law of Watercourses*, 5th edition, Crayford: Shaw.

Howe, C.W. (1971) *Benefit–Cost Analysis for Water System Planning*, Water Resources Monograph 2, Washington, DC: American Geophysical Union.

Howe, C.W. and Smith, M.G. (1994) 'The value of water supply reliability in urban water systems', *Journal of Environmental Economics and Management* **26**, 19–30.

Howe, C.W., Lazo, J.K. and Weber, K.R. (1990) 'The economic impact of agriculture-to-urban water transfers on the area of origin: a case study of the Arkansas river valley in Colorado', *American Journal of Agricultural Economics* **72**(12), 1200–9.

Howe, C.W., Schurmeier, D.R. and Shaw, W.D. (1986) 'Innovations in water management from the Colorado–Big Thompson Project and Northern Colorado Water Conservancy District' in Frederick, K.D. (ed.) *Scarce Water and Institutional Change*, Washington, DC: Resources for the Future.

Huber, J. (1987) *Conjoint Analysis: How We Got Here and Where We Are*, Sequim, WA: Sawtooth Software.

Hudgins, M.D. (1984) 'Structure of the angling experience', *Transactions of the American Fisheries Society* **113**, 350–9.

Hudson, N.W. (1987) *Soil and Water Conservation in Semi-arid Areas*, Rome: FAO.

Huisman, P. (2000) 'How the Dutch pay the water management bill', paper given at the World Water Forum, The Hague.

Huisman, P., Cramer, W., van Ee, G. and Hooghart, J.C. (1998) *Water in the Netherlands*, Delft: Netherlands Hydrological Society.

Hull, J.C., Moore, P.G. and Thomas, H. (1987) 'Utility and its measurement', *Journal of the Royal Statistical Society A* **136**, part 2, 226–47.

Hurd, B., Callaway, M., Smith, J. and Kirshen, P. (1996) *Economic Effects of Climate Change on US Water Resources*, Report to the Electric Power Research Institute, Boulder, CO: Hagler Bailly Consulting Inc.

Husain, M.S. (1978) 'The effect of the 1976 drought on industry and commerce in England and Wales' in Doornkamp, J.C., Gregory, K.J. and Burn, A.S. (eds) (1980) *Atlas of the Drought in Britain 1975–76*, London: Institute of British Geographers.

Idelovitch, E. and Ringskog, K. (1997) *Wastewater Treatment in Latin America – Old and New Options*, Washington, DC: World Bank.

IEA (International Energy Agency) (2000) *World Energy Outlook*, Paris: International Energy Agency.

IFPRI n.d. *Women: The Key to Food Security*, Washington, DC: International Food Policy Research Institute.

Imber, D., Stevenson, G. and Wilks, L. (1991) *A Contingent Valuation Study of the Kakadu Conservation Zone*, Resource Assessment Commission Research Paper No. 3, Canberra: Australian Government Printing Service.

Imhoff, K.R. (1992) 'Treatment standards and wastewater discharge fee in Germany', *Water Science and Technology* **26**(7–8), 1897–903.

Imperial, M.T. and Hennessey, T. (2000) 'Environmental governance in watersheds: the importance of collaboration to institutional performance' in National Academy of Public Administration, *Learning from Innovations in Environmental Protection*, Washington, DC: National Academy of Public Administration.

Imura, H. (1999) *The Use of Voluntary Approaches in Japan – An Initial Survey*, Paris: OECD.

Ingelhart, R. (1997) *Modernization and Postmodernization: Cultural, Economic, and Political Change in 43 Societies*, Princeton, NJ: Princeton University Press.

Ingold, N.I. and Stonebridge, N.G. (1987) 'Trade-effluent charging – the Mogden formula', *Water Pollution Control*, 172–83.

International Commission for the Protection of the Rhine n.d. *Action Plan on Flood Defence* (http://www.iksr.org/icpr).

IOH (Institute of Hydrology) (1999) *Flood Estimation Handbook*, Wallingford: Institute of Hydrology.

IPTRID (2000) *Treadle Pumps for Irrigation in Africa*, Knowledge synthesis report, International Programme for Technology and Research in Irrigation and Drainage, Rome: FAO.

Isaksson, M.T. (1998) 'Tunnelling in poor ground – choice of shield method based on reliability' in Mari, B., Lisac, Z. and Szavits-Nossan, A. (eds), Proc. XI Danube – European Conference on Soil Mechanics and Geotechnical Engineering, Croatia, 25–29 May (1998), Rotterdam: Balkema.

Isaksson, M.T. (2001) personal communication.

Iwasada, K., Murakami, M., Ikezawa, R. and Fujiwara, K. (2000) 'Flood disaster of Kochi in 1998 and paradigm shift of river works in Japan', paper given at Water 2000, Melbourne.

IWMI (International Water Management Institute) (2000) *World Water Supply and Demand 1995 to 2025*, Colombo: IWMI.

IWMI-TATA (2002) 'Innovations in groundwater recharge', *Water Policy Briefing*, Colombo: IWMI.

Jacobs, G. and Asokan, N. (2000) 'Knowledge for development: Vision 2020', presentation to the Planning Commission, Government of India.

Janssen, R. (1992) *Multiobjective Decision Support for Environmental Management*, Dordrecht: Kluwer Academic Publishers.

Jayne, T.S. (1993) *Sources and Effects of Price Instability in the World Rice Market*, MSU International Development Working Paper No. 13, East Lansing: Michigan State University.

Jeffrey, D.A. (1986) *Leeds Water Emergency Incident: Inquiry Report*, Leeds: Yorkshire Water Authority.

Jelin, E. (1991) 'Social relations of consumption: the urban popular household' in Jelin, E. (ed.) *Family, Household and Gender Relations in Developing Countries*, London/Paris: Kegan Paul.

Jochem, E. (2000) 'Energy end-use efficiency' in UNDP *World Energy Assessment*, New York: United Nations Development Programme.

Jodha, N.S. (1992) *Common Property Resources: A Missing Dimension of Development Strategies*, Washington, DC: World Bank.

Johansson, R.C. n.d. *Pricing Irrigation Water: A Literature Survey*, Washington DC, World Bank.

John, Olaf Nelson Water Resources Management (1998) *City of Rohnert Park 1997 Toilet Replacement Program*, Petaluma CA: John Olaf Nelson Water Resources Management.

Johnson, C. (1999) 'Changes in design – changes in expectations: tertiary intervention in the Muda irrigation scheme, Peninsula Malaysia', paper presented at Rivers '99: Towards Sustainable Development, Penang.

Johnson, C. (2001), personal communication.

Johnson, F.R., Desvouges, W.H., Fries, E.E. and Wood, L.L. (1995) *Conjoint Analysis of Individual and Aggregate Environmental Preferences*, TER Technical Working Paper No. T-9502, Triangle Economic Research.

Johnson, M. (2002), personal communication.

Johnston, N. (1994) *Waste Minimisation: A Route to Profit and Cleaner Production – An Interim Report on the Aire and Calder Project*, London: Centre for Exploitation of Science and Technology.

Jones-Lee, M. (1993) personal communication.

Judd, P.H. (1993) *How Much is Enough? Controlling Water Demand in Apartment Buildings*, Denver, CO: American Water Works Association.

Kant, I. (1785) *Fundamental Principles of the Metaphysics of Morals*, trans. T.K. Abbott (gopher://gopher.vt.edu: 10010/02/10715).

Karl, T.R. and Knight, R.W. (1998) 'Secular trends of precipitation amount, frequency, and intensity in the USA', *Bulletin of the American Meteorological Society* **79**, 231–41.

Katko, T.S. (1992) *The Development of Water Supply Associations in Finland and its Significance for Developing Countries*, DP Number 8, Washington, DC: The World Bank.

Kaufmann, A. (1972) *Reliability – A Mathematical Approach* (trans. A. Graham), London: Transworld.

Keller, A., Skathivadivel, R. and Seckler, D. (2000) *Water Scarcity and the Role of Storage in Development*, Research Report 39, Colombo: International Water Management Institute.

Kelly, G.A. (1955) *The Psychology of Personal Constructs*, New York: WW Norton.

Kemp, T. (1978) *Historical Patterns of Industrialization*, London: Longman.

KGS Group (1999) *Flood Protection for Winnepeg*, International Joint Commission for the Red River (www.ijc.org).

Khalid, F. and O'Brien, J. (eds) (1992) *Islam and Ecology*, London: Cassell.

King, G. n.d. *Livestock Production Efficiency*, Department of Animal and Poultry Science, University of Guelph.

Kirchler, E. (1993) 'Spouses' joint purchase decisions: determinants of influence tactics for muddling through the process', *Journal of Economic Psychology* **14**, 405–38.

Kirschner, D. and Moore, D. (1989) 'The Effect of San Francisco Bay water quality on adjacent property values', *Journal of Environmental Management* **27**, 263–74.

Klaus, J., Pflugner, W., Schmidtke, R., Wind, H. and Green, C. (1994) 'Models for flood hazard assessment and management' in Penning-Rowsell, E. and Fordham, M. (eds) *Floods across Europe: Flood Hazard Assessment, Modelling and Management*, London: Middlesex University Press.

Kloezen, W.H. and Garces-Restrepo, C. (1998) *Assessing Irrigation Performance with Comparative Indicators: The Case of the Alto Rio Lerma Irrigation District, Mexico*, Research Report 22, Colombo: IWMI.

Knapp, M.R.J. (1978) 'Economies of scale in sewerage purification and disposal', *Journal of Industrial Economics* **27**(2), 163–84.

Kneese, A.V. and Bower, B.T. (1968) *Managing Water Quality: Economics, Technology and Institutions*, Washington DC: Resources for the Future.

Knosche, R., Schreckenbacj, K., Pfeifer, M. and Weissenbach, H. (1998) 'Balances of phosphorus and nitrogen in carp ponds' in European Inland Fisheries Advisory Commission 1998 *Report of the Symposium on Water for Sustainable Inland Fisheries and Aquaculture*, Rome: FAO.

Kohler, S. (2000) 'Traditions as a burden for agricultural development. The impact of ancient and traditional water-rights on the agricultural crisis in Yemen', paper given at The Place of Ancient Agricultural Practices and Techniques in Yemen Today: Problems and Perspectives, Sanaa.

Komives, K. n.d. *Designing Pro-Poor Water and Sewer Concessions: Early Lessons from Bolivia*, Washington, DC: World Bank.

Kopelman, S., Weber, J.M. and Messick, D.M. (2000) 'Commons dilemma management: recent experimental results', paper given at the 8th Biennial Conference of IASCP, Indiana.

Kosmin, R. (1988) 'A paper on house prices and the retail price index' in Fairlight Coastal Preservation Association Fairlight Cove Benefit–Cost Analysis, Fairlight Bay.

Krivoshey, R.M. (1994) *Juries: Formation and Behavior*, Garland.

Krueger, R.A. (1988) *Focus Groups: A Practical Guide for Applied Research*, Beverly Hills: Sage.

Krutilla, J.A. (1967) 'Conservation reconsidered', *American Economic Review* **57**(4), 77–86.

Kuchenrither, R.D., Houck, C.P., Ingram, C.W., Grimes, M.M. and Elmund, G.K. (1983) 'Variable effluent nitrification: economic efficiency and water quality preservation', *Journal of the Water Pollution Control Federation* **57**(7), 1489–96.

Kuik, O., Jansen, H. and Opschoor, J. (1991) 'The Netherlands' in Barde, J.-P. and Pearce, D.W. (eds) *Valuing the Environment*, London: Earthscan.

Lakoff, G. (1987) *Women, Fire, And Dangerous Things*, Chicago: University of Chicago Press.

Lallana, C., Krinner, W., Estrela, T., Nixon, S., Leonard, J. and Berland, J.M. (2001) *Sustainable Water Use in Europe Part 2: Demand Management*, Environmental issue report No. 19, Copenhagen: European Environment Agency.

Lamb, J.C. and Hull, D.B. (1985) 'Current status in use of flexible effluent standards', *Journal of the Water Pollution Control Federation* **57**(10), 993–8.

Lambert, A. (2002) 'Making leakage management into a science', *Demand Management Bulletin* **52**, 4–5.

Lancaster, K.J. (1966) 'A new approach to consumer theory', *Journal of Political Economy* **74**, 132–57.

Land and Water Resources Research and Development Corporation (1998) *National Dryland Salinity Management Plan 1998–2003*, Canberra: Land and Water Resources Research and Development Corporation.

Landry, C.J. (1998) *Saving Our Stream Through Water Market: A Practical Guide*, Bozemand MT: Political Economy Research Centre.

Lane, J. (1996) 'Key issues in improving people's health through water and sanitation' in Howsam, P. and Carter, R. (eds) *Water Policy: Allocation and Management in Practice*, London: Spon.

Langbein, L.L. and Lichtman, A.J. (1978) *Ecological Inference*, Beverly Hills: Sage.

Lauria, D.T., Whittington, D., Choe, K., Turingan, C. and Abiad, V. (1999) 'Household demand for improved sanitation services: a case study of Calamba, the Philippines' in Bateman, I.J. and Willis, K.G. (eds) *Valuing Environmental Preferences*, Oxford: Oxford University Press.

Lavee, H., Poesen, J. and Yair, A. (1997) 'Evidence of high efficiency water-harvesting by ancient farmers in the Negev Desert, Israel', *Journal of Arid Environment* **35**, 341–8.

Law Commission (1999) *Juries in Criminal Trials Part 2 – A Discussion Paper*, Preliminary Paper 37 – Volume 1, Wellington: Law Commission.

Lawrence, R.L., Daniels, S.E. and Stankey, G.H. (1997) 'Procedural justice and public involvement in natural resource decision making', *Society and Natural Resources* **10**, 577–89.

LEAD – Pakistan n.d. Country Report – Micro Hydropower Potential (http://www/lead.org.cn/Training/Materials/mid/ushu.html).

Leopold, L.B. (1969) 'Quantitative comparison of some aesthetic factors among rivers', *US Geological Circular 620*, Washington, DC: US Geological Survey.

Leopold, L., Clarke, F.E., Hanshaw, B.B. and Balsley, J.R. (1971) *A Procedure for Evaluating Environmental Impact*, US Geological Survey Circular 645, Washington, DC: US Geological Survey.

Leung, G. (1996) 'Reclamation and sediment control in the Middle Yellow River Valley', *Water International* **21**(1).

Lewis, N. (1994) *Safe Womanhood: A Discussion Paper*, Toronto: International Federation of Institutes for Advanced Study.

Lichfield, N. (1964) 'Cost–benefit analysis in plan evaluation', *Town Planning Review* **35**(2), 159–69.

Lightfoot, D. (2000) 'The origin and diffusion of qanats in Arabia: new evidence from the Northern and Southern Peninsula', *The Geographical Journal* **166**(3).

Lindsey, G. (1990) 'Charges for urban runoff: issues in implementation', *Water Resources Bulletin* **26**(1), 117–25.

Lipsey, R.G. (1971) *An Introduction to Positive Economics*, London: Weidenfeld and Nicolson.

Lipsey, R.G. and Lancaster, K. (1956–7) 'The general theory of second best', *Review of Economic Studies* **24**, 11–32.

Littlefair, K. (1998) *Willingness to Pay for Water at the Household Level: Individual Financial Responsibility for Water Consumption*, MEWEREW Occasional Paper No. 26, London: SOAS.

Lloyd, D. (1991) *The Idea of Law*, Harmondsworth: Penguin.

Lobina, E. (2000) *Cochabamba – Water War*, London: Public Services International Research Unit, University of Greenwich.

Locke, J. (1960) *Two Treatises of Government*, edited by Peter Laslett, Cambridge: Cambridge University Press.

Loomis, J., Sorg, C. and Dommelly, D. (1986) 'Economic losses to recreational fisheries due to small-head hydro-power development: a case study of the Henry's Fork in Idaho', *Journal of Environmental Management* **22**, 85–94.

Ludwig, D., Walker, B. and Holling, C.S. (1997) 'Sustainability, stability, and resilience', *Conservation Ecology* **1**(1) (http://www.consecol.org/).

Lyons, D. (1984) *Ethics and the Rule of Law*, Cambridge: Cambridge University Press.

Maalel, K., Bergaoui, Z.K. and Khrouf, L.M. (1987) 'Roof runoff storage tanks rehabilitation in Tunisia' in Yen, B.C. (ed.) *Topics in Urban Drainage Hydraulics and Hydrology*, Lausanne: Ecole Polytechnique Federale.

Maas, A. and Anderson, R.L. (1978) *And the Desert Shall Rejoice: Conflict, Growth and Justice in Arid Environments*, Cambridge, MA: MIT.

MacKay, D.M. (1969) *Information, Mechanism and Meaning*, Cambridge, MA: MIT.

MacKay, K.T. (ed.) (1995) *Rice–Fish Culture in China*, Ottawa: IDRC.

MacRae, D. and Whittington, D. (1988) 'Assessing preferences in cost–benefit analysis: reflections on rural water supply evaluation in Haiti', *Journal of Policy Analysis and Management* **7**(2), 246–63.

MAFF (Ministry of Agriculture, Fisheries and Food) 2000 *Conservation Grants for Farmers 2000*, London: MAFF (http://www.maff.gov.uk).

Maharaj, N., Athukorala, K., Vargas, M.G. and Richardson, G. (1999) *Mainstreaming Gender in Water Resources Management*, World Water Vision.

Malmsten, U.G.H., Milsom, I., Molander, U. and Norlen, L.J. (1997) 'Urinary incontinence and lower urinary tract symptoms: an epidemiological study of men aged 45 to 99 years', *Journal of Urology* **158**, 1733–7.

Maltby, E. (1986) *Waterlogged Wealth*, London: Earthscan.

Mantymaa, E. (1996) personal communication.

Marchand, M. (1987) 'The productivity of the African floodplains', *International Journal of Environmental Studies* **29**, 201–11.

Margolis, H. (1982) '*Selfishness, altruism and rationality*', Chicago: Chicago University Press.

Marshall, A. (1920) *Principles of Economics*, London: Macmillan.

Marshall, C. (1999) *Final Report: Results of Water-Based Trading Simulations*, Washington DC: USEPA (http://www.epa.gov/owow/).

Marshall, G.R. (2000) 'Voluntary cooperation in the Commons? Evidence from a survey of farmers in the Murray region's land and water management planning districts', paper given at the 44th Annual Conference of the Australian Agricultural and Resource Economics Society, Sydney.

Martin, W.E. and Thomas, J.F. (1986) 'Policy relevance in studies of urban residential water demand', *Water Resources Research* **22**, 1735–41.

Marwell, G. and Ames, R.E. (1981) 'Economists free ride, does anyone else? Experiments on the provision of public goods, IV', *Journal of Public Economics* **15**, 295–310.

Maskell, A.D. and Sheriff, J.D.F. (1992) *Scope for Control of Urban Runoff, Volume 2: A Review of Present Methods and Practice*, CIRIA Report 124, London: CIRIA.

Mathews, P.J. (1986) 'Consents – a philosophy for the late twentieth century', *Water Pollution Control*, 408–19.

Mathieson, I.K., Know, J.W., Weatherhead, E.K., Morris, J., Jones, D.O. and Yates, A.J. (1998) *Optimum Use of Water for Industry and Agriculture Dependent on Direct Abstraction: Best Practice Manual*, R&D Technical Report W157, Swindon: Environment Agency.

Mawdsley, J.A., Bell, D.B., Adeloye, A.J. and Johnson, P. (1988) *The Value of Data in Streamflow Network Evaluation*, Newcastle-upon-Tyne: Department of Civil Engineering.

Maxwell Stamp (1998) *Incidence Effects of Charging for Domestic Water and Sewerage Services*, London: Department of the Environment, Transport and Regions.

McLuhan, T.C. (1972) *Touch the Earth: A Self-Portrait of Indian Existence*, New York: Pocket Books.

McMahon, T.A., Finlayson, B.L., Haines, A.T. and Srikanthan, R. (1992) *Global Runoff – Continental Comparisons of Annual Flows and Peak Discharges*, Cremlingen-Destedt: Catena.

McPhail, A. (1993) 'Overlooked market for water connections in Rabat's shantytowns', *Journal of Water Resources Management* **119**(3), 388–404.

McPherson, H.J. and McGarry, M.G. (1987) 'User participation and implementation strategies in water and sanitation projects', *Water Resources Development* **3**(1), 23–30.

Mehta, L. n.d. *Water, Difference and Power: Kutch and the Sardar Sarovar (Narmada) Project*, IDS Working Paper 54, Brighton: Institute of Development Studies, University of Sussex.

Meinzen-Dick, R., Brown, L.R., Sims Feldstein, H. and Quisumbing, A.R. (1997) *Gender, Property Rights, and Natural Resources*, Washington, DC: International Food Policy Research Institute.

Melbourne Water (2001) *Infostream: The Water Supply System*, Melbourne: Melbourne Water.

Mendiluce, J.M.M. and del Rio, J.P.P. n.d. *Key Policy Implications under Different Predicaments. High Water Stress – Good Coping Capability. Spain*, Madrid: Centre de Estudios Hdrograficosa.

Mendis, D.L.O. (1999) 'Lessons from the history of the rise and fall of Sri Lanka ancient irrigation', *Water Nepal* **7**(1) (http://www.lib.mrt.ac.lk/resources/traditional.html).

Merrett, S. (1997) *An Introduction to Hydroeconomics: Political Economy, Water and the Environment*, London: UCL Press.

Milgrom, P. (1992) 'Is sympathy an economic value? Philosophy, economics and the contingent valuation method' in Cambridge Economics Inc. (eds) *Contingent Valuation: A Critical Assessment*, Cambridge, MA: Cambridge Economics Inc.

Mill, J.S. (1844) 'On the definition of political economy; and on the method of investigation proper to it', *Essays on Some Unsettled Questions of Political Economy*, Bristol: Thoemmes ((1992) reprint of 1844 edition).

Mill, J.S. (1848) *Principles of Political Economy*, Harmondsworth: Penguin.

Miller, B.A. and Reidinger, R.B. (1998) *Comprehensive River Basin Development – The Tennessee Valley Authority*, World Bank Technical Paper 416, Washington, DC: World Bank.

Miller, G.A. (1956) 'The magical number seven plus or minus two: some limits on our capacity for processing information', *Psychological Review* **63**, 81–97.

Mills, A. (1994) 'The economic consequences of malaria for households: a case-study in Nepal', *Health Policy* **24**, 209–27.

Ministry of Transport, Public Works and Water Management (1996) *Landscape Planning of the River Rhine in the Netherlands*, Lelystad: RIZA.

Ministry of Water Resources (1995) *The Standard of Annual Operation Cost Rate for Water Conservancy Projects*, SL 281-95, Beijing: Ministry of Water Resources (in Chinese).

Ministry of Water Resources (1998) *Regulation for Economic Benefit Analysis Calculation and Evaluation of Existing Flood Control Projects*, SL206-98, Beijing: Ministry of Water Resources (in Chinese).

Mishan, E.J. (1993) *The Costs of Economic Growth*, revised edition, London: Weidenfeld and Nicolson.

Mitchell, G., Tetlock, P.E., Mellers, B.A. and Ordonez, L.D. (1993) 'Judgments of social justice: compromises between equality and efficiency', *Journal of Personality and Social Psychology* **65**(4), 629–39.

Mitchell, R.C. and Carson, R.T. (1981) *An Experiment in Determining Willingness to Pay for National Water Quality Improvements*, Washington DC: US Environmental Protection Agency.

Mitchell, R.C. and Carson, R.T. (1989) *Using Surveys to Value Public Goods: The Contingent Valuation Method*, Washington, DC: Resources for the Future.

Moehl, J. (2000) 'Aquaculture in Africa: perspectives from the FAO Regional Office for Africa', *FAO Aquaculture Newsletter* **23**, 38–41.

Moench, M., Burke, J. and Moench, Y. (2001) *Through a Different Lens: The Question of Groundwater, Food Security, Uncertainty, Variability and Risk*, Rome: FAO.

Momsen, J.H. (1991) *Women and Development in the Third World*, London: Routledge.

Moore, P.G. and Thomas, H. (1988) *The Anatomy of Decisions*, London: Penguin.

Morawetz, T. (1980) *The Philosophy of Law*, New York: Macmillan.

Morris, J. (1994) *Les couts entraines par les inondations des terres agricoles en Ile de France estimation approximative*, Enfield: Flood Hazard Research Centre.

Moris, J. n.d. *The Economics of Water Supplies for Irrigation: An Economist's Viewpoint*, Silsoe; Silsoe College.

Morris, J. and Hess, T. (1986) *Evaluating Farmer Response to Land Drainage Improvement*, Silsoe: Silsoe College.

Morris, J., Hess, T. and Yates, M. (1984) 'Drainage evaluation and farmer uptake' paper given at the Cranfield Conference of River Engineers, Cranfield.

Morris, J., Weatherhead, E.K., Know, J.W., Gowing, D.J.G., Green, C.H. and Tunstall, S.M. (1997) *Practical Implications of Introducing Tradeable Permits for Water Abstraction*, Sandy: Royal Society for the Protection of Birds.

Mostert, E., van Beck, E., Bouman, N.W.M., Hey, E., Savenije, H.H.G. and Thissen, W.A.H. (1999) 'River basin management and planning', keynote address given at the International Workshop on River Basin Management, The Hague.

Munsinger, G.M., Weber, J.E. and Hansen, R.W. (1975) 'Joint home purchasing decisions by husbands and wives', *Journal of Consumer Research* **1**, 60–6.

Muraro, G. (1974) 'Economic costs and benefits of an antipollution project in Italy' in *Environmental Damage Costs*, Paris: OECD.

Musgrave, W.F. (2000) 'Australia' in Dinar, A. (ed.) *The Political Economy of Water Pricing Reforms*, Washington, DC: World Bank.

Naess, A. (1993) 'The deep ecological movement: some philosophical aspects' in Armstrong, S.J. and Botzler, R.G. (eds) *Environmental Ethics – Divergence and Convergence*, New York: McGraw-Hill.

Nash, C., Pearce, D.W. and Stanley, J. (1975) 'Criteria for evaluating project evaluation techniques', *Journal of the American Institute of Planners*, 83–9.

National Drought Mitigation Center (1996) *Basics of Drought Planning*, Lincoln NE: University of Nebraska-Lincoln.

National Research Council (1985) *Safety of Dams: Flood and Earthquake Criteria*, Washington, DC: National Research Council.

National Research Council (1995) *Mexico City's Water Supply: Improving the Outlook for Sustainability*, Washington DC: National Research Council.

National Rivers Authority (1995a) *National Angling Survey 1994*, Fisheries Technical Report 5, London: HMSO.

National Rivers Authority (1995b) *Saving Water*, Worthing: Demand Management Centre.

National Statistics n.d. *Family Expenditure Survey*, London: National Statistics (www.statistics.gov.uk).

Navrud, S. (ed.) (1992) *Pricing the European Environment*, Oslo: Scandinavian University Press.

Navrud, S. and Bergland, O. (2001) *Value Transfer and Environmental Policy*, Policy Research Brief No. 8, Cambridge: Cambridge Research for the Environment.

Ndubiwa, M. (1996) *Problems due to Restricted Water Supplies: The City of Bulawayo's Experience*, Bulawayo: Office of the Town Clerk.

Neal, J. and Parker, D.J. (1988) *Flood Warnings in the Severn Trent Water Authority Area: An Investigation of Standards of Service, Effectiveness and Customer Service*, Enfield: Flood Hazard Research Centre.

Nemec, J. and Schaake, J.C. (1982) 'Sensitivity of water resource systems to climate variation', *Hydrological Sciences Journal* **27**, 327–43.

NERA (1999) *Capital Structure, Interest Coverage and Optimal Credit Ratings*, London: Water UK.

NERC (1975) *Flood Studies Report*, London: National Environment Research Council.

Netting, R.M. (1981) *Balancing on an Alp: Ecological Change and Continuity in a Swiss Mountain Community*, Cambridge: Cambridge University Press.

New South Wales Government (1986) *Floodplain Development Manual*, PWD 86010, Government of New South Wales.

Newson, M. (1997) *Land, Water and Development*, 2nd edition, London: Routledge.

Niemi, E., Fifield, A. and Whitelaw, E. (2001) *Coping with Competition for Water: Irrigation, Economic Growth, and the Ecosystem in the Upper Klamath Basin*, Eugene, OR: ECONorthwest.

Nixon, S. (2000) 'Review of the impacts of agriculture on water resources', paper given at Implementing the EU Water Framework Directive: A Seminar Series on Water. Seminar 1: Water and Agriculture, Brussels: WWF International, European Freshwater Programme.

NOAA (National Oceanic and Atmospheric Administration) (1993) 'Report of the NOAA Panel on contingent valuation', *Federal Register* **58**(10), 4601–14.

North Carolina Department of Environment and Natural Resources (1998) *Water Efficiency Manual*, Asheville, NC: Land-of-Sky Regional Council.

North, J.H. and Griffin, C.C. (1993) 'Water source as a housing characteristic: hedonic property valuation and willingness to pay for water', *Water Resources Research* **29**(7), 1923–9.

Noznick, R. (1974) *Anarchy, State and Utopia*, Oxford: Blackwell.

Null, R. (1995) 'User fees – the key to managing stormwater costs', *Public Works*.

O'Riordan, T. and Cameron, J. (eds) (1994) *Interpreting the Precautionary Principle*, London: Earthscan.

O'Riordan, T. and Paget, G. (1978) *Sharing Rivers and Canals*, Sports Council Study 16, London: The Sports Council.

Odeyemi, O.S. (1998) *A Sustainable Water Culture: Social-Christian Religious and Institutional Factors*, unpublished MA thesis, Enfield: Middlesex University.

OECD (1993) *Coastal Zone Management: Integrated Policies*, Paris: OECD.

Office of Water (1995) *Economic Benefits of Runoff Controls*, EPA 841-S-95-002, Washington, DC: US Environmental Protection Agency.

Office of Water (1999) *Storm Water Technology Fact Sheet: Porous Pavement*, EPA 832-F-99-023, Washington, DC: US Environmental Protection Agency.

OFWAT (1998) *Setting the Quality Framework*, Birmingham: OFWAT (http://www.ofwat.gov.uk).

OFWAT (1999) *Inset Appointments: Guidance for Applicants*, Birmingham: OFWAT.

OFWAT (2000a) *Approval of Companies' Charges Schemes 2001–2002*, Birmingham: Office of Water Services.

OFWAT (2000) *Comparing the Performance of the Water Companies in England and Wales in 1998-99 with Water Enterprises in Other Industrialised Countries*, Birmingham: OFWAT.

OFWAT (2000c) *The Proposed Acquisition of Dwr Cymru Cyfyngedig by Glas Cymru Cyfyngedig*, Birmingham: OFWAT.

OFWAT (2002a) *Maintaining Water and Sewerage Systems in England and Wales*, Birmingham: Office of Water Services.

OFWAT (2002b) *Water and Regulation: Facts and Figures*, Birmingham: Office of Water Services.

Operations Evaluation Department (1996) *India – Water Supply and Waste Water Services in Bombay: First, Second and Third Bombay Water-Supply and Sewerage Projects*, Impact Evaluation Report 15849, Washington, DC: World Bank.

Opschoor, J.B. and Vos, H.B. (1989) *Economic Instruments for Environmental Protection*, Paris: OECD.

Ormerod, P. (1994) *The Death of Economics*, London: Faber and Faber.

Ostrom, E. (1990) *Governing the Commons: The Evolution of Institutions for Collective Action*, New York: Cambridge University Press.

Otis, R.J. and Mara, D.D. (1985) *Diseno de Alcantarillado de Pequeno Diametro*, Nota Tecnica Numero 14, Washington, DC: World Bank.

Ourworld n.d. 'Micro-hydropower plants in Laos' (http://ourworld.compuserve.com/homepages/allen_inversin/Laos.htm).

Oweis, T., Hachum, A. and Kijne, J. (1999) *Water Harvesting and Supplemental Irrigation for Improved Water Use Efficiency in Dry Areas*, SWIM Paper 7, Colombo: IWMI.

Pahl, J. (1983) 'The allocation of money within marriage', *Sociological Review* **32**, 237–64.

Pahl, J. (1989) *Money and Marriage*, London: Macmillan.

Parker, D.J., Green, C.H. and Thompson, P.M. (1987) *Urban Flood Protection Benefits: A Project Appraisal Guide*, Aldershot: Gower.

Patmore, J.A. (1983) *Recreation and Resources*, Oxford: Basil Blackwell.

Paul, B.M. (1984) 'Perception of and agricultural adjustment to floods in Jamuna Floodplain, Bangladesh', *Human Ecology* **12**(1), 3–19.

Pearce, D.W. and Turner, R.K. (1990) *Economics of Natural Resources and the Environment*, Hemel Hempstead: Harvester Wheatsheaf.

Pearce, F. (1998) 'Ministry of not-so-funny walks', *The Guardian online*, July 9th, 1–3.

Penning-Rowsell, E.C. and Chatterton, J.B. (1977) *The Benefits of Flood Alleviation*, Aldershot, UK: Gower Technical Press.

Penning-Rowsell, E.C., Green, C.H., Thompson, P.M., Coker, A.C., Tunstall, S.M., Richards, C. and Parker, D.J. (1992) *The Economics of Coastal Management: A Manual of Assessment Techniques*, London: Belhaven.

Penning-Rowsell, E.C., Tunstall, S.M., Tapsell, S.M. and Parker, D.J. (2000). 'The benefits of flood warnings: real but elusive, and politically significant', *Journal of the Institution of Water and Environmental Management*, **14**, 7–14.

Penning-Rowsell, E.C., Winchester, P. and Bossman-Aggrey, P. (1987) *Flood Alleviation for Maidenhead: An Evaluation of Three Levels of Non-structural Approach*, Centre Internal Publication. Enfield: Middlesex Polytechnic.

Perry, C.J. (1996) *Alternative Approaches to Cost Sharing for Water Services to Agriculture in Egypt*, Colombo: IWMI.

Personett, M.L. (2001) *Convening Paper for the Development of a New Comprehensive Plan for the Delaware River Basin*, West Trenton: Delaware River Basin Commission.

Pettit, P. (1980) *Judging Justice: An Introduction to Contemporary Political Philosophy*, London: Routledge.

Pezzey, J. (1989) *Economic Analysis of Sustainable Growth and Sustainable Development*. Environment Department Working Paper No. 15, Washington, DC: World Bank.

Phipps, A.G. (1983) 'Utility function switching during residential search', *Goegrafiska Annaler 65B*, 23–38.

Pickford, J. (1995) *Low-cost Sanitation*, London: Centre for Intermediate Technology.

Pigram, J.J. (1999) 'Towards upstream-downstream hydrosolidarity: Australia's Murray–Darling River Basin', paper given at the Stockholm Water Symposium, Stockholm.

Pigram, J.J., Delforce, R.J., Cowell, M.L., Norris, V., Anthony G.M., Anderson, R.L. and Misgrave, W.F. (1992) *Transferable Water Entitlements in Australia*, Centre for Water Policy Research, Armidale: University of New England.

Pinkham, R. (2000) *Daylighting: New Life for Buried Streams*, Old Snowmass, CO; Rocky Mountain Institute.

Pinkham, R. n.d. *21st Century Water Systems: Scenarios, Visions and Drivers*, Old Snowmass, CO; Rocky Mountain Institute.

Pinkham, R., Ferguson, B. and Collin, T. (1999) *Re-Evaluating Stormwater: The Nine Mile Run Model for Restoration*, Snowmass: Rocky Mountain Institute.

Pinstrup-Andersen, Pandya-Lorch, R. and Rosegrant, M.W. (1999) *World Food Prospects: Critical Issues for the Early Twenty-First Century*, Washington: International Food Policy Research Institute.

Podmaniczky, L. (1999) personal communication.

Pohoryles, S. (2000) 'Program for Efficient Water Use in Middle East Agriculture', *Water for Peace in the Middle East and Southern Africa*, Geneva: Green Cross International.

Pohoryles, S. n.d. 'Efficiency of water use in agriculture: a crucial factor of water equilibrium', Geneva: Green Cross International.

Polak, P., Nanes, B. and Adhikari, D. (1998) *A Low-Cost Drip Irrigation System for Small Farmers in Developing Countries*, Lakewood, CO: International Development Enterprises (http://www.ideorg.org/lcstdrip.htm).

Porter, M.E. and van der Linde, C. (1995) 'Toward a new conception of the environment–competitiveness relationship', *Journal of Economic Perspectives* **9**(4), 97–131.

Postel, S. (1992) *The Last Oasis: Facing Water Scarcity*, London: Earthscan.

Postel, S. (1993) 'Water and agriculture' in Gleick, P.H. (ed.) *Water in Crisis: A Guide to the World's Fresh Water Resources*, Oxford: Oxford University Press.

Poulton, E.C. (1979) 'Biases in quantitative judgements', *Applied Ergonomics* **13**(1), 31–42.

Poulton, E.C. (1989) *Bias in Quantifying Judgments*, Hove: Lawrence Erlbaum.

Primen 2001 *The Cost of Power Disturbances to Industrial and Digital Economy Companies*, Palo Alto: Electric Power Research Institute.

Priscoli, J.D. (1996) *Conflict Management, Collaboration and Management in International Water Resources Issues*, IWR Working Paper 96-ADR-WP-6, Fort Belvoir, VA: Institute for Water Resources, US Army Corps of Engineers.

Pritchard, S. (2001) 'It didn't start with Edwards', *International Water Power and Dam Construction* **53**(8), 36–7.

Pugh, C.A. and Tomlinson, J.J. (1999) 'High-efficiency washing machine demonstration, Bern, Kansas', paper given at Conserv 99, Knoxville: Oak Ridge National Laboratory.

Purseglove, J. (1988) *Taming the Flood*, Oxford: Oxford University Press.

Putnam, Hayes and Bartlett Inc. (1980) *Comparisons of Estimated and Actual Pollution Control Capital Expenditures for Selected Industries*, Report to the Office of Planning and Evaluation, USA.

Quimby, A. and Watts, G. (1981) *Human Factors and Driving Performance*, TRRL Laboratory Report 1004, Crowthorne: Transport and Road Research Laboratory.

Rana, K. (1997) 'Recent trends in global aquaculture production: 1984–1995', *FAO Aquaculture Newsletter* **16**, 14–19.

Ras Gharib, Hurghada, Safaga, Quseir, Marsa Alam, Shalatein, Abu Ramad and Halaib (1997) *Hazard Assessment and Mitigative Measures of Flash Flooding on the Red Sea Towns, Egypt*, NARSS Special Publication No. 1, Cairo: National Authority for Remote Sensing and Space Sciences (in Arabic).

Rathgeber, E. (1996) 'Women, men, and water-resource management in Africa' in Rached, E., Rathgeber, E. and Brooks, D.B. (1996) *Water Management in Africa and the Middle East*, Ottawa: IDRC.

Rawls, J. (1971) *A Theory of Justice*, Cambridge, MA: Belknap.

Rayment, M., Bartram, H. and Curtoys, J. (1998) *Pesticide Taxes: A Discussion Paper*, Sandy: Royal Society for the Protection of Birds.

Rayner, M.J., Mathias, C.H. and Green, C.H. (1984) 'Soar Valley – a note', *ECOS* **5**(3), 33–6.

Read, G.F. and Vickridge, I. (1990) *The Environmental Impact of Sewerage Replacement and Renovation*, NO-DIG 90, ISTT, Rotterdam.

Reed, R.A. (1995) *Sustainable Sewerage: Guidelines for Community Schemes*, London: Centre for Intermediate Technology.

Rees, J. (1969) *Industrial Demand for Water: A Study of South-east England*, London: Weidenfeld and Nicolson.

Rees, J.A., Williams, S., Atkins, J.P., Hammond, C.J. and Trotter, S.D. (1993) *Economics of Water Resource Management*, R&D Note 128, Marlow: Foundation for Water Research.

Rees, Y., Mobbs, P., Barraque, B., Cambon, S., Kraemer, R.A. and Nowell-Smith, H. (1996) *International Comparison of the Demand for Water*, Birmingham: OFWAT.

Reisner, M. (1993) *Cadillac Desert: The American West and its Disappearing Water*, New York: Viking.

Reiter, P. (2000) *International Methods of Risk Analysis, Damage Evaluation and Social Impact Studies concerning Dam-Break Accidents*, Helsinki: PR Water Consulting.

Renwick, M., Green, R. and McCorkle, C. (1998) *Measuring the Price Responsiveness of Residential Water Demand in California's Urban Areas*, Sacramento: California Department of Water Resources.

Repetto, R. (1986) *Skimming the Water*, Washington, DC: World Resources Institute.

Reppert, R. (1992) *National Wetland Mitigation Banking Study*, IWR Report 92-WMB-1, Alexandria, VA: Institute for Water Resources, US Army Corps of Engineers.

Revenga, C., Brunner, J., Henninger, N., Kassem, K. and Payne, R. (2000) *Pilot Analysis of Global Ecosystems: Freshwater Systems*, Washington, DC: World Resources Institute.

Riley, A.L. (1998) *Restoring Streams in Cities: A Guide for Planners, Policymakers and Citizens*, Washington, DC: Island Press.

Rittel, H. and Webber, M.M. (1974) 'Wicked problems' in Cross, N., Elliott, D. and Roy, R. (eds) *Man-Made Futures*, London: Hutchinson.

River Planning Division (1990) *Investigation of River Economy*, Tokyo: River Bureau, Ministry of Construction.

Robbins, L. (1935) *An Essay on the Nature and Significance of Economic Science*, 2nd edition, London: Macmillan.

Roberts, P. (1991) 'Anthropological perspectives on the household', *IDS Bulletin* **22**, 60–6.

Rockstrom, J., Gordon, L., Folke, C., Falkenmark, M. and Engwall, M. (1999) 'Linkages among water vapor flows, food production, and terrestrial ecosystem services', *Conservation Ecology* **3**(2).

Rogers, P., Bhatia, R. and Huber, A. (1998) *Water as a Social and Economic Good: How to Put the Principle into Practice*, TAC Background Papers No. 2, Stockholm: Global Water Partnership.

Rogers, P., Lydon, P. and Seckler, D. (1989) *Eastern Waters Study: Strategies to Manage Flood and Drought in the Ganges-Brahmaputra Basin*, Washington, DC: USAID.

Rokeach, M. (1973) *The Nature of Human Value*, New York: Free Press.

Romer, P. (1990) 'Endogenous technological change', *Journal of Political Economy* **98**(5), 574–5.

Romer, P. (1994) 'The origins of endogenous growth', *Journal of Economic Perspectives* **8**(1), 3–22.

Rose, G.D. (1999) *Community-Based Technologies for Domestic Wastewater Treatment and Reuse: Options for urban agriculture*, Cities Feeding People Series – Report 27, Ottawa: International Development Research Centre.

Rosegrant, M.W. and Perez, N.D. n.d. *Water Resources Development in Africa: A Review and Synthesis of Issues, Potentials, and Strategies for the Future.*

Rosegrant, M.W. and Ringler, C. (1998) *Impact on Food Security and Rural Development of Reallocating Water from Agriculture to Other Uses*, Background paper 176, New York: United Nations Commission on Sustainable Development.

Rosen, S. (1974) 'Hedonic prices and implicit markets: product differentiation in pure competition', *Journal of Political Economy* **82**, 34–55.

Rosser, R. (1994) *Cognitive Development: Psychological and Biological Perspectives*, Boston: Allyn and Bacon.

Royal Commission on Environmental Pollution (2000) *Energy – the Changing Climate*, London: Royal Commission on Environmental Pollution.

RPA (Risk and Policy Analysts) (2000) *Economic Instruments in Relation to Water Abstraction*, London: Department for the Environment, Food and Rural Affairs.

Russell, B. (1954) *Human Society in Ethics and Politics*, London: Allen and Unwin.

Russell, C.S., Arey, D.G. and Kates, R.W. (1970) *Drought and Water Supply: Implications of the Massachusetts Experience for Municipal Planning*, Baltimore: Johns Hopkins University Press.

Russell, C.S., Vaughan, W.J., Clark, C.D., Rodriguez, D.J. and Darling, A.H. (2001) *Investing in Water Quality*, Washington, DC: Inter-American Development Bank.

Ryan, M.J. and Bonfield, E.H. (1975) 'The Fishbein extended model and consumer behavior', *Journal of Consumer Research* **2**, 111–36.

Sackman, H. (1975) *Delphi Critique*, Lexington: Lexington Books.

SACTRA (1994) *Trunk Roads and the Generation of Traffic*, London: Standing Advisory Committee on Trunk Road Assessment.

SACTRA (2000) *Transport Investment, Transport Intensity and Economic Growth: Interim Report*, London: Standing Advisory Committee on Trunk Road Assessment.

Sagoff, M. (1988) *The Economy of the Earth*, Cambridge: University Press.

Sala, L. and Millet, X. (1997) *Aspectos bāsicos de la reutilización de las aquas residuales regeneradas para el riego de campos de golf*, Apuntes de las Jornadas Tecnicas del Golf, Madrid: Consorci de la Costa Brava.

Saleh, R.M. and Dinar, A. (1999) *Evaluating Water Institutions and Water Sector Performance*, World Bank Technical Paper No. 447, Washington, DC: World Bank.

Sally, D. (1995) 'Conversation and cooperation in social dilemmas: a meta analysis of experiments from 1958 to 1992', *Rationality and Society* **7**(1), 58–92.

Samuelson, P.A. (1954) 'The pure theory of public expenditure', *Review of Economics and Statistics* **36**, 387–9.

Samuelson, P.A. (1970) *Economics*, 8th edition, New York: McGraw-Hill.

Sandstrom, K. (1995) 'Modeling the effects of rainfall variability on groundwater recharge in semi-arid Tanzania', *Nordic Hydrology* **26**, 313–20.

Sanmugnathan, K., Heuperman, A., Hussain, K., Prinz, D., Salas, P.A., Thakker, H., Shevah, Y. and Smith, L. (2000) *Assessment of Irrigation Options*, Cape Town: World Commission on Dams.

Savage, G. (2001) *Charges Dropped! Admission Fees to Cultural Attractions*, Sydney: Environmetrics (www.environmentrics.com.au).

Saywell, D. (1999) *Micro-credit for Sanitation*, WELL Technical Brief, Loughborough: WELL.

Schlager, E. and Ostrom, E. (1992) 'Property-rights regimes and natural resources: a conceptual analysis', *Land Economics* **68**(3), 249–62.

Schlemmer, L., Steward, J. and Whittles, J. (1989) *Socio-economic Effects of Water Restrictions on Local Authorities, Selected Industrial and Commercial Establishments and Other Private Agencies*, Report No. 68/1/89, Pretoria: Water Research Commission.

Schmitz, M. (2001) *Crop Protection: Costs and Benefits to Society and the Economy*, Agribusiness Institute, University of Giessen.

Schoeffel, P. (1995) 'Cultural and institutional issues in the appraisal of projects in developing countries: South Pacific water resources', *Project Appraisal* **10**(3), 155–61.

Schueler, T. (1995) 'Crafting better urban watershed protection plans', *Watershed Protection Techniques* **2**(2) (http://www.pipeline.com/~mrunoff/).

Schwartz, M. and Thompson, M. (1990) *Divided We Stand: Redefining Politics, Technology and Social Choice*, London: Harvester Wheatsheaf.

Schwartz, P. (1966) 'John Stuart Mill and laissez faire: London Water', *Economica*, 71–83.

Scott, C.A., Zarazua, J.A. and Levine, G. (2000) *Urban Wastewater Reuse for Crop Production in the Water-Short Guanajuato River Basin, Mexico*, Research Report 41, Colombo: IWMI.

Scott, R. (1995) *Flooding of Central and East Rand Gold Mines: An Investigation into Controls over the Inflow Rate, Water Quality and its Predicted Impacts of Flooded Mines*, report to the Water Research Commission, WRC Report No. 4861/95, Institute for Groundwater Studies, University of the Orange Free State.

Scott, R.W. (1995) *Institutions and Organisations*, London: Sage.

Scottish Natural Heritage (1993) *Visitor Monitoring Training Manual*, Edinburgh: Scottish Natural Heritage.

Seattle Public Utilities (1998) *Water Conservation Potential Assessment: Executive Summary*, Seattle: Seattle Public Utilities.

Seckler, D. (1996) *The New Era of Water Resources Management: From 'Dry' to 'Wet' Water Savings*, Research Report 1, Colombo: IWMI.

Seckler, D. (2000) *Revisiting the 'IWMI Paradigm': Increasing the Efficiency and Productivity of Water Use*, IWMI Water Brief 2, Colombo: International Water Management Institute.

Seckler, D., Barker, R. and Amarasinghe, U. (1999) 'Water scarcity in the twenty-first century', *Water Resources Development* **15**, 29–42.

Seckler, D., Molden, D. and Barker, R. (1999) *Water Scarcity in the Twenty-First Century*, IWMI Water Brief, Colombo: International Water Management Institute.

Seligman, C., Syme, G.J. and Kirby, A. (1994) 'The role of values and ethical principles in judgments of environmental dilemmas', *Journal of Social Issues* **59**(3), 105–19.

Sen, A.K. (1987) *On Ethics and Economics*, Oxford: Basil Blackwell.

Sen, A.K. (1977) 'Rational fools: a critique of the behavioral foundation of economic theory', *Journal of Philosophy and Public Affairs* **6**, 317–44.

Sen, A.K. (1990) 'Gender and cooperative conflicts' in Tinker, I. (ed.) *Peasant Inequalities*, Oxford: Oxford University Press.

Sen, A.K. (1992) *Inequality Re-examined*, Oxford: Clarendon.

Seyam, I.M., Hoekstra, A.Y., Ngabirano, G.S. and Savenije, H.H.G. (2001) 'The value of freshwater wetlands in the Zambezi basin', paper given at the AWRA/IWLRI conference, Dundee.

Shackleton, S., Shackleton, C. and Cousins, B. (2000) *Re-evaluating the Communal Lands of Southern Africa: New Understandings of Rural Livelihoods*, Natural Resource Perspectives 62, London: Overseas Development Institute.

Shah, T. (1993) *Groundwater Market and Irrigation Development: Political Economy and Practical Policy*, Bombay: Oxford University Press.

Shah, T., Molden, D., Sakthivadivel, R. and Seckler, D. (2000) *The Global Groundwater Situation: Overview of Opportunities and Challenges*, Colombo: IWMI.

Shaw, B.D. (1984) 'Water and society in the ancient Maghrib: technology, property and development', *Antiquites Africaines* **20**, 121–73.

Shevah, Y. (2000) *Irrigation and Agriculture Experience and Options in Israel*, Cape Town: World Commission on Dams.

Shewarega, F. (1999) 'Micro hydropower – a neglected resource in Ethiopia', *Addis Tribune*, 20 August.

Shiklomanov, I.A. (1998) *World Water Resources: A New Appraisal and Assessment for the 21st* Century, Paris: UNESCO.

Shirley, M.M., Xu, L.C. and Zuluaga, A.M. (2000) *Reforming the Urban Water System in Santiago, Chile*, Policy Research Working Paper 2294, Washington, DC: World Bank.

Shorter, F. (1989) 'Cairo's leap forward – people, households, and dwelling space', *Cairo Papers in Social Science 12, Monograph 1*, Cairo: The American University in Cairo Press.

Shucksmith, D.M. (1979) 'The demand for angling at the Derwent Reservoir 1970 to 1976', *Journal of Agricultural Economics* **30**, 25–37.

Shuval, H.I., Adin, A., Fattal, B., Rawitz, E. and Yekutiel, P. (1986) *Wastewater Irrigation in Developing Countries: Health Effects and Technical Solutions*, World Bank Technical Paper Number 51, Washington, DC: World Bank.

Shuval, H., Adin, A., Fattal, B., Rawitz, E. and Yekutiel, P. (1990) *Integrated Resource Recovery. Wastewater Irrigation in Developing Countries, Health Effects and Technical Solutions*, Washington, DC: World Bank.

Silva, W., Klijn, F. and Dijkman, J. (2001) *Room for the Rhine Branches in the Netherlands*, Delft: RIZA, WL/Delft Hydraulics.

Simmonds, A. (1976) *The Recreational Value of Beaches*, East Anglian Coastal Research Programme, Report No. 4, Norwich: University of East Anglia.

Simmons, I.G. (1989) *Changing the Face of the Earth*, Oxford: Basil Blackwell.

Simon, H.A. (1986) 'Rationality in psychology and economics' in Hogarth, R.M. and Reder, M.W. (eds) *Choice: The Contrast between Economics and Psychology*, Chicago: Chicago University Press.

Slovic, P., Lichtenstein, S. and Fischhoff, B. (1976) *Cognitive Processes and Societal Risk Taking*, ORI research monograph **15**(2), Oregon: Oregon Research Institute.

Smedley, P.L. and Kinniburgh, D.G. (2002) 'A review of the source, behaviour and distribution of arsenic in natural waters', *Applied Geochemistry* **17**, 517–68.

Smith, A. (1986) *The Wealth of Nations Books I-III*, Harmondsworth: Penguin.

Smith, D.I. (1998) *Water in Australia Resources and Management*, Oxford: Oxford University Press.

Smith, D.M. (1979) *Where the Grass is Greener: Living in an Unequal World*, Harmondsworth: Penguin.

Smith, M. (1992) *CROPWAT – A Computer Program for Irrigation Planning and Management*, FAO Irrigation and Drainage Paper No. 49, Rome: FAO.

Smith, M., Allen, R. and Pereira, L. (1990) *Revised FAO Methodology for Crop Water Requirements*, Rome: FAO.

Smith, P. (1990) *A Chaotic Model of Price Determination*, Manchester: IDPM, University of Manchester.

Smith, R. and Kavanagh, N. (1969) 'Measurements of the benefits of trout fishing', *Journal of Leisure Research* **1**(4), 316–32.

Smith, V.K. and Desvouges, W.H. (1986) *Measuring Water Quality Benefits*, Boston: Kluwer-Nijhoff.

Smith, V.K., Van Houtven, G.L., Pattanayek, S. and Bingham, T.H. (2000) *Improving the Practice of Benefit Transfer: A Preference Calibration Approach*, Washington: Office of Water, US Environmental Protection Agency.

Smith, V.K., Zhang, X. and Palmquist, R.B. (1995) *Marine Debris, Beach Quality and Non-Market Values*, Discussion Paper 96-07, Washington, DC: Resources for the Future.

Smithson, M. (1985) 'Toward a social theory of ignorance', *Journal for the Theory of Social Behaviour* **15**, 151–72.

Solanes, M. (1999) *Institutional and Legal Issues Relevant to the Implementation of Water Markets*, Economic Commission for Latin America and the Caribbean.

Sorensen, J.H. (1988) *Evaluation of Warning and Protective Action Implementation Times for Chemical Weapons Accidents* ORNL/TM-10437, Oak Ridge: Oak Ridge National Laboratory.

Soule, G. (1955) *Time for Living*, New York: Viking.

South East Region (1999) *Water for India's Poor: Who Pays the Price for Broken Promises?*, New Delhi: UNDP-World Bank Water and Sanitation Program.

Spash, C.L. (1997) 'Ethics and environmental attitudes with implications for economic valuation', *Journal of Environmental Management* **50**, 403–16.

Spash, C.L. (2000) 'Multiple value expression in contingent valuation: economics and ethics', *Environmental Science and Technology* **34**(8), 1433–8.

Sprey, J. (1969) 'The family as a system in conflicts', *Journal of Marriage and Family* **31**, 699–706.

Squire, L. and van der Tak, H. (1975) *Economic Analysis of Projects*, Baltimore: Johns Hopkins.

Stabler, M.J. and Ash, S.E. (1978) *The Amenity Demand for Inland Waterways*, Reading: Amenity Waterways Study Unit, University of Reading.

Stanners, D. and Bourdeau, P. (eds) (1995) *Europe's Environment. The Dobris Assessment*, Copenhagen: European Environment Agency.

Stern, P.C., Dietz, T., Abel T., Guagnano, G.A. and Kalof, L. (1999) 'A value-belief-norm theory of support for social movements', *Human Ecology Review* **6**(2), 81–97.

Stevens, A.S. (1988) 'Pueblo water rights in New Mexico', *Natural Resources Journal* **28**, 535–83.

Stevens, S.S. (1975) *Psychophysics: Introduction to its Perceptual, Neural, and Social Prospects*, New York: Wiley.

Stewart, I. (1990) *Does God Play Dice? The Mathematics of Chaos*, Harmondsworth: Penguin.

Stomal, B. and Weigel, J.-Y. n.d. *Aquaculture Economics in Africa and the Middle East*, Rome: FAO.

Stroessner, S.J. and Heuer, L.B. (1996) 'Cognitive bias in procedural justice: formation and implications of illusory correlations in perceived intergroup fairness', *Journal of Personality and Social Psychology* **71**(4), 717–28.

Sturtevant, L.A., Johnson, F.R. and Desvouges, W.H. (1995) *A Meta-analysis of Recreational Fishing*, Durham, NC: Triangle Economic Research.

Sundquist, B. (2000) *Irrigated Lands Degradation: A Global Perspective* (http://www.alltel.net?~bsundquist1/ir0.html).

Sunstein, C.R. (1999) *The Law of Group Polarization*, Chicago: Law School, University of Chicago.

Surendran, S.S. (2001) The Development of an In-House Grey and Roof Water Reclamation and Recycling System for Large Institutions, unpublished PhD thesis, Dept of Civil and Building Engineering, Loughborough University.

Surr, M., Starmer, A., Watson, D., Young, D., Green, C. and Potts, E. (1993) *Cairo Wastewater Project, Egypt: Interim Evaluation*, London: Overseas Development Administration.

Sutawan, N. (1989) *Farmer-Managed Irrigation Systems and the Impact of Government Assistance: A Note from Bali, Indonesia*, Colombo: IWMI.

Swedish Environmental Protection Agency (1996) *The Public Access – Right and Wrong in the Countryside*, Stockholm: Swedish Environmental Protection Agency.

Sweeney, D.V. (2000) 'Affidavit of Donald C Sweeney' Washington, DC: Taxpayers for Common Sense.

Sweet, L. (1999) 'Margins of hope', *IDRC Briefing* **1**, June.

Sydney Water Board n.d. *Hard Rain*, Sydney: Sydney Water Board.

Syme, G.J. and Nancarrow, B.E. (1997) 'The determinants of perception of fairness in the allocation of water to multiple uses', *Water Resources Research* **33**(9), 2143–52.

Tahseen, J. n.d. 'Women, human capital and livelihoods: an ergonomics perspective', *Natural Resources Perspectives* **54**.

Tannen, D. (1991) *You Just Don't Understand: Women and Men in Conversation*, London: Virago.

Tapsell, S.M., Fordham, M., Tunstall, S.M., Rivilla, M.J., Garner, J.L. and Portou, J. (1995) *River Skerne Public Perception Survey: Stage 2 – The River Restoration Project*, RRP 1995, Report to the River Restoration Project, Enfield: Flood Hazard Research Centre.

Tardieu, H. n.d. 'Water management for irrigation and environment in a water-stressed basin in south-west France: charging is an important tool, but is it sufficient?' Colombo: International Water Management Institute.

Tate, D.M. (1986) 'Structural change implications for industrial water use', *Water Resources Research* **22**(11), 1526–30.

Tate, D.M. (1989) 'Water demand management in Canada: a review and assessment', *Canadian Water Resources Journal* **14**(4), 71–82.

Tate, D.M., Renzetti, S. and Shaw, H.A. (1992) *Economic Instruments for Water Management: The Case for Industrial Water Pricing*, Social Science Series 26, Ottawa, ON: Economics and Conservation Branch, Environment Canada.

Tate, D.M. and Scharf, D.N. (1985) *Water Use in Canadian Industry, 1981, Social Science Series* No. 19, Water Planning and Management Branch, Ottawa: Inland Waters Directorate, Environment Canada.

Tate, J.C. (1968) Social Cost/Benefit Analysis and Rural Water Supply – Evaluation of a Proposed Project in the West Midlands, MA thesis submitted to the University of Lancaster.

Taylor, A.J. (1972) *Laissez-faire and State Intervention in Nineteenth-Century Britain*, London: Macmillan.

Taylor Binnie and Partners (1977) *Cairo Wastewater Project Final Master Plan*, Redhill: Taylor Binnie and Partners.

Texas Water Development Board (1997) *Texas Guide to Rainwater Harvesting*. Austin, TX: Texas Water Development Board.

Thackrey, J.E., Cocker, V. and Archibald, C. (1978a) 'The Malvern and Mansfield studies of domestic water usage: Part 1', *Proceedings of the Institution of Civil Engineers* **64**, 37–61.

Thackrey, J.E., Cocker, V. and Archibald, C. (1978b) 'The Malvern and Mansfield studies of domestic water usage: Part 2', *Proceedings of the Institution of Civil Engineers* **64**, 403–32.

Thibaut, J. and Walker, L. (1975) *Procedural Justice: A Psychological Analysis*, Hillsdale, NJ: Erlbaum.

Thomas, J.F. and Syme, G.J. (1988) 'Estimating residential price elasticity of demand for water: a contingent valuation approach', *Water Resources Research* **24**(11), 1847–57.

Thomas-Slayter, B. and Rocheleau, D. (1995) *Gender, Environment and Development in Kenya. A Grassroots Perspective*, London: Lynee Reinner.

Timmermans, H.J.P. (1984) 'Decompostional multiattribute preference models in spatial choice analysis: a review of recent developments', *Progress in Human Geography* **8**, 189–221.

Timmermans, H.J.P. and Veldhuisen, K.J. (1981) 'Behavioural models and spatial planning: some methodological considerations and empirical tests', *Environment and Planning A13*, 1485–98.

Tomlinson, J.J. and Rizy, D.T. (1998) *Bern Clothes Washer Study Final Report*, ORNL/M-6382, Knoxville: Oak Ridge National Laboratory.

Torterotot, J.-P. (1992) *Analyse des reponse a l'annonce de crue et impact sur les dommages dus aux inondations dans plusieurs region de France*, Noisy-le-Grand: CERGRENE.

Torterotot, J.-P. (1993) *Review of Best Practice in European Strategic Land Use Planning*, report for the National Rivers Authority, Noisy-le-Grand: CERGRENE.

Tourism and Recreation Research Unit (1983) *Recreation Site Survey Manual: Methods and Techniques for Conducting Visitor Surveys*, London: Spon.

Tunstall, S.M. (1995) *Public Perceptions of Rivers and River Water Quality: Results from a Focus Group Study*, report to the Foundation for Water Research, Enfield: Flood Hazard Research Centre.

Tunstall, S.M., Green, C.H., Fordham, M.H. and House, M.A. (1997) 'Public perception of freshwater quality with particular reference to rivers in England and Wales' in Boon, P.J. and Howell, D. (eds) *Freshwater Quality: Defining the Indefinable?* Edinburgh: The Stationery Office.

Turton, A.R. and Ohlsson, L. (1999) *Water Scarcity and Social Adaptive Capacity: Towards an Understanding of the Social Dynamics of Managing Water Scarcity in Developing Countries*, paper given at the 9th Stockholm Water Symposium, Stockholm.

Turton, C. and Farrington, J. (1998) 'Enhancing rural livelihoods through participatory watershed development in India', *Natural Resource Perspectives* **34**.

Tversky, A. and Kahneman, D. (1973) 'Availability: a heuristic for judging frequency and probability', *Cognitive Psychology* **5**, 207–32.

Tversky, A. and Kahneman, D. (1981) 'The framing of decisions and the psychology of choice', *Science* **211**, 453–8.

Tyler, T.R. and Degoey, P. (1995) 'Collective restraint in social dilemmas: procedural justice and social identification effects on support for authorities', *Journal of Personality and Social Psychology* **69**(3), 482–97.

UKWIR (2001) *Understanding Burst Rate Patterns of Water Pipes*, London: UKWIR.

UNDP (1995) *Human Development Report 1995*, Oxford: Oxford University Press.

UNDR (United Nations Disaster Relief Co-ordinator) (1984) *Disaster Prevention and Mitigation* vol. 11, Geneva: UNDR.

UNEP (2000) *Sourcebook of Alternative Technologies for Freshwater Augmentation in Some Countries in Asia*, Tokyo: International Environmental Technology Centre.

UNESCO (1979) *World Map Of Arid Zones*, Paris: UNESCO.

US General Accounting Office (1994) *Water Markets: Increasing Federal Revenues through Water Transfers*, GAO/RCED-94-164, Washington, DC: United States General Accounting Office.

US General Accounting Office (1996) *Bureau of Reclamation: Information on Allocation and Repayment of Costs of Constructing Water Projects*, GAO/RCED-96-109, Washington, DC: United States General Accounting Office.

US AID (1982) *Methods of Developing Sources of Ground Water*, RWS. 2.M, LIFEWATER (http://www.lifewater.org/wfw/wfwindex.htm).

US Congress, Office of Technology Assessment (1993) *Preparing for an Uncertain Climate* – Vol 1, OTA-O-567, Washington, DC: US Government Printing Office.

US Department of Health and Human Services (1999) *Targeting Arthritis: The Nation's Leading Cause of Disability*, Atlanta, GA: Centers for Disease Control and Prevention.

US Water Resources Council (1983) *Economic and Environmental Principles and Guidelines for Water and Related Land Resources Implementation Studies*, Washington, DC: US Government Printing Office.

USACE (US Army Corps of Engineers) (1994) *Managing Water For Drought*, IWR Report 94-NDS-8, Fort Belvoir, VA: Institute for Water Resources.

USACE (US Army Corps of Engineers) (1995) *National Study of Water Management During Drought: The Report to the US Congress*, IWR Report 94-NDS-12, Fort Belvoir, VA: Institute for Water Resources, US Army Corps of Engineers.

USACE (United States Army Corps of Engineers (1998) *Flood Proofing Performance – Successes and Failures*, National Flood Proofing Committee (http://www/usace.army.mil/inet/functions/cw/cecwp/nfpc.htm).

USDA (2001) *Historical Track Records*, Washington, DC: National Agricultural Statistics Service, US Department of Agriculture.

US EPA (United States Environmental Protection Agency) (2000) *Guidelines for Preparing Economic Analyses*, EPA- 240-R-00-003, Washington, DC: US EPA.

US EPA (US Environment Protection Agency) (1995) *Cleaner Water through Conservation*, Washington, DC: United States Environmental Protection Agency.

US EPA (US Environment Protection Agency) (1998) *Water Conservation Plan Guidelines*, Washington, DC: US EPA.

US EPA (US Environment Protection Agency) (2000a) *Storm Water Phase II Final Rule – Illicit Discharge Detection and Elimination Minimum Control Measure*, EPA 833-F-00-007, Fact Sheet 2.5, Washington, DC: US EPA.

US EPA (US Environment Protection Agency) (2000b) *The Quality of Our Nation's Waters*, EPA841-S-00-001, Washington, DC: US EPA.

USGS (US Geological Survey) n.d. *The Quality of Our Nation's Waters; Nutrients and Pesticides*, US Geological Survey Circular 1225, Washington, DC: United States Geological Survey.

van Beukering, P., van Drumen, M., Dorland, K., Jansen, H., Ozdemiroglu, E. and Pearce, D. (1998) *External Economic Benefits and Costs in Water and Solid Waste Investments*, Report R98/11, Amsterdam: vrije Universiteit.

van der Merwe, B. (1999) 'Reuse of water in Windhoek, Namibia', paper given at the 9th Stockholm Water Symposium, Stockholm.

van Koppen, B. n.d. 'Stakeholder identification and participation', paper given at an IWMI workshop, Colombo: IWMI.

van Liere, K.D. and Dunlap, R.E. (1981) 'Environmental concern: does it make a difference how it's measured?', *Environment and Behavior* **13**(6), 651–76.

van Wesemael, B., Posen, J., Benet, A.S., Barrionuevos, L.C. and Pulgdefabregas, J. (1998) 'Collection and storage of runoff from hillslopes in a semi-arid environment: geomorphic and hydrologic aspects of the alijbe system in Almeria Province, Spain', *Journal of Arid Environments* **40**(1), 1–14.

van Wijk-Sijbesma, C. (1985) *Participation of Women in Water Supply and Sanitation – Roles and Realities*, Technical Paper 22, The Hague: International Reference Centre for Community Water Supply and Sanitation.

Veck and Bill (1998) *Estimation of the Residential Price Elasticity of Demand for Water by means of a Contingent Valuation Approach*, Report 790/1/00, Pretoria: Water Research Commission.

Vermillon, D.L. (1997) *Impacts of Irrigation Management Transfer: A Review of the Evidence*, Research Report 11, Colombo: IWMI.

VEWIN (2001) *Reflections on Performance 2000: Benchmarking in the Dutch Drinking Water Industry*, Rijswijk: VEWIN.

Vickerman, R.W. (1975) *The Economics of Leisure and Recreation*, London: Macmillan.

Vickers, A. (2001) *Handbook of Water Use and Conservation*, WaterPlow Press.

Vicory, A.H. (2001) 'Applying integrated river basin management concepts within the U.S.', paper given at the IWEX 2001 Seminar 'Integrated River Basin Management – An Overview of Policy, Costs and Benefits', Birmingham.

Villarejo, D. (1996) *93640 at Risk: Farmers, Workers and Townspeople in an Era of Water Uncertainty*, Publication 16, California Institute for Rural Studies.

von Braun, J., Teklu, T. and Webb, P. (1999) *Famine in Africa: Causes, Responses and Prevention*, Baltimore: Johns Hopkins.

Von Weizsacker, E., Lovins, A.B. and Lovins, L.H. (1997) *Factor Four: Doubling Wealth, Halving Resource Use*, London: Earthscan.

von Winterfeldt, D. and Edwards, W. (1986) *Decision Analysis and Behavioral Research*, Cambridge: Cambridge University Press.

Wagret, P. (1967) *Polderlands*, London: Methuen.

Walsh, R.G. (1986) *Recreation Economic Decisions: Comparing Benefits and Costs*, State College PA: Venture.

Walsh, R.G., Johnson, D.M. and McKean, J.R. (1992) "Benefit transfer of outdoor recreation demand studies, 1968–1988', *Water Resources Research* **28**(3), 707–13.

Walters, C. (1986) *Adaptive Management of Renewable Resources*, New York: McGraw-Hill.

Water and Sanitation Program n.d. *An Anthropological View of Sanitation Issues in Rural Bolivia. A Summary*, Washington, DC: World Bank.

Water Research Centre (1985) *Cost Information for Water Supply and Sewage Disposal*, TR61, Swindon: Water Research Centre.

Water Research Commission (2000) *An Economic and Technical Evaluation of Regional Treatment Options for Point Source Gold Mine Effluents Entering the Vaal Barrage Catchment*, Report No. 800/1/00, Pretoria: Water Research Commission.

Water Research Commission (2001) 'A comparison of the water use of wattle-invaded and indigenous riparian plant communities', Report 808/1/01, Pretoria: Water Research Commission.

Water Services Corporation (1994) *Annual Report 1994*, Luqa, Malta: Water Services Corporation.

Water U.K. (2001) *The Cost of Pesticide Use in Agriculture*, London: Water UK.

Watson, G. (1995) *Good Sewers Cheap? Agency Customer Interactions in Low-Cost Urban Sanitation in Brazil*, Washington, DC: World Bank.

Watson, I.A. (1989) 'The relationship between human factors, reliability and management' in van der Staal, and van Vught, F.A. (eds) *Impact Forecasting and Assessment*, Delft: Delft University Press.

WCD (World Commission on Dams) (2000) *Dams and Development – A New Framework for Decision-Making*, London: Earthscan.

Weatherhead, E.K., Price, A.J., Morris, J. and Burton, M. (1994) *Demand for Irrigation Water*, National Rivers Authority R&D Report 14, London: HMSO.

Webb, P. and Iskandarani, M. (1998) *Water Insecurity and the Poor*, Bonn: ZEF Bonn.

Wester, P., Burton, M. and Mestre-Rodriquez, E. n.d. 'Managing the water transition in the Lerma-Chapala Basin, Mexico' Colombo: International Water Management Institute.

Wheaton, E.E. and Arthur, L.M. (eds) (1989) *Environmental and Economic Impacts of the 1988 Drought: With Emphasis on Saskatchewan and Manitoba*, Saskatoon: Saskatchewan Research Council.

Wheeler, D. *et al.*(2000) *Greening Industry: New Roles for Communities, Markets, and Governments*, Oxford: Oxford University Press.

White, G.F., Bradley, D.J. and White, A.U. (1972) *Drawers of Water: Domestic Water Use in East Africa*, Chicago, IL: University of Chicago.

White, I., Heath, L. and Melville, M. (1999) 'Ecological impacts of flood mitigation and drainage in coastal lowlands', *Australian Journal of Emergency Management*, Spring, 9–15.

White, L. (1982) *Medieval Technology and Social Change*, Oxford: Oxford University Press.

White, T.A. (1997) 'Private exchange and social capital: multiple functions of collective action in Haiti' in Swallow, B.M., Meinzen-Dick, R.S., Jackson, L.A., Williams, T.O. and White, T.A. *Multiple Functions of Common Property Regimes*, EPTD Workshop Summary Paper 5, Washington, DC: International Food Policy Technology Division.

Whittington, D. (1996) *Administering Contingent Valuation Surveys in Developing Countries*, Singapore: International Development Research Centre (www.indc.org.sg).

WHO (World Health Organisation) (1987) *Wastewater Stabilisation Ponds: Principles of Planning and Practice*, WHO EMRO Technical Publication No. 10, Alexandria: WHO.

Wicke, L. (1986) *Die Okologischen Milliarden*, Berlin.

Williams, N. (1967) *Linear and Non-Linear Programming in Industry*, London: Pitman.

Williams, P. and Kilroy, D. (2000) *Calibrating Price in ACA: The ACA Price Effect and How to Manage It*, Sequim, WA: Sawtooth Software.

Williams, P.R. (1997) *The Role of Disaster in the Development of Agriculture and the Evolution of Social Complexity in the South-Central Andes*, unpublished PhD thesis, University of Florida.

Willis, K., Beale, N., Calder, N. and Freer, D. (1993) *Paying for Heritage: What Price For Durham Cathedral?*, Working Paper 43, Newcastle-upon-Tyne: ESRC Countryside Change Initiative.

Wilson, D., Payne, D. and Gentleman, H. (1993) *Domestic Water Consumption in Scotland in 1991; Volume 1 – The Main Study Report*, Marlow: Foundation for Water Research.

Wilson, G. (1991) 'Thoughts on the cooperative conflict model of the household in relation to economic method', *IDS Bulletin* **22**(1), 31–6.

Wilson, G. (1995) *Good Sewers Cheap? Agency–Customer Interactions in Low-Cost Urban Sanitation in Brazil*, Washington, DC: World Bank.

Winje, D., Homann, H., Luhr, H.-P. and Butow, E. (1991) *Der Einfluss der Gewasserverscgmutzung auf die Kisten der Wasserversorgung in der Bundesrepublik Deutschland*, Berichte 2/91, Berlin: Erich Schmidt.

Winpenny, J. (1994) *Managing Water as an Economic Resource*, London: Routledge.

Winpenny, J.T. n.d. '*Managing water scarcity for water security*' (http://WWW.fao.org/ag/agl/aglw/webpub/scarcity.htm).

Wittink, D.R., Vriens, M. and Burhenne, W. (1994) 'Commercial use of conjoint analysis in Europe: results and critical reflections', *International Journal of Research in Marketing* **11**, 41–52.

Wolfenden, J., Gill, R. and van der Lee, J. (2001) *A Social and Economic Assessment of the Likely Impacts Resulting from Changes to Irrigation Water Allocations in the Gwydir Valley*, Armidale: Centre for Ecological Economics and Water Policy Research, University of New England.

Wolff, T.F. (1997) 'Geotechnical reliability of levees' in Burnham, M.W. and Davis, D.W. (eds) *Hydrology and Hydraulics Workshop on Risk-Based Analysis for Flood Damage Reduction Studies*, SP-28, Davis, CA: US Army Corps of Engineers Hydrologic Engineering Center.

Wood, G.D., Palmer-Jones, R., Ahmed, Q.F., Mandal, M.A.S. and Dutta, S.C. (1990) *The Water Sellers: A Cooperative Venture by the Rural Poor*, London: Intermediate Technology Publications.

Wood, S., Sebastian, K. and Scherr, S.J. (2000) *Pilot Analysis of Global Ecosystems: Agroecosystems*, Washington, DC: World Resources Institute.

Woodcock, A. and Davis, M. (1980) *Catastrophe Theory*, Harmondsworth: Penguin.

Woolcock, M. (1998) 'Social capital and economic development: toward a theoretical synthesis and policy framework', *Theory and Society* **27**(2), 151–208.

Woolcock, M. and Narayan, D. (2000) 'Social capital: implications for development theory, research, and policy', *The World Bank Research Observer* **15**(2), 225–49.

Working Group on National Weather Radar Coverage 1983 *Report of the Working Group on National Weather Radar Coverage*, London: National Water Council/Meteorological Office.

World Bank (1991) *Environmental Assessment Sourcebook*, Washington, DC: World Bank.

World Bank (1993) *Water Resource Management*, Washington, DC: World Bank.

World Bank (1996a) *Public Participation: Sourcebook*, Washington, DC: World Bank.

World Bank (1996b) *Rural Energy and Development: Improving Energy Supplies for Two Billion People*, Washington, DC: World Bank.

World Bank (1997) *Staff Appraisal Report – China: Wanjiazhai Water Transfer Project*, Report No. 15999-CHA, Washington, DC: World Bank.

World Bank (1999a) *Benchmarking Water and Sanitation Utilities: A Start-up Kit*, Washington, DC: Water and Sanitation Division.

World Bank (1999b) *Second Loess Plateau Watershed Rehabilitation Project*, Project Appraisal Document, Washington, DC: World Bank.

World Bank (2001) *Water Resource Sector Strategy: Concept Note for Discussion with CODE*, Washington, DC: World Bank.

World Bank n.d. *Reduction of Unit Transportation Cost in Using Larger Size Vessel (Economic Cost)*, Washington, DC: Inland Water Transport, World Bank.

World Commission on Environment and Development (1987) *Our Common Future*, Oxford: Oxford University Press.

World Water Council (2000) *World Water Vision*, London: Earthscan.

Wouters, P. (ed.) (1997) *International Water Law: Selected Writings of Professor Charles B Bourne*, London: Kluwer.

WRc/OXERA/FHRC (1996) *Assessing the Benefits of Surface Water Quality Improvements: Manual*, Marlow: Foundation for Water Research.

Wright, K.R. (ed.) (1990) *Water Rights of the Fifty States and Territories*, Denver, CO: American Water Works Association.

Wrightsman, L.S. (1978) 'The American trial jury on trial: empirical evidence and procedural modifications', *Journal of Social Issues* **34**(4), 137–64.

Xie, M., Kuffner, U. and Le Moigne, G. (1993) *Using Water Efficiently*, World Bank Technical Paper 205, Washington, DC: World Bank.

Yang, X. (2001) *Water Resources Conservation in Taiyuan, China*, Athens: Ohio University.

Yapa, K.A.S. (2001) *The American Way: Past and Present* (wysiwyg://31/http://kyapa.tripod.com/agengineering/gwateruse/gwateruse.htm).

Yepes, G. (1995) *Reduction of Unaccounted for Water*, ESD Water and Sanitation Division, Washington, DC: World Bank.

Yepes, G. (1999) *Do Cross-Subsidies Help the Poor to Benefit from Water and Wastewater Services? Lessons from Guayaquil*, Water and Sanitation Program, Washington DC: World Bank.

Young, R.A. (1996) *Measuring Economic Benefits for Water Investment and Policies*, Technical Paper No. 338, Washington DC: World Bank.

Young, W., Cameron, N. and Tinsley, Y. (1999) *Juries in Criminal Trials Part 2 – A Summary of the Research Findings*, Preliminary Paper 37 – Volume 2, Wellington: Law Commission.

Zaidi, A. (2001) *From the Lane to the City: The Impact of the Orangi Pilot Project's Low Cost Sanitation Model*, London: WaterAid.

Zhu, Z., Cai, M., Warg, S. and Jiang, Y. (eds) (1991) *Agroforestry Systems in China*, Ottawa: IDRC.

Zockler, C. (2000) *Wise Use of Floodplains*, Cambridge: World Wide Fund.

Zorkoczy, Z. (1993) 'Flood defence organisation and management in Hungary' in Hegedus, M. (ed.) *Proceedings of the British–Hungarian Workshop on Flood Defence*, Budapest: Vituki.

Zwarteveen, M. (1997) *A Plot of One's Own: Gender Relations and Irrigated Land Allocation Policies in Burkina Faso*, Colombo: International Irrigation Management Institute (http://www.cgiar.org/iimi).

Index

Handbook of Water Economics: Principles and Practice. C. Green
© 2003 John Wiley & Sons, Ltd ISBN: 0-471-98571-6